Geometry
Concepts & Connections

Ron Larson
Paul Battaglia

Erie, Pennsylvania
BigIdeasLearning.com

Big Ideas Learning, LLC
1762 Norcross Road
Erie, PA 16510-3838
USA

For product information and customer support, contact Big Ideas Learning at **1-877-552-7766** or visit us at ***BigIdeasLearning.com***.

Cover Image
ESA/Webb, NASA & CSA, J. Lee and the PHANGS-JWST Team.

Copyright © 2025 by Big Ideas Learning, LLC. All rights reserved.

No part of this work may be reproduced or transmitted in any form or by any means, electronic or mechanical, including, but not limited to, photocopying and recording, or by any information storage or retrieval system, without prior written permission of Big Ideas Learning, LLC unless such copying is expressly permitted by copyright law. Address inquiries to Permissions, Big Ideas Learning, LLC, 1762 Norcross Road, Erie, PA 16510.

Big Ideas Learning are registered trademarks of Larson Texts, Inc.

Printed in the U.S.A.

ISBN 13: 979-8-88802-870-4

1 2 3 4 5 6 7 8 9—27 26 25 24 23

Why Big Ideas Learning?

Because Math Is What We Do!

With a singular focus on mathematics, we are uniquely qualified and committed to supporting you at every step along your journey. Written by renowned author, Dr. Ron Larson, and his expert authorship team, this program is a seamless and comprehensive curriculum with cohesive math progressions

Ron Larson, Ph.D., is a highly acclaimed and award-winning math textbook author whose K–12, plus Higher Ed, student-friendly programs are known for their clarity, focus, coherence, rigor, and student self-reflection. Ron's enduring commitment to making math accessible and relevant to all students is his singular purpose.

Ron Larson

Paul Battaglia holds a Masters degree in Curriculum and Instruction and has taught high school math for 25 years. In addition to teaching, he is an educational consultant, award-winning textbook author, and is regularly invited to speak at national and international conferences. Paul's work involves efforts to inject relevance into the classroom so teachers can connect and engage more deeply with all students. For his efforts, Paul has been nominated for the Princeton Prize for Distinguished Secondary School Teaching.

Paul Battaglia

Meet the Team!

Get to know the amazing authorship team through exclusive online videos. The authors discuss many topics including their inspiration, proudest moment as an educator, and the meaning behind this program. Learn more online about the educators, experts, and community members who informed this program and how they support all aspects of the learning experience.

BigIdeasLearning.com

What Does Your Math Journey Look Like?

Investigate & Learn

Watch a STEM Career Video
Begin every chapter discovering a National Geographic Explorer's STEM research. Hear from each Explorer in the *Everyday Explorations Videos*.

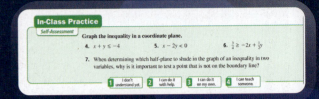

Try It and Self-Assess
Try *In-Class Practice* with feedback to help guide your learning. Rate your understanding along the way.

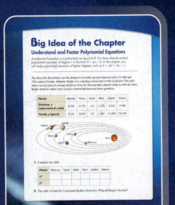

Investigate
Work with a partner to *investigate* concepts that you will be learning in each section.

Think About the Big Idea
Relate the *Big Idea of the Chapter* with an investigative real-life data context.

Get Ready
Refresh the skills you will need for the chapter before you begin.

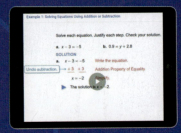

Learn and Build
Learn *Key Concepts* and interact with Examples to build your conceptual understanding.

The Road Doesn't End Here!

This program is more than just pages in a textbook. Go online to explore all the additional tools that will help you learn math this year. Watch videos of real people like an astronomer, engineer, scientist, and biologist describing how they use math every day. The learning doesn't have to stop once you leave the classroom, with online activities to get you and your family involved with your journey at home!

BigIdeasLearning.com

Connect the Big Ideas
As you learn math, you are building and connecting ideas across different pathways of thinking. Each chapter is part of your bigger math journey.

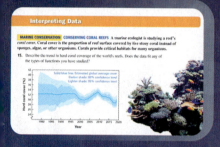

Connect to Real Life
See how the math connects to the world around you.

Get Vocabulary Help
Access vocabulary *Flash Cards* and a *Multi-Language Glossary* to strengthen your language skills.

Find Support
Access solution videos, math tools, extra practice, and more.
CalcChat and CalcView

Revisit the STEM Career
Analyze a real-life data display in the field of the National Geographic Explorer and apply chapter concepts in the *Performance Task*.

Practice
Apply the concepts you are learning and connect them to a data display in the *Practice* and *Interpreting Data*.

Practice & Apply

1 Basics of Geometry

Chapter Opener 0
    CAREER: *Large Carnivore Ecologist*
    Big Idea of the Chapter: *Construct Figures and Find Measurements* ... 1
    Getting Ready for Chapter 1 with CalcChat 2
Section 1.1   Points, Lines, and Planes 3
Section 1.2   Measuring and Constructing Segments 11
Section 1.3   Using Midpoint and Distance Formula 19
Section 1.4   Perimeter and Area in the Coordinate Plane 27
Section 1.5   Measuring and Constructing Angles 35
Section 1.6   Describing Pairs of Angles 45
Chapter Review with CalcChat 53
Performance Task: *Tiger Tales* 56

2 Reasoning and Proofs

Chapter Opener 58
    CAREER: *Geologist*
    Big Idea of the Chapter: *Understand Deductive and Inductive
    Reasoning* 59
    Getting Ready for Chapter 2 with CalcChat 60
Section 2.1   Conditional Statements 61
Section 2.2   Inductive and Deductive Reasoning 71
Section 2.3   Postulates and Diagrams 79
Section 2.4   Algebraic Reasoning 85
Section 2.5   Proving Statements about Segments and Angles 93
Section 2.6   Proving Geometric Relationships 99
Chapter Review with CalcChat 109
Performance Task: *The Greenhouse Effect* 112

3 Parallel and Perpendicular Lines

Chapter Opener 114
    CAREER: *Conservationist*
    Big Idea of the Chapter: *Understand Parallel and Perpendicular Lines* 115
    Getting Ready for Chapter 3 with Calc Chat 116
Section 3.1   **Pairs of Lines and Angles** 117
Section 3.2   **Parallel Lines and Transversals** 123
Section 3.3   **Proofs with Parallel Lines** 131
Section 3.4   **Proofs with Perpendicular Lines** 139
Section 3.5   **Equations of Parallel and Perpendicular Lines** 149
Chapter Review with Calc Chat 157
Performance Task: *Geothermal Energy* 160
Connecting Big Ideas: *Hopewell Culture Complexes* 162

4 Transformations

Chapter Opener 164
    CAREER: *Biologist*
    Big Idea of the Chapter: *Understand and Use Transformations* 165
    Getting Ready for Chapter 4 with Calc Chat 166
Section 4.1   **Translations** 167
Section 4.2   **Reflections** 175
Section 4.3   **Rotations** 183
Section 4.4   **Congruence and Transformations** 191
Section 4.5   **Dilations** 199
Section 4.6   **Similarity and Transformations** 207
Chapter Review with Calc Chat 213
Performance Task: *The Butterfly Effect* 216

5 Congruent Triangles

Chapter Opener 218
      CAREER: *Engineer*
    Big Idea of the Chapter: *Use Congruent Triangles* 219
    Getting Ready for Chapter 5 with Calc Chat 220
Section 5.1   Angles of Triangles 221
Section 5.2   Congruent Polygons 229
Section 5.3   Proving Triangle Congruence by SAS 235
Section 5.4   Equilateral and Isosceles Triangles 243
Section 5.5   Proving Triangle Congruence by SSS 251
Section 5.6   Proving Triangle Congruence by ASA and AAS 259
Section 5.7   Using Congruent Triangles 267
Section 5.8   Coordinate Proofs 273
Chapter Review with Calc Chat 279
Performance Task: *Bacteriophages* 284

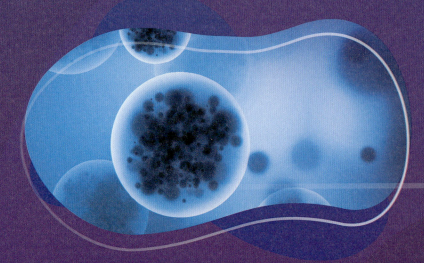

Diagnostic Technologies
In the Performance Task, students analyze a drawing of a virus known as a *bacteriophage*.

6 Relationships Within Triangles

Chapter Opener 286
    CAREER: *Archaeologist*
    Big Idea of the Chapter: *Find Relationships within Triangles* 287
    Getting Ready for Chapter 6 with Calc Chat 288
Section 6.1   Perpendicular and Angle Bisectors 289
Section 6.2   Bisectors of Triangles 297
Section 6.3   Medians and Altitudes of Triangles 307
Section 6.4   The Triangle Midsegment Theorem 315
Section 6.5   Indirect Proof and Inequalities in One Triangle 321
Section 6.6   Inequalities in Two Triangles 329
Chapter Review with Calc Chat 335
Performance Task: *Archaeology* 338
Connecting Big Ideas: *A Matter of Perspective* 340

7 Quadrilaterals and Other Polygons

Chapter Opener 342
    CAREER: *Astronomer*
    Big Idea of the Chapter: *Understand Quadrilaterals* 343
    Getting Ready for Chapter 7 with Calc Chat 344
Section 7.1   Angles of Polygons 345
Section 7.2   Properties of Parallelograms 355
Section 7.3   **Proving That a Quadrilateral Is a Parallelogram** 363
Section 7.4   Properties of Special Parallelograms 373
Section 7.5   Properties of Trapezoids and Kites 383
Chapter Review with Calc Chat 393
Performance Task: *Starstruck* 396

8 Similarity

Chapter Opener 398
    CAREER: *Biological Anthropologist*
    Big Idea of the Chapter: *Use Similar Polygons* 399
    Getting Ready for Chapter 8 with CalcChat 400
Section 8.1   Similar Polygons 401
Section 8.2   Proving Triangle Similarity by AA 411
Section 8.3   Proving Triangle Similarity by SSS and SAS 417
Section 8.4   Proportionality Theorems 427
Chapter Review with CalcChat 435
Performance Task: *African Burial Ground National Monument* 438

9 Right Triangles and Trigonometry

Chapter Opener 440
    CAREER: *Evolutionary Molecular Biologist*
    Big Idea of the Chapter: *Use Right Triangle Relationships* 441
    Getting Ready for Chapter 9 with CalcChat 442
Section 9.1   The Pythagorean Theorem 443
Section 9.2   Special Right Triangles 451
Section 9.3   Similar Right Triangles 457
Section 9.4   The Tangent Ratio 465
Section 9.5   The Sine and Cosine Ratios 471
Section 9.6   SSolving Right Triangles 479
Section 9.7   Law of Sines and Law of Cosines 485
Chapter Review with CalcChat 495
Performance Task: *Engineering a Mammoth* 500
Connecting Big Ideas: *Map out the Way* 502

10 Circles

Chapter Opener 504
    CAREER: *Anthropologist*
    Big Idea of the Chapter: Find Measurements in Circles 505
    Getting Ready for Chapter 10 with Calc Chat 506
Section 10.1 Lines and Segments That Intersect Circles 507
Section 10.2 Finding Arc Measures 515
Section 10.3 Using Chords 523
Section 10.4 Inscribed Angles and Polygons 531
Section 10.5 Angle Relationships in Circles 539
Section 10.6 Segment Relationships in Circles 547
Section 10.7 Circles in the coordinate Plane 553
Section 10.8 Focus of a Parabola 559
Chapter Review with Calc Chat 567
Performance Task: *Stonehenge* 572

Bioarchaeology
In the Performance Task, students find geometric relationships in Stonehenge and analyze their possible significance.

11 Circumference and Area

Chapter Opener 574
    CAREER: *Cultural Anthropologist*
    Big Idea of the Chapter: *Understand Circumference and Area* 575
    Getting Ready for Chapter 11 with Calc Chat 576
Section 11.1   Circumference and Arc Length 577
Section 11.2   Areas of Circles and Sectors 585
Section 11.3   Areas of Polygons 591
Section 11.4   Modeling with Area 599
Chapter Review with Calc Chat 605
Performance Task: *Center-Pivot Irrigation* 608

12 Surface Area and Volume

Chapter Opener 610
    CAREER: *Biologist*
    Big Idea of the Chapter: *Find Surface Area and Volume* 611
    Getting Ready for Chapter 12 with Calc Chat 612
Section 12.1   Cross Sections of Solids 613
Section 12.2   Volumes of Prisms and Cylinders 621
Section 12.3   Volumes of Pyramids 629
Section 12.4   Surface Areas and Volumes of Cones 635
Section 12.5   Surface Areas and Volumes of Spheres 641
Section 12.6   Modeling with Surface Area and Volume 649
Section 12.7   Solids of Revolution 655
Chapter Review with Calc Chat 661
Performance Task: *White-Nose Syndrome* 666

13 Probability

Chapter Opener 668
  CAREER: *Prehistoric Archaeologist*
  Big Idea of the Chapter: *Understand and Find Probabilities* 669
  Getting Ready for Chapter 13 with Calc Chat 670
Section 13.1 Sample Spaces and Probability 671
Section 13.2 Two-Way Tables and Probability 679
Section 13.3 Conditional Probability 685
Section 13.4 Independent and Dependent Events 693
Section 13.5 Probability of Disjoint and Overlapping Events 701
Section 13.6 Permutations and Combinations 707
Section 13.7 Binomial Distributions 715
Chapter Review with Calc Chat 721
Performance Task: *Buried Treasures* 724
Connecting Big Ideas: *Volcanoes!* 726

Selected Answers A1
English-Spanish Glossary A55
Index A69
Postulates and Theorems A85
My Guide to the Standards for Mathematical Practice A93
My Guide to Problem Solving A94
Quick Reference A95

1 Basics of Geometry

1.1 Points, Lines, and Planes
1.2 Measuring and Constructing Segments
1.3 Using Midpoint and Distance Formulas
1.4 Perimeter and Area in the Coordinate Plane
1.5 Measuring and Constructing Angles
1.6 Describing Pairs of Angles

NATIONAL GEOGRAPHIC EXPLORER
Rae Wynn-Grant — LARGE CARNIVORE ECOLOGIST

Dr. Rae Wynn-Grant is an ecologist who uses statistical modeling to investigate how anthropogenic factors can influence the spatial patterns of carnivore behavior and ecology. She studies the ecological and social drivers of human-carnivore conflict.

- What is a carnivore? Name several large carnivores that live in North America.
- Ecology is the branch of biology that deals with relationships among animals. Give several examples of predator-prey relationships in North America.

PERFORMANCE TASK
When a carnivore's habitat is diminished, the likelihood of human-carnivore conflict increases. In the Performance Task on pages 56 and 57, you will design a wildlife reservation to provide a protected habitat for a tiger population.

Ecology

Big Idea of the Chapter
Construct Figures and Find Measurements

Coordinate geometry is the study of geometric figures by plotting them in the coordinate plane. Points are defined by ordered pairs, (x, y), and other figures are defined by equations involving x and y.

Euclid and René Descartes are two of the most important figures in the history of geometry. Euclid's *Elements*, written around 300 BCE, established the foundations of modern geometry. Descartes's work led to the discovery of coordinate geometry, which allowed algebraic relationships to be represented graphically.

The map shows the range of polar bears. Light green represents the part of the range over ocean or sea ice; dark green represents the part over land.

1. What measurements do you need in order to find the area of the Arctic Circle?

2. The diameter of the Arctic Circle is 9,900 miles. Estimate the area of the range of polar bears.

3. Which countries intersect the range of polar bears?

4. There is one region in the world that has more polar bears than people. Where do you think this is?

Getting Ready for Chapter 1

Finding Absolute Value

EXAMPLE 1 Simplify $|-7-1|$.

$|-7-1| = |-7 + (-1)|$ Add the opposite of 1.

$= |-8|$ Add.

$= 8$ Find the absolute value.

▶ $|-7-1| = 8$

Simplify the expression.

1. $|8 - 12|$
2. $|-6 - 5|$
3. $|13 + (-4)|$
4. $|6 - (-2)|$
5. $|5 - (-1)|$
6. $|-8 - (-7)|$

Finding the Area of a Triangle

EXAMPLE 2 Find the area of the triangle.

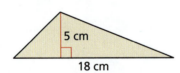

$A = \frac{1}{2}bh$ Write the formula for area of a triangle.

$= \frac{1}{2}(18)(5)$ Substitute 18 for b and 5 for h.

$= \frac{1}{2}(90)$ Multiply 18 and 5.

$= 45$ Multiply $\frac{1}{2}$ and 90.

▶ The area of the triangle is 45 square centimeters.

Find the area of the triangle.

7.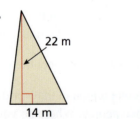
8.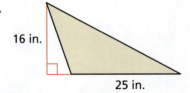
9.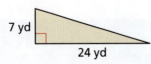
10.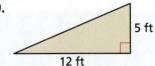

1.1 Points, Lines, and Planes

> **Learning Target:** Use defined terms and undefined terms.
>
> **Success Criteria:**
> - I can describe a point, a line, and a plane.
> - I can define and name segments and rays.
> - I can sketch intersections of lines and planes.

INVESTIGATE Using Technology

1. **Work with a partner.** Use technology to draw several points. Also, draw some lines, line segments, and rays. How would you describe a line? a point? Write your own definitions for a line segment and a ray, based on how they relate to a line.

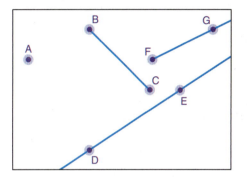

INVESTIGATE Describing Planes and Intersections

2. **Work with a partner.** The diagram shows plane P and plane Q intersecting. How would you describe a plane?

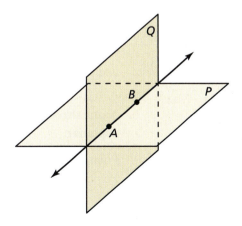

3. **SMP.5** Describe the ways in which each of the following can intersect and not intersect. Provide a sketch or use real-life objects to model each type of intersection.

   a. two lines   b. a line and a plane   c. two planes

1.1 Points, Lines, and Planes   3

Vocabulary
undefined terms
point
line
plane
collinear points
coplanar points
defined terms
line segment, or segment
endpoints
ray
opposite rays
intersection

Using Undefined Terms

In geometry, the words *point*, *line*, and *plane* are **undefined terms**. These words do not have formal definitions, but there is agreement about what they mean.

Key Concept

Undefined Terms: Point, Line, and Plane

Point A **point** has no dimension. A dot represents a point.

point A

Line A **line** has one dimension. It is represented by a line with two arrowheads, but it extends without end. Through any two points, there is exactly one line. You can use any two points on a line to name it.

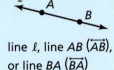

line ℓ, line AB ($\overleftrightarrow{AB}$), or line BA ($\overleftrightarrow{BA}$)

Plane A **plane** has two dimensions. It is represented by a shape that looks like a floor or a wall, but it extends without end. Through any three points not on the same line, there is exactly one plane. You can use three points that are not all on the same line to name a plane.

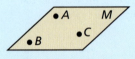

plane M, or plane ABC

Collinear points are points that lie on the same line. **Coplanar points** are points that lie in the same plane.

EXAMPLE 1 Naming Points, Lines, and Planes

a. Give two other names for $\overleftrightarrow{PQ}$ and plane R.

Other names for $\overleftrightarrow{PQ}$ are $\overleftrightarrow{QP}$ and line n. Other names for plane R are plane SVT and plane PTV.

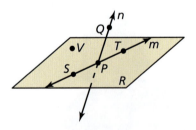

b. Name three points that are collinear. Name four points that are coplanar.

Points S, P, and T lie on the same line, so they are collinear.
Points S, P, T, and V lie in the same plane, so they are coplanar.

In-Class Practice

Self-Assessment

1. Use the diagram in Example 1. Give two other names for $\overleftrightarrow{ST}$. Name a point that is *not* coplanar with points Q, S, and T.

Using Defined Terms

In geometry, terms that can be described using known words such as *point* or *line* are called **defined terms**.

Key Concept

Defined Terms: Segment and Ray

The diagrams below use the points A and B and parts of the line AB.

Segment A **line segment**, or **segment**, is a part of a line that consists of two **endpoints** and all points on the line between the endpoints.

Ray A **ray** is a part of a line that consists of an endpoint and all points on the line on one side of the endpoint.

Opposite Rays Two rays that have the same endpoint and form a line are **opposite rays**.

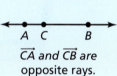

STUDY TIP
Note that $\overrightarrow{AB}$ and $\overrightarrow{BA}$ are different rays.

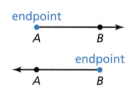

Segments and rays are collinear when they lie on the same line. Lines, segments, and rays are coplanar when they lie in the same plane.

EXAMPLE 2 — Naming Segments, Rays, and Opposite Rays

a. Give another name for $\overline{GH}$.

Another name for $\overline{GH}$ is $\overline{HG}$.

b. Name all rays with endpoint J. Which of these rays are opposite rays?

The rays with endpoint J are $\overrightarrow{JE}$, $\overrightarrow{JG}$, $\overrightarrow{JF}$, and $\overrightarrow{JH}$. The pairs of opposite rays with endpoint J are $\overrightarrow{JE}$ and $\overrightarrow{JF}$, and $\overrightarrow{JG}$ and $\overrightarrow{JH}$.

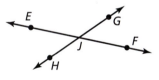

In-Class Practice

Self-Assessment

Use the diagram.

2. Give another name for $\overline{KL}$.

3. Are $\overrightarrow{KP}$ and $\overrightarrow{PK}$ the same ray? Are $\overrightarrow{NP}$ and $\overrightarrow{NM}$ the same ray? Explain.

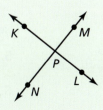

 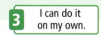

1.1 Points, Lines, and Planes

Sketching Intersections

Two or more geometric figures *intersect* when they have one or more points in common. The **intersection** of the figures is the set of points the figures have in common.

EXAMPLE 3 Sketching Intersections of Lines and Planes

a. Sketch a plane and a line that is in the plane.

b. Sketch a plane and a line that does not intersect the plane.

c. Sketch a plane and a line that intersects the plane at a point.

a.  b. 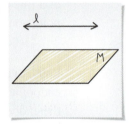 c.

EXAMPLE 4 Sketching an Intersection of Planes

Sketch two planes that intersect in a line.

Draw a vertical plane. Shade the plane.

Draw a second plane that is horizontal. Shade this plane a different color. Use dashed lines to show where planes are hidden.

Draw the line of intersection.

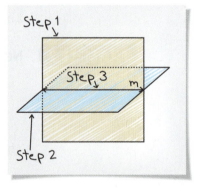

In-Class Practice

Self-Assessment

4. Sketch two different lines that intersect a plane at the same point.

Use the diagram.

5. Name the intersection of plane A and plane B.

6. Name the intersection of line k and plane A.

Chapter 1 Basics of Geometry

Connections to Real Life

EXAMPLE 5 Naming Planes that Contain Lines

The diagram shows a model of a molecule of sulfur hexafluoride, the most potent greenhouse gas in the world. Name two different planes that contain line *r*.

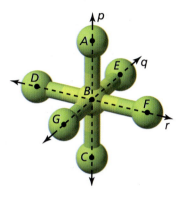

To name a plane that contains line *r*, use two points on line *r* and one point not on line *r*. Points *D* and *F* lie on line *r*. Points *C* and *E* do not lie on line *r*.

▶ So, plane *DEF* and plane *CDF* both contain line *r*.

Check The question asks for two *different* planes. Check whether plane *DEF* and plane *CDF* are two unique planes or the same plane named differently. Because point *C* does not lie in plane *DEF*, plane *DEF* and plane *CDF* are different planes.

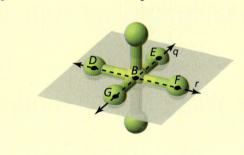 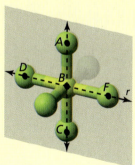

In-Class Practice

Self-Assessment

Use the diagram that shows a model of a molecule of phosphorus pentachloride.

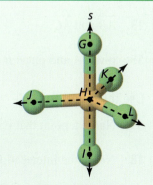

7. Name two different planes that contain line *s*.

8. Name three different planes that contain point *K*.

9. Name two different planes that contain $\overrightarrow{HJ}$.

1 I don't understand yet. **2** I can do it with help. **3** I can do it on my own. **4** I can teach someone.

1.1 Points, Lines, and Planes

1.1 Practice

Use the diagram. (See Example 1.)

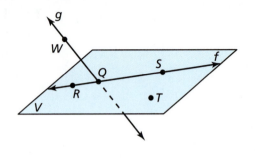

1. Give two other names for $\overleftrightarrow{WQ}$.

2. Give another name for plane V.

3. Name three points that are collinear. Then name a fourth point that is not collinear with these three points.

4. Name a point that is not coplanar with R, S, and T.

Use the diagram. (See Example 2.)

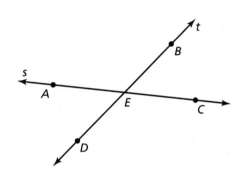

5. What is another name for $\overleftrightarrow{BD}$?

6. What is another name for $\overleftrightarrow{AC}$?

7. Name two pairs of opposite rays.

8. Name one pair of rays that are not opposite rays.

SMP.3 ERROR ANALYSIS Describe and correct the error in naming opposite rays in the diagram.

9.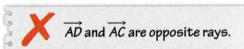

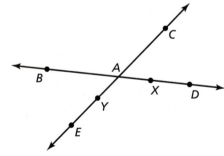

10.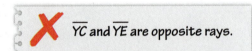

Sketch the figure described. (See Examples 3 and 4.)

11. plane P and line ℓ intersecting at one point

12. plane M and $\overrightarrow{NB}$ intersecting at point B

13. $\overrightarrow{AB}$ and $\overleftrightarrow{AC}$

14. $\overrightarrow{MN}$ and $\overrightarrow{NX}$

15. plane A and plane B not intersecting

16. plane C and plane D intersecting at $\overleftrightarrow{XY}$

Use the diagram.

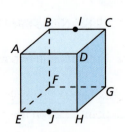

17. Name a point that is collinear with points E and H.

18. Name the intersection of plane BGF and plane HDG.

CONNECTION TO REAL LIFE Use the diagram. (See Example 5.)

19. Name two points that are collinear with P.

20. Name two planes that contain J.

21. CONNECTION TO REAL LIFE When two trucks traveling in different directions approach an intersection at the same time, one of the trucks must change its speed or direction to avoid a collision. Explain why two airplanes can travel in different directions and cross paths without colliding.

22. Given two points on a line and a third point not on the line, explain whether it is possible to draw a plane that includes the line and the third point.

23. Explain whether it is possible to draw two planes that intersect at one point.

24. You and your friend walk in opposite directions, forming opposite rays. You were originally on the corner of Apple Avenue and Cherry Court. Your friend claims he went north on Cherry Court, and you went east on Apple Avenue. Make an argument for why you know this could not have happened.

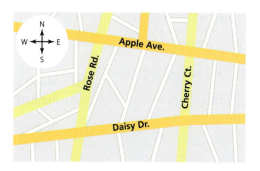

25. CONNECT CONCEPTS Graph $-7 \leq x \leq 4$ on a number line. Identify the geometric object the graph represents.

26. **SMP.7** How many intersection points could exist between four coplanar lines? Explain.

27. Is it possible for three planes to never intersect? to intersect in one line? to intersect in one point? Sketch the possible situations.

1.1 Points, Lines, and Planes

Interpreting Data

OPTICAL ILLUSIONS M.C. Escher was a Dutch graphic artist who created mathematically inspired art. His work features mathematical objects such as impossible objects and optical illusions.

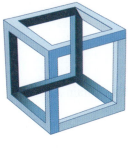
Illusion 1

Illusion 2

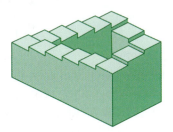
Illusion 3

28. Describe the optical illusion in Illusion 1 using vocabulary you learned in this section.

29. Would it be possible to arrange 9 cubes as shown in Illusion 2? Explain your reasoning.

30. Illusion 3 is known as the Penrose stairs, or the impossible staircase. Imagine you are walking up the stairs. You walk around twice. Do you get any higher? Explain your reasoning.

Review & Refresh

Determine which of the lines, if any, are parallel or perpendicular.

31. Line a passes through $(1, 3)$ and $(-2, -3)$.

Line b passes through $(-1, -5)$ and $(0, -3)$.

Line c passes through $(3, 2)$ and $(1, 0)$.

32. Line a: $y + 4 = \frac{1}{2}x$

Line b: $2y = -4x + 6$

Line c: $y = 2x - 1$

33. You bike at a constant speed of 10 miles per hour. You plan to bike 30 miles, plus or minus 5 miles. Write and solve an equation to find the minimum and maximum numbers of hours you bike.

Evaluate the expression.

34. $\sqrt[3]{8^5}$

35. $36^{1/2}$

Use zeros to graph the function.

36. $y = 2x(x - 5)(x + 8)$

37. $y = 4x^3 - 64x$

38. $y = 3x^3 + 3x^2 - 6x$

39. Make a box-and-whisker plot that represents the data.

Scores on a test: 76, 90, 84, 97, 82, 100, 92, 90, 88

Solve the equation.

40. $18 + x = 43$ **41.** $x - 23 = 19$

Solve the inequality. Graph the solution.

42. $a + 18 < 7$ **43.** $\frac{z}{4} \leq 12$

1.2 Measuring and Constructing Segments

Learning Target: Measure and construct line segments.

Success Criteria:
- I can copy a line segment.
- I can measure a line segment.
- I can explain and use the Segment Addition Postulate.

INVESTIGATE Measuring Line Segments

Work with a partner. A *straightedge* is a tool that you can use to draw a straight line. An example of a straightedge is a ruler.

1. Use a straightedge to draw a line segment that has a length of 6 inches.

2. **SMP.6** Use a standard-sized paper clip to measure the length of your line segment. Explain how you measured the line segment in "paper clips."

3. You measure the length and width of a rectangle in paper clips. Can you use the Pythagorean Theorem to find the length of the diagonal? Explain why or why not.

INVESTIGATE Construction: Copying a Segment

Work with a partner. A **construction** is a geometric drawing that uses a limited set of tools, usually a compass and straightedge.

Construction

Copying a Segment

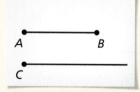  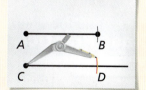

Draw a segment longer than $\overline{AB}$ using a straightedge. Label point C.

Set your compass at the length of $\overline{AB}$.

Place the compass at C. Mark point D. $\overline{CD}$ has the same length as $\overline{AB}$.

4. **SMP.5** Create a copy of the line segment in Exercise 1. What tools did you use?

Vocabulary
construction
postulate
axiom
coordinate
distance between two points
congruent segments
between

Using the Ruler Postulate

A rule that is accepted without proof is called a **postulate** or an **axiom**. A rule that can be proved is called a *theorem*, as you will see later.

Postulate 1.1

Ruler Postulate

The points on a line can be matched one to one with the real numbers. The real number that corresponds to a point is the **coordinate** of the point.

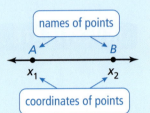

The **distance** between points A and B, written as AB, is the absolute value of the difference of the coordinates of A and B.

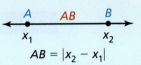

$AB = |x_2 - x_1|$

EXAMPLE 1 Using the Ruler Postulate

Measure the length of $\overline{ST}$ to the nearest tenth of a centimeter.

Align one mark of a metric ruler with S. Then estimate the coordinate of T. For example, when you align S with 2, T appears to align with 5.4.

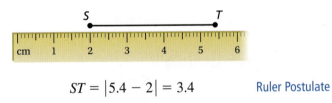

$ST = |5.4 - 2| = 3.4$ Ruler Postulate

▶ So, the length of $\overline{ST}$ is about 3.4 centimeters.

In-Class Practice

Self-Assessment

Use a ruler to measure the length of the segment to the nearest $\frac{1}{8}$ inch.

1. M————————N
2. P————————Q
3. U————V
4. W——————X

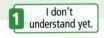 I don't understand yet.
 I can do it with help.
 I can do it on my own.
4 I can teach someone.

12   Chapter 1   Basics of Geometry

Comparing Congruent Segments

> **Key Concept**
>
> **Congruent Segments**
>
> Line segments that have the same length are called **congruent segments**. You can say "the length of $\overline{AB}$ is equal to the length of $\overline{CD}$," or you can say "$\overline{AB}$ is *congruent* to $\overline{CD}$." The symbol ≅ means "is congruent to."
>
> 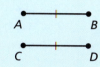 Lengths are equal.   Segments are congruent.
>
> $AB = CD$ $\qquad$ $\overline{AB} \cong \overline{CD}$
>
>
>
> "is equal to" $\qquad$ "is congruent to"

The red tick marks indicate that the segments are congruent.

EXAMPLE 2 — Comparing Segments for Congruence

Plot $J(-3, 4)$, $K(2, 4)$, $L(1, 3)$, and $M(1, -2)$ in a coordinate plane. Then determine whether $\overline{JK}$ and $\overline{LM}$ are congruent.

Plot the points.

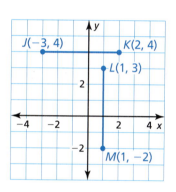

To find the length of a horizontal segment, find the absolute value of the difference of the *x*-coordinates of the endpoints.

$JK = |2 - (-3)| = 5$ **Ruler Postulate**

To find the length of a vertical segment, find the absolute value of the difference of the *y*-coordinates of the endpoints.

$LM = |-2 - 3| = 5$ **Ruler Postulate**

▶ $\overline{JK}$ and $\overline{LM}$ have the same length. So, $\overline{JK} \cong \overline{LM}$.

In-Class Practice

Self-Assessment

5. Plot $A(-2, 4)$, $B(3, 4)$, $C(0, 2)$, and $D(0, -2)$ in a coordinate plane. Then determine whether $\overline{AB}$ and $\overline{CD}$ are congruent.

1 I don't understand yet.   **2** I can do it with help.   **3** I can do it on my own.   **4** I can teach someone.

1.2 Measuring and Constructing Segments

Using the Segment Addition Postulate

When three points are collinear, you can say that one point is **between** the other two.

Point *B* is between points *A* and *C*.

Point *E* is not between points *D* and *F*.

Postulate 1.2

Segment Addition Postulate

If *B* is between *A* and *C*, then $AB + BC = AC$.

If $AB + BC = AC$, then *B* is between *A* and *C*.

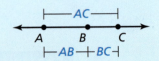

EXAMPLE 3 Using the Segment Addition Postulate

a. Find *DF*.

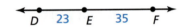

Use the Segment Addition Postulate to write an equation. Then solve the equation to find *DF*.

$DF = DE + EF$ Segment Addition Postulate
$DF = 23 + 35$ Substitute 23 for *DE* and 35 for *EF*.
$DF = 58$ Add.

b. Find *GH*.

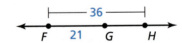

Use the Segment Addition Postulate to write an equation. Then solve the equation to find *GH*.

$FH = FG + GH$ Segment Addition Postulate
$36 = 21 + GH$ Substitute 36 for *FH* and 21 for *FG*.
$15 = GH$ Subtract 21 from each side.

In-Class Practice

Self-Assessment

Use the diagram.

6. Find *XZ*.

7. In the diagram, $WY = 30$. Can you use the Segment Addition Postulate to find the distance between points *W* and *Z*?

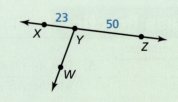

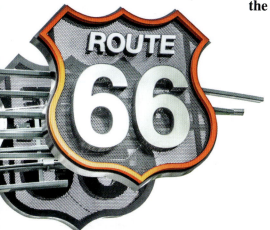

EXAMPLE 4 **Using the Segment Addition Postulate**

The cities shown on the map lie approximately in a straight line. Find the distance from Tulsa, Oklahoma, to St. Louis, Missouri.

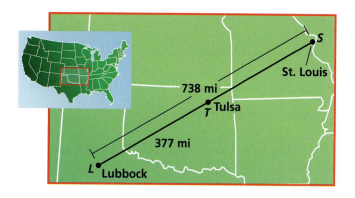

Use the Segment Addition Postulate to write an equation. Then solve the equation to find *TS*.

$LS = LT + TS$ Segment Addition Postulate
$738 = 377 + TS$ Substitute 738 for *LS* and 377 for *LT*.
$361 = TS$ Subtract 377 from each side.

▶ So, the distance from Tulsa to St. Louis is about 361 miles.

Check The distance from Lubbock to St. Louis is 738 miles. By the Segment Addition Postulate, the distance from Lubbock to Tulsa plus the distance from Tulsa to St. Louis should equal 738 miles.

$377 + 361 = 738$ ✓

In-Class Practice
Self-Assessment

8. The cities shown on the map lie approximately in a straight line. Find the distance from Albuquerque, New Mexico, to Provo, Utah.

1.2   Measuring and Constructing Segments   **15**

1.2 Practice

Use a ruler to measure the length of the segment to the nearest tenth of a centimeter. (See Example 1.)

1. •————————•

2. •————————————————•

3. •——————————————•

4. •————————————————————•

CONSTRUCTION Use a compass and straightedge to construct a copy of the segment.

5. Copy the segment in Exercise 3.

6. Copy the segment in Exercise 4.

Plot the points in a coordinate plane. Then determine whether $\overline{AB}$ and $\overline{CD}$ are congruent. (See Example 2.)

7. $A(-4, 5), B(-4, 8), C(2, -3), D(2, 0)$

8. $A(6, -1), B(1, -1), C(2, -3), D(4, -3)$

9. $A(8, 3), B(-1, 3), C(5, 10), D(5, 3)$

10. $A(6, -8), B(6, 1), C(7, -2), D(-2, -2)$

Find *FH*. (See Example 3.)

11. F—8—G—14—H

12.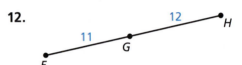

13.

14.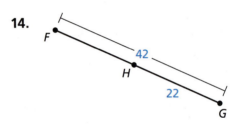

ERROR ANALYSIS Describe and correct the error in finding the length of $\overline{AB}$.

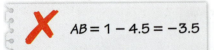

15. ✗ $AB = 1 - 4.5 = -3.5$

16. ✗ $AB = |1 + 4.5| = 5.5$

17. **SMP.6** The diagram shows an insect called a walking stick. Estimate the length of the abdomen and the length of the thorax to the nearest $\frac{1}{4}$ inch. How much longer is the walking stick's abdomen than its thorax? How many times longer is its abdomen than its thorax?

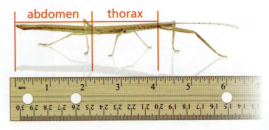

16 Chapter 1 Basics of Geometry

18. **CONNECTION TO REAL LIFE** The map shows a remote-controlled model airplane's position at three different points during a nonstop flight across the Atlantic Ocean. Point *A* represents Cape Spear, Newfoundland, point *B* represents the approximate position after 1 day, and point *C* represents Mannin Bay, Ireland. The airplane left from Cape Spear and landed in Mannin Bay. (See Example 4.)

   a. Find the total distance the model airplane flew.
   b. The flight lasted nearly 38 hours. Estimate the airplane's average speed in miles per hour.

19. Explain whether each statement is *true* or *false*.

   a. *B* is between *A* and *C*.
   b. *C* is between *B* and *E*.
   c. *D* is between *A* and *H*.
   d. *E* is between *C* and *F*.

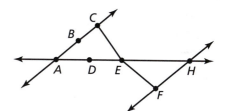

20. Point *S* is between points *R* and *T* on $\overline{RT}$. Find *RS*, *ST*, and *RT*.

   a. $RS = 2x + 10$
      $ST = x - 4$
      $RT = 21$

   b. $RS = 4x - 9$
      $ST = 19$
      $RT = 8x - 14$

21. **CONNECT CONCEPTS** The points (a, b) and (c, b) form a segment, and the points (d, e) and (d, f) form a segment. The segments are congruent. Write an equation that represents the relationship among the variables.

22. **CONNECT CONCEPTS** In the diagram, $\overline{AB} \cong \overline{BC}$, and $\overline{AC} \cong \overline{CD}$, and $AD = 12$. You choose one of the segments at random. What is the probability that the length of the segment is greater than 3?

23. Points *A*, *B*, and *C* lie on a line where $AB = 35$ and $AC = 93$. What are the possible values of *BC*?

24. **SMP.1 DIG DEEPER** Explain whether it is possible to use the Segment Addition Postulate to show (a) $FB > CB$ and (b) $AC > DB$.

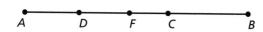

Interpreting Data

SQUARE FOOTAGE The median square footage of a single family house in the United States increased between 2000 and 2015. It reached its peak of 2,467 square feet in 2015 before falling to 2,301 square feet by 2022.

25. The square footage of the house in the floor plan only counts the yellow regions. Why?

26. Compare the square footage of this house to the median square footage in 2022.

27. Write a question about the house you would need to use the Segment Addition Postulate to answer. Then answer the question.

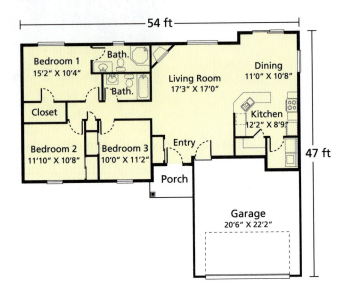

Review & Refresh

Solve the equation.

28. $3 + y = 12$

29. $5x + 7 = 9x - 17$

30. Sketch plane P and $\overleftrightarrow{YZ}$ intersecting at point Z.

31. Use intercepts to graph $-2x + 4y = -16$. Label the points corresponding to the intercepts.

Solve the inequality. Graph the solution.

32. $x - 6 \leq 13$

33. $6 - v < 8$ or $-4v \geq 40$

34. Write an inequality that represents the graph.

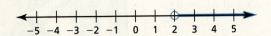

35. Graph $f(x) = 2^x - 3$. Identify the asymptote. Find the domain and range of f.

36. Is there a correlation between amusement park attendance and the wait times for rides? If so, is there a causal relationship?

37. Determine whether the relation is a function.

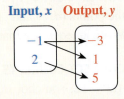

38. A football team scores a total of 7 touchdowns and field goals in a game. The team scores an extra point with each touchdown, so each touchdown is worth 7 points and each field goal is worth 3 points. The team scores a total of 41 points. How many touchdowns does the team score? How many field goals?

Write an equation in slope-intercept form of the line that passes through the given points.

39. $(0, 3), \left(\frac{1}{2}, 0\right)$

40. $(-8, -8), (12, -3)$

1.3 Using Midpoint and Distance Formulas

Learning Target: Find midpoints and lengths of segments.

Success Criteria:
- I can find lengths of segments.
- I can construct a segment bisector.
- I can find the midpoint of a segment.

INVESTIGATE Finding the Midpoint of a Line Segment

Work with a partner. Use centimeter graph paper.

1. Graph $\overline{AB}$, where the points A and B are shown.

2. Explain how to *bisect* $\overline{AB}$, that is, to divide $\overline{AB}$ into two congruent line segments. Then bisect $\overline{AB}$ and use the result to find the *midpoint M* of $\overline{AB}$.

3. What are the coordinates of the midpoint M?

4. Compare the x-coordinates of A, B, and M. Compare the y-coordinates of A, B, and M. How are the coordinates of the midpoint M related to the coordinates of A and B?

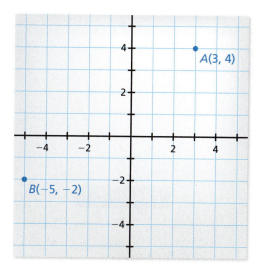

INVESTIGATE Finding the Length of a Line Segment

Work with a partner. Use centimeter graph paper.

5. Add point C to your graph as shown.

6. Use the Pythagorean Theorem to find the length of $\overline{AB}$.

7. Use a centimeter ruler to verify the length you found in Exercise 6.

8. Use the Pythagorean Theorem and point M from Exercise 3 to find the lengths of $\overline{AM}$ and $\overline{MB}$. What can you conclude?

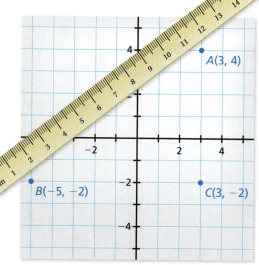

1.3 Using Midpoint and Distance Formulas   19

Vocabulary
midpoint
segment bisector

Midpoints and Segment Bisectors

> ### Key Concept
>
> **Midpoints and Segment Bisectors**
>
> The **midpoint** of a segment is the point that divides the segment into two congruent segments.
>
>
>
> M is the midpoint of $\overline{AB}$.
> So, $\overline{AM} \cong \overline{MB}$ and $AM = MB$.
>
> A **segment bisector** is a ray, line, line segment, or plane that intersects the segment at its midpoint. A midpoint or a segment bisector *bisects* a segment.
>
>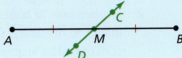
>
> $\overleftrightarrow{CD}$ is a segment bisector of $\overline{AB}$.
> So, $\overline{AM} \cong \overline{MB}$ and $AM = MB$.

EXAMPLE 1 Finding Segment Lengths

In the skateboard design, $XT = 39.9$ cm. Identify the segment bisector of $\overline{XY}$. Then find XY.

The design shows that $\overline{XT} \cong \overline{TY}$. So, point T is the midpoint of $\overline{XY}$ and $XT = TY = 39.9$ cm. Because $\overline{VW}$ intersects $\overline{XY}$ at its midpoint T, $\overline{VW}$ bisects $\overline{XY}$. Find XY.

$XY = XT + TY$	Segment Addition Postulate
$= 39.9 + 39.9$	Substitute.
$= 79.8$	Add.

▶ $\overline{VW}$ is the segment bisector of $\overline{XY}$, and XY is 79.8 centimeters.

In-Class Practice

Self-Assessment

Identify the segment bisector of $\overline{PQ}$. Then find PQ.

1.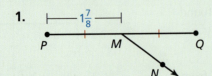

2.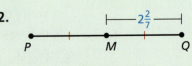

3. If a point, ray, line, line segment, or plane intersects a segment at its midpoint, then what does it do to the segment?

EXAMPLE 2 **Using Algebra with Segment Lengths**

Identify the segment bisector of $\overline{VW}$. Then find VM.

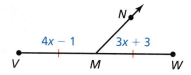

The figure shows that $\overline{VM} \cong \overline{MW}$. So, point M is the midpoint of $\overline{VW}$ and $VM = MW$. Because $\overrightarrow{MN}$ intersects $\overline{VW}$ at its midpoint M, $\overrightarrow{MN}$ bisects $\overline{VW}$.

Write and solve an equation to find VM.

$VM = MW$	Write the equation.
$4x - 1 = 3x + 3$	Substitute.
$x - 1 = 3$	Subtract $3x$ from each side.
$x = 4$	Add 1 to each side.

Evaluate the expression for VM when $x = 4$.

$$VM = 4x - 1 = 4(4) - 1 = 15$$

▶ $\overrightarrow{MN}$ is the segment bisector of $\overline{VW}$, and VM is 15.

Construction

Bisecting a Segment

Construct a segment bisector of $\overline{AB}$ by paper folding. Then label the midpoint M of $\overline{AB}$.

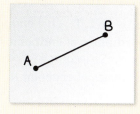  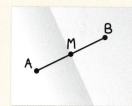

Draw a segment using a straightedge.   **Fold the paper** so that B is on top of A.   **Label the midpoint.**

In-Class Practice
Self-Assessment

4. Identify the segment bisector of $\overline{PQ}$. Then find MQ.

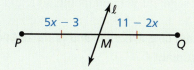

5. Identify the segment bisector of $\overline{RS}$. Then find RS.

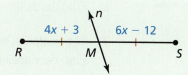

1 I don't understand yet. **2** I can do it with help. **3** I can do it on my own. **4** I can teach someone.

1.3 Using Midpoint and Distance Formulas

Using the Midpoint Formula

> **Key Concept**
>
> **The Midpoint Formula**
>
> The coordinates of the midpoint of a segment are the averages of the x-coordinates and of the y-coordinates of the endpoints.
>
> If $A(x_1, y_1)$ and $B(x_2, y_2)$ are points in a coordinate plane, then the midpoint M of $\overline{AB}$ has coordinates
>
> $$\left(\frac{x_1 + x_2}{2}, \frac{y_1 + y_2}{2}\right).$$

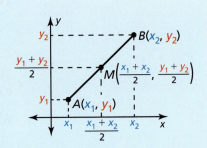

EXAMPLE 3 Using the Midpoint Formula

a. The endpoints of $\overline{RS}$ are $R(1, -3)$ and $S(4, 2)$. Find the coordinates of the midpoint M.

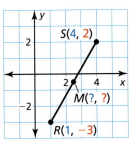

Use the Midpoint Formula.

$$M\left(\frac{1 + 4}{2}, \frac{-3 + 2}{2}\right) = M\left(\frac{5}{2}, -\frac{1}{2}\right)$$

▶ The coordinates of the midpoint M are $\left(\frac{5}{2}, -\frac{1}{2}\right)$.

b. The midpoint of $\overline{JK}$ is $M(2, 1)$. One endpoint is $J(1, 4)$. Find the coordinates of endpoint K.

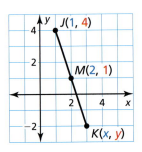

Let (x, y) be the coordinates of endpoint K. Use the Midpoint Formula.

Find x.

$$\frac{1 + x}{2} = 2$$
$$1 + x = 4$$
$$x = 3$$

Find y.

$$\frac{4 + y}{2} = 1$$
$$4 + y = 2$$
$$y = -2$$

▶ The coordinates of endpoint K are $(3, -2)$.

In-Class Practice

Self-Assessment

6. Find the midpoint M of a line segment with endpoints $A(1, 2)$ and $B(7, 8)$.

7. The midpoint of a line segment $\overline{TU}$ is $M(2, 4)$. One of the endpoints is $T(1, 1)$. Find the coordinates of the endpoint U.

1 I don't understand yet.   **2** I can do it with help.   **3** I can do it on my own.   **4** I can teach someone.

Using the Distance Formula

You can use the Distance Formula to find the distance between two points in a coordinate plane.

Pythagorean Theorem

$$c^2 = a^2 + b^2$$

Distance Formula

$$(AB)^2 = (x_2 - x_1)^2 + (y_2 - y_1)^2$$

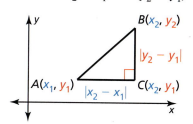

Key Concept

The Distance Formula

If $A(x_1, y_1)$ and $B(x_2, y_2)$ are points in a coordinate plane, then the distance between A and B is

$$AB = \sqrt{(x_2 - x_1)^2 + (y_2 - y_1)^2}.$$

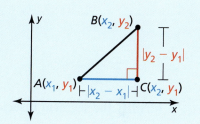

EXAMPLE 4   Using the Distance Formula

Your school is 4 miles east and 1 mile south of your apartment. A recycling center is 2 miles east and 3 miles north of your apartment. Estimate the distance between the recycling center and your school.

You can model the situation using a coordinate plane with your apartment at the origin. The coordinates of the recycling center and the school are $R(2, 3)$ and $S(4, -1)$, respectively. Use the Distance Formula. Let $(x_1, y_1) = (2, 3)$ and $(x_2, y_2) = (4, -1)$.

$RS = \sqrt{(x_2 - x_1)^2 + (y_2 - y_1)^2}$ Distance Formula
$= \sqrt{(4 - 2)^2 + (-1 - 3)^2}$ Substitute.
$= \sqrt{2^2 + (-4)^2}$ Subtract.
$= \sqrt{4 + 16}$ Evaluate powers.
$= \sqrt{20}$ Add.
≈ 4.5 Use technology.

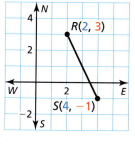

▶ So, the distance between the recycling center and your school is about 4.5 miles.

In-Class Practice

Self-Assessment

8. In Example 4, a park is 3 miles east and 4 miles south of your apartment. Estimate the distance between the park and your school.

1.3 Practice

Identify the segment bisector of $\overline{RS}$. Then find RS. (See Example 1.)

1.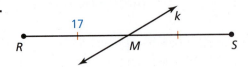

2.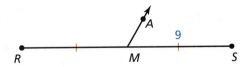

Identify the segment bisector of $\overline{JK}$. Then find JM. (See Example 2.)

3.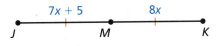

4.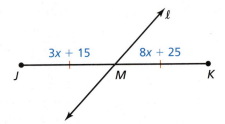

Identify the segment bisector of $\overline{XY}$. Then find XY. (See Example 2.)

5.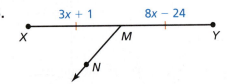

6.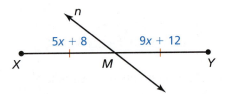

CONSTRUCTION Copy the segment and construct a segment bisector by paper folding. Then label the midpoint M.

7.

8.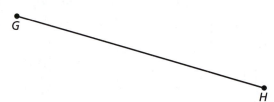

The endpoints of $\overline{CD}$ are given. Find the coordinates of the midpoint M. (See Example 3.)

9. $C(3, -5)$ and $D(7, 9)$

10. $C(-8, -6)$ and $D(-4, 10)$

The midpoint M and one endpoint of $\overline{GH}$ are given. Find the coordinates of the other endpoint. (See Example 3.)

11. $G(5, -6)$ and $M(4, 3)$

12. $H(-2, 9)$ and $M(8, 0)$

Find the distance between the two points. (See Example 4.)

13. $A(13, 2)$ and $B(7, 10)$

14. $C(-6, 5)$ and $D(-3, 1)$

15. $E(3, 7)$ and $F(6, 5)$

16. $L(7, -1)$ and $M(-2, 4)$

24   Chapter 1   Basics of Geometry

17. **SMP.3 ERROR ANALYSIS** Describe and correct the error in finding the distance between $A(6, 2)$ and $B(1, -4)$.

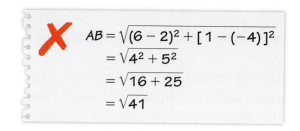

The endpoints of two segments are given. Find the length of each segment. Tell whether the segments are congruent. If they are not congruent, tell which segment is longer.

18. $\overline{AB}$: $A(0, 2)$, $B(-3, 8)$ and $\overline{CD}$: $C(-2, 2)$, $D(0, -4)$

19. $\overline{EF}$: $E(1, 4)$, $F(5, 1)$ and $\overline{GH}$: $G(-3, 1)$, $H(1, 6)$

20. **CONNECTION TO REAL LIFE** In baseball, the strike zone is the region a baseball needs to pass through for the umpire to declare it a strike when the batter does not swing. The bottom of the strike zone is a horizontal plane passing through a point just below the kneecap. The top of the strike zone is a horizontal plane passing through the midpoint of the top of the batter's shoulders and the top of the uniform pants when the player is in a batting stance. Find the height of T.

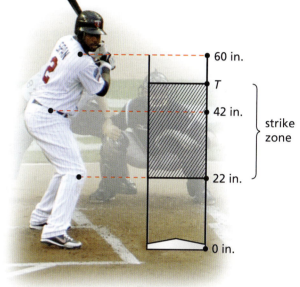

21. The endpoints of a segment are located at (a, c) and (b, c). Find the coordinates of the midpoint and the length of the segment in terms of a, b, and c.

22. **ECOLOGY PREDATOR-PREY RELATIONSHIP** Two wolves spot a deer in a field. The positions of the animals are shown. Which wolf is closer to the deer?

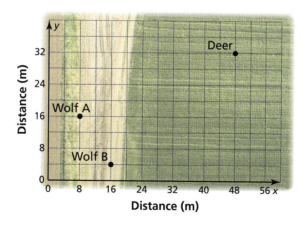

23. The length of $\overline{XY}$ is 24 centimeters. The midpoint of $\overline{XY}$ is M, and point C lies on $\overline{XM}$ so that XC is $\frac{2}{3}$ of XM. Point D lies on $\overline{MY}$ so that MD is $\frac{3}{4}$ of MY. What is the length of $\overline{CD}$?

24. **DIG DEEPER** The endpoints of $\overline{AB}$ are $A(2x, y - 1)$ and $B(y + 3, 3x + 1)$. The midpoint of $\overline{AB}$ is $M\left(-\frac{7}{2}, -8\right)$. What is the length of $\overline{AB}$?

Interpreting Data

BALLPARK DIMENSIONS Although Major League Baseball parks vary in their dimensions, some of the distances are regulated. The four bases must form a square with side lengths of 90 feet as shown.

25. Is the pitcher's mound the midpoint between home base and second base? Explain why or why not.

26. Find the distance between first base and third base.

27. A pitcher throws a ball at a speed of 100 miles per hour. Estimate the time it takes the ball to reach home plate.

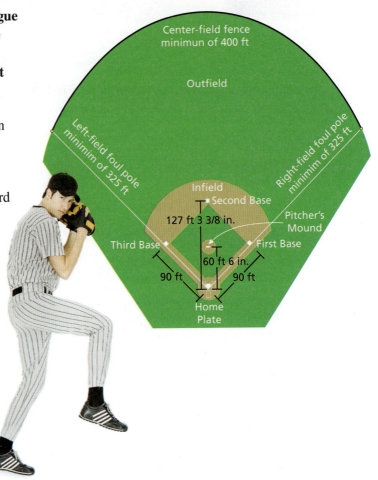

Review & Refresh

Factor the polynomial.

28. $3x^2 - 36x$

29. $n^2 + 3n - 70$

30. Name two pairs of opposite rays in the diagram.

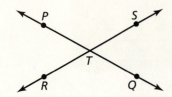

31. Solve the literal equation $5x + 15y = -30$ for y.

32. Find the average rate of change of $f(x) = 3^x$ over the interval $[1, 3]$.

33. Plot $A(-3, 3)$, $B(1, 3)$, $C(3, 2)$, and $D(3, -2)$ in a coordinate plane. Then determine whether $\overline{AB}$ and $\overline{CD}$ are congruent.

34. The function $p(x) = 80 - 2x$ represents the number of points earned on a test with x incorrect answers.

    a. How many points are earned with 2 incorrect answers?

    b. How many incorrect answers are there when 68 points are earned?

Simplify the expression. Write your answer using only positive exponents.

35. $\dfrac{b^4 \cdot b^{-2}}{b^{10}}$

36. $\left(\dfrac{2}{5t^4}\right)^{-3}$

1.4 Perimeter and Area in the Coordinate Plane

Learning Target: Find perimeters and areas of polygons in the coordinate plane.

Success Criteria:
- I can classify and describe polygons.
- I can find perimeters of polygons in the coordinate plane.
- I can find areas of polygons in the coordinate plane.

INVESTIGATE Finding the Perimeter and Area of a Quadrilateral

Work with a partner.

1. Use a piece of graph paper to draw a quadrilateral $ABCD$ in a coordinate plane. At most two sides of your quadrilateral can be horizontal or vertical. Plot and label the vertices of $ABCD$.

2. Make several observations about quadrilateral $ABCD$. Can you use any other names to classify your quadrilateral?

3. Explain how you can find the perimeter of quadrilateral $ABCD$. Then find the perimeter. Compare your method with those of your classmates.

4. Repeat Exercise 3 for the area of quadrilateral $ABCD$.

5. Find the perimeter and area of the polygon below.

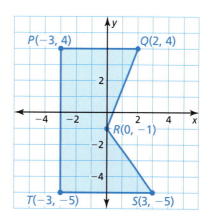

Classifying Polygons

Key Concept

Polygons

A figure that lies in a plane is a *plane figure*. Recall that a *polygon* is a closed plane figure formed by three or more line segments called *sides*. Each side intersects exactly two sides, one at each *vertex*, so that no two sides with a common vertex are collinear.

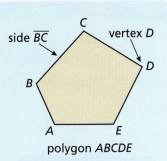
polygon ABCDE

Number of sides	Type of polygon
3	Triangle
4	Quadrilateral
5	Pentagon
6	Hexagon
7	Heptagon
8	Octagon
9	Nonagon
10	Decagon
12	Dodecagon
n	n-gon

The number of sides determines the type of polygon, as shown in the table. You can also name a polygon using the term *n-gon*, where *n* is the number of sides. For instance, a 14-gon is a polygon with 14 sides.

A polygon is *convex* when no line that contains a side of the polygon contains a point in the interior of the polygon. A polygon that is not convex is *concave*.

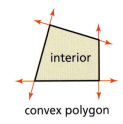
convex polygon

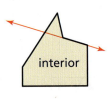
concave polygon

EXAMPLE 1 Classifying Polygons

Classify each polygon by the number of sides. Tell whether it is *convex* or *concave*.

a.

The polygon has four sides.
So, it is a quadrilateral.
The polygon is concave.

b.

The polygon has six sides.
So, it is a hexagon.
The polygon is convex.

In-Class Practice

Self-Assessment

Classify the polygon by the number of sides. Tell whether it is *convex* or *concave*.

1.
2.
3.

 I don't understand yet. 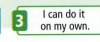 I can do it with help.   I can do it on my own. I can teach someone.

Finding Perimeter and Area in the Coordinate Plane

You can use the formulas below and the Distance Formula to find perimeters and areas of polygons in the coordinate plane.

Triangle

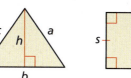

$P = a + b + c$
$A = \frac{1}{2}bh$

Square

$P = 4s$
$A = s^2$

Rectangle

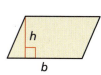

$P = 2\ell + 2w$
$A = \ell w$

Parallelogram

$A = bh$

EXAMPLE 2 Finding Perimeter in the Coordinate Plane

Find the perimeter of $\triangle DEF$ with vertices $D(1, 3)$, $E(4, -3)$, and $F(-4, -3)$.

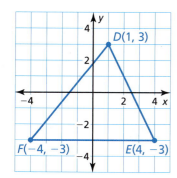

Draw the triangle in a coordinate plane by plotting the vertices and connecting them. Then find the length of each side.

$\overline{DE}$ Let $(x_1, y_1) = (1, 3)$ and $(x_2, y_2) = (4, -3)$.

$DE = \sqrt{(x_2 - x_1)^2 + (y_2 - y_1)^2}$ Distance Formula

$= \sqrt{(4 - 1)^2 + (-3 - 3)^2}$ Substitute.

$= \sqrt{3^2 + (-6)^2}$ Subtract.

$= \sqrt{45}$ Simplify.

$\overline{EF}$ $EF = |-4 - 4| = |-8| = 8$ Ruler Postulate

$\overline{FD}$ Let $(x_1, y_1) = (-4, -3)$ and $(x_2, y_2) = (1, 3)$.

$FD = \sqrt{(x_2 - x_1)^2 + (y_2 - y_1)^2}$ Distance Formula

$= \sqrt{[1 - (-4)]^2 + [3 - (-3)]^2}$ Substitute.

$= \sqrt{5^2 + 6^2}$ Subtract.

$= \sqrt{61}$ Simplify.

Find the sum of the side lengths.

$DE + EF + FD = \sqrt{45} + 8 + \sqrt{61} \approx 22.52$ units

▶ So, the perimeter of $\triangle DEF$ is about 22.52 units.

In-Class Practice

Self-Assessment

Find the perimeter of the polygon with the given vertices.

4. $G(-3, 2)$, $H(2, 2)$, $J(-1, -3)$

5. $Q(-4, -1)$, $R(1, 4)$, $S(4, 1)$, $T(-1, -4)$

| 1 I don't understand yet. | 2 I can do it with help. | 3 I can do it on my own. | 4 I can teach someone. |

EXAMPLE 3 **Finding Area in the Coordinate Plane**

Find the area of ▱JKLM with vertices $J(-3, 5)$, $K(1, 5)$, $L(2, -1)$, and $M(-2, -1)$.

> **READING**
> You can read the notation ▱JKLM as "parallelogram J K L M."

Draw the parallelogram in a coordinate plane by plotting the vertices and connecting them.

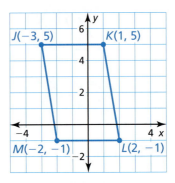

Find the lengths of the base and the height.

Base: Let $\overline{JK}$ be the base. Use the Ruler Postulate to find the length of $\overline{JK}$.

$JK = |1 - (-3)| = |4| = 4$ Ruler Postulate

Height: Let the height be the distance from point M to $\overline{JK}$. By counting grid lines, you can determine that the height is 6 units.

Substitute the values for the base and height into the formula for the area of a parallelogram.

$A = bh$ Write the formula for area of a parallelogram.

$ = 4(6)$ Substitute.

$ = 24$ Multiply.

▶ So, the area of ▱JKLM is 24 square units.

In-Class Practice

Self-Assessment

Find the area of the polygon.

6.
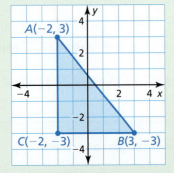

7.
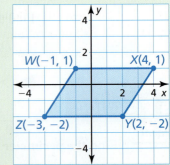

1 I don't understand yet.   2 I can do it with help.   3 I can do it on my own.   4 I can teach someone.

Connections to Real Life

EXAMPLE 4   **Finding Perimeter and Area**

You are building a shed. The diagram shows the four vertices of the shed floor. Find the perimeter and the area of the floor of the shed.

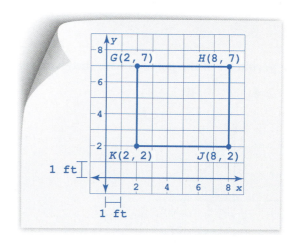

Find the length and the width.

Length $GH = |8 - 2| = 6$ Ruler Postulate

Width $KG = |7 - 2| = 5$ Ruler Postulate

The shed has a length of 6 feet and a width of 5 feet.

Substitute the values for the length and width into the formulas for the perimeter P and area A of a rectangle.

$P = 2\ell + 2w$	Write formulas.	$A = \ell w$
$= 2(6) + 2(5)$	Substitute.	$= 6(5)$
$= 22$	Evaluate.	$= 30$

▶ The perimeter of the floor of the shed is 22 feet and the area is 30 square feet.

In-Class Practice

Self-Assessment

8. You are building a patio. The diagram shows the four vertices of the patio. Find the perimeter and the area of the patio.

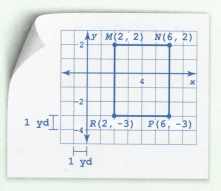

1.4   Perimeter and Area in the Coordinate Plane

1.4 Practice

Classify the polygon by the number of sides. Tell whether it is *convex* or *concave*. (See Example 1.)

1.
2.
3.
4.

Find the perimeter of the polygon with the given vertices. (See Example 2.)

5. $U(-2, 4)$, $V(3, 4)$, $W(3, -4)$

6. $Q(-3, 2)$, $R(1, 2)$, $S(1, -2)$, $T(-3, -2)$

7. 8.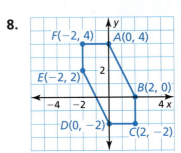

Find the area of the polygon with the given vertices. (See Example 3.)

9. $E(3, 1)$, $F(3, -2)$, $G(-2, -2)$

10. $J(-3, 4)$, $K(4, 4)$, $L(3, -3)$

11. $W(0, 0)$, $X(0, 3)$, $Y(-3, 3)$, $Z(-3, 0)$

12. $N(-4, 1)$, $P(1, 1)$, $Q(3, -1)$, $R(-2, -1)$

Use the diagram to find the perimeter and the area of the polygon.

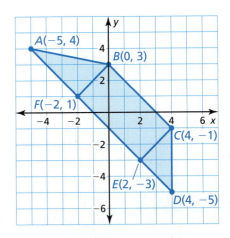

13. △CDE

14. △ABF

15. rectangle BCEF

16. quadrilateral ABCD

17. quadrilateral BCDF

18. **ERROR ANALYSIS** Describe and correct the error in finding the area of the triangle.

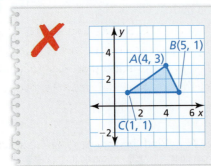

$b = |5 - 1| = 4$

$h = \sqrt{(5-4)^2 + (1-3)^2} = \sqrt{5}$

$A = \frac{1}{2}bh = \frac{1}{2}(4)(\sqrt{5}) = 2\sqrt{5}$

The area is $2\sqrt{5}$ square units.

19. **CONNECTION TO REAL LIFE** You are creating street art. The vertices of the mural are $Q(-5, 3)$, $R(7, 3)$, $S(7, -2)$, and $T(-5, -2)$. Each unit in the coordinate plane represents 1 foot. Find the perimeter and the area of the mural. *(See Example 4.)*

20. **ECOLOGY ANIMAL SANCTUARY** The diagram shows the vertices of a lion sanctuary. Each unit in the coordinate plane represents 100 feet. Find the perimeter and the area.

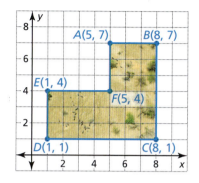

21. You and your friend hike to a waterfall that is 4 miles east of where you left your bikes. You then hike to a lookout point that is 2 miles north of your bikes. From the lookout point, you return to your bikes. About how far do you hike? Assume you travel along straight paths.

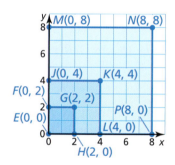

22. **SMP.8** Find the perimeter and area of each square at the left. What happens to the area of a square when its perimeter increases by a factor of n?

23. **OPEN-ENDED** Two vertices of a triangle are 4 units apart. Find possible vertices of the triangle when its area is 4 square units.

24. Connect the midpoints of the sides of square *LMNP* to make a quadrilateral. Find the perimeter and the area of this quadrilateral. What do you notice?

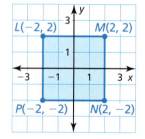

25. **CONNECT CONCEPTS** The given lines intersect to form the sides of a right triangle. Find the perimeter and the area of the triangle.

$$y = 2x - 6 \qquad y = -3x + 4 \qquad y = -\tfrac{1}{2}x + 4$$

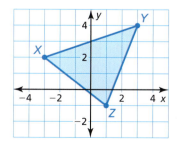

26. **PERFORMANCE TASK** Create a company logo that includes at least two different polygons and has an area of at least 50 square units. Draw your logo in a coordinate plane and record its perimeter and area. Describe the company and create a proposal explaining how your logo relates to the company.

27. **SMP.1 DIG DEEPER** Find the area of $\triangle XYZ$. Explain your method.

1.4 Perimeter and Area in the Coordinate Plane

Interpreting Data

TEN LARGEST STATES The map shows the ranking of the 10 states with the greatest areas.

28. On a coordinate plane in which each unit represents 1 mile, Colorado can be represented by the vertices (0, 0), (0, 280), (380, 280), and (380, 0). Estimate its area.

29. The area of California is about 1.6 times the area of Colorado. Estimate the area of California.

30. Estimate the area of Alaska. Explain your method.

Review & Refresh

31. Does the table represent a *linear* or *nonlinear* function?

x	−1	0	1	2	3
y	−9	−7	−5	−3	−1

Solve the equation.

32. $4 = 9 + 5x$

33. $\dfrac{x+1}{2} = 4x - 3$

Use the diagram.

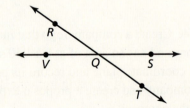

34. Give another name for $\overline{RT}$.

35. Name two pairs of opposite rays.

36. The endpoints of a segment are $J(4, 3)$ and $K(2, -3)$. Find the coordinates of the midpoint M and the length of $\overline{JK}$.

37. Use a compass and straightedge to construct a copy of the line segment.

38. You deposit $200 into a savings account that earns 5% annual interest compounded quarterly. Write a function that represents the balance y (in dollars) after t years.

Graph the function. Then describe the transformations from the graph of $f(x) = |x|$ to the graph of the function.

39. $g(x) = |x| + 5$

40. $h(x) = |x + 1|$

1.5 Measuring and Constructing Angles

Learning Target: Measure, construct, and describe angles.

Success Criteria:
- I can measure and classify angles.
- I can construct congruent angles.
- I can find angle measures.
- I can construct an angle bisector.

You can classify angles according to their measures.

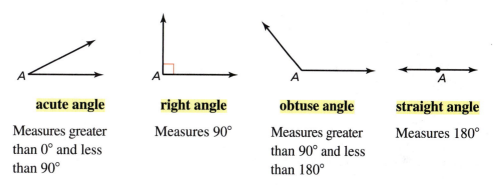

acute angle	right angle	obtuse angle	straight angle
Measures greater than 0° and less than 90°	Measures 90°	Measures greater than 90° and less than 180°	Measures 180°

INVESTIGATE Measuring and Classifying Angles

Work with a partner. Find the degree measure of each angle. Classify each angle as acute, right, or obtuse.

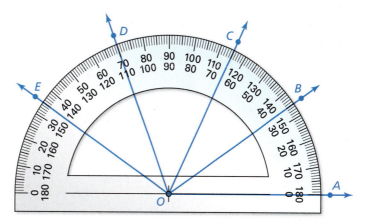

1. ∠AOB
2. ∠AOC
3. ∠BOC
4. ∠BOE
5. ∠COE
6. ∠COD
7. ∠BOD
8. AOE

9. **SMP.5 CONSTRUCTION** Construct a copy of an angle from the diagram above. Explain your method.

10. Construct each of the following. Explain your method.

    a. An angle that is twice the measure of the angle in Exercise 9.

    b. Separate the angle in Exercise 9 into two angles with the same measure.

Vocabulary

acute angle
right angle
obtuse angle
straight angle
angle
vertex
sides of an angle
interior of an angle
exterior of an angle
measure of an angle
congruent angles
angle bisector

Naming Angles

An **angle** is a set of points consisting of two different rays that have the same endpoint, called the **vertex**. The rays are the **sides** of the angle.

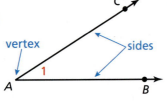

You can name an angle in several different ways. The symbol ∠ represents an angle.

Use its vertex, such as ∠A.

Use a point on each ray and the vertex, such as ∠BAC or ∠CAB. The vertex is the middle letter.

Use a number, such as ∠1.

The region that contains all the points between the sides of the angle is the **interior of the angle**. The region that contains all the points outside the angle is the **exterior of the angle**.

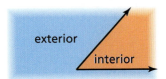

EXAMPLE 1 Naming Angles

You measure the angles formed by the lighthouse at point *M* and three boats. Name three angles shown in the diagram.

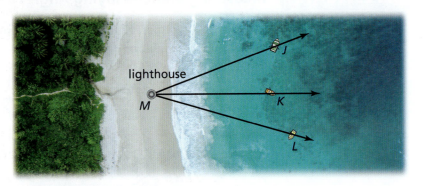

▶ ∠JMK or ∠KMJ

∠KML or ∠LMK

∠JML or ∠LMJ

In-Class Practice

Self-Assessment

Write three names for the angle.

1.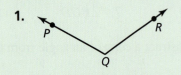

2.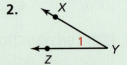

3.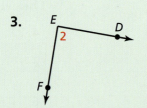

| 1 | I don't understand yet. | 2 | I can do it with help. | 3 | I can do it on my own. | 4 | I can teach someone. |

36 Chapter 1 Basics of Geometry

Measuring and Classifying Angles

> ### Postulate 1.3
>
> **Protractor Postulate**
>
> Consider $\overleftrightarrow{OB}$ and a point A on one side of $\overleftrightarrow{OB}$. The rays of the form $\overrightarrow{OA}$ can be matched one to one with the real numbers from 0 to 180.
>
>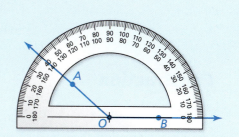
>
> The **measure** of $\angle AOB$, which can be written as $m\angle AOB$, is equal to the absolute value of the difference between the real numbers matched with $\overrightarrow{OA}$ and $\overrightarrow{OB}$ on a protractor.

EXAMPLE 2 **Measuring and Classifying Angles**

Find the measure of each angle. Then classify the angle.

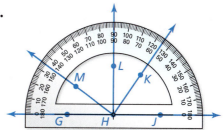

a. $\angle GHK$

$\overrightarrow{HG}$ lines up with 0° on the outer scale of the protractor. $\overrightarrow{HK}$ passes through 125° on the outer scale. So, $m\angle GHK = 125°$. It is an *obtuse* angle.

b. $\angle JHL$

$\overrightarrow{HJ}$ lines up with 0° on the inner scale of the protractor. $\overrightarrow{HL}$ passes through 90°. So, $m\angle JHL = 90°$. It is a *right* angle.

c. $\angle LHK$

$\overrightarrow{HL}$ passes through 90°. $\overrightarrow{HK}$ passes through 55° on the inner scale. So, $m\angle LHK = |90 - 55| = 35°$. It is an *acute* angle.

In-Class Practice

Self-Assessment

Find the measure of the angle. Then classify the angle.

4. $\angle CBD$

5. $\angle ABE$

6. $\angle EBD$

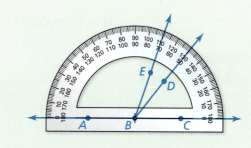

| 1 | I don't understand yet. | 2 | I can do it with help. | 3 | I can do it on my own. | 4 | I can teach someone. |

Using Congruent Angles

Two angles are **congruent angles** when they have the same measure. In the construction below, ∠A and ∠D are congruent angles.

m∠A = m∠D The measure of angle A is *equal to* the measure of angle D.

∠A ≅ ∠D Angle A is *congruent to* angle D.

Construction

Copying an Angle

In this construction, the *center* of an arc is the point where the compass point rests. The *radius* of an arc is the distance from the center of the arc to a point on the arc drawn by the compass.

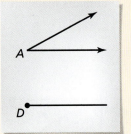 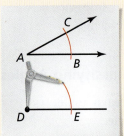 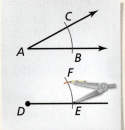 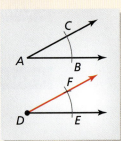

Draw a segment to copy ∠A. Label point D on the segment.

Draw arcs with centers A and D using the same radius. Label B, C, and E.

Draw an arc with radius BC and center E. Label the intersection F.

Draw a ray, $\overrightarrow{DF}$. ∠D has the same measure as ∠A.

EXAMPLE 3 Using Congruent Angles

Assume m∠ADC = 140°. What is m∠EFG?

The red arcs indicate that

∠ABC ≅ ∠FGH

and

∠ADC ≅ ∠EFG.

Because ∠ADC ≅ ∠EFG, m∠ADC = m∠EFG.

▶ So, m∠EFG = 140°.

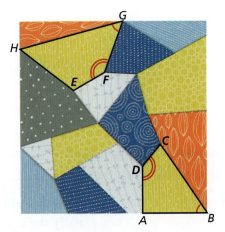

In-Class Practice

Self-Assessment

7. Without measuring, explain whether ∠DAB and ∠FEH in Example 3 appear to be congruent. Use a protractor to verify your answer.

1 I don't understand yet.   **2** I can do it with help.   **3** I can do it on my own.   **4** I can teach someone.

Using the Angle Addition Postulate

Postulate 1.4

Angle Addition Postulate

Words If P is in the interior of ∠RST, then the measure of ∠RST is equal to the sum of the measures of ∠RSP and ∠PST.

Symbols If P is in the interior of ∠RST, then

$m\angle RST = m\angle RSP + m\angle PST$.

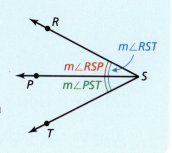

EXAMPLE 4 Finding Angle Measures

Given that $m\angle LKN = 145°$, find $m\angle LKM$ and $m\angle MKN$.

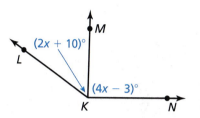

Write and solve an equation to find the value of x.

$m\angle LKN = m\angle LKM + m\angle MKN$	Angle Addition Postulate
$145° = (2x + 10)° + (4x - 3)°$	Substitute angle measures.
$145 = 6x + 7$	Combine like terms.
$138 = 6x$	Subtract 7 from each side.
$23 = x$	Divide each side by 6.

Evaluate the given expressions when $x = 23$.

$m\angle LKM = (2x + 10)° = (2 \cdot 23 + 10)° = 56°$

$m\angle MKN = (4x - 3)° = (4 \cdot 23 - 3)° = 89°$

▶ So, $m\angle LKM = 56°$ and $m\angle MKN = 89°$.

In-Class Practice

Self-Assessment

Find the indicated angle measures.

8. Given that ∠KLM is a straight angle, find $m\angle KLN$ and $m\angle NLM$.

9. Given that ∠EFG is a right angle, find $m\angle EFH$ and $m\angle HFG$.

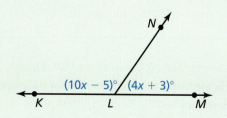

| **1** I don't understand yet. | **2** I can do it with help. | **3** I can do it on my own. | **4** I can teach someone. |

Bisecting Angles

An **angle bisector** is a ray that divides an angle into two angles that are congruent. In the figure, $\overrightarrow{YW}$ bisects $\angle XYZ$, so $\angle XYW \cong \angle ZYW$.

You can use a compass and straightedge to bisect an angle.

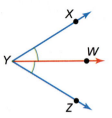

Construction

Bisecting an Angle

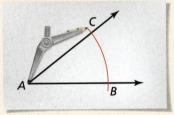 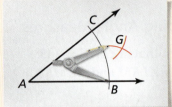 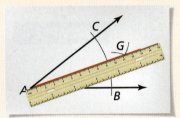

Draw an arc with center A that intersects both sides of $\angle A$. Label the intersections B and C.

Draw arcs with centers C and B using the same radius. Label the intersection G.

Draw a ray, $\overrightarrow{AG}$. $\overrightarrow{AG}$ bisects $\angle A$.

EXAMPLE 5 Using a Bisector to Find Angle Measures

$\overrightarrow{QS}$ bisects $\angle PQR$, and $m\angle PQS = 24°$. Find $m\angle PQR$.

Draw a diagram.

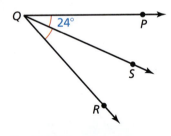

Because $\overrightarrow{QS}$ bisects $\angle PQR$, $m\angle PQS = m\angle RQS$. So, $m\angle RQS = 24°$. Use the Angle Addition Postulate to find $m\angle PQR$.

$m\angle PQR = m\angle PQS + m\angle RQS$	Angle Addition Postulate
$= 24° + 24°$	Substitute angle measures.
$= 48°$	Add.

▸ So, $m\angle PQR = 48°$.

In-Class Practice

Self-Assessment

10. Angle MNP is a straight angle, and $\overrightarrow{NQ}$ bisects $\angle MNP$. Draw $\angle MNP$ and $\overrightarrow{NQ}$. Use matching arcs to indicate congruent angles in your diagram. Find the angle measures of these congruent angles.

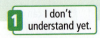

1.5 Practice

Write three names for the angle.

1.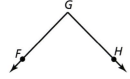

2.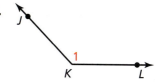

Name three different angles in the diagram. (See Example 1.)

3.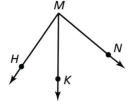

4.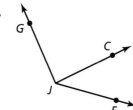

Find the angle measure. Then classify the angle. (See Example 2.)

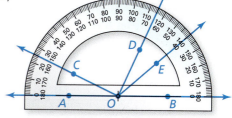

5. $m\angle BOD$

6. $m\angle AOE$

7. $m\angle COE$

8. $m\angle COD$

SMP.3 ERROR ANALYSIS Describe and correct the error in finding the angle measure in the diagram at the right.

9.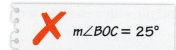

10.

CONSTRUCTION Use a compass and straightedge to copy the angle.

11.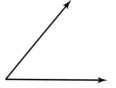

12.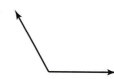

In the diagram, $m\angle AED = 34°$ and $m\angle EAD = 112°$. (See Example 3.)

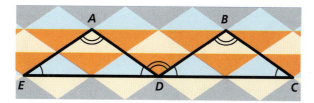

13. Identify the angles congruent to $\angle AED$.

14. Identify the angles congruent to $\angle EAD$.

15. Find $m\angle BDC$.

16. Find $m\angle ADB$.

1.5 Measuring and Constructing Angles   41

Find the indicated angle measure.

17. Find $m\angle ABC$.

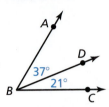

18. $\angle GHK$ is a straight angle. Find $m\angle LHK$.

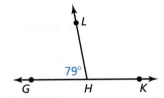

Find the indicated angle measures. (See Example 4.)

19. $m\angle ABC = 95°$. Find $m\angle ABD$ and $m\angle DBC$.

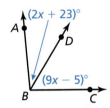

20. $m\angle XYZ = 117°$. Find $m\angle XYW$ and $m\angle WYZ$.

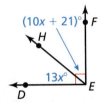

21. $\angle LMN$ is a straight angle. Find $m\angle LMP$ and $m\angle NMP$.

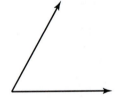

22. Find $m\angle DEH$ and $m\angle FEH$.

CONSTRUCTION Copy the angle. Then construct the angle bisector with a compass and straightedge.

23.

24.

25. CONNECTION TO REAL LIFE The map shows the intersections of three roads. Malcom Way intersects Sydney Street at an angle of 162°. Park Road intersects Sydney Street at an angle of 87°. Find the angle at which Malcom Way intersects Park Road.

26. In the sculpture shown, the measure of $\angle LMN$ is 76°, and the measure of $\angle PMN$ is 36°. What is the measure of $\angle LMP$?

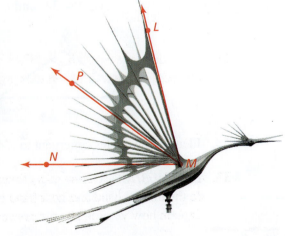

$\overrightarrow{FH}$ **bisects** ∠*EFG*. **Find the indicated angle measures.** (See Example 5.)

27. *m*∠*EFH* = 63°. Find *m*∠*GFH* and *m*∠*EFG*.

28. *m*∠*GFH* = 71°. Find *m*∠*EFH* and *m*∠*EFG*.

▶ **29.** *m*∠*EFG* = 124°. Find *m*∠*EFH* and *m*∠*GFH*.

30. *m*∠*EFG* = 119°. Find *m*∠*EFH* and *m*∠*GFH*.

$\overrightarrow{BD}$ **bisects** ∠*ABC*. **Find** *m*∠*ABD*, *m*∠*CBD*, **and** *m*∠*ABC*.

31.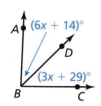

32. *m*∠*ABC* = (2 − 16*x*)°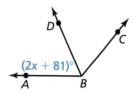

33. In the diagram of the roof truss, ∠*DGF* is a straight angle, and $\overrightarrow{GB}$ bisects ∠*DGF*. Find *m*∠*DGE* and *m*∠*FGE*.

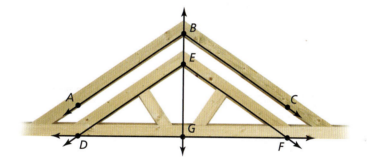

34. In a coordinate plane, the ray from the origin through (4, 0) forms one side of an angle. Use the numbers below as *x*- and *y*-coordinates to create each type of angle.

   a. acute angle   **b.** right angle   **c.** obtuse angle   **d.** straight angle

35. Classify the angles that result from bisecting each type of angle.

   a. acute angle   **b.** right angle   **c.** obtuse angle   **d.** straight angle

36. In the diagram, *m*∠*AGC* = 38°, *m*∠*CGD* = 71°, and *m*∠*FGC* = 147°. Find each angle measure.

   a. *m*∠*AGB*   **b.** *m*∠*DGF*

   c. *m*∠*AGF*   **d.** *m*∠*BGD*

37. **SMP.1 DIG DEEPER** How many times between 12 A.M. and 12 P.M. do the minute hand and hour hand of a clock form a right angle? Explain how you found your answer.

Interpreting Data

ROOF PITCH Roof pitch is the measure of a roof's vertical rise divided by its horizontal run. In the U.S., a run of 12 inches is used. Outside of the U.S., an angle is typically used.

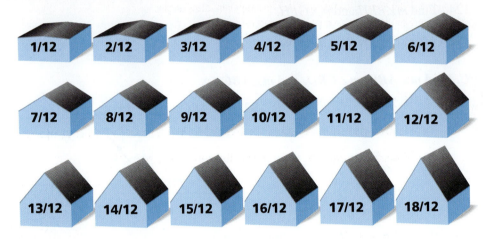

38. Describe several of the pitches above using an angle measure. Which angle did you use?

39. Explain how the pitch that is used for a roof affects the cost of building the roof.

40. Explain which pitches are best in snowy regions and which are best in regions with high winds.

Review & Refresh

41. Find the perimeter and the area of $\triangle ABC$ with vertices $A(-1, 1)$, $B(2, 1)$, and $C(1, -2)$.

42. Point Y is between points X and Z on $\overline{XZ}$. $XY = 27$ and $YZ = 8$. Find XZ.

Solve the equation.

43. $3x + 15 + 4x - 9 = 90$

44. $3(6 - 8x) = 2(-12x + 9)$

Simplify the expression.

45. $\sqrt{160}$

46. $\sqrt[3]{135}$

47. $\sqrt{\dfrac{21}{100}}$

48. $\dfrac{\sqrt{11}}{\sqrt{5}}$

49. Graph $y < -\dfrac{1}{3}x + 2$ in a coordinate plane.

50. Graph $y = \begin{cases} -x, & \text{if } x \leq -1 \\ 2x - 3, & \text{if } x > -1 \end{cases}$. Find the domain and range.

51. The positions of three players during a game are shown. Player A throws a ball to Player B, who then throws the ball to Player C.

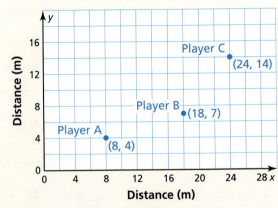

  a. Who throws the ball farther, Player A or B?

  b. How far is it from Player A to Player C?

Solve the system using any method.

52. $2x + 3y = 3$
     $x = y - 11$

53. $3x - 4y = 24$
     $-5x + 2y = -26$

1.6 Describing Pairs of Angles

> **Learning Target:** Identify and use pairs of angles.
>
> **Success Criteria:**
> - I can identify complementary and supplementary angles.
> - I can identify linear pairs and vertical angles.
> - I can find angle measures in pairs of angles.

INVESTIGATE Identifying Pairs of Angles

Work with a partner. A square is divided by its diagonals into four triangles.

1. What do you notice about the following angle pairs?

   $a°$ and $b°$

   $c°$ and $d°$

   $c°$ and $e°$

2. Find the values of the indicated variables. Do not use a protractor to measure the angles.

   $c =$

   $d =$

   $e =$

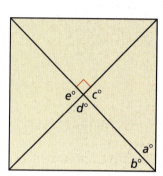

3. Explain how you obtained each answer in Exercise 2.

INVESTIGATE Identifying Pairs of Angles

Work with a partner. The five-pointed star has a regular pentagon at its center.

4. What do you notice about the following angle pairs?

   $x°$ and $y°$

   $y°$ and $z°$

   $x°$ and $z°$

5. Find the values of the indicated variables. Do not use a protractor to measure the angles.

   $x =$

   $y =$

   $z =$

   $w =$

   $v =$

6. Explain how you obtained each answer in Exercise 5.

Using Complementary and Supplementary Angles

Vocabulary
adjacent angles
complementary angles
supplementary angles
linear pair
vertical angles

Key Concept

Adjacent Angles

Adjacent angles are two angles that share a common vertex and side, but have no common interior points.

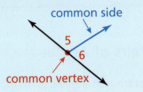
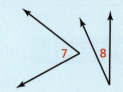

∠5 and ∠6 are adjacent angles. | ∠7 and ∠8 are *nonadjacent* angles.

Complementary and Supplementary Angles

The measures of **complementary angles** have a sum of 90°.

The measures of **supplementary angles** have a sum of 180°.

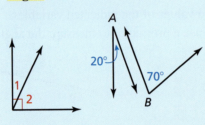
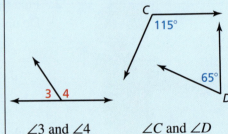

∠1 and ∠2   ∠A and ∠B | ∠3 and ∠4   ∠C and ∠D

EXAMPLE 1   **Identifying Pairs of Angles**

In the diagram, name a pair of adjacent angles, a pair of complementary angles, and a pair of supplementary angles.

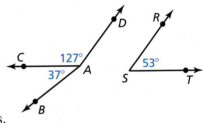

∠BAC and ∠CAD share a common vertex and side, but have no common interior points. So, they are adjacent angles.

Because 37° + 53° = 90°, ∠BAC and ∠RST are complementary angles.

Because 127° + 53° = 180°, ∠CAD and ∠RST are supplementary angles.

In-Class Practice

Self-Assessment

1. Name a pair of adjacent angles, a pair of complementary angles, and a pair of supplementary angles.

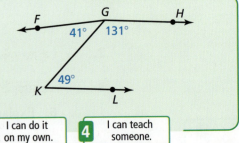

| **1** I don't understand yet. | **2** I can do it with help. | **3** I can do it on my own. | **4** I can teach someone. |

EXAMPLE 2 **Finding Angle Measures**

a. ∠1 is a complement of ∠2, and $m\angle 1 = 62°$. Find $m\angle 2$.

Draw a diagram with complementary adjacent angles to illustrate the relationship.

$m\angle 2 = 90° - m\angle 1 = 90° - 62° = 28°$

b. ∠3 is a supplement of ∠4, and $m\angle 4 = 47°$. Find $m\angle 3$.

Draw a diagram with supplementary adjacent angles to illustrate the relationship.

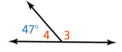

$m\angle 3 = 180° - m\angle 4 = 180° - 47° = 133°$

EXAMPLE 3 **Finding Angle Measures**

When viewed from the side, the frame of a ball-return net forms a pair of supplementary angles with the ground. Find $m\angle BCE$ and $m\angle ECD$.

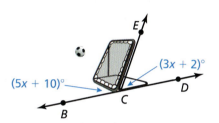

Use the fact that the sum of the measures of supplementary angles is 180°.

$m\angle BCE + m\angle ECD = 180°$	Write an equation.
$(5x + 10)° + (3x + 2)° = 180°$	Substitute angle measures.
$8x + 12 = 180$	Combine like terms.
$x = 21$	Solve for x.

Evaluate the given expressions when $x = 21$.

$m\angle BCE = (5x + 10)° = (5 \cdot 21 + 10)° = 115°$

$m\angle ECD = (3x + 2)° = (3 \cdot 21 + 2)° = 65°$

▶ So, $m\angle BCE = 115°$ and $m\angle ECD = 65°$.

In-Class Practice

Self-Assessment

2. ∠1 is a complement of ∠2, and $m\angle 2 = 5°$. Find $m\angle 1$.

3. ∠3 is a supplement of ∠4, and $m\angle 3 = 148°$. Find $m\angle 4$.

1 I don't understand yet.   **2** I can do it with help.   **3** I can do it on my own.   **4** I can teach someone.

1.6 Describing Pairs of Angles

Using Other Angle Pairs

Key Concept

Linear Pairs and Vertical Angles

Two adjacent angles are a **linear pair** when their noncommon sides are opposite rays. The angles in a linear pair are supplementary angles.

∠1 and ∠2 are a linear pair.

Two angles are **vertical angles** when their sides form two pairs of opposite rays.

∠3 and ∠6 are vertical angles.
∠4 and ∠5 are vertical angles.

EXAMPLE 4 Identifying Angle Pairs

Identify all the linear pairs and all the vertical angles in the diagram.

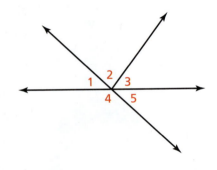

To find linear pairs, look for adjacent angles whose noncommon sides are opposite rays.

▶ ∠1 and ∠4 are a linear pair. ∠4 and ∠5 are also a linear pair.

To find vertical angles, look for pairs of opposite rays.

▶ ∠1 and ∠5 are vertical angles.

In-Class Practice

Self-Assessment

4. Identify all the linear pairs and all the vertical angles in the diagram.

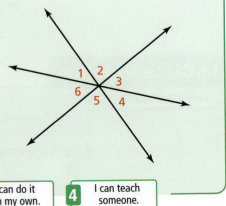

1 I don't understand yet. **2** I can do it with help. **3** I can do it on my own. **4** I can teach someone.

Chapter 1 Basics of Geometry

EXAMPLE 5 Finding Angle Measures in a Linear Pair

Two angles form a linear pair. The measure of one angle is five times the measure of the other angle. Find the measure of each angle.

Draw a diagram. Let $x°$ be the measure of one angle. The measure of the other angle is $5x°$.

Use the fact that the angles of a linear pair are supplementary to write an equation.

$x° + 5x° = 180°$	Write an equation.
$6x = 180$	Combine like terms.
$x = 30$	Divide each side by 6.

▶ The measures of the angles are 30° and 5(30°) = 150°.

Concept Summary

Interpreting a Diagram

There are some things you can conclude from a diagram, and some you cannot. For example, here are some things you *can* conclude from the diagram.

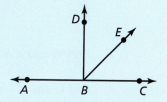

YOU CAN CONCLUDE

- All points shown are coplanar.
- Points A, B, and C are collinear, and B is between A and C.
- $\overleftrightarrow{AC}$, $\overrightarrow{BD}$, and $\overrightarrow{BE}$ intersect at point B.
- $\angle DBE$ and $\angle EBC$ are adjacent angles, and $\angle ABC$ is a straight angle.
- Point E lies in the interior of $\angle DBC$.

Here are some things you *cannot* conclude from the diagram above.

YOU CANNOT CONCLUDE

- $\overline{AB} \cong \overline{BC}$
- $\angle DBE \cong \angle EBC$
- $\angle ABD$ is a right angle.

To make such conclusions, the information in the diagram at the right must be given.

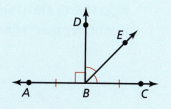

In-Class Practice

Self-Assessment

5. Two angles form a linear pair. The measure of one angle is $1\frac{1}{2}$ times the measure of the other angle. Find the measure of each angle.

 I don't understand yet.   I can do it with help.   I can do it on my own.   I can teach someone.

1.6 Practice

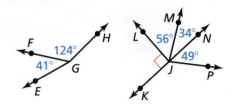

Use the diagrams. (See Example 1.)

1. Name a pair of adjacent complementary angles.

2. Name a pair of nonadjacent complementary angles.

Find the angle measure. (See Example 2.)

3. $\angle 1$ is a complement of $\angle 2$, and $m\angle 1 = 23°$. Find $m\angle 2$.

4. $\angle 7$ is a supplement of $\angle 8$, and $m\angle 7 = 109°$. Find $m\angle 8$.

Find the measure of each angle. (See Example 3.)

5.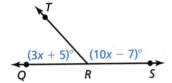

6.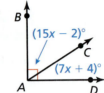

7. $\angle UVW$ and $\angle XYZ$ are complementary angles, $m\angle UVW = (x - 10)°$, and $m\angle XYZ = (4x - 10)°$.

8. $\angle EFG$ and $\angle LMN$ are supplementary angles, $m\angle EFG = (3x + 17)°$, and $m\angle LMN = \left(\frac{1}{2}x - 5\right)°$.

Use the diagram. (See Example 4.)

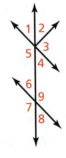

9. Identify all the linear pairs that include $\angle 1$.

10. Identify all the linear pairs that include $\angle 7$.

11. Are $\angle 6$ and $\angle 8$ vertical angles?

12. Are $\angle 2$ and $\angle 5$ vertical angles?

SMP.3 ERROR ANALYSIS Describe and correct the error in identifying pairs of angles in the diagram.

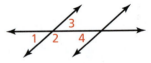

13.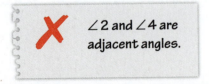

14.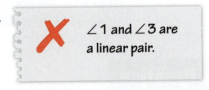

Find the measure of each angle. (See Example 5.)

15. Two angles form a linear pair. The measure of one angle is twice the measure of the other angle.

16. The measure of an angle is $\frac{1}{4}$ the measure of its complement.

50   Chapter 1   Basics of Geometry

CONNECTION TO REAL LIFE The picture shows the Alamillo Bridge in Seville, Spain. In the picture, $m\angle 1 = 58°$ and $m\angle 2 = 24°$.

STEM Video: Alamillo Bridge

17. Find the measure of the supplement of $\angle 1$.

18. Find the measure of the supplement of $\angle 2$.

19. CONSTRUCTION Construct a linear pair where one angle measure is 115°.

20. CONSTRUCTION Construct a pair of adjacent angles that have angle measures of 45° and 97°.

CONNECT CONCEPTS Write and solve an algebraic equation to find the measure of each angle described.

21. The measure of an angle is 3° more than $\frac{1}{2}$ the measure of its supplement.

22. Two angles form a linear pair. The measure of one angle is 15° less than $\frac{2}{3}$ the measure of the other angle.

23. Determine whether you can conclude each statement from the diagram. Explain your reasoning.

   a. $\overline{CA} \cong \overline{AF}$
   b. Points C, A, and F are collinear.
   c. $\angle CAD \cong \angle EAF$
   d. $\overline{BA} \cong \overline{AE}$
   e. $\angle DAE$ is a right angle.

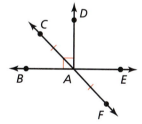

24. **SMP.7** $\angle KJL$ and $\angle LJM$ are complements, and $\angle MJN$ and $\angle LJM$ are complements. Explain whether you can show that $\angle KJL \cong \angle MJN$.

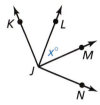

25. CONNECT CONCEPTS Let $m\angle 1 = x°$, $m\angle 2 = y°$, and $m\angle 3 = z°$. $\angle 2$ is the complement of $\angle 1$, and $\angle 3$ is the supplement of $\angle 1$.

   a. Write equations for y as a function of x and z as a function of x. What is the domain of each function? Explain.
   b. Graph each function and find its range.

1.6   Describing Pairs of Angles

Interpreting Data

n-POINTED STARS Star shapes are named by the number of points they contain. Several stars are shown below. Each star's points are all congruent, and have the same angle measures.

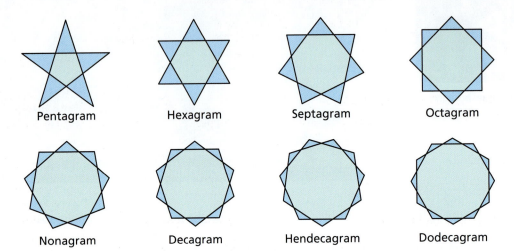

Pentagram   Hexagram   Septagram   Octagram

Nonagram   Decagram   Hendecagram   Dodecagram

26. Find the internal angle measure of each point on (a) a pentagram and (b) a hexagram.

27. **SMP.8** Continue to find the internal angle measures of the points of n-pointed stars for n = 7, 8, 9, 10, 11, and 12. Describe the pattern.

28. Are any of the internal angle measures of the stars complements or supplements to the internal angle measures of other stars?

Review & Refresh

Find the area of the polygon with the given vertices.

29. $K(-3, 4)$, $L(1, 4)$, $M(-4, -2)$, $N(0, -2)$

30. $X(-1, 2)$, $Y(-1, -3)$, $Z(4, -3)$

31. The midpoint of $\overline{JK}$ is $M(0, 1)$. One endpoint is $J(-6, 3)$. Find the coordinates of endpoint K.

32. Identify the segment bisector of $\overline{RS}$. Then find RS.

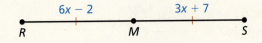

Solve the equation. Graph the solution(s), if possible.

33. $|t + 5| = 3$

34. $\left|\frac{1}{4}d - 1\right| + 2 = 5$

35. Given that $m\angle EFG = 126°$, find $m\angle EFH$ and $m\angle HFG$.

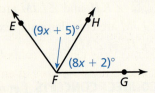

Find the slope and the y-intercept of the graph of the linear equation.

36. $y = -5x + 2$

37. $y + 7 = \frac{3}{2}x$

1 Chapter Review

Rate your understanding of each section.

1 I don't understand yet. 2 I can do it with help. 3 I can do it on my own. 4 I can teach someone.

1.1 Points, Lines, and Planes (pp. 3–10)

Learning Target: Use defined terms and undefined terms.

Vocabulary
undefined terms
point
line
plane
collinear points
coplanar points
defined terms
line segment, or segment
endpoints
ray
opposite rays
intersection

Use the diagram.

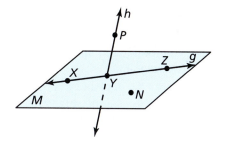

1. Give another name for plane M.
2. Name a line in plane M.
3. Name a line intersecting plane M.
4. Name two rays.
5. Name a pair of opposite rays.
6. Name a point not in plane M.
7. Is it possible for the intersection of two planes to be a segment? a line? a ray? Sketch the possible situations.

1.2 Measuring and Constructing Segments (pp. 11–18)

Learning Target: Measure and construct line segments.

Vocabulary
construction
postulate
axiom
coordinate
distance between two points
congruent segments
between

Find XZ.

8.

9.

10. Plot $A(8, -4)$, $B(3, -4)$, $C(7, 1)$, and $D(7, -3)$ in a coordinate plane. Then determine whether $\overline{AB}$ and $\overline{CD}$ are congruent.

11. You pass by school and the library on a walk from home to the bookstore, as shown below. How far from school is the library? How long does it take you to walk from home to the bookstore at an average speed of 68 meters per minute?

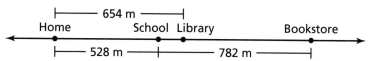

Chapter 1   Chapter Review   53

1.3 Using Midpoint and Distance Formulas (pp. 19–26)

Learning Target: Find midpoints and lengths of segments.

Vocabulary
midpoint
segment bisector

The endpoints of $\overline{ST}$ are given. Find the coordinates of the midpoint M. Then find the length of $\overline{ST}$.

12. $S(-2, 4)$ and $T(3, 9)$

13. $S(6, -3)$ and $T(7, -2)$

14. The midpoint of $\overline{JK}$ is $M(6, 3)$. One endpoint is $J(14, 9)$. Find the coordinates of endpoint K.

15. Point M is the midpoint of $\overline{AB}$, where $AM = 3x + 8$ and $MB = 6x - 4$. Find AB.

16. The coordinate plane shows distances (in feet) on a standard little league baseball infield. The pitcher's plate is about 3.5 feet farther from home plate than the midpoint between home plate and second base is to home plate. Estimate the distance between home plate and the pitcher's plate. Explain how you found your answer.

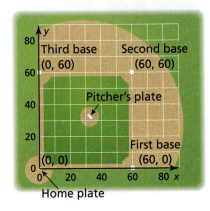

17. The endpoints of $\overline{DE}$ are $D(-3, y)$ and $E(x, 6)$. The midpoint of $\overline{DE}$ is $M(4, 2)$. What is the length of $\overline{DE}$?

1.4 Perimeter and Area in the Coordinate Plane (pp. 27–34)

Learning Target: Find perimeters and areas of polygons in the coordinate plane.

Classify the polygon by the number of sides. Tell whether it is *convex* or *concave*.

18.

19.

Find the perimeter and area of the polygon with the given vertices.

20. $W(5, 6)$, $X(5, -1)$, $Y(2, -1)$, $Z(2, 6)$

21. $E(6, -2)$, $F(6, 5)$, $G(-1, 5)$

22. Two polygons are shown. Compare the area and perimeter of the concave polygon with the area and perimeter of the convex polygon.

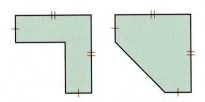

23. Find the perimeter of quadrilateral $RSTU$ in the coordinate plane at the right.

24. Find the area of quadrilateral $RSTU$.

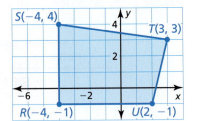

1.5 Measuring and Constructing Angles (pp. 35–44)

Learning Target: Measure, construct, and describe angles.

Vocabulary
acute angle
right angle
obtuse angle
straight angle
angle
vertex
sides of an angle
interior of an angle
exterior of an angle
measure of an angle
congruent angles
angle bisector

Find $m\angle ABD$ and $m\angle CBD$.

25. $m\angle ABC = 77°$

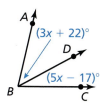

26. $m\angle ABC = 111°$

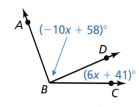

27. Find the measure of the angle using a protractor.

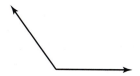

28. Given that P is in the interior of $\angle ABC$, $m\angle PBC = 30°$, $\angle DBC$ is a right angle, and $m\angle ABD = 26°$, what are the possible measures of $\angle ABP$?

1.6 Describing Pairs of Angles (pp. 45–52)

Learning Target: Identify and use pairs of angles.

Vocabulary
adjacent angles
complementary angles
supplementary angles
linear pair
vertical angles

$\angle 1$ and $\angle 2$ are complementary angles. Given $m\angle 1$, find $m\angle 2$.

29. $m\angle 1 = 12°$

30. $m\angle 1 = 83°$

$\angle 3$ and $\angle 4$ are supplementary angles. Given $m\angle 3$, find $m\angle 4$.

31. $m\angle 3 = 116°$

32. $m\angle 3 = 56°$

33. Construct a linear pair, where one angle measure is 35°. Label the measures of both angles.

34. The measure of an angle is 4 times the measure of its supplement. Find the measures of both angles.

35. Find the measures of $\angle ADB$ and $\angle BDC$ formed between the escalators.

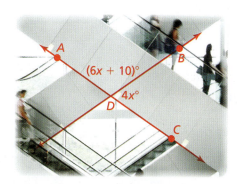

1 PERFORMANCE TASK
SMP.4 SMP.5

Tiger Tales

Conflict between humans and wild animals is a major threat to both humans and animals. Causes of human-tiger conflict include the following:

- **WILD PREY AVAILABILITY**
- **HABITAT AVAILABILITY**
- **HUMAN BEHAVIOR**
- **IMPROPER LIVESTOCK MANAGEMENT**
- **SOCIOECONOMIC FACTORS**

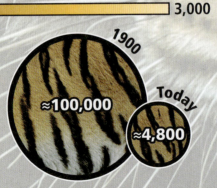

Estimated Wild Tiger Populations

- India: 3,000
- Russia: 500
- Indonesia: 400
- Nepal: 350
- Malaysia: 300
- Other: 250

1900: ≈100,000
Today: ≈4,800

The wild tiger population has decreased about 95% since 1900.

Analyzing Data

Use the information on the previous page to complete the following exercises.

1. Explain what is shown in the data display. What do you notice? What do you wonder?

2. Construct a circle graph that represents the data in the display.

3. Are any of the angles in your circle graph supplementary? complementary?

WILDLIFE REFUGE

You propose a new wildlife refuge in an attempt to limit human-tiger conflict. Use points and line segments to sketch the outline of your refuge in a coordinate plane. Name each point and line segment in your sketch.

A local government requires several details before considering your proposal. Provide the following information:
- the length of each side of the refuge
- the area of the refuge
- the measures of the angles formed by the sides of the refuge
- the coordinates of at least three gates, located at midpoints of the sides of the refuge

2 Reasoning and Proofs

2.1 Conditional Statements
2.2 Inductive and Deductive Reasoning
2.3 Postulates and Diagrams
2.4 Algebraic Reasoning
2.5 Proving Statements about Segments and Angles
2.6 Proving Geometric Relationships

NATIONAL GEOGRAPHIC EXPLORER
Caroline Quanbeck — GEOLOGIST

Caroline Quanbeck is a geologist whose research aims to reconstruct the evolution of sea level rise in Western Australia during the Last Interglacial, a warm period 125,000 years ago when temperatures were similar to today but global average sea level was 20 to 30 feet higher.

- What causes rising sea levels?
- Explain some of the effects of rising sea levels on coastal communities.

PERFORMANCE TASK

Greenhouse gases are major contributors to climate change. In the Performance Task on pages 112 and 113, you will see how greenhouse gases warm the planet. Then you will research some of the effects of climate change and write conditional statements based on your research.

Climate Change

Big Idea of the Chapter
Understand Deductive and Inductive Reasoning

Deductive reasoning begins with a hypothesis that is proven through logic. Inductive reasoning extracts a likely (but not certain) premise from specific observations.

Climate change refers to long-term shifts in temperatures and weather patterns. These changes occur naturally over time, but human activities have been the main cause of climate change since the 1800s. This is primarily due to the burning of fossil fuels, which produces heat-trapping gases. The graph shows how average global surface temperature has varied from 1880 to 2023.

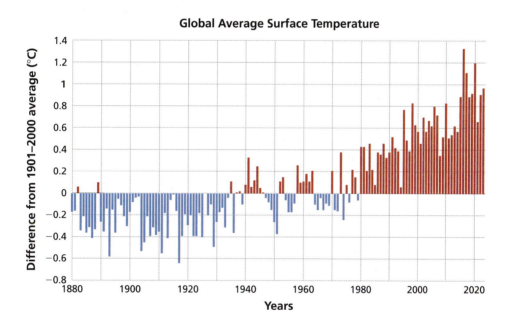

Use the graph to answer the questions.

1. You conclude that the average global surface temperature will continue to increase. Is this an example of deductive or inductive reasoning? Explain.

2. At any time, the highest and lowest temperatures on Earth are likely to vary by more than 55°C. How do you think scientists measure global average surface temperature?

3. What do you think humans can do to lessen the increase in the global average surface temperature?

Getting Ready for Chapter 2

Finding the nth Term of an Arithmetic Sequence

EXAMPLE 1 Write an equation for the nth term of the arithmetic sequence 2, 5, 8, 11, ... Then find a_{20}.

The first term is 2, and the common difference is 3.

$a_n = a_1 + (n - 1)d$ Equation for an arithmetic sequence

$a_n = 2 + (n - 1)3$ Substitute 2 for a_1 and 3 for d.

$a_n = 3n - 1$ Simplify.

Use the equation to find the 20th term.

$a_n = 3n - 1$ Write the equation.

$a_{20} = 3(20) - 1$ Substitute 20 for n.

$= 59$ Simplify.

▶ The 20th term of the arithmetic sequence is 59.

Write an equation for the nth term of the arithmetic sequence. Then find a_{50}.

1. 3, 9, 15, 21, . . .   **2.** $-29, -12, 5, 22, \ldots$ **3.** 2.8, 3.4, 4.0, 4.6, . . .

Rewriting Literal Equations

EXAMPLE 2 Solve the literal equation $3x + 6y = 24$ for y.

$3x + 6y = 24$ Write the equation.

$3x - 3x + 6y = 24 - 3x$ Subtraction Property of Equality

$6y = 24 - 3x$ Simplify.

$\dfrac{6y}{6} = \dfrac{24 - 3x}{6}$ Division Property of Equality

$y = 4 - \dfrac{1}{2}x$ Simplify.

▶ The rewritten literal equation is $y = 4 - \dfrac{1}{2}x$.

Solve the literal equation for x.

4. $2y - 2x = 10$ **5.** $20y + 5x = 15$

6. $4y - 5 = 4x + 7$ **7.** $y = 8x - x$

8. $y = 4x + zx + 6$ **9.** $z = 2x + 6xy$

2.1 Conditional Statements

Learning Target: Understand and write conditional statements.

Success Criteria:
- I can write conditional statements.
- I can write biconditional statements.
- I can determine if conditional statements are true by using truth tables.

A *conditional statement*, symbolized by $p \rightarrow q$, can be written as an "if-then statement" that contains a *hypothesis p* and a *conclusion q*. Here is an example.

If a polygon is a triangle, then the sum of its angle measures is 180°.

hypothesis, *p*   conclusion, *q*

INVESTIGATE Determining Whether Statements Are True or False

Work with a partner. A hypothesis can be either true or false. The same is true of a conclusion. When a conditional statement is true, the hypothesis and conclusion do not necessarily both have to be true. Determine whether each conditional statement is true or false. Justify your answer.

1. If yesterday was Wednesday, then today is Thursday.

2. If an angle is acute, then it has a measure of 30°.

3. If a month has 30 days, then it is June.

4. If an even number is not divisible by 2, then 9 is a perfect cube.

INVESTIGATE Determining Whether Statements Are True or False

Work with a partner. Use the points in the coordinate plane to determine whether each statement is true or false. Justify your answer.

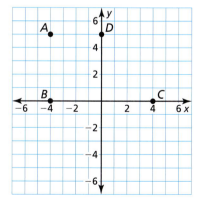

5. $\triangle ABC$ is a right triangle.

6. $\triangle BDC$ is an equilateral triangle.

7. $\triangle BDC$ is an isosceles triangle.

8. Quadrilateral $ABCD$ is a trapezoid.

9. Quadrilateral $ABCD$ is a parallelogram.

INVESTIGATE Determining Whether Statements Are True or False

Work with a partner. Determine whether each conditional statement is true or false. Justify your answer.

10. If $\triangle ADC$ is a right triangle, then the Pythagorean Theorem is valid for $\triangle ADC$.

11. If $\angle A$ and $\angle B$ are complementary, then the sum of their measures is 180°.

Vocabulary
conditional statement
if-then form
hypothesis
conclusion
negation
converse
inverse
contrapositive
equivalent statements
perpendicular lines
biconditional statement
truth value
truth table

Writing Conditional Statements

Key Concept

Conditional Statement

A **conditional statement** is a logical statement that has two parts, a *hypothesis p* and a *conclusion q*. When a conditional statement is written in **if-then form**, the "if" part contains the **hypothesis** and the "then" part contains the **conclusion**.

Words   If p, then q.   **Symbols** $p \rightarrow q$ (read as "p implies q")

Negation

The **negation** of a statement is the *opposite* of the original statement. To write the negation of a statement p, you write the symbol for negation ($\sim$) before the letter.

Words   not p **Symbols** $\sim p$ (read as "not p")

EXAMPLE 1   Rewriting a Statement in If-Then Form

Identify the hypothesis and the conclusion. Then rewrite the conditional statement in if-then form.

a. All birds have feathers.

   All birds have feathers.
   hypothesis   conclusion

   ▶ If an animal is a bird, then it has feathers.

b. You are in Texas if you are in Houston.

   You are in Texas if you are in Houston.
   conclusion   hypothesis

   ▶ If you are in Houston, then you are in Texas.

EXAMPLE 2   Writing a Negation

Write the negation of each statement.

a. The ball is red.

   ▶ The ball is not red.

b. The cat is not black.

   ▶ The cat is black.

In-Class Practice

Self-Assessment

Identify the hypothesis and the conclusion. Then rewrite the conditional statement in if-then form.

1. All 30° angles are acute angles.
2. $2x + 7 = 1$, because $x = -3$.

Write the negation of the statement.

3. The shirt is green.
4. The shoes are not red.

 I don't understand yet.   I can do it with help.   I can do it on my own.   I can teach someone.

62   Chapter 2   Reasoning and Proofs

> **Key Concept**
>
> ### Related Conditionals
>
> Consider the conditional statement below.
>
> **Words** If p, then q.   **Symbols** $p \to q$
>
> **Converse** To write the **converse** of a conditional statement, exchange the hypothesis and the conclusion.
>
> **Words** If q, then p.   **Symbols** $q \to p$
>
> **Inverse** To write the **inverse** of a conditional statement, negate both the hypothesis and the conclusion.
>
> **Words** If not p, then not q.   **Symbols** $\sim p \to \sim q$
>
> **Contrapositive** To write the **contrapositive** of a conditional statement, first write the converse. Then negate both the hypothesis and the conclusion.
>
> **Words** If not q, then not p.   **Symbols** $\sim q \to \sim p$
>
> A conditional statement and its contrapositive are either both true or both false. Similarly, the converse and inverse of a conditional statement are either both true or both false. In general, when two statements are both true or both false, they are called **equivalent statements**.

EXAMPLE 3 Writing Related Conditional Statements

Consider the conditional statement "If you are a guitar player, then you are a musician." Let p be the hypothesis and q be the conclusion. Write each statement in words. Then describe whether it is true or false.

a. the converse $q \to p$

Converse: If you are a musician, then you are a guitar player.
false; Not all musicians play the guitar.

b. the inverse $\sim p \to \sim q$

Inverse: If you are not a guitar player, then you are not a musician.
false; Even if you do not play the guitar, you can still be a musician.

c. the contrapositive $\sim q \to \sim p$

Contrapositive: If you are not a musician, then you are not a guitar player.
true; A person who is not a musician cannot be a guitar player.

In-Class Practice
Self-Assessment

5. Repeat Example 3 when p is "the stars are visible" and q is "it is night."

 I don't understand yet.   I can do it with help.   I can do it on my own.   I can teach someone.

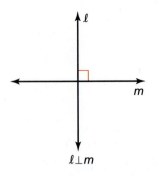

$\ell \perp m$

You can write a definition as a conditional statement in if-then form or as its converse. Both the conditional statement and its converse are true for definitions. For example, consider the definition of *perpendicular lines*.

If two lines intersect to form a right angle, then they are **perpendicular lines**.

You can also write the definition using the converse: If two lines are perpendicular lines, then they intersect to form a right angle.

You can write "line ℓ is perpendicular to line m" as $\ell \perp m$.

EXAMPLE 4 Using Definitions

Decide whether each statement about the diagram is true. Explain your answer using the definitions you have learned.

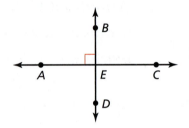

a. $\overleftrightarrow{AC} \perp \overleftrightarrow{BD}$

This statement is *true*. The right angle symbol in the diagram indicates that the lines intersect to form a right angle. So, you can say the lines are perpendicular.

b. $\angle AEB$ and $\angle CEB$ are a linear pair.

This statement is *true*. By definition, if the noncommon sides of adjacent angles are opposite rays, then the angles are a linear pair. Because $\overrightarrow{EA}$ and $\overrightarrow{EC}$ are opposite rays, $\angle AEB$ and $\angle CEB$ are a linear pair.

c. $\overrightarrow{EA}$ and $\overrightarrow{EB}$ are opposite rays.

This statement is *false*. The rays have the same endpoint, but they do not form a line. So, the rays are not opposite rays.

In-Class Practice

Self-Assessment

Decide whether the statement is true. Explain your answer using the definitions you have learned.

6. $\angle JMF$ and $\angle FMG$ are supplementary.

7. Point M is the midpoint of $\overline{FH}$.

8. $\angle JMF$ and $\angle HMG$ are vertical angles.

9. $\overleftrightarrow{FH} \perp \overleftrightarrow{JG}$

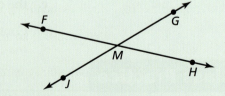

Writing Biconditional Statements

> ### Key Concept
>
> **Biconditional Statement**
>
> When a conditional statement and its converse are both true, you can write them as a single *biconditional statement*. A **biconditional statement** is a statement that contains the phrase "if and only if."
>
> **Words** p if and only if q **Symbols** $p \leftrightarrow q$
>
> Any definition can be written as a biconditional statement.

EXAMPLE 5 Writing a Biconditional Statement

Rewrite the definition of perpendicular lines as a biconditional statement.

Definition If two lines intersect to form a right angle, then they are perpendicular lines.

Let p be "two lines intersect to form a right angle," and let q be "they are perpendicular lines." Write the definition $p \rightarrow q$.

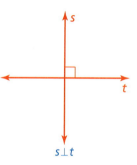

$s \perp t$

Definition If two lines intersect to form a right angle, then they are perpendicular lines.

Write the converse $q \rightarrow p$.

Converse If two lines are perpendicular lines, then they intersect to form a right angle.

Use the definition and its converse to write the biconditional statement $p \leftrightarrow q$.

▶ **Biconditional** Two lines intersect to form a right angle if and only if they are perpendicular lines.

In-Class Practice

Self-Assessment

10. Rewrite the definition of a right angle as a single biconditional statement.

   Definition If an angle is a right angle, then its measure is 90°.

11. Rewrite the statements as a biconditional statement:

   If you are taking theater class, then you will be in the fall play.
   If you are in the fall play, then you must be taking theater class.

2.1 Conditional Statements

Making Truth Tables

The **truth value** of a statement is either true (T) or false (F). You can determine the conditions under which a conditional statement is true by using a **truth table**. The truth table below shows the truth values for hypothesis p and conclusion q.

The conditional statement $p \rightarrow q$ is false only when a true hypothesis produces a false conclusion.

Two statements are *logically equivalent* when they have the same truth table.

Conditional		
p	q	$p \rightarrow q$
T	T	T
T	F	F
F	T	T
F	F	T

EXAMPLE 6 Making a Truth Table

Use the truth table above to make truth tables for the converse, inverse, and contrapositive of a conditional statement $p \rightarrow q$.

Converse		
p	q	$q \rightarrow p$
T	T	T
T	F	T
F	T	F
F	F	T

Inverse				
p	q	$\sim p$	$\sim q$	$\sim p \rightarrow \sim q$
T	T	F	F	T
T	F	F	T	T
F	T	T	F	F
F	F	T	T	T

Notice that the converse and the inverse are logically equivalent because they have the same truth table.

Contrapositive				
p	q	$\sim q$	$\sim p$	$\sim q \rightarrow \sim p$
T	T	F	F	T
T	F	T	F	F
F	T	F	T	T
F	F	T	T	T

Notice that a conditional statement and its contrapositive are logically equivalent because they have the same truth table.

In-Class Practice

Self-Assessment

Create a truth table for the logical statement.

12. $p \rightarrow \sim q$

13. $\sim(p \rightarrow q)$

2.1 Practice

Identify the hypothesis and the conclusion.

1. If you run, then you are fast.
2. If you like math, then you like science.

Rewrite the conditional statement in if-then form. (See Example 1.)

3. $9x + 5 = 23$, because $x = 2$.
4. Today is Friday, so tomorrow is the weekend.
5. When a glacier melts, the sea level rises.
6. Two right angles are supplementary angles.

Write the negation of the statement. (See Example 2.)

7. The sky is blue.
8. The lake is cold.
9. The ball is not pink.
10. The dog is not a Labrador retriever.

Write the conditional statement $p \to q$, the converse $q \to p$, the inverse $\sim p \to \sim q$, and the contrapositive $\sim q \to \sim p$ in words. Then decide whether each statement is *true* or *false*. (See Example 3.)

11. Let p be "two angles are supplementary," and let q be "the measures of the angles sum to 180°."

12. Let p be "you are not an only child," and let q be "you have a sibling."

13. Let p be "it does not snow," and let q be "I will run outside."

14. Let p be "the Sun is out," and let q be "it is daytime."

15. Let p be "$3x - 7 = 20$," and let q be "$x = 9$."

16. Let p be "it is Valentine's Day," and let q be "it is February."

Decide whether the statement about the diagram is true. Explain your answer using the definitions you have learned. (See Example 4.)

17. $m\angle ABC = 90°$

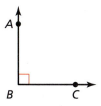

18. $\angle S \cong \angle T$

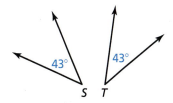

19. $m\angle 2 + m\angle 3 = 180°$

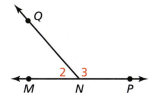

20. M is the midpoint of $\overline{AB}$.

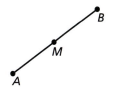

Rewrite the definition of the italicized term as a biconditional statement. (See Example 5.)

▶ **21.** The *midpoint* of a segment is the point that divides the segment into two congruent segments.

22. Two angles are *vertical angles* when their sides form two pairs of opposite rays.

23. *Adjacent angles* are two angles that share a common vertex and side but have no common interior points.

24. Two angles are *supplementary angles* when the sum of their measures is 180°.

Rewrite the statements as a biconditional statement.

25. If a polygon has three sides, then it is a triangle. If a polygon is a triangle, then it has three sides.

26. If a polygon has four sides, then it is a quadrilateral. If a polygon is a quadrilateral, then it has four sides.

Create a truth table for the logical statement. (See Example 6.)

▶ **27.** $\sim p \to q$ **28.** $\sim q \to p$ **29.** $\sim(\sim p \to \sim q)$

30. $\sim(p \to \sim q)$ **31.** $q \to \sim p$ **32.** $\sim(q \to p)$

33. **SMP.3 ERROR ANALYSIS** Describe and correct the error in writing the converse of the conditional statement.

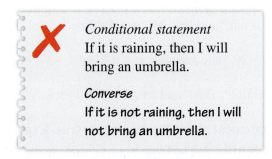

Conditional statement
If it is raining, then I will bring an umbrella.

Converse
If it is not raining, then I will not bring an umbrella.

34. You know that the contrapositive of a statement is true. Does that help you determine whether the statement can be rewritten as a true biconditional statement? Explain your reasoning.

35. **SMP.2** Use the conditional statement to identify the if-then statement as the converse, inverse, or contrapositive of the conditional statement. Then use the symbols to represent both statements.

Conditional statement
If I rode my bike to school, then I did not walk to school.

If-then statement
If I did not ride my bike to school, then I walked to school.

36. CONNECT CONCEPTS Explain whether the statement "If $x = 4$, then $x^2 - 10 = x + 2$" can be combined with its converse to form a true biconditional statement.

37. The Venn diagram represents all the musicians at a high school. Write three conditional statements in if-then form describing the relationships between the various groups of musicians.

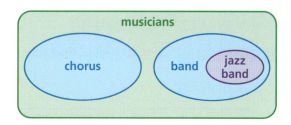

38. **SMP.4** Create a Venn diagram representing each conditional statement. Write the converse of each conditional statement. Then explain whether each conditional statement and its converse are true or false.

   a. If you see a lion at the zoo, then you will see a cat.

   b. If you play a sport, then you wear a helmet.

   c. If this month has 31 days, then it is not February.

39. OPEN-ENDED Advertising slogans such as "Buy these shoes! They will make you a better athlete!" often imply conditional statements. Find an advertisement or write your own slogan. Then write it as a conditional statement.

40. Write a series of if-then statements that allow you to find the measure of each angle, given that $m\angle 1 = 90°$.

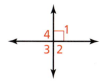

41. CONNECTION TO REAL LIFE The largest natural arch in the United States is Landscape Arch, located in Thompson, Utah. It spans 290 feet.

   a. Use the information to write at least two true conditional statements.

   b. Which type of related conditional statement must also be true? Write the related conditional statements.

   c. What are the other two types of related conditional statements? Write the related conditional statements. Then determine their truth values. Explain your reasoning.

42. One example of a true conditional statement involving dates is "If today is August 31, then tomorrow is September 1." Write a conditional statement using dates so that the truth value depends on when the statement is read.

43. **SMP.1 DIG DEEPER** Can the converse and the contrapositive of a conditional statement both have truth values that are false? Justify your answer.

Interpreting Data

LOGICAL FALLACIES A logical fallacy is an error in reasoning that makes an argument invalid. All logical fallacies are arguments in which a conclusion doesn't follow logically from what preceded it.

44. Research a causal fallacy. Then give an example of the fallacy in real life. How is a causal fallacy similar to content you learned in this section?

45. Research three other logical fallacies from the list shown. Then give a real-life example of each.

Circular Argument	Strawman Argument	Equivocation
Hasty Generalization	Appeal to Ignorance	Appeal to Pity
Red Herring Fallacy	False Dilemma	Bandwagon Fallacy
Appeal to Hypocrisy	Slippery Slope Fallacy	Appeal to Authority
Appeal to Tradition	Fallacy of Sunk Costs	Ad Hominem

Review & Refresh

46. Determine whether the graph represents a function.

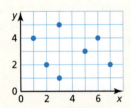

47. Find the measure of each angle.

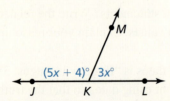

48. The average distance from Earth to the moon is 3.844×10^5 kilometers. Write this number in standard form.

49. In the diagram, $\overrightarrow{WY}$ bisects $\angle XWZ$, and $m\angle YWZ = 49°$. Find $m\angle XWY$ and $m\angle XWZ$.

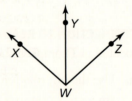

Perform the operation.

50. $3x^2(-x + 7)$

51. $(z - 1)(z + 8)$

52. $(5b^2 - 6b + 3) - (4b - 2)$

53. $(-4n^3 - n^2 + 8) + (6n^2 + 5n - 9)$

54. Write an inequality that represents the graph.

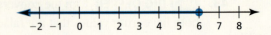

2.2 Inductive and Deductive Reasoning

Learning Target: Use inductive and deductive reasoning.

Success Criteria:
- I can use inductive reasoning to make conjectures.
- I can use deductive reasoning to verify conjectures.
- I can distinguish between inductive and deductive reasoning.

INVESTIGATE Writing a Conjecture

Work with a partner. A *conjecture* is an unproven statement based on observations. Write a conjecture about the pattern. Then use your conjecture to draw the 10th object in the pattern.

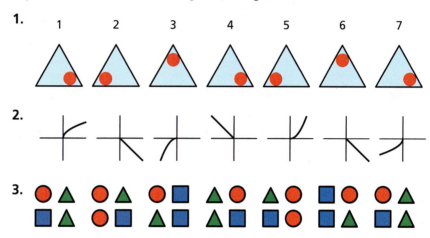

INVESTIGATE Using a Venn Diagram

Work with a partner. Use the Venn diagram to determine whether the statement is true or false. Assume that no region of the Venn diagram is empty.

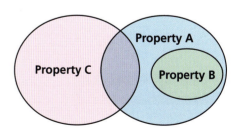

4. If an item has Property B, then it has Property A.

5. If an item has Property A, then it has Property B.

6. If an item has Property A, then it has Property C.

7. Some items that have Property A do not have Property B.

8. If an item has Property C, then it does not have Property B.

9. Some items have both Properties A and C.

10. Some items have both Properties B and C.

Vocabulary
conjecture
inductive reasoning
counterexample
deductive reasoning

Using Inductive Reasoning

Key Concept

Inductive Reasoning

A **conjecture** is an unproven statement that is based on observations. You use **inductive reasoning** when you find a pattern in specific cases and then write a conjecture for the general case.

EXAMPLE 1 Describing Visual Patterns

Describe how to sketch the fourth figure in each pattern. Then sketch the fourth figure.

a.

Each successive circle is divided into two more equal regions. Sketch the fourth figure by dividing a circle into eighths. Shade the section just above the horizontal segment at the left.

b.

  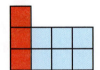

Each successive figure has one more column of blue squares. Sketch the fourth figure by adding a fourth column of blue squares.

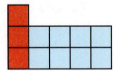

In-Class Practice

Self-Assessment

1. Describe how to sketch the fourth figure in the pattern. Then sketch the fourth figure.

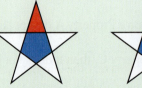

1 I don't understand yet. **2** I can do it with help. **3** I can do it on my own. **4** I can teach someone.

72 Chapter 2 Reasoning and Proofs

EXAMPLE 2   Making and Testing a Conjecture

Consecutive integers follow each other in order, such as 3, 4, and 5.
Make and test a conjecture about the sum of any three consecutive integers.

Find a pattern using a few groups of small numbers.

$3 + 4 + 5 = 12 = 4 \cdot 3$ $\qquad$ $7 + 8 + 9 = 24 = 8 \cdot 3$

$10 + 11 + 12 = 33 = 11 \cdot 3$ $\qquad$ $16 + 17 + 18 = 51 = 17 \cdot 3$

Make a conjecture.

Conjecture The sum of any three consecutive integers is three times the second number.

Test your conjecture using other numbers. For example, test that it works with the groups $-1, 0, 1$ and $100, 101, 102$.

$-1 + 0 + 1 = 0 = 0 \cdot 3$ ✓

$100 + 101 + 102 = 303 = 101 \cdot 3$ ✓

Key Concept

Counterexample

To show that a conjecture is true, you must show that it is true for all cases. To show that a conjecture is false, find a *counterexample*. A **counterexample** is a specific case for which the conjecture is false.

EXAMPLE 3   Finding a Counterexample

A student makes the following conjecture about the sum of two numbers. Find a counterexample to disprove the student's conjecture.

Conjecture *The sum of two numbers is always more than the greater number.*

To find a counterexample, find a sum that is less than the greater number.

$-2 + (-3) = -5$

$-5 \not> -2$

▶ Because a counterexample exists, the conjecture is false.

In-Class Practice

Self-Assessment

2. Make and test a conjecture about the sum of any five consecutive integers.

3. Find a counterexample to show that the conjecture is false.
   Conjecture *The value of x^2 is always greater than the value of x.*

2.2   Inductive and Deductive Reasoning

Using Deductive Reasoning

> ### Key Concept
>
> **Deductive Reasoning**
>
> **Deductive reasoning** uses facts, definitions, accepted properties, and the laws of logic to form a logical argument.
>
> **Laws of Logic**
>
> **Law of Detachment**
>
> If the hypothesis of a true conditional statement is true, then the conclusion is also true.
>
> **Law of Syllogism**
>
> If hypothesis p, then conclusion q.
> If hypothesis q, then conclusion r. } If these statements are true,
>
> If hypothesis p, then conclusion r. ← then this statement is true.

EXAMPLE 4 Using the Law of Detachment

If two segments have the same length, then they are congruent. You know that $BC = XY$. Use the Law of Detachment to make a statement.

Because $BC = XY$ satisfies the hypothesis of a true conditional statement, the conclusion is also true.

▶ So, $\overline{BC} \cong \overline{XY}$.

EXAMPLE 5 Using the Law of Syllogism

Use the Law of Syllogism to write a new conditional statement that follows from the pair of true statements.

If $x^2 > 25$, then $x^2 > 20$.   If $x > 5$, then $x^2 > 25$.

The conclusion of the second statement is the hypothesis of the first statement. So, you can write the following new statement.

▶ If $x > 5$, then $x^2 > 20$.

In-Class Practice

Self-Assessment

4. If $90° < m\angle R < 180°$, then $\angle R$ is obtuse. The measure of $\angle R$ is 155°. Use the Law of Detachment to make a statement.

5. Use the Law of Syllogism to write a new conditional statement that follows from the pair of true statements.

   If you get an A on your math test, then you can go to the movies.
   If you go to the movies, then you can watch your favorite actor.

EXAMPLE 6 Using Inductive and Deductive Reasoning

What conclusion can you make about the product of an even integer and any other integer?

Look for a pattern in several examples. Use inductive reasoning to make a conjecture.

$(-2)(2) = -4$ $(-1)(2) = -2$ $2(2) = 4$ $3(2) = 6$

$(-2)(-4) = 8$ $(-1)(-4) = 4$ $2(-4) = -8$ $3(-4) = -12$

Conjecture Even integer • Any integer = Even integer

Let n and m each be any integer. Use deductive reasoning to show that the conjecture is true.

$2n$ is an even integer because any integer multiplied by 2 is even.

$2nm$ represents the product of an even integer $2n$ and any integer m.

$2nm$ is the product of 2 and an integer nm. So, $2nm$ is an even integer.

▶ The product of an even integer and any integer is an even integer.

EXAMPLE 7 Comparing Inductive and Deductive Reasoning

Decide whether inductive reasoning or deductive reasoning is used to reach each conclusion.

a. **Each time Monica kicks a ball up in the air, it returns to the ground. So, the next time Monica kicks a ball up in the air, it will return to the ground.**

Inductive reasoning, because a pattern is used to reach the conclusion.

b. **All reptiles are cold-blooded. Parrots are not cold-blooded. Sue's pet parrot is not a reptile.**

Deductive reasoning, because facts about animals and the laws of logic are used to reach the conclusion.

In-Class Practice

Self-Assessment

6. Use inductive reasoning to make a conjecture about the sum of a number and itself. Then use deductive reasoning to show that the conjecture is true.

7. Explain whether inductive reasoning or deductive reasoning is used to reach the conclusion.

   All multiples of 8 are divisible by 4.
   64 is a multiple of 8.
   So, 64 is divisible by 4.

2.2 Inductive and Deductive Reasoning

2.2 Practice

Describe the pattern. Then write or draw the next two numbers, letters, or figures. (See Example 1.)

1. 1, −2, 3, −4, 5, . . .

2. A, D, G, J, M, . . .

3.

4.

Make and test a conjecture about the given quantity. (See Example 2.)

5. the sum of an even integer and an odd integer

6. the product of any two even integers

7. the quotient of a number and its reciprocal

8. the quotient of two negative integers

Find a counterexample to show that the conjecture is false. (See Example 3.)

9. The product of two positive numbers is always greater than either number.

10. If n is a nonzero integer, then $\dfrac{n+1}{n}$ is always greater than 1.

11. If two angles are supplements of each other, then one of the angles must be acute.

12. **CLIMATE CHANGE GREENLAND** The graph shows the total mass loss of the Greenland ice sheet since 2002. Write a conjecture using the graph.

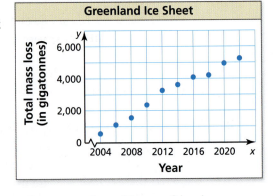

Use the Law of Detachment to determine what you can conclude from the given information, if possible. (See Example 4.)

13. If you download a GIF, then your device crashes. You download a GIF.

14. If your cousin lets you borrow a car, then you will go to the mountains with your friend. You will go to the mountains with your friend.

15. If a point divides a line segment into two congruent line segments, then the point is a midpoint. Point P divides $\overline{LH}$ into two congruent line segments.

Use the Law of Syllogism to write a new conditional statement that follows from the pair of true statements, if possible. (See Example 5.)

16. If $a = 3$, then $5a = 15$. If $\frac{1}{2}a = 1\frac{1}{2}$, then $a = 3$.

17. If $x < -2$, then $|x| > 2$. If $x > 2$, then $|x| > 2$.

18. If a figure is a rhombus, then the figure is a parallelogram. If a figure is a parallelogram, then the figure has two pairs of opposite sides that are parallel.

76   Chapter 2   Reasoning and Proofs

Use inductive reasoning to make a conjecture about the given quantity. Then use deductive reasoning to show that the conjecture is true. (See Example 6.)

19. the sum of two odd integers

20. the product of two odd integers

Explain whether inductive reasoning or deductive reasoning is used to reach the conclusion. (See Example 7.)

21. Each time you go to bed, you charge your electronic devices. So, the next time you go to bed, you will charge your electronic devices.

22. Even numbers are divisible by 2. Odd numbers are not divisible by 2. So, 4 is an even number.

23. All photosynthetic organisms produce oxygen. Phytoplankton are photosynthetic organisms. So, phytoplankton produce oxygen.

24. **CONNECTION TO REAL LIFE** The table shows the average weights of several subspecies of tigers. What conjecture can you make about the relation between the weights of female tigers and the weights of male tigers?

STEM Video: Tiger

	Weight of female (pounds)	Weight of male (pounds)
Siberian	370	660
Bengal	300	480
South China	240	330
Sumatran	200	270
Indo-Chinese	250	400

25. **SMP.7 OPEN-ENDED** The first two terms of a sequence are $\frac{1}{4}$ and $\frac{1}{2}$. Describe three different possible patterns for the sequence. List the first five terms for each sequence.

26. **SMP.8** Each figure is made of squares that are 1 unit by 1 unit. Predict the perimeter of the 20th figure.

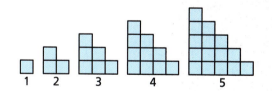

27. Geologists use the Mohs scale to determine a mineral's hardness. Using the scale, a mineral with a higher rating will leave a scratch on a mineral with a lower rating. Testing a mineral's hardness can help identify the mineral.

Mineral	Talc	Gypsum	Calcite	Fluorite
Mohs rating	1	2	3	4

a. The four minerals are randomly labeled A, B, C, and D. Mineral A is scratched by Mineral B. Mineral C is scratched by all three of the other minerals. What can you conclude?

b. How can you identify *all* the minerals in part (a)?

28. **CONNECT CONCEPTS** Use inductive reasoning to write a formula for the sum of the first n positive even integers.

Interpreting Data

SOLAR SYSTEM BODIES In 2006, the International Astronomical Union defined a planet to be a celestial body that

(1) orbits a star,

(2) has enough gravity to make it spherical, and

(3) has cleared away objects of similar size near its orbit.

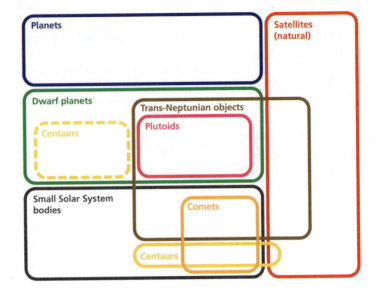

29. Determine whether each statement is true or false.

  a. If an object is a trans-Neptunian object, then it is a dwarf planet.

  b. If an object is a plutoid, then it is a dwarf planet.

30. Which of the three conditions for being a planet do you think Pluto does not satisfy?

Review & Refresh

31. Identify the hypothesis and the conclusion. Then rewrite the conditional statement in if-then form.

  Storm surge causes the erosion of coastline.

32. Classify the polygon by the number of sides. Tell whether it is *convex* or *concave*.

33. Write a recursive rule for the sequence.

n	1	2	3	4
a_n	4	11	18	25

34. Write an equation of the line that passes through the points (3, 2) and (0, 8).

35. $\angle 3$ is a complement of $\angle 4$, and $m\angle 3 = 19°$. Find $m\angle 4$.

36. Determine whether the equation $y = x^2 + 5$ represents a *linear* or *nonlinear* function.

37. Solve the equation $-6x + 5 = x - 9$.

38. Determine which postulate is illustrated by the statement $m\angle DAC = m\angle DAE + m\angle EAB$.

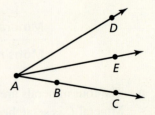

39. Find $(2n^2 - n - 6) + (-5n^2 - 4n + 8)$.

40. Solve $3^{x+4} = 3^8$.

2.3 Postulates and Diagrams

Learning Target: Interpret and sketch diagrams.

Success Criteria:
- I can identify postulates represented by diagrams.
- I can sketch a diagram given a verbal description.
- I can interpret a diagram.

INVESTIGATE Interpreting Diagrams

Work with a partner.

1. On a piece of paper, draw two perpendicular lines. Label them $\overleftrightarrow{AB}$ and $\overleftrightarrow{CD}$. Look at the diagram from different angles. Do the lines appear perpendicular regardless of the angle at which you look at them? Describe *all* the angles at which you can look at the lines and have them appear perpendicular.

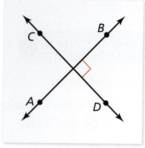
view from above

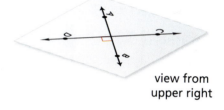
view from upper right

INVESTIGATE Interpreting a Diagram

SMP.6 Work with a partner.

2. When you draw a diagram, you are communicating with others. It is important that you include sufficient information in the diagram. Use the diagram below to determine which of the following statements you can assume to be true.

    a. Points *D*, *G*, and *I* are collinear.

    b. Points *A*, *C*, and *H* are collinear.

    c. $\overleftrightarrow{EG}$ and $\overleftrightarrow{AH}$ are perpendicular.

    d. $\overleftrightarrow{AF}$ and $\overleftrightarrow{BD}$ are perpendicular.

    e. $\overleftrightarrow{AF}$ and $\overleftrightarrow{BD}$ are coplanar.

    f. $\overleftrightarrow{EG}$ and $\overleftrightarrow{BD}$ do not intersect.

    g. $\overleftrightarrow{AF}$ and $\overleftrightarrow{BD}$ intersect.

    h. $\overleftrightarrow{AC}$ and $\overleftrightarrow{FH}$ are the same line.

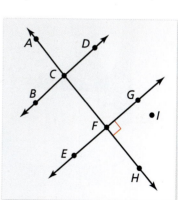

Vocabulary
line perpendicular to a plane

Identifying Postulates

Postulates 2.1 and 2.2

2.1 Two Point Postulate

Through any two points, there exists exactly one line.

2.2 Line-Point Postulate

A line contains at least two points.

Through points A and B, there is exactly one line ℓ. Line ℓ contains at least two points.

Postulate 2.3

Line Intersection Postulate

If two lines intersect, then their intersection is exactly one point.

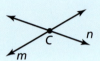

Postulates 2.4 and 2.5

2.4 Three Point Postulate

Through any three noncollinear points, there exists exactly one plane.

2.5 Plane-Point Postulate

A plane contains at least three noncollinear points.

Through points D, E, and F, there is exactly one plane, plane R. Plane R contains at least three noncollinear points.

Postulate 2.6

Plane-Line Postulate

If two points lie in a plane, then the line containing them lies in the plane.

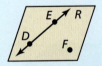

Points D and E lie in plane R, so $\overleftrightarrow{DE}$ lies in plane R.

Postulate 2.7

Plane Intersection Postulate

If two planes intersect, then their intersection is a line.

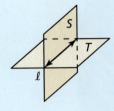

EXAMPLE 1 **Identifying a Postulate Using a Diagram**

State the postulate illustrated by the diagram.

a.

▶ **Line Intersection Postulate** If two lines intersect, then their intersection is exactly one point.

b.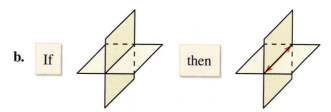

▶ **Plane Intersection Postulate** If two planes intersect, then their intersection is a line.

EXAMPLE 2 **Identifying Postulates from a Diagram**

Use the diagram to write examples of the Plane-Point Postulate and the Plane-Line Postulate.

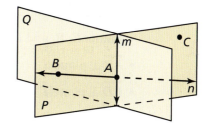

Plane-Point Postulate Plane P contains at least three noncollinear points, A, B, and C.

Plane-Line Postulate Point A and point B lie in plane P. So, line n containing points A and B also lies in plane P.

In-Class Practice

Self-Assessment

1. In the diagram in Example 2, which postulate allows you to say that the intersection of plane P and plane Q is a line?

2. Use the diagram in Example 2 to write an example of each postulate.
   a. Two Point Postulate
   b. Line-Point Postulate
   c. Line Intersection Postulate

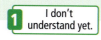

Sketching and Interpreting Diagrams

EXAMPLE 3 **Sketching a Diagram**

Sketch a diagram showing $\overleftrightarrow{TV}$ intersecting $\overline{PQ}$ at point W, so that $\overline{TW} \cong \overline{WV}$.

Draw $\overleftrightarrow{TV}$ and label points T and V.

Draw point W at the midpoint of $\overline{TV}$. Mark the congruent segments.

Draw $\overline{PQ}$ through W.

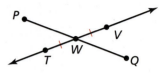

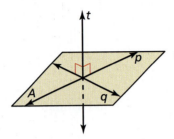

A line is a **line perpendicular to a plane** if and only if the line intersects the plane in a point and is perpendicular to every line in the plane that intersects it at that point.

In a diagram, a line perpendicular to a plane must be marked with a right angle symbol, as shown.

EXAMPLE 4 **Interpreting a Diagram**

Which of the following statements *cannot* be assumed from the diagram?

- Points A, B, and F are collinear.
- Points E, B, and D are collinear.
- $\overleftrightarrow{AB} \perp$ plane S
- $\overleftrightarrow{CD} \perp$ plane T
- $\overleftrightarrow{AF}$ intersects $\overleftrightarrow{BC}$ at point B.

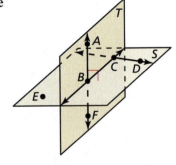

No drawn line connects points E, B, and D. So, you cannot assume they are collinear. With no right angle marked, you cannot assume $\overleftrightarrow{CD} \perp$ plane T.

In-Class Practice

Self-Assessment

Use the diagram in Example 3.

3. If it is given that $\overline{PW}$ and $\overline{QW}$ are congruent, how can you indicate this in the diagram?

4. Name a pair of supplementary angles in the diagram.

Use the diagram in Example 4.

5. Explain whether you can assume that plane S intersects plane T at $\overleftrightarrow{BC}$.

6. Explain how you know that $\overleftrightarrow{AB} \perp \overleftrightarrow{BC}$.

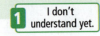

2.3 Practice

State the postulate illustrated by the diagram. (See Example 1.)

1.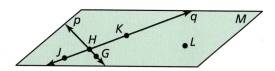

2. If [plane] then [plane with points A, B, C]

Use the diagram to write an example of the postulate. (See Example 2.)

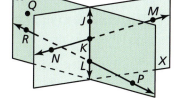

3. Line-Point Postulate

4. Line Intersection Postulate

5. Three Point Postulate

6. Plane-Line Postulate

Sketch a diagram of the description. (See Example 3.)

7. plane P and line m perpendicular to plane P

8. $\overline{XY}$ in plane P, $\overline{XY}$ bisected by point A, and point C not on $\overline{XY}$

9. $\overline{XY}$ intersecting $\overline{WV}$ at point A, so that $XA = VA$

10. $\overline{AB}$, $\overline{CD}$, and $\overline{EF}$ are all in plane P, and point X is the midpoint of all three segments.

SMP.6 **Use the diagram to determine whether you can assume the statement.** (See Example 4.)

11. Planes W and X intersect at $\overleftrightarrow{KL}$.

12. Points K, L, M, and N are coplanar.

13. $\overleftrightarrow{MN}$ and $\overleftrightarrow{RP}$ intersect.

14. $\angle PLK$ is a right angle.

15. $\angle NKJ$ and $\angle JKM$ are supplementary angles.

16. **CONNECT CONCEPTS** One way to graph a linear equation is to draw a line through two points whose coordinates satisfy the equation. Which postulate guarantees this works for any linear equation?

17. If two lines intersect, then they intersect in exactly one point by the Line Intersection Postulate. Do the two lines have to be in the same plane? Draw a picture to support your answer.

18. Points E, F, and G all lie in plane P and in plane Q. What must be true about points E, F, and G so that planes P and Q are different planes? What must be true about points E, F, and G to force planes P and Q to be the same plane? Make sketches to support your answers.

Interpreting Data

PERSPECTIVE IN ART In 1435, Leon Battista Alberti composed a theory of linear perspective in which he used mathematics to create art. Alberti's techniques had a large impact on European artists and is still used by artists today.

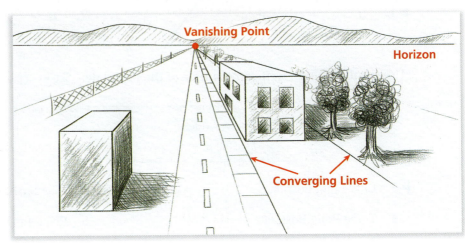

Prior to the 15th century, artists often made distant objects smaller and overlapped objects to create a sense of depth.

19. In real life, are converging lines intersecting or parallel?

20. In the drawing, are the converging lines intersecting or parallel?

21. Why does converging lines at a point on the horizon create an illusion of three dimensionality?

Review & Refresh

22. Find a counterexample to show that the conjecture is false.

If a figure has four sides, then it is a rectangle.

Solve the equation.

23. $t - 6 = -4$ **24.** $5 = \dfrac{x}{7}$

25. Find $m\angle 1$.

26. Find the perimeter and the area of $\square ABCD$ with vertices $A(3, 5)$, $B(6, 5)$, $C(4, -1)$, and $D(1, -1)$.

27. A locker in the shape of a rectangular prism has a width of 12 inches. Its height is four times its depth. The volume of the locker is 10,800 cubic inches. Find the height and depth of the locker.

28. Write the next three terms of the geometric sequence.

$\dfrac{5}{2}, 10, 40, 160, \ldots$

29. Rewrite the statements as a single biconditional statement.

If you can vote, then you are at least 18 years old. If you are at least 18 years old, then you can vote.

84 Chapter 2 Reasoning and Proofs

2.4 Algebraic Reasoning

Learning Target: Use properties of equality to solve problems.

Success Criteria:
- I can identify algebraic properties of equality.
- I can use algebraic properties of equality to solve equations.
- I can use properties of equality to solve for geometric measures.

INVESTIGATE Justifying Steps in a Solution

1. **Work with a partner.** In previous courses, you studied different properties, such as the properties of equality and the Distributive, Commutative, and Associative Properties. Write the property that justifies each of the following solution steps.

Algebraic Step	Justification
$2(x + 3) - 5 = 5x + 4$	Write given equation.
$2x + 6 - 5 = 5x + 4$	
$2x + 1 = 5x + 4$	
$2x - 2x + 1 = 5x - 2x + 4$	
$1 = 3x + 4$	
$1 - 4 = 3x + 4 - 4$	
$-3 = 3x$	
$\dfrac{-3}{3} = \dfrac{3x}{3}$	
$-1 = x$	
$x = -1$	

INVESTIGATE Justifying Steps in a Solution

2. **Work with a partner.** The symbols ♦ and • represent addition and multiplication (not necessarily in that order). Determine which symbol represents which operation. Justify your answer. Then state each algebraic property being illustrated.

Example of Property	Name of Property
$5 ♦ 6 = 6 ♦ 5$	
$4 • (5 • 6) = (4 • 5) • 6$	
$0 ♦ 5 = 0$	
$0 • 5 = 5$	
$1 ♦ 5 = 5$	
$4 ♦ (5 • 6) = 4 ♦ 5 • 4 ♦ 6$	

Using Algebraic Properties

Key Concept

Algebraic Properties

Let a, b, and c be real numbers.

Addition Property of Equality	If $a = b$, then $a + c = b + c$.
Subtraction Property of Equality	If $a = b$, then $a - c = b - c$.
Multiplication Property of Equality	If $a = b$, then $a \cdot c = b \cdot c$, $c \neq 0$.
Division Property of Equality	If $a = b$, then $\dfrac{a}{c} = \dfrac{b}{c}$, $c \neq 0$.
Substitution Property of Equality	If $a = b$, then a can be substituted for b (or b for a) in any equation or expression.
Distributive Property	**Sum** $\quad a(b + c) = ab + ac$
	Difference $\quad a(b - c) = ab - ac$

EXAMPLE 1 Justifying Steps

Solve $3x + 2 = 23 - 4x$. Justify each step.

Equation	Explanation	Reason
$3x + 2 = 23 - 4x$	Write the equation.	Given
$3x + 2 + 4x = 23 - 4x + 4x$	Add $4x$ to each side.	Addition Property of Equality
$7x + 2 = 23$	Combine like terms.	Simplify.
$7x + 2 - 2 = 23 - 2$	Subtract 2 from each side.	Subtraction Property of Equality
$7x = 21$	Combine constant terms.	Simplify.
$x = 3$	Divide each side by 7.	Division Property of Equality

▶ The solution is $x = 3$.

Check

$3x + 2 = 23 - 4x$

$3(3) + 2 \stackrel{?}{=} 23 - 4(3)$

$9 + 2 \stackrel{?}{=} 23 - 12$

$11 = 11$ ✓

In-Class Practice

Self-Assessment

Solve the equation. Justify each step.

1. $6x - 11 = -35$
2. $-2p - 9 = 10p - 17$
3. $39 - 5z = -1 + 5z$
4. $3(3x + 14) = -3$

1 I don't understand yet. **2** I can do it with help. **3** I can do it on my own. **4** I can teach someone.

EXAMPLE 2 Justifying Steps

Solve $-5(7w + 8) = 30$. Justify each step.

Equation	Explanation	Reason
$-5(7w + 8) = 30$	Write the equation.	Given
$-35w - 40 = 30$	Multiply.	Distributive Property
$-35w = 70$	Add 40 to each side.	Addition Property of Equality
$w = -2$	Divide each side by -35.	Division Property of Equality

▶ The solution is $w = -2$.

EXAMPLE 3 Finding an Increase in Hourly Wage

You get a raise at your part-time job. To write your raise as a percent, use the formula $p(r + 1) = n$, where p is your previous wage, r is the percent increase (as a decimal), and n is your new wage. Solve the formula for r. What is your raise written as a percent when your hourly wage increases from $15.50 to $17.05 per hour?

Solve for r in the formula $p(r + 1) = n$.

Equation	Explanation	Reason
$p(r + 1) = n$	Write the equation.	Given
$pr + p = n$	Multiply.	Distributive Property
$pr = n - p$	Subtract p from each side.	Subtraction Property of Equality
$r = \dfrac{n - p}{p}$	Divide each side by p.	Division Property of Equality

Evaluate $r = \dfrac{n - p}{p}$ when $n = 17.05$ and $p = 15.50$.

$$r = \frac{n - p}{p} = \frac{17.05 - 15.5}{15.5} = \frac{1.55}{15.5} = 0.1$$

▶ Your raise is 10%.

In-Class Practice

Self-Assessment

Solve the equation. Justify each step.

5. $4 = -10b + 6(2 - b)$

6. $-3(2r - 5) = 2(9 - 4r)$

7. Solve the formula $A = \frac{1}{2}bh$ for b. Justify each step. Then find the base of a triangle whose area is 952 square feet and whose height is 56 feet.

2.4 Algebraic Reasoning

Using Other Properties of Equality

Key Concept

Reflexive, Symmetric, and Transitive Properties of Equality

	Real Numbers	Segment Lengths	Angle Measures
Reflexive Property	$a = a$	$AB = AB$	$m\angle A = m\angle A$
Symmetric Property	If $a = b$, then $b = a$.	If $AB = CD$, then $CD = AB$.	If $m\angle A = m\angle B$, then $m\angle B = m\angle A$.
Transitive Property	If $a = b$ and $b = c$, then $a = c$.	If $AB = CD$ and $CD = EF$, then $AB = EF$.	If $m\angle A = m\angle B$ and $m\angle B = m\angle C$, then $m\angle A = m\angle C$.

EXAMPLE 4 Using Properties of Equality with Angle Measures

You reflect the beam of a spotlight off a mirror lying flat on a stage, as shown. Determine whether $m\angle DBA = m\angle EBC$.

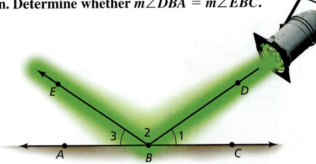

Equation	Explanation	Reason
$m\angle 1 = m\angle 3$	Marked in diagram.	Given
$m\angle DBA = m\angle 3 + m\angle 2$	Add measures of adjacent angles.	Angle Addition Postulate
$m\angle DBA = m\angle 1 + m\angle 2$	Substitute $m\angle 1$ for $m\angle 3$.	Substitution Property of Equality
$m\angle 1 + m\angle 2 = m\angle EBC$	Add measures of adjacent angles.	Angle Addition Postulate
$m\angle DBA = m\angle EBC$	Both measures are equal to the sum $m\angle 1 + m\angle 2$.	Transitive Property of Equality

In-Class Practice

Self-Assessment

Name the property of equality that the statement illustrates.

8. If $m\angle 6 = m\angle 7$, then $m\angle 7 = m\angle 6$.

9. If $JK = KL$ and $KL = 16$, then $JK = 16$.

1 I don't understand yet.   **2** I can do it with help.   **3** I can do it on my own.   **4** I can teach someone.

Connections to Real Life

EXAMPLE 5 Using Properties of Equality with Segment Lengths

A park, a shoe store, a pizza shop, and a movie theater are located, in that order, on a city street. The distance between the park and the shoe store is the same as the distance between the pizza shop and the movie theater. Show that the distance between the park and the pizza shop is the same as the distance between the shoe store and the movie theater.

Sketch the order of the four shops.

Modify your diagram by letting the points P, S, Z, and M represent the park, the shoe store, the pizza shop, and the movie theater, respectively. Show any mathematical relationships.

Use the Segment Addition Postulate to show that $PZ = SM$.

Equation	Explanation	Reason
$PS = ZM$	Marked in diagram.	Given
$PZ = PS + SZ$	Add lengths of adjacent segments.	Segment Addition Postulate
$SM = SZ + ZM$	Add lengths of adjacent segments.	Segment Addition Postulate
$PS + SZ = ZM + SZ$	Add SZ to each side of $PS = ZM$.	Addition Property of Equality
$PZ = SM$	Substitute PZ for $PS + SZ$ and SM for $ZM + SZ$.	Substitution Property of Equality

Look Back Reread the problem. Make sure your diagram is drawn precisely using the given information. Check the steps in your solution.

In-Class Practice

Self-Assessment

10. In Example 5, a hot dog stand is located halfway between the shoe store and the pizza shop, at point H. Show that $PH = HM$.

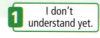

2.4 Algebraic Reasoning

2.4 Practice

Write the property that justifies each step.

1. $3x - 12 = 7x + 8$ Given
   $-4x - 12 = 8$ _____
   $-4x = 20$ _____
   $x = -5$ _____

2. $5(x - 1) = 4x + 13$ Given
   $5x - 5 = 4x + 13$ _____
   $x - 5 = 13$ _____
   $x = 18$ _____

Solve the equation. Justify each step. (See Examples 1 and 2.)

3. $2x - 8 = 6x - 20$

4. $5(3x - 20) = -10$

5. $3(2x + 11) = 9$

6. $2(-x - 5) = 12$

7. $44 - 2(3x + 4) = -18x$

8. $4(5x - 9) = -2(x + 7)$

SMP.3 ERROR ANALYSIS Describe and correct the error in solving the equation and justifying each step.

9.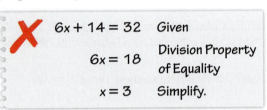

10.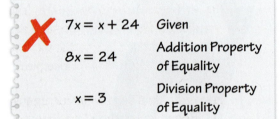

Solve the equation for y. Justify each step.

11. $5x + y = 18$

12. $-4x + 2y = 8$

13. $2y + 0.5x = 16$

14. $\frac{1}{2}x - \frac{3}{4}y = -2$

15. $12 - 3y = 30x + 6$

16. $3x + 7 = -7 + 9y$

Solve the formula for the given variable. Justify each step.

17. $C = 2\pi r$; r

18. $I = Prt$; P

19. $S = 2\pi r^2 + 2\pi rh$; h

20. The formula for the perimeter P of a rectangle is

    $P = 2\ell + 2w$

    where ℓ is the length and w is the width. Solve the formula for ℓ. Justify each step. Then find the length of a rectangular lawn with a perimeter of 32 meters and a width of 5 meters. (See Example 3.)

21. The formula for the area A of a trapezoid is

    $A = \frac{1}{2}h(b_1 + b_2)$

    where h is the height and b_1 and b_2 are the lengths of the two bases. Solve the formula for b_1. Justify each step. Then find the length of one of the bases of the trapezoid when the area of the trapezoid is 91 square meters, the height is 7 meters, and the length of the other base is 20 meters.

Name the property of equality that the statement illustrates.

22. If $x = y$, then $3x = 3y$.

23. If $AM = MB$, then $AM + 5 = MB + 5$.

24. $x = x$

25. If $x = y$, then $y = x$.

26. If $AB = LM$, then $LM = AB$.

27. If $BC = XY$ and $XY = 8$, then $BC = 8$.

Use the diagrams. (See Example 4.)

28. Show that $m\angle 1 = m\angle 3$ when $m\angle ABD = m\angle CBE$.

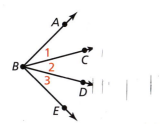

29. Show that $m\angle 2 = m\angle 3$.

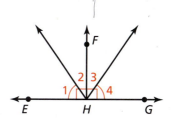

30. **CONNECTION TO REAL LIFE** You run a road race with two water stops. The distance between the starting line and the second water stop is the same as the distance between the first water stop and the finish line. Show that the distance between the starting line and the first water stop is the same as the distance between the second water stop and the finish line. (See Example 5.)

31. **SMP.6** At least how many segment lengths or angle measures are needed to demonstrate the Reflexive Property? the Symmetric Property? the Transitive Property? Explain your reasoning.

Show that the perimeter of △ABC is equal to the perimeter of △ADC.

32.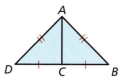

33.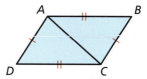

34. **CONNECT CONCEPTS** In the figure, $\overline{ZY} \cong \overline{XW}$, $ZX = 5x + 17$, $YW = 10 - 2x$, and $YX = 3$. Find ZY and XW.

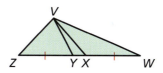

35. The formula to convert a temperature in degrees Fahrenheit (°F) to degrees Celsius (°C) is $C = \frac{5}{9}(F - 32)$.

   a. Solve the formula for F. Justify each step.

   b. Make a table that shows the conversion to Fahrenheit for each temperature: 0°C, 20°C, 32°C, and 41°C.

   c. Use your table to graph the temperature in degrees Fahrenheit as a function of the temperature in degrees Celsius. Is this a linear function?

Interpreting Data

SPHERICAL GEOMETRY Euclidean geometry can be used to model flat regions as planes. Spherical geometry can be used to model spherical regions, such as the surface of the Earth.

36. In spherical geometry, a great circle is similar to a line in Euclidean geometry. A great circle is any circle on the surface of a sphere whose center is also the center of the sphere. In how many points can two great circles intersect?

37. In Euclidean geometry, two perpendicular lines form four right angles. How many right angles are formed by two perpendicular great circles? Explain.

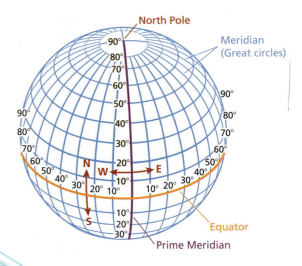

Review & Refresh

Name the definition, property, or postulate that is represented by the diagram.

38.

    X   Y   Z

    $XY + YZ = XZ$

39.

    M, N, P, L (angles)

Rewrite the conditional statement in if-then form.

40. When it storms, soccer practice is canceled.

41. People taller than 4 feet are allowed to ride the roller coaster.

Solve the inequality. Graph the solution, if possible.

42. $|d - 3| > 7$

43. $16 < 2|5w + 4|$

44. Use inductive reasoning to make a conjecture about the difference of two even integers. Then use deductive reasoning to show that the conjecture is true.

45. Sketch a diagram of $\overleftrightarrow{XY}$ intersecting $\overline{WV}$ at point Z, so that $\overline{XZ} \cong \overline{ZY}$.

46. Approximate when the function is positive, negative, increasing, or decreasing.

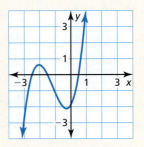

2.5 Proving Statements about Segments and Angles

Learning Target: Prove statements about segments and angles.

Success Criteria:
- I can explain the structure of a two-column proof.
- I can write a two-column proof.
- I can identify properties of congruence.

A **proof** is a logical argument that uses deductive reasoning to show that a statement is true.

INVESTIGATE Completing Proofs

Work with a partner.

1. Complete the statements to prove that $AB = BC$.

   Given $AC = AB + AB$

   Prove $AB = BC$

   You are given that $AC = $ _____. By the _____, $AB + BC = AC$. $AB + BC = AB + AB$ by the _____. Then by the _____, $AB = BC$.

2. Seven steps of a proof are shown. Complete the statements to prove that $\overleftrightarrow{JM} \perp \overleftrightarrow{LN}$.

   Given $\angle JKL \cong \angle MKL$
   Prove $\overleftrightarrow{JM} \perp \overleftrightarrow{LN}$

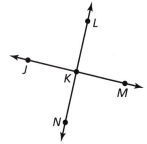

STATEMENTS	REASONS
1. $\angle JKL \cong \angle MKL$	1. Given
2. $m\angle JKL = m\angle MKL$	2. _____
3. $m\angle JKL + m\angle MKL = 180°$	3. _____
4. $m\angle JKL +$ _____ $= 180°$	4. Substitution Property of Equality
5. $2(m\angle JKL) = 180°$	5. _____
6. _____	6. Division Property of Equality
7. $\overleftrightarrow{JM} \perp \overleftrightarrow{LN}$	7. _____

Vocabulary
proof
two-column proof
theorem

Writing Two-Column Proofs

A **proof** is a logical argument that uses deductive reasoning to show that a statement is true.

A **two-column proof** has numbered statements and corresponding reasons that show an argument in a logical order. Each statement in the left-hand column is either given information or the result of applying a known property or fact to statements already made. Each reason in the right-hand column is an explanation for the corresponding statement.

EXAMPLE 1 Writing a Two-Column Proof

Write a two-column proof for the situation in Example 4 of Section 2.4.

Given $m\angle 1 = m\angle 3$

Prove $m\angle DBA = m\angle EBC$

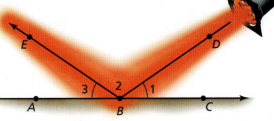

STATEMENTS	REASONS
1. $m\angle 1 = m\angle 3$	1. Given
2. $m\angle DBA = m\angle 3 + m\angle 2$	2. Angle Addition Postulate
3. $m\angle DBA = m\angle 1 + m\angle 2$	3. Substitution Property of Equality
4. $m\angle 1 + m\angle 2 = m\angle EBC$	4. Angle Addition Postulate
5. $m\angle DBA = m\angle EBC$	5. Transitive Property of Equality

In-Class Practice
Self-Assessment

1. Complete the proof.

   Given T is the midpoint of $\overline{SU}$.
   Prove $x = 5$

STATEMENTS	REASONS
1. T is the midpoint of $\overline{SU}$.	1. _____
2. $\overline{ST} \cong \overline{TU}$	2. Definition of midpoint
3. $ST = TU$	3. Definition of congruent segments
4. $7x = 3x + 20$	4. _____
5. _____	5. Subtraction Property of Equality
6. $x = 5$	6. _____

Using Properties of Congruence

A **theorem** is a statement that can be proven. The reasons used in a proof can include definitions, properties, postulates, and theorems. Once you have proven a theorem, you can use the theorem as a reason in other proofs.

Theorem 2.1

Properties of Segment Congruence

Segment congruence is reflexive, symmetric, and transitive.

Reflexive   For any segment AB, $\overline{AB} \cong \overline{AB}$.
Symmetric If $\overline{AB} \cong \overline{CD}$, then $\overline{CD} \cong \overline{AB}$.
Transitive If $\overline{AB} \cong \overline{CD}$ and $\overline{CD} \cong \overline{EF}$, then $\overline{AB} \cong \overline{EF}$.

Prove this Theorem Exercise 7, page 97

EXAMPLE 2 — Proving a Property of Segment Congruence

Write a two-column proof for the Symmetric Property of Segment Congruence.

Given $\overline{LM} \cong \overline{NP}$
Prove $\overline{NP} \cong \overline{LM}$

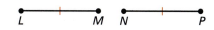

STATEMENTS	REASONS
1. $\overline{LM} \cong \overline{NP}$	1. Given
2. $LM = NP$	2. Definition of congruent segments
3. $NP = LM$	3. Symmetric Property of Equality
4. $\overline{NP} \cong \overline{LM}$	4. Definition of congruent segments

In-Class Practice

Self-Assessment

2. Complete the proof.
Given $\overline{LM} \cong \overline{NP}, \overline{NP} \cong \overline{QR}$
Prove $\overline{LM} \cong \overline{QR}$

STATEMENTS	REASONS
1. $\overline{LM} \cong \overline{NP}, \overline{NP} \cong \overline{QR}$	1. _____
2. _____	2. Definition of congruent segments
3. $LM = QR$	3. _____
4. _____	4. Definition of congruent segments

2.5   Proving Statements about Segments and Angles

Theorem 2.2

Properties of Angle Congruence

Angle congruence is reflexive, symmetric, and transitive.

Reflexive   For any angle A, $\angle A \cong \angle A$.
Symmetric   If $\angle A \cong \angle B$, then $\angle B \cong \angle A$.
Transitive If $\angle A \cong \angle B$ and $\angle B \cong \angle C$, then $\angle A \cong \angle C$.

Prove this Theorem Exercises 6 and 8, page 97; Exercise 31, page 111.

EXAMPLE 3   Identifying Properties of Congruence

Name the property that each statement illustrates.

a. If $\angle T \cong \angle V$ and $\angle V \cong \angle R$, then $\angle T \cong \angle R$.

▶ Transitive Property of Angle Congruence

b. If $\overline{JL} \cong \overline{YZ}$, then $\overline{YZ} \cong \overline{JL}$.

▶ Symmetric Property of Segment Congruence

EXAMPLE 4   Writing a Two-Column Proof

Prove this property of angle bisectors: If you know that $\overrightarrow{AC}$ bisects $\angle BAD$, prove that two times $m\angle BAC$ equals $m\angle BAD$.

Given $\overrightarrow{AC}$ bisects $\angle BAD$.

Prove $2m\angle BAC = m\angle BAD$

STATEMENTS	REASONS
1. $\overrightarrow{AC}$ bisects $\angle BAD$.	1. Given
2. $\angle BAC \cong \angle DAC$	2. Definition of angle bisector
3. $m\angle BAC = m\angle DAC$	3. Definition of congruent angles
4. $m\angle BAC + m\angle DAC = m\angle BAD$	4. Angle Addition Postulate
5. $m\angle BAC + m\angle BAC = m\angle BAD$	5. Substitution Property of Equality
6. $2m\angle BAC = m\angle BAD$	6. Distributive Property

In-Class Practice

Self-Assessment

Name the property that the statement illustrates.

3. $\overline{GH} \cong \overline{GH}$

4. If $\angle K \cong \angle P$, then $\angle P \cong \angle K$.

5. **WHAT IF?** In Example 4, you want to prove that $m\angle CAD = \frac{1}{2}m\angle BAD$ instead. How would the proof be different?

2.5 Practice

1. Complete the proof. (See Example 1.)

   Given $PQ = RS$
   Prove $PR = QS$

   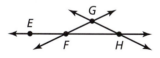

STATEMENTS	REASONS
1. $PQ = RS$	1. _____
2. $PQ + QR = RS + QR$	2. _____
3. _____	3. Segment Addition Postulate
4. $RS + QR = QS$	4. Segment Addition Postulate
5. $PR = QS$	5. _____

PROVING A THEOREM Write a two-column proof for the property. (See Example 2.)

2. Symmetric Property of Angle Congruence

3. Reflexive Property of Segment Congruence

4. Transitive Property of Angle Congruence

Name the property that the statement illustrates. (See Example 3.)

5. If $\overline{PQ} \cong \overline{ST}$ and $\overline{ST} \cong \overline{UV}$, then $\overline{PQ} \cong \overline{UV}$.

6. $\angle F \cong \angle F$

7. If $\overline{XY} \cong \overline{UV}$, then $\overline{UV} \cong \overline{XY}$.

8. If $\angle L \cong \angle M$ and $\angle M \cong \angle N$, then $\angle L \cong \angle N$.

PROOF Write a two-column proof. (See Example 4.)

9. **Given** $\angle GFH \cong \angle GHF$
   Prove $\angle EFG$ and $\angle GHF$ are supplementary.

10. **Given** $\overline{AB} \cong \overline{FG}$,
    $\overleftrightarrow{BF}$ bisects $\overline{AC}$ and $\overline{DG}$.
    Prove $\overline{BC} \cong \overline{DF}$

    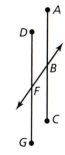

11. **CONNECTION TO REAL LIFE** Prove that the distance from the restaurant to the movie theater is the same as the distance from the café to the dry cleaners.

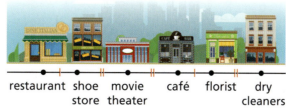

restaurant   shoe store   movie theater   café   florist   dry cleaners

12. **SMP.6 DIG DEEPER** Fold two corners of a piece of paper so their edges match, as shown. Write a two-column proof to show that the angle measure at the top of the page where the folds meet is always the same no matter how you make the folds.

Interpreting Data

GOLDBACH'S CONJECTURE In 1742, German mathematician Christian Goldbach proposed that every even number greater than 2 is the sum of two prime numbers. The conjecture has been shown to hold true for all even numbers less than 4,000,000,000,000,000,000.

13. Use the diagram to find two even numbers that can be written as the sum of two prime numbers in four different ways. Write the ways.

14. Write the numbers 110, 112, and 114 as the sum of two prime numbers.

15. Supercomputers have shown that the conjecture is true for all numbers less than 4 quintillion. Why isn't this a deductive proof?

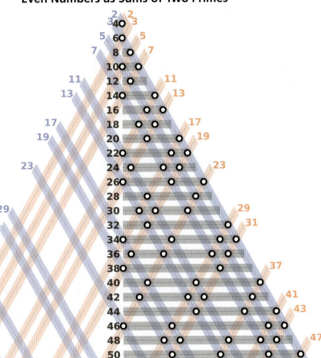

In 2020, a prize of 1 million dollars was offered to anyone who proved Goldbach's Conjecture within the next two years. The prize went unclaimed.

Review & Refresh

Solve the equation using any method.

16. $4x^2 - 87 = 109$

17. $3x^2 - 2x - 7 = 0$

18. Does the table represent a *linear* or *nonlinear* function?

x	2	4	6	8	10
y	$\frac{1}{2}$	1	2	4	8

Find the angle measure.

19. $\angle 1$ is a complement of $\angle 4$, and $m\angle 1 = 33°$. Find $m\angle 4$.

20. $\angle 3$ is a supplement of $\angle 2$, and $m\angle 2 = 147°$. Find $m\angle 3$.

21. Use inductive reasoning to make a conjecture about the sum of two negative integers. Then use deductive reasoning to show that the conjecture is true.

22. Solve the equation. Justify each step.

$$-3(6x - 1) = 6x - 9$$

23. A fitness center charges members an initial fee of $10 and a monthly fee of $21.99. Find the total cost of 1 year of membership.

24. Sketch a diagram showing $\overline{AB}$ intersecting $\overleftrightarrow{CD}$ at point K, so that $\overline{AK} \cong \overline{KB}$ and $\overline{CK} \cong \overline{KD}$.

98 Chapter 2 Reasoning and Proofs

2.6 Proving Geometric Relationships

Learning Target: Prove geometric relationships.

Success Criteria:
- I can prove geometric relationships by writing flowchart proofs.
- I can prove geometric relationships by writing paragraph proofs.

INVESTIGATE — Matching Reasons in a Flowchart Proof

1. Work with a partner. Match each reason with the correct step in the flowchart.

Given $AC = AB + AB$

Prove $AB = BC$

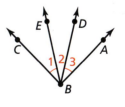

Flowchart:
- $AC = AB + AB$
- $AB + BC = AC$ → $AB + BC = AB + AB$ → $AB = BC$

a. Segment Addition Postulate   b. Given
c. Transitive Property of Equality   d. Subtraction Property of Equality

INVESTIGATE — Matching Reasons in a Flowchart Proof

2. Work with a partner. Match each reason with the correct step in the flowchart.

Given $m\angle 1 = m\angle 3$

Prove $m\angle EBA = m\angle CBD$

Flowchart:
- $m\angle 1 = m\angle 3$
- $m\angle EBA = m\angle 2 + m\angle 3$ → $m\angle EBA = m\angle 2 + m\angle 1$ → $m\angle EBA = m\angle 1 + m\angle 2$
- $m\angle 1 + m\angle 2 = m\angle CBD$ → $m\angle EBA = m\angle CBD$

a. Angle Addition Postulate   b. Transitive Property of Equality
c. Substitution Property of Equality   d. Angle Addition Postulate
e. Given   f. Commutative Prop. of Addition

RESOURCES

Vocabulary
flowchart proof, or flow proof
paragraph proof

Writing Flowchart Proofs

A **flowchart proof**, or **flow proof**, uses boxes and arrows to show the flow of a logical argument. Each reason is below the statement it justifies.

Theorem 2.3

Right Angles Congruence Theorem

All right angles are congruent.

EXAMPLE 1 Proving the Right Angles Congruence Theorem

Use the given flowchart proof to write a two-column proof of the Right Angles Congruence Theorem.

Given $\angle 1$ and $\angle 2$ are right angles.

Prove $\angle 1 \cong \angle 2$

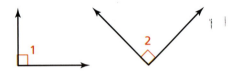

Flowchart Proof

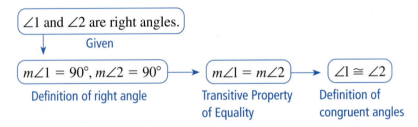

Two-Column Proof

STATEMENTS	REASONS
1. $\angle 1$ and $\angle 2$ are right angles.	1. Given
2. $m\angle 1 = 90°$, $m\angle 2 = 90°$	2. Definition of right angle
3. $m\angle 1 = m\angle 2$	3. Transitive Property of Equality
4. $\angle 1 \cong \angle 2$	4. Definition of congruent angles

In-Class Practice

Self-Assessment

1. Complete the flowchart proof. Then write a two-column proof.

   Given $\overline{AB} \perp \overline{BC}$, $\overline{DC} \perp \overline{BC}$

   Prove $\angle B \cong \angle C$

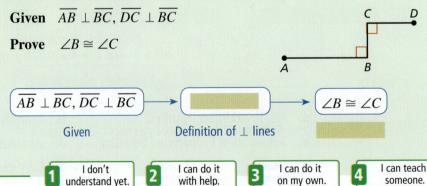

1. I don't understand yet.   2. I can do it with help.   3. I can do it on my own.   4. I can teach someone.

Theorem 2.4

Congruent Supplements Theorem

If two angles are supplementary to the same angle (or to congruent angles), then they are congruent.

If ∠1 and ∠2 are supplementary and ∠3 and ∠2 are supplementary, then ∠1 ≅ ∠3.

Prove this Theorem Exercise 16 (case 2), page 107

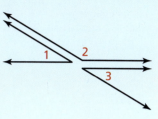

EXAMPLE 2 — Proving a Case of the Congruent Supplements Theorem

Use the given two-column proof to write a flowchart proof that proves that two angles supplementary to the same angle are congruent.

Given ∠1 and ∠2 are supplementary.
∠3 and ∠2 are supplementary.

Prove ∠1 ≅ ∠3

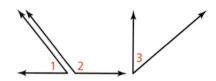

Two-Column Proof

STATEMENTS	REASONS
1. ∠1 and ∠2 are supplementary. ∠3 and ∠2 are supplementary.	1. Given
2. $m\angle 1 + m\angle 2 = 180°$, $m\angle 3 + m\angle 2 = 180°$	2. Definition of supplementary angles
3. $m\angle 1 + m\angle 2 = m\angle 3 + m\angle 2$	3. Transitive Property of Equality
4. $m\angle 1 = m\angle 3$	4. Subtraction Property of Equality
5. ∠1 ≅ ∠3	5. Definition of congruent angles

Flowchart Proof

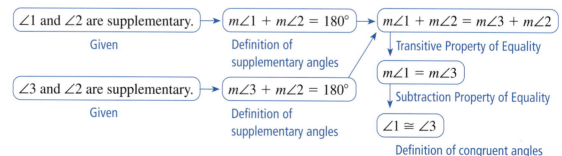

In-Class Practice

Self-Assessment

2. Use the two-column proof in Example 2 of Section 2.5 to write a flowchart proof for the Symmetric Property of Segment Congruence.

1 I don't understand yet. **2** I can do it with help. **3** I can do it on my own. **4** I can teach someone.

2.6 Proving Geometric Relationships

Theorem 2.5

Congruent Complements Theorem

If two angles are complementary to the same angle (or to congruent angles), then they are congruent.

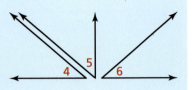

If ∠4 and ∠5 are complementary and ∠6 and ∠5 are complementary, then ∠4 ≅ ∠6.

Prove this Theorem Exercise 15 (case 1), page 106

EXAMPLE 3 — Proving a Case of the Congruent Complements Theorem

Write a flowchart proof that proves that if two angles are complementary to congruent angles, then they are congruent.

Given ∠1 and ∠2 are complementary.
∠3 and ∠4 are complementary.
∠2 ≅ ∠3

Prove ∠1 ≅ ∠4

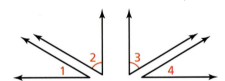

Flowchart Proof

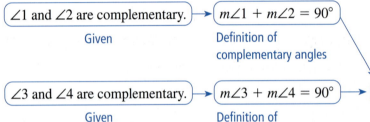

∠1 and ∠2 are complementary. → $m\angle 1 + m\angle 2 = 90°$
Given — Definition of complementary angles

∠3 and ∠4 are complementary. → $m\angle 3 + m\angle 4 = 90°$ → $m\angle 1 + m\angle 2 = m\angle 3 + m\angle 4$
Given — Definition of complementary angles — Transitive Property of Equality

∠2 ≅ ∠3 → $m\angle 2 = m\angle 3$ → $m\angle 1 + m\angle 3 = m\angle 3 + m\angle 4$
Given — Definition of congruent angles — Substitution Property of Equality

$m\angle 1 = m\angle 4$
Subtraction Property of Equality

∠1 ≅ ∠4
Definition of congruent angles

In-Class Practice

Self-Assessment

3. Write a flowchart proof.

   Given $AB = DE$, $BC = CD$
   Prove $\overline{AC} \cong \overline{CE}$

   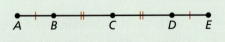

 I don't understand yet.
 I can do it with help.
 I can do it on my own.
4 I can teach someone.

Writing Paragraph Proofs

Another proof format is a **paragraph proof**, which presents the statements and reasons of a proof as sentences in a paragraph. It uses words to explain the logical flow of the argument.

Postulate 2.8

Linear Pair Postulate

If two angles form a linear pair, then they are supplementary.

∠1 and ∠2 form a linear pair, so ∠1 and ∠2 are supplementary and $m\angle 1 + m\angle 2 = 180°$.

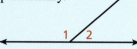

Theorem 2.6

Vertical Angles Congruence Theorem

Vertical angles are congruent.

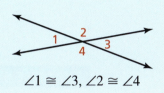

∠1 ≅ ∠3, ∠2 ≅ ∠4

EXAMPLE 4 Proving the Vertical Angles Congruence Theorem

Write a paragraph proof of the Vertical Angles Congruence Theorem.

Given ∠5 and ∠7 are vertical angles.

Prove ∠5 ≅ ∠7

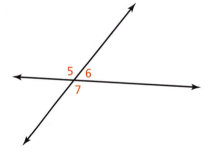

Paragraph Proof

∠5 and ∠7 are vertical angles formed by intersecting lines. As shown in the diagram, ∠5 and ∠6 are a linear pair, and ∠6 and ∠7 are a linear pair. Then, by the Linear Pair Postulate, ∠5 and ∠6 are supplementary and ∠6 and ∠7 are supplementary. So, by the Congruent Supplements Theorem, ∠5 ≅ ∠7.

In-Class Practice

Self-Assessment

4. Write a paragraph proof.

   Given ∠1 is a right angle.

   Prove ∠2 is a right angle.

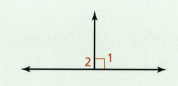

2.6 Proving Geometric Relationships

EXAMPLE 5 Using Angle Relationships

Find the value of x.

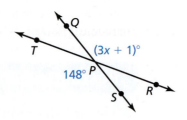

∠TPS and ∠QPR are vertical angles. By the Vertical Angles Congruence Theorem, the angles are congruent. Use this to write and solve an equation.

$m\angle TPS = m\angle QPR$	Definition of congruent angles
$148° = (3x + 1)°$	Substitute angle measures.
$147 = 3x$	Subtract 1 from each side.
$49 = x$	Divide each side by 3.

▶ So, the value of x is 49.

EXAMPLE 6 Using the Vertical Angles Congruence Theorem

Write a paragraph proof.

Given ∠1 ≅ ∠4

Prove ∠2 ≅ ∠3

Paragraph Proof

∠1 and ∠4 are congruent. By the Vertical Angles Congruence Theorem, ∠1 ≅ ∠2 and ∠3 ≅ ∠4. By the Transitive Property of Angle Congruence, ∠2 ≅ ∠4. Using the Transitive Property of Angle Congruence once more, ∠2 ≅ ∠3.

In-Class Practice

Self-Assessment

5. Find the value of w.

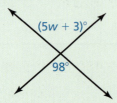

6. Find the values of a and b.

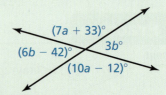

7. In Example 6, prove that ∠1 ≅ ∠4 when it is given that ∠2 ≅ ∠3.

1 I don't understand yet. **2** I can do it with help. **3** I can do it on my own. **4** I can teach someone.

2.6 Practice

Identify the pair(s) of congruent angles in the figures. Explain how you know they are congruent.

▶ 1.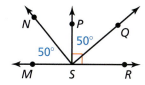

2. $\angle ABC$ is supplementary to $\angle CBD$.
$\angle CBD$ is supplementary to $\angle DEF$.

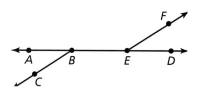

Use the diagram and the given angle measure to find the other three measures.

▶ 3. $m\angle 1 = 143°$

4. $m\angle 3 = 159°$

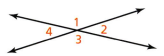

5. $m\angle 2 = 34°$

6. A pair of scissors are painted on a side of the Matilija Dam. Of the angles formed by the scissors, one measures about 75°. What are the measures of the other three angles?

The removal of the obsolete Matilija Dam has been delayed for decades.

Find the value of each variable. (See Example 5.)

▶ 7.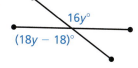

8.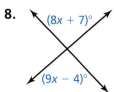

9.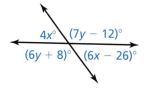

10. 2(5x − 5)°, (5y + 5)°, (3x − 5)°, 20y°

11. **SMP.3 ERROR ANALYSIS** Describe and correct the error in using the diagram to find the value of x.

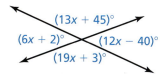

$(13x + 45)° + (19x + 3)° = 180°$
$32x + 48 = 180$
$32x = 132$
$x = 4.125$

2.6 Proving Geometric Relationships 105

12. **SMP.7** Find the measure of each angle in the diagram.

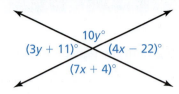

13. **PROOF** Complete the flowchart proof. Then write a two-column proof. (See Example 1.)

    Given ∠1 ≅ ∠3
    Prove ∠2 ≅ ∠4

    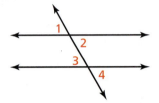

    ∠1 ≅ ∠3 → ∠1 ≅ ∠2, ∠3 ≅ ∠4 → ∠2 ≅ ∠3 → ∠2 ≅ ∠4
    Given   Vertical Angles
                   Congruence Theorem

14. **PROOF** Complete the two-column proof. Then write a flowchart proof. (See Examples 2 and 3.)

    Given ∠ABD is a right angle.
              ∠CBE is a right angle.
    Prove ∠ABC ≅ ∠DBE

    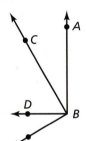

STATEMENTS	REASONS
1. ∠ABD is a right angle. ∠CBE is a right angle.	1. _____
2. ∠ABC and ∠CBD are complementary.	2. Definition of complementary angles
3. ∠DBE and ∠CBD are complementary.	3. _____
4. ∠ABC ≅ ∠DBE	4. _____

15. **PROVING THEOREM 2.5** Complete the paragraph proof for the Congruent Complements Theorem. Then write a two-column proof. (See Example 4.)

    Given ∠1 and ∠2 are complementary.
              ∠1 and ∠3 are complementary.
    Prove ∠2 ≅ ∠3

    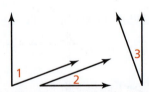

    ∠1 and ∠2 are complementary, and ∠1 and ∠3 are complementary. By the definition of _____ angles, $m\angle 1 + m\angle 2 = 90°$ and _____ = 90°. By the _____, $m\angle 1 + m\angle 2 = m\angle 1 + m\angle 3$. By the Subtraction Property of Equality, _____. So, ∠2 ≅ ∠3 by the definition of _____.

16. **PROVING THEOREM 2.4** Complete the two-column proof for the Congruent Supplements Theorem. Then write a paragraph proof. (See Example 6.)

Given ∠1 and ∠2 are supplementary.
∠3 and ∠4 are supplementary.
∠1 ≅ ∠4

Prove ∠2 ≅ ∠3

STATEMENTS	REASONS
1. ∠1 and ∠2 are supplementary. ∠3 and ∠4 are supplementary. ∠1 ≅ ∠4	1. Given
2. $m\angle 1 + m\angle 2 = 180°$, $m\angle 3 + m\angle 4 = 180°$	2. _____
3. _____ $= m\angle 3 + m\angle 4$	3. Transitive Property of Equality
4. $m\angle 1 = m\angle 4$	4. Definition of congruent angles
5. $m\angle 1 + m\angle 2 =$ _____	5. Substitution Property of Equality
6. $m\angle 2 = m\angle 3$	6. _____
7. _____	7. _____

17. **SMP.6** Explain why you do not use inductive reasoning when writing a proof.

PROOF Write a proof using any format.

18. **Given** ∠QRS and ∠PSR are supplementary.
    Prove ∠QRL ≅ ∠PSR

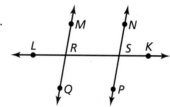

19. **Given** $\overline{JK} \perp \overline{JM}, \overline{KL} \perp \overline{ML}, \angle J \cong \angle M, \angle K \cong \angle L$
    Prove $\overline{JM} \perp \overline{ML}$ and $\overline{JK} \perp \overline{KL}$

20. **Given** ∠AEB ≅ ∠DEC
    Prove ∠AEC ≅ ∠DEB

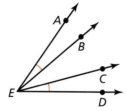

21. Is the converse of the Linear Pair Postulate true? If so, write a biconditional statement. If not, explain why not.

22. **SMP.5 OPEN-ENDED** Draw three lines all intersecting at the same point. Label two of the angle measures so that you can find the remaining four angle measures. Explain what tools you used and how you chose which angle measures to label.

2.6 Proving Geometric Relationships

Interpreting Data

NICOMACHUS'S THEOREM Nicomachus of Gerasa was a mathematician who was born in the Roman province of Syria, in what is now Jordan in the first century AD. His *Introduction to Arithmetic* laid the groundwork for the following theorem about the sum of the cubes of the first n numbers:

$$1^3 + 2^3 + 3^3 + \ldots + n^3 = (1 + 2 + 3 + \ldots + n)^2$$

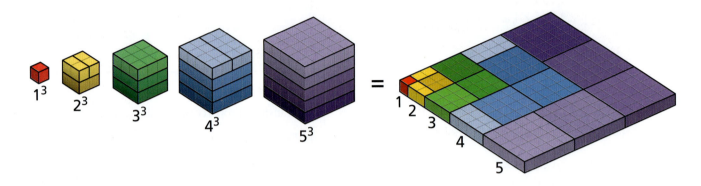

23. The figure shows that the theorem is true for $n = 5$. Explain whether this *visual proof* convinces you that the theorem is true for all values of n.

24. Extend the figure to include $n = 6$. Is the theorem still valid?

Review & Refresh

25. Complete the statement. Name the property you use.

If $\overline{RS} \cong \overline{TU}$ and $\overline{TU} \cong \overline{VW}$, then ▨ $\cong$ ▨.

Use the cube.

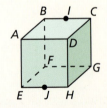

26. Name three collinear points.

27. Write an example of the Three Point Postulate.

28. Name two planes containing $\overline{BC}$.

29. The final velocity v_f of an object is given by the formula $v_f = v_i + at$, where v_i is the initial velocity, a is the acceleration, and t is the time.

   a. Solve the formula for t. Justify each step.

   b. A car with an initial velocity of 14 meters per second accelerates at a constant rate of 2.5 meters per second squared. How many seconds does it take the car to reach a final velocity of 29 meters per second?

30. Complete the square for $x^2 - 14x$. Then factor the trinomial.

Graph the function.

31. $y = (x + 2)(x - 4)$

32. $y = -3(x - 1)^2 + 4$

2 Chapter Review

Rate your understanding of each section.
1. I don't understand yet.
2. I can do it with help.
3. I can do it on my own.
4. I can teach someone.

2.1 Conditional Statements (pp. 61–70)

Learning Target: Understand and write conditional statements.

Vocabulary
conditional statement
if-then form
hypothesis
conclusion
negation
converse
inverse
contrapositive
equivalent statements
perpendicular lines
biconditional statement
truth value
truth table

Write the if-then form, the converse, the inverse, the contrapositive, and the biconditional of the conditional statement.

1. Two lines intersect in a point.
2. $4x + 9 = 21$ because $x = 3$.
3. The measures of supplementary angles sum to 180°.
4. The measure of a right angle is 90°.

Decide whether the statement about the diagram is true. Explain your answer using the definitions you have learned.

5. S is the midpoint of $\overline{EF}$.
6. $\overline{ES} \cong \overline{ST}$
7. $\overrightarrow{ST}$ is a segment bisector of $\overline{EF}$.

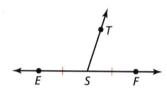

2.2 Inductive and Deductive Reasoning (pp. 71–78)

Learning Target: Use inductive and deductive reasoning.

Vocabulary
conjecture
inductive reasoning
counterexample
deductive reasoning

8. Make and test a conjecture about the difference of any two odd integers.

9. If an angle is a right angle, then the angle measures 90°. ∠B is a right angle. Using the Law of Detachment, what statement can you make?

10. Use the Law of Syllogism to write a new conditional statement that follows from the pair of true statements: If $x = 3$, then $2x = 6$. If $4x = 12$, then $x = 3$.

Decide whether inductive reasoning or deductive reasoning is used to reach the conclusion. Explain your reasoning.

11. The wolf population in a park has increased each year for the last 10 years. So, the wolf population will increase again next year.

12. The dew point is the warmest temperature at which the relative humidity reaches 100 percent. On a given night, the relative humidity reaches 100 percent at the moment the temperature drops to 72°. So, the dew point is 72°.

Chapter 2 Chapter Review 109

2.3 Postulates and Diagrams (pp. 79–84)

Learning Target: Interpret and sketch diagrams.

Vocabulary
line perpendicular to a plane

13. State the postulate illustrated by the diagram.

 If then

Sketch a diagram of the description.

14. $\angle ABC$, an acute angle, is bisected by $\overrightarrow{BE}$.

15. $\angle CDE$, a straight angle, is bisected by $\overleftrightarrow{DK}$.

16. Plane P intersects plane R at $\overleftrightarrow{XY}$. $\overline{ZW}$ lies in plane P. Plane $P \perp$ plane R.

Use the diagram at the right to determine whether you can assume the statement.

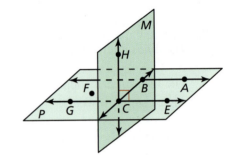

17. Points A, B, C, and E are coplanar.

18. $\overleftrightarrow{HC} \perp \overleftrightarrow{GE}$

19. Points F, B, and G are collinear.

20. $\overleftrightarrow{AB} \parallel \overleftrightarrow{GE}$

21. $\overleftrightarrow{AB}$ lies in plane S. Points A, B, and C lie in plane R. Point C does not lie in S. Describe the intersection of plane R and plane S. Make a sketch to support your answer. State three postulates that support your answer.

2.4 Algebraic Reasoning (pp. 85–92)

Learning Target: Use properties of equality to solve problems.

Solve the equation. Justify each step.

22. $-9x - 21 = -20x - 87$

23. $5x + 2(2x - 23) = -154$

Name the property of equality that the statement illustrates.

24. If $LM = RS$ and $RS = 25$, then $LM = 25$.

25. If $3XY = 36$, then $XY = 12$.

26. A formula for the volume V (in gallons) of a cylinder with a diameter of 22.5 inches is

$$V = \frac{11.25^2 \pi h}{231}$$

where h is the height of the cylinder in inches. Solve the formula for h. Justify each step. Then find the height of the 55-gallon steel drum.

2.5 Proving Statements about Segments and Angles (pp. 93–98)

Vocabulary
proof
two-column proof
theorem

Learning Target: Prove statements about segments and angles.

Name the property that the statement illustrates.

27. If $\angle ABC \cong \angle LMN$ and $\angle LMN \cong \angle XYZ$, then $\angle ABC \cong \angle XYZ$.

28. If $\angle DEF \cong \angle JKL$, then $\angle JKL \cong \angle DEF$.

29. $\angle C \cong \angle C$

30. If $MN = PQ$ and $PQ = RS$, then $MN = RS$.

31. Write a two-column proof for the Reflexive Property of Angle Congruence.

32. A ramp at a skate park is constructed with $\angle BAD \cong \angle CDA$, as pictured. Prove that $\angle EAB \cong \angle FDC$.

2.6 Proving Geometric Relationships (pp. 99–108)

Vocabulary
flowchart proof, or flow proof
paragraph proof

Learning Target: Prove geometric relationships.

33. Complete the flowchart proof. Then write a two-column proof.

   Given $\angle 3$ and $\angle 2$ are complementary.
   $m\angle 1 + m\angle 2 = 90°$

   Prove $\angle 3 \cong \angle 1$

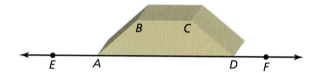

| $m\angle 1 + m\angle 2 = 90°$ | → | $\angle 1$ and $\angle 2$ are complementary. | → | $\angle 3$ and $\angle 2$ are complementary. | → | $\angle 3 \cong \angle 1$ |

Given   Definition of complementary angles

34. Write a paragraph proof.

   Given $m\angle ABC = 48°$, $m\angle ABD = 24°$

   Prove $\overrightarrow{BD}$ bisects $\angle ABC$.

2 PERFORMANCE TASK
SMP.1

The Greenhouse Effect

1. Solar radiation reaches Earth. Some of this radiation is reflected back into space.
2. The rest of the radiation is absorbed by oceans, land, and the atmosphere, which heats Earth.
3. Some of this heat is released into space, and some is trapped by greenhouse gases in the atmosphere, keeping Earth warm enough to sustain life.
4. Earth radiates heat.

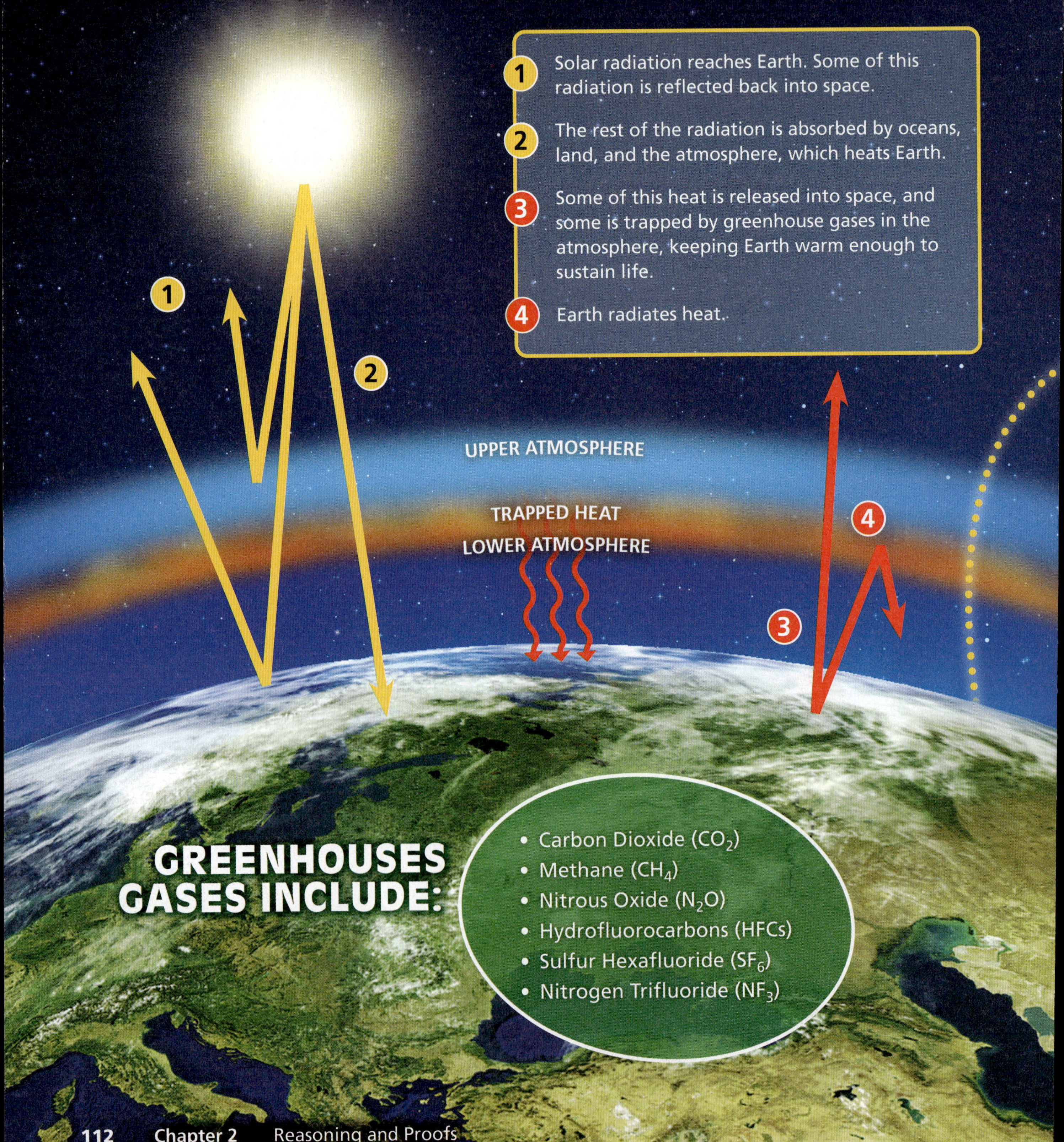

UPPER ATMOSPHERE

TRAPPED HEAT
LOWER ATMOSPHERE

GREENHOUSES GASES INCLUDE:
- Carbon Dioxide (CO_2)
- Methane (CH_4)
- Nitrous Oxide (N_2O)
- Hydrofluorocarbons (HFCs)
- Sulfur Hexafluoride (SF_6)
- Nitrogen Trifluoride (NF_3)

Analyzing Data

Use the information on the previous page to complete the following exercises.

1 Explain what is shown in the data display. What do you notice? What do you wonder?

2 Your friend writes the conditional statement, "If a substance is a greenhouse gas, then it is carbon dioxide." Is this conditional statement true? Is the converse true? the inverse? the contrapositive?

3 Write a conditional statement about the greenhouse effect. Write the converse, inverse, and contrapositive of the statement. Then tell if each statement is true.

CLIMATE CHANGE CONDITIONALS

Greenhouse gases are a major contributor to climate change. Use the Internet or other resources to research the effects of climate change.

- Write three conditional statements based on your research.

- Write the converse, inverse, and contrapositive of each statement. Then explain whether each statement is *true* or *false*.

- Find a conjecture about climate change, and a counterexample that shows that the conjecture is false.

3 Parallel and Perpendicular Lines

- 3.1 Pairs of Lines and Angles
- 3.2 Parallel Lines and Transversals
- 3.3 Proofs with Parallel Lines
- 3.4 Proofs with Perpendicular Lines
- 3.5 Equations of Parallel and Perpendicular Lines

NATIONAL GEOGRAPHIC EXPLORER
Andrés Ruzo CONSERVATIONIST

Andrés Ruzo is a geothermal scientist known for his work at the world's largest documented thermal river, the Boiling River of the Amazon. He is the founder and director of the Boiling River Project, conducting scientific research and conservation work in the Boiling River area. Andres is also heavily involved in education. He serves on the boards of a high school and a university in Costa Rica, and is a Student Independent Research Teacher at schools in the United States.

- What is geothermal science?
- How can geothermal energy be used to generate electricity? What percent of the electricity used in the United States is geothermal?
- What is the typical temperature of Earth's crust at a depth of 1 mile? 2 miles?

PERFORMANCE TASK
Geothermal power plants harness the heat within the earth and use it to generate electricity. In the Performance Task on pages 160 and 161, you will find a location for a new power plant that will provide electricity to several cities.

Geothermal Science

Big Idea of the Chapter
Understand Parallel and Perpendicular Lines

Parallel lines are lines in a plane that are always the same distance apart. Parallel lines do not intersect. Perpendicular lines are lines that intersect at a right angle.

Earth is divided into four major components.

- An *inner core* of solid iron that is about 2,440 kilometers in diameter
- An *outer core* of molten rock (magma) that is about 2,300 kilometers thick
- A *mantle* of magma and rock that is about 3,000 kilometers thick
- A *crust* of solid rock that forms the continents and ocean floors that is as many as 70 kilometers thick on land, and as few as 5 kilometers thick under the ocean floor

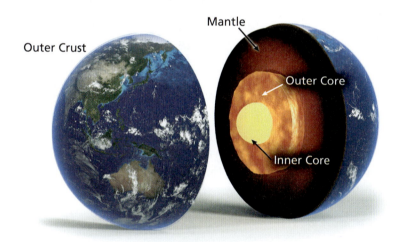

1. In general, as you travel towards Earth's core, the temperature of the crust increases by about 25°C per kilometer. Complete the table.

Depth (km)	0	0.5	1	1.5	2	2.5	3
Temperature (°C)	15						

2. When you are drilling down into Earth's crust, how can you tell that you are drilling straight down toward Earth's center?

Getting Ready for Chapter 3

Finding the Slope of a Line

EXAMPLE 1 Find the slope of the line.

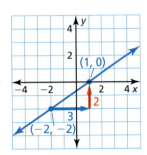

Let $(x_1, y_1) = (-2, -2)$ and $(x_2, y_2) = (1, 0)$.

$$\text{slope} = \frac{y_2 - y_1}{x_2 - x_1} \quad \text{Write formula for slope.}$$

$$= \frac{0 - (-2)}{1 - (-2)} \quad \text{Substitute.}$$

$$= \frac{2}{3} \quad \text{Simplify.}$$

Find the slope of the line.

1.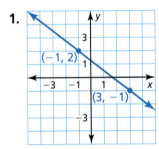
2.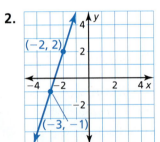
3.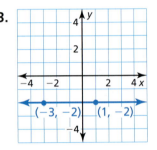

Writing Equations of Lines

EXAMPLE 2 Write an equation of the line that passes through the point $(-4, 5)$ and has a slope of $\frac{3}{4}$.

$y = mx + b$ Write the slope-intercept form.

$5 = \frac{3}{4}(-4) + b$ Substitute $\frac{3}{4}$ for m, -4 for x, and 5 for y.

$5 = -3 + b$ Simplify.

$8 = b$ Solve for b.

▶ So, an equation is $y = \frac{3}{4}x + 8$.

Write an equation of the line that passes through the given point and has the given slope.

4. $(6, 1); m = -3$
5. $(-3, 8); m = -2$
6. $(-1, 5); m = 4$
7. $(2, -4); m = \frac{1}{2}$
8. $(-8, -5); m = -\frac{1}{4}$
9. $(0, 9); m = \frac{2}{3}$

3.1 Pairs of Lines and Angles

> **Learning Target:** Understand lines, planes, and pairs of angles.
>
> **Success Criteria:**
> - I can identify lines and planes.
> - I can identify parallel and perpendicular lines.
> - I can identify pairs of angles formed by transversals.

INVESTIGATE Points of Intersection

1. **Work with a partner.** Write the number of points of intersection of each pair of coplanar lines.

   a. parallel lines
   b. intersecting lines
   c. coincident lines

INVESTIGATE Classifying Pairs of Lines

2. **Work with a partner.** The figure shows a *right rectangular prism*. All its angles are right angles. Classify each of the following pairs of lines as *parallel*, *intersecting*, *coincident*, or *skew*. (Two lines are *skew lines* when they do not intersect and are not coplanar.)

   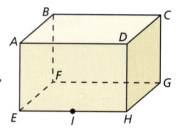

   a. $\overleftrightarrow{AB}$ and $\overleftrightarrow{BC}$
   b. $\overleftrightarrow{AD}$ and $\overleftrightarrow{BC}$
   c. $\overleftrightarrow{EI}$ and $\overleftrightarrow{IH}$
   d. $\overleftrightarrow{BF}$ and $\overleftrightarrow{EH}$
   e. $\overleftrightarrow{EF}$ and $\overleftrightarrow{CG}$
   f. $\overleftrightarrow{AB}$ and $\overleftrightarrow{GH}$

INVESTIGATE Classifying Pairs of Angles

3. **Work with a partner.** In the figure, two parallel lines are intersected by a third line called a *transversal*.

   a. Identify all the pairs of vertical angles.

   b. Identify all the linear pairs of angles.

   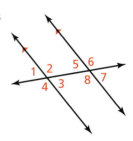

Vocabulary
parallel lines
skew lines
parallel planes
transversal
corresponding angles
alternate interior angles
alternate exterior angles
consecutive interior angles

Identifying Lines and Planes

Key Concept

Parallel Lines, Skew Lines, and Parallel Planes

Two lines that do not intersect are either *parallel lines* or *skew lines*.
Two lines are **parallel lines** when they do not intersect and are coplanar.
Two lines are **skew lines** when they do not intersect and are not coplanar.
Two planes that do not intersect are **parallel planes**.

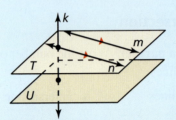

Lines m and n are parallel lines ($m \parallel n$).

Lines m and k are skew lines.

Planes T and U are parallel planes ($T \parallel U$).

Lines k and n are intersecting lines, and there is a plane (not shown) containing them.

Small directed arrows, as shown in red on lines m and n above, are used to show that lines are parallel. The symbol $\parallel$ means "is parallel to," as in $m \parallel n$.

Segments and rays are parallel when they lie in parallel lines. A line is parallel to a plane when the line is in a plane parallel to the given plane.

EXAMPLE 1 Identifying Lines and Planes

Consider the lines that contain the segments in the figure and the planes that contain the faces of the figure. Which line(s) or plane(s) appear to fit each description?

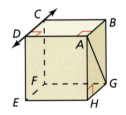

a. line(s) parallel to $\overleftrightarrow{CD}$ and containing point A

$\overleftrightarrow{AB}$, $\overleftrightarrow{HG}$, and $\overleftrightarrow{EF}$ all appear parallel to $\overleftrightarrow{CD}$, but only $\overleftrightarrow{AB}$ contains point A.

b. line(s) skew to $\overleftrightarrow{CD}$ and containing point A

Both $\overleftrightarrow{AG}$ and $\overleftrightarrow{AH}$ appear skew to $\overleftrightarrow{CD}$ and contain point A.

c. plane(s) parallel to plane EFG and containing point A

Plane ABC appears parallel to plane EFG and contains point A.

In-Class Practice

Self-Assessment

Use the diagram in Example 1.

1. Name the line(s) through point F that appear skew to $\overleftrightarrow{EH}$.

2. Name the line(s) through point A that appear perpendicular to $\overleftrightarrow{GH}$.

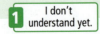

Identifying Parallel and Perpendicular Lines

Two lines in the same plane are either parallel or intersect at a point.

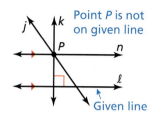

Through a point not on a given line, there are infinitely many lines. Exactly one of these lines is parallel to the given line, and exactly one of them is perpendicular to the given line.

Postulate 3.1

3.1 Parallel Postulate

If there is a line and a point not on the line, then there is exactly one line through the point parallel to the given line.

Postulate 3.2

3.2 Perpendicular Postulate

If there is a line and a point not on the line, then there is exactly one line through the point perpendicular to the given line.

EXAMPLE 2 Identifying Parallel and Perpendicular Lines

The map shows how the roads in a town are related to one another.

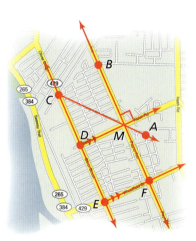

a. **Name a pair of parallel lines.**
$\overleftrightarrow{MD} \parallel \overleftrightarrow{FE}$

b. **Name a pair of perpendicular lines.**
$\overleftrightarrow{MD} \perp \overleftrightarrow{BF}$

c. **Is $\overleftrightarrow{FE} \parallel \overleftrightarrow{AC}$? Explain.**
$\overleftrightarrow{FE}$ is not parallel to $\overleftrightarrow{AC}$, because $\overleftrightarrow{MD}$ is parallel to $\overleftrightarrow{FE}$, and by the Parallel Postulate, there is exactly one line parallel to $\overleftrightarrow{FE}$ through M.

In-Class Practice

Self-Assessment

3. In Example 2, explain whether you can use the Perpendicular Postulate to show that $\overleftrightarrow{CE}$ is *not* perpendicular to $\overleftrightarrow{BF}$.

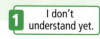

Identifying Pairs of Angles

A **transversal** is a line that intersects two or more coplanar lines at different points.

Key Concept

Angles Formed by Transversals

Two angles are **corresponding angles** when they have corresponding positions.

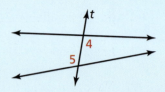

Two angles are **alternate interior angles** when they lie between the two lines and on opposite sides of the transversal t.

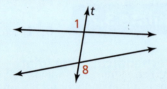

Two angles are **alternate exterior angles** when they lie outside the two lines and on opposite sides of the transversal t.

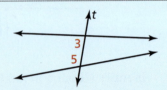

Two angles are **consecutive interior angles** when they lie between the two lines and on the same side of the transversal t.

EXAMPLE 3 Identifying Pairs of Angles

Identify all pairs of angles of the given type.

a. corresponding

∠1 and ∠5, ∠2 and ∠6, ∠3 and ∠7, ∠4 and ∠8

b. alternate interior

∠2 and ∠7, ∠4 and ∠5

c. alternate exterior

∠1 and ∠8, ∠3 and ∠6

d. consecutive interior

∠2 and ∠5, ∠4 and ∠7

In-Class Practice

Self-Assessment

Classify the pair of numbered angles.

4.

5.

 I don't understand yet.   I can do it with help.   I can do it on my own.   I can teach someone.

3.1 Practice

Consider the lines that contain the segments in the figure and the planes that contain the faces of the figure. All angles are right angles. Which line(s) or plane(s) contain point *B* and appear to fit the description? (See Example 1.)

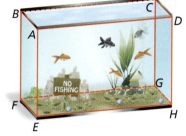

▶ 1. line(s) parallel to $\overleftrightarrow{CD}$

2. line(s) skew to $\overleftrightarrow{CD}$

3. plane(s) parallel to plane *CDH*

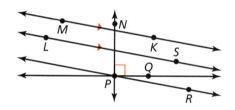

Use the diagram. (See Example 2.)

4. Name a pair of perpendicular lines.

▶ 5. Is $\overleftrightarrow{PN} \parallel \overleftrightarrow{KM}$? Explain.

6. Is $\overleftrightarrow{PR} \perp \overleftrightarrow{NP}$? Explain.

Identify all pairs of angles of the given type. (See Example 3.)

▶ 7. corresponding

8. alternate interior

9. alternate exterior

10. consecutive interior

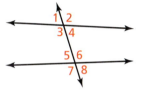

SMP.7 Classify the angle pair as *corresponding*, *alternate interior*, *alternate exterior*, or *consecutive interior* angles.

▶ 11. ∠5 and ∠1

12. ∠11 and ∠13

13. ∠6 and ∠13

14. ∠2 and ∠11

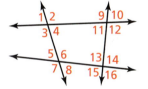

15. **GEOTHERMAL SCIENCE** **VOLCANO** Explain whether the line containing the *main vent* is skew to the line containing the *secondary vent*.

STEM Video: Tree House

16. **CONNECTION TO REAL LIFE** Use the photo to decide whether the statement is true or false. Explain.

   a. The plane containing the floor of the tree house is parallel to the ground.

   b. All the lines containing the balusters, such as $\overleftrightarrow{CD}$, are perpendicular to the plane containing the floor of the tree house.

Interpreting Data

PARALLEL POSTULATES Euclid's *Elements* defines what is now called *Euclidean geometry*. In Euclidian geometry, the Parallel Postulate is true, but it was eventually discovered that there are other types of geometry where it does not apply. In non-Euclidean geometries, such as spherical geometry and hyperbolic geometry, the theorems you will study in this course are not always true.

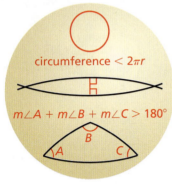

Spherical Geometry

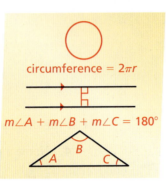

Euclidean Geometry

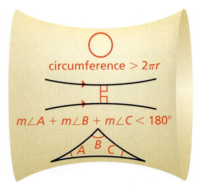

Hyperbolic Geometry

17. Compare the circumferences of circles with the same radius for these geometries.

18. What can you say about parallel lines in each of these geometries?

19. Compare the sums of the angle measures of a triangle for these geometries.

Review & Refresh

20. Copy the segment and construct a segment bisector by paper folding. Then label the midpoint *M*.

21. Solve the inequality $t - (-3) \geq 7$. Graph the solution.

22. Name the property that the statement $\overline{FG} \cong \overline{FG}$ illustrates.

Solve the system.

23. $y = \frac{1}{6}x + 1$
$y = \frac{1}{3}x + 2$

24. $-0.5x - 1.5y = -7$
$3.5x + 1.5y = 4$

25. Use the Transitive Property of Equality to complete the statement. If $m\angle 3 = m\angle 5$ and $m\angle 5 = m\angle 7$, then _____.

26. Write a proof using any format.

Given $\angle 1$ and $\angle 3$ are complementary.
$\angle 2$ and $\angle 4$ are complementary.

Prove $\angle 1 \cong \angle 4$

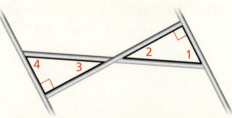

27. Write an equation of the line that passes through the point (1, 3) and has a slope of -2.

28. Evaluate $\sqrt[3]{-125}$.

29. Find the volume of a cylinder with a radius of 5 inches and a height of 2 inches.

3.2 Parallel Lines and Transversals

Learning Target: Prove and use theorems about parallel lines.

Success Criteria:
• I can use properties of parallel lines to find angle measures.
• I can prove theorems about parallel lines.

INVESTIGATE Making Conjectures about Parallel Lines

1. **SMP.5** **Work with a partner.** Draw two parallel lines. Draw a third line that intersects both parallel lines. Find the measures of the eight angles that are formed. What can you conclude?

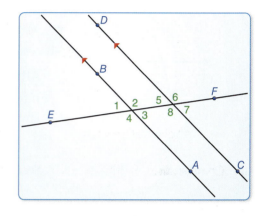

INVESTIGATE Writing Conjectures

2. **Work with a partner.** Use the results of Exercise 1 to write conjectures about the following pairs of angles formed by two parallel lines and a transversal.

   a. corresponding angles

   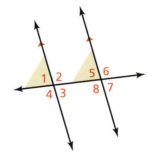

   b. alternate interior angles

   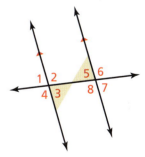

   c. consecutive interior angles

   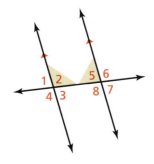

   d. alternate exterior angles

   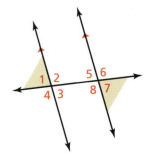

Using Properties of Parallel Lines

Theorem 3.1

Corresponding Angles Theorem

If two parallel lines are cut by a transversal, then the pairs of corresponding angles are congruent.

Examples ∠1 ≅ ∠5, ∠2 ≅ ∠6, ∠3 ≅ ∠7, and ∠4 ≅ ∠8

Prove this Theorem Exercise 27, page 173

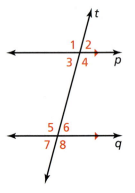

Theorem 3.2

Alternate Interior Angles Theorem

If two parallel lines are cut by a transversal, then the pairs of alternate interior angles are congruent.

Examples ∠3 ≅ ∠6 and ∠4 ≅ ∠5

Prove this Theorem Exercise 13, page 128

EXAMPLE 1 Identifying Angles

Identify the numbered angles that have a measure of 120°.

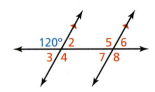

Using the Corresponding Angles Theorem, $m\angle 5 = 120°$.

∠5 and ∠8 are vertical angles. Using the Vertical Angles Congruence Theorem, $m\angle 8 = 120°$.

∠5 and ∠4 are alternate interior angles. Using the Alternate Interior Angles Theorem, $m\angle 4 = 120°$.

▶ So, the numbered angles that have a measure of 120° are ∠4, ∠5, and ∠8.

In-Class Practice

Self-Assessment

1. Given $m\angle 1 = 105°$, find $m\angle 4$, $m\angle 5$, and $m\angle 8$. Explain which theorems you used.

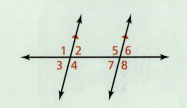

 I don't understand yet.   I can do it with help.   I can do it on my own.   I can teach someone.

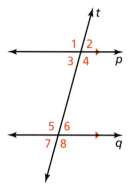

> ### Theorem 3.3
>
> **Alternate Exterior Angles Theorem**
>
> If two parallel lines are cut by a transversal, then the pairs of alternate exterior angles are congruent.
>
> **Examples** ∠1 ≅ ∠8 and ∠2 ≅ ∠7
>
> *Proof* Example 3, page 126

> ### Theorem 3.4
>
> **Consecutive Interior Angles Theorem**
>
> If two parallel lines are cut by a transversal, then the pairs of consecutive interior angles are supplementary.
>
> **Examples** ∠3 and ∠5 are supplementary, and
> ∠4 and ∠6 are supplementary
>
> *Prove this Theorem* Exercise 14, page 128

EXAMPLE 2 **Using Properties of Parallel Lines**

Find the value of x.

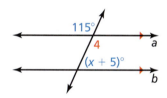

By the Vertical Angles Congruence Theorem, $m\angle 4 = 115°$. Lines a and b are parallel, so you can use theorems about parallel lines.

$m\angle 4 + (x + 5)° = 180°$	Consecutive Interior Angles Theorem
$115° + (x + 5)° = 180°$	Substitute 115° for $m\angle 4$.
$x + 120 = 180$	Combine like terms.
$x = 60$	Subtract 120 from each side.

▶ So, the value of x is 60.

In-Class Practice

Self-Assessment

2. Given $m\angle 3 = 68°$ and $m\angle 8 = (2x + 4)°$, what is the value of x?

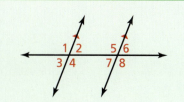

| 1 I don't understand yet. | 2 I can do it with help. | 3 I can do it on my own. | 4 I can teach someone. |

3.2 Parallel Lines and Transversals

Proving Theorems about Parallel Lines

EXAMPLE 3 Proving the Alternate Exterior Angles Theorem

Prove that if two parallel lines are cut by a transversal, then the pairs of alternate exterior angles are congruent.

Draw a diagram. Label a pair of alternate exterior angles as ∠1 and ∠2.

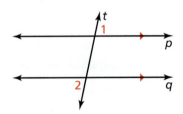

You are looking for an angle that is related to both ∠1 and ∠2. Notice that one angle is a vertical angle with ∠2 and a corresponding angle with ∠1. Label it ∠3.

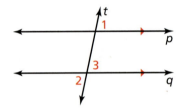

Given $p \parallel q$

Prove ∠1 ≅ ∠2

STATEMENTS	REASONS
1. $p \parallel q$	1. Given
2. ∠1 ≅ ∠3	2. Corresponding Angles Theorem
3. ∠3 ≅ ∠2	3. Vertical Angles Congruence Theorem
4. ∠1 ≅ ∠2	4. Transitive Property of Angle Congruence

In-Class Practice

Self-Assessment

3. Write an alternative proof for the Alternate Exterior Angles Theorem using the diagram shown.

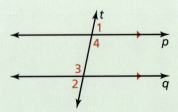

1 I don't understand yet.   **2** I can do it with help.   **3** I can do it on my own.   **4** I can teach someone.

126   Chapter 3   Parallel and Perpendicular Lines

Connections to Real Life

EXAMPLE 4 Using Properties of Parallel Lines

When sunlight enters a drop of rain, different colors of light leave the drop at different angles. This process is what makes a rainbow. For violet light, $m\angle 2 = 40°$. What is $m\angle 1$?

The Sun's rays are parallel, and ∠1 and ∠2 are alternate interior angles. By the Alternate Interior Angles Theorem, ∠1 ≅ ∠2.

▶ So, by the definition of congruent angles, $m\angle 1 = m\angle 2 = 40°$.

In-Class Practice
Self-Assessment

4. **WHAT IF?** In Example 4, $m\angle 2 = 41°$ for yellow light. What is $m\angle 1$? How do you know?

5. You are climbing between trees at an adventure park using ropes. What is $m\angle 1$?

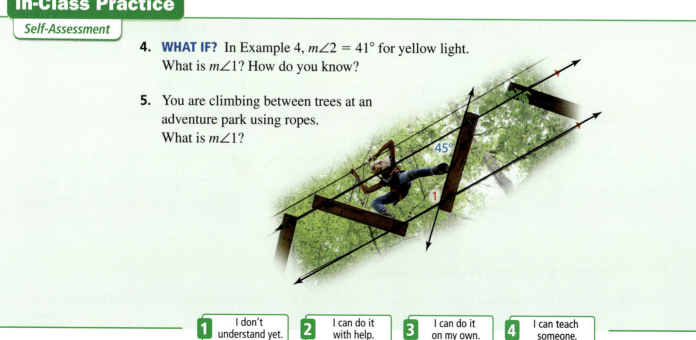

| **1** I don't understand yet. | **2** I can do it with help. | **3** I can do it on my own. | **4** I can teach someone. |

3.2 Practice

Find $m\angle 1$ and $m\angle 2$. Explain which theorems you used. (See Example 1.)

1.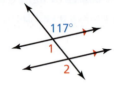

2.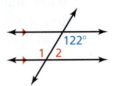

Find the value of x. (See Example 2.)

3.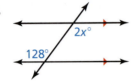

4.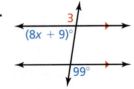

5.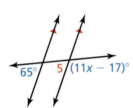

6.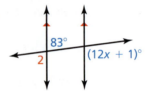

Find $m\angle 1$, $m\angle 2$, and $m\angle 3$.

7.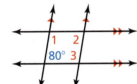

8.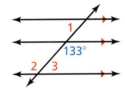

9.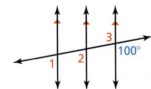

10.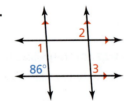

SMP.3 ERROR ANALYSIS Describe and correct the error in the student's reasoning.

11.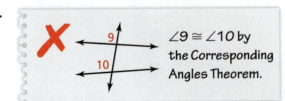

12.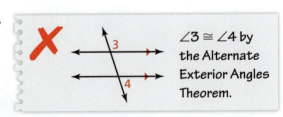

PROVING A THEOREM Prove the theorem. (See Example 3.)

13. Alternate Interior Angles Theorem

14. Consecutive Interior Angles Theorem

15. **CONNECTION TO REAL LIFE** A group of campers tie up their food between two parallel trees, as shown. The rope is pulled taut, forming a straight line. Find $m\angle 2$. (See Example 4.)

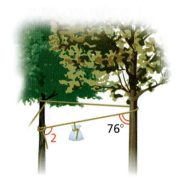

16. **CONNECTION TO REAL LIFE** You are designing a box like the one shown.

   a. The measure of $\angle 1$ is 70°. Find $m\angle 2$ and $m\angle 3$.

   b. Explain why $\angle ABC$ is a straight angle.

   c. If $m\angle 1$ is 60°, will $\angle ABC$ still be a straight angle? Explain whether the opening of the box will be *more steep* or *less steep*.

17. Explain whether it is possible for consecutive interior angles to be congruent.

CONNECT CONCEPTS Write and solve a system of linear equations to find the values of *x* and *y*.

18.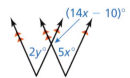

19.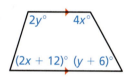

20. In the diagram, $\angle 4 \cong \angle 5$, and $\overline{SE}$ bisects $\angle RSF$. Find $m\angle 1$.

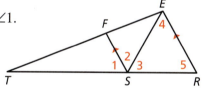

21. **SMP.6** Your friend claims to be able to make the pool shot shown in the diagram by hitting the cue ball so that $m\angle 1 = 25°$. Explain whether your friend is correct.

22. **SMP.1** **DIG DEEPER** The postulates and theorems in this book represent Euclidean geometry. In spherical geometry, a great circle is similar to a line in Euclidean geometry. A great circle is any circle of a sphere whose diameter is equal to the diameter of the sphere. In spherical geometry, explain whether it is possible that a transversal intersects two parallel lines.

Interpreting Data

AIRPORT RUNWAY DESIGN Boston Logan Airport has 6 runways. Runway numbers are determined by the direction in which a plane using the runway is traveling. A plane would travel north on runway 36, east on runway 9, south on runway 18, and west on runway 27.

23. Use the compass to explain how to name a runway. Then explain why runway 22R is also called 4L.

24. Are runways 22R and 22L parallel? How can you tell?

25. Find the measures of the angles formed where runway 15R intersects runways 22R and 22L.

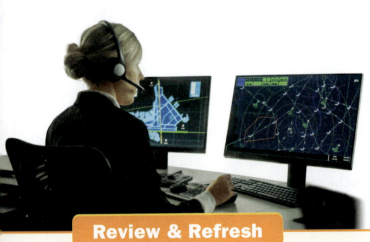

Logan Airport
Boston, Massachussetts

Review & Refresh

Use the diagram.

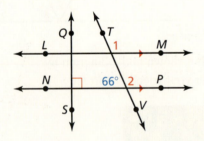

26. Name a pair of perpendicular lines.

27. Name a pair of parallel lines.

Name the property that the statement illustrates.

28. If $\angle F \cong \angle G$ and $\angle G \cong \angle H$, then $\angle F \cong \angle H$.

29. If $\overline{WX} \cong \overline{YZ}$, then $\overline{YZ} \cong \overline{WX}$.

Factor the polynomial completely.

30. $t^3 - 5t^2 + 3t - 15$ 31. $4x^4 - 36x^2$

32. Find the x- and y-intercepts of the graph of $7x - 4y = 28$.

33. A square painting is surrounded by a frame with uniform width. The painting has a side length of $(x - 3)$ inches. The side length of the frame is $(x + 2)$ inches. Write an expression for the area of the square frame. Then find the area of the frame when $x = 12$.

34. Find the value of x in the diagram.

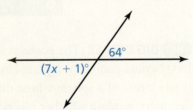

130   Chapter 3   Parallel and Perpendicular Lines

3.3 Proofs with Parallel Lines

Learning Target: Prove and use theorems about identifying parallel lines.

Success Criteria:
- I can use theorems to identify parallel lines.
- I can construct parallel lines.
- I can prove theorems about identifying parallel lines.

INVESTIGATE Exploring Converses

Work with a partner. Write the converse of each conditional statement. Draw a diagram to represent the converse. Explain whether the converse is true.

1. **Corresponding Angles Theorem**
   If two parallel lines are cut by a transversal, then the pairs of corresponding angles are congruent.

   Converse

   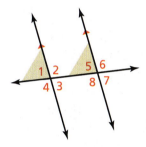

2. **Alternate Interior Angles Theorem**
   If two parallel lines are cut by a transversal, then the pairs of alternate interior angles are congruent.

   Converse

   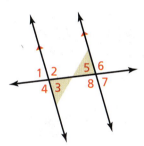

3. **Alternate Exterior Angles Theorem**
   If two parallel lines are cut by a transversal, then the pairs of alternate exterior angles are congruent.

   Converse

   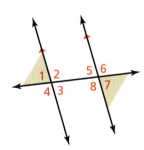

4. **Consecutive Interior Angles Theorem**
   If two parallel lines are cut by a transversal, then the pairs of consecutive interior angles are supplementary.

   Converse

   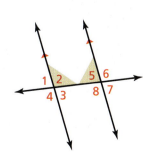

Using Converses of Theorems

The theorem below is the converse of the Corresponding Angles Theorem. Similarly, the other theorems about angles formed when parallel lines are cut by a transversal have true converses. Remember that the converse of a true conditional statement is not necessarily true, so you must prove each converse of a theorem.

Theorem 3.5

Corresponding Angles Converse

If two lines are cut by a transversal so the corresponding angles are congruent, then the lines are parallel.

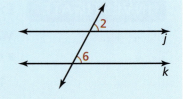

Prove this Theorem Exercise 27, page 173

EXAMPLE 1 Using the Corresponding Angles Converse

Find the value of x that makes $m \parallel n$.

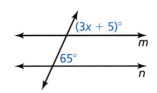

Lines m and n are parallel when the marked corresponding angles are congruent.

$(3x + 5)° = 65°$ Use the Corresponding Angles Converse to write an equation.

$3x = 60$ Subtract 5 from each side.

$x = 20$ Divide each side by 3.

▶ So, lines m and n are parallel when $x = 20$.

Check Verify that the angles have the same measure when $x = 20$.

$(3x + 5)° = (3(20) + 5)°$ Substitute 20 for x.

$= (60 + 5)°$ Multiply.

$= 65°$ ✓   Add.

In-Class Practice

Self-Assessment

1. Find the value of x that makes $m \parallel n$.

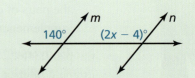

Construction

Constructing Parallel Lines

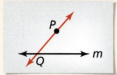

Draw a point P and a line m. Choose a point Q on line m and draw $\overleftrightarrow{QP}$.

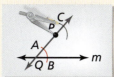

Draw an arc with center Q that crosses both lines. Use the same compass setting to draw an arc with center P. Label points A, B, and C.

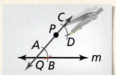

Draw an arc with radius AB and center A. Use the same compass setting to draw an arc with center C. Label point D.

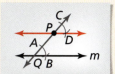

Draw $\overleftrightarrow{PD}$. This line is parallel to line m.

Theorem 3.6

Alternate Interior Angles Converse

If two lines are cut by a transversal so the alternate interior angles are congruent, then the lines are parallel.

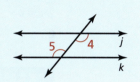

EXAMPLE 2   Proving the Alternate Interior Angles Converse

Prove that if two lines are cut by a transversal so the alternate interior angles are congruent, then the lines are parallel.

Given $\angle 4 \cong \angle 5$

Prove $g \parallel h$

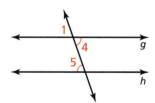

STATEMENTS	REASONS
1. $\angle 4 \cong \angle 5$	1. Given
2. $\angle 1 \cong \angle 4$	2. Vertical Angles Congruence Theorem
3. $\angle 1 \cong \angle 5$	3. Transitive Property of Angle Congruence
4. $g \parallel h$	4. Corresponding Angles Converse

In-Class Practice

Self-Assessment

2. In Example 2, let $\angle 2$ and $\angle 5$ be vertical angles. Write an alternative proof for the Alternate Interior Angles Converse using $\angle 2$.

Theorem 3.7

Alternate Exterior Angles Converse

If two lines are cut by a transversal so the alternate exterior angles are congruent, then the lines are parallel.

Prove this Theorem Exercise 6, page 136

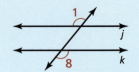

Theorem 3.8

Consecutive Interior Angles Converse

If two lines are cut by a transversal so the consecutive interior angles are supplementary, then the lines are parallel.

Prove this Theorem Exercise 7, page 136

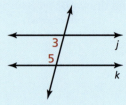

If ∠3 and ∠5 are supplementary, then j ∥ k.

EXAMPLE 3 Determining Whether Lines Are Parallel

In the diagram, r ∥ s and ∠1 is congruent to ∠3. Prove p ∥ q.

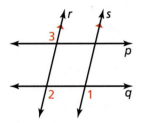

Look at the diagram to make a plan. The diagram suggests that you look at angles 1, 2, and 3. Also, you may find it helpful to focus on one pair of lines and one transversal at a time.

Plan for Proof
  a. Look at ∠1 and ∠2. ∠1 ≅ ∠2 because r ∥ s.
  b. Look at ∠2 and ∠3. If ∠2 ≅ ∠3, then p ∥ q.

Plan in Action
  a. It is given that r ∥ s, so by the Corresponding Angles Theorem, ∠1 ≅ ∠2.
  b. It is also given that ∠1 ≅ ∠3. Then ∠2 ≅ ∠3 by the Transitive Property of Angle Congruence.

▶ So, by the Alternate Exterior Angles Converse, p ∥ q.

In-Class Practice

Self-Assessment

3. In the diagram, j ∥ k and ∠2 is congruent to ∠3. Prove m ∥ n.

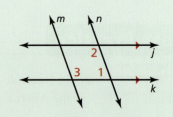

Using the Transitive Property of Parallel Lines

Theorem 3.9

Transitive Property of Parallel Lines

If two lines are parallel to the same line, then they are parallel to each other.

Prove this Theorem Exercise 26, page 137;
Exercise 29, page 155

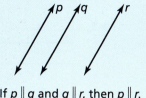

If $p \parallel q$ and $q \parallel r$, then $p \parallel r$.

EXAMPLE 4 Using the Transitive Property of Parallel Lines

The flag of the United States has 13 alternating red and white stripes. Each stripe is parallel to the stripe immediately below it. Explain why the top stripe is parallel to the bottom stripe.

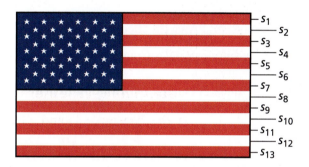

You can name the stripes from top to bottom as $s_1, s_2, s_3, \ldots, s_{13}$. Each stripe is parallel to the one immediately below it, so $s_1 \parallel s_2$, $s_2 \parallel s_3$, and so on. Then $s_1 \parallel s_3$ by the Transitive Property of Parallel Lines. Similarly, because $s_3 \parallel s_4$, it follows that $s_1 \parallel s_4$. By continuing this reasoning, $s_1 \parallel s_{13}$.

▶ So, the top stripe is parallel to the bottom stripe by the Transitive Property of Parallel Lines.

In-Class Practice
Self-Assessment

4. Each step is parallel to the step immediately above it. The bottom step is parallel to the ground. Explain why the top step is parallel to the ground.

| **1** I don't understand yet. | **2** I can do it with help. | **3** I can do it on my own. | **4** I can teach someone. |

3.3 Practice

Find the value of *x* that makes *m* ∥ *n*. (See Example 1.)

1.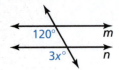

2.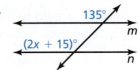

3.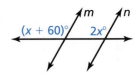

CONSTRUCTION Trace line *m* and point *P*. Then use a compass and straightedge to construct a line through point *P* that is parallel to line *m*.

4.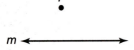

5.

PROVING A THEOREM Prove the theorem. (See Example 2.)

6. Consecutive Interior Angles Converse

7. Alternate Exterior Angles Converse

Decide whether there is enough information to prove that *m* ∥ *n*. If so, state the theorem you can use. (See Example 3.)

8.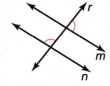

9.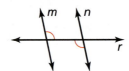

10.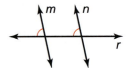

Find the value of *x* that makes *m* ∥ *n*.

11.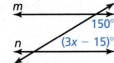

12.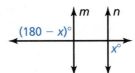

13.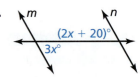

SMP.3 ERROR ANALYSIS Describe and correct the error in the reasoning.

14.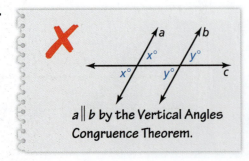

15.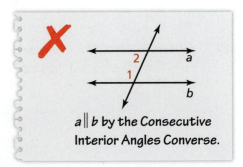

136 Chapter 3 Parallel and Perpendicular Lines

Explain whether $\overleftrightarrow{AC}$ and $\overleftrightarrow{DF}$ are parallel.

16.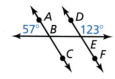

17.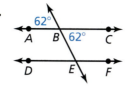

18.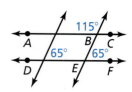

▶ 19. **SMP.8 CONNECTION TO REAL LIFE** Each rung of the ladder is parallel to the rung directly above it. Explain why the top rung is parallel to the bottom rung. (See Example 4.)

20. **CONNECTION TO REAL LIFE** The map shows part of Denver, Colorado. Use the markings on the map. Explain whether the numbered streets are parallel to one another.

21. Explain which rays are parallel and which rays are not parallel.

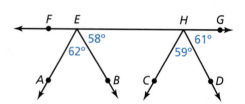

PROOF Write a proof.

22. **Given** ∠1 and ∠3 are supplementary.

    Prove $m \parallel n$

    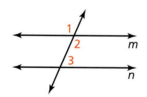

23. **Given** ∠1 ≅ ∠2, ∠3 ≅ ∠4

    Prove $\overline{AB} \parallel \overline{CD}$

    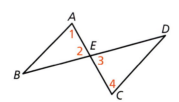

24. **Given** $a \parallel b$, ∠2 ≅ ∠3

    Prove $c \parallel d$

    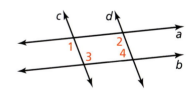

25. **CONNECT CONCEPTS** Can r be parallel to s and can p be parallel to q at the same time?

    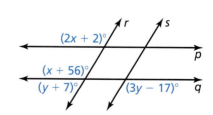

26. **PROVING THEOREM 3.9** Prove the Transitive Property of Parallel Lines Theorem.

3.3 Proofs with Parallel Lines

Interpreting Data

OREGON COUNTRY From 1818 to 1846, Great Britain and the U.S. jointly occupied the region known as Oregon Country. In 1846, the Oregon Treaty divided the region between the countries along the 49th *parallel*.

27. Lines of latitude, or parallels, are about 111 kilometers apart. Estimate the area of Oregon Country between the 42nd and 49th parallels.

28. Today, the 42nd parallel forms the border between which two coastal states?

29. Do latitudes intersect? Are latitudes best described using Euclidean geometry or spherical geometry?

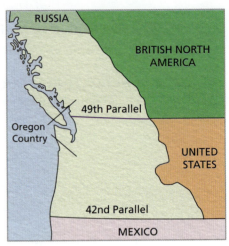

Map of Oregon Country in 1840

Only about 80,000 of an estimated 400,000 Oregon Trail emigrants settled near the end of the trail, in Oregon's Willamette Valley.

Review & Refresh

30. Find the value of *x*.

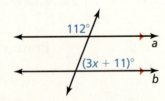

Use the diagram.

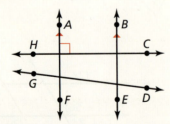

31. Name a pair of perpendicular lines.

32. Is $\overleftrightarrow{HC} \parallel \overleftrightarrow{GD}$?

Find the distance between the two points.

33. $(5, -4)$ and $(0, 8)$

34. $(13, 1)$ and $(9, -4)$

35. Evaluate the function when $x = -2, 3,$ and 5.
$$f(x) = -3x + 5$$

36. Write a proof using any format.

    Given $\angle 1 \cong \angle 3$

    Prove $\angle 2 \cong \angle 4$

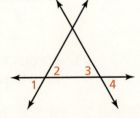

37. The height (in feet) of a T-shirt *t* seconds after it is launched into a crowd can be represented by $h(t) = -16t^2 + 96t + 4$. Estimate and interpret the maximum value of the function.

138 Chapter 3 Parallel and Perpendicular Lines

3.4 Proofs with Perpendicular Lines

> **Learning Target:** Prove and use theorems about perpendicular lines.
>
> **Success Criteria:**
> - I can find the distance from a point to a line.
> - I can construct perpendicular lines and perpendicular bisectors.
> - I can prove theorems about perpendicular lines.

INVESTIGATE Constructing Perpendicular Lines

Work with a partner.

1. Use a piece of paper.

   a. Fold and crease the piece of paper, as shown. Label the ends of the crease as A and B.

   b. Fold the paper again so that point A coincides with point B. Crease the paper on that fold.

   c. Unfold the paper and examine the four angles formed by the two creases. What can you conclude about the four angles?

INVESTIGATE Constructing Perpendicular Lines

Work with a partner.

2. Use a new piece of paper and repeat the first step of Exercise 1.

   a. Unfold the paper and draw a point not on the crease, as shown. Label the point C.

   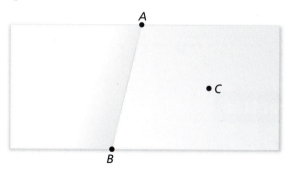

   b. Fold the paper so that the existing crease lies on top of itself and point C lies on the new fold. Crease the paper on the new fold.

   c. Unfold the paper and examine the four angles formed by the two creases. What can you conclude about the four angles?

   d. Explain whether you can find a line segment that connects $\overline{AB}$ and C that is shorter than the one on the new fold.

Finding the Distance from a Point to a Line

Vocabulary
distance from a point to a line
perpendicular bisector

The **distance from a point to a line** is the least distance between the point and any point on the line. You can find this distance by finding the length of the perpendicular segment from the point to the line. For example, the distance between point A and line k is AB.

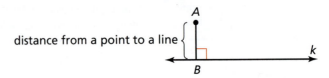

EXAMPLE 1   Finding the Distance from a Point to a Line

Find the distance from point A to $\overleftrightarrow{BD}$.

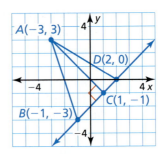

Because $\overline{AC} \perp \overleftrightarrow{BD}$, the distance from point A to $\overleftrightarrow{BD}$ is AC. Use the Distance Formula.

$AC = \sqrt{(x_2 - x_1)^2 + (y_2 - y_1)^2}$ Distance Formula

$AC = \sqrt{[1-(-3)]^2 + (-1-3)^2}$ Substitute.

$ = \sqrt{4^2 + (-4)^2}$ Simplify.

$ = \sqrt{32}$ Simplify.

$ \approx 5.7$ Approximate.

▶ So, the distance from point A to $\overleftrightarrow{BD}$ is about 5.7 units.

In-Class Practice

Self-Assessment

1. Find the distance from point E to $\overleftrightarrow{FH}$.

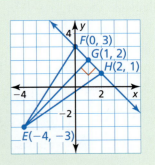

   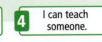

Constructing Perpendicular Lines

Construction

Constructing a Perpendicular Line

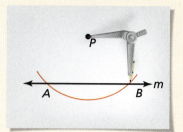
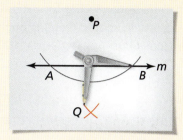
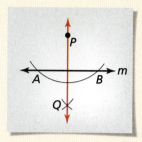

Draw an arc with center P that intersects the line twice.

Draw intersecting arcs with the same radius and centers A and B.

Draw $\overleftrightarrow{PQ}$. This line is perpendicular to line m.

The **perpendicular bisector** of a line segment $\overline{PQ}$ is the line n with the following two properties.

- $n \perp \overline{PQ}$
- n passes through the midpoint M of $\overline{PQ}$.

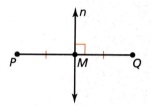

Construction

Constructing a Perpendicular Bisector

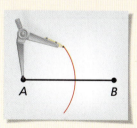
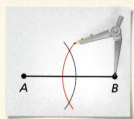
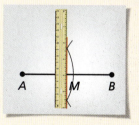

Draw an arc with center A using a compass setting that is greater than half the length of $\overline{AB}$.

Keep the same compass setting. Place the compass at B. Draw an arc.

Draw a line through the two points of intersection. This line is the perpendicular bisector.

In-Class Practice

Self-Assessment

2. Trace $\overline{AB}$. Then use a compass and straightedge to construct a perpendicular bisector of $\overline{AB}$.

3.4 Proofs with Perpendicular Lines   141

Proving Theorems about Perpendicular Lines

Theorem 3.10

3.10 Linear Pair Perpendicular Theorem

If two lines intersect to form a linear pair of congruent angles, then the lines are perpendicular.

If ∠1 ≅ ∠2, then g ⊥ h.

Prove this Theorem Exercise 7, page 145

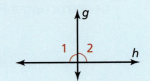

Theorem 3.11

3.11 Perpendicular Transversal Theorem

In a plane, if a transversal is perpendicular to one of two parallel lines, then it is perpendicular to the other line.

If h ∥ k and j ⊥ h, then j ⊥ k.

Prove this Theorem Exercise 3, page 142

EXAMPLE 2 Proving the Perpendicular Transversal Theorem

Use the diagram to prove the Perpendicular Transversal Theorem.

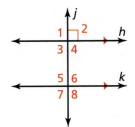

Given h ∥ k, j ⊥ h

Prove j ⊥ k

STATEMENTS	REASONS
1. h ∥ k, j ⊥ h	1. Given
2. m∠2 = 90°	2. Definition of perpendicular lines
3. ∠2 ≅ ∠6	3. Corresponding Angles Theorem
4. m∠2 = m∠6	4. Definition of congruent angles
5. m∠6 = 90°	5. Transitive Property of Equality
6. j ⊥ k	6. Definition of perpendicular lines

In-Class Practice

Self-Assessment

3. Prove the Perpendicular Transversal Theorem using the diagram in Example 2 and the Alternate Exterior Angles Theorem.

Theorem 3.12

3.12 Lines Perpendicular to a Transversal Theorem

In a plane, if two lines are perpendicular to the same line, then they are parallel to each other.

If $m \perp p$ and $n \perp p$, then $m \parallel n$.

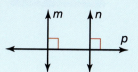

Prove this Theorem Exercise 8, page 145; Exercise 28, page 155

EXAMPLE 3 Using the Lines Perpendicular to a Transversal Theorem

Use the diagram.

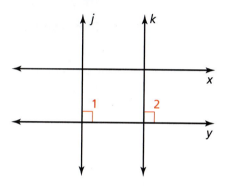

a. Name two pairs of perpendicular lines.

$\angle 1$ and $\angle 2$ are right angles. So, $j \perp y$ and $k \perp y$ by the definition of perpendicular lines.

b. Explain which lines, if any, are parallel.

Because both lines j and k are perpendicular to y, $j \parallel k$ by the Lines Perpendicular to a Transversal Theorem.

In-Class Practice

Self-Assessment

Use the diagram.

4. Explain which lines, if any, are parallel.

5. Explain which lines, if any, are perpendicular.

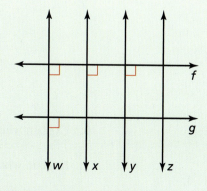

1 I don't understand yet.   **2** I can do it with help.   **3** I can do it on my own.   **4** I can teach someone.

3.4 Proofs with Perpendicular Lines

Connections to Real Life

EXAMPLE 4 **Using a Theorem**

The photo shows the layout of a neighborhood. Explain which lines, if any, must be parallel.

Lines p and q are both perpendicular to s, so by the Lines Perpendicular to a Transversal Theorem, $p \parallel q$. Also, lines s and t are both perpendicular to q, so by the Lines Perpendicular to a Transversal Theorem, $s \parallel t$.

▶ So, from the diagram you can conclude $p \parallel q$ and $s \parallel t$.

In-Class Practice

Self-Assessment

Use the lines marked in the photo.

6. Explain whether $b \parallel a$.

7. Explain whether $b \perp c$.

3.4 Practice

Find the distance from point A to $\overleftrightarrow{XZ}$. (See Example 1.)

1.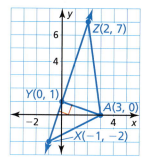

2.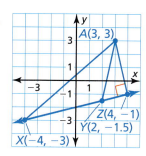

CONSTRUCTION Trace line m and point P. Then use a compass and straightedge to construct a line perpendicular to line m through point P.

3.

4.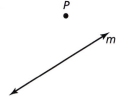

CONSTRUCTION Trace $\overline{AB}$. Then use a compass and straightedge to construct the perpendicular bisector of $\overline{AB}$.

5.

6.

PROVING A THEOREM Prove the theorem. (See Examples 2 and 3).

7. Linear Pair Perpendicular Theorem

8. Lines Perpendicular to a Transversal Theorem

Explain which lines, if any, must be parallel. (See Example 4.)

9.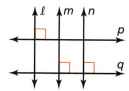

10.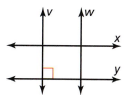

11.

12.

3.4 Proofs with Perpendicular Lines 145

SMP.3 ERROR ANALYSIS Describe and correct the error in the statement about the diagram.

13.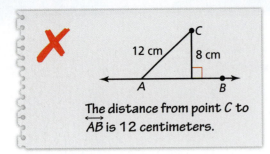

14.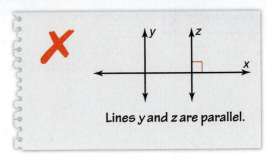

15. You are trying to cross a stream from point A. Explain which point you should jump to in order to jump the shortest distance.

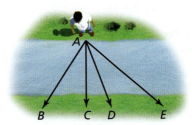

PROOF Use the diagram to write a proof of the statement.

16. If two intersecting lines are perpendicular, then they intersect to form four right angles.

    Given $a \perp b$
    Prove $\angle 1, \angle 2, \angle 3,$ and $\angle 4$ are right angles.

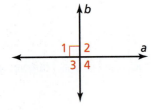

17. If two sides of two adjacent acute angles are perpendicular, then the angles are complementary.

    Given $\overrightarrow{BA} \perp \overrightarrow{BC}$
    Prove $\angle 1$ and $\angle 2$ are complementary.

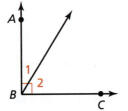

18. **SMP.7** Find all the unknown angle measures in the diagram. Justify your answer for each angle measure.

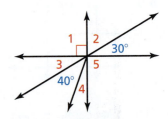

19. **SMP.3** Your friend claims that because you can find the distance from a point to a line, you should be able to find the distance between any two lines. Explain whether your friend is correct.

20. In the diagram, $a \perp b$. Find the value of x that makes $b \parallel c$.

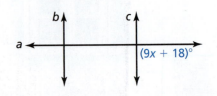

146 Chapter 3 Parallel and Perpendicular Lines

21. **GEOTHERMAL SCIENCE** GEYSER You propose a boardwalk design that passes a geyser. Your proposed design is shown. The boardwalk must be at least 100 feet from the center of the geyser at point G. Explain whether the design meets the requirement.

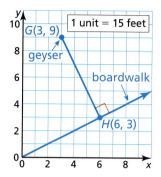

22. The painted line segments that form the path of a crosswalk can be painted as shown, or they can be perpendicular to the two parallel lines of the crosswalk. Explain which type of pattern requires less paint if both types use lines of equal thickness.

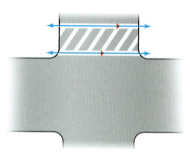

23. **CONSTRUCTION** Construct a square of side length AB.

24. Two lines, a and b, are perpendicular to line c. Line d is parallel to line c. The distance between lines a and b is x meters. The distance between lines c and d is y meters. What shape is formed by the intersections of the four lines?

25. **CONNECT CONCEPTS** Let C be a point on line n. Explain whether the area of △ABC depends on the location of C.

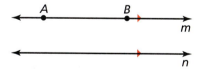

26. **SMP.1** The postulates and theorems in this book represent Euclidean geometry. In spherical geometry, a great circle is similar to a line in Euclidean geometry. A great circle is any circle of a sphere whose diameter is equal to the diameter of the sphere. In spherical geometry, how many right angles are formed by two perpendicular lines? Justify your answer.

27. **SMP.1** Describe how you can find the distance from a point to a plane. Can you find the distance from a line to a plane? Explain your reasoning.

Interpreting Data

CARBON ALLOTROPES The atoms of carbon can bond together in different ways, resulting in allotropes such as diamond, graphite, and hollow meshes called fullerenes. The physical properties of carbon vary widely with the allotrope. For example, diamond is the hardest natural substance and graphite is soft enough to use in pencils.

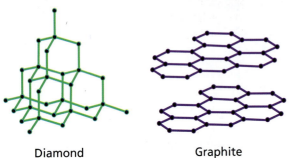

Diamond   Graphite   Buckminsterfullerene

28. Can you identify any perpendicular segments in the bonds of the three allotropes?

29. A single molecule of buckminsterfullerene is called a buckeyball. What popular sport has a ball with a similar structure?

30. Why do you think diamond is the hardest natural substance?

Review & Refresh

Find the slope and the *y*-intercept of the graph of the linear equation.

31. $y = \frac{1}{6}x - 8$ 32. $-3x + y = 9$

33. Two angles form a linear pair. The measure of one angle is 77°. Find the measure of the other angle.

34. The post office and the grocery store are both on the same straight road between the school and your house. The distance from the school to the post office is 376 yards, the distance from the post office to your house is 929 yards, and the distance from the grocery store to your house is 513 yards.

   a. What is the distance from the post office to the grocery store?

   b. What is the distance from the school to your house?

35. Find the slope of the line that passes through $(-4, 3)$ and $(6, 8)$.

36. Is there enough information to prove that $r \parallel s$? If so, state the theorem you can use.

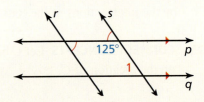

Consider the lines that contain the segments in the figure and the planes that contain the faces of the figure. Which line(s) or plane(s) contain point *G* and appear to fit the description?

37. line(s) parallel to $\overleftrightarrow{EF}$

38. line(s) perpendicular to $\overleftrightarrow{EF}$

39. line(s) skew to $\overleftrightarrow{EF}$

40. plane(s) parallel to plane *ADE*

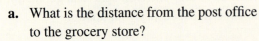

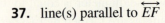

3.5 Equations of Parallel and Perpendicular Lines

Learning Target: Partition line segments and understand slopes of parallel and perpendicular lines.

Success Criteria:
- I can partition directed line segments using slope.
- I can use slopes to identify parallel and perpendicular lines.
- I can write equations of parallel and perpendicular lines.
- I can find the distance from a point to a line.

INVESTIGATE Slopes of Parallel and Perpendicular Lines

1. **Work with a partner.** Write an equation of the line that is parallel or perpendicular to the given line and passes through the given point. What is the relationship between the slopes?

   a.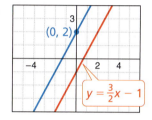

   b.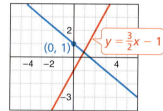

   c.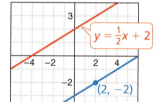

   d.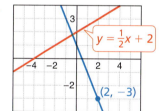

   e.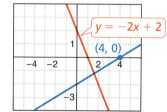

INVESTIGATE Slopes of Parallel and Perpendicular Lines

2. **Work with a partner.** Write the equations of the parallel or perpendicular lines. Use technology to check your answer.

   a.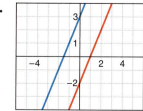

   b.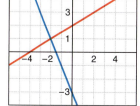

3.5 Equations of Parallel and Perpendicular Lines   149

> **Vocabulary**
> directed line segment

Partitioning a Directed Line Segment

A **directed line segment** AB is a segment that represents moving from point A to point B. The following example shows how to use slope to find a point on a directed line segment that partitions the segment in a given ratio.

EXAMPLE 1 **Partitioning a Directed Line Segment**

Find the coordinates of point P along the directed line segment AB so that the ratio of AP to PB is 3 to 2.

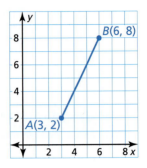

To divide the segment in the ratio 3 to 2, *partition* it into $3 + 2 = 5$ congruent pieces. Point $P(x, y)$ is $\frac{3}{5}$ of the way from point A to point B. Find x and y.

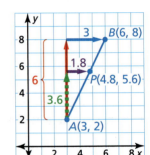

$x = 3 + \frac{3}{5}(6 - 3)$ Add $\frac{3}{5}$ of the horizontal distance (run) between A and B.
$ = 3 + \frac{9}{5}$ Simplify.
$ = \frac{24}{5}$ Add.

$y = 2 + \frac{3}{5}(8 - 2)$ Add $\frac{3}{5}$ of the vertical distance (rise) between A and B.
$ = 2 + \frac{18}{5}$ Simplify.
$ = \frac{28}{5}$ Add.

▶ So, the coordinates of point P are $\left(\frac{24}{5}, \frac{28}{5}\right)$, or $(4.8, 5.6)$.

Check $AP = \sqrt{(4.8 - 3)^2 + (5.6 - 2)^2} = \sqrt{16.2}$
$PB = \sqrt{(6 - 4.8)^2 + (8 - 5.6)^2} = \sqrt{7.2}$
$\dfrac{AP}{PB} = \sqrt{\dfrac{16.2}{7.2}} = 1.5 = \dfrac{3}{2}$ ✓

In-Class Practice

Self-Assessment

1. Find the coordinates of point P along the directed line segment AB so that the ratio of AP to PB is 4 to 1.

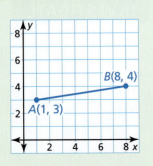

1 I don't understand yet.   **2** I can do it with help.   **3** I can do it on my own.   **4** I can teach someone.

150   Chapter 3   Parallel and Perpendicular Lines

Identifying Parallel and Perpendicular Lines

Theorem 3.13

Slopes of Parallel Lines

In a coordinate plane, two nonvertical lines are parallel if and only if they have the same slope.

Any two vertical lines are parallel.

Proof page 421
Prove this Theorem Exercise 23, page 424

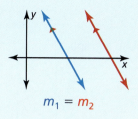

$m_1 = m_2$

Theorem 3.14

Slopes of Perpendicular Lines

In a coordinate plane, two nonvertical lines are perpendicular if and only if the product of their slopes is -1.

Horizontal lines are perpendicular to vertical lines.

Prove this Theorem Exercise 25, page 424
Exercise 26, page 425

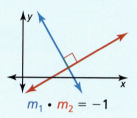

$m_1 \cdot m_2 = -1$

EXAMPLE 2 Identifying Parallel and Perpendicular Lines

Determine which lines are parallel and which lines are perpendicular.

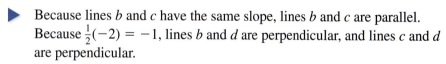

Find the slope of each line.

Line a: $m = \dfrac{3-2}{0-(-3)} = \dfrac{1}{3}$

Line b: $m = \dfrac{0-(-1)}{2-0} = \dfrac{1}{2}$

Line c: $m = \dfrac{-4-(-5)}{1-(-1)} = \dfrac{1}{2}$

Line d: $m = \dfrac{2-0}{-3-(-2)} = -2$

▶ Because lines b and c have the same slope, lines b and c are parallel. Because $\frac{1}{2}(-2) = -1$, lines b and d are perpendicular, and lines c and d are perpendicular.

In-Class Practice

Self-Assessment

2. Determine which lines are parallel and which lines are perpendicular.

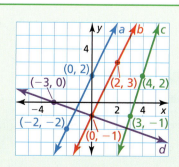

| 1 I don't understand yet. | 2 I can do it with help. | 3 I can do it on my own. | 4 I can teach someone. |

3.5 Equations of Parallel and Perpendicular Lines

Writing Equations of Parallel and Perpendicular Lines

EXAMPLE 3 — Writing an Equation of a Parallel Line

Write an equation of the line passing through the point $(-1, 1)$ that is parallel to the line $y = 2x - 3$.

The line $y = 2x - 3$ has a slope of 2. By the Slopes of Parallel Lines Theorem, a line parallel to this line also has a slope of 2. So, $m = 2$.

Find the y-intercept b by using $m = 2$ and $(x, y) = (-1, 1)$.

$y = mx + b$	Use slope-intercept form.
$1 = 2(-1) + b$	Substitute for m, x, and y.
$3 = b$	Solve for b.

▶ Because $m = 2$ and $b = 3$, an equation of the line is $y = 2x + 3$.

Check Use a graph.

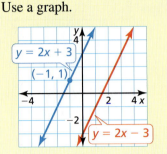

EXAMPLE 4 — Writing an Equation of a Perpendicular Line

Write an equation of the line passing through the point $(2, 3)$ that is perpendicular to the line $2x + y = 2$.

The line $2x + y = 2$, or $y = -2x + 2$, has a slope of -2. Use the Slopes of Perpendicular Lines Theorem to find the slope m of the perpendicular line.

| $-2 \cdot m = -1$ | The product of the slopes of ⊥ lines is -1. |
| $m = \frac{1}{2}$ | Divide each side by -2. |

Find the y-intercept b by using $m = \frac{1}{2}$ and $(x, y) = (2, 3)$.

$y = mx + b$	Use slope-intercept form.
$3 = \frac{1}{2}(2) + b$	Substitute for m, x, and y.
$2 = b$	Solve for b.

▶ Because $m = \frac{1}{2}$ and $b = 2$, an equation of the line is $y = \frac{1}{2}x + 2$.

Check Use a graph.

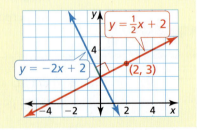

In-Class Practice

Self-Assessment

3. Write an equation of the line that passes through the point $(1, 5)$ and is (a) parallel to the line $y = 3x - 5$ and (b) perpendicular to the line $y = 3x - 5$.

1 I don't understand yet.   **2** I can do it with help.   **3** I can do it on my own.   **4** I can teach someone.

Finding the Distance from a Point to a Line

EXAMPLE 5 Finding the Distance from a Point to a Line

Find the distance from the point (1, 0) to the line $y = -x + 3$.

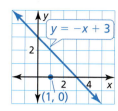

The distance from a point to a line is the length of the perpendicular segment from the point to the line. Find an equation of the line perpendicular to $y = -x + 3$ that passes through the point (1, 0).

> The given line has a slope of -1. So, a line perpendicular to it has a slope of 1.

$y - 0 = 1(x - 1)$ Use point-slope form.
$y = x - 1$ Simplify.

Find the intersection of the perpendicular lines.

$y = -x + 3$ Equation 1
$y = x - 1$ Equation 2

The graph shows that the perpendicular lines intersect at (2, 1).

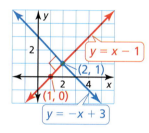

Use the Distance Formula to find the distance from (1, 0) to (2, 1).

$\text{distance} = \sqrt{(2-1)^2 + (1-0)^2}$ Distance Formula
$= \sqrt{1^2 + 1^2}$ Simplify.
$= \sqrt{2}$ Simplify.
≈ 1.4 Use technology.

▶ So, the distance from the point (1, 0) to the line $y = -x + 3$ is about 1.4 units.

In-Class Practice

Self-Assessment

4. Find the distance from the point (6, 4) to the line $y = x + 4$.

5. Find the distance from the point $(-1, 6)$ to the line $y = -2x$.

| 1 I don't understand yet. | 2 I can do it with help. | 3 I can do it on my own. | 4 I can teach someone. |

3.5   Equations of Parallel and Perpendicular Lines

3.5 Practice

Find the coordinates of point P along the directed line segment AB so that AP to PB is the given ratio. (See Example 1.)

1. $A(8, 0)$, $B(3, -2)$; 1 to 4
2. $A(-2, -4)$, $B(6, 1)$; 3 to 2
3. $A(1, 6)$, $B(-2, -3)$; 5 to 1
4. $A(-3, 2)$, $B(5, -4)$; 2 to 6

Determine which of the lines are parallel and which of the lines are perpendicular. (See Example 2.)

5.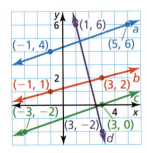
6.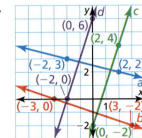

Write an equation of the line passing through point P that is (a) parallel to the given line and (b) perpendicular to the given line. (See Examples 3 and 4.)

7. $P(0, 1)$, $y = -2x + 3$
8. $P(-2, 6)$, $x = -5$
9. $P(4, 0)$, $-x + 2y = 12$
10. $P(2, 3)$, $y + 2 = -2x$

Find the distance from point A to the given line. (See Example 5.)

11. $A(-1, 7)$, $y = 3x$
12. $A(-9, -3)$, $y = x - 6$
13. $A(15, -21)$, $5x + 2y = 4$
14. $A\left(-\frac{1}{4}, 5\right)$, $-x + 2y = 14$

Write an equation of the line that passes through the midpoint of $\overline{PQ}$ and is perpendicular to $\overline{PQ}$.

15. $P(-5, -5)$, $Q(3, 3)$
16. $P(0, 2)$, $Q(6, -2)$

Find the distance between the parallel lines.

17.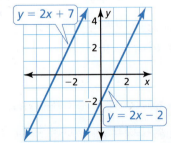
18.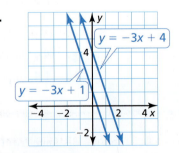

19. **SMP.7** Point P divides the directed line segment XY so that the ratio of XP to PY is 3 to 5. Describe the point that divides the directed line segment YX so that the ratio of YP to PX is 5 to 3.

154 Chapter 3 Parallel and Perpendicular Lines

20. Explain whether triangle *LMN* is a right triangle.

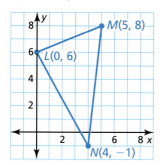

21. Explain whether quadrilateral *QRST* is a parallelogram.

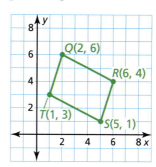

22. **SMP.7** The slope of line ℓ is greater than 0 and less than 1. Write an inequality for the slope of a line perpendicular to ℓ.

23. **SMP.4 CONNECTION TO REAL LIFE** A bike path is constructed perpendicular to a street starting at point $P(2, 2)$. An equation of the line representing the street is $y = -\frac{2}{3}x$. Represent the situation in a coordinate plane. Approximately how far is the starting point from the street when each unit represents 10 feet?

24. **GEOTHERMAL SCIENCE HOT SPRINGS** You plan to hike the path shown between two hot springs. Approximate your minimum distance from each hot spring when each unit represents 100 yards.

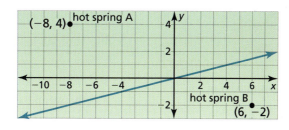

25. **SMP.6 PERFORMANCE TASK** Utility mapping involves positioning underground pipes and cables. Sewer pipes intersect the gas pipe at right angles in front of each residence. Lampposts must be installed at least 5 feet from the nearest gas or sewer pipe. Represent a neighborhood of at least 6 residences on a coordinate plane.

26. Consider the line shown and the line through $(-1, k)$ and $(-6, 2)$. What is the value of k when the lines are parallel? perpendicular? neither?

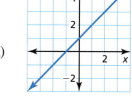

27. **SMP.8 DIG DEEPER** Write a formula for the distance from the point (x_0, y_0) to the line $ax + by = 0$. Check your formula using a point and a line.

PROVING A THEOREM Use the slopes of lines to write a paragraph proof of the theorem.

28. Lines Perpendicular to a Transversal Theorem: In a plane, if two lines are perpendicular to the same line, then they are parallel to each other.

29. Transitive Property of Parallel Lines Theorem: If two lines are parallel to the same line, then they are parallel to each other.

Interpreting Data

GEOGRAPHIC CENTER OF THE U.S. The geographic center of the 48 contiguous states was determined in 1918 by the United States Coast and Geodetic Survey. It was determined to be at 39°50′N 98°35′W, about 4 kilometers northwest of the center of Lebanon, Kansas.

30. The distance between Earth's parallels is about 111 kilometers. What is the distance between the center of the U.S. and the 49th parallel?

31. The southernmost point of the 48 contiguous states is in Key West, Florida. Approximate the distance between the center of the U.S. and Key West.

32. If you cut out a cardboard map of the U.S. and balanced it on one finger, explain where you would expect the balance point to be.

Review & Refresh

33. Find the value of x that makes $m \parallel n$.

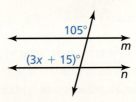

34. Make and test a conjecture about the product of three consecutive odd numbers.

35. Find the perimeter of the triangle with the vertices $(0, 1)$, $(3, 6)$, and $(4, 1)$.

36. Determine which lines, if any, must be parallel.

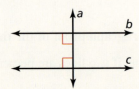

37. Solve $x^2 - 9x = 0$.

38. A chute forms a line between two parallel supports, as shown. Find $m\angle 2$.

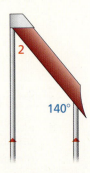

39. Solve the inequality $2w - 3 > 2w + w - 7$. Graph the solution.

Solve the system.

40. $6x + 3y = 24$
    $2x - 3y = -16$

41. $-y = 3$
    $2x - 3y = 11$

42. Graph the quadratic function
    $$y = (x - 1)(x + 2).$$
    Label the vertex, axis of symmetry, and x-intercepts. Find the domain and range of the function.

3 Chapter Review

Rate your understanding of each section.

1. I don't understand yet.
2. I can do it with help.
3. I can do it on my own.
4. I can teach someone.

3.1 Pairs of Lines and Angles (pp. 117–122)

⦿ **Learning Target:** Understand lines, planes, and pairs of angles.

Vocabulary
parallel lines
skew lines
parallel planes
transversal
corresponding angles
alternate interior angles
alternate exterior angles
consecutive interior angles

Consider the lines that contain the segments in the figure and the planes that contain the faces of the figure. All angles are right angles. Which line(s) or plane(s) contain point *N* and appear to fit the description?

1. line(s) perpendicular to $\overleftrightarrow{QR}$

2. line(s) parallel to $\overleftrightarrow{QR}$

3. line(s) skew to $\overleftrightarrow{QR}$

4. plane(s) parallel to plane *LMQ*

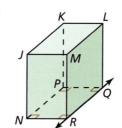

Identify all pairs of angles of the given type.

5. consecutive interior

6. alternate interior

7. corresponding

8. alternate exterior

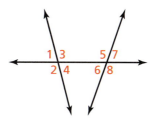

3.2 Parallel Lines and Transversals (pp. 123–130)

⦿ **Learning Target:** Prove and use theorems about parallel lines.

Find the values of *x* and *y*.

9.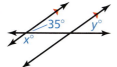

10.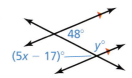

11.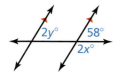

12.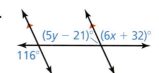

Chapter 3 Chapter Review 157

3.3 Proofs with Parallel Lines (pp. 131–138)

Learning Target: Prove and use theorems about identifying parallel lines.

Find the value of x that makes $m \parallel n$.

13.

14.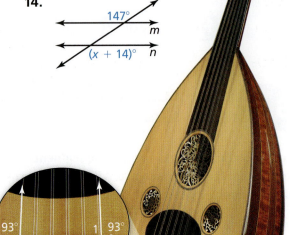

15.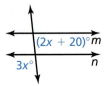

16.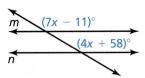

17. The strings of a musical instrument called an *oud* are shown. Explain whether the outer strings of the oud are parallel.

3.4 Proofs with Perpendicular Lines (pp. 139–148)

Learning Target: Prove and use theorems about perpendicular lines.

Vocabulary
distance from a point to a line
perpendicular bisector

Explain which lines, if any, must be parallel.

18.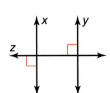

19.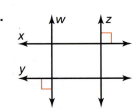

20.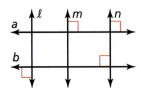

21.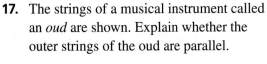

22. Use the diagram to write a proof.

   Given $\angle 1 \cong \angle 2$, $h \perp k$

   Prove $g \parallel h$

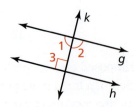

158 Chapter 3 Parallel and Perpendicular Lines

3.5 Equations of Parallel and Perpendicular Lines (pp. 149–156)

⊙ **Learning Target:** Partition line segments and understand slopes of parallel and perpendicular lines.

Find the coordinates of point P along the directed line segment AB so that AP to PB is the given ratio.

23. $A(-3, 2)$, $B(5, 5)$; 1 to 3

24. $A(-2, 4)$, $B(4, -3)$; 3 to 2

25. Determine which of the lines are parallel and which of the lines are perpendicular.

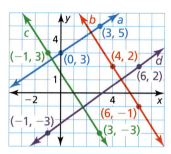

Write an equation of the line passing through point A that is parallel to the given line.

26. $A(3, -4)$, $y = -x + 8$

27. $A(-6, 5)$, $y = \frac{1}{2}x - 7$

Write an equation of the line passing through point A that is perpendicular to the given line.

28. $A(6, -1)$, $y = -2x + 8$

29. $A(-1, 5)$, $y = \frac{1}{7}x + 4$

30. Explain whether quadrilateral JKLM is a square.

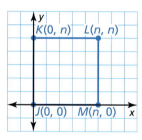

Find the distance from point A to the given line.

31.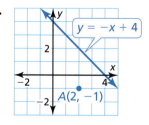

32.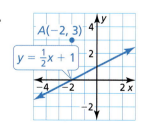

33. A coordinate plane is superimposed on a property map. Each unit in the coordinate plane represents 1 foot. The location of a tree on the property is given by the point (12, 6). How close is the tree to a property line modeled by the line $y = \frac{1}{4}x - 14$?

3 PERFORMANCE TASK
SMP.2 SMP.4

GEOTHERMAL ENERGY

Geothermal Energy: Energy produced by Earth's internal heat

- Heat is produced when radioactive particles slowly decay in Earth's core.
- Magma comes close to the surface in areas where the crust is thin, faulted, or fractured by plate tectonics.
- The heat from this magma is transferred to underground water, which produces geothermal energy.

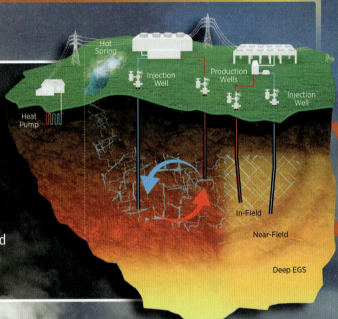

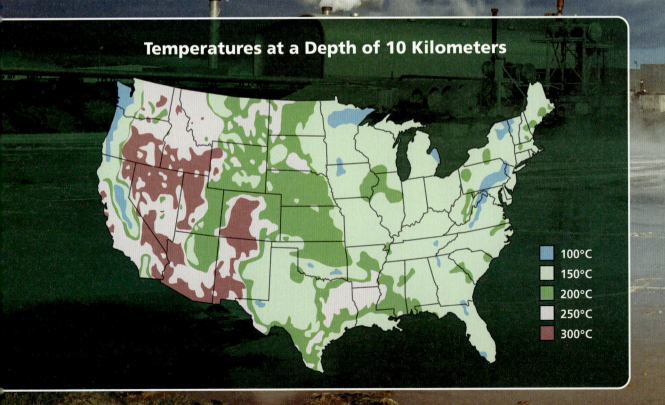

Temperatures at a Depth of 10 Kilometers

- 100°C
- 150°C
- 200°C
- 250°C
- 300°C

Analyzing Data

Use the information on the previous page to complete the following exercises.

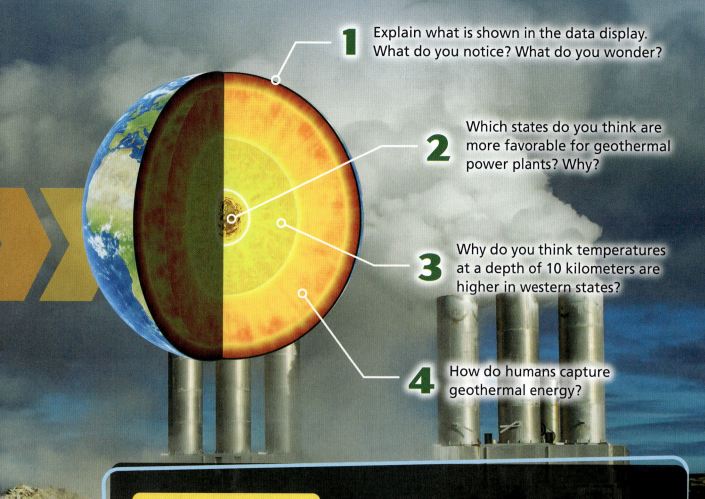

1 Explain what is shown in the data display. What do you notice? What do you wonder?

2 Which states do you think are more favorable for geothermal power plants? Why?

3 Why do you think temperatures at a depth of 10 kilometers are higher in western states?

4 How do humans capture geothermal energy?

NEW POWER PLANT

You work for an energy company that wants to build a new geothermal power plant.

- Choose a state for the power plant. Did any factors other than ground temperature affect your decision? Explain the method you would use to harness geothermal energy.
- Plot the approximate locations of two cities in the state in a coordinate plane and connect them with a line segment. Then construct the perpendicular bisector of the segment. Explain where the power plant could be located so that it is equidistant from the two cities.
- Plot the location of a third city in the coordinate plane. Show how to find a location for the power plant that is equidistant from all three cities.

Connecting Big Ideas

For use after Chapter 3.
SMP.4 SMP.7

Hopewell Culture Complexes

Around 2,000 years ago in what is now southern Ohio, American Indians used precise geometric measurements to build complexes consisting of earthen exclosures and mounds. These complexes were used for feasts, funerals, rituals, and rites of passage.

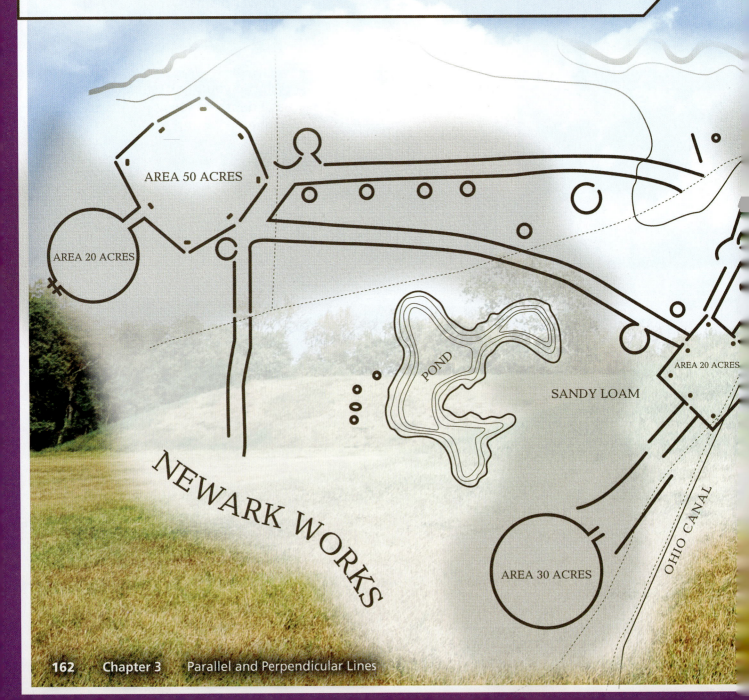

1
What do you notice? What do you wonder?

2
The circle attached to the octagon in the map has an area of about 20 acres. There are 43,560 square feet per acre. Estimate the radius of the circle.

3
You can use alternate corners of the octagon to form a square with side lengths equal to the diameter of the circle. Plot the square in a coordinate plane. Prove that the points you plotted form a square.

4
Research other Hopewell Culture complexes. Describe the geometric shapes and relationships present. How did they use parallel lines?

THINKING ABOUT THE BIG IDEAS
How can **Finding Measurements** help you prove that the points you plotted form a square?

Chapter 3   Connecting Big Ideas

4 Transformations

4.1 Translations
4.2 Reflections
4.3 Rotations
4.4 Congruence and Transformations
4.5 Dilations
4.6 Similarity and Transformations

NATIONAL GEOGRAPHIC EXPLORER
Aaron Pomerantz BIOLOGIST

Aaron Pomerantz is an entomologist whose research aims to discover the genetic basis of color and wing transparency in butterflies. He has also applied novel technology such as origami-based portable microscopes and handheld gene sequencers to conduct fieldwork in remote tropical rainforests.

- What is entomology? What is lepidopterology?
- How many wings do all butterflies have?
- What is metamorphosis? What are the stages of a butterfly's life?

PERFORMANCE TASK
Entomologists often sketch insects that they find in nature. Sketches can be dilated to enlarge certain physical features. In the Performance Task on pages 216 and 217, you will sketch a butterfly species and show how to construct a dilation of your sketch.

Entomology

Big Idea of the Chapter
Understand and Use Transformations

In geometry, there are four basic transformations: translations, reflections in a line, rotations about a point, and dilations in which you enlarge or reduce a figure.

There are two common types of metamorphosis in insects, incomplete metamorphosis and complete metamorphosis. There are four stages in complete metamorphosis: egg, larva, pupa, and adult.

Butterfly Life Cycle

Grasshoppers, crickets, dragonflies, and cockroaches go through incomplete metamorphosis, where the young usually look like small adults but lack wings. On the other hand, butterflies, moths, beetles, flies, and bees go through complete metamorphosis, where the young (called larva) look very different from the adults.

1. There are about 17,500 species of butterflies in the world, and about 750 species in the United States. How many can you name?

2. State insects are designated by 48 of the 50 states. Iowa and Michigan are the only two states without a designated state insect. Can you name your state's insect?

3. The most common commercial use of the stages of metamorphosis is the production of silk from a silk moth. Explain how a silk moth's life cycle is used to produce silk.

Getting Ready for Chapter 4

Identifying Transformations

EXAMPLE 1 Tell whether the red figure is a *translation*, *reflection*, *rotation*, or *dilation* of the blue figure.

a.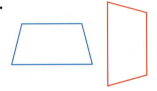

The red figure is a rotation of the blue figure.

b.

The red figure is a reflection of the blue figure.

Tell whether the red figure is a *translation*, *reflection*, *rotation*, or *dilation* of the blue figure.

1.

2.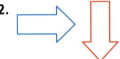

3.

Translating Figures in the Coordinate Plane

EXAMPLE 2 A triangle has vertices $A(-1, 0)$, $B(0, 3)$, and $C(2, 2)$. Draw the triangle and its image after a translation 2 units left and 4 units down. What are the coordinates of the image?

Draw the triangle. Then move each vertex 2 units left and 4 units down.

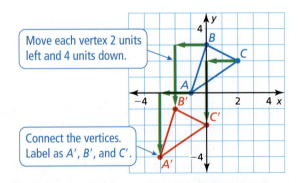

▶ The coordinates of the image are $A'(-3, -4)$, $B'(-2, -1)$, and $C'(0, -2)$.

Draw the figure and its image after the given translation. What are the coordinates of the image?

4. $A(-3, -3)$, $B(0, 0)$, $C(1, -2)$; 3 units right and 3 units up

5. $A(-1, -4)$, $B(-3, -3)$, $C(3, 0)$, $D(4, -2)$; 1 unit left and 6 units up

4.1 Translations

Learning Target: Understand translations of figures.

Success Criteria:
- I can translate figures using translation vectors.
- I can translate figures in the coordinate plane.
- I can explain what a rigid motion is.
- I can perform a composition of translations on a figure.

A **transformation** is a function that moves or changes a figure in some way to produce a new figure called an **image**. Another name for the original figure is the **preimage**. The points on the preimage are the inputs for the transformation, and the points on the image are the outputs.

INVESTIGATE Translating a Polygon

Work with a partner.

1. The diagram shows the *translation* of $\triangle DEF$ to $\triangle D'E'F'$ (read as "triangle D prime, E prime, F prime"). How would you define a translation?

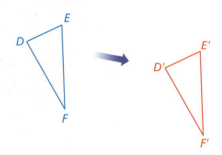

INVESTIGATE Translating a Polygon

Work with a partner.

2. Use technology to draw any triangle and label it $\triangle ABC$.

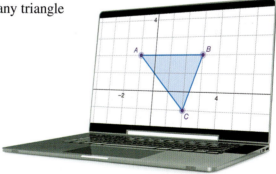

3. Translate the triangle to form a new triangle, called $\triangle A'B'C'$. What do you observe about the side lengths, angle measures, and coordinates of the vertices of the two triangles?

4. The point (x, y) is translated a units horizontally and b units vertically. Write a rule to determine the coordinates of the image of (x, y).

   $(x, y) \rightarrow (,)$

5. Based on your results in Exercises 2–4, is there anything you would like to change or include in your definition in Exercise 1?

Vocabulary
transformation
image
preimage
translation
translation vector
component form
rigid motion
composition of transformations

Performing Translations

A **translation** is a transformation that moves every point of a figure the same distance in the same direction. The preimage is translated along a **translation vector** which describes the direction and *magnitude*, or size, of the translation.

Key Concept

Translations

A translation *maps* the points P and Q of a plane figure along a translation vector to the points P' and Q', so that one of the following statements is true.

- $PP' = QQ'$ and $\overline{PP'} \parallel \overline{QQ'}$ or
- $PP' = QQ'$, and $\overline{PP'}$ and $\overline{QQ'}$ are collinear.

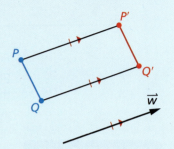

translation vector w

EXAMPLE 1 Drawing a Translation

Translate △ABC along translation vector w.

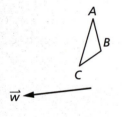

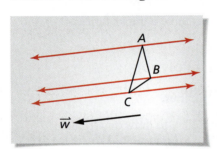

Draw a line through each vertex that is parallel to $\vec{w}$.

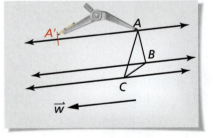

Set a compass to the length of $\vec{w}$. Starting at A, mark this distance along the line in the same direction as the vector to find A'.

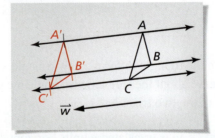

Repeat to find B' and C'. Connect the vertices to form the translated image, △$A'B'C'$.

In-Class Practice

Self-Assessment

1. Translate △ABC along translation vector w.

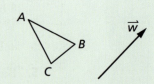

Key Concept

Translations in the Coordinate Plane

You can represent vectors in the coordinate plane by an arrow drawn from one point to another. The **component form** of a vector combines the horizontal and vertical components. So, the component form of $\vec{PQ}$ is $\langle 5, 3 \rangle$.

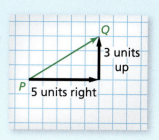

EXAMPLE 2 Using a Translation Vector in the Coordinate Plane

The vertices of $\triangle ABC$ are $A(0, 3)$, $B(2, 4)$, and $C(1, 0)$. Translate $\triangle ABC$ using the translation vector $\langle 5, -1 \rangle$.

First, graph $\triangle ABC$. Use $\langle 5, -1 \rangle$ to move each vertex 5 units right and 1 unit down. Label the image vertices and draw $\triangle A'B'C'$.

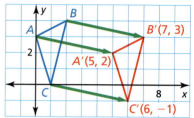

You can also express a translation along $\langle a, b \rangle$ using a rule, which has the notation $(x, y) \rightarrow (x + a, y + b)$.

EXAMPLE 3 Translating a Figure in the Coordinate Plane

Graph quadrilateral $ABCD$ with vertices $A(-1, 2)$, $B(-1, 5)$, $C(4, 6)$, and $D(4, 2)$ and its image after the translation $(x, y) \rightarrow (x + 3, y - 1)$.

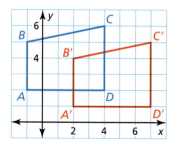

Graph quadrilateral $ABCD$. To find the coordinates of the vertices of the image, add 3 to the x-coordinates and subtract 1 from the y-coordinates of the vertices of the preimage. Then graph the image, as shown at the left.

$(x, y) \rightarrow (x + 3, y - 1)$

$A(-1, 2) \rightarrow A'(2, 1)$

$B(-1, 5) \rightarrow B'(2, 4)$

$C(4, 6) \rightarrow C'(7, 5)$

$D(4, 2) \rightarrow D'(7, 1)$

In-Class Practice

Self-Assessment

2. The vertices of $\triangle LMN$ are $L(2, 2)$, $M(5, 3)$, and $N(9, 1)$. Translate $\triangle LMN$ using the translation vector $\langle -2, 6 \rangle$.

3. Graph $\triangle RST$ with vertices $R(2, 2)$, $S(5, 2)$, and $T(3, 5)$ and its image after the translation $(x, y) \rightarrow (x + 1, y + 2)$.

4.1 Translations

Performing Compositions

A **rigid motion** is a transformation that preserves length and angle measure. A rigid motion maps lines to lines, rays to rays, and segments to segments.

Postulate 4.1

Translation Postulate

A translation is a rigid motion.

When two or more transformations are combined to form a single transformation, the result is a **composition of transformations**.

Theorem 4.1

Composition Theorem

The composition of two (or more) rigid motions is a rigid motion.

Prove this Theorem Exercise 26, page 173

EXAMPLE 4 **Performing a Composition of Translations**

Graph $\overline{RS}$ with endpoints $R(-8, 5)$ and $S(-6, 8)$ and its image after the composition.

Translation: $(x, y) \to (x + 5, y - 2)$

Translation: $(x, y) \to (x - 4, y - 2)$

Graph $\overline{RS}$.

Translate $\overline{RS}$ 5 units right and 2 units down. $\overline{R'S'}$ has endpoints $R'(-3, 3)$ and $S'(-1, 6)$.

Translate $\overline{R'S'}$ 4 units left and 2 units down. $\overline{R''S''}$ has endpoints $R''(-7, 1)$ and $S''(-5, 4)$.

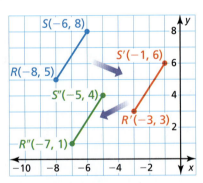

In-Class Practice

Self-Assessment

4. Graph $\overline{VW}$ with endpoints $V(-6, -4)$ and $W(-3, 1)$ and its image after the composition.

Translation: $(x, y) \to (x + 3, y + 1)$

Translation: $(x, y) \to (x - 6, y - 4)$

1 I don't understand yet.   **2** I can do it with help.   **3** I can do it on my own.   **4** I can teach someone.

Connections to Real Life

EXAMPLE 5 **Rewriting a Composition of Translations**

You use floor tiles to help you learn a new dance move. You move 1 tile right and 3 tiles down. Then you move 2 tiles left and 1 tile up. Rewrite the composition as a single translation.

Let your starting position be an arbitrary point $A(x, y)$ on a coordinate plane where each grid square represents 1 tile.

After the first translation, the coordinates of your position are

$A'(x + 1, y - 3)$.

The second translation maps $A'(x + 1, y - 3)$ to

$A''(x + 1 - 2, y - 3 + 1) = A''(x - 1, y - 2)$.

▶ The single translation rule for the composition is $(x, y) \rightarrow (x - 1, y - 2)$. So, your final position is 1 tile left and 2 tiles down from your starting position.

Check Test a point to check that the rule is correct. For instance, let $A(0, 0)$ be your starting position.

Apply the two translations to $A(0, 0)$.

$A(0, 0) \rightarrow A'(0 + 1, 0 - 3) = A'(1, -3)$

$A'(1, -3) \rightarrow A''(1 - 2, -3 + 1) = A''(-1, -2)$

Check that the single translation rule gives the same result.

$A(0, 0) \rightarrow A''(0 - 1, 0 - 2) = A''(-1, -2)$ ✓

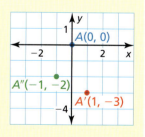

In-Class Practice
Self-Assessment

5. In Example 5, you move 2 tiles right and 3 tiles up. Then you move 1 tile left and 1 tile down. Rewrite the composition as a single translation.

4.1 Practice

Translate the figure along translation vector w. (See Example 1.)

1.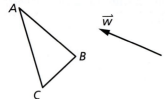

2.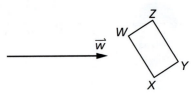

The vertices of △DEF are D(2, 5), E(6, 3), and F(4, 0). Translate △DEF using the given translation vector. Graph △DEF and its image. (See Example 2.)

3. ⟨6, 0⟩
4. ⟨5, −1⟩
5. ⟨−3, −7⟩
6. ⟨−2, −4⟩

Find the component form of the translation vector that translates P(−3, 6) to P′.

7. P′(0, 1)
8. P′(−4, 8)

Write a rule for the translation of △LMN to △L′M′N′.

9.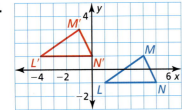

10.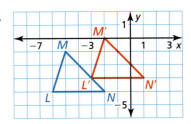

Use the translation rule $(x, y) \rightarrow (x - 8, y + 4)$ to answer the question.

11. What is the image of A(2, 6)?
12. What is the preimage of D′(4, −3)?

Graph quadrilateral PQRS with vertices P(−2, 3), Q(1, 2), R(3, −1), and S(−2, −1) and its image after the translation. (See Example 3.)

13. $(x, y) \rightarrow (x + 4, y + 6)$
14. $(x, y) \rightarrow (x + 9, y - 2)$
15. $(x, y) \rightarrow (x - 2, y - 5)$
16. $(x, y) \rightarrow (x - 1, y + 3)$

Graph △XYZ with vertices X(2, 4), Y(6, 0), and Z(7, 2) and its image after the composition. (See Example 4.)

17. Translation: $(x, y) \rightarrow (x + 12, y + 4)$
    Translation: $(x, y) \rightarrow (x - 5, y - 9)$

18. Translation: $(x, y) \rightarrow (x - 6, y)$
    Translation: $(x, y) \rightarrow (x + 2, y + 7)$

19. **SMP.3 ERROR ANALYSIS** Describe and correct the error in graphing the image of △ABC after the translation $(x, y) \rightarrow (x - 3, y + 2)$.

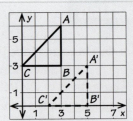

Write rules for the composition of translations.

20.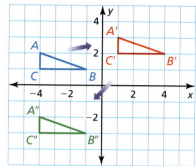

21.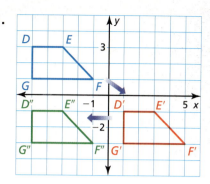

22. **ENTOMOLOGY SILVERFISH** A study determines whether silverfish can learn a complex maze. The insect first moves 3 inches right and 2 inches down. Then it moves is 5 inches left and 1 inch down. Rewrite the composition as a single translation. (See Example 5.)

23. You are studying an amoeba through a microscope. The amoeba moves on a grid-indexed microscope slide in a straight line from square B3 to square G7. Describe the translation. How far does the amoeba travel if the side length of each grid square is 2 millimeters?

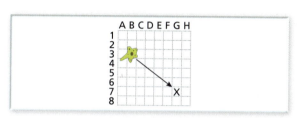

CONNECT CONCEPTS A translation maps the blue figure to the red figure. Find the value of each variable.

24.

25.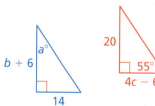

26. **PROVING THEOREM 4.1** Prove the Composition Theorem.

27. **PROVING A THEOREM** Use properties of translations to prove each theorem.

    a. Corresponding Angles Theorem

    b. Corresponding Angles Converse

28. **SMP.6** A translation maps $\overline{GH}$ to $\overline{G'H'}$. Your friend claims that if you draw segments connecting G to G' and H to H', then the resulting quadrilateral is a parallelogram. Explain whether your friend is correct.

29. **SMP.7** The vertices of $\triangle ABC$ are $A(2, 2)$, $B(4, 2)$, and $C(3, 4)$. Graph the image of $\triangle ABC$ after the transformation $(x, y) \rightarrow (x + y, y)$. Explain whether this transformation is a translation.

4.1   Translations   173

Interpreting Data

CHESS MOVES The game of chess has 6 types of pieces: king, queen, bishop, rook, knight, and pawn. Each chess move is a translation on an 8-by-8 chess board. Each piece is allowed only specific types of translations.

The 5 Best Chess Moves of All Time
(ranked by Chess.com)
1. Shirov's Jaw-Dropping Bishop Sacrifice
2. Meier's Spectacular Sacrifice
3. Marshall's Legendary Move
4. Vladimirov's Thunderbolt
5. Geller's Rook And Pawn Endgame

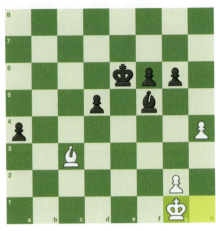

Shirov's Jaw-Dropping Bishop Sacrifice

30. Describe all the moves a knight can make using translations.

31. Describe all the moves a rook can make using translations.

32. Research and describe one of the chess moves listed above.

Review & Refresh

33. Decide whether there is enough information to prove that $m \parallel n$. If so, state the theorem you can use.

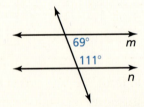

Write an equation of the line passing through point P that is perpendicular to the given line.

34. $P(4, -1)$, $y - 3 = -4(x + 7)$

35. $P(-3, 5)$, $5x - 2y = 8$

Write an equation for the nth term of the arithmetic sequence. Then find a_{10}.

36. $4, 1, -2, -5, \ldots$ 37. $\frac{4}{5}, \frac{3}{5}, \frac{2}{5}, \frac{1}{5}, \ldots$

38. Solve $6x^3 - 12x^2 = 0$.

39. Graph $p(x) = -\frac{7}{2}x^2$. Compare the graph to the graph of $f(x) = x^2$.

40. Which lines, if any, must be parallel?

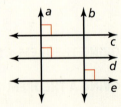

41. The function $h(x) = -16x^2 + 48x + 6$ models the height h (in feet) of a ball ejected from a ball launcher after x seconds. When does the ball reach a height of 30 feet?

42. Find the inverse of the function $f(x) = -\frac{1}{2}x + \frac{5}{2}$. Then graph the function and its inverse.

4.2 Reflections

Learning Target: Understand reflections of figures.

Success Criteria:
- I can reflect figures.
- I can perform compositions with reflections.
- I can identify line symmetry in polygons.

INVESTIGATE — Defining a Reflection

Work with a partner.

1. The diagram shows the *reflection* of △DEF to △D′E′F′. How would you define a reflection?

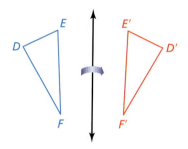

INVESTIGATE — Reflecting a Polygon

Work with a partner.

2. Use technology to draw any triangle and label it △ABC.

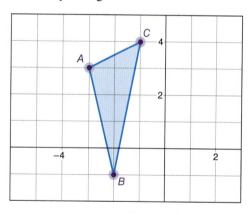

3. Reflect the triangle in the y-axis to form △A′B′C′. What do you observe about the side lengths, angle measures, and coordinates of the vertices of the two triangles?

4. How do your observations in Exercise 3 change when you reflect △ABC in the x-axis?

5. Write rules to determine the coordinates of the image of (x, y) when it is reflected in the x-axis or the y-axis.

   Reflection in x-axis: **Reflection in y-axis:**

   $(x, y) \rightarrow (\;\;\;,\;\;\;)$ $(x, y) \rightarrow (\;\;\;,\;\;\;)$

6. Based on your results in Exercises 2–5, is there anything you would like to change or include in your definition in Exercise 1?

Vocabulary
reflection
line of reflection
glide reflection
line symmetry
line of symmetry

Performing Reflections

A **reflection** is a transformation that uses a line like a mirror to reflect a figure. This line is called the **line of reflection**.

Key Concept

Reflections

A reflection in a line m maps every point P in the plane to a point P', such that:

- If P is not on m, then m is the perpendicular bisector of $\overline{PP'}$, or
- If P is on m, then $P = P'$.

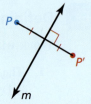

point P not on m point P on m

EXAMPLE 1   Reflecting in Horizontal and Vertical Lines

Graph $\triangle ABC$ with vertices $A(1, 3)$, $B(5, 2)$, and $C(2, 1)$ and its image after each reflection.

a. in the line m: $y = 1$

Point A is 2 units above line m, so A' is 2 units below line m at $(1, -1)$. Similarly, B' is 1 unit below line m at $(5, 0)$. Because point C is on line m, you know that $C = C'$.

b. in the line n: $x = 3$

Point A is 2 units left of line n, so its reflection A' is 2 units right of line n at $(5, 3)$. Similarly, B' is 2 units left of line n at $(1, 2)$, and C' is 1 unit right of line n at $(4, 1)$.

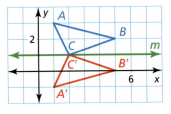 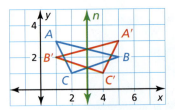

In-Class Practice

Self-Assessment

Graph $\triangle DEF$ and its image after a reflection in the given line.

1. $x = 1$ **2.** $y = 3$

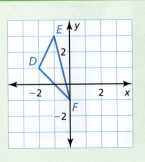

 I don't understand yet.   I can do it with help.   3 I can do it on my own.   I can teach someone.

EXAMPLE 2 **Reflecting in the Line $y = x$**

Graph $\overline{FG}$ with endpoints $F(-1, 2)$ and $G(1, 2)$ and its image after a reflection in the line $y = x$.

Graph the line $y = x$. Then plot $F(-1, 2)$ and $G(1, 2)$.

Reflect $F(-1, 2)$ to $F'(2, -1)$.

Reflect $G(1, 2)$ to $G'(2, 1)$.

Draw the line segments.

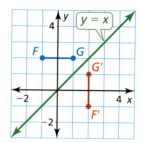

Key Concept

Coordinate Rules for Reflections

- If (a, b) is reflected in the x-axis, then its image is the point $(a, -b)$.
- If (a, b) is reflected in the y-axis, then its image is the point $(-a, b)$.
- If (a, b) is reflected in the line $y = x$, then its image is the point (b, a).
- If (a, b) is reflected in the line $y = -x$, then its image is the point $(-b, -a)$.

EXAMPLE 3 **Reflecting in the Line $y = -x$**

Graph $\overline{JK}$ with endpoints $J(0, 3)$ and $K(3, 3)$ and its image after a reflection in the line $y = -x$.

Graph $\overline{JK}$ and the line $y = -x$. Use the coordinate rule for reflecting in the line $y = -x$ to find the coordinates of the endpoints of the image. Then graph the image.

$(a, b) \rightarrow (-b, -a)$

$J(0, 3) \rightarrow J'(-3, 0)$

$K(3, 3) \rightarrow K'(-3, -3)$

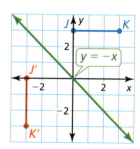

In-Class Practice

Self-Assessment

The vertices of $\triangle JKL$ are $J(1, 3)$, $K(4, 4)$, and $L(3, 1)$. Graph $\triangle JKL$ and its image after a reflection in the given line.

3. x-axis

4. y-axis

5. $y = x$

6. $y = -x$

| **1** I don't understand yet. | **2** I can do it with help. | **3** I can do it on my own. | **4** I can teach someone. |

Performing Glide Reflections

Postulate 4.2

Reflection Postulate

A reflection is a rigid motion.

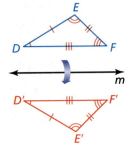

Because a reflection is a rigid motion, and a rigid motion preserves length and angle measure, the following statements are true for the reflection shown.

$DE = D'E'$ $EF = E'F'$ $FD = F'D'$

$m\angle D = m\angle D'$ $m\angle E = m\angle E'$ $m\angle F = m\angle F'$

A **glide reflection** is a transformation involving a translation followed by a reflection in which every point P is mapped to a point P'' by the following steps.

First, a translation maps P to P'.

Then a reflection in a line k parallel to the direction of the translation maps P' to P''.

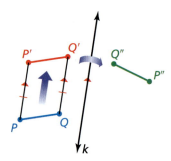

EXAMPLE 4 Performing a Glide Reflection

Graph $\triangle ABC$ with vertices $A(3, 2)$, $B(6, 3)$, and $C(7, 1)$ and its image after the glide reflection.

Translation: $(x, y) \to (x - 12, y)$

Reflection: in the x-axis

Begin by graphing $\triangle ABC$. Then graph $\triangle A'B'C'$ after a translation 12 units left. Finally, graph $\triangle A''B''C''$ after a reflection in the x-axis.

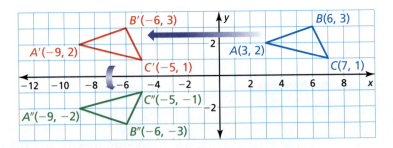

In-Class Practice
Self-Assessment

7. **WHAT IF?** In Example 4, $\triangle ABC$ is translated 4 units down and then reflected in the y-axis. Graph $\triangle ABC$ and its image after the glide reflection.

Identifying Lines of Symmetry

A figure in the plane has **line symmetry** when the figure can be mapped onto itself by a reflection in a line. This line of reflection is a **line of symmetry**, such as line *m* at the right.

A figure can have more than one line of symmetry.

EXAMPLE 5 Identifying Line Symmetry

Determine whether each polygon has line symmetry. If so, draw the line(s) of symmetry and describe any reflections that map the polygon onto itself.

a. trapezoid

The trapezoid has line symmetry. The line of symmetry is shown. A reflection in the line of symmetry maps the trapezoid onto itself.

b. regular hexagon

The regular hexagon has line symmetry. The 6 lines of symmetry are shown. A reflection in any of the lines of symmetry maps the hexagon onto itself.

c. parallelogram

The parallelogram does not have line symmetry because the figure cannot be mapped onto itself by a reflection in a line.

In-Class Practice

Self-Assessment

Determine whether the polygon has line symmetry. If so, draw the line(s) of symmetry and describe any reflections that map the polygon onto itself.

8. rectangle

9. regular pentagon

10. isosceles triangle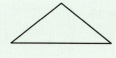

1 I don't understand yet.   **2** I can do it with help.   **3** I can do it on my own.   **4** I can teach someone.

4.2 Reflections

4.2 Practice

Determine whether the coordinate plane shows a reflection in the *x*-axis, *y*-axis, or *neither*.

1.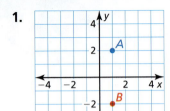

2.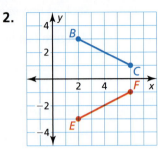

Graph the polygon with the given vertices and its image after a reflection in the given line. (See Example 1.)

▶ 3. $J(2, -4)$, $K(3, 7)$, $L(6, -1)$; *x*-axis

4. $J(5, 3)$, $K(1, -2)$, $L(-3, 4)$; *y*-axis

5. $J(2, -1)$, $K(4, -5)$, $L(3, 1)$; $x = -1$

6. $J(1, -1)$, $K(3, 0)$, $L(0, -4)$; $x = 2$

7. $J(2, 4)$, $K(-4, -2)$, $L(-1, 0)$; $y = 1$

8. $J(3, -5)$, $K(4, -1)$, $L(0, -3)$; $y = -3$

Graph the polygon with the given vertices and its image after a reflection in the line $y = x$. (See Example 2.)

▶ 9. $A(6, -3)$, $B(1, -2)$, $C(4, 1)$

10. $A(0, -3)$, $B(2, 2)$, $C(5, 0)$

11. $A(-2, 4)$, $B(1, 4)$, $C(1, 2)$, $D(-2, 2)$

12. $A(2, -1)$, $B(-1, 2)$, $C(2, 3)$, $D(4, 2)$

Graph the polygon with the given vertices and its image after a reflection in the line $y = -x$. (See Example 3.)

▶ 13. $A(1, 2)$, $B(4, 2)$, $C(3, -2)$

14. $A(-2, -3)$, $B(-2, 0)$, $C(0, 1)$

15. $A(-3, 2)$, $B(1, -1)$, $C(-2, -2)$, $D(-4, -1)$

16. $A(2, 0)$, $B(3, 4)$, $C(6, 4)$, $D(5, 0)$

Graph △*RST* with vertices $R(4, 1)$, $S(7, 3)$, and $T(6, 4)$ and its image after the glide reflection. (See Example 4.)

▶ 17. **Translation:** $(x, y) \rightarrow (x, y - 1)$
    Reflection: in the *y*-axis

18. **Translation:** $(x, y) \rightarrow (x - 3, y)$
    Reflection: in the line $y = -1$

Determine whether the figure has line symmetry. If so, draw the line(s) of symmetry and describe any reflections that map the figure onto itself. (See Example 5.)

▶ 19.

20.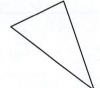

21.

180   Chapter 4   Transformations

22. Describe the line symmetry (if any) of each word.

   a. LOOK

   b. OX

23. **SMP.3 ERROR ANALYSIS** Identify and correct the error in describing the transformation.

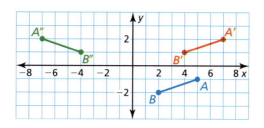

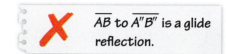

24. CONNECT CONCEPTS The line $y = 3x + 2$ is reflected in the line $y = -1$. What is the equation of the image?

Point B' is the image of point B after a reflection in a line. Write an equation of the line.

25. $B(0, 3)$, $B'(0, -1)$

26. $B(2, -4)$, $B'(6, -4)$

27. CONSTRUCTION Follow the steps below to construct a reflection of $\triangle ABC$ in the line m. Use a compass and straightedge.

- Draw $\triangle ABC$ and line m.
- Use a compass and straightedge to find a point A' such that line m is a perpendicular bisector of the segment AA'.
- Repeat to find points B' and C'. Draw $\triangle A'B'C'$.

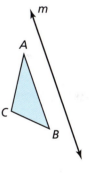

28. **SMP.5** Use a reflective device to verify your construction in Exercise 27.

29. OPEN-ENDED Draw a line segment in Quadrant III. Identify a glide reflection that maps the line segment entirely to Quadrant I.

30. Is the composition of a translation and a reflection commutative? (In other words, do you obtain the same image regardless of the order?) Justify your answer.

31. DIG DEEPER Explain how to reflect $\triangle MNQ$ in the line $y = -2x$.

32. DIG DEEPER Point $B'(1, 4)$ is the image of $B(3, 2)$ after a reflection in line c. Write an equation of line c.

4.2 Reflections 181

Interpreting Data

KALEIDOSCOPES Kaleidoscopes were invented in 1816 by the Scottish inventor David Brewster. He observed that objects placed near a pair of mirrors created elaborate patterns.

33. How many lines of symmetry does the hexagonal pattern have?

34. How many lines of symmetry does the octagonal pattern have?

35. A traditional kaleidoscope is made using 2 mirrors that meet at an angle of 60°, which produces hexagonal images. At what angle should the mirrors meet to produce octagonal images?

Hexagonal Pattern

Octagonal Pattern

Review & Refresh

36. Find the distance from point A to $\overleftrightarrow{XZ}$.

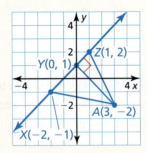

Solve the equation by graphing.

37. $|2x| = |x + 6|$ 38. $5x - 7 = 2(x + 1)$

39. A subway train travels at a speed of 30 miles per hour. What is the speed of the subway train in feet per second?

40. Find the distance from the point $(-3, 6)$ to the line $y = -\frac{3}{2}x - 5$.

41. Evaluate $h(x) = -3x + 7$ when $x = -1$.

42. Solve $A = \frac{1}{2}h(b_1 + b_2)$ for b_2.

43. Use the translation $(x, y) \to (x, y + 4)$ to find the image of $A(0, -4)$.

44. Factor $-2t^2 + 9t - 7$.

45. Make a scatter plot of the data. Then describe the relationship between the data.

x	0.3	0.6	0.8	1.2	1.4	1.9	2.0	2.1
y	1.1	1.4	1.7	2.3	2.6	3.0	3.1	3.3

46. Name the property that "If $\angle A \cong \angle B$ and $\angle B \cong \angle C$, then $\angle A \cong \angle C$." illustrates.

4.3 Rotations

Learning Target: Understand rotations of figures.

Success Criteria:
- I can rotate figures.
- I can perform compositions with rotations.
- I can identify rotational symmetry in polygons.

INVESTIGATE Defining a Rotation

Work with a partner.

1. The diagram shows a *rotation* of △DEF to △D'E'F'. How would you define a rotation?

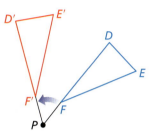

INVESTIGATE Rotating a Polygon

Work with a partner.

2. Use technology to draw any triangle and label it △ABC.

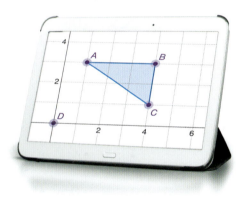

3. Rotate the triangle 90° counterclockwise about the origin to form △A'B'C'. What do you observe about the side lengths, angle measures, and coordinates of the vertices of the two triangles?

4. Write rules to determine the coordinates of the image of (x, y) when it is rotated 90°, 180°, and 270° counterclockwise about the origin.

90° Rotation:	**180° Rotation:**	**270° Rotation:**
$(x, y) \rightarrow (\ \ \ ,\ \ \ )$	$(x, y) \rightarrow (\ \ \ ,\ \ \ )$	$(x, y) \rightarrow (\ \ \ ,\ \ \ )$

5. Based on your results in Exercises 2–4, is there anything you would like to change or include in your definition in Exercise 1?

6. Is a rotation a rigid motion? Explain.

Vocabulary
rotation
center of rotation
angle of rotation
rotational symmetry
center of symmetry

Performing Rotations

A **rotation** is a transformation in which a figure is turned about a fixed point called the **center of rotation**. Rays drawn from the center of rotation to a point and its image form the **angle of rotation**.

> **STUDY TIP**
> The figure to the right shows a 40° counterclockwise rotation. Rotations can be clockwise or counterclockwise. In this book, all rotations are counterclockwise unless otherwise noted.

Key Concept

Rotations

A rotation about a point P through an angle of $x°$ maps every point Q in the plane to a point Q' such that:

- If Q is not the center of rotation P, then $QP = Q'P$ and $m\angle QPQ' = x°$, or

- If Q is the center of rotation P, then $Q = Q'$.

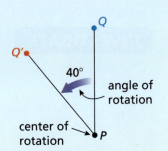

EXAMPLE 1 Drawing a Rotation

Draw a 120° rotation of △ABC about point P.

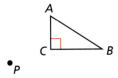

Draw a segment from P to A.

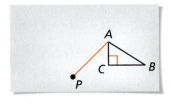

Draw a ray to form a 120° angle with $\overline{PA}$.

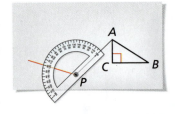

Draw A' so that $PA' = PA$.

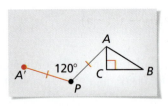

Repeat the previous 3 steps for each remaining vertex. Draw △$A'B'C'$.

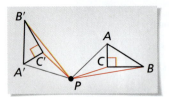

In-Class Practice

Self-Assessment

1. Trace △DEF and point P. Then draw a 50° rotation of △DEF about point P.

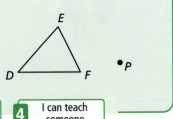

You can rotate a figure more than 180°. The diagram shows rotations of point A 130°, 220°, and 310° about the origin. Notice that point A and its images all lie on the same circle. A rotation of 360° maps a figure onto itself.

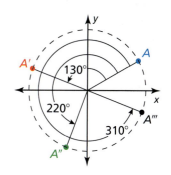

You can use coordinate rules to find the coordinates of a point after a rotation of 90°, 180°, or 270° about the origin.

Key Concept

Coordinate Rules for Rotations about the Origin

When a point (a, b) is rotated counterclockwise about the origin, the following are true.

- For a rotation of 90°, $(a, b) \to (-b, a)$.
- For a rotation of 180°, $(a, b) \to (-a, -b)$.
- For a rotation of 270°, $(a, b) \to (b, -a)$.

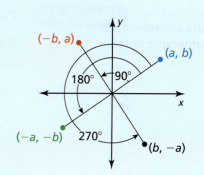

EXAMPLE 2 Rotating a Figure in the Coordinate Plane

Graph quadrilateral RSTU with vertices $R(3, 1)$, $S(5, 1)$, $T(5, -3)$, and $U(2, -1)$ and its image after a 270° rotation about the origin.

Use the coordinate rule for a 270° rotation to find the coordinates of the vertices of the image. Then graph quadrilateral RSTU and its image.

$(a, b) \to (b, -a)$

$R(3, 1) \to R'(1, -3)$

$S(5, 1) \to S'(1, -5)$

$T(5, -3) \to T'(-3, -5)$

$U(2, -1) \to U'(-1, -2)$

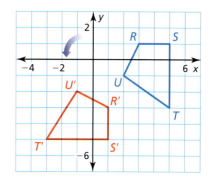

In-Class Practice

Self-Assessment

2. Graph △JKL with vertices $J(3, 0)$, $K(4, 3)$, and $L(6, 0)$ and its image after a 90° rotation about the origin.

| 1 I don't understand yet. | 2 I can do it with help. | 3 I can do it on my own. | 4 I can teach someone. |

Performing Compositions with Rotations

> **Postulate 4.3**
>
> **Rotation Postulate**
>
> A rotation is a rigid motion.

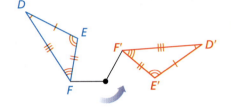

Because a rotation is a rigid motion, and a rigid motion preserves length and angle measure, the following statements are true for the rotation shown.

$DE = D'E'$ $EF = E'F'$ $FD = F'D'$

$m\angle D = m\angle D'$ $m\angle E = m\angle E'$ $m\angle F = m\angle F'$

EXAMPLE 3 **Performing a Composition**

Graph $\overline{RS}$ with endpoints $R(1, -3)$ and $S(2, -6)$ and its image after the composition.

    Reflection: in the y-axis

    Rotation: $90°$ about the origin

Graph $\overline{RS}$. Reflect $\overline{RS}$ in the y-axis. $\overline{R'S'}$ has endpoints $R'(-1, -3)$ and $S'(-2, -6)$.

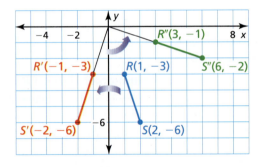

Rotate $\overline{R'S'}$ $90°$ about the origin. $\overline{R''S''}$ has endpoints $R''(3, -1)$ and $S''(6, -2)$.

In-Class Practice

Self-Assessment

3. Graph $\overline{AB}$ with endpoints $A(-4, 4)$ and $B(-1, 7)$ and its image after the composition.

   Translation: $(x, y) \rightarrow (x - 2, y - 1)$

   Rotation: $90°$ about the origin

4. Graph $\triangle TUV$ with vertices $T(1, 2)$, $U(3, 5)$, and $V(6, 3)$ and its image after the composition.

   Rotation: $180°$ about the origin

   Reflection: in the x-axis

Identifying Rotational Symmetry

A figure in a plane has **rotational symmetry** when the figure can be mapped onto itself by a rotation of 180° or less about a point on the figure. This point is the **center of symmetry**. Note that the rotation can be either clockwise or counterclockwise.

The figure below has rotational symmetry, because a rotation of either 90° or 180° maps the figure onto itself (although a rotation of 45° does not).

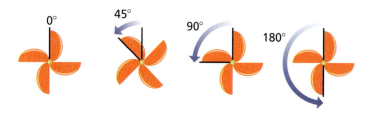

EXAMPLE 4 Identifying Rotational Symmetry

Determine whether each polygon has rotational symmetry. If so, describe any rotations that map the polygon onto itself.

a. parallelogram

b. regular octagon

c. trapezoid

The parallelogram has rotational symmetry. The center is the intersection of the diagonals. A 180° rotation about the center maps the parallelogram onto itself.

The regular octagon has rotational symmetry. The center is the intersection of the diagonals. Rotations of 45°, 90°, 135°, or 180° about the center all map the octagon onto itself.

The trapezoid does not have rotational symmetry because no rotation of 180° or less maps the trapezoid onto itself.

In-Class Practice

Self-Assessment

Determine whether the polygon has rotational symmetry. If so, describe any rotations that map the polygon onto itself.

5. rhombus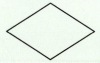

6. octagon

7. right triangle

4.3 Practice

Trace the polygon and point *P*. Then draw a rotation of the polygon about point *P* using the given number of degrees. (See Example 1.)

▶ **1.** 150°

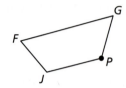

2. 130°

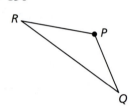

Graph the polygon with the given vertices and its image after a rotation of the given number of degrees about the origin. (See Example 2.)

▶ **3.** $A(-3, 2)$, $B(2, 4)$, $C(3, 1)$; 90°

4. $D(-3, -1)$, $E(-1, 2)$, $F(4, -2)$; 180°

5. $J(1, 4)$, $K(5, 5)$, $L(7, 2)$, $M(2, 2)$; 180°

6. $Q(-6, -3)$, $R(-5, 0)$, $S(-3, 0)$, $T(-1, -3)$; 270°

SMP.3 ERROR ANALYSIS The endpoints of $\overline{CD}$ are $C(-1, 1)$ and $D(2, 3)$. Describe and correct the error in finding the coordinates of the endpoints of the image after a rotation of 270° about the origin.

7.
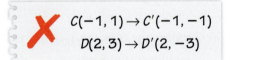

8.
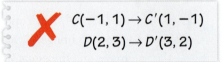

Graph $\overline{XY}$ with endpoints $X(-3, 1)$ and $Y(4, -5)$ and its image after the composition. (See Example 3.)

▶ **9.** **Translation:** $(x, y) \rightarrow (x, y + 2)$
  Rotation: 90° about the origin

10. **Rotation:** 180° about the origin
  Translation: $(x, y) \rightarrow (x - 1, y + 1)$

Graph $\triangle LMN$ with vertices $L(1, 6)$, $M(-2, 4)$, and $N(3, 2)$ and its image after the composition.

11. **Rotation:** 90° about the origin
  Translation: $(x, y) \rightarrow (x - 3, y + 2)$

12. **Reflection:** in the *x*-axis
  Rotation: 270° about the origin

Determine whether the figure has rotational symmetry. If so, describe any rotations that map the figure onto itself. (See Example 4.)

▶ **13.**

14.

15.

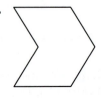

16. **CONSTRUCTION** Follow these steps to construct a rotation of △ABC by angle D about a point O. Use a compass and straightedge.

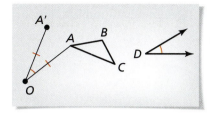

- Draw △ABC, ∠D, and O (the center of rotation).
- Draw $\overline{OA}$. Use the construction for copying an angle to copy ∠D at O, as shown. Then draw A′ so that OA′ = OA.
- Repeat to find points B′ and C′. Draw △A′B′C′.

17. **SMP.2** You enter a revolving door.

    a. You rotate the door 180°. Explain what this means in the context of the situation.

    b. You rotate the door 360°. Explain what this means in the context of the situation.

STEM Video: Revolving Door

18. **CONNECT CONCEPTS** Use the graph of $y = 2x - 3$.

    a. Rotate the line 90°, 180°, and 270° about the origin. Write the equation of the line for each image. Describe the relationship between the equation of the preimage and the equation of each image.

    b. Explain whether the relationships you described in part (a) are true for any line that is not vertical or horizontal.

19. The endpoints of $\overline{JK}$ are $J(-5, -4)$ and $K(-3, -1)$. What are the coordinates of the endpoints of the image after a rotation of 630° about the origin? 900° about the origin?

20. **SMP.7** Explain whether it is possible for a figure to have 90° rotational symmetry but not 180° rotational symmetry.

21. The vertices of a quadrilateral after a reflection in the line $y = -x$, followed by a rotation of 90° about the origin, are $D''(-1, -2)$, $E''(4, -1)$, $F''(3, 2)$, and $G''(1, 1)$. What are the vertices of quadrilateral DEFG?

22. **OPEN-ENDED** Draw a figure that has rotational symmetry but not line symmetry.

23. **DIG DEEPER** △XYZ has vertices $X(2, 5)$, $Y(3, 1)$, and $Z(0, 2)$. Rotate △XYZ 90° about the point $P(-2, -1)$.

24. **SMP.1** Can rotations of 90°, 180°, 270°, and 360° be written as the compositions of two reflections? Justify your answers.

Interpreting Data

SYMMETRY IN NATURE Two types of symmetry found in living organisms are line symmetry and rotational symmetry.

Daisy   Lime   Starfish   Clover

25. Describe the rotational symmetry of the four objects shown.

26. Describe other living organisms that have rotational symmetry.

27. In nature, different shapes sometimes evolve because they provide survival advantages to organisms. What advantages do you think rotational symmetry provides to a living organism?

Review & Refresh

$\overrightarrow{DF}$ **bisects** $\angle CDE$. **Find the indicated angle measures.**

28. $m\angle CDF = 43°$. Find $m\angle EDF$ and $m\angle CDE$.

29. $m\angle CDE = 102°$. Find $m\angle CDF$ and $m\angle EDF$.

30. The figures are congruent. Name the corresponding angles and the corresponding sides.

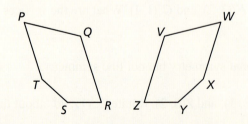

31. The endpoints of the directed line segment AB are $A(1, 2)$ and $B(10, 5)$. Find the coordinates of point P along segment AB so that the ratio of AP to PB is 1 to 2.

32. Graph the system. Identify a solution.

$y < x + 3$

$y \geq \frac{1}{2}x + 1$

33. Explain whether the table represents a *linear* or an *exponential* function.

x	−1	0	1	2	3
y	0.5	2	8	32	128

Graph the polygon with the given vertices and its image after the indicated transformation.

34. $A(-4, 1)$, $B(-3, 3)$, $C(-1, 2)$

Reflection: in the *x*-axis

35. $J(-2, -3)$, $K(-1, 1)$, $L(2, 0)$, $M(1, -4)$

Translation: $(x, y) \to (x + 3, y - 2)$

4.4 Congruence and Transformations

Learning Target: Understand congruence transformations.

Success Criteria:
- I can identify congruent figures.
- I can describe congruence transformations.
- I can use congruence transformations to solve problems.

INVESTIGATE Reflecting Figures in Lines

Work with a partner. Use technology to draw any scalene triangle and label it $\triangle ABC$. Draw any line, $\overleftrightarrow{DE}$, and another line that is parallel to $\overleftrightarrow{DE}$.

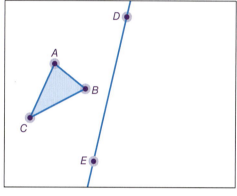

1. Reflect $\triangle ABC$ in $\overleftrightarrow{DE}$, followed by a reflection in the other line to form $\triangle A''B''C''$. What do you notice?

2. Is there a single transformation that maps $\triangle ABC$ to $\triangle A''B''C''$?

3. Using the same triangle and line $\overleftrightarrow{DE}$, draw line $\overleftrightarrow{DF}$ that intersects $\overleftrightarrow{DE}$ at point D so that $\angle EDF$ is an acute or right angle. Then reflect $\triangle ABC$ in $\overleftrightarrow{DE}$, followed by a reflection in $\overleftrightarrow{DF}$ to form $\triangle A''B''C''$. What do you notice?

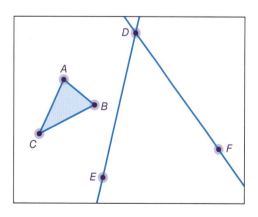

4. Is there a single transformation that maps $\triangle ABC$ to $\triangle A''B''C''$? Explain.

5. Repeat Exercises 3 and 4 with other figures. What do you notice?

> **Vocabulary**
> congruent figures
> congruence transformation

Identifying Congruent Figures

Two geometric figures are **congruent figures** if and only if there is a rigid motion or a composition of rigid motions that maps one of the figures to the other. Congruent figures have the same size and same shape.

Congruent

same size and same shape

Not congruent

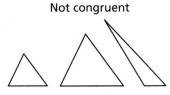

different sizes or shapes

You can identify congruent figures in the coordinate plane by identifying the rigid motion or composition of rigid motions that maps one of the figures to the other. Recall that translations, reflections, rotations, and compositions of these transformations are rigid motions.

EXAMPLE 1 Identifying Congruent Figures

Identify any congruent figures in the coordinate plane. Explain.

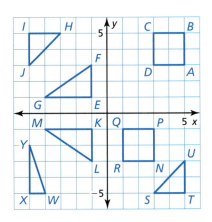

Square $NPQR$ is a translation of square $ABCD$ 2 units left and 6 units down. So, square $ABCD$ and square $NPQR$ are congruent.

$\triangle KLM$ is a reflection of $\triangle EFG$ in the x-axis. So, $\triangle EFG$ and $\triangle KLM$ are congruent.

$\triangle STU$ is a 180° rotation of $\triangle HIJ$. So, $\triangle HIJ$ and $\triangle STU$ are congruent.

In-Class Practice

Self-Assessment

1. Identify any congruent figures in the coordinate plane. Explain.

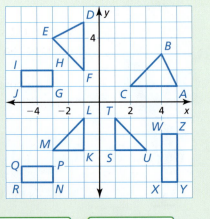

| 1 I don't understand yet. | 2 I can do it with help. | 3 I can do it on my own. | 4 I can teach someone. |

192 Chapter 4 Transformations

Congruence Transformations

Another name for a rigid motion or a combination of rigid motions is a **congruence transformation** because the preimage and image are congruent. The terms *rigid motion* and *congruence transformation* are interchangeable.

EXAMPLE 2 **Describing a Congruence Transformation**

Describe a congruence transformation that maps □ABCD to □EFGH.

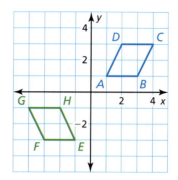

Two sides of □ABCD rise from left to right, and the corresponding sides of □EFGH fall from left to right. If you reflect □ABCD in the y-axis, as shown, then the image, □A'B'C'D', will have the same orientation as □EFGH.

Then you can map □A'B'C'D' to □EFGH using a translation 4 units down.

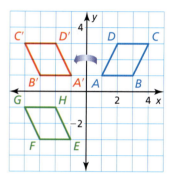

▶ So, a congruence transformation that maps □ABCD to □EFGH is a reflection in the y-axis, followed by a translation 4 units down.

In-Class Practice

Self-Assessment

2. In Example 2, describe another congruence transformation that maps □ABCD to □EFGH.

3. Describe a congruence transformation that maps △JKL to △MNP.

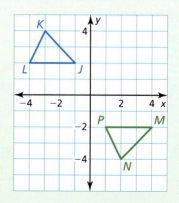

| 1 I don't understand yet. | 2 I can do it with help. | 3 I can do it on my own. | 4 I can teach someone. |

4.4 Congruence and Transformations 193

Using Theorems about Congruence Transformations

Compositions of two reflections result in either a translation or a rotation.

Theorem 4.2

Reflections in Parallel Lines Theorem

If lines k and m are parallel, then a reflection in line k followed by a reflection in line m is the same as a translation.

If A'' is the image of A, then

1. $\overline{AA''}$ is perpendicular to k and m, and
2. $AA'' = 2d$, where d is the distance between k and m.

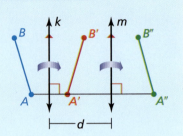

Prove this Theorem Exercise 19, page 197

EXAMPLE 3   Using the Reflections in Parallel Lines Theorem

A reflection in line k maps $\overline{GH}$ to $\overline{G'H'}$. A reflection in line m maps $\overline{G'H'}$ to $\overline{G''H''}$. Also, $HB = 9$ and $H''D = 4$.

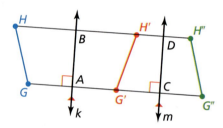

a. Name any segments congruent to each segment: $\overline{GH}, \overline{HB},$ and $\overline{GA}$.

$\overline{GH} \cong \overline{G'H'}$, and $\overline{GH} \cong \overline{G''H''}$.
$\overline{HB} \cong \overline{H'B}. \overline{GA} \cong \overline{G'A}$.

b. **Does $AC = BD$? Explain.**

Yes, $\overline{GG''}$ and $\overline{HH''}$ are perpendicular to both k and m. So, $ABDC$ is a rectangle because it has four right angles. $\overline{AC}$ and $\overline{BD}$ are opposite sides of rectangle $ABDC$, so $AC = BD$.

c. **What is the length of $\overline{GG''}$?**

By the properties of reflections, $H'B = 9$ and $H'D = 4$. The Reflections in Parallel Lines Theorem implies that $GG'' = HH'' = 2 \cdot BD$, so the length of $\overline{GG''}$ is $2(9 + 4) = 26$ units.

In-Class Practice

Self-Assessment

Use the figure. The distance between line k and line m is 1.6 centimeters.

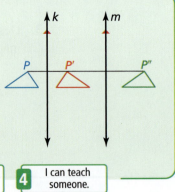

4. The preimage is reflected in line k, then in line m. Describe a single transformation that maps the blue figure to the green figure.

5. What is the relationship between $\overline{PP'}$ and line k? Explain.

Theorem 4.3

Reflections in Intersecting Lines Theorem

If lines k and m intersect at point P, then a reflection in line k followed by a reflection in line m is the same as a rotation about point P.

The angle of rotation is $2x°$, where $x°$ is the measure of the acute or right angle formed by lines k and m.

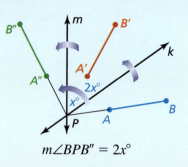

$m\angle BPB'' = 2x°$

Prove this Theorem Exercise 22, page 241

EXAMPLE 4 Using the Reflections in Intersecting Lines Theorem

In the diagram, the figure is reflected in line k. The image is then reflected in line m. Describe a single transformation that maps F to F''.

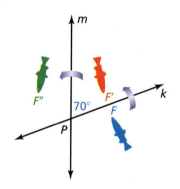

By the Reflections in Intersecting Lines Theorem, a reflection in line k followed by a reflection in line m is the same as a rotation about point P. The measure of the acute angle formed by lines k and m is 70°. So, by the Reflections in Intersecting Lines Theorem, the angle of rotation is $2(70°) = 140°$.

▶ A single transformation that maps F to F'' is a 140° rotation about point P. You can check that this is correct by tracing lines k and m and point F, then rotating the point 140°.

In-Class Practice

Self-Assessment

6. In the diagram, the preimage is reflected in line k, then in line m. Describe a single transformation that maps the blue figure to the green figure.

7. A rotation of 76° maps C to C'. To map C to C' using two reflections, what is the measure of the angle formed by the intersecting lines of reflection?

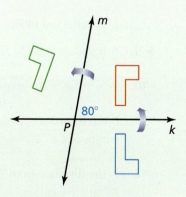

4.4 Practice

Identify any congruent figures in the coordinate plane. Explain. (See Example 1.)

▶ 1.
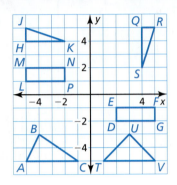

2.
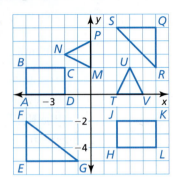

Describe a congruence transformation that maps the blue preimage to the green image.
(See Example 2.)

▶ 3.
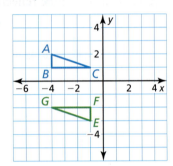

4.
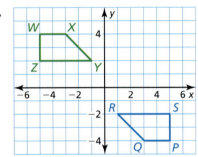

Determine whether the polygons with the given vertices are congruent. Use transformations to explain your reasoning.

5. $Q(2, 4)$, $R(5, 4)$, $S(4, 1)$ and $T(6, 4)$, $U(9, 4)$, $V(8, 1)$

6. $W(-3, 1)$, $X(2, 1)$, $Y(4, -4)$, $Z(-5, -4)$ and $C(-1, -3)$, $D(-1, 2)$, $E(4, 4)$, $F(4, -5)$

7. $J(1, 1)$, $K(3, 2)$, $L(4, 1)$ and $M(6, 1)$, $N(5, 2)$, $P(2, 1)$

8. $A(0, 0)$, $B(1, 2)$, $C(4, 2)$, $D(3, 0)$ and $E(0, -5)$, $F(-1, -3)$, $G(-4, -3)$, $H(-3, -5)$

△ABC **is reflected in line** k, **and** △A'B'C' **is reflected in line** m. (See Example 3.)

▶ 9. A translation maps △ABC to which triangle?

10. Which lines are perpendicular to $\overline{AA''}$?

11. If the distance between k and m is 2.6 inches, what is the length of $\overline{CC''}$?

12. Is the distance from B' to m the same as the distance from B'' to m? Explain.

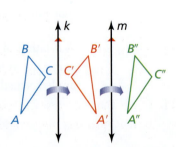

Describe a single transformation that maps A to A″. (See Example 4.)

13.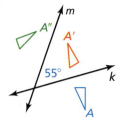

14.

15. **SMP.3 ERROR ANALYSIS** Describe and correct the error in using the Reflections in Intersecting Lines Theorem.

A 72° rotation about point P maps the blue figure to the green figure.

16. Use the Reflections in Parallel Lines Theorem to explain how you can make a glide reflection using three reflections. How are the lines of reflection related?

CONSTRUCTION Use a compass and straightedge to construct two lines of reflection that produce a composition of reflections resulting in the given transformation.

17. **Translation:** △ABC → △A″B″C″

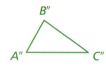

18. **Rotation about P:** △XYZ → △X″Y″Z″

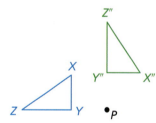

19. **PROVING A THEOREM** Prove the Reflections in Parallel Lines Theorem.

   Given A reflection in line ℓ maps $\overline{JK}$ to $\overline{J'K'}$, a reflection in line m maps $\overline{J'K'}$ to $\overline{J''K''}$, and $\ell \parallel m$.

   Prove a. $\overline{JJ''}$ is perpendicular to ℓ and m.

   b. $JJ'' = 2d$, where d is the distance between ℓ and m.

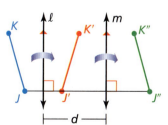

20. You reflect a figure in each of two parallel lines. Explain whether the order of the reflections is important.

21. **SMP.7** Describe a sequence of two or more different transformations where the order of the transformations does not affect the final image.

22. **SMP.1 DIG DEEPER** Are any two rays congruent? If so, describe a congruence transformation that maps a ray to any other ray. If not, explain why not.

Interpreting Data

IDEAL VERSUS PERCEIVED Humanistic psychology divides the self into two categories, the perceived self (how you see yourself) and the ideal self (how you would like to be). Congruence occurs when the perceived self and the ideal self overlap significantly.

23. Compare how the word *congruence* is used in psychology to how it is used in geometry.

24. Psychologists tend to believe that it is not possible for your ideal self to be identical to your perceived self. Do you agree?

Review & Refresh

Graph quadrilateral *QRST* with vertices $Q(2, -1)$, $R(5, -2)$, $S(5, -4)$, and $T(2, -4)$ and its image after the composition.

25. Translation: $(x, y) \to (x - 5, y + 3)$
   Reflection: in the line $y = -3$

26. Reflection: in the *x*-axis
   Rotation: $90°$ about the origin

Graph the linear equation. Identify the *x*-intercept.

27. $y = -\frac{3}{4}x + 2$ **28.** $3x + y = -5$

29. Write an inequality that represents the graph.

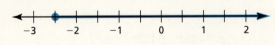

Explain whether the sequence is *arithmetic*, *geometric*, or *neither*.

30. $\frac{2}{3}$, 2, 6, 18, . . .   **31.** $-4, -1, 2, 5, . . .$

Solve the equation.

32. $12 + 6m = 2m$

33. $-2(8 - y) = -6y$

34. $7(2n + 1) = \frac{1}{3}(6n - 15)$

Find the value of *x*.

35. 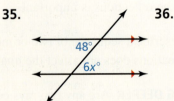   **36.**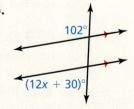

4.5 Dilations

Learning Target: Understand dilations of figures.

Success Criteria:
- I can identify dilations.
- I can dilate figures.
- I can solve real-life problems involving scale factors and dilations.

INVESTIGATE Dilating Figures

Work with a partner.

1. The diagram shows a *dilation* of △DEF to △D′E′F′. How would you define a dilation?

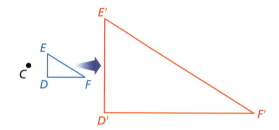

INVESTIGATE Dilating Figures

Work with a partner.

2. Use technology to draw any line segment, $\overline{PQ}$, and a point C not on the line segment.

   a. Dilate $\overline{PQ}$ using a *scale factor* of 2 and the *center of dilation* C to form $\overline{P'Q'}$. What do you notice? Make several observations.

   b. Choose two other scale factors, where one scale factor is greater than 1 and the other scale factor is between 0 and 1. What conclusions can you make?

3. Use technology to draw any △PQR and a point C not in △PQR.

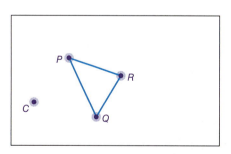

   a. Dilate △PQR using the center of dilation C and several different scale factors to form △P′Q′R′. Compare △PQR and △P′Q′R′.

   b. Make a conjecture about the side lengths and angle measures of the image of △PQR after a dilation with a scale factor of k.

4. Based on your results in Exercises 2 and 3, is there anything you would like to change or include in your definition in Exercise 1?

5. Explain whether a dilation is a rigid motion.

4.5   Dilations   199

Vocabulary
dilation
center of dilation
scale factor
enlargement
reduction

Identifying and Performing Dilations

A **dilation** is a transformation in which a figure is enlarged or reduced with respect to a fixed point C called the **center of dilation** and a **scale factor** k, which is the ratio of the lengths of the corresponding sides of the image and the preimage. When $k > 1$, a dilation is an **enlargement**. When $0 < k < 1$, a dilation is a **reduction**.

Key Concept

Dilations

A dilation with center of dilation C and scale factor k maps every point P in a figure to a point P' so that the following are true.

- If P is the center of dilation C, then $P = P'$.
- If P is not the center of dilation C, then the image point P' lies on $\overrightarrow{CP}$. The scale factor k is a positive number such that $k = \dfrac{CP'}{CP}$.
- Angle measures are preserved.

A dilation does not change any line that passes through the center of dilation. A dilation maps a line that does not pass through the center of dilation to a parallel line. In the figure above, $\overleftrightarrow{PR} \parallel \overleftrightarrow{P'R'}$, $\overleftrightarrow{PQ} \parallel \overleftrightarrow{P'Q'}$, and $\overleftrightarrow{QR} \parallel \overleftrightarrow{Q'R'}$.

EXAMPLE 1 Identifying Dilations

Find the scale factor of the dilation. Then tell whether the dilation is a *reduction* or an *enlargement*.

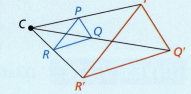

Because $\dfrac{CP'}{CP} = \dfrac{12}{8}$, the scale factor is $k = \dfrac{3}{2}$.

▶ So, the dilation is an enlargement.

In-Class Practice

Self-Assessment

1. Find the scale factor of the dilation. Then tell whether the dilation is a *reduction* or an *enlargement*.

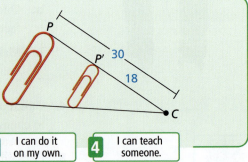

STUDY TIP

In this chapter, for all dilations in the coordinate plane, the center of dilation is the origin unless otherwise noted.

Key Concept

Coordinate Rule for Dilations

If $P(x, y)$ is the preimage of a point, then its image after a dilation centered at the origin $(0, 0)$ with scale factor k is the point $P'(kx, ky)$.

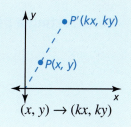

$(x, y) \rightarrow (kx, ky)$

EXAMPLE 2 — Dilating a Figure in the Coordinate Plane

Graph $\triangle ABC$ with vertices $A(2, 1)$, $B(4, 1)$, and $C(4, -1)$ and its image after a dilation with a scale factor of 2.

Use the coordinate rule for a dilation with $k = 2$ to find the coordinates of the vertices of the image. Then graph $\triangle ABC$ and its image.

$(x, y) \rightarrow (2x, 2y)$

$A(2, 1) \rightarrow A'(4, 2)$

$B(4, 1) \rightarrow B'(8, 2)$

$C(4, -1) \rightarrow C'(8, -2)$

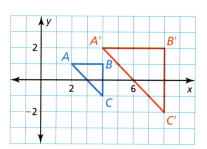

EXAMPLE 3 — Dilating a Figure in the Coordinate Plane

Graph quadrilateral $KLMN$ with vertices $K(-3, 6)$, $L(0, 6)$, $M(3, 3)$, and $N(-3, -3)$ and its image after a dilation with a scale factor of $\frac{1}{3}$.

Use the coordinate rule for a dilation with $k = \frac{1}{3}$ to find the coordinates of the vertices of the image. Then graph quadrilateral $KLMN$ and its image.

$(x, y) \rightarrow \left(\frac{1}{3}x, \frac{1}{3}y\right)$

$K(-3, 6) \rightarrow K'(-1, 2)$

$L(0, 6) \rightarrow L'(0, 2)$

$M(3, 3) \rightarrow M'(1, 1)$

$N(-3, -3) \rightarrow N'(-1, -1)$

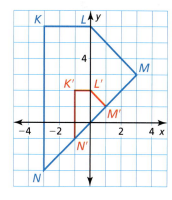

In-Class Practice

Self-Assessment

Graph $\triangle PQR$ and its image after a dilation with scale factor k.

2. $P(-2, -1)$, $Q(-1, 0)$, $R(0, -1)$; $k = 4$

3. $P(5, -5)$, $Q(10, -5)$, $R(10, 5)$; $k = 0.4$

1 I don't understand yet. **2** I can do it with help. **3** I can do it on my own. **4** I can teach someone.

Construction

Constructing a Dilation

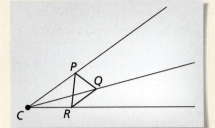
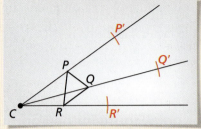
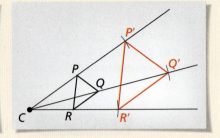

Draw △PQR and center of dilation C outside the triangle. Draw rays from C through the vertices of the triangle.

Use a compass to make a mark on each ray that is twice the distance from the center to the vertex. Label P′, Q′, and R′.

Connect the points to form △P′Q′R′.

Scale factors can be negative numbers. When this occurs, the figure rotates 180°. So, when $k > 0$, a dilation with a scale factor of k is the same as the composition of a dilation with a scale factor of k followed by a rotation of 180° about the center of dilation.

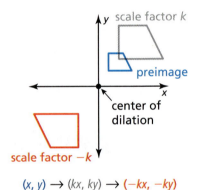

$(x, y) \rightarrow (kx, ky) \rightarrow (-kx, -ky)$

EXAMPLE 4 Using a Negative Scale Factor

Graph △FGH with vertices $F(-4, -2)$, $G(-2, 4)$, and $H(-2, -2)$ and its image after a dilation with a scale factor of $-\frac{1}{2}$.

Use the coordinate rule for a dilation with $k = -\frac{1}{2}$ to find the coordinates of the vertices of the image. Then graph △FGH and its image.

$(x, y) \rightarrow \left(-\frac{1}{2}x, -\frac{1}{2}y\right)$

$F(-4, -2) \rightarrow F'(2, 1)$

$G(-2, 4) \rightarrow G'(1, -2)$

$H(-2, -2) \rightarrow H'(1, 1)$

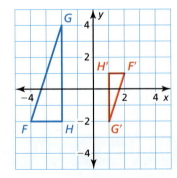

In-Class Practice

Self-Assessment

4. Graph △PQR with vertices $P(1, 2)$, $Q(3, 1)$, and $R(1, -3)$ and its image after a dilation with a scale factor of -2.

Connections to Real Life

EXAMPLE 5 **Finding a Scale Factor**

You are making your own photo stickers. Your photo is 4 inches by 4 inches. The image on the stickers is 1.1 inches by 1.1 inches. What is the scale factor of this dilation?

The scale factor is the ratio of a side length of the sticker image to a side length of the original photo, or $\frac{1.1 \text{ in.}}{4 \text{ in.}}$.

▶ So, in simplest form, the scale factor is $\frac{11}{40}$.

EXAMPLE 6 **Finding the Length of an Image**

You are using a magnifying glass that shows the image of an object as six times the object's actual size. Determine the length of the image of the spider seen through the magnifying glass.

1.5 cm

$\frac{\text{cm} \to \text{image length}}{\text{cm} \to \text{actual length}} = k$ — Write ratio of corresponding lengths.

$\frac{x}{1.5} = 6$ — Substitute values.

$x = 9$ — Multiply each side by 1.5.

▶ So, the image length seen through the magnifying glass is 9 centimeters.

In-Class Practice
Self-Assessment

5. An optometrist dilates the pupils of a patient's eyes to get a better look at the back of the eyes. A pupil dilates from 4.5 millimeters to 8 millimeters. What is the scale factor of this dilation?

12.6 cm

6. The image of another spider seen through the magnifying glass in Example 6 is shown at the right. Find the actual length of the spider.

 I don't understand yet.
 I can do it with help.
 I can do it on my own.
 I can teach someone.

4.5 Dilations

4.5 Practice

Find the scale factor of the dilation. Then tell whether the dilation is a *reduction* or an *enlargement*. (See Example 1.)

▶ 1.

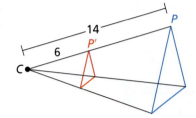

2.

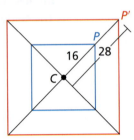

CONSTRUCTION Copy the diagram. Then use a compass and straightedge to construct a dilation of quadrilateral *RSTU* with the given center and scale factor *k*.

3. Center P, $k = 2$

4. Center C, $k = 3$

5. Center C, $k = 75\%$

6. Center R, $k = 0.25$

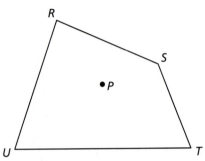

Graph the polygon with the given vertices and its image after a dilation with scale factor *k*. (See Examples 2, 3, and 4.)

▶ 7. $X(6, -1)$, $Y(-2, -4)$, $Z(1, 2)$; $k = 3$

8. $A(0, 5)$, $B(-10, -5)$, $C(5, -5)$; $k = 120\%$

9. $J(4, 0)$, $K(-8, 4)$, $L(0, -4)$, $M(12, -8)$; $k = 0.25$

10. $T(9, -3)$, $U(6, 0)$, $V(3, 9)$, $W(0, 0)$; $k = \frac{2}{3}$

▶ 11. $B(-5, -10)$, $C(-10, 15)$, $D(0, 5)$; $k = -\frac{1}{5}$

12. $R(-7, -1)$, $S(2, 5)$, $T(-2, -3)$, $U(-3, -3)$; $k = -4$

▶ 13. **CONNECTION TO REAL LIFE** Your wallet-sized school photo is 2.5 inches by 3.5 inches. You want to dilate the photo to 5 inches by 7 inches. What is the scale factor of this dilation? (See Example 5.)

The red figure is the image of the blue figure after a dilation with center *C*. Find the scale factor of the dilation. Then find the value of the variable.

14.

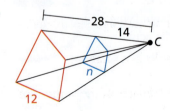

15.

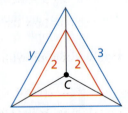

204 Chapter 4 Transformations

ENTOMOLOGY INSECTS You are using a magnifying glass. Use the actual length of the insect and the magnification level to determine the length of the image of the insect seen through the magnifying glass. (See Example 6.)

16. ladybug
    Magnification: 10×

4.5 mm

▶ 17. emperor moth
    Magnification: 5×

60 mm

18. dragonfly
    Magnification: 20×

47 mm

19. carpenter ant
    Magnification: 15×

12 mm

20. You perform a dilation in which the center of dilation is outside the figure and the scale factor is 0.1. Is the dilated figure or the original figure closer to the center of dilation? How do you know?

21. **CONNECTION TO REAL LIFE** You have a 4-inch by 6-inch photo from the school dance. You have an 8-inch by 10-inch frame. Can you enlarge the photo without cropping to fit the frame?

Graph △ABC with vertices $A(-3, 4)$, $B(-4, 2)$, and $C(0, -4)$ and its image after the transformation. Then explain whether the transformation is (a) a dilation and (b) a rigid motion.

22. $(x, y) \rightarrow (2x, y)$

23. $(x, y) \rightarrow (x, 3y)$

24. **CONNECT CONCEPTS** The larger triangle at the right is a dilation of the smaller triangle. Find the values of x and y.

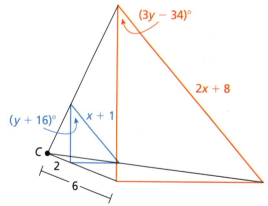

25. **SMP.8 OPEN-ENDED** Graph any rectangle in a coordinate plane.

    a. Find the perimeter and the area of the rectangle.
    b. Dilate the rectangle using a scale factor greater than 1. Find the perimeter and the area of the image. Compare the perimeters and the areas of the rectangles. What do you notice?
    c. Repeat part (b) using a scale factor greater than 0 and less than 1.
    d. Make conjectures for how the perimeter and area change when a figure is dilated.

26. **SMP.6** Explain why a dilation with a negative scale factor results in a rotation.

27. △ABC has vertices $A(4, 2)$, $B(4, 6)$, and $C(7, 2)$. Find the coordinates of the vertices of the image after a dilation with center $(4, 0)$ and scale factor 2.

Interpreting Data

EYELASH MITES An optometrist is studying eyelash mites, which are small bugs found at the bases of eyelashes. They are about $\frac{1}{3}$ millimeter long.

28. Estimate the magnification of the photograph.

29. If you looked at an eyelash mite in a $100\times$ microscope, how long would the mite appear to be?

30. How do optical microscopes magnify things?

Review & Refresh

Graph the polygon with the given vertices and its image after the indicated transformation.

31. $A(2, -1)$, $B(0, 4)$, $C(-3, 5)$
    Translation: $(x, y) \to (x - 1, y + 3)$

32. $A(-5, 6)$, $B(-7, 8)$, $C(-3, 11)$
    Reflection: in the x-axis

33. $D(-3, 2)$, $E(-1, 4)$, $F(1, 2)$, $G(1, -1)$
    Rotation: $270°$ about the origin

34. Simplify $\dfrac{4^{-2}b^{-3}}{2^{-1}a^0 b^{-4}}$.

35. You are painting a rectangular canvas that is 30 inches wide and 40 inches long. Your friend is painting a rectangular canvas, where the width and length are each x inches shorter. When $x = 3$, what is the area of your friend's canvas?

36. Describe a congruence transformation that maps the blue preimage to the green image.

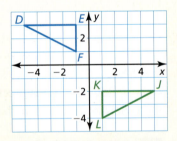

37. Graph $g(x) = 3(x - 1)^2 + 7$. Compare the graph to the graph of $f(x) = x^2$.

Find the product.

38. $(3x - 4)^2$

39. $(w - 5)(6 + 2w)$

Solve the system using any method.

40. $y = -3x + 5$
    $2x + 4y = 15$

41. $0.6y + 0.5x = 1$
    $0.25x = -0.5y + 2$

4.6 Similarity and Transformations

Learning Target: Understand similarity transformations.

Success Criteria:
- I can perform similarity transformations.
- I can describe similarity transformations.
- I can prove that figures are similar.

Two figures are *similar figures* when they have the same shape but not necessarily the same size.

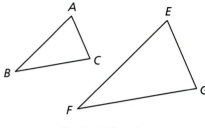

Similar Triangles

INVESTIGATE   Transforming Figures and Determining Similarity

Work with a partner. Use technology to draw any triangle and label it △ABC.

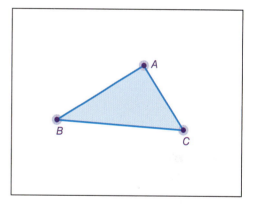

1. Translate △ABC several times using different translations. Explain whether the images are similar to the preimage.

2. Reflect △ABC several times using different lines of reflection. Explain whether the images are similar to the preimage.

3. Rotate △ABC several times using different centers of rotation and angles of rotation. Explain whether the images are similar to the preimage.

4. Dilate △ABC several times using different scale factors and centers of dilation. Explain whether the images are similar to the preimage.

5. A figure undergoes a composition of transformations, which includes translations, reflections, rotations, and dilations. Explain whether the image is similar to the preimage.

6. Explain the difference between congruent figures and similar figures.

Vocabulary
similarity transformation
similar figures

Performing Similarity Transformations

Dilations are nonrigid motions because they preserve shape but not necessarily size. A **similarity transformation** is a dilation or a composition of rigid motions and dilations. Two geometric figures are **similar figures** if and only if there is a similarity transformation that maps one of the figures to the other.

Unlike congruence transformations that preserve length and angle measure, similarity transformations preserve angle measure only, unless the dilations have scale factors of 1 or −1. So, similar figures have the same shape but not necessarily the same size.

EXAMPLE 1 Performing a Similarity Transformation

Graph △ABC with vertices $A(-4, 1)$, $B(-2, 2)$, and $C(-2, 1)$ and its image after the similarity transformation.

Translation: $(x, y) \rightarrow (x + 5, y + 1)$

Dilation: $(x, y) \rightarrow (2x, 2y)$

Graph △ABC. Translate △ABC 5 units right and 1 unit up. △A′B′C′ has vertices $A'(1, 2)$, $B'(3, 3)$, and $C'(3, 2)$.

Dilate △A′B′C′ using a scale factor of 2. △A″B″C″ has vertices $A''(2, 4)$, $B''(6, 6)$, and $C''(6, 4)$.

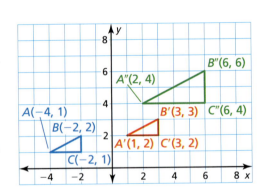

In-Class Practice

Self-Assessment

1. Graph $\overline{CD}$ with endpoints $C(-2, 2)$ and $D(2, 2)$ and its image after the similarity transformation.

   Rotation: 90° about the origin
   Dilation: $(x, y) \rightarrow \left(\frac{1}{2}x, \frac{1}{2}y\right)$

2. Graph △FGH with vertices $F(1, 2)$, $G(4, 4)$, and $H(2, 0)$ and its image after the similarity transformation.

   Reflection: in the x-axis
   Dilation: $(x, y) \rightarrow (1.5x, 1.5y)$

Describing Similarity Transformations

EXAMPLE 2 Describing a Similarity Transformation

Describe a similarity transformation that maps trapezoid *PQRS* to trapezoid *WXYZ*.

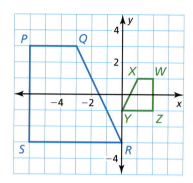

$\overline{QR}$ falls from left to right, and $\overline{XY}$ rises from left to right. If you reflect trapezoid *PQRS* in the *y*-axis, then the image, trapezoid *P'Q'R'S'*, will have the same orientation as trapezoid *WXYZ*.

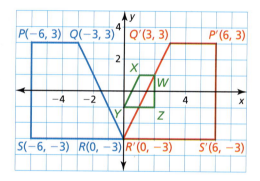

Trapezoid *WXYZ* appears to be about one-third as large as trapezoid *P'Q'R'S'*. Dilate trapezoid *P'Q'R'S'* using a scale factor of $\frac{1}{3}$.

$$P'(6, 3) \rightarrow P''(2, 1) \qquad R'(0, -3) \rightarrow R''(0, -1)$$
$$Q'(3, 3) \rightarrow Q''(1, 1) \qquad S'(6, -3) \rightarrow S''(2, -1)$$

The vertices of trapezoid *P"Q"R"S"* match the vertices of trapezoid *WXYZ*.

▶ So, a similarity transformation that maps trapezoid *PQRS* to trapezoid *WXYZ* is a reflection in the *y*-axis, followed by a dilation with a scale factor of $\frac{1}{3}$.

In-Class Practice
Self-Assessment

3. In Example 2, describe another similarity transformation that maps trapezoid *PQRS* to trapezoid *WXYZ*.

Proving Figures Are Similar

To prove that two figures are similar, you must prove that a similarity transformation maps one of the figures to the other.

EXAMPLE 3 **Proving That Two Squares Are Similar**

Prove that square *ABCD* is similar to square *EFGH*.

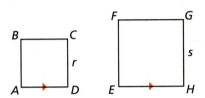

Given Square *ABCD* with side length r, square *EFGH* with side length s, $\overline{AD} \parallel \overline{EH}$

Prove Square *ABCD* is similar to square *EFGH*.

Translate square *ABCD* so that point *A* maps to point *E*.

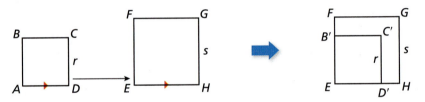

Next, dilate square $EB'C'D'$ using the center of dilation E. Choose the scale factor to be the ratio of the side lengths of *EFGH* and $EB'C'D'$, which is $\frac{s}{r}$.

▶ A similarity transformation maps square *ABCD* to square *EFGH*. So, square *ABCD* is similar to square *EFGH*.

In-Class Practice
Self-Assessment

4. Prove that $\triangle JKL$ is similar to $\triangle MNP$.

Given Right isosceles $\triangle JKL$ with leg length t, right isosceles $\triangle MNP$ with leg length v, $\overline{LJ} \parallel \overline{PM}$

Prove $\triangle JKL$ is similar to $\triangle MNP$.

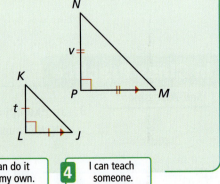

4.6 Practice

Graph △FGH with vertices F(−2, 2), G(−2, −4), and H(−4, −4) and its image after the similarity transformation. (See Example 1.)

1. **Dilation:** $(x, y) \rightarrow \left(\frac{3}{4}x, \frac{3}{4}y\right)$
   Reflection: in the x-axis

2. **Rotation:** 90° about the origin
   Dilation: $(x, y) \rightarrow (3x, 3y)$

Describe a similarity transformation that maps the blue preimage to the green image. (See Example 2.)

3.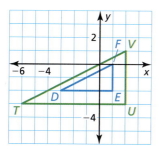

4.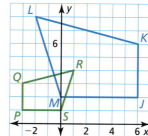

Prove that the figures are similar. (See Example 3.)

5. **Given** Right isosceles △ABC with leg length j, right isosceles △RST with leg length k, $\overline{CA} \parallel \overline{RT}$
   Prove △ABC is similar to △RST.

 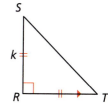

6. **Given** Rectangle JKLM with side lengths x and y, rectangle QRST with side lengths 2x and 2y
   Prove Rectangle JKLM is similar to rectangle QRST.

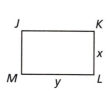 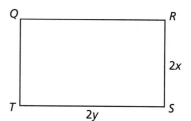

7. **CONNECTION TO REAL LIFE** The stop sign and the stop sign sticker are regular octagons. Explain whether they are similar.

12.6 in.

4 in.

8. △ABC can be mapped to △DEF by a translation 3 units right and 2 units up, followed by a dilation with a scale factor of $\frac{1}{2}$. Describe a similarity transformation that maps △DEF to △ABC.

9. **SMP.8** △QRS has vertices Q(1, 1), R(1, 5), and S(7, 1).
   a. Graph △QRS. Then connect the midpoints of the sides of △QRS to make another triangle. Are the triangles similar? Justify your answer.
   b. Repeat part (a) for several other triangles. What conjecture can you make?

Interpreting Data

BODY PROPORTIONS As humans grow, their body proportions change. A baby's head is large in proportion to the rest of their body. As a child grows up, their head becomes smaller in proportion to the rest of their body. This tends to not be true for reptiles, as shown in the chart.

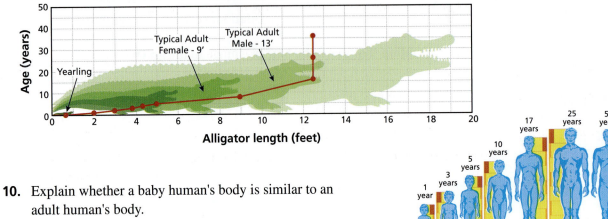

10. Explain whether a baby human's body is similar to an adult human's body.

11. Explain whether a baby alligator's body is similar to an adult alligator's body.

12. Compare the portions of a human's height that are taken up by the head as the human grows.

13. Compare the portions of an alligator's height that are taken up by the head as the alligator grows.

Review & Refresh

Graph $\triangle DEF$ with vertices $D(4, -6)$, $E(4, -2)$, and $F(8, -2)$ and its image after the transformation.

14. a dilation with a scale factor of 2.5

15. a 270° rotation about the origin

16. Write an equation of the line passing through $(2, 3)$ that is perpendicular to the line $y = -\frac{1}{4}x + 1$.

17. Determine whether the quadrilaterals with vertices $J(-4, -2)$, $K(-1, -1)$, $L(-1, -7)$, $M(-4, -5)$ and $W(6, 2)$, $X(3, 3)$, $Y(3, -3)$, $Z(6, -1)$ are congruent.

Solve the inequality. Graph the solution.

18. $4m - 1 > 9 + 2m$ 19. $-1 < 4z - 5 < 19$

20. Solve $9x - 2 = 13 + 6x$. Justify each step.

Classify the angle.

21.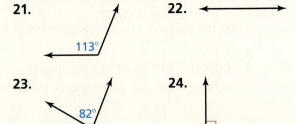

22.

23.

24.

25. The linear function $m = 60 - 5c$ represents the amount of time m (in minutes) that you have left to escape a room in a game after receiving c clues.

   a. Find the domain of the function. Is the domain *discrete* or *continuous*?

   b. Graph the function using its domain.

4 Chapter Review with CalcChat

Rate your understanding of each section.

1 I don't understand yet. **2** I can do it with help. **3** I can do it on my own. **4** I can teach someone.

4.1 Translations (pp. 167–174)

⊙ **Learning Target:** Understand translations of figures.

Vocabulary
transformation
image
preimage
translation
translation vector
component form
rigid motion
composition of transformations

The vertices of △XYZ are X(2, 3), Y(−3, 2), and Z(−4, −3). Translate △XYZ using the given translation vector or rule. Graph △XYZ and its image.

1. ⟨0, 2⟩

2. ⟨−3, 4⟩

3. $(x, y) \to (x + 3, y - 1)$

4. $(x, y) \to (x + 4, y + 1)$

Graph △PQR with vertices P(0, −4), Q(1, 3), and R(2, −5) and its image after the composition.

5. **Translation:** $(x, y) \to (x + 1, y + 2)$
   Translation: $(x, y) \to (x - 4, y + 1)$

6. **Translation:** $(x, y) \to (x, y + 3)$
   Translation: $(x, y) \to (x - 1, y + 1)$

7. A translation maps △ABC to △A′B′C′ using the translation vector ⟨−3, 5⟩. A second translation maps △A′B′C′ to △A″B″C″ using the translation vector ⟨4, −2⟩. Write a rule for translating △ABC to △A″B″C″.

4.2 Reflections (pp. 175–182)

⊙ **Learning Target:** Understand reflections of figures.

Vocabulary
reflection
line of reflection
glide reflection
line symmetry
line of symmetry

Graph the polygon and its image after a reflection in the given line.

8. $x = 4$

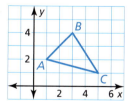

9. $y = 3$

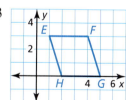

10. Graph $\overline{RS}$ with endpoints R(2, 3) and S(4, −1) and its image after the glide reflection.

    Translation: $(x, y) \to (x, y + 3)$

    Reflection: in the y-axis

11. How many lines of symmetry does the figure have?

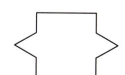

4.3 Rotations (pp. 183–190)

Learning Target: Understand rotations of figures.

Vocabulary
rotation
center of rotation
angle of rotation
rotational symmetry
center of symmetry

Graph the polygon with the given vertices and its image after a rotation of the given number of degrees about the origin.

12. $A(-3, -1)$, $B(2, 2)$, $C(3, -3)$; 90°

13. $W(-2, -1)$, $X(-1, 3)$, $Y(3, 3)$, $Z(3, -3)$; 180°

14. Graph $\overline{XY}$ with endpoints $X(5, -2)$ and $Y(3, -3)$ and its image after the composition.

    Reflection: in the x-axis

    Rotation: 270° about the origin

Determine whether the figure has rotational symmetry. If so, describe any rotations that map the figure onto itself.

15.

16.

17. The diagram shows a game in which you use the pieces at the top to form solid rows at the bottom. Using only translations and rotations, describe the transformations of the pieces at the top that will form two solid rows at the bottom.

18. Can a figure that does not have 90° rotational symmetry be mapped onto itself by a rotation of 270°?

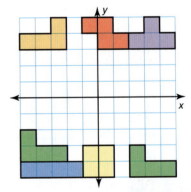

4.4 Congruence and Transformations (pp. 191–198)

Learning Target: Understand congruence transformations.

Vocabulary
congruent figures
congruence transformation

19. Identify any congruent figures in the coordinate plane at the right.

20. Which transformation is the same as reflecting a figure in two parallel lines? in two intersecting lines?

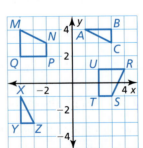

21. In a marching band maneuver, the marcher at the left spins 180° in place with arms spread, and hands the horn to the marcher at the right, who spins 180° with arms spread, and stops.

    a. How far from the initial position is the horn?

    b. What composition maps the horn from the initial position to the final position?

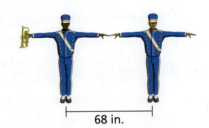

214   Chapter 4   Transformations

4.5 Dilations (pp. 199–206)

⊙ **Learning Target:** Understand dilations of figures.

Vocabulary
dilation
center of dilation
scale factor
enlargement
reduction

22. Find the scale factor of the dilation. Then tell whether the dilation is a *reduction* or an *enlargement*.

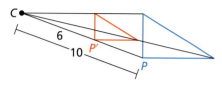

Graph the triangle with the given vertices and its image after a dilation with scale factor k.

23. $P(2, 2)$, $Q(4, 4)$, $R(8, 2)$; $k = \frac{1}{2}$

24. $X(-3, 2)$, $Y(2, 3)$, $Z(1, -1)$; $k = -3$

25. You are using a magnifying glass that shows the image of an object as four times the object's actual size. The image has a length of 15.2 centimeters. Find the actual length of the object.

26. Use the given actual and magnified lengths to determine whether the following insects were seen using the same magnification level.

grasshopper
Actual: 2 in.
Magnified: 15 in.

honeybee
Actual: $\frac{5}{8}$ in.
Magnified: $\frac{75}{16}$ in.

4.6 Similarity and Transformations (pp. 207–212)

⊙ **Learning Target:** Understand similarity transformations.

Vocabulary
similarity transformation
similar figures

27. Graph △DEF with vertices $D(-3, 4)$, $E(3, 4)$, and $F(1, 2)$ and its image after the similarity transformation.

Translation: $(x, y) \to (x + 1, y - 2)$
Dilation: $(x, y) \to \left(\frac{3}{2}x, \frac{3}{2}y\right)$

Describe a similarity transformation that maps △ABC to △RST.

28. $A(1, 0)$, $B(-2, -1)$, $C(-1, -2)$ and $R(-3, 0)$, $S(6, -3)$, $T(3, -6)$

29. $A(6, 4)$, $B(-2, 0)$, $C(-4, 2)$ and $R(2, 3)$, $S(0, -1)$, $T(1, -2)$

30. $A(3, -2)$, $B(0, 4)$, $C(-1, -3)$ and $R(-4, -6)$, $S(8, 0)$, $T(-6, 2)$

31. The original photograph shown is 4 inches by 6 inches.

    a. What transformations produce the new photograph?

    b. The scale factor of the dilation involved in producing the new photograph is $\frac{1}{2}$. What are the dimensions of the new photograph?

    c. You have a frame that holds photos that are 8.5 inches by 11 inches. Explain whether you can enlarge the original photograph without cropping to fit the frame.

original

new

4 PERFORMANCE TASK
SMP.5

The Butterfly Effect

Citrus Swallowtail

$3\frac{1}{2}$–$4\frac{3}{8}$ in.

Zebra Swallowtail

$2\frac{1}{2}$–4 in.

Mexican Yellow

$1\frac{3}{4}$–$2\frac{1}{2}$ in.

Desert Orangetip

1–$1\frac{1}{2}$ in.

Green-Underside Blue

1–$1\frac{1}{2}$ in.

Arctic Skipper

1–$1\frac{1}{4}$ in.

European Peacock

2–$2\frac{1}{2}$ in.

Emerald Swallowtail

3–4 in.

Spicebush Swallowtail

3–4 in.

The Apollo

$2\frac{1}{2}$–$3\frac{3}{4}$ in.

Eastern Tiger Swallowtail

$2\frac{1}{2}$–$4\frac{1}{2}$ in.

Monarch

$3\frac{3}{8}$–$4\frac{7}{8}$ in.

Analyzing Data

Use the information on the previous page to complete the following exercises.

Explain what is shown in the display. What do you notice? What do you wonder?

Which butterflies could have a wingspan of 2 feet when under 5× magnification?

The butterflies have been dilated to appear the same size. Which have been reduced?

Do all the butterflies have line symmetry? Do any have rotational symmetry?

BUTTERFLY RESEARCH

Entomologists often create illustrations of the insects they are studying. Research one of the butterfly species shown. Create a life-size illustration of the species and show any lines of symmetry. Then construct a dilation that shows how the species would look under a magnifying glass. State the magnification level that you used. Finally, give information about how to identify the species, its habitat, and its diet.

5 Congruent Triangles

- 5.1 Angles of Triangles
- 5.2 Congruent Polygons
- 5.3 Proving Triangle Congruence by SAS
- 5.4 Equilateral and Isosceles Triangles
- 5.5 Proving Triangle Congruence by SSS
- 5.6 Proving Triangle Congruence by ASA and AAS
- 5.7 Using Congruent Triangles
- 5.8 Coordinate Proofs

NATIONAL GEOGRAPHIC EXPLORER
Aydogan Ozcan ENGINEER

Dr. Aydogan Ozcan's research focuses on the use of computation to create new optical microscopy, sensing, and diagnostic technologies. He pioneered the use of smartphone biomedical tools such as diagnostic test readers, bacteria sensors, blood analyzers, and allergen detectors, all integrated with mobile phones using compact interfaces.

- What is microscopy?
- What is an allergen detector? How can you use an allergen detector to determine what allergies you might have?
- Name some types of bacteria that are beneficial to humans. Name some types that are harmful to humans.

PERFORMANCE TASK
Scientists draw diagrams of bacteria and viruses in order to document their features. In the Performance Task on pages 284 and 285, you will analyze a drawing of a virus known as a *bacteriophage*.

Diagnostic Technologies

Big Idea of the Chapter
Use Congruent Triangles

Triangles have the unique property that if each side of a triangle is congruent to a different side of another triangle, then the triangles must be congruent. No other polygon has this property. You can use other relationships between sides and angles to determine whether triangles are congruent.

A difference between bacteria and viruses is that bacteria are living cells, while viruses are non-living collections of molecules that need a host to reproduce. Many bacteria are helpful, such as those in our digestive system and those that decompose organic materials in soil. Similarly, viruses can be helpful. Some can infect and kill dangerous bacteria, and others can trigger an immune response that provides protection against more dangerous viruses.

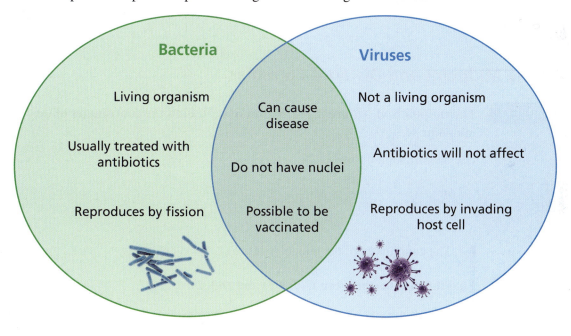

1. A nanometer (nm) is one billionth of a meter. How many bacteria that are 2,000 nanometers long can fit end to end in a meter? How many viruses that are 100 nanometers long can fit end to end in a meter?

2. A typical human hosts about 3×10^{13} bacteria cells and approximately the same number of human cells. Which weigh more? How do you know?

3. Typically when a virus replicates itself, the new virus is congruent to the original. When new viruses are not congruent, a new strain of virus is created. Why does this complicate the treatment of a viral infection?

Getting Ready for Chapter 5

Solving Equations with Variables on Both Sides

EXAMPLE 1 Solve $2 - 5x = -3x$.

$2 - 5x = -3x$	Write the equation.
$+5x \quad +5x$	Addition Property of Equality
$2 = 2x$	Simplify.
$\dfrac{2}{2} = \dfrac{2x}{2}$	Division Property of Equality
$1 = x$	Simplify.

▶ The solution is $x = 1$.

Solve the equation.

1. $7x + 12 = 3x$
2. $5p + 10 = 8p + 1$
3. $z - 2 = 4 + 9z$

Using the Midpoint and Distance Formulas

EXAMPLE 2 The endpoints of $\overline{AB}$ are $A(-2, 3)$ and $B(4, 7)$. Find the coordinates of the midpoint M.

Use the Midpoint Formula.

$$M\left(\dfrac{-2 + 4}{2}, \dfrac{3 + 7}{2}\right) = M\left(\dfrac{2}{2}, \dfrac{10}{2}\right)$$
$$= M(1, 5)$$

▶ The coordinates of the midpoint M are $(1, 5)$.

EXAMPLE 3 Find the distance between $C(0, -5)$ and $D(3, 2)$.

$CD = \sqrt{(x_2 - x_1)^2 + (y_2 - y_1)^2}$	Distance Formula
$= \sqrt{(3 - 0)^2 + [2 - (-5)]^2}$	Substitute.
$= \sqrt{3^2 + 7^2}$	Subtract.
$= \sqrt{9 + 49}$	Evaluate powers.
$= \sqrt{58}$	Add.
≈ 7.6	Use technology.

▶ The distance between $C(0, -5)$ and $D(3, 2)$ is about 7.6.

Find the coordinates of the midpoint M of the segment with the given endpoints. Then find the distance between the endpoints.

4. $P(-4, 1)$ and $Q(0, 7)$
5. $G(3, 6)$ and $H(9, -2)$

5.1 Angles of Triangles

Learning Target: Prove and use theorems about angles of triangles.

Success Criteria:
- I can classify triangles by sides and by angles.
- I can find interior and exterior angle measures of triangles.

INVESTIGATE Analyzing Angle Measures of Triangles

Work with a partner.

1. Use technology to draw a triangle. Rotate the triangle 180° about the midpoints of two of its sides.

2. Repeat Exercise 1 for several triangles. What do you notice about the angles at the vertex where the three triangles meet? Make a conjecture.

INVESTIGATE Analyzing Angle Measures of Triangles

Work with a partner.

3. Use technology to draw a triangle and an exterior angle. Find the measures of the interior angles and exterior angle.

4. Repeat Exercise 3 for several triangles. What do you notice about the measures of the interior angles and exterior angles? Make a conjecture.

5.1 Angles of Triangles 221

Vocabulary
interior angles
exterior angles
corollary to a theorem

Classifying Triangles by Sides and by Angles

Key Concept

Classifying Triangles by Sides

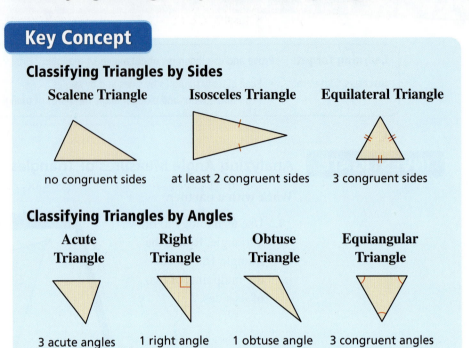

Classifying Triangles by Angles

EXAMPLE 1 Classifying Triangles by Sides and by Angles

Classify the triangular shape of the support beams in the photo by its sides and by measuring its angles.

The triangle has a pair of congruent sides, so it is isosceles. By measuring, you can determine that the angles are 55°, 55°, and 70°.

▶ So, it is an acute isosceles triangle.

In-Class Practice

Self-Assessment

1. Classify the triangle by its sides and by measuring its angles.

2. Draw an obtuse isosceles triangle and an acute scalene triangle.

Chapter 5 Congruent Triangles

EXAMPLE 2 **Classifying a Triangle in the Coordinate Plane**

Classify △OPQ by its sides. Then determine whether it is a right triangle.

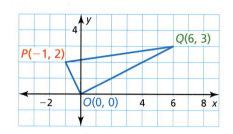

Use the Distance Formula to find the side lengths.

$OP = \sqrt{(x_2 - x_1)^2 + (y_2 - y_1)^2}$ Distance Formula

$= \sqrt{(-1 - 0)^2 + (2 - 0)^2}$ Substitute.

$= \sqrt{5} \approx 2.2$ Simplify.

$OQ = \sqrt{(x_2 - x_1)^2 + (y_2 - y_1)^2}$ Distance Formula

$= \sqrt{(6 - 0)^2 + (3 - 0)^2}$ Substitute.

$= \sqrt{45} \approx 6.7$ Simplify.

$PQ = \sqrt{(x_2 - x_1)^2 + (y_2 - y_1)^2}$ Distance Formula

$= \sqrt{[6 - (-1)]^2 + (3 - 2)^2}$ Substitute.

$= \sqrt{50} \approx 7.1$ Simplify.

Because no sides are congruent, △OPQ is a scalene triangle.

Check for right angles.

The slope of $\overline{OP}$ is $\dfrac{2 - 0}{-1 - 0} = -2$.

The slope of $\overline{OQ}$ is $\dfrac{3 - 0}{6 - 0} = \dfrac{1}{2}$.

The product of the slopes is $-2\left(\dfrac{1}{2}\right) = -1$.

So, $\overline{OP} \perp \overline{OQ}$ and ∠POQ is a right angle.

▶ △OPQ is a right scalene triangle.

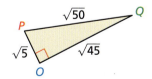

In-Class Practice
Self-Assessment

3. △ABC has vertices A(0, 0), B(3, 3), and C(−3, 3). Classify the triangle by its sides. Then determine whether it is a right triangle.

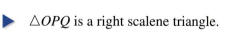

5.1 Angles of Triangles

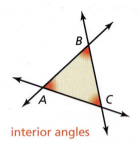
interior angles

Finding Angle Measures of Triangles

When the sides of a polygon are extended, other angles are formed. The original angles are the **interior angles**. The angles that form linear pairs with the interior angles are the **exterior angles**.

exterior angles

Theorem 5.1

Triangle Sum Theorem

The sum of the measures of the interior angles of a triangle is 180°.

Prove this Theorem Exercise 29, page 227

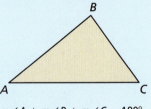

$m\angle A + m\angle B + m\angle C = 180°$

Theorem 5.2

Exterior Angle Theorem

The measure of an exterior angle of a triangle is equal to the sum of the measures of the two nonadjacent interior angles.

Prove this Theorem Exercise 22, page 227

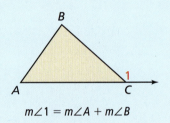

$m\angle 1 = m\angle A + m\angle B$

EXAMPLE 3 Finding an Angle Measure

Find $m\angle JKM$.

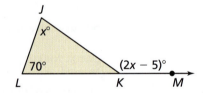

Write and solve an equation to find the value of x.

$(2x - 5)° = 70° + x°$ Apply the Exterior Angle Theorem.

$x = 75$ Solve for x.

Substitute 75 for x in $2x - 5$ to find $m\angle JKM$.

$2x - 5 = 2 \cdot 75 - 5 = 145$

▶ So, the measure of $\angle JKM$ is 145°.

In-Class Practice

Self-Assessment

4. Find $m\angle 1$.

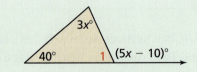

 I don't understand yet.   I can do it with help.   I can do it on my own.   I can teach someone.

A **corollary to a theorem** is a statement that can be proved easily using the theorem. The corollary below follows from the Triangle Sum Theorem.

Corollary 5.1

Corollary to the Triangle Sum Theorem

The acute angles of a right triangle are complementary.

Prove this Corollary Exercise 21, page 227

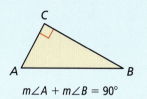

$m\angle A + m\angle B = 90°$

EXAMPLE 4 Finding Angle Measures

You are designing doors for a new building. The doors are right triangles. For each door, the measure of one acute angle in the triangle is twice the measure of the other. Find the measure of each acute angle for one door.

Sketch a diagram of the situation. Let the measure of the smaller acute angle be $x°$. Then the measure of the larger acute angle is $2x°$.

The Corollary to the Triangle Sum Theorem states that the acute angles of a right triangle are complementary. Write and solve an equation to find the value of x.

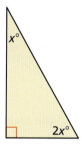

$x° + 2x° = 90°$ Corollary to the Triangle Sum Theorem

$x = 30$ Solve for x.

▶ So, the measures of the acute angles are 30° and 2(30°) = 60°.

Check Add the two angle measures and check that their sum satisfies the Corollary to the Triangle Sum Theorem.

$30° + 60° = 90°$ ✓

In-Class Practice

Self-Assessment

5. Find the measure of each acute angle.

6. **WHAT IF?** In Example 4, find the measure of each acute angle when the measure of one acute angle in the triangle is three times the measure of the other.

5.1 Angles of Triangles   **225**

5.1 Practice

Classify the triangle by its sides and by measuring its angles. (See Example 1.)

1.
2.
3.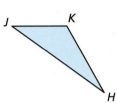

Classify △ABC by its sides. Then determine whether it is a right triangle. (See Example 2.)

4. $A(3, 3), B(6, 9), C(6, -3)$
5. $A(2, 3), B(6, 3), C(2, 7)$
6. $A(1, 9), B(4, 8), C(2, 5)$
7. $A(-2, 3), B(0, -3), C(3, -2)$

Find $m\angle 1$. Then classify the triangle by its angles.

8.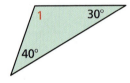
9.
10.

Find the measure of the exterior angle. (See Example 3.)

11.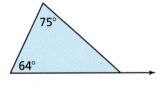
12.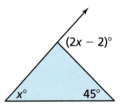
13.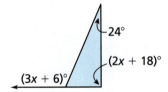

14. **SMP.3 ERROR ANALYSIS** Describe and correct the error in finding $m\angle 1$.

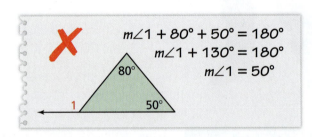

Find the measure of each acute angle in the right triangle. (See Example 4.)

15. The measure of one acute angle is 5 times the measure of the other acute angle.

16. The measure of one acute angle is 3 times the sum of the measure of the other acute angle and 8.

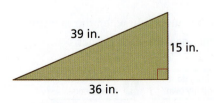

17. **SMP.5 OPEN-ENDED** Construct a triangle with an exterior angle measure of 110°.

18. **CONNECTION TO REAL LIFE** A face of a ramp is shown. Classify the triangle by its sides and by its angles.

19. Find the measure of each numbered angle.

20. You are bending a strip of metal into an isosceles triangle for a sculpture. The strip of metal is 20 inches long. The first bend is made 6 inches from one end. Describe two ways you could complete the triangle.

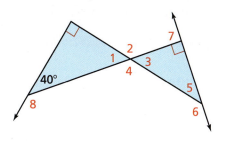

21. **PROVING COROLLARY 5.1** Prove the Corollary to the Triangle Sum Theorem.

    Given △ABC is a right triangle.

    Prove ∠A and ∠B are complementary.

    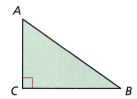

22. **PROVING THEOREM 5.2** Prove the Exterior Angle Theorem

    Given △ABC, exterior ∠BCD

    Prove $m\angle A + m\angle B = m\angle BCD$

    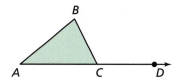

23. Is it possible to draw a right isosceles triangle? a right equilateral triangle? If so, provide an example. If not, explain why it is not possible.

24. **CONNECT CONCEPTS** △ABC is isosceles, $AB = x$, and $BC = 2x - 4$.

    a. Find two possible values for x when the perimeter of △ABC is 32.

    b. How many possible values are there for x when the perimeter of △ABC is 12?

25. **SMP.7** Let the measures of the exterior angles of a triangle, one angle at each vertex, be $x°$, $y°$, and $z°$, as shown. What can you prove?

CONNECT CONCEPTS Find the values of x and y.

26.

27.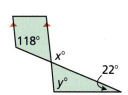

28. **SMP.6** Your friend claims the measure of an exterior angle will always be greater than each interior angle measure. Explain whether your friend is correct.

29. **PROVING THEOREM 5.1** Use each diagram to write a proof of the Triangle Sum Theorem.

    a.   b.

    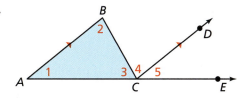

5.1   Angles of Triangles   227

Interpreting Data

BERMUDA TRIANGLE The Bermuda Triangle covers about 500,000 square miles of the Atlantic Ocean. The area is known for strong and unexpected storms, which build up and dissipate quickly.

30. Classify the Bermuda Triangle by its angles and by its sides.

31. Use the given area of the Bermuda Triangle to estimate the lengths of its sides.

32. One of the deepest ocean trenches in the world is found in the Bermuda Triangle. Use a resource to find the depth of this trench.

Review & Refresh

33. Determine whether the triangles with the vertices $Q(1, 1)$, $R(2, 4)$, $S(5, 1)$ and $T(3, 0)$, $U(4, 3)$, $V(7, 0)$ are congruent. Use transformations to explain your reasoning.

Solve the equation.

34. $|2b - 5| = 9$

35. $x + 6 = -2x$

36. Find the scale factor of the dilation. Then tell whether the dilation is a *reduction* or an *enlargement*.

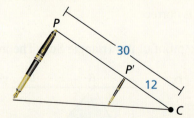

37. Determine whether $y = 2(0.5)^t$ represents *exponential growth* or *exponential decay*. Identify the percent rate of change.

38. Describe a similarity transformation that maps $\angle DEF$ to $\angle TUV$.

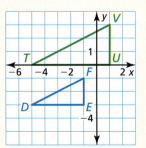

Use the diagram.

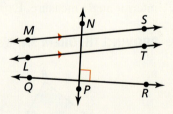

39. Name a pair of parallel lines.

40. Name a pair of perpendicular lines.

228 Chapter 5 Congruent Triangles

5.2 Congruent Polygons

Learning Target: Understand congruence in terms of rigid motions.

Success Criteria:
- I can identify corresponding parts of congruent polygons.
- I can use rigid motions to show that two triangles are congruent.
- I can use congruent polygons to solve problems.

INVESTIGATE Describing Rigid Motions

1. **Work with a partner.** Of the four transformations you studied in Chapter 4, which are rigid motions? Explain why the image of a triangle under a rigid motion is always congruent to the original triangle.

Translation   Reflection   Rotation   Dilation

INVESTIGATE Finding a Composition of Rigid Motions

2. **Work with a partner.** Describe a composition of rigid motions that maps $\triangle ABC$ to $\triangle DEF$. Use dynamic geometry software to verify your answer.

a.
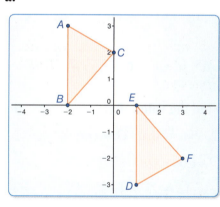

b.
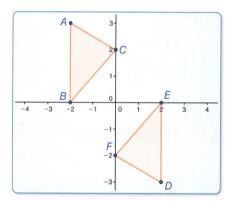

c.
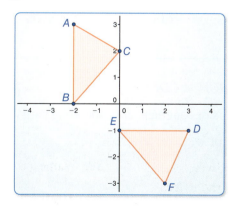

d.
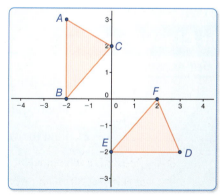

Vocabulary
corresponding parts

Identifying and Using Corresponding Parts

Two geometric figures are congruent if and only if a rigid motion or a composition of rigid motions maps one of the figures onto the other. A rigid motion maps each part of a figure to a **corresponding part** of its image. Because rigid motions preserve length and angle measure, corresponding parts of congruent figures are congruent.

EXAMPLE 1 Identifying Corresponding Parts

Write a congruence statement for the triangles. Identify all pairs of congruent corresponding parts.

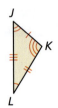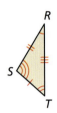

The diagram indicates that △JKL ≅ △TSR.

Corresponding angles ∠J ≅ ∠T, ∠K ≅ ∠S, ∠L ≅ ∠R

Corresponding sides $\overline{JK} \cong \overline{TS}, \overline{KL} \cong \overline{SR}, \overline{LJ} \cong \overline{RT}$

EXAMPLE 2 Using Properties of Congruent Figures

In the diagram, DEFG ≅ SPQR.

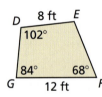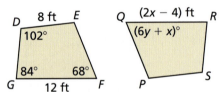

a. Find the value of x.

You know that $\overline{FG} \cong \overline{QR}$.

$FG = QR$

$12 = 2x - 4$

$16 = 2x$

$8 = x$

b. Find the value of y.

You know that ∠F ≅ ∠Q.

$m\angle F = m\angle Q$

$68° = (6y + x)°$

$68 = 6y + 8$

$10 = y$

In-Class Practice

Self-Assessment

In the diagram, ABGH ≅ CDEF.

1. Identify all pairs of congruent corresponding parts.
2. Find the value of x.

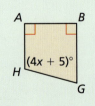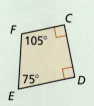

When all the corresponding parts of two triangles are congruent, you can use rigid motions to show that the triangles are congruent.

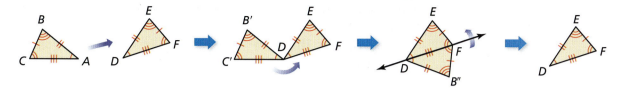

So, to show that two triangles are congruent, it is sufficient to show that their corresponding parts are congruent. In general, this is true for all polygons.

EXAMPLE 3 **Showing that Figures Are Congruent**

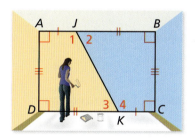

You divide a wall into orange and blue sections along $\overline{JK}$. Explain whether the sections of the wall will be the same size and shape.

By the Lines Perpendicular to a Transversal Theorem, $\overline{AB} \parallel \overline{DC}$. Then $\angle 1 \cong \angle 4$ and $\angle 2 \cong \angle 3$ by the Alternate Interior Angles Theorem. By the Reflexive Property of Segment Congruence, $\overline{JK} \cong \overline{KJ}$. Use these and the information given in the diagram to show that $AJKD \cong CKJB$ because all corresponding parts are congruent.

▶ Yes, the two sections will be the same size and shape.

Theorem 5.3

Properties of Triangle Congruence

Triangle congruence is reflexive, symmetric, and transitive.

Reflexive For any triangle △ABC, △ABC ≅ △ABC.
Symmetric If △ABC ≅ △DEF, then △DEF ≅ △ABC.
Transitive If △ABC ≅ △DEF and △DEF ≅ △JKL, then △ABC ≅ △JKL.

Proof Available online

In-Class Practice
Self-Assessment

3. In the diagram at the right, show that △PTS ≅ △RTQ.

4. Name the property that the statement illustrates.
   If △MNP ≅ △QRS, then △QRS ≅ △MNP.

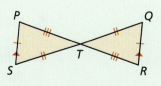

Using the Third Angles Theorem

Theorem 5.4

Third Angles Theorem

If two angles of one triangle are congruent to two angles of another triangle, then the third angles are also congruent.

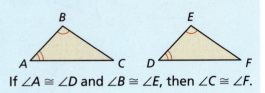

If $\angle A \cong \angle D$ and $\angle B \cong \angle E$, then $\angle C \cong \angle F$.

Prove this Theorem Exercise 10, page 233

EXAMPLE 4 Using the Third Angles Theorem

Find $m\angle BDC$.

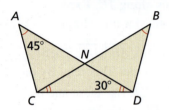

$\angle A \cong \angle B$ and $\angle ADC \cong \angle BCD$, so by the Third Angles Theorem, $\angle ACD \cong \angle BDC$. By the Triangle Sum Theorem, $m\angle ACD = 180° - 45° - 30° = 105°$.

▶ So, $m\angle BDC = m\angle ACD = 105°$ by the definition of congruent angles.

EXAMPLE 5 Proving that Triangles Are Congruent

Use the information in the figure to prove that $\triangle ACD \cong \triangle CAB$.

Given $\overline{AD} \cong \overline{CB}, \overline{DC} \cong \overline{BA}, \angle ACD \cong \angle CAB,$
$\angle CAD \cong \angle ACB$

Prove $\triangle ACD \cong \triangle CAB$

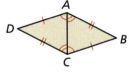

STATEMENTS	REASONS
1. $\overline{AD} \cong \overline{CB}$, $\overline{DC} \cong \overline{BA}$	1. Given
2. $\overline{AC} \cong \overline{CA}$	2. Reflexive Property of Segment Congruence
3. $\angle ACD \cong \angle CAB$, $\angle CAD \cong \angle ACB$	3. Given
4. $\angle B \cong \angle D$	4. Third Angles Theorem
5. $\triangle ACD \cong \triangle CAB$	5. All corresponding parts are congruent.

In-Class Practice

Self-Assessment

Use the diagram.

5. Find $m\angle DCN$.

6. What additional information is needed to conclude that $\triangle NDC \cong \triangle NSR$?

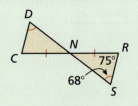

5.2 Practice

Write a congruence statement for the polygons. Identify all pairs of congruent corresponding parts. (See Example 1.)

1.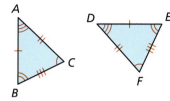

2.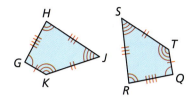

Find the values of *x* and *y*. (See Example 2.)

3. $ABCD \cong EFGH$

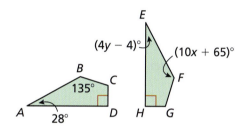

4. $\triangle MNP \cong \triangle TUS$

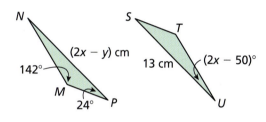

Explain whether the polygons are congruent. (See Example 3.)

5.

6.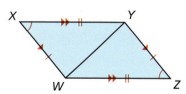

Find $m\angle 1$. (See Example 4.)

7.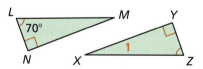

8.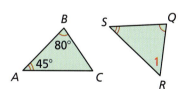

9. **PROOF** Triangular postage stamps, like the ones shown, are highly valued by stamp collectors. Prove that $\triangle AEB \cong \triangle CED$. (See Example 5.)

   Given $\overline{AB} \parallel \overline{DC}$, $\overline{AB} \cong \overline{DC}$, E is the midpoint of $\overline{AC}$ and $\overline{BD}$.

   Prove $\triangle AEB \cong \triangle CED$

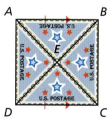

10. **PROVING A THEOREM** Prove the Third Angles Theorem by using the Triangle Sum Theorem.

11. **PROOF** Prove that the criteria for congruent triangles are equivalent to the definition of congruence in terms of rigid motions.

Interpreting Data

TRUSS BRIDGE A truss bridge is composed of a series of triangles called *trusses*. Trusses stabilize the bridge, allowing it to support heavy loads over a large span.

Truss Bridge Types

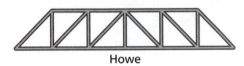
Howe

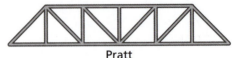
Pratt

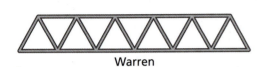
Warren

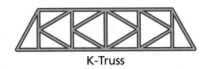
K-Truss

12. Which types of truss bridge appear to be composed entirely of congruent triangles?

13. Truss bridges are common for spans of up to 250 feet. What types of bridges are better for very long spans?

14. Explain why truss bridges are composed of triangles instead of quadrilaterals.

Review & Refresh

15. Find the measure of the exterior angle.

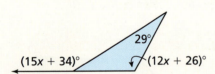

Graph △FGH with vertices $F(-6, 3)$, $G(3, 0)$, and $H(3, -6)$ and its image after the similarity transformation.

16. Translation: $(x, y) \rightarrow (x + 2, y - 1)$

Dilation: $(x, y) \rightarrow (2x, 2y)$

17. Dilation: $(x, y) \rightarrow \left(\frac{1}{3}x, \frac{1}{3}y\right)$

Reflection: in the y-axis

18. You design a logo for your soccer team. The logo is 3 inches by 5 inches. You decide to dilate the logo to 1.5 inches by 2.5 inches. What is the scale factor of this dilation?

Factor the polynomial.

19. $t^2 + 7t + 10$

20. $2x^2 + 5x - 12$

Use the graphs of f and g to describe the transformation from the graph of f to the graph of g.

21. $f(x) = 2x$; $g(x) = -4x + 1$

22. $f(x) = x^2$; $g(x) = \frac{1}{2}x^2 - 5$

23. Write a piecewise function represented by the graph.

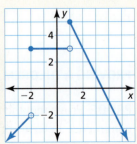

234 Chapter 5 Congruent Triangles

5.3 Proving Triangle Congruence by SAS

Learning Target: Prove and use the Side-Angle-Side Congruence Theorem.

Success Criteria:
- I can use rigid motions to prove the SAS Congruence Theorem.
- I can use the SAS Congruence Theorem.

INVESTIGATE Reasoning about Triangles

Work with a partner.

1. Use technology to construct two circles with different radii and the same center. Draw an angle that has a measure less than 180° with its vertex at the center of the circles. Label the vertex A.

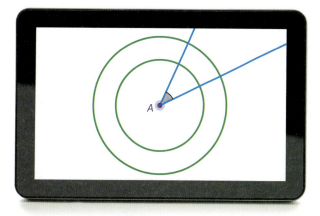

2. Locate the point where one side of $\angle A$ intersects the smaller circle and label this point B. Locate the point where the other side of $\angle A$ intersects the larger circle and label this point C. Then draw $\triangle ABC$.

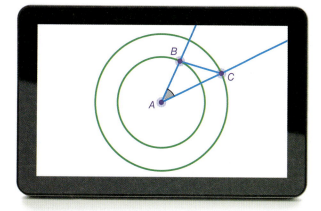

3. Find BC, $m\angle B$, and $m\angle C$.

4. **SMP.8** Repeat Exercises 1–3 several times, redrawing $\angle A$ in different orientations. Use the same two radii and the same measure of $\angle A$ each time. What do you notice? Make a conjecture.

5. Can you prove your conjecture in Exercise 4? If so, write your proof.

5.3 Proving Triangle Congruence by SAS 235

Using the Side-Angle-Side Congruence Theorem

> ### Theorem 5.5
>
> **Side-Angle-Side (SAS) Congruence Theorem**
>
> If two sides and the included angle of one triangle are congruent to two sides and the included angle of a second triangle, then the two triangles are congruent.
>
> If $\overline{AB} \cong \overline{DE}$, $\angle A \cong \angle D$, and $\overline{AC} \cong \overline{DF}$, then $\triangle ABC \cong \triangle DEF$.
>
>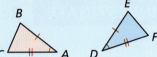

PROOF   **Side-Angle-Side (SAS) Congruence Theorem**

Given $\overline{AB} \cong \overline{DE}$, $\angle A \cong \angle D$, $\overline{AC} \cong \overline{DF}$

Prove $\triangle ABC \cong \triangle DEF$

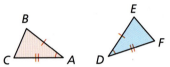

Translate $\triangle ABC$ so that point A maps to point D.

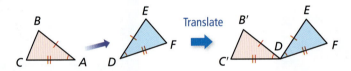

Rotate $\triangle DB'C'$ through $\angle C'DF$ so that the image of $\overrightarrow{DC'}$ coincides with $\overrightarrow{DF}$.

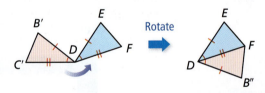

Reflect $\triangle DB''F$ in the line through points D and F.

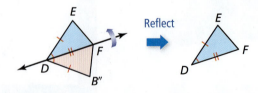

Because a reflection preserves angle measure and $\angle B''DF \cong \angle EDF$, the reflection maps $\overrightarrow{DB''}$ to $\overrightarrow{DE}$. Because $\overline{DB''} \cong \overline{DE}$, the reflection maps point B'' to point E. So, this reflection maps $\triangle DB''F$ to $\triangle DEF$.

Because you can map $\triangle ABC$ to $\triangle DEF$ using a composition of rigid motions, $\triangle ABC \cong \triangle DEF$.

EXAMPLE 1 Using the SAS Congruence Theorem

Write a proof.

Given $\overline{BC} \cong \overline{DA}, \overline{BC} \parallel \overline{AD}$

Prove $\triangle ABC \cong \triangle CDA$

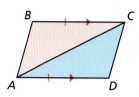

	STATEMENTS	REASONS
S	1. $\overline{BC} \cong \overline{DA}$	1. Given
	2. $\overline{BC} \parallel \overline{AD}$	2. Given
A	3. $\angle BCA \cong \angle DAC$	3. Alternate Interior Angles Theorem
S	4. $\overline{AC} \cong \overline{CA}$	4. Reflexive Property of Segment Congruence
	5. $\triangle ABC \cong \triangle CDA$	5. SAS Congruence Theorem

EXAMPLE 2 Using SAS and Properties of Shapes

In the diagram, $\overline{QS}$ and $\overline{RP}$ pass through the center M of the circle. What can you conclude about $\triangle MRS$ and $\triangle MPQ$?

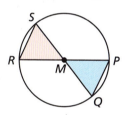

Because they are vertical angles, $\angle PMQ \cong \angle RMS$. All points on a circle are the same distance from the center, so $\overline{MP}, \overline{MQ}, \overline{MR}$, and $\overline{MS}$ are all congruent.

▶ So, $\triangle MRS$ and $\triangle MPQ$ are congruent by the SAS Congruence Theorem.

In-Class Practice

Self-Assessment

1. Use rigid motions to prove that $\triangle JKL \cong \triangle MNP$.

In the diagram, $ABCD$ is a square and $R, S, T,$ and U are the midpoints of the sides of $ABCD$. Also, $\overline{RT} \perp \overline{SU}$ and $\overline{SV} \cong \overline{VU}$.

2. Prove that $\triangle SVR \cong \triangle UVR$.

3. Prove that $\triangle BSR \cong \triangle DUT$.

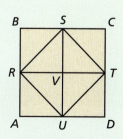

Connections to Real Life

EXAMPLE 3 **Proving Triangle Congruence**

You are making a canvas sign to hang on the triangular portion of the building shown in the photo. You think you can use two identical triangular sheets of canvas. You know that

$\overline{RP} \perp \overline{QS}$ and $\overline{PQ} \cong \overline{PS}$.

Use the SAS Congruence Theorem to prove that △PQR ≅ △PSR.

It is given that $\overline{PQ} \cong \overline{PS}$. By the Reflexive Property of Segment Congruence, $\overline{RP} \cong \overline{RP}$. By the definition of perpendicular lines, both ∠RPQ and ∠RPS are right angles, so they are congruent by the Right Angles Congruence Theorem. So, two pairs of sides and their included angles are congruent.

▶ △PQR and △PSR are congruent by the SAS Congruence Theorem.

In-Class Practice

Self-Assessment

4. You are designing the window shown. You want to make △DRA congruent to △DRG. You design the window so that $\overline{DA} \cong \overline{DG}$ and ∠ADR ≅ ∠GDR. Use the SAS Congruence Theorem to prove △DRA ≅ △DRG.

1 I don't understand yet.   **2** I can do it with help.   **3** I can do it on my own.   **4** I can teach someone.

5.3 Practice

Explain whether enough information is given to prove that the triangles are congruent using the SAS Congruence Theorem.

1. △ABD, △CDB

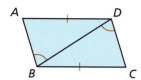

2. △LMN, △NQP

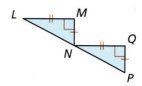

3. △EFH, △GHF

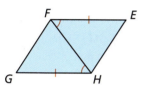

4. △KLM, △MNK

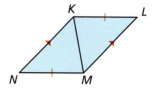

PROOF Write a proof. (See Example 1.)

▶ 5. **Given** C is the midpoint of $\overline{AE}$ and $\overline{BD}$.
   Prove △ABC ≅ △EDC

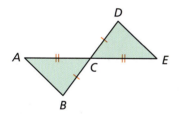

6. **Given** $\overline{PT} \cong \overline{RT}, \overline{QT} \cong \overline{ST}$
   Prove △PQT ≅ △RST

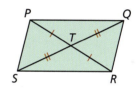

7. **Given** $\overline{PQ}$ bisects ∠SPT, $\overline{SP} \cong \overline{TP}$
   Prove △SPQ ≅ △TPQ

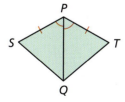

8. **Given** $\overline{AB} \cong \overline{CD}, \overline{AB} \parallel \overline{CD}$
   Prove △ABC ≅ △CDA

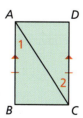

9. **SMP.6** Your friend says that △YXZ ≅ △WXZ by the SAS Congruence Theorem. Explain whether your friend is correct.

10. What additional information do you need to prove that △ABC ≅ △DBC?

Use the given information to name two triangles that are congruent. Explain why the triangles are congruent. (See Example 2.)

▶ **11.** ABCD is a square.

12. RSTUV is a regular pentagon.

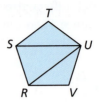

13. ∠SRT ≅ ∠URT, and R is the center of the circle.

14. $\overline{MK} \perp \overline{MN}$, $\overline{KL} \perp \overline{NL}$, and M and L are centers of circles.

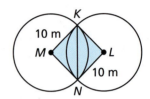

Construction

Copying a Triangle Using SAS

Construct a triangle that is congruent to △ABC using the SAS Congruence Theorem. Use a compass and straightedge.

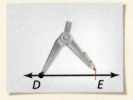

Construct $\overline{DE}$ so that it is congruent to $\overline{AB}$.

Construct ∠D so that it is congruent to ∠A.

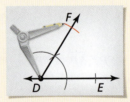

Construct $\overline{DF}$ so that it is congruent to $\overline{AC}$.

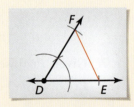

Draw △DEF. By the SAS Congruence Theorem, △ABC ≅ △DEF.

SMP.5 CONSTRUCTION Construct a triangle that is congruent to △ABC using the SAS Congruence Theorem.

15.

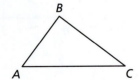

16.

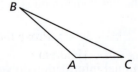

17. **CONNECTION TO REAL LIFE** The *epidemiologic triangle* is a model used to understand what causes an infectious disease (agent), how the disease is transmitted (vector), who carries the disease (host), and where the disease is likely to be transmitted (environment). In the model, △AHE is equilateral and $\overline{HV}$ bisects ∠AHE. Use the SAS Congruence Theorem to prove that △AHV ≅ △EHV. (See Example 3.)

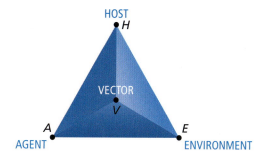

18. **CONNECTION TO REAL LIFE** The rug is made of isosceles triangles. You know ∠B ≅ ∠D. Use the SAS Congruence Theorem to prove that △ABC ≅ △CDE.

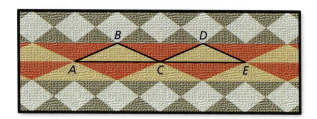

19. **CONNECT CONCEPTS** Prove that △ABC ≅ △DEC. Then find the values of x and y.

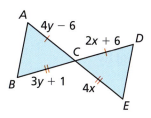

20. Is it possible to prove that two triangles are congruent when you know that two corresponding sides and a non-included angle are congruent? (In other words, is SSA a valid congruence theorem?) If so, write a proof. If not, provide a counterexample.

21. **SMP.1** The two isosceles triangles shown have congruent legs and at least one pair of congruent angles. Explain whether there is enough information to prove that the triangles are congruent.

22. **PROVING THEOREM 4.3** Prove the Reflections in Intersecting Lines Theorem.

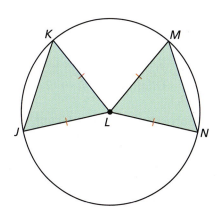

5.3 Proving Triangle Congruence by SAS

Interpreting Data

GEODESIC DOME A geodesic dome is a polyhedron. The triangles that make up the dome are rigid, making it able to withstand heavy loads. The first geodesic dome was designed by Walther Bauersfeld in the 1920s. It housed a planetarium.

23. Research how geodesic dome designs are based on regular icosahedra. Summarize your findings.

24. Is a geodesic dome composed entirely of congruent equilateral triangles? Explain why or why not.

Planetarium
Jena, Germany 1922

Geodesic Dome

Review & Refresh

Classify the triangle by its sides and by measuring its angles.

25.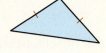

26.

27. Graph $\triangle JKL$ with vertices $J(1, -2)$, $K(3, -1)$, and $L(4, -4)$ and its image after the similarity transformation.

Reflection: in the line $y = x$

Dilation: $(x, y) \rightarrow (2x, 2y)$

Solve the inequality. Graph the solution.

28. $2d + 7 \leq 25$

29. $|b + 9| > 4$

30. Find the values of x and y when $\triangle MNP \cong \triangle QRS$.

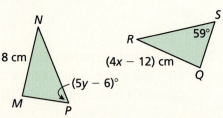

31. You want to determine the number of students in your school who know how to drive. You survey fifty students at random. Sixteen students know how to drive, and thirty-four do not. So, you conclude that 32% of the students in your school know how to drive. Is your conclusion valid?

32. Evaluate $g(x) = 14 - \frac{1}{2}x$ when $x = -4, 0,$ and 8.

5.4 Equilateral and Isosceles Triangles

Learning Target: Prove and use theorems about isosceles and equilateral triangles.

Success Criteria:
- I can prove and use theorems about isosceles triangles.
- I can prove and use theorems about equilateral triangles.

INVESTIGATE Reasoning about Isosceles Triangles

Work with a partner.

1. **SMP.5** Construct several circles. For each circle, draw a triangle with one vertex at the center of the circle and two vertices on the circle. Explain why the triangles are isosceles.

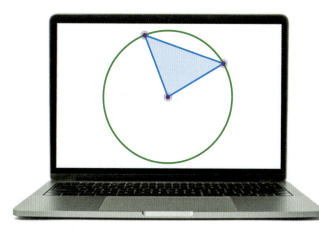
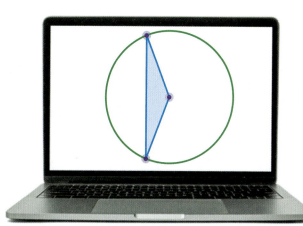

2. Measure the angles of the triangle. What do you notice? Make a conjecture about the angle measures of an isosceles triangle.

3. $\triangle ABC$ is an isosceles triangle. Given that $\overline{AB} \cong \overline{AC}$, show that $\angle B \cong \angle C$ when

   a. $\overline{AD}$ bisects $\angle CAB$.

   b. $\overline{AD}$ is the perpendicular bisector of $\overline{BC}$.

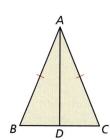

5.4 Equilateral and Isosceles Triangles   243

Using the Base Angles Theorem

Vocabulary
legs of an isosceles triangle
vertex angle
base
base angles of an isosceles triangle

A triangle is isosceles when it has at least two congruent sides. When an isosceles triangle has exactly two congruent sides, these two sides are the **legs**. The angle formed by the legs is the **vertex angle**. The third side is the **base** of the isosceles triangle. The two angles adjacent to the base are called **base angles**.

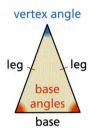

Theorem 5.6

Base Angles Theorem

If two sides of a triangle are congruent, then the angles opposite them are congruent.

If $\overline{AB} \cong \overline{AC}$, then $\angle B \cong \angle C$.

Prove this Theorem Investigate Exercise 3, page 243

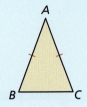

Theorem 5.7

Converse of the Base Angles Theorem

If two angles of a triangle are congruent, then the sides opposite them are congruent.

If $\angle B \cong \angle C$, then $\overline{AB} \cong \overline{AC}$.

Prove this Theorem Exercise 14, page 265

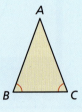

EXAMPLE 1 Using the Base Angles Theorem

In $\triangle DEF$, $\overline{DE} \cong \overline{DF}$. Name two congruent angles.

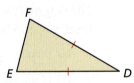

▶ $\overline{DE} \cong \overline{DF}$, so by the Base Angles Theorem, $\angle E \cong \angle F$.

In-Class Practice

Self-Assessment

Complete the statement.

1. If $\overline{HG} \cong \overline{HK}$, then $\angle\_\_\_ \cong \angle\_\_\_$.

2. If $\angle KHJ \cong \angle KJH$, then $\_\_\_ \cong \_\_\_$.

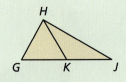

Corollary 5.2

Corollary to the Base Angles Theorem

If a triangle is equilateral, then it is equiangular.

Prove this Corollary Exercise 21, page 249

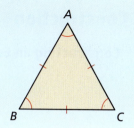

Corollary 5.3

Corollary to the Converse of the Base Angles Theorem

If a triangle is equiangular, then it is equilateral.

Prove this Corollary Exercise 22, page 249

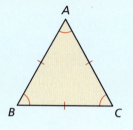

EXAMPLE 2 **Finding Measures in a Triangle**

Find the measures of $\angle P$, $\angle Q$, and $\angle R$.

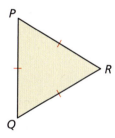

The diagram shows that $\triangle PQR$ is equilateral. So, by the Corollary to the Base Angles Theorem, $\triangle PQR$ is equiangular. So, $m\angle P = m\angle Q = m\angle R$.

$3(m\angle P) = 180°$ Triangle Sum Theorem

$m\angle P = 60°$ Divide each side by 3.

▶ The measures of $\angle P$, $\angle Q$, and $\angle R$ are all 60°.

In-Class Practice

Self-Assessment

3. Find the length of $\overline{ST}$ for the triangle.

5.4 Equilateral and Isosceles Triangles

Using Isosceles and Equilateral Triangles

Construction

Constructing an Equilateral Triangle

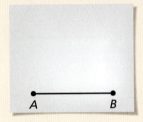
Copy $\overline{AB}$.

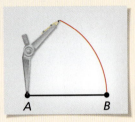
Draw an arc with center A and radius AB.

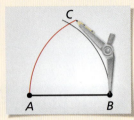
Draw an arc with center B and radius AB. Label the intersection of the arcs from Steps 2 and 3 as C.

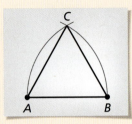
Draw $\triangle ABC$.

EXAMPLE 3 Using Isosceles and Equilateral Triangles

Find the values of x and y in the diagram.

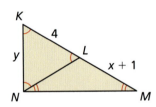

Because $\triangle KLN$ is equiangular, it is also equilateral and $\overline{KN} \cong \overline{KL}$. So, $y = 4$.

Because $\angle LNM \cong \angle LMN$, $\overline{LN} \cong \overline{LM}$, and $\triangle LMN$ is isosceles. You also know that $LN = 4$ because $\triangle KLN$ is equilateral.

$LN = LM$	Definition of congruent segments
$4 = x + 1$	Substitute 4 for LN and $x + 1$ for LM.
$3 = x$	Subtract 1 from each side.

▶ So, $y = 4$ and $x = 3$.

In-Class Practice

Self-Assessment

Find the values of x and y in the diagram.

4.

5.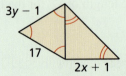

6.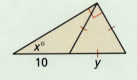

| **1** I don't understand yet. | **2** I can do it with help. | **3** I can do it on my own. | **4** I can teach someone. |

EXAMPLE 4   Using Isosceles Triangles

In the lifeguard tower, $\overline{PS} \cong \overline{QR}$ and $\angle QPS \cong \angle PQR$.

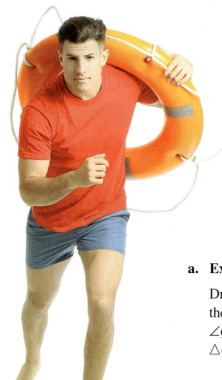

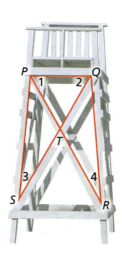

a. **Explain how to prove that $\triangle QPS \cong \triangle PQR$.**

Draw and label $\triangle QPS$ and $\triangle PQR$ so that they do not overlap. By the Reflexive Property, $\overline{PQ} \cong \overline{QP}$. It is given that $\overline{PS} \cong \overline{QR}$, and $\angle QPS \cong \angle PQR$. So, by the SAS Congruence Theorem, $\triangle QPS \cong \triangle PQR$.

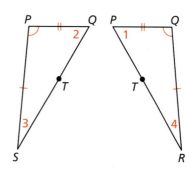

b. **Explain why $\triangle PQT$ is isosceles.**

From part (a), you know that $\angle 1 \cong \angle 2$ because corresponding parts of congruent triangles are congruent. By the Converse of the Base Angles Theorem, $\overline{PT} \cong \overline{QT}$, and $\triangle PQT$ is isosceles.

In-Class Practice
Self-Assessment

7. In Example 4, show that $\triangle PTS \cong \triangle QTR$.

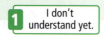

5.4   Equilateral and Isosceles Triangles

5.4 Practice

Complete the statement. State which theorem you used. (See Example 1.)

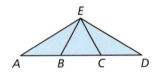

1. If $\overline{AE} \cong \overline{DE}$, then $\angle$___ $\cong \angle$___.

2. If $\overline{AB} \cong \overline{EB}$, then $\angle$___ $\cong \angle$___.

▶ 3. If $\angle D \cong \angle CED$, then ___ $\cong$ ___.

4. If $\angle EBC \cong \angle ECB$, then ___ $\cong$ ___.

Find the value of x. (See Example 2.)

▶ 5.

6.

7.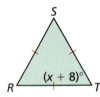

8.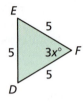

CONSTRUCTION Construct an equilateral triangle whose sides are the given length.

9. 3 inches

10. 1.25 inches

Find the values of x and y. (See Example 3.)

▶ 11.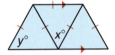

12.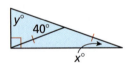

13. **SMP.3 ERROR ANALYSIS** Describe and correct the error in finding the length of $\overline{BC}$.

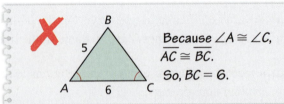

14. **CONNECTION TO REAL LIFE** The diagram represents part of the exterior of the Bow Tower in Calgary. In the diagram, $\triangle ABD$ and $\triangle CBD$ are congruent equilateral triangles. (See Example 4.)

   a. Explain why $\triangle ABC$ is isosceles.
   b. Explain why $\angle BAE \cong \angle BCE$.
   c. Show that $\triangle ABE$ and $\triangle CBE$ are congruent.
   d. Find the measure of $\angle BAE$.

15. Use the image of the purse shown.

    a. Explain why △ABE ≅ △DCE.
    b. Name the isosceles triangles in the purse.
    c. Name three angles that are congruent to ∠EAD.

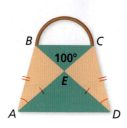

Find the perimeter of the triangle.

16.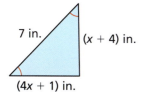

17.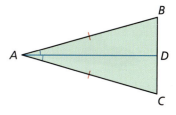

18. **SMP.7 CONNECT CONCEPTS** The lengths of the sides of a triangle are $3t$, $5t - 12$, and $t + 20$. Find the values of t that make the triangle isosceles. Explain your reasoning.

19. **CONNECT CONCEPTS** The measure of an exterior angle of an isosceles triangle is $x°$. Write expressions representing the possible angle measures of the triangle in terms of x.

20. **PROOF** Use the diagram to prove the Base Angles Theorem.

    Given $\overline{AB} \cong \overline{AC}$
    Prove $\angle B \cong \angle C$

21. **PROVING A COROLLARY** Prove that the Corollary to the Base Angles Theorem follows from the Base Angles Theorem.

22. **PROVING A COROLLARY** Prove that the Corollary to the Converse of the Base Angles Theorem follows from the Converse of the Base Angles Theorem.

23. **SMP.3** The coordinates of two points are $T(0, 6)$ and $U(6, 0)$. Explain whether the points T, U, and V will always be the vertices of an isosceles triangle when V is any point on the line $y = x$.

24. **CONNECT CONCEPTS** Use the construction of an equilateral triangle and rotations to draw a hexagon whose sides are 2 inches long. Explain your process.

25. **PROOF** Use the diagram to prove that △DEF is equilateral.

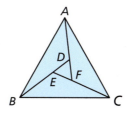

Given △ABC is equilateral.
    $\angle CAD \cong \angle ABE \cong \angle BCF$
Prove △DEF is equilateral.

5.4 Equilateral and Isosceles Triangles

Interpreting Data

SUMMER TRIANGLE The Summer Triangle consists of three bright stars in three different constellations. These stars are Vega, Deneb, and Altair. It is most prominent in the northern summer season.

26. Describe the shape of the triangle in this view.

27. Vega, Deneb, and Altair are in the constellations Lyra, Cygnus, and Aquilla. Which of these constellations represents a swan?

Review & Refresh

Use the given property to complete the statement.

28. Reflexive Property of Segment Congruence:
    ____ ≅ $\overline{SE}$

29. Symmetric Property of Segment Congruence:
    If ____ ≅ ____, then $\overline{RS} \cong \overline{JK}$.

30. Transitive Property of Segment Congruence:
    If $\overline{EF} \cong \overline{PQ}$, and $\overline{PQ} \cong \overline{UV}$, then ____ ≅ ____.

31. Find $m\angle 1$.

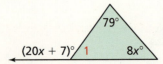

32. Find the distance from the point $(-4, -7)$ to the line $y = -\frac{1}{2}x - 4$.

33. In the diagram, $ABCD \cong JKLM$. Find $m\angle L$ and JK.

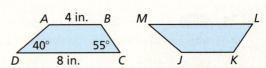

34. The figure shows a stained glass window. Explain whether there is enough information given to prove that $\triangle 1 \cong \triangle 2$.

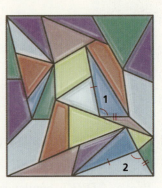

5.5 Proving Triangle Congruence by SSS

Learning Target: Use the Side-Side-Side Congruence Theorem.

Success Criteria:
- I can use the SSS Congruence Theorem.
- I can use the Hypotenuse-Leg Congruence Theorem.

INVESTIGATE Reasoning about Triangles

Work with a partner.

1. Use technology to construct circles with center A and radii of 2 units and 3 units.

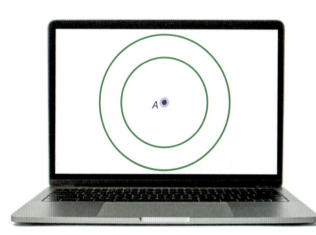

2. Draw $\overline{BC}$ so that $BC = 4$, B is on the smaller circle, and C is on the larger circle. Then draw $\triangle ABC$.

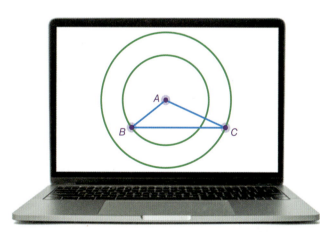

3. Explain why the side lengths of $\triangle ABC$ are 2, 3, and 4 units.

4. Find $m\angle A$, $m\angle B$, and $m\angle C$.

5. **SMP.8** Repeat Exercises 2–4 several times, redrawing $\overline{BC}$ in different locations. What do you notice? Make a conjecture.

6. Can you prove your conjecture in Exercise 5? If so, write your proof.

5.5 Proving Triangle Congruence by SSS 251

Vocabulary
legs of a right triangle
hypotenuse

Using the Side-Side-Side Congruence Theorem

Theorem 5.8

Side-Side-Side (SSS) Congruence Theorem

If three sides of one triangle are congruent to three sides of a second triangle, then the two triangles are congruent.

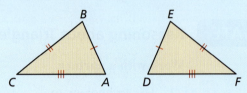

If $\overline{AB} \cong \overline{DE}$, $\overline{BC} \cong \overline{EF}$, and $\overline{AC} \cong \overline{DF}$, then $\triangle ABC \cong \triangle DEF$.

Prove this Theorem Exercise 26, page 257
Proof Available online

EXAMPLE 1 Using the SSS Congruence Theorem

Write a proof.

Given $\overline{KL} \cong \overline{NL}$, $\overline{KM} \cong \overline{NM}$

Prove $\triangle KLM \cong \triangle NLM$

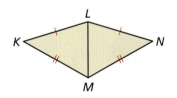

STATEMENTS	REASONS
S 1. $\overline{KL} \cong \overline{NL}$	1. Given
S 2. $\overline{KM} \cong \overline{NM}$	2. Given
S 3. $\overline{LM} \cong \overline{LM}$	3. Reflexive Property of Segment Congruence
4. $\triangle KLM \cong \triangle NLM$	4. SSS Congruence Theorem

In-Class Practice

Self-Assessment

1. Write a proof.

   Given $\overline{JK} \cong \overline{KL} \cong \overline{LM} \cong \overline{MJ}$

   Prove $\triangle JKL \cong \triangle LMJ$

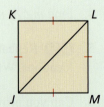

 I don't understand yet.
 I can do it with help.
 I can do it on my own.
 I can teach someone.

Using the Hypotenuse-Leg Congruence Theorem

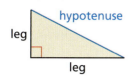

In a right triangle, the sides adjacent to the right angle are called the **legs**. The side opposite the right angle is called the **hypotenuse** of the right triangle.

Theorem 5.9

Hypotenuse-Leg (HL) Congruence Theorem

If the hypotenuse and a leg of a right triangle are congruent to the hypotenuse and a leg of a second right triangle, then the two triangles are congruent.

If $\overline{AB} \cong \overline{DE}$, $\overline{AC} \cong \overline{DF}$, and $m\angle C = m\angle F = 90°$, then $\triangle ABC \cong \triangle DEF$.

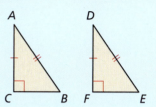

Prove this Theorem Exercise 22, page 449
Proof Available online

EXAMPLE 2 — Using the Hypotenuse-Leg Congruence Theorem

Write a proof.

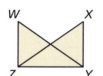

Given $\overline{WY} \cong \overline{XZ}$, $\overline{WZ} \perp \overline{ZY}$, $\overline{XY} \perp \overline{ZY}$

Prove $\triangle WYZ \cong \triangle XZY$

Redraw the triangles so they are side by side with corresponding parts in the same position. Mark the given information in the diagram.

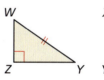

STATEMENTS	REASONS
H 1. $\overline{WY} \cong \overline{XZ}$	1. Given
2. $\overline{WZ} \perp \overline{ZY}$, $\overline{XY} \perp \overline{ZY}$	2. Given
3. $\angle Z$ and $\angle Y$ are right angles.	3. Definition of $\perp$ lines
4. $\triangle WYZ$ and $\triangle XZY$ are right triangles.	4. Definition of a right triangle
L 5. $\overline{ZY} \cong \overline{YZ}$	5. Reflexive Property of Segment Congruence
6. $\triangle WYZ \cong \triangle XZY$	6. HL Congruence Theorem

In-Class Practice

Self-Assessment

2. Use the information in the diagram to prove that $\triangle ABD \cong \triangle CDB$.

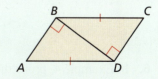

5.5 Proving Triangle Congruence by SSS

Connections to Real Life

EXAMPLE 3 Using the SSS Congruence Theorem

Explain why the bench with the diagonal support is stable, while the one without the support can collapse.

The bench with the diagonal support forms triangles with fixed side lengths. By the SSS Congruence Theorem, any triangles with three congruent sides are congruent. So, each triangle has only one possible shape, which makes the bench stable. The bench without the diagonal support is not stable because there are many possible quadrilaterals with the given side lengths.

EXAMPLE 4 Using the Hypotenuse-Leg Congruence Theorem

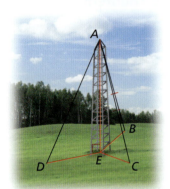

The television antenna is perpendicular to the plane containing points B, C, D, and E. Each of the cables running from the top of the antenna to B, C, and D has the same length. Prove that $\triangle AEB \cong \triangle AEC$.

Given $\overline{AE} \perp \overline{EB}$, $\overline{AE} \perp \overline{EC}$, $\overline{AE} \perp \overline{ED}$, $\overline{AB} \cong \overline{AC} \cong \overline{AD}$

Prove $\triangle AEB \cong \triangle AEC$

You are given that $\overline{AE} \perp \overline{EB}$ and $\overline{AE} \perp \overline{EC}$. So, $\angle AEB$ and $\angle AEC$ are right angles by the definition of perpendicular lines. By definition, $\triangle AEB$ and $\triangle AEC$ are right triangles.

You are given that the hypotenuses of these two triangles, $\overline{AB}$ and $\overline{AC}$, are congruent. Also, $\overline{AE}$ is a leg for both triangles, and $\overline{AE} \cong \overline{AE}$ by the Reflexive Property of Segment Congruence.

▶ So, by the Hypotenuse-Leg Congruence Theorem, $\triangle AEB \cong \triangle AEC$.

In-Class Practice

Self-Assessment

Explain whether the figure is stable.

3.

4.

5.

6. In Example 4, prove that $\triangle AEB \cong \triangle AEC \cong \triangle AED$.

5.5 Practice

Explain whether enough information is given to prove that the triangles are congruent using the SSS Congruence Theorem or HL Congruence Theorem.

1. △ABC, △DBE

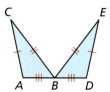

2. △PQS, △RQS

3. △ABC, △FED

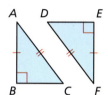

4. △PQT, △SRT

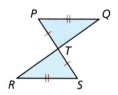

Explain whether the congruence statement is true.

5. △RST ≅ △TQP

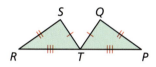

6. △ABD ≅ △CDB

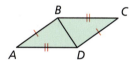

Write a proof. (See Example 1.)

▶ 7. Given $\overline{LM} \cong \overline{JK}$, $\overline{MJ} \cong \overline{KL}$

Prove △LMJ ≅ △JKL

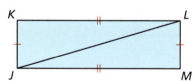

8. Given $\overline{WX} \cong \overline{VZ}$, $\overline{WY} \cong \overline{VY}$, $\overline{YZ} \cong \overline{YX}$

Prove △VWX ≅ △WVZ

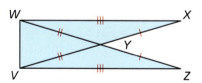

Redraw the triangles so they are side by side with corresponding parts in the same position. Then write a proof. (See Example 2.)

▶ 9. Given $\overline{AC} \cong \overline{BD}$, $\overline{AB} \perp \overline{AD}$, $\overline{CD} \perp \overline{AD}$

Prove △BAD ≅ △CDA

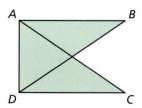

10. Given G is the midpoint of $\overline{EH}$, $\overline{FG} \cong \overline{GI}$, ∠E and ∠H are right angles.

Prove △EFG ≅ △HIG

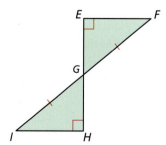

11. **SMP.3 ERROR ANALYSIS** Describe and correct the error in identifying congruent triangles.

12. Describe how to determine whether two triangles are congruent using only a piece of string.

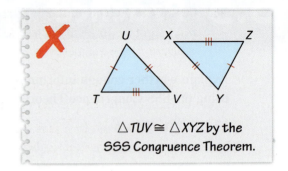

△TUV ≅ △XYZ by the SSS Congruence Theorem.

Construction

Copying a Triangle Using SSS

Construct a triangle that is congruent to △ABC using the SSS Congruence Theorem. Use a compass and straightedge.

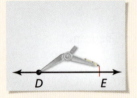
Construct $\overline{DE}$ so that it is congruent to $\overline{AB}$.

Draw an arc with radius AC and center D.

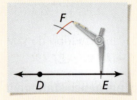
Draw an intersecting arc with radius BC and center E. Label F.

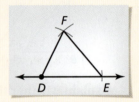
Draw △DEF. By the SSS Congruence Theorem, △ABC ≅ △DEF.

SMP.5 CONSTRUCTION Construct a triangle that is congruent to △QRS using the SSS Congruence Theorem.

13.

14.

Explain whether the figure is stable. (See Example 3.)

▶ 15.

16.

▶ 17. **CONNECTION TO REAL LIFE** The distances between consecutive bases on a softball field are the same. The distance from home plate to second base is the same as the distance from first base to third base. The angles created at each base are 90°. Prove △HFS ≅ △FST ≅ △STH. (See Example 4.)

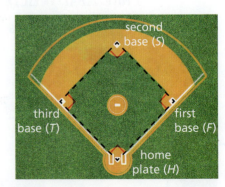

256   Chapter 5   Congruent Triangles

18. **CONNECTION TO REAL LIFE** To support a tree, you attach wires from the trunk of the tree to stakes in the ground, as shown in the diagram.

    a. What additional information do you need to use the HL Congruence Theorem to prove that △JKL ≅ △MKL?

    b. The midpoint of $\overline{JM}$ is K. Name a theorem you can use to prove that △JKL ≅ △MKL.

19. **SMP.6** Use the photo of the phone case, where $\overline{AB} \cong \overline{DE}$ and $\overline{AC} \cong \overline{CE}$.

    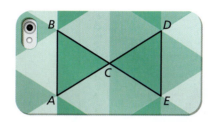

    a. What additional information do you need to use the SSS Congruence Theorem to prove that △ABC ≅ △EDC?

    b. What additional information do you need to use the SAS Congruence Theorem to prove that △ABC ≅ △EDC?

Use the given coordinates to determine whether △ABC ≅ △DEF.

20. $A(-2, -2)$, $B(4, -2)$, $C(4, 6)$, $D(5, 7)$, $E(5, 1)$, $F(13, 1)$

21. $A(-5, 7)$, $B(-5, 2)$, $C(0, 2)$, $D(0, 6)$, $E(0, 1)$, $F(4, 1)$

22. **PERFORMANCE TASK** Research camping supplies such as chairs, tents, and grills. Describe aspects of the designs that make them stable. Then write a letter that you could send to the manufacturer with suggestions for improving the stability of one item.

SMP.5 Use the given information to sketch △LMN and △STU. Mark the triangles with the given information. Then prove that △LMN ≅ △STU.

23. $\overline{LM} \perp \overline{MN}$, $\overline{ST} \perp \overline{TU}$, $\overline{LM} \cong \overline{NM} \cong \overline{UT} \cong \overline{ST}$

24. $\overline{LM} \perp \overline{MN}$, $\overline{ST} \perp \overline{TU}$, $\overline{LM} \cong \overline{ST}$, $\overline{LN} \cong \overline{SU}$

25. **CONNECT CONCEPTS** Find all values of x that make the triangles congruent.

    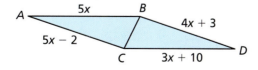

26. **PROOF** Use rigid motions to prove that △DFG ≅ △HJK.

    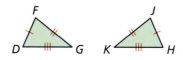

Interpreting Data

NUTRITION RECOMMENDATIONS The food pyramid was introduced in 1992. The most recent nutrition recommendations, displayed in the MyPlate, were introduced in 2011. Each presents the recommended number of servings to be eaten each day from basic food groups.

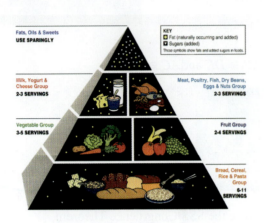

1992 Food Pyramid   2011 MyPlate

27. About what percentage of the total area of the triangular face is represented by each category?

28. Research the 2011 MyPlate diagram. Why do you think the nutrition recommendations were revised?

29. SMP.2 SMP.4 Create a diagram using triangles that presents the recommended number of servings to be eaten each day from the food groups. Are any of your triangles congruent? What would this mean in real life?

Review & Refresh

30. Determine whether $\overleftrightarrow{AC}$ and $\overleftrightarrow{DF}$ are parallel.

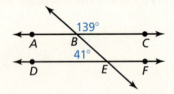

31. Find the values of x and y in the diagram of the magnet.

32. Graph the polygon given by $J(0, 3)$, $K(2, -2)$, $L(1, -4)$ and its image after a reflection in the y-axis.

33. Write a proof.

Given $\overline{AE} \cong \overline{DE}$,
$\overline{BE} \cong \overline{CE}$,
$\angle AEB$ and $\angle DEC$ are vertical angles.

Prove $\triangle AEB \cong \triangle DEC$

34. Graph $y \leq 4 - x$ in a coordinate plane.

35. Find $m\angle 1$.

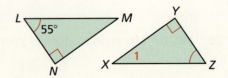

258   Chapter 5   Congruent Triangles

5.6 Proving Triangle Congruence by ASA and AAS

Learning Target: Prove and use the Angle-Side-Angle Congruence Theorem and the Angle-Angle-Side Congruence Theorem.

Success Criteria:
- I can use rigid motions to prove the ASA Congruence Theorem.
- I can prove the AAS Congruence Theorem.
- I can use the ASA and AAS Congruence Theorems.

INVESTIGATE — Determining Valid Congruence Theorems

Work with a partner.

1. Use technology to construct a circle with center A.

2. Draw an angle that has a measure less than 180° with vertex A. Label one of the points where a side of the angle intersects the circle as B. Label the other point of intersection as D.

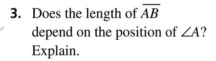

3. Does the length of $\overline{AB}$ depend on the position of $\angle A$? Explain.

4. Draw an angle with vertex B and side $\overrightarrow{BA}$ so that the other side intersects $\overrightarrow{AD}$. Label the point where the other side of the angle intersects $\overrightarrow{AD}$ as C.

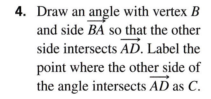

5. Find $m\angle ACB$, BC, and AC.

6. Repeat Exercises 1–5 several times, redrawing $\angle A$ in different orientations. Use the same angle measure for $\angle A$, the same radius for the circle, and the same angle measure for $\angle B$. What do you notice? Make a conjecture.

7. Explain whether each of the following is a valid triangle congruence theorem.

   a. Angle-Angle-Side (AAS)

   b. Angle-Angle-Angle (AAA)

Using the ASA and AAS Congruence Theorems

Theorem 5.10

Angle-Side-Angle (ASA) Congruence Theorem

If two angles and the included side of one triangle are congruent to two angles and the included side of a second triangle, then the two triangles are congruent.

If $\angle A \cong \angle D$, $\overline{AC} \cong \overline{DF}$, and $\angle C \cong \angle F$, then $\triangle ABC \cong \triangle DEF$.

Prove this Theorem Exercise 1, page 261

PROOF Angle-Side-Angle (ASA) Congruence Theorem

Given $\angle A \cong \angle D$, $\overline{AC} \cong \overline{DF}$, $\angle C \cong \angle F$

Prove $\triangle ABC \cong \triangle DEF$

Translate $\triangle ABC$ so that point A maps to point D.

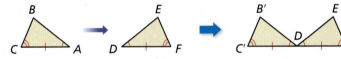

Rotate $\triangle DB'C'$ through $\angle C'DF$ so that the image of $\overrightarrow{DC'}$ coincides with $\overrightarrow{DF}$

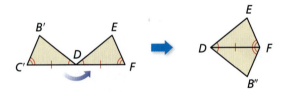

Reflect $\triangle DB''F$ in the line through points D and F.

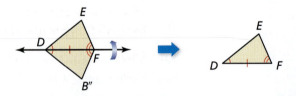

Because a reflection preserves angle measure and $\angle B''DF \cong \angle EDF$, the reflection maps $\overrightarrow{DB''}$ to $\overrightarrow{DE}$. Because $\angle B''FD \cong \angle EFD$, the reflection maps $\overrightarrow{FB''}$ to $\overrightarrow{FE}$. The image of B'' lies on $\overrightarrow{DE}$ and $\overrightarrow{FE}$. Because $\overrightarrow{DE}$ and $\overrightarrow{FE}$ have only point E in common, the image of B'' must be E. So, this reflection maps $\triangle DB''F$ to $\triangle DEF$.

Because you can map $\triangle ABC$ to $\triangle DEF$ using a composition of rigid motions, $\triangle ABC \cong \triangle DEF$.

Theorem 5.11

Angle-Angle-Side (AAS) Congruence Theorem

If two angles and a non-included side of one triangle are congruent to two angles and the corresponding non-included side of a second triangle, then the two triangles are congruent.

If $\angle A \cong \angle D$, $\angle C \cong \angle F$, and $\overline{BC} \cong \overline{EF}$, then $\triangle ABC \cong \triangle DEF$.

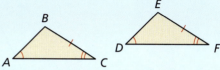

PROOF Angle-Angle-Side (AAS) Congruence Theorem

Given $\angle A \cong \angle D$, $\angle C \cong \angle F$, $\overline{BC} \cong \overline{EF}$

Prove $\triangle ABC \cong \triangle DEF$

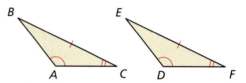

You are given $\angle A \cong \angle D$ and $\angle C \cong \angle F$. By the Third Angles Theorem, $\angle B \cong \angle E$. You are given $\overline{BC} \cong \overline{EF}$. So, two pairs of angles and their included sides are congruent. By the ASA Congruence Theorem, $\triangle ABC \cong \triangle DEF$.

EXAMPLE 1 Identifying Congruent Triangles

Can the triangles be proven congruent with the information given in the diagram? If so, state the theorem you can use.

a.  b. 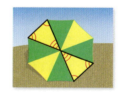 c.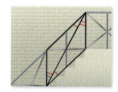

a. The vertical angles are congruent, so two pairs of angles and a pair of non-included sides are congruent. The triangles are congruent by the AAS Congruence Theorem.

b. There is not enough information to prove the triangles are congruent, because no sides are known to be congruent.

c. Two pairs of angles and their included sides are congruent. The triangles are congruent by the ASA Congruence Theorem.

In-Class Practice

Self-Assessment

1. Can the triangles be proven congruent with the information given in the diagram? If so, state the theorem you can use.

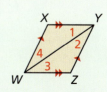

 I don't understand yet. 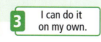 I can do it with help.   I can do it on my own. **4** I can teach someone.

5.6 Proving Triangle Congruence by ASA and AAS

Construction

Copying a Triangle Using ASA

Construct a triangle that is congruent to △ABC using the ASA Congruence Theorem. Use a compass and straightedge.

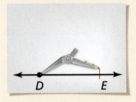  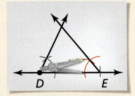 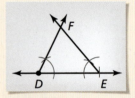

Construct $\overline{DE}$ so that it is congruent to $\overline{AB}$.

Construct ∠D with vertex D and side $\overrightarrow{DE}$ so that it is congruent to ∠A.

Construct ∠E with vertex E and side $\overrightarrow{ED}$ so that it is congruent to ∠B.

Label the intersection of the sides of ∠D and ∠E that you constructed in Steps 2 and 3 as F. By the ASA Congruence Theorem, △ABC ≅ △DEF.

EXAMPLE 2 Using the ASA Congruence Theorem

Write a proof.

Given $\overline{AD} \parallel \overline{EC}$, $\overline{BD} \cong \overline{BC}$

Prove △ABD ≅ △EBC

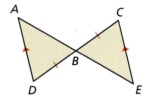

	STATEMENTS	REASONS
	1. $\overline{AD} \parallel \overline{EC}$	1. Given
A	2. ∠D ≅ ∠C	2. Alternate Interior Angles Theorem
S	3. $\overline{BD} \cong \overline{BC}$	3. Given
A	4. ∠ABD ≅ ∠EBC	4. Vertical Angles Congruence Theorem
	5. △ABD ≅ △EBC	5. ASA Congruence Theorem

In-Class Practice

Self-Assessment

2. In the diagram, $\overline{AB} \perp \overline{AD}$, $\overline{DE} \perp \overline{AD}$, and $\overline{AC} \cong \overline{DC}$. Prove △ABC ≅ △DEC.

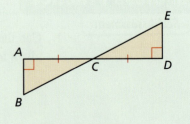

 I don't understand yet.   I can do it with help.   I can do it on my own.   I can teach someone.

Concept Summary

Triangle Congruence Theorems

You have learned five methods for proving that triangles are congruent.

SAS	SSS	HL (right △ only)	ASA	AAS
Two sides and the included angle are congruent.	All three sides are congruent.	The hypotenuse and one of the legs are congruent.	Two angles and the included side are congruent.	Two angles and a non-included side are congruent.

In the Exercises, you will prove three additional theorems about the congruence of right triangles: **Hypotenuse-Angle, Leg-Leg,** and **Angle-Leg.**

EXAMPLE 3 Using the AAS Congruence Theorem

Write a proof.

Given $\overline{HF} \parallel \overline{GK}$, $\angle F$ and $\angle K$ are right angles.

Prove △HFG ≅ △GKH

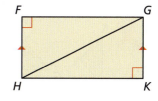

	STATEMENTS	REASONS
	1. $\overline{HF} \parallel \overline{GK}$	1. Given
A	2. $\angle GHF \cong \angle HGK$	2. Alternate Interior Angles Theorem
	3. $\angle F$ and $\angle K$ are right angles.	3. Given
A	4. $\angle F \cong \angle K$	4. Right Angles Congruence Theorem
S	5. $\overline{HG} \cong \overline{GH}$	5. Reflexive Property of Segment Congruence
	6. △HFG ≅ △GKH	6. AAS Congruence Theorem

In-Class Practice

Self-Assessment

3. In the diagram, $\angle S \cong \angle U$ and $\overline{RS} \cong \overline{VU}$. Prove △RST ≅ △VUT.

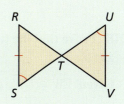

 I don't understand yet.   I can do it with help.   I can do it on my own.   I can teach someone.

5.6   Proving Triangle Congruence by ASA and AAS

5.6 Practice

Decide whether enough information is given to prove that the triangles are congruent. If so, state the theorem you can use. (See Example 1.)

▶ 1. △ABC, △QRS

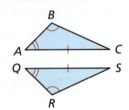

2. △RSV, △UTV

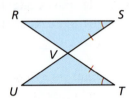

CONSTRUCTION Construct a triangle that is congruent to the given triangle using the ASA Congruence Theorem. Use a compass and straightedge.

3.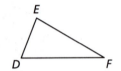

4.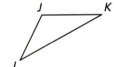

SMP.3 ERROR ANALYSIS Describe and correct the error.

5.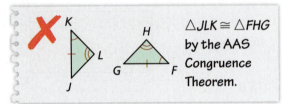

6.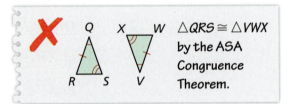

PROOF Prove that the triangles are congruent using the ASA Congruence Theorem. (See Example 2.)

▶ 7. Given M is the midpoint of $\overline{NL}$.
$\overline{NL} \perp \overline{NQ}$, $\overline{NL} \perp \overline{MP}$, $\overline{QM} \parallel \overline{PL}$

  Prove △NQM ≅ △MPL

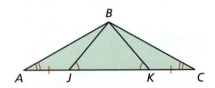

8. Given $\overline{AJ} \cong \overline{KC}$, ∠BJK ≅ ∠BKJ, ∠A ≅ ∠C

  Prove △ABK ≅ △CBJ

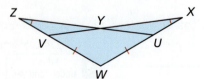

PROOF Prove that the triangles are congruent using the AAS Congruence Theorem. (See Example 3.)

▶ 9. Given $\overline{VW} \cong \overline{UW}$, ∠X ≅ ∠Z

  Prove △XWV ≅ △ZWU

264   Chapter 5   Congruent Triangles

10. **Given** ∠NKM ≅ ∠LMK, ∠L ≅ ∠N

    Prove △NMK ≅ △LKM

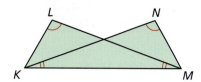

PROVING A THEOREM Write a paragraph proof for the theorem about right triangles.

11. **Hypotenuse-Angle (HA) Congruence Theorem** If an acute angle and the hypotenuse of a right triangle are congruent to an acute angle and the hypotenuse of a second right triangle, then the triangles are congruent.

12. **Leg-Leg (LL) Congruence Theorem** If the legs of a right triangle are congruent to the legs of a second right triangle, then the triangles are congruent.

13. **Angle-Leg (AL) Congruence Theorem** If an acute angle and a leg of a right triangle are congruent to an acute angle and the corresponding leg of a second right triangle, then the triangles are congruent.

14. **PROVING A THEOREM** Prove the Converse of the Base Angles Theorem. (*Hint*: Draw an auxiliary line inside the triangle.)

15. **CONNECT CONCEPTS** The toy contains △ABC and △DBC. Explain whether you can conclude that △ABC ≅ △DBC from the given angle measures.

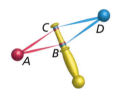

    $m\angle ABC = (8x - 32)°$ $m\angle DBC = (4y - 24)°$

    $m\angle BCA = (5x + 10)°$ $m\angle BCD = (3y + 2)°$

    $m\angle CAB = (2x - 8)°$ $m\angle CDB = (y - 6)°$

16. **CONNECTION TO REAL LIFE** When a light ray from an object meets a mirror, it is reflected back to your eye. For example, in the diagram, a light ray from point C is reflected at point D and travels to point A. The *law of reflection* states that the angle of incidence, ∠CDB, is congruent to the angle of reflection, ∠ADB.

    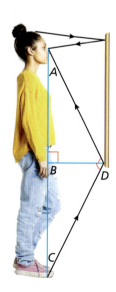

    a. Prove that △ABD is congruent to △CBD.

       Given ∠CDB ≅ ∠ADB, $\overline{DB} \perp \overline{AC}$

       Prove △ABD ≅ △CBD

    b. Verify that △ACD is isosceles.

    c. Explain whether moving away from a mirror has any effect on the amount of your reflection you can see.

17. **SMP.1** In △ABC and △DEF, $m\angle A = 68°$, $m\angle C = m\angle F = 59°$, $m\angle E = 53°$, and AB = DE = 8 units. Can you prove that △ABC ≅ △DEF? If so, write a proof. If not, explain why not.

18. Explain whether it is possible to rewrite any proof that uses the AAS Congruence Theorem as a proof that uses the ASA Congruence Theorem.

Interpreting Data

KING POST TRUSS A king post is a central vertical post used in making trusses for roofs. King posts were used in Roman buildings, and in medieval architecture.

19. Use the Internet to find an image of a roof that uses king post trusses. Label the types of triangles in the image.

20. Why do you think triangles are used in the construction of roofs?

21. Use the Internet to describe the difference between a king post truss and a queen post truss.

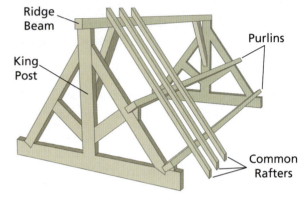

Review & Refresh

Decide whether enough information is given to prove that the triangles are congruent. If so, state the theorem you can use.

22. △BAD, △DCB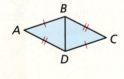

23. △EFH, △GFH

24. Copy the angle using a compass and straightedge.

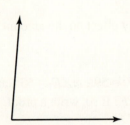

25. Find the coordinates of the midpoint of the line segment with endpoints $J(-2, 3)$ and $K(4, -1)$.

26. **DIAGNOSTIC TECHNOLOGIES**
MICROSCOPY You are using a microscope that shows the image of an object as 100 times the object's actual size. Use the actual length of the bacterium to determine the length of its image seen through the microscope.

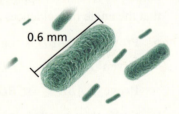

Complete the statement. State which theorem you use.

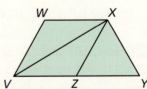

27. If $\overline{VW} \cong \overline{WX}$, then $\angle$____ $\cong \angle$____.

28. If $\angle XYZ \cong \angle ZXY$, then ____ $\cong$ ____.

266 Chapter 5 Congruent Triangles

5.7 Using Congruent Triangles

Learning Target: Use congruent triangles in proofs and to measure distances.

Success Criteria:
- I can use congruent triangles to prove statements.
- I can use congruent triangles to solve real-life problems.
- I can use congruent triangles to prove that constructions are valid.

INVESTIGATE Measuring the Width of a River

Work with a partner.

1. The figure shows how a surveyor can measure the width of a river by making measurements on only one side of the river.

   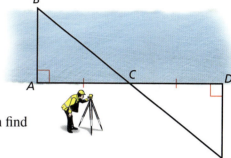

   a. Explain how the surveyor can find the width of the river.

   b. Write a proof to verify that the method you described in part (a) is valid.

   Given ∠A is a right angle, ∠D is a right angle, $\overline{AC} \cong \overline{CD}$

   c. Exchange proofs with another group and discuss the reasoning used.

2. One of Napoleon's officers estimated the width of a river as follows. The officer stood on the bank of the river and lowered the visor on his cap until the farthest thing visible was the edge of the bank on the other side. He then turned and noted the point on his side that was in line with the tip of his visor and his eye. The officer then paced the distance to this point and concluded that distance was the width of the river.

   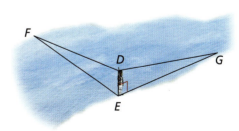

   a. Explain how the officer concluded that the width of the river is *EG*.

   b. Write a proof to verify that the conclusion the officer made is correct.

   Given ∠DEG is a right angle, ∠DEF is a right angle, ∠EDG ≅ ∠EDF

   c. Exchange proofs with another group and discuss the reasoning used.

Using Congruent Triangles

If you can prove that two triangles are congruent, then you know that their corresponding parts must be congruent as well.

EXAMPLE 1 **Using Congruent Triangles**

Explain how you can use the given information to prove that the hang glider parts are congruent.

Given $\angle 1 \cong \angle 2$, $\angle RTQ \cong \angle RTS$

Prove $\overline{QT} \cong \overline{ST}$

STEM Video:
Hang Glider Challenge

If you can show that $\triangle QRT \cong \triangle SRT$, then you will know that $\overline{QT} \cong \overline{ST}$. First, copy the diagram and mark the given information. Then mark the information that you can deduce. In this case, $\angle RQT$ and $\angle RST$ are supplementary to congruent angles, so $\angle RQT \cong \angle RST$. Also, $\overline{RT} \cong \overline{RT}$ by the Reflexive Property of Segment Congruence.

Mark given information.

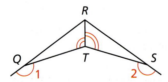

Mark deduced information.

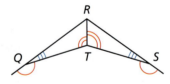

Two angle pairs and a non-included side are congruent, so by the AAS Congruence Theorem, $\triangle QRT \cong \triangle SRT$.

▶ Because corresponding parts of congruent triangles are congruent, $\overline{QT} \cong \overline{ST}$.

In-Class Practice

Self-Assessment

1. Explain how you can prove that $\angle A \cong \angle C$.

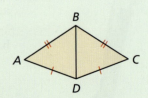

EXAMPLE 2 **Using Congruent Triangles for Measurement**

Explain how the following method allows you to find the distance across San Francisco Bay, from point N to point P.

- Find a point K on the near side so that $\overline{NK} \perp \overline{NP}$.
- Find M, the midpoint of $\overline{NK}$.
- Locate the point L so that $\overline{NK} \perp \overline{KL}$ and L, P, and M are collinear.

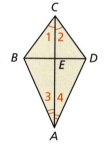

Map Data: Google, © 2023 / San Francisco Bay

Because $\overline{NK} \perp \overline{NP}$ and $\overline{NK} \perp \overline{KL}$, $\angle N$ and $\angle K$ are congruent right angles. Because M is the midpoint of $\overline{NK}$, $\overline{NM} \cong \overline{KM}$. The vertical angles $\angle KML$ and $\angle NMP$ are congruent. So, $\triangle MLK \cong \triangle MPN$ by the ASA Congruence Theorem. Then because corresponding parts of congruent triangles are congruent, $\overline{KL} \cong \overline{NP}$. So, you can find the distance NP across the river by measuring $\overline{KL}$.

EXAMPLE 3 **Planning a Proof Involving Pairs of Triangles**

Use the given information to write a plan for proof.

Given $\angle 1 \cong \angle 2$, $\angle 3 \cong \angle 4$

Prove $\angle BCE \cong \triangle DCE$

In $\triangle BCE$ and $\triangle DCE$, you know that $\angle 1 \cong \angle 2$ and $\overline{CE} \cong \overline{CE}$. If you can show that $\overline{CB} \cong \overline{CD}$, then you can use the SAS Congruence Theorem.

To prove that $\overline{CB} \cong \overline{CD}$, you can first prove that $\triangle CBA \cong \triangle CDA$. You are given $\angle 1 \cong \angle 2$ and $\angle 3 \cong \angle 4$. $\overline{CA} \cong \overline{CA}$ by the Reflexive Property of Segment Congruence. You can use the ASA Congruence Theorem to prove that $\triangle CBA \cong \triangle CDA$.

▶ **Plan for Proof** Use the ASA Congruence Theorem to prove that $\triangle CBA \cong \triangle CDA$. Then state that $\overline{CB} \cong \overline{CD}$. Use the SAS Congruence Theorem to prove that $\triangle BCE \cong \triangle DCE$.

In-Class Practice

Self-Assessment

2. In Example 2, explain whether it matters how far from point N you place a stake at point K.

3. Write a plan to prove that $\triangle PTU \cong \triangle UQP$.

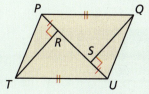

1 I don't understand yet. 2 I can do it with help. 3 I can do it on my own. 4 I can teach someone.

5.7 Using Congruent Triangles

Proving Constructions

You can use congruent triangles to prove that the construction below for copying an angle is valid.

Construction

Copying an Angle

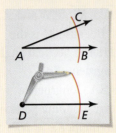
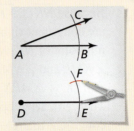
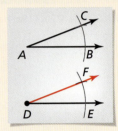

Draw a segment with initial point D. Draw arcs with centers A and D using the same radius. Label B, C, and E.

Draw an arc with radius BC and center E. Label the intersection F.

Draw a ray, $\overrightarrow{DF}$. In Example 4, you will prove that $\angle D \cong \angle A$.

EXAMPLE 4 Proving a Construction

Write a proof to verify that the construction for copying an angle is valid.

Add $\overline{BC}$ and $\overline{EF}$ to the diagram. In the construction, one compass setting determines $\overline{AB}$, $\overline{DE}$, $\overline{AC}$, and $\overline{DF}$, and another compass setting determines $\overline{BC}$ and $\overline{EF}$. So, you can use the following as given statements.

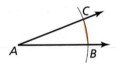
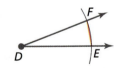

Given $\overline{AB} \cong \overline{DE}$, $\overline{AC} \cong \overline{DF}$, $\overline{BC} \cong \overline{EF}$

Prove $\angle D \cong \angle A$

STATEMENTS	REASONS
1. $\overline{AB} \cong \overline{DE}, \overline{AC} \cong \overline{DF}, \overline{BC} \cong \overline{EF}$	1. Given
2. $\triangle DEF \cong \triangle ABC$	2. SSS Congruence Theorem
3. $\angle D \cong \angle A$	3. Corresponding parts of congruent triangles are congruent.

In-Class Practice

Self-Assessment

4. Write a proof to verify that the construction of an angle bisector on page 40 is valid.

5.7 Practice

Explain how to prove that the statement is true. (See Example 1.)

1. ∠A ≅ ∠D

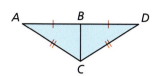

2. $\overline{AC} \cong \overline{DB}$

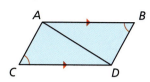

3. **SMP.4 CONNECTION TO REAL LIFE** Explain how to find DE. (See Example 2.)

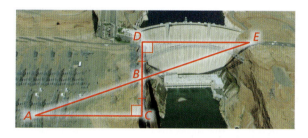

Write a plan to prove that ∠1 ≅ ∠2. (See Example 3.)

4.

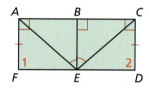

5.

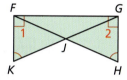

Write a proof to verify that the construction is valid. (See Example 4.)

6. Line perpendicular to a line through a point on the line

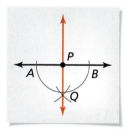

7. Line perpendicular to a line through a point not on the line (page 141)

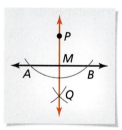

8. CONNECT CONCEPTS Determine whether each conditional statement is true or false. If the statement is false, rewrite it as a true statement using the converse, inverse, or contrapositive.

  a. If two triangles have the same perimeter, then they are congruent.

  b. If two triangles are congruent, then they have the same area.

9. Which triangles can you prove are congruent to △ABC? Select all that apply.

Interpreting Data

EUCLID'S PROOF The diagram shows a portion of Euclid's proof of the Pythagorean Theorem.

Elucid

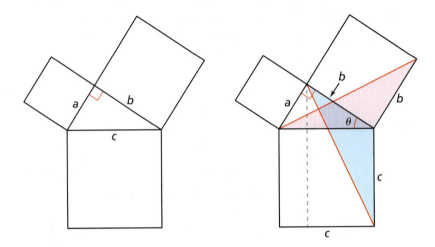

10. How does the diagram on the left demonstrate the Pythagorean Theorem?

11. In the diagram on the right, Euclid proved that the red triangle is congruent to the blue triangle. Describe a proof to show this.

12. **SMP.1** After proving that the red and blue triangles are congruent, explain how you think Euclid went on to prove the Pythagorean Theorem.

Review & Refresh

Find the perimeter of the polygon with the given vertices.

13. $A(-1, 1)$, $B(4, 1)$, $C(4, -2)$, $D(-1, -2)$

14. $J(-5, 3)$, $K(-2, 1)$, $L(3, 4)$

15. Find the value of x.

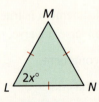

16. There are 380 students at your school. The number of students is increasing at an annual rate of 2%. Write and graph an exponential function to model the number of students at your school as a function of number of years.

17. Simplify $(3y - 2) + (-y + 4)$.

Decide whether enough information is given to prove that the triangles are congruent. If so, state the theorem you can use.

18. $\triangle TUV$, $\triangle XYZ$

19. $\triangle JKM$, $\triangle LKM$

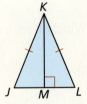

5.8 Coordinate Proofs

Learning Target: Use coordinates to write proofs.

Success Criteria:
- I can place figures in a coordinate plane.
- I can write plans for coordinate proofs.
- I can write coordinate proofs.

INVESTIGATE Writing a Proof Using Coordinates

SMP.5 Work with a partner.

1. Draw $\overline{AB}$ with endpoints $A(-3, 0)$ and $B(3, 0)$. Then draw $\triangle ABC$ so that C lies on the y-axis.

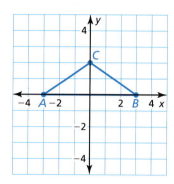

2. Classify $\triangle ABC$ by its sides.

3. Repeat Exercises 1 and 2, drawing C at different points on the y-axis. What do you notice?

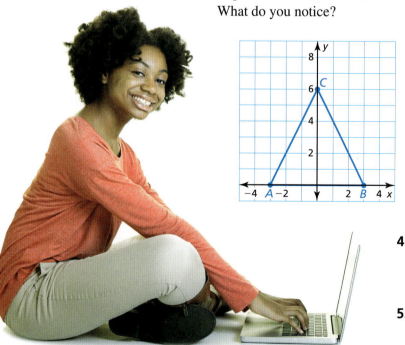

4. How can you prove that if C lies on the y-axis, then $\triangle ABC$ is an isosceles triangle?

5. What coordinates of C make $\triangle ABC$ an equilateral triangle?

5.8 Coordinate Proofs 273

Vocabulary
coordinate proof

Placing Figures in a Coordinate Plane

A **coordinate proof** involves placing geometric figures in a coordinate plane.

EXAMPLE 1   Placing a Figure in a Coordinate Plane

Place each figure in a coordinate plane in a way that is convenient for finding side lengths. Assign coordinates to each vertex.

a. a rectangle

Let h represent the length and k represent the width.

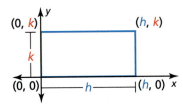

b. a triangle

Notice that you need to use three different variables.

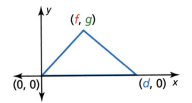

EXAMPLE 2   Applying Variable Coordinates

Place an isosceles right triangle in a coordinate plane. Then find the length of the hypotenuse and the coordinates of its midpoint M.

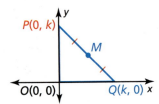

Place $\triangle PQO$ with the right angle at the origin. Let the length of the legs be k. Then the vertices are located at $P(0, k)$, $Q(k, 0)$, and $O(0, 0)$.

Find PQ, the length of the hypotenuse.

$PQ = \sqrt{(k-0)^2 + (0-k)^2}$ Distance Formula

$\quad = \sqrt{k^2 + (-k)^2}$ Simplify.

$\quad = \sqrt{k^2 + k^2}$ Simplify.

$\quad = \sqrt{2k^2}$ Combine like terms.

$\quad = k\sqrt{2}$ Simplify.

Use the Midpoint Formula to find the midpoint M of the hypotenuse.

$$M\left(\frac{0+k}{2}, \frac{k+0}{2}\right) = M\left(\frac{k}{2}, \frac{k}{2}\right)$$

▶ So, the length of the hypotenuse is $k\sqrt{2}$ and its midpoint is $\left(\frac{k}{2}, \frac{k}{2}\right)$.

In-Class Practice

Self-Assessment

1. Show another way to place the rectangle in Example 1 part (a) that is convenient for finding side lengths. Assign new coordinates.

2. Graph the points $O(0, 0)$, $H(m, n)$, and $J(m, 0)$. What kind of triangle is $\triangle OHJ$? Find each side length and the coordinates of the midpoint of each side.

EXAMPLE 3 Writing a Plan for a Coordinate Proof

Write a plan to prove that $\overrightarrow{SO}$ bisects $\angle PSR$.

Given Coordinates of vertices of $\triangle POS$ and $\triangle ROS$

Prove $\overrightarrow{SO}$ bisects $\angle PSR$.

Plan for Proof Use the Distance Formula to find the side lengths of $\triangle POS$ and $\triangle ROS$. Then use the SSS Congruence Theorem to show that $\triangle POS \cong \triangle ROS$. Finally, use the fact that corresponding parts of congruent triangles are congruent to conclude that $\angle PSO \cong \angle RSO$, which implies that $\overrightarrow{SO}$ bisects $\angle PSR$.

EXAMPLE 4 Writing a Coordinate Proof

Write a coordinate proof.

Given Coordinates of vertices of quadrilateral $OTUV$

Prove $\triangle OTU \cong \triangle UVO$

Segments $\overline{OV}$ and $\overline{UT}$ have the same length.

$OV = |h - 0| = h$

$UT = |(m + h) - m| = h$

Horizontal segments $\overline{UT}$ and $\overline{OV}$ each have a slope of 0, which implies that they are parallel. Segment $\overline{OU}$ intersects $\overline{UT}$ and $\overline{OV}$ to form congruent alternate interior angles, $\angle TUO$ and $\angle VOU$. By the Reflexive Property of Segment Congruence, $\overline{OU} \cong \overline{UO}$.

▶ So, $\triangle OTU \cong \triangle UVO$ by the SAS Congruence Theorem.

In-Class Practice

Self-Assessment

3. Write a plan for the proof.

   Given $\overrightarrow{GJ}$ bisects $\angle OGH$.

   Prove $\triangle GJO \cong \triangle GJH$

4. Write a coordinate proof.

   Given Coordinates of vertices of $\triangle NPO$ and $\triangle NMO$

   Prove $\triangle NPO \cong \triangle NMO$

1 I don't understand yet.   **2** I can do it with help.   **3** I can do it on my own.   **4** I can teach someone.

5.8   Coordinate Proofs

Connections to Real Life

EXAMPLE 5 Writing a Coordinate Proof

You buy a tall, four-legged plant stand. When you place a plant on the stand, the stand appears to be unstable under the weight of the plant. The diagram shows a coordinate plane superimposed on one pair of the plant stand's legs. The legs are extended to form $\triangle OBC$. Prove that $\triangle OBC$ is a scalene triangle. Explain why the plant stand may be unstable.

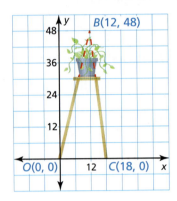

First, find the side lengths of $\triangle OBC$.

$OB = \sqrt{(12 - 0)^2 + (48 - 0)^2}$ Distance Formula

$ = \sqrt{2{,}448} \approx 49.5$ in. Simplify and approximate.

$BC = \sqrt{(18 - 12)^2 + (0 - 48)^2}$ Distance Formula

$ = \sqrt{2{,}340} \approx 48.4$ in. Simplify and approximate.

$OC = |18 - 0|$ Distance Formula

$ = 18$ in. Simplify.

▶ Because $\triangle OBC$ has no congruent sides, $\triangle OBC$ is a scalene triangle by definition. The plant stand may be unstable because $\overline{OB}$ is longer than $\overline{BC}$, so the plant stand is leaning to the right.

In-Class Practice

Self-Assessment

5. **SMP.2** You design the front of a phone tripod using a coordinate plane on a computer program. The coordinates of the vertices of the triangle at the front of the tripod are $A(0, 0)$, $B(12, 16)$, and $C(22, 0)$. One unit in the coordinate plane represents one inch. Prove that $\triangle ABC$ is a scalene triangle. Describe how to adjust point C to improve stability.

 I don't understand yet.
 I can do it with help.
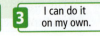 I can do it on my own.
 I can teach someone.

5.8 Practice

Place the figure in a coordinate plane in a convenient way. Assign coordinates to each vertex. Explain the advantages of your placement. (See Example 1.)

1. a right triangle with leg lengths of 3 units and 2 units

2. a square with a side length of 3 units

Place the figure in a coordinate plane and find the indicated length. (See Example 2.)

3. a right triangle with leg lengths of 7 and 9 units; Find the length of the hypotenuse.

4. a square with side length n; Find the length of the diagonal.

Write a plan for the proof. (See Example 3.)

5. **Given** Coordinates of vertices of $\triangle OPM$ and $\triangle ONM$

   Prove $\triangle OPM$ and $\triangle ONM$ are isosceles.

   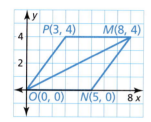

6. **Given** G is the midpoint of $\overline{HF}$.

   Prove $\triangle GHJ \cong \triangle GFO$

   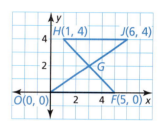

PROOF Write a coordinate proof. (See Example 4.)

7. **Given** Coordinates of vertices of $\triangle DEC$ and $\triangle BOC$

   Prove $\triangle DEC \cong \triangle BOC$

   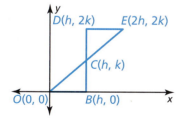

8. **Given** Coordinates of vertices of $\triangle DEA$, H is the midpoint of $\overline{DA}$, G is the midpoint of $\overline{EA}$.

   Prove $\overline{DG} \cong \overline{EH}$

   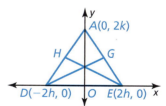

9. **CONNECTION TO REAL LIFE** A manufacturer cuts a piece of metal for a microscope. The resulting piece of metal can be represented in a coordinate plane by a triangle with $A(0, 0)$, $B(5, 12)$, and $C(10, 0)$. One unit in the coordinate plane represents one millimeter. Prove that $\triangle ABC$ is isosceles. (See Example 5.)

10. **OPEN-ENDED** Choose one of the theorems you have encountered that is easier to prove with a coordinate proof than with another type of proof. Then write a coordinate proof.

11. **SMP.7 DIG DEEPER** Write algebraic expressions for the coordinates of each endpoint of a line segment whose midpoint is the origin.

Interpreting Data

THE PENTAGON The Pentagon is the world's largest office building. It has 6.6 million square feet of floor space. Each side of the regular pentagon is about 920 feet long. Typically, more than 20,000 people work in the building.

12. What is the interior angle measure at each vertex?

13. **SMP.5** Represent the vertices of the Pentagon in a coordinate plane. What tools did you use?

14. Use coordinate geometry to approximate the area of the building.

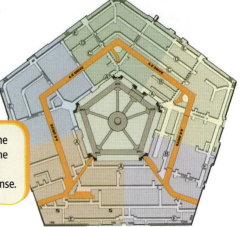

The Pentagon is the headquarters of the United States Department of Defense.

Review & Refresh

Solve the equation.

15. $6x + 13 = -5$

16. $3(x - 1) = -(x + 10)$

17. Factor the polynomial $14a^2 + 23a + 3$.

18. Explain how to prove that $\angle J \cong \angle L$.

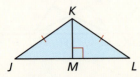

19. Decide whether enough information is given to prove that the $\triangle DEF$ and $\triangle JKL$ are congruent. If so, state the theorem you can use.

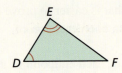
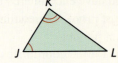

20. Write a proof.

    Given $\overline{XY} \cong \overline{ZY}, \overline{WY} \cong \overline{VY}, \overline{VW} \cong \overline{ZX}$

    Prove $\triangle VWZ \cong \triangle ZXV$

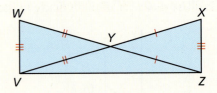

Find the value of x.

21.

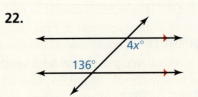

22.

278 Chapter 5 Congruent Triangles

5 Chapter Review with

Rate your understanding of each section.

1 I don't understand yet. **2** I can do it with help. **3** I can do it on my own. **4** I can teach someone.

5.1 Angles of Triangles (pp. 221–228)

◉ **Learning Target:** Prove and use theorems about angles of triangles.

Vocabulary
interior angles
exterior angles
corollary to a theorem

Classify the triangle by its sides and by measuring its angles.

1.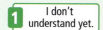

2.

Classify △ABC by its sides. Then determine whether it is a right triangle.

3. $A(-2, 3)$, $B(3, 4)$, $C(1, -1)$

4. $A(2, 3)$, $B(6, 3)$, $C(2, 7)$

Find the measure of the exterior angle.

5.

6.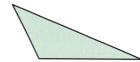

Find the measure of each acute angle.

7.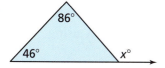

8.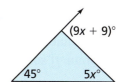

9.

10.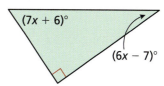

11. In a right triangle, the measure of one acute angle is 4 times the difference of the measure of the other acute angle and 5. Find the measure of each acute angle in the triangle.

12. Is it possible to draw an obtuse isosceles triangle? an obtuse equilateral triangle? If so, provide an example. If not, explain why it is not possible.

5.2 Congruent Polygons (pp. 229–234)

Learning Target: Understand congruence in terms of rigid motions.

Vocabulary
corresponding parts

13. In the diagram, $GHJK \cong LMNP$. Identify all pairs of congruent corresponding parts. Then write another congruence statement for the quadrilaterals.

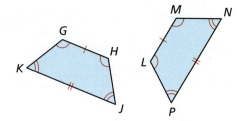

14. Find $m\angle V$.

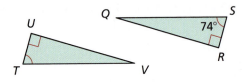

15. The figure shows the flag of the Czech Republic. Write a congruence statement for two of the polygons. Then show that those polygons are congruent.

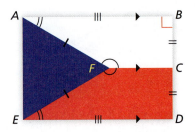

5.3 Proving Triangle Congruence by SAS (pp. 235–242)

Learning Target: Prove and use the Side-Angle-Side Congruence Theorem.

Decide whether enough information is given to prove that $\triangle WXZ \cong \triangle YZX$ using the SAS Congruence Theorem. If so, write a proof. If not, explain why.

16.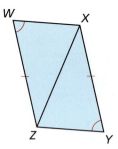

17.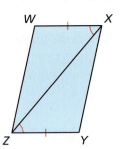

18. Construct a triangle that is congruent to $\triangle RST$ using the SAS Congruence Theorem.

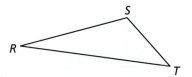

19. In the pyramid-shaped picture frame shown, $AD = CD$ and $\angle ADB \cong \angle CDB$. Use the SAS Congruence Theorem to prove that $\triangle ADB \cong \triangle CDB$.

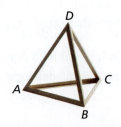

280 Chapter 5 Congruent Triangles

5.4 Equilateral and Isosceles Triangles (pp. 243–250)

⊙ **Learning Target:** Prove and use theorems about isosceles and equilateral triangles.

Vocabulary
legs of an isosceles triangle
vertex angle
base
base angles of an isosceles triangle

Complete the statement. State which theorem you used.

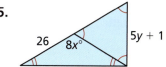

20. If $\overline{QP} \cong \overline{QR}$, then $\angle\underline{\ \ } \cong \angle\underline{\ \ }$.

21. If $\angle TRV \cong \angle TVR$, then $\underline{\ \ } \cong \underline{\ \ }$.

22. If $\overline{RQ} \cong \overline{RS}$, then $\angle\underline{\ \ } \cong \angle\underline{\ \ }$.

23. If $\angle SRV \cong \angle SVR$, then $\underline{\ \ } \cong \underline{\ \ }$.

Find the values of x and y.

24.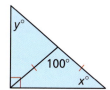

25.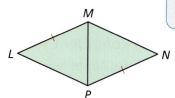

5.5 Proving Triangle Congruence by SSS (pp. 251–258)

⊙ **Learning Target:** Use the Side-Side-Side Congruence Theorem.

Vocabulary
legs of a right triangle
hypotenuse

26. Decide whether enough information is given to use the SSS Congruence Theorem to prove that $\triangle LMP \cong \triangle NPM$. If so, write a proof. If not, explain why.

27. Decide whether enough information is given to use the HL Congruence Theorem to prove that $\triangle WXZ \cong \triangle YZX$. If so, write a proof. If not, explain why.

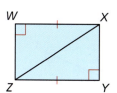

28. The photo shows two triangular windows.

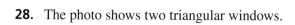

a. What additional information do you need to prove that $\triangle ABD \cong \triangle CBD$ using the HL Congruence Theorem?

b. What additional information do you need to prove that $\triangle ABD \cong \triangle CBD$ using the SSS Congruence Theorem?

5.6 Proving Triangle Congruence by ASA and AAS (pp. 259–266)

Learning Target: Prove and use the Angle-Side-Angle Congruence Theorem and the Angle-Angle-Side Congruence Theorem.

Decide whether enough information is given to prove that the triangles are congruent using the AAS Congruence Theorem. If so, write a proof. If not, explain why.

29. △EFG, △HJK

30. △TUV, △QRS

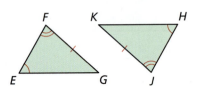
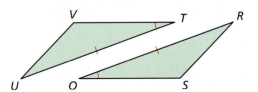

Decide whether enough information is given to prove that the triangles are congruent using the ASA Congruence Theorem. If so, write a proof. If not, explain why.

31. △LPN, △LMN

32. △WXZ, △YZX

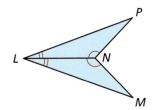
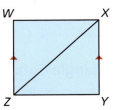

5.7 Using Congruent Triangles (pp. 267–272)

Learning Target: Use congruent triangles in proofs and to measure distances.

Explain how to prove that the statement is true.

33. ∠K ≅ ∠N

34. $\overline{AD} \cong \overline{CB}$

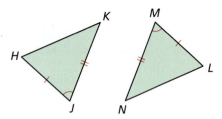
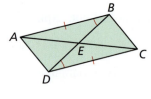

35. The diagram shows the shortest route around the buoys at points A, B, C, and D for a boat race. Use the information in the diagram to prove that ∠D ≅ ∠B.

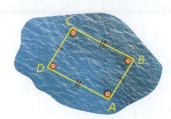

282   Chapter 5   Congruent Triangles

5.8 Coordinate Proofs (pp. 273–278)

Learning Target: Use coordinates to write proofs.

Vocabulary
coordinate proof

Place the figure in a coordinate plane in a convenient way. Assign coordinates to each vertex. Explain the advantages of your placement.

36. an isosceles triangle

37. a trapezoid with a pair of adjacent right angles

38. A rectangle has vertices (0, 0), (2k, 0), and (0, k). Find the fourth vertex.

39. A square has vertices (−k, 0), (0, k), and (k, 0). Find the fourth vertex.

40. Write a coordinate proof.
    Given Coordinates of vertices of △ODB and △BDC
    Prove △ODB ≅ △BDC

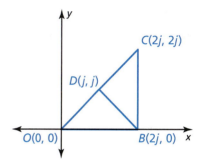

41. Write a coordinate proof.
    Given Coordinates of vertices of quadrilateral OPQR
    Prove △OPQ ≅ △QRO

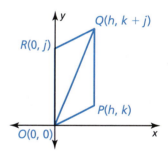

42. Write a coordinate proof to show that the triangles created by the keyboard stand are congruent.

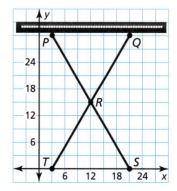

5 PERFORMANCE TASK
SMP.1

BACTERIOPHAGES

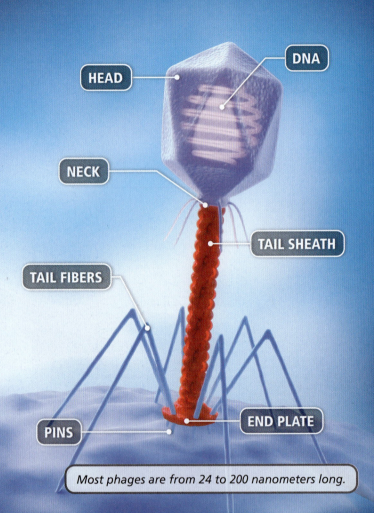

- HEAD
- DNA
- NECK
- TAIL SHEATH
- TAIL FIBERS
- PINS
- END PLATE

Most phages are from 24 to 200 nanometers long.

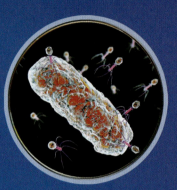

1 A phage lands on a bacterium.

2 The phage uses its pins to inject its DNA into the bacterium.

3 The DNA is copied and new phages assemble inside the bacterium.

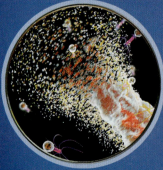

4 The new phages produce chemicals that rupture the bacterium, killing it in the process.

Analyzing Data

Use the information on the previous page to complete the following exercises.

1 Explain what is shown in the data display. What do you notice? What do you wonder?

2 A scientist views a bacteriophage under a microscope and draws a net of the head as shown. All line segments that appear parallel are parallel. Identify any triangles that appear to be congruent in the diagram.

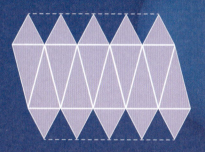

3 If possible, prove that the triangles you identified in Exercise 2 are congruent. If not possible, explain what additional information is needed.

GOING VIRAL

Enlarge the net in Exercise 2 by a scale factor, cut it out, and fold it to make a 20-sided polyhedron called an *icosahedron*. Are the same triangles still congruent? Use the Internet to find the net of another polyhedron made of triangles. Then repeat Exercises 2 and 3 for the net of that polyhedron.

6 Relationships Within Triangles

6.1 Perpendicular and Angle Bisectors
6.2 Bisectors of Triangles
6.3 Medians and Altitudes of Triangles
6.4 The Triangle Midsegment Theorem
6.5 Indirect Proof and Inequalities in One Triangle
6.6 Inequalities in Two Triangles

NATIONAL GEOGRAPHIC EXPLORER

Amy E. Gusick ARCHAEOLOGIST

Dr. Amy E. Gusick is an associate curator of archaeology and chair of the Department of Anthropology at the Natural History Museum of Los Angeles. Her research is centered in Alta and Baja, California, home to some of the earliest-known human occupation in the New World. One of Amy's interests is human coastal migration and settlement of the late Pleistocene and early Holocene epochs. She uses both land and underwater methods in her research.

- What does an archaeologist do?
- What is the Pacific Rim?
- When did the Pleistocene epoch end? When did the Holocene epoch begin?
- Humans who lived in these eras are classified as hunter-gatherers. What is a hunter-gatherer?

PERFORMANCE TASK
When archaeologists discover artifact fragments, they try to piece them together to determine the size and shape of the original object. In the Performance Task on pages 338 and 339, you will use a fragment to find the diameter of an ancient plate.

Archaeology

Big Idea of the Chapter
Find Relationships within Triangles

You are familiar with the vertices, angles, and sides of a triangle. In this chapter, you will study other special features of a triangle such as medians, altitudes, and midsegments.

In Greece, the Temple of Poseidon, the Temple of Aphaia, and the Temple of Hephaestus appear to form an isosceles triangle. A second triangle appears to be formed by the Temple of Apollo, the Parthenon, and the Temple of Aphaia.

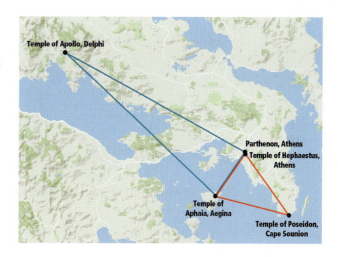

1. How might have the ancient Greeks measured the distances of the sides of the isosceles triangles?

2. Compare the locations of each temple and the dates of construction given below. Use the Internet to research each temple and determine if there are any historical causes for its construction.

   Temple of Poseidon: around 450 BC   Temple of Hephaestus: around 450 BC

   Temple of Aphaia: around 500 BC   Temple of Apollo: around 510 BC

   Temple of Athena (Parthenon): around 450 BC

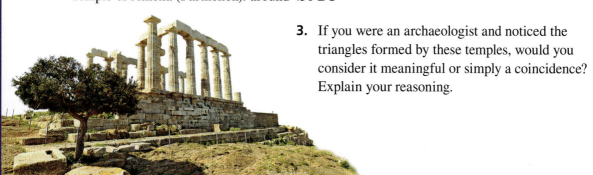

3. If you were an archaeologist and noticed the triangles formed by these temples, would you consider it meaningful or simply a coincidence? Explain your reasoning.

Getting Ready for Chapter 6

Writing an Equation of a Perpendicular Line

EXAMPLE 1 Write an equation of the line passing through the point $(-2, 0)$ that is perpendicular to the line $y = 2x + 8$.

The line $y = 2x + 8$ has a slope of 2. Use the Slopes of Perpendicular Lines Theorem.

$2 \cdot m = -1$ The product of the slopes of $\perp$ lines is -1.

$m = -\frac{1}{2}$ Divide each side by 2.

Find the y-intercept b by using $m = -\frac{1}{2}$ and $(x, y) = (-2, 0)$.

$y = mx + b$ Use slope-intercept form.

$0 = -\frac{1}{2}(-2) + b$ Substitute for m, x, and y.

$-1 = b$ Solve for b.

▶ Because $m = -\frac{1}{2}$ and $b = -1$, an equation of the line is $y = -\frac{1}{2}x - 1$.

Write an equation of the line passing through point P that is perpendicular to the given line.

1. $P(3, 1)$, $y = \frac{1}{3}x - 5$

2. $P(4, -3)$, $y = -x - 5$

Writing Compound Inequalities

EXAMPLE 2 Write each sentence as an inequality.

a. A number x is greater than or equal to -1 and less than 6.

A number x is greater than or equal to -1 and less than 6.

$x \geq -1$ and $x < 6$

▶ An inequality is $-1 \leq x < 6$.

b. A number y is at most 4 or at least 9.

A number y is at most 4 or at least 9.

$y \leq 4$ or $y \geq 9$

▶ An inequality is $y \leq 4$ or $y \geq 9$.

Write the sentence as an inequality.

3. A number w is at least -3 and no more than 8.

4. A number d is fewer than -1 or no less than 5.

6.1 Perpendicular and Angle Bisectors

Learning Target: Use theorems about perpendicular and angle bisectors.

Success Criteria:
- I can identify a perpendicular bisector and an angle bisector.
- I can use theorems about bisectors to find measures in figures.
- I can write equations of perpendicular bisectors.

INVESTIGATE Drawing Perpendicular and Angle Bisectors

Work with a partner.

1. Use technology to draw any segment and its perpendicular bisector. What do you notice about the distances between any point on the perpendicular bisector and the endpoints of the line segment? Explain why this is true.

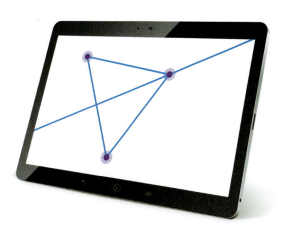

2. Use technology to draw any angle and its angle bisector. What do you notice about the distances between any point on the angle bisector and the sides of the angle? Explain why this is true.

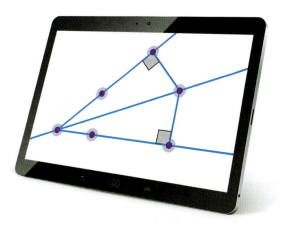

3. What conjectures can you make using your results in Exercises 1 and 2? Write your conjectures as conditional statements written in if-then form.

Vocabulary
equidistant

Using Perpendicular Bisectors

Recall that a *perpendicular bisector* of a line segment is the line that is perpendicular to the segment at its midpoint.

A point is **equidistant** from two figures when the point is the *same distance* from each figure.

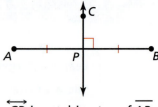

$\overleftrightarrow{CP}$ is a ⊥ bisector of $\overline{AB}$.

Theorem 6.1

Perpendicular Bisector Theorem

In a plane, if a point lies on the perpendicular bisector of a segment, then it is equidistant from the endpoints of the segment.

If $\overleftrightarrow{CP}$ is the ⊥ bisector of $\overline{AB}$, then $CA = CB$.

Prove this Theorem Exercise 19, page 295

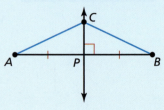

Theorem 6.2

Converse of the Perpendicular Bisector Theorem

In a plane, if a point is equidistant from the endpoints of a segment, then it lies on the perpendicular bisector of the segment.

If $DA = DB$, then point D lies on the ⊥ bisector of $\overline{AB}$.

Prove this Theorem Exercise 20, page 295

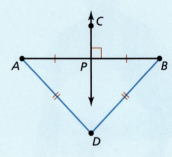

EXAMPLE 1 Using a Diagram

Is there enough information in the diagram to conclude that point N lies on the perpendicular bisector of $\overline{KM}$?

It is given that $\overline{KL} \cong \overline{ML}$. So, $\overline{LN}$ is a segment bisector of $\overline{KM}$. You do not know whether $\overline{LN}$ is perpendicular to $\overline{KM}$ because it is not indicated in the diagram.

▶ So, you cannot conclude that point N lies on the perpendicular bisector of $\overline{KM}$.

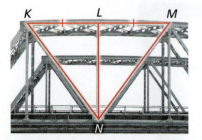

In-Class Practice

Self-Assessment

1. **WHAT IF?** Assume that $KN = MN$. Is there enough information to conclude that point N lies on the perpendicular bisector for $\overline{KM}$?

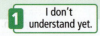

EXAMPLE 2 **Using the Perpendicular Bisector Theorems**

Find each measure.

a. *RS*

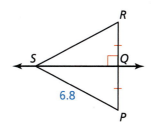

From the figure, $\overleftrightarrow{SQ}$ is the perpendicular bisector of $\overline{PR}$. By the Perpendicular Bisector Theorem, $PS = RS$.

▶ So, $RS = PS = 6.8$.

b. *EG*

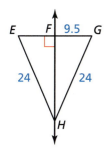

Because $EH = GH$ and $\overleftrightarrow{HF} \perp \overline{EG}$, $\overleftrightarrow{HF}$ is the perpendicular bisector of $\overline{EG}$ by the Converse of the Perpendicular Bisector Theorem. So, F is the midpoint of $\overline{EG}$, and $EF = GF$.

▶ So, $EG = EF + GF = 9.5 + 9.5 = 19$.

c. *AD*

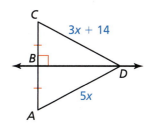

From the figure, $\overleftrightarrow{BD}$ is the perpendicular bisector of $\overline{AC}$.

$AD = CD$	Perpendicular Bisector Theorem
$5x = 3x + 14$	Substitute.
$x = 7$	Solve for x.

▶ So, $AD = 5x = 5(7) = 35$.

In-Class Practice

Self-Assessment

Use the figure and the given information to find the indicated measure.

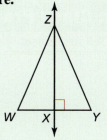

2. $\overleftrightarrow{ZX}$ is the perpendicular bisector of $\overline{WY}$, and $YZ = 13.75$. Find WZ.

3. $\overleftrightarrow{ZX}$ is the perpendicular bisector of $\overline{WY}$, $WZ = 4n - 13$, and $YZ = n + 17$. Find YZ.

4. Find WX when $WZ = 20.5$, $WY = 14.8$, and $YZ = 20.5$.

1 I don't understand yet. **2** I can do it with help. **3** I can do it on my own. **4** I can teach someone.

6.1 Perpendicular and Angle Bisectors

Using Angle Bisectors

Recall that an *angle bisector* is a ray that divides an angle into two congruent adjacent angles and that the *distance from a point to a line* is the length of the perpendicular segment from the point to the line.

Theorem 6.3

Angle Bisector Theorem

If a point lies on the bisector of an angle, then it is equidistant from the two sides of the angle.

If $\overrightarrow{AD}$ bisects $\angle BAC$ and $\overrightarrow{DB} \perp \overrightarrow{AB}$ and $\overrightarrow{DC} \perp \overrightarrow{AC}$, then $DB = DC$.

Prove this Theorem Exercise 21(a), page 295

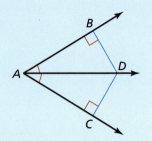

Theorem 6.4

Converse of the Angle Bisector Theorem

If a point is in the interior of an angle and is equidistant from the two sides of the angle, then it lies on the bisector of the angle.

If $\overrightarrow{DB} \perp \overrightarrow{AB}$ and $\overrightarrow{DC} \perp \overrightarrow{AC}$ and $DB = DC$, then $\overrightarrow{AD}$ bisects $\angle BAC$.

Prove this Theorem Exercise 21(b), page 295

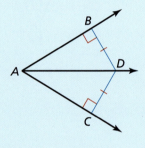

EXAMPLE 3 Using an Angle Bisector Theorem

Find RS.

From the figure, $\overrightarrow{QS}$ is the angle bisector of $\angle PQR$.

$PS = RS$	Angle Bisector Theorem
$5x = 6x - 5$	Substitute.
$5 = x$	Solve for x.

▶ So, $RS = 6x - 5 = 6(5) - 5 = 25$.

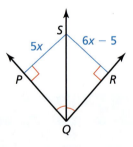

In-Class Practice

Self-Assessment

Use the figure and the given information to find the indicated measure.

5. $\overrightarrow{BD}$ bisects $\angle ABC$, $AD = 3z + 7$, and $CD = 2z + 11$. Find CD.

6. Find $m\angle ABC$ when $AD = 3.2$, $CD = 3.2$, and $m\angle DBC = 39°$.

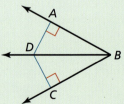

Writing Equations of Perpendicular Bisectors

EXAMPLE 4 Writing an Equation of a Bisector

Write an equation of the perpendicular bisector of the segment with endpoints $P(-2, 3)$ and $Q(4, 1)$.

Graph $\overline{PQ}$. By definition, the perpendicular bisector of $\overline{PQ}$ is perpendicular to $\overline{PQ}$ at its midpoint.

Find the midpoint M of $\overline{PQ}$.

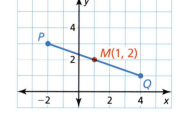

$$M\left(\frac{-2+4}{2}, \frac{3+1}{2}\right) = M\left(\frac{2}{2}, \frac{4}{2}\right) = M(1, 2)$$

Find the slope of $\overline{PQ}$.

$$\text{slope of } \overline{PQ} = \frac{1-3}{4-(-2)} \qquad \text{Use slope formula.}$$

$$= \frac{-2}{6} = -\frac{1}{3} \qquad \text{Simplify.}$$

Because the slopes of perpendicular lines are negative reciprocals, the slope of the perpendicular bisector is 3.

Write an equation. The perpendicular bisector of $\overline{PQ}$ has slope 3 and passes through $(1, 2)$.

$$y = mx + b \qquad \text{Use slope-intercept form.}$$
$$2 = 3(1) + b \qquad \text{Substitute for } m, x, \text{ and } y.$$
$$-1 = b \qquad \text{Solve for } b.$$

▶ So, an equation of the perpendicular bisector of $\overline{PQ}$ is $y = 3x - 1$.

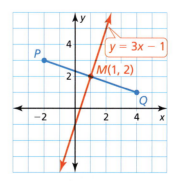

In-Class Practice

Self-Assessment

7. Write an equation of the perpendicular bisector of the segment with endpoints $(-1, -5)$ and $(3, -1)$.

| **1** I don't understand yet. | **2** I can do it with help. | **3** I can do it on my own. | **4** I can teach someone. |

6.1 Perpendicular and Angle Bisectors

6.1 Practice

Explain whether the information in the figure allows you to conclude that point *P* lies on the perpendicular bisector of $\overline{LM}$. (See Example 1.)

1.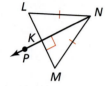

2.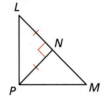

3.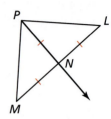

Find the indicated measure. (See Example 2.)

4. *GH*

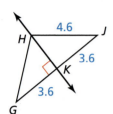

5. *AB*

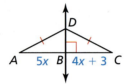

6. *UW*

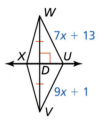

Explain whether the information in the figure allows you to make the given conclusion.

7.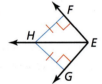

Conclusion: $\overrightarrow{EH}$ bisects $\angle FEG$.

8.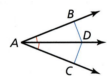

Conclusion: $DB = DC$

Find the indicated measure. (See Example 3.)

9. $m\angle ABD$

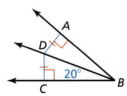

10. *FG*

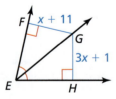

11. $m\angle KJL$

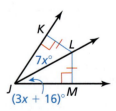

12. **ERROR ANALYSIS** Describe and correct the error in the student's reasoning.

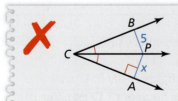

By the Angle Bisector Theorem, $x = 5$.

294 Chapter 6 Relationships Within Triangles

Write an equation of the perpendicular bisector of the segment with the given endpoints.
(See Example 4.)

▶ **13.** $M(1, 5), N(7, -1)$ **14.** $Q(-2, 0), R(6, 12)$ **15.** $U(-3, 4), V(9, 8)$

16. CONNECTION TO REAL LIFE In the diagram, the road is perpendicular to the support beam and $\overline{AB} \cong \overline{CB}$. Explain whether you can conclude that $\overline{AD} \cong \overline{CD}$.

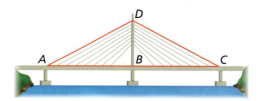

17. SMP.2 CONNECTION TO REAL LIFE $\overrightarrow{BL}$ and $\overrightarrow{BR}$ are the paths from a soccer ball to the goalposts. Explain where it makes sense for the goalie to stand to block the shot.

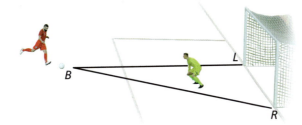

18. SMP.5 CONSTRUCTION Construct a copy of $\overline{XY}$. Then construct a perpendicular bisector and plot a point Z on the bisector so that the distance between point Z and $\overline{XY}$ is 3 centimeters. Measure $\overline{XZ}$ and $\overline{YZ}$. Which theorem does this construction demonstrate?

19. PROVING THEOREM 6.1 Prove the Perpendicular Bisector Theorem.
Given $AP = BP$
Prove Point C lies on the perpendicular bisector of $\overline{AB}$.

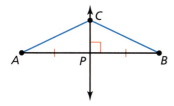

20. PROVING THEOREM 6.2 Prove the Converse of the Perpendicular Bisector Theorem.
(*Hint:* Use an auxiliary line.)
Given $CA = CB$
Prove Point C lies on the perpendicular bisector of $\overline{AB}$.

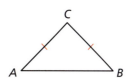

21. PROVING A THEOREM Use a congruence theorem to prove each theorem.
  a. Angle Bisector Theorem
  b. Converse of the Angle Bisector Theorem

22. SMP.1 DIG DEEPER In the figures at the right, $\triangle J'K'L'$ is a rotation of $\triangle JKL$. Explain how to find the center of rotation.

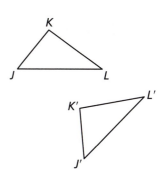

23. PROOF In the figure at the left, plane P is a perpendicular bisector of $\overline{XZ}$ at point Y. Prove that $\angle VXW \cong \angle VZW$.

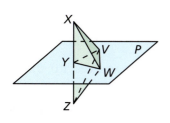

Interpreting Data

LEAF VENATION Within each leaf of a plant, the vascular tissue forms veins. The veins transport water to the leaf in a similar way to how an animal's veins transport oxygen to its cells. The arrangement of veins in a leaf is called the *venation pattern*.

Hazelnut Leaf   Currant Leaf   Strawberry Leaf

24. Describe the venation pattern of each leaf.

25. Describe the relationship between the secondary veins and the central vein.

26. Describe how the venation pattern helps ensure a plant's survival. Is it important that the central vein is an angle bisector of the secondary veins?

Review & Refresh

Classify the triangle by its sides.

27.   28.

Classify the triangle by its angles.

29.    30.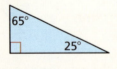

31. A wooden gate is designed as shown. Find $m\angle 2$.

32. Use the given information to write a plan for proof.

    Given $\overline{AD} \cong \overline{CD}, \overline{AE} \cong \overline{CE}$

    Prove $\triangle BDA \cong \triangle BDC$

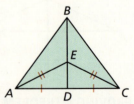

33. In $\triangle RST$ and $\triangle XYZ$, $\overline{RS} \cong \overline{XY}$ and $\angle R \cong \angle X$. What is the third congruence statement that is needed to prove that $\triangle RST \cong \triangle XYZ$ using the ASA Congruence Theorem? the AAS Congruence Theorem?

34. Graph the square with the vertices $A(0, 0)$, $B(0, k)$, $C(k, k)$, and $D(k, 0)$. Then find the coordinates of the midpoint of each side.

296   Chapter 6   Relationships Within Triangles

6.2 Bisectors of Triangles

Learning Target: Use bisectors of triangles.

Success Criteria:
- I can find the circumcenter and incenter of a triangle.
- I can circumscribe a circle about a triangle.
- I can inscribe a circle within a triangle.
- I can use points of concurrency to solve real-life problems.

INVESTIGATE Analyzing Bisectors of Triangles

Work with a partner.

1. Use technology to draw any triangle and the perpendicular bisectors of all three sides of the triangle. What do you notice? What happens when you move the vertices of the triangle?

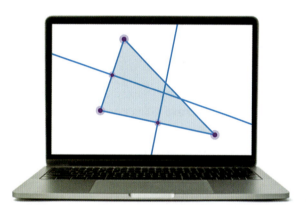

2. Draw the circle with its center at the intersection of the perpendicular bisectors that passes through a vertex of the triangle. What do you notice? What does this mean?

3. Use technology to draw a different triangle and the angle bisectors of all three angles of the triangle. What do you notice? What happens when you move the vertices of the triangle?

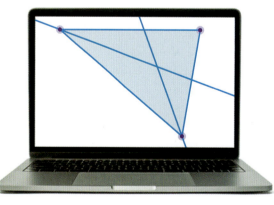

4. Find the distance r between the intersection of the angle bisectors and one of the sides of the triangle. Draw the circle with its center at the intersection of the angle bisectors and radius r. What do you notice? What does this mean?

5. What conjectures can you make using your results in Exercises 1–4? Write your conjectures as conditional statements written in if-then form.

Using the Circumcenter of a Triangle

Vocabulary
concurrent
point of concurrency
circumcenter
incenter

When three or more lines, rays, or segments intersect in the same point, they are called **concurrent** lines, rays, or segments. The point of intersection of the lines, rays, or segments is called the **point of concurrency**.

In a triangle, the three perpendicular bisectors are concurrent. The point of concurrency is the **circumcenter** of the triangle.

Theorem 6.5

Circumcenter Theorem

The circumcenter of a triangle is equidistant from the vertices of the triangle.

If $\overline{PD}$, $\overline{PE}$, and $\overline{PF}$ are perpendicular bisectors, then $PA = PB = PC$.

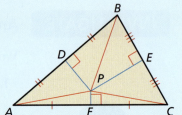

PROOF Circumcenter Theorem

Given △ABC; the perpendicular bisectors of $\overline{AB}$, $\overline{BC}$, and $\overline{AC}$

Prove The perpendicular bisectors intersect in a point; that point is equidistant from A, B, and C.

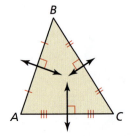

STATEMENTS	REASONS
1. △ABC; the perpendicular bisectors of $\overline{AB}$, $\overline{BC}$, and $\overline{AC}$	1. Given
2. The perpendicular bisectors of $\overline{AB}$ and $\overline{BC}$ intersect at some point P.	2. Because the sides of a triangle cannot be parallel, these perpendicular bisectors must intersect in some point. Call it P.
3. Draw $\overline{PA}$, $\overline{PB}$, and $\overline{PC}$.	3. Two Point Postulate
4. $PA = PB$, $PB = PC$	4. Perpendicular Bisector Theorem
5. $PA = PC$	5. Transitive Property of Equality
6. P is on the perpendicular bisector of $\overline{AC}$.	6. Converse of the Perpendicular Bisector Theorem
7. $PA = PB = PC$. So, P is equidistant from the vertices of the triangle.	7. From the results of Steps 4 and 5, and the definition of equidistant

298   Chapter 6   Relationships Within Triangles

EXAMPLE 1 **Using the Circumcenter Theorem**

Three snack carts sell frozen yogurt at points A, B, and C in a city. Each of the three carts is the same distance from the frozen yogurt distributor. Find the location of the distributor.

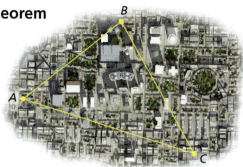

The Circumcenter Theorem shows that you can find a point equidistant from three points by using the perpendicular bisectors of the triangle formed by the three points.

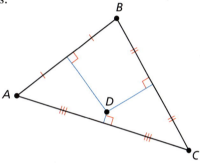

▶ Copy points A, B, and C and connect them to draw $\triangle ABC$. Then use a compass and straightedge to draw the three perpendicular bisectors of $\triangle ABC$. The circumcenter D is the location of the distributor.

The circumcenter P is equidistant from the three vertices, so P is the center of a circle that passes through all three vertices. As shown below, the location of P depends on the type of triangle. The circle with center P is said to be *circumscribed* about the triangle.

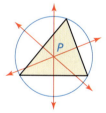 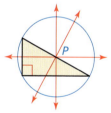 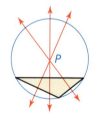

Acute triangle P is inside triangle. Right triangle P is on triangle. Obtuse triangle P is outside triangle.

In-Class Practice

Self-Assessment

1. Three snack carts sell hot pretzels at points D, E, and F. Each of the three carts is the same distance from the pretzel distributor. Find the location of the distributor.

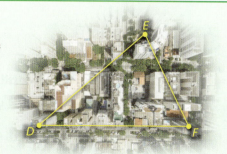

| **1** I don't understand yet. | **2** I can do it with help. | **3** I can do it on my own. | **4** I can teach someone. |

6.2 Bisectors of Triangles

Construction

Circumscribing a Circle About a Triangle

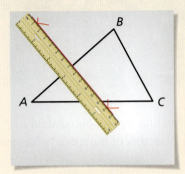

Draw the perpendicular bisector of $\overline{AB}$.

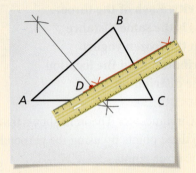

Draw the perpendicular bisector of $\overline{BC}$. Label the intersection of the bisectors D. This is the circumcenter.

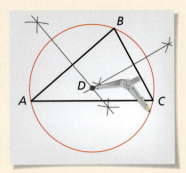

Place the compass at D. Set the width by using any vertex of the triangle. This is the radius of the *circumcircle*. Draw the circle.

EXAMPLE 2   Finding the Circumcenter of a Triangle

Find the coordinates of the circumcenter of $\triangle ABC$ with vertices $A(0, 3)$, $B(0, -1)$, and $C(6, -1)$.

Graph $\triangle ABC$.

Find equations of two perpendicular bisectors. Use the Slopes of Perpendicular Lines Theorem, which states that horizontal lines are perpendicular to vertical lines.

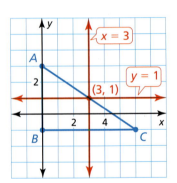

The midpoint of $\overline{AB}$ is $(0, 1)$. The line through $(0, 1)$ that is perpendicular to $\overline{AB}$ is $y = 1$.

The midpoint of $\overline{BC}$ is $(3, -1)$. The line through $(3, -1)$ that is perpendicular to $\overline{BC}$ is $x = 3$.

The lines $x = 3$ and $y = 1$ intersect at $(3, 1)$.

▶ So, the coordinates of the circumcenter are $(3, 1)$.

In-Class Practice

Self-Assessment

Find the coordinates of the circumcenter of the triangle with the given vertices.

2. $R(-2, 5)$, $S(-6, 5)$, $T(-2, -1)$
3. $W(-1, 4)$, $X(1, 4)$, $Y(1, -6)$

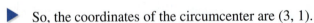

Using the Incenter of a Triangle

Just as a triangle has three perpendicular bisectors, it also has three angle bisectors. The angle bisectors of a triangle are also concurrent. This point of concurrency is the **incenter** of the triangle. For any triangle, the incenter always lies inside the triangle.

Theorem 6.6

Incenter Theorem

The incenter of a triangle is equidistant from the sides of the triangle.

If $\overline{AP}$, $\overline{BP}$, and $\overline{CP}$ are angle bisectors of $\triangle ABC$, then $PD = PE = PF$.

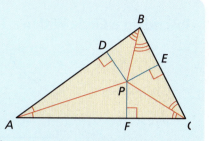

Prove this Theorem Exercise 27, page 305

EXAMPLE 3 Using the Incenter of a Triangle

In the figure shown, $ND = 5x - 1$ and $NE = 2x + 11$.

a. Find NF.

Point N is the incenter of $\triangle ABC$ because it is the point of concurrency of the three angle bisectors. So, by the Incenter Theorem, $ND = NE = NF$.

Solve for x.

$ND = NE$	Incenter Theorem
$5x - 1 = 2x + 11$	Substitute.
$x = 4$	Solve for x.

Find ND (or NE).

$ND = 5x - 1 = 5(4) - 1 = 19$

▶ So, because $ND = NF$, $NF = 19$.

b. Can NG be equal to 18? Explain your reasoning.

Recall that the shortest distance between a point and a line is the length of a perpendicular segment. In this case, the perpendicular segment is $\overline{NF}$, which has a length of 19. Because $18 < 19$, NG cannot be equal to 18.

In-Class Practice

Self-Assessment

4. In the figure shown, $QM = 3x + 8$ and $QN = 7x + 2$. Find QP.

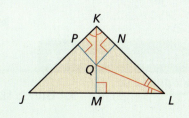

6.2   Bisectors of Triangles

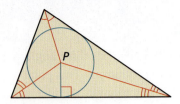

Because the incenter *P* is equidistant from the three sides of the triangle, a circle drawn using *P* as the center and the distance to one side of the triangle as the radius will just touch the other two sides of the triangle. The circle is said to be *inscribed* within the triangle.

Construction

Inscribing a Circle Within a Triangle

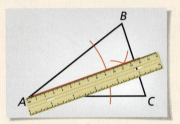

Draw the angle bisector of ∠A.

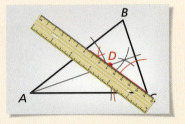

Draw the angle bisector of ∠C. Label the intersection of the bisectors *D*. This is the incenter.

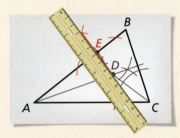

Draw the perpendicular line from *D* to $\overline{AB}$. Label the point where it intersects $\overline{AB}$ as *E*.

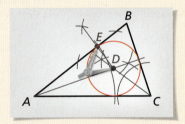

Place the compass at *D*. Set the width to *DE*. This is the radius of the *incircle*. Draw the circle.

EXAMPLE 4 Modeling Real Life

City officials want to place a lamppost near the streets shown so that the lamppost is the same distance from all three streets. Should the lamppost be at the *circumcenter* or *incenter* of the triangular piece of land?

Because the shape of the land is an obtuse triangle, the circumcenter lies outside the triangle and is not equidistant from the sides of the triangle. By the Incenter Theorem, the incenter of the triangle is equidistant from the sides of the triangle.

▶ So, the lamppost should be at the incenter of the triangular piece of land.

In-Class Practice

Self-Assessment

5. Draw a sketch to show the location *L* of the lamppost in Example 4.

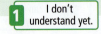

6.2 Practice

1. **CONNECTION TO REAL LIFE** You and two friends plan to walk your dogs together. You want the meeting place to be the same distance from each person's residence. Explain how you can use the diagram to locate the meeting place. (See Example 1.)

2. **CONNECTION TO REAL LIFE** You are camping in Joshua Tree National Park. You plan to set up camp the same distance from each of the mines shown. Use the diagram to determine the location of your campsite.

The angle bisectors of △XYZ intersect at point *P* and are shown in red. Find the indicated measure.

3. *PB*

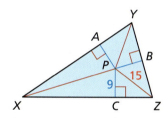

4. *HP*

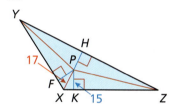

Find the coordinates of the circumcenter of the triangle with the given vertices. (See Example 2.)

5. $A(0, 0)$, $B(0, 8)$, $C(6, 0)$

6. $A(2, 2)$, $B(2, 4)$, $C(8, 4)$

7. $H(-10, 7)$, $J(-6, 3)$, $K(-2, 3)$

8. $L(3, -6)$, $M(5, -3)$, $N(8, -6)$

Point *N* is the incenter of △*ABC*. Use the given information to find the indicated measure. (See Example 3.)

9. $ND = 6x - 2$
   $NE = 3x + 7$
   Find *NF*.

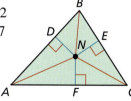

10. $NG = x + 3$
    $NH = 2x - 3$
    Find *NJ*.

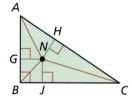

11. $NK = 2x - 2$
    $NL = -x + 10$
    Find *NM*.

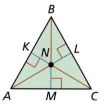

12. $NQ = 2x$
    $NR = 3x - 2$
    Find *NS*.

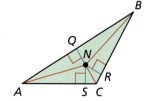

6.2 Bisectors of Triangles 303

CONSTRUCTION Copy the triangle with the given angle measures. Find the incenter. Then construct the inscribed circle.

13.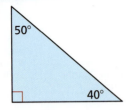

14.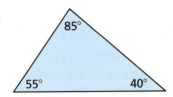

SMP.3 ERROR ANALYSIS Describe and correct the error in identifying equal distances.

15.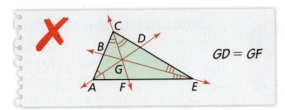

16.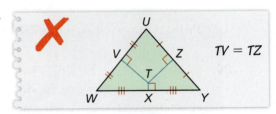

17. **CONNECTION TO REAL LIFE** You are placing a fountain in a triangular koi pond. You want the fountain to be the same distance from each side of the pond. Should the fountain be at the *circumcenter* or *incenter* of the triangular pond? (See Example 4.)

18. **CONNECTION TO REAL LIFE** A marching band director wants a soloist to be the same distance from each side of the triangular formation shown below. Should the soloist be at the *cirumcenter* or *incenter* of the triangular formation?

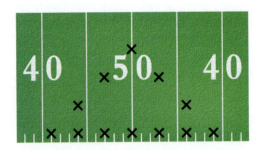

SMP.6 Complete the statement with *always*, *sometimes*, or *never*. Explain your reasoning.

19. The circumcenter of a scalene triangle is _____ inside the triangle.

20. If the perpendicular bisector of one side of a triangle intersects the opposite vertex, then the triangle is _____ isosceles.

21. The perpendicular bisectors of a triangle intersect at a point that is _____ equidistant from the midpoints of the sides of the triangle.

22. The angle bisectors of a triangle intersect at a point that is _____ equidistant from the sides of the triangle.

304 Chapter 6 Relationships Within Triangles

SMP.7 Find the value of x that makes point N the incenter of the triangle.

23.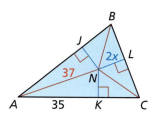

24.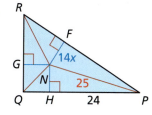

25. **PROVING A THEOREM** Write a proof of the Incenter Theorem.

   Given $\triangle ABC$, $\overline{AD}$ bisects $\angle CAB$, $\overline{BD}$ bisects $\angle CBA$, $\overline{DE} \perp \overline{AB}$, $\overline{DF} \perp \overline{BC}$, and $\overline{DG} \perp \overline{CA}$.

   Prove The angle bisectors intersect at D, which is equidistant from $\overline{AB}$, $\overline{BC}$, and $\overline{CA}$.

26. **ARCHAEOLOGY** **FIRE PIT** Archaeologists find three stones. They believe that the stones were once part of a circle of stones with a community fire pit at its center. They mark the locations of stones A, B, and C on a coordinate plane, where distances are measured in feet.

   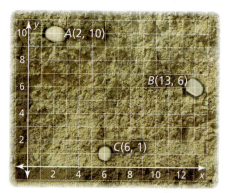

   a. Explain how archaeologists can use a sketch to estimate the center of the circle of stones.

   b. Copy the diagram and find the approximate coordinates of the point at which the archaeologists should look for the fire pit.

27. **SMP.6** Is it possible for the incenter and the circumcenter of a triangle to be the same point? Use diagrams to support your reasoning.

28. The arms of the windmill are the angle bisectors of the red triangle. What point of concurrency is the point that connects the three arms?

29. **SMP.6** Explain why the incenter of a triangle is always located inside the triangle.

30. **SMP.8** Use reflections to show that the three lines of symmetry of an equilateral triangle are perpendicular bisectors of the sides of the triangle.

31. **SMP.5** Cut the largest circle possible from an isosceles triangle made of paper whose sides are 8 inches, 12 inches, and 12 inches. Find the radius of the circle. State whether you used perpendicular bisectors or angle bisectors.

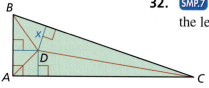

32. **SMP.7** Point D is the incenter of $\triangle ABC$. Write an expression for the length x in terms of the three side lengths AB, AC, and BC.

Interpreting Data

BALANCING POINT You have already studied the *circumcenter* and the *incenter* of a triangle. In the next lesson, you will study the *centroid*. The centroid is the intersection of the *medians* of a triangle. A median is a segment from a vertex to the midpoint of the opposite side. Cut 3 identical acute triangles out of cardboard. Find the circumcenter on the first triangle, the incenter on the second triangle, and the centroid on the third triangle.

33. Does your triangle balance on any of the three points?

34. Cut out a piece of cardboard in an irregular shape. Experimentally find its balancing point. What do you observe?

35. Describe a real-life application of the balancing point of an object.

Balance on the circumcenter?

Balance on the incenter?

Balance on the centroid?

Review & Refresh

36. Find $m\angle ABD$.

37. For $h(x) = -7x$, find the value of x for which $h(x) = 42$.

38. Determine whether the table represents a *linear* or *nonlinear* function. Explain.

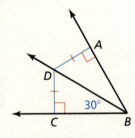

39. A triangle has vertices $A(0, 0)$, $B(8, 12)$, and $C(16, 0)$. Prove that $\triangle ABC$ is isosceles.

40. The endpoints of $\overline{AB}$ are $A(-3, 5)$ and $B(3, 5)$. Find the coordinates of the midpoint M. Then find AB.

41. Find the distance from point A to $\overleftrightarrow{XZ}$.

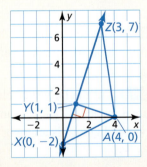

42. The largest concentrated solar power plant in the world is the Noor Complex, located in the Sahara Desert. It cost 3.9 billion dollars to construct. Use this information to write two true conditional statements.

6.3 Medians and Altitudes of Triangles

Learning Target: Use medians and altitudes of triangles.

Success Criteria:
- I can draw medians and altitudes of triangles.
- I can find the centroid of a triangle.
- I can find the orthocenter of a triangle.

INVESTIGATE Drawing Medians and Altitudes of Triangles

Work with a partner. A *median* of a triangle is a segment from a vertex to the midpoint of the opposite side. An *altitude* of a triangle is the perpendicular segment from a vertex to the opposite side or to the line that contains the opposite side.

1. Use technology to draw any triangle. Construct the medians of the triangle. What do you notice? What happens when you move the vertices of the triangle?

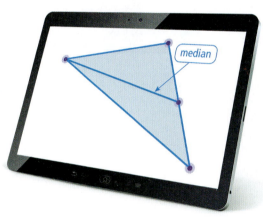

2. In Exercise 1, the point of concurrency divides each median into two segments. Find a relationship between the lengths of the segments.

3. Use technology to draw any triangle. Construct the altitudes of the triangle. What do you notice? What happens when you move the vertices of the triangle?

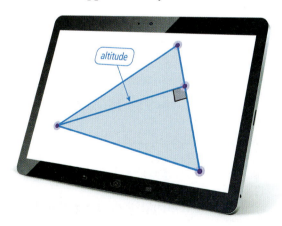

4. **SMP.8** What conjectures can you make using your results in Exercises 1–3?

Vocabulary
median of a triangle
centroid
altitude of a triangle
orthocenter

Using the Median of a Triangle

A **median of a triangle** is a segment from a vertex to the midpoint of the opposite side. The three medians of a triangle are concurrent. The point of concurrency, called the **centroid**, is inside the triangle.

Theorem 6.7

Centroid Theorem

The centroid of a triangle is two-thirds of the distance from each vertex to the midpoint of the opposite side.

The medians of $\triangle ABC$ meet at point P, and $AP = \frac{2}{3}AE$, $BP = \frac{2}{3}BF$, and $CP = \frac{2}{3}CD$.

Proof Available online
Prove this Theorem Exercise 32, page 313

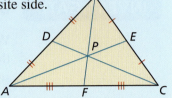

EXAMPLE 1 Using the Centroid of a Triangle

In $\triangle RST$, point Q is the centroid, and $SQ = 8$. Find QW and SW.

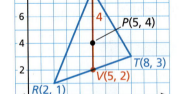

$SQ = \frac{2}{3}SW$ Centroid Theorem

$8 = \frac{2}{3}SW$ Substitute 8 for SQ.

$12 = SW$ Multiply each side by $\frac{3}{2}$.

Then $QW = SW - SQ = 12 - 8 = 4$.

▶ So, $QW = 4$ and $SW = 12$.

EXAMPLE 2 Finding the Centroid of a Triangle

Find the centroid of $\triangle RST$ with vertices $R(2, 1)$, $S(5, 8)$, and $T(8, 3)$.

Graph $\triangle RST$. Find the midpoint V of $\overline{RT}$, and sketch median $\overline{SV}$.

$$V\left(\frac{2+8}{2}, \frac{1+3}{2}\right) = V(5, 2)$$

The centroid is two-thirds of the distance from each vertex to the midpoint of the opposite side. The distance from $S(5, 8)$ to $V(5, 2)$ is $8 - 2 = 6$ units. So, the centroid is $\frac{2}{3}(6) = 4$ units down from vertex S on $\overline{SV}$.

▶ So, the coordinates of the centroid P are $(5, 8 - 4)$, or $(5, 4)$.

In-Class Practice

Self-Assessment

1. In Example 1, $RQ = 12$. Find QV and RV.

Find the centroid of the triangle with the given vertices.

2. $F(2, 5)$, $G(4, 9)$, $H(6, 1)$
3. $X(-3, 3)$, $Y(1, 5)$, $Z(-1, -2)$

Using the Altitude of a Triangle

An **altitude of a triangle** is the perpendicular segment from a vertex to the opposite side or to the line that contains the opposite side.

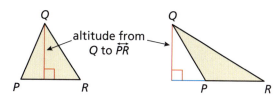

Key Concept

Orthocenter

The lines containing the altitudes of a triangle are concurrent. This point of concurrency is the **orthocenter** of the triangle.

The lines containing $\overline{AF}$, $\overline{BD}$, and $\overline{CE}$ meet at the orthocenter G of $\triangle ABC$.

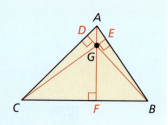

The location of the orthocenter P of a triangle depends on the type of triangle.

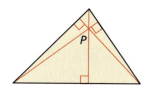
Acute triangle
P is inside triangle.

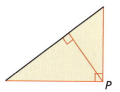
Right triangle
P is on triangle.

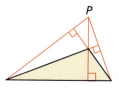
Obtuse triangle
P is outside triangle.

EXAMPLE 3 — Locating the Orthocenter of a Triangle

Tell whether the orthocenter of the triangle with vertices $P(-3, -1)$, $Q(0, 1)$, and $R(3, 0)$ is *inside*, *on*, or *outside* the triangle.

Graph $\triangle PQR$.

Notice that $\angle PQR$ is obtuse.

▶ So, $\triangle PQR$ is obtuse and the orthocenter is outside the triangle.

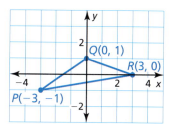

In-Class Practice

Self-Assessment

Tell whether the orthocenter of the triangle with the given vertices is *inside*, *on*, or *outside* the triangle.

4. $D(0, 0)$, $E(0, -4)$, $F(4, 0)$

5. $A(-2, 3)$, $B(2, 4)$, $C(1, -4)$

EXAMPLE 4 **Finding the Orthocenter of a Triangle**

Find the orthocenter of $\triangle XYZ$ with vertices $X(-5, -1)$, $Y(-2, 4)$, and $Z(3, -1)$.

Graph $\triangle XYZ$.

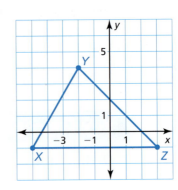

Find an equation of the line that contains the altitude from Y to $\overline{XZ}$. Because $\overline{XZ}$ is horizontal, the altitude is vertical. The line that contains the altitude is $x = -2$ because it passes through $Y(-2, 4)$.

Find an equation of the line that contains the altitude from X to $\overline{YZ}$. The altitude is perpendicular to $\overline{YZ}$, so find the slope of $\overline{YZ}$.

$$\text{slope of } \overline{YZ} = \frac{-1 - 4}{3 - (-2)} = -1$$

Because the product of the slopes of two perpendicular lines is -1, the slope of a line perpendicular to $\overline{YZ}$ is 1. The line passes through $X(-5, -1)$.

$y = mx + b$	Use slope-intercept form.
$-1 = 1(-5) + b$	Substitute -1 for y, 1 for m, and -5 for x.
$4 = b$	Solve for b.

So, an equation of the line is $y = x + 4$.

Find the point of intersection of the graphs of $x = -2$ and $y = x + 4$.

Substitute -2 for x in the equation $y = x + 4$. Then solve for y.

$y = x + 4$	Write equation.
$y = -2 + 4$	Substitute -2 for x.
$y = 2$	Add.

▶ So, the coordinates of the orthocenter are $(-2, 2)$.

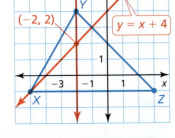

In-Class Practice

Self-Assessment

Tell whether the orthocenter of the triangle with the given vertices is *inside*, *on*, or *outside* the triangle. Then find the orthocenter.

6. $A(0, 3)$, $B(0, -2)$, $C(6, -3)$

7. $J(-3, -4)$, $K(-3, 4)$, $L(5, 4)$

| 1 | I don't understand yet. | 2 | I can do it with help. | 3 | I can do it on my own. | 4 | I can teach someone. |

310 Chapter 6 Relationships Within Triangles

Concept Summary

Segments, Lines, Rays, and Points in Triangles

	Example	Point of Concurrency	Property	Example
perpendicular bisector		circumcenter	The circumcenter *P* of a triangle is equidistant from the vertices of the triangle.	
angle bisector		incenter	The incenter *I* of a triangle is equidistant from the sides of the triangle.	
median		centroid	The centroid *R* of a triangle is two-thirds of the distance from each vertex to the midpoint of the opposite side.	
altitude		orthocenter	The lines containing the altitudes of a triangle are concurrent at the orthocenter *O*.	

EXAMPLE 5   Proving a Property of Isosceles Triangles

Prove that the median from the vertex angle to the base of an isosceles triangle is an altitude.

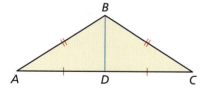

Given △*ABC* is isosceles, with base $\overline{AC}$. $\overline{BD}$ is the median to base $\overline{AC}$.

Prove $\overline{BD}$ is an altitude of △*ABC*.

Paragraph Proof Legs $\overline{AB}$ and $\overline{BC}$ of isosceles △*ABC* are congruent. $\overline{CD} \cong \overline{AD}$ because $\overline{BD}$ is the median to $\overline{AC}$. Also, $\overline{BD} \cong \overline{BD}$ by the Reflexive Property of Segment Congruence. So, △*ABD* ≅ △*CBD* by the SSS Congruence Theorem. ∠*ADB* ≅ ∠*CDB* because corresponding parts of congruent triangles are congruent. Also, ∠*ADB* and ∠*CDB* are a linear pair. $\overline{BD}$ and $\overline{AC}$ intersect to form a linear pair of congruent angles, so $\overline{BD} \perp \overline{AC}$ by the Linear Pair Perpendicular Theorem, and $\overline{BD}$ is an altitude of △*ABC*.

In-Class Practice

Self-Assessment

8. **WHAT IF?** In Example 5, you want to show that median $\overline{BD}$ is also an angle bisector. How would your proof be different?

6.3 Practice

Point P is the centroid of △LMN. Find PN and QP. (See Example 1.)

1. $QN = 9$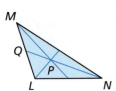
2. $QN = 21$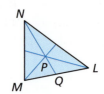
3. $QN = 30$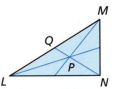

Point G is the centroid of △ABC. BG = 6, AF = 12, and AE = 15. Find the length of the segment.

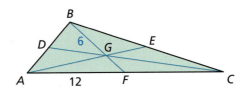

4. $\overline{FC}$
5. $\overline{BF}$
6. $\overline{AG}$
7. $\overline{GE}$

8. **SMP.3 ERROR ANALYSIS** Describe and correct the error in finding DE. Point D is the centroid.

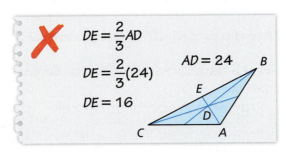

Find the centroid of the triangle with the given vertices. (See Example 2.)

9. $A(2, 3), B(8, 1), C(5, 7)$
10. $F(1, 5), G(-2, 7), H(-6, 3)$

Tell whether the orthocenter of the triangle with the given vertices is *inside*, *on*, or *outside* the triangle. Then find the orthocenter. (See Examples 3 and 4.)

11. $L(0, 5), M(3, 1), N(8, 1)$
12. $X(-3, 2), Y(5, 2), Z(-3, 6)$
13. $A(-4, 0), B(1, 0), C(-1, 3)$
14. $T(-2, 1), U(2, 1), V(0, 4)$

SMP.5 CONSTRUCTION Draw the indicated triangle and find its centroid and orthocenter.

15. right isosceles triangle
16. obtuse scalene triangle

PROOF Write a proof of the statement. (See Example 5.)

17. The angle bisector from the vertex angle to the base of an isosceles triangle is a median.

18. The altitude from the vertex angle to the base of an isosceles triangle is a perpendicular bisector.

SMP.6 Complete the statement with *always*, *sometimes*, or *never*.

19. The centroid is _____ on the triangle.

20. The orthocenter is _____ outside the triangle.

21. The centroid is _____ formed by the intersection of the three medians.

22. CONNECTION TO REAL LIFE Find the area of the triangular part of the paper airplane wing that is outlined in red. Which special segment of the triangle did you use?

23. Complete the statement for △DEF with centroid K and medians $\overline{DH}, \overline{EJ}$, and $\overline{FG}$.

a. $EJ = $ ____ KJ

b. $DK = $ ____ KH

c. $FG = $ ____ FK

d. $KG = $ ____ FG

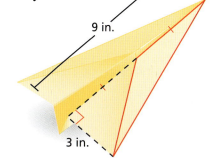

24. CONNECT CONCEPTS Graph the lines on the same coordinate plane. Find the centroid of the triangle formed by their intersections.

$y_1 = 3x - 4$ $y_2 = \frac{3}{4}x + 5$ $y_3 = -\frac{3}{2}x - 4$

25. **SMP.5** **CONSTRUCTION** Use a compass and straightedge to construct a triangle and find its centroid.

CONNECT CONCEPTS Point D is the centroid of △ABC. Use the given information to find the value of x.

26. $BD = 4x + 5$ and $BF = 9x$

27. $DG = 2x - 8$ and $CG = 3x + 3$

28. PROOF Prove that a median of an equilateral triangle is an angle bisector, a perpendicular bisector, and an altitude.

29. PROOF Prove the statements in parts (a)–(c).

Given $\overline{LP}$ and $\overline{MQ}$ are medians of scalene △LMN. Point R is on $\overrightarrow{LP}$ such that $\overline{LP} \cong \overline{PR}$. Point S is on $\overrightarrow{MQ}$ such that $\overline{MQ} \cong \overline{QS}$.

Prove a. $\overline{NS} \cong \overline{NR}$

b. $\overline{NS}$ and $\overline{NR}$ are both parallel to $\overline{LM}$.

c. R, N, and S are collinear.

30. **SMP.1** **DIG DEEPER** Construct an acute scalene triangle. Find the orthocenter, centroid, and circumcenter. What can you conclude?

31. PROOF In the figure, $\overline{AE}, \overline{BF}$, and $\overline{CD}$ are the medians of △ABC. How can you show that all three medians intersect at point G? Prove that the three medians of any triangle are concurrent.

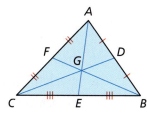

6.3   Medians and Altitudes of Triangles   313

Interpreting Data

CENTER OF GRAVITY A center of gravity is the point that represents the average location of an object's weight. The center of gravity is useful in predicting the behavior of a moving body when acted on by gravity.

32. Which has a higher center of gravity, an SUV or a sedan? Describe the consequences of having a higher center of gravity when driving.

33. Which has a higher center of gravity, a horse or a pig? Describe the consequences of having a higher center of gravity when transporting animals.

34. How is center of gravity related to the centroid of a triangle?

Suspend the mug from any point. A vertical line from the point of suspension passes through the center of gravity.

Next, suspend the mug from a different point. A vertical line from this point of suspension intersects the first line at the center of gravity.

Center of gravity (inside the mug)

Review & Refresh

35. Find $m\angle GJK$.

36. Find the coordinates of the circumcenter of the triangle with vertices $D(3, 5)$, $E(7, 9)$, and $F(11, 5)$.

Determine whether $\overline{AB}$ is parallel to $\overline{CD}$.

37. $A(5, 6)$, $B(-1, 3)$ and $C(-4, 9)$, $D(-16, 3)$

38. $A(-3, 6)$, $B(5, 4)$ and $C(-14, -10)$, $D(-2, -7)$

39. Graph $g(x) = \frac{1}{3}(x - 4)^2 + 7$. Compare the graph to the graph of $f(x) = x^2$.

Solve the system.

40. $x - 3y = -6$
    $5y = 2 + 3x$

41. $2x = 11 - 5y$
    $0.5x + 7y = 20$

Solve the equation.

42. $3x^2 + 48 = 0$

43. $x^2 - 8x = -4$

44. You conduct a survey that asks 146 juniors and seniors in your school whether they plan to participate in the school talent show. Of the 21 students who plan to participate, 13 are seniors. Of the juniors surveyed, 63 do not plan to participate. Organize the results in a two-way table. Include the marginal frequencies.

45. Write a plan for the proof.

    Given $\overline{EG}$ bisects $\angle DEF$.
    Prove $\triangle EGD \cong \triangle EGF$

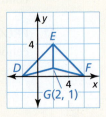

6.4 The Triangle Midsegment Theorem

Learning Target: Find and use midsegments of triangles.

Success Criteria:
- I can use midsegments of triangles in the coordinate plane to solve problems.
- I can solve real-life problems involving midsegments.

INVESTIGATE Drawing Midsegments of a Triangle

Work with a partner. Use technology.

1. Draw any △ABC. Plot and connect the midpoints of two sides of △ABC. Why is this called a *midsegment* of △ABC?

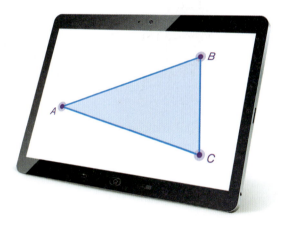

2. Analyze the midsegments and sides of △ABC. What do you notice?

3. Move the vertices of △ABC to form different triangles. Then write a conjecture about the relationships between the midsegments and sides of a triangle.

4. Label the triangle formed by the midsegments of △ABC as shown. Analyze and compare △ABC and △DEF. What do you notice? Make several observations.

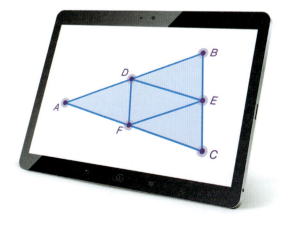

Vocabulary
midsegment of a triangle

Using the Midsegment of a Triangle

A **midsegment of a triangle** is a segment that connects the midpoints of two sides of the triangle. Every triangle has three midsegments, which form the *midsegment triangle*.

The midsegments of △ABC at the right are $\overline{MP}, \overline{MN},$ and $\overline{NP}$. Midsegment $\overline{MP}$ can be called "the midsegment opposite $\overline{AC}$." The *midsegment triangle* is △MNP.

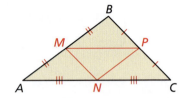

EXAMPLE 1 Using a Midsegment in the Coordinate Plane

In △JKL, show that midsegment $\overline{MN}$ is parallel to $\overline{JL}$ and that $MN = \frac{1}{2}JL$.

Find the coordinates of M and N by finding the midpoints of $\overline{JK}$ and $\overline{KL}$.

$$M\left(\frac{-6 + (-2)}{2}, \frac{1 + 5}{2}\right) = M\left(\frac{-8}{2}, \frac{6}{2}\right) = M(-4, 3)$$

$$N\left(\frac{-2 + 2}{2}, \frac{5 + (-1)}{2}\right) = N\left(\frac{0}{2}, \frac{4}{2}\right) = N(0, 2)$$

Find and compare the slopes of $\overline{MN}$ and $\overline{JL}$.

$$\text{slope of } \overline{MN} = \frac{2 - 3}{0 - (-4)} = -\frac{1}{4} \qquad \text{slope of } \overline{JL} = \frac{-1 - 1}{2 - (-6)} = -\frac{2}{8} = -\frac{1}{4}$$

▶ Because the slopes are the same, $\overline{MN}$ is parallel to $\overline{JL}$.

Find and compare the lengths of $\overline{MN}$ and $\overline{JL}$.

$$MN = \sqrt{[0 - (-4)]^2 + (2 - 3)^2} = \sqrt{16 + 1} = \sqrt{17}$$

$$JL = \sqrt{[2 - (-6)]^2 + (-1 - 1)^2} = \sqrt{64 + 4} = \sqrt{68} = 2\sqrt{17}$$

▶ Because $\sqrt{17} = \frac{1}{2}(2\sqrt{17})$, $MN = \frac{1}{2}JL$.

In-Class Practice

Self-Assessment

Use the graph of △ABC.

1. Show that midsegment $\overline{DE}$ is parallel to $\overline{AC}$ and that $DE = \frac{1}{2}AC$.

2. Find the coordinates of the endpoints of midsegment $\overline{EF}$, which is opposite $\overline{AB}$. Show that $\overline{EF} \parallel \overline{AB}$ and that $EF = \frac{1}{2}AB$.

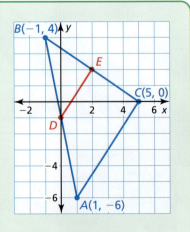

1 I don't understand yet. **2** I can do it with help. **3** I can do it on my own. **4** I can teach someone.

Using the Triangle Midsegment Theorem

Theorem 6.8

Triangle Midsegment Theorem

The segment connecting the midpoints of two sides of a triangle is parallel to the third side and is half as long as that side.

$\overline{DE}$ is a midsegment of $\triangle ABC$, $\overline{DE} \parallel \overline{AC}$, and $DE = \frac{1}{2}AC$.

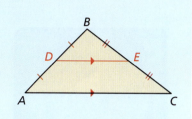

Prove this Theorem Exercise 3, page 317; Exercise 5, page 319

EXAMPLE 2   Proving the Triangle Midsegment Theorem

Write a coordinate proof of the Triangle Midsegment Theorem for one midsegment.

Given $\overline{DE}$ is a midsegment of $\triangle OBC$.

Prove $\overline{DE} \parallel \overline{OC}$ and $DE = \frac{1}{2}OC$

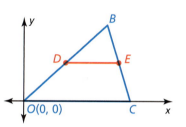

Assign coordinates to $\triangle OBC$ in the coordinate plane. Because you are finding midpoints, use $2p$, $2q$, and $2r$. Then find the coordinates of D and E.

$$D\left(\frac{2q + 0}{2}, \frac{2r + 0}{2}\right) = D(q, r)$$

$$E\left(\frac{2q + 2p}{2}, \frac{2r + 0}{2}\right) = E(q + p, r)$$

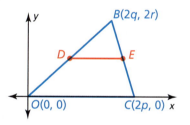

The y-coordinates of D and E are the same, so $\overline{DE}$ has a slope of 0. $\overline{OC}$ is on the x-axis, so its slope is 0.

▶ Because their slopes are the same, $\overline{DE} \parallel \overline{OC}$.

Use the Ruler Postulate to find DE and OC.

$$DE = |(q + p) - q| = p \qquad OC = |2p - 0| = 2p$$

▶ Because $p = \frac{1}{2}(2p)$, $DE = \frac{1}{2}OC$.

In-Class Practice

Self-Assessment

3. Use the diagram from Example 2 to prove the Triangle Midsegment Theorem for midsegment $\overline{FE}$, where F is the midpoint of $\overline{OC}$.

Connections to Real Life

EXAMPLE 3 Using the Triangle Midsegment Theorem

$\overline{UV}$ and $\overline{VW}$ are midsegments of $\triangle RST$. Find UV and RS.

STEM Video: Roof Truss

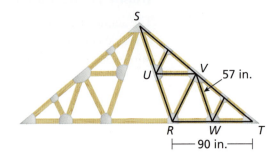

$UV = \frac{1}{2} \cdot RT = \frac{1}{2}(90 \text{ in.}) = 45 \text{ in.}$ $RS = 2 \cdot VW = 2(57 \text{ in.}) = 114 \text{ in.}$

▶ So, $UV = 45$ inches and $RS = 115$ inches.

EXAMPLE 4 Using the Triangle Midsegment Theorem

Elm Street intersects Cherry Street and Peach Street at their midpoints. Your home is at point P. You leave your home and jog down Cherry Street to Oak Street, over Oak Street to Peach Street, up Peach Street to Elm Street, over Elm Street to Cherry Street, and then back home up Cherry Street. About how many miles do you jog?

length of Elm Street $= \frac{1}{2} \cdot$ (length of Oak St.) $= \frac{1}{2}(1.4 \text{ mi}) = 0.7$ mi

length of Cherry Street $= 2 \cdot$ (length from P to Elm St.) $= 2(1.3 \text{ mi}) = 2.6$ mi

distance along your route: $2.6 + 1.4 + \frac{1}{2}(2.25) + 0.7 + 1.3 = 7.125$

▶ So, you jog about 7 miles.

Check Reasonableness Use compatible numbers to check that your answer is reasonable.

Total distance:

$2.6 + 1.4 + \frac{1}{2}(2.25) + 0.7 + 1.3 \approx 2.5 + 1.5 + 1 + 0.5 + 1.5 = 7$ ✓

In-Class Practice

Self-Assessment

4. Copy the diagram in Example 3. Draw and name the third midsegment. Then find the length of $\overline{VS}$ when the length of the third midsegment is 81 inches.

5. **WHAT IF?** In Example 4, you leave your home and jog down Peach Street to Oak Street, over Oak Street to Cherry Street, up Cherry Street to Elm Street, over Elm Street to Peach Street, and then back home up Peach Street. Explain which jogging route is longer.

6.4 Practice

Use the graph of △ABC with midsegments $\overline{DE}, \overline{EF}$, and $\overline{DF}$. (See Example 1.)

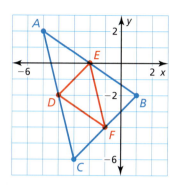

1. Find the coordinates of points D, E, and F.

2. Show that $\overline{DE} \parallel \overline{CB}$ and that $DE = \frac{1}{2}CB$.

▶ 3. Show that $\overline{EF} \parallel \overline{AC}$ and that $EF = \frac{1}{2}AC$.

4. Show that $\overline{DF} \parallel \overline{AB}$ and that $DF = \frac{1}{2}AB$.

▶ 5. **PROVING A THEOREM** Use the diagram from Example 2 to prove the Triangle Midsegment Theorem for midsegment $\overline{DF}$, where F is the midpoint of $\overline{OC}$. (See Example 2.)

6. **PROOF** Write a proof.

   Given $\overline{MN}, \overline{MP}$, and $\overline{PN}$ are midsegments of △QRS.

   Prove △QMP ≅ △MRN

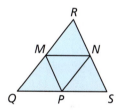

$\overline{DE}$ is a midsegment of △ABC. Find the value of x. (See Example 3.)

▶ 7.

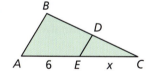

8.

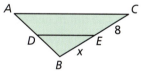

▶ 9. **CONNECTION TO REAL LIFE** The distance between consecutive bases on a baseball field is 90 feet. The pitcher fields a ball halfway between first base and third base. Find the distance between the shortstop and the pitcher. (See Example 4.)

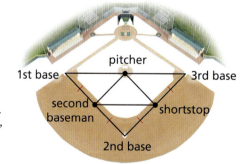

10. **CONNECT CONCEPTS** In △GHJ, A is the midpoint of $\overline{GH}$, $\overline{CB}$ is a midsegment, and $\overline{CB} \parallel \overline{GH}$. What is GA when $GH = 7z - 1$ and $CB = 4z - 3$?

11. **SMP.1 DIG DEEPER** The midpoints of the sides of a triangle are given. Find the vertices of the original triangle. Explain your process and how you can check your answer.

    a. P(2, 1), Q(4, 5), R(7, 4)

    b. T(4, 12), U(5, 15), V(6.4, 10.8)

6.4 The Triangle Midsegment Theorem   319

Interpreting Data

CHICHEN ITZA El Castillo is a Mesoamerican pyramid built by the Maya civilization around 1000 AD. The pyramid is the central structure of the Chichen Itza archaeological site in Yucatan, Mexico. It is one of the tallest Mayan structures.

12. Describe how the Triangle Midsegment Theorem can be used to estimate the widths of the terraces of the pyramid.

13. El Castillo stands 99 feet tall and has a square base with a length of 181 feet. Estimate the volume of El Castillo.

14. A cubic foot of limestone weighs about 165 pounds. Estimate the weight of El Castillo.

Review & Refresh

15. Find a counterexample to show that the conjecture is false.

    Conjecture The difference of two numbers is always less than the greater number.

16. Find UV.

    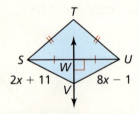

17. Find the coordinates of the centroid of $\triangle MNP$ with vertices $M(-8, -6)$, $N(-4, -2)$, and $P(0, -4)$.

20. Write a piecewise function that represents the total cost y (in dollars) of going to the trampoline park for x minutes. Then determine the total cost for 75 minutes.

21. The incenter of $\triangle ABC$ is point N. $NQ = 2x + 1$ and $NR = 4x - 9$. Find NS.

    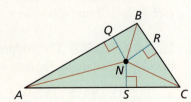

Determine whether the equation represents a *linear* or *nonlinear* function.

18. $y = -|x + 1|$
19. $y = \frac{1}{3}x + 2$

6.5 Indirect Proof and Inequalities in One Triangle

Learning Target: Write indirect proofs and understand inequalities in a triangle.

Success Criteria:
- I can write indirect proofs.
- I can order the angles of a triangle given the side lengths.
- I can order the side lengths of a triangle given the angle measures.
- I can determine possible side lengths of triangles.

INVESTIGATE   Analyzing Angle Measures and Side Lengths of Triangles

Work with a partner.

1. Use technology to draw any scalene △ABC. Find the side lengths and angle measures of the triangle.

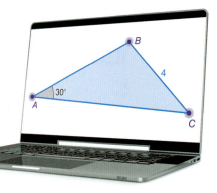

2. Order the side lengths of △ABC from shortest to longest. Order the angle measures from smallest to largest. What do you notice? What happens when you move the vertices of the triangle?

3. Write a conjecture about the relationship between side lengths and angle measures of a triangle.

4. Use technology to draw a side $\overline{DE}$ of a triangle that has a length of 5 units. Then draw a circle with center D that has a radius of 2 units. Choose a point F that lies on the circle. Find the side lengths of △DEF.

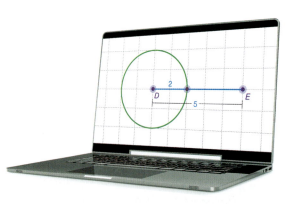

5. Move F around the circle to form new triangles. Describe the possible values of EF. Make observations about the side lengths of △DEF.

Vocabulary
indirect proof

Writing an Indirect Proof

In an **indirect proof**, you start by making the temporary assumption that the desired conclusion is false. By then showing that this assumption leads to a logical impossibility, you prove the original statement true *by contradiction*.

Key Concept

How to Write an Indirect Proof (Proof by Contradiction)

- Identify the statement you want to prove. Assume temporarily that this statement is false by assuming that its opposite is true.
- Reason logically until you reach a contradiction.
- Point out that the desired conclusion must be true because the contradiction proves the temporary assumption false.

EXAMPLE 1 Writing an Indirect Proof

Write an indirect proof that in a given triangle, there can be at most one right angle.

Given $\triangle ABC$

Prove $\triangle ABC$ can have at most one right angle.

Assume temporarily that $\triangle ABC$ has two right angles. Then assume $\angle A$ and $\angle B$ are right angles.

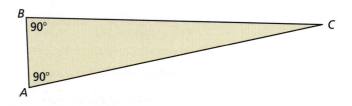

By the definition of right angle, $m\angle A = m\angle B = 90°$.

$m\angle A + m\angle B + m\angle C = 180°$	Triangle Sum Theorem
$90° + 90° + m\angle C = 180°$	Substitution Property of Equality
$m\angle C = 0°$	Subtraction Property of Equality

A triangle cannot have an angle measure of 0°. This contradicts the given information. So, the assumption that $\triangle ABC$ has two right angles must be false, which proves that $\triangle ABC$ can have at most one right angle.

In-Class Practice

Self-Assessment

1. Write an indirect proof that a scalene triangle cannot have two congruent angles.

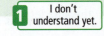 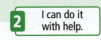

Relating Sides and Angles of a Triangle

Theorem 6.9

Triangle Longer Side Theorem

If one side of a triangle is longer than another side, then the angle opposite the longer side is larger than the angle opposite the shorter side.

Prove this Theorem Exercise 22, page 327

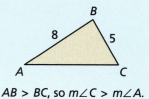

$AB > BC$, so $m\angle C > m\angle A$.

Theorem 6.10

Triangle Larger Angle Theorem

If one angle of a triangle is larger than another angle, then the side opposite the larger angle is longer than the side opposite the smaller angle.

Prove this Theorem Exercise 23, page 327

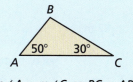

$m\angle A > m\angle C$, so $BC > AB$.

EXAMPLE 2 Comparing Side Lengths and Angle Measures

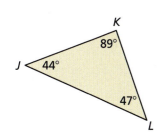

a. Compare the measures of $\angle B$ and $\angle C$.

The side opposite $\angle B$ is $\overline{AC}$, which has a length of 9. The side opposite $\angle C$ is $\overline{AB}$, which has a length of 14.

▶ Because $AB > AC$, $m\angle C > m\angle B$ by the Triangle Longer Side Theorem.

b. Compare JK and KL.

The angle opposite $\overline{JK}$ is $\angle L$, which has a measure of 47°. The angle opposite $\overline{KL}$ is $\angle J$, which has a measure of 44°.

▶ Because $m\angle L > m\angle J$, $JK > KL$ by the Triangle Larger Angle Theorem.

In-Class Practice

Self-Assessment

Compare the measures of the given sides or angles.

2. $\angle H$ and $\angle G$

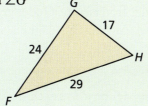

3. $\overline{PQ}$ and $\overline{QR}$

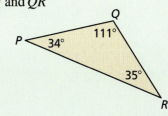

1 I don't understand yet.   **2** I can do it with help.   **3** I can do it on my own.   **4** I can teach someone.

6.5 Indirect Proof and Inequalities in One Triangle

EXAMPLE 3 **Ordering Angle Measures of a Triangle**

An archaeologist finds pottery that is 82 meters away from tools and 89 meters away from drawings. The tools and drawings are 96 meters apart. List the angles of △TPD in order from smallest to largest.

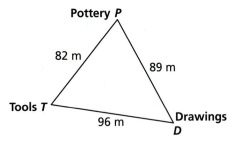

Draw the triangle that represents the situation. Label the side lengths.

The sides from shortest to longest are $\overline{TP}$, $\overline{PD}$, and $\overline{TD}$. The angles opposite these sides are ∠D, ∠T, and ∠P, respectively.

▶ So, by the Triangle Longer Side Theorem, the angles from smallest to largest are ∠D, ∠T, and ∠P.

EXAMPLE 4 **Ordering Side Lengths of a Triangle**

List the sides of △DEF in order from shortest to longest.

Find m∠F.

$m\angle D + m\angle E + m\angle F = 180°$	Triangle Sum Theorem
$51° + 47° + m\angle F = 180°$	Substitute angle measures.
$m\angle F = 82°$	Solve for $m\angle F$.

The angles from smallest to largest are ∠E, ∠D, and ∠F. The sides opposite these angles are $\overline{DF}$, $\overline{EF}$, and $\overline{DE}$, respectively.

▶ So, by the Triangle Larger Angle Theorem, the sides from shortest to longest are $\overline{DF}$, $\overline{EF}$, and $\overline{DE}$.

In-Class Practice

Self-Assessment

4. List the angles of △PQR in order from smallest to largest.

5. List the sides of △RST in order from shortest to longest.

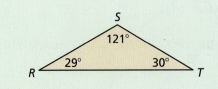

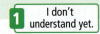

Using the Triangle Inequality Theorem

Not every group of three segments can be used to form a triangle. For example, three attempted triangle constructions using segments with given lengths are shown below. Only the first group of segments forms a triangle.

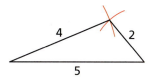 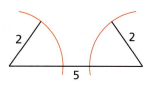 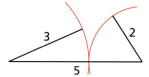

Theorem 6.11

Triangle Inequality Theorem

The sum of the lengths of any two sides of a triangle is greater than the length of the third side.

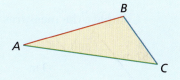

$AB + BC > AC \qquad AC + BC > AB \qquad AB + AC > BC$

Prove this Theorem Exercise 24, page 327

EXAMPLE 5 Finding Possible Side Lengths

A triangle has one side of length 14 and another side of length 9. Describe the possible lengths of the third side.

Let x represent the length of the third side. Draw diagrams to help visualize the small and large values of x. Then use the Triangle Inequality Theorem to write and solve inequalities.

Small values of x

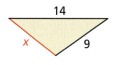

$x + 9 > 14$

$x > 5$

Large values of x

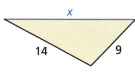

$9 + 14 > x$

$23 > x$, or $x < 23$

▶ The length of the third side must be greater than 5 and less than 23.

In-Class Practice

Self-Assessment

6. A triangle has one side of length 12 inches and another side of length 20 inches. Describe the possible lengths of the third side.

Explain whether it is possible to construct a triangle with the given side lengths.

7. 4 ft, 9 ft, 10 ft
8. 8 m, 9 m, 18 m
9. 5 cm, 7 cm, 12 cm

1 I don't understand yet. **2** I can do it with help. **3** I can do it on my own. **4** I can teach someone.

6.5 Practice

Write the first step in an indirect proof of the statement.

1. If *x* and *y* are odd integers, then *xy* is odd.

2. In △ABC, if m∠A = 100°, then ∠B is not a right angle.

3. **PROOF** Write an indirect proof that an odd number is not divisible by 4. (See Example 1.)

4. **PROOF** Write an indirect proof of the statement "In △QRS, if m∠Q + m∠R = 90°, then m∠S = 90°."

Compare the measures of the given sides or angles. (See Example 2.)

5. ∠J and ∠K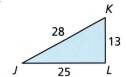

6. $\overline{YZ}$ and $\overline{XY}$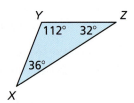

List the angles of the triangle in order from smallest to largest. (See Example 3.)

7.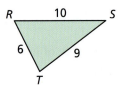

8.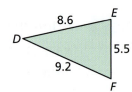

List the sides of the triangle in order from shortest to longest. (See Example 4.)

9.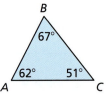

10.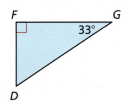

Describe the possible lengths of the third side of the triangle given the lengths of the other two sides. (See Example 5.)

11. 5 inches, 12 inches

12. 12 feet, 18 feet

13. 25 meters, 25 meters

Explain whether it is possible to construct a triangle with the given side lengths.

14. 6, 7, 11

15. 3, 6, 9

16. 28, 17, 46

17. **CONNECTION TO REAL LIFE** You construct a stage prop of a triangular mountain. $\overline{JL}$ is about 32 feet long, $\overline{JK}$ is about 24 feet long, and $\overline{KL}$ is about 26 feet long. List the angles of △JKL in order from smallest to largest.

18. **SMP.3** Your friend claims to have seen you at noon yesterday in Providence, Rhode Island. You have a receipt that shows you were at a restaurant in Baltimore, Maryland at that time. Explain how to use indirect reasoning to prove your friend is mistaken.

19. **CONNECTION TO REAL LIFE** You travel from Fort Peck Lake to Glacier National Park and from Glacier National Park to Granite Peak.

    a. Describe the possible distances from Granite Peak back to Fort Peck Lake.

    b. How is your answer to part (a) affected if you know that $m\angle 2 < m\angle 1$ and $m\angle 2 < m\angle 3$?

20. The Exterior Angle Inequality Theorem states the following:

    The measure of an exterior angle of a triangle is greater than the measure of either of the nonadjacent interior angles.

    Explain how you know that $m\angle 1 > m\angle A$ and $m\angle 1 > m\angle B$ in $\triangle ABC$ with exterior angle $\angle 1$.

21. **CONNECT CONCEPTS** Explain why the hypotenuse of a right triangle must always be longer than either leg.

22. **PROVING THEOREM 6.9** Use the diagram to prove the Triangle Longer Side Theorem.

    Given $BC > AB$, $BD = BA$

    Prove $m\angle BAC > m\angle C$

    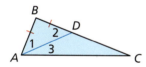

23. **PROVING THEOREM 6.10** Prove the Triangle Larger Angle Theorem.

    Given $m\angle A > m\angle C$

    Prove $BC > AB$

    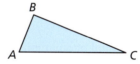

24. **PROVING THEOREM 6.11** Prove the Triangle Inequality Theorem.

    Given $\triangle ABC$

    Prove $AB + BC > AC$, $AC + BC > AB$, and $AB + AC > BC$

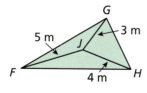

25. **SMP.6** The perimeter of $\triangle HGF$ must be between what two measurements? Explain how you know your answer is correct.

26. **SMP.7** The length of the base of an isosceles triangle is ℓ. Describe the possible lengths of each leg.

27. **SMP.1 DIG DEEPER** The longest side of a triangle has length z. You randomly choose lesser positive numbers x and y. Use the Triangle Inequality Theorem and the graph to find the probability that x, y, and z represent the side lengths of a triangle.

Interpreting Data

ARCHAEOLOGY POTTERY In archaeology, fragments that were once part of a larger whole are common. Archaeologists examine multiple fragments to determine the shape of the original object.

28. Does it appear that the pottery fragments below were from the same object?

29. Explain whether it is possible for a triangular fragment to have one side length of 1.3 inches and a perimeter of 2.4 inches.

30. What types of information do archaeologists document when finding ancient artifacts?

Ancient Native American (Anasazi) pottery fragments

Review & Refresh

31. $\triangle XYZ$ has vertices $X(-5, -2)$, $Y(-3, 4)$, and $Z(3, 0)$. Find the coordinates of the vertices of the midsegment triangle of $\triangle XYZ$.

32. You have a digital photograph that is 960 pixels by 720 pixels. You reduce the size of the photograph to 240 pixels by 180 pixels to post it on a website. What is the scale factor of this dilation?

33. The incenter of $\triangle ABC$ is point N. $NU = -3x + 6$ and $NV = -5x$. Find NT.

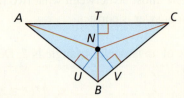

34. Tell whether the orthocenter of $\triangle TUV$ with vertices $T(-2, 5)$, $U(0, 1)$, and $V(2, 5)$ is *inside*, *on*, or *outside* the triangle. Then find its coordinates.

35. Graph $\overline{XY}$ with endpoints $X(-1, 3)$ and $Y(6, -2)$ and its image after a rotation of 270° about the origin, followed by a reflection in the x-axis.

Decide whether enough information is given to prove that the triangles are congruent. If so, state the theorem you would use.

36. $\triangle FGJ$, $\triangle HGJ$

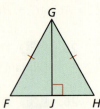

37. $\triangle KLM$, $\triangle KNM$

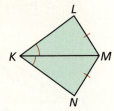

38. Find the value of x.

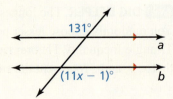

6.6 Inequalities in Two Triangles

> **Learning Target:** Understand inequalities in two triangles.
> **Success Criteria:**
> - I can explain the Hinge Theorem.
> - I can compare measures in triangles.
> - I can solve real-life problems using the Hinge Theorem.

INVESTIGATE Comparing Measures in Triangles

Work with a partner. Use technology to draw any △ABC. Then draw a circle with center B through vertex A.

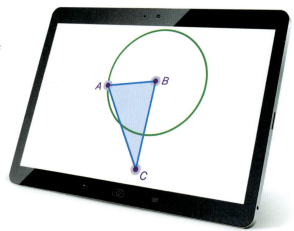

1. Draw △DBC so that D is a point on the circle. Then compare the side lengths of △ABC and △DBC.

2. Compare the lengths of $\overline{AC}$ and $\overline{DC}$ and the measures of ∠ABC and ∠DBC. What do you notice?

3. Move point D to several locations on the circle. At each location, repeat Exercise 2. Record your results in the table. Then write a conjecture that summarizes your observations.

	AB	BC	AC	DC	m∠ABC	m∠DBC
1.						
2.						
3.						
4.						
5.						

4. If two sides of one triangle are congruent to two sides of another triangle, what can you say about the included angles and the third sides of the triangles?

Comparing Measures in Triangles

Imagine a gate between fence posts *A* and *B* that has hinges at *A* and swings open at *B*.

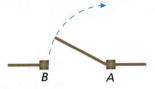

As the gate swings open, you can think of △*ABC*, with side $\overline{AC}$ formed by the gate itself, side $\overline{AB}$ representing the distance between the fence posts, and side $\overline{BC}$ representing the opening between post *B* and the outer edge of the gate.

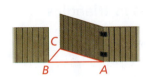 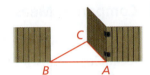 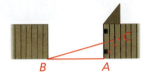

Theorem 6.12

Hinge Theorem

If two sides of one triangle are congruent to two sides of another triangle, and the included angle of the first is larger than the included angle of the second, then the third side of the first is longer than the third side of the second.

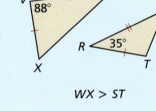

WX > ST

Prove this Theorem Exercise 9, page 333

EXAMPLE 1 Using the Hinge Theorem

Given that $\overline{JK} \cong \overline{LK}$, how does *JM* compare to *LM*?

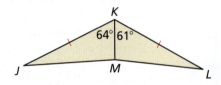

You are given that $\overline{JK} \cong \overline{LK}$, and you know that $\overline{KM} \cong \overline{KM}$ by the Reflexive Property of Segment Congruence. Because 64° > 61°, *m∠JKM > m∠LKM*. So, two sides of △*JKM* are congruent to two sides of △*LKM*, and the included angle of △*JKM* is larger.

▶ By the Hinge Theorem, *JM > LM*.

In-Class Practice

Self-Assessment

1. **WHAT IF?** In Example 1, how does *JM* compare to *LM* when *m∠JKM < m∠LKM*?

   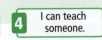

Theorem 6.13

Converse of the Hinge Theorem

If two sides of one triangle are congruent to two sides of another triangle, and the third side of the first is longer than the third side of the second, then the included angle of the first is larger than the included angle of the second.

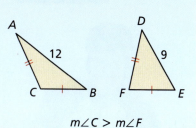

$m\angle C > m\angle F$

Proof page 331

PROOF **Converse of the Hinge Theorem**

Given $\overline{AB} \cong \overline{DE}, \overline{BC} \cong \overline{EF}, AC > DF$

Prove $m\angle B > m\angle E$

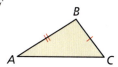

Indirect Proof

Assume temporarily that $m\angle B \not> m\angle E$. Then it follows that either $m\angle B < m\angle E$ or $m\angle B = m\angle E$.

If $m\angle B < m\angle E$, then $AC < DF$ by the Hinge Theorem.

If $m\angle B = m\angle E$, then $\angle B \cong \angle E$. So, $\triangle ABC \cong \triangle DEF$ by the SAS Congruence Theorem and $AC = DF$.

Both conclusions contradict the given statement that $AC > DF$. So, the temporary assumption that $m\angle B \not> m\angle E$ cannot be true. This proves that $m\angle B > m\angle E$.

EXAMPLE 2 Using the Converse of the Hinge Theorem

Given that $\overline{ST} \cong \overline{PR}$, how does $m\angle PST$ compare to $m\angle SPR$?

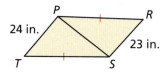

You are given that $\overline{ST} \cong \overline{PR}$, and you know that $\overline{PS} \cong \overline{PS}$ by the Reflexive Property of Segment Congruence. Because 24 inches > 23 inches, $PT > SR$. So, two sides of $\triangle STP$ are congruent to two sides of $\triangle PRS$ and the third side of $\triangle STP$ is longer.

▶ By the Converse of the Hinge Theorem, $m\angle PST > m\angle SPR$.

In-Class Practice

Self-Assessment

Use the diagram.

2. If $PR = PS$ and $m\angle QPR > m\angle QPS$, which is longer, $\overline{SQ}$ or $\overline{RQ}$?

3. If $PR = PS$ and $RQ < SQ$, which is larger, $\angle RPQ$ or $\angle SPQ$?

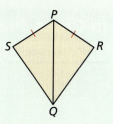

Connections to Real Life

EXAMPLE 3 Using the Hinge Theorem

Two groups of bikers leave the same camp heading in opposite directions. Each group travels 2 miles, then changes direction and travels 1.2 miles. Group A starts due east and then turns 45° toward north. Group B starts due west and then turns 30° toward south. Which group is farther from camp?

Draw a diagram that represents the situation.

Use linear pairs to find the included angles formed by the paths that the groups take.

Group A: 180° − 45° = 135°   **Group B:** 180° − 30° = 150°

The included angles are 135° and 150°.

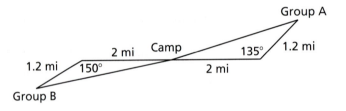

Because 150° > 135°, Group B's distance from camp is greater than Group A's distance from camp by the Hinge Theorem.

▶ So, Group B is farther from camp.

Look Back Because the turn toward north for Group A is greater than the turn toward south for Group B, you can reason that Group A would be closer to camp than Group B. So, Group B is farther from camp.

In-Class Practice

Self-Assessment

4. WHAT IF? In Example 3, Group C leaves camp and travels 2 miles due north, then turns 40° toward east and travels 1.2 miles. Compare the distances from camp for all three groups.

6.6 Practice

Complete the statement with < or >. Explain your reasoning. (See Example 1.)

1. AC ____ DC

2. MN ____ LK

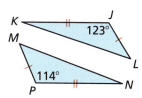

Complete the statement with < or >. Explain your reasoning. (See Example 2.)

3. $m\angle 1$ ____ $m\angle 2$

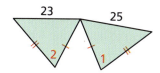

4. $m\angle 1$ ____ $m\angle 2$

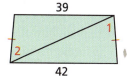

SMP.4 CONNECTION TO REAL LIFE Two flights leave from the same airport. Determine which flight is farther from the airport. Explain your reasoning. (See Example 3.)

5. **Flight 1:** Flies 100 miles due west, then turns 20° toward north and flies 50 miles.

   Flight 2: Flies 100 miles due north, then turns 30° toward east and flies 50 miles.

6. **Flight 1:** Flies 210 miles due south, then turns 70° toward west and flies 80 miles.

   Flight 2: Flies 80 miles due north, then turns 50° toward east and flies 210 miles.

7. **CONNECT CONCEPTS** Find the possible values of x in the figure. Explain your reasoning.

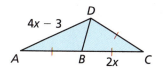

8. $\overline{NR}$ is a median of $\triangle NPQ$, and $NQ > NP$. Explain why $\angle NRQ$ is obtuse.

9. **PROVING THEOREM 6.12** Use the Plan for Proof to prove the Hinge Theorem.

   Given $\overline{AB} \cong \overline{DE}, \overline{BC} \cong \overline{EF}, m\angle ABC > m\angle DEF$
   Prove $AC > DF$

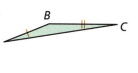

   Plan for Proof

   1. Because $m\angle ABC > m\angle DEF$, you can locate a point P in the interior of $\angle ABC$ so that $\angle CBP \cong \angle FED$ and $\overline{BP} \cong \overline{ED}$. Draw $\overline{BP}$ and show that $\triangle PBC \cong \triangle DEF$.

   2. Locate a point H on $\overline{AC}$ so that $\overrightarrow{BH}$ bisects $\angle PBA$, and show that $\triangle ABH \cong \triangle PBH$.

   3. Begin with the statement $AC = AH + HC$. Then show that $AC > DF$.

Interpreting Data

HELICOPTER NAVIGATION Navigating a small helicopter is very different than navigating a light plane. Helicopters have more visibility and are more maneuverable than fixed-wing aircraft. The diagram shows the distances of two different helicopters from a heliport.

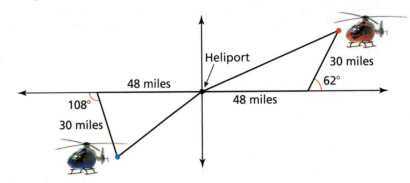

10. Explain how the pilots can use the Hinge Theorem to determine which helicopter is farther from the heliport.

11. Explain whether you are given enough information to determine how many miles the helicopters are from each other.

12. Why might it be important for a helicopter pilot to know geometry?

Review & Refresh

Find the value of x.

13.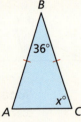

14. $\overline{ST}$ is a midsegment of $\triangle PQR$.

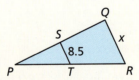

15. Graph quadrilateral $ABCD$ with vertices $A(-8, 2)$, $B(-6, 8)$, $C(-2, 6)$, and $D(-4, 2)$ and its image after the similarity transformation.

    Reflection: in the x-axis
    Dilation: $(x, y) \rightarrow (0.5x, 0.5y)$

16. Explain whether it is possible to construct a triangle with side lengths of 9 inches, 11 inches, and 21 inches?

17. The Deer County Parks Committee plans to build a park. The committee sketches one possible location of the park represented by point P.

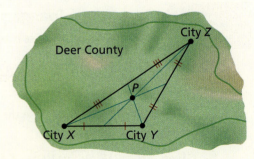

a. Which point of concurrency did the committee use in the sketch as the location of the park?

b. The committee wants the park to be equidistant from the three cities. Should the point of concurrency in the sketch be the location of the park? If not, which point of concurrency should the committee use?

334 Chapter 6 Relationships Within Triangles

6 Chapter Review

Rate your understanding of each section.
1. I don't understand yet.
2. I can do it with help.
3. I can do it on my own.
4. I can teach someone.

6.1 Perpendicular and Angle Bisectors (pp. 289–296)

Learning Target: Use theorems about perpendicular and angle bisectors.

Vocabulary
equidistant

Find the indicated measure.

1. DC

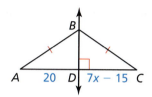

2. RS

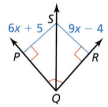

3. $m\angle JFH$

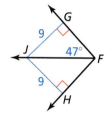

4. Is there enough information in the diagram to find ST? If so, find the length. If not, explain why not.

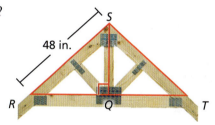

6.2 Bisectors of Triangles (pp. 297–306)

Learning Target: Use bisectors of triangles.

Vocabulary
concurrent
point of concurrency
circumcenter
incenter

Find the coordinates of the circumcenter of the triangle with the given vertices.

5. $T(-6, -5)$, $U(0, -1)$, $V(0, -5)$

6. $X(-2, 1)$, $Y(2, -3)$, $Z(6, -3)$

7. Point D is the incenter of $\triangle LMN$. Find the value of x.

8. Draw an acute $\triangle ABC$. Construct the circumscribed circle about $\triangle ABC$.

9. Draw an obtuse $\triangle DEF$. Construct the inscribed circle within $\triangle DEF$.

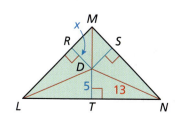

Chapter 6 Chapter Review 335

6.3 Medians and Altitudes of Triangles (pp. 307–314)

⊙ **Learning Target:** Use medians and altitudes of triangles.

Vocabulary
median of a triangle
centroid
altitude of a triangle
orthocenter

Point D is the centroid of △ABC. Find ED and DC.

10. $EC = 18$

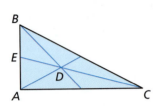

11. $EC = 27$

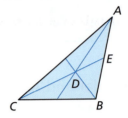

Find the centroid of the triangle with the given vertices.

12. $A(-10, 3), B(-4, 5), C(-4, 1)$

13. $D(2, -8), E(2, -2), F(8, -2)$

Tell whether the orthocenter of the triangle with the given vertices is *inside*, *on*, or *outside* the triangle. Then find the orthocenter.

14. $G(1, 6), H(5, 6), J(3, 1)$

15. $K(-8, 5), L(-6, 3), M(0, 5)$

16. The centroid of △ABC lies on one of the altitudes of △ABC. What can you conclude about △ABC?

17. Draw a triangle so that one of its vertices is the orthocenter. Explain how you drew the triangle to meet this condition.

6.4 The Triangle Midsegment Theorem (pp. 315–320)

⊙ **Learning Target:** Find and use midsegments of triangles.

Vocabulary
midsegment of a triangle

Find the coordinates of the vertices of the midsegment triangle for the triangle with the given vertices.

18. $A(-6, 8), B(-6, 4), C(0, 4)$

19. $D(-3, 1), E(3, 5), F(1, -5)$

$\overline{DE}$ **is a midsegment of △ABC. Find the value of x.**

20.

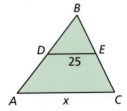

21.

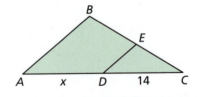

22. The diagram shows your first lap in mowing the triangular field. How far do you travel in this lap?

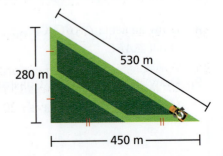

336   Chapter 6   Relationships Within Triangles

6.5 Indirect Proof and Inequalities in One Triangle (pp. 321–328)

Learning Target: Write indirect proofs and understand inequalities in a triangle.

Vocabulary
indirect proof

23. Write an indirect proof of the statement "In △XYZ, if XY = 4 and XZ = 8, then YZ > 4."

List the sides of the triangle in order from shortest to longest.

24.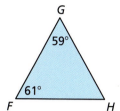

25.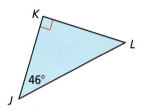

Describe the possible lengths of the third side of the triangle given the lengths of the other two sides.

26. 4 inches, 8 inches

27. 6 meters, 9 meters

28. The widest adjustment possible for a wakeboarder's feet on a wakeboard is x = 24 inches. Write an indirect proof that there can be at most two congruent angles of the triangle formed by the wakeboarder's legs and the wakeboard.

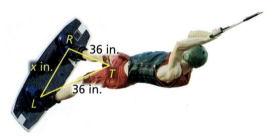

6.6 Inequalities in Two Triangles (pp. 329–334)

Learning Target: Understand inequalities in two triangles.

Use the diagram.

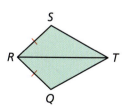

29. If RQ = RS and m∠QRT > m∠SRT, then how does $\overline{QT}$ compare to $\overline{ST}$?

30. If RQ = RS and QT > ST, then how does ∠QRT compare to ∠SRT?

31. Two boats leave the same island. The first boat travels 20 miles due south, then turns 20° toward east and travels 15 miles. The second boat travels 15 miles due east, then turns 10° toward north and travels 20 miles. Explain which boat is farther from the island.

6 PERFORMANCE TASK
SMP.4 SMP.5

Archaeology

Archaeology is the study of human past through material remains.

THE ARCHAEOLOGICAL PROCESS

Selecting an Excavation Site
A site is selected by consulting historic records, conducting field surveys, and sometimes by accidentally discovering artifacts.

Conducting Research
Archaeologists find reliable sources to learn about a specific people, place, and time period.

Excavating the Site
Archaeologists make a detailed map and establish a physical grid over the site. Each grid square is then excavated one layer at a time. As artifacts are discovered, their grid coordinates and layer numbers are recorded.

Cleaning and Cataloging Artifacts
Artifacts are cleaned carefully to avoid inflicting damage. Then they are sorted into categories, and fragments are pieced together.

Reporting the Results
The final step is to analyze and interpret the findings, which are reported in publications, reports, lectures, and exhibitions.

In archaeology, broken pieces of pottery are called *sherds*, and broken pieces of glass are called *shards*.

Analyzing Data

Use the information on the previous page to complete the following exercises.

1 Explain what is shown in the display. What do you notice? What do you wonder?

2 Explain whether a triangular sherd can have side lengths of 1 inch, 2 inches, and 3 inches.

3 A triangular shard has side lengths of 2 centimeters, 2 centimeters, and $\sqrt{8}$ centimeters. Classify the triangle.

4 The shard in Exercise 3 breaks into two triangular shards. List a set of possible side lengths for each shard.

RECONSTRUCTING THE PAST

You are an archaeologist learning about the daily lives of an ancient civilization. You discover the fragments of a circular plate shown above. Use one of the fragments and the mathematical relationships in this chapter to find the diameter of the original plate. Explain each step so that other archaeologists can replicate your method.

Connecting Big Ideas

For use after Chapter 6.
SMP.5 SMP.6

A MATTER OF PERSPECTIVE

For a photograph to accurately represent the distance between two objects, it must be taken at a position equidistant from each object. The OSIRIS-REx spacecraft took this photograph of Earth and the moon.

Earth

Diameter: 12,756 km

In this photograph, this line is about 30 centimeters long.

TOP-DOWN VIEW OF WHERE PHOTOGRAPH WAS TAKEN

Moon

Earth

390,000 km

5,420,000 km

5,120,000 km

Spacecraft

340 Connecting Big Ideas

1 What do you notice? What do you wonder?

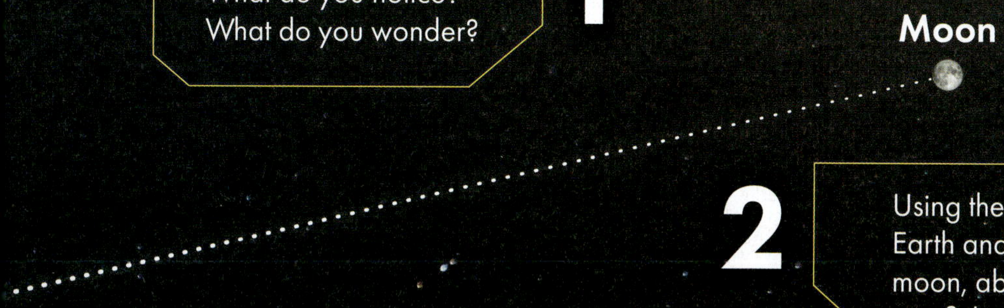

Moon

2 Using the actual diameter of Earth and its distance from the moon, about how many Earths can fit between it and the moon?

3 Explain whether the photo accurately represents the distance between Earth and the moon.

4 This diagram shows the moon's orbit around Earth. Copy the locations of Earth and the moon. Show the locations where a photograph can be taken from within the moon's orbit to accurately represent the distance between the objects.

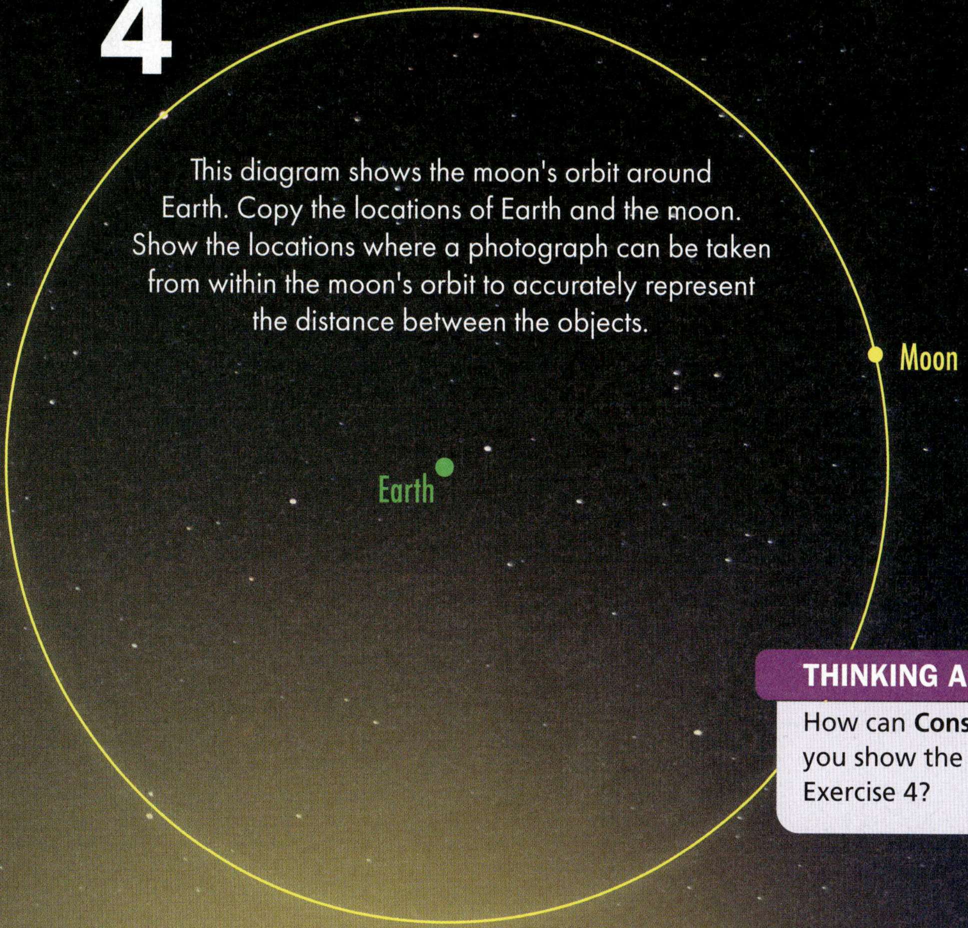

Moon

Earth

THINKING ABOUT THE BIG IDEAS

How can **Constructing Figures** help you show the desired locations in Exercise 4?

Connecting Big Ideas

7 Quadrilaterals and Other Polygons

- 7.1 Angles of Polygons
- 7.2 Properties of Parallelograms
- 7.3 Proving That a Quadrilateral Is a Parallelogram
- 7.4 Properties of Special Parallelograms
- 7.5 Properties of Trapezoids and Kites

NATIONAL GEOGRAPHIC EXPLORER
Brendan Lawrence Mullan ASTRONOMER

Dr. Brendan Lawrence Mullan is an astronomer who believes that people are fascinated by the night sky, space missions, and photos of planets and galaxies. Dr. Mullan says that "human beings want to connect with some cosmic context greater than themselves. I want to give them that chance." He believes that inspiring a new generation of scientists is crucial to solving the 21st-century problems that humanity faces.

- What is astronomy?
- What does *terrestrial* mean? What does *extraterrestrial* mean?
- Do you think there is intelligent life on planets in other parts of the universe? If so, do you think they have communicated with humans?
- What is a UFO? Do you think humans have had experiences with UFOs?

PERFORMANCE TASK
Humans have identified constellations in the night sky for millennia. In the Performance Task on pages 396 and 397, you will use angle measures and side lengths to investigate polygons found in several different constellations.

Astrobiology

Big Idea of the Chapter
Understand Quadrilaterals

There are several special types of quadrilaterals. These include squares, rectangles, parallelograms, and trapezoids. In this chapter you will study the characteristics of each type.

There are many places in the United States overcome by light pollution, which makes it difficult to fully observe the night sky or see it as brightly as in the photograph below. Artificial lighting obscures the natural light of the stars. People have identified shapes and patterns in the night sky for thousands of years, some of which have been used as tools for navigation or to create stories about mythological creatures.

When viewed from Earth, stars often appear as if they lie in the same two-dimensional plane. You want to know whether the stars shown form a parallelogram.

1. What is a parallelogram?

2. What relationship can you use to determine whether points in a coordinate plane form a parallelogram?

3. Use the relationship you described in Exercise 2 to determine whether the stars form a parallelogram.

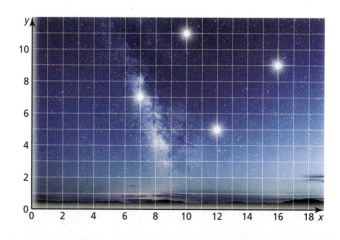

RESOURCES

343

Getting Ready for Chapter 7

Using Structure to Solve a Multi-Step Equation

EXAMPLE 1 Solve $3(2 + x) = -9$.

$3(2 + x) = -9$	Write the equation.
$\dfrac{3(2 + x)}{3} = \dfrac{-9}{3}$	Division Property of Equality
$2 + x = -3$	Simplify.
$\underline{-2 \qquad -2}$	Subtraction Property of Equality
$x = -5$	Simplify.

Solve the equation.

1. $4(7 - x) = 16$
2. $7(1 - x) + 2 = -19$

Identifying Parallel and Perpendicular Lines

EXAMPLE 2 Determine which lines are parallel and which are perpendicular.

Find the slope of each line.

Line a: $m = \dfrac{3 - (-3)}{-4 - (-2)} = -3$

Line b: $m = \dfrac{-1 - (-4)}{1 - 2} = -3$

Line c: $m = \dfrac{2 - (-2)}{3 - 4} = -4$

Line d: $m = \dfrac{2 - 0}{2 - (-4)} = \dfrac{1}{3}$

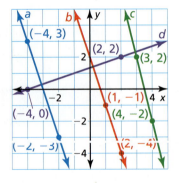

▶ Lines a and b have slopes of -3, so they are parallel. Line d has a slope of $\frac{1}{3}$, the negative reciprocal of -3, so it is perpendicular to lines a and b.

Determine which lines are parallel and which are perpendicular.

3.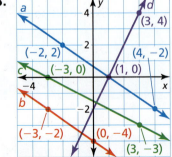

4.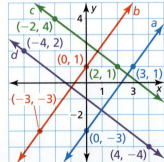

7.1 Angles of Polygons

Learning Target: Find angle measures of polygons.

Success Criteria:
- I can find the sum of the interior angle measures of a polygon.
- I can find interior angle measures of polygons.
- I can find exterior angle measures of polygons.

INVESTIGATE Finding Sums of Interior Angle Measures of Polygons

Work with a partner.

1. Draw a quadrilateral and a pentagon. Use what you know about the interior angle measures of triangles to find the sum of the interior angle measures of each polygon.

2. Draw other convex polygons and find the sums of the measures of their interior angles using the method in Exercise 1. Record your results in the table below.

Number of sides, n	3	4	5	6	7	8	9
Number of triangles							
Sum of angle measures, S							

3. **SMP.2 SMP.8** Write an equation that represents S as a function of n. Explain what the function represents.

4. Use the function you found in Exercise 3 to write a new function that represents the measure A of one interior angle in a polygon with n congruent sides and n congruent angles.

5. Explain whether the function in Exercise 3 applies to the polygon below.

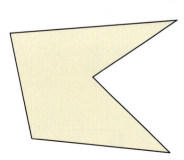

Vocabulary
diagonal
equilateral polygon
equiangular polygon
regular polygon

Using Interior Angle Measures of Polygons

In a polygon, two vertices that are endpoints of the same side are called *consecutive vertices*. A **diagonal** of a polygon is a segment that joins two *nonconsecutive vertices*.

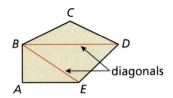

The diagonals from one vertex divide a polygon into triangles. Dividing a polygon with n sides into $(n-2)$ triangles shows that the sum of the measures of the interior angles of a polygon is a multiple of 180°.

Theorem 7.1

Polygon Interior Angles Theorem

The sum of the measures of the interior angles of a convex n-gon is $(n-2) \cdot 180°$.

$$m\angle 1 + m\angle 2 + \cdots + m\angle n = (n-2) \cdot 180°$$

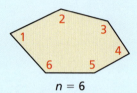

$n = 6$

Proof page 350
Prove this Theorem Exercise 37 (for pentagons), page 353

EXAMPLE 1 — Finding the Sum of Angle Measures in a Polygon

Find the sum of the measures of the interior angles of the polygon.

The polygon is a convex octagon. It has 8 sides. Use the Polygon Interior Angles Theorem.

$(n - 2) \cdot 180° = (8 - 2) \cdot 180°$ Substitute 8 for n.

$= 6 \cdot 180°$ Subtract.

$= 1{,}080°$ Multiply.

▶ The sum of the measures of the interior angles of the polygon is 1,080°.

In-Class Practice

Self-Assessment

1. The shape on the coin is an 11-gon. Find the sum of the measures of the interior angles.

EXAMPLE 2 Finding the Number of Sides of a Polygon

The sum of the measures of the interior angles of a convex polygon is 900°. Classify the polygon by the number of sides.

Use the Polygon Interior Angles Theorem to write an equation involving the number of sides n. Then solve the equation to find the number of sides.

$(n - 2) \cdot 180° = 900°$ Polygon Interior Angles Theorem
$n - 2 = 5$ Divide each side by 180°.
$n = 7$ Add 2 to each side.

▶ The polygon has 7 sides. It is a heptagon.

Corollary 7.1

Corollary to the Polygon Interior Angles Theorem

The sum of the measures of the interior angles of a quadrilateral is 360°.

Prove this Corollary Exercise 38, page 353

EXAMPLE 3 Finding an Unknown Interior Angle Measure

Find the value of x in the diagram.

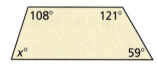

The polygon is a quadrilateral. Use the Corollary to the Polygon Interior Angles Theorem to write an equation involving x. Then solve the equation.

$x° + 108° + 121° + 59° = 360°$ Corollary to the Polygon Interior Angles Theorem
$x + 288 = 360$ Combine like terms.
$x = 72$ Subtract 288 from each side.

▶ The value of x is 72.

In-Class Practice

Self-Assessment

2. The sum of the measures of the interior angles of a convex polygon is 1,440°. Classify the polygon by the number of sides.

3. Find the value of x in the diagram.

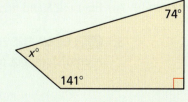

  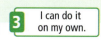

Equilateral and equiangular both share the prefix *equi-*, which means "equal." An **equilateral polygon** has sides with equal lengths. An **equiangular polygon** has angles with equal measures. A convex polygon that is both equilateral and equiangular is a **regular polygon**.

Equilateral

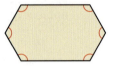
Equiangular

Regular

EXAMPLE 4 **Finding Angle Measures in Polygons**

A home plate for a baseball field is shown.

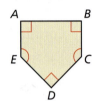

a. **Explain whether the polygon is regular.**

The polygon is not equilateral or equiangular. So, the polygon is not regular.

b. **Find the measures of ∠C and ∠E.**

Find the sum of the measures of the interior angles.

$(n - 2) \cdot 180° = (5 - 2) \cdot 180° = 540°$ Polygon Interior Angles Theorem

Let $x° = m\angle C = m\angle E$. Write an equation involving x and solve the equation.

$x° + x° + 90° + 90° + 90° = 540°$ Write an equation.

$2x + 270 = 540$ Combine like terms.

$x = 135$ Solve for x.

▶ So, $m\angle C = m\angle E = 135°$.

In-Class Practice
Self-Assessment

4. Find $m\angle S$ and $m\angle T$ in the diagram.

5. **SMP.5** **OPEN-ENDED** Construct a pentagon that is equilateral but not equiangular.

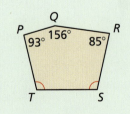

Using Exterior Angle Measures of Polygons

Unlike the sum of the interior angle measures of a convex polygon, the sum of the exterior angle measures does *not* depend on the number of sides of the polygon. The diagrams suggest that the sum of the measures of the exterior angles, one angle at each vertex, of a pentagon is 360°. In general, this sum is 360° for any convex polygon.

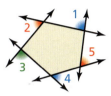
Shade one exterior angle at each vertex.

Cut out the exterior angles.

Arrange the exterior angles to form 360°.

Theorem 7.2

Polygon Exterior Angles Theorem

The sum of the measures of the exterior angles of a convex polygon, one angle at each vertex, is 360°.

$$m\angle 1 + m\angle 2 + \cdots + m\angle n = 360°$$

Prove this Theorem Exercise 42, page 353

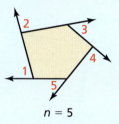
$n = 5$

EXAMPLE 5   Finding an Unknown Exterior Angle Measure

Find the value of x in the diagram.

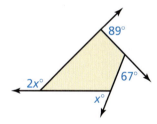

Use the Polygon Exterior Angles Theorem to write and solve an equation.

$x° + 2x° + 89° + 67° = 360°$	Polygon Exterior Angles Theorem
$3x + 156 = 360$	Combine like terms.
$x = 68$	Solve for x.

▶ The value of x is 68.

In-Class Practice

Self-Assessment

6. A convex hexagon has exterior angles with measures 34°, 49°, 58°, 67°, and 75°. What is the measure of an exterior angle at the sixth vertex?

 I don't understand yet.   I can do it with help.   I can do it on my own.   I can teach someone.

Proving by Mathematical Induction

> ### Key Concept
>
> **Mathematical Induction**
>
> Some statements can be proven using *mathematical induction*. A proof by mathematical induction has two steps:
>
> **Base Case:** Show that the statement P_n is true for the first case.
>
> **Inductive Step:** Prove that if P_k is true, then P_{k+1} is true.

EXAMPLE 6   **Proving by Mathematical Induction**

Prove the Polygon Interior Angles Theorem.

Base case: Show that the theorem is true for $n = 3$.

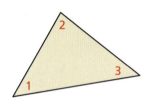

$m\angle 1 + m\angle 2 + m\angle 3 = (3 - 2) \cdot 180°$	Substitute 3 for n.
$= 180°$ ✓	Simplify.

The statement is true by the Triangle Sum Theorem.

Inductive Step: When $k \geq 3$, prove that if the sum of the interior angle measures of a k-gon is $(k - 2) \cdot 180°$, then the sum of the interior angle measures of a $(k + 1)$-gon is

$$[(k + 1) - 2] \cdot 180° = (k - 1) \cdot 180°.$$

Let A be a convex polygon with $k + 1$ sides and vertices $V_1, V_2, V_3, \ldots, V_k,$ and V_{k+1}. By taking any three consecutive vertices and connecting the first to the third, you create polygon B with k sides and triangle C.

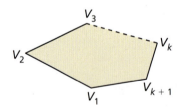 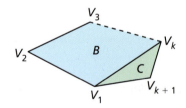

The sum of the interior angle measures in polygon A is equal to the sum of the angles in polygon B and Triangle C, which is

     Polygon B   **Triangle C**

$$(k - 2) \cdot 180° + 180° = (k - 1) \cdot 180°.$$

This completes the proof for the inductive step.

▶ So, the theorem is true for polygons with 3 more more sides.

In-Class Practice

Self-Assessment

7. Use mathematical induction to prove that $1 + 2 + 3 + \cdots + n = \dfrac{n(n + 1)}{2}$ for all natural numbers $n \geq 1$.

7.1 Practice

with Calc Chat and Calc View

Find the sum of the measures of the interior angles of the indicated convex polygon. (See Example 1.)

▶ 1. nonagon 2. 14-gon 3. 16-gon 4. 20-gon

The sum of the measures of the interior angles of a convex polygon is given. Classify the polygon by the number of sides. (See Example 2.)

▶ 5. 720° 6. 1,080° 7. 2,520° 8. 3,240°

Find the value of x. (See Example 3.)

▶ 9.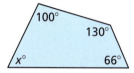

10.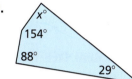

11.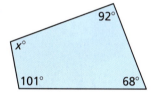

12.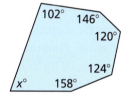

13. **ERROR ANALYSIS** Describe and correct the error in finding the value of x.

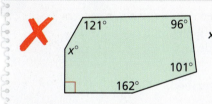

Find the measures of $\angle X$ and $\angle Y$. (See Example 4.)

14.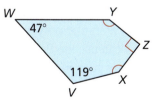

▶ 15.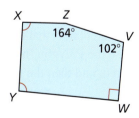

16.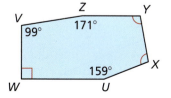

17.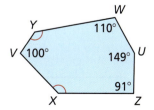

7.1 Angles of Polygons 351

Find the value of *x*. (See Example 5.)

18. 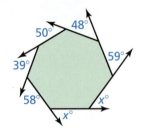   19. 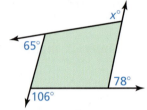   20.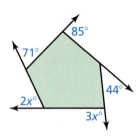

Find the measure of each interior angle and each exterior angle of the indicated regular polygon.

21. pentagon   22. 18-gon   23. 45-gon

24. **CONNECTION TO REAL LIFE** The base of a jewelry box is shaped like a regular octagon. What is the measure of each interior angle of the jewelry box base?

25. **CONNECTION TO REAL LIFE** NASA's InSight is a robotic lander designed to study the deep interior of Mars. The solar panels on InSight are shaped like regular decagons. Find the measure of each interior angle of the solar panels. Then find the measure of each exterior angle.

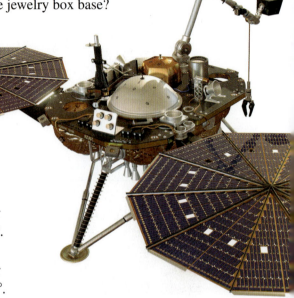

26. Write a formula to find the number n of sides in a regular polygon given that the measure of one interior angle is $x°$.

27. Write a formula to find the number of sides n in a regular polygon given that the measure of one exterior angle is $x°$.

Find the number of sides for the regular polygon described.

28. Each interior angle has a measure of 156°.   29. Each interior angle has a measure of 165°.

30. Each exterior angle has a measure of 9°.   31. Each exterior angle has a measure of 6°.

32. **SMP.6** Your friend claims that to find the interior angle measures of a regular polygon, you do not have to use the Polygon Interior Angles Theorem. Instead you can use the Polygon Exterior Angles Theorem and then the Linear Pair Postulate. Explain whether your friend is correct.

33. Find the measures of all the interior angles of the polygon.

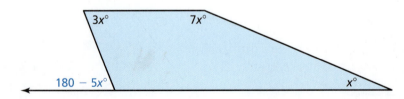

34. Explain whether the hexagon is a regular hexagon.

PROOF Use mathematical induction to prove the statement. (See Example 6.)

▶ **35.** $1^2 + 2^2 + 3^2 + \cdots + n^2 = \dfrac{n(n+1)(2n+1)}{6}$

36. $1^3 + 2^3 + 3^3 + \cdots + n^3 = \dfrac{n^2(n+1)^2}{4}$

37. PROVING A THEOREM Write a paragraph proof of the Polygon Interior Angles Theorem for the case when $n = 5$.

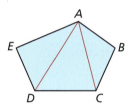

38. PROVING COROLLARY 7.1 Write a paragraph proof of the Corollary to the Polygon Interior Angles Theorem.

39. SMP.2 CONNECT CONCEPTS The formula for the measure of each interior angle in a regular polygon can be written in function notation.

  a. Write a function h that represents the measure of any interior angle in a regular polygon with n sides.

  b. Find $h(9)$. Then find n when $h(n) = 150°$.

  c. Plot the points for $n = 3, 4, 5, 6, 7,$ and 8. What happens to $h(n)$ as n gets larger?

40. SMP.1 DIG DEEPER Write an expression to find the sum of the measures of the interior angles for a concave polygon. Explain how you know your expression is correct.

41. For a concave polygon, is it true that at least one of the interior angle measures must be greater than 180°? If not, give an example. If so, explain your reasoning.

42. PROVING THEOREM 7.2 Write a paragraph proof of the Polygon Exterior Angles Theorem.

43. Polygon $ABCDEFGH$ is a regular octagon. The line containing $\overline{AB}$ intersects the line containing $\overline{CD}$ at point P. Find $m\angle BPC$.

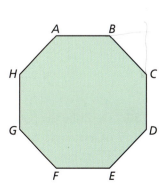

Interpreting Data

COLUMNAR JOINTING Columnar jointing is a geological feature where sets of fractures, referred to as joints, result in the formation of a regular array of polygonal prisms.

44. Describe the type of polygon shown in the photographs. Do any of them appear to be regular?

45. Find the sum of the interior angle measures of the polygon(s) described in Exercise 44.

46. Why does columnar jointing take place? Is it common?

Review & Refresh

Find the value of x.

47.

48.

49. Which is greater, $m\angle 1$ or $m\angle 2$?

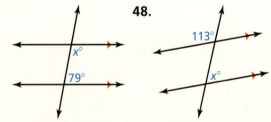

50. Describe the possible lengths of the third side of a triangle with side lengths of 4 inches and 17 inches.

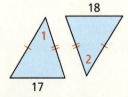

51. Write an equation of the line that passes through (3, −4) and is perpendicular to $y = \frac{1}{2}x + 7$.

52. $\overline{DE}$ is the midsegment of $\triangle ABC$. Find the value of x.

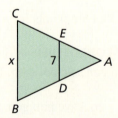

53. Factor $x^2 + 4x - 21$.

54. Find the measure of the exterior angle.

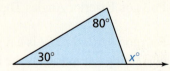

7.2 Properties of Parallelograms

Learning Target: Prove and use properties of parallelograms.

Success Criteria:
- I can use properties of parallelograms.
- I can prove properties of parallelograms.
- I can solve problems involving parallelograms in the coordinate plane.

INVESTIGATE   Discovering Properties of Parallelograms

Work with a partner. A *parallelogram* is a quadrilateral with both pairs of opposite sides parallel.

1. Use technology to construct any parallelogram. Explain your process.

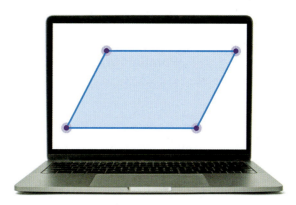

2. Find the angle measures and side lengths of the parallelogram. What do you observe?

3. Repeat Exercises 1 and 2 for several other parallelograms. Use your results to make conjectures about the angle measures and side lengths of a parallelogram. Explain how to prove your conjectures.

4. Use technology to draw the diagonals of any parallelogram. Make a conjecture about any parallelogram that involves its diagonals. Provide examples to support your reasoning.

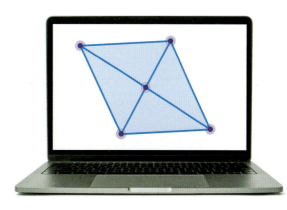

Vocabulary
parallelogram

Using Properties of Parallelograms

A **parallelogram** is a quadrilateral with both pairs of opposite sides parallel. In ▱PQRS, $\overline{PQ} \parallel \overline{RS}$ and $\overline{QR} \parallel \overline{PS}$ by definition.

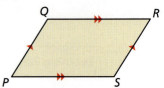

Theorem 7.3

Parallelogram Opposite Sides Theorem

If a quadrilateral is a parallelogram, then its opposite sides are congruent.

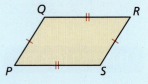

If PQRS is a parallelogram, then $\overline{PQ} \cong \overline{RS}$ and $\overline{QR} \cong \overline{SP}$.

Proof Available online

Theorem 7.4

Parallelogram Opposite Angles Theorem

If a quadrilateral is a parallelogram, then its opposite angles are congruent.

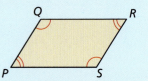

If PQRS is a parallelogram, then $\angle P \cong \angle R$ and $\angle Q \cong \angle S$.

Prove this Theorem Exercise 18, page 361

EXAMPLE 1 Using Properties of Parallelograms

Find the values of x and y.

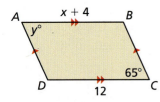

ABCD is a parallelogram by the definition of a parallelogram. Use the Parallelogram Opposite Sides Theorem to find the value of x.

$AB = CD$	Opposite sides of a parallelogram are congruent.
$x + 4 = 12$	Substitute $x + 4$ for AB and 12 for CD.
$x = 8$	Subtract 4 from each side.

By the Parallelogram Opposite Angles Theorem, $\angle A \cong \angle C$, or $m\angle A = m\angle C$. So, $y° = 65°$.

▶ In ▱ABCD, $x = 8$ and $y = 65$.

In-Class Practice

Self-Assessment

1. Find the values of x and y.

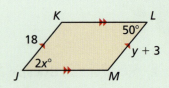

Theorem 7.5

Parallelogram Consecutive Angles Theorem

If a quadrilateral is a parallelogram, then its consecutive angles are supplementary.

If *PQRS* is a parallelogram, then $x° + y° = 180°$.

Prove this Theorem Exercise 19, page 361

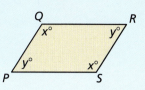

Theorem 7.6

Parallelogram Diagonals Theorem

If a quadrilateral is a parallelogram, then its diagonals bisect each other.

If *PQRS* is a parallelogram, then $\overline{QM} \cong \overline{SM}$ and $\overline{PM} \cong \overline{RM}$.

Proof page 358
Prove this Theorem Exercise 20, page 361

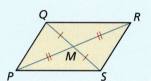

EXAMPLE 2 Using Properties of a Parallelogram

As shown, part of the extending arm of a desk lamp is a parallelogram. The angles of the parallelogram change as the lamp is raised and lowered. Find $m\angle C$ when $m\angle D = 110°$.

By the Parallelogram Consecutive Angles Theorem, the consecutive angle pairs in ▱*ABCD* are supplementary. So, $m\angle D + m\angle C = 180°$. Because $m\angle D = 110°$, $m\angle C = 180° - 110° = 70°$.

In-Class Practice
Self-Assessment

2. **WHAT IF?** In Example 2, find $m\angle C$ when $m\angle D$ is twice the measure of $\angle C$.

| 1 I don't understand yet. | 2 I can do it with help. | 3 I can do it on my own. | 4 I can teach someone. |

7.2   Properties of Parallelograms

PROOF: PARALLELOGRAM DIAGONALS THEOREM

Given $PQRS$ is a parallelogram. Diagonals $\overline{PR}$ and $\overline{QS}$ intersect at point M.

Prove M bisects $\overline{QS}$ and $\overline{PR}$.

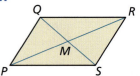

STATEMENTS	REASONS
1. $PQRS$ is a parallelogram.	1. Given
2. $\overline{PQ} \parallel \overline{RS}$	2. Definition of a parallelogram
3. $\angle QPR \cong \angle SRP$, $\angle PQS \cong \angle RSQ$	3. Alternate Interior Angles Theorem
4. $\overline{PQ} \cong \overline{RS}$	4. Parallelogram Opposite Sides Theorem
5. $\triangle PMQ \cong \triangle RMS$	5. ASA Congruence Theorem
6. $\overline{QM} \cong \overline{SM}$, $\overline{PM} \cong \overline{RM}$	6. Corresponding parts of congruent triangles are congruent.
7. M bisects $\overline{QS}$ and $\overline{PR}$.	7. Definition of segment bisector

EXAMPLE 3 Writing a Two-Column Proof

Write a two-column proof.

Given $ABCD$ and $GDEF$ are parallelograms.

Prove $\angle B \cong \angle F$

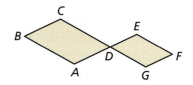

STATEMENTS	REASONS
1. $ABCD$ and $GDEF$ are parallelograms.	1. Given
2. $\angle CDA \cong \angle B$, $\angle EDG \cong \angle F$	2. Parallelogram Opposite Angles Theorem
3. $\angle CDA \cong \angle EDG$	3. Vertical Angles Congruence Theorem
4. $\angle B \cong \angle F$	4. Transitive Property of Angle Congruence

In-Class Practice

Self-Assessment

3. Using the figure and the given statement in Example 3, prove that $\angle C$ and $\angle F$ are supplementary angles.

Using Parallelograms in the Coordinate Plane

EXAMPLE 4 Using Parallelograms in the Coordinate Plane

Find the coordinates of the intersection of the diagonals of ▱LMNO with vertices L(1, 4), M(7, 4), N(6, 0), and O(0, 0).

By the Parallelogram Diagonals Theorem, the diagonals of a parallelogram bisect each other. So, the coordinates of the intersection are the midpoints of diagonals $\overline{LN}$ and $\overline{OM}$. You can use either diagonal to find the coordinates of the intersection. Use $\overline{OM}$ to simplify the calculation because one endpoint is (0, 0).

coordinates of midpoint of $\overline{OM} = \left(\dfrac{7+0}{2}, \dfrac{4+0}{2}\right) = \left(\dfrac{7}{2}, 2\right)$ **Midpoint Formula**

▶ The coordinates of the intersection of the diagonals are $\left(\dfrac{7}{2}, 2\right)$.

EXAMPLE 5 Using Parallelograms in the Coordinate Plane

Three vertices of ▱WXYZ are W(−1, −3), X(−3, 2), and Z(4, −4). Find the coordinates of vertex Y.

Graph the vertices W, X, and Z.

Find the slope of $\overline{WX}$.

$$\text{slope of } \overline{WX} = \dfrac{2-(-3)}{-3-(-1)} = \dfrac{5}{-2}$$

Start at Z(4, −4). Use the rise and run to find vertex Y.

A rise of 5 represents a change of 5 units up. A run of −2 represents a change of 2 units left. So, plot the point that is 5 units up and 2 units left from Z(4, −4). The point is (2, 1). Label it as vertex Y.

▶ So, the coordinates of vertex Y are (2, 1).

Check Find the slopes of $\overline{XY}$ and $\overline{WZ}$ to verify that they are parallel.

slope of $\overline{XY} = \dfrac{1-2}{2-(-3)} = \dfrac{-1}{5} = -\dfrac{1}{5}$ slope of $\overline{WZ} = \dfrac{-4-(-3)}{4-(-1)} = \dfrac{-1}{5} = -\dfrac{1}{5}$

In-Class Practice
Self-Assessment

4. Find the coordinates of the intersection of the diagonals of ▱STUV with vertices S(−2, 3), T(1, 5), U(6, 3), and V(3, 1).

5. Three vertices of ▱ABCD are A(2, 4), B(5, 2), and C(3, −1). Find the coordinates of vertex D.

  I don't understand yet.   2 I can do it with help.   3 I can do it on my own.   4 I can teach someone.

7.2 Practice

Find the value of each variable in the parallelogram. (See Example 1.)

1.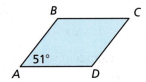

2.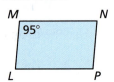

Find the measure of the indicated angle in the parallelogram. (See Example 2.)

3. Find $m\angle B$.

4. Find $m\angle N$.

SMP.3 ERROR ANALYSIS Describe and correct the error in using properties of parallelograms.

5.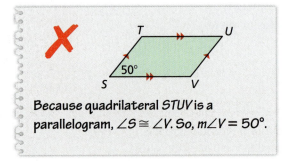

6.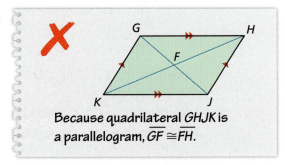

PROOF Write a two-column proof. (See Example 3.)

7. Given $ABCD$ and $CEFD$ are parallelograms.

   Prove $\overline{AB} \cong \overline{FE}$

   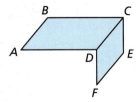

8. Given $ABCD$, $EBGF$, and $HJKD$ are parallelograms.

   Prove $\angle 2 \cong \angle 3$

   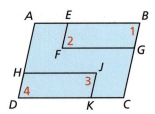

Find the coordinates of the intersection of the diagonals of the parallelogram with the given vertices. (See Example 4.)

9. $W(-2, 5)$, $X(2, 5)$, $Y(4, 0)$, $Z(0, 0)$

10. $Q(-1, 3)$, $R(5, 2)$, $S(1, -2)$, $T(-5, -1)$

Three vertices of $\square DEFG$ are given. Find the coordinates of the remaining vertex. (See Example 5.)

11. $D(0, 2)$, $E(-1, 5)$, $G(4, 0)$

12. $D(-2, -4)$, $F(0, 7)$, $G(1, 0)$

13. $D(-4, -2)$, $E(-3, 1)$, $F(3, 3)$

14. $E(-1, 4)$, $F(5, 6)$, $G(8, 0)$

Find the measure of each angle.

15. The measure of one interior angle of a parallelogram is 0.25 times the measure of another angle.

16. The measure of one interior angle of a parallelogram is 50° more than 4 times the measure of another angle.

17. **ASTROBIOLOGY** **BINOCULARS** Part of the mount for the pair of astronomy binoculars shown is a parallelogram. The angles of the parallelogram change as the mount is adjusted. Find $m\angle R$, $m\angle S$, and $m\angle T$ when $m\angle Q = 66°$.

PROVING A THEOREM Use the diagram to write a two-column proof of the theorem.

18. Parallelogram Opposite Angles Theorem.

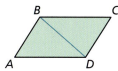

Given ABCD is a parallelogram.

Prove $\angle A \cong \angle C$, $\angle B \cong \angle D$

19. Parallelogram Consecutive Angles Theorem

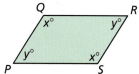

Given PQRS is a parallelogram.

Prove $x° + y° = 180°$

20. **PROVING THEOREM 7.6** WXYZ is a parallelogram. Diagonals $\overline{WY}$ and $\overline{XZ}$ intersect at point V. Write a paragraph proof of the Parallelogram Diagonals Theorem.

21. **SMP.7** In ▱LMNP, the ratio of LM to MN is 4 : 3. Find LM when the perimeter of ▱LMNP is 28.

22. **SMP.7** Points (1, 2), (3, 6), and (6, 4) are three vertices of a parallelogram. How many parallelograms can be created using these three vertices? Find the coordinates of each point that could be the fourth vertex.

23. **CONNECT CONCEPTS** In ▱STUV, $m\angle TSU = 32°$, $m\angle USV = (x^2)°$, $m\angle TUV = 12x°$, and $\angle TUV$ is an acute angle. Find $m\angle USV$.

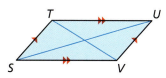

24. **PROOF** Prove the *Congruent Parts of Parallel Lines Corollary:* If three or more parallel lines cut off congruent segments on one transversal, then they cut off congruent segments on every transversal.

Given $\overleftrightarrow{GH} \parallel \overleftrightarrow{JK} \parallel \overleftrightarrow{LM}, \overline{GJ} \cong \overline{JL}$

Prove $\overline{HK} \cong \overline{KM}$

(*Hint:* Draw $\overline{KP}$ and $\overline{MQ}$ such that quadrilateral GPKJ and quadrilateral JQML are parallelograms.)

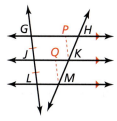

7.2 Properties of Parallelograms 361

Interpreting Data

PARALLELOGRAM OFFICE The architectural firm Bothe Richter Teherani designed an office building in Hamburg, Germany. The front of the building has a base of 123 meters and a height of 23 meters. The building won the Leaf Award for Best Structural Design in 2005.

25. Describe how to estimate the area of the front of the building.

26. Trace the front of the building, including any beams that are parallel to the sides. How many parallelograms do you see?

27. Describe other geometric figures that an architect could use when designing a building.

Review & Refresh

28. List the sides of △DEF in order from shortest to longest.

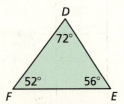

29. Find the value of x.

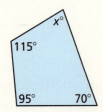

30. The coordinates of a point and its image after a reflection are shown. What is the line of reflection?

$$(7, -5) \rightarrow (-7, -5)$$

31. Decide whether there is enough information to prove that $\ell \parallel m$. If so, state the theorem you can use.

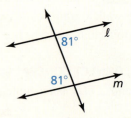

32. The path from E to F is longer than the path from E to D. The path from G to D is the same length as the path from G to F. What can you conclude about $\angle DGE$ and $\angle EGF$?

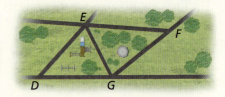

7.3 Proving That a Quadrilateral Is a Parallelogram

Learning Target: Prove that a quadrilateral is a parallelogram.

Success Criteria:
- I can prove that a quadrilateral is a parallelogram.
- I can find missing measures that make a quadrilateral a parallelogram.
- I can show that a quadrilateral in the coordinate plane is a parallelogram.

INVESTIGATE Proving That a Quadrilateral Is a Parallelogram

Work with a partner. Use technology.

1. Construct any quadrilateral whose opposite sides are congruent. Is the quadrilateral a parallelogram? Explain how you know.

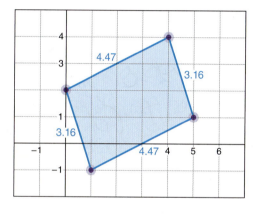

2. Repeat Exercise 1 for several other quadrilaterals. Make a conjecture based on your results.

3. Write the converse of your conjecture. Is the converse true? Explain.

4. Construct any quadrilateral whose opposite angles are congruent. Is the quadrilateral a parallelogram? Explain how you know.

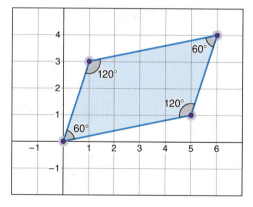

5. Repeat Exercise 4 for several other quadrilaterals. Make a conjecture based on your results.

6. Write the converse of your conjecture in Exercise 5. Is the converse true? Explain.

7. Use congruent triangles to prove that *ABCD* is a parallelogram.

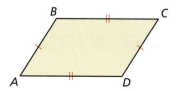

Identifying and Verifying Parallelograms

Theorem 7.7

Parallelogram Opposite Sides Converse

If both pairs of opposite sides of a quadrilateral are congruent, then the quadrilateral is a parallelogram.

If $\overline{AB} \cong \overline{CD}$ and $\overline{BC} \cong \overline{DA}$, then ABCD is a parallelogram.

Prove this Theorem Investigate Exercise 1, page 363

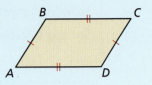

Theorem 7.8

Parallelogram Opposite Angles Converse

If both pairs of opposite angles of a quadrilateral are congruent, then the quadrilateral is a parallelogram.

If $\angle A \cong \angle C$ and $\angle B \cong \angle D$, then ABCD is a parallelogram.

Prove this Theorem Exercise 24, page 371

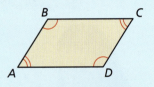

PROOF PARALLELOGRAM OPPOSITE SIDES CONVERSE

Given $\overline{AB} \cong \overline{CD}, \overline{BC} \cong \overline{DA}$

Prove ABCD is a parallelogram.

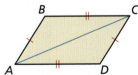

STATEMENTS	REASONS
1. $\overline{AB} \cong \overline{CD}, \overline{BC} \cong \overline{DA}$	1. Given
2. Draw $\overline{AC}$.	2. Through any two points, there exists exactly one line.
3. $\overline{AC} \cong \overline{CA}$	3. Reflexive Property of Segment Congruence
4. $\triangle ABC \cong \triangle CDA$	4. SSS Congruence Theorem
5. $\angle BAC \cong \angle DCA$, $\angle BCA \cong \angle DAC$	5. Corresponding parts of congruent triangles are congruent.
6. $\overline{AB} \parallel \overline{CD}, \overline{BC} \parallel \overline{DA}$	6. Alternate Interior Angles Converse
7. ABCD is a parallelogram.	7. Definition of parallelogram

EXAMPLE 1 Identifying a Parallelogram

An amusement park ride has a moving platform attached to four swinging arms. In the diagram, $\overline{AD}$ and $\overline{BC}$ represent two of the swinging arms, and $\overline{DC}$ is parallel to the ground (line ℓ). Explain why the moving platform represented by $\overline{AB}$ is always parallel to the ground.

Both pairs of opposite sides are congruent, so $ABCD$ is a parallelogram by the Parallelogram Opposite Sides Converse.

By the definition of a parallelogram, $\overline{AB} \parallel \overline{DC}$. Because $\overline{DC}$ is parallel to line ℓ, $\overline{AB}$ is also parallel to line ℓ by the Transitive Property of Parallel Lines. So, the moving platform is parallel to the ground.

EXAMPLE 2 Finding Side Lengths of a Parallelogram

For what values of x and y is quadrilateral $PQRS$ a parallelogram?

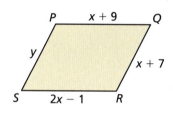

By the Parallelogram Opposite Sides Converse, if both pairs of opposite sides of a quadrilateral are congruent, then the quadrilateral is a parallelogram. Find x so that $\overline{PQ} \cong \overline{SR}$.

$PQ = SR$	Set the segment lengths equal.
$x + 9 = 2x - 1$	Substitute $x + 9$ for PQ and $2x - 1$ for SR.
$10 = x$	Solve for x.

When $x = 10$, $PQ = 10 + 9 = 19$ and $SR = 2(10) - 1 = 19$. Find y so that $\overline{PS} \cong \overline{QR}$.

$PS = QR$	Set the segment lengths equal.
$y = x + 7$	Substitute y for PS and $x + 7$ for QR.
$y = 10 + 7$	Substitute 10 for x.
$y = 17$	Add.

When $x = 10$ and $y = 17$, $PS = 17$ and $QR = 10 + 7 = 17$.

▶ Quadrilateral $PQRS$ is a parallelogram when $x = 10$ and $y = 17$.

In-Class Practice

Self-Assessment

1. In quadrilateral $WXYZ$, $m\angle W = 42°$, $m\angle X = 138°$, and $m\angle Y = 42°$. Find $m\angle Z$. Explain whether $WXYZ$ a parallelogram.

2. For what values of x and y is quadrilateral $ABCD$ a parallelogram?

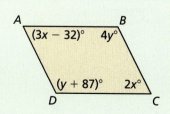

 I don't understand yet.
 I can do it with help.
 I can do it on my own.
 I can teach someone.

Theorem 7.9

Opposite Sides Parallel and Congruent Theorem

If one pair of opposite sides of a quadrilateral are parallel and congruent, then the quadrilateral is a parallelogram.

If $\overline{BC} \parallel \overline{AD}$ and $\overline{BC} \cong \overline{AD}$, then $ABCD$ is a parallelogram.

Prove this Theorem Exercise 25, page 371

Theorem 7.10

Parallelogram Diagonals Converse

If the diagonals of a quadrilateral bisect each other, then the quadrilateral is a parallelogram.

If $\overline{BD}$ and $\overline{AC}$ bisect each other, then $ABCD$ is a parallelogram.

Prove this Theorem Exercise 26, page 371

EXAMPLE 3 Identifying a Parallelogram

The door shown is installed in a building that has leaned sideways over time. Explain how you know that $SV = TU$.

In the photograph, $\overline{ST} \parallel \overline{UV}$ and $\overline{ST} \cong \overline{UV}$. By the Opposite Sides Parallel and Congruent Theorem, quadrilateral $STUV$ is a parallelogram. By the Parallelogram Opposite Sides Theorem, you know that opposite sides of a parallelogram are congruent.

▶ So, $SV = TU$.

In-Class Practice
Self-Assessment

State the theorem you can use to show that the quadrilateral is a parallelogram.

3.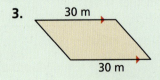

4.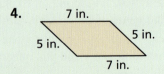

5.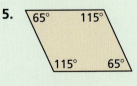

 I don't understand yet.
 I can do it with help.
 I can do it on my own.
 I can teach someone.

366 Chapter 7 Quadrilaterals and Other Polygons

Concept Summary

Ways to Prove a Quadrilateral Is a Parallelogram

1. Show that both pairs of opposite sides are parallel. (*Definition*)

2. Show that both pairs of opposite sides are congruent. (*Parallelogram Opposite Sides Converse*)

3. Show that both pairs of opposite angles are congruent. (*Parallelogram Opposite Angles Converse*)

4. Show that one pair of opposite sides are parallel and congruent. (*Opposite Sides Parallel and Congruent Theorem*)

5. Show that the diagonals bisect each other. (*Parallelogram Diagonals Converse*)

EXAMPLE 4 Finding Diagonal Lengths of a Parallelogram

For what value of x is quadrilateral $CDEF$ a parallelogram?

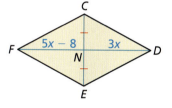

By the Parallelogram Diagonals Converse, if the diagonals of $CDEF$ bisect each other, then it is a parallelogram. You are given that $\overline{CN} \cong \overline{EN}$. Find x so that $\overline{FN} \cong \overline{DN}$.

$FN = DN$	Set the segment lengths equal.
$5x - 8 = 3x$	Substitute $5x - 8$ for FN and $3x$ for DN.
$-8 = -2x$	Subtract $5x$ from each side.
$4 = x$	Divide each side by -2.

When $x = 4$, $FN = 5(4) - 8 = 12$ and $DN = 3(4) = 12$.

▶ Quadrilateral $CDEF$ is a parallelogram when $x = 4$.

In-Class Practice

Self-Assessment

6. For what value of x is quadrilateral $MNPQ$ a parallelogram? Explain your reasoning.

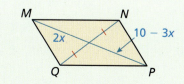

Using Coordinate Geometry

EXAMPLE 5 Identifying a Parallelogram in the Coordinate Plane

Show that quadrilateral ABCD is a parallelogram.

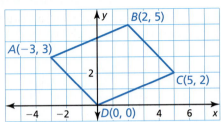

Method 1 Show that a pair of sides are parallel and congruent. Then apply the Opposite Sides Parallel and Congruent Theorem.

First, use the slope formula to show that $\overline{AB} \parallel \overline{CD}$.

$$\text{slope of } \overline{AB} = \frac{5-3}{2-(-3)} = \frac{2}{5} \qquad \text{slope of } \overline{CD} = \frac{2-0}{5-0} = \frac{2}{5}$$

Because $\overline{AB}$ and $\overline{CD}$ have the same slope, they are parallel.

Then use the Distance Formula to show that $\overline{AB}$ and $\overline{CD}$ are congruent.

$$AB = \sqrt{[2-(-3)]^2 + (5-3)^2} = \sqrt{29}$$
$$CD = \sqrt{(5-0)^2 + (2-0)^2} = \sqrt{29}$$

Because $AB = CD = \sqrt{29}$, $\overline{AB} \cong \overline{CD}$.

▶ $\overline{AB}$ and $\overline{CD}$ are parallel and congruent. So, ABCD is a parallelogram by the Opposite Sides Parallel and Congruent Theorem.

Method 2 Show that opposite sides are congruent. Then apply the Parallelogram Opposite Sides Converse. In Method 1, you already have shown that because $AB = CD = \sqrt{29}$, $\overline{AB} \cong \overline{CD}$. Now find AD and BC.

$$AD = \sqrt{(-3-0)^2 + (3-0)^2} = 3\sqrt{2}$$
$$BC = \sqrt{(2-5)^2 + (5-2)^2} = 3\sqrt{2}$$

Because $AD = BC = 3\sqrt{2}$, $\overline{AD} \cong \overline{BC}$.

▶ $\overline{AB} \cong \overline{CD}$ and $\overline{AD} \cong \overline{BC}$. So, ABCD is a parallelogram by the Parallelogram Opposite Sides Converse.

In-Class Practice

Self-Assessment

7. Show that quadrilateral JKLM is a parallelogram.

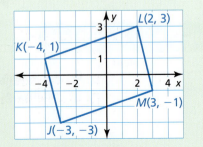

| **1** I don't understand yet. | **2** I can do it with help. | **3** I can do it on my own. | **4** I can teach someone. |

Chapter 7 Quadrilaterals and Other Polygons

7.3 Practice

State which theorem you can use to show that the quadrilateral is a parallelogram. (See Examples 1 and 3.)

1.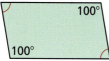

2.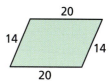

3.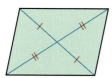

4.

Find the values of x and y that make the quadrilateral a parallelogram. (See Example 2.)

5.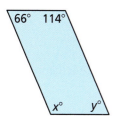

6.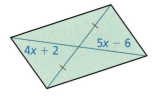

Find the value of x that makes the quadrilateral a parallelogram. (See Example 4.)

7.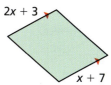

8.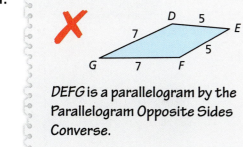

Show that the quadrilateral is a parallelogram. (See Example 5.)

9. $A(0, 1)$, $B(4, 4)$, $C(12, 4)$, $D(8, 1)$

10. $E(-3, 0)$, $F(-3, 4)$, $G(3, -1)$, $H(3, -5)$

SMP.3 ERROR ANALYSIS Describe and correct the error in identifying a parallelogram.

11.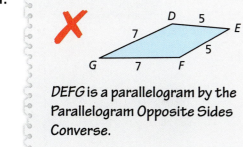

12.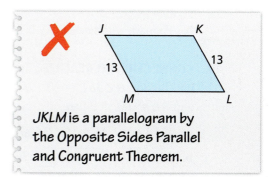

7.3 Proving That a Quadrilateral Is a Parallelogram

13. **SMP.7** Find the value of *x* that makes the quadrilateral a parallelogram.

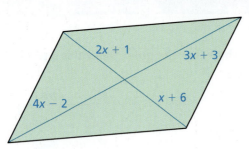

14. **CONNECT CONCEPTS** Find the value of *x* such that the quadrilateral is a parallelogram. Then find the perimeter of the parallelogram.

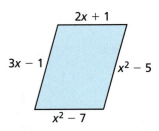

Write the indicated theorems as a biconditional statement.

15. Parallelogram Opposite Sides Theorem and Parallelogram Opposite Sides Converse

16. Parallelogram Diagonals Theorem and Parallelogram Diagonals Converse

17. **CONSTRUCTION** Follow the steps below to construct a parallelogram. Use a theorem to explain why this method works.

    Use a ruler to draw two segments that intersect at their midpoints.

    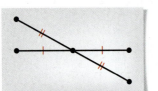

    Then connect the endpoints of the segments to form a parallelogram.

    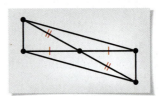

18. **CONNECTION TO REAL LIFE** You shoot a pool ball, and it rolls back to where it started, as shown in the diagram. The ball bounces off each wall at the same angle at which it hits the wall. The ball hits the first wall at an angle of 63°. So, $m\angle AEF = 63°$.

    a. Find $m\angle AFE$.

    b. Explain whether *EFGH* is a parallelogram.

    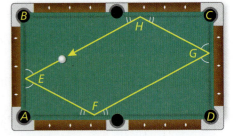

19. **CONNECTION TO REAL LIFE** In the diagram of the parking lot, $m\angle JKL = 60°$, $JK = LM = 21$ feet, and $KL = JM = 9$ feet.

    a. Find $m\angle JML$, $m\angle KJM$, and $m\angle KLM$.

    b. $\overline{LM} \parallel \overline{NO}$ and $\overline{NO} \parallel \overline{PQ}$. Which theorem can you use to show that $\overline{JK} \parallel \overline{PQ}$?

370   Chapter 7   Quadrilaterals and Other Polygons

Describe how to prove that *ABCD* is a parallelogram.

20.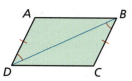

21.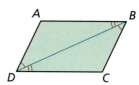

22.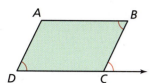

23.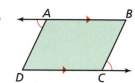

24. **PROVING THEOREM 7.8** Parallelogram Opposite Angles Converse

    Given $\angle A \cong \angle C, \angle B \cong \angle D$

    Prove *ABCD* is a parallelogram.

    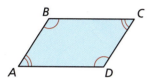

25. **PROVING THEOREM 7.9** Opposite Sides Parallel and Congruent Theorem

    Given $\overline{QR} \parallel \overline{PS}, \overline{QR} \cong \overline{PS}$

    Prove *PQRS* is a parallelogram.

    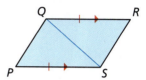

26. **PROVING THEOREM 7.10** Parallelogram Diagonals Converse

    Given Diagonals $\overline{JL}$ and $\overline{KM}$ bisect each other.

    Prove *JKLM* is a parallelogram.

    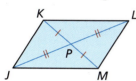

27. **PROOF** Write a proof.

    Given *DEBF* is a parallelogram. $AE = CF$

    Prove *ABCD* is a parallelogram.

    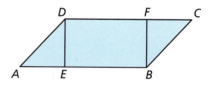

28. In the diagram, *ABCD* is a parallelogram, $BF = DE = 12$, and $CF = 8$. Find *AE*.

    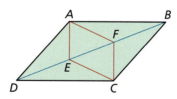

29. **SMP.6** Show that if *ABCD* is a parallelogram with its diagonals intersecting at *E*, then you can connect the midpoints *F*, *G*, *H*, and *J* of $\overline{AE}, \overline{BE}, \overline{CE},$ and $\overline{DE}$, respectively, to form another parallelogram, *FGHJ*.

    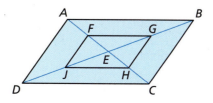

7.3 Proving That a Quadrilateral Is a Parallelogram

Interpreting Data

PARALLELOGRAM LAW OF FORCES The parallelogram law of forces states that if two forces acting simultaneously on an object are represented in magnitude and direction by the adjacent sides of a parallelogram, then their resultant force can be represented in magnitude and direction by the diagonal of the parallelogram which passes through their point of intersection.

30. Draw the resultant force indicated by the drawing.

31. Estimate the number of pounds of the resultant force.

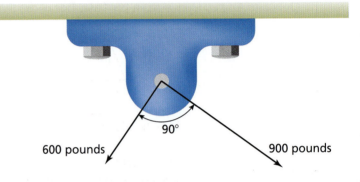

Review & Refresh

△XYZ ≅ △MNL. **Complete the statement.**

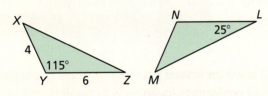

32. $m\angle M =$ _____   33. $MN =$ _____

34. Find the value of x.

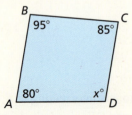

35. Find the distance between $A(4, 2)$ and $B(7, 11)$.

36. Three vertices of ▱DEFG are $D(1, 1)$, $E(5, 2)$, and $F(1, 8)$. Find the coordinates of the remaining vertex.

37. Graph the triangle with vertices $X(2, -2)$, $Y(-4, -6)$, and $Z(0, 8)$ and its image in the coordinate plane after a dilation with scale factor $k = 0.5$.

38. Find the value of x.

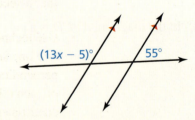

39. Complete the statement AD _____ CD with < or >.

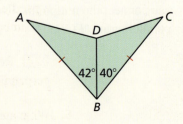

7.4 Properties of Special Parallelograms

Learning Target: Explain the properties of special parallelograms.

Success Criteria:
- I can explain how special parallelograms are related.
- I can identify special quadrilaterals.
- I can find missing measures of special parallelograms.
- I can identify special parallelograms in a coordinate plane.

INVESTIGATE Analyzing Diagonals of Quadrilaterals

Work with a partner. Recall the three types of parallelograms shown below.

Rhombus Rectangle Square

1. Use the diagrams to define each type of quadrilateral.

2. Use technology to construct two congruent line segments that bisect each other. Draw a quadrilateral by connecting the endpoints.

3. Is the quadrilateral you drew a parallelogram? a rectangle? a rhombus? a square?

4. **SMP.8** Repeat Exercises 2 and 3 for several pairs of congruent line segments that bisect each other. Make conjectures based on your results.

5. Use technology to construct two line segments that are perpendicular bisectors of each other. Draw a quadrilateral by connecting the endpoints.

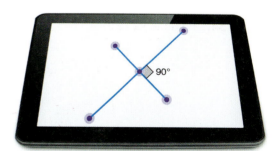

6. Is the quadrilateral you drew a parallelogram? a rectangle? a rhombus? a square?

7. **SMP.8** Repeat Exercises 5 and 6 for several other line segments that are perpendicular bisectors of each other. Make conjectures based on your results.

8. What are some properties of the diagonals of rectangles, rhombuses, and squares?

Vocabulary
rhombus
rectangle
square

Using Properties of Special Parallelograms

Key Concept

Rhombuses, Rectangles, and Squares

A **rhombus** is a parallelogram with four congruent sides.

A **rectangle** is a parallelogram with four right angles.

A **square** is a parallelogram with four congruent sides and four right angles.

The Venn diagram illustrates some important relationships among parallelograms, rhombuses, rectangles, and squares.

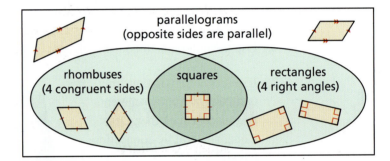

EXAMPLE 1 Using Properties of Special Quadrilaterals

For any rhombus $QRST$, decide whether the statement is *always* or *sometimes* true. Draw a diagram and explain your reasoning.

a. $\angle Q \cong \angle S$

By definition, a rhombus is a parallelogram with four congruent sides. By the Parallelogram Opposite Angles Theorem, opposite angles of a parallelogram are congruent. So, $\angle Q \cong \angle S$. The statement is *always* true.

b. $\angle Q \cong \angle R$

If rhombus $QRST$ is a square, then all four angles are congruent right angles. So, $\angle Q \cong \angle R$ when $QRST$ is a square. Because not all rhombuses are also squares, the statement is *sometimes* true.

In-Class Practice

Self-Assessment

1. For any square $JKLM$, explain whether it is *always* or *sometimes* true that $\overline{JK} \perp \overline{KL}$.

  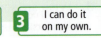

Corollary 7.2

Rhombus Corollary

A quadrilateral is a rhombus if and only if it has four congruent sides.

$ABCD$ is a rhombus if and only if $\overline{AB} \cong \overline{BC} \cong \overline{CD} \cong \overline{AD}$.

Prove this Corollary Exercise 51, page 381

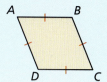

Corollary 7.3

Rectangle Corollary

A quadrilateral is a rectangle if and only if it has four right angles.

$ABCD$ is a rectangle if and only if $\angle A$, $\angle B$, $\angle C$, and $\angle D$ are right angles.

Prove this Corollary Exercise 52, page 381

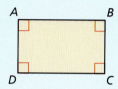

Corollary 7.4

Square Corollary

A quadrilateral is a square if and only if it is a rhombus and a rectangle.

$ABCD$ is a square if and only if $\overline{AB} \cong \overline{BC} \cong \overline{CD} \cong \overline{AD}$ and $\angle A$, $\angle B$, $\angle C$, and $\angle D$ are right angles.

Prove this Corollary Exercise 53, page 381

EXAMPLE 2 — Classifying Special Quadrilaterals

Classify the special quadrilateral.

The quadrilateral has four congruent sides. By the Rhombus Corollary, the quadrilateral is a rhombus. Because one of the angles is not a right angle, the rhombus cannot be a square.

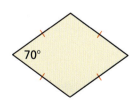

In-Class Practice

Self-Assessment

2. A quadrilateral has four congruent sides and three angles that measure 90°. Sketch the quadrilateral and classify it.

Using Properties of Diagonals

Theorems 7.11

Rhombus Diagonals Theorem

A parallelogram is a rhombus if and only if its diagonals are perpendicular.

▱ABCD is a rhombus if and only if $\overline{AC} \perp \overline{BD}$.

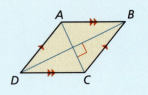

Proof Available online
Prove this Theorem Exercise 48, page 381

Theorems 7.12

Rhombus Opposite Angles Theorem

A parallelogram is a rhombus if and only if each diagonal bisects a pair of opposite angles.

▱ABCD is a rhombus if and only if
$\overline{AC}$ bisects ∠BCD and ∠BAD, and
$\overline{BD}$ bisects ∠ABC and ∠ADC.

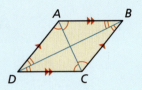

Prove this Theorem Exercises 49 and 50, page 381

EXAMPLE 3 Finding Angle Measures in a Rhombus

Find the measures of the numbered angles in rhombus ABCD.

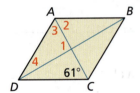

Use the Rhombus Diagonals Theorem and the Rhombus Opposite Angles Theorem to find the angle measures.

$m\angle 1 = 90°$	The diagonals of a rhombus are perpendicular.
$m\angle 2 = 61°$	Alternate Interior Angles Theorem
$m\angle 3 = 61°$	Each diagonal of a rhombus bisects a pair of opposite angles, and $m\angle 2 = 61°$.
$m\angle 1 + m\angle 3 + m\angle 4 = 180°$	Triangle Sum Theorem
$90° + 61° + m\angle 4 = 180°$	Substitute 90° for $m\angle 1$ and 61° for $m\angle 3$.
$m\angle 4 = 29°$	Solve for $m\angle 4$.

▶ So, $m\angle 1 = 90°$, $m\angle 2 = 61°$, $m\angle 3 = 61°$, and $m\angle 4 = 29°$.

In-Class Practice

Self-Assessment

3. In Example 3, find $m\angle ADC$ and $m\angle BCD$.

4. Find the measures of the numbered angles in rhombus DEFG.

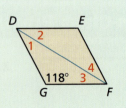

 I don't understand yet.   I can do it with help. 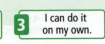 I can do it on my own.   I can teach someone.

Theorem 7.13

Rectangle Diagonals Theorem

A parallelogram is a rectangle if and only if its diagonals are congruent.

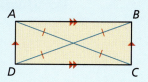

▱ABCD is a rectangle if and only if $\overline{AC} \cong \overline{BD}$.

Prove this Theorem Exercises 59 and 60, page 382

EXAMPLE 4 — Identifying a Rectangle

You are building a frame for a window. The window will be installed in the opening shown in the diagram.

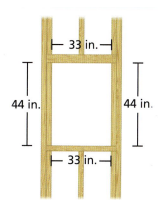

a. The opening must be a rectangle. Given the measurements in the diagram, can you assume that it is?

No, you cannot. Opposite boards are the same length, so they form a parallelogram. But you do not know whether the angles are right angles.

b. You measure the diagonals of the opening. They are 54.8 inches and 55.3 inches. What can you conclude about the shape of the opening?

By the Rectangle Diagonals Theorem, the diagonals of a rectangle are congruent. The diagonals of the quadrilateral formed by the boards are not congruent, so the boards do not form a rectangle.

EXAMPLE 5 — Finding Diagonal Lengths in a Rectangle

In rectangle $QRST$, $QS = 5x - 31$ and $RT = 2x + 11$. Find the lengths of the diagonals of $QRST$.

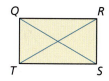

By the Rectangle Diagonals Theorem, the diagonals of a rectangle are congruent. Find x so that $\overline{QS} \cong \overline{RT}$.

$QS = RT$	Set the diagonal lengths equal.
$5x - 31 = 2x + 11$	Substitute $5x - 31$ for QS and $2x + 11$ for RT.
$x = 14$	Simplify.

When $x = 14$, $QS = 5(14) - 31 = 39$ and $RT = 2(14) + 11 = 39$.

▶ Each diagonal has a length of 39 units.

In-Class Practice
Self-Assessment

5. WHAT IF? The diagonals of the window opening in Example 4 have the same measure. Explain whether you can conclude that the opening is a rectangle.

6. In rectangle $WXYZ$, $WY = 4x - 15$ and $XZ = 3x + 8$. Find the lengths of the diagonals of $WXYZ$.

7.4 Properties of Special Parallelograms

Using Coordinate Geometry

EXAMPLE 6 Identifying a Parallelogram in the Coordinate Plane

Decide whether ▱ABCD with vertices $A(-2, 6)$, $B(6, 8)$, $C(4, 0)$, and $D(-4, -2)$ is a *rectangle*, a *rhombus*, or a *square*. Give all names that apply.

Graph the parallelogram.

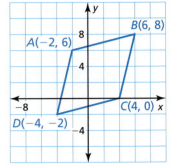

From the graph, it appears that all four sides are congruent and there are no right angles. Check the lengths and slopes of the diagonals of ▱ABCD.

Use the Distance Formula to find AC and BD.

$$AC = \sqrt{(-2-4)^2 + (6-0)^2} = \sqrt{72} = 6\sqrt{2}$$

$$BD = \sqrt{[6-(-4)]^2 + [8-(-2)]^2} = \sqrt{200} = 10\sqrt{2}$$

Because $6\sqrt{2} \neq 10\sqrt{2}$, the diagonals are not congruent. So, ▱ABCD is not a rectangle. Because it is not a rectangle, it also cannot be a square.

Use the slope formula to find the slopes of the diagonals $\overline{AC}$ and $\overline{BD}$.

$$\text{slope of } \overline{AC} = \frac{6-0}{-2-4} = \frac{6}{-6} = -1 \qquad \text{slope of } \overline{BD} = \frac{8-(-2)}{6-(-4)} = \frac{10}{10} = 1$$

Because the product of the slopes of the diagonals is -1, the diagonals are perpendicular.

▶ So, ▱ABCD is a rhombus.

Check Each side of ▱ABCD has a length of $2\sqrt{17}$ units, so ▱ABCD is a rhombus. Check the slopes of two consecutive sides.

$$\text{slope of } \overline{AB} = \frac{8-6}{6-(-2)} = \frac{2}{8} = \frac{1}{4} \qquad \text{slope of } \overline{BC} = \frac{8-0}{6-4} = \frac{8}{2} = 4$$

Because the product of these slopes is not -1, $\overline{AB}$ is not perpendicular to $\overline{BC}$. So, $\angle ABC$ is not a right angle, and ▱ABCD is not a rectangle or a square. ✓

In-Class Practice

Self-Assessment

7. Decide whether ▱PQRS with vertices $P(-5, 2)$, $Q(0, 4)$, $R(2, -1)$, and $S(-3, -3)$ is a *rectangle*, a *rhombus*, or a *square*. Give all names that apply.

1 I don't understand yet. **2** I can do it with help. **3** I can do it on my own. **4** I can teach someone.

7.4 Practice

For any rhombus *JKLM*, decide whether the statement is *always* or *sometimes* true. Draw a diagram and explain your reasoning. (See Example 1.)

1. $\angle L \cong \angle M$
2. $\angle K \cong \angle M$
▶ 3. $\overline{JM} \cong \overline{KL}$
4. $\overline{JL} \cong \overline{KM}$

Classify the quadrilateral. (See Example 2.)

▶ 5.

6.

7.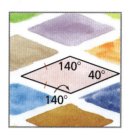

Find the measures of the numbered angles in rhombus *DEFG*. (See Example 3.)

8.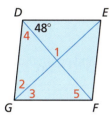

▶ 9.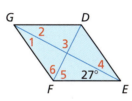

10.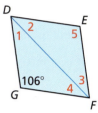

For any rectangle *WXYZ*, decide whether the statement is *always* or *sometimes* true. Draw a diagram and explain your reasoning.

11. $\angle W \cong \angle X$
12. $\overline{WX} \cong \overline{YZ}$
13. $\overline{WX} \cong \overline{XY}$
14. $\overline{WY} \perp \overline{XZ}$

Explain whether the quadrilateral is a rectangle. (See Example 4.)

▶ 15.

16.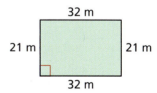

Find the lengths of the diagonals of rectangle *WXYZ*. (See Example 5.)

▶ 17. $WY = 6x - 7$
$XZ = 3x + 2$

18. $WY = 14x + 10$
$XZ = 11x + 22$

19. $WY = 24x - 8$
$XZ = -18x + 13$

20. **SMP.3 ERROR ANALYSIS** Quadrilateral *PQRS* is a rhombus. Describe and correct the error in finding the value of *x*.

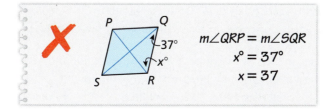

7.4 Properties of Special Parallelograms

The diagonals of rhombus *ABCD* intersect at *E*. Given that *m∠BAC* = 53°, *DE* = 8, and *EC* = 6, find the indicated measure.

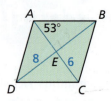

21. *m∠DAC*   **22.** *m∠AED*

23. *DB*   **24.** *AE*

The diagonals of rectangle *QRST* intersect at *P*. Given that *m∠PTS* = 34° and *QS* = 10, find the indicated measure.

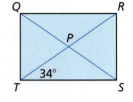

25. *m∠QTR*   **26.** *m∠QRT*

27. *QP*   **28.** *RT*

The diagonals of square *LMNP* intersect at *K*. Given that *LK* = 1, find the indicated measure.

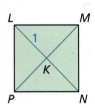

29. *m∠MKN*   **30.** *m∠LMK*

31. *KN*   **32.** *LN*

Name each quadrilateral—*parallelogram*, *rectangle*, *rhombus*, or *square*—for which the statement is always true.

33. It is equiangular.

34. It is equiangular and equilateral.

35. The diagonals are perpendicular.

36. Opposite sides are congruent.

Explain whether ▱*JKLM* is a rectangle, a rhombus, or a square. Give all names that apply. (See Example 6.)

37. *J*(−4, 2), *K*(0, 3), *L*(1, −1), *M*(−3, −2)

38. *J*(−2, 7), *K*(7, 2), *L*(−2, −3), *M*(−11, 2)

39. *J*(3, 1), *K*(3, −3), *L*(−2, −3), *M*(−2, 1)

40. *J*(−1, 4), *K*(−3, 2), *L*(2, −3), *M*(4, −1)

SMP.6 Complete each statement with *always*, *sometimes*, or *never*.

41. A square is _____ a rhombus.

42. A rectangle is _____ a square.

43. The diagonals of a square _____ bisect its angles.

44. A rhombus _____ has four congruent angles.

45. **SMP.5** You want to mark off a square region for chalk art on a sidewalk. You use a tape measure to mark off a quadrilateral. Each side of the quadrilateral is 2.5 meters long. Explain how you can use the tape measure to determine whether the quadrilateral is a square.

46. **CONNECTION TO REAL LIFE** In the window, $\overline{BD} \cong \overline{DF} \cong \overline{BH} \cong \overline{HF}$. Also, ∠*HAB*, ∠*BCD*, ∠*DEF*, and ∠*FGH* are right angles.

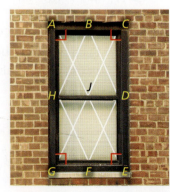

a. Classify *HBDF* and *ACEG*.

b. *BD* = 25 inches and *AE* = 50 inches. What is the total length of the material used to create the white grid on the window?

47. Which quadrilateral can be called a regular quadrilateral?

48. PROVING THEOREM 7.11 Use the plan for proof to write a paragraph proof for one part of the Rhombus Diagonals Theorem.

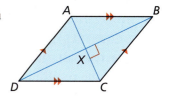

Given ABCD is a parallelogram. $\overline{AC} \perp \overline{BD}$

Prove ABCD is a rhombus.

Plan for Proof Because ABCD is a parallelogram, its diagonals bisect each other at X. Use $\overline{AC} \perp \overline{BD}$ to show that △BXC ≅ △DXC. Then show that $\overline{BC} \cong \overline{DC}$. Use the properties of a parallelogram to show that ABCD is a rhombus.

PROVING THEOREM 7.12 Write a proof for part of the Rhombus Opposite Angles Theorem.

49. Given PQRS is a parallelogram.

$\overline{PR}$ bisects ∠SPQ and ∠QRS.

$\overline{SQ}$ bisects ∠PSR and ∠RQP.

Prove PQRS is a rhombus.

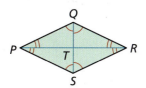

50. Given WXYZ is a rhombus.

Prove $\overline{WY}$ bisects ∠ZWX

$\overline{ZX}$ bisects ∠WZY

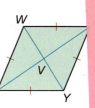

PROVING A COROLLARY Write the corollary as a conditional statement and its converse. Then explain why each statement is true.

51. Rhombus Corollary   **52.** Rectangle Corollary   **53.** Square Corollary

54. Explain whether it is possible for a rhombus to have congruent diagonals.

55. Explain whether (a) all rhombuses are similar and (b) all squares are similar.

56. SMP.7 CONNECT CONCEPTS Explain why every rhombus has at least two lines of symmetry.

57. PROOF Write a proof.

Given △XYZ ≅ △XWZ, ∠XYW ≅ ∠ZWY

Prove WXYZ is a rhombus.

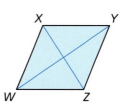

58. SMP.1 DIG DEEPER The length of one diagonal of a rhombus is 4 times the length of the other diagonal. Write an expression that represents the perimeter of the rhombus. Explain what the variable in your expression represents.

PROVING THEOREM 7.13 Write a proof for part of the Rectangle Diagonals Theorem.

59. Given PQRS is a rectangle.

Prove $\overline{PR} \cong \overline{SQ}$

60. Given PQRS is a parallelogram. $\overline{PR} \cong \overline{SQ}$

Prove PQRS is a rectangle.

Interpreting Data

NATURAL CRYSTALS Most minerals occur naturally as crystals. The atoms in a crystal have a specific internal pattern. When new atoms are deposited in a crystal, they continue the pattern. The shape of the resulting crystal is dependent on this pattern.

61. Describe the faces of the crystals shown below.

62. The mineral below is called amethyst. Name other minerals that grow naturally in the form of crystals.

63. Explain why some minerals form as crystals and some do not.

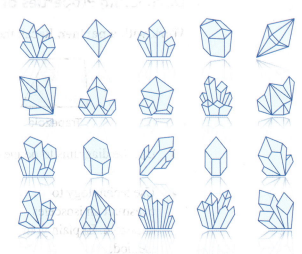

Review & Refresh

64. $\overline{DE}$ is a midsegment of △ABC. Find the values of x and y.

65. Find the values of x and y in the parallelogram.

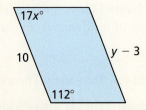

66. Find the measure of each interior angle and each exterior angle of a regular 24-gon.

67. Find the perimeter and area of △PQR with vertices P(3, −2), Q(3, 4), and R(6, 2).

68. State which theorem you can use to show that the quadrilateral is a parallelogram.

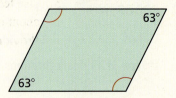

69. Find the length of $\overline{AB}$.

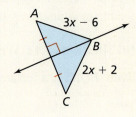

382 Chapter 7 Quadrilaterals and Other Polygons

7.5 Properties of Trapezoids and Kites

Learning Target: Use properties of trapezoids and kites to find measures.

Success Criteria:
- I can identify trapezoids and kites.
- I can use properties of trapezoids and kites to solve problems.
- I can find the length of the midsegment of a trapezoid.
- I can explain the hierarchy of quadrilaterals.

INVESTIGATE Discovering Properties of Trapezoids and Kites

Work with a partner. Recall the types of quadrilaterals shown.

Trapezoid   Isosceles Trapezoid   Kite

1. Use the diagrams to define each type of quadrilateral.

2. Use technology to construct an isosceles trapezoid. Explain your method.

3. Find the angle measures and diagonal lengths of the trapezoid. What do you observe?

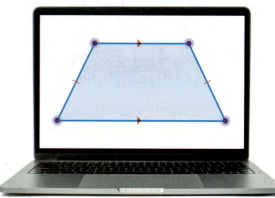

4. Repeat Exercises 2 and 3 for several other isosceles trapezoids. Make conjectures based on your results.

5. Use technology to construct a kite. Explain your method. Make a conjecture about interior angle measures and a conjecture about the diagonals of the kite. Provide examples to support your reasoning.

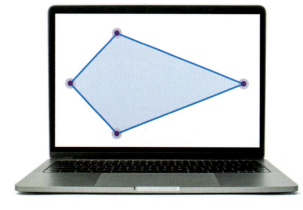

Vocabulary
- trapezoid
- bases
- base angles
- legs
- isosceles trapezoid
- midsegment of a trapezoid
- kite

Using Properties of Trapezoids

A **trapezoid** is a quadrilateral with exactly one pair of parallel sides. The parallel sides are the **bases**.

Base angles of a trapezoid are two consecutive angles whose common side is a base. A trapezoid has two pairs of base angles. For example, in trapezoid ABCD, ∠A and ∠D are one pair of base angles, and ∠B and ∠C are the second pair. The nonparallel sides are the **legs** of the trapezoid.

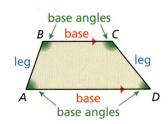

If the legs of a trapezoid are congruent, then the trapezoid is an **isosceles trapezoid**.

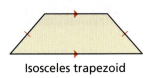

Isosceles trapezoid

EXAMPLE 1 Identifying a Trapezoid in the Coordinate Plane

Show that ORST is a trapezoid. Then decide whether it is isosceles.

Compare the slopes of opposite sides.

slope of $\overline{RS} = \dfrac{4-3}{2-0} = \dfrac{1}{2}$ slope of $\overline{OT} = \dfrac{2-0}{4-0} = \dfrac{2}{4} = \dfrac{1}{2}$

The slopes of $\overline{RS}$ and $\overline{OT}$ are the same, so $\overline{RS} \parallel \overline{OT}$.

slope of $\overline{ST} = \dfrac{2-4}{4-2} = \dfrac{-2}{2} = -1$ slope of $\overline{RO} = \dfrac{3-0}{0-0} = \dfrac{3}{0}$ Undefined

The slopes of $\overline{ST}$ and $\overline{RO}$ are not the same, so $\overline{ST}$ is not parallel to $\overline{RO}$.

▶ Because ORST has exactly one pair of parallel sides, it is a trapezoid.

Compare the lengths of legs $\overline{RO}$ and $\overline{ST}$.

$RO = |3-0| = 3$ $ST = \sqrt{(2-4)^2 + (4-2)^2} = \sqrt{8} \approx 2.83$

Because $RO \neq ST$, legs $\overline{RO}$ and $\overline{ST}$ are *not* congruent.

▶ So, ORST is not an isosceles trapezoid.

Make theorems on graph post-it

In-Class Practice
Self-Assessment

Use trapezoid ABCD.

1. Show that ABCD is a trapezoid. Then decide whether it is isosceles.

2. Vertex B moves to B(1, 3). Explain whether ABCD is a trapezoid.

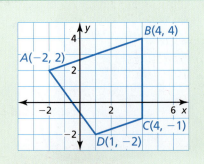

| 1 I don't understand yet. | 2 I can do it with help. | 3 I can do it on my own. | 4 I can teach someone. |

384   Chapter 7   Quadrilaterals and Other Polygons

Theorem 7.14

Isosceles Trapezoid Base Angles Theorem

If a trapezoid is isosceles, then each pair of base angles is congruent.

If trapezoid ABCD is isosceles, then ∠A ≅ ∠D and ∠B ≅ ∠C.

Prove this Theorem Exercise 25, page 390

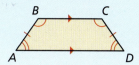

Theorem 7.15

Isosceles Trapezoid Base Angles Converse

If a trapezoid has a pair of congruent base angles, then it is an isosceles trapezoid.

If ∠A ≅ ∠D (or if ∠B ≅ ∠C), then trapezoid ABCD is isosceles.

Prove this Theorem Exercise 26, page 390

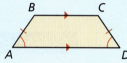

Theorem 7.16

Isosceles Trapezoid Diagonals Theorem

A trapezoid is isosceles if and only if its diagonals are congruent.

Trapezoid ABCD is isosceles if and only if $\overline{AC} \cong \overline{BD}$.

Prove this Theorem Exercise 34, page 391

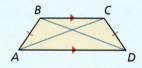

EXAMPLE 2 Using Properties of Isosceles Trapezoids

Incan architecture often features trapezoidal doorways and windows. Find $m\angle M$, $m\angle K$, and $m\angle L$ in the doorway.

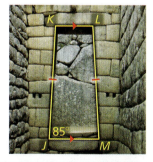

Because ∠J and ∠M are a pair of base angles, they are congruent. So, $m\angle M = m\angle J = 85°$. Because ∠J and ∠K are consecutive interior angles formed by $\overleftrightarrow{JK}$ intersecting two parallel lines, they are supplementary. So, $m\angle K = 180° - 85° = 95°$. Because ∠K and ∠L are a pair of base angles, they are congruent. So, $m\angle L = m\angle K = 95°$.

▶ So, $m\angle M = 85°$, $m\angle K = 95°$, and $m\angle L = 95°$.

In-Class Practice

Self-Assessment

3. If $m\angle HEF = 70°$ and $m\angle FGH = 110°$, is trapezoid EFGH isosceles? Explain.

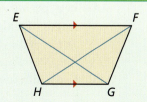

7.5 Properties of Trapezoids and Kites

Using the Trapezoid Midsegment Theorem

Recall that a midsegment of a triangle is a segment that connects the midpoints of two sides of the triangle. The **midsegment of a trapezoid** is the segment that connects the midpoints of its legs. The theorem below is similar to the Triangle Midsegment Theorem.

Theorem 7.17

Trapezoid Midsegment Theorem

The midsegment of a trapezoid is parallel to each base, and its length is one-half the sum of the lengths of the bases.

If $\overline{MN}$ is the midsegment of trapezoid $ABCD$, then $\overline{MN} \parallel \overline{AB}$, $\overline{MN} \parallel \overline{DC}$, and $MN = \frac{1}{2}(AB + CD)$.

Prove this Theorem Exercise 33, page 391

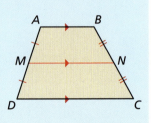

EXAMPLE 3 Using the Midsegment of a Trapezoid

In the diagram, $\overline{MN}$ is the midsegment of trapezoid $PQRS$. Find MN.

$MN = \frac{1}{2}(PQ + SR)$ Trapezoid Midsegment Theorem

$= \frac{1}{2}(12 + 28)$ Substitute 12 for PQ and 28 for SR.

$= 20$ Simplify.

▶ So, MN is 20 inches.

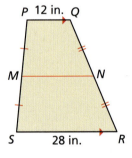

EXAMPLE 4 Using a Midsegment in the Coordinate Plane

Find the length of midsegment $\overline{YZ}$ in trapezoid $STUV$.

Find the lengths of $\overline{SV}$ and $\overline{TU}$.

$SV = \sqrt{(0-2)^2 + (6-2)^2} = \sqrt{20} = 2\sqrt{5}$

$TU = \sqrt{(8-12)^2 + (10-2)^2} = \sqrt{80} = 4\sqrt{5}$

Use the Trapezoid Midsegment Theorem.

$YZ = \frac{1}{2}(SV + TU) = \frac{1}{2}(2\sqrt{5} + 4\sqrt{5}) = \frac{1}{2}(6\sqrt{5}) = 3\sqrt{5}$

▶ So, the length of $\overline{YZ}$ is $3\sqrt{5}$ units.

In-Class Practice

Self-Assessment

4. In trapezoid $JKLM$, $\angle J$ and $\angle M$ are right angles, and $JK = 9$ centimeters. The length of midsegment $\overline{NP}$ of trapezoid $JKLM$ is 12 centimeters. Sketch trapezoid $JKLM$ and its midsegment. Find ML.

5. Use a different method to find the length of $\overline{YZ}$ in Example 4.

Using Properties of Kites

A **kite** is a quadrilateral that has two pairs of consecutive congruent sides, but opposite sides are not congruent.

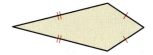

Theorem 7.18

Kite Diagonals Theorem

If a quadrilateral is a kite, then its diagonals are perpendicular.

If quadrilateral ABCD is a kite, then $\overline{AC} \perp \overline{BD}$.

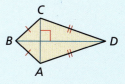

Prove this Theorem Exercise 32, page 391

Theorem 7.19

Kite Opposite Angles Theorem

If a quadrilateral is a kite, then exactly one pair of opposite angles are congruent.

If quadrilateral ABCD is a kite and $\overline{BC} \cong \overline{BA}$, then $\angle A \cong \angle C$ and $\angle B \not\cong \angle D$.

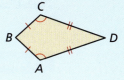

Prove this Theorem Exercise 31, page 391

EXAMPLE 5 Finding Angle Measures in a Kite

Find $m\angle D$ in the kite shown.

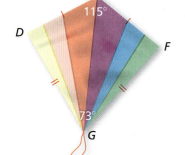

By the Kite Opposite Angles Theorem, DEFG has exactly one pair of congruent opposite angles. Because $\angle E \not\cong \angle G$, $\angle D$ and $\angle F$ must be congruent. So, $m\angle D = m\angle F$. Write and solve an equation to find $m\angle D$.

$m\angle D + m\angle F + 115° + 73° = 360°$ Corollary to the Polygon Interior Angles Theorem

$m\angle D + m\angle D + 115° + 73° = 360°$ Substitute $m\angle D$ for $m\angle F$.

$2(m\angle D) + 188° = 360°$ Combine like terms.

$m\angle D = 86°$ Solve for $m\angle D$.

▶ So, $m\angle D = 86°$.

In-Class Practice

Self-Assessment

6. In a kite, the measures of a pair of opposite angles are 50° and 108°. Find the measure of one of the other angles in the kite.

Identifying Special Quadrilaterals

The diagram shows relationships among the special quadrilaterals you have studied in this chapter. Each shape in the diagram has the properties of the shapes linked above it. For example, a rhombus has the properties of a parallelogram and a quadrilateral.

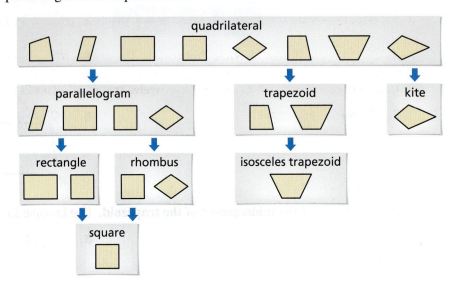

EXAMPLE 6 **Identifying a Quadrilateral**

What is the most specific name for quadrilateral *ABCD*?

The diagram shows $\overline{AE} \cong \overline{CE}$ and $\overline{BE} \cong \overline{DE}$. So, the diagonals bisect each other. By the Parallelogram Diagonals Converse, *ABCD* is a parallelogram.

Rectangles, rhombuses, and squares are also parallelograms. However, there is no information given about the side lengths or angle measures of *ABCD*. So, you cannot determine whether it is a rectangle, a rhombus, or a square.

▶ So, the most specific name for *ABCD* is a parallelogram.

In-Class Practice

Self-Assessment

Give the most specific name for the quadrilateral.

7.

8.

9.

7.5 Practice

Show that the quadrilateral with the given vertices is a trapezoid. Then decide whether it is isosceles. (See Example 1.)

▶ 1. $W(1, 4), X(1, 8), Y(-3, 9), Z(-3, 3)$

2. $D(-3, 3), E(-1, 1), F(1, -4), G(-3, 0)$

3. $M(-2, 0), N(0, 4), P(5, 4), Q(8, 0)$

4. $H(1, 9), J(4, 2), K(5, 2), L(8, 9)$

Find the measure of each angle in the isosceles trapezoid. (See Example 2.)

▶ 5.

6.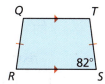

Find the length of the midsegment of the trapezoid. (See Example 3.)

▶ 7.

8.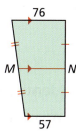

Find AB.

9.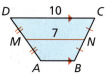

10.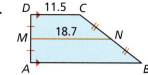

Find the length of the midsegment of the trapezoid with the given vertices. (See Example 4.)

▶ 11. $S(0, 0), T(2, 7), U(6, 10), V(8, 6)$

12. $A(0, 3), B(2, 5), C(6, 4), D(2, 0)$

13. $A(2, 0), B(8, -4), C(12, 2), D(0, 10)$

14. $S(-2, 4), T(-2, -4), U(3, -2), V(13, 10)$

Find $m\angle G$. (See Example 5.)

▶ 15.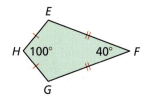

16.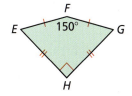

Give the most specific name for the quadrilateral. (See Example 6.)

▶ 17.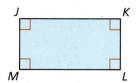

18.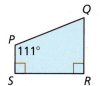

SMP.7 Find the value of x.

19.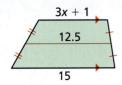

20.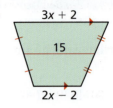

21. CONNECT CONCEPTS You use 94 inches of plastic to frame the perimeter of a kite. One side of the kite has a length of 18 inches. Find the length of each of the three remaining sides.

22. PROOF Write a proof.
Given $\overline{JL} \cong \overline{LN}, \overline{KM}$ is a midsegment of $\triangle JLN$.
Prove Quadrilateral $JKMN$ is an isosceles trapezoid.

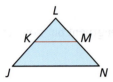

23. PROOF Write a proof.
Given $ABCD$ is a kite.
$\overline{AB} \cong \overline{CB}, \overline{AD} \cong \overline{CD}$
Prove $\overline{CE} \cong \overline{AE}$

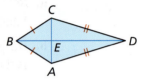

24. CONNECTION TO REAL LIFE Scientists are researching solar sails, which move spacecraft using radiation pressure from sunlight. What is the area of the solar sail shown?

PROVING A THEOREM Use the diagram to prove the given theorem. In the diagram, $\overline{EC}$ is drawn parallel to $\overline{AB}$.

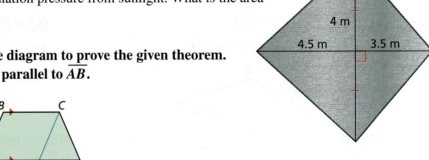

25. Isosceles Trapezoid Base Angles Theorem
Given $ABCD$ is an isosceles trapezoid.
$\overline{BC} \parallel \overline{AD}$
Prove $\angle A \cong \angle D, \angle B \cong \angle BCD$

26. Isosceles Trapezoid Base Angles Converse
Given $ABCD$ is a trapezoid.
$\angle A \cong \angle D, \overline{BC} \parallel \overline{AD}$
Prove $ABCD$ is an isosceles trapezoid.

27. CONNECT CONCEPTS The bases of a trapezoid lie on the lines $y = 2x + 7$ and $y = 2x - 5$. Write the equation of the line that contains the midsegment of the trapezoid.

28. PROOF Write a proof.
Given $QRST$ is an isosceles trapezoid.
Prove $\angle TQS \cong \angle SRT$

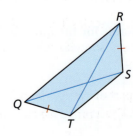

29. **CONNECTION TO REAL LIFE** A plastic web is made in the shape of a regular dodecagon (12-sided polygon). $\overline{AB} \parallel \overline{PQ}$, and X is equidistant from the vertices of the dodecagon.

   a. Are you given enough information to prove that ABPQ is an isosceles trapezoid?

   b. What is the measure of each interior angle of ABPQ?

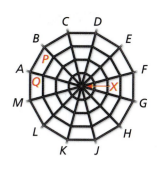

30. One of the earliest shapes used for cut diamonds is called the *table cut*, as shown in the figure. Each face of a cut gem is called a *facet*.

STEM Video: Diamond

   a. $\overline{BC} \parallel \overline{AD}$, and $\overline{AB}$ and $\overline{DC}$ are not parallel. What shape is the facet labeled ABCD?

   b. $\overline{DE} \parallel \overline{GF}$, and $\overline{DG}$ and $\overline{EF}$ are congruent but not parallel. What shape is the facet labeled DEFG?

31. **PROVING THEOREM 7.19** Use the diagram to prove the Kite Opposite Angles Theorem.

    Given EFGH is a kite.
    $\overline{EF} \cong \overline{FG}, \overline{EH} \cong \overline{GH}$
    Prove $\angle E \cong \angle G, \angle F \not\cong \angle H$

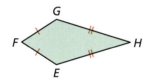

32. **PROVING THEOREM 7.18** Use the diagram to prove the Kite Diagonals Theorem.

    Given ABCD is a kite.
    $\overline{BC} \cong \overline{BA}, \overline{DC} \cong \overline{DA}$
    Prove $\overline{AC} \perp \overline{BD}$

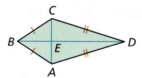

33. **PROVING THEOREM 7.17** In the diagram below, $\overline{BG}$ is the midsegment of $\triangle ACD$, and $\overline{GE}$ is the midsegment of $\triangle ADF$. Use the diagram to prove the Trapezoid Midsegment Theorem.

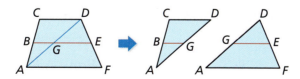

34. **PROVING THEOREM 7.16** To prove the biconditional statement in the Isosceles Trapezoid Diagonals Theorem, you must prove both parts separately.

   a. Prove part of the Isosceles Trapezoid Diagonals Theorem.

      Given JKLM is an isosceles trapezoid, $\overline{KL} \parallel \overline{JM}$, and $\overline{JK} \cong \overline{LM}$.
      Prove $\overline{JL} \cong \overline{KM}$

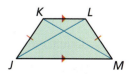

   b. Write the other part of the Isosceles Trapezoid Diagonals Theorem as a conditional. Then prove the statement is true.

7.5   Properties of Trapezoids and Kites

Interpreting Data

TRAPEZOIDAL ESTIMATION Trapezoids are often used to estimate the area of irregular shapes. In calculus, the trapezoidal rule is a formal method of estimating the area of a figure using trapezoids. In the map below, the area of Tennessee is approximated by 3 geometric shapes.

35. Estimate the area of the left section of Tennessee.

36. Estimate the area of the central section of Tennessee.

37. Estimate the total area of Tennessee.

Review & Refresh

38. Find the distance from $(-4, 7)$ to the line $y = 2x$.

39. Classify the quadrilateral.

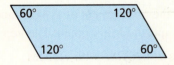

40. Find the measure of $\overline{LP}$ in $\square LMNQ$.

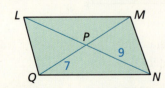

41. Graph $\overline{MN}$ with endpoints $M(1, 3)$ and $N(3, 5)$ and its image after a translation 2 units right, followed by a rotation 90° about the origin.

42. Sketch a diagram showing $\overline{AB}$ in plane P and $\overleftrightarrow{CD}$ not in plane P, such that $\overleftrightarrow{CD}$ bisects $\overline{AB}$.

43. State which theorem you can use to show that the quadrilateral is a parallelogram.

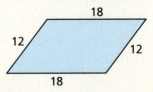

44. Decide whether enough information is given to prove that the triangles are congruent using the HL Congruence Theorem.

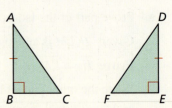

7 Chapter Review with CalcChat

Rate your understanding of each section.

1. I don't understand yet.
2. I can do it with help.
3. I can do it on my own.
4. I can teach someone.

7.1 Angles of Polygons (pp. 345–354)

○ **Learning Target:** Find angle measures of polygons.

Vocabulary
diagonal
equilateral polygon
equiangular polygon
regular polygon

1. Find the sum of the measures of the interior angles of a regular 30-gon. Then find the measure of each interior angle and each exterior angle.

Find the value of x.

2.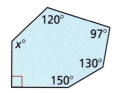

3.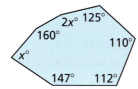

4.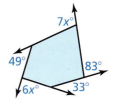

7.2 Properties of Parallelograms (pp. 355–362)

○ **Learning Target:** Prove and use properties of parallelograms.

Vocabulary
parallelogram

Find the value of each variable in the parallelogram.

5.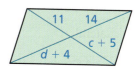

6. (parallelogram with diagonals labeled 11, 14, $c+5$, $d+4$)

7. Find the coordinates of the intersection of the diagonals of ▱QRST with vertices $Q(-8, 1)$, $R(2, 1)$, $S(4, -3)$, and $T(-6, -3)$.

8. Three vertices of ▱JKLM are $J(1, 4)$, $K(5, 3)$, and $L(6, -3)$. Find the coordinates of vertex M.

9. Three vertices of a parallelogram are located at $(-4, 3)$, $(1, -2)$, and $(-1, 4)$. What are two possible locations of the fourth vertex?

10. The figure shown is composed of two parallelograms. Find x.

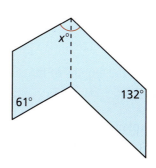

7.3 Proving That a Quadrilateral Is a Parallelogram (pp. 363–372)

◉ **Learning Target:** Prove that a quadrilateral is a parallelogram.

State which theorem you can use to show that the quadrilateral is a parallelogram.

11.

12.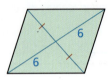

13.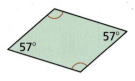

14. Find the values of x and y that make the quadrilateral a parallelogram.

    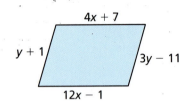

15. Find the value of x that makes the quadrilateral a parallelogram.

    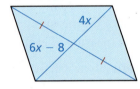

16. In the diagram of the staircase shown, $\overline{QT} \parallel \overline{RS}$, $QT = RS = 9$ feet, $QR = 3$ feet, and $m\angle QRS = 123°$.

    a. Which theorem can you use to show that $QRST$ is a parallelogram?

    b. Find ST, $m\angle QTS$, $m\angle TQR$, and $m\angle TSR$.

17. Show that quadrilateral $WXYZ$ with vertices $W(-1, 6)$, $X(2, 8)$, $Y(1, 0)$, and $Z(-2, -2)$ is a parallelogram.

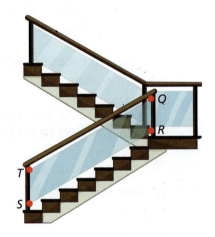

7.4 Properties of Special Parallelograms (pp. 373–382)

◉ **Learning Target:** Explain the properties of special parallelograms.

Vocabulary
rhombus
rectangle
square

Classify the quadrilateral.

18.

19.

20.

21. Find the lengths of the diagonals of rectangle $WXYZ$ where $WY = -2x + 34$ and $XZ = 3x - 26$.

22. Explain whether ▱$JKLM$ with vertices $J(5, 8)$, $K(9, 6)$, $L(7, 2)$, and $M(3, 4)$ is a rectangle, a rhombus, or a square. Give all names that apply.

7.5 Properties of Trapezoids and Kites (pp. 383–392)

⊙ **Learning Target:** Use properties of trapezoids and kites to find measures.

Vocabulary
trapezoid
bases
base angles
legs
isosceles trapezoid
midsegment of a trapezoid
kite

23. Find the measure of each angle in the isosceles trapezoid *WXYZ*.

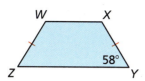

24. Find the length of the midsegment of trapezoid *ABCD*.

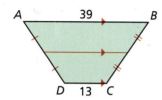

25. Find the length of the midsegment of trapezoid *JKLM* with vertices *J*(6, 10), *K*(10, 6), *L*(8, 2), and *M*(2, 2).

26. A kite has angle measures of $7x°$, 65°, 85°, and 105°. Find the value of *x*. Which of the angles are opposite angles?

27. Quadrilateral *WXYZ* is a trapezoid with a pair of opposite supplementary angles. Explain whether *WXYZ* is an isosceles trapezoid.

Give the most specific name for the quadrilateral.

28.

29.

30.

31.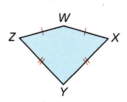

32. You are building a plant stand with three equally spaced circular shelves. The diagram shows a vertical cross section through the diameters of the shelves. What is the diameter of the middle shelf?

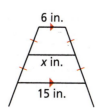

7 PERFORMANCE TASK
SMP.5 SMP.7

STARSTRUCK

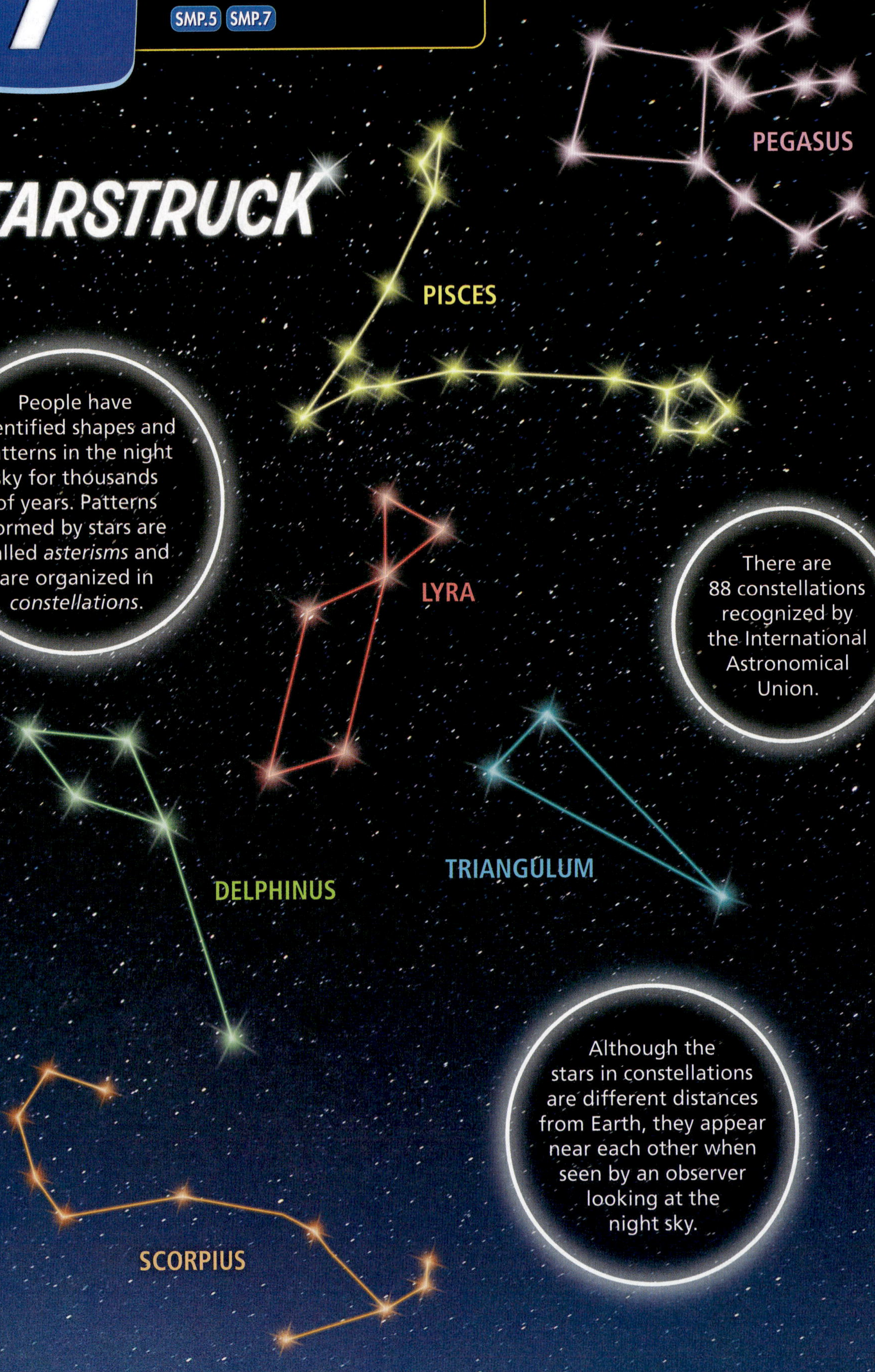

PEGASUS

PISCES

People have identified shapes and patterns in the night sky for thousands of years. Patterns formed by stars are called *asterisms* and are organized in *constellations*.

LYRA

There are 88 constellations recognized by the International Astronomical Union.

DELPHINUS

TRIANGULUM

Although the stars in constellations are different distances from Earth, they appear near each other when seen by an observer looking at the night sky.

SCORPIUS

Analyzing Data

Use the information on the previous page to complete the following exercises.

1 Explain what is shown in the display. What do you notice? What do you wonder?

URSA MINOR

2 Which constellation shown includes a shape closest to a parallelogram? a kite?

URSA MAJOR

3 What are the sums of the interior angle measures of the polygons in Pisces?

REACH FOR THE STARS

Research the constellation Sagittarius. What is the name of its brightest star? What was the Wow! signal and how does it relate to Sagittarius?

Draw the *asterism* in Sagittarius known as "the Teapot" in a coordinate plane. Identify any polygons in your drawing and find the sum(s) of the the interior angle measures. Then classify each polygon using coordinate geometry.

8 Similarity

8.1 Similar Polygons
8.2 Proving Triangle Similarity by AA
8.3 Proving Triangle Similarity by SSS and SAS
8.4 Proportionality Theorems

NATIONAL GEOGRAPHIC EXPLORER

Carter Clinton — BIOLOGICAL ANTHROPOLOGIST

Dr. Carter Clinton studies soil taken from the New York African Burial Ground. The burial ground contains the remains of more than 15,000 free and enslaved Africans buried from the middle 1630s to 1795. In 1991, the graves were excavated, and the soil was carefully stored. Dr. Clinton analyzes bacterial DNA in the soil to learn about the lives of the people buried at the site.

- What is DNA? How can scientists obtain a sample of a person's DNA?
- What is genomics?
- The human genome is composed of about 3 billion *base pairs*. What are base pairs?

PERFORMANCE TASK

Artists often create scale drawings of monuments and historical sites for educational materials. In the Performance Task on pages 438 and 439, you will create a brochure for the African Burial Ground National Monument that includes a scale drawing of the site.

DNA and Genomes

Big Idea of the Chapter
Use Similar Polygons

You have learned that two figures are similar when there exists a similarity transformation that maps one onto the other. In this chapter, you will learn other ways to prove similarity. You will also study properties of similar figures.

Deoxyribonucleic acid (DNA) is a molecule found in the cells of all living things. An organism's DNA contains the information needed to build it. Most cells in an organism contain a complete copy of the organism's DNA.

DNA also plays a primary role in heredity. When an organism reproduces, a portion of its DNA is passed to its offspring. This is why offspring resemble their parents or grandparents.

DNA is composed of two chains of *nucleotides*. Each nucleotide consists of a sugar molecule (deoxyribose) and a phosphate group that link to neighboring nucleotides. Nucleotides also include a nitrogen-containing *base*. Each base connects to a *complementary base* on the other chain of nucleotides, causing the two chains to wrap around one another. The resulting shape is a *double-helix*, resembling a twisted ladder with rungs that are composed of the following base pairs.

1. Consider two siblings who have the same biological parents. Explain whether you would expect the offspring to resemble one another.

2. Your friend says that it makes sense to call an infant and a teenager with the same parents *similar* because their DNA means they have the same shape, but are different sizes. Explain whether you think this makes sense.

Getting Ready for Chapter 8

Determining Whether Ratios Form a Proportion

EXAMPLE 1 Tell whether $\frac{2}{8}$ and $\frac{3}{12}$ form a proportion.

Compare the ratios in simplest form.

$$\frac{2}{8} = \frac{2 \div 2}{8 \div 2} = \frac{1}{4}$$

$$\frac{3}{12} = \frac{3 \div 3}{12 \div 3} = \frac{1}{4}$$

The ratios are equivalent.

▶ So, $\frac{2}{8}$ and $\frac{3}{12}$ form a proportion.

Tell whether the ratios form a proportion.

1. $\frac{5}{3}, \frac{35}{21}$
2. $\frac{9}{24}, \frac{24}{64}$
3. $\frac{8}{56}, \frac{6}{28}$
4. $\frac{18}{4}, \frac{27}{9}$
5. $\frac{15}{21}, \frac{55}{77}$
6. $\frac{26}{8}, \frac{39}{12}$

Finding a Scale Factor

EXAMPLE 2 Find the scale factor of each dilation.

a.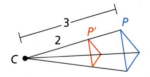

b.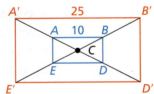

▶ Because $\frac{CP'}{CP} = \frac{2}{3}$, the scale factor is $k = \frac{2}{3}$.

▶ Because $\frac{A'B'}{AB} = \frac{25}{10}$, the scale factor is $k = \frac{25}{10} = \frac{5}{2}$.

Find the scale factor of the dilation.

7.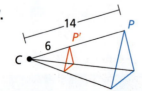

8.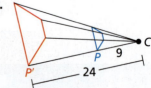

8.1 Similar Polygons

Learning Target: Understand the relationship between similar polygons.

Success Criteria:
- I can use similarity statements.
- I can find corresponding lengths in similar polygons.
- I can find perimeters and areas of similar polygons.
- I can decide whether polygons are similar.

INVESTIGATE Comparing a Figure to Its Dilation

Work with a partner. Use technology.

1. Construct any quadrilateral. Dilate it to form a similar quadrilateral using any scale factor k and any center of dilation.

2. Compare the corresponding angles of the original quadrilateral and its image. What do you observe?

3. Find the ratios of the side lengths of the image to the corresponding side lengths of the original quadrilateral. What do you observe?

4. Compare the perimeters and areas of the original quadrilateral and its image. What do you observe?

5. Repeat Exercises 1–4 for several other polygons, scale factors, and centers of dilation. Do you obtain similar results?

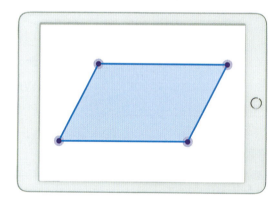

6. Explain, in your own words, how similar polygons are related.

8.1 Similar Polygons 401

Using Similarity Statements

Recall from Section 4.6 that two geometric figures are similar figures if and only if there is a similarity transformation that maps one figure onto the other.

> ### Key Concept
>
> **Corresponding Parts of Similar Polygons**
>
> In the diagram below, $\triangle ABC$ is similar to $\triangle DEF$. You can write "$\triangle ABC$ is similar to $\triangle DEF$" as $\triangle ABC \sim \triangle DEF$. A similarity transformation preserves angle measure. So, corresponding angles are congruent. A similarity transformation also enlarges or reduces side lengths by a scale factor k. So, corresponding side lengths are proportional.
>
>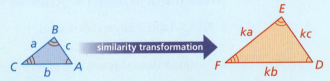
>
> **Corresponding angles**   **Ratios of corresponding side lengths**
>
> $\angle A \cong \angle D, \angle B \cong \angle E, \angle C \cong \angle F$ $\dfrac{DE}{AB} = \dfrac{EF}{BC} = \dfrac{FD}{CA} = k$

EXAMPLE 1 Using Similarity Statements

In the diagram, $\triangle RST \sim \triangle XYZ$.

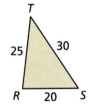

a. Find the scale factor from $\triangle RST$ to $\triangle XYZ$.

$$\dfrac{XY}{RS} = \dfrac{12}{20} = \dfrac{3}{5} \qquad \dfrac{YZ}{ST} = \dfrac{18}{30} = \dfrac{3}{5} \qquad \dfrac{ZX}{TR} = \dfrac{15}{25} = \dfrac{3}{5}$$

▶ So, the scale factor is $\dfrac{3}{5}$.

b. List all pairs of congruent angles.

▶ $\angle R \cong \angle X$, $\angle S \cong \angle Y$, and $\angle T \cong \angle Z$.

c. Write the ratios of the corresponding side lengths in a *statement of proportionality*.

▶ Because the ratios in part (a) are equal, $\dfrac{XY}{RS} = \dfrac{YZ}{ST} = \dfrac{ZX}{TR}$.

In-Class Practice

Self-Assessment

1. In the diagram, $\triangle JKL \sim \triangle PQR$.

   a. Find the scale factor from $\triangle JKL$ to $\triangle PQR$.
   b. List all pairs of congruent angles.
   c. Write the ratios of the corresponding side lengths in a statement of proportionality.

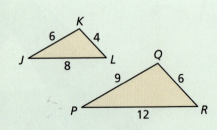

 I don't understand yet.   I can do it with help.   I can do it on my own.   I can teach someone.

Finding Corresponding Lengths in Similar Polygons

> **Key Concept**
>
> **Corresponding Lengths in Similar Polygons**
>
> If two polygons are similar, then the ratio of any two corresponding lengths in the polygons is equal to the scale factor of the similar polygons.

EXAMPLE 2 **Finding a Corresponding Length**

In the diagram, $\triangle DEF \sim \triangle MNP$. Find the value of x.

The triangles are similar, so the corresponding side lengths are proportional.

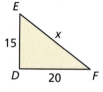

$\dfrac{MN}{DE} = \dfrac{NP}{EF}$ Write proportion.

$\dfrac{18}{15} = \dfrac{30}{x}$ Substitute.

$18x = 450$ Cross Products Property

$x = 25$ Divide each side by 18.

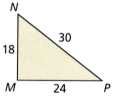

▶ The value of x is 25.

EXAMPLE 3 **Finding a Corresponding Length**

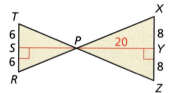

In the diagram, $\triangle TPR \sim \triangle XPZ$. Find the length of the altitude $\overline{PS}$.

First, find the scale factor from $\triangle XPZ$ to $\triangle TPR$.

$\dfrac{TR}{XZ} = \dfrac{6+6}{8+8} = \dfrac{12}{16} = \dfrac{3}{4}$

Because the ratio of the lengths of the altitudes in similar triangles is equal to the scale factor, you can write the following proportion.

$\dfrac{PS}{PY} = \dfrac{3}{4}$ Write proportion.

$\dfrac{PS}{20} = \dfrac{3}{4}$ Substitute 20 for PY.

$PS = 15$ Multiply each side by 20.

▶ The length of the altitude $\overline{PS}$ is 15.

In-Class Practice

Self-Assessment

2. Find the value of x.

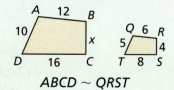

ABCD ~ QRST

3. Find KM.

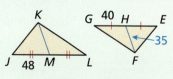

$\triangle JKL \sim \triangle EFG$

Finding Perimeters and Areas of Similar Polygons

Theorem 8.1

Perimeters of Similar Polygons

If two polygons are similar, then the ratio of their perimeters is equal to the ratios of their corresponding side lengths.

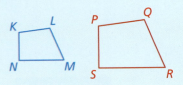

If $KLMN \sim PQRS$, then

$$\frac{PQ + QR + RS + SP}{KL + LM + MN + NK} = \frac{PQ}{KL} = \frac{QR}{LM} = \frac{RS}{MN} = \frac{SP}{NK}.$$

Prove this Theorem Exercise 23, page 409

EXAMPLE 4 Finding Perimeters

STEM Video: Scale Model of a Pool

A town plans to build a new swimming pool. An Olympic-sized pool is rectangular with a length of 50 meters and a width of 25 meters. The new pool will be similar in shape to an Olympic-sized pool but will have a length of 40 meters. Find the perimeters of an Olympic-sized pool and the new pool.

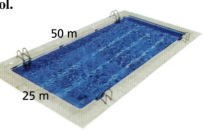

Because the new pool will be similar to an Olympic-sized pool, the scale factor is the ratio of the lengths, $\frac{40}{50} = \frac{4}{5}$. The perimeter of an Olympic-sized pool is $2(50) + 2(25) = 150$ meters. Write and solve a proportion to find the perimeter x of the new pool.

$\frac{x}{150} = \frac{4}{5}$ Perimeters of Similar Polygons Theorem

$x = 120$ Multiply each side by 150.

▶ So, the perimeter of an Olympic-sized pool is 150 meters, and the perimeter of the new pool is 120 meters.

In-Class Practice

Self-Assessment

4. The two gazebos shown are similar pentagons. Find the perimeter of Gazebo A.

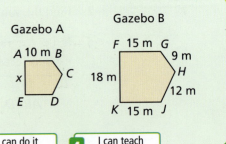

| 1 I don't understand yet. | 2 I can do it with help. | 3 I can do it on my own. | 4 I can teach someone. |

404   Chapter 8   Similarity

Theorem 8.2

Areas of Similar Polygons

If two polygons are similar, then the ratio of their areas is equal to the squares of the ratios of their corresponding side lengths.

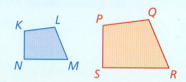

If $KLMN \sim PQRS$, then

$$\frac{\text{Area of } PQRS}{\text{Area of } KLMN} = \left(\frac{PQ}{KL}\right)^2 = \left(\frac{QR}{LM}\right)^2 = \left(\frac{RS}{MN}\right)^2 = \left(\frac{SP}{NK}\right)^2.$$

Prove this Theorem Exercise 32, page 409

EXAMPLE 5 — Finding Areas of Similar Polygons

$\triangle ABC \sim \triangle DEF$. Find the area of $\triangle DEF$.

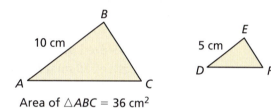

Area of $\triangle ABC = 36$ cm²

Because the triangles are similar, the ratio of the area of $\triangle ABC$ to the area of $\triangle DEF$ is equal to the square of the ratio of AB to DE. Write and solve a proportion to find the area of $\triangle DEF$. Let A represent the area of $\triangle DEF$.

$\dfrac{\text{Area of } \triangle ABC}{\text{Area of } \triangle DEF} = \left(\dfrac{AB}{DE}\right)^2$ Areas of Similar Polygons Theorem

$\dfrac{36}{A} = \left(\dfrac{10}{5}\right)^2$ Substitute.

$\dfrac{36}{A} = \dfrac{100}{25}$ Square the right side of the equation.

$900 = 100A$ Cross Products Property

$9 = A$ Divide.

▶ The area of $\triangle DEF$ is 9 square centimeters.

In-Class Practice

Self-Assessment

5. In the diagram, $GHJK \sim LMNP$. Find the area of $LMNP$.

Area of $GHJK = 84$ m²

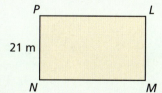

Deciding Whether Polygons Are Similar

EXAMPLE 6 **Deciding Whether Polygons Are Similar**

Decide whether *ABCDE* and *KLQRP* are similar. Explain your reasoning.

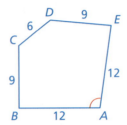 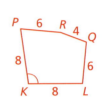

Corresponding sides of the pentagons are proportional with a scale factor of $\frac{2}{3}$. However, this does not necessarily mean the pentagons are similar. Use a similarity transformation to decide whether the pentagons are similar. A dilation with center *A* and scale factor $\frac{2}{3}$ moves *ABCDE* onto *AFGHJ*. Then a reflection moves *AFGHJ* onto *KLMNP*.

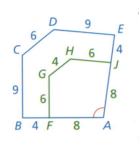 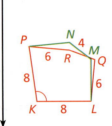

KLMNP does not exactly coincide with *KLQRP*, because not all the corresponding angles are congruent. (Only ∠*A* and ∠*K* are congruent.)

▶ Because angle measure is not preserved, the two pentagons are not similar.

In-Class Practice
Self-Assessment

Refer to the floor tile designs below. In each design, the red outer shape is a regular hexagon.

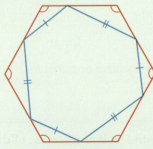 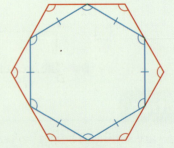

Tile Design 1   Tile Design 2

6. Explain whether the hexagons in Tile Design 1 are similar.

7. Explain whether the hexagons in Tile Design 2 are similar.

8.1 Practice

Find the scale factor. Then list all pairs of congruent angles and write the ratios of the corresponding side lengths in a statement of proportionality. (See Example 1.)

▶ 1. △ABC ~ △LMN

2. DEFG ~ PQRS

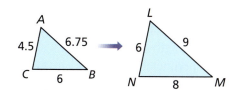
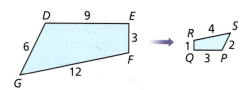

The polygons are similar. Find the value of x. (See Example 2.)

▶ 3.

4.

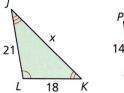
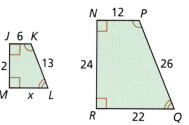

The triangles are similar. Find the value of the variable. (See Example 3.)

▶ 5.

6.

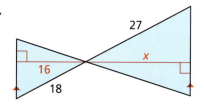
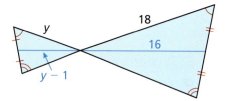

RSTU ~ ABCD. **Find the ratio of their perimeters.**

7.

8.

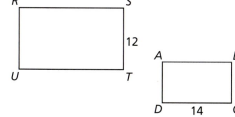
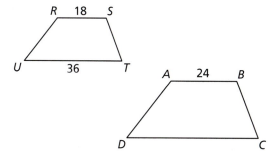

Two polygons are similar. The perimeter of one polygon and the ratio of the corresponding side lengths are given. Find the perimeter of the other polygon.

9. perimeter of smaller polygon: 48 cm; ratio: $\frac{2}{3}$

10. perimeter of smaller polygon: 66 ft; ratio: $\frac{3}{4}$

11. **CONNECTION TO REAL LIFE** Scientists rope off two excavation sites. Site A is rectangular with a length of 60 meters and a width of 40 meters. Site B is similar in shape to Site A but has a length of 45 meters. How much rope is needed for both sites? (See Example 4.)

12. **CONNECTION TO REAL LIFE** A family decides to put a rectangular patio in their backyard, similar to the shape of the backyard. The backyard has a length of 45 feet and a width of 20 feet. The length of the new patio is 18 feet. Find the perimeter of the backyard and the perimeter of the patio.

The polygons are similar. The area of one polygon is given. Find the area of the other polygon. (See Example 5.)

13.

14.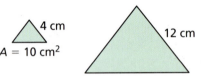

15. **SMP.3 ERROR ANALYSIS** Describe and correct the error in finding the perimeter of triangle B. The triangles are similar.

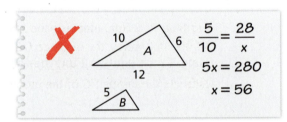

16. **SMP.3 ERROR ANALYSIS** Describe and correct the error in finding the area of rectangle B. The rectangles are similar.

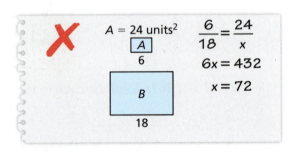

Decide whether the red and blue polygons are similar. (See Example 6.)

17.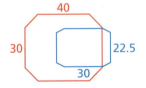

18.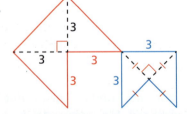

19. In table tennis, the table is a rectangle 9 feet long and 5 feet wide. A tennis court is a rectangle 78 feet long and 36 feet wide. Are the two surfaces similar? Explain. If so, find the scale factor of the tennis court to the table.

20. **SMP.3** If the side lengths of two rectangles are proportional, must the two rectangles be similar? Explain your reasoning.

SMP.6 The figures are similar. Find the missing corresponding side length.

21. Figure A has a perimeter of 24 inches. Figure B has a perimeter of 36 inches and one of the side lengths is 12 inches.

22. Figure A has an area of 48 square feet and one of the side lengths is 6 feet. Figure B has an area of 75 square feet.

23. **PROVING THEOREM 8.1** Prove the Perimeters of Similar Polygons Theorem for similar rectangles. Include a diagram in your proof.

SMP.6 Tell whether the polygons are *always*, *sometimes*, or *never* similar.

24. two isosceles triangles

25. two isosceles trapezoids

26. two rhombuses

27. two squares

28. two regular polygons

29. a right triangle and an equilateral triangle

30. **CONNECTION TO REAL LIFE** During a total solar eclipse, the moon passes directly between Earth and the Sun, blocking the Sun's rays. The distance DA between Earth and the Sun is 93,000,000 miles, the distance DE between Earth and the moon is 240,000 miles, and the radius AB of the Sun is 432,500 miles. Use the diagram and the given measurements to estimate the radius EC of the moon.

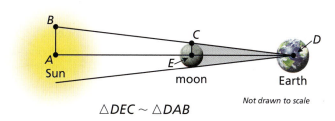

$\triangle DEC \sim \triangle DAB$

31. **CONNECT CONCEPTS** The equations of the lines shown are $y = \frac{4}{3}x + 4$ and $y = \frac{4}{3}x - 8$. Show that $\triangle AOB \sim \triangle COD$.

32. **PROVING THEOREM 8.2** Prove the Areas of Similar Polygons Theorem for similar rectangles. Include a diagram in your proof.

33. **DIG DEEPER** In the diagram, $PQRS$ is a square, and $PLMS \sim LMRQ$. Find the exact value of x. This value is called the *golden ratio*. Golden rectangles have their length and width in this ratio. Show that the similar rectangles in the diagram are golden rectangles.

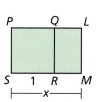

8.1 Similar Polygons

Interpreting Data

THE KOCH SNOWFLAKE A fractal is a complicated pattern that remains complicated even when viewed at different scales. Some fractals can be created by repeating a process over and over. For example, the Koch Snowflake is one of the first fractals to have been described. The Koch Snowflake is self-similar. If you magnify the edge of the snowflake, the magnified image will appear similar to the original image. You can construct the Koch Snowflake in stages, the first 5 of which are shown below.

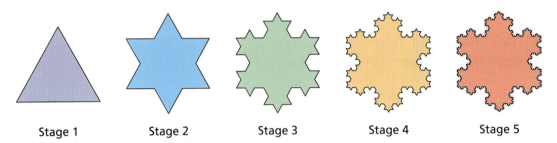

Stage 1   Stage 2   Stage 3   Stage 4   Stage 5

34. Describe the pattern used to create the Koch Snowflake.

35. The perimeter of the triangle in Stage 1 is 3 units. Find the perimeters of the other four stages.

36. Use the Internet to find examples of fractals in nature.

Review & Refresh

Find the value of x.

37.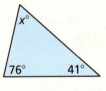

38.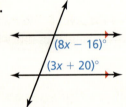

39.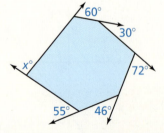

40. In rectangle $ABCD$, $AC = 6x - 15$ and $BD = -2x + 17$. Find the lengths of the diagonals of $ABCD$.

Solve the equation.

41. $2^{x+3} = 8^x$

42. $4x^2 - 16 = 8$

43. You are making a blueprint of a house. You measure the lengths of the walls of a room to be 11 feet by 12 feet. When you draw the room on the blueprint, the lengths of the walls are 8.25 inches by 9 inches. What scale factor dilates the room to the blueprint?

Find the inverse of the function. Then graph the function and its inverse.

44. $f(x) = 2x^3 - 4$

45. $f(x) = \frac{1}{5}x^2, x \geq 0$

46. Tell whether the table of values represents a *linear*, an *exponential*, or a *quadratic* function.

x	−2	−1	0	1	2
y	2	3	4.5	6.75	10.125

47. The incenter of $\triangle ABC$ is point N, $NZ = 4x - 10$, and $NY = 3x - 1$. Find NW.

410   Chapter 8   Similarity

8.2 Proving Triangle Similarity by AA

Learning Target: Understand and use the Angle-Angle Similarity Theorem.

Success Criteria:
- I can prove triangle similarity using the Angle-Angle Similarity Theorem.
- I can solve real-life problems using similar triangles.

INVESTIGATE Comparing Triangles

SMP.5 Work with a partner.

1. Construct any $\triangle ABC$. Find $m\angle A$ and $m\angle B$.

2. Construct $\triangle DEF$ so that each of the following is true. Explain your method.
   - $m\angle D = m\angle A$
   - $m\angle E = m\angle B$
   - $\triangle DEF$ is not congruent to $\triangle ABC$.

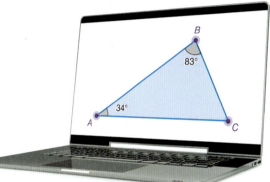

3. Explain whether the two triangles are similar.

4. Repeat Exercises 1–3 for several different triangles. Describe your results. Can you construct two triangles in this way that are *not* similar?

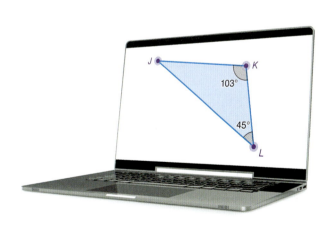

5. **SMP.8** Make a conjecture about any two triangles with two pairs of congruent angles. Use transformations to support your answer.

8.2 Proving Triangle Similarity by AA   411

Using the Angle-Angle Similarity Theorem

Theorem 8.3

Angle-Angle (AA) Similarity Theorem

If two angles of one triangle are congruent to two angles of another triangle, then the two triangles are similar.

If $\angle A \cong \angle D$ and $\angle B \cong \angle E$, then $\triangle ABC \sim \triangle DEF$.

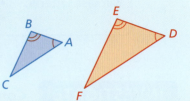

Prove this Theorem Exercise 12, page 415
Proof Available online

EXAMPLE 1 Using the AA Similarity Theorem

Determine whether the triangles are similar. If they are, write a similarity statement.

a.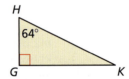

Because they are both right angles, $\angle D$ and $\angle G$ are congruent.

By the Triangle Sum Theorem, $26° + 90° + m\angle E = 180°$, so $m\angle E = 64°$. So, $\angle E$ and $\angle H$ are congruent.

▶ So, $\triangle CDE \sim \triangle KGH$ by the AA Similarity Theorem.

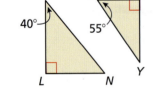

b. Because they are both right angles, $\angle L$ and $\angle X$ are congruent.

By the Triangle Sum Theorem,

$40° + 90° + m\angle N = 180°$, so $m\angle N = 50°$ and

$55° + 90° + m\angle K = 180°$, so $m\angle K = 35°$.

The triangles only share one pair of congruent angles.

▶ So, the triangles are not similar.

In-Class Practice

Self-Assessment

1. Explain whether the triangles are similar. If they are, write a similarity statement.

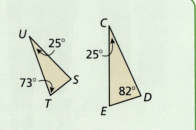

412 Chapter 8 Similarity

EXAMPLE 2 **Using the AA Similarity Theorem**

Show that the two triangles are similar and write a similarity statement.

a. △ABE and △ACD

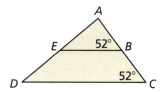

Because m∠ABE and m∠C both equal 52°, ∠ABE ≅ ∠C. By the Reflexive Property of Angle Congruence, ∠A ≅ ∠A.

▶ So, △ABE ~ △ACD by the AA Similarity Theorem.

b. △SVR and △UVT

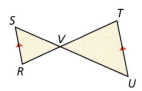

You know ∠SVR ≅ ∠UVT by the Vertical Angles Congruence Theorem. The diagram shows $\overline{RS} \parallel \overline{UT}$, so ∠S ≅ ∠U by the Alternate Interior Angles Theorem.

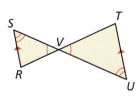

▶ So, △SVR ~ △UVT by the AA Similarity Theorem.

In-Class Practice

Self-Assessment

Show that the triangles are similar and write a similarity statement.

2. △FGH and △RQS

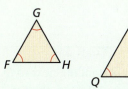

3. △CDF and △DEF

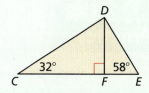

4. **WHAT IF?** In Example 2(b), $\overline{SR} \not\parallel \overline{TU}$. Explain whether the triangles can still be similar.

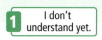

8.2 Proving Triangle Similarity by AA

Connections to Real Life

Previously, you learned a way to use congruent triangles to find measurements indirectly. Another useful way to find measurements indirectly is by using similar triangles.

EXAMPLE 3   Finding a Missing Side Length

A free-fall ride casts a shadow that is 80 feet long. At the same time, a person standing nearby who is 5 feet 5 inches tall casts a shadow that is 34 inches long. How tall is the free-fall ride?

The Sun's rays hit the ride and the person at the same angle. The ride and the person form sides of two right triangles with their shadows on the ground.

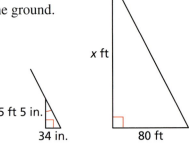

There are two pairs of congruent angles, so the triangles are similar by the AA Similarity Theorem. Use a proportion to find the height x. Write 5 feet 5 inches as 65 inches so that you can form two ratios of feet to inches.

$$\frac{x \text{ ft}}{65 \text{ in.}} = \frac{80 \text{ ft}}{34 \text{ in.}}$$ Write proportion of side lengths.

$$x = \frac{5{,}200}{34}$$ Multiply each side by 65.

$$x \approx 152.94$$ Divide.

▶ So, the free-fall ride is about 153 feet tall.

Check Check that your answer is reasonable in the context of the problem. You can estimate that a fifteen-story building is about

$$15(10 \text{ feet}) = 150 \text{ feet},$$

so it is reasonable that a free-fall ride can be 153 feet tall.

In-Class Practice
Self-Assessment

5. **WHAT IF?** A child who is 52 inches tall is standing next to the person in Example 3. Show two different ways to find the length of the child's shadow.

6. You stand outside and measure the lengths of the shadows cast by both you and a tree. Write a proportion showing how you can find the height of the tree.

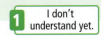

414   Chapter 8   Similarity

8.2 Practice

with Calc Chat and Calc Chat

Explain whether the triangles are similar. If they are, write a similarity statement.
(See Example 1.)

1.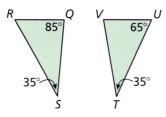

2.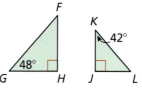

Show that the two triangles are similar and write a similarity statement. (See Example 2.)

3.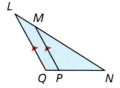

4.

5. **SMP.2 CONNECTION TO REAL LIFE** A saguaro cactus casts a shadow that is 30 feet long. At the same time, a person standing nearby who is 5 feet 10 inches tall casts a shadow that is 50 inches long. How tall is the cactus? (See Example 3.)

6. **CONNECTION TO REAL LIFE** You can measure the width of the lake using a surveying technique, as shown in the diagram. Find the width of the lake, WX.

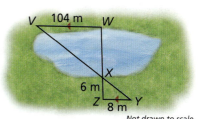

7. Explain why all equilateral triangles are similar.

8. **SMP.3 CONNECT CONCEPTS** Explain how you can use similar triangles to show that any two points on a line can be used to find its slope.

9. Explain whether (a) AAA and (b) AAAA are valid methods of showing that two quadrilaterals are similar.

10. **PROOF** Prove that if the lengths of two sides of a triangle are a and b, respectively, then the lengths of the corresponding altitudes to those sides are in the ratio b to a.

11. **SMP.1 DIG DEEPER** A portion of an amusement park ride is shown. Find EF. Justify your answer.

12. Use transformations to prove that $\triangle PQR \sim \triangle STU$.

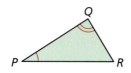

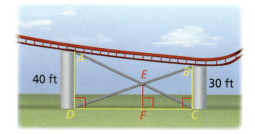

Interpreting Data

INCLINED PLANE The rate at which an object slides down an inclined plane depends on the slope of the plane. The diagram below shows that the gravitational force of the weight is separated into two components. One is parallel to the inclined plane and one is perpendicular to the inclined plane.

13. Find and copy three triangles in the diagram. Label the vertices.

14. Name a pair of similar triangles. How do you know they are similar?

15. Is there a triangle that is not similar to the other two? How do you know?

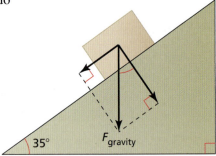

Object Sliding Down an Inclined Plane

Review & Refresh

16. Decide whether enough information is given to prove that the triangles are congruent. If so, state the theorem you can use.

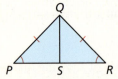

17. A stop sign is shaped like a regular octagon. Find the measure of each (a) interior angle and (b) exterior angle.

18. Find $m\angle S$.

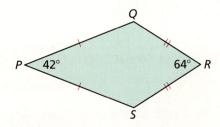

19. In the diagram, $ABCD \sim EFGH$. The area of $ABCD$ is 288 square meters. Find the area of $EFGH$.

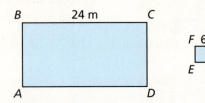

20. Decide whether ▱$WXYZ$ with vertices $W(-4, 2)$, $X(-1, 5)$, $Y(1, 3)$, and $Z(-2, 0)$ is a *rectangle*, a *rhombus*, or a *square*. Give all names that apply.

416 Chapter 8 Similarity

8.3 Proving Triangle Similarity by SSS and SAS

Learning Target: Understand and use additional triangle similarity theorems.

Success Criteria:
- I can use the SSS and SAS Similarity Theorems to determine whether triangles are similar.
- I can use similar triangles to prove theorems about slopes of parallel and perpendicular lines.

INVESTIGATE Deciding Whether Triangles Are Similar

Work with a partner. Use technology.

1. Construct any $\triangle ABC$. Find AB, AC, and BC.

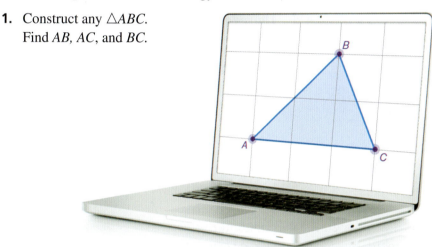

2. Choose any positive rational number k and construct $\triangle DEF$ so that $DE = k \cdot AB$, $DF = k \cdot AC$, and $EF = k \cdot BC$. Explain whether $\triangle DEF$ is similar to $\triangle ABC$.

3. **SMP.8** Repeat parts Exercises 1 and 2 several times by changing $\triangle ABC$ and k. Make a conjecture about the similarity of two triangles based on their side lengths.

4. If an angle of one triangle is congruent to an angle of a second triangle and the lengths of the sides including these angles are proportional, are the triangles similar? Provide examples to support your reasoning.

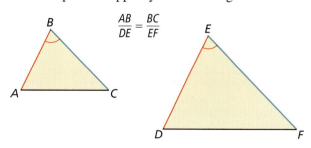

$$\frac{AB}{DE} = \frac{BC}{EF}$$

8.3 Proving Triangle Similarity by SSS and SAS 417

Using the Side-Side-Side Similarity Theorem

In addition to using congruent corresponding angles to show that two triangles are similar, you can use proportional corresponding side lengths.

Theorem 8.4

Side-Side-Side (SSS) Similarity Theorem

If the corresponding side lengths of two triangles are proportional, then the triangles are similar.

If $\dfrac{AB}{RS} = \dfrac{BC}{ST} = \dfrac{CA}{TR}$, then $\triangle ABC \sim \triangle RST$.

Proof page 419

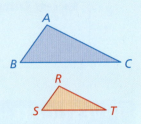

EXAMPLE 1 Using the SSS Similarity Theorem

Is either $\triangle DEF$ or $\triangle GHJ$ similar to $\triangle ABC$? If so, write a similarity statement.

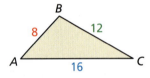
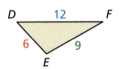
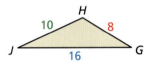

Compare $\triangle ABC$ and $\triangle DEF$ by finding ratios of corresponding side lengths.

Shortest sides	Longest sides	Remaining sides
$\dfrac{AB}{DE} = \dfrac{8}{6} = \dfrac{4}{3}$	$\dfrac{CA}{FD} = \dfrac{16}{12} = \dfrac{4}{3}$	$\dfrac{BC}{EF} = \dfrac{12}{9} = \dfrac{4}{3}$

▶ All the ratios are equal, so $\triangle ABC \sim \triangle DEF$.

Compare $\triangle ABC$ and $\triangle GHJ$ by finding ratios of corresponding side lengths.

Shortest sides	Longest sides	Remaining sides
$\dfrac{AB}{GH} = \dfrac{8}{8} = 1$	$\dfrac{CA}{JG} = \dfrac{16}{16} = 1$	$\dfrac{BC}{HJ} = \dfrac{12}{10} = \dfrac{6}{5}$

▶ The ratios are not all equal, so $\triangle ABC$ and $\triangle GHJ$ are not similar.

In-Class Practice

Self-Assessment

1. Which of the three triangles are similar? Write a similarity statement.

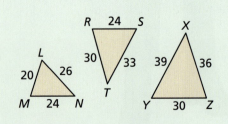

 I don't understand yet.
 I can do it with help.
 I can do it on my own.
4 I can teach someone.

PROOF **SSS Similarity Theorem**

Given $\dfrac{RS}{JK} = \dfrac{ST}{KL} = \dfrac{TR}{LJ}$

Prove $\triangle RST \sim \triangle JKL$

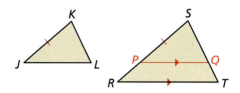

Construct $\overline{PQ}$ so that $PS = JK$ and $\overline{PQ} \parallel \overline{RT}$. Because $\angle R \cong \angle SPQ$ and $\angle T \cong \angle SQP$ by the Corresponding Angle Theorem, $\triangle RST \sim \triangle PSQ$ by the AA Similarity Theorem. Side lengths of similar triangles are proportional, so $\dfrac{RS}{PS} = \dfrac{ST}{SQ} = \dfrac{TR}{QP}$. Use this proportion and the fact that $PS = JK$ to deduce that $SQ = KL$ and $QP = LJ$. So, $\triangle PSQ \cong \triangle JKL$ by the SSS Congruence Theorem. Because corresponding parts of congruent triangles are congruent, you can also prove that $\triangle RST \sim \triangle JKL$ using the AA Similarity Theorem.

EXAMPLE 2 Using the SSS Similarity Theorem

Find the value of x that makes $\triangle ABC \sim \triangle DEF$.

 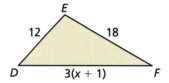

Find the value of x that makes corresponding side lengths proportional.

$\dfrac{AB}{DE} = \dfrac{BC}{EF}$	Write proportion.
$\dfrac{4}{12} = \dfrac{x-1}{18}$	Substitute.
$6 = x - 1$	Multiply each side by 18.
$7 = x$	Add 1 to each side.

Check that the side lengths are proportional when $x = 7$.

$BC = 7 - 1 = 6$ $DF = 3(7 + 1) = 24$

$\dfrac{AB}{DE} \stackrel{?}{=} \dfrac{BC}{EF} \;\Rightarrow\; \dfrac{4}{12} = \dfrac{6}{18}$ ✓ $\dfrac{AB}{DE} \stackrel{?}{=} \dfrac{AC}{DF} \;\Rightarrow\; \dfrac{4}{12} = \dfrac{8}{24}$ ✓

▶ When $x = 7$, the triangles are similar by the SSS Similarity Theorem.

In-Class Practice
Self-Assessment

2. Find the value of x that makes $\triangle ABC \sim \triangle DEF$.

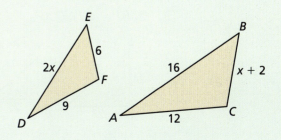

Using the Side-Angle-Side Similarity Theorem

Theorem 8.5

Side-Angle-Side (SAS) Similarity Theorem

If an angle of one triangle is congruent to an angle of a second triangle and the lengths of the sides including these angles are proportional, then the triangles are similar.

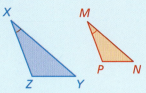

If $\angle X \cong \angle M$ and $\dfrac{ZX}{PM} = \dfrac{XY}{MN}$, then $\triangle XYZ \sim \triangle MNP$.

Prove this Theorem Exercise 18, page 423

EXAMPLE 3 Using the SAS Similarity Theorem

Can the right end of the lean-to shelter be similar to the left end using the angle measure and lengths shown?

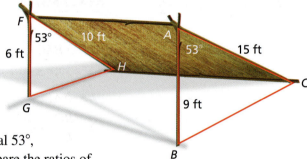

Both $m\angle A$ and $m\angle F$ equal 53°, so $\angle A \cong \angle F$. Next, compare the ratios of the lengths of the sides that include $\angle A$ and $\angle F$.

Shorter sides
$\dfrac{AB}{FG} = \dfrac{9}{6} = \dfrac{3}{2}$

Longer sides
$\dfrac{AC}{FH} = \dfrac{15}{10} = \dfrac{3}{2}$

The lengths of the sides that include $\angle A$ and $\angle F$ are proportional. So, by the SAS Similarity Theorem, $\triangle ABC \sim \triangle FGH$.

▶ Yes, the right end of the shelter can be similar to the left end using the given angle measure and lengths.

In-Class Practice
Self-Assessment

Explain how to show that the indicated triangles are similar.

3. $\triangle SRT \sim \triangle PNQ$

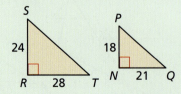

4. $\triangle XZW \sim \triangle YZX$

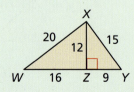

Proving Slope Criteria Using Similar Triangles

You can use similar triangles to prove the Slopes of Parallel Lines Theorem. Because the theorem is biconditional, you must prove both parts. The first part is proved below. The second part is proved in the exercises.

PROOF **Part of Slopes of Parallel Lines Theorem**

Given $\ell \parallel n$, ℓ and n are nonvertical.

Prove $m_\ell = m_n$

First, consider the case where ℓ and n are horizontal. Because all horizontal lines are parallel and have a slope of 0, the statement is true for horizontal lines.

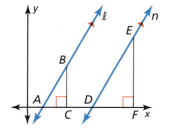

For the case of nonhorizontal, nonvertical lines, draw two such parallel lines. Draw vertical segments parallel to the y-axis to form triangles as shown. Because vertical and horizontal lines are perpendicular, $\angle BCA$ and $\angle EFD$ are right angles.

STATEMENTS	REASONS
1. $\ell \parallel n$	1. Given
2. $\angle BAC \cong \angle EDF$	2. Corresponding Angles Theorem
3. $\angle BCA \cong \angle EFD$	3. Right Angles Congruence Theorem
4. $\triangle ABC \sim \triangle DEF$	4. AA Similarity Theorem
5. $\dfrac{BC}{EF} = \dfrac{AC}{DF}$	5. Corresponding sides of similar figures are proportional.
6. $\dfrac{BC}{AC} = \dfrac{EF}{DF}$	6. Rewrite proportion.
7. $m_\ell = \dfrac{BC}{AC}$, $m_n = \dfrac{EF}{DF}$	7. Definition of slope
8. $m_n = \dfrac{BC}{AC}$	8. Substitution Property of Equality
9. $m_\ell = m_n$	9. Transitive Property of Equality

Concept Summary

Triangle Similarity Theorems

AA Similarity Theorem   SSS Similarity Theorem   SAS Similarity Theorem

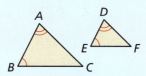 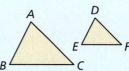 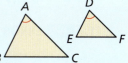

If $\angle A \cong \angle D$ and $\angle B \cong \angle E$, then $\triangle ABC \sim \triangle DEF$.

If $\dfrac{AB}{DE} = \dfrac{BC}{EF} = \dfrac{AC}{DF}$, then $\triangle ABC \sim \triangle DEF$.

If $\angle A \cong \angle D$ and $\dfrac{AB}{DE} = \dfrac{AC}{DF}$, then $\triangle ABC \sim \triangle DEF$.

8.3 Practice

Determine whether △JKL or △RST is similar to △ABC. (See Example 1.)

1.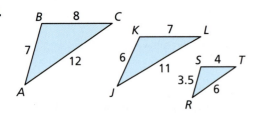

2.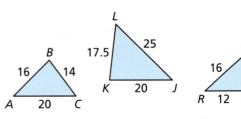

Find the value of x that makes △DEF ~ △XYZ. (See Example 2.)

3.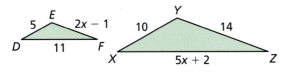

4.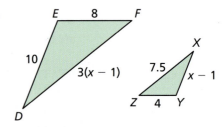

Determine whether the two triangles are similar. If they are similar, write a similarity statement and find the scale factor of triangle B to triangle A. (See Example 3.)

5.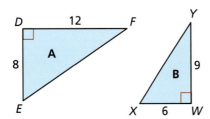

6.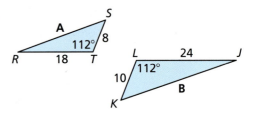

Verify that △ABC ~ △DEF. Find the scale factor of △ABC to △DEF.

7. △ABC: BC = 18, AB = 15, AC = 12
   △DEF: EF = 12, DE = 10, DF = 8

8. △ABC: AB = 10, BC = 16, CA = 20
   △DEF: DE = 25, EF = 40, FD = 50

Show that the triangles are similar and write a similarity statement.

9.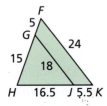

10.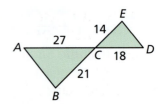

11. **SMP.3 ERROR ANALYSIS** Describe and correct the error in writing a similarity statement.

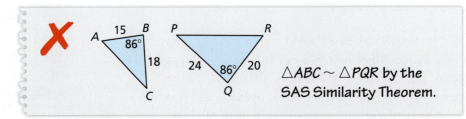

△ABC ~ △PQR by the SAS Similarity Theorem.

422   Chapter 8   Similarity

12. The shortest side of a triangle similar to △XYZ is 20 units long. Find the other side lengths of the triangle.

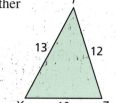

13. **SMP.7** The side lengths of △ABC are 24, 8x, and 48. The side lengths of △DEF are 15, 25, and 6x. Explain whether it is possible that the triangles are similar.

14. You are given two right triangles in which one pair of corresponding legs and the pair of hypotenuses are proportional.

    a. The lengths of the given pair of corresponding legs are 6 and 18, and the lengths of the hypotenuses are 10 and 30. Find the lengths of the other pair of corresponding legs.

    b. Are these triangles similar? Explain whether this suggests a Hypotenuse-Leg Similarity Theorem for right triangles.

15. **CONNECTION TO REAL LIFE** In the portion of the shuffleboard court shown, $\frac{BC}{AC} = \frac{BD}{AE}$. Determine the additional information you need to show that △BCD ~ △ACE using the (a) SSS Similarity Theorem and (b) SAS Similarity Theorem.

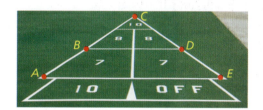

16. **DNA AND GENOMES MOLECULES** In the drawing of a DNA molecule, $WX = XY = 0.8$ inch, $VW = YZ = 0.6$ inch, and $WY = 1.0$ inch. Find the width, VZ, of the DNA molecule in the drawing.

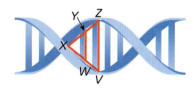

17. **PROOF** Given that △BAC is a right triangle and D, E, and F are midpoints of the sides, prove that △DEF is a right triangle.

18. **PROVING THEOREM 8.5** Write a two-column proof of the SAS Similarity Theorem.

    Given $\angle A \cong \angle D, \frac{AB}{DE} = \frac{AC}{DF}$

    Prove △ABC ~ △DEF

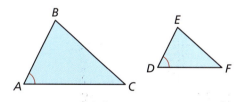

19. **SMP.6** For △JKL and △MNP, $\frac{JK}{MN} = \frac{KL}{NP}$. Without using the SAS Similarity Theorem, explain why $m\angle K$ must equal $m\angle N$ for the triangles to be similar.

20. Explain whether any two right triangles are similar.

21. **SMP.4** You want to create a stained glass window for the opening shown. Show how you can arrange four congruent pieces of glass to create the window. Then show that each piece of stained glass is similar to the opening, and state the side lengths and angle measures of each piece of glass.

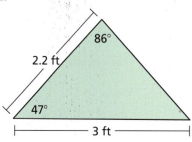

8.3   Proving Triangle Similarity by SSS and SAS   423

22. **CONNECT CONCEPTS** Explain whether △ABC with vertices A(−5, 4), B(−2, 8), and C(1, 6) is similar to △XYZ with vertices X(−4, −6), Y(2, 2), and Z(8, −2).

23. **PROVING THEOREM 3.13** Prove the second part of the Slopes of Parallel Lines Theorem from page 421.

    Given $m_\ell = m_n$, ℓ and n are nonvertical.
    Prove $\ell \parallel n$

    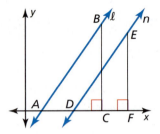

24. Explain why it is not necessary to have an Angle-Side-Angle Similarity Theorem.

25. **PROVING THEOREM 3.14** Complete the partial two-column proof of one part of the Slopes of Perpendicular Lines Theorem. Then finish the proof.

    Given $\ell \perp n$, ℓ and n are nonvertical.
    Prove $m_\ell m_n = -1$

    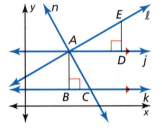

STATEMENTS	REASONS
1. $\ell \perp n$	1. Given
2. $m\angle CAE = 90°$	2. _____
3. $m\angle CAE = m\angle DAE + m\angle CAD$	3. _____
4. _____	4. Transitive Property of Equality
5. $\angle BCA \cong \angle CAD$	5. _____
6. _____	6. Definition of congruent angles
7. $m\angle DAE + m\angle BCA = 90°$	7. _____
8. _____	8. Solve statement 7 for $m\angle DAE$.
9. $m\angle BCA + m\angle BAC + 90° = 180°$	9. _____
10. _____	10. Solve statement 9 for $m\angle BAC$.
11. _____	11. Transitive Property of Equality
12. _____	12. Definition of congruent angles
13. $\angle ABC \cong \angle ADE$	13. _____
14. _____	14. AA Similarity Theorem

26. **PROVING THEOREM 3.14** Complete the partial two-column proof of the other part of the Slopes of Perpendicular Lines Theorem. Then finish the proof.

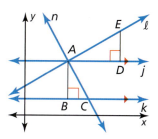

Given $m_\ell m_n = -1$, ℓ and n are nonvertical.

Prove $\ell \perp n$

STATEMENTS	REASONS
1. $m_\ell m_n = -1$	1. Given
2. _____	2. Definition of slope
3. $\dfrac{DE}{AD} \cdot \left(-\dfrac{AB}{BC}\right) = -1$	3. _____
4. $\dfrac{DE}{AD} = \dfrac{BC}{AB}$	4. _____
5. _____	5. Rewrite proportion.
6. _____	6. Right Angles Congruence Theorem
7. _____	7. _____
8. _____	8. Corresponding angles of similar figures are congruent.
9. _____	9. Alternate Interior Angles Theorem
10. $m\angle BAC = m\angle DAE$, $m\angle BCA = m\angle CAD$	10. _____
11. $m\angle BAC + m\angle BCA + 90° = 180°$	11. _____
12. _____	12. Subtraction Property of Equality
13. $m\angle CAD + m\angle DAE = 90°$	13. _____

27. **SMP.1 DIG DEEPER** Explain whether each is a valid method of showing that two quadrilaterals are similar.

    a. SASA

    b. SASAS

    c. SSSS

    d. SSSAS

28. Use a diagram to show why there is no Side-Side-Angle Similarity Theorem.

Interpreting Data

ARCHITECTURE The building pictured below incorporates hundreds of triangles in its design. The entrance to the building consists of three equilateral triangles. The two smaller triangles are congruent. The ratio of the side lengths of the larger triangle to the side lengths of the smaller triangles is 4 : 3.

29. What theorems can you use to prove the triangles are similar?

30. What can you determine about the two triangles created by the overlap of the three triangles?

31. Why do you think the designer used equilateral triangles? What types of triangles would you use?

Review & Refresh

32. In the diagram, ▱*QRST* is similar to ▱*WXYZ*. Find the value of *x*.

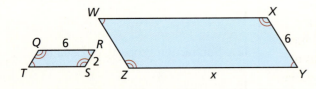

33. Show that the triangles are similar and write a similarity statement.

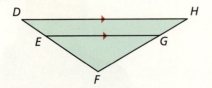

34. Find the coordinates of point *P* along the directed line segment *AB* with vertices $A(-3, -5)$ and $B(9, -1)$ so that the ratio of *AP* to *PB* is 1 to 3.

35. Write an equation of the perpendicular bisector of the segment with endpoints $R(-1, -2)$ and $S(5, 2)$.

Graph △*LMN* with vertices $L(-3, -2)$, $M(-1, 1)$, and $N(2, -3)$ and its image after the composition.

36. **Translation:** $(x, y) \rightarrow (x - 4, y + 3)$
    Rotation: 180° about the origin

37. **Rotation:** 90° about the origin
    Reflection: in the *y*-axis

Decide whether enough information is given to prove that the triangles are congruent. If so, state the theorem you can use.

38. △*JKL*, △*LMJ*

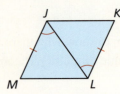

39. △*QRS*, △*QTS*

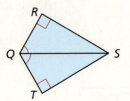

8.4 Proportionality Theorems

Learning Target: Understand and use proportionality theorems.

Success Criteria:
- I can use proportionality theorems to find lengths in triangles.
- I can find lengths when two transversals intersect three parallel lines.
- I can find lengths when a ray bisects an angle of a triangle.

INVESTIGATE Discovering Proportionality Relationships

Work with a partner. Use technology.

1. Construct any $\triangle ABC$. Construct $\overline{DE}$ parallel to $\overline{BC}$ with endpoints on $\overline{AB}$ and $\overline{AC}$, respectively.

2. Find a relationship among AD, BD, AE, and CE. Is the relationship true when you construct $\overline{DE}$ in other locations parallel to $\overline{BC}$?

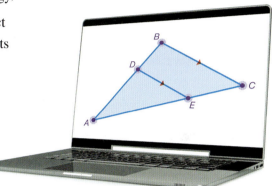

3. Change $\triangle ABC$ and repeat Exercises 1 and 2 several times. Write a conjecture that summarizes your results.

4. A line that bisects an angle of a triangle divides the opposite side into two segments. How are the lengths of these segments related to the lengths of the other two sides of the triangle? Provide examples to support your reasoning.

Using the Triangle Proportionality Theorem

Theorem 8.6

Triangle Proportionality Theorem

If a line parallel to one side of a triangle intersects the other two sides, then it divides the two sides proportionally.

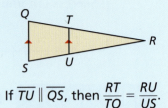

If $\overline{TU} \parallel \overline{QS}$, then $\dfrac{RT}{TQ} = \dfrac{RU}{US}$.

Prove this Theorem Exercise 12, page 432

Theorem 8.7

Converse of the Triangle Proportionality Theorem

If a line divides two sides of a triangle proportionally, then it is parallel to the third side.

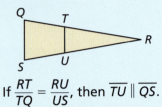

If $\dfrac{RT}{TQ} = \dfrac{RU}{US}$, then $\overline{TU} \parallel \overline{QS}$.

Prove this Theorem Exercise 13, page 432

EXAMPLE 1 Finding the Length of a Segment

Find the length of $\overline{RQ}$.

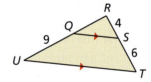

The diagram shows that $\overline{QS} \parallel \overline{UT}$. So, $\overline{QS}$ divides $\overline{RU}$ and $\overline{RT}$ proportionally. Use the Triangle Proportionality Theorem to write a proportion.

$\dfrac{RQ}{QU} = \dfrac{RS}{ST}$ Triangle Proportionality Theorem

$\dfrac{RQ}{9} = \dfrac{4}{6}$ Substitute.

$RQ = 6$ Multiply each side by 9.

▶ The length of $\overline{RQ}$ is 6 units.

In-Class Practice

Self-Assessment

1. Find the length of $\overline{YZ}$.

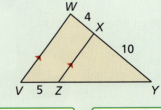

The theorems on the previous page also imply the following.

Contrapositive of the Triangle Proportionality Theorem

If $\dfrac{RT}{TQ} \neq \dfrac{RU}{US}$, then $\overline{TU} \nparallel \overline{QS}$.

Inverse of the Triangle Proportionality Theorem

If $\overline{TU} \nparallel \overline{QS}$, then $\dfrac{RT}{TQ} \neq \dfrac{RU}{US}$.

EXAMPLE 2 Using the Converse of the Triangle Proportionality Theorem

On the shoe rack, $BA = 33$ centimeters, $CB = 27$ centimeters, $CD = 44$ centimeters, and $DE = 25$ centimeters. Explain why the shelf is not parallel to the floor.

Find and simplify the ratios of the lengths.

$$\dfrac{CD}{DE} = \dfrac{44}{25} \qquad \dfrac{CB}{BA} = \dfrac{27}{33} = \dfrac{9}{11}$$

▶ Because $\dfrac{44}{25} \neq \dfrac{9}{11}$, $\overleftrightarrow{BD}$ is not parallel to $\overleftrightarrow{AE}$. So, the shelf is not parallel to the floor.

Construction

Constructing a Point along a Directed Line Segment

Construct the point L on $\overline{AB}$ so that the ratio of AL to LB is 3 to 1.

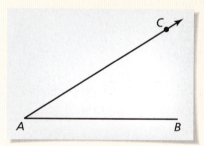
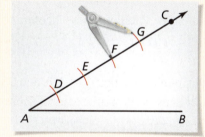
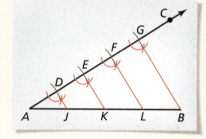

Draw $\overline{AB}$ of any length. Choose any point C not on $\overleftrightarrow{AB}$. Draw $\overline{AC}$.

Place the point of a compass at A and make successive arcs with the same radius. Label the points of intersection E, F, and G.

Draw $\overline{GB}$. Copy $\angle AGB$ and construct congruent angles at D, E, and F with sides that intersect $\overline{AB}$ at J, K, and L.

In-Class Practice

Self-Assessment

2. Determine whether $\overline{PS} \parallel \overline{QR}$.

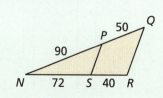

8.4 Proportionality Theorems **429**

Using Other Proportionality Theorems

Theorem 8.8

Three Parallel Lines Theorem

If three parallel lines intersect two transversals, then they divide the transversals proportionally.

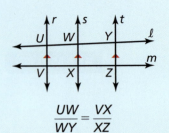

$$\frac{UW}{WY} = \frac{VX}{XZ}$$

Prove this Theorem Exercise 16, page 433

EXAMPLE 3 Using the Three Parallel Lines Theorem

Find the distance HF between Main Street and South Main Street.

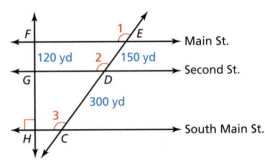

Because ∠1, ∠2, and ∠3 are all congruent, you can use the Corresponding Angles Converse to determine that $\overleftrightarrow{FE}$, $\overleftrightarrow{GD}$, and $\overleftrightarrow{HC}$ are parallel. These parallel lines divide the transversals proportionally. Find HF.

Use the Three Parallel Lines Theorem to write a proportion.

$\dfrac{HG}{GF} = \dfrac{CD}{DE}$ Three Parallel Lines Theorem

$\dfrac{HG}{120} = \dfrac{300}{150}$ Substitute.

$HG = 240$ Multiply each side by 120.

By the Segment Addition Postulate, $HF = HG + GF = 240 + 120 = 360$.

▶ So, the distance between Main Street and South Main Street is 360 yards.

In-Class Practice

Self-Assessment

Find the length of the given line segment.

3. $\overline{BD}$

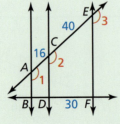

4. $\overline{JM}$

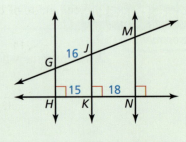

| 1 | I don't understand yet. | 2 | I can do it with help. | 3 | I can do it on my own. | 4 | I can teach someone. |

Theorem 8.9

Triangle Angle Bisector Theorem

If a ray bisects an angle of a triangle, then it divides the opposite side into segments whose lengths are proportional to the lengths of the other two sides.

Prove this Theorem Exercise 17, page 433

$$\frac{AD}{DB} = \frac{CA}{CB}$$

EXAMPLE 4 Using the Triangle Angle Bisector Theorem

Find the length of $\overline{RS}$.

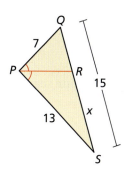

Because $\angle QPR \cong \angle SPR$, $\overrightarrow{PR}$ is an angle bisector of $\angle QPS$. So, you can apply the Triangle Angle Bisector Theorem. Use the fact that $RQ = 15 - x$.

$$\frac{RQ}{RS} = \frac{PQ}{PS} \quad \text{Triangle Angle Bisector Theorem}$$

$$\frac{15 - x}{x} = \frac{7}{13} \quad \text{Substitute.}$$

$$195 - 13x = 7x \quad \text{Cross Products Property}$$

$$9.75 = x \quad \text{Solve for } x.$$

▶ So, the length of $\overline{RS}$ is 9.75 units.

In-Class Practice

Self-Assessment

Find the value of the variable.

5.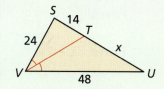

6.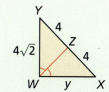

8.4 Proportionality Theorems

8.4 Practice

Find the length of $\overline{AB}$. (Example 1.)

▶ 1.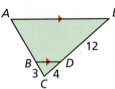

2.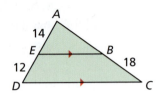

Determine whether $\overline{KM} \parallel \overline{JN}$. (Example 2.)

▶ 3.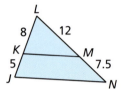

4.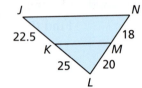

Find the length of the indicated line segment. (Example 3.)

▶ 5. $\overline{VX}$

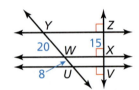

6. $\overline{SU}$

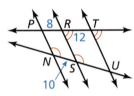

Find the value of the variable. (Example 4.)

▶ 7.

8.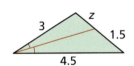

9.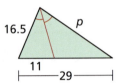

SMP.7 Find the value of x for which $\overline{PQ} \parallel \overline{RS}$.

10.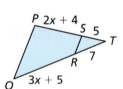

11.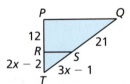

12. **PROVING THEOREM 8.6** Prove the Triangle Proportionality Theorem.

   Given $\overline{QS} \parallel \overline{TU}$

   Prove $\dfrac{QT}{TR} = \dfrac{SU}{UR}$

   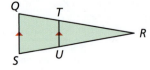

13. **PROVING THEOREM 8.7** Prove the Converse of the Triangle Proportionality Theorem.

   Given $\dfrac{ZY}{YW} = \dfrac{ZX}{XV}$

   Prove $\overline{YX} \parallel \overline{WV}$

14. **CONNECTION TO REAL LIFE** The real estate term lake *frontage* refers to the distance along the edge of a piece of property that touches a lake.

    a. Find the lake frontage of each lot shown.
    b. In general, the more lake frontage a lot has, the higher its selling price. Which lot(s) should be listed for the highest price?
    c. The least expensive lot is $250,000. Find the prices of the other lots when the lot prices are in the same ratio as the lake frontages.

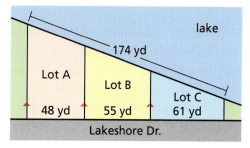

15. **SMP.8** Find the values of x and y.

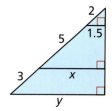

16. **PROVING THEOREM 8.8** Use the diagram with the auxiliary line drawn to write a paragraph proof of the Three Parallel Lines Theorem.

    Given $k_1 \parallel k_2 \parallel k_3$

    Prove $\dfrac{CB}{BA} = \dfrac{DE}{EF}$

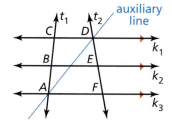

17. **PROVING THEOREM 8.9** Use the diagram with the auxiliary lines drawn to write a paragraph proof of the Triangle Angle Bisector Theorem.

    Given $\angle YXW \cong \angle WXZ$

    Prove $\dfrac{YW}{WZ} = \dfrac{XY}{XZ}$

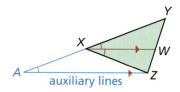

18. **SMP.1** Explain how the Triangle Midsegment Theorem is related to the Triangle Proportionality Theorem.

19. **CONSTRUCTION** Given segments with lengths r, s, and t, construct a segment of length x, such that $\dfrac{r}{s} = \dfrac{t}{x}$.

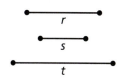

20. **PROOF** Prove Ceva's Theorem: If P is any point inside $\triangle ABC$, then $\dfrac{AY}{YC} \cdot \dfrac{CX}{XB} \cdot \dfrac{BZ}{ZA} = 1$.

    (Hint: Draw segments parallel to $\overline{BY}$ through A and C, as shown. Apply the Triangle Proportionality Theorem to $\triangle ACM$.)

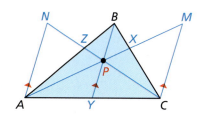

8.4 Proportionality Theorems

Interpreting Data

COSMIC TRIANGLE Cosmology is the study of the universe. The cosmic triangle displays different models of the universe. The location of a model in the triangle depends on the answers to three questions: How much matter is in the universe? Is the expansion of the universe accelerating or decelerating? Is the universe flat?

21. The lines that appear to be parallel in the cosmic triangle are parallel. Use the Triangle Proportionality Theorem to make several statements about the data display.

22. Recent observations suggests that the universe is flat, and its expansion rate is accelerating. Which model of the universe matches these observations?

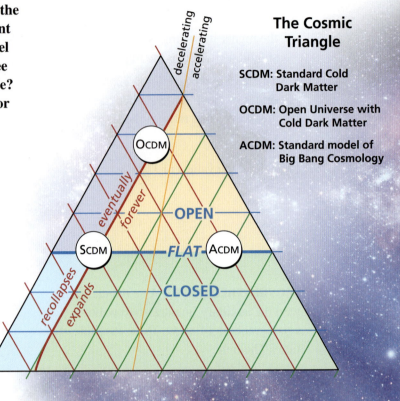

The Cosmic Triangle

SCDM: Standard Cold Dark Matter

OCDM: Open Universe with Cold Dark Matter

ACDM: Standard model of Big Bang Cosmology

Review & Refresh

23. Graph △FGH with vertices $F(-4, -2)$, $G(-2, 0)$, and $H(-4, -4)$ and its image after the similarity transformation.

    Translation: $(x, y) \rightarrow (x + 2, y + 4)$

    Dilation: $(x, y) \rightarrow \left(\frac{1}{2}x, \frac{1}{2}y\right)$

24. You want to install a public mailbox. The public mailbox should be the same distance from each of the three apartment buildings shown. Use the diagram to determine the location of the public mailbox.

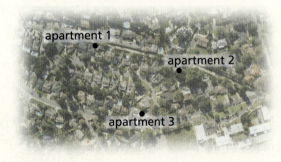

25. Find the value of x when △DEF ~ △MNP.

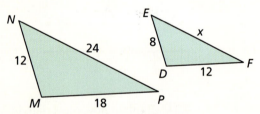

26. Solve the equation $A = \dfrac{pq}{2}$ for p.

27. Show that the triangles are similar. Write a similarity statement.

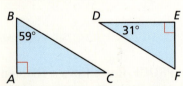

28. The side lengths of △ABC are 10, 6x, and 20, and the side lengths of △DEF are 25, 30, and 50. Find the value of x that makes △ABC ~ △DEF.

434   Chapter 8   Similarity

8 Chapter Review

Rate your understanding of each section.

 I don't understand yet.
 I can do it with help.
 I can do it on my own.
I can teach someone.

8.1 Similar Polygons (pp. 401–410)

⊙ **Learning Target:** Understand the relationship between similar polygons.

Find the scale factor. Then list all pairs of congruent angles and write the ratios of the corresponding side lengths in a statement of proportionality.

1. $ABCD \sim EFGH$

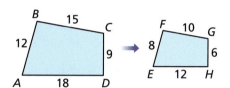

2. $\triangle XYZ \sim \triangle RPQ$

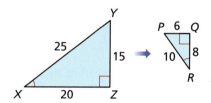

3. The polygons are similar. Find the value of x.

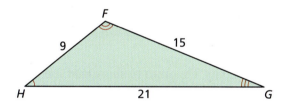

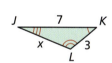

Decide whether the two polygons are similar.

4.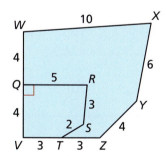

5.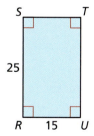

6. A square piece of cloth with an area of 324 square inches is folded in half twice to form the napkin shown. What is the area of the folded napkin?

8.2 Proving Triangle Similarity by AA (pp. 411–416)

Learning Target: Understand and use the Angle-Angle Similarity Theorem.

Explain whether the triangles are similar. If they are, write a similarity statement.

7.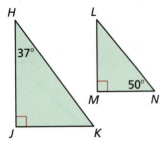

8.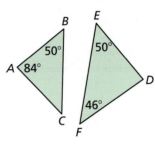

Show that the triangles are similar and write a similarity statement.

9.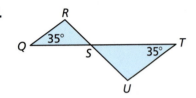

10.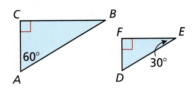

11. A cell tower casts a shadow that is 72 feet long, while a nearby tree that is 27 feet tall casts a shadow that is 6 feet long. How tall is the tower?

8.3 Proving Triangle Similarity by SSS and SAS (pp. 417–426)

Learning Target: Understand and use additional triangle similarity theorems.

Use the SSS Similarity Theorem or the SAS Similarity Theorem to show that the triangles are similar and to write a similarity statement.

12.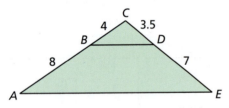

13.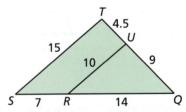

14. Find the value of x that makes $\triangle ABC \sim \triangle DEF$.

 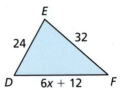

15. The side lengths of $\triangle LMN$ are 20, $8x$, and 60. The side lengths of $\triangle RST$ are 25, 50, and $15x$. Explain whether it is possible that the triangles are similar.

16. $\triangle ABC$ is an isosceles triangle that has an angle with a measure of 50°. $\triangle DEF$ is an isosceles triangle that has an angle with a measure of 40°. Explain whether it is possible that the triangles are similar.

8.4 Proportionality Theorems (pp. 427–434)

Learning Target: Understand and use proportionality theorems.

Determine whether $\overline{AB} \parallel \overline{CD}$.

17.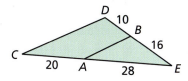

18.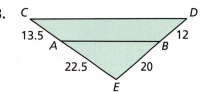

19. Find the length of $\overline{YB}$.

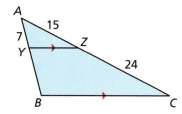

20. List two possible sets of values for *VX* and *XZ*.

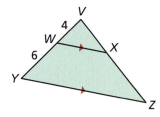

Find the length of $\overline{AB}$.

21.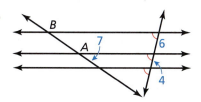

22.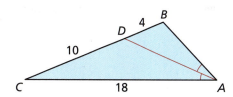

23. Find the distance *AC* between First Street and Third Street.

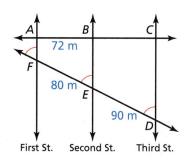

24. Draw $\overline{AB}$ with a length of at least 2 inches. Construct a segment that divides $\overline{AB}$ in the ratio 2 to 3.

8 PERFORMANCE TASK
SMP.5

African Burial Ground
NATIONAL MONUMENT

In 1991, archaeologists found human skeletal remains at a site in New York City. A total of 419 bodies were uncovered while excavating the northern portion of the site. Dating from the middle 1630s to 1795, the site is the nation's earliest and largest African burial ground rediscovered in the United States. The site was designated as the nation's 123rd National Monument on February 27, 2006.

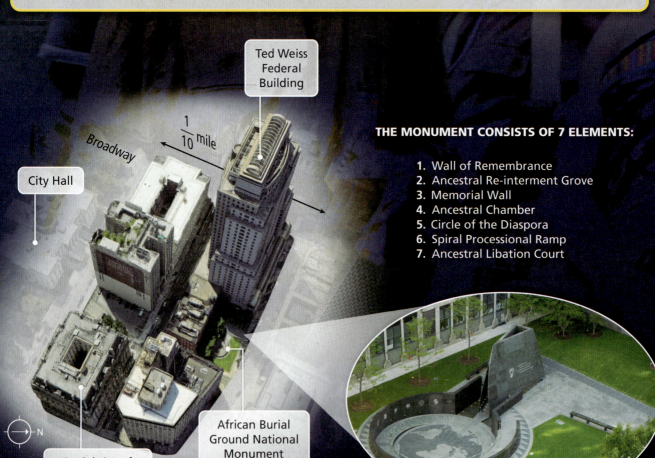

Ted Weiss Federal Building

$\frac{1}{10}$ mile

Broadway

City Hall

African Burial Ground National Monument

Burial site of an estimated 15,000–20,000 people

THE MONUMENT CONSISTS OF 7 ELEMENTS:

1. Wall of Remembrance
2. Ancestral Re-interment Grove
3. Memorial Wall
4. Ancestral Chamber
5. Circle of the Diaspora
6. Spiral Processional Ramp
7. Ancestral Libation Court

Analyzing Data

Use the information on the previous page to complete the following exercises.

1 Explain what is shown in the display. What do you notice? What do you wonder?

2 An overhead view of the Ancestral Chamber at the African Burial Ground National Monument is shown. What do the two red triangles represent?

3 Explain how you know that the triangles are similar, and approximate the value of x.

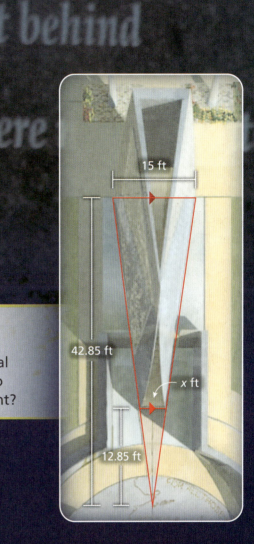

CREATING A BROCHURE

Create a brochure for the monument. Your brochure should include information about the seven elements of the monument, the cultural and historical importance of the site, and a scale drawing of the Ancestral Chamber and the Circle of the Diaspora. Indicate the scale factor that you used to create your drawing.

9 Right Triangles and Trigonometry

9.1 The Pythagorean Theorem
9.2 Special Right Triangles
9.3 Similar Right Triangles
9.4 The Tangent Ratio
9.5 The Sine and Cosine Ratios
9.6 Solving Right Triangles
9.7 Law of Sines and Law of Cosines

NATIONAL GEOGRAPHIC EXPLORER

Beth Shapiro   **EVOLUTIONARY MOLECULAR BIOLOGIST**

Dr. Beth Shapiro researches how populations and species change through time by studying genetic material extracted from fossils and other remains. She wrote *How to Clone a Mammoth*, a book describing the scientific techniques needed and challenges that must be overcome to revive an extinct species.

- What does de-extinction mean?
- What does cloning mean? Have any animals been cloned?
- Where did woolly mammoths live? When did they become extinct?
- What is a mastodon? How are mammoths and mastodons related to modern-day elephants?

PERFORMANCE TASK
Animal skeletons are often assembled and put on display in museums. In the Performance Task on pages 500 and 501, you will work on a new woolly mammoth exhibit at a museum.

Extinct Species

Big Idea of the Chapter
Use Right Triangle Relationships

There are several special relationships in right triangles. You have already used right triangles to find distances in the coordinate plane. In this chapter, you will use concepts involving right triangles, such as the Pythagorean Theorem and trigonometric ratios.

Between 15,000 and 20,000 years ago, wolves were domesticated. They developed a more docile disposition and learned to read human facial expressions. Their skulls, teeth, and paws shrank. To study the history of the domestication of dogs, scientists compared the jawbone fossils of canines found in different parts of the world. The 6 jawbone fossils shown below are from 3 domesticated dogs and 3 wolves.

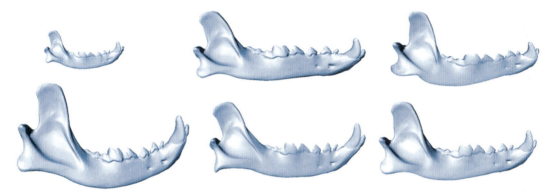

One way to compare the shapes of the jawbones is to associate each one with a right triangle. The height and base of each triangle represents the height and base of the jawbone.

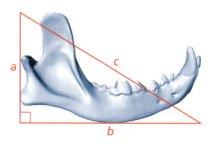

1. Trace each of the six jawbones. For each, draw the right triangle that represents the height and base of the jawbone.

2. Find the ratio $a : b$ for each of the triangles you drew. What can you conclude?

3. Which of the jawbones shown above do you think are from wolves? Why?

Getting Ready for Chapter 9

Solving Proportions

EXAMPLE 1 Solve $\dfrac{x}{10} = \dfrac{3}{2}$.

$\dfrac{x}{10} = \dfrac{3}{2}$ Write the proportion.

$x \cdot 2 = 10 \cdot 3$ Cross Products Property

$2x = 30$ Multiply.

$\dfrac{2x}{2} = \dfrac{30}{2}$ Division Property of Equality

$x = 15$ Simplify.

Solve the proportion.

1. $\dfrac{x}{12} = \dfrac{3}{4}$
2. $\dfrac{x}{3} = \dfrac{5}{2}$
3. $\dfrac{4}{x} = \dfrac{7}{56}$
4. $\dfrac{10}{23} = \dfrac{4}{x}$
5. $\dfrac{x+1}{2} = \dfrac{21}{14}$
6. $\dfrac{9}{3x-15} = \dfrac{3}{12}$

Using Properties of Radicals

EXAMPLE 2 Simplify $\sqrt{128}$.

$\sqrt{128} = \sqrt{64 \cdot 2}$ Factor using the greatest perfect square factor.

$= \sqrt{64} \cdot \sqrt{2}$ Product Property of Square Roots

$= 8\sqrt{2}$ Simplify.

EXAMPLE 3 Simplify $\dfrac{4}{\sqrt{5}}$.

$\dfrac{4}{\sqrt{5}} = \dfrac{4}{\sqrt{5}} \cdot \dfrac{\sqrt{5}}{\sqrt{5}}$ Multiply by $\dfrac{\sqrt{5}}{\sqrt{5}}$.

$= \dfrac{4\sqrt{5}}{\sqrt{25}}$ Product Property of Square Roots

$= \dfrac{4\sqrt{5}}{5}$ Simplify.

Simplify the expression.

7. $\sqrt{75}$
8. $\sqrt{270}$
9. $\sqrt{135}$
10. $\dfrac{2}{\sqrt{7}}$
11. $\dfrac{5}{\sqrt{2}}$
12. $\dfrac{12}{\sqrt{6}}$

9.1 The Pythagorean Theorem

Learning Target: Understand and apply the Pythagorean Theorem.

Success Criteria:
- I can list common Pythagorean triples.
- I can find missing side lengths of right triangles.
- I can classify a triangle as *acute*, *right*, or *obtuse* given its side lengths.

INVESTIGATE Proving the Pythagorean Theorem

Work with a partner. In 1876, James Garfield, a sitting member of the United States Congress, discovered a new proof of the Pythagorean Theorem. To prove the theorem, Garfield arranged two congruent right triangles to create the trapezoid shown.

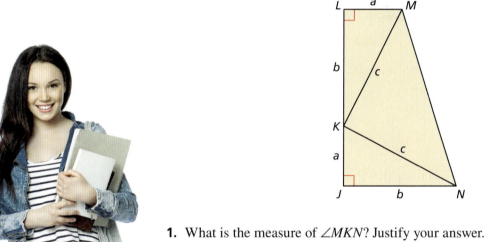

1. What is the measure of ∠MKN? Justify your answer.

2. Write two different expressions that represent the total area of the trapezoid.

3. Use your expressions in Exercise 2 to write an equation relating a, b, and c.

4. Use the equation you found in Exercise 3 to find the missing side lengths of the triangles below.

   a.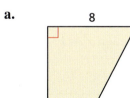
   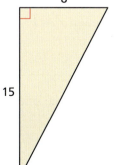

   b.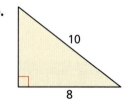

RESOURCES

9.1 The Pythagorean Theorem 443

Vocabulary
Pythagorean triple

Using the Pythagorean Theorem

Theorem 9.1

Pythagorean Theorem

In a right triangle, the square of the length of the hypotenuse is equal to the sum of the squares of the lengths of the legs.

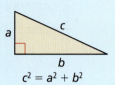

$c^2 = a^2 + b^2$

Prove this Theorem Investigate, page 443; Exercise 23, page 449

A **Pythagorean triple** is a set of three positive integers a, b, and c that satisfy the equation $c^2 = a^2 + b^2$.

Key Concept

Common Pythagorean Triples and Some of Their Multiples

3, 4, 5	5, 12, 13	8, 15, 17	7, 24, 25
6, 8, 10	10, 24, 26	16, 30, 34	14, 48, 50
9, 12, 15	15, 36, 39	24, 45, 51	21, 72, 75
$3x, 4x, 5x$	$5x, 12x, 13x$	$8x, 15x, 17x$	$7x, 24x, 25x$

After the first row, the triples are multiples of the boldfaced triple above it.

EXAMPLE 1 Using the Pythagorean Theorem

Find the value of x. Then tell whether the side lengths form a Pythagorean triple.

$c^2 = a^2 + b^2$	Pythagorean Theorem
$x^2 = 5^2 + 12^2$	Substitute.
$x^2 = 25 + 144$	Multiply.
$x^2 = 169$	Add.
$x = 13$	Take the positive square root of each side.

▶ The value of x is 13. Because the side lengths 5, 12, and 13 are integers that satisfy the equation $c^2 = a^2 + b^2$, they form a Pythagorean triple.

In-Class Practice

Self-Assessment

1. Find the value of x. Then tell whether the side lengths form a Pythagorean triple.

EXAMPLE 2 Using the Pythagorean Theorem

Find the value of x. Then tell whether the side lengths form a Pythagorean triple.

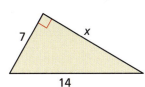

$$c^2 = a^2 + b^2$$ Pythagorean Theorem
$$14^2 = 7^2 + x^2$$ Substitute.
$$196 = 49 + x^2$$ Multiply.
$$147 = x^2$$ Subtract 49 from each side.
$$\sqrt{147} = x$$ Take the positive square root of each side.
$$7\sqrt{3} = x$$ Simplify.

▶ The value of x is $7\sqrt{3}$. Because $7\sqrt{3}$ is not an integer, the side lengths do not form a Pythagorean triple.

EXAMPLE 3 Finding a Missing Length

The skyscrapers are connected by a skywalk with support beams. Find the length of each support beam.

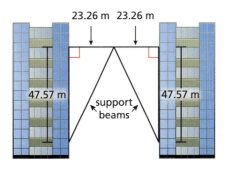

Each support beam forms the hypotenuse of a right triangle. Use the Pythagorean Theorem to find the length x (in meters) of each support beam.

$$x^2 = (23.26)^2 + (47.57)^2$$ Pythagorean Theorem
$$x = \sqrt{(23.26)^2 + (47.57)^2}$$ Take the positive square root of each side.
$$x \approx 52.95$$ Use technology.

▶ The length of each support beam is about 52.95 meters.

In-Class Practice
Self-Assessment

2. Find the value of x. Then tell whether the side lengths form a Pythagorean triple.

3. An *anemometer* is a device used to measure wind speed. The anemometer shown is attached to the top of a pole. Support wires are attached to the pole 5 feet above the ground. Each support wire is 6 feet long. How far from the base of the pole is each wire attached to the ground?

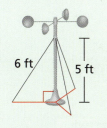

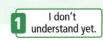

9.1 The Pythagorean Theorem

Using the Converse of the Pythagorean Theorem

The converse of the Pythagorean Theorem is also true. You can use it to determine whether a triangle with given side lengths is a right triangle.

Theorem 9.2

Converse of the Pythagorean Theorem

If the square of the length of the longest side of a triangle is equal to the sum of the squares of the lengths of the other two sides, then the triangle is a right triangle.

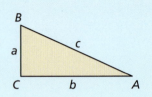

If $c^2 = a^2 + b^2$, then $\triangle ABC$ is a right triangle.

Prove this Theorem Exercise 25, page 449

EXAMPLE 4 **Verifying Right Triangles**

Tell whether each triangle is a right triangle.

a.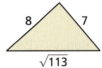

b.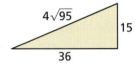

Let c represent the length of the longest side of the triangle. Check to see whether the side lengths satisfy the equation $c^2 = a^2 + b^2$.

a.
$$c^2 = a^2 + b^2$$
$$(\sqrt{113})^2 \stackrel{?}{=} 7^2 + 8^2$$
$$113 \stackrel{?}{=} 49 + 64$$
$$113 = 113 \checkmark$$

▶ The triangle is a right triangle.

b.
$$c^2 = a^2 + b^2$$
$$(4\sqrt{95})^2 \stackrel{?}{=} 15^2 + 36^2$$
$$4^2 \cdot (\sqrt{95})^2 \stackrel{?}{=} 15^2 + 36^2$$
$$16 \cdot 95 \stackrel{?}{=} 225 + 1{,}296$$
$$1{,}520 \neq 1{,}521 \; ✗$$

▶ The triangle is *not* a right triangle.

In-Class Practice
Self-Assessment

Tell whether the triangle is a right triangle.

4.

5.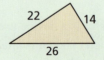

6.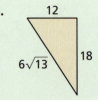

Classifying Triangles

You can use the *Pythagorean Inequalities Theorem* to determine whether a triangle is acute or obtuse.

Theorem 9.3

Pythagorean Inequalities Theorem

For any $\triangle ABC$, where c is the length of the longest side, the following statements are true.

If $c^2 < a^2 + b^2$, then $\triangle ABC$ is acute.

If $c^2 > a^2 + b^2$, then $\triangle ABC$ is obtuse.

$c^2 < a^2 + b^2$

$c^2 > a^2 + b^2$

Prove this Theorem Exercises 26 and 27, page 449

EXAMPLE 5 Classifying Triangles

Determine whether segments with lengths of 4.3 feet, 5.2 feet, and 6.1 feet form a triangle. If so, is the triangle *acute*, *right*, or *obtuse*?

Use the Triangle Inequality Theorem to determine whether the segments form a triangle.

$4.3 + 5.2 \overset{?}{>} 6.1$ $4.3 + 6.1 \overset{?}{>} 5.2$ $5.2 + 6.1 \overset{?}{>} 4.3$

$9.5 > 6.1$ ✓ $10.4 > 5.2$ ✓ $11.3 > 4.3$ ✓

So, these segments form a triangle. Classify the triangle by comparing the square of the length of the longest side with the sum of the squares of the lengths of the other two sides.

$c^2 \;\square\; a^2 + b^2$ Compare c^2 with $a^2 + b^2$.

$6.1^2 \;\square\; 4.3^2 + 5.2^2$ Substitute.

$37.21 \;\square\; 18.49 + 27.04$ Simplify.

$37.21 < 45.53$ Add.

▶ Because $c^2 < a^2 + b^2$, the segments with lengths of 4.3 feet, 5.2 feet, and 6.1 feet form an acute triangle.

In-Class Practice

Self-Assessment

Determine whether the segment lengths form a triangle. If so, is the triangle *acute*, *right*, or *obtuse*?

7. 3, 4, 6
8. 2.1, 2.8, 3.5
9. 4.6, 2.8, 7.4

1 I don't understand yet. **2** I can do it with help. **3** I can do it on my own. **4** I can teach someone.

9.1 The Pythagorean Theorem

9.1 Practice

Find the value of x. Then tell whether the side lengths form a Pythagorean triple. (See Examples 1 and 2.)

▶ 1.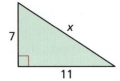

2.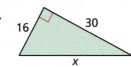

▶ 3.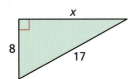

4.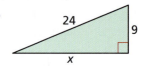

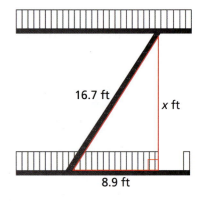

5. **CONNECTION TO REAL LIFE** Find the distance between the two platforms of the fire escape. (See Example 3.)

6. **CONNECTION TO REAL LIFE** Television sizes are measured by the lengths of their diagonals. You want to purchase a television that is at least 40 inches. Should you purchase a television that is 20.25 inches tall and 36 inches wide?

Tell whether the triangle is a right triangle. (See Example 4.)

7.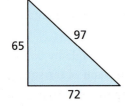

8.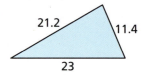

▶ 9.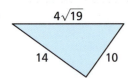

10.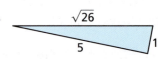

Determine whether the segment lengths form a triangle. If so, is the triangle *acute*, *right*, or *obtuse*? (See Example 5.)

▶ 11. 10, 11, and 14

12. 6, 8, and 14

13. 12, 16, and 20

14. 15, 20, and 26

15. 5.3, 6.7, and 7.8

16. 10, 15, and $5\sqrt{13}$

17. **SMP.5** You are making a frame for a painting. The rectangular painting will be 24 inches long and 18 inches wide. Without measuring angles, describe how you can use a tool to be certain that the corners of the frame are 90°.

Find the area of the isosceles triangle.

18.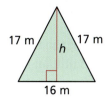

19.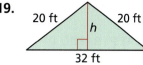

20. The side lengths of a triangle are 9, 12, and x. What values of x make the triangle a right triangle? an acute triangle? an obtuse triangle?

21. You make a kite for International Kite Day on January 14th. Binding for the perimeter of a kite comes in lengths of two yards. How many lengths should you buy for the kite shown?

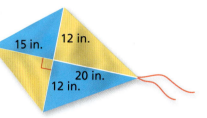

22. **PROVING THEOREM 5.9** Prove the Hypotenuse-Leg (HL) Congruence Theorem.

23. **PROVING THEOREM 9.1** Explain why $\triangle ABC$, $\triangle ACD$, and $\triangle CBD$ are similar. Then use the similar triangles to prove the Pythagorean Theorem.

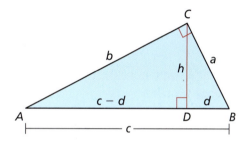

24. **SMP.8** Consider two positive integers m and n, where $m > n$. Do the following expressions produce a Pythagorean triple? If so, prove your answer. If not, give a counterexample.

$$2mn,\ m^2 - n^2,\ m^2 + n^2$$

25. **PROVING THEOREM 9.2** Prove the Converse of the Pythagorean Theorem. (*Hint*: Draw $\triangle ABC$ with side lengths a, b, and c, where c is the length of the longest side. Then draw a right triangle with side lengths a, b, and x, where x is the length of the hypotenuse. Compare lengths c and x.)

26. **PROVING THEOREM 9.3** Prove the Pythagorean Inequalities Theorem when $c^2 < a^2 + b^2$.

    Given In $\triangle ABC$, $c^2 < a^2 + b^2$, where c is the length of the longest side. $\triangle PQR$ has side lengths a, b, and x, where x is the length of the hypotenuse, and $\angle R$ is a right angle.

    Prove $\triangle ABC$ is an acute triangle.

27. **PROVING THEOREM 9.3** Prove the Pythagorean Inequalities Theorem when $c^2 > a^2 + b^2$.

28. **SMP.6 CONNECT CONCEPTS** Let $ABCD$ be a square in the coordinate plane with vertices that have integer coordinates. If possible, draw $ABCD$ so that it has the given area, and show that $ABCD$ is a square. If not possible, explain why not.

    a. 5 square units
    b. 6 square units
    c. 8 square units

Interpreting Data

GREAT PYRAMID OF GIZA Archaeologists have determined that the Great Pyramid of Giza was built about 4,500 years ago. It contains about 2.3 million blocks. Each side of its square base is 756 meters long and its height is 147 meters.

29. Use right triangles and the Pythagorean Theorem to find the length of the edge labeled below.

30. If it took 20 years to build the pyramid, about how many blocks had to be put in place each day?

Review & Refresh

31. Find the value of x.

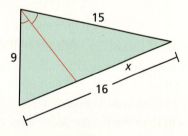

Graph the polygon with the given vertices and its image after the indicated transformation.

32. $A(-4, 1)$, $B(5, -2)$, $C(2, 4)$

   Translation: $(x, y) \rightarrow (x - 2, y - 3)$

33. $J(-3, -1)$, $K(1, 2)$, $L(1, -1)$, $M(-3, -4)$

   Dilation: scale factor $k = 3$

34. Explain how to find $m\angle ABD$ when you are given $m\angle ABC$ and $m\angle CBD$.

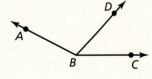

35. Find the coordinates of the centroid of $\triangle JKL$ with vertices $J(-1, 2)$, $K(5, 6)$, and $L(5, -2)$.

36. Two different tent sizes made by the same company are shown. Determine whether the triangular faces of the tents are similar.

37. Find $m\angle 1$, $m\angle 2$, and $m\angle 3$.

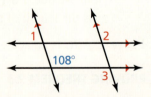

38. $WXYZ$ is an isosceles trapezoid, where $\overline{XY} \parallel \overline{WZ}$, $\overline{WX} \cong \overline{YZ}$, and $m\angle W = 54°$. Find $m\angle X$, $m\angle Y$, and $m\angle Z$.

9.2 Special Right Triangles

> **Learning Target:** Understand and use special right triangles.
> **Success Criteria:**
> - I can find side lengths in 45°-45°-90° triangles.
> - I can find side lengths in 30°-60°-90° triangles.
> - I can use special right triangles to solve real-life problems.

INVESTIGATE Finding Side Ratios of Special Right Triangles

SMP.5 **Work with a partner.**

1. One type of special right triangle is a 45°-45°-90° triangle.

   a. Construct a right triangle with acute angle measures of 45°.

   b. Find the exact ratios of the side lengths.

   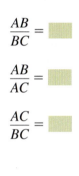
   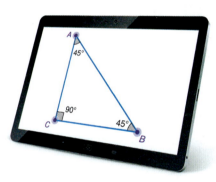

   c. **SMP.8** Repeat parts (a) and (b) for several other 45°-45°-90° triangles. Use your results to write a conjecture about the ratios of the side lengths of 45°-45°-90° triangles.

2. Another type of special right triangle is a 30°-60°-90° triangle.

   a. Construct a right triangle with acute angle measures of 30° and 60°.

   b. Find the exact ratios of the side lengths.

   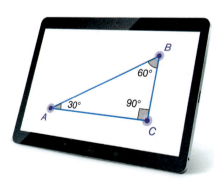

   c. **SMP.8** Repeat parts (a) and (b) for several other 30°-60°-90° triangles. Use your results to write a conjecture about the ratios of the side lengths of 30°-60°-90° triangles.

Finding Side Lengths in Special Right Triangles

A 45°-45°-90° triangle is an *isosceles right triangle* that can be formed by cutting a square in half diagonally.

Theorem 9.4

45°-45°-90° Triangle Theorem

In a 45°-45°-90° triangle, the hypotenuse is $\sqrt{2}$ times as long as each leg.

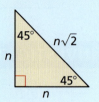

hypotenuse = leg · $\sqrt{2}$

Prove this Theorem Exercise 11, page 455

EXAMPLE 1 Finding Side Lengths in 45°-45°-90° Triangles

Find the value of x.

a.

b.

a. By the Triangle Sum Theorem, the measure of the third angle must be 45°, so the triangle is a 45°-45°-90° triangle.

$\text{hypotenuse} = \text{leg} \cdot \sqrt{2}$ 45°-45°-90° Triangle Theorem
$x = 8 \cdot \sqrt{2}$ Substitute.
$x = 8\sqrt{2}$ Simplify.

b. By the Base Angles Theorem and the Corollary to the Triangle Sum Theorem, the triangle is a 45°-45°-90° triangle.

$\text{hypotenuse} = \text{leg} \cdot \sqrt{2}$ 45°-45°-90° Triangle Theorem
$5\sqrt{2} = x \cdot \sqrt{2}$ Substitute.
$5 = x$ Divide each side by $\sqrt{2}$.

In-Class Practice

Self-Assessment

Find the missing side length(s).

1.

2.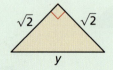

Theorem 9.5

30°-60°-90° Triangle Theorem

In a 30°-60°-90° triangle, the hypotenuse is twice as long as the shorter leg, and the longer leg is $\sqrt{3}$ times as long as the shorter leg.

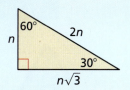

hypotenuse = shorter leg · 2
longer leg = shorter leg · $\sqrt{3}$

Prove this Theorem Exercise 12, page 455

EXAMPLE 2 — Finding Side Lengths in a 30°-60°-90° Triangle

Find the values of x and y.

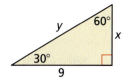

Find the value of x.

longer leg = shorter leg · $\sqrt{3}$	30°-60°-90° Triangle Theorem
$9 = x \cdot \sqrt{3}$	Substitute.
$\dfrac{9}{\sqrt{3}} = x$	Divide each side by $\sqrt{3}$.
$\dfrac{9}{\sqrt{3}} \cdot \dfrac{\sqrt{3}}{\sqrt{3}} = x$	Multiply by $\dfrac{\sqrt{3}}{\sqrt{3}}$.
$\dfrac{9\sqrt{3}}{3} = x$	Multiply fractions.
$3\sqrt{3} = x$	Simplify.

Find the value of y.

hypotenuse = shorter leg · 2	30°-60°-90° Triangle Theorem
$y = 3\sqrt{3} \cdot 2$	Substitute.
$y = 6\sqrt{3}$	Simplify.

▶ The value of x is $3\sqrt{3}$, and the value of y is $6\sqrt{3}$.

In-Class Practice

Self-Assessment

Find the missing side length(s).

3.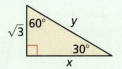

4.

9.2 Special Right Triangles

Connections to Real Life

EXAMPLE 3 **Finding the Area of a Figure**

36 in.

The caution sign shown is shaped like an equilateral triangle. Estimate the area of the sign.

Find the height h of the triangle by dividing it into two 30°-60°-90° triangles. The length of the longer leg of one of these triangles is h. The length of the shorter leg is 18 inches.

$h = 18 \cdot \sqrt{3} = 18\sqrt{3}$ 30°-60°-90° Triangle Theorem

Use the base and height to find the area of the triangle.

Area $= \frac{1}{2}bh = \frac{1}{2}(36)(18\sqrt{3}) \approx 561.18$

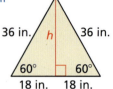

▶ The area of the sign is about 561 square inches.

EXAMPLE 4 **Finding a Missing Side Length**

A tipping platform is a ramp used to unload trucks. How high is the end of an 80-foot ramp when the tipping angle is 30°? 45°?

When the tipping angle is 30°, the height h of the ramp is the length of the shorter leg of a 30°-60°-90° triangle. The length of the hypotenuse is 80 feet.

$80 = 2h$ 30°-60°-90° Triangle Theorem
$40 = h$ Divide each side by 2.

When the tipping angle is 45°, the height is the length of a leg of a 45°-45°-90° triangle. The length of the hypotenuse is 80 feet.

$80 = h \cdot \sqrt{2}$ 45°-45°-90° Triangle Theorem
$\dfrac{80}{\sqrt{2}} = h$ Divide each side by $\sqrt{2}$.
$56.57 \approx h$ Use technology.

▶ When the tipping angle is 30°, the ramp height is 40 feet. When the tipping angle is 45°, the height is about 57 feet.

In-Class Practice

Self-Assessment

5. A recycling sticker resembles an equilateral triangle with side lengths of 6 centimeters. Approximate the area of the sticker.

6. The body of a dump truck rests on a frame. The body is raised to empty a load of sand. How far from the frame is the front of the 14-foot-long body when it is tipped upward by a 60° angle?

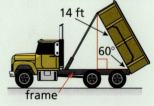

 I don't understand yet.   I can do it with help.   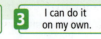 I can do it on my own.   I can teach someone.

9.2 Practice

Find the value of x. (See Example 1.)

1.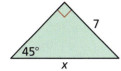
2.
3.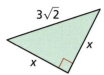

Find the values of x and y. (See Example 2.)

4.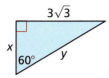
5.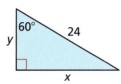
6.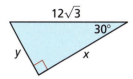

Find the area of the figure. (See Example 3.)

7.
8.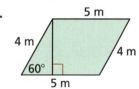

9. **CONNECTION TO REAL LIFE** How high does the drawbridge rise when x is 30°? 45°? 60°? (See Example 4.)

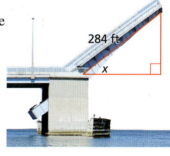

10. **CONNECTION TO REAL LIFE** The nut is shaped like a regular hexagon. Find the value of x.

11. **PROVING THEOREM 9.4** Write a paragraph proof of the 45°-45°-90° Triangle Theorem.

    Given $\triangle DEF$ is a 45°-45°-90° triangle.

    Prove The hypotenuse is $\sqrt{2}$ times as long as each leg.

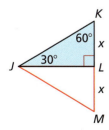

12. **PROVING THEOREM 9.5** Write a paragraph proof of the 30°-60°-90° Triangle Theorem. (*Hint*: Construct $\triangle JML$ congruent to $\triangle JKL$.)

    Given $\triangle JKL$ is a 30°-60°-90° triangle.

    Prove The hypotenuse is twice as long as the shorter leg, and the longer leg is $\sqrt{3}$ times as long as the shorter leg.

13. Find the side length of an equilateral triangle with an area of $3\sqrt{3}$ square units.

14. **DIG DEEPER** $\triangle TUV$ is a 30°-60°-90° triangle. Two vertices are $U(3, -1)$ and $V(-3, -1)$, $\overline{UV}$ is the hypotenuse, and point T is in Quadrant I. Find the coordinates of T. How do you know your answer is correct?

9.2 Special Right Triangles 455

Interpreting Data

SPIRAL OF THEODORUS The Spiral of Theodorus is comprised of right triangles placed as shown. The spiral starts with an isosceles right triangle with leg lengths of 1, and every triangle after that has a shorter leg length of 1.

Ammonite Fossil

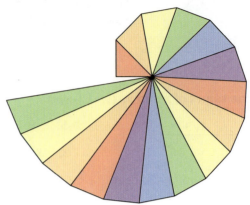

Spiral of Theodorus

15. Find the hypotenuse for several of the right triangles in the spiral. Describe the pattern.

16. How many of the right triangles are 45°-45°-90° triangles?

17. How many of the right triangles are 30°-60°-90° triangles?

Review & Refresh

18. In the diagram, $\triangle DEF \sim \triangle LMN$. Find the value of x.

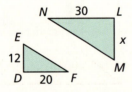

19. Determine whether segments with lengths of 2.6 feet, 4.8 feet, and 6.0 feet form a triangle. If so, is the triangle *acute*, *right*, or *obtuse*?

20. Find the length of $\overline{DC}$.

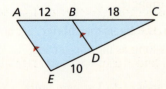

21. The endpoints of $\overline{CD}$ are $C(-2, 9)$ and $D(3, -1)$. Find the coordinates of the midpoint M.

22. Use the vertices to determine whether $\triangle DEF$ and $\triangle MNP$ are congruent.

$D(3, 5), E(8, 0), F(4, -3)$

$M(-5, 3), N(0, 8), P(3, 4)$

23. Which pieces of stained glass, if any, are similar?

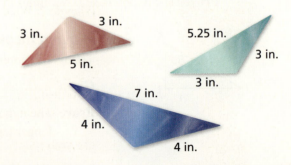

24. Three vertices of $\square JKLM$ are $J(0, 5), K(4, 5),$ and $M(3, 0)$. Find the coordinates of vertex L.

9.3 Similar Right Triangles

Learning Target: Use proportional relationships in right triangles.

Success Criteria:
- I can explain the Right Triangle Similarity Theorem.
- I can find the geometric mean of two numbers.
- I can find missing dimensions in right triangles.

INVESTIGATE Analyzing Similarity in Right Triangles

SMP.5 Work with a partner.

1. Construct two congruent right scalene triangles.

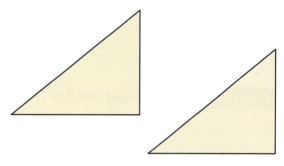

2. Construct an altitude to the hypotenuse in one of the right triangles. Use the altitude to form two smaller triangles. Label the three triangles as shown.

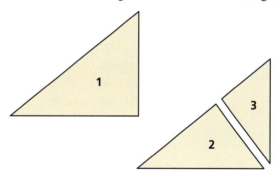

3. Compare the angle measures of Triangle 1 with the angle measures of Triangle 2. What can you conclude about the two triangles?

4. Repeat Exercise 3 for Triangles 1 and 3, and for Triangles 2 and 3.

5. When you draw an altitude to the hypotenuse of a right triangle, what is the relationship between the two smaller triangles that are formed? How are each of the smaller triangles related to the larger triangle?

6. Use your results in Exercise 5 to find x. Explain your method.

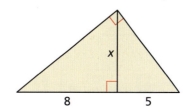

9.3 Similar Right Triangles 457

Vocabulary
geometric mean

Identifying Similar Triangles

When the altitude is drawn to the hypotenuse of a right triangle, the two smaller triangles are similar to the original triangle and to each other.

Theorem 9.6

Right Triangle Similarity Theorem

If the altitude is drawn to the hypotenuse of a right triangle, then the two triangles formed are similar to the original triangle and to each other.

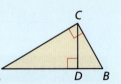

△CBD ~ △ABC, △ACD ~ △ABC, and △CBD ~ △ACD.

Prove this Theorem Exercise 22, page 463

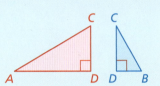

EXAMPLE 1 Identifying Similar Triangles

Identify the similar triangles.

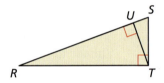

△RST is a right triangle with altitude $\overline{TU}$ drawn to the hypotenuse. By the Right Triangle Similarity Theorem, the two triangles formed by $\overline{TU}$ are similar to △RST and to each other. Sketch the three similar right triangles so that the corresponding angles and sides have the same orientation.

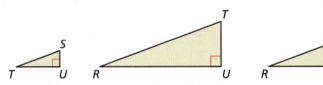

▶ △TSU ~ △RTU ~ △RST

In-Class Practice

Self-Assessment

Identify the similar triangles.

1.

2.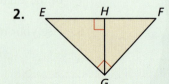

| **1** I don't understand yet. | **2** I can do it with help. | **3** I can do it on my own. | **4** I can teach someone. |

Connections to Real Life

EXAMPLE 2 **Using Similar Triangles**

A roof has a cross section that is a right triangle. The diagram shows the approximate dimensions of this cross section. Find the height h of the roof.

$\overline{YW}$ is the altitude of $\triangle XZY$ drawn to the hypotenuse. By the Right Triangle Similarity Theorem, the two triangles formed by $\overline{YW}$ are similar to $\triangle XZY$ and to each other. Sketch the three similar right triangles so that the corresponding angles and sides have the same orientation.

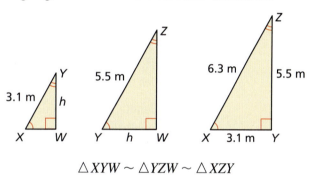

$$\triangle XYW \sim \triangle YZW \sim \triangle XZY$$

Because $\triangle XYW \sim \triangle XZY$, you can write a proportion.

$\dfrac{YW}{ZY} = \dfrac{XY}{XZ}$ Corresponding side lengths of similar triangles are proportional.

$\dfrac{h}{5.5} = \dfrac{3.1}{6.3}$ Substitute.

$h \approx 2.7$ Multiply each side by 5.5.

▶ The height of the roof is about 2.7 meters.

In-Class Practice

Self-Assessment

Find the value of x.

3.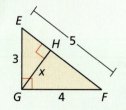

4.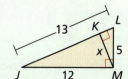

9.3   Similar Right Triangles

Using a Geometric Mean

The **geometric mean** of two positive numbers a and b is the positive number x that satisfies $\frac{a}{x} = \frac{x}{b}$. So, $x^2 = ab$ and $x = \sqrt{ab}$.

EXAMPLE 3 Finding a Geometric Mean

Find the geometric mean of 24 and 48.

$x^2 = ab$	Definition of geometric mean
$x^2 = 24 \cdot 48$	Substitute 24 for a and 48 for b.
$x = \sqrt{24 \cdot 48}$	Take the positive square root of each side.
$x = \sqrt{24 \cdot 24 \cdot 2}$	Factor.
$x = 24\sqrt{2}$	Simplify.

▶ The geometric mean of 24 and 48 is $24\sqrt{2} \approx 33.9$.

Theorem 9.7

Geometric Mean (Altitude) Theorem

In a right triangle, the altitude to the hypotenuse divides the hypotenuse into two segments.

The length of the altitude is the geometric mean of the lengths of the two segments of the hypotenuse.

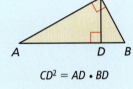

$CD^2 = AD \cdot BD$

Prove this Theorem Exercise 20, page 463

Theorem 9.8

Geometric Mean (Leg) Theorem

In a right triangle, the altitude to the hypotenuse divides the hypotenuse into two segments.

The length of each leg of the right triangle is the geometric mean of the lengths of the hypotenuse and the segment of the hypotenuse that is adjacent to that leg.

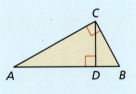

$CB^2 = DB \cdot AB$
$AC^2 = AD \cdot AB$

Prove this Theorem Exercise 21, page 463

In-Class Practice

Self-Assessment

Find the geometric mean of the two numbers.

5. 12 and 27   **6.** 18 and 54   **7.** 16 and 18

EXAMPLE 4 Using a Geometric Mean

Find the value of each variable.

a.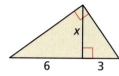

Apply the Geometric Mean (Altitude) Theorem.

$x^2 = 6 \cdot 3$
$x^2 = 18$
$x = \sqrt{18}$
$x = \sqrt{9} \cdot \sqrt{2}$
$x = 3\sqrt{2}$

▶ The value of x is $3\sqrt{2}$.

b.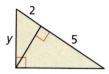

Apply the Geometric Mean (Leg) Theorem.

$y^2 = 2 \cdot (5 + 2)$
$y^2 = 2 \cdot 7$
$y^2 = 14$
$y = \sqrt{14}$

▶ The value of y is $\sqrt{14}$.

EXAMPLE 5 Using Indirect Measurement

STEM Video: Height of a Rock Wall

To find the cost of installing a rock wall in your school gymnasium, you need to find the height of the gym wall. You use a cardboard square to line up the top and bottom of the gym wall with your eye. Your friend measures the vertical distance from the ground to your eye and the horizontal distance from you to the gym wall. Find the height of the gym wall.

By the Geometric Mean (Altitude) Theorem, you know that 8.5 is the geometric mean of w and 5.

$8.5^2 = w \cdot 5$ Geometric Mean (Altitude) Theorem
$72.25 = 5w$ Multiply.
$14.45 = w$ Divide each side by 5.

▶ The height of the wall is $5 + w = 5 + 14.45 = 19.45$ feet.

In-Class Practice
Self-Assessment

8. Find the value of x in the triangle at the right.

9. **WHAT IF?** In Example 5, the vertical distance from the ground to your eye is 5.5 feet, and the distance from you to the gym wall is 9 feet. Find the height of the gym wall.

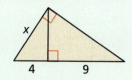

9.3 Similar Right Triangles 461

9.3 Practice

Identify the similar triangles. (See Example 1.)

1.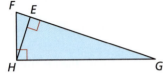

2.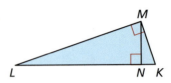

Find the value of x. (See Example 2.)

3.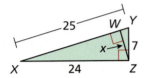

4.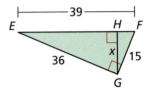

5.

6.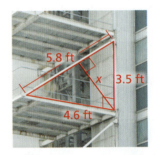

Find the geometric mean of the two numbers. (See Example 3.)

7. 8 and 32

8. 9 and 16

9. 24 and 45

Find the value of the variable. (See Example 4.)

10.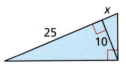

11.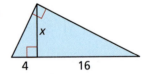

12.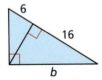

13.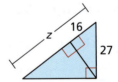

14. **SMP.3 ERROR ANALYSIS** Describe and correct the error in applying the Geometric Mean (Leg) Theorem.

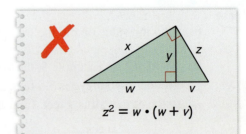

$z^2 = w \cdot (w + v)$

CONNECTION TO REAL LIFE Use the diagram to answer the questions. (See Example 5.)

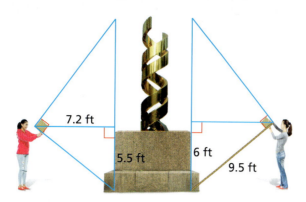

▶ **15.** You use a cardboard square to line up the top and bottom of the DNA sculpture with your eye, as shown on the left of the diagram. Approximate the height of the sculpture.

16. Your friend stakes a piece of rope at the base of the monument, as shown on the right of the diagram. Your friend extends the rope to the cardboard square lined up to the top and bottom of the monument. Use the measurements to approximate the height of the monument. Explain whether you get the same answer as you did in Exercise 15.

SMP.7 Find the value(s) of the variable(s).

17. 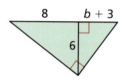   **18.** 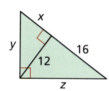   **19.**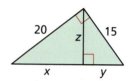

Use the given statements to prove the theorem.

  Given $\triangle ABC$ is a right triangle.
    Altitude $\overline{CD}$ is drawn to hypotenuse $\overline{AB}$.

20. PROVING THEOREM 9.7 Prove the Geometric Mean (Altitude) Theorem by showing that $CD^2 = AD \cdot BD$.

21. PROVING THEOREM 9.8 Prove the Geometric Mean (Leg) Theorem by showing that $CB^2 = DB \cdot AB$ and $AC^2 = AD \cdot AB$.

22. PROVING THEOREM 9.6 Prove the Right Triangle Similarity Theorem.

  Given $\triangle ABC$ is a right triangle.
    Altitude $\overline{CD}$ is drawn to hypotenuse $\overline{AB}$.
  Prove $\triangle CBD \sim \triangle ABC$,
    $\triangle ACD \sim \triangle ABC$,
    $\triangle CBD \sim \triangle ACD$

23. SMP.1 DIG DEEPER The arithmetic mean and geometric mean of two nonnegative numbers x and y are shown. Write an inequality that relates these two means. Justify your answer.

  arithmetic mean $= \dfrac{x + y}{2}$ geometric mean $= \sqrt{xy}$

Interpreting Data

GEOMETRIC MEAN To find the arithmetic mean of n numbers, divide the sum of the numbers by n. To find the geometric mean of n numbers, find the nth root of the product of the numbers. The areas of 15 squares are shown.

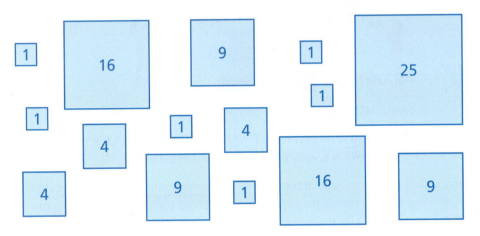

24. Find the arithmetic mean and geometric mean of the areas of the 15 squares.

25. Which mean would you use to describe the 15 areas? Why?

Review & Refresh

26. $\overline{DE}$ is a midsegment of $\triangle ABC$. Find the value of x.

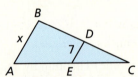

27. Find BC.

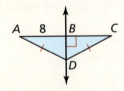

28. How long is the ramp?

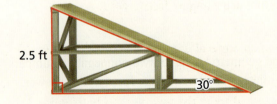

29. Tell whether the triangle is a right triangle.

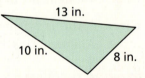

30. Find the value of y.

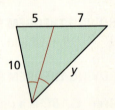

31. Determine whether the triangles are similar. If so, write a similarity statement.

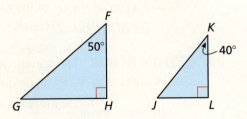

464 Chapter 9 Right Triangles and Trigonometry

9.4 The Tangent Ratio

Learning Target: Understand and use the tangent ratio.

Success Criteria:
- I can explain the tangent ratio.
- I can find tangent ratios.
- I can use tangent ratios to solve real-life problems.

INVESTIGATE Calculating a Tangent Ratio

Work with a partner. Use technology.

1. Construct right scalene $\triangle ABC$, in which $\overline{AC}$ is a horizontal segment, and $\overline{BC}$ is a vertical segment. Find $m\angle A$ and $m\angle B$.

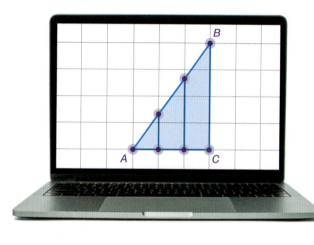

2. Construct several segments perpendicular to $\overline{AC}$ to form right triangles that share vertex A. Explain how the triangles are related.

3. Use the definition below to find tan A for each right triangle in Exercise 2. Compare the values. Then find the tangent of the other acute angle in each triangle. Compare your results with those of other students.

   Let $\triangle ABC$ be a right triangle with acute $\angle A$. The *tangent* of $\angle A$ (written as tan A) is defined as follows.

   $$\tan A = \frac{\text{length of leg opposite } \angle A}{\text{length of leg adjacent to } \angle A} = \frac{BC}{AC}$$

   a. Does the size of a right triangle affect the value of the tangent of either acute angle? Justify your conclusion.

   b. Does the measure of an angle affect the value of the tangent of the angle? Explain your reasoning.

4. Summarize what you learned about the tangent ratio in Exercise 3.

Vocabulary
trigonometric ratio
tangent
angle of elevation

Using the Tangent Ratio

A **trigonometric ratio** is a ratio of the lengths of two sides in a right triangle. All right triangles with a given acute angle are similar by the AA Similarity Theorem. So, $\triangle JKL \sim \triangle XYZ$, and you can write $\dfrac{KL}{YZ} = \dfrac{JL}{XZ}$. This can be rewritten as $\dfrac{KL}{JL} = \dfrac{YZ}{XZ}$, which is a trigonometric ratio. So, trigonometric ratios are constant for a given angle measure.

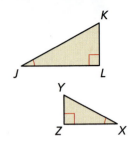

The **tangent** ratio is a trigonometric ratio for acute angles that involves the lengths of the legs of a right triangle.

READING
Remember the following abbreviations.
tangent → tan
opposite → opp
adjacent → adj

Key Concept

Tangent Ratio

Let $\triangle ABC$ be a right triangle with acute $\angle A$.
The tangent of $\angle A$ (written as tan A) is defined as follows.

$$\tan A = \dfrac{\text{length of leg opposite } \angle A}{\text{length of leg adjacent to } \angle A} = \dfrac{BC}{AC}$$

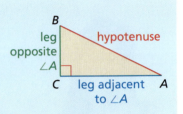

You can use the same diagram to find the tangent of $\angle B$. Notice that the leg adjacent to $\angle A$ is the leg *opposite* $\angle B$ and the leg opposite $\angle A$ is the leg *adjacent* to $\angle B$.

EXAMPLE 1 Finding Tangent Ratios

Find tan S and tan R.

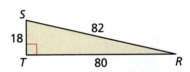

$$\tan S = \dfrac{\text{opp } \angle S}{\text{adj to } \angle S} = \dfrac{RT}{ST} = \dfrac{80}{18} = \dfrac{40}{9} \approx 4.4444$$

$$\tan R = \dfrac{\text{opp } \angle R}{\text{adj to } \angle R} = \dfrac{ST}{RT} = \dfrac{18}{80} = \dfrac{9}{40} = 0.225$$

In-Class Practice

Self-Assessment

Find tan J and tan K.

1.
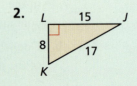

2.

[1] I don't understand yet. [2] I can do it with help. [3] I can do it on my own. [4] I can teach someone.

EXAMPLE 2 Finding a Leg Length

Find the value of x.

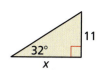

Use the tangent of an acute angle to find a leg length.

$\tan 32° = \dfrac{\text{opp}}{\text{adj}}$ Write ratio for tangent of 32°.

$\tan 32° = \dfrac{11}{x}$ Substitute.

$x \cdot \tan 32° = 11$ Multiply each side by x.

$x = \dfrac{11}{\tan 32°}$ Divide each side by tan 32°.

$x \approx 17.6$ Use technology.

▶ The value of x is about 17.6.

EXAMPLE 3 Using a Special Right Triangle to Find a Tangent

Use a special right triangle to find the tangent of a 60° angle.

Because all 30°-60°-90° triangles are similar, you can simplify your calculations by choosing 1 as the length of the shorter leg. Use the 30°-60°-90° Triangle Theorem to find the length of the longer leg.

longer leg = shorter leg • $\sqrt{3}$ 30°-60°-90° Triangle Theorem

$= 1 \cdot \sqrt{3}$ Substitute.

$= \sqrt{3}$ Simplify.

Find tan 60°.

$\tan 60° = \dfrac{\text{opp}}{\text{adj}}$ Write ratio for tangent of 60°.

$\tan 60° = \dfrac{\sqrt{3}}{1}$ Substitute.

$\tan 60° = \sqrt{3}$ Simplify.

▶ The tangent of any 60° angle is $\sqrt{3}$, or about 1.7321.

In-Class Practice

Self-Assessment

Find the value of x.

3.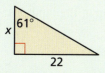

4.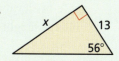

5. **WHAT IF?** In Example 3, the length of the shorter leg is 5 instead of 1. Show that the tangent of 60° is still equal to $\sqrt{3}$.

1 I don't understand yet. 2 I can do it with help. 3 I can do it on my own. 4 I can teach someone.

9.4 The Tangent Ratio

Connections to Real Life

An **angle of elevation** is an angle formed by a horizontal line and a line of sight *up* to an object.

EXAMPLE 4 Using the Angle of Elevation

You measure your distance from a tree and the angle of elevation from the ground to the top of the tree. Find the height of the tree.

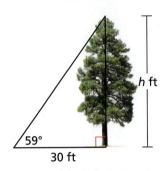

$\tan 59° = \dfrac{\text{opp}}{\text{adj}}$ Write ratio for tangent of 59°.

$\tan 59° = \dfrac{h}{30}$ Substitute.

$30 \cdot \tan 59° = h$ Multiply each side by 30.

$49.9 \approx h$ Use technology.

▶ The tree is about 50 feet tall.

Check Because 59° is close to 60°, you can use the legs of a 30°-60°-90° triangle to check your answer.

longer leg = shorter leg · $\sqrt{3}$ 30°-60°-90° Triangle Theorem

= 30 · $\sqrt{3}$ Substitute.

≈ 51.2   Use technology.

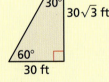

51.2 is close to the value of *h*. ✓

In-Class Practice

Self-Assessment

6. You measure your distance from a lamppost and the angle of elevation from the ground to the top of the lamppost. Find the height of the lamppost.

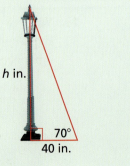

 I don't understand yet.   I can do it with help.   I can do it on my own.   I can teach someone.

9.4 Practice

Find the tangents of the acute angles in the right triangle. (See Example 1.)

1.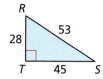
2.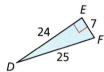
3.

Find the value of x. (See Example 2.)

4.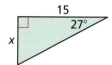
5.
6.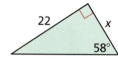

Use a special right triangle to find the tangent of the given angle measure. (See Example 3.)

7. 45°
8. 30°

9. **CONNECTION TO REAL LIFE** You measure your distance from the base of the Washington Monument and the angle of elevation from the ground to the top of the monument. Find the height h of the Washington Monument. (See Example 4.)

10. **CONNECTION TO REAL LIFE** Scientists can measure the depths of craters on the moon by looking at photos of shadows. Estimate the depth d of the crater.

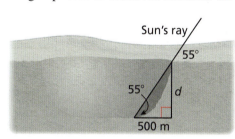

11. **SMP.7** Find the tangent of the smaller acute angle in a right triangle with side lengths 5, 12, and 13.

12. **SMP.7** How does the tangent of an acute angle in a right triangle change as the angle measure increases? Justify your answer.

13. Write expressions for the tangent of each acute angle in the right triangle. Explain how the tangent of one acute angle is related to the tangent of the other acute angle. What kind of angle pair is $\angle A$ and $\angle B$?

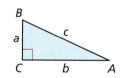

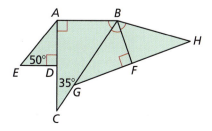

14. **DIG DEEPER** Find the perimeter of the figure, where $AC = 26$, $AD = BF$, and D is the midpoint of $\overline{AC}$.

Interpreting Data

ANGLE OF CLIMB Similar to the angle of elevation, the angle of climb is the angle between a horizontal plane representing Earth's surface and the actual flight path of the aircraft during its ascent. A pilot needs to be aware of the angle of climb while operating an aircraft.

15. A typical angle of climb is between 15° and 25°. Estimate the angle of climb shown in the diagram.

16. An angle of climb is usually expressed as a percent (tan C). Estimate the percent for the angle of climb shown in the diagram.

17. A plane is climbing at a rate of 350 miles per hour at its angle of climb to an altitude of 30,000 feet. If it maintains its angle of climb, when will it reach its desired altitude?

Review & Refresh

18. Find the value of x. Tell whether the side lengths form a Pythagorean triple.

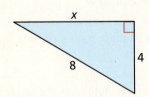

19. Find the geometric mean of 18 and 26.

20. Find the area of the polygon with vertices $(1, 1)$, $(2, -2)$, and $(-3, -2)$.

21. Graph $\overline{XY}$ with endpoints $X(-4, 2)$ and $Y(1, -3)$ and its image after a rotation 180° about the origin, followed by a reflection in the x-axis.

22. Find the coordinates of the circumcenter of the triangle with vertices $A(-1, 2)$, $B(-1, -2)$, and $C(5, -2)$.

Find the value of x.

23. 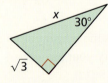   **24.**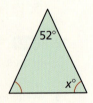

25. The horizontal boards of a fence are parallel. Find $m\angle 2$.

470   Chapter 9   Right Triangles and Trigonometry

9.5 The Sine and Cosine Ratios

Learning Target: Understand and use the sine and cosine ratios.

Success Criteria:
- I can explain the sine and cosine ratios.
- I can find sine and cosine ratios.
- I can use sine and cosine ratios to solve real-life problems.

INVESTIGATE Calculating Sine and Cosine Ratios

Work with a partner. Use technology.

1. Construct right scalene $\triangle ABC$, in which $\overline{AC}$ is a horizontal segment and $\overline{BC}$ is a vertical segment. Find $m\angle A$ and $m\angle B$. Then construct several segments perpendicular to $\overline{AC}$ to form right triangles that share vertex A.

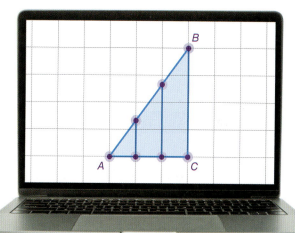

2. Use the definitions below to find $\sin A$ and $\cos A$ for each right triangle in Exercise 1.

   Let $\triangle ABC$ be a right triangle with acute $\angle A$. The *sine* of $\angle A$ and *cosine* of $\angle A$ are defined as follows.

   $$\sin A = \frac{\text{length of leg opposite } \angle A}{\text{length of hypotenuse}} = \frac{BC}{AB}$$

   $$\cos A = \frac{\text{length of leg adjacent to } \angle A}{\text{length of hypotenuse}} = \frac{AC}{AB}$$

   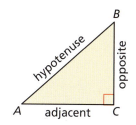

   a. Does the size of a right triangle affect the value of the sine and cosine of an acute angle?

   b. Does the measure of an angle affect the value of the sine and cosine of the angle?

3. What is the relationship between the measures of $\angle A$ and $\angle B$? Find $\sin B$ and $\cos B$.

4. Summarize what you learned about the sine and cosine ratios in Exercises 2 and 3.

Vocabulary
sine
cosine
angle of depression

Using the Sine and Cosine Ratios

The **sine** and **cosine** ratios are trigonometric ratios for acute angles that involve the lengths of a leg and the hypotenuse of a right triangle.

Key Concept

Sine and Cosine Ratios

Let $\triangle ABC$ be a right triangle with acute $\angle A$. The sine of $\angle A$ and cosine of $\angle A$ (written as sin A and cos A) are defined as follows.

$$\sin A = \frac{\text{length of leg opposite } \angle A}{\text{length of hypotenuse}} = \frac{BC}{AB}$$

$$\cos A = \frac{\text{length of leg adjacent to } \angle A}{\text{length of hypotenuse}} = \frac{AC}{AB}$$

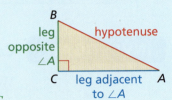

EXAMPLE 1 — Finding Sine and Cosine Ratios

Find sin S, sin R, cos S, and cos R.

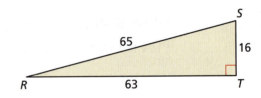

$$\sin S = \frac{\text{opp } \angle S}{\text{hyp}} = \frac{RT}{SR} = \frac{63}{65} \approx 0.9692$$

$$\sin R = \frac{\text{opp } \angle R}{\text{hyp}} = \frac{ST}{SR} = \frac{16}{65} \approx 0.2462$$

$$\cos S = \frac{\text{adj to } \angle S}{\text{hyp}} = \frac{ST}{SR} = \frac{16}{65} \approx 0.2462$$

$$\cos R = \frac{\text{adj to } \angle R}{\text{hyp}} = \frac{RT}{SR} = \frac{63}{65} \approx 0.9692$$

In-Class Practice

Self-Assessment

1. Find sin D, sin F, cos D, and cos F.

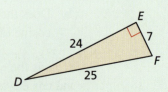

> **Key Concept**
>
> **Sine and Cosine of Complementary Angles**
>
> The sine of an acute angle is equal to the cosine of its complement.
> The cosine of an acute angle is equal to the sine of its complement.
>
> Let A and B be complementary angles. Then the following statements are true.
>
> $\sin A = \cos(90° - A) = \cos B \qquad \sin B = \cos(90° - B) = \cos A$
> $\cos A = \sin(90° - A) = \sin B \qquad \cos B = \sin(90° - B) = \sin A$

EXAMPLE 2 **Rewriting Trigonometric Expressions**

Write $\sin 56°$ in terms of cosine.

Use the fact that the sine of an acute angle is equal to the cosine of its complement.

$$\sin 56° = \cos(90° - 56°) = \cos 34°$$

▶ The sine of 56° is the same as the cosine of 34°.

EXAMPLE 3 **Finding Leg Lengths**

Find the values of x and y using sine and cosine.

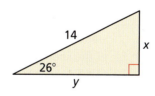

Use a sine ratio to find the value of x and a cosine ratio to find the value of y.

$\sin 26° = \dfrac{\text{opp}}{\text{hyp}}$	Write ratios.	$\cos 26° = \dfrac{\text{adj}}{\text{hyp}}$
$\sin 26° = \dfrac{x}{14}$	Substitute.	$\cos 26° = \dfrac{y}{14}$
$14 \cdot \sin 26° = x$	Multiply each side by 14.	$14 \cdot \cos 26° = y$
$6.1 \approx x$	Use technology.	$12.6 \approx y$

▶ The value of x is about 6.1, and the value of y is about 12.6.

In-Class Practice

Self-Assessment

2. Write $\cos 23°$ in terms of sine.

3. Find the values of u and t using sine and cosine.

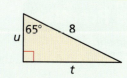

| **1** I don't understand yet. | **2** I can do it with help. | **3** I can do it on my own. | **4** I can teach someone. |

Finding Sine and Cosine in Special Right Triangles

EXAMPLE 4   **Finding the Sine and Cosine of 45°**

Find the sine and cosine of a 45° angle.

Begin by sketching a 45°-45°-90° triangle. Because all such triangles are similar, you can simplify your calculations by choosing 1 as the length of each leg. Using the 45°-45°-90° Triangle Theorem, the length of the hypotenuse is $\sqrt{2}$.

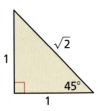

$\sin 45° = \dfrac{\text{opp}}{\text{hyp}}$ Write ratios for sine and cosine of 45°. $\cos 45° = \dfrac{\text{adj}}{\text{hyp}}$

$= \dfrac{1}{\sqrt{2}}$ Substitute. $= \dfrac{1}{\sqrt{2}}$

$= \dfrac{\sqrt{2}}{2}$ Multiply each side by $\dfrac{\sqrt{2}}{2}$. $= \dfrac{\sqrt{2}}{2}$

≈ 0.7071 Simplify. ≈ 0.7071

▶ So, $\sin 45° \approx 0.7071$ and $\cos 45° \approx 0.7071$.

EXAMPLE 5   **Finding the Sine and Cosine of 30°**

Find the sine and cosine of a 30° angle.

Begin by sketching a 30°-60°-90° triangle. Because all such triangles are similar, you can simplify your calculations by choosing 1 as the length of the shorter leg. Using the 30°-60°-90° Triangle Theorem, the length of the longer leg is $\sqrt{3}$ and the length of the hypotenuse is 2.

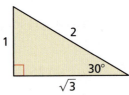

$\sin 30° = \dfrac{\text{opp}}{\text{hyp}}$ Write ratios for sine and cosine of 30°. $\cos 30° = \dfrac{\text{adj}}{\text{hyp}}$

$= \dfrac{1}{2}$ Substitute. $= \dfrac{\sqrt{3}}{2}$

$= 0.5$ Simplify. ≈ 0.8660

▶ So, $\sin 30° = 0.5$ and $\cos 30° \approx 0.8660$.

In-Class Practice

Self-Assessment

4. Find the sine and cosine of a 60° angle.

1 I don't understand yet.   **2** I can do it with help.   **3** I can do it on my own.   **4** I can teach someone.

Connections to Real Life

Recall from the previous lesson that an *angle of elevation* is an angle formed by a horizontal line and a line of sight *up* to an object. An **angle of depression** is an angle formed by a horizontal line and a line of sight *down* to an object.

EXAMPLE 6 **Finding Unknown Distances**

You are skiing on a mountain. Find the distance x from you to the base of the mountain.

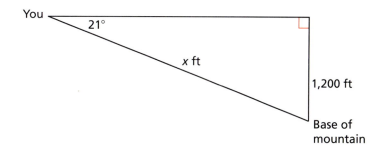

Write a trigonometric ratio for the sine of the angle of depression involving the distance x. Then solve for x.

$\sin 21° = \dfrac{\text{opp}}{\text{hyp}}$ Write ratio for sine of 21°.

$\sin 21° = \dfrac{1{,}200}{x}$ Substitute.

$x \cdot \sin 21° = 1{,}200$ Multiply each side by x.

$x = \dfrac{1{,}200}{\sin 21°}$ Divide each side by sin 21°.

$x \approx 3{,}348.5$ Use technology.

▶ The distance from you to the base of the mountain is about 3,349 feet.

Check

The value of sin 21° is about 0.3584. Substitute for x in the sine ratio and compare the values.

$\dfrac{1{,}200}{x} \approx \dfrac{1{,}200}{3{,}348.5} \approx 0.3584$

This value is approximately the same as the value of sin 21°. ✓

In-Class Practice
Self-Assessment

5. WHAT IF? In Example 6, the angle of depression is 28°. Find the distance from you to the base of the mountain.

1 I don't understand yet.   **2** I can do it with help.   **3** I can do it on my own.   **4** I can teach someone.

9.5   The Sine and Cosine Ratios

9.5 Practice with Calc Chat and Calc View

Find sin D, sin E, cos D, and cos E. (See Example 1.)

1.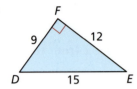

2.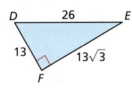

3.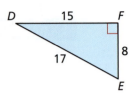

Write the expression in terms of cosine. (See Example 2.)

4. $\sin 81°$

5. $\sin 37°$

6. $\sin 29°$

Write the expression in terms of sine.

7. $\cos 59°$

8. $\cos 42°$

9. $\cos 73°$

Find the value of each variable using sine and cosine. (See Example 3.)

10.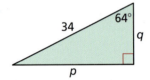

11.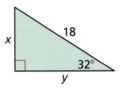

12.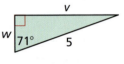

13. Which ratio(s) are equal to sin X? Select all that apply. (See Example 4.)

    $\cos X$ $\sin Z$ $\cos Z$

    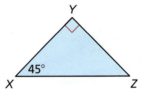

14. Explain how to tell which side of a right triangle is adjacent to an acute angle and which side is the hypotenuse.

15. Which ratios are equal to $\frac{1}{2}$? Select all that apply. (See Example 5.)

    $\sin L$ $\cos L$ $\sin J$ $\cos J$

    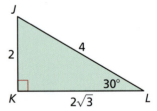

16. Explain what you must know about a triangle to use the sine ratio or the cosine ratio.

17. **CONNECTION TO REAL LIFE** Find the length of the slide. (See Example 6.)

    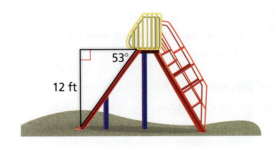

476 Chapter 9 Right Triangles and Trigonometry

18. **CONNECTION TO REAL LIFE** Find the height of the roller coaster using two different methods. Explain.

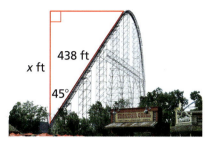

19. You fly a kite using a 20-foot-long string. The angle of elevation from your hands to the kite is 67°. Your hands are 5 feet above the ground.

    a. How far above the ground is the kite?

    b. As the angle of elevation increases, does the height of your kite change at a constant rate? Justify your answer.

20. **CONNECT CONCEPTS** $\triangle EQU$ is equilateral and $\triangle RGT$ is a right triangle with $RG = 2$, $RT = 1$, and $m\angle T = 90°$. Show that $\sin E = \cos G$.

21. **SMP.7** Using only the given information, explain whether you would use a sine ratio or a cosine ratio to find the length of the hypotenuse.

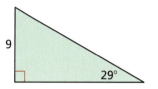

22. Let A be any acute angle of a right triangle. Show that (a) $\tan A = \dfrac{\sin A}{\cos A}$ and (b) $(\sin A)^2 + (\cos A)^2 = 1$.

23. **CONNECTION TO REAL LIFE** Sonar systems use sound to detect underwater objects. Submarines use sonar systems to detect obstacles.

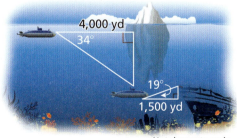

Not drawn to scale

    a. The sonar system of a submarine detects an iceberg ahead. How many yards must the submarine descend to pass under the iceberg?

    b. The sonar system then detects a sunken ship 1,500 yards ahead, with an angle of elevation of 19° to the highest part of the sunken ship. How many yards must the submarine rise to pass over the sunken ship?

24. **SMP.7** Explain why the area of $\triangle ABC$ in the diagram can be found using the formula Area $= \tfrac{1}{2}ab \sin C$. Then calculate the area when $a = 4$, $b = 7$, and $m\angle C = 40°$.

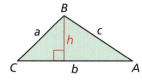

Interpreting Data

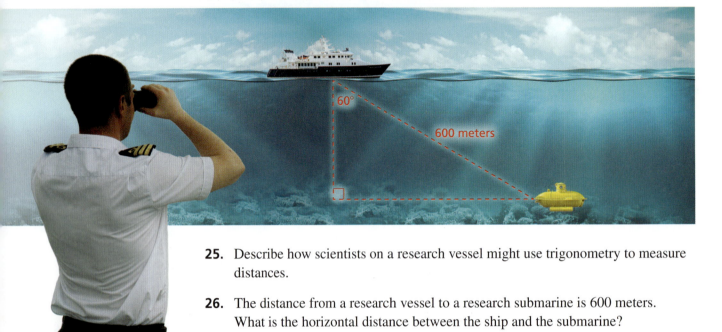

RESEARCH VESSEL A research vessel is a ship designed to carry out research at sea. Research vessels are sometimes constructed around an icebreaker hull, allowing them to operate in polar waters.

25. Describe how scientists on a research vessel might use trigonometry to measure distances.

26. The distance from a research vessel to a research submarine is 600 meters. What is the horizontal distance between the ship and the submarine?

27. Find the depth of the submarine.

Review & Refresh

Find the value of x. Tell whether the side lengths form a Pythagorean triple.

28.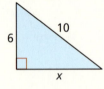

29.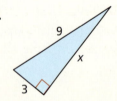

30. Find the value of x.

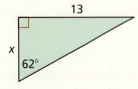

31. Find the measures of each interior angle and each exterior angle of a regular 21-gon.

32. Determine whether AC is *less than*, *greater than*, or *equal to* DF.

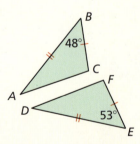

33. The polygons are congruent. Find the values of x and y.

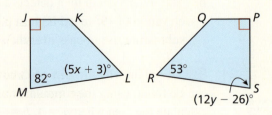

9.6 Solving Right Triangles

Learning Target: Find unknown side lengths and angle measures of right triangles.

Success Criteria:
- I can explain inverse trigonometric ratios.
- I can use inverse trigonometric ratios to approximate angle measures.
- I can solve right triangles.
- I can solve real-life problems by solving right triangles.

INVESTIGATE Solving Right Triangles

Work with a partner.

1. Use what you know about sine and cosine in special right triangles to find the measure of $\angle A$.

   a. $\sin A = \dfrac{\sqrt{2}}{2}$ b. $\cos A = \dfrac{1}{2}$

   c. $\cos A = \dfrac{\sqrt{2}}{2}$ d. $\cos A = \dfrac{\sqrt{3}}{2}$

   e. $\sin A = \dfrac{\sqrt{3}}{2}$ f. $\sin A = \dfrac{1}{2}$

2. Show how you can use technology to verify your answers in Exercise 1.

3. Explain how you can use technology to find the measure of an angle if you know the value of sine, cosine, or tangent of the angle.

4. The figure shows a ladder that firefighters use to enter a window of a building. The ladder leans against the building to form a right triangle with the building and the ground. Find the values of $\sin D$ and $\cos E$.

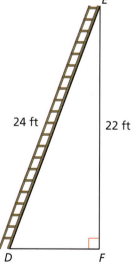

5. Find all missing measures of $\triangle DEF$. The ideal climbing angle for a ladder is 75°. How close is the ladder to the ideal climbing angle?

6. When you know the lengths of the sides of a right triangle, how can you find the measures of the two acute angles?

Using Inverse Trigonometric Ratios

Vocabulary
- inverse tangent
- inverse sine
- inverse cosine
- solve a right triangle

Key Concept

Inverse Trigonometric Ratios

Let ∠A be an acute angle in a right triangle.

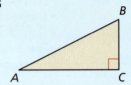

Inverse Tangent If $\tan A = x$, then $\tan^{-1} x = m\angle A$. $\tan^{-1}\dfrac{BC}{AC} = m\angle A$

Inverse Sine If $\sin A = y$, then $\sin^{-1} y = m\angle A$. $\sin^{-1}\dfrac{BC}{AB} = m\angle A$

Inverse Cosine If $\cos A = z$, then $\cos^{-1} z = m\angle A$. $\cos^{-1}\dfrac{AC}{AB} = m\angle A$

The expression "$\tan^{-1} x$" is read as "the inverse tangent of x."

EXAMPLE 1 Finding Angle Measures

Let ∠A, ∠B, and ∠C be acute angles. Use technology to approximate the measures of ∠A, ∠B, and ∠C.

a. $\tan A = 0.75$

   $m\angle A = \tan^{-1} 0.75 \approx 36.9°$

b. $\sin B = 0.87$

   $m\angle B = \sin^{-1} 0.87 \approx 60.5°$

c. $\cos C = 0.15$

   $m\angle C = \cos^{-1} 0.15 \approx 81.4°$

In-Class Practice

Self-Assessment

1. The sine of which angle in the diagram is $\frac{12}{13}$? The tangent of which angle is $\frac{5}{12}$?

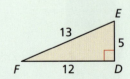

Let ∠G, ∠H, and ∠K be acute angles. Use technology to approximate the measures of ∠G, ∠H, and ∠K.

2. $\tan G = 0.43$
3. $\sin H = 0.68$
4. $\cos K = 0.94$

1 I don't understand yet. **2** I can do it with help. **3** I can do it on my own. **4** I can teach someone.

Solving Right Triangles

To **solve a right triangle** means to find all unknown side lengths and angle measures. You can solve a right triangle when you know either of the following.

- two side lengths
- one side length and the measure of one acute angle

EXAMPLE 2 Solving a Right Triangle

Solve the right triangle.

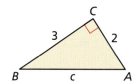

Use the Pythagorean Theorem to find the length of the hypotenuse.

$c^2 = a^2 + b^2$ Pythagorean Theorem

$c^2 = 3^2 + 2^2$ Substitute.

$c^2 = 13$ Simplify.

$c = \sqrt{13}$ Take the positive square root of each side.

$c \approx 3.6$ Use technology.

Find $m\angle B$.

$m\angle B = \tan^{-1}\frac{2}{3} \approx 33.7°$ Use technology.

Find $m\angle A$.

Because $\angle A$ and $\angle B$ are complements, you can write

$m\angle A = 90° - m\angle B$

$\approx 90° - 33.7°$

$= 56.3°$.

▶ In $\triangle ABC$, $c \approx 3.6$, $m\angle B \approx 33.7°$, and $m\angle A \approx 56.3°$.

In-Class Practice
Self-Assessment

Solve the right triangle.

5.

6.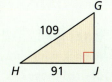

7.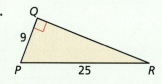

9.6 Solving Right Triangles 481

EXAMPLE 3 Solving a Right Triangle

Solve the right triangle.

Use trigonometric ratios to find the values of g and h.

$\sin H = \dfrac{\text{opp}}{\text{hyp}}$ Write ratios. $\cos H = \dfrac{\text{adj}}{\text{hyp}}$

$\sin 25° = \dfrac{h}{13}$ Substitute. $\cos 25° = \dfrac{g}{13}$

$13 \cdot \sin 25° = h$ Multiply each side by 13. $13 \cdot \cos 25° = g$

$5.5 \approx h$ Use technology. $11.8 \approx g$

Because $\angle H$ and $\angle G$ are complements, you can write

$m\angle G = 90° - m\angle H = 90° - 25° = 65°$.

▶ In $\triangle GHJ$, $h \approx 5.5$, $g \approx 11.8$, and $m\angle G = 65°$.

EXAMPLE 4 Finding an Angle Measure

Your school is building a *raked stage*. The stage visible to the audience will be 30 feet long from front to back, with a total rise of 2 feet. You want the *rake* (angle of elevation) to be 5° or less for safety. Is the rake within your desired range?

Draw a diagram that represents the situation. Let $x°$ be the rake.

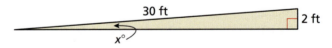

Use the inverse sine ratio to find the degree measure x of the rake.

$x = \sin^{-1}\dfrac{2}{30} \approx 3.8$

▶ The rake is about 3.8°, so it is within your desired range of 5° or less.

In-Class Practice
Self-Assessment

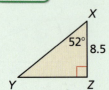

8. Solve $\triangle XYZ$.

9. **WHAT IF?** In Example 4, the raked stage is 20 feet long from front to back with a total rise of 2 feet. Is the raked stage within your desired range?

1 I don't understand yet.   **2** I can do it with help.   **3** I can do it on my own.   **4** I can teach someone.

9.6 Practice

Let ∠D be an acute angle. Use technology to approximate m∠D. (See Example 1.)

▶ **1.** sin D = 0.75

2. cos D = 0.33

3. tan D = 0.28

Solve the right triangle. (See Examples 2 and 3.)

4.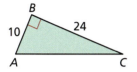

▶ **5.**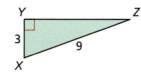

6.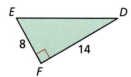

▶ **7.**

8.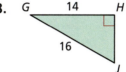

9.

10. SMP.3 ERROR ANALYSIS Describe and correct the error in using an inverse trigonometric ratio.

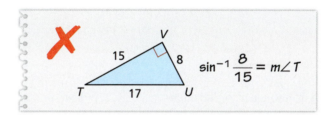

11. CONNECTION TO REAL LIFE In order to unload clay easily, the body of a dump truck must be elevated to at least 45°. The front of the body of a dump truck that is 14 feet long has been raised 8 feet. Explain whether the clay will pour out easily. (See Example 4.)

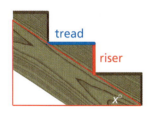

12. OPEN-ENDED The recommended riser-to-tread ratio for steps is 7 : 11. You want to build stairs that are less steep than this recommendation. Give an example of a riser-to-tread ratio that you can use. Find the value of x for your stairs.

13. SMP.4 An access ramp must not have an incline greater than 4.76°. You want to build a ramp with a vertical rise of 8 inches. You want to minimize the horizontal distance taken up by the ramp. Draw a diagram showing the approximate dimensions of your ramp.

14. The cosine of which angle in △ABC is $\frac{4}{5}$? The tangent of which angle is $\frac{4}{3}$?

15. CONNECT CONCEPTS Find the measure of the acute angle formed by $y = 3x$ and the x-axis. Then approximate the angle measure.

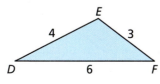

16. DIG DEEPER Without measuring, find $m\angle D$, $m\angle E$, and $m\angle F$.

Interpreting Data

GLIDE ANGLE In aviation, commercial pilots often use the *rule of three*. This rule states that 3 nautical miles should be allowed for every 1,000 feet of descent. A nautical mile is about 1.151 miles.

17. Estimate the glide angle.

18. How many miles from the runway should a pilot start descending from a height of 30,000 feet?

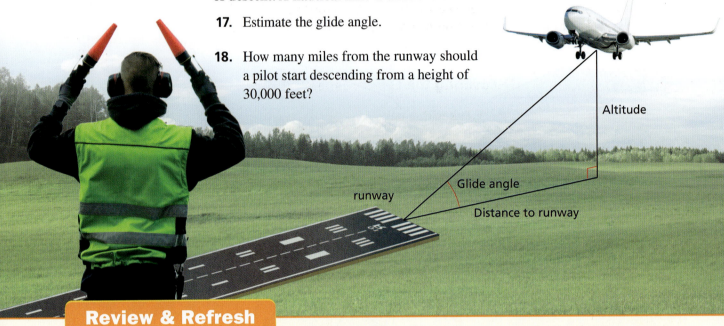

Review & Refresh

19. Find sin *Y*, cos *Y*, and tan *Y*. Write each answer as a fraction and as a decimal.

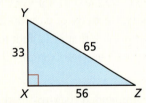

20. Identify the similar right triangles. Then find the value of *y*.

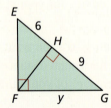

21. In the diagram, △*DEF* ≅ △*QRS*. Find the values of *x* and *y*.

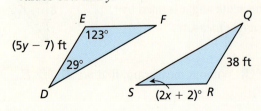

22. Find $m\angle 1$. Tell which theorem you use.

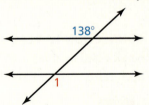

23. Determine whether the molecular model has rotational symmetry. If so, describe any rotations that map the model onto itself.

Solve the proportion.

24. $\dfrac{13}{9} = \dfrac{x}{18}$

25. $\dfrac{5.6}{12.7} = \dfrac{4.9}{x}$

26. Find the measure of the exterior angle.

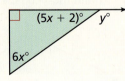

9.7 Law of Sines and Law of Cosines

Learning Target: Find unknown side lengths and angle measures of triangles.

Success Criteria:
- I can find areas of triangles using formulas that involve sine.
- I can solve triangles using the Law of Sines.
- I can solve triangles using the Law of Cosines.

INVESTIGATE | Discovering the Law of Sines

SMP.5 Work with a partner.

1. Construct any acute $\triangle ABC$. Construct the altitude from vertex B to $\overline{AC}$ and label it as h. Then write a formula for the area of $\triangle ABC$.

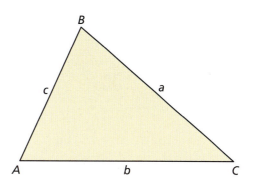

2. Rewrite your area formula for $\triangle ABC$ so that it contains $\sin C$.

3. Rewrite your area formula for $\triangle ABC$ so that it contains $\sin A$.

4. Show that $\dfrac{\sin A}{a} = \dfrac{\sin C}{c}$.

5. **SMP.8** Draw several other acute triangles and find their side lengths and angle measures. Write a conjecture about the relationship between the sines of the angles and the lengths of the sides of a triangle.

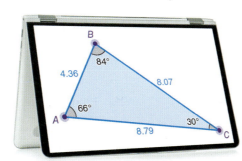
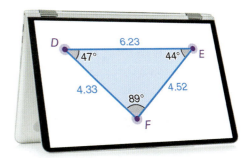

9.7 Law of Sines and Law of Cosines 485

Vocabulary
Law of Sines
Law of Cosines

Finding Areas of Triangles

Key Concept

Area of a Triangle

The area of any triangle is given by one-half the product of the lengths of two sides times the sine of their included angle. For $\triangle ABC$ shown, there are three ways to calculate the area.

Area = $\frac{1}{2}bc \sin A$ Area = $\frac{1}{2}ac \sin B$ Area = $\frac{1}{2}ab \sin C$

EXAMPLE 1 Finding the Area of a Triangle

Find the area of the triangle.

a.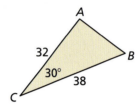

b.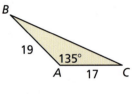

a. Area = $\frac{1}{2}ab \sin C$ Write formula for area.

$= \frac{1}{2}(38)(32) \sin 30°$ Substitute for a, b, and C.

$= \frac{1}{2}(38)(32)\left(\frac{1}{2}\right)$ Evaluate sin 30°.

$= 304$ Multiply.

▶ The area of the triangle is 304 square units.

b. Area = $\frac{1}{2}bc \sin A$ Write formula for area.

$= \frac{1}{2}(17)(19) \sin 135°$ Substitute for b, c, and A.

≈ 114.2 Use technology.

> Use technology to find trigonometric ratios for obtuse angles.
> sin 135° ≈ 0.7071

▶ The area of the triangle is about 114.2 square units.

In-Class Practice

Self-Assessment

Find the area of $\triangle ABC$ with the given side lengths and included angle.

1.

2.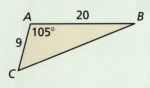

1 I don't understand yet.   2 I can do it with help.   3 I can do it on my own.   4 I can teach someone.

Using the Law of Sines

You can use the **Law of Sines** to solve triangles when two angles and the length of any side are known (AAS or ASA cases), or when the lengths of two sides and an angle opposite one of the two sides are known (SSA case).

Theorem 9.9

Law of Sines

The Law of Sines can be written in either of the following forms for $\triangle ABC$ with sides of length a, b, and c.

$$\frac{\sin A}{a} = \frac{\sin B}{b} = \frac{\sin C}{c} \qquad \frac{a}{\sin A} = \frac{b}{\sin B} = \frac{c}{\sin C}$$

Prove this Theorem Exercise 32, page 493

EXAMPLE 2 Using the Law of Sines (SSA Case)

Solve the triangle.

Use the Law of Sines to find $m\angle B$.

$$\frac{\sin B}{b} = \frac{\sin A}{a} \qquad \text{Law of Sines}$$

$$\frac{\sin B}{11} = \frac{\sin 115°}{20} \qquad \text{Substitute.}$$

$$\sin B = \frac{11 \sin 115°}{20} \qquad \text{Multiply each side by 11.}$$

$$m\angle B \approx 29.9° \qquad \text{Use technology.}$$

By the Triangle Sum Theorem, $m\angle C \approx 180° - 115° - 29.9° = 35.1°$.

Use the Law of Sines again to find the remaining side length c of the triangle.

$$\frac{c}{\sin C} = \frac{a}{\sin A} \qquad \text{Law of Sines}$$

$$\frac{c}{\sin 35.1°} = \frac{20}{\sin 115°} \qquad \text{Substitute.}$$

$$c = \frac{20 \sin 35.1°}{\sin 115°} \qquad \text{Multiply each side by } \sin 35.1°.$$

$$c \approx 12.7 \qquad \text{Use technology.}$$

▶ In $\triangle ABC$, $m\angle B \approx 29.9°$, $m\angle C \approx 35.1°$, and $c \approx 12.7$.

In-Class Practice

Self-Assessment

Solve the triangle.

3.

4.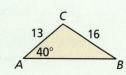

1 I don't understand yet. **2** I can do it with help. **3** I can do it on my own. **4** I can teach someone.

EXAMPLE 3 **Using the Law of Sines (AAS Case)**

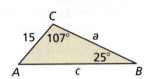

Solve the triangle.

By the Triangle Sum Theorem, $m\angle A = 180° - 107° - 25° = 48°$.

By the Law of Sines, you can write $\dfrac{a}{\sin 48°} = \dfrac{15}{\sin 25°} = \dfrac{c}{\sin 107°}$.

$\dfrac{a}{\sin 48°} = \dfrac{15}{\sin 25°}$ Write two equations, each with one variable. $\dfrac{c}{\sin 107°} = \dfrac{15}{\sin 25°}$

$a = \dfrac{15 \sin 48°}{\sin 25°}$ Solve for each variable. $c = \dfrac{15 \sin 107°}{\sin 25°}$

$a \approx 26.4$ Use technology. $c \approx 33.9$

▶ In $\triangle ABC$, $m\angle A = 48°$, $a \approx 26.4$, and $c \approx 33.9$.

EXAMPLE 4 **Using the Law of Sines (ASA Case)**

The distance between consecutive bases on a baseball field is 90 feet. A player catches a ball at point A and wants to throw the ball directly to third base. How far must the player throw the ball?

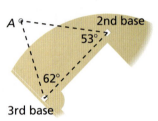

In the diagram, let b represent the distance from point A to third base. So, b represents how far the player must throw the ball.

By the Triangle Sum Theorem, $m\angle A = 180° - 62° - 53° = 65°$.

Use the Law of Sines to write an equation involving b.

$\dfrac{90}{\sin 65°} = \dfrac{b}{\sin 53°}$ $\qquad$ $\dfrac{a}{\sin A} = \dfrac{b}{\sin B}$

$\dfrac{90 \sin 53°}{\sin 65°} = b$ Multiply each side by $\sin 53°$.

$79.3 \approx b$ Use technology.

▶ The player must throw the ball about 79 feet.

In-Class Practice

Self-Assessment

Solve the triangle.

5.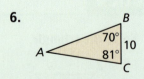

6.

7. **WHAT IF?** The player in Example 4 decides to throw the ball to second base instead of third base. Which throw is longer and by how much?

1 I don't understand yet. **2** I can do it with help. **3** I can do it on my own. **4** I can teach someone.

Using the Law of Cosines

You can use the **Law of Cosines** to solve triangles when two sides and the included angle are known (SAS case), or when all three sides are known (SSS case).

Theorem 9.10

Law of Cosines

If $\triangle ABC$ has sides of length a, b, and c, as shown, then the following are true.

$$a^2 = b^2 + c^2 - 2bc \cos A$$
$$b^2 = a^2 + c^2 - 2ac \cos B$$
$$c^2 = a^2 + b^2 - 2ab \cos C$$

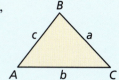

Prove this Theorem Exercise 36, page 493

EXAMPLE 5 Using the Law of Cosines (SAS Case)

Solve the triangle.

Use the Law of Cosines to find side length b.

$b^2 = a^2 + c^2 - 2ac \cos B$	Law of Cosines
$b^2 = 11^2 + 14^2 - 2(11)(14) \cos 34°$	Substitute.
$b^2 = 317 - 308 \cos 34°$	Simplify.
$b = \sqrt{317 - 308 \cos 34°}$	Take the positive square root of each side.
$b \approx 7.9$	Use technology.

Use the Law of Sines to find $m\angle A$.

$\dfrac{\sin A}{11} = \dfrac{\sin 34°}{\sqrt{317 - 308 \cos 34°}}$	$\dfrac{\sin A}{a} = \dfrac{\sin B}{b}$
$\sin A = \dfrac{11 \sin 34°}{\sqrt{317 - 308 \cos 34°}}$	Multiply each side by 11.
$m\angle A \approx 51.6°$	Use technology.

By the Triangle Sum Theorem, $m\angle C \approx 180° - 34° - 51.6° = 94.4°$.

▶ In $\triangle ABC$, $b \approx 7.9$, $m\angle A \approx 51.6°$, and $m\angle C \approx 94.4°$.

In-Class Practice

Self-Assessment

Solve the triangle.

8.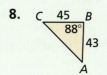

9.

| 1 | I don't understand yet. | 2 | I can do it with help. | 3 | I can do it on my own. | 4 | I can teach someone. |

EXAMPLE 6 **Using the Law of Cosines (SSS Case)**

Solve the triangle.

First, find the angle opposite the longest side, $\overline{AC}$. So, find $m\angle B$.

$b^2 = a^2 + c^2 - 2ac \cos B$ Law of Cosines

$27^2 = 12^2 + 20^2 - 2(12)(20) \cos B$ Substitute.

$\dfrac{27^2 - 12^2 - 20^2}{-2(12)(20)} = \cos B$ Solve for cos B.

$m\angle B \approx 112.7°$ Use technology.

Now, use the Law of Sines to find $m\angle A$.

$\dfrac{\sin A}{12} = \dfrac{\sin 112.7°}{27}$ $\dfrac{\sin A}{a} = \dfrac{\sin B}{b}$

$\sin A = \dfrac{12 \sin 112.7°}{27}$ Multiply each side by 12.

$m\angle A \approx 24.2°$ Use technology.

By the Triangle Sum Theorem, $m\angle C \approx 180° - 24.2° - 112.7° = 43.1°$.

▶ In $\triangle ABC$, $m\angle A \approx 24.2°$, $m\angle B \approx 112.7°$, and $m\angle C \approx 43.1°$.

EXAMPLE 7 **Finding an Angle Measure**

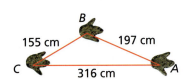

EXTINCT SPECIES **DINOSAURS** An organism's step angle is a measure of walking efficiency. The closer the angle is to 180°, the more efficiently the organism walked. Find the step angle B shown by the dinosaur footprints.

$b^2 = a^2 + c^2 - 2ac \cos B$ Law of Cosines

$316^2 = 155^2 + 197^2 - 2(155)(197) \cos B$ Substitute.

$\dfrac{316^2 - 155^2 - 197^2}{-2(155)(197)} = \cos B$ Solve for cos B.

$127.3° \approx m\angle B$ Use technology.

▶ The step angle B is about 127.3°.

In-Class Practice

Self-Assessment

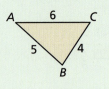

10. Solve the triangle at the left.

11. Determine whether the dinosaur whose footprints are shown at the right walked more efficiently than the dinosaur in Example 7.

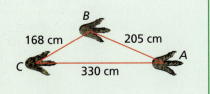

9.7 Practice

Use technology to find the trigonometric ratio.

1. sin 98° **2.** cos 139° **3.** tan 165°

Find the area of the triangle. (See Example 1.)

4. 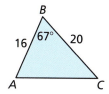   **5.**   **6.**

Solve the triangle. (See Examples 2, 3, and 4.)

7. 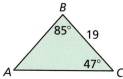   **8.** 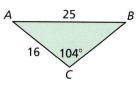   **9.**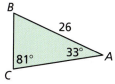

10. 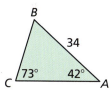   **11.** 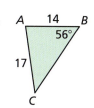   **12.**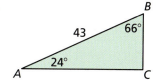

Solve the triangle. (See Examples 5 and 6.)

13. 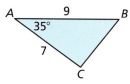   **14.** 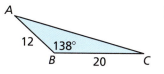   **15.**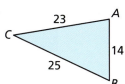

16. 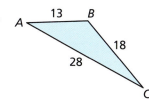   **17.** 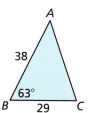   **18.**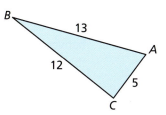

19. SMP.3 ERROR ANALYSIS Describe and correct the error in finding $m\angle A$ in $\triangle ABC$ when $a = 19$, $b = 21$, and $c = 11$.

$$\cos A = \frac{a^2 - b^2 - c^2}{-2(a)(b)}$$

$$\cos A = \frac{19^2 - 21^2 - 11^2}{-2(19)(21)}$$

$$m\angle A \approx 75.4°$$

Tell whether you would use the Law of Sines, the Law of Cosines, or the Pythagorean Theorem and trigonometric ratios to solve the triangle with the given information. Then solve the triangle.

20. $m\angle A = 72°, m\angle B = 44°, b = 14$

21. $m\angle B = 98°, m\angle C = 37°, a = 18$

22. $m\angle C = 65°, a = 12, b = 21$

23. $m\angle B = 90°, a = 15, c = 6$

24. **SMP.6** Your friend says that the Law of Sines can be used to find JK. Your cousin says that the Law of Cosines can be used to find JK. Explain whether either person is incorrect.

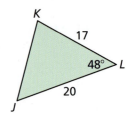

▶ **25. CONNECTION TO REAL LIFE** You bounce a basketball to your friend, as shown in the diagram. What is the distance between you and your friend? (See Example 7.)

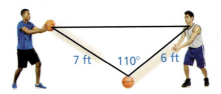

26. CONNECTION TO REAL LIFE A zip line is constructed across a valley, as shown in the diagram. What is the width w of the valley?

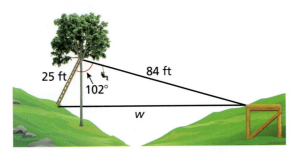

27. **SMP.4** You are on the observation deck of the Empire State Building looking at the Chrysler Building. When you turn 145° clockwise, you see the Statue of Liberty. Use the distances between the given buildings to draw a diagram to represent this situation. Estimate the distance between the Empire State Building and the Statue of Liberty.

- Chrysler Building and Empire State Building: ≈0.6 mi
- Chrysler Building and Statue of Liberty: ≈5.6 mi

28. The Leaning Tower of Pisa has a height of 183 feet. In 1990, the tower stood about 5.5° off vertical until it was stabilized a few years later, and now stands 4° off vertical. In terms of horizontal distance, how much farther was the top of the tower off vertical in 1990 when compared with the tower today?

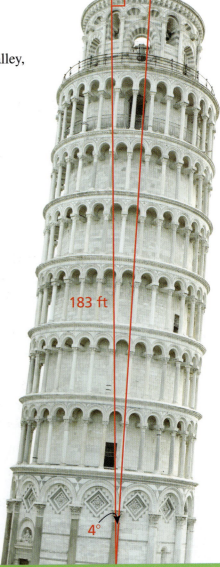

29. **CONNECTION TO REAL LIFE** A golfer hit a drive 260 yards on a hole that is 400 yards long. The shot was 15° off target.

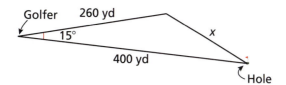

a. **SMP.2** Find and interpret x in the diagram.

b. The golfer hit the next shot precisely the distance found in part (a). What is the maximum angle by which the shot can be off target in order to land no more than 10 yards from the hole?

30. The *ambiguous case* of the Law of Sines occurs when you are given the measure of one acute angle, the length of one adjacent side, and the length of the side opposite that angle, which is less than the length of the adjacent side. This results in two possible triangles. Using the given information, find two possible solutions for $\triangle ABC$. Draw a diagram for each triangle.

a. $m\angle A = 40°, a = 13, b = 16$

b. $m\angle A = 21°, a = 17, b = 32$

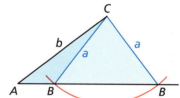

31. **SMP.7** Simplify the Law of Cosines for when the given angle is a right angle.

32. **PROVING THEOREM 9.9** Use the formula for area of a triangle to prove the Law of Sines. Justify each step.

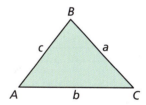

33. **SMP.1 DIG DEEPER** Consider any triangle with side lengths of a, b, and c. Calculate the value of s, which is half the perimeter of the triangle. What measurement of the triangle is represented by $\sqrt{s(s-a)(s-b)(s-c)}$? How do you know?

34. Use the Law of Cosines to show that the measure of each angle of an equilateral triangle is 60°.

35. An airplane flies 55° east of north from City A to City B, a distance of 470 miles. Another airplane flies 7° north of east from City A to City C, a distance of 890 miles. What is the distance between Cities B and C?

36. **PROVING THEOREM 9.10** Use the given information to write a proof of the Law of Cosines.

Given $\overline{BD}$ is an altitude of $\triangle ABC$.

Prove $a^2 = b^2 + c^2 - 2bc \cos A$

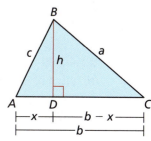

9.7 Law of Sines and Law of Cosines

Interpreting Data

ROCK AND ROLL The Rock and Roll Hall of Fame is in Cleveland, Ohio. The building was designed by architect I. M. Pei. It was dedicated on September 1, 1995.

37. The front face of the building is an isosceles triangle. The length of the base is 229.5 feet. What other measurements do you need to know to find the area of the face?

38. If the front face is an isosceles right triangle, how can you find its area?

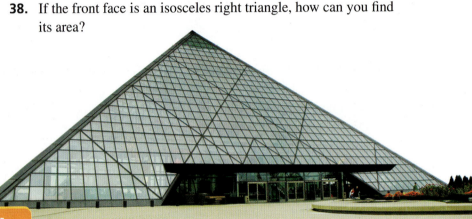

Review & Refresh

Find the value of *x*.

39.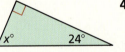

40.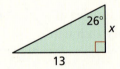

44. $ABCD \cong EFGH$. Find the values of *x* and *y*.

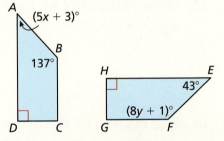

41. A triangle has one side length of 8 inches and another side length of 15 inches. Describe the possible lengths of the third side.

42. Find the values of *x* and *y*.

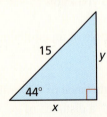

45. You draw a map of the path from your home to your school on a coordinate plane. The park is halfway between your home and the school. Your home is located at the point (1, 2) and your school is located at the point (5, 6). What point represents the location of the park?

43. State which theorem you can use to show that the quadrilateral is a parallelogram.

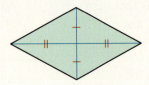

46. Solve the triangle.

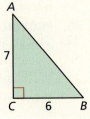

9 Chapter Review with CalcChat

Rate your understanding of each section.
1 I don't understand yet. 2 I can do it with help. 3 I can do it on my own. 4 I can teach someone.

9.1 The Pythagorean Theorem (pp. 443–450)

Learning Target: Understand and apply the Pythagorean Theorem.

Vocabulary
Pythagorean triple

Find the value of x. Then tell whether the side lengths form a Pythagorean triple.

1.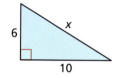

2.

3.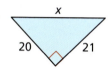

4.

Tell whether the triangle is a right triangle.

5.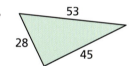

6.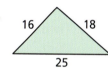

7.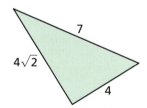

8.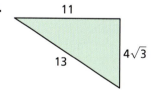

Determine whether the segment lengths form a triangle. If so, is the triangle *acute*, *right*, or *obtuse*?

9. 6, 8, and 9

10. 10, $2\sqrt{2}$, and $6\sqrt{3}$

11. 13, 18, and $3\sqrt{55}$

12. Do the integers 12, 35, and 37 form a Pythagorean triple? If so, use multiples of these integers to write two more Pythagorean triples. If not, explain why not.

13. The integers 9, 40, and 41 form a Pythagorean triple. Without calculating, explain whether a triangle with side lengths of 10 feet, 40 feet, and 41 feet is *acute*, *right*, or *obtuse*.

9.2 Special Right Triangles (pp. 451–456)

⊙ **Learning Target:** Understand and use special right triangles.

Find the values of x and y.

14.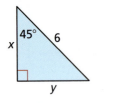

15.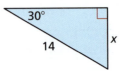

16.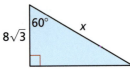

17.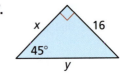

18. Find the area and perimeter of △ABC.

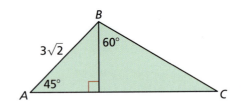

9.3 Similar Right Triangles (pp. 457–464)

⊙ **Learning Target:** Use proportional relationships in right triangles.

Vocabulary
geometric mean

Identify the similar triangles. Then find the value of x.

19.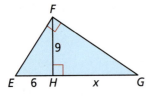

20.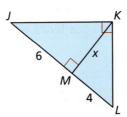

21.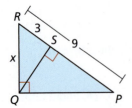

22.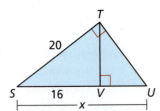

Find the geometric mean of the two numbers.

23. 9 and 25

24. 36 and 48

25. Use the information in the diagram to find the height of the traffic light.

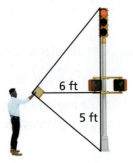

9.4 The Tangent Ratio (pp. 465–470)

Learning Target: Understand and use the tangent ratio.

Vocabulary
trigonometric ratio
tangent
angle of elevation

Find the tangents of the acute angles in the right triangle.

26.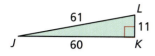

27.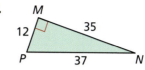

28.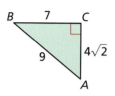

29.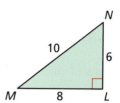

Find the value of x.

30.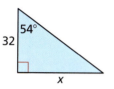

31.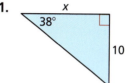

32.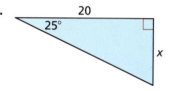

33.

34. The angle of elevation from the bottom of a fence to the top of a tree that is 4 feet from the fence is 75°.

   a. How tall is the tree?

   b. The angle of elevation from the bottom of the fence to the first limb on the the tree is 62°. How high is the limb?

   c. The angle of elevation from the top of the fence to the top of the tree is 70°. How tall is the fence?

35. You stand next to a trampoline. Your eyes are 3 feet above the trampoline and you are 7 feet from its center, where your friend jumps. The angle of elevation from your eyes to your friend is 35°. How high above the trampoline is your friend?

36. Find the tangent of the smaller acute angle in a right triangle with side lengths 8, 15, and 17.

37. The tangent of an acute angle in a right triangle is $\frac{3}{4}$. Explain whether the sides of the right triangle all have integer lengths.

9.5 The Sine and Cosine Ratios (pp. 471–478)

Learning Target: Understand and use the sine and cosine ratios.

Vocabulary
sine
cosine
angle of depression

Find sin X, sin Z, cos X, and cos Z.

38.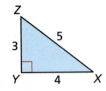

39.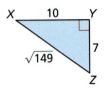

40.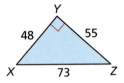

41. Write sin 72° in terms of cosine.

42. Write cos 29° in terms of sine.

Find the value of each variable using sine and cosine.

43.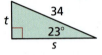

44.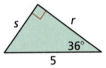

45. The Niagara Falls Incline Railway has an angle of elevation of 30° and a total length of 196 feet. How many feet does the Niagara Falls Incline Railway rise vertically?

9.6 Solving Right Triangles (pp. 479–484)

Learning Target: Find unknown side lengths and angle measures of right triangles.

Vocabulary
inverse tangent
inverse sine
inverse cosine
solve a right triangle

Determine which of the two acute angles has the given trigonometric ratio.

46. The cosine of the angle is $\frac{3}{5}$.

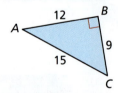

47. The tangent of the angle is $\frac{24}{7}$.

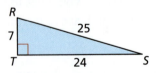

Let $\angle Q$ be an acute angle. Use technology to approximate the measure of $\angle Q$.

48. cos Q = 0.32

49. sin Q = 0.91

50. tan Q = 0.04

Solve the right triangle.

51.

52.

53.

54. You look up at a drone at an angle of elevation of 23°. Your eyes are 5 feet above the ground, and the distance to the drone is 210 feet. What is the altitude of the drone?

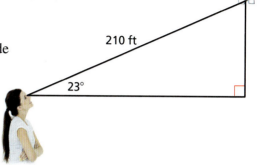

9.7 Law of Sines and Law of Cosines (pp. 485–494)

○ **Learning Target:** Find unknown side lengths and angle measures of triangles.

Vocabulary
Law of Sines
Law of Cosines

Use technology to find the trigonometric ratio.

55. sin 136° **56.** cos 124° **57.** tan 155°

Find the area of △ABC with the given side lengths and included angle.

58.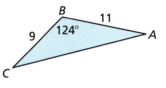

59.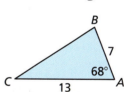

Solve △ABC.

60.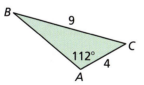

61.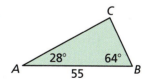

62. $m\angle C = 48°$, $b = 20$, $c = 28$

63. $m\angle B = 25°$, $a = 8$, $c = 3$

64. $m\angle B = 102°$, $m\angle C = 43°$, $b = 21$

65. $a = 10$, $b = 3$, $c = 12$

66. You are sealing a triangular blacktop surface. One side of the triangle is 36 feet long, and another side is 28 feet long. The angle opposite the 28-foot side is 42°.

 a. Draw a diagram to represent this situation.

 b. Use the Law of Sines to solve the triangle from part (a).

 c. One gallon of sealant covers 80 square feet. How many gallons of sealant do you need to apply two coats to the blacktop surface?

9 PERFORMANCE TASK
SMP.6

Engineering a Mammoth

As Arctic permafrost thaws, large quantities of harmful carbon dioxide and methane gases are released into the atmosphere. Some scientists believe that cloning woolly mammoths could help keep the permafrost frozen. However, because there are no living woolly mammoth cells to clone, scientists instead aim to engineer elephants with mammoth-like characteristics that can thrive in cold environments.

STEP 1:
Extract DNA from mammoth bones.

Researchers have sequenced the complete genome of the woolly mammoth. Enough DNA bases were recovered from a single 700,000-year-old tooth to account for 70-80% of the genome.

STEP 2:
Combine several DNA samples and use technology to sequence a mammoth's genome.

STEP 3:
Compare the mammoth's genome to an elephant's genome and identify key differences.

STEP 4:
Retrieve cells from an elephant and use technology to edit the DNA to look more like mammoth DNA in key areas.

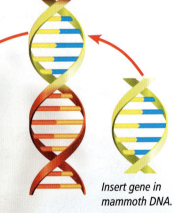

Remove gene in elephant DNA.

Insert gene in mammoth DNA.

STEP 5:
Perform the cloning process using these new mammoth-like cells.

Analyzing Data

Use the information on the previous page to complete the following exercises.

1 Explain what is shown in the display. What do you notice? What do you wonder?

2 Researchers believe a full woolly mammoth genome contains over 4 billion DNA bases. About how many DNA bases were recovered from the 700,000-year-old tooth?

A MAMMOTH TASK

You work on an exhibit featuring a woolly mammoth skeleton. Standing 15 feet from the assembled skeleton, the angle of elevation from your eyes to the top of the shoulder is 16°. Write your height as a percent of the mammoth's height. Then conduct research to estimate the total length of the mammoth from front to back.

Create an informational display about woolly mammoths that includes the following information:
- typical shoulder heights and weights of woolly mammoths
- the shoulder height of the particular mammoth on display
- habitat and diet
- reasons that the Arctic permafrost is thawing
- how engineering mammoths could help keep the permafrost frozen

Connecting Big Ideas

For use after Chapter 9.
SMP.2

Map out the Way

A map of several streets of a town is shown.

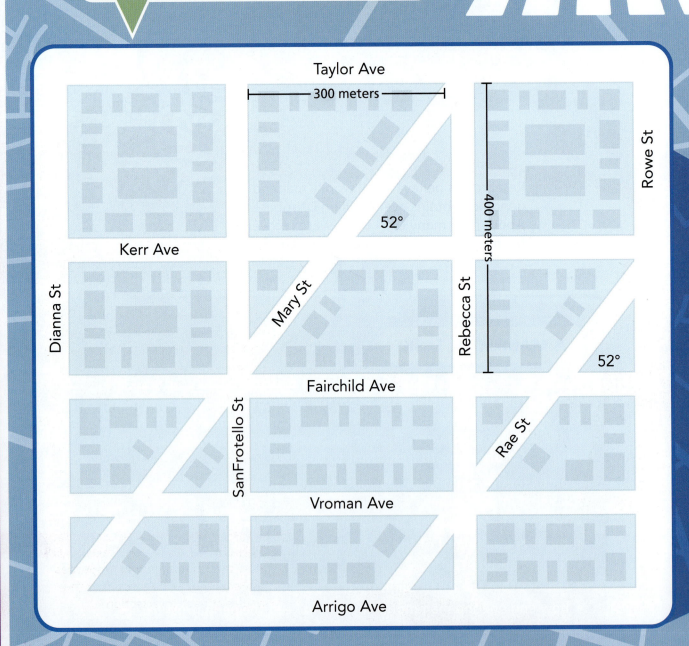

1. What do you notice? What do you wonder?

2. The streets arranged in a grid intersect at right angles. A surveyor is mapping out the angles of several intersections shown on the map. Explain which roads intersect Mary Street at a 52° angle.

3. Is Mary Street parallel to Rae Street? Justify your answer.

4. Identify any similar triangles created by the map.

5. If you walk on Mary Street from the corner of SanFrotello Street and Fairchild Avenue to the corner of Rebecca Street and Taylor Avenue, what distance do you walk?

THINKING ABOUT THE BIG IDEAS

How can **Understanding Properties of Parallel Lines** help you find the angles at each intersection?

Connecting Big Ideas

10 Circles

10.1 Lines and Segments That Intersect Circles
10.2 Finding Arc Measures
10.3 Using Chords
10.4 Inscribed Angles and Polygons
10.5 Angle Relationships in Circles
10.6 Segment Relationships in Circles
10.7 Circles in the Coordinate Plane
10.8 Focus of a Parabola

NATIONAL GEOGRAPHIC EXPLORER
Christine Lee ANTHROPOLOGIST

Dr. Christine Lee is an anthropologist who studies human remains. She looks for physical clues about people's lives, such as what they did for work, what illnesses they had, what traumas they suffered, and their age. In Mongolia, she excavated a royal cemetery for the Xiongnu people, who prompted China to build the Great Wall.

- What other aspects of people's lives can you learn about through anthropology?
- When was the Great Wall of China built? How long is the Great Wall?

PERFORMANCE TASK
Archaeologists often try to discern the purpose of structures by analyzing their geometric properties. In the Performance Task on pages 572 and 573, you will find geometric relationships in Stonehenge and analyze their possible significance.

Anthropology

Big Idea of the Chapter
Find Measurements in Circles

You are familiar with circles and several of their features: radius, diameter, circumference, and area. In this chapter, you will study the properties of segments and lines that intersect circles, such as chords, secants, and tangents.

Stonehenge is a prehistoric monument in England. It is thought to have been constructed around 3000 BC. The monument consists of an outer ring of vertical stones, each around 13 feet high and 7 feet wide. Inside is a ring of smaller stones. Archaeologists think that Stonehenge could have been a burial ground; cremated remains found buried in its vicinity date to the time of its construction.

1. The diameter of the outer ring of stones at Stonehenge is about 100 meters. Estimate the area enclosed by the outer ring.

2. Use the aerial photograph above to estimate the diameter of the inner ring of stones.

Getting Ready for Chapter 10

Solving Quadratic Equations by Completing the Square

EXAMPLE 1 Solve $x^2 + 8x - 3 = 0$ by completing the square.

$x^2 + 8x - 3 = 0$	Write original equation.
$x^2 + 8x = 3$	Add 3 to each side.
$x^2 + 8x + 4^2 = 3 + 4^2$	Complete the square by adding $\left(\frac{8}{2}\right)^2$, or 4^2, to each side.
$(x + 4)^2 = 19$	Write the left side as a square of a binomial.
$x + 4 = \pm\sqrt{19}$	Take the square root of each side.
$x = -4 \pm \sqrt{19}$	Subtract 4 from each side.

▶ The solutions are $x = -4 + \sqrt{19}$ and $x = -4 - \sqrt{19}$.

Solve the equation by completing the square.

1. $x^2 - 2x = 5$
2. $r^2 + 10r = -7$
3. $w^2 - 8w = 9$
4. $p^2 + 10p - 4 = 0$
5. $k^2 - 4k - 7 = 0$
6. $-z^2 + 2z = 1$

Multiplying Binomials

EXAMPLE 2 Find the product $(x + 3)(2x - 1)$.

$$(x + 3)(2x - 1) = \overset{\text{First}}{x(2x)} + \overset{\text{Outer}}{x(-1)} + \overset{\text{Inner}}{3(2x)} + \overset{\text{Last}}{(3)(-1)} \quad \text{FOIL Method}$$
$$= 2x^2 + (-x) + 6x + (-3) \quad \text{Multiply.}$$
$$= 2x^2 + 5x - 3 \quad \text{Simplify.}$$

▶ The product is $2x^2 + 5x - 3$.

Find the product.

7. $(x + 7)(x + 4)$
8. $(a + 1)(a - 5)$
9. $(q - 9)(3q - 4)$
10. $(2v - 7)(5v + 1)$
11. $(4h + 3)(2 + h)$
12. $(8 - 6b)(5 - 3b)$

10.1 Lines and Segments That Intersect Circles

Learning Target: Identify lines and segments that intersect circles and use them to solve problems.

Success Criteria:
- I can identify special segments and lines that intersect circles.
- I can draw and identify common tangents.
- I can use properties of tangents to solve problems.

INVESTIGATE Investigating Lines and Segments That Intersect Circles

Work with a partner.

1. Use two pencils and a paper clip to draw a circle by placing a pencil in each end of the paper clip. Anchor one pencil on a piece of paper. Use the other pencil to apply slight pressure to the edge of the paper clip and draw a circle. How would you define a *circle*?

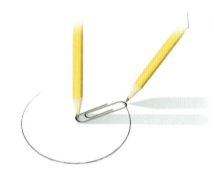

2. **SMP.6** The drawing below shows different types of lines or segments that intersect a circle. In your own words, write a definition for each type of line or segment.

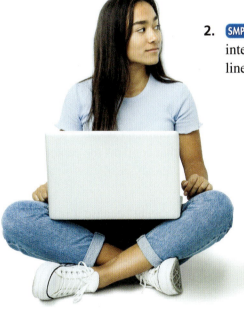

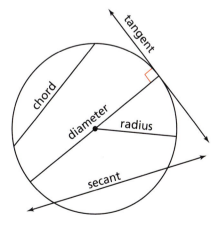

3. Of the five types of lines and segments in Exercise 2, explain which one is a subset of another.

4. **SMP.5** Draw a circle with center O and a radius $\overline{OA}$. Construct a line m that passes through A and is perpendicular to $\overline{OA}$. What do you notice about line m?

Vocabulary
circle
center
radius
chord
diameter
secant
tangent
point of tangency
tangent circles
concentric circles
common tangent

Identifying Special Segments and Lines

A **circle** is the set of all points in a plane that are equidistant from a given point called the **center** of the circle. So, given a point C and a positive number r, a circle is the set of all points P in the plane such that $|CP| = r$.

circle C, or $\odot C$

Key Concept

Lines and Segments That Intersect Circles

A segment whose endpoints are the center and any point on a circle is a **radius**.

A **chord** is a segment whose endpoints are on a circle. A **diameter** is a chord that contains the center of the circle.

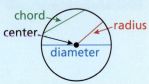

A **secant** is a line that intersects a circle in two points.

A **tangent** is a line in the plane of a circle that intersects the circle in exactly one point, the **point of tangency**. $\overrightarrow{BA}$ and $\overrightarrow{AB}$ are also called tangents.

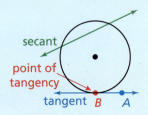

EXAMPLE 1 Identifying Special Segments and Lines

Tell whether each line, ray, or segment is best described as a *radius*, *chord*, *diameter*, *secant*, or *tangent* of $\odot C$.

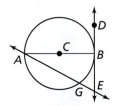

a. $\overline{AC}$

$\overline{AC}$ is a radius because C is the center and A is a point on the circle.

b. $\overline{AB}$

$\overline{AB}$ is a diameter because it is a chord that contains the center C.

c. $\overrightarrow{BE}$

$\overrightarrow{BE}$ is a tangent because it intersects the circle in exactly one point.

d. $\overleftrightarrow{AE}$

$\overleftrightarrow{AE}$ is a secant because it is a line that intersects the circle in two points.

In-Class Practice

Self-Assessment

1. In Example 1, what word best describes $\overline{AG}$? $\overline{CB}$?

2. In Example 1, name a tangent line.

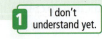

Drawing and Identifying Common Tangents

> ### Key Concept
>
> **Coplanar Circles and Common Tangents**
>
> In a plane, two circles can intersect in two points, one point, or no points. Coplanar circles that intersect in one point are called **tangent circles**. Coplanar circles that have a common center are called **concentric circles**.
>
> 2 points of intersection
>
> 1 point of intersection (tangent circles)
>
> no points of intersection
>
> concentric circles
>
> A line that is tangent to two coplanar circles is called a **common tangent**. A *common internal tangent* intersects the segment that joins the centers of the two circles. A *common external tangent* does not intersect the segment that joins the centers of the two circles.

EXAMPLE 2   **Drawing and Identifying Common Tangents**

Tell how many common tangents the circles have and draw them. State whether the tangents are *external tangents* or *internal tangents*.

a.   b.  c.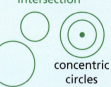

Draw the segment that joins the centers of the two circles. Then draw the common tangents.

a. 4 common tangents: 2 internal, 2 external
b. 3 common tangents: 1 internal, 2 external
c. 2 common tangents: 2 external

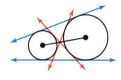 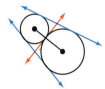

In-Class Practice

Self-Assessment

Tell how many common tangents the circles have and draw them. State whether the tangents are *external tangents* or *internal tangents*.

3.   4.   5.

1 I don't understand yet. **2** I can do it with help. **3** I can do it on my own. **4** I can teach someone.

10.1   Lines and Segments That Intersect Circles

Using Properties of Tangents

Theorem 10.1

Tangent Line to Circle Theorem

In a plane, a line is tangent to a circle if and only if the line is perpendicular to a radius of the circle at its endpoint on the circle.

Prove this Theorem Exercise 26, page 513

Theorem 10.2

External Tangent Congruence Theorem

Segments that are tangents to a circle and have a common external point are congruent.

Prove this Theorem Exercise 25, page 513

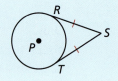

EXAMPLE 3   Verifying a Tangent to a Circle

Is $\overline{ST}$ tangent to $\odot P$?

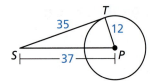

Use the Converse of the Pythagorean Theorem. Because $12^2 + 35^2 = 37^2$, $\triangle PTS$ is a right triangle and $\overline{ST} \perp \overline{PT}$. So, $\overline{ST}$ is perpendicular to a radius of $\odot P$ at its endpoint on $\odot P$.

▶ By the Tangent Line to Circle Theorem, $\overline{ST}$ is tangent to $\odot P$.

EXAMPLE 4   Finding the Radius of a Circle

In the diagram, point B is a point of tangency. Find the radius r of $\odot C$.

You know from the Tangent Line to Circle Theorem that $\overline{AB} \perp \overline{BC}$, so $\triangle ABC$ is a right triangle. You can use the Pythagorean Theorem.

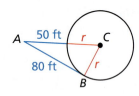

$(r + 50)^2 = r^2 + 80^2$	Use the Pythagorean Theorem.
$r^2 + 100r + 2{,}500 = r^2 + 6{,}400$	Multiply.
$100r = 3{,}900$	Subtract r^2 and 2,500 from each side.
$r = 39$ ft	Divide each side by 100.

In-Class Practice

Self-Assessment

6. Is $\overline{DE}$ tangent to $\odot C$?

7. In Example 4, find r when AB is 70 feet.

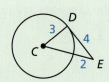

1 I don't understand yet.   **2** I can do it with help.   **3** I can do it on my own.   **4** I can teach someone.

Construction

Constructing a Tangent to a Circle

Construct a line tangent to ⊙C that passes through point A.

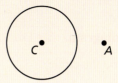

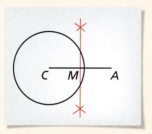

Draw $\overline{AC}$. Construct the bisector of $\overline{AC}$ and label the midpoint M.

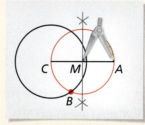

Construct ⊙M with radius MA. Label one of the intersections as point B.

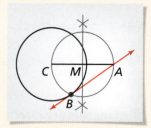

Draw the tangent line $\overleftrightarrow{AB}$.

EXAMPLE 5   Using Properties of Tangents

$\overline{RS}$ is tangent to ⊙C at S, and $\overline{RT}$ is tangent to ⊙C at T. Find the value of x.

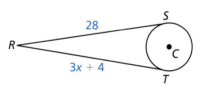

Because $\overline{RS}$ and $\overline{RT}$ are tangents to ⊙C from a common external point, they are congruent by the External Tangent Congruence Theorem.

$RS = RT$	External Tangent Congruence Theorem
$28 = 3x + 4$	Substitute.
$24 = 3x$	Subtract 4 from each side.
$8 = x$	Divide each side by 3.

▶ The value of x is 8.

In-Class Practice

Self-Assessment

8. Points M and N are points of tangency. Find the value(s) of x.

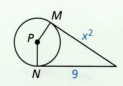

10.1   Lines and Segments That Intersect Circles   511

10.1 Practice

with Calc Chat and Calc View

1–14
15 or 16 (pick)
17–22, 24, 27
Tue & Wed

Use the diagram. (See Example 1.)

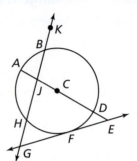

1. Name the circle.

2. Name two radii and a diameter.

▶ 3. Name two chords.

4. Name a secant, a tangent line, and a point of tangency.

Copy the diagram. Tell how many common tangents the circles have and draw them. State whether the tangents are *external tangents* or *internal tangents*. (See Example 2.)

▶ 5.

6.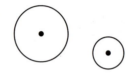

7.

Explain whether $\overline{AB}$ is tangent to $\odot C$. (See Example 3.)

8.

▶ 9.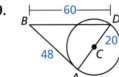

10.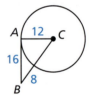

Point B is a point of tangency. Find the radius r of $\odot C$. (See Example 4.)

▶ 11.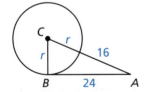

12.

13.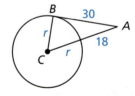

14. **SMP.3 ERROR ANALYSIS** Describe and correct the error in determining whether $\overline{XY}$ is tangent to $\odot Z$.

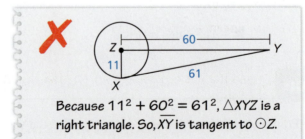

Because $11^2 + 60^2 = 61^2$, $\triangle XYZ$ is a right triangle. So, $\overline{XY}$ is tangent to $\odot Z$.

SMP.5 CONSTRUCTION Construct $\odot C$ with the given radius and point A outside of $\odot C$. Then construct a line tangent to $\odot C$ that passes through A.

15. $r = 2$ in.

16. $r = 4.5$ cm

Points B and D are points of tangency. Find the value(s) of x. (See Example 5.)

▶17.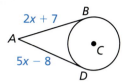

18.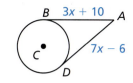

19.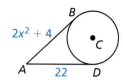

20. Explain what you can determine about the points of tangency when two lines tangent to the same circle do not intersect.

21. **SMP.6** Explain why the diameter of a circle is the longest chord of the circle.

22. **CONNECT CONCEPTS** In $\odot C$, radii $\overline{CA}$ and $\overline{CB}$ are perpendicular. $\overleftrightarrow{BD}$ and $\overleftrightarrow{AD}$ are tangent to $\odot C$. What type of quadrilateral is *CADB*?

23. **CONNECTION TO REAL LIFE** A bicycle chain is pulled tightly so that $\overline{MN}$ is a common tangent of the gears. Find the distance between the centers of the gears.

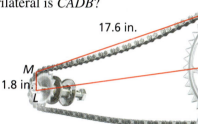
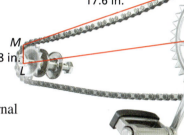

24. **PROOF** In the diagram, $\overline{RS}$ is a common internal tangent to $\odot A$ and $\odot B$. Prove that $\dfrac{AC}{BC} = \dfrac{RC}{SC}$.

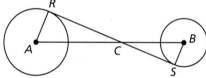

25. **PROVING THEOREM 10.2** Prove the External Tangent Congruence Theorem.

    Given $\overline{SR}$ and $\overline{ST}$ are tangent to $\odot P$.
    Prove $\overline{SR} \cong \overline{ST}$

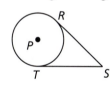

26. **PROVING THEOREM 10.1** Use the diagram to prove each part of the biconditional in the Tangent Line to Circle Theorem.

    a. Prove indirectly that if a line is tangent to a circle, then it is perpendicular to a radius.

       Given Line *m* is tangent to $\odot Q$ at point *P*.
       Prove $m \perp \overline{QP}$

    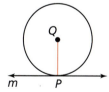

    b. Prove indirectly that if a line is perpendicular to a radius at its endpoint, then the line is tangent to the circle.

       Given $m \perp \overline{QP}$
       Prove Line *m* is tangent to $\odot Q$.

27. **DIG DEEPER** In the diagram, $AB = AC = 12$, $BC = 8$, and each of the three segments intersects $\odot P$ in exactly one point. What is the radius of $\odot P$? Justify your answer.

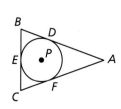

Interpreting Data

DISCUS THROW The discus throw is an event in which athletes attempt to throw a discus farther than their competitors. The athlete spins around one and a half times through a circle, then releases the discus.

28. What is the radius of the circular path?

29. When the discus is released, explain whether it continues to travel in a circular path.

30. If the released discus travels in a straight path, is the path tangent to the circular path?

Review & Refresh

Solve the triangle.

31.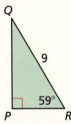

32.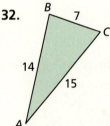

Tell whether the lines through the given points are *parallel*, *perpendicular*, or *neither*.

33. Line 1: $(-5, -3), (0, 1)$
    Line 2: $(4, 2), (8, 7)$

34. Line 1: $(-6, -2), (-3, -6)$
    Line 2: $(2, 1), (8, -7)$

35. Point P is the centroid of $\triangle LMN$. Find LP and PQ when $LQ = 36$.

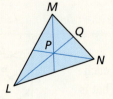

36. $\angle J$ and $\angle K$ are consecutive angles in a parallelogram, $m\angle J = (3x + 7)°$, and $m\angle K = (5x - 11)°$. Find each angle measure.

37. Find the horizontal distance covered by the steps of the escalator.

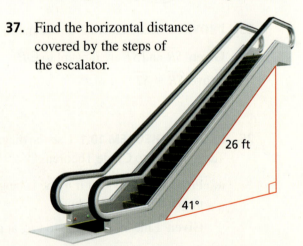

38. Find the length of the midsegment of the trapezoid.

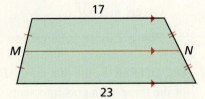

514 Chapter 10 Circles

10.2 Finding Arc Measures

> **Learning Target:** Understand arc measures and similar circles.
> **Success Criteria:**
> • I can find arc measures.
> • I can identify congruent arcs.
> • I can prove that all circles are similar.

A **central angle** of a circle is an angle that is formed by two radii and has a vertex at the center of the circle. A *circular arc* is a portion of a circle that is between two radii. The measure of a circular arc is the measure of its central angle.

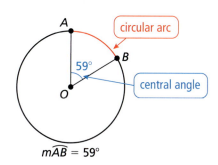

$m\widehat{AB} = 59°$

INVESTIGATE Measuring Circular Arcs

Work with a partner. In each Ferris wheel shown, the passenger cars are equally spaced.

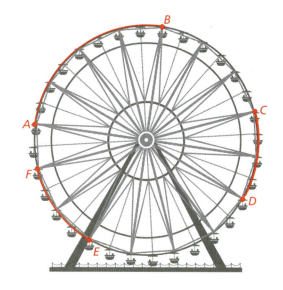

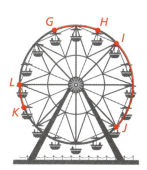

1. Compare the Ferris wheels. Explain whether they represent *congruent circles*.

2. Find the measure of each circular arc shown. Explain your reasoning.

3. Are any of the arcs *similar arcs*? *congruent arcs*? Explain.

4. Explain whether the size of the circle affects the measure of a circular arc.

10.2 Finding Arc Measures 515

Vocabulary
central angle
minor arc
major arc
semicircle
measure of a minor arc
measure of a major arc
adjacent arcs
congruent circles
congruent arcs
similar arcs

Finding Arc Measures

A **central angle** of a circle is an angle that is formed by two radii and has a vertex at the center of the circle. In the diagram, ∠ACB is a central angle of ⊙C.

If m∠ACB is less than 180°, then the points on ⊙C that lie in the interior of ∠ACB form a **minor arc** with endpoints A and B. The points on ⊙C that do not lie on the minor arc AB form a **major arc** with endpoints A and B. A **semicircle** is an arc with endpoints that are the endpoints of a diameter.

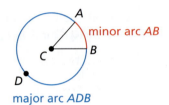

Key Concept

Measuring Arcs

The **measure of a minor arc** is the measure of its central angle. The expression $m\widehat{AB}$ is read as "the measure of arc AB."

The measure of the entire circle is 360°. The **measure of a major arc** is the difference of 360° and the measure of the related minor arc. The measure of a semicircle is 180°.

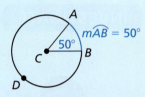

$m\widehat{AB} = 50°$

$m\widehat{ADB} = 360° - 50° = 310°$

EXAMPLE 1 Finding Measures of Arcs

Find the measure of each arc of ⊙P, where $\overline{RT}$ is a diameter.

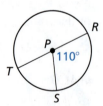

a. $\widehat{RS}$

$\widehat{RS}$ is a minor arc, so $m\widehat{RS} = m\angle RPS = 110°$.

b. $\widehat{RTS}$

$\widehat{RTS}$ is a major arc, so $m\widehat{RTS} = 360° - m\widehat{RS} = 360° - 110° = 250°$.

In-Class Practice

Self-Assessment

1. In Example 1, find $m\widehat{RST}$.

Two arcs of the same circle are **adjacent arcs** when they intersect at exactly one point. You can add the measures of two adjacent arcs.

> ### Postulate 10.1
>
> **Arc Addition Postulate**
>
> The measure of an arc formed by two adjacent arcs is the sum of the measures of the two arcs.
>
>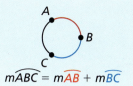
>
> $m\widehat{ABC} = m\widehat{AB} + m\widehat{BC}$

EXAMPLE 2 Using the Arc Addition Postulate

Find the measure of each arc.

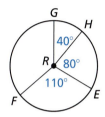

a. $\widehat{GE}$

$m\widehat{GE} = m\widehat{GH} + m\widehat{HE} = 40° + 80° = 120°$

b. $\widehat{GEF}$

$m\widehat{GEF} = m\widehat{GE} + m\widehat{EF} = 120° + 110° = 230°$

c. $\widehat{GF}$

$m\widehat{GF} = 360° - m\widehat{GEF} = 360° - 230° = 130°$

EXAMPLE 3 Finding Measures of Arcs

A recent survey asked teenagers whether they would rather meet a famous musician, athlete, actor, inventor, or other person. The circle graph shows the results. Find the indicated arc measures.

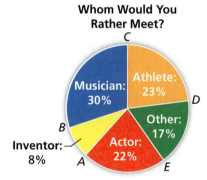

Whom Would You Rather Meet?

a. $m\widehat{AC}$

By the Arc Addition Postulate, $m\widehat{AC} = m\widehat{AB} + m\widehat{BC}$. $\widehat{AB}$ represents 8% of the circle, so $m\widehat{AB} = 0.08(360°) = 28.8°$. $\widehat{BC}$ represents 30% of the circle, so $m\widehat{BC} = 0.3(360°) = 108°$.

▶ So, $m\widehat{AC} = 28.8° + 108° = 136.8°$.

b. $m\widehat{ACD}$

By the Arc Addition Postulate, $m\widehat{ACD} = m\widehat{AC} + m\widehat{CD}$. $\widehat{CD}$ represents 23% of the circle, so $m\widehat{CD} = 0.23(360°) = 82.8°$.

▶ So, $m\widehat{ACD} = 136.8° + 82.8° = 219.6°$.

In-Class Practice

Self-Assessment

2. Find $m\widehat{QRT}$.

3. In Example 3, find $m\widehat{EBD}$.

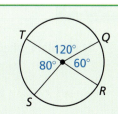

| 1 I don't understand yet. | 2 I can do it with help. | 3 I can do it on my own. | 4 I can teach someone. |

10.2 Finding Arc Measures

Identifying Congruent Arcs

Two circles are **congruent circles** if and only if a rigid motion or a composition of rigid motions maps one circle onto the other. Two arcs are **congruent arcs** if and only if they have the same measure and they are arcs of the same circle or of congruent circles.

Theorem 10.3

Congruent Circles Theorem

Two circles are congruent circles if and only if they have the same radius.

Prove this Theorem Exercise 19, page 521

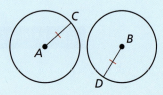

⊙A ≅ ⊙B if and only if $\overline{AC} \cong \overline{BD}$.

Theorem 10.4

Congruent Central Angles Theorem

In the same circle, or in congruent circles, two minor arcs are congruent if and only if their corresponding central angles are congruent.

Prove this Theorem Exercise 20, page 521

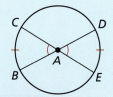

$\widehat{BC} \cong \widehat{DE}$ if and only if ∠BAC ≅ ∠DAE.

EXAMPLE 4 Identifying Congruent Arcs

Explain whether $\widehat{UV}$ and $\widehat{YZ}$ are congruent.

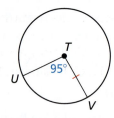 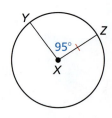

▶ $\widehat{UV} \cong \widehat{YZ}$ by the Congruent Central Angles Theorem because they are arcs of congruent circles and they have congruent central angles, ∠UTV ≅ ∠YXZ.

In-Class Practice

Self-Assessment

4. Explain whether $\widehat{MN}$ and $\widehat{PQ}$ are congruent.

| 1 I don't understand yet. | 2 I can do it with help. | 3 I can do it on my own. | 4 I can teach someone. |

Proving Circles Are Similar

Theorem 10.5

Similar Circles Theorem

All circles are similar.

Prove this Theorem Exercise 5, page 519

PROOF Similar Circles Theorem

Given ⊙C with center C and radius r,
⊙D with center D and radius s

Prove ⊙C ~ ⊙D

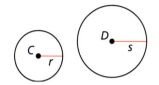

First, translate ⊙C so that point C maps to point D. The image of ⊙C is ⊙C′ with center D. So, ⊙C′ and ⊙D are concentric circles.

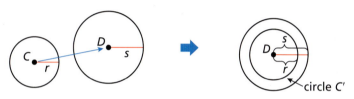

⊙C′ is the set of all points that are r units from point D. Dilate ⊙C′ using center of dilation D and scale factor $\frac{s}{r}$.

▶ Because a similarity transformation maps ⊙C to ⊙D, ⊙C ~ ⊙D.

Two arcs are **similar arcs** if and only if they have the same measure. All congruent arcs are similar, but not all similar arcs are congruent.

In-Class Practice

Self-Assessment

5. Write a coordinate proof of the Similar Circles Theorem.

Given ⊙O with center O(0, 0) and radius r,
⊙A with center A(a, b) and radius s

Prove ⊙O ~ ⊙A

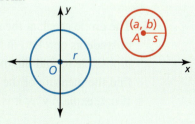

10.2 Finding Arc Measures 519

10.2 Practice

Name the minor arc and find its measure. Then name the major arc and find its measure.

1.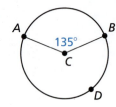
2.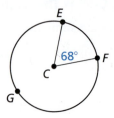
3.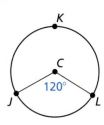

Identify the given arc as a *major arc*, *minor arc*, or *semicircle*. Then find the measure of the arc. (See Example 1.)

4. $\overarc{AB}$
5. $\overarc{AC}$
6. $\overarc{FG}$
7. $\overarc{EG}$

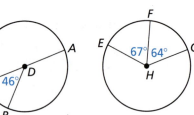

Find the measure of each arc. (See Example 2.)

8. a. $\overarc{RS}$
   b. $\overarc{QRS}$
   c. $\overarc{QST}$
   d. $\overarc{QT}$

9. a. $\overarc{JL}$
   b. $\overarc{KM}$
   c. $\overarc{JLM}$
   d. $\overarc{JM}$

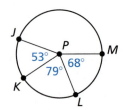

10. **CONNECTION TO REAL LIFE** A recent survey asked high school students their favorite type of music. The results are shown in the circle graph. Find each indicated arc measure. (See Example 3.)

    a. $m\overarc{AE}$
    b. $m\overarc{ACE}$
    c. $m\overarc{GDC}$
    d. $m\overarc{BHC}$
    e. $m\overarc{FD}$
    f. $m\overarc{FBD}$

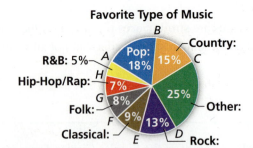

11. The circle graph at the right shows the percentages of students enrolled in fall sports at a high school. Is it possible to find the measure of each minor arc? If so, find the measure of the arc for each category shown. If not, explain why it is not possible.

Explain whether the red arcs are congruent. (See Example 4.)

12. 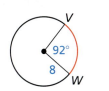   13.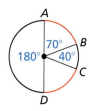

14. **SMP.3 ERROR ANALYSIS** Describe and correct the error in naming the red arc.

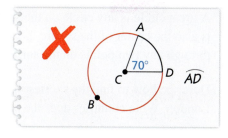

CONNECT CONCEPTS Find the value of x. Then find the measure of the red arc.

15. 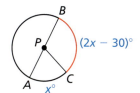   16.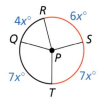

17. **SMP.6** Two diameters of $\odot P$ are $\overline{AB}$ and $\overline{CD}$. Find $m\widehat{ACD}$ and $m\widehat{AC}$ when $m\widehat{AD} = 20°$.

18. **CONNECTION TO REAL LIFE** Time zone wheels can be used to find the time in different locations around the world. To use the wheel shown to find the time in Tokyo when it is 4 P.M. in San Francisco, rotate the small wheel until 4 P.M. and San Francisco line up, as shown. Then look at Tokyo to see that it is 9 A.M. there.

    a. What is the arc measure between each time zone on the wheel?
    b. What is the measure of the minor arc from the Tokyo zone to the Anchorage zone?
    c. If two locations differ by 180° on the wheel, and it is 3 P.M. at one location, what time is it at the other location?

19. **PROVING THEOREM 10.3** Use the diagram on page 518 to prove each part of the biconditional in the Congruent Circles Theorem.

    a. **Given** $\overline{AC} \cong \overline{BD}$
       Prove $\odot A \cong \odot B$

    b. **Given** $\odot A \cong \odot B$
       Prove $\overline{AC} \cong \overline{BD}$

20. **PROVING THEOREM 10.4** Use the diagram to prove each part of the biconditional in the Congruent Central Angles Theorem.

    a. **Given** $\angle BAC \cong \angle DAE$
       Prove $\widehat{BC} \cong \widehat{DE}$

    b. **Given** $\widehat{BC} \cong \widehat{DE}$
       Prove $\angle BAC \cong \angle DAE$

Interpreting Data

GREAT CIRCLE ROUTE In flying, a *great circle route* is the shortest route between two points on the surface of a sphere. The distance of the route is the length of the arc between the two points. When plotted on a flat map, a great circle route usually appears curved.

21. A great circle is any circle on the surface of a sphere whose center is also the center of the sphere. Is there a great circle that passes through any two points on the surface of a sphere?

22. Describe how to find the shortest flight path between Seattle and London. What countries does the path pass over?

23. What is the maximum flying distance between two points on Earth's surface?

String stretch between two points: Appears curved.

Tilt globe to look directly over route. Now, the route appears straight.

Review & Refresh

24. Points B and D are points of tangency. Find the value(s) of x.

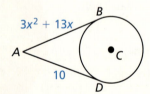

Solve the triangle.

25.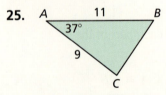

26.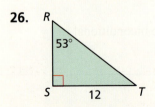

27. Find the geometric mean of 4 and 64.

28. Show that the two triangles are similar.

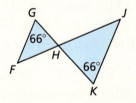

Find the value of x.

29.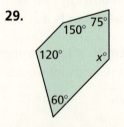

30.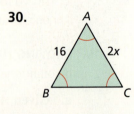

Graph the polygon with the given vertices and its image after the indicated transformation.

31. $A(-1, 5)$, $B(-4, 1)$, $C(2, 1)$
    Reflection: in the y-axis

32. $E(2, 1)$, $F(2, 5)$, $G(5, 4)$, $H(5, 0)$
    Translation: $(x, y) \rightarrow (x + 2, y - 3)$

10.3 Using Chords

> **Learning Target:** Understand and apply theorems about chords.
>
> **Success Criteria:**
> - I can use chords of circles to find arc measures.
> - I can use chords of circles to find lengths.
> - I can describe the relationship between a diameter and a chord perpendicular to a diameter.
> - I can find the center of a circle given three points on the circle.

INVESTIGATE Making Conjectures about Chords

Work with a partner. Use technology.

1. Construct a chord $\overline{BC}$ of a circle A. Then construct a chord on the perpendicular bisector of $\overline{BC}$. What do you notice?

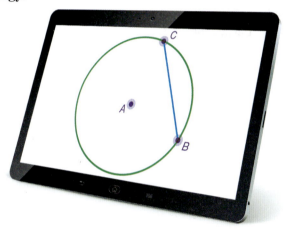

2. **SMP.8** In Exercise 1, what happens when you move the endpoints of $\overline{BC}$? What happens when you resize the circle? Make a conjecture about the perpendicular bisector of a chord.

3. Construct a diameter $\overline{BC}$ of a circle A. Then construct a chord $\overline{DE}$ perpendicular to $\overline{BC}$ at a point F. What do you notice?

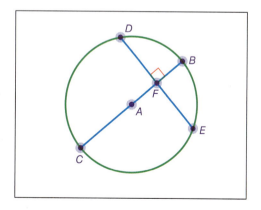

4. **SMP.8** In Exercise 3, what happens when you move point F to a different position on $\overline{BC}$? when you resize the circle? Make a conjecture about a chord that is perpendicular to a diameter of a circle.

10.3 Using Chords 523

Using Chords of Circles

A diameter divides a circle into two semicircles. Any other chord divides a circle into a minor arc and a major arc.

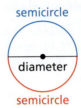

Theorem 10.6

Congruent Corresponding Chords Theorem

In the same circle, or in congruent circles, two minor arcs are congruent if and only if their corresponding chords are congruent.

Prove this Theorem Exercise 14, page 529

$\widehat{AB} \cong \widehat{CD}$ if and only if $\overline{AB} \cong \overline{CD}$.

EXAMPLE 1 Using Congruent Chords

Find $m\widehat{FG}$.

The circles have the same radius. By the Congruent Circles Theorem, $\odot P \cong \odot Q$. Because $\overline{FG}$ and $\overline{JK}$ are congruent chords in congruent circles, the corresponding minor arcs $\widehat{FG}$ and $\widehat{JK}$ are congruent by the Congruent Corresponding Chords Theorem.

▶ So, $m\widehat{FG} = m\widehat{JK} = 80°$.

In-Class Practice

Find the measure of the red arc or chord.

1.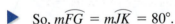

2.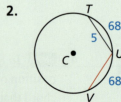

524   Chapter 10   Circles

Theorem 10.7

Perpendicular Chord Bisector Theorem

If a diameter of a circle is perpendicular to a chord, then the diameter bisects the chord and its arc.

If $\overline{EG}$ is a diameter and $\overline{EG} \perp \overline{DF}$, then $\overline{HD} \cong \overline{HF}$ and $\overset{\frown}{GD} \cong \overset{\frown}{GF}$.

Prove this Theorem Exercise 15, page 529

EXAMPLE 2 Using a Diameter

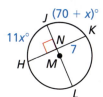

a. Find HK.

Diameter $\overline{JL}$ is perpendicular to $\overline{HK}$. So, by the Perpendicular Chord Bisector Theorem, $\overline{JL}$ bisects $\overline{HK}$, and $HN = NK$.

▶ So, $HK = 2(NK) = 2(7) = 14$.

b. Find $m\overset{\frown}{HK}$.

Diameter $\overline{JL}$ is perpendicular to $\overline{HK}$. So, by the Perpendicular Chord Bisector Theorem, $\overline{JL}$ bisects $\overset{\frown}{HK}$, and $m\overset{\frown}{HJ} = m\overset{\frown}{JK}$.

$m\overset{\frown}{HJ} = m\overset{\frown}{JK}$	Perpendicular Chord Bisector Theorem
$11x° = (70 + x)°$	Substitute.
$10x = 70$	Subtract x from each side.
$x = 7$	Divide each side by 10.

So, $m\overset{\frown}{HJ} = m\overset{\frown}{JK} = (70 + x)° = (70 + 7)° = 77°$, and $m\overset{\frown}{HK} = 2(m\overset{\frown}{HJ}) = 2(77°) = 154°$.

▶ The measure of $\overset{\frown}{HK}$ is 154°.

In-Class Practice

Self-Assessment

Find the measure of the red arc or chord.

3.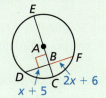

4.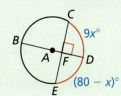

| 1 | I don't understand yet. | 2 | I can do it with help. | 3 | I can do it on my own. | 4 | I can teach someone. |

10.3 Using Chords 525

> ### Theorem 10.8
>
> **Perpendicular Chord Bisector Converse**
> If one chord of a circle is a perpendicular bisector of another chord, then the first chord is a diameter.
>
>
>
> If $\overline{QS}$ is a perpendicular bisector of $\overline{TR}$, then $\overline{QS}$ is a diameter of the circle.
>
> *Prove this Theorem* Exercise 17, page 529

EXAMPLE 3 **Using Perpendicular Bisectors**

Three bushes are arranged in a garden, as shown. Where should you place a sprinkler so that it is the same distance from each bush?

Place the sprinkler at the center of the circle that passes through the bushes.

Construction

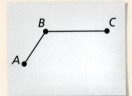	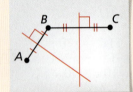	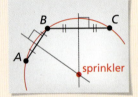
Label the bushes as shown. Draw $\overline{AB}$ and $\overline{BC}$.	Draw the perpendicular bisectors of $\overline{AB}$ and $\overline{BC}$. By the Perpendicular Chord Bisector Converse, these lie on diameters of the circle containing A, B, and C.	Find the intersection of the perpendicular bisectors. This is the center of the circle.

In-Class Practice

Self-Assessment

5. In Example 3, you want to plant a fourth bush so that it is equidistant from the sprinkler. Describe the possible locations where you can plant the bush.

6. **OPEN-ENDED** Plot any three noncollinear points in a coordinate plane. Find the point that is the same distance from each of the three plotted points.

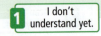

Theorem 10.9

Equidistant Chords Theorem

In the same circle, or in congruent circles, two chords are congruent if and only if they are equidistant from the center.

Prove this Theorem Exercise 19, page 529

$\overline{AB} \cong \overline{CD}$ if and only if $EF = EG$.

EXAMPLE 4 Using Congruent Chords to Find the Radius of a Circle

In the diagram, $QR = ST = 16$. Find the radius of $\odot C$.

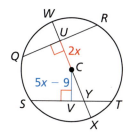

Because $\overline{CQ}$ is a segment whose endpoints are the center and a point on the circle, it is a radius of $\odot C$. Because $\overline{CU} \perp \overline{QR}$, $\triangle QUC$ is a right triangle.

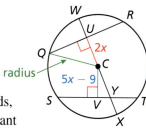

Find CU. Because $\overline{QR}$ and $\overline{ST}$ are congruent chords, $\overline{QR}$ and $\overline{ST}$ are equidistant from C by the Equidistant Chords Theorem. So, $CU = CV$.

$CU = CV$ Equidistant Chords Theorem

$2x = 5x - 9$ Substitute.

$x = 3$ Solve for x.

So, $CU = 2x = 2(3) = 6$.

Find QU. Because diameter $\overline{WX} \perp \overline{QR}$, $\overline{WX}$ bisects $\overline{QR}$ by the Perpendicular Chord Bisector Theorem.

So, $QU = \frac{1}{2}QR = \frac{1}{2}(16) = 8$.

Find CQ. The lengths of the legs of right $\triangle QUC$ are $CU = 6$ and $QU = 8$. Because the integers 6, 8, and 10 form a Pythagorean triple, $CQ = 10$.

▶ So, the radius of $\odot C$ is 10 units.

In-Class Practice

Self-Assessment

Use the diagram and the given measures to find the radius of $\odot N$.

7. $JK = LM = 24$, $NP = 3x$, $NQ = 7x - 12$

8. $NP = NQ = 5$, $JK = 5x - 1$, $LM = 7x - 11$

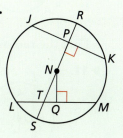

10.3 Practice

with Calc Chat and Calc View

Find the measure of the red arc or chord in ⊙C. (See Example 1.)

1.

2.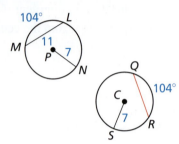

3.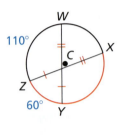

Find the value of x. (See Example 2.)

4.

5.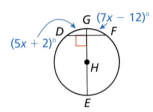

6.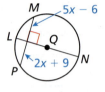

7. **CONNECTION TO REAL LIFE** Three tables are arranged on a patio, as shown. Explain how to place a patio heater so that it is the same distance from each table. (See Example 3.)

8. An archaeologist finds part of a circular plate. What was the diameter of the plate? Justify your answer.

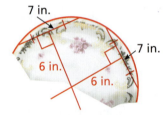

Explain whether $\overline{AB}$ is a diameter of the circle.

9.

10.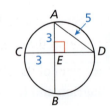

Find the radius of ⊙Q. (See Example 4.)

11.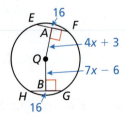

12.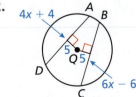

13. **SMP.3 ERROR ANALYSIS** $AB = DE = 24$. Describe and correct the error in finding the radius of $\odot C$.

    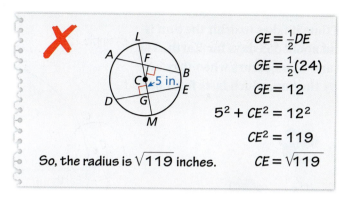

14. **PROVING THEOREM 10.6** Use the diagram to prove each part of the biconditional in the Congruent Corresponding Chords Theorem.

    a. **Given** $\overline{AB} \cong \overline{CD}$
       Prove $\widehat{AB} \cong \widehat{CD}$

    b. **Given** $\widehat{AB} \cong \widehat{CD}$
       Prove $\overline{AB} \cong \overline{CD}$

    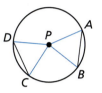

15. **PROVING THEOREM 10.7** Use congruent triangles to prove the Perpendicular Chord Bisector Theorem.

    Given $\overline{EG}$ is a diameter of $\odot L$.
    $\overline{EG} \perp \overline{DF}$

    Prove $\overline{DC} \cong \overline{FC}, \widehat{DG} \cong \widehat{FG}$

16. In the diagram, point C is a point of tangency. $\overline{AB}$ is parallel to line n. Explain whether $\overline{CD}$ bisects $\widehat{AB}$.

    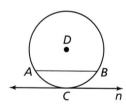

17. **PROVING THEOREM 10.8** Write a proof of the Perpendicular Chord Bisector Converse.

    Given $\overline{QS}$ is the perpendicular bisector of $\overline{RT}$.
    Prove $\overline{QS}$ is a diameter of the circle.

    (*Hint:* Let C be the center of the circle. Show that C must lie on $\overline{QS}$.)

18. **DIG DEEPER** In $\odot P$, the lengths of the parallel chords are 20, 16, and 12. Find $m\widehat{AB}$.

19. **PROVING THEOREM 10.9** Prove both parts of the biconditional of the Equidistant Chords Theorem.

10.3 Using Chords 529

Interpreting Data

SOLAR CONJUNCTION The time it takes to orbit the Sun is about 687 days for Mars and about 365 days for Earth. The solar conjunction of Earth and Mars occurs when they are obscured from each other by the Sun, which lasts for a period of about two weeks.

Mars Curiosity rover

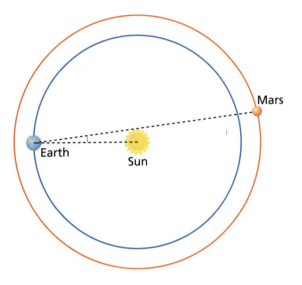

20. Why is communication between NASA and a rover on Mars not possible during a solar conjunction?

21. Describe the solar conjunction of Earth and Mars in terms of chords of Earth's orbit around the Sun.

22. Explain why Earth and Mars are occasionally on opposite sides of the Sun. How often does this occur?

Review & Refresh

23. In the diagram, point B is a point of tangency. Find the radius x of $\odot C$.

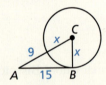

24. A surveyor takes measurements to determine the length of a bridge to be built from the North Picnic Area to the South Picnic Area. Find the length of the bridge.

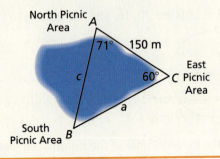

Find the missing interior angle measure.

25. Quadrilateral $JKLM$ has angle measures $m\angle J = 32°$, $m\angle K = 125°$, and $m\angle L = 44°$. Find $m\angle M$.

26. Pentagon $PQRST$ has angle measures $m\angle P = 85°$, $m\angle Q = 134°$, $m\angle R = 97°$, and $m\angle S = 102°$. Find $m\angle T$.

27. Explain whether the red arcs are congruent, similar, or neither.

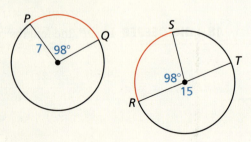

530 Chapter 10 Circles

10.4 Inscribed Angles and Polygons

Learning Target: Use properties of inscribed angles and inscribed polygons.

Success Criteria:
- I can find measures of inscribed angles and intercepted arcs.
- I can find angle measures of inscribed polygons.
- I can construct a square inscribed in a circle.

INVESTIGATE Constructing Inscribed Angles and Central Angles

Work with a partner.

1. Use the diagram to write definitions for an *inscribed angle* and an *intercepted arc*.

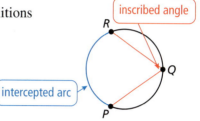

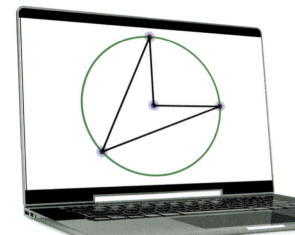

2. Use technology to construct an inscribed angle of a circle. Then construct the corresponding central angle.

3. Measure both angles. What do you notice?

4. **SMP.8** What happens to the angle measures when you change the inscribed angle? What happens to the angle measures when you change the size of the circle? Make a conjecture about the relationship between the measure of an inscribed angle and the measure of its intercepted arc.

5. Each vertex of a quadrilateral lies on a circle. Use technology to find a relationship among the measures of the interior angles of the quadrilateral. Make a conjecture that summarizes your results. Provide examples to support your reasoning.

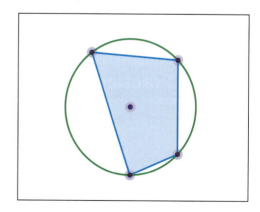

10.4 Inscribed Angles and Polygons 531

Vocabulary
inscribed angle
intercepted arc
subtend
inscribed polygon
circumscribed circle

Using Inscribed Angles

An **inscribed angle** is an angle whose vertex lies on a circle and whose sides contain chords of the circle. An arc that lies between two lines, rays, or segments is called an **intercepted arc**. If the endpoints of a chord or arc lie on the sides of an inscribed angle, then the chord or arc is said to **subtend** the angle.

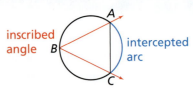

$\angle B$ intercepts $\overset{\frown}{AC}$.
$\overset{\frown}{AC}$ subtends $\angle B$.
$\overline{AC}$ subtends $\angle B$.

Theorem 10.10

Measure of an Inscribed Angle Theorem

The measure of an inscribed angle is one-half the measure of its intercepted arc.

Prove this Theorem Exercise 17, page 537

$m\angle ADB = \frac{1}{2}(m\overset{\frown}{AB})$

EXAMPLE 1 Using Inscribed Angles

Find (a) $m\angle T$ and (b) $m\overset{\frown}{QR}$.

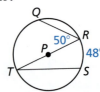

a. Use the Measure of an Inscribed Angle Theorem to find $m\angle T$.

$m\angle T = \frac{1}{2}(m\overset{\frown}{RS}) = \frac{1}{2}(48°) = 24°$

b. Use the Measure of an Inscribed Angle Theorem to find $m\overset{\frown}{TQ}$. Then use the fact that $\overset{\frown}{TQR}$ is a semicircle to find $m\overset{\frown}{QR}$.

$\frac{1}{2}(m\overset{\frown}{TQ}) = m\angle R$ $m\overset{\frown}{QR} = 180° - m\overset{\frown}{TQ}$
$\frac{1}{2}(m\overset{\frown}{TQ}) = 50°$ $\phantom{m\overset{\frown}{QR}} = 180° - 100°$
$m\overset{\frown}{TQ} = 100°$ $\phantom{m\overset{\frown}{QR}} = 80°$

In-Class Practice

Self-Assessment

Find the indicated measure.

1. $m\angle G$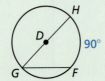

2. $m\overset{\frown}{TV}$

1 I don't understand yet.   **2** I can do it with help.   **3** I can do it on my own.   **4** I can teach someone.

EXAMPLE 2 Finding the Measure of an Intercepted Arc

Find $m\overset{\frown}{RS}$ and $m\angle STR$. What do you notice about $\angle STR$ and $\angle RUS$?

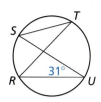

From the Measure of an Inscribed Angle Theorem, $\frac{1}{2}(m\overset{\frown}{RS}) = m\angle RUS$. So, $m\overset{\frown}{RS} = 2(m\angle RUS) = 2(31°) = 62°$.

Also, $m\angle STR = \frac{1}{2}(m\overset{\frown}{RS}) = \frac{1}{2}(62°) = 31°$.

▶ So, $m\overset{\frown}{RS} = 62°$, $m\angle STR = 31°$, and $\angle STR \cong \angle RUS$.

Theorem 10.11

Inscribed Angles of a Circle Theorem

If two inscribed angles of a circle intercept the same arc, then the angles are congruent.

Prove this Theorem Exercise 18, page 537

$\angle ADB \cong \angle ACB$

EXAMPLE 3 Finding the Measure of an Angle

Find $m\angle F$.

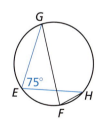

Both $\angle E$ and $\angle F$ intercept $\overset{\frown}{GH}$. So, $\angle E \cong \angle F$ by the Inscribed Angles of a Circle Theorem.

▶ So, $m\angle F = m\angle E = 75°$.

In-Class Practice

Self-Assessment

3. Find $m\angle X$.

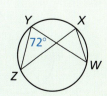

| 1 I don't understand yet. | 2 I can do it with help. | 3 I can do it on my own. | 4 I can teach someone. |

10.4 Inscribed Angles and Polygons

Using Inscribed Polygons

A polygon is an **inscribed polygon** when all its vertices lie on a circle. The circle that contains the vertices is a **circumscribed circle**.

Theorem 10.12

Inscribed Right Triangle Theorem

If a right triangle is inscribed in a circle, then the hypotenuse is a diameter of the circle. Conversely, if one side of an inscribed triangle is a diameter of the circle, then the triangle is a right triangle and the angle opposite the diameter is the right angle.

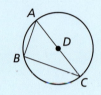

$m\angle ABC = 90°$ if and only if $\overline{AC}$ is a diameter of the circle.

Prove this Theorem Exercise 19, page 537

Theorem 10.13

Inscribed Quadrilateral Theorem

A quadrilateral can be inscribed in a circle if and only if its opposite angles are supplementary.

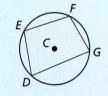

D, E, F, and G lie on ⊙C if and only if $m\angle D + m\angle F = m\angle E + m\angle G = 180°$.

Proof BigIdeasMath.com
Prove this Theorem Exercise 20, page 537

EXAMPLE 4 Using Inscribed Polygons

Find the value of each variable.

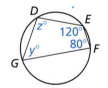

DEFG is inscribed in a circle, so opposite angles are supplementary by the Inscribed Quadrilateral Theorem.

$m\angle D + m\angle F = 180°$ $\qquad$ $m\angle E + m\angle G = 180°$

$z + 80 = 180$ $\qquad\qquad$ $120 + y = 180$

$z = 100$ $\qquad\qquad\qquad$ $y = 60$

▶ The value of z is 100 and the value of y is 60.

In-Class Practice
Self-Assessment

Find the value of each variable.

4.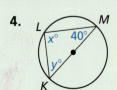

5. (Circle with B, C, D, A; angles 68°, x°, 82°, y°)

6.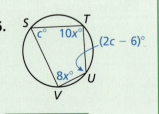

1 I don't understand yet.　　2 I can do it with help.　　3 I can do it on my own.　　4 I can teach someone.

Construction

Constructing a Square Inscribed in a Circle

Given ⊙C, construct a square inscribed in a circle.

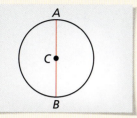

Draw any diameter. Label the endpoints A and B.

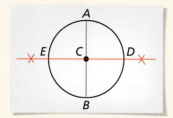

Construct the perpendicular bisector of the diameter. Label the points where it intersects ⊙C as points D and E.

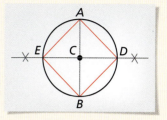

Connect points A, D, B, and E to form a square.

EXAMPLE 5 Using a Circumscribed Circle

Your camera has a 90° field of vision, and you want to photograph the front of a statue. You stand at a location in which the front of the statue fits perfectly within your camera's field of vision, as shown. You want to change your location. Where else can you stand so that the front of the statue fits perfectly within your camera's field of vision?

From the Inscribed Right Triangle Theorem, you know that if a right triangle is inscribed in a circle, then the hypotenuse of the triangle is a diameter of the circle. So, draw the circle that has the front of the statue as a diameter.

▶ The statue fits perfectly within your camera's 90° field of vision from any point on the semicircle in front of the statue.

In-Class Practice

Self-Assessment

7. In Example 5, explain how to find locations where the left side of the statue fits perfectly within your camera's field of vision.

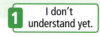 I don't understand yet.   I can do it with help.   I can do it on my own.   I can teach someone.

10.4 Practice

Find the indicated measure. (See Examples 1, 2, and 3.)

1. $m\angle A$

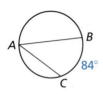

2. $m\angle G$

3. $m\widehat{VU}$

4. $m\widehat{WX}$

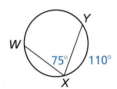

5. $m\angle EHF$

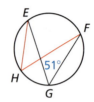

6. $m\widehat{PS}$

Find the value of each variable. (See Example 4.)

7.

8.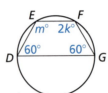

9.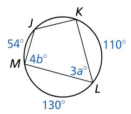

10. **SMP.3 ERROR ANALYSIS** Describe and correct the error in finding the value of x.

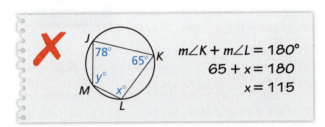

11. **CONNECTION TO REAL LIFE** A *carpenter's square* is an L-shaped tool used to draw right angles. You need to cut a circular piece of wood into two semicircles. How can you use the carpenter's square to draw a diameter on the circular piece of wood? (See Example 5.)

CONNECT CONCEPTS Find the values of x and y. Then find the measures of the interior angles of the polygon.

12.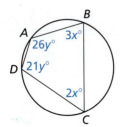

13.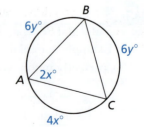

536 Chapter 10 Circles

14. **SMP.6** Explain whether every polygon of the given type can be inscribed inside a circle.

    a. right triangle
    b. kite
    c. rhombus
    d. isosceles trapezoid

15. **CONSTRUCTION** Construct an equilateral triangle inscribed in a circle.

16. **CONSTRUCTION** The side length of an inscribed regular hexagon is equal to the radius of the circumscribed circle. Use this fact to construct a regular hexagon inscribed in a circle.

17. **PROVING THEOREM 10.10** If an angle is inscribed in $\odot Q$, the center Q can be on a side of the inscribed angle, inside the inscribed angle, or outside the inscribed angle. Prove each case of the Measure of an Inscribed Angle Theorem.

    a. **Case 1**

    Given $\angle ABC$ is inscribed in $\odot Q$. Let $m\angle B = x°$. Center Q lies on $\overline{BC}$.

    Prove $m\angle ABC = \frac{1}{2}m\widehat{AC}$

    (*Hint*: Show that $\triangle AQB$ is isosceles. Then write $m\widehat{AC}$ in terms of x.)

    b. **Cases 2 and 3** Use the diagrams and auxiliary lines to write a proof for Cases 2 and 3.

    Case 2   Case 3

18. **PROVING THEOREM 10.11** Write a proof of the Inscribed Angles of a Circle Theorem.

19. **PROVING THEOREM 10.12** The Inscribed Right Triangle Theorem is written as a conditional statement and its converse. Write a proof for each statement.

20. **PROVING THEOREM 10.13** Copy and complete the paragraph proof for one part of the Inscribed Quadrilateral Theorem.

    Given $\odot C$ with inscribed quadrilateral $DEFG$

    Prove $m\angle D + m\angle F = 180°$, $m\angle E + m\angle G = 180°$

    By the Arc Addition Postulate, $m\widehat{EFG} + \_\_\_ = 360°$ and $m\widehat{FGD} + m\widehat{DEF} = 360°$. Using the $_____$ Theorem, $m\widehat{EDG} = 2(m\angle F)$, $m\widehat{EFG} = 2(m\angle D)$, $m\widehat{DEF} = 2(m\angle G)$, and $m\widehat{FGD} = 2(m\angle E)$. By the Substitution Property of Equality, $2(m\angle D) + \_\_\_ = 360°$, so $\_\_\_$. Similarly, $\_\_\_$.

21. **SMP.1 DIG DEEPER** If you draw the smallest possible circle through C tangent to $\overline{AB}$, the circle will intersect $\overline{AC}$ at J and $\overline{BC}$ at K. Explain how to find the exact length of $\overline{JK}$.

    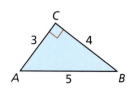

Interpreting Data

INSCRIBED POLYGON Stonehenge's outer ring forms a 56-sided regular polygon inscribed in a circle. It is believed that the builders of Stonehenge may have constructed this shape by inscribing congruent squares inside the main circle. The vertices of the polygon seem to correspond with the eclipses of the moon.

22. How might the ancient builders have laid out the vertices of the inscribed polygon?

23. The upright stones at Stonehenge weigh about 25 tons each. How might the builders have quarried and moved these stones 5,000 years ago?

24. Some archaeologists think that Stonehenge was built as a calendar. Why do you think this is?

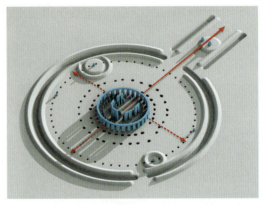

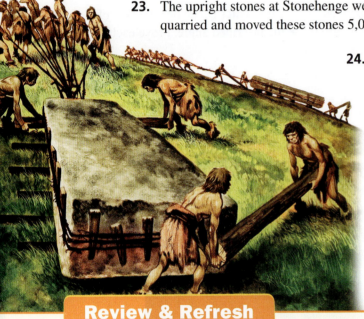

Review & Refresh

25. Describe a congruence transformation that maps $\triangle ABC$ to $\triangle DEF$.

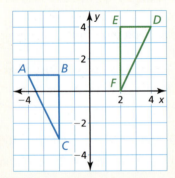

26. Find the radius of $\odot Q$.

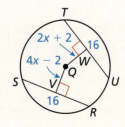

Identify the given arc as a *major arc*, *minor arc*, or *semicircle*. Then find the measure of the arc.

27. $\overset{\frown}{BC}$

28. $\overset{\frown}{AC}$

29. $\overset{\frown}{AB}$

30. $\overset{\frown}{ABC}$

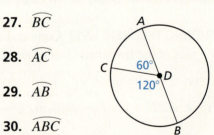

31. Tell whether $\overline{AB}$ is tangent to $\odot C$.

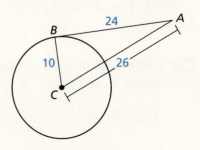

10.5 Angle Relationships in Circles

Learning Target: Understand angles formed by chords, secants, and tangents.

Success Criteria:
- I can identify angles and arcs determined by chords, secants, and tangents.
- I can find angle measures and arc measures involving chords, secants, and tangents.
- I can use circumscribed angles to solve problems.

INVESTIGATE   Investigating Angles in Circles

Work with a partner. Use technology.

1. Construct a chord in a circle. Then construct a tangent line to the circle at one of the endpoints of the chord.

2. Find the measures of the angles and arcs determined by the chord and the tangent line. What do you notice?

3. **SMP.8** How do the measures of the angles and circular arcs change when you move an endpoint of the chord? How do these measures change when you resize the circle? Use your results to make a conjecture.

4. Construct two chords that intersect inside a circle. Make a conjecture about the measures of the angles and arcs determined by the chords. Provide examples to support your reasoning.

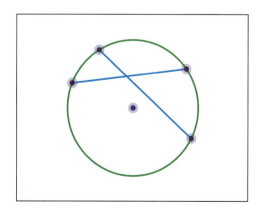

10.5   Angle Relationships in Circles   539

Vocabulary

circumscribed angle

Finding Angle and Arc Measures

Theorem 10.14

Tangent and Intersected Chord Theorem

If a tangent and a chord intersect at a point on a circle, then the measure of each angle formed is one-half the measure of its intercepted arc.

$m\angle 1 = \frac{1}{2}(m\widehat{AB})$
$m\angle 2 = \frac{1}{2}(m\widehat{BCA})$

Prove this Theorem Exercise 14, page 545

EXAMPLE 1 Finding Angle and Arc Measures

Line *m* is tangent to the circle. Find the indicated measure.

a. $m\angle 1$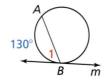

b. $m\widehat{KJL}$

Use the Tangent and Intersected Chord Theorem.

$m\angle 1 = \frac{1}{2}(m\widehat{AB})$

▶ So, $m\angle 1 = \frac{1}{2}(130°) = 65°$.

Use the Tangent and Intersected Chord Theorem.

$\frac{1}{2}(m\widehat{KJL}) = m\angle KLN$

▶ So, $m\widehat{KJL} = 2(125°) = 250°$.

If two nonparallel lines intersect a circle, there are three places where the lines can intersect.

on the circle

inside the circle

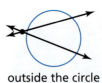
outside the circle

In-Class Practice

Self-Assessment

Line *m* is tangent to the circle. Find the indicated measure.

1. $m\angle 1$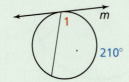

2. $m\widehat{XY}$

 I don't understand yet.   I can do it with help.   I can do it on my own.   I can teach someone.

Theorem 10.15

Angles Inside the Circle Theorem

If two chords intersect *inside* a circle, then the measure of each angle is one-half the *sum* of the measures of the arcs intercepted by the angle and its vertical angle.

$m\angle 1 = \frac{1}{2}(m\widehat{DC} + m\widehat{AB})$
$m\angle 2 = \frac{1}{2}(m\widehat{AD} + m\widehat{BC})$

Prove this Theorem Exercise 15, page 545

Theorem 10.16

Angles Outside the Circle Theorem

If a tangent and a secant, two tangents, or two secants intersect *outside* a circle, then the measure of the angle formed is one-half the *difference* of the measures of the intercepted arcs.

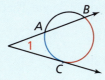 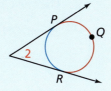 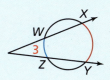

$m\angle 1 = \frac{1}{2}(m\widehat{BC} - m\widehat{AC})$ $m\angle 2 = \frac{1}{2}(m\widehat{PQR} - m\widehat{PR})$ $m\angle 3 = \frac{1}{2}(m\widehat{XY} - m\widehat{WZ})$

Prove this Theorem Exercise 17, page 545

EXAMPLE 2   Finding Angle Measures

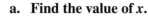

a. Find the value of x.

The chords $\overline{JL}$ and $\overline{KM}$ intersect inside the circle. Use the Angles Inside the Circle Theorem.

$x° = \frac{1}{2}(m\widehat{JM} + m\widehat{LK})$
$x° = \frac{1}{2}(130° + 156°)$
$x = 143$

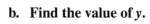

b. Find the value of y.

The tangent $\overrightarrow{CD}$ and the secant $\overrightarrow{CB}$ intersect outside the circle. Use the Angles Outside the Circle Theorem.

$m\angle BCD = \frac{1}{2}(m\widehat{AD} - m\widehat{BD})$
$y° = \frac{1}{2}(178° - 76°)$
$y = 51$

In-Class Practice

Self-Assessment

Find the value of the variable.

3.

4.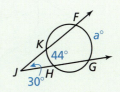

| 1 I don't understand yet. | 2 I can do it with help. | 3 I can do it on my own. | 4 I can teach someone. |

10.5   Angle Relationships in Circles

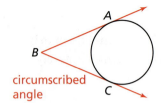

Using Circumscribed Angles

A **circumscribed angle** is an angle whose sides are tangent to a circle.

Theorem 10.17

Circumscribed Angle Theorem

The measure of a circumscribed angle is equal to 180° minus the measure of the central angle that intercepts the same arc.

Prove this Theorem Exercise 18, page 545

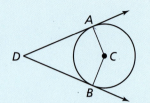

$m\angle ADB = 180° - m\angle ACB$

EXAMPLE 3 Finding Angle Measures

Find the value of x.

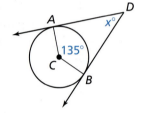

a. Use the Circumscribed Angle Theorem to find $m\angle ADB$.

$$m\angle ADB = 180° - m\angle ACB \quad \text{Circumscribed Angle Theorem}$$
$$x° = 180° - 135° \quad \text{Substitute.}$$
$$x = 45 \quad \text{Subtract.}$$

▶ So, the value of x is 45.

b. Use the Measure of an Inscribed Angle Theorem and the Circumscribed Angle Theorem to find $m\angle EJF$.

$$m\angle EJF = \tfrac{1}{2}(m\widehat{EF}) \quad \text{Measure of an Inscribed Angle Theorem}$$
$$m\angle EJF = \tfrac{1}{2}(m\angle EGF) \quad \text{Definition of measure of a minor arc}$$
$$m\angle EJF = \tfrac{1}{2}(180° - m\angle EHF) \quad \text{Circumscribed Angle Theorem}$$
$$x° = \tfrac{1}{2}(180° - 30°) \quad \text{Substitute.}$$
$$x = 75 \quad \text{Simplify.}$$

▶ So, the value of x is 75.

In-Class Practice

Self-Assessment

Find the value of x.

5.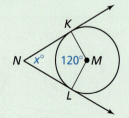

6.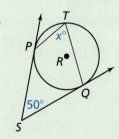

EXAMPLE 4   Finding an Arc Measure

The diagram shows the portion of Earth visible to a satellite in orbit 300 miles above Earth at point C. Earth's radius is approximately 4,000 miles. Find $m\widehat{BD}$.

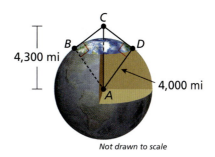

Not drawn to scale

Find $m\angle BCD$. Then use the Circumscribed Angle Theorem to find $m\angle BAD$ and $m\widehat{BD}$.

Because $\overline{AB}$ and $\overline{AD}$ are radii of a sphere, $\overline{AB} \cong \overline{AD}$. Also, $\overline{CA} \cong \overline{CA}$ by the Reflexive Property of Segment Congruence. So, $\triangle ABC \cong \triangle ADC$ by the Hypotenuse-Leg Congruence Theorem. Because corresponding parts of congruent triangles are congruent, $\angle BCA \cong \angle DCA$. Solve right $\triangle CBA$ to find that $m\angle BCA \approx 68.5°$. So, $m\angle BCD \approx 2(68.5°) = 137°$.

$m\angle BCD = 180° - m\angle BAD$	Circumscribed Angle Theorem
$m\angle BCD = 180° - m\widehat{BD}$	Definition of measure of a minor arc
$137° \approx 180° - m\widehat{BD}$	Substitute.
$m\widehat{BD} \approx 43°$	Solve for $m\widehat{BD}$.

▶ So, the measure of $\widehat{BD}$ is about 43°.

Check You can use inverse trigonometric ratios to find $m\angle BAC$ and $m\angle DAC$.

$$m\angle BAC = \cos^{-1}\left(\frac{4{,}000}{4{,}300}\right) \approx 21.5° \qquad m\angle DAC = \cos^{-1}\left(\frac{4{,}000}{4{,}300}\right) \approx 21.5°$$

So, $m\angle BAD \approx 21.5° + 21.5° = 43°$, and therefore $m\widehat{BD} \approx 43°$.

In-Class Practice

Self-Assessment

7. The diagram shows the portion of Earth you can see when you are on top of Mount Rainier on a clear day. You are about 2.73 miles above sea level at point B. Find $m\widehat{CD}$.

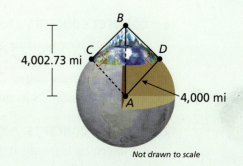

Not drawn to scale

1 I don't understand yet.   2 I can do it with help.   3 I can do it on my own.   4 I can teach someone.

10.5   Angle Relationships in Circles

10.5 Practice with CalcChat and CalcView

Line t is tangent to the circle. Find the indicated measure. (See Example 1.)

1. $m\widehat{AB}$

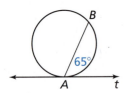

2. $m\angle 1$

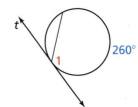

Find the value of x. (See Examples 2 and 3.)

3.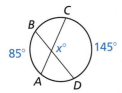

4.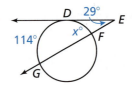

5.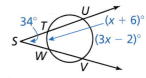

6.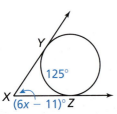

7.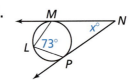

8.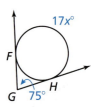

9. **CONNECTION TO REAL LIFE** The diagram shows the portion of Earth visible from a hot air balloon 1.2 miles above the ground at point W. Earth's radius is about 4,000 miles. Find $m\widehat{ZX}$. (See Example 4.)

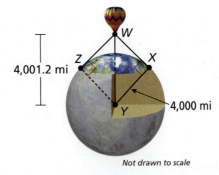

Not drawn to scale

10. **CONNECT CONCEPTS** Use the diagram at the right to write an algebraic expression for c in terms of a and b.

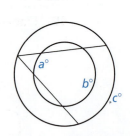

11. **SMP.6** Your friend claims that it is possible for a circumscribed angle to have the same measure as its intercepted arc. Explain whether your friend is correct.

12. **CONNECT CONCEPTS** $\triangle XYZ$ is an equilateral triangle inscribed in $\odot P$. $\overline{AB}$ intersects $\odot P$ only at point X, $\overline{BC}$ intersects $\odot P$ only at point Y, and $\overline{AC}$ intersects $\odot P$ only at point Z. Draw a diagram that illustrates this situation. Then classify $\triangle ABC$ by its angles and sides. Justify your answer.

544 Chapter 10 Circles

13. In the diagram, $\overrightarrow{PL}$ is tangent to the circle, and $\overline{KJ}$ is a diameter. What is the range of possible angle measures of $\angle LPJ$?

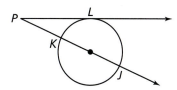

14. **PROVING THEOREM 10.14** To prove the Tangent and Intersected Chord Theorem, you must prove three cases.

   a. The diagram shows the case where $\overline{AB}$ contains the center of the circle. Use the Tangent Line to Circle Theorem to write a proof for this case.

   b. Draw diagrams and write proofs for the other two cases: where the center of the circle is in the (1) interior and (2) exterior of $\angle CAB$.

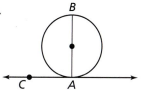

15. **PROVING THEOREM 10.15** Write a proof of the Angle Inside the Circle Theorem.

   Given Chords $\overline{AC}$ and $\overline{BD}$ intersect inside a circle.
   Prove $m\angle 1 = \frac{1}{2}(m\widehat{DC} + m\widehat{AB})$

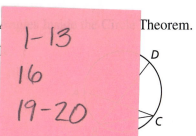

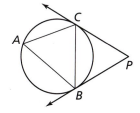

16. **SMP.1 DIG DEEPER** In the diagram, lines are tangent to the circle. Point A is any point on the major arc formed by the endpoints of the chord $\overline{BC}$. Label all congruent angles in the figure. Explain how you know the angles are congruent.

17. **PROVING THEOREM 10.16** Use the diagram at the right to prove the Angles Outside the Circle Theorem for the case of a tangent and a secant. Then copy the diagrams for the other two cases on page 541 and draw appropriate auxiliary segments. Use your diagrams to prove each case.

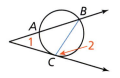

18. **PROVING THEOREM 10.17** Prove that the Circumscribed Angle Theorem follows from the Angles Outside the Circle Theorem.

Find the indicated measure(s). Justify your answer.

19. Find $m\angle P$ when $m\widehat{WZY} = 200°$.

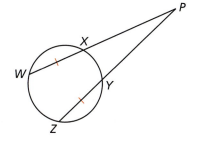

20. Find $m\widehat{AB}$ and $m\widehat{ED}$.

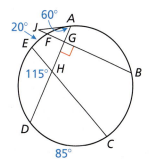

Interpreting Data

GLOBAL POSITIONING SYSTEM The Global Positioning System (GPS) consists of satellites orbiting Earth. To find your location using GPS, you must have unobstructed lines of sight to four or more GPS satellites.

21. The GPS coordinates of the White House are 38° 53′ 53″ N, 77° 2′ 12″ W. What does this mean?

22. GPS satellites are in orbit about 12,000 miles from Earth's surface. Why are they so far away?

23. **SMP.1** Estimate the number of GPS satellites that are needed to provide coverage to every location on Earth's surface. Explain your method.

Review & Refresh

24. Find the perimeter and area of the triangle with vertices $P(-3, -7)$, $Q(-3, 8)$, and $R(5, 8)$.

25. An amusement park ride swings back and forth along a circular arc as shown, where $m\angle EAB = 145°$ and $m\angle DAC = 80°$. Find $m\widehat{BC}$.

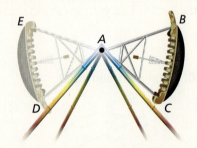

26. A triangle has one side of length 18 and another side of length 11. Describe the possible lengths of the third side.

Find the indicated measure.

27. $m\angle B$

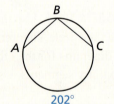

28. $m\widehat{JK}$

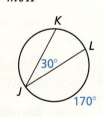

29. Explain whether $\overline{WY}$ is a diameter of the circle.

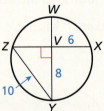

30. Graph $\triangle ABC$ with vertices $A(-8, 6)$, $B(4, 2)$, and $C(-2, -4)$ and its image after a dilation with a scale factor of $\frac{1}{2}$.

10.6 Segment Relationships in Circles

Learning Target: Use theorems about segments of chords, secants, and tangents.

Success Criteria:
- I can find lengths of segments of chords.
- I can identify segments of secants and tangents.
- I can find lengths of segments of secants and tangents.

INVESTIGATE Investigating Segments of Chords and Secants

Work with a partner. Use technology.

1. Construct two chords $\overline{BC}$ and $\overline{DE}$ that intersect in the interior of a circle at a point F.

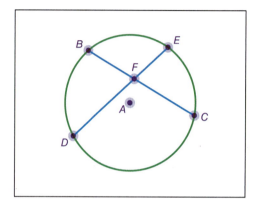

   a. Find the segment lengths BF, CF, DF, and EF. How are BF and CF related to DF and EF?

   b. **SMP.8** How do the segment lengths change when you move endpoints of the chords? How do the segment lengths change when you resize the circle? Use your results to make a conjecture.

2. Construct two secants $\overleftrightarrow{BC}$ and $\overleftrightarrow{BD}$ that intersect at a point B outside a circle.

   a. Find the segment lengths BE, BC, BF, and BD. How are BE and BC related to BF and BD?

   b. How do the segment lengths change when you move the secants? How do the segment lengths change when you resize the circle? Use your results to make a conjecture.

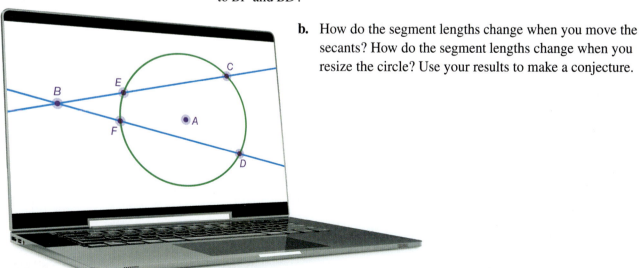

Vocabulary

segments of a chord
tangent segment
secant segment
external segment

Using Segments of Chords, Tangents, and Secants

When two chords intersect in the interior of a circle, each chord is divided into two segments that are called **segments of the chord**.

Theorem 10.18

Segments of Chords Theorem

If two chords intersect in the interior of a circle, then the product of the lengths of the segments of one chord is equal to the product of the lengths of the segments of the other chord.

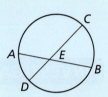

Prove this Theorem Exercise 12, page 551

$EA \cdot EB = EC \cdot ED$

EXAMPLE 1 Using Segments of Chords

Find *ML* and *JK*.

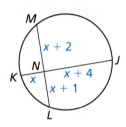

Use the Segments of Chords Theorem to find the value of *x*.

$NK \cdot NJ = NL \cdot NM$	Segments of Chords Theorem
$x \cdot (x + 4) = (x + 1) \cdot (x + 2)$	Substitute.
$x^2 + 4x = x^2 + 3x + 2$	Simplify.
$4x = 3x + 2$	Subtract x^2 from each side.
$x = 2$	Subtract $3x$ from each side.

Find *ML* and *JK* by substitution.

$ML = (x + 2) + (x + 1)$ $JK = x + (x + 4)$

$= 2 + 2 + 2 + 1$ $= 2 + 2 + 4$

$= 7$ $= 8$

▶ So, $ML = 7$ and $JK = 8$.

In-Class Practice

Self-Assessment

Find the value of *x*.

1.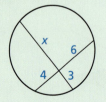
2.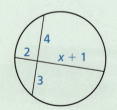
3.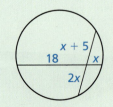

1 I don't understand yet.	**2** I can do it with help.	**3** I can do it on my own.	**4** I can teach someone.

A **tangent segment** is a segment that is tangent to a circle at an endpoint. A **secant segment** is a segment that contains a chord of a circle and has exactly one endpoint outside the circle. The part of a secant segment that is outside the circle is called an **external segment**.

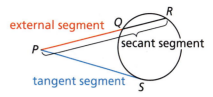

$\overline{PS}$ is a tangent segment.
$\overline{PR}$ is a secant segment.
$\overline{PQ}$ is the external segment of $\overline{PR}$.

Theorem 10.19

Segments of Secants Theorem

If two secant segments share the same endpoint outside a circle, then the product of the lengths of one secant segment and its external segment equals the product of the lengths of the other secant segment and its external segment.

Prove this Theorem Exercise 10, page 551

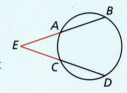

$EA \cdot EB = EC \cdot ED$

EXAMPLE 2 Using Segments of Secants

Find the value of x.

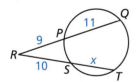

$RP \cdot RQ = RS \cdot RT$	Segments of Secants Theorem
$9 \cdot (11 + 9) = 10 \cdot (x + 10)$	Substitute.
$180 = 10x + 100$	Simplify.
$80 = 10x$	Subtract 100 from each side.
$8 = x$	Divide each side by 10.

▶ The value of x is 8.

In-Class Practice

Self-Assessment

Find the value of x.

4.

5.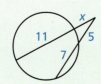

6.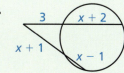

1 I don't understand yet. **2** I can do it with help. **3** I can do it on my own. **4** I can teach someone.

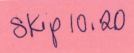
Skip 10.20

Theorem 10.20

Segments of Secants and Tangents Theorem

If a secant segment and a tangent segment share an endpoint outside a circle, then the product of the lengths of the secant segment and its external segment equals the square of the length of the tangent segment.

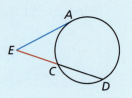

$EA^2 = EC \cdot ED$

Prove this Theorem Exercises 13, page 551

EXAMPLE 3 Using Segments of Secants and Tangents

Find *RS*.

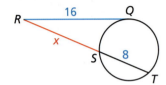

$RQ^2 = RS \cdot RT$	Segments of Secants and Tangents Theorem
$16^2 = x \cdot (x + 8)$	Substitute.
$256 = x^2 + 8x$	Simplify.
$0 = x^2 + 8x - 256$	Write in standard form.
$x = \dfrac{-8 \pm \sqrt{8^2 - 4(1)(-256)}}{2(1)}$	Use Quadratic Formula.
$x = -4 \pm 4\sqrt{17}$	Simplify.

Use the positive solution because lengths cannot be negative.

▶ So, $RS = -4 + 4\sqrt{17}$, or about 12.49.

EXAMPLE 4 Finding the Radius of a Circle

Find the radius of the aquarium tank.

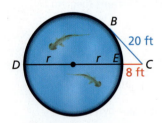

$CB^2 = CE \cdot CD$	Segments of Secants and Tangents Theorem
$20^2 = 8 \cdot (2r + 8)$	Substitute.
$400 = 16r + 64$	Simplify.
$336 = 16r$	Subtract 64 from each side.
$21 = r$	Divide each side by 16.

▶ So, the radius of the tank is 21 feet.

In-Class Practice

Self-Assessment

Find the value of x.

7.   8.   9.

10. **WHAT IF?** In Example 4, $CB = 35$ feet and $CE = 14$ feet. Find the radius of the tank.

10.6 Practice

Find the value of x. (See Example 1.)

1.

2.

3.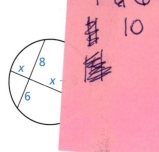

Find the value of x. (See Example 2.)

4.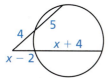

5.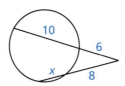

6.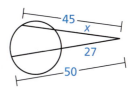

Find the value of x. (See Example 3.)

7.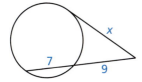

8.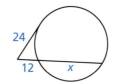

9.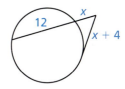

10. **PROVING THEOREM 10.19** Prove the Segments of Secants Theorem. (*Hint*: Draw a diagram and add auxiliary line segments to form similar triangles.)

11. **CONNECTION TO REAL LIFE** The *Cassini* spacecraft conducted a series of missions in Saturn's orbit from 2004 to 2017. Three of Saturn's moons, Tethys, Calypso, and Telesto, have nearly circular orbits of radius 295,000 kilometers. The diagram shows the positions of the moons and the spacecraft on one of *Cassini*'s missions. Find the distance $\overline{DB}$ from *Cassini* to Tethys when $\overline{AD}$ is tangent to the circular orbit. (See Example 4.)

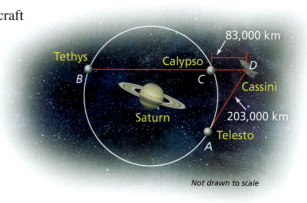

12. **PROVING THEOREM 10.18** Write a proof of the Segments of Chords Theorem.

    Plan for Proof Use the diagram from page 548. Draw $\overline{AC}$ and $\overline{DB}$. Show that $\triangle EAC$ and $\triangle EDB$ are similar. Use the fact that corresponding side lengths in similar triangles are proportional.

13. **PROVING THEOREM 10.20** Prove the Segments of Secants and Tangents Theorem. Then use the Tangent Line to Circle Theorem to prove the Segments of Secants and Tangents Theorem for the special case when the secant segment contains the center of the circle.

14. In the figure, $AB = 12$, $BC = 8$, $DE = 6$, $PD = 4$, and A is a point of tangency. Find the radius of $\odot P$.

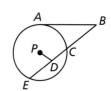

Interpreting Data

ROUNDABOUTS A roundabout is a circular intersection in which road traffic is permitted to flow in one direction around a circular island without stopping. Compared to stop signs, roundabouts reduce the severity of collisions.

15. Why do you think roundabouts reduce the severity of collisions?

16. Compare the distance traveled in a roundabout to the distance traveled in a normal intersection.

17. Your GPS system tells you to take the third exit in the roundabout below. Are you turning left, turning right, or going straight? Explain.

Review & Refresh

18. In the diagram, $AC = FD = 30$, $PG = x + 5$, and $PJ = 3x - 1$. Find the radius of $\odot P$.

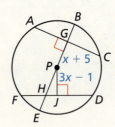

19. You are 60 feet from a radio tower and the angle of elevation from the ground to the top of the tower is 69°. Find the height of the radio tower.

20. Find $m\widehat{WY}$.

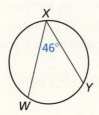

21. Show that the two triangles are similar.

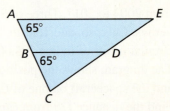

22. Find the value of x that makes $m \parallel n$.

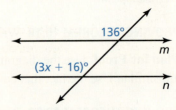

23. Find $m\widehat{WZY}$.

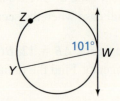

10.7 Circles in the Coordinate Plane

Learning Target: Understand equations of circles.

Success Criteria:
- I can write equations of circles.
- I can find the center and radius of a circle.
- I can graph equations of circles.
- I can solve real-life problems involving circles.

INVESTIGATE Deriving Equations of Circles

Work with a partner.

1. Let (0, 0) be the center of a circle with radius 4. Use the Pythagorean Theorem to write an equation that represents the distance between the center of the circle and a point (x, y) on the circle.

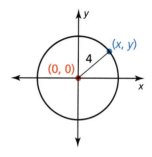

2. How does the equation in Exercise 1 change when the center of the circle is (1, 1)? Write the equation.

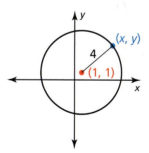

3. What is an equation of a circle with center (h, k) and radius r in the coordinate plane?

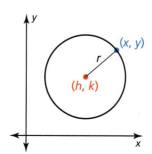

10.7 Circles in the Coordinate Plane 553

Vocabulary
standard equation of a circle

Writing and Graphing Equations of Circles

Let (x, y) represent any point on a circle with center at the origin and radius r. By the Pythagorean Theorem,

$$x^2 + y^2 = r^2.$$

This is the equation of a circle with center at the origin and radius r.

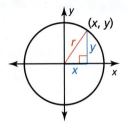

Key Concept

Standard Equation of a Circle

Let (x, y) represent any point on a circle with center (h, k) and radius r. By the Pythagorean Theorem,

$$(x - h)^2 + (y - k)^2 = r^2.$$

This is the **standard equation of a circle** with center (h, k) and radius r.

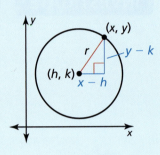

EXAMPLE 1 Writing the Standard Equation of a Circle

Write the standard equation of each circle.

a. the circle shown at the left

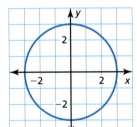

The radius is 3, and the center is at the origin.

$(x - h)^2 + (y - k)^2 = r^2$	Standard equation of a circle
$(x - 0)^2 + (y - 0)^2 = 3^2$	Substitute $(h, k) = (0, 0)$ and $r = 3$.
$x^2 + y^2 = 9$	Simplify.

▶ The standard equation of the circle is $x^2 + y^2 = 9$.

b. the circle with center $(0, -9)$ and radius 4.2

$(x - h)^2 + (y - k)^2 = r^2$	Standard equation of a circle
$(x - 0)^2 + [y - (-9)]^2 = 4.2^2$	Substitute $(h, k) = (0, -9)$ and $r = 4.2$.
$x^2 + (y + 9)^2 = 17.64$	Simplify.

▶ The standard equation of the circle is $x^2 + (y + 9)^2 = 17.64$.

In-Class Practice

Self-Assessment

Write the standard equation of the circle with the given center and radius.

1. center: $(0, 0)$, radius: 2.5
2. center: $(-2, 5)$, radius: 7

| 1 I don't understand yet. | 2 I can do it with help. | 3 I can do it on my own. | 4 I can teach someone. |

EXAMPLE 2 Writing the Standard Equation of a Circle

Write the standard equation of the circle shown.

The center is $(-1, 3)$, and a point on the circle is $(-5, 6)$. To find the radius r, find the distance between $(-1, 3)$ and $(-5, 6)$.

$r = \sqrt{[-5 - (-1)]^2 + (6 - 3)^2}$ Distance Formula

$ = \sqrt{(-4)^2 + 3^2}$ Simplify.

$ = 5$ Simplify.

Substitute the values of h, k, and r into the standard equation of a circle.

$(x - h)^2 + (y - k)^2 = r^2$ Standard equation of a circle

$[x - (-1)]^2 + (y - 3)^2 = 5^2$ Substitute $(h, k) = (-1, 3)$ and $r = 5$.

$(x + 1)^2 + (y - 3)^2 = 25$ Simplify.

▶ The standard equation of the circle is $(x + 1)^2 + (y - 3)^2 = 25$.

EXAMPLE 3 Graphing a Circle

The equation of a circle is $x^2 + y^2 - 8x + 4y - 16 = 0$. Find the center and the radius of the circle. Then graph the circle.

You can write the equation in standard form by completing the square on the x-terms and the y-terms.

$x^2 + y^2 - 8x + 4y - 16 = 0$ Equation of circle

$x^2 - 8x + y^2 + 4y = 16$ Isolate constant. Group terms.

$x^2 - 8x + 16 + y^2 + 4y + 4 = 16 + 16 + 4$ Complete the square twice.

$(x - 4)^2 + (y + 2)^2 = 36$ Factor left side. Simplify right side.

$(x - 4)^2 + [y - (-2)]^2 = 6^2$ Rewrite the equation.

▶ The center is $(4, -2)$, and the radius is 6.

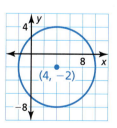

In-Class Practice

Self-Assessment

3. The point $(3, 4)$ is on a circle with center $(1, 4)$. Write the standard equation of the circle.

4. The equation of a circle is $x^2 + y^2 - 8x + 6y + 9 = 0$. Find the center and the radius of the circle. Then graph the circle.

1 I don't understand yet. **2** I can do it with help. **3** I can do it on my own. **4** I can teach someone.

10.7 Circles in the Coordinate Plane

Connections to Real Life

EXAMPLE 4 Using Circles to Model Real Life

The epicenter of an earthquake is the point on Earth's surface directly above the earthquake's origin. A seismograph can be used to determine the distance to the epicenter of an earthquake. Seismographs are needed in three different places to locate an earthquake's epicenter.

Use the seismograph readings from points A, B, and C to find the epicenter of an earthquake.

- The epicenter is 7 miles away from point A.
- The epicenter is 4 miles away from point B.
- The epicenter is 5 miles away from point C.

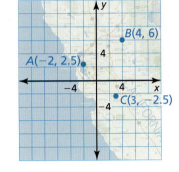

The set of all points equidistant from a given point is a circle, so the epicenter is located on each of the following circles.

⊙A with center $(-2, 2.5)$ and radius 7

⊙B with center $(4, 6)$ and radius 4

⊙C with center $(3, -2.5)$ and radius 5

To find the epicenter, graph the circles on a coordinate plane where each unit corresponds to one mile. Find the point of intersection of the three circles.

STEM Video: Seismographs and Earthquake Epicenters

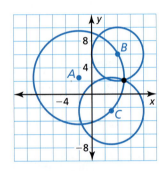

▶ The epicenter is at about $(5, 2)$.

In-Class Practice

Self-Assessment

5. Telecommunication towers can be used to transmit cellular phone calls. A graph shows towers at points $(0, 0)$, $(0, 5)$, and $(6, 3)$ with units measured in kilometers. Each tower has a range of 3 kilometers.

   a. Sketch a graph and locate the towers. Explain whether there are any locations that may receive calls from more than one tower.

   b. The center of City A is located at $(-2, 2.5)$, and the center of City B is located at $(5, 4)$. Each city has a radius of 1.5 kilometers. Which city seems to have better cell phone coverage? Why?

556 Chapter 10 Circles

10.7 Practice

Write the standard equation of the circle. (See Example 1.)

1.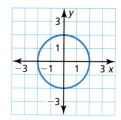

2.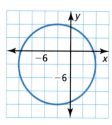

▶ 3. the circle with center (0, 0) and radius 7

4. the circle with center (3, −5) and radius 11

Use the given information to write the standard equation of the circle. (See Example 2.)

5. The center is (0, 0), and a point on the circle is (0, 6).

6. The center is (−7, −2), and a point on the circle is (1, −8).

▶ 7. The center is (1, 2), and a point on the circle is (4, 2).

8. The endpoints of a diameter of the circle are (0, −1) and (−5, −6).

Find the center and radius of the circle. Then graph the circle. (See Example 3.)

9. $x^2 + y^2 = 49$

10. $(x + 5)^2 + (y - 3)^2 = 9$

▶ 11. $x^2 + y^2 - 6x = 7$

12. $x^2 + y^2 + 4x + 12y + 15 = 0$

Prove or disprove the statement.

13. The point (2, 3) lies on the circle centered at the origin with radius 8.

14. The point $(\sqrt{6}, 2)$ lies on the circle centered at the origin and containing the point (3, −1).

15. **SMP.4 CONNECTION TO REAL LIFE** Zone 1 of a city's commuter system serves people living within 3 miles of the city's center. Zone 2 serves those between 3 and 7 miles from the center. Zone 3 serves those more than 7 miles from the center. (See Example 4.)

   a. Graph this situation on a coordinate plane where each unit corresponds to 1 mile. Locate the city's center at the origin.

   b. Determine which zone serves people whose homes are represented by (3, 4), (6, 5), (1, 2), (0, 3), and (1, 6).

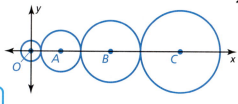

16. **SMP.1 DIG DEEPER** Four tangent circles are centered on the x-axis. The radius of ⊙A is twice the radius of ⊙O. The radius of ⊙B is three times the radius of ⊙O. The radius of ⊙C is four times the radius of ⊙O. All circles have integer radii, and the point (63, 16) is on ⊙C. Write an equation of ⊙A.

Interpreting Data

EPICENTER OF AN EARTHQUAKE Seismologists need data from at least three seismographs to determine the location of an earthquake's epicenter. The map shows the locations of the epicenters of earthquakes that took place between 1963 and 1998.

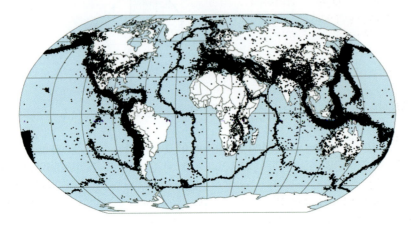

17. Earthquake epicenters tend to occur at fault lines in Earth's crust. Use the map to describe the locations of Earth's fault lines.

18. There are 7 major tectonic plates in Earth's crust. Use the map to describe the locations of these plates.

19. How does a seismologist locate the epicenter of an earthquake?

Review & Refresh

Find the value of x.

20.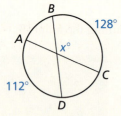

21.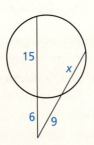

27. Find $m\angle N$.

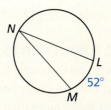

Identify the arc as a *major arc*, *minor arc*, or *semicircle*. Then find the measure of the arc.

22. $\overset{\frown}{RS}$

23. $\overset{\frown}{PR}$

24. $\overset{\frown}{ST}$

25. $\overset{\frown}{PRT}$

26. $\overset{\frown}{RST}$

28. The vertical supports on a staircase are parallel. Find $m\angle 2$.

558   Chapter 10   Circles

10.8 Focus of a Parabola

> **Learning Target:** Graph and write equations of parabolas.
>
> **Success Criteria:**
> - I can explain the relationships among the focus, the directrix, and the graph of a parabola.
> - I can graph parabolas using characteristics.
> - I can write equations of parabolas using characteristics.

INVESTIGATE Analyzing Graphs of Parabolas

Work with a partner.

1. Use dashes along the bottom of a piece of lined paper to mark and number equidistant points from -5 to 5 as shown. These dashes represent the units along the x-axis. Plot a point $F(0, 2)$, using the same scale, that is two units above 0. Draw a line through F to represent the y-axis.

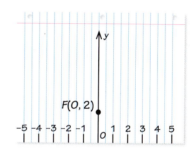

2. Fold the paper so the origin is on top of point F. Unfold the paper and describe the line represented by the fold you made.

3. Repeat the process in Exercise 1 with the points $(1, 0)$, $(-1, 0)$, $(2, 0)$, and $(-2, 0)$, and so on. The diagrams below show the fold for $(1, 0)$. After you are done, examine the folds. What do you notice?

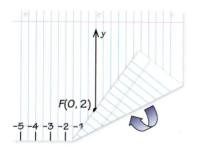 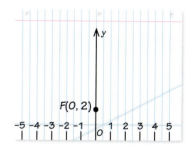

4. For each fold, use the Pythagorean Theorem to find and label a point (x, y) that is equidistant from F and the x-axis. Then find an equation that represents the curve that passes through these points.

Vocabulary
focus
directrix

Exploring the Focus and Directrix

A parabola can be defined as the set of all points (x, y) in a plane that are equidistant from a fixed point called the **focus** and a fixed line called the **directrix**.

- The focus is in the interior of the parabola and lies on the axis of symmetry.
- The vertex lies halfway between the focus and the directrix.
- The directrix is perpendicular to the axis of symmetry.

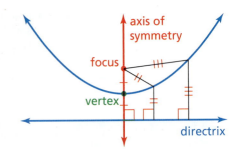

EXAMPLE 1 Deriving an Equation

Write an equation of the parabola with focus $F(0, 2)$ and directrix $y = -2$.

The vertex is halfway between the focus and the directrix, at $(0, 0)$. Notice the line segments drawn from point F to point P and from point P to point D. By the definition of a parabola, these line segments, PD and PF, must be congruent.

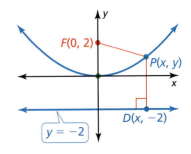

$PD = PF$	Definition of a parabola
$\lvert y - (-2) \rvert = \sqrt{x^2 + (2 - y)^2}$	Write expressions for the lengths of the line segments.
$(y + 2)^2 = x^2 + (2 - y)^2$	Square each side.
$y^2 + 4y + 4 = x^2 + 4 - 4y + y^2$	Expand.
$8y = x^2$	Combine like terms.
$y = \frac{1}{8}x^2$	Divide each side by 8.

▶ So, an equation of the parabola is $y = \frac{1}{8}x^2$.

In-Class Practice

Self-Assessment

1. Write an equation of the parabola with focus $F(0, -3)$ and directrix $y = 3$.

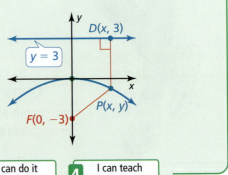

1 I don't understand yet. **2** I can do it with help. **3** I can do it on my own. **4** I can teach someone.

Key Concept

Standard Equations of a Parabola with Vertex at the Origin

Vertical axis of symmetry ($x = 0$)

Equation: $y = \dfrac{1}{4p}x^2$

Focus: $(0, p)$

Directrix: $y = -p$

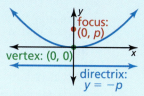
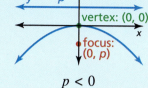

Horizontal axis of symmetry ($y = 0$)

Equation: $x = \dfrac{1}{4p}y^2$

Focus: $(p, 0)$

Directrix: $x = -p$

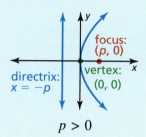
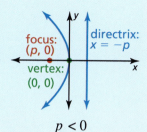

EXAMPLE 2 Writing and Graphing an Equation of a Parabola

Write an equation of the parabola with vertex $(0, 0)$ and directrix $x = 1$. Then graph the parabola.

Notice that the directrix is a vertical line and $p = -1$.

$x = \dfrac{1}{4p}y^2$ Write the equation of a parabola.

$x = \dfrac{1}{4(-1)}y^2$ Substitute -1 for p.

$x = -\dfrac{1}{4}y^2$ Simplify.

Use a table of values to graph the parabola. Notice that opposite y-values result in the same x-value.

y	x
±1	−0.25
±2	−1
±3	−2.25
±4	−4

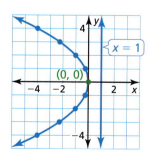

In-Class Practice

Self-Assessment

2. Write an equation of the parabola with vertex $(0, 0)$ and focus $F\left(0, \dfrac{1}{2}\right)$. Then graph the parabola.

Key Concept

Standard Equations of a Parabola with Vertex at (h, k)

Vertical axis of symmetry ($x = h$)

Equation: $y = \dfrac{1}{4p}(x - h)^2 + k$

Focus: $(h, k + p)$
Directrix: $y = k - p$

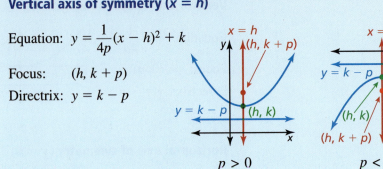
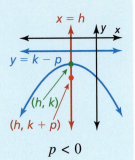

Horizontal axis of symmetry ($y = k$)

Equation: $x = \dfrac{1}{4p}(y - k)^2 + h$

Focus: $(h + p, k)$
Directrix: $x = h - p$

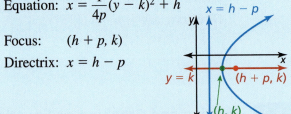
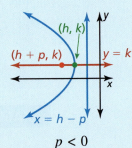

EXAMPLE 3 — Writing and Graphing the Equation of a Translated Parabola

Write an equation of the parabola with vertex $(6, 2)$ and focus $F(10, 2)$. Then graph the parabola.

Notice that the vertex and the focus lie on the same horizontal line.

y	x
6	7
4	6.25
2	6
0	6.25
−2	7

$x = \dfrac{1}{4p}(y - k)^2 + h$ Write the equation of a parabola.

$x = \dfrac{1}{4(4)}(y - 2)^2 + 6$ Substitute 6 for h, 2 for k, and 4 for p.

$x = \dfrac{1}{16}(y - 2)^2 + 6$ Simplify.

Use a table of values to graph the parabola.

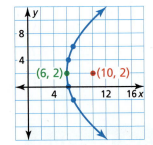

In-Class Practice

Self-Assessment

3. Write an equation of a parabola with vertex $(-1, 4)$ and directrix $y = 6$. Then graph the parabola.

1 I don't understand yet.   **2** I can do it with help.   **3** I can do it on my own.   **4** I can teach someone.

Connections to Real Life

Parabolic reflectors have parabolic cross sections that can reflect sound, light, or other energy. Waves that hit a parabolic reflector parallel to the axis of symmetry are directed to the focus. Waves that come from the focus and then hit the parabolic reflector are directed parallel to the axis of symmetry.

EXAMPLE 4 Using the Equation of a Parabola

An electricity-generating dish uses a parabolic reflector to concentrate sunlight onto a high-frequency engine located at the focus of the reflector. The sunlight heats helium to 650°C to power the engine. Write an equation that represents the cross section of the dish shown with its vertex at (0, 0). What is the depth of the dish?

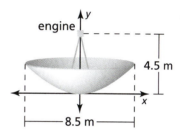

Because the vertex is at the origin, and the axis of symmetry is vertical, the equation has the form $y = \dfrac{1}{4p}x^2$. The engine is at the focus, which is 4.5 meters above the vertex. So, $p = 4.5$. Substitute 4.5 for p to write the equation.

$$y = \dfrac{1}{4(4.5)}x^2 = \dfrac{1}{18}x^2$$

The depth of the dish is the y-value at the dish's outside edge. The dish extends $\dfrac{8.5}{2} = 4.25$ meters to either side of the vertex (0, 0), so find y when $x = 4.25$.

$$y = \dfrac{1}{18}(4.25)^2 \approx 1$$

▶ The depth of the dish is about 1 meter.

In-Class Practice

Self-Assessment

4. A parabolic microwave antenna is 16 feet in diameter. Write an equation that represents the cross section of the antenna with its vertex at (0, 0) and its focus 10 feet to the right of the vertex. What is the depth of the antenna?

| **1** I don't understand yet. | **2** I can do it with help. | **3** I can do it on my own. | **4** I can teach someone. |

10.8 Practice

Write an equation of the parabola. (See Example 1.)

1.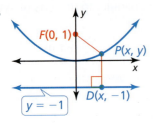

2.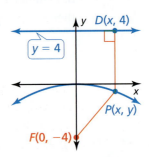

Write an equation of the parabola with the given characteristics. Then graph the parabola. (See Example 2.)

3. focus: $(-7, 0)$
   directrix: $x = 7$

4. focus: $\left(\frac{2}{3}, 0\right)$
   vertex: $(0, 0)$

5. directrix: $y = \frac{8}{3}$
   vertex: $(0, 0)$

6. focus: $\left(0, \frac{6}{7}\right)$
   vertex: $(0, 0)$

Write an equation of the parabola with the given characteristics. Then graph the parabola. (See Example 3.)

7. directrix: $y = 12$
   vertex: $(2, 3)$

8. directrix: $x = 4$
   vertex: $(-7, -5)$

9. focus: $\left(\frac{5}{4}, -1\right)$
   directrix: $x = \frac{3}{4}$

10. focus: $\left(-3, \frac{11}{2}\right)$
    directrix: $y = -\frac{3}{2}$

11. Identify the vertex, focus, directrix, and axis of symmetry of $g(x) = \frac{1}{8}(x - 3)^2 + 2$. Then describe the transformations of the graph of $f(x) = \frac{1}{4}x^2$ to the graph of g.

12. **CONNECTION TO REAL LIFE** A device simulates the clicking sound of a bottlenose dolphin and emits it from the focus of a parabolic reflector used to study echolocation. Write an equation that represents the cross section of the reflector shown, with its vertex at $(0, 0)$. What is the depth of the reflector? (See Example 4.)

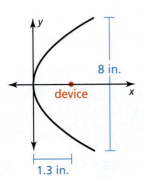

Write an equation of the parabola.

13.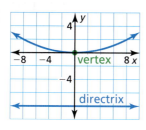

14.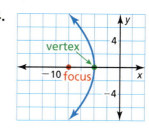

15. **SMP.2** **SOLAR ENERGY** Solar energy can be concentrated using a long trough that has a parabolic cross section, as shown in the figure. Write an equation that represents the cross section of the trough with its vertex at (0, 0). What are the domain and range in this situation? What do they represent?

16. Explain how the width of the graph of the equation $y = \dfrac{1}{4p}x^2$ changes as $|p|$ increases.

17. The graph shows the path of a volleyball served from an initial height of 6 feet as it travels over a net.

    a. Which point represents the vertex? focus? a point on the directrix?

    b. An underhand serve follows the same parabolic path but is hit from a height of 3 feet. How does this affect the focus? the directrix?

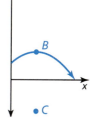

18. **SMP.1** **SMP.8** Derive the equation of a parabola that opens to the right with vertex (0, 0), focus $(p, 0)$, and directrix $x = -p$. Explain whether you can use the same method to derive the equation for a similar parabola that opens left, up, or down.

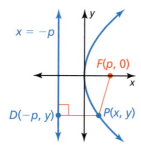

19. **SMP.5** **PERFORMANCE TASK** You can make a solar hot dog cooker by shaping foil-lined poster board into a trough that has a parabolic cross section and passing a wire through each end piece. Design and construct your own hot dog cooker. Explain your process.

10.8   Focus of a Parabola   565

Interpreting Data

SUSPENSION BRIDGES Civil engineers design suspension bridge cables in a parabolic shape to lessen tension on the supporting towers. The dimensions of the Golden Gate Bridge, which was once the largest suspension bridge in the world, are shown. Let (0, 0) represent the position of the center of the main cable.

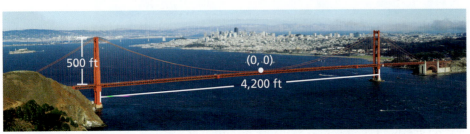

20. Write an equation of the parabola that represents the main cable of the Golden Gate Bridge.

21. Describe the location of the focus of the parabola.

22. How far above the roadway is the cable when it is 150 feet from the center of the bridge?

Review & Refresh

Find the value of x.

23.

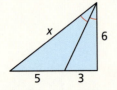

24.

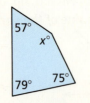

29. Triangle ABC has vertices $A(4, 6)$, $B(8, 8)$, and $C(8, 2)$. Find the circumcenter.

30. Find the values of x and y.

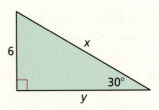

25. **26.**

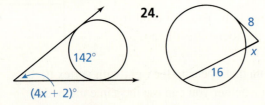

31. Find the geometric mean of 6 and 54.

27. Find the center and the radius of the circle with equation $x^2 + y^2 - 10x + 2y = 23$. Then graph the circle.

Graph quadrilateral $PQRS$ with vertices $P(1, -1)$, $Q(4, -2)$, $R(3, -4)$, and $S(1, -3)$ and its image after the composition.

28. Find the measure of each angle.

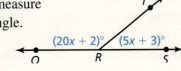

32. **Translation:** $(x, y) \rightarrow (x - 3, y + 4)$
Rotation: 90° about the origin

33. **Dilation:** $(x, y) \rightarrow \left(\frac{1}{4}x, \frac{1}{4}y\right)$
Reflection: in the y-axis

10 Chapter Review

Rate your understanding of each section.

1. I don't understand yet.
2. I can do it with help.
3. I can do it on my own.
4. I can teach someone.

10.1 Lines and Segments That Intersect Circles (pp. 507–514)

Learning Target: Identify lines and segments that intersect circles and use them to solve problems.

Vocabulary
circle
center
radius
chord
diameter
secant
tangent
point of tangency
tangent circles
concentric circles
common tangent

Tell whether the line, ray, or segment is best described as a *radius*, *chord*, *diameter*, *secant*, or *tangent* of ⊙P.

1. $\overline{PK}$
2. $\overline{NM}$
3. $\overrightarrow{JL}$
4. $\overline{KN}$
5. $\overleftrightarrow{NL}$
6. $\overline{PN}$

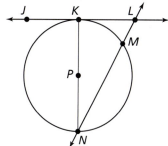

Tell how many common tangents the circles have and draw them. State whether the tangents are *external tangents* or *internal tangents*.

7.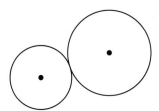

8.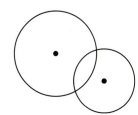

Points Y and Z are points of tangency. Find the value of the variable.

9.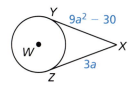

10.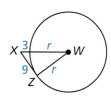

11. Explain whether $\overline{AB}$ is tangent to ⊙C.

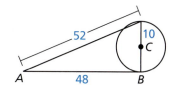

Chapter 10 Chapter Review 567

10.2 Finding Arc Measures (pp. 515–522)

Learning Target: Understand arc measures and similar circles.

Vocabulary
central angle
minor arc
major arc
semicircle
measure of a minor arc
measure of a major arc
adjacent arcs
congruent circles
congruent arcs
similar arcs

Find the measure of the indicated arc.

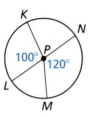

12. $\widehat{KL}$ 13. $\widehat{LM}$

14. $\widehat{KM}$ 15. $\widehat{KN}$

Explain whether the red arcs are congruent.

16. 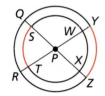   17.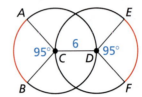

18. A survey asked high school seniors what they intend to do after graduating. The circle graph shows the results. Find each indicated arc measure.

   a. $\widehat{AB}$ b. $\widehat{AC}$
   c. $\widehat{BD}$ d. $\widehat{ABF}$

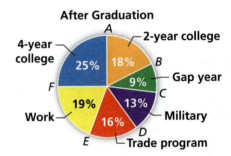

10.3 Using Chords (pp. 523–530)

Learning Target: Understand and apply theorems about chords.

Find the measure of $\widehat{AB}$.

19. 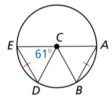   20. 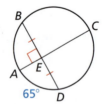   21.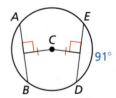

22. In the diagram, $QN = QP = 10$, $JK = 4x$, and $LM = 6x - 24$. Find the radius of $\odot Q$.

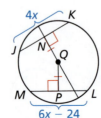

568   Chapter 10   Circles

10.4 Inscribed Angles and Polygons (pp. 531–538)

Learning Target: Use properties of inscribed angles and inscribed polygons.

Vocabulary
inscribed angle
intercepted arc
subtend
inscribed polygon
circumscribed circle

Find the value(s) of the variable(s).

23.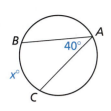

24.

25.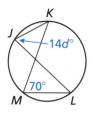

26.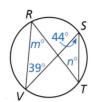

27. Construct a 30°-60°-90° right triangle inscribed in a circle. Justify your construction.

10.5 Angle Relationships in Circles (pp. 539–546)

Learning Target: Understand angles formed by chords, secants, and tangents.

Vocabulary
circumscribed angle

Find the value of x.

28.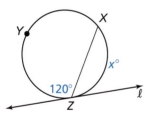

29.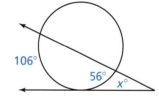

30.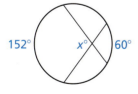

31.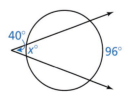

32. In the diagram, $\overrightarrow{AC}$ and $\overrightarrow{AD}$ are tangent to the circle and $m\angle A = \frac{1}{2} m\angle B$. Find $m\angle COD$.

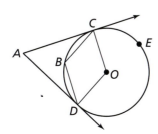

10.6 Segment Relationships in Circles (pp. 547–552)

⊙ **Learning Target:** Use theorems about segments of chords, secants, and tangents.

Vocabulary
segments of a chord
tangent segment
secant segment
external segment

Find the value of x.

33.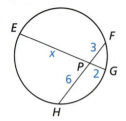

34.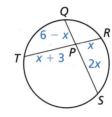

35.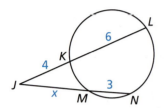

36.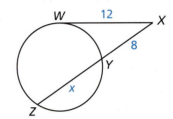

37. Newgrange is a large tomb in Ireland consisting of a circular mound with a diameter of 250 feet. A 62-foot-long passage leads toward the mound's center. Find the perpendicular distance x from the end of the passage to either side of the mound.

10.7 Circles in the Coordinate Plane (pp. 553–558)

⊙ **Learning Target:** Understand equations of circles.

Vocabulary
standard equation of a circle

Write the standard equation of the circle.

38.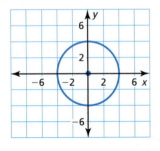

39.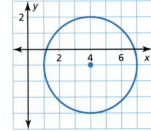

40. the circle with center (0, 0) and radius 9

41. the circle with center (6, 21) and radius 4

42. The center is (−7, 6), and a point on the circle is (−7, 1).

43. The equation of a circle is $x^2 + y^2 - 12x + 8y + 48 = 0$. Find the center and the radius of the circle. Then graph the circle.

10.8 Focus of a Parabola (pp. 559–566)

Learning Target: Graph and write equations of parabolas.

Vocabulary
focus
directrix

Write an equation of the parabola with the given characteristics.

44. vertex: (0, 0)
directrix: $x = 2$

45. focus: (2, 2)
vertex: (2, 6)

Identify the focus, directrix, and axis of symmetry of the parabola. Graph the equation.

46. $36y = x^2$

47. $64x + 8y^2 = 0$

Write an equation of the parabola.

48.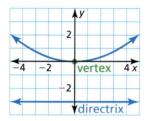

49.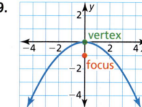

50.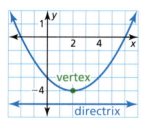

51.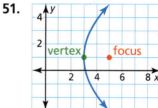

52. Parabolic microphones use a microphone at the focal point of a parabolic dish to amplify and record sound. One such device has a diameter of 20 inches and a depth of 6 inches. Describe the location of the microphone.

10 PERFORMANCE TASK
SMP.2

STONEHENGE

Stonehenge is a prehistoric monument in Wiltshire, England. The first monument at the site was constructed about 5,000 years ago.

POSSIBLE FUNCTIONS AND PURPOSES

Human remains as much as 5,000 years old have been found at the site.

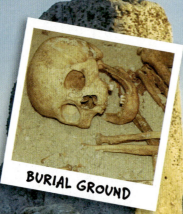

BURIAL GROUND

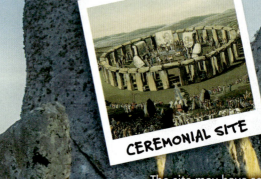

CEREMONIAL SITE

The site may have served as the location of religious rituals and ceremonies.

SCIENTIFIC OBSERVATORY

A PLACE OF HEALING

Skeletons at the site show signs of illness or injury. This indicates that ancient peoples may have traveled to the region believing that the stones contained healing powers.

The geometry of Stonehenge suggests that it may have been built to observe and predict the patterns of the moon and the Sun.

A *megalith* is a large stone used to construct a structure or monument. Some researchers believe that a unit of length called a *megalithic yard* (MY) was used in the construction of Stonehenge.

1 MY ≈ 0.829 m

572   Chapter 10   Circles

Analyzing Data

Use the information on the previous page to complete the following exercises.

1 Explain what is shown in the data display. What do you notice? What do you wonder?

2 Use the Internet or another resource to research and describe every component in the diagram below.

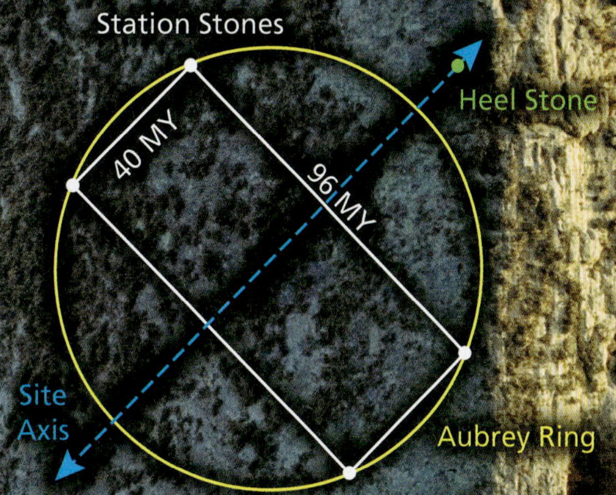

Station Stones
40 MY
96 MY
Heel Stone
Site Axis
Aubrey Ring

3 The four Station Stones approximately form a rectangle with the given dimensions (in megalithic yards). Use these dimensions to approximate the diameter of the Aubrey ring.

4 Find the measure of each arc subtended by adjacent Station Stones.

CREATE A MODEL

Use what you have found about Stonehenge to create a scale model of the monument. Some archaeologists believe that the Station Stones are the remaining vertices of a different formation of stones arranged in a regular polygon inscribed in the Aubrey Ring. Describe a possible polygon. Then use the Internet or another resource to find the possible significance of the polygon.

11 Circumference and Area

- 11.1 Circumference and Arc Length
- 11.2 Areas of Circles and Sectors
- 11.3 Areas of Polygons
- 11.4 Modeling with Area

NATIONAL GEOGRAPHIC EXPLORER
Alizé Carrère CULTURAL ANTHROPOLOGIST

Alizé Carrère has a bachelor's degree in environmental sciences and international development, and a master's degree in bioresource engineering. She has worked in the Middle East on water resource management and electronic waste between Israel and Palestine. She has also conducted research in Madagascar, studying farmers who adapted to severe deforestation by using erosional gullies as farmland.

- What is bioresource engineering?
- Where is Madagascar? How large is it? What is unique about this island?
- What percent of the species of animals living in Madagascar are not found anywhere else on Earth?

PERFORMANCE TASK
One focus of bioresource engineering is irrigation. In the 1940s Frank Zybach invented the center-pivot system in order to irrigate crops more effectively. In the Performance Task on pages 608 and 609, you will design your own center-pivot irrigation system.

Bioresource Engineering

Big Idea of the Chapter
Understand Circumference and Area

The circumference of a circle is the distance around the circle. The area of a figure is the region bounded by the figure. Area is measured in square units, such as square feet.

One cow can eat up to 24 pounds of hay a day. This means that livestock farmers need to be able to store large quantities of hay between harvests. Farmers will often wrap round bales of hay in white plastic and store them outside. The plastic covering keeps the hay dry and aids in proper fermentation. Hay can also be wrapped in twine or netting, but these are not suitable for outside storage.

Use the cylinder-shaped hay bale shown.

1. The area of a circle with radius r is $A = \pi r^2$. Find the area of one of the bases of the bale.

2. The circumference C of a cylinder with radius r is $C = 2\pi r$. Find the circumference of one of the bases of the bale.

3. The surface area A of a cylinder with radius r and height h is $A = 2\pi r^2 + 2\pi rh$. A farmer has 4,500 square feet of plastic leftover from last season. How many more square feet of plastic must the farmer purchase to completely cover 65 bales?

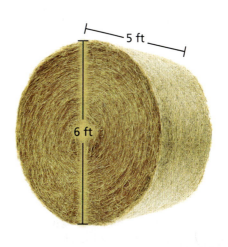

Getting Ready for Chapter 11

Finding Areas of Triangles

EXAMPLE 1   A triangle has a base of 8 inches and a height of 7 inches. Find the area of the triangle.

$A = \frac{1}{2}bh$ Write formula for area of a triangle.

$= \frac{1}{2}(8)(7)$ Substitute 8 for b and 7 for h.

$= 28$ Multiply.

▶ The area of the triangle is 28 square inches.

Find the area of the triangle.

1.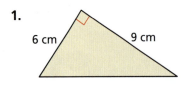

2.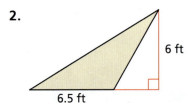

Finding a Missing Dimension

EXAMPLE 2   A rectangle has a perimeter of 10 meters and a length of 3 meters. What is the width of the rectangle?

$P = 2\ell + 2w$ Write formula for perimeter of a rectangle.

$10 = 2(3) + 2w$ Substitute 10 for P and 3 for ℓ.

$10 = 6 + 2w$ Multiply 2 and 3.

$4 = 2w$ Subtract 6 from each side.

$2 = w$ Divide each side by 2.

▶ The width is 2 meters.

Find the missing dimension.

3. A rectangle has a perimeter of 28 inches and a width of 5 inches. What is the length of the rectangle?

4. A triangle has an area of 12 square centimeters and a height of 12 centimeters. What is the base of the triangle?

5. A rectangle has an area of 84 square feet and a width of 7 feet. What is the length of the rectangle?

11.1 Circumference and Arc Length

Learning Target: Understand circumference, arc length, and radian measure.

Success Criteria:
- I can use the formula for the circumference of a circle to find measures.
- I can find arc lengths and use arc lengths to find measures.
- I can solve real-life problems involving circumference.
- I can explain radian measure and convert between degree and radians.

INVESTIGATE Finding the Length of a Circular Arc

Work with a partner. A roundabout at a playground has a radius of 10 feet. As it rotates, a person can ride the roundabout at different distances from the center of the circular ride.

1. Find the distance that each person travels along the red circular arc.

    a. one full rotation

    b. one-fourth of a rotation

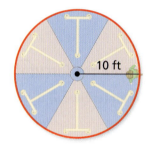
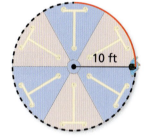

    c. one-third of a rotation

    d. five-eighths of a rotation

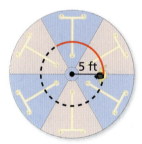
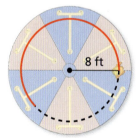

2. A person standing 8 feet from the center of the roundabout travels one-fourth of a rotation. Without performing any calculations, who travels farther, this person or the person in Exercise 1(b)? How do you know?

3. For what fraction of a rotation would a person standing 10 feet from the center of the roundabout travel the same distance as the person in Exercise 1(d)? Explain your reasoning.

4. Explain how to find the length of any circular arc.

Vocabulary
circumference
arc length
radian

Using the Formula for Circumference

The **circumference** of a circle is the distance around the circle. Consider a regular polygon inscribed in a circle. As the number of sides increases, the polygon approximates the circle, and the ratio of the perimeter of the polygon to the diameter of the circle approaches $\pi \approx 3.14159\ldots$.

For all circles, the ratio of the circumference C to the diameter d is $\dfrac{C}{d} = \pi$.

Key Concept

Circumference of a Circle

The circumference C of a circle is $C = \pi d$ or $C = 2\pi r$, where d is the diameter of the circle and r is the radius of the circle.

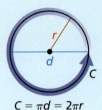

$C = \pi d = 2\pi r$

EXAMPLE 1 — Using the Formula for Circumference

a. Find the circumference of a circle with a radius of 9 centimeters.

$C = 2\pi r$ Write formula for circumference.
$ = 2 \cdot \pi \cdot 9$ Substitute 9 for r.
$ = 18\pi$ Multiply.
$ \approx 56.55$ Use technology.

▶ The circumference is about 56.55 centimeters.

b. Find the radius of a circle with a circumference of 26 meters.

$C = 2\pi r$ Write formula for circumference.
$26 = 2\pi r$ Substitute 26 for C.
$\dfrac{26}{2\pi} = r$ Divide each side by 2π.
$4.14 \approx r$ Use technology.

▶ The radius is about 4.14 meters.

In-Class Practice

Self-Assessment

1. Find the circumference of a circle with a diameter of 5 inches.

2. Find the diameter of a circle with a circumference of 17 feet.

Finding and Using Arc Lengths

An **arc length** is a portion of the circumference of a circle. You can use the measure of the arc (in degrees) to find its length (in linear units).

Key Concept

Arc Length

In a circle, the ratio of the length of a given arc to the circumference is equal to the ratio of the measure of the arc to 360°.

$$\frac{\text{Arc length of } \widehat{AB}}{2\pi r} = \frac{m\widehat{AB}}{360°}, \text{ or}$$

$$\text{Arc length of } \widehat{AB} = \frac{m\widehat{AB}}{360°} \cdot 2\pi r$$

EXAMPLE 2 Finding and Using Arc Lengths

Find each indicated measure.

a. arc length of $\widehat{AB}$ **b.** $m\widehat{RS}$

Arc length of $\widehat{AB} = \frac{60°}{360°} \cdot 2\pi(8)$

$= \frac{1}{6} \cdot 16\pi$

≈ 8.38 cm

$\frac{\text{Arc length of } \widehat{RS}}{2\pi r} = \frac{m\widehat{RS}}{360°}$

$\frac{44}{2\pi(15.28)} = \frac{m\widehat{RS}}{360°}$

$360° \cdot \frac{44}{2\pi(15.28)} = \frac{m\widehat{RS}}{360°} \cdot 360°$

$165° \approx m\widehat{RS}$

In-Class Practice

Self-Assessment

Find the indicated measure.

3. circumference of $\odot N$ **4.** radius of $\odot G$

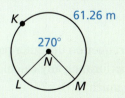 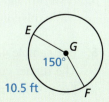

11.1 Circumference and Arc Length

Connections to Real Life

EXAMPLE 3 **Using Circumference to Find Distance Traveled**

How many feet does the tire shown travel when it makes 15 revolutions?

The diameter of the tire is $d = 15 + 2(5.5) = 26$ in.

The circumference of the tire is $C = \pi d = \pi \cdot 26 = 26\pi$ in.

In one revolution, the tire travels a distance equal to its circumference. So, in 15 revolutions, the tire travels a distance equal to 15 times its circumference.

$$\text{Distance traveled} = \text{Number of revolutions} \cdot \text{Circumference}$$

$$= 15 \cdot 26\pi$$

$$\approx 1{,}225.2 \text{ in.}$$

Use unit analysis to convert 1,225.2 inches to feet.

$$1{,}225.2 \text{ in.} \cdot \frac{1 \text{ ft}}{12 \text{ in.}} = 102.1 \text{ ft}$$

▶ The tire travels about 102 feet.

EXAMPLE 4 **Using Arc Length to Find Distances**

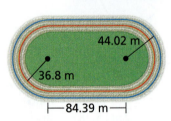

The curves at the ends of the track shown are 180° arcs of circles. The radius of the arc for a runner on the inner path shown in the diagram is 36.8 meters. About how far does the runner travel in one lap?

The path of the runner is made of two straight sections and two semicircles. Find the sum of the lengths of each part.

$$\text{Distance} = 2 \cdot \text{Length of each straight section} + 2 \cdot \text{Length of each semicircle}$$

$$= 2(84.39) + 2\left(\tfrac{1}{2} \cdot 2\pi \cdot 36.8\right)$$

$$\approx 400.0$$

▶ The runner travels about 400 meters.

In-Class Practice

Self-Assessment

5. A car tire has a diameter of 28 inches. How many revolutions does the tire make while traveling 500 feet?

6. In Example 4, the radius of the arc for a runner on the outer path is 44.02 meters. The runner completes one lap. Without performing any calculations, how do you know which runner travels farther? How much farther?

Measuring Angles in Radians

You have encountered angle measures written using degrees, but there are other units of angle measure. **Radians** are a unit of angle measure that are based on the length of the arc subtended by a central angle in a circle of radius 1. Because a circle of radius 1 has a diameter of 2π, 2π radians is equivalent to 360°.

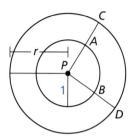

Because $m\widehat{CD} = m\widehat{AB}$, $\widehat{CD}$ and $\widehat{AB}$ are similar. So, $\dfrac{\text{Arc length of } \widehat{CD}}{\text{Arc length of } \widehat{AB}} = \dfrac{r}{1}$, which implies the arc length of $\widehat{CD}$ is $r \cdot \dfrac{m\widehat{AB}}{360°} \cdot 2\pi$.

This form of the equation shows that the arc length associated with central angle CPD is *proportional to the radius* of the circle. The constant of proportionality, $\dfrac{m\widehat{AB}}{360°} \cdot 2\pi$, is defined to be the radian measure of the central angle associated with the arc.

Key Concept

Converting between Degrees and Radians

Degrees to radians Multiply degree measure by $\dfrac{2\pi \text{ radians}}{360°}$, or $\dfrac{\pi \text{ radians}}{180°}$.

Radians to degrees Multiply radian measure by $\dfrac{360°}{2\pi \text{ radians}}$, or $\dfrac{180°}{\pi \text{ radians}}$.

EXAMPLE 5 Converting between Degree and Radian Measure

a. Convert 45° to radians.

$$45° \cdot \dfrac{\pi \text{ radians}}{180°} = \dfrac{\pi}{4} \text{ radian}$$

▶ So, $45° = \dfrac{\pi}{4}$ radian.

b. Convert $\dfrac{3\pi}{2}$ radians to degrees.

$$\dfrac{3\pi}{2} \text{ radians} \cdot \dfrac{180°}{\pi \text{ radians}} = 270°$$

▶ So, $\dfrac{3\pi}{2}$ radians = 270°.

In-Class Practice

Self-Assessment

7. Convert 15° to radians.

8. Convert $\dfrac{4\pi}{3}$ radians to degrees.

1 I don't understand yet. **2** I can do it with help. **3** I can do it on my own. **4** I can teach someone.

11.1 Practice

Find the indicated measure. (See Example 1.)

1. circumference of a circle with a radius of 6 inches

2. circumference of a circle with a diameter of 5 inches

3. diameter of a circle with a circumference of 63 feet

4. radius of a circle with a circumference of 28π

Find the indicated measure. (See Example 2.)

5. arc length of $\widehat{AB}$

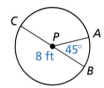

6. $m\widehat{DE}$

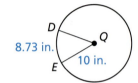

7. radius of $\odot R$

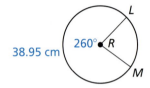

8. **ERROR ANALYSIS** Describe and correct the error in finding the circumference of $\odot C$.

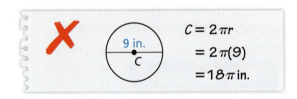

9. **CONNECTION TO REAL LIFE** A measuring wheel is used to calculate the length of a path. The diameter of the wheel is 8 inches. The wheel makes 87 complete revolutions along the length of the path. How many feet long is the path? (See Example 3.)

Find the perimeter of the shaded region. (See Example 4.)

10.

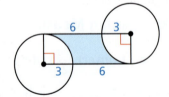

11.

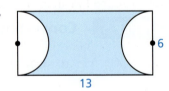

Convert the angle measure. (See Example 5.)

12. Convert 300° to radians.

13. Convert 70° to radians.

14. Convert $\dfrac{11\pi}{12}$ radians to degrees.

15. Convert $\dfrac{\pi}{8}$ radian to degrees.

16. A semicircle has endpoints $(-2, 5)$ and $(2, 8)$. Find the arc length of the semicircle.

582 Chapter 11 Circumference and Area

Find the circumference of the circle represented by the given equation. Write the circumference in terms of π.

17. $x^2 + y^2 = 16$

18. $(x + 2)^2 + (y - 3)^2 = 9$

19. How many revolutions does the smaller gear complete during a single revolution of the larger gear?

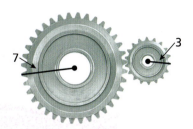

20. Use the diagram to show that the length of $\widehat{PQ}$ is proportional to the radius r.

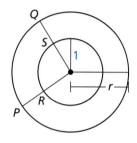

21. **SMP.6** The Greek scholar Eratosthenes estimated Earth's circumference by assuming that the Sun's rays were parallel. He chose a day when the Sun shone straight down into a well in the city of Syene. At noon, he measured the angle the Sun's rays made with a vertical stick in the city of Alexandria. Eratosthenes assumed that the distance from Syene to Alexandria was about 575 miles. Explain how Eratosthenes was able to use this information to estimate Earth's circumference. Then estimate Earth's circumference.

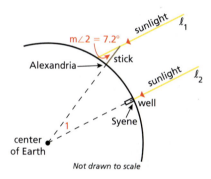

22. Find the circumference of each circle.

    a. a circle circumscribed about a square with a side length of 6 centimeters

    b. a circle inscribed in an equilateral triangle with a side length of 9 inches

23. **PROOF** The circles in the diagram to the right are concentric and $\overline{FG} \cong \overline{GH}$. Prove that $\widehat{JK}$ and $\widehat{NG}$ have the same length.

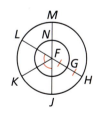

24. **SMP.8** $\overline{AB}$ is divided into congruent segments, each of which is the diameter of a semicircle.

    a. What is the sum of the arc lengths?

    b. What is the sum of the arc lengths when $\overline{AB}$ is divided into 8 congruent segments? 16 congruent segments? n congruent segments?

Interpreting Data

BIORESOURCE ENGINEERING **PIVOT IRRIGATION** A center-pivot irrigation system consists of sprinkler equipment that rotates around a central pivot point to irrigate a circular region. Pivot irrigation uses less water than the traditional flooding irrigation method and also reduces fertilizer loss. The figures show square fields with side lengths of 120 feet.

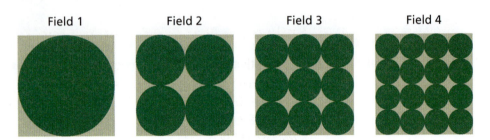

25. What percent of Field 1 is covered by the circle?

26. A farmer wants to cover more of the field by using 4 circles, as shown in Field 2. Explain whether this strategy works.

27. Find the percent of Fields 3 and 4 that are covered by circles. What do you notice?

Review & Refresh

28. Find the value of x that makes $\triangle PQR \sim \triangle XYZ$.

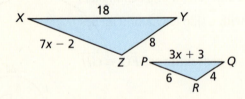

29. Find the area of the polygon with vertices $L(-3, 1)$, $M(4, 1)$, $N(4, -5)$ and $P(-3, -5)$.

30. Find the value of x.

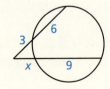

31. L'Umbracle is an open-air gallery and garden in Valencia, Spain. The structure is composed of 55 parabolic arches. One of the arches can be represented by a parabola with focus $(0, 5.5)$ and vertex $(0, 18)$. Write an equation for the parabola.

32. Find the length of the midsegment of the trapezoid.

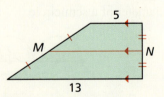

33. Find the center and radius of the circle $x^2 + y^2 = 16$. Then graph the circle.

584   Chapter 11   Circumference and Area

11.2 Areas of Circles and Sectors

Learning Target: Find areas of circles and areas of sectors of circles.

Success Criteria:
- I can use the formula for area of a circle to find measures.
- I can find areas of sectors of circles.
- I can solve problems involving areas of sectors.

INVESTIGATE   Finding the Area of a Sector of a Circle

Work with a partner. The concentrated beam from the light in a lighthouse can be seen from many miles away. These beams are produced using a *Fresnel lens*, invented in the early 18th century by French engineer Augustin-Jean Fresnel. Fresnel's invention has been referred to as "the invention that saved a million ships."

1. A *sector of a circle* is the region bounded by two radii of the circle and their intercepted arc. The figures below show four different lighthouses. Find the area of the shaded circle or sector of a circle that is covered by the light beam from each lighthouse.

    a. one full rotation

    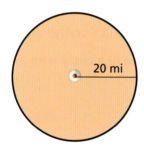

    b. one-fourth of a rotation

    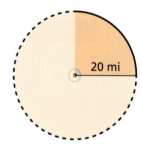

    c. one-third of a rotation

    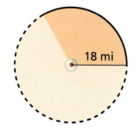

    d. five-eighths of a rotation

    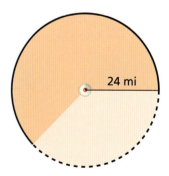

2. For what fraction of a rotation would the lighthouse in Exercise 1(b) cover the same area as the lighthouse in Exercise 1(d)? Explain your reasoning.

3. Explain, in your own words, how you can find the area of a sector of a circle.

Vocabulary

sector of a circle

Using the Formula for the Area of a Circle

You can divide a circle into congruent sections and rearrange the sections to form a figure that resembles a parallelogram. Increasing the number of congruent sections increases the figure's resemblance to a parallelogram.

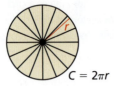
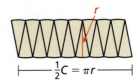

The base of the parallelogram that the figure approaches is half of the circumference, so $b = \frac{1}{2}C = \frac{1}{2}(2\pi r) = \pi r$. The height is the radius, so $h = r$. So, the area of the parallelogram is $A = bh = (\pi r)(r) = \pi r^2$.

Key Concept

Area of a Circle

The area of a circle is

$$A = \pi r^2$$

where r is the radius of the circle.

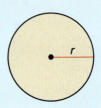

EXAMPLE 1 Using the Formula for the Area of a Circle

a. Find the area of a circle with a radius of 2.5 centimeters.

$A = \pi r^2$	Write formula for area of a circle.
$= \pi \cdot (2.5)^2$	Substitute 2.5 for r.
≈ 19.63	Use technology.

▶ The area of the circle is about 19.63 square centimeters.

b. Find the diameter of a circle with an area of 113.1 square meters.

$A = \pi r^2$	Write formula for area of a circle.
$113.1 = \pi r^2$	Substitute 113.1 for A.
$\dfrac{113.1}{\pi} = r^2$	Divide each side by π.
$6 \approx r$	Take the positive square root of each side.

▶ The radius is about 6 meters, so the diameter is about 12 meters.

In-Class Practice

Self-Assessment

1. Find the area of a circle with a radius of 4.5 meters.

2. Find the radius of a circle with an area of 176.7 square feet.

Finding Areas of Sectors

A **sector of a circle** is the region bounded by two radii of the circle and their intercepted arc. In the diagram below, sector APB is bounded by $\overline{AP}$, $\overline{BP}$, and $\overparen{AB}$.

> ### Key Concept
>
> **Area of a Sector**
>
> The ratio of the area of a sector of a circle to the area of the whole circle (πr^2) is equal to the ratio of the measure of the intercepted arc to 360°.
>
> $$\frac{\text{Area of sector } APB}{\pi r^2} = \frac{m\overparen{AB}}{360°}, \quad \text{or}$$
>
> $$\text{Area of sector } APB = \frac{m\overparen{AB}}{360°} \cdot \pi r^2$$

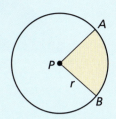

EXAMPLE 2 Finding Areas of Sectors

Find the areas of the sectors formed by ∠UTV.

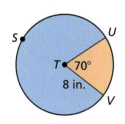

Find the measures of the minor and major arcs.

Because $m\angle UTV = 70°$, $m\overparen{UV} = 70°$ and $m\overparen{USV} = 360° - 70° = 290°$.

Find the areas of the small and large sectors.

$\text{Area of small sector} = \dfrac{m\overparen{UV}}{360°} \cdot \pi r^2$ Write formula for area of a sector.

$\qquad = \dfrac{70°}{360°} \cdot \pi \cdot 8^2$ Substitute.

$\qquad \approx 39.10$ Use technology.

$\text{Area of large sector} = \dfrac{m\overparen{USV}}{360°} \cdot \pi r^2$ Write formula for area of a sector.

$\qquad = \dfrac{290°}{360°} \cdot \pi \cdot 8^2$ Substitute.

$\qquad \approx 161.97$ Use technology.

▶ The areas of the small and large sectors are about 39.10 square inches and about 161.97 square inches, respectively.

In-Class Practice

Self-Assessment

3. Find the areas of the sectors formed by ∠KJL.

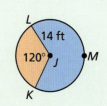

Connections to Real Life

EXAMPLE 3 Using the Area of a Sector

A fragment of a Mayan plate is shown. Find the area of $\odot C$.

To find the area of $\odot C$, use the formula for the area of a sector.

$$\text{Area of sector } BCD = \frac{m\widehat{BD}}{360°} \cdot \text{Area of } \odot C \quad \text{Write formula for area of a sector.}$$

$$94.2 = \frac{48°}{360°} \cdot \text{Area of } \odot C \quad \text{Substitute.}$$

$$706.5 = \text{Area of } \odot C \quad \text{Solve for area of } \odot C.$$

▶ The area of $\odot C$ is 706.5 square centimeters.

EXAMPLE 4 Finding the Area of a Region

A rectangular wall has an entrance cut into it. You want to paint the wall. What is the area of the region you need to paint?

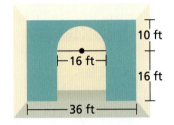

The area you need to paint is the area of the rectangle minus the area of the entrance. The shape of the entrance can be decomposed into a semicircle and a square.

$$\text{Area of wall} = \text{Area of rectangle} - (\text{Area of semicircle} + \text{Area of square})$$

$$= 36(26) - \left[\frac{180°}{360°} \cdot (\pi \cdot 8^2) + 16^2\right]$$

$$= 936 - (32\pi + 256)$$

$$\approx 579.47$$

▶ The area you need to paint is about 579 square feet.

In-Class Practice

Self-Assessment

4. Find the area of $\odot H$.

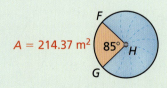

$A = 214.37 \text{ m}^2$, 85°

5. Find the area of the figure.

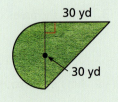

30 yd, 30 yd

| 1 I don't understand yet. | 2 I can do it with help. | 3 I can do it on my own. | 4 I can teach someone. |

588 Chapter 11 Circumference and Area

11.2 Practice

with Calc Chat and Calc View

Find the indicated measure. (See Example 1.)

1. area of a circle with a radius of 5 inches

2. radius of a circle with an area of 89 square feet

3. diameter of a circle with an area of 676π square centimeters

Find the areas of the sectors formed by $\angle DFE$. (See Example 2.)

4.

5.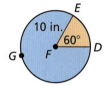

6.

The area of the shaded sector is shown. Find the indicated measure. (See Example 3.)

7. area of $\odot M$

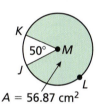

8. radius of $\odot M$

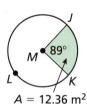

9. diameter of $\odot M$

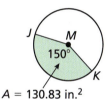

Find the area of the shaded region. (See Example 4.)

10.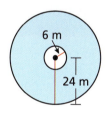

11.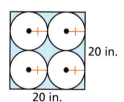

12.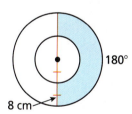

13. **CONNECTION TO REAL LIFE** The diagram shows the shape of a putting green at a miniature golf course. One part of the green is a sector of a circle. Find the area of the putting green.

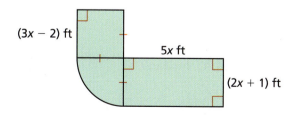

14. **DIG DEEPER** The radius of each circle is 6 inches. Find the area between the three congruent tangent circles. Explain your method.

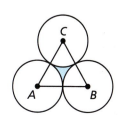

11.2 Areas of Circles and Sectors 589

Interpreting Data

RADAR IMAGES A radar emits energy which strikes objects in the air. This energy is reflected in all directions, including back to the radar. The strength of the returned energy is measured and used to determine precipitation levels. In general, the more energy that returns to the radar, the heavier the precipitation.

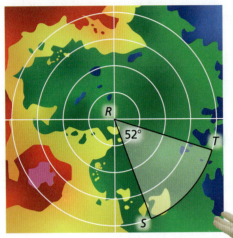

15. The area of sector *TRS* is 3,858 square kilometers. Find the area of ⊙*R*.

16. Estimate the percent of ⊙*R* that is green.

17. Research what each color shown on the radar represents.

Review & Refresh

18. Find the circumference of ⊙*M*.

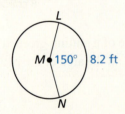

19. Point *D* is the centroid of △*ABC*. Find *CD* and *CE* when *DE* = 7.

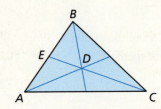

20. Find the distance from the point (−6, 4) to the line $y = 3x - 1$.

21. An agility A-frame is used to test the agility of dogs. Prove that the distance up both sides of the ramp is the same.

22. Find the lengths of the diagonals of rectangle *JKLM* when $JL = 4x + 2$ and $KM = 3x + 12$.

590 Chapter 11 Circumference and Area

11.3 Areas of Polygons

> **Learning Target:** Find angle measures and areas of regular polygons.
>
> **Success Criteria:**
> - I can find areas of rhombuses and kites.
> - I can find angle measures in regular polygons.
> - I can find areas of regular polygons.
> - I can explain how the area of a triangle is related to the area formulas for rhombuses, kites, and regular polygons.

The *center of a regular polygon* is the center of its circumscribed circle.

The distance from the center to any side of a regular polygon is called the *apothem of a regular polygon*.

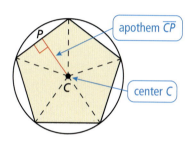

INVESTIGATE

Finding the Area of a Regular Polygon

SMP.5 Work with a partner.

1. Construct an equilateral triangle and find its area. Explain your method.

2. Find the apothem of the triangle you constructed in Exercise 1 and use it to find the area of the triangle. Explain your method. Compare your answer with the area you found in Exercise 1.

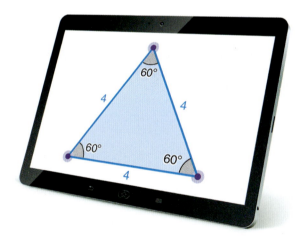

3. Construct the regular polygons below using any side length. Then use the apothem of each polygon to find its area. Explain your method.

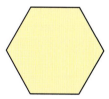 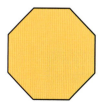

4. Use your answers to Exercise 3 to develop a strategy to find the area of any regular polygon, regardless of the number of sides. Then write a formula for the area of any regular polygon.

Vocabulary
center of a regular polygon
radius of a regular polygon
apothem of a regular polygon
central angle of a regular polygon

Finding Areas of Rhombuses and Kites

You can decompose a rhombus or kite with diagonals d_1 and d_2 into two congruent triangles with base d_1 and height $\frac{1}{2}d_2$. The area of one of these triangles is $\frac{1}{2}d_1\left(\frac{1}{2}d_2\right) = \frac{1}{4}d_1d_2$. So, the area of a rhombus or kite is $2\left(\frac{1}{4}d_1d_2\right) = \frac{1}{2}d_1d_2$.

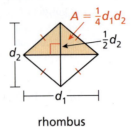
rhombus

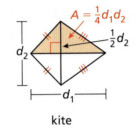
kite

Key Concept

Area of a Rhombus or Kite

The area of a rhombus or kite is one-half the product of the diagonals d_1 and d_2.

$A = \frac{1}{2}d_1d_2$

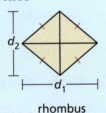
rhombus

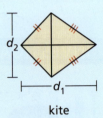
kite

EXAMPLE 1 Finding the Area of a Rhombus or Kite

Find the area of each rhombus or kite.

a.

$A = \frac{1}{2}d_1d_2$

$= \frac{1}{2}(6)(8)$

$= 24$

▶ So, the area is 24 square meters.

b.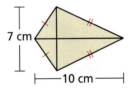

$A = \frac{1}{2}d_1d_2$

$= \frac{1}{2}(10)(7)$

$= 35$

▶ So, the area is 35 square centimeters.

In-Class Practice
Self-Assessment

1. Find the area of a rhombus with diagonals $d_1 = 4$ feet and $d_2 = 5$ feet.

2. Find the area of a kite with diagonals $d_1 = 12$ inches and $d_2 = 9$ inches.

Finding Angle Measures in Regular Polygons

The **center of a regular polygon** and the **radius of a regular polygon** are the center and the radius of its circumscribed circle.

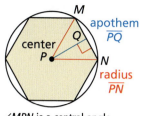

The distance from the center to any side of a regular polygon is the **apothem of a regular polygon**. The apothem is the altitude of an isosceles triangle that has two radii as legs.

∠MPN is a central angle.

A **central angle of a regular polygon** is an angle formed by two radii drawn to consecutive vertices of the polygon. To find the measure of each central angle, divide 360° by the number of sides of the polygon.

EXAMPLE 2 — Finding Angle Measures in a Regular Polygon

ABCDE is a regular pentagon inscribed in ⊙*F*. Find each angle measure.

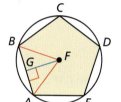

a. *m∠AFB*

∠AFB is a central angle of *ABCDE*, which has 5 sides.

▶ So, $m\angle AFB = \dfrac{360°}{5} = 72°$.

b. *m∠AFG*

$\overline{FG}$ is an apothem, which makes it an altitude of isosceles △AFB. So, $\overline{FG}$ bisects ∠AFB and $m\angle AFG = \frac{1}{2}(m\angle AFB)$.

$$m\angle AFG = \tfrac{1}{2}(m\angle AFB) = \tfrac{1}{2}(72°) = 36°$$

▶ So, *m∠AFG* = 36°.

c. *m∠GAF*

By the Triangle Sum Theorem, the sum of the angle measures of right △GAF is 180°.

$$m\angle GAF = 180° - 90° - 36° = 54°$$

▶ So, *m∠GAF* = 54°.

In-Class Practice

Self-Assessment

In the diagram, *WXYZ* is a square inscribed in ⊙*P*.

3. Identify the center, a radius, an apothem, and a central angle of *WXYZ*.

4. Find *m∠XPY*, *m∠XPQ*, and *m∠PXQ*.

11.3 Areas of Polygons

Finding Areas of Regular Polygons

> **Key Concept**
>
> **Area of a Regular Polygon**
>
> The area of a regular n-gon with side length s is one-half the product of the apothem a and the perimeter P.
>
> $A = \frac{1}{2}aP$, or $A = \frac{1}{2}a \cdot ns$

EXAMPLE 3 Finding the Area of a Regular Polygon

A regular nonagon is inscribed in a circle with a radius of 4 units. Find the area of the nonagon.

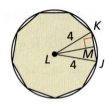

The measure of central $\angle JLK$ is $\dfrac{360°}{9}$, or 40°. Apothem $\overline{LM}$ bisects the central angle, so $m\angle KLM$ is 20°. To find the lengths of the legs, use trigonometric ratios for right $\triangle KLM$.

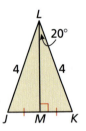

$$\sin 20° = \frac{MK}{LK} \qquad \cos 20° = \frac{LM}{LK}$$

$$\sin 20° = \frac{MK}{4} \qquad \cos 20° = \frac{LM}{4}$$

$$4 \sin 20° = MK \qquad 4 \cos 20° = LM$$

The regular nonagon has side length $s = 2(MK) = 2(4 \sin 20°) = 8 \sin 20°$, and apothem $a = LM = 4 \cos 20°$.

Find the area A of the regular nonagon.

$A = \frac{1}{2}a \cdot ns$ Write formula for area of a regular polygon.

$= \frac{1}{2}(4 \cos 20°) \cdot (9)(8 \sin 20°)$ Substitute.

≈ 46.3 Use technology.

▶ So, the area of the nonagon is about 46.3 square units.

In-Class Practice

Self-Assessment

5. A regular 15-gon is inscribed in a circle with a radius of 9 units. Find the area of the 15-gon.

Connections to Real Life

EXAMPLE 4 Finding the Area of a Regular Polygon

You are decorating the top of a table by covering it with small ceramic tiles. The tabletop is a regular octagon with 15-inch sides and a radius of about 19.6 inches. What is the area you are covering?

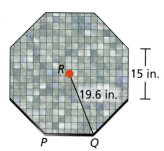

Find the perimeter P of the tabletop. An octagon has 8 sides, so $P = 8(15) = 120$ inches.

Find the apothem a. The apothem is height RS of $\triangle PQR$.

Because $\triangle PQR$ is isosceles, altitude $\overline{RS}$ bisects $\overline{QP}$.

So, $QS = \frac{1}{2}(QP) = \frac{1}{2}(15) = 7.5$ inches.

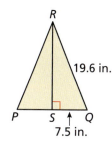

To find RS, use the Pythagorean Theorem for $\triangle RQS$.

$$a = RS = \sqrt{19.6^2 - 7.5^2} = \sqrt{327.91}$$

Find the area A of the tabletop.

$A = \frac{1}{2}aP$ Write formula for area of a regular polygon.

$= \frac{1}{2}(\sqrt{327.91})(120)$ Substitute.

≈ 1086.5 Use technology.

▶ The area you are covering with tiles is about 1086.5 square inches.

In-Class Practice

Self-Assessment

Find the area of the regular polygon.

6.

7.

11.3 Practice

with CalcChat and CalcView

Find the area of the kite or rhombus. (See Example 1.)

1.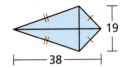
2.
3.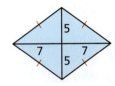

Find the measure of a central angle of a regular polygon with the given number of sides.

4. 10 sides
5. 18 sides
6. 7 sides

Find the given angle measure for regular octagon ABCDEFGH. (See Example 2.)

7. $m\angle GJH$
8. $m\angle GJK$
9. $m\angle KGJ$
10. $m\angle EJH$

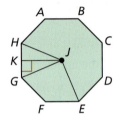

Find the area of the regular polygon. (See Example 3.)

11.
12.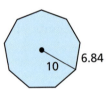
13.

14. a pentagon with an apothem of 5 units
15. an octagon with a radius of 11 units

Find the area of the shaded region.

16.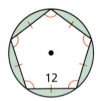
17.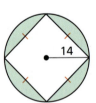
18.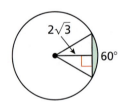

19. **CONNECTION TO REAL LIFE** Basaltic columns are geological formations that result from rapidly cooling lava. Giant's Causeway in Ireland contains many hexagonal basaltic columns. The top of one of the columns is in the shape of a regular hexagon with a radius of 8 inches. Find the area of the top of the column. (See Example 4.)

20. **CONNECTION TO REAL LIFE** A watch has a circular surface on a background that is a regular octagon. Find the area of the octagon. Then find the area of the silver border around the circular face.

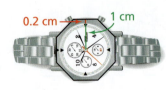

21. **SMP.1** Explain what happens to the area of a kite when you double the length of one of the diagonals. Then explain what happens when you double the lengths of both diagonals.

22. **CONNECT CONCEPTS** One diagonal of a rhombus is four times the length of the other diagonal. The area of the rhombus is 98 square feet. Write and solve an equation to find the length of each diagonal.

23. **SMP.1** The perimeter of a regular nonagon, or 9-gon, is 18 inches. Is this enough information to find the area? If so, find the area and explain your reasoning. If not, explain why not.

24. **PROOF** Prove that the area of any quadrilateral with perpendicular diagonals is $A = \frac{1}{2}d_1d_2$, where d_1 and d_2 are the lengths of the diagonals.

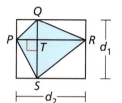

25. **SMP.7** Three vertices of kite *WXYZ* are *W*(1, 1), *X*(3, 4), and *Y*(5, 1). Find a possible set of coordinates for *Z*. Then find the perimeter and area of kite *WXYZ*.

26. The area of a regular pentagon is 72 square centimeters. Find the length of one side.

27. The area of a regular dodecagon, or 12-gon, is 140 square inches. Find the apothem of the polygon.

28. **SMP.7** Each polygon in the diagram is regular. Find the approximate area of the entire shaded region.

29. Find the area of regular hexagon *ABCDEF* by using the formula $A = \frac{1}{2}aP$, or $A = \frac{1}{2}a \cdot ns$. Then find the area by adding the areas of the triangles. Check that both methods yield the same area. Explain which method you prefer.

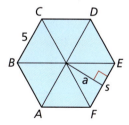

30. **SMP.8** The area of a regular *n*-gon is given by $A = \frac{1}{2}aP$. As *n* approaches infinity, what does the *n*-gon approach? What does *P* approach? What does *a* approach? What can you conclude?

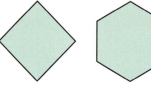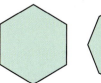

Interpreting Data

SOCCER BALL SURFACE AREA The standard design of a soccer ball is stitched from 32 regular polygons: 12 pentagons and 20 hexagons.

31. What is the sum of the 3 angle measures that meet at each vertex? Why do you think this is?

32. The pentagons and hexagons on the soccer ball have side lengths of 2 inches. Estimate the area of each pentagon and each hexagon.

33. Estimate the surface area of a soccer ball.

Review & Refresh

Find the indicated measure.

34. area of ⊙N

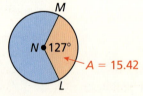

35. arc length of $\widehat{AB}$

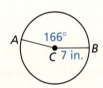

40. Solve the right triangle.

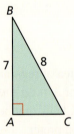

36. Write an equation of a parabola with focus $F(0, 1)$ and directrix $y = -3$.

37. △ABC has vertices $A(-2, 1)$, $B(0, 3)$, and $C(4, 1)$. △DEF has vertices $D(1, -1)$, $E(3, 1)$, and $F(7, -1)$. Are the triangles similar?

41. Find the value of x that makes $m \parallel n$.

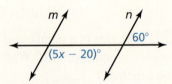

Find the value of x.

38.

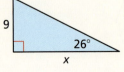

39.

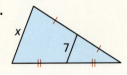

42. Find the measure of the exterior angle.

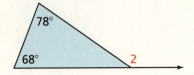

11.4 Modeling with Area

> **Learning Target:** Understand the concept of population density and modeling with area.
>
> **Success Criteria:**
> - I can explain what population density means.
> - I can find and use population densities.
> - I can use area formulas to solve problems.

INVESTIGATE Analyzing Population and Area

Work with a partner.

1. Use the Internet to find the population and land area of each county in Florida given below. Then find the number of people per square mile for each county.

   a. Indian River County   b. St. Lucie County   c. Martin County

   d. Palm Beach County   e. Broward County   f. Miami-Dade County

      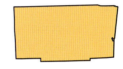   

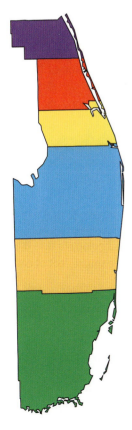

2. Without calculating, how do you expect the number of people per square mile in the entire six-county region to compare to the values for each individual county in Exercise 1? Justify your answer.

3. Collier County is the largest county in Florida by land area, but when the counties in Florida are ordered by population, it falls outside the top 10. How do you expect the number of people per square mile in Exercise 1 to change when Collier County is included? Why? Justify your answer.

4. How can you use the population and area of a region to describe how densely the region is populated?

Vocabulary
population density

Using Area Formulas

The **population density** of a city, county, or state is a measure of how many people live within a given area.

$$\text{Population density} = \frac{\text{number of people}}{\text{area of land}}$$

Population density is usually given in terms of square miles but can be expressed using other units, such as city blocks.

EXAMPLE 1 Finding a Population Density

The state of Nevada has a population of about 3.1 million people. Find the population density in people per square mile.

Estimate the area of Nevada. It is approximately shaped like a trapezoid.

$$A = \frac{1}{2}h(b_1 + b_2) = \frac{1}{2}(320)(200 + 490) = 110{,}400 \text{ mi}^2$$

Find the population density.

$$\text{Population density} = \frac{\text{number of people}}{\text{area of land}} = \frac{3{,}100{,}000}{110{,}400} \approx 28$$

▶ The population density is about 28 people per square mile.

EXAMPLE 2 Using the Formula for Population Density

A circular region has a population of 430,000 people and a population density of 5,475 people per square mile. Find the radius of the region.

Use the formula for population density. Let r represent the radius of the region.

STEM Video: Seismographs and Earthquake Epicenters

$\text{Population density} = \dfrac{\text{number of people}}{\text{area of land}}$	Formula for population density
$5{,}475 = \dfrac{430{,}000}{\pi r^2}$	Substitute.
$5{,}475\pi r^2 = 430{,}000$	Multiply each side by πr^2.
$r^2 = \dfrac{430{,}000}{5{,}475\pi}$	Divide each side by $5{,}475\pi$.
$r \approx 5$	Use technology to take the positive square root of each side.

▶ The radius of the region is about 5 miles.

In-Class Practice

Self-Assessment

1. About 58,000 people live in a circular region with a 2-mile radius. Find the population density in people per square mile.

2. A circular region has a population of about 175,000 people and a population density of about 1,318 people per square mile. Find the radius of the region.

1 I don't understand yet.   **2** I can do it with help.   **3** I can do it on my own.   **4** I can teach someone.

EXAMPLE 3 **Using Perimeter and Area to Solve a Design Problem**

You are designing a rectangular corral with an area of 450 square meters. A barn will form one side of the corral. You want to minimize the amount of fencing that you need for the other three sides of the corral. This will include an opening that is 3 meters wide where a gate will be placed. How many meters of fencing do you need?

Let the corral have area A, length ℓ, and width w. Write an expression for the perimeter of the three sides that need fencing.

$A = \ell w$ Area of corral

$450 = \ell w$ Substitute 450 for A.

$\dfrac{450}{w} = \ell$ Divide each side by w.

Let ℓ represent the length of the side of the corral against the barn. So, $2w + \ell$ represents the perimeter of the three sides that need fencing.

$2w + \ell = 2w + \dfrac{450}{w}$ Substitute $\dfrac{450}{w}$ for ℓ.

Use technology to create tables of values to find the width w that minimizes the value of $2w + \dfrac{450}{w}$. You may need to decrease the increment for the independent variable, as shown.

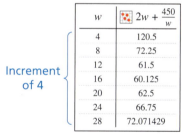

Increment of 4:
w	$2w + \dfrac{450}{w}$
4	120.5
8	72.25
12	61.5
16	60.125
20	62.5
24	66.75
28	72.071429

Increment of 0.5:
w	$2w + \dfrac{450}{w}$
13.5	60.333333
14	60.142857
14.5	60.034483
15	60
15.5	60.032258
16	60.125
16.5	60.272727

The width that minimizes the value of $2w + \dfrac{450}{w}$ is 15 meters.

So, the length of the corral is $\ell = \dfrac{450}{w} = \dfrac{450}{15} = 30$ meters.

Sketch a diagram of the corral that includes the gate opening, as shown. You need $2w + \ell - 3$ feet of fencing.

$2w + \ell - 3 = 2(15) + 30 - 3$ Substitute 15 for w and 30 for ℓ.

$= 57$ Simplify.

▶ So, you need 57 meters of fencing.

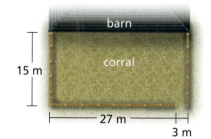

In-Class Practice

Self-Assessment

3. WHAT IF? In Example 3, you want the corral to have an area of 800 square meters. How many meters of fencing do you need?

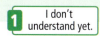 I don't understand yet.   I can do it with help.   I can do it on my own.   I can teach someone.

EXAMPLE 4 **Solving a Density Problem**

Magnetic computer tape was first used to record and store data in 1951. The magnetic tape drive recorded data at 768 bits per inch on $\frac{1}{2}$-inch tape.

a. *Areal density* is a measurement of the amount of data that can be stored on a given unit of storage space. The 6-inch segment of magnetic tape stores 4,608 bits of data. Find the areal density in bits per square inch.

0.5 in.

6 in.

Find the area A of the segment of magnetic tape.

$$A = \ell w = (6 \text{ in.})(0.5 \text{ in.}) = 3 \text{ in.}^2$$

Divide to find the areal density in bits per square inch.

$$\frac{4{,}608 \text{ bits}}{3 \text{ in.}^2} = \frac{1{,}536 \text{ bits}}{1 \text{ in.}^2} \qquad \text{Divide numerator and denominator by 3.}$$

▶ The areal density is 1,536 bits per square inch.

b. Data storage technology has improved dramatically since 1951. A 4-inch segment of $\frac{1}{2}$-inch magnetic tape can store 402 gigabits of data. About how many times more data per square inch can be stored on this 4-inch segment of tape than on the 6-inch segment in part (a)? (One gigabit contains 1 billion bits.)

Find the areal density of the 4-inch segment of magnetic tape. The area is $(4 \text{ in.})(0.5 \text{ in.}) = 2$ square inches.

$$\frac{402 \text{ gigabits}}{2 \text{ in.}^2} = \frac{201 \text{ gigabits}}{1 \text{ in.}^2} \qquad \text{Divide numerator and denominator by 2.}$$

The areal density is 201 gigabits per square inch. Because 1 gigabit contains 1 billion bits, the areal density is 201 billion bits per square inch. Divide to compare the segments of magnetic tape.

$$\frac{201{,}000{,}000{,}000 \text{ bits/in.}^2}{1{,}536 \text{ bits/in.}^2} = 130{,}859{,}375$$

▶ So, about 131 million times more data per square inch can be stored on the 4-inch segment of tape than the 6-inch segment of tape.

In-Class Practice

Self-Assessment

4. The segment of tape in Example 4(a) is a portion of a tape reel that is 1,200 feet long. How much data can be stored on the entire reel?

5. **WHAT IF?** A 6-inch segment of $\frac{1}{2}$-inch tape stores 20.1 gigabits of data. Compare the storage of this tape segment with the other segments in Example 4.

 I don't understand yet.   I can do it with help.   I can do it on my own.   I can teach someone.

11.4 Practice

with Calc Chat and Calc View

1. The state of Kansas has a population of about 2.91 million people. Find the population density in people per square mile. (See Example 1.)

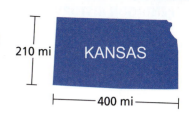

2. Yellowstone National Park has an area of about 2.22 million acres. The table shows the estimated park populations for several animals. Find the population density in animals per acre for each animal.

Animal	Grizzly bear	Elk	Mule deer	Bighorn sheep
Population	200	20,000	1,900	345

3. About 79,000 people live in a circular region with a population density of about 513 people per square mile. Find the radius of the region. (See Example 2.)

4. A circular region with a 4-mile radius has a population density of 6,366 people per square mile. Find the number of people who live in the region.

5. **CONNECTION TO REAL LIFE** A zoo wants to create a rectangular giraffe exhibit with an area of 2,500 square feet. What dimensions minimize the amount of fencing needed to enclose the exhibit? (See Example 3.)

6. **SMP.4 SMP.7** A field of length ℓ and width w has a perimeter of 320 yards.

   a. Write an expression that represents the area of the field in terms of ℓ.

   b. Use your expression from part (a) to determine the dimensions of the field that maximize the area. What do you notice?

7. **CONNECTION TO REAL LIFE** One measure of rug quality is *knot density*. Higher-quality rugs have a greater knot density. The rug shown is made of 345,600 knots. (See Example 4.)

   a. Find the knot density per square inch.

   b. Another rug is 3 feet by 4 feet and is made of 604,800 knots. Explain which is the better-quality rug.

8. The two islands with the given areas have the same population. Explain which has the greater population density.

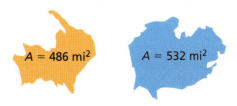

9. **SMP.2 OPEN-ENDED** Write a real-life problem involving density and area. Show how the area affects the density.

11.4 Modeling with Area 603

Interpreting Data

PENTAGON HISTORY The Pentagon was completed in January 1943. About 1,000 architects and 14,000 construction workers worked 3 shifts around the clock to finish the building. It has 7 stories, 2 of which are underground.

10. **SMP.1** Estimate the land area beneath the building, not including the center courtyard. Explain your method.

11. Use the area in Exercise 10 to estimate the population density when staffed with 25,000 employees.

12. Why do you think the architects used a regular-pentagonal design?

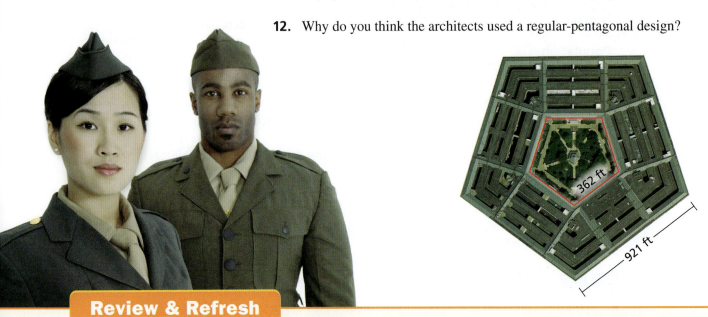

Review & Refresh

Find the indicated measure.

13. $m\widehat{EF}$

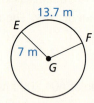

14. area of each sector

15. In the diagram, *RSTUVWXY* is a regular octagon inscribed in $\odot C$. The radius of the circle is 8 units. Find the area of the octagon.

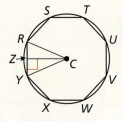

16. A school gymnasium is being remodeled. The basketball court will be similar to an NCAA basketball court, which has a length of 94 feet and a width of 50 feet. The school plans to make the width of the new court 45 feet. Find the perimeters of an NCAA court and the new court.

17. Find the value of each variable using sine and cosine.

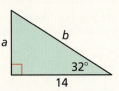

18. Find the sum of the measures of the interior angles of a 17-gon.

19. Find the geometric mean of 4 and 25.

11 Chapter Review

Rate your understanding of each section.

1 I don't understand yet. **2** I can do it with help. **3** I can do it on my own. **4** I can teach someone.

11.1 Circumference and Arc Length (pp. 577–584)

Learning Target: Understand circumference, arc length, and radian measure.

Vocabulary
circumference
arc length
radian

Find the indicated measure.

1. diameter of ⊙P

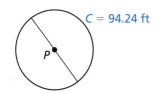

2. circumference of ⊙F

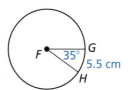

3. arc length of $\widehat{AB}$

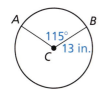

4. $m\widehat{QR}$

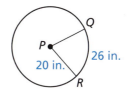

Find the perimeter of the shaded region.

5.

6.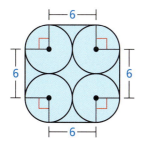

Convert the angle measure.

7. Convert 15° to radians.

8. Convert $\dfrac{3\pi}{5}$ radians to degrees.

9. A mountain bike tire has a diameter of 26 inches. How far does the tire travel when it makes 32 revolutions?

11.2 Areas of Circles and Sectors (pp. 585–590)

Learning Target: Find areas of circles and areas of sectors of circles.

Vocabulary
sector of a circle

Find the area of the shaded region.

10.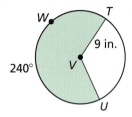

11.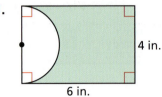

12. A slice of pizza with an area of 38 square inches has been removed from the pizza. What is the diameter of the whole pizza?

11.3 Areas of Polygons (pp. 591–598)

Learning Target: Find angle measures and areas of regular polygons.

Vocabulary
center of a regular polygon
radius of a regular polygon
apothem of a regular polygon
central angle of a regular polygon

Find the area of the kite or rhombus.

13.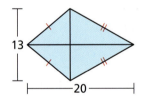

14.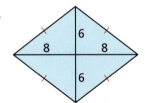

Find the area of the regular polygon.

15.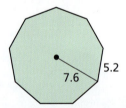

16.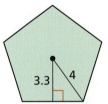

17. Find the measure of a central angle of a regular polygon with 11 sides.

18. A gazebo is in the shape of a regular octagon with a side length of 6 feet. Find the area covered by the gazebo.

19. What regular polygon with a side length of 1 foot can be inscribed in a circle with a diameter of 2 feet?

11.4 Modeling with Area (pp. 599–604)

Learning Target: Understand the concept of population density and modeling with area.

Vocabulary
population density

20. About 1.75 million people live in a circular region with a 15-mile diameter. Find the population density in people per square mile.

21. About 650,000 people live in a circular region with a 6-mile radius. Find the population density in people per square mile.

22. A circular region has a population of about 15,500 people and a population density of about 775 people per square kilometer. Find the radius of the region.

23. Central Park in New York City is rectangular with a length of 2.5 miles and a width of 0.5 mile. During an afternoon, its population density is about 15 people per acre. Find the number of people in the park that afternoon. One acre is equal to $\frac{1}{640}$ square mile.

24. You are using 48 feet of portable fencing to enclose a dance area along the front of a stage. What is the greatest rectangular dance area possible with the stage forming one of the sides?

25. A farmer wants to plant corn so that there are 36,000 plants per acre in the field shown. How many seeds does the farmer need? (1 acre = 43,560 ft²)

11 PERFORMANCE TASK
SMP.4

Center-Pivot Irrigation

Sprinklers are placed along sections of pipe, which are joined together and supported by trusses, and mounted on wheeled towers. Most systems are less than 500 meters long.

A center-pivot irrigation system contains a pipe structure that rotates about a **pivot point**. Water enters the system at the pivot point and then exits through sprinklers along the system. These systems typically complete one full revolution every three days.

The sprinklers in a central-pivot irrigation system must overlap to achieve a more uniform distribution of water. Too much overlap leads to over watering. Not enough overlap leads to dry spots.

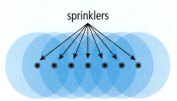
sprinklers

Analyzing Data

Use the information on the previous page to complete the following exercises.

1. Explain what is shown in the display. What do you notice? What do you wonder?

2. A system of center-pivot irrigation sprinklers is 150 meters long. Find the circumference and area of the field that is watered by the system.

IRRIGATION DESIGN

Design a center-pivot irrigation system. Determine each of the following:

- total radius of the system
- spacing between sprinklers
- number of wheeled towers
- throw radius of each sprinkler
- number of sprinklers
- rotation speed of the system

What happens to the area irrigated by a sprinkler as the distance from the pivot point increases? Provide examples to support your answer. Using this information, explain how you can modify your system to achieve a more uniform distribution of water.

What area can be irrigated by your system in 1 hour? in 1 day?

12 Surface Area and Volume

12.1 Cross Sections of Solids
12.2 Volumes of Prisms and Cylinders
12.3 Volumes of Pyramids
12.4 Surface Areas and Volumes of Cones
12.5 Surface Areas and Volumes of Spheres
12.6 Modeling with Surface Area and Volume
12.7 Solids of Revolution

NATIONAL GEOGRAPHIC EXPLORER
Daniela A. Cafaggi — BIOLOGIST

Daniela Cafaggi is a biologist who studies the diversity and conservation of bats in the archaeological zones of Yucatán, Mexico. Her team has identified more than 20 different species of bats in the region. She promotes coexistence between humans and bats, and highlights the importance of bats in ancient and current Mayan culture.

- Name several famous archaeological zones of the Yucatán Peninsula in Mexico.
- When did the ancient Mayans build El Castillo at Chichén Itzá?

PERFORMANCE TASK
Conservationists use artificial bat caves to combat white-nose syndrome. In the Performance Task on pages 666 and 667, you will design an artificial bat cave and estimate the number of hibernating bats that it can accommodate.

Conservation Biology

Big Idea of the Chapter
Find Surface Area and Volume

You already know how to find the perimeter and area of a two-dimensional figure. In this chapter, you will learn how to find the surface area and volume of solid figures such as prisms, pyramids, cylinders, cones, and spheres.

Most bats are nocturnal, flying and hunting at night. During the day, bats sleep, often hanging from ceilings of caves to avoid predators. Some species of bats live in large colonies that can have millions of members. Most bats use a process called *echolocation* to find food and avoid obstacles. To echolocate, bats produce high-frequency sounds which bounce off objects and return to the bat. The bat is able to use these echoes to understand its surroundings.

1. The ceiling of a cave is rectangular with a width of 100 feet and a length of 200 feet. What is the area of the ceiling?

2. For one species, each bat needs 8 square inches of ceiling space. How many bats can hang from the ceiling of the cave in Exercise 1?

3. A bat box is an artificial shelter designed to encourage bats to live in areas where there are few natural places for bats to find shelter. You construct a bat box with a ceiling that is 6 inches wide and 18 inches long. How many bats can live in the bat box?

Getting Ready for Chapter 12

Finding Surface Area

EXAMPLE 1 Find the surface area of the prism.

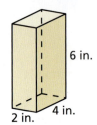

$S = 2\ell w + 2\ell h + 2wh$	Write formula for surface area of a rectangular prism.
$= 2(2)(4) + 2(2)(6) + 2(4)(6)$	Substitute 2 for ℓ, 4 for w, and 6 for h.
$= 88$	Simplify.

▶ The surface area is 88 square inches.

Find the surface area of the prism.

1.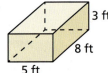

2.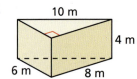

Finding Areas of Similar Polygons

EXAMPLE 2 In the diagram, $\triangle JKL \sim \triangle MNP$. Find the area of $\triangle MNP$.

Because the triangles are similar, the ratio of the area of $\triangle JKL$ to the area of $\triangle MNP$ is equal to the square of the ratio of KL to NP. Let A represent the area of $\triangle MNP$.

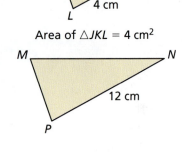

Area of $\triangle JKL = 4$ cm²

$\dfrac{\text{Area of }\triangle JKL}{\text{Area of }\triangle MNP} = \left(\dfrac{KL}{NP}\right)^2$	Areas of Similar Polygons Theorem
$\dfrac{4}{A} = \left(\dfrac{4}{12}\right)^2$	Substitute.
$36 = A$	Simplify.

▶ The area of $\triangle MNP$ is 36 square centimeters.

The figures are similar. Find the area of the figure on the right.

3.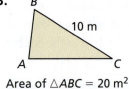

Area of $\triangle ABC = 20$ m²

4.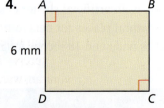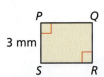

Area of $ABCD = 48$ mm²

12.1 Cross Sections of Solids

> **Learning Target:** Describe and draw cross sections.
>
> **Success Criteria:**
> - I can classify solids.
> - I can describe and draw cross sections.
> - I can solve real-life problems involving cross sections.

INVESTIGATE Describing Cross Sections

Work with a partner. When a plane intersects a solid, the intersection is called a *cross section*.

1. For each food, describe its shape. If you can cut the food into two congruent pieces, what shape would the cross section be? Compare your results with those of your classmates.

    a. wheel of cheese

    b. watermelon

    c. stick of butter

    d. cucumber

2. Describe how you can slice the wedge of cheese so that the cross section formed is the given shape.

    a. triangle
    b. rectangle
    c. trapezoid

3. Explain whether there is more than one way to slice the wedge of cheese in Exercise 2 to form a triangular cross section. Use drawings to support your answer.

Vocabulary
polyhedron
face
edge
vertex
cross section

Classifying Solids

A three-dimensional figure, or *solid*, is bounded by flat or curved surfaces that enclose a single region of space. A **polyhedron** is a solid that is bounded by polygons, called **faces**. An **edge** of a polyhedron is a line segment formed by the intersection of two faces. A **vertex** of a polyhedron is a point where three or more edges meet. The plural of polyhedron is *polyhedra* or *polyhedrons*.

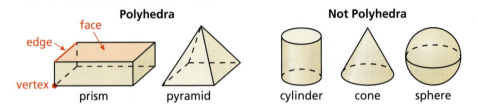

To name a prism or pyramid, use the shape of the *base*. The two bases of a prism are congruent polygons in parallel planes.

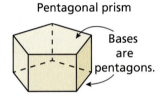
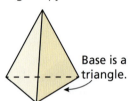

EXAMPLE 1   Classifying Solids

Tell whether each solid is a polyhedron. If it is, name the polyhedron.

a.   b.   c.

a. The solid is formed by polygons, so it is a polyhedron. The two parallel bases are congruent rectangles, so it is a rectangular prism.

b. The solid is formed by polygons, so it is a polyhedron. The base is a hexagon, so it is a hexagonal pyramid.

c. The cone has a curved surface, so it is not a polyhedron.

In-Class Practice

Self-Assessment

Tell whether the solid is a polyhedron. If it is, name the polyhedron.

1. 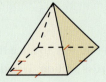   2. 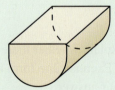   3.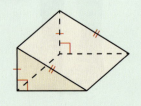

1 I don't understand yet.   **2** I can do it with help.   **3** I can do it on my own.   **4** I can teach someone.

Describing Cross Sections

Imagine a plane slicing through a solid. The intersection of the plane and the solid is a **cross section**. Here are three different cross sections of a cube.

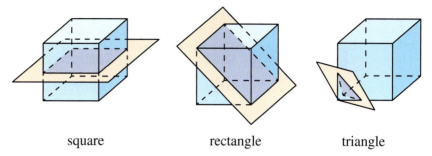

square   rectangle   triangle

EXAMPLE 2   **Describing Cross Sections**

Describe the shape formed by the intersection of the plane and the solid.

a. 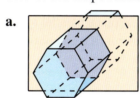   b. 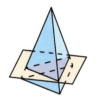   c.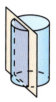

d.    e. 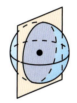   f.

a. The cross section of the prism is a hexagon.

b. The cross section the pyramid is a triangle.

c. The cross section the cylinder is a rectangle.

d. The cross section the cone is a circle.

e. The cross section the sphere is a circle.

f. The cross section the prism is a trapezoid.

In-Class Practice

Self-Assessment

Describe the shape formed by the intersection of the plane and the solid.

4.   5.   6.

1 I don't understand yet.   **2** I can do it with help.   **3** I can do it on my own.   **4** I can teach someone.

12.1   Cross Sections of Solids

Drawing Cross Sections

The Plane Intersection Postulate states that if two planes intersect, then their intersection is a line. This postulate can help you when drawing a cross section.

EXAMPLE 3 **Drawing a Cross Section**

Draw the cross section formed by a plane parallel to the base that contains the red line segment drawn on the square pyramid. What is the shape of the cross section?

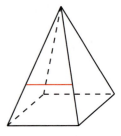

Visualize a horizontal plane parallel to the base that intersects the lateral face and passes through the red line segment.

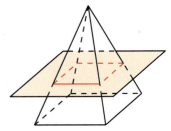

The horizontal plane is parallel to the base of the pyramid. So, draw each pair of parallel line segments where the plane intersects the lateral faces of the pyramid.

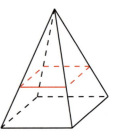

Shade the cross section.

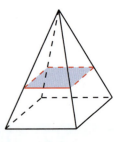

▶ The cross section is a square.

In-Class Practice

Self-Assessment

7. **WHAT IF?** Draw the cross section formed by a plane perpendicular to the base that contains the vertex of the square pyramid in Example 3. What is the shape of the cross section?

8. Describe how a plane can intersect the pyramid in Example 3 so that it forms a cross section that is (a) a trapezoid and (b) a line segment.

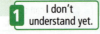

616   Chapter 12   Surface Area and Volume

Connections to Real Life

EXAMPLE 4 Finding the Perimeter and Area of a Cross Section

A machine at a sawmill cuts a 4-inch by 4-inch piece of wood lengthwise along its diagonal, as shown. Find the perimeter and area of the cross section formed by the cut.

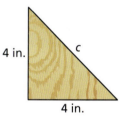
8.5 ft

Draw a diagram of the cross section.

It is a rectangle with a length of 8.5 feet, or 102 inches. Use the Pythagorean Theorem to find its width. The length and width of the end of the piece of wood is 4 inches.

$c^2 = a^2 + b^2$	Pythagorean Theorem
$c^2 = 4^2 + 4^2$	Substitute.
$c^2 = 16 + 16$	Multiply.
$c^2 = 32$	Add.
$c = \sqrt{32}$	Take the positive square root of each side.

The width of the rectangular cross section is $\sqrt{32}$ inches.

Perimeter of cross section

$P = 2\ell + 2w$

$= 2(102) + 2(\sqrt{32})$

≈ 215.31

Area of cross section

$A = \ell w$

$= 102 \cdot \sqrt{32}$

≈ 577

▶ The perimeter of the cross section is about 215.31 inches, and the area of the cross section is about 577 square inches.

Check Estimate to check that your answer is reasonable. The length of the cross section is about 9 feet, and its width is about 6 inches, or 0.5 foot.

Perimeter: $P = 2\ell + 2w = 2(9) + 2(0.5) = 19$ ft $= 228$ in. ✓

Area: $A = \ell w = 9 \cdot 0.5 = 4.5$ ft² $= 648$ in.² ✓

In-Class Practice

Self-Assessment

9. A 6-inch by 6-inch piece of wood that is 10.25 feet long is cut lengthwise along its diagonal. Find the perimeter and area of the cross section formed by the cut.

1 I don't understand yet. **2** I can do it with help. **3** I can do it on my own. **4** I can teach someone.

12.1 Practice with Calc Chat and Calc View

Tell whether the solid is a polyhedron. If it is, name the polyhedron. (See Example 1.)

1.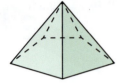
2.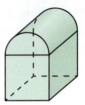
3.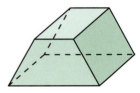

Sketch the polyhedron.

4. triangular prism
5. hexagonal prism
6. pentagonal pyramid

Name the figure that is described.

7. a pyramid with 6 faces
8. a prism with 10 faces
9. a prism with 9 edges

Describe the shape formed by the intersection of the plane and the solid. (See Example 2.)

10.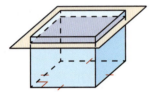
11.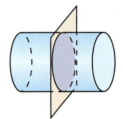
12.

13. **SMP.3 ERROR ANALYSIS** Describe and correct the error in identifying the solid.

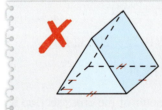

The base is a rectangle, so the solid is a rectangular pyramid.

14. **OPEN-ENDED** Give an example of a solid from which a triangular, hexagonal, and trapezoidal cross section can be formed.

Draw the cross section formed by the described plane that contains the red line segment drawn on the solid. What is the shape of the cross section? (See Example 3.)

15. plane is perpendicular to base

16. plane is parallel to bottom face

    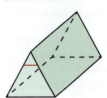

17. plane is perpendicular to bottom face

    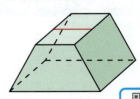

Draw the cross section formed by a vertical plane that divides the solid into two congruent parts. Is there more than one way to use a vertical plane to divide the figure into two congruent parts? If so, explain whether the cross section changes.

18.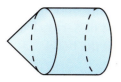

19.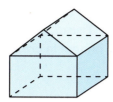

20.

21. **CONNECTION TO REAL LIFE** You cut the cake vertically into two congruent parts. (See Example 4.)

a. Find the perimeter and area of the cross section formed by the cut.

b. Find the surface area of the cake that is not frosted before the cut. How does the unfrosted surface area change after the cut?

c. Can the cake be cut into two congruent parts another way? If so, find the perimeter and area of the cross section formed by the cut.

22. **CONNECTION TO REAL LIFE** A mason uses a concrete saw to cut a block in the shape of a rectangular prism along a diagonal of a base, as shown. Describe the shape of the cross section formed by the cut. Explain whether the two pieces formed by the cut are congruent.

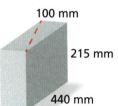

23. **SMP.8** Find the number of faces, edges, and vertices for each solid. Then write an equation that relates F, E, and V. Verify that your equation is true for several other solids in this section.

Solid	tetrahedron	cube	octahedron	dodecahedron	icosahedron
Faces, F					
Edges, E					
Vertices, V					

24. **SMP.6** Describe a solid that can be intersected by a plane to form the cross section shown. Explain how you form the cross section.

25. Can every plane that intersects a sphere form a circular cross section? Explain why or why not.

26. **SMP.1 DIG DEEPER** A plane that intersects a sphere is 7 meters from the center of the sphere. The radius of the sphere is 25 meters. Draw a diagram of this situation. Find the area of the cross section.

Interpreting Data

CT SCAN A computerized tomography (CT) scan is an imaging technique used to obtain detailed internal images of a body. During a CT scan, a machine takes a series of X-rays from different angles. A computer processes these images to create cross sections of the body.

27. Describe the X-ray images shown below.

28. Estimate the distance between successive cross sections.

29. How does a CT scan differ from an MRI scan?

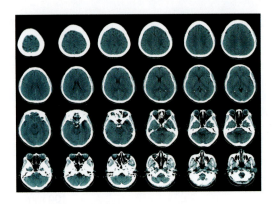

Review & Refresh

30. Explain how to prove that $\overline{AB} \cong \overline{CB}$.

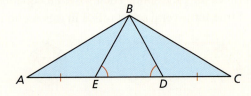

31. Tailors want to know the density of fabric when deciding what material to use when making clothing. A rectangular piece that is 36 inches long and 30 inches wide weighs 10 ounces. Find the density of the fabric in ounces per square yard.

32. Explain whether $\overline{AB}$ is tangent to $\odot C$.

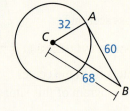

33. Solve the right triangle.

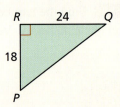

34. Verify that the segment lengths 39, 52, and 64 form a triangle. Is the triangle *acute*, *right*, or *obtuse*?

35. Find the area of the quadrilateral.

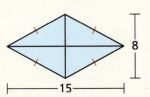

36. Find the area of a circle with a diameter of 13 centimeters.

12.2 Volumes of Prisms and Cylinders

Learning Target: Find and use volumes of prisms and cylinders.

Success Criteria:
- I can find volumes of prisms and cylinders.
- I can solve real-life problems involving volumes of prisms and cylinders.
- I can find surface areas and volumes of similar solids.

INVESTIGATE Finding Volumes of Prisms and Cylinders

Work with a partner. Recall that the *volume* of a right prism or a right cylinder is equal to the product of the area of a base and the height.

right prism 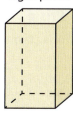   right cylinder

1. What does the volume of a solid represent?

2. Consider a deck of 52 cards. Each card is about $\frac{1}{100}$ inch thick. What is the volume of the deck of cards?

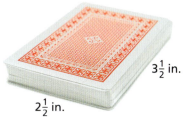

$3\frac{1}{2}$ in.

$2\frac{1}{2}$ in.

3. Consider two stacks of coins. Each coin has a diameter of 22 millimeters and a thickness of 1.78 millimeters. Compare the volumes of the stacks.

4. How can you find the volume of a prism or cylinder that is not a right prism or right cylinder?

Vocabulary
volume
Cavalieri's Principle
similar solids

Finding Volumes of Prisms and Cylinders

The **volume** of a solid is the number of cubic units contained in its interior. **Cavalieri's Principle**, named after Bonaventura Cavalieri (1598–1647), states that if two solids have the same height and the same cross-sectional area at every level, then they have the same volume. The prisms below have the same volume.

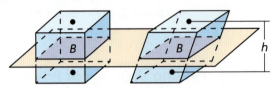

Key Concept

Volume of a Prism

The volume V of a prism is

$$V = Bh$$

where B is the area of a base and h is the height.

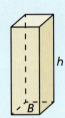 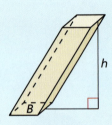

EXAMPLE 1 — Finding the Volume of a Prism

Find the volume of the prism.

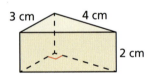

The area of a triangular base is $B = \frac{1}{2}(3)(4) = 6$ cm² and the height is $h = 2$ cm.

$V = Bh$ Formula for volume of a prism

$ = 6(2)$ Substitute.

$ = 12$ Simplify.

▶ The volume is 12 cubic centimeters.

In-Class Practice

Self-Assessment

1. Find the volume of the prism.

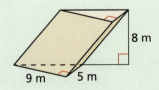

 I don't understand yet.   I can do it with help.   I can do it on my own.   I can teach someone.

Consider a cylinder with height h and base radius r, and a rectangular prism with the same height that has a square base with sides of length $r\sqrt{\pi}$.

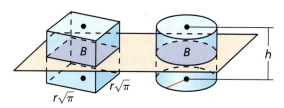

The cylinder and the prism have the same cross-sectional area, πr^2, at every level and the same height. By Cavalieri's Principle, the prism and the cylinder have the same volume. The volume of the prism is $V = Bh = \pi r^2 h$, so the volume of the cylinder is also $V = Bh = \pi r^2 h$.

Key Concept

Volume of a Cylinder

The volume V of a cylinder is

$$V = Bh = \pi r^2 h$$

where B is the area of a base, h is the height, and r is the radius of a base.

 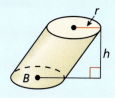

EXAMPLE 2 Finding the Volume of a Cylinder

Find the volume of the cylinder.

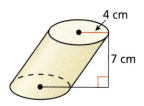

The dimensions of the cylinder are $r = 4$ cm and $h = 7$ cm.

$$V = \pi r^2 h = \pi(4)^2(7) = 112\pi \approx 351.86$$

▶ The volume is about 351.86 cubic centimeters.

In-Class Practice

Self-Assessment

Find the volume of the cylinder.

2. 5 in., 12.5 in.

3. 8 ft, 14 ft

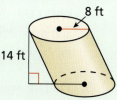

 I don't understand yet.
 I can do it with help.
 I can do it on my own.
4 I can teach someone.

12.2   Volumes of Prisms and Cylinders

Using Volumes of Prisms

EXAMPLE 3 **Finding the Height of a Rectangular Prism**

The rectangular chest has a volume of 72 cubic feet. What is the height of the chest?

The area of a rectangular base is $B = 6(4) = 24$ ft² and the volume is $V = 72$ ft³.

$V = Bh$	Formula for volume of a prism
$72 = 24h$	Substitute.
$3 = h$	Divide each side by 24.

▶ The height of the chest is 3 feet.

EXAMPLE 4 **Finding the Volume of a Composite Solid**

Find the volume of the concrete block.

The small rectangles are congruent. To find the area of the base, subtract two times the area of a small rectangle from the area of the large rectangle.

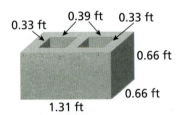

$$B = \text{Area of large rectangle} - 2 \cdot \text{Area of small rectangle}$$

$$= 1.31(0.66) - 2(0.33)(0.39)$$

$$= 0.6072$$

Using the formula for the volume of a prism, the volume is

$$V = Bh = 0.6072(0.66) \approx 0.40.$$

▶ The volume is about 0.40 cubic foot.

In-Class Practice

Self-Assessment

4. **WHAT IF?** In Example 3, you want the height to be 2.5 feet and the volume to be 25 cubic feet. What should the area of the base be? Give a possible length and width.

5. Find the volume of the composite solid.

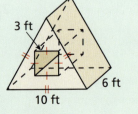

 I don't understand yet.   I can do it with help.   I can do it on my own.   I can teach someone.

Finding Surface Areas and Volumes of Similar Solids

Two solids of the same type with equal ratios of corresponding linear measures, such as heights or radii, are called **similar solids**. The ratio of the corresponding linear measures of two similar solids is called the *scale factor*. If two similar solids have a scale factor of k, then

- the ratio of their surface areas is equal to k^2.
- the ratio of their volumes is equal to k^3.

EXAMPLE 5   Finding the Surface Area and Volume of a Similar Solid

Cylinder A and cylinder B are similar. Find the surface area and volume of cylinder B.

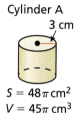
Cylinder A
3 cm
$S = 48\pi$ cm^2
$V = 45\pi$ cm^3

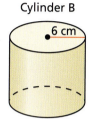
Cylinder B
6 cm

The scale factor is $k = \dfrac{\text{Radius of cylinder B}}{\text{Radius of cylinder A}}$

$= \dfrac{6}{3} = 2.$

Use the scale factor to find the surface area of cylinder B.

$\dfrac{\text{Surface area of cylinder B}}{\text{Surface area of cylinder A}} = k^2$ The ratio of the surface areas is k^2.

$\dfrac{\text{Surface area of cylinder B}}{48\pi} = 2^2$ Substitute.

Surface area of cylinder B $= 192\pi$ Multiply each side by 48π.

Use the scale factor to find the volume of cylinder B.

$\dfrac{\text{Volume of cylinder B}}{\text{Volume of cylinder A}} = k^3$ The ratio of the volumes is k^3.

$\dfrac{\text{Volume of cylinder B}}{45\pi} = 2^3$ Substitute.

Volume of cylinder B $= 360\pi$ Multiply each side by 45π.

▶ The surface area of cylinder B is 192π square centimeters. The volume of cylinder B is 360π cubic centimeters.

In-Class Practice

Self-Assessment

6. Prism C and prism D are similar. Find the surface area and volume of prism D.

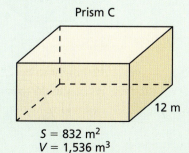
Prism C
12 m
$S = 832$ m^2
$V = 1,536$ m^3

Prism D
3 m

 I don't understand yet.   I can do it with help.   I can do it on my own.   I can teach someone.

12.2 Practice

with CalcChat and CalcView

Find the volume of the prism. (See Example 1.)

1.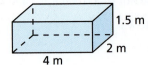

2.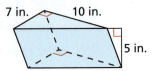

Find the volume of the cylinder. (See Example 2.)

3.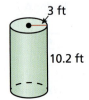

4.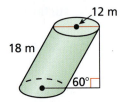

Find the missing dimension of the prism or cylinder. (See Example 3.)

5. Volume = 560 ft^3

6. Volume = 80 cm^3

7. Volume = 72.66 in.^{3}

8. Volume = 1,696.5 m^3

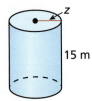

Find the volume of the composite solid. (See Example 4.)

9.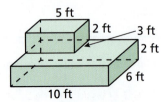

10.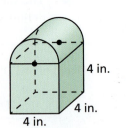

11.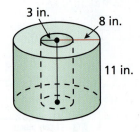

12.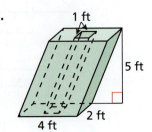

626   Chapter 12   Surface Area and Volume

The solids are similar. Find the surface area and volume of solid B. (See Example 5.)

13. Prism A 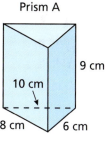 Prism B

S = 264 cm²
V = 216 cm³

14. Cylinder A  Cylinder B

S = 1,056π in.²
V = 4,608π in.³

15. **CONNECTION TO REAL LIFE** The Great Blue Hole is a cylindrical trench located off the coast of Belize. It is approximately 1,000 feet wide and 400 feet deep. About how many gallons of water does the Great Blue Hole contain? (1 ft³ ≈ 7.48 gallons)

16. **CONNECTION TO REAL LIFE** You melt a rectangular block of wax to make candles. How many candles of the given shape can you make using a block that measures 10 centimeters by 9 centimeters by 20 centimeters?

STEM Video: Paper Measurements

17. An aquarium shaped like a rectangular prism has a length of 30 inches, a width of 10 inches, and a height of 20 inches. You fill the aquarium $\frac{3}{4}$ full with water. When you submerge a rock in the aquarium, the water level rises 0.25 inch. Find the volume of the rock. How many rocks of this size can you place in the aquarium before water spills out?

18. **SMP.7** How can you change the edge length of a cube so that the volume is reduced by 40%?

19. **SMP.1 DIG DEEPER** Estimate the volume of the bag of yellow onions shown. Explain your method.

20. **SMP.6** The height of cylinder X is twice the height of cylinder Y. The radius of cylinder X is half the radius of cylinder Y. Compare the surface areas and volumes of cylinder X and cylinder Y. Justify your answer.

21. **CONNECT CONCEPTS** Find the volume of the solid shown. The bases are sectors of circles.

 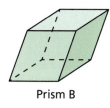

Prism A   Prism B

22. The two rectangular prisms have the same height, and the bases of prism A are congruent to the bases of prism B. Do the prisms have the same volume? the same surface area? Explain.

Interpreting Data

CRUDE OIL TANK Crude oil is the naturally occurring liquid form of petroleum. Crude oil is refined into other fuels and oil products. It is often stored in cylindrical oil tanks.

23. The tank shown has a height and diameter of 20 meters. Estimate the volume of the tank.

24. A common measure of volume used for oil is a *barrel*. A cubic meter is equivalent to 6.29 barrels. Estimate the volume of the tank in terms of barrels.

25. A barrel is equivalent to 42 gallons. How many gallons can the tank hold?

Review & Refresh

26. In the diagram, $JKLM \cong PQRS$. Find the values of x and y.

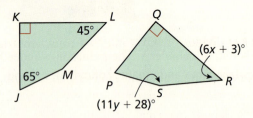

Tell whether the solid is a polyhedron. If it is, name the polyhedron.

27.

28.

29. Find the value of x.

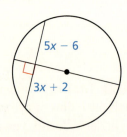

30. The state of Colorado has a population of about 5.77 million people. Find the population density in people per square mile.

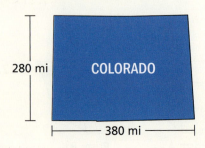

12.3 Volumes of Pyramids

> **Learning Target:** Find and use volumes of pyramids.
>
> **Success Criteria:**
> - I can find volumes of pyramids.
> - I can use volumes of pyramids to find measures.
> - I can find volumes of similar pyramids.
> - I can find volumes of composite solids containing pyramids.

INVESTIGATE Finding the Volume Formula for Pyramids

SMP.1 Work with a partner. Consider a triangular prism with parallel, congruent bases $\triangle JKL$ and $\triangle MNP$. You can divide this triangular prism into three triangular pyramids.

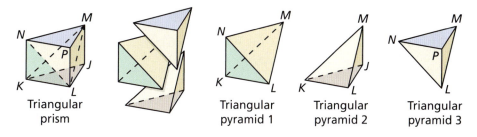

1. You can combine triangular pyramids 1 and 2 to form pyramid Q. Explain why its base is a parallelogram.

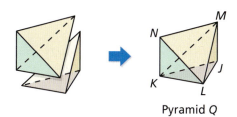

Pyramid Q

2. Explain why diagonal $\overline{KM}$ divides $\square JKNM$ into two congruent triangles.

3. You can divide any cross section parallel to $\square JKNM$ into two congruent triangles that are the cross sections of triangular pyramids 1 and 2. What can you use Cavalieri's Principle to conclude?

4. You can combine triangular pyramids 1 and 3 to form pyramid R. Use pyramid R to show that triangular pyramids 1 and 3 have the same volume.

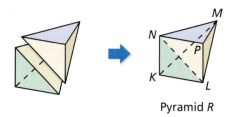

Pyramid R

5. Use your results to write a formula for the volume of a pyramid.

Finding Volumes of Pyramids

> ## Key Concept
>
> **Volume of a Pyramid**
>
> The volume V of a pyramid is
>
> $$V = \tfrac{1}{3}Bh$$
>
> where B is the area of the base and h is the height.

 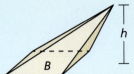

EXAMPLE 1 Finding Volume of a Pyramid

a. Find the volume of the pyramid.

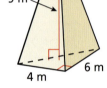

$V = \tfrac{1}{3}Bh$ Write formula for volume of a pyramid.

$= \tfrac{1}{3}\left(\tfrac{1}{2} \cdot 4 \cdot 6\right)(9)$ Substitute.

$= \tfrac{1}{3}(12)(9)$ Multiply.

$= 36$ Multiply.

▶ The volume is 36 cubic meters.

b. Find the volume of the pyramid.

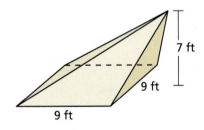

$V = \tfrac{1}{3}Bh$ Write formula for volume of a pyramid.

$= \tfrac{1}{3}(9 \cdot 9)(7)$ Substitute.

$= \tfrac{1}{3}(81)(7)$ Multiply.

$= 189$ Multiply.

▶ The volume is 189 cubic feet.

In-Class Practice

Self-Assessment

Find the volume of the pyramid.

1.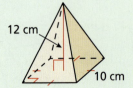

2.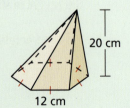

 I don't understand yet.   I can do it with help.   I can do it on my own.   I can teach someone.

Using Volumes of Pyramids

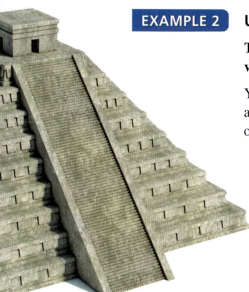

EXAMPLE 2   **Using the Volume of a Pyramid**

The Mayan pyramid El Castillo has a height of about 30 meters and a volume of about 30,580 cubic meters. Find the side length of the base.

You can see in the photo that El Castillo is approximately shaped like a square pyramid. So, let the side length of the base be x. Then the area of the base is x^2.

$V = \frac{1}{3}Bh$	Write formula for volume of a pyramid.
$30{,}580 \approx \frac{1}{3}x^2(30)$	Substitute.
$30{,}580 \approx 10x^2$	Simplify.
$3{,}058 \approx x^2$	Divide each side by 10.
$55.3 \approx x$	Take the positive square root of each side.

▶ The side length of the base is about 55 meters.

EXAMPLE 3   **Using the Volume of a Pyramid**

Find the height of the triangular pyramid.

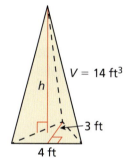

The area of the base is $B = \frac{1}{2}(4)(3) = 6$ ft^2 and the volume is $V = 14$ ft^3.

$V = \frac{1}{3}Bh$	Write formula for volume of a pyramid.
$14 = \frac{1}{3}(6)h$	Substitute.
$7 = h$	Solve for h.

▶ The height is 7 feet.

In-Class Practice

Self-Assessment

3. The volume of a square pyramid is 75 cubic meters and the height is 9 meters. Find the side length of the base.

4. Find the height of the triangular pyramid at the right.

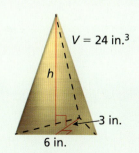

Finding Volumes of Similar Solids and Composites

EXAMPLE 4 Finding the Volume of a Similar Solid

Pyramid A and pyramid B are similar. Find the volume of pyramid B.

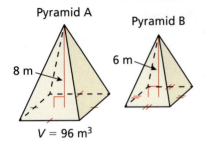

The scale factor is $k = \dfrac{\text{Height of pyramid B}}{\text{Height of pyramid A}} = \dfrac{6}{8} = \dfrac{3}{4}$.

Use the scale factor to find the volume of pyramid B.

$\dfrac{\text{Volume of pyramid B}}{\text{Volume of pyramid A}} = k^3$ The ratio of the volumes is k^3.

$\dfrac{\text{Volume of pyramid B}}{96} = \left(\dfrac{3}{4}\right)^3$ Substitute.

Volume of pyramid B $= 40.5$ Multiply each side by 96.

▶ The volume of pyramid B is 40.5 cubic meters.

EXAMPLE 5 Finding the Volume of a Composite Solid

Find the volume of the composite solid.

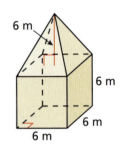

$\begin{aligned}\boxed{\text{Volume of solid}} &= \boxed{\text{Volume of cube}} + \boxed{\text{Volume of pyramid}}\end{aligned}$

$= s^3 + \tfrac{1}{3}Bh$ Write formulas.

$= 6^3 + \tfrac{1}{3}(6)^2 \cdot 6$ Substitute.

$= 216 + 72$ Simplify.

$= 288$ Add.

▶ The volume is 288 cubic meters.

In-Class Practice

Self-Assessment

5. Pyramid C and pyramid D are similar. Find the volume of pyramid D.

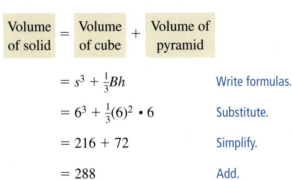

6. Find the volume of the composite solid.

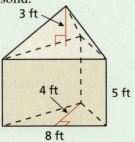

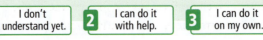

12.3 Practice

Find the volume of the pyramid. (See Example 1.)

1.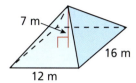

2.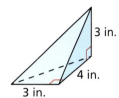

Find the value of x. (See Examples 2 and 3.)

3. Volume = 120 m³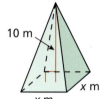

4. Volume = 480 in.³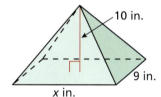

5. Volume = 198 yd³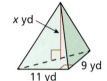

6. Volume = 15 ft³

The pyramids are similar. Find the volume of pyramid B. (See Example 4.)

7.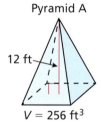

8.

Find the volume of the composite solid. (See Example 5.)

9.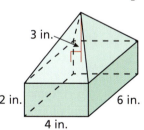

10.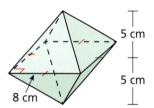

11. **CONNECTION TO REAL LIFE** Nautical deck prisms were once used as a safe way to illuminate decks on ships. This prism is composed of three solids: a regular hexagonal prism with an edge length of 3.5 inches and a height of 1.5 inches, a regular hexagonal prism with an edge length of 3.25 inches and a height of 0.25 inch, and a regular hexagonal pyramid with an edge length of 3.25 inches and a height of 3 inches. Find the volume of the deck prism.

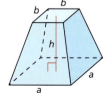

12. **SMP.1 DIG DEEPER** A *frustum* of a pyramid is the part of the pyramid that lies between the base and a plane parallel to the base, as shown. Write a formula for the volume of the frustum of a square pyramid in terms of a, b, and h. Explain your method.

Interpreting Data

The Mona Lisa by Leonardo da Vinci has been on display at the Louvre since 1797. It is one of the most famous and valuable paintings in the world.

LOUVRE PYRAMID The Louvre Pyramid in Paris is 71 feet tall and has a square base with side lengths of 112 feet. It has a total of 673 pieces of glass, of which 603 are rhombuses and 70 are triangles. It is similar to the Great Pyramid of Giza and the Luxor Pyramid in Las Vegas.

13. Find the volume of the Louvre Pyramid.

14. The side lengths of the square base of the Great Pyramid of Giza are 756 feet. Find its volume.

15. The Luxor Pyramid in Las Vegas has a height of 350 feet. Find its volume.

Review & Refresh

Find the value of x.

16.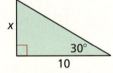

17.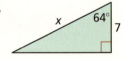

18. Find the volume of the cylinder.

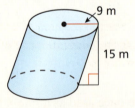

19. Describe the shape formed by the intersection of the plane and the solid.

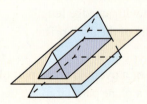

20. The diagram shows the location of a campsite and a hiking trail. You want to choose a campsite that is at least 100 feet from the trail. Explain whether this campsite meets your requirement.

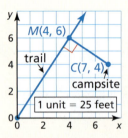

21. Let p be "it is Thanksgiving" and let q be "it is November." Write the conditional statement $p \rightarrow q$ and the contrapositive $\sim q \rightarrow \sim p$ in words. Then decide whether each statement is true or false.

22. A circular region has a population of about 175,000 people and a population density of about 580 people per square mile. Find the radius of the region.

634   Chapter 12   Surface Area and Volume

12.4 Surface Areas and Volumes of Cones

Learning Target: Find and use surface areas and volumes of cones.

Success Criteria:
- I can find surface areas of cones.
- I can find volumes of cones.
- I can find the volumes of similar cones.
- I can find the volumes of composite solids containing cones.

INVESTIGATE Finding the Volume Formula for Cones

Work with a partner.

1. The base of a pyramid is a regular polygon that is inscribed in the base of a cone. The pyramid and the cone also share the same vertex. How does the volume of the pyramid compare to the volume of the cone?

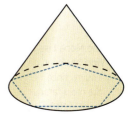

2. Describe what happens to the pyramid as you increase the number of sides of the polygon inscribed in the base of the cone.

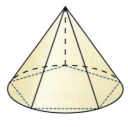 

3. Use your observations in Exercise 2 to write a formula for the volume V of a cone in terms of r, the radius of the base. Explain your reasoning.

4. The ratio of the area of a sector to the area of a circle is equal to the ratio of the arc length to the circumference of the circle. Use a proportion to find the area of the sector in the net.

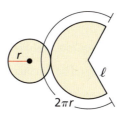

5. Use the formula for area of a circle and the formula for area of a sector to write a formula for the surface area of a cone.

Vocabulary

lateral surface of a cone

Finding Surface Areas of Right Cones

A *circular cone*, or *cone*, has a circular *base* and a *vertex* that is not in the same plane as the base. The *altitude*, or *height*, is the perpendicular distance between the vertex and the base. In a *right cone*, the height meets the base at its center and the *slant height* is the distance between the vertex and a point on the base edge.

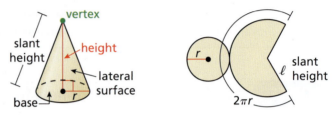

The **lateral surface of a cone** consists of all segments that connect the vertex with points on the base edge. When you cut along the slant height and lay the right cone flat, you get the net shown above.

Key Concept

Surface Area of a Right Cone

The surface area S of a right cone is

$$S = \pi r^2 + \pi r \ell$$

where r is the radius of the base and ℓ is the slant height.

EXAMPLE 1 Finding Surface Areas of Right Cones

Find the surface area of the right cone.

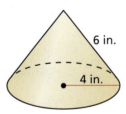

$S = \pi r^2 + \pi r \ell$ Write formula for surface area of a cone.

$= \pi \cdot 4^2 + \pi(4)(6)$ Substitute.

$= 40\pi$ Simplify.

≈ 125.66 Use technology.

▶ The surface area is about 125.66 square inches.

In-Class Practice

Self-Assessment

1. Find the surface area of the right cone.

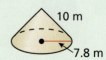

 I don't understand yet.   I can do it with help.   I can do it on my own.   I can teach someone.

636   Chapter 12   Surface Area and Volume

Finding Volumes of Cones

Consider a cone with a regular polygon inscribed in the base. The pyramid with the same vertex as the cone has volume $V = \frac{1}{3}Bh$. As you increase the number of sides of the polygon, it approaches the base of the cone and the pyramid approaches the cone. The volume approaches $\frac{1}{3}\pi r^2 h$ as the base area B approaches πr^2.

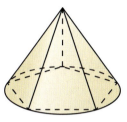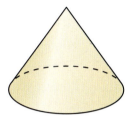

Key Concept

Volume of a Cone

The volume V of a cone is

$$V = \tfrac{1}{3}Bh = \tfrac{1}{3}\pi r^2 h$$

where B is the area of the base, h is the height, and r is the radius of the base.

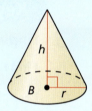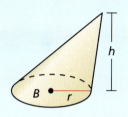

EXAMPLE 2 Finding the Volume of a Cone

Find the volume of the cone.

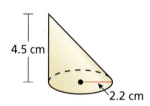

$V = \tfrac{1}{3}\pi r^2 h$ Write formula for volume of a cone.

$= \tfrac{1}{3}\pi \cdot (2.2)^2 \cdot 4.5$ Substitute.

$= 7.26\pi$ Simplify.

≈ 22.81 Use technology.

▶ The volume is about 22.81 cubic centimeters.

In-Class Practice

Self-Assessment

Find the volume of the cone.

2.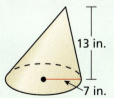

3.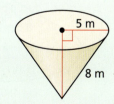

 I don't understand yet.   I can do it with help.   I can do it on my own.   I can teach someone.

12.4 Surface Areas and Volumes of Cones

Using Similar Solids and Composite Solids

EXAMPLE 3 **Finding the Surface Area and Volume of a Similar Solid**

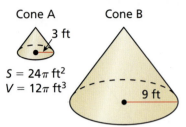

Cone A
3 ft
$S = 24\pi$ ft^2
$V = 12\pi$ ft^3

Cone B
9 ft

Cone A and cone B are similar. Find the surface area and volume of cone B.

The scale factor is $k = \dfrac{\text{Radius of cone B}}{\text{Radius of cone A}} = \dfrac{9}{3} = 3$.

Use the scale factor to find the surface area and volume of cone B.

$\dfrac{\text{Surface area of cone B}}{\text{Surface area of cone A}} = k^2$ Write equations. $\dfrac{\text{Volume of cone B}}{\text{Volume of cone A}} = k^3$

$\dfrac{\text{Surface area of cone B}}{24\pi} = 3^2$ Substitute. $\dfrac{\text{Volume of cone B}}{12\pi} = 3^3$

Surface area of cone B $= 216\pi$ Solve. Volume of cone B $= 324\pi$

▶ The surface area of cone B is 216π square feet. The volume of cone B is 324π cubic feet.

EXAMPLE 4 **Finding the Volume of a Composite Solid**

Find the volume of the composite solid.

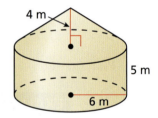

4 m
5 m
6 m

Let h_1 be the height of the cylinder and let h_2 be the height of the cone.

$\begin{aligned}
\text{Volume of solid} &= \text{Volume of cylinder} + \text{Volume of cone} \\
&= \pi r^2 h_1 + \tfrac{1}{3}\pi r^2 h_2 & \text{Write formulas.} \\
&= \pi \cdot 6^2 \cdot 5 + \tfrac{1}{3}\pi \cdot 6^2 \cdot 4 & \text{Substitute.} \\
&= 180\pi + 48\pi & \text{Simplify.} \\
&= 228\pi & \text{Add.} \\
&\approx 716.28 & \text{Use technology.}
\end{aligned}$

▶ The volume is about 716.28 cubic meters.

In-Class Practice

Self-Assessment

4. Cone C and cone D are similar. Find the surface area and volume of cone D.

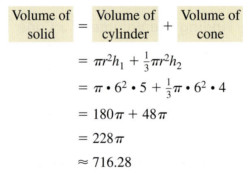

Cone C
8 cm
$S = 480\pi$ cm^2
$V = 600\pi$ cm^3

Cone D
2 cm

5. Find the volume of the composite solid.

5 cm
10 cm
3 cm

| 1 | I don't understand yet. | 2 | I can do it with help. | 3 | I can do it on my own. | 4 | I can teach someone. |

12.4 Practice

Find the surface area of the right cone. (See Example 1.)

▶ **1.** A right cone has a radius of 8 inches and a slant height of 16 inches.

2. A right cone has a diameter of 11.2 feet and a height of 9.2 feet.

Find the volume of the cone. (See Example 2.)

▶ **3.** A right cone has a radius of 10 millimeters and a height of 13 millimeters.

4. A cone has a diameter of 11.5 inches and a height of 15.2 inches.

The cones are similar. Find the surface area and volume of cone B. (See Example 3.)

▶ **5.**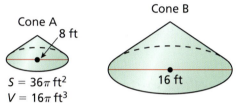

6.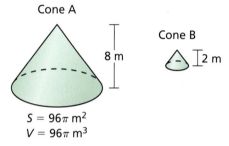

Find the volume of the composite solid. (See Example 4.)

▶ **7.**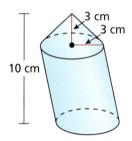

8.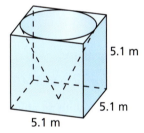

9. **SMP.7** A cone has height h and a base with radius r. You want to change the cone so its volume is doubled. What is the new height if you change only the height? What is the new radius if you change only the radius? Explain.

10. **SMP.3** In the figure, the two cylinders are congruent. The combined height of the two smaller cones equals the height of the larger cone. Does this mean the total volume of the two smaller cones is equal to the volume of the larger cone? Justify your answer.

11. A *frustum* of a cone is the part of the cone that lies between the base and a plane parallel to the base, as shown. Write a formula for the volume of the frustum of a cone in terms of a, b, and h.

Interpreting Data

HOURGLASS An hourglass is an instrument used to measure time. It consists of two glass bulbs connected vertically by a narrow neck that allows a regulated flow of sand from the upper bulb to the lower one.

12. Find the volume of the sand in the upper cone when $t = 0$ minutes.

13. It takes 60 minutes for all the sand to fall from the upper cone to the lower cone. After 30 minutes the sand in the upper cone is a perfect cone shape. Find the height of this shape.

Review & Refresh

Find the indicated measure.

14. area of a circle with a radius of 7 feet

15. diameter of a circle with an area of 256π square meters

16. Find the volume of the cylinder.

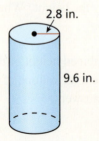

17. Two polygons are similar. The perimeter of one polygon is 54 inches. The ratio of corresponding side lengths is $\frac{2}{3}$. Find two possible perimeters of the other polygon.

18. You cut an orange in half. Find the perimeter and area of the cross section formed by the cut.

19. Find the volume of the pyramid.

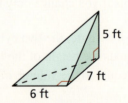

20. Tell whether $\widehat{JM} \cong \widehat{KL}$.

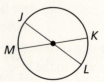

640 Chapter 12 Surface Area and Volume

12.5 Surface Areas and Volumes of Spheres

Learning Target: Find and use surface areas and volumes of spheres.

Success Criteria:
- I can find surface areas of spheres.
- I can find volumes of spheres.
- I can find the volumes of composite solids.

INVESTIGATE Finding a Surface Area Formula for Spheres

Work with a partner.

1. Two identical pieces of material make up the covering of a baseball with radius r. Use the circle with radius r and the covering of the ball to estimate the surface area S of the ball in terms of r.

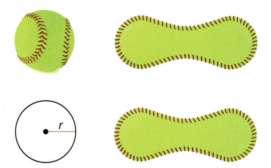

INVESTIGATE Finding a Volume Formula for Spheres

SMP.1 Work with a partner. The figure shows a hemisphere and a cylinder with a cone removed. A plane parallel to their bases intersects the solids z units above their bases.

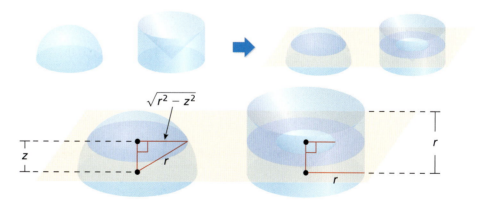

2. Use the AA Similarity Theorem to show that the radius of the cross section of the cone at height z is z.

3. Show that the area of the cross section formed by the plane is $\pi(r^2 - z^2)$ for both solids. What can you conclude using Cavalieri's Principle?

4. Write a formula for the volume V of a sphere with radius r.

Vocabulary
chord of a sphere
great circle

Finding Surface Areas of Spheres

A *sphere* is the set of all points in space equidistant from a given point. This point is called the *center* of the sphere. A *radius* of a sphere is a segment from the center to a point on the sphere. A **chord of a sphere** is a segment whose endpoints are on the sphere. A *diameter* of a sphere is a chord that contains the center.

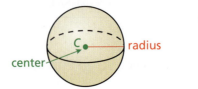
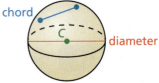

If a plane intersects a sphere, then the intersection is either a single point or a circle. If the plane contains the center of the sphere, then the intersection is a **great circle** of the sphere. The circumference of a great circle is the circumference of the sphere. Every great circle of a sphere separates the sphere into two congruent halves called *hemispheres*.

Key Concept

Surface Area of a Sphere

The surface area S of a sphere is

$$S = 4\pi r^2$$

where r is the radius of the sphere.

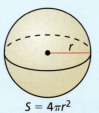

$S = 4\pi r^2$

EXAMPLE 1   Finding the Surface Area of a Sphere

Find the surface area of the sphere.

$S = 4\pi r^2$	Formula for surface area of a sphere
$= 4\pi(8)^2$	Substitute 8 for r.
$= 256\pi$	Simplify.
≈ 804.25	Use technology.

▶ The surface area is about 804.25 square inches.

In-Class Practice

Self-Assessment

Find the surface area of the sphere with the given radius or diameter.

1. radius = 6 yd
2. diameter = 40 ft

EXAMPLE 2 Finding the Surface Area of a Sphere

Find the surface area of the sphere.

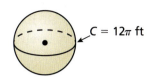

The circumference is 12π feet, so the radius of the sphere is $\dfrac{12\pi}{2\pi} = 6$ feet.

$S = 4\pi r^2$ Formula for surface area of a sphere

$ = 4\pi(6)^2$ Substitute 6 for r.

$ = 144\pi$ Simplify.

$ \approx 452.39$ Use technology.

▶ The surface area is about 452.39 square feet.

EXAMPLE 3 Finding a Length in a Sphere

Find the diameter of the sphere.

$S = 20.25\pi$ cm²

$S = 4\pi r^2$ Formula for surface area of a sphere

$20.25\pi = 4\pi r^2$ Substitute 20.25π for S.

$5.0625 = r^2$ Divide each side by 4π.

$2.25 = r$ Take the positive square root of each side.

▶ The diameter is $2r = 2 \cdot 2.25 = 4.5$ centimeters.

In-Class Practice
Self-Assessment

Find the surface area of the sphere.

3.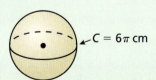

4.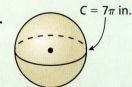

5. A sphere has a surface area of 30π square meters. Find the radius of the sphere.

12.5   Surface Areas and Volumes of Spheres

Finding Volumes of Spheres

In the Investigate, you used a hemisphere and cone to find a formula for the volume of a sphere. You can also use a sphere and a cylinder that has a pair of cones removed. Each solid has the same height and the same cross-sectional area at every level. So, by Cavalieri's Principle, they have the same volume.

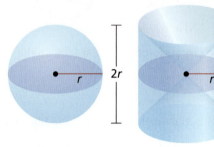

$$V = \pi r^2(2r) - 2\left(\frac{1}{3}\pi r^2 \cdot r\right)$$
$$= 2\pi r^3 - \frac{2}{3}\pi r^3$$
$$= \frac{4}{3}\pi r^3$$

Key Concept

Volume of a Sphere

The volume V of a sphere is

$$V = \frac{4}{3}\pi r^3$$

where r is the radius of the sphere.

EXAMPLE 4 Finding the Volume of a Sphere

Find the volume of the soccer ball.

4.5 in.

$V = \frac{4}{3}\pi r^3$	Formula for volume of a sphere
$= \frac{4}{3}\pi(4.5)^3$	Substitute 4.5 for r.
$= 121.5\pi$	Simplify.
≈ 381.70	Use technology.

▶ The volume of the soccer ball is about 381.70 cubic inches.

In-Class Practice

Self-Assessment

Find the volume of the sphere.

6. 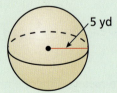 5 yd

7.  36 in.

| 1 | I don't understand yet. | 2 | I can do it with help. | 3 | I can do it on my own. | 4 | I can teach someone. |

EXAMPLE 5 Finding the Volume of a Sphere

The surface area of a sphere is 324π square centimeters. Find the volume of the sphere.

Use the surface area to find the radius.

$S = 4\pi r^2$ — Formula for surface area of a sphere

$324\pi = 4\pi r^2$ — Substitute 324π for S.

$81 = r^2$ — Divide each side by 4π.

$9 = r$ — Take the positive square root of each side.

The radius is 9 centimeters. Use the radius to find the volume.

$V = \frac{4}{3}\pi r^3$ — Formula for volume of a sphere

$= \frac{4}{3}\pi(9)^3$ — Substitute 9 for r.

$= 972\pi$ — Simplify.

$\approx 3{,}053.63$ — Use technology.

▶ The volume is about 3,053.63 cubic centimeters.

EXAMPLE 6 Finding the Volume of a Composite Solid

Find the volume of the composite solid.

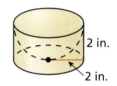

Volume of solid = Volume of cylinder − Volume of hemisphere

$= \pi r^2 h - \frac{1}{2}\left(\frac{4}{3}\pi r^3\right)$ — Write formulas.

$= \pi(2)^2(2) - \frac{1}{2}\left(\frac{4}{3}\pi(2)^3\right)$ — Substitute 2 for r and 2 for h.

$= 8\pi - \frac{16}{3}\pi$ — Multiply.

$= \frac{24}{3}\pi - \frac{16}{3}\pi$ — Rewrite using a common denominator.

$= \frac{8}{3}\pi$ — Subtract.

≈ 8.38 — Use technology.

▶ The volume is about 8.38 cubic inches.

In-Class Practice

Self-Assessment

8. The surface area of a sphere is 576π square centimeters. Find the volume of the sphere.

9. Find the volume of the composite solid at the right.

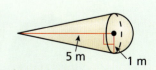

 I don't understand yet.   I can do it with help.   I can do it on my own.   I can teach someone.

12.5 Surface Areas and Volumes of Spheres

12.5 Practice

Find the surface area of the sphere. (See Examples 1 and 2.)

1.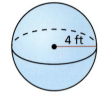

2.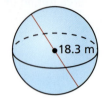

3.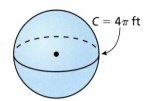

Find the indicated measure. (See Example 3.)

4. Find the radius of a sphere with a surface area of 4π square feet.

5. Find the diameter of a sphere with a surface area of 900π square meters.

6. Find the radius and diameter of a sphere with a surface area of 196π square centimeters.

Find the volume of the sphere. (See Example 4.)

7.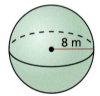

8.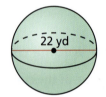

9.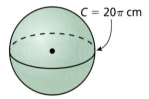

10. **SMP.3 ERROR ANALYSIS** Describe and correct the error in finding the volume of the sphere.

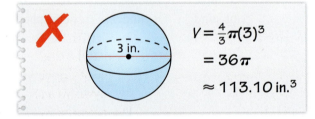

Find the surface area and volume of the hemisphere.

11.

12.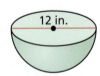

13.

Approximate the surface area and volume of the ball.

14. bowling ball

$d = 8.5$ in.

15. softball

$C = 12$ in.

16. golf ball

$d = 1.7$ in.

Find the volume of the sphere with the given surface area. (See Example 5.)

▶ **17.** Surface area = 16π ft²

18. Surface area = 484π cm²

Find the volume of the composite solid. (See Example 6.)

▶ **19.**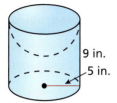

20.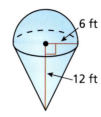

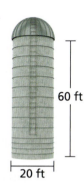

21. **CONNECTION TO REAL LIFE** A silo has the dimensions shown. The top of the silo is a hemisphere. Find the volume of the silo.

22. Three tennis balls are stored in a cylindrical container with a height of 8 inches and a radius of 1.43 inches. The circumference of a tennis ball is 8 inches. Find the amount of space within the cylinder not taken up by the tennis balls.

23. **SMP.8 CONNECT CONCEPTS** Copy and complete the table shown for a sphere. Compare the ratios of the surface areas. Then compare the ratios of the volumes. Explain whether spheres are *always*, *sometimes*, or *never* similar.

Radius	Surface area	Volume
3 in.	36π in.²	36π in.³
4 in.		
5 in.		
6 in.		

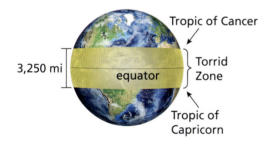

24. **CONNECTION TO REAL LIFE** The Torrid Zone on Earth is the area between the Tropic of Cancer and the Tropic of Capricorn. A meteorite is equally likely to hit anywhere on Earth. Estimate the probability that the meteorite will land in the Torrid Zone. (The radius of Earth is about 4,000 miles.)

25. **PERFORMANCE TASK** The propane tank shown is used as the primary heat source for your residence. Research to estimate the amount of propane that you will use each year. Then estimate your average monthly propane cost. About how often will the tank need to be refilled?

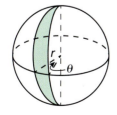

26. **DIG DEEPER** A *spherical lune* is the region between two great circles of a sphere. Find the formula for the surface area of a lune.

27. **DIG DEEPER** A sphere with a radius of 2 inches is inscribed in a right cone with a height of 6 inches. Find the surface area and the volume of the cone.

Interpreting Data

THE BLUE PLANET Earth is called the "Blue Planet" due to the abundant water on its surface. Human bodies are mostly made of water. While humans often take liquid water for granted, it is a rare commodity in our solar system.

28. The radius of Earth is about 4,000 miles. Estimate its surface area.

29. Use the circle graph to estimate the surface area of Earth that is covered by (a) water and (b) mountains.

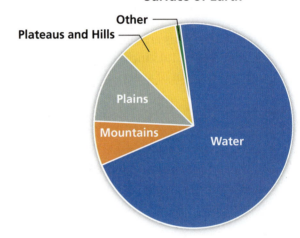

Review & Refresh

30. The pyramids are similar. Find the volume of pyramid B.

$V = 120$ in.^{3}

31. Find the missing dimension of the cylinder.

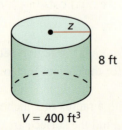

$V = 400$ ft^3

32. In rectangle *WXYZ*, $WY = 4x + 7$ and $XZ = 6x - 3$. Find the lengths of the diagonals of *WXYZ*.

33. Explain whether $\overline{KM} \parallel \overline{JN}$.

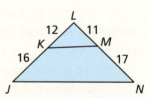

34. Find the surface area and the volume of the cone.

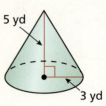

12.6 Modeling with Surface Area and Volume

Learning Target: Understand the concept of density and modeling with volume.

Success Criteria:
- I can explain what density means.
- I can use the formula for density to solve problems.
- I can use geometric shapes to model objects.
- I can solve modeling problems.

INVESTIGATE   Finding Densities

Work with a partner.

1. Approximate the volume of each object with the given mass. Then find the mass per unit of volume, or *density,* of each object.

   a. Brick: 2.3 kg

   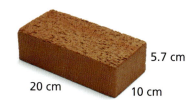

   b. Log: 18.1 kg

   c. Golf ball: 45.9 g

   d. Cork: 2.6 g

2. Objects with a density greater than 1 gram per cubic centimeter will sink in fresh water. The objects with a density less than 1 gram per cubic centimeter will float in fresh water. Which of the object(s) in Exercise 1 will float in fresh water?

3. An egg sinks in fresh water, but it floats in saltwater. Why is this?

Vocabulary
density

Using Volume Formulas

Density is the amount of matter that an object has in a given unit of volume. The density of an object is calculated by dividing its mass by its volume.

$$\text{Density} = \frac{\text{Mass}}{\text{Volume}}$$

Different materials have different densities, so density can be used to distinguish between materials that look similar. For example, table salt and sugar look alike. However, table salt has a density of 2.16 grams per cubic centimeter, while sugar has a density of 1.58 grams per cubic centimeter.

EXAMPLE 1 Using the Formula for Density

The diagram shows the dimensions of a standard gold bar at Fort Knox. Gold has a density of about 19.3 grams per cubic centimeter. Find the mass of the gold bar.

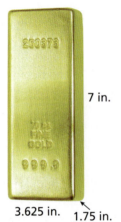

7 in.
3.625 in.   1.75 in.

Convert the dimensions to centimeters using 1 inch = 2.54 centimeters.

Length: $7 \text{ in.} \cdot \dfrac{2.54 \text{ cm}}{1 \text{ in.}} = 17.78 \text{ cm}$

Width: $3.625 \text{ in.} \cdot \dfrac{2.54 \text{ cm}}{1 \text{ in.}} = 9.2075 \text{ cm}$

Height: $1.75 \text{ in.} \cdot \dfrac{2.54 \text{ cm}}{1 \text{ in.}} = 4.445 \text{ cm}$

Let x represent the mass (in grams) of the gold bar. Use the formula for density to find x. Because the gold bar is shaped like a rectangular prism, use $V = Bh = \ell wh$ for the volume.

$\text{Density} = \dfrac{\text{Mass}}{\text{Volume}}$ .... Formula for density

$19.3 \approx \dfrac{x}{17.78(9.2075)(4.445)}$ .... Substitute.

$14{,}044 \approx x$ .... Solve for x.

▶ The mass of the gold bar is about 14,044 grams.

In-Class Practice

Self-Assessment

1. A concrete cylinder has a radius of 24 inches and a height of 32 inches. The density of concrete is 2.3 grams per cubic centimeter. Find the mass of the concrete cylinder.

 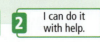

EXAMPLE 2 **Using a Volume Formula**

CONSERVATION BIOLOGY **TREE GROWTH** A conservation group estimates the trunk of a sequoia tree to have a height of about 50 meters and a base diameter of about 0.8 meter.

a. The wood of a sequoia tree has a density of about 450 kilograms per cubic meter. Find the mass of the trunk.

Let x represent the mass (in kilograms) of the trunk. Use the formula for density to find x. Because the trunk is approximately cylindrical, use $V = Bh = \pi r^2 h$ for the volume. The radius is $\frac{0.8}{2} = 0.4$ meter.

$$\text{Density} = \frac{\text{Mass}}{\text{Volume}} \qquad \text{Formula for density}$$

$$450 \approx \frac{x}{\pi(0.4)^2(50)} \qquad \text{Substitute.}$$

$$3600\pi \approx x \qquad \text{Solve for } x.$$

$$11{,}310 \approx x \qquad \text{Use technology.}$$

▶ The mass of the trunk is about 11,310 kilograms.

b. Each year, the tree trunk forms new cells that arrange themselves in concentric circles called *growth rings*. These rings indicate how much wood the tree produces annually. The conservation group estimates that the trunk will put on a growth ring of about 1 centimeter thick and its height will increase by about 0.25 meter this year. How many cubic meters of wood does the tree trunk produce this year? If the tree grows at these same rates for the next five years, will it produce the same amount of wood each year?

Make a table that shows the trunk dimensions and volume for five years.

Year	0	1	2	3	4	5
Height (meters)	50	50.25	50.5	50.75	51	51.25
Base radius (meters)	0.4	0.41	0.42	0.43	0.44	0.45
Volume (cubic meters)	25.13	26.54	27.99	29.48	31.02	32.60

+ 1.41   + 1.45   + 1.49   + 1.54   + 1.58

▶ The tree will produce about 26.54 − 25.13 = 1.41 cubic meters of wood in the first year. The tree will not produce the same amount of wood each year for five years because the differences between the volumes from year to year are increasing.

In-Class Practice
Self-Assessment

2. **WHAT IF?** The conservation group makes the same growth estimates for the trunk of a sequoia tree that has a height of about 40 meters and a base diameter of about 0.75 meter. (a) Find the mass of the trunk. (b) How many cubic meters of wood will the trunk gain after four years?

1 I don't understand yet. **2** I can do it with help. **3** I can do it on my own. **4** I can teach someone.

Using Surface Area Formulas

EXAMPLE 3   **Estimating the Thickness of a Can**

The density of aluminum is about 2.7 grams per cubic centimeter. The mass of the empty aluminum can is about 14.9 grams. Estimate the thickness of the aluminum.

Estimate the volume of aluminum in the can.

$$\text{Volume} = \frac{\text{Mass}}{\text{Density}} \quad \text{Write formula.}$$

$$\approx \frac{14.9}{2.7} \quad \text{Substitute.}$$

$$\approx 5.5 \text{ cm}^3 \quad \text{Divide.}$$

Estimate the surface area of the can. The aluminum can is approximately cylindrical. Assume that the thickness of the aluminum is uniform throughout the can. The radius is $\frac{6.8}{2} = 3.4$ centimeters.

$$S = 2\pi r^2 + 2\pi rh \quad \text{Formula for surface area of a cylinder}$$

$$= 2\pi(3.4)^2 + 2\pi(3.4)(12.2) \quad \text{Substitute.}$$

$$= 106.08\pi \quad \text{Simplify.}$$

$$\approx 333 \text{ cm}^2 \quad \text{Use technology.}$$

Estimate the thickness x of the can.

$$\boxed{\text{Surface area}} \times \boxed{\text{Thickness}} \approx \boxed{\text{Volume of aluminum}}$$

$$333x \approx 5.5$$

$$x \approx 0.017$$

▶ So, the thickness of the aluminum is about 0.017 centimeter, or about 0.17 millimeter.

In-Class Practice

Self-Assessment

3. The mass of the empty aluminum lunch box is about 700 grams. Estimate the thickness of the aluminum.

 I don't understand yet.   I can do it with help.   I can do it on my own.   I can teach someone.

12.6 Practice

1. **CONNECTION TO REAL LIFE** The diagram shows the dimensions of a block of ice. Ice has a density of about 0.92 gram per cubic centimeter. Find the mass of the block of ice. (See Example 1.)

   3.5 in.
   7.5 in.
   11.5 in.

2. **CONNECTION TO REAL LIFE** The United States has minted one-dollar silver coins called American Eagle Silver Bullion Coins since 1986. Each coin has a diameter of 40.6 millimeters and is 2.98 millimeters thick. The density of silver is 10.5 grams per cubic centimeter. Find the mass of an American Eagle Silver Bullion Coin.

3. **CONNECTION TO REAL LIFE** An apple growing on a tree has a circumference of 6 inches. (See Example 2.)

   a. The apple has a density of 0.46 gram per cubic centimeter. Find the mass of the apple.

   b. The radius of the apple increases $\frac{1}{8}$ inch per week for the next five weeks. Explain how the volume changes during the five-week period.

4. **CONNECTION TO REAL LIFE** The height of a tree trunk is 20 meters and the base diameter is 0.5 meter.

   a. The wood has a density of 380 kilograms per cubic meter. Find the mass of the trunk.

   b. For each of the next 5 years, the trunk puts on a growth ring 4 millimeters thick. In the first year, the height increases by 0.2 meter. The tree produces the same amount of wood each year. What is the height of the trunk after 5 years?

5. **CONNECTION TO REAL LIFE** The density of steel is approximately 7.8 grams per cubic centimeter. An empty steel can with a mass of 76 grams has a radius of 6.1 centimeters and a height of 6.3 centimeters. Estimate the thickness of the steel. (See Example 3.)

6. **SMP.8** Links of a chain are made from cylindrical metal rods with a diameter of 6 millimeters. The density of the metal is about 8 grams per cubic centimeter.

   27 mm
   9 mm
   15 mm

   a. To approximate the length of a rod used to make a link, should you use the perimeter around the inside of the link? the outside? the average of these perimeters? Explain your reasoning. Then approximate the mass of a chain with 100 links.

   b. Approximate the length of a taut chain with 100 links. Explain your procedure.

Interpreting Data

STRENGTH VERSUS DENSITY The chart below compares the strength and density of different building materials. Less dense materials that are weak are on the bottom left. Denser materials that are strong are on the top right.

7. Describe the chart. Explain whether the scales on the axes are linear.

8. Why do you think wood is used so often as a building material?

9. About how many times stronger is glass than wood? Explain.

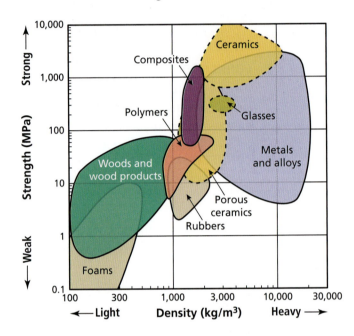

Review & Refresh

10. Show that a quadrilateral with vertices $P(3, 5)$, $Q(6, 4)$, $R(7, -1)$, and $S(1, 1)$ is a trapezoid. Then decide whether it is isosceles.

11. Find the surface area and the volume of the sphere.

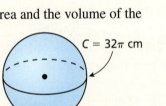

$C = 32\pi$ cm

14. Decide whether enough information is given to prove that $\triangle ABC$ and $\triangle DCB$ are congruent.

15. The pyramids are similar. Find the volume of pyramid B.

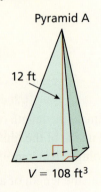
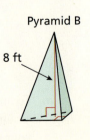

Pyramid A — 12 ft, $V = 108$ ft³

Pyramid B — 8 ft

Find the value of x. Write your answer in simplest form.

12.

13.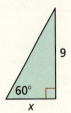

654 Chapter 12 Surface Area and Volume

12.7 Solids of Revolution

Learning Target: Sketch and use solids of revolution.

Success Criteria:
- I can sketch and describe solids of revolution.
- I can find surface areas and volumes of solids of revolution.
- I can form solids of revolution in the coordinate plane.

INVESTIGATE Modeling Solids of Revolution

Work with a partner.

1. Tape 3-inch by 5-inch index cards to pencils as shown. When you rotate each pencil, describe the solid modeled by the rotating index card.

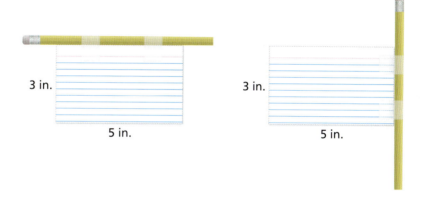

2. Do the solids in Exercise 1 have the same surface area? the same volume?

3. Tape the straight side of a protractor to a pencil. When you rotate the pencil, describe the solid modeled by the rotating protractor.

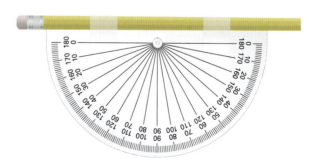

4. Find the surface area and volume of the solid in Exercise 3. Explain how you found your answers.

5. Can you tape an object to a pencil and rotate the pencil to model a cone? a cube? Explain why or why not.

Vocabulary
solid of revolution
axis of revolution

Sketching and Describing Solids of Revolution

A **solid of revolution** is a three-dimensional figure that is formed by rotating a two-dimensional shape around an axis. The line around which the shape is rotated is called the **axis of revolution**.

The figures above show that when you rotate a rectangle around a line that contains one of its sides, the solid of revolution that is produced is a cylinder.

EXAMPLE 1 Sketching and Describing Solids of Revolution

Sketch the solid produced by rotating the figure around the given axis. Then identify and describe the solid.

a.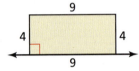

b.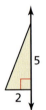

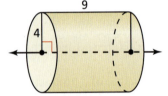

▶ The solid is a cylinder with a height of 9 units and a radius of 4 units.

▶ The solid is a cone with a height of 5 units and a radius of 2 units.

In-Class Practice

Self-Assessment

Sketch the solid produced by rotating the figure around the given axis. Then identify and describe the solid.

1. 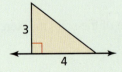   2.   3.

Surface Areas and Volumes of Solids of Revolution

EXAMPLE 2 Finding Surface Area and Volume of a Solid of Revolution

Sketch and describe the solid produced by rotating the figure around the given axis. Then find its surface area and volume.

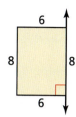

The solid is a cylinder with a height of 8 units and a radius of 6 units.

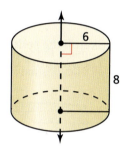

Surface area:
$S = 2\pi r^2 + 2\pi rh$ Write formula.
$= 2\pi(6)^2 + 2\pi(6)(8)$ Substitute 6 for r and 8 for h.
$= 168\pi$ Simplify.
≈ 527.79 Use technology.

Volume:
$V = \pi r^2 h$ Write formula.
$= \pi(6)^2(8)$ Substitute 6 for r and 8 for h.
$= 288\pi$ Simplify.
≈ 904.78 Use technology.

▶ The cylinder has a surface area of about 527.79 square units and a volume of about 904.78 cubic units.

In-Class Practice

Self-Assessment

4. Sketch and describe the solid produced by rotating the figure around the given axis. Then find its surface area and volume.

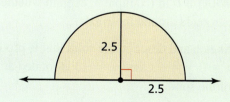

| 1 I don't understand yet. | 2 I can do it with help. | 3 I can do it on my own. | 4 I can teach someone. |

12.7   Solids of Revolution   657

Forming Solids of Revolution in the Coordinate Plane

EXAMPLE 3 Forming a Solid of Revolution

Sketch and describe the solid that is produced when the region enclosed by $y = 0$, $y = x$, and $x = 5$ is rotated around the y-axis. Then find the volume of the solid.

Graph each equation.

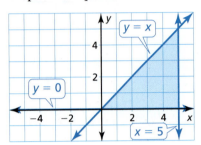

Reflect the region in the y-axis.

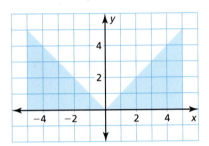

Connect the vertices of the of triangles using curved lines.

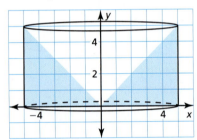

The composite solid consists a cylinder with a cone removed.

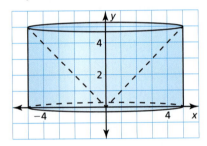

Find the volume of the composite solid. The cylinder and the cone both have a height of 5 units and a radius of 5 units.

$$\text{Volume of solid} = \text{Volume of cylinder} - \text{Volume of cone}$$

$$= \pi r^2 h - \tfrac{1}{3}\pi r^2 h \qquad \text{Write formulas.}$$
$$= \pi \cdot 5^2 \cdot 5 - \tfrac{1}{3}\pi \cdot 5^2 \cdot 5 \qquad \text{Substitute 5 for } r \text{ and 5 for } h.$$
$$= 125\pi - \tfrac{125}{3}\pi \qquad \text{Simplify.}$$
$$\approx 261.80 \qquad \text{Use technology.}$$

▶ The volume of the solid is about 261.80 cubic units.

In-Class Practice
Self-Assessment

5. **WHAT IF?** In Example 3, explain whether the solid changes when the region is rotated around the x-axis.

6. Sketch and describe the solid that is produced when the region enclosed by $x = 0$, $y = -x$, and $y = -3$ is rotated around the x-axis. Then find the volume of the solid.

1 I don't understand yet. **2** I can do it with help. **3** I can do it on my own. **4** I can teach someone.

12.7 Practice with Calc Chat and Calc View

Sketch the solid produced by rotating the figure around the given axis. Then identify and describe the solid. (See Example 1.)

1.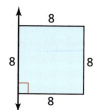

2.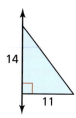

3.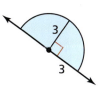

Sketch the solid of revolution. Then identify and describe the solid.

4. a rectangle with length 6 and width 3 rotated around one of its shorter sides

5. a right triangle with legs of lengths 6 and 9 rotated around its longer leg

Sketch and describe the solid produced by rotating the figure around the given axis. Then find its surface area and volume. (See Example 2.)

6.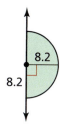

7.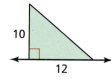

8.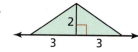

Sketch and describe the solid that is produced when the region enclosed by the given equations is rotated around the given axis. Then find the volume of the solid. (See Example 3.)

9. $x = 0, y = 0, y = x + 3$; x-axis

10. $x = 3, y = 0, y = \frac{1}{2}x$; y-axis

11. **CONNECT CONCEPTS** The figure shows the graph of a function f on an interval $[a, b]$. Sketch the solid produced when the region enclosed by the graph of f and the equations $x = a$, $x = b$, and $y = 0$ is rotated around the x-axis.

12. A right triangle has sides with lengths 15, 20, and 25. Describe the three solids formed when the triangle is rotated around each of its sides. Then find the volumes of the solids in terms of π.

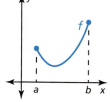

13. **SMP.7 OPEN-ENDED** Write a system of equations whose enclosed region, when rotated around the x-axis or y-axis, produces the same solid with the same dimensions.

14. The solid shown is a type of *torus*. Sketch a two-dimensional shape and an axis of revolution that forms the torus.

15. **DIG DEEPER** A 30°-30°-120° isosceles triangle has two legs of length 4 units. When it is rotated around an axis that contains one leg, what is the volume of the solid of revolution?

Interpreting Data

NUCLEAR COOLING TOWERS Nuclear reactors use energy from splitting atoms to boil water. The steam produced spins turbines, which then generate electricity. The function of the cooling towers often used by nuclear power plants is to remove excess heat from this water.

16. Sketch a two-dimensional shape and an axis of revolution that forms a solid resembling a cooling tower.

17. **SMP.4** A nuclear cooling tower is 400 feet tall. Estimate its surface area and its volume. Explain your method.

Review & Refresh

18. A circular region has a population of about 2.5 million people and a population density of about 9,824 people per square mile. Find the radius of the region.

19. The diagram shows the radius of a titanium ball. Titanium has a density of about 4.51 grams per cubic centimeter. Find the mass of the titanium ball.

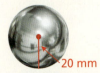

20. Find the value of x. Tell whether the side lengths form a Pythagorean Triple.

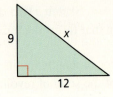

21. Find the surface area of the sphere.

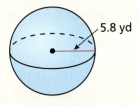

22. Find the volume of the cone.

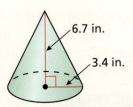

23. You are running on a circular path at a constant rate of 8.8 feet per second. The path is one mile in diameter. How long will it take you to run two complete laps?

24. Write an equation of a parabola with focus $F(3, 0)$ and directrix $x = -3$.

12 Chapter Review with CalcChat

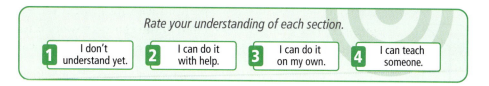

Rate your understanding of each section.

1 I don't understand yet. **2** I can do it with help. **3** I can do it on my own. **4** I can teach someone.

12.1 Cross Sections of Solids (pp. 613–620)

○ **Learning Target:** Describe and draw cross sections.

Vocabulary
polyhedron
face
edge
vertex
cross section

Describe the shape formed by the intersection of the plane and the solid.

1.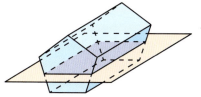

2.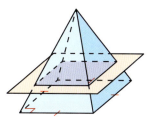

3.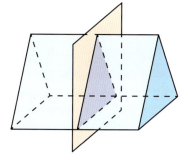

4.

Draw the cross section formed by the described plane that contains the red line segment drawn on the solid. What is the shape of the cross section?

5. plane is parallel to base

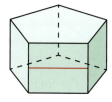

6. plane is parallel to bottom face

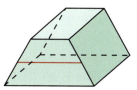

7. Describe and draw two cross sections that can be formed by a plane intersecting the solid in Exercise 5. The shapes of the cross sections should be different than the shape of the cross section in Exercise 5.

12.2 Volumes of Prisms and Cylinders (pp. 621–628)

⊙ **Learning Target:** Find and use volumes of prisms and cylinders.

Vocabulary
volume
Cavalieri's Principle
similar solids

Find the volume of the solid.

8.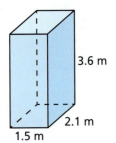

9.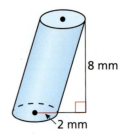

10.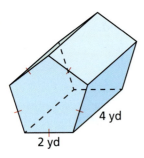

11.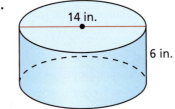

12. You are designing a rectangular planter box. You want the length to be 6 times the width, the height to be 5 inches, and the volume to be 1,080 cubic inches. What should the length be?

Find the volume of the composite solid.

13.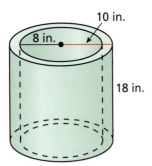

14.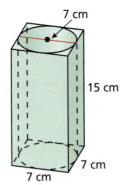

15. Cylinder A and cylinder B are similar. Find the surface area and volume of cylinder B.

Cylinder A

$S = 56\pi$ ft^2
$V = 48\pi$ ft^3

Cylinder B
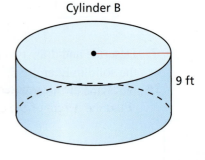

12.3 Volumes of Pyramids (pp. 629–634)

⊙ **Learning Target:** Find and use volumes of pyramids.

Find the volume of the pyramid.

16.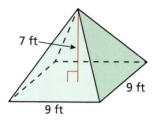

17.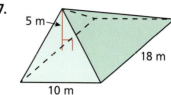

18. The largest pyramid at the Nima Sand Museum in Japan has a height of 21 meters and a square base with side lengths of 17 meters. Find the volume of the pyramid.

19. The volume of a square pyramid is 60 cubic inches and the height is 15 inches. Find the side length of the square base.

Find the volume of the composite solid.

20.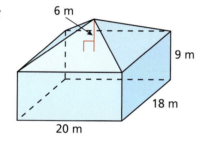

21.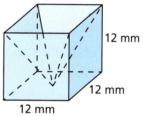

12.4 Surface Areas and Volumes of Cones (pp. 635–640)

⊙ **Learning Target:** Find and use surface areas and volumes of cones.

Vocabulary
lateral surface of a cone

Find the surface area and the volume of the cone.

22.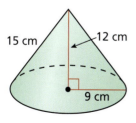

23.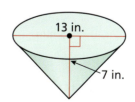

24. A cone with a diameter of 16 centimeters has a volume of 320π cubic centimeters. Find the height of the cone.

12.5 Surface Areas and Volumes of Spheres (pp. 641–648)

Learning Target: Find and use surface areas and volumes of spheres.

Vocabulary
chord of a sphere
great circle

Find the surface area and the volume of the sphere.

25.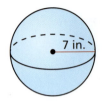

26.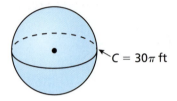

27. The shape of Mercury can be approximated by a sphere with a diameter of 4,880 kilometers. Find the surface area and the volume of Mercury.

28. A solid is composed of a cube with a side length of 6 meters and a hemisphere with a diameter of 6 meters. Find the volume of the composite solid.

12.6 Modeling with Surface Area and Volume (pp. 649–654)

Learning Target: Understand the concept of density and modeling with volume.

Vocabulary
density

29. A part for a toy train is made by drilling a hole that has a diameter of 0.6 centimeter through a wooden ball that has a diameter of 4 centimeters.

   a. Estimate the volume of the wooden ball after the hole is made.

   b. Do the surface area and volume of the wood decrease after the hole is made?

30. The diagram shows the dimensions of a bar of platinum. Platinum has a density of 21.4 grams per cubic centimeter. Find the mass of the bar.

31. The density of porcelain is about 2.4 grams per cubic centimeter. The mass of the mug is about 378 grams. Estimate the thickness of the porcelain.

12.7 Solids of Revolution (pp. 655–660)

Learning Target: Sketch and use solids of revolution.

Vocabulary
solid of revolution
axis of revolution

Sketch and describe the solid produced by rotating the figure around the given axis. Then find its surface area and volume.

32.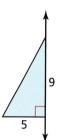

33.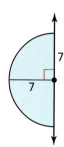

34.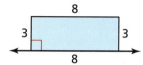

35.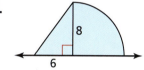

Sketch a two-dimensional shape and an axis of revolution that forms the object shown.

36.

37.

38. Sketch and describe the solid that is produced when the region enclosed by $y = 0$, $y = x$, and $x = 2$ is rotated around the y-axis. Then find the volume of the solid.

39. Your friend says when you rotate the figure shown around either the x-axis or the y-axis, the resulting solid is a sphere. Is your friend correct?

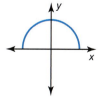

40. Which is greater, the volume of the solid produced by rotating the rectangle shown around the x-axis or the y-axis?

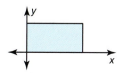

12 PERFORMANCE TASK
SMP.2 SMP.4

White-Nose Syndrome

What Is White-Nose Syndrome?
White-nose syndrome (WNS) is a fungal disease that affects hibernating bats. The fungus looks like white fuzz on a bat's nose.

WNS causes bats to become overactive and burn up fat needed during the winter. As a result, many bats starve to death before spring.

The fungus that causes WNS has spread to at least 36 states in the United States.

What Is Being Done?
Some conservationists build artificial bat caves that can be easily disinfected. In some artificial caves, mesh materials are used to line the walls so that the bats can grip on to the surface. Wood panels can also be installed to accommodate crevice-dwelling bats.

WHY SHOULD WE CARE?
Bats bring many benefits to their ecosystems, such as:
- Insect Control
- Pollination
- Seed Dispersal
- Fertilization

Analyzing Data

Use the information on the previous page to complete the following exercises.

1. Explain what is shown in the display. What do you notice? What do you wonder?

2. A bat with WNS is kept in a rectangular prism-shaped bat box for observation. The box has base side lengths of 8 inches and a height of 3 feet. Find the volume of the bat box.

3. The entrance of an artificial bat cave is a circle. Must every cross section of the cave be a circle? Explain why or why not.

DESIGN A BAT CAVE

Research the approximate number of bats that roost in Bracken Cave in Comal County, Texas. Then research an appropriate volume for an artificial bat cave. Design an artificial cave that can be used to accommodate the bats in Bracken Cave. Provide a sketch of your cave and describe the shape of the cave, the thickness of the walls, and the size and shape of the cave opening. Then determine the amount of mesh material that you will need to line the inner walls of your cave.

Finally, conduct research to estimate the maximum number of roosting bats that your cave can accommodate. About how many of these artificial caves are needed to accommodate all of the bats in Bracken Cave?

13 Probability

13.1 Sample Spaces and Probability
13.2 Two-Way Tables and Probability
13.3 Conditional Probability
13.4 Independent and Dependent Events
13.5 Probability of Disjoint and Overlapping Events
13.6 Permutations and Combinations
13.7 Binomial Distributions

NATIONAL GEOGRAPHIC EXPLORER

Jeffrey Ian Rose PREHISTORIC ARCHAEOLOGIST

Dr. Jeffrey Ian Rose is a prehistoric archaeologist specializing in the Paleolithic and Neolithic periods of the Arabian Peninsula. His areas of interest include modern human origins, Neolithization, stone tool technology, human genetics, rock art, geoarchaeology, underwater archaeology, and comparative religions.

- When did the Paleolithic and Neolithic periods occur?
- Which modern countries are in the Arabian Peninsula?
- Describe different types of stone tools that have been discovered from the Neolithic period. Are these different from the stone tools that have been discovered from the Paleolithic period?

PERFORMANCE TASK

Archaeologists use probability to help determine where to excavate. In the Performance Task on pages 724 and 725, you will help a team of archaeologists choose between three potential excavation sites.

Prehistoric Archaeology

Big Idea of the Chapter
Understand and Find Probabilities

A probability is a number between 0 and 1 that describes how likely it is that an event will occur. For instance, a probability of 0.5 means that an event occurs about half the time.

An archaeological site is any place that contains physical remains of past human activities. Sites without a written record are considered prehistoric archaeological sites, which may include villages, rock art, ancient cemeteries, and megalithic stone monuments.

Work with a partner. An archaeologist is asked about the experimental probabilities of finding several different objects during past expeditions. The answers are recorded in the table.

Object	Probability
tools	*"about nine times out of ten"*
pottery	*"about 70 percent of the time"*
religious objects	*"about three tenths of the time"*
bones	*"one hundred percent"*
intact human skeleton	*"less than one percent"*
walls or other parts of structures	*"about one out of four times"*

1. Describe the likelihood of each event in the table.

2. Order the objects by probability from least to greatest.

3. Compare the probability of finding religious objects with the probability of *not* finding pottery.

Getting Ready for Chapter 13

Using the Percent Proportion

EXAMPLE 1 What percent of 12 is 9?

$\dfrac{a}{w} = \dfrac{p}{100}$ 　　Write the percent proportion.

$\dfrac{9}{12} = \dfrac{p}{100}$ 　　Substitute 9 for *a* and 12 for *w*.

$100 \cdot \dfrac{9}{12} = 100 \cdot \dfrac{p}{100}$ 　　Multiplication Property of Equality

$75 = p$ 　　Simplify.

▶ So, 9 is 75% of 12.

Write and solve a proportion to answer the question.

1. What percent of 30 is 6?
2. What number is 68% of 25?

Making a Histogram

EXAMPLE 2 The frequency table shows the ages of people at a gym. Display the data in a histogram.

Draw and label the axes. Then draw a bar to represent the frequency of each interval.

Age	Frequency
10–19	7
20–29	12
30–39	6
40–49	4
50–59	0
60–69	3

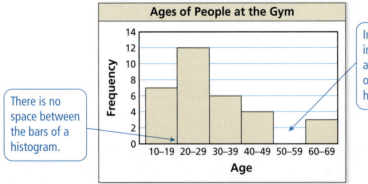

There is no space between the bars of a histogram.

Include any interval with a frequency of 0. The bar height is 0.

3. Display the data in a histogram.

Movies Watched per Week			
Movies	0–1	2–3	4–5
Frequency	35	11	6

670

13.1 Sample Spaces and Probability

Learning Target: Find sample spaces and probabilities of events.

Success Criteria:
- I can list the possible outcomes in a sample space.
- I can find theoretical probabilities.
- I can find experimental probabilities.

INVESTIGATE Finding Sample Spaces and Describing Events

Work with a partner.

1. Describe the set of all possible outcomes for each experiment.

   a. Two coins are flipped.

   b. Three coins are flipped.

   c. One six-sided die is rolled.

   d. Two six-sided dice are rolled.

2. Use your results in Exercise 1 to describe the likelihood that the given event will occur.

   a. You flip two tails.
   b. You flip three tails.
   c. You roll an odd number.
   d. You roll a sum greater than 3.

3. Use your results in Exercise 1 to determine which event is more likely to occur.

   a. Event *A*: flip exactly one heads
      Event *B*: flip two heads

   b. Event *A*: flip exactly two heads
      Event *B*: flip three heads

   c. Event *A*: roll an even number
      Event *B*: roll a number less than 3

   d. Event *A*: roll "doubles"
      Event *B*: roll a sum less than 6

4. Describe a real-life situation where it is important to know the likelihood of an event.

RESOURCES

13.1 Sample Spaces and Probability   671

Vocabulary

probability experiment
outcome
event
sample space
probability of an event
theoretical probability
experimental probability

Sample Spaces

A **probability experiment** is an action, or trial, that has varying results. The possible results of a probability experiment are **outcomes**. A collection of one or more outcomes is an **event**. The set of all possible outcomes is called a **sample space**.

Probability experiment: rolling a six-sided die
Sample space: 1, 2, 3, 4, 5, 6
Event: rolling an even number
Outcome: rolling a 4

EXAMPLE 1   Finding a Sample Space

You flip a coin and roll a six-sided die. How many possible outcomes are in the sample space? List the possible outcomes.

Use a tree diagram to find the outcomes in the sample space.

```
Coin flip      Die roll      Outcomes
                  1 ........ (H, 1)
                  2 ........ (H, 2)
                  3 ........ (H, 3)
  Heads           4 ........ (H, 4)
                  5 ........ (H, 5)
                  6 ........ (H, 6)

                  1 ........ (T, 1)
                  2 ........ (T, 2)
                  3 ........ (T, 3)
  Tails           4 ........ (T, 4)
                  5 ........ (T, 5)
                  6 ........ (T, 6)
```

▶ The sample space has 12 possible outcomes. They are listed below.

Heads, 1   Heads, 2   Heads, 3   Heads, 4   Heads, 5   Heads, 6
Tails, 1   Tails, 2   Tails, 3   Tails, 4   Tails, 5   Tails, 6

In-Class Practice

Self-Assessment

Find the number of possible outcomes in the sample space. Then list the possible outcomes.

1. You flip two coins.

2. You flip two coins and roll a six-sided die.

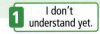

Theoretical Probabilities

The **probability of an event** is a measure of the likelihood, or chance, that the event will occur. Probability is a number from 0 to 1, including 0 and 1, and can be expressed as a decimal, fraction, or percent.

The outcomes for a specified event are called *favorable outcomes*. When all outcomes are equally likely, the **theoretical probability** of the event can be found using the following equation.

$$\text{Theoretical probability} = \frac{\text{Number of favorable outcomes}}{\text{Total number of outcomes}}$$

The probability of event A is written as $P(A)$.

EXAMPLE 2 Finding a Theoretical Probability

A student taking a quiz randomly guesses the answers to four true-false questions. What is the probability of the student guessing exactly two correct answers?

Let C represent a correct answer and I represent an incorrect answer.

Number correct	Outcome
0	IIII
1	CIII ICII IICI IIIC
2	IICC ICIC ICCI CIIC CICI CCII
3	ICCC CICC CCIC CCCI
4	CCCC

> Of the 16 possible outcomes, there are 6 favorable outcomes with exactly two correct.

$$P(\text{exactly two correct answers}) = \frac{\text{Number of favorable outcomes}}{\text{Total number of outcomes}}$$

$$= \frac{6}{16} = \frac{3}{8}$$

▶ The probability of guessing exactly two correct answers is $\frac{3}{8}$, or 37.5%.

In-Class Practice

Self-Assessment

3. You flip a coin and roll a six-sided die. What is the probability that the coin shows tails and the die shows 4?

1 I don't understand yet.   **2** I can do it with help.   **3** I can do it on my own.   **4** I can teach someone.

13.1   Sample Spaces and Probability

The sum of the probabilities of all outcomes in a sample space is 1. So, when you know the probability of event A, you can find the probability of the *complement* of event A. The *complement* of event A consists of all outcomes that are not in A and is denoted by $\overline{A}$. The notation $\overline{A}$ is read as "A bar."

Key Concept

Probability of the Complement of an Event

The probability of the complement of event A is

$$P(\overline{A}) = 1 - P(A).$$

EXAMPLE 3 Finding Probabilities of Complements

When two six-sided dice are rolled, there are 36 possible outcomes, as shown. Find the probability of each event.

a. The sum is *not* 6.

$$P(\text{sum is not 6}) = 1 - P(\text{sum is 6}) = 1 - \tfrac{5}{36} = \tfrac{31}{36} \approx 0.861$$

b. The sum is less than or equal to 10.

$$P(\text{sum} \leq 10) = 1 - P(\text{sum} > 10) = 1 - \tfrac{3}{36} = \tfrac{33}{36} = \tfrac{11}{12} \approx 0.917$$

c. You roll two different numbers.

$$P(\text{different numbers}) = 1 - P(\text{doubles}) = 1 - \tfrac{6}{36} = \tfrac{30}{36} = \tfrac{5}{6} \approx 0.833$$

In-Class Practice

Self-Assessment

Use the information in Example 3 to find the probability of each event.

4. The sum is *not* 11.

5. The sum is greater than 3.

Experimental Probabilities

An **experimental probability** is based on repeated *trials* of a probability experiment. The number of trials is the number of times the probability experiment is performed. Each trial in which a favorable outcome occurs is called a *success*.

$$\text{Experimental probability} = \frac{\text{Number of successes}}{\text{Number of trials}}$$

EXAMPLE 4 Finding an Experimental Probability

The central angles of the sections of the spinner are congruent. The spinner is spun 20 times. The table shows the results. For which color is the experimental probability of stopping on the color the same as the theoretical probability?

Spinner Results

red	green	blue	yellow
5	9	3	3

The theoretical probability of stopping on each of the four colors is $\frac{1}{4}$. Use the outcomes in the table to find the experimental probabilities.

$$P(\text{red}) = \frac{5}{20} = \frac{1}{4} \qquad P(\text{green}) = \frac{9}{20} \qquad P(\text{blue}) = \frac{3}{20} \qquad P(\text{yellow}) = \frac{3}{20}$$

▶ The experimental probability of stopping on red is the same as the theoretical probability.

EXAMPLE 5 Finding an Experimental Probability

A research team finds that 368 out of 490 crustaceans have ingested plastic. The types of crustaceans that ingested plastic are shown. The team randomly selects a crustacean that ingested plastic to demonstrate their findings. What is the probability that they choose a crayfish?

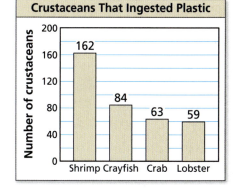

The number of trials is the number of crustaceans that ingested plastic, 368. A success is a crustacean that ingested plastic is a crayfish. From the figure, there are 84 crayfish.

$$P(\text{crustacean that ingested plastic is a crayfish}) = \frac{84}{368} = \frac{21}{92} \approx 0.228$$

▶ The probability that they choose a crayfish is about 23%.

In-Class Practice
Self-Assessment

6. In Example 4, for which color is the experimental probability of stopping on the color greater than the theoretical probability?

7. WHAT IF? In Example 5, what is the probability that they randomly select a lobster?

 I don't understand yet.   I can do it with help.   I can do it on my own.   I can teach someone.

13.1 Practice

Find the number of possible outcomes in the sample space. Then list the possible outcomes. (See Example 1.)

▶ 1. You flip a coin and draw a marble at random from a bag containing two purple marbles and one white marble.

2. You flip four coins.

3. You randomly choose a letter from A to F and a whole number from 1 to 3.

4. You draw two marbles without replacement from a bag containing three green marbles and three black marbles.

▶ 5. A game show airs five days per week. Each day, a prize is randomly placed behind one of two doors. The contestant wins the prize by selecting the correct door. What is the probability that exactly two of the five contestants win a prize during a week? (See Example 2.)

6. Your friend has two standard decks of 52 playing cards and asks you to randomly draw one card from each deck. What is the probability that you will draw two spades?

▶ 7. When two six-sided dice are rolled, there are 36 possible outcomes. Find the probability that (a) the sum is *not* 4 and (b) the sum is greater than 5. (See Example 3.)

8. The age distribution of guests at a cultural festival is shown. Find the probability that (a) a person chosen at random is at least 15 years old and (b) a person chosen at random is *not* 25 to 44 years old.

9. **CONNECTION TO REAL LIFE** You lose your earbuds while walking home from school. The earbuds are equally likely to be at any point along the path shown. What is the probability that the earbuds are on Cherry Street?

10. **SMP.3 ERROR ANALYSIS** A student randomly guesses the answers to two true-false questions. Describe and correct the error in finding the probability of the student guessing both answers correctly.

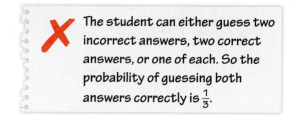

> ✗ The student can either guess two incorrect answers, two correct answers, or one of each. So the probability of guessing both answers correctly is $\frac{1}{3}$.

▶ 11. You roll a six-sided die 60 times. The table shows the results. For which number is the experimental probability of rolling the number the same as the theoretical probability? *(See Example 4.)*

Six-sided Die Results					
⚀	⚁	⚂	⚃	⚄	⚅
11	14	7	10	6	12

12. **PREHISTORIC ARCHAEOLOGY ARTIFACTS** An archaeologist uncovers the artifacts shown in the bar graph. An artifact is randomly selected for display. What is the probability that a piece of pottery is selected? *(See Example 5.)*

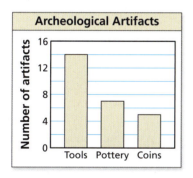

13. A survey of 140 teenagers asked what type of food they like best. The results are shown. What is the probability that a randomly selected teenager from the survey likes Mexican food best?

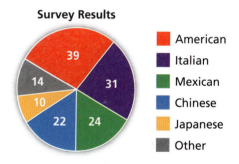

14. **SMP.7 DIG DEEPER** A test contains n true-false questions. A student randomly guesses the answer to each question. Write an expression that gives the probability of correctly answering all n questions.

15. **SMP.5** The table shows a simulation of rolling two six-sided dice three times. Use a random number generator to simulate rolling two six-sided dice 50 times. Compare the experimental probabilities of rolling each possible sum with the theoretical probabilities.

	A	B	C
1	First Die	Second Die	Sum
2	4	6	10
3	3	5	8
4	1	6	7

16. **CONNECT CONCEPTS** A sphere fits inside a cube so that it touches each face, as shown. What is the probability a point chosen at random inside the cube is also inside the sphere?

17. **PERFORMANCE TASK** You are in charge of designing a game of chance for a fundraiser. You expect about 200 people to play. Write a proposal in which you describe your game. Be sure to include how much you will charge to play, how much each winner will receive, the theoretical probability of winning, and how much you expect to raise (after prizes are deducted).

Interpreting Data

WORLD REGIONS The countries of the world are often divided into 4 regions: The Americas, Asia-Pacific, Europe, and Africa. In the map, the 4 colors represent the 4 regions and the area of each circle indicates the size of the population of a country.

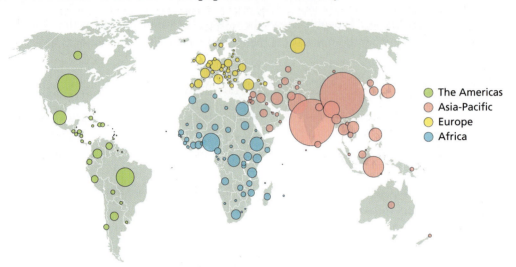

- The Americas
- Asia-Pacific
- Europe
- Africa

18. A person is randomly chosen from the Americas. Estimate the probability that the person lives in the United States.

19. A person is randomly chosen from Asia-Pacific. Estimate the probability that the person lives in India.

Review & Refresh

20. Sketch the solid produced by rotating the figure around the given axis. Then identify and describe the solid.

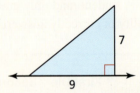

21. A sidewalk square is 5 feet wide and 4 inches thick. The density of concrete is 2,400 kilograms per cubic meter. Find the mass of the sidewalk square.

22. Find the surface area and volume of the hemisphere.

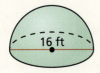

23. Write the standard equation for a circle with center (2, 3) that passes through the point (6, 0). Then graph the circle.

24. Find the value of x that makes $\triangle ABC \sim \triangle XYZ$.

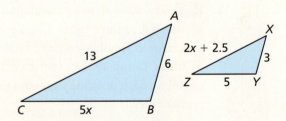

25. Find the value of x.

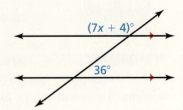

13.2 Two-Way Tables and Probability

Learning Target: Use two-way tables to represent data and find probabilities.

Success Criteria:
- I can make two-way tables.
- I can find and interpret relative frequencies and conditional relative frequencies.
- I can use conditional relative frequencies to find probabilities.

INVESTIGATE   Finding Probabilities Using a Two-Way Table

Work with a partner. A survey of 80 students at a high school asks whether they participate in outside of school activities and whether they participate in inside of school activities. The results are shown in the Venn diagram.

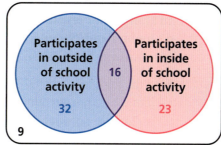

1. Show how you can represent the data in the Venn diagram using a single table.

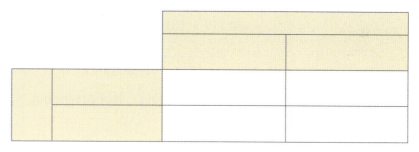

2. One student is selected at random from the 80 students who took the survey. Find the probability that the student

   a. participates in an outside of school activity.

   b. participates in an outside of school activity and participates in an inside of school activity.

   c. participates in an outside of school activity and does not participate in an inside of school activity.

3. Conduct a survey of the students in your class. Choose two categories that are different from those given above. Then summarize the results in both a Venn diagram and a table similar to the one above. Discuss your results and find a probability using your table.

Vocabulary
two-way table
joint frequency
marginal frequency
joint relative frequency
marginal relative frequency
conditional relative frequency

Making Two-Way Tables

A **two-way table** is a frequency table that displays data collected from one source that belong to two different categories. One category of data is represented by rows and the other is represented by columns. The two-way table below shows the results of a survey that asked freshmen and sophomores whether they are attending a school concert.

Each entry in the table is called a **joint frequency**. The sums of the rows and columns are called **marginal frequencies**.

		Attendance	
		Attending	Not Attending
Class	Freshman	25	44
	Sophomore	80	32

joint frequency

EXAMPLE 1 Making a Two-Way Table

In another survey, 106 juniors and 114 seniors respond. Of those, 42 juniors and 77 seniors plan on attending. Organize these results in a two-way table. Then find and interpret the marginal frequencies.

Find the joint frequencies. Because 42 of the 106 juniors are attending, 64 juniors are not attending. Because 77 of the 114 seniors are attending, 37 seniors are not attending.

Find the marginal frequencies. Create a new column and row for the sums. Then add the entries and interpret the results.

Find the sums of the marginal frequencies. Notice the sums 106 + 114 = 220 and 119 + 101 = 220 are equal. Place this value at the bottom right.

		Attendance		
		Attending	Not Attending	Total
Class	Junior	42	64	106
	Senior	77	37	114
	Total	119	101	220

- 106 juniors responded.
- 114 seniors responded.
- 220 students were surveyed.
- 119 students are attending.
- 101 students are not attending.

In-Class Practice

Self-Assessment

1. You randomly survey people about whether they are in favor of planting a community garden at school. Of 96 students surveyed, 61 are in favor. Of 88 teachers surveyed, 17 are against. Organize the results in a two-way table. Then find and interpret the marginal frequencies.

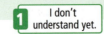

Finding Joint and Marginal Relative Frequencies

You can display values in a two-way table as frequency counts or as *relative frequencies*.

> **Key Concept**
>
> **Relative Frequencies**
>
> A **joint relative frequency** is the ratio of a joint frequency to the total number of values or observations.
>
> A **marginal relative frequency** is the sum of the joint relative frequencies in a row or a column.

EXAMPLE 2 Finding Joint and Marginal Relative Frequencies

Use the survey results in Example 1 to make a two-way table that shows the joint and marginal relative frequencies. Interpret one of the joint relative frequencies and one of the marginal relative frequencies.

To find the joint relative frequencies, divide each frequency by the total number of students in the survey. Then find the sum of each row and each column to find the marginal relative frequencies.

		Attendance		
		Attending	Not Attending	Total
Class	Junior	$\frac{42}{220} \approx 0.191$	$\frac{64}{220} \approx 0.291$	0.482
	Senior	$\frac{77}{220} = 0.35$	$\frac{37}{220} \approx 0.168$	0.518
	Total	0.541	0.459	1

▶ The joint relative frequency 0.291 means that about 29.1% of the students in the survey are juniors who are not attending the concert. So, the probability that a randomly selected student from the survey is a junior who is not attending the concert is about 29.1%.

The marginal relative frequency 0.518 means that about 51.8% of the students in the survey are seniors. So, the probability that a randomly selected student from the survey is a senior is about 51.8%.

In-Class Practice

Self-Assessment

2. Use the survey results in Exercise 1 to make a two-way table that shows the joint and marginal relative frequencies. Interpret one of the joint relative frequencies and one of the marginal relative frequencies.

Finding Conditional Relative Frequencies

A **conditional relative frequency** is the ratio of a joint relative frequency to a marginal relative frequency. You can find a conditional relative frequency using a row total or a column total of a two-way table.

EXAMPLE 3 Finding Conditional Relative Frequencies

Use the survey results in Example 1. Make a two-way table that shows the conditional relative frequencies based on (a) the row totals and (b) the column totals. Interpret one of the conditional relative frequencies.

a. Use the marginal relative frequency of each *row* in Example 2 to calculate the conditional relative frequencies.

		Attendance	
		Attending	Not Attending
Class	Junior	$\frac{0.191}{0.482} \approx 0.396$	$\frac{0.291}{0.482} \approx 0.604$
	Senior	$\frac{0.35}{0.518} \approx 0.676$	$\frac{0.168}{0.518} \approx 0.324$

▶ The conditional relative frequency 0.604 means that about 60.4% of the juniors in the survey are not attending the concert. So, the probability that a randomly selected junior from the survey is not attending the concert is about 60.4%.

b. Use the marginal relative frequency of each *column* in Example 2 to calculate the conditional relative frequencies.

		Attendance	
		Attending	Not Attending
Class	Junior	$\frac{0.191}{0.541} \approx 0.353$	$\frac{0.291}{0.459} \approx 0.634$
	Senior	$\frac{0.35}{0.541} \approx 0.647$	$\frac{0.168}{0.459} \approx 0.366$

▶ The conditional relative frequency 0.634 means that of the students in the survey who are not attending the concert, about 63.4% are juniors. So, given that a randomly selected student in the survey is not attending the concert, the probability that the student is a junior is about 63.4%.

In-Class Practice

Self-Assessment

3. Use the survey results in Exercise 1 to make a two-way table that shows the conditional relative frequencies based on the column totals. Interpret one of the conditional relative frequencies.

13.2 Practice with Calc Chat and Calc View

1. You survey 171 children and 180 adults at Grand Central Station in New York City. Of those, 132 children and 151 adults wash their hands after using the public restrooms. Organize these results in a two-way table. Then find and interpret the marginal frequencies. (See Example 1.)

2. A survey asks 80 seniors and 66 juniors whether they have a curfew. Of those, 59 seniors and 28 juniors say they have a curfew. Organize these results in a two-way table. Then find and interpret the marginal frequencies.

3. Use the survey results from Exercise 1 to make a two-way table that shows the joint and marginal relative frequencies. Interpret one of the joint relative frequencies and one of the marginal relative frequencies. (See Example 2.)

4. A survey asks teenagers and adults about whether their state should increase the minimum driving age. The two-way table shows the results.

   a. What does 120 represent?
   b. What does 925 represent?
   c. What does 1,501 represent?

		Age Group		
		Teenager	Adult	Total
Response	Yes	45	880	925
	No	456	120	576
	Total	501	1,000	1,501

5. A survey finds that 73 people like horror movies and 87 people do not. Of those who like horror movies, 39 people have visited a haunted house. Of those who do not like horror movies, 42 people have visited a haunted house. Make a two-way table that shows the conditional relative frequencies based on (a) the horror movie totals and (b) the haunted house totals. Interpret one of the conditional relative frequencies. (See Example 3.)

6. **CONNECTION TO REAL LIFE** You ask students in a college cafeteria whether they prefer buffets or ordering meals. Of the 14 commuters and 17 on-campus students in the cafeteria, 8 commuters prefer ordering meals and 9 on-campus students prefer buffets. Find the probability that a randomly selected student from the cafeteria is a commuter who prefers buffets.

7. Use the survey results in Exercise 2 to find the probability that a randomly selected senior from the survey has a curfew.

8. **OPEN-ENDED** Create and conduct a survey in your class. Organize the results in a two-way table. Then create a two-way table that shows the joint and marginal relative frequencies. Use the relative frequencies to find a probability.

9. **SMP.7** Provide an example of a three-way table. Explain how you can find conditional relative frequencies for the data in the table. Then find and interpret one of the conditional relative frequencies.

Interpreting Data

THE TITANIC The Titanic was an ocean liner meant to transport passengers across the Atlantic Ocean. At the time of its completion in 1912, it was the largest ship in existence. During its first voyage, the ship struck an iceberg and was destroyed, killing over 1,500 people.

		Survived		
		Yes	No	Total
Ticket class	First	202	123	325
	Second	118	167	285
	Third	178	528	706
	Total	498	818	1,316

10. Use the two-way table to answer each question.

   a. What does 118 represent?   **b.** What 706 represent?

11. What is the probability that a randomly chosen first class passenger on the Titanic survived the accident? a third class passenger?

12. Use the two-way table shown to make a two-way table that shows the conditional relative frequencies based on the row totals. Interpret one of the conditional relative frequencies.

Review & Refresh

13. When two six-sided dice are rolled, there are 36 possible outcomes. Find the probability that the sum is *not* 7.

14. Sketch and describe the solid produced by rotating the figure around the given axis. Then find its surface area and volume.

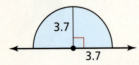

15. A steel cube has side lengths of 0.5 meter. Steel has a density of about 7,700 kilograms per cubic meter. Find the mass of the cube.

16. Find $m\widehat{RS}$.

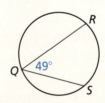

17. Find the value of x that makes the quadrilateral a parallelogram.

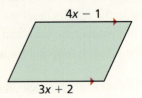

684 Chapter 13 Probability

13.3 Conditional Probability

Learning Target: Find and use conditional probabilities.

Success Criteria:
- I can explain the meaning of conditional probability.
- I can find conditional probabilities.
- I can make decisions using probabilities.

INVESTIGATE Finding Conditional Probabilities

Work with a partner. Six pieces of paper, numbered 1 through 6, are placed in a bag. You draw two pieces of paper one at a time without replacing the first.

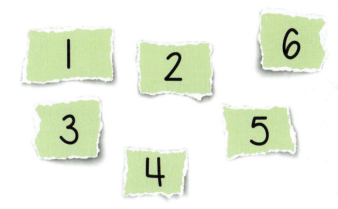

1. Use a tree diagram to find the outcomes in the sample space.

2. What is the probability that you draw two odd numbers?

3. When the first number you draw is odd, what is the probability that the second number you draw is also odd?

4. Compare and contrast the questions in Exercises 2 and 3.

5. The probability in Exercise 3 is called a *conditional probability*. How would you define conditional probability?

6. The probability that event B occurs given that event A has occurred is called the conditional probability of B given A and is written as $P(B|A)$. The probability that both events A and B occur is written as $P(A \text{ and } B)$.

   Find $P(B|A)$, $P(A \text{ and } B)$, and $P(A)$ for the following pair of events.

   Event A: The first number is divisible by 3.

   Event B: The second number is greater than 2.

7. Use your answers in Exercise 6 to write a formula for $P(B|A)$ in terms of $P(A \text{ and } B)$ and $P(A)$.

> **Vocabulary**
> conditional probability

Understanding Conditional Probability

The probability that event B occurs given that event A has occurred is called the **conditional probability** of B given A and is written as $P(B|A)$. You can use sample spaces and two-way tables to find conditional probabilities.

EXAMPLE 1 Using a Sample Space to Find a Conditional Probability

A family has two dogs and two cats. They randomly select a pet to get brushed and then randomly select a different pet to get a treat. Find the probability that they select a cat to get a treat given that they selected a dog to get brushed.

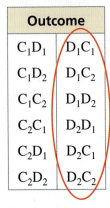

Let C_1 and C_2 represent the two cats, and D_1 and D_2 represent the two dogs. Use a table to list the outcomes in the sample space.

Use the sample space to find $P(\text{cat second}\,|\,\text{dog first})$. There are 6 outcomes for choosing a dog first. A cat is second in 4 of these 6 outcomes.

▶ So, $P(\text{cat second}\,|\,\text{dog first}) = \frac{4}{6} = \frac{2}{3} \approx 0.667$, or about 66.7%.

EXAMPLE 2 Using a Two-Way Table to Find Conditional Probabilities

A quality-control inspector checks for defective parts. The two-way table shows the results. Find each probability.

		Result	
		Pass	Fail
Part Type	Defective	3	36
	Non-defective	450	11

a. $P(\text{pass}\,|\,\text{defective})$

Find the probability that a defective part passes.

$$P(\text{pass}\,|\,\text{defective}) = \frac{\text{Number of defective parts passed}}{\text{Total number of defective parts}}$$

$$= \frac{3}{3+36} = \frac{3}{39} = \frac{1}{13} \approx 0.077, \text{ or about } 7.7\%$$

b. $P(\text{fail}\,|\,\text{non-defective})$

Find the probability that a non-defective part fails.

$$P(\text{fail}\,|\,\text{non-defective}) = \frac{\text{Number of non-defective parts failed}}{\text{Total number of non-defective parts}}$$

$$= \frac{11}{450+11} = \frac{11}{461} \approx 0.024, \text{ or about } 2.4\%$$

In-Class Practice

Self-Assessment

1. In Example 1, what is the probability that they select a dog to get a treat given that they selected a dog to get brushed?

2. In Example 2, find (a) the probability that a non-defective part passes, and (b) the probability that a defective part fails.

Key Concept

Conditional Probability Formula

Words For two events A and B, the conditional probability of the second event given the first event is the probability that both events occur divided by the probability of the first event.

Symbols $P(B|A) = \dfrac{P(A \text{ and } B)}{P(A)}$

EXAMPLE 3 Using a Formula to Find a Conditional Probability

Find the probability in Example 2(a) using the formula for conditional probability.

Find the joint and marginal relative frequencies. There are a total of 500 parts in the two-way table.

		Result		
		Pass	Fail	Total
Part Type	Defective	$\dfrac{3}{500} = 0.006$	$\dfrac{36}{500} = 0.072$	0.078
	Non-defective	$\dfrac{450}{500} = 0.9$	$\dfrac{11}{500} = 0.022$	0.922
	Total	0.906	0.094	1

Use the formula for conditional probability. Let event A be "part is defective" and let event B be "part passes."

$P(B|A) = \dfrac{P(A \text{ and } B)}{P(A)}$ Write formula for conditional probability.

$= \dfrac{0.006}{0.078}$ Substitute 0.006 for $P(A \text{ and } B)$ and 0.078 for $P(A)$.

$= \dfrac{6}{78}$ Rewrite fraction.

$= \dfrac{1}{13} \approx 0.077$ Simplify.

▶ So, the probability that a defective part passes is about 7.7%.

In-Class Practice
Self-Assessment

3. Find the probability in Example 2(b) using the formula for conditional probability.

EXAMPLE 4   **Finding Conditional Probabilities**

At a school, 60% of students buy a school lunch, 18% of students buy a dessert, and 10% of students buy a lunch and a dessert.

a. What is the probability that a student who buys lunch also buys dessert?

Let event A be "buys lunch" and let event B be "buys dessert."

You are given $P(A) = 0.6$ and $P(A \text{ and } B) = 0.1$. Use the formula to find $P(B|A)$.

$P(B|A) = \dfrac{P(A \text{ and } B)}{P(A)}$ Write formula for conditional probability.

$= \dfrac{0.1}{0.6}$ Substitute 0.1 for $P(A \text{ and } B)$ and 0.6 for $P(A)$.

$= \dfrac{1}{6}$ Rewrite fraction.

≈ 0.167 Simplify.

▶ So, the probability that a student who buys lunch also buys dessert is about 16.7%.

b. What is the probability that a student who buys dessert also buys lunch?

Using the same events A and B from part (a), you are given $P(B) = 0.18$ and $P(A \text{ and } B) = 0.1$. Use the formula to find $P(A|B)$.

$P(A|B) = \dfrac{P(A \text{ and } B)}{P(B)}$ Write formula for conditional probability.

$= \dfrac{0.1}{0.18}$ Substitute 0.1 for $P(A \text{ and } B)$ and 0.18 for $P(B)$.

$= \dfrac{10}{18}$ Rewrite fraction.

$= \dfrac{5}{9} \approx 0.556$ Simplify.

▶ So, the probability that a student who buys dessert also buys lunch is about 55.6%.

In-Class Practice

Self-Assessment

4. At a coffee shop, 80% of customers order coffee, 15% of customers order coffee and a bagel, and 20% of customers order coffee and a sandwich.

  a. What is the probability that a customer who orders coffee also orders a bagel?

  b. What is the probability that a customer who orders coffee also orders a sandwich?

  c. Explain what information you need to find the probability that a customer who orders a bagel also orders coffee.

1 I don't understand yet.   **2** I can do it with help.   **3** I can do it on my own.   **4** I can teach someone.

Make Decisions Using Conditional Probabilities

EXAMPLE 5 Using Conditional Probabilities to Make a Decision

You want to burn a certain number of calories during a workout. You map out three possible jogging routes. Before each workout, you randomly select a route. Afterward, you use a fitness tracker to determine whether you reach your goal. The table shows your data. Which route should you use from now on?

Route	Reaches Goal	Does Not Reach Goal
A	|||| ||||		||||	
B	|||| ||||		||||
C	|||| |||| ||	||||	

Use the data to make a two-way table that shows the joint and marginal relative frequencies. There are a total of 50 observations in the table.

Find the conditional probabilities by dividing each joint relative frequency in the "Reaches Goal" column by the marginal relative frequency in its corresponding row.

	Reaches Goal?		
Route	Yes	No	Total
A	0.22	0.12	0.34
B	0.22	0.08	0.30
C	0.24	0.12	0.36
Total	0.68	0.32	1

$$P(\text{reaches goal} \mid \text{Route A}) = \frac{P(\text{Route A and reaches goal})}{P(\text{Route A})} = \frac{0.22}{0.34} \approx 0.647$$

$$P(\text{reaches goal} \mid \text{Route B}) = \frac{P(\text{Route B and reaches goal})}{P(\text{Route B})} = \frac{0.22}{0.30} \approx 0.733$$

$$P(\text{reaches goal} \mid \text{Route C}) = \frac{P(\text{Route C and reaches goal})}{P(\text{Route C})} = \frac{0.24}{0.36} \approx 0.667$$

▶ Based on the sample, the probability that you reach your goal is greatest when you use Route B. So, you should use Route B from now on.

In-Class Practice

Self-Assessment

5. Over time, a manager records whether three employees meet or exceed expectations on their tasks. Explain which employee is most deserving of a pay increase based on the results in the table.

Employee	Exceed Expectations	Meet Expectations
A	|||| ||||	||||	
B	|||| |||| ||	|||| |||
C	|||| ||||		|||| ||

13.3 Practice

1. A school lunch offers three different fruits and two different vegetables as side dishes. You are served two different side dishes at random. Find the probability that you are served a vegetable second given that you were served a fruit first. (See Example 1.)

2. You have two beaches and three trails you are interested in exploring during a visit to a national park. You randomly select two of the five to explore. Find the probability that you select a beach to explore second given that you randomly selected a beach to explore first.

3. A teacher administers two different versions of a test to students. The two-way table shows the results. Find (a) $P(\text{pass} \mid \text{Test A})$ and (b) $P(\text{Test B} \mid \text{fail})$. (See Example 2.)

		Grade	
		Pass	Fail
Test	A	49	7
	B	34	12

4. The two-way table shows the numbers of tropical cyclones that formed during hurricane season over a 12-year period. Find (a) $P(\text{hurricane} \mid \text{Northern Hemisphere})$ and (b) $P(\text{Southern Hemisphere} \mid \text{hurricane})$.

		Location	
		Northern Hemisphere	Southern Hemisphere
Type of Tropical Cyclone	Tropical depression	100	107
	Tropical storm	342	487
	Hurricane	379	525

5. Find the probability in Exercise 3(a) using the formula for conditional probability. (See Example 3.)

6. Find the probability in Exercise 4(a) using the formula for conditional probability.

7. **CONNECTION TO REAL LIFE** At a school, 43% of students attend the homecoming football game, 48% of students attend the homecoming dance, and 23% of students attend the game and the dance. (See Example 4.)

   a. What is the probability that a student who attends the football game also attends the dance?
   b. What is the probability that a student who attends the dance also attends the football game?

8. **CONNECTION TO REAL LIFE** Of all the residents in a city that commuted to work on a given day, 54% took the subway, 10% took the subway and a bus, and 5% took the subway and a taxi.

   a. What is the probability that a resident who took the subway also took a bus?
   b. What is the probability that a resident who took the subway also took a taxi?

▶ 9. You want to find the quickest route to school. You map out three routes. Before school, you randomly select a route and record whether you are late or on time. The table shows your findings. Assuming you leave at the same time each morning, explain which route you should use. *(See Example 5.)*

Route	On Time	Late
A	7	4
B	11	3
C	12	4

10. A teacher is assessing three groups of students in order to award one group a prize. Over a period of time, the teacher records whether the groups meet or exceed expectations on their assigned tasks. The table shows the results. Explain which group should be awarded the prize.

Group	Exceed Expectations	Meet Expectations
1	12	4
2	8	5
3	9	6

11. **SMP.7** Show that $P(B|A) \cdot P(A) = P(A|B) \cdot P(B)$.

12. In a survey, 53% of respondents have a music streaming subscription, 68% have a video streaming subscription, and 47% of respondents who have video streaming also have music streaming. What is the probability that a person from the survey has both video and music streaming?

13. **CONNECT CONCEPTS** The Venn diagram shows the results of a survey. Use the Venn diagram to construct a two-way table. Then find the probability that a randomly selected person from the survey who owns a dog also owns a cat.

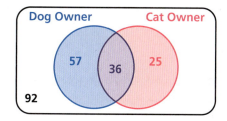

14. **CONNECT CONCEPTS** The Venn diagram represents the sample space S for two events X and Y. The area of each region is proportional to the number of outcomes within the region. Explain whether $P(X|Y) > P(Y|X)$ is *true* or *false*.

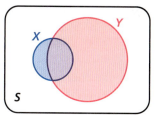

15. Use a two-way table to write an example of Bayes' Theorem, which is given by

$$P(A|B) = \frac{P(B|A) \cdot P(A)}{P(B)}.$$

16. **SMP.1 DIG DEEPER** A company creates a new recipe for a snack and tests it against its current recipe. The table shows the results. The company is deciding whether it should change the snack's recipe, and to whom the snack should be marketed. Use probability to explain the decisions the company should make when the total size of the snack's market is expected to (a) change very little, and (b) expand very rapidly.

		Recipe Preference	
		Current	New
Current Consumer of Snack	Yes	72	46
	No	52	114

13.3 Conditional Probability 691

Interpreting Data

STAR RATING SYSTEM A website allows users to rate movies on a 5-star scale. The lowest rating is 1 star and the highest rating is 5 stars. The graph compares the average ratings of 1,700 movies to the number of reviewers of each movie.

17. Describe the graph. How is the rating related to the number of reviewers?

18. Explain whether you would rather have many or few reviewers if you made a movie.

19. SMP.1 Estimate the probability that a movie with an average rating of 4 had 50 or more reviewers. Explain your method.

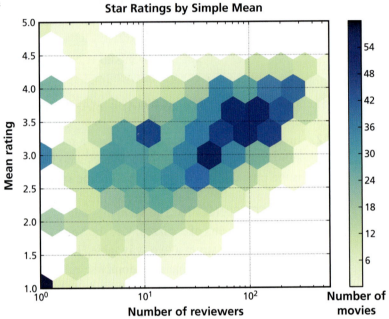

Review & Refresh

20. Use the data to create a two-way table that shows the joint and marginal relative frequencies.

		Dominant Hand		
		Left	Right	Total
Grade	10th	16	99	115
	11th	24	92	116
	Total	40	191	231

21. You roll a six-sided die 30 times. A 5 is rolled 8 times. What is the theoretical probability of rolling a 5? What is the experimental probability of rolling a 5?

22. Find the circumference of a circle with radius of 7 inches.

23. Find the value of x.

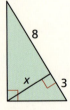

24. Sketch and describe the solid that is produced when the region enclosed by the graphs of the equations $x = -3$, $y = 0$, and $y = -2x + 1$ is rotated around the x-axis. Then find the volume of the solid.

692 Chapter 13 Probability

13.4 Independent and Dependent Events

> **Learning Target:** Understand and find probabilities of independent and dependent events.
>
> **Success Criteria:**
> - I can explain how independent events and dependent events are different.
> - I can determine whether events are independent.
> - I can find probabilities of independent and dependent events.

INVESTIGATE — Identifying Independent and Dependent Events

Work with a partner.

1. Two events are either *independent* or *dependent*. Which pair of events below are independent? Which are dependent?

    a. You roll a six-sided die twice.

    Event A: The first number is even.

    Event B: The second number is a 6.

    b. Six pieces of paper, numbered 1 through 6, are placed in a bag. Two pieces of paper are selected one at a time without replacement.

    Event A: The first number is even.

    Event B: The second number is a 6.

2. Complete the table for each set of events in Exercise 1.

Experiment	Rolling Die	Selecting Papers
$P(A)$		
$P(B)$		
$P(B \mid A)$		
$P(A \text{ and } B)$		

3. Write a formula that relates $P(A \text{ and } B)$, $P(B \mid A)$, and $P(A)$.

    $P(A \text{ and } B) = $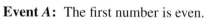

Determining Whether Events Are Independent

Vocabulary
independent events
dependent events

Two events are **independent events** when the occurrence of one event does not affect the occurrence of the other event.

Key Concept

Probability of Independent Events

Words Two events A and B are independent events if and only if the probability that both events occur is the product of the probabilities of the events.

Symbols $P(A \text{ and } B) = P(A) \cdot P(B)$

EXAMPLE 1 Determining Whether Events Are Independent

A student randomly guesses the answers to four true-false questions. Use a sample space to determine whether guessing correctly on Question 1 and guessing correctly on Question 2 are independent events.

Use a table to list the outcomes in the sample space.

Outcomes			
IIII	IIIC	CIIC	CICC
CIII	IICC	CICI	CCIC
ICII	ICIC	CCII	CCCI
IICI	ICCI	ICCC	CCCC

$P(\text{correct on Question 1}) = \frac{8}{16} = \frac{1}{2}$ $P(\text{correct on Question 2}) = \frac{8}{16} = \frac{1}{2}$

$P(\text{correct on Question 1 and correct on Question 2}) = \frac{4}{16} = \frac{1}{4}$

▶ Because $\frac{1}{2} \cdot \frac{1}{2} = \frac{1}{4}$, the events are independent.

EXAMPLE 2 Determining Whether Events Are Independent

A group of three students includes one junior and two seniors. Use a sample space to determine whether randomly selecting a senior first and randomly selecting a senior second are independent events.

Let J represent the junior. Let S_1 and S_2 represent the two seniors. Use a table to list the outcomes in the sample space.

Number of seniors	Outcome	
1	S_1J	JS_1
1	S_2J	JS_2
2	S_1S_2	S_2S_1

$P(\text{senior first}) = \frac{4}{6} = \frac{2}{3}$ $P(\text{senior second}) = \frac{4}{6} = \frac{2}{3}$

$P(\text{senior first and senior second}) = \frac{2}{6} = \frac{1}{3}$

▶ Because $\frac{2}{3} \cdot \frac{2}{3} \neq \frac{1}{3}$, the events are not independent.

In-Class Practice

Self-Assessment

1. In Example 1, determine whether guessing Question 1 incorrectly and guessing Question 2 correctly are independent events.

2. In Example 2, determine whether randomly selecting a senior first and randomly selecting a junior second are independent events.

 I don't understand yet.
 I can do it with help.
 I can do it on my own.
 I can teach someone.

You can also determine whether two events are independent using conditional probabilities.

> ### Key Concept
>
> **Conditional Probability and Independent Events**
>
> **Words** When two events A and B are independent, the conditional probability of A given B is equal to the probability of A, and the conditional probability of B given A is equal to the probability of B.
>
> **Symbols** $P(A|B) = P(A)$ and $P(B|A) = P(B)$

EXAMPLE 3 Determining Whether Events Are Independent

Use conditional probabilities to determine whether the events are independent in (a) Example 1 and (b) Example 2.

a. Determine whether $P(B|A) = P(B)$.

$$P(\text{correct on Question 2} | \text{correct on Question 1}) = \frac{4}{8}$$
$$= \frac{1}{2}$$

$$P(\text{correct on Question 2}) = \frac{8}{16}$$
$$= \frac{1}{2}$$

▶ Being correct on the first question does not affect the probability of being correct on the second question. Because $P(B|A) = P(B)$, the events are independent.

b. Determine whether $P(B|A) = P(B)$.

$$P(\text{senior second} | \text{senior first}) = \frac{2}{4}$$
$$= \frac{1}{2}$$

$$P(\text{senior second}) = \frac{4}{6}$$
$$= \frac{2}{3}$$

▶ The first selection affects the outcome of the second selection. Because $P(B|A) \neq P(B)$, the events are not independent.

In-Class Practice

Self-Assessment

3. Five out of eight tiles in a bag have numbers on them. You randomly draw a tile, set it aside, and then randomly draw another tile. Use a conditional probability to determine whether selecting a numbered tile first and a numbered tile second are independent events.

1 I don't understand yet. **2** I can do it with help. **3** I can do it on my own. **4** I can teach someone.

EXAMPLE 4 **Using a Two-Way Table to Determine Independence**

A satellite TV provider surveys customers in three cities. The survey asks whether they would recommend the TV provider to a friend. The results, given as joint relative frequencies, are shown in the two-way table.

		Location		
		Glendale	Santa Monica	Long Beach
Response	Yes	0.29	0.27	0.32
	No	0.05	0.03	0.04

a. Determine whether recommending the provider to a friend and living in Long Beach are independent events.

Use the formula $P(B) = P(B|A)$ and compare $P(\text{Long Beach})$ and $P(\text{Long Beach}|\text{yes})$.

$$P(\text{Long Beach}) = 0.32 + 0.04 = 0.36$$

$$P(\text{Long Beach}|\text{yes}) = \frac{P(\text{yes and Long Beach})}{P(\text{yes})}$$

$$= \frac{0.32}{0.29 + 0.27 + 0.32} \approx 0.36$$

▶ Because $P(\text{Long Beach}) \approx P(\text{Long Beach}|\text{yes})$, the two events are independent.

b. Determine whether *not* recommending the provider to a friend and living in Glendale are independent events.

Use the formula $P(B) = P(B|A)$ and compare $P(\text{Glendale})$ and $P(\text{Glendale}|\text{no})$.

$$P(\text{Glendale}) = 0.29 + 0.05 = 0.34$$

$$P(\text{Glendale}|\text{no}) = \frac{P(\text{no and Glendale})}{P(\text{no})}$$

$$= \frac{0.05}{0.05 + 0.03 + 0.04} \approx 0.42$$

▶ Because $P(\text{Glendale}) \neq P(\text{Glendale}|\text{no})$, the two events are not independent.

In-Class Practice

Self-Assessment

4. In Example 4, determine whether recommending the provider to a friend and living in Santa Monica are independent events.

Finding Probabilities of Events

In Example 1, it makes sense that the events are independent because the second guess should not be affected by the first guess. In Example 2, however, the selection of the second person *depends* on the selection of the first person because the same person cannot be selected twice. These events are *dependent*. Two events are **dependent events** when the occurrence of one event *does* affect the occurrence of the other event.

> ### Key Concept
> **Probability of Dependent Events**
>
> **Words** If two events A and B are dependent events, then the probability that both events occur is the product of the probability of the first event and the conditional probability of the second event given the first event.
>
> **Symbols** $P(A \text{ and } B) = P(A) \cdot P(B|A)$

EXAMPLE 5 Finding the Probability of Dependent Events

A bag contains twenty \$1 bills and five \$10 bills. You randomly draw a bill from the bag, set it aside, and then randomly draw another bill from the bag. Find the probability that both events A and B will occur.

Event A: The first bill is \$10.

Event B: The second bill is \$10.

The events are dependent because there is one less bill in the bag on your second draw than on your first draw. Find $P(A)$ and $P(B|A)$. Then multiply the probabilities.

$P(A) = \frac{5}{25}$ 5 of the 25 bills are \$10 bills.

$P(B|A) = \frac{4}{24}$ When the first bill is \$10, 4 of the remaining 24 bills are \$10 bills.

$P(A \text{ and } B) = P(A) \cdot P(B|A) = \frac{5}{25} \cdot \frac{4}{24} = \frac{1}{5} \cdot \frac{1}{6} = \frac{1}{30} \approx 0.033$

▶ So, the probability that you draw two \$10 bills is about 3.3%.

In-Class Practice

Self-Assessment

5. In Example 5, what is the probability that both bills are \$1 bills?

6. A spinner is divided into equal parts. Find the probability that you get a 5 on your first spin and a number greater than 3 on your second spin.

 I don't understand yet.
 I can do it with help.
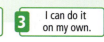 I can do it on my own.
 I can teach someone.

13.4 Practice

Use a sample space to determine whether the events are independent. (See Examples 1 and 2.)

▶ 1. You play a game that involves spinning the spinner shown. The central angles of the sections of the spinner are congruent. Determine whether randomly spinning blue and then green are independent events.

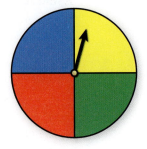

2. There are three green apples and one red apple in a bowl. You randomly select one apple to eat now and another apple to eat with lunch. Determine whether randomly selecting a green apple first and randomly selecting a green apple second are independent events.

▶ 3. You randomly select two gift cards from a bag that contains three restaurant gift cards and two department store gift cards. Determine whether randomly selecting a restaurant gift card first and randomly selecting a department store gift card second are independent events.

4. You roll a six-sided die two times. Determine whether getting a 6 and then getting a 1 are independent events.

Use a conditional probability to determine whether the events are independent. (See Example 3.)

▶ 5. You have six solid and three striped cell phone cases. You randomly select a case, set it aside, and then randomly select another case. Determine whether randomly selecting a striped case first and a striped case second are independent events.

6. You flip a coin and roll a six-sided die. Determine whether getting tails and getting a 4 are independent events.

▶ 7. Three different local hospitals in New York surveyed their patients. The survey asked whether the patient's physician communicated efficiently. The results, given as joint relative frequencies, are shown in the two-way table. Determine whether being satisfied with the communication of the physician and living in Saratoga are independent events. (See Example 4.)

		Location		
		Glens Falls	Saratoga	Albany
Response	Yes	0.123	0.289	0.338
	No	0.042	0.095	0.113

8. **SMP.3 ERROR ANALYSIS** Events A and B are independent. Describe and correct the error in finding $P(A$ and $B)$.

✗
$P(A) = 0.6$
$P(B) = 0.2$
$P(A$ and $B) = 0.6 + 0.2 = 0.8$

698 Chapter 13 Probability

9. **CONNECTION TO REAL LIFE** A bag contains 12 movie tickets and 8 concert tickets. You randomly choose 1 ticket and do not replace it. Then you randomly choose another ticket. Find the probability that both events A and B will occur. (See Example 5.)

   Event A: The first ticket is a concert ticket.

   Event B: The second ticket is a concert ticket.

10. You play a game that involves spinning the money wheel shown. You spin the wheel twice. Find the probability that you get more than $500 on your first spin and then go bankrupt on your second spin.

11. A bag contains one red marble and one blue marble. The diagrams show the possible outcomes of randomly choosing two marbles using different methods. For each method, determine whether the marbles were selected with or without replacement.

    a. 1st Draw   2nd Draw
    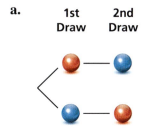

    b. 1st Draw   2nd Draw
    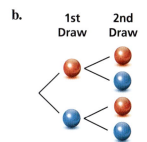

12. A meteorologist claims that there is a 70% chance of rain. When it rains, there is a 75% chance that your softball game will be rescheduled. Explain whether the game is more likely to be rescheduled than played.

13. Two six-sided dice are rolled once. Events A and B are represented by the diagram. Describe each event. Explain whether the two events are dependent or independent.

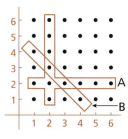

14. **SMP.7** Events A and B are independent. Explain whether $P(A \text{ and } B)$ can also be defined as $P(B) \cdot P(A|B)$.

15. **SMP.1 DIG DEEPER** A football team losing by 14 points manages to score two touchdowns (worth 6 points each) before the end of the game. The other team does not score again. After each touchdown, the coach must decide whether to go for 1 point with a kick (which is successful 99% of the time) or 2 points with a run or pass (which is successful 45% of the time). Develop a strategy so that the team has a probability of winning the game that is greater than the probability of losing. Explain your strategy and calculate the probabilities of winning and losing the game.

Interpreting Data

RURAL POPULATION About 97% of the United States is considered rural, but only 20% of the U.S. population lives in rural areas. The display shows the percents of the populations of different countries that lived in rural areas in 2021.

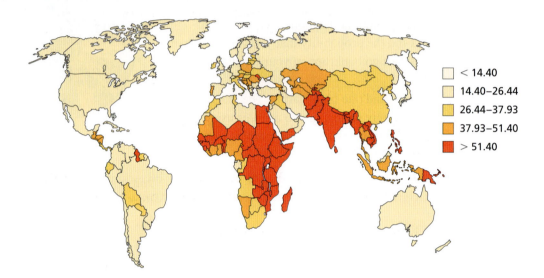

< 14.40
14.40–26.44
26.44–37.93
37.93–51.40
> 51.40

16. Estimate the number of countries with a rural population that is over 51.4% of the total population.

17. You randomly select a country on the map with a rural population that is over 51.4% of the total population. Estimate the probability that the country you chose is in Africa.

Review & Refresh

18. You roll a six-sided die and flip a coin. Find the probability that you get a 2 when rolling the die and heads when flipping the coin.

19. Find the measures of the numbered angles in rhombus *DEFG*.

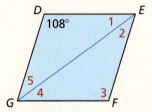

20. Find the coordinates of the centroid of △*XYZ* with vertices $X(0, 3)$, $Y(6, -3)$, and $Z(-2, -5)$.

21. Find the distance from the point $A(2, -4)$ to the line $y = x + 1$.

22. A survey asks 68 adults and 57 teenagers whether they have been to an escape room. Complete the two-way table. Then interpret the marginal frequencies.

		Escape Room		
		Yes	No	Total
Age	Adult	35		
	Teenager		28	
	Total			

13.5 Probability of Disjoint and Overlapping Events

Learning Target: Find probabilities of disjoint and overlapping events.

Success Criteria:
- I can explain how disjoint events and overlapping events are different.
- I can find probabilities of disjoint events.
- I can find probabilities of overlapping events.
- I can solve real-life problems using more than one probability rule.

INVESTIGATE Identifying Overlapping and Disjoint Events

Work with a partner.

1. You roll two six-sided dice. Which pair of events below are *overlapping*? Which are *disjoint*? Use Venn diagrams to support your answers.

   a. **Event A:** The sum is an even number.
      Event B: The sum is 7.

   b. **Event A:** The sum is less than 7.
      Event B: The sum is a prime number.

2. What does it mean for two events to be *overlapping*? *disjoint*?

3. Complete the table for each set of events in Exercise 1.

Experiment	Events in (a)	Events in (b)
$P(A)$		
$P(B)$		
$P(A$ and $B)$		
$P(A$ or $B)$		

4. Use the results from Exercise 3 to write general formulas for $P(A$ or $B)$.

   Events are disjoint: $P(A$ or $B) = $

   Events are overlapping: $P(A$ or $B) = $

Vocabulary
compound event
overlapping events
disjoint events

Compound Events

The union or intersection of two events is called a **compound event**.

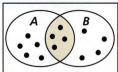

Intersection of A and B   Union of A and B   Intersection of A and B is empty.

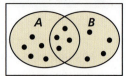

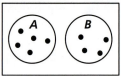

To find P(A or B) you must consider the number of outcomes in the intersection of A and B. Two events are **overlapping** when they have one or more outcomes in common. Two events are **disjoint**, or *mutually exclusive*, when they have no outcomes in common, as shown in the third diagram.

Key Concept

Probability of Compound Events

If A and B are any two events, then the probability of A or B is

$$P(A \text{ or } B) = P(A) + P(B) - P(A \text{ and } B).$$

If A and B are disjoint events, then $P(A \text{ and } B) = 0$ and the probability of A or B is

$$P(A \text{ or } B) = P(A) + P(B).$$

EXAMPLE 1 Finding the Probability of Disjoint Events

A card is randomly selected from a standard deck of 52 playing cards. What is the probability that it is a 10 *or* a face card?

Let event A be selecting a 10 and event B be selecting a face card. Event A has 4 outcomes and event B has 12 outcomes. Because A and B are disjoint, use the disjoint probability formula.

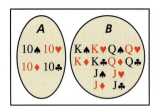

$P(A \text{ or } B) = P(A) + P(B)$ Write disjoint probability formula.

$= \dfrac{4}{52} + \dfrac{12}{52}$ Substitute known probabilities.

$= \dfrac{16}{52}$ Add.

$= \dfrac{4}{13} \approx 0.308$ Simplify and use technology.

▶ So, the probability that a randomly selected card is a 10 or a face card is about 30.8%.

In-Class Practice

Self-Assessment

1. A card is randomly selected from a standard deck of 52 playing cards. Find the probability of selecting an ace *or* an 8.

 I don't understand yet.   I can do it with help.   I can do it on my own.   I can teach someone.

EXAMPLE 2 **Finding the Probability of Overlapping Events**

A card is randomly selected from a standard deck of 52 playing cards. What is the probability that it is a face card *or* a spade?

Let event A be selecting a face card and event B be selecting a spade. Event A has 12 outcomes and event B has 13 outcomes. Of these, 3 outcomes are common to A and B. Find $P(A \text{ or } B)$.

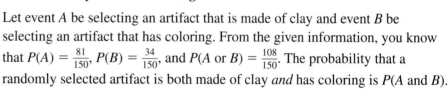

$P(A \text{ or } B) = P(A) + P(B) - P(A \text{ and } B)$ — Write general formula.

$= \frac{12}{52} + \frac{13}{52} - \frac{3}{52}$ — Substitute known probabilities.

$= \frac{22}{52}$ — Add.

$= \frac{11}{26} \approx 0.423$ — Simplify and use technology.

EXAMPLE 3 **Finding the Probability of Overlapping Events**

PREHISTORIC ARCHAEOLOGY **ARTIFACTS** An archaeology lab receives 150 artifacts for processing. Of those, 108 are either made of clay or have coloring. There are 81 artifacts made of clay and 34 artifacts that have coloring. What is the probability that a randomly selected artifact is made of clay *and* has coloring?

Let event A be selecting an artifact that is made of clay and event B be selecting an artifact that has coloring. From the given information, you know that $P(A) = \frac{81}{150}$, $P(B) = \frac{34}{150}$, and $P(A \text{ or } B) = \frac{108}{150}$. The probability that a randomly selected artifact is both made of clay *and* has coloring is $P(A \text{ and } B)$.

$P(A \text{ or } B) = P(A) + P(B) - P(A \text{ and } B)$ — Write general formula.

$\frac{108}{150} = \frac{81}{150} + \frac{34}{150} - P(A \text{ and } B)$ — Substitute known probabilities.

$P(A \text{ and } B) = \frac{81}{150} + \frac{34}{150} - \frac{108}{150}$ — Solve for $P(A \text{ and } B)$.

$P(A \text{ and } B) = \frac{7}{150}$ — Simplify.

$P(A \text{ and } B) \approx 0.047$ — Use technology.

▶ So, the probability that a randomly selected artifact is both made of clay *and* has coloring is about 4.7%.

In-Class Practice

Self-Assessment

2. A card is randomly selected from a standard deck of 52 playing cards. Find the probability of selecting a 10 *or* a diamond.

3. Out of 200 students in a senior class, 113 students are either varsity athletes or on the honor roll. There are 74 seniors who are varsity athletes and 51 seniors who are on the honor roll. What is the probability that a randomly selected senior is both a varsity athlete *and* on the honor roll?

Using More Than One Probability Rule

EXAMPLE 4 **Finding the Probability of Compound Events**

The American Diabetes Association estimates that 9.4% of people in the United States have diabetes. A medical lab has developed a simple diagnostic test for diabetes that is 98% accurate for people who have the disease and 95% accurate for people who do not have it. The medical lab gives the test to a randomly selected person. What is the probability that the diagnosis is correct?

Let event A be "person has diabetes" and event B be "correct diagnosis." Notice that the probability of B depends on the occurrence of A, so the events are dependent. When A occurs, $P(B) = 0.98$. When A does not occur, $P(B) = 0.95$.

A probability tree diagram, where the probabilities are given along the branches, can help you see the different ways to obtain a correct diagnosis. Use the complements of events A and B to complete the diagram, where $\overline{A}$ is "person does not have diabetes" and $\overline{B}$ is "incorrect diagnosis." Notice that the probabilities for all branches from the same point must sum to 1.

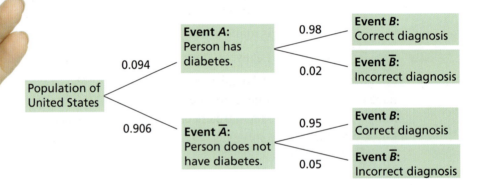

To find the probability that the diagnosis is correct, follow the branches leading to event B.

$P(B) = P(A \text{ and } B) + P(\overline{A} \text{ and } B)$ Use tree diagram.

$\quad = P(A) \cdot P(B|A) + P(\overline{A}) \cdot P(B|\overline{A})$ Probability of dependent events

$\quad = (0.094)(0.98) + (0.906)(0.95)$ Substitute.

$\quad \approx 0.953$ Use technology.

▶ The probability that the diagnosis is correct is about 0.953, or 95.3%.

In-Class Practice

Self-Assessment

4. In Example 4, what is the probability that a randomly selected person diagnosed with diabetes actually has the disease?

13.5 Practice

Each section of the spinner shown has the same area. Find the probability of the event.
(See Examples 1 and 2.)

1. spinning blue *or* a 1
2. spinning green *or* a multiple of 4
3. spinning red *or* an odd number
4. spinning yellow *or* a number less than 5
5. spinning a factor of 6 *or* a number greater than 9
6. spinning an even number *or* a prime number

SMP.3 ERROR ANALYSIS Describe and correct the error in finding the probability of randomly drawing the given card from a standard deck of 52 playing cards.

7. ✗ $P(\text{heart or face card})$
   $= P(\text{heart}) + P(\text{face card})$
   $= \frac{13}{52} + \frac{12}{52} = \frac{25}{52}$

8. ✗ $P(\text{club or 9})$
   $= P(\text{club}) + P(9) + P(\text{club and 9})$
   $= \frac{13}{52} + \frac{4}{52} + \frac{1}{52} = \frac{9}{26}$

9. **CONNECTION TO REAL LIFE** A group of 40 trees in a forest are not growing properly. A botanist determines that 34 of the trees have a disease or are being damaged by insects, with 18 trees having a disease and 20 being damaged by insects. What is the probability that a randomly selected tree has both a disease *and* is being damaged by insects? (See Example 3.)

STEM Video: Tree Growth

10. **CONNECTION TO REAL LIFE** Out of 55 teenagers enrolled in dance classes, 30 teenagers take either hip-hop or jazz classes. There are 13 teenagers who take hip-hop classes and 24 teenagers who take jazz classes. What is the probability that a randomly selected teenager takes both hip-hop *and* jazz classes?

11. A company is focus testing a new type of fruit drink. The focus group is 47% male. Of the responses, 40% of the males and 54% of the females said they would buy the fruit drink. What is the probability that a randomly selected person would buy the fruit drink? (See Example 4.)

12. You take a bus from your neighborhood to a store. The express bus arrives at your neighborhood at a random time between 7:30 and 7:36 A.M. The local bus arrives at your neighborhood at a random time between 7:30 and 7:40 A.M. You arrive at the bus stop at 7:33 A.M. Find the probability that you miss the express bus *or* the local bus.

13. Write a general rule for finding $P(A \text{ or } B \text{ or } C)$ for (a) disjoint and (b) overlapping events A, B, and C.

Interpreting Data

POPULATION OF LOS ANGELES COUNTY Los Angeles County contains 88 cities and has a population of over 10 million. To match this population in Middle America, it would take 298 counties covering an area of 471,941 square miles.

14. A person is randomly selected from the United States. What is the probability that the person lives in Los Angeles County?

15. A person is randomly selected from the United States. What is the probability that the person lives in one of the counties shown in Middle America or Los Angeles County?

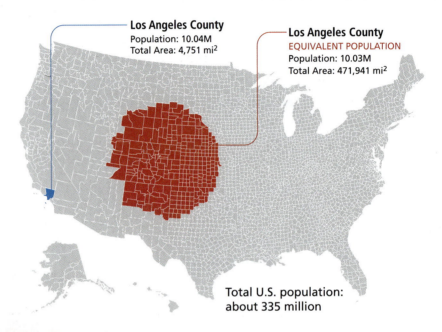

Review & Refresh

16. You randomly draw a card from a standard deck of 52 playing cards, set it aside, and then randomly draw another card from the deck. Find the probability that both cards are hearts.

17. A cat eats half a cup of food, twice per day. Will the automatic pet feeder hold enough food for 10 days? (1 cup ≈ 14.4 in.³)

Find the measure of each arc where $\overline{AC}$ is a diameter.

18. $\overset{\frown}{ABC}$

19. $\overset{\frown}{ABE}$

20. $\overset{\frown}{AE}$

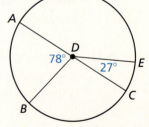

21. Find the value of each variable using sine and cosine.

706 Chapter 13 Probability

13.6 Permutations and Combinations

Learning Target: Count permutations and combinations.

Success Criteria:
- I can explain the difference between permutations and combinations.
- I can find numbers of permutations and combinations.
- I can find probabilities using permutations and combinations.

INVESTIGATE   Counting Outcomes

Work with a partner.

1. A fair conducts three obstacle course races. In how many different orders can the dogs finish in each race? Justify your answers.

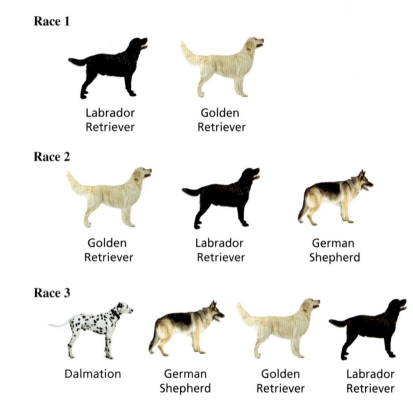

2. For each race in Exercise 1, in how many different ways can the dogs finish first and second? Justify your answers.

3. For each race in Exercise 1, how many different pairs of dogs can you form?

4. Explain why your answers in Exercise 3 are different from your answers in Exercise 2.

Vocabulary
permutation
factorial
combination

Permutations

A **permutation** is an arrangement of objects in which order is important. For instance, the 6 possible permutations of the letters A, B, and C are shown.

| ABC | ACB | BAC |
| BCA | CAB | CBA |

EXAMPLE 1 Counting Permutations

Consider the letters in the word JULY.

a. **In how many ways can you arrange all of the letters?**

Because the order of the letters is important, use the Fundamental Counting Principle to find the number of permutations of the letters in the word JULY.

$$\text{Number of permutations} = \begin{pmatrix}\text{Choices for}\\\text{1st letter}\end{pmatrix}\begin{pmatrix}\text{Choices for}\\\text{2nd letter}\end{pmatrix}\begin{pmatrix}\text{Choices for}\\\text{3rd letter}\end{pmatrix}\begin{pmatrix}\text{Choices for}\\\text{4th letter}\end{pmatrix}$$

$$= 4 \cdot 3 \cdot 2 \cdot 1$$

$$= 24$$

▶ There are 24 ways you can arrange all of the letters in the word JULY.

b. **In how many ways can you arrange 2 of the letters?**

When arranging 2 letters of the word JULY, you have 4 choices for the first letter and 3 choices for the second letter.

$$\text{Number of permutations} = \begin{pmatrix}\text{Choices for}\\\text{1st letter}\end{pmatrix}\begin{pmatrix}\text{Choices for}\\\text{2nd letter}\end{pmatrix}$$

$$= 4 \cdot 3$$

$$= 12$$

▶ There are 12 ways you can arrange 2 of the letters in the word JULY.

Check

| JU | JL | JY | UJ | UL | UY |
| LJ | LU | LY | YJ | YU | YL |

In-Class Practice

Self-Assessment

1. Consider the letters in the word MARCH. In how many ways can you arrange (a) all of the letters and (b) 3 of the letters?

1 I don't understand yet. **2** I can do it with help. **3** I can do it on my own. **4** I can teach someone.

In Example 1(a), you evaluated the expression 4 • 3 • 2 • 1. This expression can be written as 4! and is read "4 *factorial*." For any positive integer *n*, the product of the integers from 1 to *n* is called a **factorial** and is written as

$$n! = n \cdot (n-1) \cdot (n-2) \cdot \cdots \cdot 3 \cdot 2 \cdot 1.$$

As a special case, the value of 0! is defined to be 1.

In Example 1(b), you found the permutations of 4 objects taken 2 at a time. You can also find the number of permutations using the following formula.

Key Concept

Permutations

Formula

The number of permutations of *n* objects taken *r* at a time, where $r \leq n$, is given by

$$_nP_r = \frac{n!}{(n-r)!}.$$

Example

The number of permutations of 4 objects taken 2 at a time is

$$_4P_2 = \frac{4!}{(4-2)!} = \frac{4 \cdot 3 \cdot 2!}{2!} = 12.$$

EXAMPLE 2 Using Permutations

You ride on a float with your soccer team in a parade. There are 12 floats in the parade, and their order is chosen at random. Find the probability that your float is first and the float with the school chorus is second.

Write the number of possible ways that two of the floats can be first and second as the number of permutations of the 12 floats taken 2 at a time.

$$_{12}P_2 = \frac{12!}{(12-2)!} \qquad \text{Permutations formula}$$

$$= \frac{12!}{10!} \qquad \text{Subtract.}$$

$$= \frac{12 \cdot 11 \cdot 10!}{10!} \qquad \text{Expand 12!. Divide out the common factor, 10!.}$$

$$= 132 \qquad \text{Simplify.}$$

Only one of the possible permutations includes your float first and the float with the school chorus second. So,

$$P(\text{soccer team is 1st, chorus is 2nd}) = \frac{1}{132}.$$

▶ The probability is $\frac{1}{132}$.

In-Class Practice

Self-Assessment

2. WHAT IF? In Example 2, there are 14 floats in the parade. Find the probability that the soccer team is first and the chorus is second.

Combinations

A **combination** is a selection of objects in which order is *not* important. For instance, in a drawing for 3 identical prizes, the order of the winners does not matter. If the prizes were different, then the order would matter.

EXAMPLE 3 **Counting Combinations**

Count the possible combinations of 2 letters chosen from A, B, C, D.

List all of the permutations of 2 letters from the list A, B, C, D. Because order is not important in a combination, cross out any duplicate pairs.

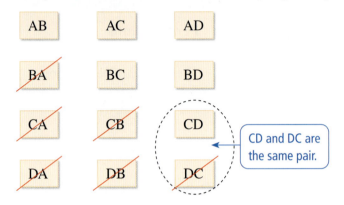

CD and DC are the same pair.

▶ There are 6 possible combinations of 2 letters from the list A, B, C, D.

In Example 3, you found the number of combinations of objects by making an organized list. You can also find the number of combinations using the following formula.

Key Concept

Combinations

Formula

The number of combinations of n objects taken r at a time, where $r \leq n$, is given by

$$_nC_r = \frac{n!}{(n-r)! \cdot r!}.$$

Example

The number of combinations of 4 objects taken 2 at a time is

$$_4C_2 = \frac{4!}{(4-2)! \cdot 2!} = \frac{4 \cdot 3 \cdot 2!}{2! \cdot (2 \cdot 1)} = 6.$$

In-Class Practice

Self-Assessment

Count the possible combinations of r letters chosen from the given list.

3. L, M, N, O; $r = 2$
4. A, B, C, D, E; $r = 3$

EXAMPLE 4 **Using Combinations**

A yearbook editor has selected 14 photos, including one of you and one of your friend, to use in a collage for the yearbook. The photos are placed at random. There is room for 2 photos at the top of the page. What is the probability that your photo and your friend's photo are the 2 placed at the top of the page?

The order in which the photos are chosen is not important. Write the number of possible outcomes as the number of combinations of 14 photos taken 2 at a time, or $_{14}C_2$.

$_{14}C_2 = \dfrac{14!}{(14-2)! \cdot 2!}$ Combinations formula

$= \dfrac{14!}{12! \cdot 2!}$ Subtract.

$= \dfrac{14 \cdot 13 \cdot \cancel{12!}}{\cancel{12!} \cdot (2 \cdot 1)}$ Expand 14! and 2!. Divide out the common factor, 12!.

$= 91$ Simplify.

Only one of the possible combinations includes your photo and your friend's photo. So,

$P(\text{your photo and your friend's photos are chosen}) = \dfrac{1}{91}$.

▶ The probability is $\dfrac{1}{91}$.

Check Use technology.

nCr(14,2)   = 91

In-Class Practice

Self-Assessment

5. Explain which expression does *not* belong with the other three.

$\dfrac{7!}{2! \cdot 5!}$ $_7C_5$ $_7C_2$ $\dfrac{7!}{(7-2)!}$

6. **WHAT IF?** In Example 4, there are 20 photos in the collage. Find the probability that your photo and your friend's photo are the 2 placed at the top of the page.

1 I don't understand yet. **2** I can do it with help. **3** I can do it on my own. **4** I can teach someone.

13.6 Practice

Find the number of ways you can arrange (a) all of the letters and (b) 2 of the letters in the given word. (See Example 1.)

▶ 1. ROCK
2. WATER
3. FLOWERS

Evaluate the expression.

4. $_5P_2$
5. $_9P_1$
6. $_{12}P_0$

7. Eleven students are competing in a graphic design contest. In how many different ways can the students finish first, second, and third?

8. Six friends go to a movie theater. In how many different ways can they sit together in a row of 6 empty seats?

9. **CONNECTION TO REAL LIFE** You and your friend are 2 of 8 servers working a shift in a restaurant. At the beginning of the shift, the manager randomly assigns one section to each server. Find the probability that you are assigned Section 1 and your friend is assigned Section 2. (See Example 2.)

10. You make 6 posters to hold up at a basketball game. Each poster has a letter of the word TIGERS. You and 5 friends sit next to each other in a row. The posters are distributed at random. Find the probability that TIGERS is spelled correctly when you hold up the posters.

Count the possible combinations of *r* letters chosen from the given list. (See Example 3.)

▶ 11. A, B, C, D; $r = 3$
12. U, V, W, X, Y, Z; $r = 3$
13. D, E, F, G, H; $r = 4$

Evaluate the expression.

14. $_5C_1$
15. $_9C_9$
16. $_{12}C_3$

17. A team of 25 rowers attends a rowing tournament. Five rowers compete at a time. How many combinations of 5 rowers are possible?

18. A grocery store sells 7 different flavors of vegetable dip. You have enough money to purchase 2 flavors. How many combinations of 2 flavors of vegetable dip are possible?

SMP.3 ERROR ANALYSIS Describe and correct the error in evaluating the expression.

19.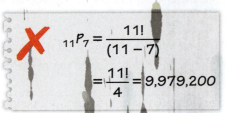

$$_{11}P_7 = \frac{11!}{(11-7)}$$
$$= \frac{11!}{4} = 9{,}979{,}200$$

20.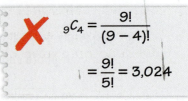

$$_9C_4 = \frac{9!}{(9-4)!}$$
$$= \frac{9!}{5!} = 3{,}024$$

21. **CONNECTION TO REAL LIFE** You and your friend are in the studio audience on a game show. From an audience of 300 people, 2 people are randomly selected as contestants. What is the probability that you and your friend are chosen? (See Example 4.)

22. You work 5 evenings each week. Your supervisor assigns you 5 evenings at random from the 7 possibilities. What is the probability that your schedule does not include working on the weekend?

23. **SMP.8** Complete the table for each given value of r. Then write an inequality relating $_nP_r$ and $_nC_r$.

	$r=0$	$r=1$	$r=2$	$r=3$
$_3P_r$				
$_3C_r$				

24. **CONNECT CONCEPTS** A polygon is convex when no line that contains a side of the polygon contains a point in the interior of the polygon. Consider a convex polygon with n sides. Use the combinations formula to write an expression for the number of diagonals in an n-sided polygon. Then use your result to write a formula for the number of diagonals of an n-sided convex polygon.

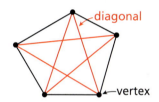

25. **SMP.6** Describe why it makes sense to define 0! as 1.

26. You are ordering a burrito with 2 main ingredients and 3 toppings. The menu below shows the possible choices. How many different burritos are possible?

27. How many integers, greater than 999 but not greater than 4,000, can be formed with the digits 0, 1, 2, 3, and 4? Repetition of digits is allowed.

28. **SMP.1 DIG DEEPER** Follow the steps below to explore a famous probability problem called the *birthday problem*. (Assume there are 365 equally likely birthdays possible.)

   a. What is the probability that at least 2 people share the same birthday in a group of 6 randomly chosen people? in a group of 10 randomly chosen people?

   b. Generalize the results from part (a) by writing a formula for the probability $P(n)$ that at least 2 people in a group of n people share the same birthday. (*Hint:* Use $_nP_r$ notation in your formula.)

   c. Use technology to determine at what group size the probability that at least 2 people share the same birthday first exceeds 50%. Explain your method.

Interpreting Data

LICENSE PLATE NUMBERS License plates assign unique patterns of letters and numbers to each car in a state. Different states use different patterns of symbols.

29. How many different identification permutations with no repeating letters or numbers are possible using (a) 3 letters followed by 3 digits and (b) 6 alphanumeric characters?

30. Which of the states shown below appear to have one of the five fewest possible unique license plates?

Review & Refresh

31. Find the value of x.

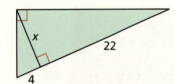

32. You spin the wheel shown. The central angles of the sections of the spinner are congruent. Use a sample space to determine whether randomly spinning red and then blue are independent events.

33. Events A and B are dependent. Find $P(B|A)$ when $P(A \text{ and } B) = 0.04$ and $P(A) = 0.16$.

34. Events A and B are disjoint. Find $P(A \text{ or } B)$ when $P(A) = 0.4$ and $P(B) = 0.6$.

35. A tire has a diameter of 22 inches. How far does the tire travel when it makes 25 revolutions?

36. Point Q is the centroid of $\triangle RST$, and $SV = 39$. Find SQ and QV.

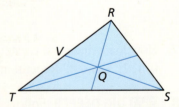

37. Find the measure of the exterior angle.

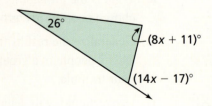

714   Chapter 13   Probability

13.7 Binomial Distributions

> **Learning Target:** Understand binomial distributions.
>
> **Success Criteria:**
> - I can explain the meaning of a probability distribution.
> - I can construct and interpret probability distributions.
> - I can find probabilities using binomial distributions.

INVESTIGATE Counting Outcomes

Work with a partner. The diagrams represent the possible outcomes when flipping n coins.

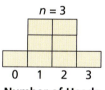

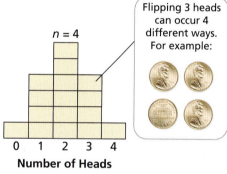

1. What is the probability of flipping 2 heads when 4 coins are flipped?

2. Draw a similar diagram that represents the possible outcomes when flipping 5 coins. What is the probability of flipping 2 heads when 5 coins are flipped?

3. Complete the table showing the numbers of ways in which 2 heads can occur when n coins are flipped.

n	2	3	4	5	6
Occurrences of 2 heads					

4. Describe the pattern shown in Exercise 3. Use the pattern to find the number of ways in which 2 heads can occur when 7 coins are flipped. Justify your answer.

Vocabulary
random variable
probability distribution
binomial distribution
binomial experiment

Probability Distributions

A **random variable** is a variable whose value is determined by the outcomes of a probability experiment. For every random variable, a *probability distribution* can be defined. A **probability distribution** is a function that gives the probability of each possible value of a random variable. The sum of all the probabilities in a probability distribution must equal 1. An example is shown.

Probability Distribution for Rolling a Six-Sided Die

x (random variable)	1	2	3	4	5	6
P(x)	$\frac{1}{6}$	$\frac{1}{6}$	$\frac{1}{6}$	$\frac{1}{6}$	$\frac{1}{6}$	$\frac{1}{6}$

EXAMPLE 1 Constructing a Probability Distribution

Let x be a random variable that represents the sum when two six-sided dice are rolled. Make a table and draw a histogram showing the probability distribution for x.

Make a table. The possible values of x are the integers from 2 to 12. The table shows how many outcomes of rolling two dice produce each value of x. Divide the number of outcomes for x by 36 to find $P(x)$.

x (sum)	2	3	4	5	5	7	8	9	10	11	12
Number of Outcomes	1	2	3	4	5	6	5	4	3	2	1
P(x)	$\frac{1}{36}$	$\frac{1}{18}$	$\frac{1}{12}$	$\frac{1}{9}$	$\frac{5}{36}$	$\frac{1}{6}$	$\frac{5}{36}$	$\frac{1}{9}$	$\frac{1}{12}$	$\frac{1}{18}$	$\frac{1}{36}$

Draw a histogram where the intervals are given by x and the relative frequencies are given by $P(x)$.

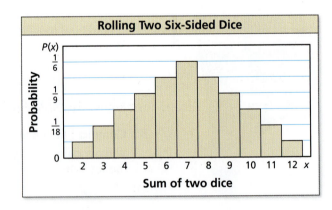

In-Class Practice

Self-Assessment

An octahedral die has eight sides numbered 1 through 8. Let x be a random variable that represents the sum when two such dice are rolled.

1. Make a table and draw a histogram showing the probability distribution for x.

716 Chapter 13 Probability

EXAMPLE 2 **Interpreting a Probability Distribution**

Use the probability distribution in Example 1 to answer each question.

a. **What is the most likely sum when rolling two six-sided dice?**

The most likely sum when rolling two six-sided dice is the value of x for which $P(x)$ is greatest. This probability is greatest for $x = 7$. So, when rolling the two dice, the most likely sum is 7.

b. **What is the probability that the sum of the two dice is at least 10?**

The probability that the sum of the two dice is at least 10 is

$$P(x \geq 10) = P(x = 10) + P(x = 11) + P(x = 12)$$
$$= \frac{3}{36} + \frac{2}{36} + \frac{1}{36}$$
$$= \frac{6}{36}$$
$$= \frac{1}{6}$$
$$\approx 0.167.$$

▶ The probability is about 16.7%.

c. **What is the probability you roll a sum of 7 twice in a row?**

The probability that the sum of the two dice is 7 twice in a row is

$$P(x = 7 \text{ twice in a row}) = P(x = 7) \cdot P(x = 7)$$
$$= \frac{1}{6} \cdot \frac{1}{6}$$
$$= \frac{1}{36}$$
$$\approx 0.028.$$

▶ The probability is about 2.8%.

In-Class Practice
Self-Assessment

Use the probability distribution in Exercise 1 to answer each question.

2. What is the most likely sum when rolling the two dice?

3. What is the probability that the sum of the two dice is at most 3?

4. What is the probability that you roll a sum of 6 twice in a row?

1 I don't understand yet.　2 I can do it with help.　3 I can do it on my own.　4 I can teach someone.

13.7 Binomial Distributions

Binomial Distributions

One type of probability distribution is a **binomial distribution**. A binomial distribution shows the probabilities of the outcomes of a *binomial experiment*.

A **binomial experiment** meets the following conditions.

- There are n independent trials.
- Each trial has only two possible outcomes: success and failure.
- The probability of success is the same for each trial. This probability is denoted by p. The probability of failure is $1 - p$.

For a binomial experiment, the probability of exactly k successes in n trials is

$$P(k \text{ successes}) = {}_nC_k \, p^k (1 - p)^{n-k}.$$

EXAMPLE 3 Constructing a Binomial Distribution

According to a survey, about 60% of teenagers ages 13 to 17 in the U.S. say they spend time with friends online daily. You ask 6 randomly chosen teenagers (ages 13 to 17) whether they spend time with friends online daily. Draw a histogram of the binomial distribution for your survey. What is the most likely outcome of your survey?

The probability that a randomly selected teenager says they spend time with friends online daily is $p = 0.6$. Because you survey 6 people, $n = 6$.

$P(k = 0) = {}_6C_0 (0.6)^0 (0.4)^6 \approx 0.004$

$P(k = 1) = {}_6C_1 (0.6)^1 (0.4)^5 \approx 0.037$

$P(k = 2) = {}_6C_2 (0.6)^2 (0.4)^4 \approx 0.138$

$P(k = 3) = {}_6C_3 (0.6)^3 (0.4)^3 \approx 0.276$

$P(k = 4) = {}_6C_4 (0.6)^4 (0.4)^2 \approx 0.311$

$P(k = 5) = {}_6C_5 (0.6)^5 (0.4)^1 \approx 0.187$

$P(k = 6) = {}_6C_6 (0.6)^6 (0.4)^0 \approx 0.047$

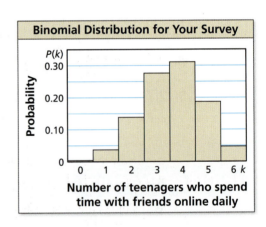

▶ The most likely outcome is that 4 of the 6 teenagers spend time with friends online daily.

In-Class Practice

Self-Assessment

According to a survey, about 26% of people ages 12 and older in the U.S. have listened to a podcast in the last month. You ask 4 randomly chosen people ages 12 and older whether they have listened to a podcast in the last month.

5. Draw a histogram of the binomial distribution for your survey. What is the most likely outcome of your survey?

1 I don't understand yet. **2** I can do it with help. **3** I can do it on my own. **4** I can teach someone.

13.7 Practice

Make a table and draw a histogram showing the probability distribution for the random variable. (See Example 1.)

▶ 1. x = the number on a table tennis ball randomly chosen from a bag that contains 5 balls labeled "1," 3 balls labeled "2," and 2 balls labeled "3."

2. $w = 1$ when a randomly chosen letter from the English alphabet is a vowel and $w = 2$ otherwise.

Use the probability distribution to determine (a) the number that is most likely to be spun on a spinner, (b) the probability of spinning an even number, and (c) the probability of spinning an odd number twice in a row. (See Example 2.)

▶ 3.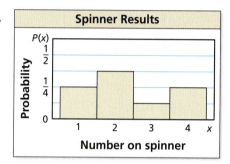

4.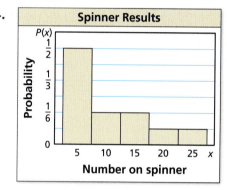

Calculate the probability of flipping a coin 20 times and getting the given number of heads.

5. 1   6. 4   ▶ 7. 18   8. 20

▶ 9. **SMP.4 CONNECTION TO REAL LIFE** In your school, 30% of students plan to attend a movie night. You ask 5 randomly chosen students from your school whether they plan to attend the movie night. (See Example 3.)

   a. Draw a histogram of the binomial distribution for your survey.
   b. What is the most likely outcome of your survey?
   c. What is the probability that at most 2 students plan to attend the movie night?

10. **SMP.2** A sound system has n speakers. Each speaker functions with probability p, independent of the other speakers. The system will function when at least 50% of its speakers function. For what values of p is a 5-speaker system more likely to function than a 3-speaker system?

11. **DIG DEEPER** How many successes might you expect from a binomial experiment with n trials and probability of success p? (Hint: Find the mean number of successes for n trials.)

12. **CONNECT CONCEPTS** On the farm shown, 7 gopher holes appear each week. Assume that a gopher hole has an equal chance of appearing at any point on the farm. What is the probability that at least one gopher hole appears in the carrot patch?

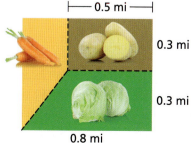

Interpreting Data

BIRTH WEIGHT The distribution shows the birthweights for about 2,500 newborn babies in Canada. Babies often lose around 10% of their weight shortly after birth. Most babies gain this weight back within the first 2 weeks after birth.

13. What would you expect the average weight to be for two-week-old babies in Canada?

14. Estimate the percent of babies whose birthweight is between 3.3 kilograms and 3.5 kilograms.

15. Estimate the percent of babies whose birthweight is greater than 3.5 kilograms.

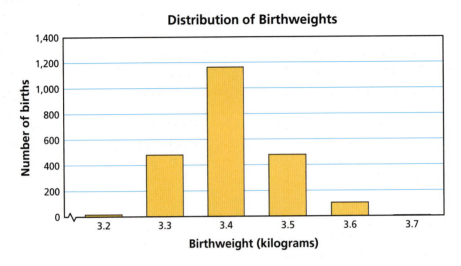

Review & Refresh

Count the possible combinations of *r* letters chosen from the given list.

16. E, F, G, H; $r = 2$

17. L, M, N, O, P; $r = 3$

18. Find the coordinates of the intersection of the diagonals of ▱MNPQ with vertices $M(2, 3)$, $N(6, 5)$, $P(8, -3)$, and $Q(4, -5)$.

19. Let $\angle G$ be an acute angle with $\sin G = 0.71$. Use technology to approximate $m\angle G$.

20. You collect data about a dog pageant. Of the 25 dogs in the pageant, 7 receive a ribbon, 18 receive a collar, and 5 receive both a ribbon and a collar. What is the probability that a dog in the pageant receives a ribbon *or* a collar?

21. A bag contains three $10 gift cards, two $20 gift cards, and a $30 gift card. You randomly select a gift card and give it away. Then you randomly select another gift card.

    Event A: You select the $10 gift card first.

    Event B: You select the $20 gift card second.

    Determine whether the events are independent or dependent.

22. Point *D* is a point of tangency. Find the radius *r* of ⊙*C*.

    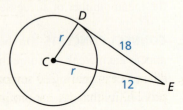

13 Chapter Review with

Rate your understanding of each section.

 I don't understand yet.   I can do it with help. 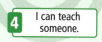 I can do it on my own. **4** I can teach someone.

13.1 Sample Spaces and Probability (pp. 671–678)

◉ **Learning Target:** Find sample spaces and probabilities of events.

Vocabulary
probability experiment
outcome
event
sample space
probability of an event
theoretical probability
experimental probability

1. You flip a coin and draw a marble at random from a bag containing two blue marbles and two green marbles. Find the number of possible outcomes in the sample space. Then list the possible outcomes.

2. A bag contains 9 tiles, one for each letter in the word HAPPINESS. You choose a tile at random. What is the probability that you choose a tile with the letter S? What is the probability that you choose a tile with a letter other than P?

3. You throw a dart at the board shown. Your dart is equally likely to hit any point inside the square board. Are you most likely to get 5 points, 10 points, or 20 points?

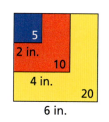

13.2 Two-Way Tables and Probability (pp. 679–684)

◉ **Learning Target:** Use two-way tables to represent data and find probabilities.

Vocabulary
two-way table
joint frequency
marginal frequency
joint relative frequency
marginal relative frequency
conditional relative frequency

4. A survey asks residents of the east and west sides of a city whether they support the construction of a mall. The results, given as joint relative frequencies, are shown in the two-way table. What is the probability that a randomly selected resident who responded no is from the west side?

		Location	
		East Side	West Side
Response	Yes	0.47	0.36
	No	0.08	0.09

5. After an assembly, 220 seniors and 270 juniors respond to a survey. Of those, 200 seniors and 230 juniors say the motivational speaker was impactful. Organize these results in a two-way table. Then find and interpret the marginal frequencies.

13.3 Conditional Probability (pp. 685–692)

Learning Target: Find and use conditional probabilities.

Vocabulary
conditional probability

6. You have two acrylic paintings and two oil paintings. You randomly select a painting to sell and then you randomly select a different painting to present at a gallery. Find the probability that you selected an acrylic painting to sell given that you randomly selected an oil painting to present at the gallery.

7. An inspector tests rotors of helicopter drones. The two-way table shows the joint and marginal relative frequencies. Find and compare $P(\text{single rotor} \mid \text{failed})$ and $P(\text{single rotor} \mid \text{passed})$.

		Result		
		Passed	Failed	Total
Type	Single Rotor	0.30	0.20	0.50
	Multi-Rotor	0.40	0.10	0.50
	Total	0.70	0.30	1

8. At a baseball game, 90% of guests receive a coupon code and 30% of guests receive a coupon code and a bobblehead. What is the probability that a guest who receives a coupon code also receives a bobblehead?

13.4 Independent and Dependent Events (pp. 693–700)

Learning Target: Understand and find probabilities of independent and dependent events.

Vocabulary
independent events
dependent events

9. As part of a board game, you need to spin the spinner, which is divided into equal parts. Find the probability that you get a 2 on your first spin and a number less than or equal to 5 on your second spin.

10. You are a DJ at a wedding. A playlist contains 10 pop songs and 20 country songs. You set the playlist to select songs at random. Once a song is played, the same song will not play again. Find the probability that the first two songs to play are both country songs.

722 Chapter 13 Probability

13.5 Probability of Disjoint and Overlapping Events (pp. 701–706)

Learning Target: Find probabilities of disjoint and overlapping events.

Vocabulary
compound event
overlapping events
disjoint events

11. Let A and B be events such that $P(A) = 0.32$, $P(B) = 0.48$, and $P(A \text{ and } B) = 0.12$. Find $P(A \text{ or } B)$.

12. Out of 100 employees in a restaurant, 92 either work part time or work 5 days each week. There are 14 employees who work part time and 80 employees who work 5 days each week. What is the probability that a randomly selected employee works both part time and 5 days each week?

13.6 Permutations and Combinations (pp. 707–714)

Learning Target: Count permutations and combinations.

Vocabulary
permutation
factorial
combination

Evaluate the expression.

13. $_7P_6$

14. $_{13}P_{10}$

15. $_6C_2$

16. $_8C_4$

17. You and your friend are two of the four winners of individual concert tickets. There is one VIP ticket, one superior ticket, one general admission ticket, and one value ticket. The tickets are given to the winners randomly. Find the probability that you get the superior ticket and your friend gets the value ticket.

18. You work in a food truck at a festival. Of the 11 food trucks, 2 are randomly selected to be placed at the entrance. What is the probability that your food truck is placed at the entrance?

13.7 Binomial Distributions (pp. 715–720)

Learning Target: Understand binomial distributions.

Vocabulary
random variable
probability distribution
binomial distribution
binomial experiment

19. Find the probability of flipping a coin 12 times and getting exactly 4 heads.

20. A basketball player makes a free throw 82.6% of the time. The player attempts 5 free throws. Draw a histogram of the binomial distribution of the number of successful free throws. What is the most likely outcome?

21. According to a survey, about 37% of Americans go online mostly using a smartphone. You ask 4 randomly chosen Americans about whether they go online mostly using a smartphone. Draw a histogram of the binomial distribution for your survey. What is the probability that two or more of the respondents go online mostly using a smartphone?

13 PERFORMANCE TASK
SMP.4

Buried Treasures

COINS
Coins are often made with words and images that provide valuable information about nations and rulers.

Archaeologists study a wide variety of artifacts in order to learn about the past.

POTTERY
Pottery, one of the most common types of archaeological discovery, gives cultural insight into ancient societies.

INSCRIPTIONS
Inscriptions and manuscripts give insight into culture, language, chronology, and much more.

TOOLS
Ancient tools demonstrate the technologies and behaviors of ancient peoples.

BONES
Bones provide information about topics such as lifestyle, health, and ages of civilizations.

Analyzing Data

Use the information on the previous page to complete the following exercises.

1 Explain what is shown in the display. What do you notice? What do you wonder?

2 You find 4 bones, 6 pieces of pottery, and 2 coins at an excavation site. You choose one of the artifacts at random to clean. List the possible outcomes.

3 Find the theoretical probability of choosing each type of artifact to clean.

CHOOSING AN EXCAVATION SITE

Archaeologists will choose one of three sites to excavate. Multiple surveys are used to determine whether each site appears likely to contain a significant number of ancient artifacts. The conclusions of the surveys are shown. Which site should the archaeologists choose? Create a presentation to convince the archaeologists to choose this site.

Site	Likely	Unlikely
A	|||| ||||		||||
B	|||| |||	|||
C	|||| ||||	||||

The site is partitioned into 9 square-shaped regions. In any given region, the probability of finding an artifact is about 45%. Draw and interpret a histogram of a probability distribution for this situation.

Connecting Big Ideas

For use after Chapter 13.
SMP.1   SMP.4

More than 80 percent of Earth's surface is of volcanic origin. The number of volcanoes in the world is shown in the map. The graph shows the number of volcanoes in each of the top 20 countries with the most volcanoes.

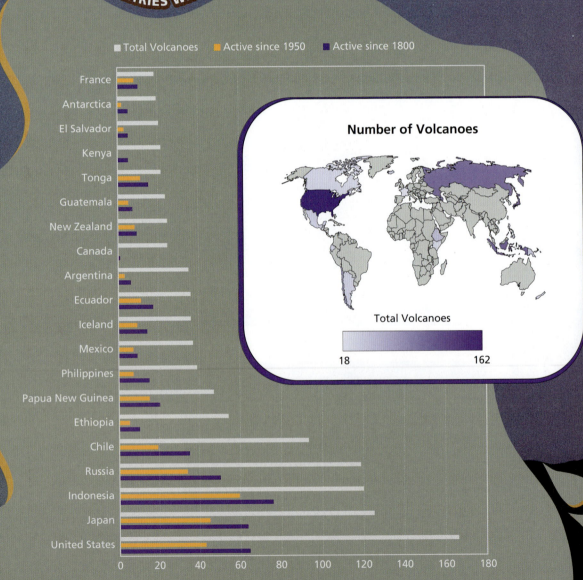

1. What do you notice?
   What do you wonder?

2. Make a two-way table with two countries that displays the number of volcanoes that have been active since 1950 and the number of volcanoes that have not been active since 1950.

3. Find and interpret the marginal frequencies of the two-way table.

4. What is the probability that a randomly selected volcano from the list of countries in the graph has been active since 1950?

5. What is the probability that a randomly selected volcano from the list of countries in the graph is located in Japan and has been active since 1800?

6. Use the Internet to research the surface area of Earth. Then create a spherical data display that shows how much of Earth's surface is of volcanic origin compared to the rest of the surface.

THINKING ABOUT THE BIG IDEAS

How can **Finding Surface Area and Volume** help you create a spherical data display?

Connecting Big Ideas

Selected Answers

Getting Ready for Chapter 1
1. 4
2. 11
3. 9
4. 8
5. 6
6. 1
7. 154 m²
8. 200 in.²
9. 84 yd²
10. 30 ft²

1.1 Practice
1. $\overleftrightarrow{QW}$, line g
3. R, Q, S; Sample answer: T
5. $\overline{DB}$
7. $\overrightarrow{EB}$ and $\overrightarrow{ED}$, $\overrightarrow{EA}$ and $\overrightarrow{EC}$
9. $\overrightarrow{AD}$ and $\overrightarrow{AC}$ are not opposite rays because A, C, and D are not collinear; Sample answer: $\overrightarrow{AD}$ and $\overrightarrow{AB}$ are opposite rays.
11. Sample answer:
13. Sample answer:
15. Sample answer:
17. J
19. K, N
21. One airplane passes above the other because they are traveling in different planes.
23. no; Two planes can intersect in a line, overlap completely, or not intersect at all.
25. segment
27. yes; yes; yes; Sample answer:
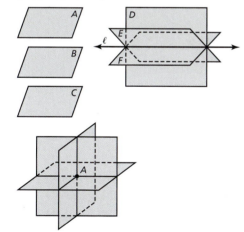
29. no; It is not possible to create a triangular figure in which any two sides are coplanar, but the entire triangle does *not* lie on one plane.

1.1 Review & Refresh
31. Lines a and b are parallel.
32. Lines a and b are perpendicular. None are parallel.
33. $|10t - 30| = 5$; 2.5 hours, 3.5 hours
34. 32
35. 6
36.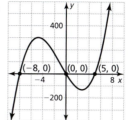
37.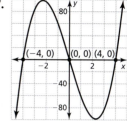
38.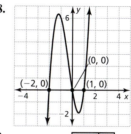
39.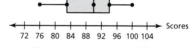
40. $x = 25$
41. $x = 42$
42. $a < -11$
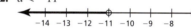
43. $z \leq 48$

1.2 Practice
1. 3.5 cm
3. 4.5 cm
5. Check students' work.
7. 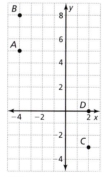 yes
9. 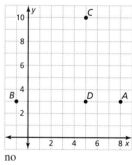 no
11. 22
13. 24
15. The absolute value should have been found; $AB = 3.5$
17. $2\frac{1}{4}$ in., $1\frac{3}{4}$ in.; about $\frac{1}{2}$ in.; about $1\frac{2}{7}$ times
19. a. true; B is on $\overleftrightarrow{AC}$ between A and C.
    b. false; B, C, and E are not collinear.
    c. true; D is on $\overleftrightarrow{AH}$ between A and H.
    d. false; C, E, and F are not collinear.
21. $|a - c| = |e - f|$
23. 58 or 128
25. Square footage only includes living area, and porches and garages are not considered living area.
27. Sample answer: What is the length of the porch?; about 11.5 ft

Selected Answers A1

1.2 Review & Refresh
28. $y = 9$
29. $x = 6$
30. Sample answer:
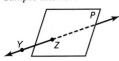
31.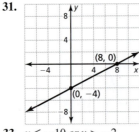
32. $x \le 19$

33. $v \le -10$ or $v > -2$
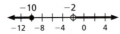
34. $x > 2$
35.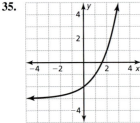

asymptote: $y = -3$; domain: all real numbers; range: $y > -3$

36. yes; yes; As more people attend an amusement park, the lines are likely to get longer.
37. not a function
38. 5 touchdowns; 2 field goals
39. $y = -6x + 3$
40. $y = \frac{1}{4}x - 6$

1.3 Practice
1. line k; 34
3. M; 40
5. $\overrightarrow{MN}$; 32
7. Check students' work.
9. (5, 2)
11. (3, 12)
13. 10 units
15. $\sqrt{13}$, or about 3.6 units
17. The y-coordinates were subtracted from the x-coordinates of each point, instead of subtracting the corresponding coordinates from each point. $AB = \sqrt{61}$
19. $EF = 5$, $GH = \sqrt{41} \approx 6.4$; no; $\overline{GH}$
21. $\left(\frac{a+b}{2}, c\right)$; $|b - a|$
23. 13 cm
25. no; The distance from home plate to the pitcher's mound is 60 feet 6 inches, but the distance from the pitcher's mound to second base is over 66 feet.
27. about 0.4 sec

1.3 Review & Refresh
28. $3x(x - 12)$
29. $(n - 7)(n + 10)$
30. $\overrightarrow{TP}$ and $\overrightarrow{TQ}$, $\overrightarrow{TR}$ and $\overrightarrow{TS}$
31. $y = -\frac{1}{3}x - 2$
32. 12
33. 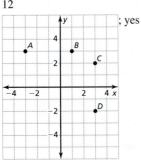 ; yes

34. a. 76 points
    b. 6 incorrect answers
35. $\dfrac{1}{b^8}$
36. $\dfrac{125t^{12}}{8}$

1.4 Practice
1. quadrilateral; concave
3. pentagon; convex
5. $13 + \sqrt{89}$, or about 22.43 units
7. $7 + 2\sqrt{10} + \sqrt{13}$, or about 16.93 units
9. 7.5 square units
11. 9 square units
13. $4 + 4\sqrt{2}$, or about 9.66 units; 4 square units
15. $12\sqrt{2}$, or about 16.97 units; 16 square units
17. $4 + 12\sqrt{2}$, or about 20.97 units; 20 square units
19. 34 ft; 60 ft²
21. about 10.47 mi
23. Sample answer: (0, 0), (0, 2), (4, 0)
25. $4\sqrt{5} + 2\sqrt{10}$, or about 15.27 units; 10 square units
27. 13 square units; Sample answer: Draw a rectangle with vertices (3, −1), (−3, −1), (−3, 4), and (3, 4). Subtract the area of the unshaded triangles inside the rectangle from the total area of the rectangle.
29. about 170,240 mi²

1.4 Review & Refresh
31. linear
32. $x = -1$
33. $x = 1$
34. $\overline{TR}$
35. $\overrightarrow{QV}$ and $\overrightarrow{QS}$, $\overrightarrow{QR}$ and $\overrightarrow{QT}$
36. (3, 0); $2\sqrt{10}$, or about 6.32 units
37. Check students' work.
38. $y = 200(1.0125)^{4t}$
39.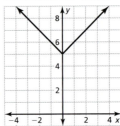

The graph of g is a vertical translation 5 units up of the graph of f.

40.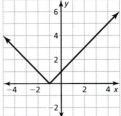

The graph of g is a horizontal translation 1 unit left of the graph of f.

1.5 Practice
1. $\angle G$, $\angle FGH$, $\angle HGF$
3. $\angle HMK$, $\angle KMN$, $\angle HMN$
5. 65°; acute
7. 115°; obtuse
9. The outer scale was used, but the inner scale should have been used because $\overrightarrow{OB}$ passes through 0° on the inner scale; $m\angle BOC = 155°$
11. Check students' work.
13. $\angle ADE$, $\angle BDC$, $\angle BCD$
15. 34°
17. 58°
19. 37°, 58°
21. 77°, 103°
23. Check students' work.
25. 75°
27. 63°, 126°
29. 62°, 62°
31. 44°, 44°, 88°
33. 90°, 90°

35. a. acute **b.** acute **c.** acute **d.** right
37. 22 times; At 12 A.M., the minute hand and the hour hand overlap, so the angle between the hands is 0°. The angle increases to 180° and decreases back to 0° when the hands overlap again. The hands will form a right angle two times during this period. So, for every time after 12 A.M. that the hands overlap, the hands formed a right angle two times. The hands overlap 11 times from 12 A.M. to 12 P.M. So, the hands form a right angle 2 • 11 = 22 times.
39. Roofs with greater pitches cost more to build because they require more shingles or other roofing materials to cover them.

1.5 Review & Refresh
41. $3 + \sqrt{10} + \sqrt{13}$, or about 9.77 units; 4.5 square units
42. 35 **43.** $x = 12$
44. all real numbers **45.** $4\sqrt{10}$
46. $3\sqrt[3]{5}$ **47.** $\frac{\sqrt{21}}{10}$ **48.** $\frac{\sqrt{55}}{5}$

49. 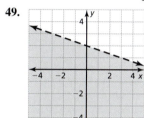 **50.**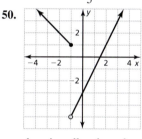
domain: all real numbers; range: $y > -5$

51. a. Player A
 b. about 18.9 m
52. $(-6, 5)$ **53.** $(4, -3)$

1.6 Practice
1. $\angle LJM, \angle MJN$ **3.** 67°
5. $m\angle QRT = 47°, m\angle TRS = 133°$
7. $m\angle UVW = 12°, m\angle XYZ = 78°$
9. $\angle 1$ and $\angle 5$ **11.** yes
13. They do not share a common vertex and side, so they are not adjacent; Sample answer: $\angle 1$ and $\angle 2$ are adjacent.
15. 60°, 120° **17.** 122°
19. Check students' work.
21. $x + (\frac{1}{2}x + 3) = 180$; 118°, 62°
23. a. yes; They are marked as congruent.
 b. yes; Point A lies on $\overleftrightarrow{CF}$.
 c. no; They do not have a special relationship, and their angle measurements are unknown.
 d. no; They are not marked as congruent
 e. yes; $\angle BAD$ and $\angle DAE$ are a linear pair, and $\angle BAD$ is marked as a right angle.
25. a. $y = 90 - x, z = 180 - x$; domain of both functions is $0 < x < 90$; $\angle 1$ and $\angle 2$ are complementary, so the measure of $\angle 1$ is between 0° and 90°.

b.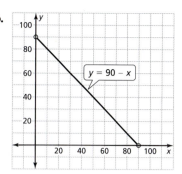

The range is $0 < y < 90$;

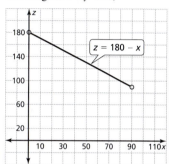

The range is $90 < z < 180$.
27. 77.1°, 90°, 100°, 72°, 81.8°, 60°

1.6 Review & Refresh
29. 24 square units **30.** 12.5 square units
31. $(6, -1)$ **32.** M; 32
33. $t = -8, t = -2$
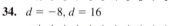
34. $d = -8, d = 16$

35. 68°, 58° **36.** $-5; 2$ **37.** $\frac{3}{2}; -7$

Chapter 1 Review
1. Sample answer: plane XYN **2.** Sample answer: line g
3. Sample answer: line h **4.** Sample answer: $\overleftrightarrow{XZ}, \overrightarrow{YP}$
5. $\overrightarrow{YX}$ and $\overrightarrow{YZ}$ **6.** P
7. no; yes; no

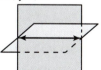

8. 41 **9.** 11
10.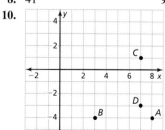

no
11. 126 m; about 19.26 min
12. $(\frac{1}{2}, \frac{13}{2}); \sqrt{50}$, or about 7.1 units
13. $(\frac{13}{2}, -\frac{5}{2}); \sqrt{2}$, or about 1.4 units

14. $(-2, -3)$
15. 40
16. about 45.9 ft; I used the Distance Formula to determine the distance from home plate to second base is about 84.85 feet. So, the midpoint is about 42.4 feet from home plate. So, the pitchers plate is 3.5 feet farther than this distance, or about 45.9 feet.
17. $2\sqrt{65}$, or about 16.1 units
18. hexagon; convex
19. octagon; concave
20. 20 units; 21 square units
21. $14 + 7\sqrt{2}$, or about 23.9 units; 24.5 square units
22. The area of the convex polygon is greater; the perimeter of the concave polygon is greater.
23. $11 + 5\sqrt{2} + \sqrt{17}$, or about 22.2 units
24. 29.5 square units
25. 49°, 28°
26. 88°, 23°
27. 127°
28. 34°, 86°
29. 78°
30. 7°
31. 64°
32. 124°
33. Check students' work.
34. 144°, 36°
35. 112°, 68°

Chapter 2

Getting Ready for Chapter 2

1. $a_n = 6n - 3$; $a_{50} = 297$
2. $a_n = 17n - 46$; $a_{50} = 804$
3. $a_n = 0.6n + 2.2$; $a_{50} = 32.2$
4. $x = y - 5$
5. $x = -4y + 3$
6. $x = y - 3$
7. $x = \dfrac{y}{7}$
8. $x = \dfrac{y - 6}{z + 4}$
9. $x = \dfrac{z}{6y + 2}$

2.1 Practice

1. hypothesis: you run; conclusion: you are fast
3. If $x = 2$, then $9x + 5 = 23$.
5. If a glacier melts, then the sea level rises.
7. The sky is not blue.
9. The ball is pink.
11. conditional: If two angles are supplementary, then the measures of the angles sum to 180°; true
converse: If the measures of two angles sum to 180°, then the angles are supplementary; true
inverse: If two angles are not supplementary, then the measures of the angles do not sum to 180°; true
contrapositive: If the measures of two angles do not sum to 180°, then the angles are not supplementary; true
13. conditional: If it does not snow, then I will run outside; false
converse: If I run outside, then it is not snowing; false
inverse: If it snows, then I will not run outside; false
contrapositive: If I do not run outside, then it is snowing; false
15. conditional: If $3x - 7 = 20$, then $x = 9$; true
converse: If $x = 9$, then $3x - 7 = 20$; true
inverse: If $3x - 7 \ne 20$, then $x \ne 9$; true
contrapositive: If $x \ne 9$, then $3x - 7 \ne 20$; true
17. true; By definition of right angle, the measure of $\angle ABC$ is 90°.
19. true; If angles form a linear pair, then the sum of their angle measures is 180°.
21. A point is the midpoint of a segment if and only if it is the point that divides the segment into two congruent segments.
23. Two angles are adjacent angles if and only if they share a common vertex and side, but have no common interior points.
25. A polygon has three sides if and only if it is a triangle.

27.

p	q	$\sim p$	$\sim p \rightarrow q$
T	T	F	T
T	F	F	T
F	T	T	T
F	F	T	F

29.

p	q	$\sim p$	$\sim q$	$\sim p \rightarrow \sim q$	$\sim(\sim p \rightarrow \sim q)$
T	T	F	F	T	F
T	F	F	T	T	F
F	T	T	F	F	T
F	F	T	T	T	F

31.

p	q	$\sim p$	$q \rightarrow \sim p$
T	T	F	F
T	F	F	T
F	T	T	T
F	F	T	T

33. The inverse was used instead of the converse; If I bring an umbrella, then it is raining.
35. inverse; $p \rightarrow q$; $\sim p \rightarrow \sim q$
37. Sample answer: If a student is in the jazz band, then the student is in the band. If a student is in chorus, then the student is not in the band. If a student is in chorus, then the student is a musician.
39. Sample answer: slogan: "This treadmill is a fat-burning machine!"; conditional statement: If you use this treadmill, then you will burn fat.
41. a. Sample answer: If a natural arch is the largest in the United States, then it is the Landscape Arch. If a natural arch is the Landscape Arch, then it spans 290 feet.
b. contrapositive; Sample answer: If a natural arch is not the Landscape Arch, then it is not the largest in the United States. If a natural arch does not span 290 feet, then it is not the Landscape Arch.
c. converse, inverse; Sample answer: converse: If a natural arch is the Landscape Arch, then it is the largest in the United States; inverse: If a natural arch is not the largest in the United States, then it is not the Landscape Arch; Both of these statements are true because there is only one arch that fits both criteria.
converse: If a natural arch spans 290 feet, then it is the Landscape Arch; inverse: If a natural arch is not the Landscape Arch, then it does not span 290 feet; Both of these statements are false because it is possible for a natural arch in another country to span 290 feet.
43. no; In the truth tables for the converse and contrapositive of $p \rightarrow q$, there are no situations where the converse $q \rightarrow p$ and the contrapositive $\sim q \rightarrow \sim p$ are both false.
45. Sample answer:
Circular argument: Maine is the best place to visit because it is better than any other state.
Strawman argument: When a principal wants to remove a school vending machine, a student says that the principal wants to remove everything that students like.
Bandwagon fallacy: All of my classmates think the solution of an equation is 12, so the solution must be 12.

2.1 Review & Refresh
46. not a function   47. 114°, 66°   48. 384,400
49. 49°, 98°   50. $-3x^3 + 21x^2$ 51. $z^2 + 7z - 8$
52. $5b^2 - 10b + 5$ 53. $-4n^3 + 5n^2 + 5n - 1$
54. $x \leq 6$

2.2 Practice
1. The absolute value of each number in the list is 1 greater than the absolute value of the previous number in the list, and the signs alternate from positive to negative; $-6, 7$
3. This is a sequence of regular polygons, each polygon having one more side than the previous polygon.

5. *Sample answer:* The sum of an even integer and an odd integer is an odd integer; $2 + 5 = 7, -4 + 9 = 5, 10 + 7 = 17$
7. *Sample answer:* The quotient of a number and its reciprocal is the square of that number;
$9 \div \frac{1}{9} = 9 \cdot 9 = 9^2, \frac{2}{3} \div \frac{3}{2} = \frac{2}{3} \cdot \frac{2}{3} = \left(\frac{2}{3}\right)^2,$
$\frac{1}{7} \div 7 = \frac{1}{7} \cdot \frac{1}{7} = \left(\frac{1}{7}\right)^2$
9. *Sample answer:* $1 \cdot 5 = 5, 5 \not> 5$
11. They could both be right angles. Then, neither are acute.
13. Your device crashes.
15. Point P is the midpoint of $\overline{LH}$.
17. not possible
19. *Sample answer:* The sum of two odd integers is an even integer; Let m and n be integers. Then $(2m + 1)$ and $(2n + 1)$ are odd integers.
$(2m + 1) + (2n + 1) = 2m + 2n + 2 = 2(m + n + 1);$
$2(m + n + 1)$ is an integer divisible by 2 and is therefore an even integer.
21. Inductive reasoning because the conjecture is based on the assumption that a pattern, observed in specific cases, will continue.
23. Deductive reasoning because the Law of Syllogism was used to draw the conclusion.
25. *Sample answer:* Each term in the sequence is twice the previous term, $\frac{1}{4}, \frac{1}{2}, 1, 2, 4$; Each term is $\frac{1}{4}$ more than the previous term, $\frac{1}{4}, \frac{1}{2}, \frac{3}{4}, 1, \frac{5}{4}$; Each term is the product of the previous term and half the reciprocal of the previous term; $\frac{1}{4}, \frac{1}{2}, \frac{1}{2}, \frac{1}{2}, \frac{1}{2}$
27. **a.** Mineral C must be Talc. Mineral A must be either Gypsum or Calcite. Mineral B must be either Calcite or Fluorite. Mineral D is not Talc.
   b. Check Mineral B and Mineral D. If Mineral D scratches Mineral B, then Mineral D is Fluorite, Mineral B is Calcite, and Mineral A is Gypsum. If Mineral B scratches Mineral D, then Mineral B is Fluorite, and you have to check Mineral D and Mineral A. The one that scratches the other has the higher hardness rating and is therefore Calcite. The one that gets scratched is Gypsum.
29. **a.** false   **b.** true

2.2 Review & Refresh
31. hypothesis: there is a storm surge; conclusion: erosion of coastline occurs; If there is a storm surge, then the erosion of the coastline will occur.

32. hexagon; convex   33. $a_1 = 4, a_n = a_{n-1} + 7$
34. $y = -2x + 8$ 35. 71°   36. nonlinear
37. $x = 2$ 38. Angle Addition Postulate
39. $-3n^2 - 5n + 2$ 40. $x = 4$

2.3 Practice
1. Two Point Postulate
3. *Sample answer:* Line q contains points J and K.
5. *Sample answer:* Through points K, H, and L, there is exactly one plane, which is plane M.

7.   9.

11. yes   13. no   15. yes
17. yes

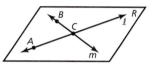

19. parallel
21. *Sample answer:* It appears to give the drawing depth and distance, which creates an illusion of three dimensionality.

2.3 Review & Refresh
22. *Sample answer:* trapezoid
23. $t = 2$ 24. $x = 35$ 25. 153°
26. $6 + 4\sqrt{10}$, or about 18.65 units; 18 square units
27. 60 in., 15 in.   28. 640, 2,560, 10,240
29. You can vote if and only if you are least 18 years old.

2.4 Practice
1. Subtraction Property of Equality; Addition Property of Equality; Division Property of Equality

3. | Equation | Explanation and Reason |
|---|---|
| $2x - 8 = 6x - 20$ | Write the equation; Given |
| $-4x - 8 = -20$ | Subtract $6x$ from each side; Subtraction Property of Equality |
| $-4x = -12$ | Add 8 to each side; Addition Property of Equality |
| $x = 3$ | Divide each side by -4; Division Property of Equality |

5. | Equation | Explanation and Reason |
|---|---|
| $3(2x + 11) = 9$ | Write the equation; Given |
| $6x + 33 = 9$ | Multiply; Distributive Property |
| $6x = -24$ | Subtract 33 from each side; Subtraction Property of Equality |
| $x = -4$ | Divide each side by 6; Division Property of Equality |

Selected Answers   A5

7.
Equation	Explanation and Reason
$44 - 2(3x + 4) = -18x$	Write the equation; Given
$44 - 6x - 8 = -18x$	Multiply; Distributive Property
$-6x + 36 = -18x$	Combine like terms; Simplify.
$36 = -12x$	Add $6x$ to each side; Addition Property of Equality
$-3 = x$	Divide each side by -12; Division Property of Equality
$x = -3$	Rewrite the solution; Symmetric Property of Equality

9. The reasons for the second and third equations are incorrect.
   $6x + 14 = 32$ Given
   $6x = 18$ Subtraction Property of Equality
   $x = 3$ Division Property of Equality

11.
Equation	Explanation and Reason
$5x + y = 18$	Write the equation; Given
$y = -5x + 18$	Subtract $5x$ from each side; Subtraction Property of Equality

13.
Equation	Explanation and Reason
$2y + 0.5x = 16$	Write the equation; Given
$2y = -0.5x + 16$	Subtract $0.5x$ from each side; Subtraction Property of Equality
$y = -0.25x + 8$	Divide each side by 2; Division Property of Equality

15.
Equation	Explanation and Reason
$12 - 3y = 30x + 6$	Write the equation; Given
$-3y = 30x - 6$	Subtract 12 from each side; Subtraction Property of Equality
$y = -10x + 2$	Divide each side by -3; Division Property of Equality

17.
Equation	Explanation and Reason
$C = 2\pi r$	Write the equation; Given
$\dfrac{C}{2\pi} = r$	Divide each side by 2π; Division Property of Equality
$r = \dfrac{C}{2\pi}$	Rewrite the equation; Symmetric Property of Equality

19.
Equation	Explanation and Reason
$S = 2\pi r^2 + 2\pi rh$	Write the equation; Given
$S - 2\pi r^2 = 2\pi rh$	Subtract $2\pi r^2$ from each side; Subtraction Property of Equality
$\dfrac{S - 2\pi r^2}{2\pi r} = h$	Divide each side by $2\pi r$; Division Property of Equality
$h = \dfrac{S - 2\pi r^2}{2\pi r}$	Rewrite the equation; Symmetric Property of Equality

21.
Equation	Explanation and Reason
$A = \tfrac{1}{2}h(b_1 + b_2)$	Write the equation; Given
$\dfrac{2A}{h} = b_1 + b_2$	Divide each side by $\tfrac{1}{2}h$; Division Property of Equality
$\dfrac{2A}{h} - b_2 = b_1$	Subtract b_2 from each side; Subtraction Property of Equality
$b_1 = \dfrac{2A}{h} - b_2$	Rewrite the equation; Symmetric Property of Equality

$b_1 = 6$ m

23. Addition Property of Equality
25. Symmetric Property of Equality
27. Transitive Property of Equality

29.
Equation	Explanation and Reason
$m\angle 1 = m\angle 4$, $m\angle EHF = 90°$, $m\angle GHF = 90°$	Marked in diagram; Given
$m\angle EHF = m\angle GHF$	$\angle EHF$ and $\angle GHF$ are both $90°$; Transitive Property of Equality
$m\angle EHF = m\angle 1 + m\angle 2$, $m\angle GHF = m\angle 3 + m\angle 4$	Add measures of adjacent angles; Angle Addition Postulate
$m\angle 1 + m\angle 2 = m\angle 3 + m\angle 4$	Substitute $m\angle 1 + m\angle 2$ for $m\angle EHF$. Substitute $m\angle 3 + m\angle 4$ for $m\angle GHF$; Substitution Property of Equality
$m\angle 1 + m\angle 2 = m\angle 3 + m\angle 1$	Substitute $m\angle 1$ for $m\angle 4$; Substitution Property of Equality
$m\angle 2 = m\angle 3$	Subtract $m\angle 1$ from each side; Subtraction Property of Equality

31. 1; 2; 3; The definition of the Reflexive Property of Equality only involves one angle or segment. The definition of the Symmetric Property of Equality involves two angles or segments. The definition of the Transitive Property of Equality involves three angles or segments.

33.
Equation	Explanation and Reason
$BC = DA$, $CD = AB$	Marked in diagram; Given
$AC = AC$	AC is equal to itself; Reflexive Property of Equality
$AC + AB + BC = AC + AB + BC$	Add $AB + BC$ to each side of $AC = AC$; Addition Property of Equality
$AC + AB + BC = AC + CD + DA$	Substitute CD for AB, and DA for BC; Substitution Property of Equality

35. a.
Equation	Explanation and Reason
$C = \tfrac{5}{9}(F - 32)$	Write the equation; Given
$\tfrac{9}{5}C = F - 32$	Multiply each side by $\tfrac{9}{5}$; Multiplication Property of Equality
$\tfrac{9}{5}C + 32 = F$	Add 32 to each side; Addition Property of Equality
$F = \tfrac{9}{5}C + 32$	Rewrite the equation; Symmetric Property of Equality

b.
Degrees Celsius (°C)	Degrees Fahrenheit (°F)
0	32
20	68
32	89.6
41	105.8

c.

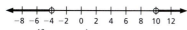

Yes, it is a linear function.

37. 8; Two perpendicular great circles have two intersection points, each creating 4 right angles.

2.4 Review & Refresh
38. Segment Addition Postulate
39. angle bisector
40. If it storms, then soccer practice is canceled.
41. If a person is taller than 4 feet, then that person is allowed to ride the roller coaster.
42. $d < -4$ or $d > 10$

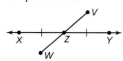

43. $w < -\frac{12}{5}$ or $w > \frac{4}{5}$

44. *Sample answer:* The difference of two even integers is an even integer; Let n and m be any integer. Then $2n$ and $2m$ are even integers because they are the product of 2 and an integer. $2n - 2m$ represents the difference of the two even integers. By the Distributive Property, $2n - 2m = 2(n - m)$, and $2(n - m)$ is an even integer because it is the product of 2 and an integer, $(n - m)$.

45. *Sample answer:*

46. The function is positive when $-2.5 < x < -1.5$ and $x > 0.5$ and is negative when $x < -2.5$ and $-1.5 < x < 0.5$. The function is increasing when $x < -2$ and $x > -0.25$ and decreasing when $-2 < x < -0.25$.

2.5 Practice
1. Given; Addition Property of Equality; $PQ + QR = PR$; Transitive Property of Equality

3.

STATEMENTS	REASONS
1. A segment exists with endpoints A and B.	1. Given
2. AB equals the length of the segment with endpoints A and B.	2. Ruler Postulate
3. $AB = AB$	3. Reflexive Property of Equality
4. $\overline{AB} \cong \overline{AB}$	4. Definition of congruent segments

5. Transitive Property of Segment Congruence
7. Symmetric Property of Segment Congruence

9.

STATEMENTS	REASONS
1. $\angle GFH \cong \angle GHF$	1. Given
2. $m\angle GFH = m\angle GHF$	2. Definition of congruent angles
3. $\angle EFG$ and $\angle GFH$ form a linear pair.	3. Given (diagram)
4. $\angle EFG$ and $\angle GFH$ are supplementary.	4. Definition of linear pair
5. $m\angle EFG + m\angle GFH = 180°$	5. Definition of supplementary angles
6. $m\angle EFG + m\angle GHF = 180°$	6. Substitution Property of Equality
7. $\angle EFG$ and $\angle GHF$ are supplementary.	7. Definition of supplementary angles

11. Let point R represent the restaurant, S represent the shoe store, M represent the movie theater, C represent the café, F represent the florist, and D represent the dry cleaners.
Given: $RS = CF$, $SM = MC = FD$; **Prove:** $RM = CD$

STATEMENTS	REASONS
1. $RS = CF$, $SM = MC = FD$	1. Given
2. $RM = RS + SM$	2. Segment Addition Postulate
3. $CF + FD = CD$	3. Segment Addition Postulate
4. $RS + SM = CD$	4. Substitution Property of Equality
5. $RM = CD$	5. Substitution Property of Equality

13. *Sample answer:* 34, 36; $17 + 17 = 34$, $11 + 23 = 34$, $5 + 29 = 34$, $3 + 31 = 34$; $17 + 19 = 36$, $13 + 23 = 36$, $7 + 29 = 36$, $5 + 31 = 36$
15. Because inductive reasoning was used.

2.5 Review & Refresh
16. $x = \pm 7$ **17.** $x = \dfrac{1 \pm \sqrt{22}}{3}$
18. nonlinear **19.** 57° **20.** 33°
21. The sum of two negative integers is negative; Let a and b be two positive integers. So $-a$ and $-b$ are two negative integers. $-a + (-b) = -(a + b)$. Because the sum of two positive numbers, $a + b$, is positive, $-(a + b)$ is negative, so the sum of two negative numbers, $-a + (-b)$, is negative.
22. *Sample answer:*

Equation	Justification
$-3(6x - 1) = 6x - 9$	Write given equation.
$-18x + 3 = 6x - 9$	Distributive Property
$-18x + 3 - 3 = 6x - 9 - 3$	Subtraction Property of Equality
$-18x = 6x - 12$	Simplify.
$-18x - 6x = 6x - 12 - 6x$	Subtraction Property of Equality
$-24x = -12$	Simplify.
$\dfrac{-24x}{-24} = \dfrac{-12}{-24}$	Division Property of Equality
$x = \dfrac{1}{2}$	Simplify.

23. $273.88
24. *Sample answer:*

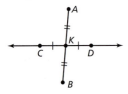

2.6 Practice
1. $\angle MSN \cong \angle PSQ$ by definition because they have the same measure; $\angle MSP \cong \angle PSR$ by the Right Angles Congruence Theorem. They form a linear pair, which means they are supplementary by the Linear Pair Postulate, and because one is a right angle, so is the other by the Subtraction Property of Equality; $\angle NSP \cong \angle QSR$ by the Congruent Complements Theorem because they are complementary to congruent angles; $\angle NSQ \cong \angle MSP$ and $\angle NSQ \cong \angle PSR$ by the Right Angles Congruence Theorem. Because $\angle MSP$ is a right angle, $\angle MSN$ and $\angle NSP$ are complementary. So, $m\angle NSP = 40°$ and $m\angle NSQ = 90°$ by the Angle Addition Postulate. So, $\angle NSQ$ is a right angle by definition.
3. $m\angle 2 = 37°$, $m\angle 3 = 143°$, $m\angle 4 = 37°$
5. $m\angle 1 = 146°$, $m\angle 3 = 146°$, $m\angle 4 = 34°$
7. $y = 9$ **9.** $x = 13$, $y = 20$
11. The expressions should have been set equal to each other because they are vertical angles;
$(13x + 45)° = (19x + 3)°$
$-6x + 45 = 3$
$-6x = -42$
$x = 7$

13. Transitive Property of Angle Congruence; Transitive Property of Angle Congruence

STATEMENTS	REASONS
1. $\angle 1 \cong \angle 3$	1. Given
2. $\angle 1 \cong \angle 2$, $\angle 3 \cong \angle 4$	2. Vertical Angles Congruence Theorem
3. $\angle 2 \cong \angle 3$	3. Transitive Property of Angle Congruence
4. $\angle 2 \cong \angle 4$	4. Transitive Property of Angle Congruence

15. complementary; $m\angle 1 + m\angle 3$; Transitive Property of Equality; $m\angle 2 = m\angle 3$; congruent angles

STATEMENTS	REASONS
1. $\angle 1$ and $\angle 2$ are complementary. $\angle 1$ and $\angle 3$ are complementary.	1. Given
2. $m\angle 1 + m\angle 2 = 90°$, $m\angle 1 + m\angle 3 = 90°$	2. Definition of complementary angles
3. $m\angle 1 + m\angle 2 = m\angle 1 + m\angle 3$	3. Transitive Property of Equality
4. $m\angle 2 = m\angle 3$	4. Subtraction Property of Equality
5. $\angle 2 \cong \angle 3$	5. Definition of congruent angles

17. The purpose of a proof is to ensure the truth of a statement with such certainty that the theorem or rule proved could be used as a justification in proving another statement or theorem. Because inductive reasoning relies on observations about patterns in specific cases, the pattern may not continue or may change. So, a conclusion reached through inductive reasoning is much less certain and, if used to justify another statement or theorem, could lead to an incorrect conclusion.
19. *Sample answer:*

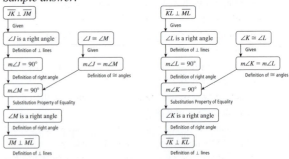

21. no; The converse would be: "If two angles are supplementary, then they are a linear pair." This is false because angles can be supplementary without being adjacent.
23. *Sample answer:* No, this uses inductive reasoning so the pattern may not hold true for all values of n.

2.6 Review & Refresh

25. $\overline{RS} \cong \overline{VW}$; Transitive Property of Segment Congruence
26. *Sample answer:* B, I, and C
27. *Sample answer:* Because E, F, and G are not collinear, there is exactly one plane through points E, F, and G.
28. *Sample answer:* plane ABC and plane BCG
29. **a.**

Equation	Justification
$v_f = v_i + at$	Write given equation.
$v_f - v_i = v_i + at - v_i$	Subtraction Property of Equality
$v_f - v_i = at$	Simplify.
$\dfrac{v_f - v_i}{a} = \dfrac{at}{a}$	Division Property of Equality
$\dfrac{v_f - v_i}{a} = t$	Simplify.

b. 6 seconds

30. $x^2 - 14x + 49 = (x - 7)^2$
31.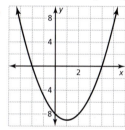
32.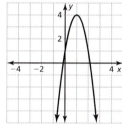

Chapter 2 Review

1. conditional: If two lines intersect, then their intersection is a point.
   converse: If two lines intersect in a point, then they are intersecting lines.
   inverse: If two lines do not intersect, then they do not intersect in a point.
   contrapositive: If two lines do not intersect in a point, then they are not intersecting lines.
   biconditional: Two lines intersect if and only if their intersection is a point.

2. conditional: If $x = 3$, then $4x + 9 = 21$.
   converse: If $4x + 9 = 21$, then $x = 3$.
   inverse: If $x \neq 3$, then $4x + 9 \neq 21$.
   contrapositive: If $4x + 9 \neq 21$, then $x \neq 3$.
   biconditional: $x = 3$ if and only if $4x + 9 = 21$.

3. conditional: If two angles are supplementary, then their measures sum to 180°.
   converse: If the measures of two angles sum to 180°, then the angles are supplementary.
   inverse: If two angles are not supplementary, then their measures do not sum to 180°.
   contrapositive: If the measures of two angles do not sum to 180°, then the angles are not supplementary.
   biconditional: Two angles are supplementary if and only if their measures sum to 180°.

4. conditional: If an angle is a right angle, then it measures 90°.
   converse: If an angle measures 90°, then it is a right angle.
   inverse: If an angle is not a right angle, then it does not measure 90°.
   contrapositive: If an angle does not measure 90°, then it is not a right angle.
   biconditional: An angle is a right angle if and only if it measures 90°.

5. yes; Definition of midpoint
6. no; The diagram does not include tick marks to show the congruence of $\overline{ES}$ and $\overline{ST}$.
7. yes; Definition of segment bisector
8. *Sample answer:* The difference of any two odd integers is an even integer; $9 - 5 = 4$, $1 - 1 = 0$, $-9 - (-7) = -2$
9. $m\angle B = 90°$
10. If $4x = 12$, then $2x = 6$.
11. inductive reasoning; The conjecture is based on the assumption that a pattern, observed in specific cases, will continue.
12. deductive reasoning; The conclusion is based on accepted scientific properties and the Law of Detachment.
13. Two Point Postulate
14. *Sample answer:*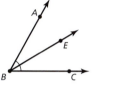
15. *Sample answer:*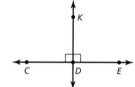
16. *Sample answer:*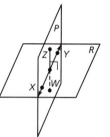
17. yes   18. yes   19. no   20. no
21. *Sample answer:* The intersection of plane R and plane S is $\overleftrightarrow{AB}$.

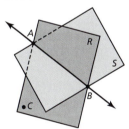

Three Point Postulate, Plane-Line Postulate, Plane Intersection Postulate

22.
Equation	Explanation and Reason
$-9x - 21 = -20x - 87$	Write the equation; Given
$11x - 21 = -87$	Add $20x$ to each side; Addition Property of Equality
$11x = -66$	Add 21 to each side; Addition Property of Equality
$x = -6$	Divide each side by 11; Division Property of Equality

23.
Equation	Explanation and Reason
$5x + 2(2x - 23) = -154$	Write the equation; Given
$5x + 4x - 46 = -154$	Multiply; Distributive Property
$9x - 46 = -154$	Combine like terms; Simplify.
$9x = -108$	Add 46 to each side; Addition Property of Equality
$x = -12$	Divide each side by 9; Division Property of Equality

Selected Answers   A9

24. Transitive Property of Equality or Substitution Property of Equality
25. Division Property of Equality
26.

Equation	Reason
$V = \dfrac{11.25^2 \pi h}{231}$	Write given equation.
$231 \cdot V = 231 \cdot \dfrac{11.25^2 \pi h}{231}$	Multiplication Property of Equality
$231V = 11.25^2 \pi h$	Simplify.
$\dfrac{231V}{11.25^2 \pi} = \dfrac{11.25^2 \pi h}{11.25^2 \pi}$	Division Property of Equality
$\dfrac{231V}{11.25^2 \pi} = h$	Simplify.
$h \approx 31.95$ in.	

27. Transitive Property of Angle Congruence
28. Symmetric Property of Angle Congruence
29. Reflexive Property of Angle Congruence
30. Transitive Property of Equality or Substitution Property of Equality
31.

STATEMENTS	REASONS
1. An angle with vertex A exists.	1. Given
2. $m\angle A$ equals the measure of the angle with vertex A.	2. Protractor Postulate
3. $m\angle A = m\angle A$	3. Reflexive Property of Equality
4. $\angle A \cong \angle A$	4. Definition of congruent angles

32.

STATEMENTS	REASONS
1. $\angle BAD \cong \angle CDA$	1. Given
2. $m\angle BAD = m\angle CDA$	2. Definition of congruent angles
3. $m\angle BAD + m\angle EAB = 180°$, $m\angle CDA + m\angle FDC = 180°$	3. Linear Pair Postulate
4. $m\angle BAD = 180° - m\angle EAB$, $m\angle CDA = 180° - m\angle FDC$	4. Subtraction Property of Equality
5. $180° - m\angle EAB = 180° - m\angle FDC$	5. Substitution Property of Equality
6. $-m\angle EAB = -m\angle FDC$	6. Subtraction Property of Equality
7. $m\angle EAB = m\angle FDC$	7. Multiplication Property of Equality
8. $\angle EAB \cong \angle FDC$	8. Definition of congruent angles

33. Given; Congruent Complements Theorem

STATEMENTS	REASONS
1. $m\angle 1 + m\angle 2 = 90°$	1. Given
2. $\angle 1$ and $\angle 2$ are complementary.	2. Definition of complementary angles
3. $\angle 3$ and $\angle 2$ are complementary.	3. Given
4. $\angle 3 \cong \angle 1$	4. Congruent Complements Theorem

34. $\angle ABD$ and $\angle DBC$ are adjacent angles. By the Angle Addition Postulate, $m\angle ABD + m\angle DBC = m\angle ABC$. From the given values, $m\angle ABD = 24°$ and $m\angle ABC = 48°$. By the Substitution Property of Equality, $24° + m\angle DBC = 48°$. By the Subtraction Property of Equality, $m\angle DBC = 24°$. Because $m\angle ABD = m\angle DBC$, $\angle ABD \cong \angle DBC$ by the definition of congruent angles. So, by the definition of an angle bisector, $\overrightarrow{BD}$ bisects $\angle ABC$.

Chapter 3

Getting Ready for Chapter 3
1. $m = -\frac{3}{4}$ 2. $m = 3$ 3. $m = 0$
4. $y = -3x + 19$ 5. $y = -2x + 2$ 6. $y = 4x + 9$
7. $y = \frac{1}{2}x - 5$ 8. $y = -\frac{1}{4}x - 7$ 9. $y = \frac{2}{3}x + 9$

3.1 Practice
1. $\overleftrightarrow{AB}$ 3. plane ABF
5. no; They are intersecting lines.
7. $\angle 1$ and $\angle 5$; $\angle 2$ and $\angle 6$; $\angle 3$ and $\angle 7$; $\angle 4$ and $\angle 8$
9. $\angle 1$ and $\angle 8$; $\angle 2$ and $\angle 7$
11. corresponding 13. consecutive interior
15. no; The lines intersect.
17. For a circle with radius r, the circumference is greatest in hyperbolic geometry and least in spherical geometry.
19. The sum of the angle measures of a triangle is greatest in spherical geometry and least in hyperbolic geometry.

3.1 Review & Refresh
20. Check students' work.
21. $t \geq 4$

22. Reflexive Property of Segment Congruence
23. $(-6, 0)$ 24. $(-1, 5)$ 25. $m\angle 3 = m\angle 7$
26. *Sample answer:* Because $\angle 1$ and $\angle 3$ are complementary and $\angle 2$ and $\angle 4$ are complementary, $m\angle 1 + m\angle 3 = 90°$ and $m\angle 2 + m\angle 4 = 90°$ by definition of complementary angles. By the Substitution Property of Equality, $m\angle 1 + m\angle 3 = m\angle 2 + m\angle 4$. By the Vertical Angles Congruence Theorem, $m\angle 3 = m\angle 2$. Then, by the Substitution Property of Equality, $m\angle 1 + m\angle 2 = m\angle 2 + m\angle 4$. So, by the Subtraction Property of Equality, $m\angle 1 = m\angle 4$, and $\angle 1 \cong \angle 4$ by the definition of congruent angles.
27. $y = -2x + 5$ 28. -5
29. about 157.1 in.^{3}

3.2 Practice

1. $m\angle 1 = m\angle 2 = 117°$; Sample answer: $m\angle 1 = 117°$ by the Vertical Angles Congruence Theorem and $m\angle 1 = m\angle 2$ by the Corresponding Angles Theorem.
3. $x = 64$
5. $x = 12$
7. $m\angle 1 = 100°, m\angle 2 = 80°, m\angle 3 = 100°$
9. $m\angle 1 = 80°, m\angle 2 = 80°, m\angle 3 = 100°$
11. In order to use the Corresponding Angles Theorem, the angles need to be formed by two parallel lines cut by a transversal, but none of the lines in this diagram appear to be parallel; $\angle 9$ and $\angle 10$ are corresponding angles.
13.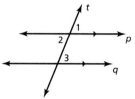

STATEMENTS	REASONS
1. $p \parallel q$	1. Given
2. $\angle 3 \cong \angle 1$	2. Corresponding Angles Theorem
3. $\angle 1 \cong \angle 2$	3. Vertical Angles Congruence Theorem
4. $\angle 3 \cong \angle 2$	4. Transitive Property of Angle Congruence

15. $m\angle 2 = 104°$
17. If two parallel lines are cut by a perpendicular transversal, then the consecutive interior angles will be congruent right angles.
19. $2x + 2y + 12 = 180$
    $4x + y + 6 = 180; x = 30, y = 54$
21. no; In order to make the shot, you must hit the cue ball so that $m\angle 1 = 65°$. The ball hits the side of the table at the same angle it bounces off, $65°$. The angle the ball hits the side of the table and $\angle 1$ are congruent by the Alternate Interior Angles Theorem.
23. A runway is named by the first two digits of the number of degrees from north a plane is traveling on the runway. Parallel runways have an L or R after the number which represents the left or right runway from the direction the plane is traveling; A plane can either travel southwest at 220° or northeast at 40°.
25. 70°; 110°; 70°; 110°; 70°; 110°; 70°; 110°

3.2 Review & Refresh

26. Sample answer: $\overleftrightarrow{LM}$ and $\overleftrightarrow{QS}$
27. $\overleftrightarrow{LM}$ and $\overleftrightarrow{NP}$
28. Transitive Property of Angle Congruence
29. Symmetric Property of Segment Congruence
30. $(t - 5)(t^2 + 3)$
31. $4x^2(x + 3)(x - 3)$
32. $(4, 0), (0, -7)$
33. $10x - 5; 115$ in.^{2}
34. $x = 9$

3.3 Practice

1. $x = 40$
3. $x = 60$
5. Check students' work.

7.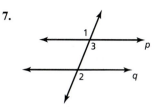

It is given that $\angle 1 \cong \angle 2$. By the Vertical Angles Congruence Theorem, $\angle 1 \cong \angle 3$. Then by the Transitive Property of Congruence, $\angle 2 \cong \angle 3$. So, by the Corresponding Angles Converse, $p \parallel q$.

9. yes; Alternate Interior Angles Converse
11. $x = 15$
13. $x = 20$
15. It would be true that $a \parallel b$ if $\angle 1$ and $\angle 2$ were supplementary, but you cannot assume that they are supplementary unless it is stated or the diagram is marked as such. You can say that $\angle 1$ and $\angle 2$ are consecutive interior angles.
17. cannot be determined; The marked angles are vertical angles. You do not know anything about the angles formed by the intersection of $\overleftrightarrow{DF}$ and $\overleftrightarrow{BE}$.
19. All of the rungs are parallel to each other by the Transitive Property of Parallel Lines.
21. $\overrightarrow{EA} \parallel \overrightarrow{HC}$ by the Corresponding Angles Converse. $\angle AEH \cong \angle CHG$ by definition because $m\angle AEH = 62° + 58° = 120°$ and $m\angle CHG = 59° + 61° = 120°$. However, $\overrightarrow{EB}$ is not parallel to $\overrightarrow{HD}$ because corresponding angles $\angle BEH$ and $\angle DHG$ do not have the same measure and are therefore not congruent.

23.

STATEMENTS	REASONS
1. $\angle 1 \cong \angle 2, \angle 3 \cong \angle 4$	1. Given
2. $\angle 2 \cong \angle 3$	2. Vertical Angles Congruence Theorem
3. $\angle 1 \cong \angle 3$	3. Transitive Property of Angle Congruence
4. $\angle 1 \cong \angle 4$	4. Transitive Property of Angle Congruence
5. $\overline{AB} \parallel \overline{CD}$	5. Alternate Interior Angles Converse

25. no
27. Sample answer: about 604,000 square kilometers
29. no; spherical

3.3 Review & Refresh

30. $x = 19$
31. Sample answer: $\overleftrightarrow{AF}$ and $\overleftrightarrow{CH}$
32. no
33. 13
34. $\sqrt{41}$
35. $f(-2) = 11; f(3) = -4; f(5) = -10$

36. Sample answer:

STATEMENTS	REASONS
1. $\angle 1 \cong \angle 3$	1. Given
2. $\angle 2 \cong \angle 1$	2. Vertical Angles Congruence Theorem
3. $\angle 2 \cong \angle 3$	3. Transitive Property of Angle Congruence
4. $\angle 3 \cong \angle 4$	4. Vertical Angles Congruence Theorem
5. $\angle 2 \cong \angle 4$	5. Transitive Property of Angle Congruence

37. 148; The T-shirt reaches a maximum height of 148 feet after 3 seconds.

3.4 Practice

1. about 3.2 units **3.** Check students' work.
5. Check students' work.
7.

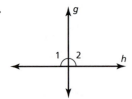

Because $\angle 1 \cong \angle 2$, by definition, $m\angle 1 = m\angle 2$. Also, by the Linear Pair Postulate, $m\angle 1 + m\angle 2 = 180°$. Then, by the Substitution Property of Equality, $m\angle 1 + m\angle 1 = 180°$, and $2(m\angle 1) = 180°$ by the Distributive Property. So, by the Division Property of Equality, $m\angle 1 = 90°$. Finally, $g \perp h$ by the definition of perpendicular lines.

9. $m \parallel n$; Because $m \perp q$ and $n \perp q$, lines m and n are parallel by the Lines Perpendicular to a Transversal Theorem.

11. $n \parallel p$; Because $k \perp n$ and $k \perp p$, lines n and p are parallel by the Lines Perpendicular to a Transversal Theorem.

13. The length of the perpendicular segment should be used; The distance from point C to $\overline{AB}$ is 8 centimeters.

15. point C; Because $\overline{AC}$ appears to be perpendicular to the water's edge, it would represent the shortest distance from point A to the line formed by the opposite edge of the stream.

17.

STATEMENTS	REASONS
1. $\overrightarrow{BA} \perp \overrightarrow{BC}$	1. Given
2. $\angle ABC$ is a right angle.	2. Definition of perpendicular lines
3. $m\angle ABC = 90°$	3. Definition of right angle
4. $m\angle 1 + m\angle 2 = m\angle ABC$	4. Angle Addition Postulate
5. $m\angle 1 + m\angle 2 = 90°$	5. Transitive Property of Equality
6. $\angle 1$ and $\angle 2$ are complementary.	6. Definition of complementary angles

19. no; The shortest distance from a point on one line to the other line will be different for different points on the line unless the lines are parallel.

21. yes; The center of the geyser is about 100.6 feet from the boardwalk at the closest point.

23. Check students' work.

25. no; The area of a triangle is $\frac{1}{2}bh$. The base of $\triangle ABC$ is AB, and the height is the distance from point C to line m. Because m and n are parallel, the distance between any point on line n and line m is the same. So, the base and height of $\triangle ABC$ are the same for every possible location of C, and the area is always the same.

27. Find the length of the segment that is perpendicular to the plane and that has one endpoint on the given point and one endpoint on the plane; You can find the distance from a line to a plane only if the line is parallel to the plane. Then you can pick any point on the line and find the distance from that point to the plane. If a line is not parallel to a plane, then the distance from the line to the plane is not defined because it would be different for each point on the line.

29. Sample answer: soccer

3.4 Review & Refresh

31. $m = \frac{1}{6}$; $b = -8$ **32.** $m = 3$; $b = 9$ **33.** $103°$
34. a. 416 yards
  b. 1,305 yards
35. $\frac{1}{2}$
36. yes; Alternate Interior Angles Converse
37. $\overleftrightarrow{HG}$ **38.** $\overleftrightarrow{FG}$ **39.** $\overleftrightarrow{CG}$ **40.** plane BCG

3.5 Practice

1. $P(7, -0.4)$ **3.** $P(-1.5, -1.5)$ **5.** $a \parallel c, b \perp d$
7. a. $y = -2x + 1$ **9. a.** $y = \frac{1}{2}x - 2$
  b. $y = \frac{1}{2}x + 1$ **b.** $y = -2x + 8$
11. about 3.2 units **13.** about 5.4 units
15. $y = -x - 2$ **17.** about 4 units
19. It is the same point.
21. yes; $\overleftrightarrow{QT} \parallel \overleftrightarrow{RS}$ because they have the same slope ($m = 3$), and $\overleftrightarrow{ST} \parallel \overleftrightarrow{QR}$ because they have the same slope $\left(m = -\frac{1}{2}\right)$.

23. 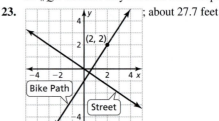 ; about 27.7 feet

25. Check students' work. **27.** $\dfrac{|ax_0 + by_0|}{\sqrt{a^2 + b^2}}$

29. If $x \parallel y$ and $y \parallel z$, then by the Slopes of Parallel Lines Theorem, $m_x = m_y$ and $m_y = m_z$. Therefore, by the Transitive Property of Equality, $m_x = m_z$. So, by the Slopes of Parallel Lines Theorem, $x \parallel z$.

31. about 2,300 kilometers

3.5 Review & Refresh

33. $x = 30$
34. Sample answer: The product of three consecutive odd numbers is odd; $1 \cdot 3 \cdot 5 = 15$; $5 \cdot 7 \cdot 9 = 315$; $9 \cdot 11 \cdot 13 = 1,287$
35. about 14.93 units **36.** $b \parallel c$
37. $x = 0$ and $x = 9$ **38.** $m\angle 2 = 40°$

39. $w < 4$

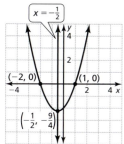

40. $(1, 6)$ **41.** $(1, -3)$

42.

domain: all real numbers; range: $y \geq -\frac{9}{4}$

Chapter 3 Review

1. $\overleftrightarrow{NR}$ 2. $\overrightarrow{NP}$ 3. $\overleftrightarrow{JN}$ 4. plane JKN
5. $\angle 3$ and $\angle 5$, $\angle 4$ and $\angle 6$ 6. $\angle 3$ and $\angle 6$, $\angle 4$ and $\angle 5$
7. $\angle 1$ and $\angle 5$, $\angle 2$ and $\angle 6$, $\angle 3$ and $\angle 7$, $\angle 4$ and $\angle 8$
8. $\angle 1$ and $\angle 8$, $\angle 2$ and $\angle 7$ 9. $x = 145$, $y = 35$
10. $x = 13$, $y = 132$ 11. $x = 61$, $y = 29$
12. $x = 14$, $y = 17$ 13. $x = 107$
14. $x = 133$ 15. $x = 32$ 16. $x = 23$
17. no; $m\angle 1 = 87° \neq 93°$, so corresponding angles are not congruent.
18. $x \parallel y$; Because $x \perp z$ and $y \perp z$, lines x and y are parallel by the Lines Perpendicular to a Transversal Theorem.
19. none; In order to say that lines are parallel, you need to know something about *both* of the intersections between the two lines and a transversal.
20. $\ell \parallel m \parallel n$, $a \parallel b$; Because $a \perp n$ and $b \perp n$, lines a and b are parallel by the Lines Perpendicular to a Transversal Theorem. Because $m \perp a$ and $n \perp a$, lines m and n are parallel by the Lines Perpendicular to a Transversal Theorem. Because $\ell \perp b$ and $n \perp b$, lines ℓ and n are parallel by the Lines Perpendicular to a Transversal Theorem. Because $\ell \parallel n$ and $m \parallel n$, lines ℓ and m are parallel by the Transitive Property of Parallel Lines.
21. $a \parallel b$; Because $a \perp n$ and $b \perp n$, lines a and b are parallel by the Lines Perpendicular to a Transversal Theorem.

22.
STATEMENTS	REASONS
1. $\angle 1 \cong \angle 2$	1. Given
2. $g \perp k$	2. Linear Pair Perpendicular Theorem
3. $h \perp k$	3. Given
4. $g \parallel h$	4. Lines Perpendicular to a Transversal Theorem

23. $(-1, 2.75)$ 24. $(1.6, -0.2)$
25. $b \parallel c$, $a \perp b$, $a \perp c$ 26. $y = -x - 1$
27. $y = \frac{1}{2}x + 8$ 28. $y = \frac{1}{2}x - 4$
29. $y = -7x - 2$
30. yes; The angles are all right angles because the sides are all formed by horizontal or vertical lines, and the length of each side is the same.
31. about 2.1 units 32. about 2.7 units
33. about 16.5 feet

Chapter 4

Getting Ready for Chapter 4

1. reflection 2. rotation 3. dilation

4.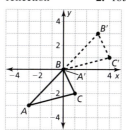

$A'(0, 0)$, $B'(3, 3)$, $C'(4, 1)$

5.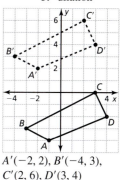

$A'(-2, 2)$, $B'(-4, 3)$, $C'(2, 6)$, $D'(3, 4)$

4.1 Practice

1. Check students' work.

3.

5.

7. $\langle 3, -5 \rangle$ 9. $(x, y) \rightarrow (x - 5, y + 2)$
11. $A'(-6, 10)$

13.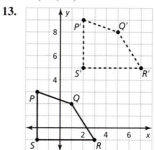

15.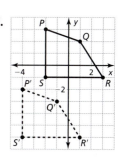

17.

19. The vertical and horizontal translations were switched.

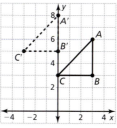

21. translation: $(x, y) \rightarrow (x + 6, y - 4)$,
translation: $(x, y) \rightarrow (x - 6, y)$

23. The amoeba moves right 5 squares and down 4 squares; about 12.8 mm
25. $a = 35, b = 14, c = 5$
27. a.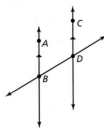

Translate $\overleftrightarrow{AB}$ and $\overrightarrow{BD}$ along $\overrightarrow{BD}$ so that point B maps to point D. Then $\overleftrightarrow{BD}$ and its image are the same line. Translations map lines to parallel lines, so $\overleftrightarrow{AB} \parallel \overleftrightarrow{A'B'}$. Because $\overleftrightarrow{A'B'}$ passes through D, by the Parallel Postulate, $\overleftrightarrow{A'B'}$ and $\overleftrightarrow{CD}$ are the same line. Translations are rigid motions which preserve angle measure, so the angles formed by $\overleftrightarrow{AB}$ and $\overleftrightarrow{BD}$ are congruent to the corresponding angles formed by $\overleftrightarrow{CD}$ and $\overleftrightarrow{BD}$.

b.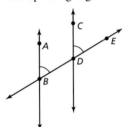

Because $\angle ABD \cong \angle CDE$, a translation along $\overrightarrow{BD}$ maps $\angle ABD$ onto $\angle CDE$. Because translations map lines to parallel lines, $\overleftrightarrow{AB} \parallel \overleftrightarrow{CD}$.

29. 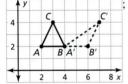 ; no; Because the value of y changes, you are not adding the same amount to each x-value.

31. A rook can translate between 1 to 7 spaces right and left, and translate between 1 to 7 spaces up and down.

4.1 Review & Refresh

33. yes; Consecutive Interior Angles Converse
34. $y = \frac{1}{4}x - 2$
35. $y = -\frac{2}{5}x + \frac{19}{5}$
36. $a_n = 7 - 3n, a_{10} = -23$
37. $a_n = 1 - \frac{1}{5}n, a_{10} = -1$
38. $x = 0$ and $x = 2$
39. 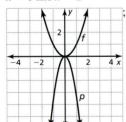 ; The graph of p is a vertical stretch by a factor of $\frac{7}{2}$ and a reflection in the x-axis of the graph of f.

40. lines c and d
41. $\frac{3 + \sqrt{3}}{2}$, or about 2.366 sec and $\frac{3 - \sqrt{3}}{2}$, or about 0.634 sec

42. $f^{-1}(x) = -2x + 5$
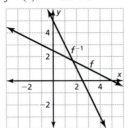

4.2 Practice

1. x-axis
3.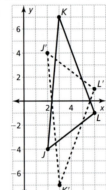
5.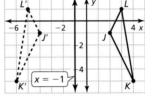
7.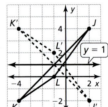
9.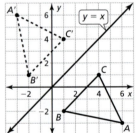
11.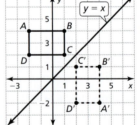
13.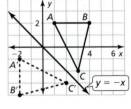
15.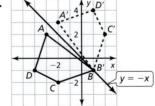

17.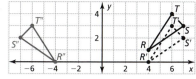

19. yes

 ; A reflection in the line of symmetry maps the square onto itself.

21. yes

 ; A reflection in the line of symmetry maps the figure onto itself.

23. The line of reflection has to be *parallel* to the direction of the translation for it to be a glide reflection; translation $(x, y) \to (x + 2, y + 3)$, reflection: in the y-axis

25. $y = 1$ **27.** Check students' work.

29. Sample answer: translation: $(x, y) \to (x, y + 6)$, reflection: in the y-axis

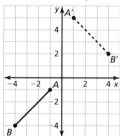

31. Sample answer: Find the perpendicular distance from each point to the line and draw the reflected point that same distance away from the line on its opposite side.

33. 6   **35.** 45°

4.2 Review & Refresh

36. $3\sqrt{2}$, or about 4.2 units   **37.** $x = -2$ and $x = 6$
38. $x = 3$ **39.** 44 ft/sec
40. $\sqrt{13}$, or about 3.6 units   **41.** $h(-1) = 10$
42. $b_2 = \dfrac{2A}{h} - b_1$ **43.** $A'(0, 0)$
44. $-(2t - 7)(t - 1)$

45. 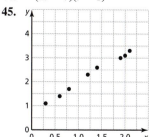 ; The data show a positive linear correlation.

46. Transitive Property of Angle Congruence

4.3 Practice

1. 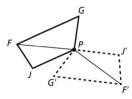   **3.**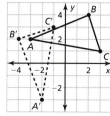

5.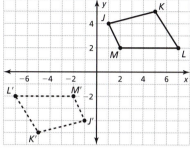

7. The rule for a 270° rotation, $(x, y) \to (y, -x)$, should have been used instead of the rule for a reflection in the x-axis; $C(-1, 1) \to C'(1, 1)$, $D(2, 3) \to D'(3, -2)$

9.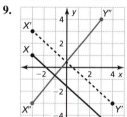

11.

13. yes; Rotations of 90° and 180° about the center map the figure onto itself.

15. no

17. **a.** If you were outside, you are now inside, or vice versa, because you have made half of a rotation.

b. You are back where you started because you have made a full rotation.

19. $J'(-4, 5), K'(-1, 3); J'(5, 4), K'(3, 1)$

21. $D(-1, 2), E(4, 1), F(3, -2), G(1, -1)$

23.

25. If the petals of the daisy were equally spaced apart it would have rotational symmetry; Rotations of about 32.7° about the center map the lime onto itself; Rotations of 72° and 144° about the center map the starfish onto itself; The clover has 90° rotational symmetry.
27. Check students' work.

4.3 Review & Refresh

28. $m\angle EDF = 43°$, $m\angle CDE = 86°$
29. $m\angle CDF = 51°$, $m\angle EDF = 51°$
30. $\angle P$ and $\angle W$, $\angle Q$ and $\angle V$, $\angle R$ and $\angle Z$, $\angle S$ and $\angle Y$, $\angle T$ and $\angle X$; $\overline{PQ}$ and $\overline{WV}$, $\overline{QR}$ and $\overline{VZ}$, $\overline{RS}$ and $\overline{ZY}$, $\overline{ST}$ and $\overline{YX}$, $\overline{TP}$ and $\overline{XW}$
31. $P(4, 3)$
32.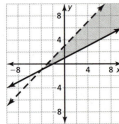

Sample answer: (2, 2)

33. exponential; As x increases by 1, y increases by a constant factor of 4.
34. 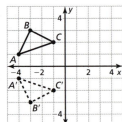   35.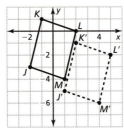

4.4 Practice

1. $\triangle HJK \cong \triangle QRS$, $\square DEFG \cong \square LMNP$; $\triangle HJK$ is a 90° rotation of $\triangle QRS$. $\square DEFG$ is a translation 7 units right and 3 units down of $\square LMNP$.
3. Sample answer: 180° rotation about the origin, followed by a translation 5 units left and 1 unit down
5. yes; $\triangle TUV$ is a translation 4 units right of $\triangle QRS$. So, $\triangle TUV \cong \triangle QRS$.
7. no; M and N are translated 2 units right of their corresponding vertices, L and K, but P is translated only 1 unit right of its corresponding vertex, J. So, this is not a rigid motion.
9. $\triangle A''B''C''$ 11. 5.2 in.
13. 110° rotation about the intersection of lines m and k
15. If $x°$ is the measure of the acute angle formed by the intersecting lines, an angle of $2x°$ should be used to describe the angle of rotation; A 144° rotation about point P maps the blue image to the green image.
17. Check students' work.

19.

STATEMENTS	REASONS
1. A reflection in line ℓ maps $\overline{JK}$ to $\overline{J'K'}$, a reflection in line m maps $\overline{J'K'}$ to $\overline{J''K''}$, and $\ell \parallel m$.	1. Given
2. If $\overline{JJ''}$ intersects line ℓ at L and line m at M, then ℓ is the perpendicular bisector of $\overline{JJ'}$, and m is the perpendicular bisector of $\overline{J'J''}$.	2. Definition of reflection
3. $\overline{J'J''}$ is perpendicular to ℓ and m, and $JL = LJ'$ and $J'M = MJ''$.	3. Definition of perpendicular bisector
4. If d is the distance between ℓ and m, then $d = LM$.	4. Ruler Postulate
5. $LM = LJ' + J'M$ and $JJ'' = JL + LJ' + J'M + MJ''$	5. Segment Addition Postulate
6. $JJ'' = LJ' + LJ' + J'M + J'M$	6. Substitution Property of Equality
7. $JJ'' = 2(LJ' + J'M)$	7. Distributive Property
8. $JJ'' = 2(LM)$	8. Substitution Property of Equality
9. $JJ'' = 2d$	9. Substitution Property of Equality

21. Sample answer: translation 2 units down, reflection in the y-axis
23. Sample answer: The word congruence is used in similar ways in psychology and geometry because they compare two things based on similarities.

4.4 Review & Refresh

25. 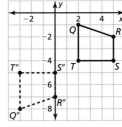   26.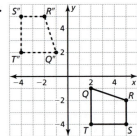

27. 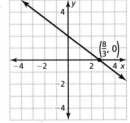   28.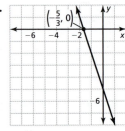

29. $x \geq -\frac{5}{2}$
30. geometric; The common ratio is 3.
31. arithmetic; The common difference is 3.
32. $m = -3$ 33. $y = 2$
34. $n = -1$ 35. $x = 8$ 36. $x = 4$

4.5 Practice

1. $\frac{3}{7}$; reduction
3. Check students' work.
5. Check students' work.
7.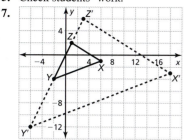
9.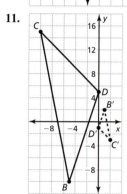
11.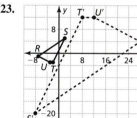
13. $k = 2$
15. $k = \frac{2}{3}$; $y = 3$
17. 300 mm
19. 180 mm
21. no
23.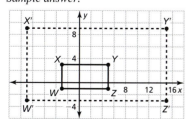

   a. no; The side lengths of the triangle do not all increase by the same factor.
   b. no; The side lengths and angles of the triangle are not equal.

25. a. Sample answer: $P = 24$ units, $A = 32$ square units
    b. Sample answer:

    (graph)

    $P = 72$ units, $A = 288$ square units; The perimeter of the dilated rectangle is three times the perimeter of the original rectangle. The area of the dilated rectangle is nine times the area of the original rectangle.

    c. Sample answer:
    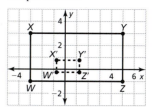

    $P = 6$ units, $A = 2$ square units; The perimeter of the dilated rectangle is $\frac{1}{4}$ the perimeter of the original rectangle. The area of the dilated rectangle is $\frac{1}{16}$ the area of the original rectangle.

    d. Sample answer: The perimeter changes by a factor of k. The area changes by a factor of k^2.

27. $A'(4, 4)$, $B'(4, 12)$, $C'(10, 4)$
29. $33\frac{1}{3}$ mm long

4.5 Review & Refresh

31.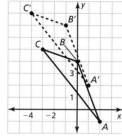
32.
33.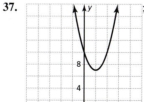
34. $\frac{b}{8}$
35. 999 in.^{2}
36. Sample answer: reflection in the y-axis, translation 5 units down
37. (graph); The graph of g is a translation 1 unit right, followed by a vertical stretch by a factor of 3, then a translation 7 units up of the graph of f.
38. $9x^2 - 24x + 16$
39. $2w^2 - 4w - 30$
40. $\left(\frac{1}{2}, \frac{7}{2}\right)$
41. $\left(-7, \frac{15}{2}\right)$

4.6 Practice

1.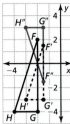

3. *Sample answer:* dilation with a scale factor of 2, followed by a translation 1 unit up

5. Reflect $\triangle ABC$ in $\overleftrightarrow{AB}$.

Then translate $\triangle ABC'$ so that point A maps to point R.

 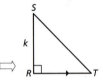

Next, dilate $\triangle RB'C''$ using center of dilation R. Choose the scale factor to be the ratio of the side lengths of $\triangle RST$ and $\triangle RB'C''$, which is $\dfrac{k}{j}$.

A similarity transformation maps $\triangle ABC$ to $\triangle RST$. So, $\triangle ABC$ is similar to $\triangle RST$.

7. yes; The stop sign sticker can be mapped to the regular-sized stop sign by translating the sticker to the left until the centers match, and then dilating the sticker with a scale factor of 3.15. Because there is a similarity transformation that maps one stop sign to the other, the sticker is similar to the regular-sized stop sign.

9. a. 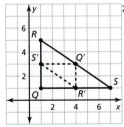 ; yes; The smaller triangle can be mapped to the larger one by a dilation with $k = -2$, followed by the translation $(x, y) \rightarrow (x + 9, y + 7)$. Because one can be mapped to the other by a similarity transformation, the triangles are similar.

b. Check students' work; The triangle formed when the midpoints of a triangle are connected is always similar to the original triangle.

11. *Sample answer:* yes; All body parts of a baby alligator can be mapped with a dilation to their corresponding parts of an adult alligator.

13. *Sample answer:* The portions of an alligator's height that is taken up by the head remains the same as they age.

4.6 Review & Refresh

14.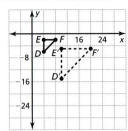

15.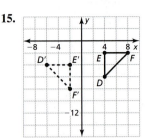

16. $y = 4x - 5$

17. The quadrilaterals are congruent.

18. $m > 5$

19. $1 < z < 6$

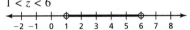

20.
Equation	Justification
$9x - 2 = 13 + 6x$	Write given equation.
$3x - 2 = 13$	Subtraction Property of Equality
$3x = 15$	Addition Property of Equality
$x = 5$	Division Property of Equality

21. obtuse 22. straight 23. acute 24. right

25. a. [0, 1, 2, ..., 10, 11, 12]; discrete

b.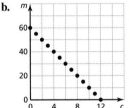

Chapter 4 Review

1.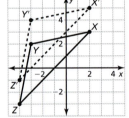

2.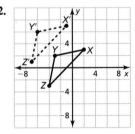

3.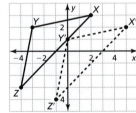

4.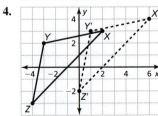

A18 Selected Answers

5. 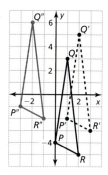 **6.**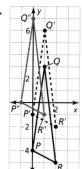

7. $(x, y) \rightarrow (x + 1, y + 3)$

8. 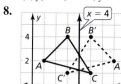 **9.**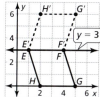

10.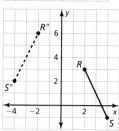

11. 2

12. 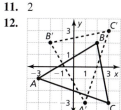 **13.**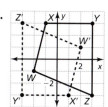

14.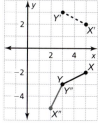

15. yes; Rotations of 60°, 120°, and 180° about the center map the figure onto itself.

16. yes; Rotations of 72° and 144° about the center map the figure onto itself.

17. *Sample answer:* orange: rotate 90° around point (−2, 3), translate 4 units right and 5 units down; red: translate 7 units down and 3 units right; purple: rotate 90° around point (2, 3), translate 3 units left and 7 units down

18. no

19. △ABC ≅ △XYZ, quadrilateral MNPQ ≅ quadrilateral RSTU

20. translation; rotation

21. **a.** 136 in.
 b. reflection in the vertical line through the center of the left marcher, followed by reflection in the vertical line through the center of the right marcher

22. $k = \frac{3}{5}$; reduction

23. 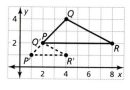 **24.**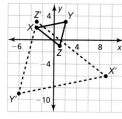

25. 3.8 cm **26.** yes

27.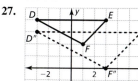

28. *Sample answer:* reflection in the *y*-axis, followed by a dilation with $k = 3$

29. *Sample answer:* dilation with $k = \frac{1}{2}$, followed by a reflection in the line $y = x$

30. *Sample answer:* 270° rotation about the origin, followed by a dilation with center at the origin and $k = 2$

31. **a.** reflection, reduction (dilation), and translation
 b. 2 in. by 3 in.
 c. no; The scale factor for the shorter sides is $\frac{17}{8}$, but the scale factor for the longer sides is $\frac{11}{6}$. So, the photo would have to be cropped or distorted in order to fit the frame.

Chapter 5

Getting Ready for Chapter 5

1. $x = -3$ **2.** $p = 3$ **3.** $z = -\frac{3}{4}$

4. $M(-2, 4)$; about 7.2 units **5.** $M(6, 2)$; 10 units

5.1 Practice

1. right isosceles **3.** obtuse scalene **5.** isosceles; right
7. scalene; right **9.** 52°; right **11.** 139°
13. 114° **15.** 15°, 75°
17. Check students' work.
19. $m\angle 1 = 50°$; $m\angle 2 = 130°$; $m\angle 3 = 50°$; $m\angle 4 = 130°$; $m\angle 5 = 40°$; $m\angle 6 = 140°$; $m\angle 7 = 90°$; $m\angle 8 = 140°$

21.

STATEMENTS	REASONS
1. △ABC is a right triangle.	1. Given
2. ∠C is a right angle.	2. Given (marked in diagram)
3. $m\angle C = 90°$	3. Definition of a right angle
4. $m\angle A + m\angle B + m\angle C = 180°$	4. Triangle Sum Theorem
5. $m\angle A + m\angle B + 90° = 180°$	5. Substitution Property of Equality
6. $m\angle A + m\angle B = 90°$	6. Subtraction Property of Equality
7. ∠A and ∠B are complementary.	7. Definition of complementary angles

Selected Answers **A19**

23. yes; no

A right equilateral triangle is not possible, because the hypotenuse must be longer than either leg in a right triangle.

25. Sample answer: $x + y + z = 360$
27. $x = 118, y = 96$
29. a.

STATEMENTS	REASONS
1. $\overleftrightarrow{AB} \parallel \overleftrightarrow{CD}$	1. Given (marked in diagram)
2. $\angle ACD$ and $\angle 5$ form a linear pair.	2. Definition of linear pair
3. $m\angle ACD + m\angle 5 = 180°$	3. Linear Pair Postulate
4. $m\angle 3 + m\angle 4 = m\angle ACD$	4. Angle Addition Postulate
5. $m\angle 3 + m\angle 4 + m\angle 5 = 180°$	5. Substitution Property of Equality
6. $\angle 1 \cong \angle 5$	6. Corresponding Angles Theorem
7. $\angle 2 \cong \angle 4$	7. Alternate Interior Angles Theorem
8. $m\angle 1 = m\angle 5, m\angle 2 = m\angle 4$	8. Definition of congruent angles
9. $m\angle 3 + m\angle 2 + m\angle 1 = 180°$	9. Substitution Property of Equality

b.

STATEMENTS	REASONS
1. $\overleftrightarrow{BD} \parallel \overleftrightarrow{AC}$	1. Given (marked in diagram)
2. $\angle ABD$ and $\angle 4$ form a linear pair.	2. Definition of linear pair
3. $m\angle 4 + m\angle ABD = 180°$	3. Linear Pair Postulate
4. $m\angle 2 + m\angle 5 = m\angle ABD$	4. Angle Addition Postulate
5. $m\angle 4 + m\angle 2 + m\angle 5 = 180°$	5. Substitution Property of Equality
6. $\angle 1 \cong \angle 4, \angle 3 \cong \angle 5$	6. Alternate Interior Angles Theorem
7. $m\angle 1 = m\angle 4, m\angle 3 = m\angle 5$	7. Definition of congruent angles
8. $m\angle 1 + m\angle 2 + m\angle 3 = 180°$	8. Substitution Property of Equality

31. 1,075 miles

5.1 Review & Refresh

33. yes; $\triangle TUV$ is a translation of $\triangle QRS$ 2 units right and 1 unit down.
34. $b = -2$ and $b = 7$
35. $x = -2$
36. $k = \frac{2}{5}$; reduction
37. exponential decay; 50%
38. Sample answer: $\triangle TUV$ is a dilation with a scale factor of $k = \frac{3}{2}$, followed by a translation 2.5 units right and 4.5 units up of $\triangle DEF$.
39. $\overleftrightarrow{MS}$ and $\overleftrightarrow{LT}$
40. $\overleftrightarrow{NP}$ and $\overleftrightarrow{QR}$

5.2 Practice

1. Sample answer: $\triangle BCA \cong \triangle EFD$; corresponding angles: $\angle A \cong \angle D, \angle B \cong \angle E, \angle C \cong \angle F$; corresponding sides: $\overline{AB} \cong \overline{DE}, \overline{BC} \cong \overline{EF}, \overline{AC} \cong \overline{DF}$
3. $x = 7, y = 8$
5. From the diagram, $\overline{WX} \cong \overline{LM}, \overline{XY} \cong \overline{MN}, \overline{YZ} \cong \overline{NJ}, \overline{VZ} \cong \overline{KJ}$, and $\overline{WV} \cong \overline{LK}$. Also from the diagram, $\angle V \cong \angle K$, $\angle W \cong \angle L, \angle X \cong \angle M, \angle Y \cong \angle N$, and $\angle Z \cong \angle J$. Because all corresponding parts are congruent, $VWXYZ \cong KLMNJ$.
7. 20°
9.

STATEMENTS	REASONS
1. $\overline{AB} \parallel \overline{DC}, \overline{AB} \cong \overline{DC}$, E is the midpoint of $\overline{AC}$ and $\overline{BD}$.	1. Given
2. $\angle AEB \cong \angle CED$	2. Vertical Angles Congruence Theorem
3. $\angle BAE \cong \angle DCE$, $\angle ABE \cong \angle CDE$	3. Alternate Interior Angles Theorem
4. $\overline{AE} \cong \overline{CE}, \overline{BE} \cong \overline{DE}$	4. Definition of midpoint
5. $\triangle AEB \cong \triangle CED$	5. All corresponding parts are congruent.

11. A rigid motion maps each part of a figure to a corresponding part of its image. Because rigid motions preserve length and angle measure, corresponding parts of congruent figures are congruent, which means that the corresponding sides and corresponding angles are congruent.
13. Sample answer: suspension bridges

5.2 Review & Refresh

15. 139°
16.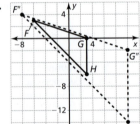
17.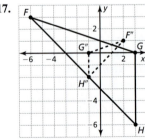
18. $k = \frac{1}{2}$
19. $(t + 5)(t + 2)$
20. $(2x - 3)(x + 4)$
21. The graph of g is a vertical stretch by a factor of 2, a reflection in the x-axis, and a vertical translation 1 unit up of the graph of f.
22. The graph of g is a vertical shrink by a factor of $\frac{1}{2}$ and a vertical translation 5 units down of the graph of f.

A20 Selected Answers

23. $f(x) = \begin{cases} x, & \text{if } x < -2 \\ 3, & \text{if } -2 \leq x < 1 \\ 7 - 2x, & \text{if } x \geq 1 \end{cases}$

5.3 Practice

1. no; The congruent angles are not the included angles.
3. yes; Two pairs of sides and the included angles are congruent.

5.
STATEMENTS	REASONS
1. C is the midpoint of $\overline{AE}$ and $\overline{BD}$.	1. Given
2. $\angle ACB \cong \angle ECD$	2. Vertical Angles Congruence Theorem
3. $\overline{AC} \cong \overline{EC}, \overline{BC} \cong \overline{DC}$	3. Definition of midpoint
4. $\triangle ABC \cong \triangle EDC$	4. SAS Congruence Theorem

7.
STATEMENTS	REASONS
1. $\overline{SP} \cong \overline{TP}$, $\overline{PQ}$ bisects $\angle SPT$.	1. Given
2. $\overline{PQ} \cong \overline{PQ}$	2. Reflexive Property of Segment Congruence
3. $\angle SPQ \cong \angle TPQ$	3. Definition of angle bisector
4. $\triangle SPQ \cong \triangle TPQ$	4. SAS Congruence Theorem

9. no; One of the congruent angles is not the included angle.
11. $\triangle BAD \cong \triangle DCB$; Because the sides of the square are congruent, $\overline{BA} \cong \overline{DC}$ and $\overline{AD} \cong \overline{CB}$. Also, because the angles of the square are congruent, $\angle A \cong \angle C$. So, $\triangle BAD$ and $\triangle DCB$ are congruent by the SAS Congruence Theorem.
13. $\triangle SRT \cong \triangle URT$; $\overline{RT} \cong \overline{RT}$ by the Reflexive Property of Congruence. Also, because all points on a circle are the same distance from the center, $\overline{RS} \cong \overline{RU}$. It is given that $\angle SRT \cong \angle URT$. So, $\triangle SRT$ and $\triangle URT$ are congruent by the SAS Congruence Theorem.
15. Check students' work.

17.
STATEMENTS	REASONS
1. $\triangle AHE$ is equilateral; $\overline{HV}$ bisects $\angle AHE$.	1. Given
2. $\overline{AH} \cong \overline{EH}$	2. Definition of equilateral triangle
3. $\overline{VH} \cong \overline{VH}$	3. Reflexive Property of Segment Congruence
4. $\angle AHV \cong \angle EHV$	4. Definition of angle bisector
5. $\triangle AHV \cong \triangle EHV$	5. SAS Congruence Theorem

19.
STATEMENTS	REASONS
1. $\overline{AC} \cong \overline{DC}$, $\overline{BC} \cong \overline{EC}$	1. Given
2. $\angle ACB \cong \angle DCE$	2. Vertical Angles Congruence Theorem
3. $\triangle ABC \cong \triangle DEC$	3. SAS Congruence Theorem

$x = 4, y = 5$

21. no; The congruent angles may not be the included angles.
23. Check students' work.

5.3 Review & Refresh

25. obtuse isosceles
26. equiangular equilateral
27.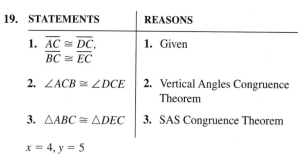

28. $d \leq 9$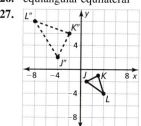
29. $b < -13$ or $b > -5$

30. $x = 5, y = 13$
31. yes
32. $g(-4) = 16$; $g(0) = 14$; $g(8) = 10$

5.4 Practice

1. A, D; Base Angles Theorem
3. $\overline{CD}, \overline{CE}$; Converse of the Base Angles Theorem
5. $x = 12$
7. $x = 52$
9. Check students' work.
11. $x = 60, y = 60$
13. When two angles of a triangle are congruent, the sides opposite the angles are congruent; Because $\angle A \cong \angle C$, $\overline{AB} \cong \overline{BC}$. So, $BC = 5$.
15. a. By the markings, $\overline{AE} \cong \overline{DE}$, $\overline{AB} \cong \overline{DC}$, and $\angle BAE \cong \angle CDE$. So, $\triangle ABE \cong \triangle DCE$ by the SAS Congruence Theorem.
    b. $\triangle AED, \triangle BEC$
    c. $\angle EDA, \angle EBC, \angle ECB$
17. 39 in.
19. $(180 - x)°, \left(\frac{x}{2}\right)°, \left(\frac{x}{2}\right)°$ or $(180 - x)°, (180 - x)°, (2x - 180)°$

21.

STATEMENTS	REASONS
1. △ABC is equilateral.	1. Given
2. $\overline{AB} \cong \overline{AC}$, $\overline{AB} \cong \overline{BC}$, $\overline{AC} \cong \overline{BC}$	2. Definition of equilateral triangle
3. ∠B ≅ ∠C, ∠A ≅ ∠C, ∠A ≅ ∠B	3. Base Angles Theorem
4. △ABC is equiangular.	4. Definition of equiangular triangle

23. no; T, U, and V will always be the vertices of an isosceles triangle except when V is collinear with T and U, which happens when the coordinates of V are (3, 3).

25.

STATEMENTS	REASONS
1. △ABC is equilateral, ∠CAD ≅ ∠ABE ≅ ∠BCF	1. Given
2. △ABC is equiangular.	2. Corollary to the Base Angles Theorem
3. ∠ABC ≅ ∠BCA ≅ ∠BAC	3. Definition of equiangular triangle
4. m∠CAD = m∠ABE = m∠BCF, m∠ABC = m∠BCA = m∠BAC	4. Definition of congruent angles
5. m∠ABC = m∠ABE + m∠EBC, m∠BCA = m∠BCF + m∠ACF, m∠BAC = m∠CAD + m∠BAD	5. Angle Addition Postulate
6. m∠ABE + m∠EBC = m∠BCF + m∠ACF = m∠CAD + m∠BAD	6. Substitution Property of Equality
7. m∠ABE + m∠EBC = m∠ABE + m∠ACF = m∠ABE + m∠BAD	7. Substitution Property of Equality
8. m∠EBC = m∠ACF = m∠BAD	8. Subtraction Property of Equality
9. ∠EBC ≅ ∠ACF ≅ ∠BAD	9. Definition of congruent angles
10. ∠FEB ≅ ∠DFC ≅ ∠EDA	10. Third Angles Theorem
11. ∠FEB and ∠FED are supplementary, ∠DFC and ∠EFD are supplementary, and ∠EDA and ∠FDE are supplementary.	11. Linear Pair Postulate
12. ∠FED ≅ ∠EFD ≅ ∠FDE	12. Congruent Supplements Theorem
13. △DEF is equiangular.	13. Definition of equiangular triangle
14. △DEF is equilateral.	14. Corollary to the Converse of the Base Angles Theorem

27. Cygnus

5.4 Review & Refresh

28. $\overline{SE}$
29. $\overline{JK}$; $\overline{RS}$
30. $\overline{EF}$; $\overline{UV}$
31. m∠1 = 53°
32. about 4.5 units
33. m∠L = 55°; JK = 4 inches
34. yes; The triangles are congruent by the SAS Congruence Theorem.

5.5 Practice

1. yes; $\overline{AB} \cong \overline{DB}$, $\overline{BC} \cong \overline{BE}$, $\overline{AC} \cong \overline{DE}$
3. yes; $\angle B$ and $\angle E$ are right angles, $\overline{AB} \cong \overline{FE}$, $\overline{AC} \cong \overline{FD}$
5. no; You are given that $\overline{RS} \cong \overline{PQ}$, $\overline{ST} \cong \overline{QT}$, and $\overline{RT} \cong \overline{PT}$. So, it should say $\triangle RST \cong \triangle PQT$ by the SSS Congruence Theorem.

7.
STATEMENTS	REASONS
1. $\overline{LM} \cong \overline{JK}$, $\overline{MJ} \cong \overline{KL}$	1. Given
2. $\overline{JL} \cong \overline{JL}$	2. Reflexive Property of Segment Congruence
3. $\triangle LMJ \cong \triangle JKL$	3. SSS Congruence Theorem

9.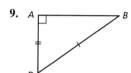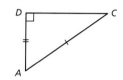

STATEMENTS	REASONS
1. $\overline{AC} \cong \overline{DB}$, $\overline{AB} \perp \overline{AD}$, $\overline{CD} \perp \overline{AD}$	1. Given
2. $\overline{AD} \cong \overline{AD}$	2. Reflexive Property of Congruence
3. $\angle BAD$ and $\angle CDA$ are right angles.	3. Definition of perpendicular lines
4. $\triangle BAD$ and $\triangle CDA$ are right triangles.	4. Definition of a right triangle
5. $\triangle BAD \cong \triangle CDA$	5. HL Congruence Theorem

11. The order of the points in the congruence statement should reflect the corresponding sides and angles; $\triangle TUV \cong \triangle ZYX$ by the SSS Congruence Theorem.
13. Check students' work.
15. yes; The diagonal supports in this figure form triangles with fixed side lengths. By the SSS Congruence Theorem, any triangles with three congruent sides are congruent. So, each triangle has only one possible shape, which makes the figure stable.

17.
STATEMENTS	REASONS
1. $\overline{HF} \cong \overline{FS} \cong \overline{ST} \cong \overline{TH}$; $\overline{FT} \cong \overline{SH}$; $\angle H$, $\angle F$, $\angle S$, and $\angle T$ are right angles.	1. Given
2. $\overline{SH} \cong \overline{SH}$	2. Reflexive Property of Segment Congruence
3. $\triangle HFS$, $\triangle FST$, and $\triangle STH$ are right triangles.	3. Definition of a right triangle
4. $\triangle HFS \cong \triangle FST \cong \triangle STH$	4. HL Congruence Theorem

19. a. $\overline{BC} \cong \overline{DC}$
    b. $\angle A \cong \angle E$ or $\overline{BC} \cong \overline{DC}$
21. no

23. Sample answer: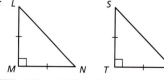

It is given that $\overline{LM} \cong \overline{ST}$ and $\overline{NM} \cong \overline{UT}$. By the definition of perpendicular lines, $m\angle LMN = m\angle STU = 90°$. $\angle LMN \cong \angle STU$ by the Right Angles Congruence Theorem. So, $\triangle LMN \cong \triangle STU$ by the SAS Congruence Theorem.

25. $x = 5$
27. Sample answer: bread, cereal, rice, and pasta: 41.5%, fruit: 14.6%, vegetable: 19.5%, meat, poultry, dry beans, eggs, and nuts: 9.8%, milk, yogurt, and cheese: 9.8%, fats, oils, and sweets: 4.8%
29. Check students' work.

5.5 Review & Refresh

30. yes
31. $x = 82$, $y = 16$
32.

33.
STATEMENTS	REASONS
1. $\overline{AE} \cong \overline{DE}$, $\overline{BE} \cong \overline{CE}$	1. Given
2. $\angle AEB \cong \angle DEC$	2. Vertical Angles Congruence Theorem
3. $\triangle AEB \cong \triangle DEC$	3. SAS Congruence Theorem

34.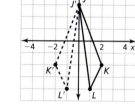

35. $m\angle 1 = 35°$

5.6 Practice

1. yes; AAS Congruence Theorem
3. Check students' work.
5. The corresponding vertices are not written in the same order; $\triangle JLK \cong \triangle GHF$ by the AAS Congruence Theorem.

7.

STATEMENTS	REASONS
1. M is the midpoint of $\overline{NL}$, $\overline{NL} \perp \overline{NQ}$, $\overline{NL} \perp \overline{MP}$, $\overline{QM} \parallel \overline{PL}$	1. Given
2. $\angle QNM$ and $\angle PML$ are right angles.	2. Definition of perpendicular lines
3. $\angle QNM \cong \angle PML$	3. Right Angles Congruence Theorem
4. $\angle QMN \cong \angle PLM$	4. Corresponding Angles Theorem
5. $\overline{NM} \cong \overline{ML}$	5. Definition of midpoint
6. $\triangle NQM \cong \triangle MPL$	6. ASA Congruence Theorem

9.

STATEMENTS	REASONS
1. $\overline{VW} \cong \overline{UW}$, $\angle X \cong \angle Z$	1. Given
2. $\angle W \cong \angle W$	2. Reflexive Property of Angle Congruence
3. $\triangle XWV \cong \triangle ZWU$	3. AAS Congruence Theorem

11. You are given two right triangles, so the triangles have congruent right angles by the Right Angles Congruence Theorem. Because another pair of angles and a pair of corresponding nonincluded sides (the hypotenuses) are congruent, the triangles are congruent by the AAS Congruence Theorem.

13. You are given two right triangles, so the triangles have congruent right angles by the Right Angles Congruence Theorem. There is also another pair of congruent corresponding angles and a pair of congruent corresponding sides. If the pair of congruent sides is the included side, then the triangles are congruent by the ASA Congruence Theorem. If the pair of congruent sides is a nonincluded pair, then the triangles are congruent by the AAS Congruence Theorem.

15. yes; When $x = 14$ and $y = 26$, $m\angle ABC = m\angle DBC = m\angle BCA = m\angle BCD = 80°$ and $m\angle CAB = m\angle CDB = 20°$. This satisfies the Triangle Sum Theorem for both triangles. Because $\overline{CB} \cong \overline{CB}$ by the Reflexive Property of Congruence, you can conclude that $\triangle ABC \cong \triangle DBC$ by the ASA Congruence Theorem or the AAS Congruence Theorem.

17. yes; By the Triangle Sum Theorem, $m\angle B = 180° - 68° - 59° = 53°$ and $m\angle D = 180° - 53° - 59° = 68°$. So, $\angle A \cong \angle D$ and $\angle B \cong \angle E$ by the definition of congruent angles and $\overline{AB} \cong \overline{DE}$ by the definition of congruent segments. So, $\triangle ABC \cong \triangle DEF$ by the ASA Congruence Theorem.

19. Check students' work.

21. *Sample answer:* A king post truss has a central beam that forms a triangular shape. A queen post truss has multiple central beams and forms a square shape.

5.6 Review & Refresh

22. yes; SSS Congruence Theorem
23. no
24. Check students' work.
25. $(1, 1)$
26. 60 mm
27. WVX, WXV; Base Angles Theorem
28. $\overline{ZX}$, $\overline{ZY}$; Converse of the Base Angles Theorem

5.7 Practice

1. By the Reflexive Property of Congruent Segments, $\overline{BC} \cong \overline{BC}$. So, all three pairs of sides are congruent. By the SSS Congruence Theorem, $\triangle ABC \cong \triangle DBC$. Because corresponding parts of congruent triangles are congruent, $\angle A \cong \angle D$.

3. Because $\overline{AC} \perp \overline{BC}$ and $\overline{ED} \perp \overline{BD}$, $\angle ACB$ and $\angle EDB$ are congruent right angles. Because B is the midpoint of $\overline{CD}$, $\overline{BC} \cong \overline{BD}$. The vertical angles $\angle ABC$ and $\angle EBD$ are congruent. So, $\triangle ABC \cong \triangle EBD$ by the ASA Congruence Theorem. Then, because corresponding parts of congruent triangles are congruent, $\overline{AC} \cong \overline{ED}$. So, you can find the distance ED across the canyon by measuring $\overline{AC}$.

5. Use the AAS Congruence Theorem to prove that $\triangle FHG \cong \triangle GKF$. Then state that $\angle FGK \cong \angle GFH$. Use the Congruent Complements Theorem to prove that $\angle 1 \cong \angle 2$.

7.

STATEMENTS	REASONS
1. $\overline{AP} \cong \overline{BP}$, $\overline{AQ} \cong \overline{BQ}$	1. Given
2. $\overline{PQ} \cong \overline{PQ}$	2. Reflexive Property of Congruence
3. $\triangle APQ \cong \triangle BPQ$	3. SSS Congruence Theorem
4. $\angle APQ \cong \angle BPQ$	4. Corresponding parts of congruent triangles are congruent.
5. $\overline{PM} \cong \overline{PM}$	5. Reflexive Property of Congruence
6. $\triangle APM \cong \triangle BPM$	6. SAS Congruence Theorem
7. $\angle AMP \cong \angle BMP$	7. Corresponding parts of congruent triangles are congruent.
8. $\angle AMP$ and $\angle BMP$ form a linear pair.	8. Definition of a linear pair
9. $\overline{MP} \perp \overline{AB}$	9. Linear Pair Perpendicular Theorem
10. $\angle AMP$ and $\angle BMP$ are right angles.	10. Definition of perpendicular lines

9. $\triangle GHJ$, $\triangle DEF$, $\triangle NPQ$

11. *Sample answer:*

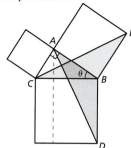

Note that ∠CBD and ∠ABE are right angles and therefore, $m\angle CBD = m\angle ABE = 90° + \theta$ and ∠ABD ≅ ∠CBE. Also note that $\overline{AB} \cong \overline{BE}$ and $\overline{CB} \cong \overline{BD}$. This means that △ABD ≅ △CBE by the SAS Congruence Theorem.

5.7 Review & Refresh
13. 16 units
14. $\sqrt{13} + \sqrt{34} + \sqrt{65}$, or about 17.5 units
15. $x = 30$
16. $y = 380(1.02)^x$

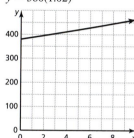

17. $2y + 2$
18. yes; ASA Congruence Theorem
19. yes; HL Congruence Theorem

5.8 Practice
1. *Sample answer:*

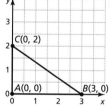

; It is easy to find the lengths of horizontal and vertical segments and distances from the origin.

3. *Sample answer:*

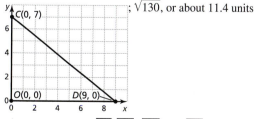

; $\sqrt{130}$, or about 11.4 units

5. Find the lengths of $\overline{OP}, \overline{PM}, \overline{MN},$ and $\overline{NO}$ to show that $\overline{OP} \cong \overline{PM}$ and $\overline{MN} \cong \overline{NO}$.

7. $DC = 2k - k = k, BC = k - 0 = k, DE = 2h - h = h, OB = h - 0 = 0, EC = \sqrt{(2h-h)^2 + (2k-k)^2} = \sqrt{h^2 + k^2}, OC = \sqrt{(h-0)^2 + (k-0)^2} = \sqrt{h^2 + k^2}$; So, $\overline{DC} \cong \overline{BC}, \overline{DE} \cong \overline{OB},$ and $\overline{EC} \cong \overline{OC}$. By the SSS Congruence Theorem, △DEC ≅ △BOC.

9. Using the Distance Formula,
$AB = \sqrt{(5-0)^2 + (12-0)^2} = 13$ mm and
$CB = \sqrt{(10-5)^2 + (0-12)^2} = 13$ mm. So $AB = CB$, $\overline{AB} \cong \overline{CB}$, and △ABC is isosceles.

11. $(-k, -m)$ and (k, m) **13.** Check students' work.

5.8 Review & Refresh
15. $x = -3$ **16.** $x = -\frac{7}{4}$
17. $(7a + 1)(2a + 3)$
18. △MKJ and △MKL are right triangles. $\overline{JK} \cong \overline{LK}$ is given and $\overline{MK} \cong \overline{MK}$ by the Reflexive Property of Congruence. So, by the HL Congruence Theorem, △MKJ ≅ △MKL. Because corresponding parts of congruent triangles are congruent, ∠J ≅ ∠L.
19. no

20.

STATEMENTS	REASONS
1. $\overline{XY} \cong \overline{ZY}, \overline{WY} \cong \overline{VY}, \overline{VW} \cong \overline{ZX}$	1. Given
2. $\overline{VZ} \cong \overline{ZV}$	2. Symmetric Property of Segment Congruence
3. $XY = ZY, WY = VY$	3. Definition of congruent segments
4. $WZ = WY + ZY, XV = XY + VY$	4. Segment Addition Postulate
5. $WZ = VY + XY$	5. Substitution Property of Equality
6. $WZ = XV$	6. Substitution Property of Equality
7. $\overline{WZ} \cong \overline{XV}$	7. Definition of congruent segments
8. △VWZ ≅ △ZXV	8. SSS Congruence Theorem

21. $x = 13$ **22.** $x = 34$

Chapter 5 Review
1. acute isosceles   **2.** obtuse scalene
3. scalene; not right   **4.** isosceles; right
5. 132°   **6.** 90°   **7.** 42°, 48°   **8.** 35°, 55°
9. 36°, 54°   **10.** 22°, 68°   **11.** 22°, 68°
12. yes; no

All equilateral triangles are also equiangular. All obtuse triangles have exactly one angle greater than 90°, so they are never equiangular.

13. corresponding sides: $\overline{GH} \cong \overline{LM}, \overline{HJ} \cong \overline{MN}, \overline{JK} \cong \overline{NP},$ and $\overline{GK} \cong \overline{LP}$; corresponding angles: ∠G ≅ ∠L, ∠H ≅ ∠M, ∠J ≅ ∠N, and ∠K ≅ ∠P; *Sample answer:* JHGK ≅ NMLP
14. 16°

15. quadrilateral $ABCF \cong$ quadrilateral $EDCF$; It is given that $\angle BAF \cong \angle DEF$, $\overline{AF} \cong \overline{EF}$, $\angle EFC \cong \angle AFC$, $\overline{BC} \cong \overline{DC}$, and $\overline{AB} \cong \overline{ED}$. Because $\overleftrightarrow{AB} \parallel \overleftrightarrow{FC}$ and $\overleftrightarrow{FC} \parallel \overleftrightarrow{ED}$, you can show that $\overleftrightarrow{AB} \perp \overleftrightarrow{BD}$, $\overleftrightarrow{FC} \perp \overleftrightarrow{BD}$, and $\overleftrightarrow{ED} \perp \overleftrightarrow{BD}$ using the Perpendicular Transversal Theorem, and that $\angle ABC \cong \angle EDC$ and $\angle FCB \cong \angle FCD$ using the definition of perpendicular lines and the Right Angles Congruence Theorem. $\overline{FC} \cong \overline{FC}$ by the Reflexive Property of Segment Congruence. Because all corresponding sides are congruent and all corresponding angles are congruent, quadrilateral $ABCF \cong$ quadrilateral $EDCF$.

16. no; There are two pairs of congruent sides and one pair of congruent angles, but the angles are not the included angles.

17. yes;

STATEMENTS	REASONS
1. $\overline{WX} \cong \overline{YZ}$, $\angle WXZ \cong \angle YZX$	1. Given
2. $\overline{XZ} \cong \overline{XZ}$	2. Reflexive Property of Congruence
3. $\triangle WXZ \cong \triangle YZX$	3. SAS Congruence Theorem

18. Check students' work.

19.

STATEMENTS	REASONS
1. $AD = CD$, $\angle ADB \cong \angle CDB$	1. Given
2. $\overline{AD} \cong \overline{CD}$	2. Definition of congruent segments
3. $\overline{DB} \cong \overline{DB}$	3. Reflexive Property of Segment Congruence
4. $\triangle ADB \cong \triangle CDB$	4. SAS Congruence Theorem

20. P; PRQ; Base Angles Theorem

21. $\overline{TR}$; $\overline{TV}$; Converse of the Base Angles Theorem

22. RQS; RSQ; Base Angles Theorem

23. $\overline{SR}$; $\overline{SV}$; Converse of the Base Angles Theorem

24. $x = 40, y = 50$ **25.** $x = 15, y = 5$

26. no; There is only enough information to conclude that two pairs of sides are congruent.

27. yes;

STATEMENTS	REASONS
1. $\overline{WX} \cong \overline{YZ}$, $\angle XWZ$ and $\angle ZYX$ are right angles.	1. Given
2. $\overline{XZ} \cong \overline{XZ}$	2. Reflexive Property of Segment Congruence
3. $\triangle WXZ$ and $\triangle YZX$ are right triangles.	3. Definition of a right triangle
4. $\triangle WXZ \cong \triangle YZX$	4. HL Congruence Theorem

28. a. $\overline{BD} \perp \overline{AC}$
    b. $\overline{AB} \cong \overline{CB}$

29. yes;

STATEMENTS	REASONS
1. $\angle E \cong \angle H$, $\angle F \cong \angle J$, $\overline{FG} \cong \overline{JK}$	1. Given
2. $\triangle EFG \cong \triangle HJK$	2. AAS Congruence Theorem

30. no; There is only enough information to conclude that one pair of angles and one pair of sides are congruent.

31. yes;

STATEMENTS	REASONS
1. $\angle PLN \cong \angle MLN$, $\angle PNL \cong \angle MNL$	1. Given
2. $\overline{LN} \cong \overline{LN}$	2. Reflexive Property of Segment Congruence
3. $\triangle LPN \cong \triangle LMN$	3. ASA Congruence Theorem

32. no; There is only enough information to conclude that one pair of angles and one pair of sides are congruent.

33. By the SAS Congruence Theorem, $\triangle HJK \cong \triangle LMN$. Because corresponding parts of congruent triangles are congruent, $\angle K \cong \angle N$.

34. By the Vertical Angles Congruence Theorem, $\angle AEB \cong \angle CED$. By the AAS Congruence Theorem, $\triangle AEB \cong \triangle CED$. Because corresponding parts of congruent triangles are congruent, $\overline{AE} \cong \overline{CE}$ and $\overline{DE} \cong \overline{BE}$. By the Vertical Angles Congruence Theorem, $\angle AED \cong \angle CEB$. So, $\triangle AED \cong \triangle CEB$ by the SAS Congruence Theorem. Because corresponding parts of congruent triangles are congruent, $\overline{AD} \cong \overline{CB}$.

35. Given: $\overline{AB} \cong \overline{CD}, \overline{BC} \cong \overline{DA}$. Construct line segment $\overline{AC}$. By the Symmetric Property of Segment Congruence, $\overline{AC} \cong \overline{CA}$. So, $\triangle CDA \cong \triangle ABC$ by the SSS Congruence Theorem. Because corresponding parts of congruent triangles are congruent, $\angle D \cong \angle B$.

36. ; Sample answer: Placing the vertices on the axes makes it easy to find the base length and the height.

37. ; Sample answer: Placing the vertices on the axes makes it easy to find the base length and the height.

38. $(2k, k)$ **39.** $(0, -k)$

40. Segments $\overline{OD}$ and $\overline{BD}$ have the same length.
$OD = \sqrt{(j-0)^2 + (j-0)^2} = \sqrt{j^2 + j^2} = \sqrt{2j^2} = j\sqrt{2}$
$BD = \sqrt{(j-2j)^2 + (j-0)^2} = \sqrt{(-j)^2 + j^2} = \sqrt{2j^2} = j\sqrt{2}$
Segments $\overline{DB}$ and $\overline{DC}$ have the same length.
$DB = BD = j\sqrt{2}$
$DC = \sqrt{(2j-j)^2 + (2j-j)^2} = \sqrt{j^2 + j^2} = \sqrt{2j^2} = j\sqrt{2}$
Segments $\overline{OB}$ and $\overline{BC}$ have the same length.
$OB = |2j - 0| = 2j$
$BC = |2j - 0| = 2j$
So, you can apply the SSS Congruence Theorem to conclude that $\triangle ODB \cong \triangle BDC$.

41. Using the Distance Formula,
$OP = \sqrt{h^2 + k^2}$, $QR = \sqrt{h^2 + k^2}$, $OR = j$,
and $QP = j$. So, $\overline{OP} \cong \overline{QR}$ and $\overline{OR} \cong \overline{QP}$. Also, by the Reflexive Property of Segment Congruence, $\overline{QO} \cong \overline{QO}$. So, you can apply the SSS Congruence Theorem to conclude that $\triangle OPQ \cong \triangle QRO$.

42. Using the Distance Formula, $PQ = 18$ and $ST = 18$. So, $\overline{PQ} \cong \overline{ST}$. Also, the horizontal segments $\overline{PQ}$ and $\overline{ST}$ each have a slope of 0, which implies that they are parallel. So, $\overline{PS}$ intersects $\overline{PQ}$ and $\overline{ST}$ to form congruent alternate interior angles, $\angle P$ and $\angle S$. By the Vertical Angles Congruence Theorem, $\angle PRQ \cong \angle SRT$. So, by the AAS Congruence Theorem, $\triangle PQR \cong \triangle STR$.

Chapter 6

Getting Ready for Chapter 6

1. $y = -3x + 10$ **2.** $y = x - 7$
3. $-3 \leq w \leq 8$ **4.** $d < -1$ or $d \geq 5$

6.1 Practice

1. yes; *Sample answer:* Because point N is equidistant from L and M, point N is on the perpendicular bisector of $\overline{LM}$ by the Converse of the Perpendicular Bisector Theorem. Because only one line can be perpendicular to $\overline{LM}$ at point K, $\overleftrightarrow{NK}$ must be the perpendicular bisector of $\overline{LM}$, and P is on $\overleftrightarrow{NK}$.

3. no; *Sample answer:* You would need to know that $\overleftrightarrow{PN} \perp \overleftrightarrow{ML}$.

5. 15

7. yes; *Sample answer:* Because H is equidistant from $\overrightarrow{EF}$ and $\overrightarrow{EG}$, $\overrightarrow{EH}$ bisects $\angle FEG$ by the Converse of the Angle Bisector Theorem.

9. 20°   **11.** 28°
13. $y = x - 2$ **15.** $y = -3x + 15$
17. on the perpendicular bisector of $\overline{LR}$

19. *Sample answer:* Because $\overleftrightarrow{CP}$ is the perpendicular bisector of $\overline{AB}$, $\overleftrightarrow{CP}$ is perpendicular to $\overline{AB}$ and point P is the midpoint of $\overline{AB}$. By the definition of midpoint, $AP = BP$, and by the definition of perpendicular lines, $m\angle CPA = m\angle CPB = 90°$. Then by the definition of segment congruence, $\overline{AP} \cong \overline{BP}$, and by the definition of angle congruence, $\angle CPA \cong \angle CPB$. By the Reflexive Property of Segment Congruence, $\overline{CP} \cong \overline{CP}$. So, $\triangle CPA \cong \triangle CPB$ by the SAS Congruence Theorem, and $\overline{CA} \cong \overline{CB}$ because corresponding parts of congruent triangles are congruent. So, $CA = CB$ by the definition of segment congruence.

21. a.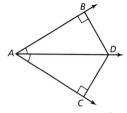

Sample answer: If $\overrightarrow{AD}$ bisects $\angle BAC$, then by definition of angle bisector, $\angle BAD \cong \angle CAD$. Also, because $\overline{DB} \perp \overline{AB}$ and $\overline{DC} \perp \overline{AC}$, by definition of perpendicular lines, $\angle ABD$ and $\angle ACD$ are right angles, and congruent to each other by the Right Angles Congruence Theorem. Also, $\overline{AD} \cong \overline{AD}$ by the Reflexive Property of Congruence. So, by the AAS Congruence Theorem, $\triangle ADB \cong \triangle ADC$. Because corresponding parts of congruent triangles are congruent, $DB = DC$. This means that point D is equidistant from each side of $\angle BAC$.

b.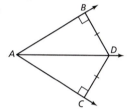

Sample answer:

STATEMENTS	REASONS
1. $\overline{DC} \perp \overrightarrow{AC}$, $\overline{DB} \perp \overrightarrow{AB}$, $BD = CD$	1. Given
2. $\angle ABD$ and $\angle ACD$ are right angles.	2. Definition of perpendicular lines
3. $\triangle ABD$ and $\triangle ACD$ are right triangles.	3. Definition of a right triangle
4. $\overline{BD} \cong \overline{CD}$	4. Definition of congruent segments
5. $\overline{AD} \cong \overline{AD}$	5. Reflexive Property of Congruence
6. $\triangle ABD \cong \triangle ACD$	6. HL Congruence Theorem
7. $\angle BAD \cong \angle CAD$	7. Corresponding parts of congruent triangles are congruent.
8. $\overrightarrow{AD}$ bisects $\angle BAC$.	8. Definition of angle bisector

23. *Sample answer:* Because $\overline{YW}$ is on plane P, and plane P is a perpendicular bisector of $\overline{XZ}$ at point Y, $\overline{YW}$ is a perpendicular bisector of $\overline{XZ}$ by definition of a plane perpendicular to a line. So, by the Perpendicular Bisector Theorem, $\overline{XW} \cong \overline{ZW}$.

Because $\overline{YV}$ is on plane P, and plane P is a perpendicular bisector of $\overline{XZ}$ at point Y, $\overline{YV}$ is a perpendicular bisector of $\overline{XZ}$ by definition of a plane perpendicular to a line. So, by the Perpendicular Bisector Theorem, $\overline{XV} \cong \overline{ZV}$.

$\overline{WV} \cong \overline{WV}$ by the Reflexive Property of Congruence. Then, because $\overline{XW} \cong \overline{ZW}$ and $\overline{XV} \cong \overline{ZV}$, $\triangle WVX \cong \triangle WVZ$ by the SSS Congruence Theorem. So, $\angle VXW \cong \angle VZW$ because corresponding parts of congruent triangles are congruent.

25. *Sample answer:* The central vein runs the entire length of the leaf and the secondary veins stem from the central vein and point outward.

6.1 Review & Refresh
27. scalene
28. equilateral
29. acute
30. right
31. $m\angle 2 = 35°$
32. *Sample answer:* Use the SSS Congruence Theorem to prove that $\triangle ADE \cong \triangle CDE$. Because corresponding parts of congruent triangles are congruent, $\angle ADE \cong \angle CDE$. Then use the SAS Congruence Theorem to prove that $\triangle BDA \cong \triangle BDC$.
33. $\angle S \cong \angle Y; \angle T \cong \angle Z$
34.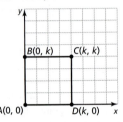

$\left(0, \frac{k}{2}\right), \left(\frac{k}{2}, k\right), \left(k, \frac{k}{2}\right), \left(\frac{k}{2}, 0\right)$

6.2 Practice
1. *Sample answer:* You could copy the positions of the three residences and connect the points to draw a triangle. Then draw the three perpendicular bisectors of the triangle. The point where the perpendicular bisectors meet, the circumcenter, should be the location of the meeting place.
3. 9
5. (3, 4)
7. (−4, 9)
9. 16
11. 6
13. Check students' work.
15. *Sample answer:* Because point G is the intersection of the angle bisectors, it is the incenter. But, because $\overline{GD}$ and $\overline{GF}$ are not necessarily perpendicular to a side of the triangle, there is not sufficient evidence to conclude that $\overline{GD}$ and $\overline{GF}$ are congruent; Point G is equidistant from the sides of the triangle.
17. incenter
19. sometimes; *Sample answer:* If the scalene triangle is obtuse or right, then the circumcenter is outside or on the triangle, respectively. However, if the scalene triangle is acute, then the circumcenter is inside the triangle.
21. sometimes; *Sample answer:* This only happens when the triangle is equilateral.
23. $x = 6$
25. *Sample answer:* Because $\overline{DE} \perp \overline{AB}, \overline{DF} \perp \overline{BC}$, and $\overline{DG} \perp \overline{CA}, \angle DFB, \angle DEB, \angle DEA$, and $\angle DGA$ are congruent right angles. Also, by definition of angle bisector, $\angle DBF \cong \angle DBE$ and $\angle DAE \cong \angle DAG$. In addition, $\overline{DB} \cong \overline{DB}$ and $\overline{DA} \cong \overline{DA}$ by the Reflexive Property of Congruence. So, $\triangle DFB \cong \triangle DEB$ and $\triangle DEA \cong \triangle DGA$ by the AAS Congruence Theorem. Next, because corresponding parts of congruent triangles are congruent, $\overline{DF} \cong \overline{DE}$ and $\overline{DG} \cong \overline{DE}$. By the Transitive Property of Congruence, $\overline{DF} \cong \overline{DE} \cong \overline{DG}$. So, point D is equidistant from $\overline{AB}, \overline{BC}$, and $\overline{CA}$. Because D is equidistant from $\overline{CA}$ and $\overline{CB}$, by the Converse of the Angle Bisector Theorem, point D is on the angle bisector of $\angle ACB$. So, the angle bisectors intersect at point D.

27. yes; In an equilateral triangle, each perpendicular bisector passes through the opposite vertex and divides the triangle into two congruent triangles. So, it is also an angle bisector.

29. *Sample answer:* If the incenter was outside the triangle, it would be closer to one or more sides of the triangle than the other(s). The Incenter Theorem says that this is not possible.
31. about 3 in.; angle bisectors
33. the centroid
35. *Sample answer:* a see-saw at the playground

6.2 Review & Refresh
36. $m\angle ABD = 30°$
37. $x = -6$
38. linear; *Sample answer:* As x increases by 2, y increases by 3.
39. *Sample answer:* Using the Distance Formula,
$AB = \sqrt{(8-0)^2 + (12-0)^2} = 4\sqrt{13}$ and
$BC = \sqrt{(16-8)^2 + (0-12)^2} = 4\sqrt{13}$. Because $AB = BC$, $\triangle ABC$ is isosceles.
40. $M(0, 5); AB = 6$
41. $\sqrt{10}$, or about 3.2 units
42. *Sample answer:* If a concentrated solar power plant is the largest in the world, then it is the Noor Complex; If a concentrated solar power plant is the Noor Complex, then it cost 3.9 billion dollars to construct.

6.3 Practice
1. 6, 3
3. 20, 10
5. 9
7. 5
9. $\left(5, \frac{11}{3}\right)$
11. outside; (0, −5)
13. inside; (−1, 2)
15. *Sample answer:*

17. *Sample answer:*

Legs $\overline{AB}$ and $\overline{BC}$ of isosceles $\triangle ABC$ are congruent. $\angle ABD \cong \angle CBD$ because $\overline{BD}$ is an angle bisector of vertex angle ABC. Also, $\overline{BD} \cong \overline{BD}$ by the Reflexive Property of Congruence. So, $\triangle ABD \cong \triangle CBD$ by the SAS Congruence Theorem. $\overline{AD} \cong \overline{CD}$ because corresponding parts of congruent triangles are congruent. So, $\overline{BD}$ is a median.
19. never
21. always
23. a. $EJ = 3KJ$
    b. $DK = 2KH$
    c. $FG = \frac{3}{2}FK$
    d. $KG = \frac{1}{3}FG$

25. Check students' work.   27. $x = 9$

29. a. *Sample answer:*

STATEMENTS	REASONS
1. $\overline{LP}$ and $\overline{MQ}$ are medians of scalene $\triangle LMN$; $\overline{LP} \cong \overline{PR}$, $\overline{MQ} \cong \overline{QS}$	1. Given
2. $\overline{NP} \cong \overline{MP}, \overline{LQ} \cong \overline{NQ}$	2. Definition of median
3. $\angle LPM \cong \angle RPN$, $\angle MQL \cong \angle SQN$	3. Vertical Angles Congruence Theorem
4. $\triangle LPM \cong \triangle RPN$, $\triangle MQL \cong \triangle SQN$	4. SAS Congruence Theorem
5. $\overline{NR} \cong \overline{LM}, \overline{NS} \cong \overline{LM}$	5. Corresponding parts of congruent triangles are congruent.
6. $\overline{NS} \cong \overline{NR}$	6. Transitive Property of Congruence

b. It was shown in part (a) that $\triangle LPM \cong \triangle RPN$ and $\triangle MQL \cong \triangle SQN$. So, $\angle LMP \cong \angle RNP$ and $\angle MLQ \cong \angle SNQ$ because corresponding parts of congruent triangles are congruent. Then, $\overline{NS} \parallel \overline{LM}$ and $\overline{NR} \parallel \overline{LM}$ by the Alternate Interior Angles Converse.

c. Because $\overline{NS}$ and $\overline{NR}$ are both parallel to the same segment, $\overline{LM}$, they would have to be parallel to each other by the Transitive Property of Parallel Lines. However, because they intersect at point N, they cannot be parallel. So, they must be collinear.

31. *Sample answer:* Let $\overline{AE}$ and $\overline{BF}$ be two medians of $\triangle ABC$ and G be their point of intersection. Draw a line segment through point F and parallel to $\overline{AE}$, and let point Q be the intersection with $\overline{BC}$.

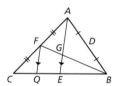

Because $\overline{FQ} \parallel \overline{AE}$, $\angle CFQ \cong \angle CAE$ and $\angle CQF \cong \angle CEA$ by the Corresponding Angles Theorem. $\triangle CFQ$ and $\triangle CAE$ also have $\angle C$ in common, so $\triangle CAE$ is a similarity transformation of $\triangle CFQ$ because the two triangles have the same shape and size. So, $CA = k_1 CF$, $CE = k_1 CQ$, and $AE = k_1 FQ$ for some scale factor k_1. Similarly, note that $\triangle BFQ$ is a similarity transformation of $\triangle BGE$, so $BF = k_2 BG$, $BQ = k_2 BE$, and $FQ = k_2 GE$ for some scale factor k_2. Because F is the midpoint of $\overline{CA}$ and $CA = k_1 CF$, $k_1 = 2$. So, $CE = 2CQ$ and Q is the midpoint of $\overline{CE}$. By the Segment Addition Postulate, $QB = QE + EB$. Because $QB = QE + EB = \frac{1}{2}CE + EB = \frac{1}{2}EB + EB = \frac{3}{2}EB$, $k_2 = \frac{3}{2}$. So, $BF = \frac{3}{2}BG$ and the intersection of medians $\overline{AE}$ and $\overline{BF}$, point G, lies on $\overline{BF}$, $\frac{2}{3}$ of the way from B to F.

Let $\overline{CD}$ be the third median of $\triangle ABC$ and H be its point of intersection with $\overline{BF}$. Draw a line segment through point F and parallel to $\overline{CD}$, and let point R be the intersection with $\overline{AB}$.

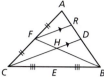

You can use the same reasoning as before to show that $BF = \frac{3}{2}BH$ and the intersection of medians $\overline{CD}$ and $\overline{BF}$, point H, lies on $\overline{BF}$, $\frac{2}{3}$ of the way from B to F.

So, points G and H are the same point, which means medians $\overline{AE}, \overline{BF}$, and $\overline{CD}$ are concurrent at that point.

33. horse; *Sample answer:* Animals with a higher center of gravity are more likely to tip over so they would need to be secured in a way to prevent this while transporting them.

6.3 Review & Refresh

35. $59°$ 36. $(7, 5)$ 37. yes   38. no

39. 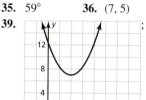 ; The graph of g is a translation 4 units right, a horizontal shrink by a factor of $\frac{1}{3}$, and a translation 7 units up of the graph of f.

40. $(6, 4)$ 41. $(-2, 3)$
42. $x = \pm 4i$ 43. $x = 4 \pm 2\sqrt{3}$

44.

		Talent Show		
		Participate	Not Participate	Total
Gender	Male	8	63	71
	Female	13	62	75
	Total	21	125	146

45. *Sample answer:* First find ED and EF using the Distance Formula. Then, $\overline{ED} \cong \overline{EF}$ by the definition of congruent segments. Use the Reflexive Property of Segment Congruence to show that $\overline{EG} \cong \overline{EG}$. $\angle DEG \cong \angle FEG$ by the definition of angle bisector. Finally, prove that $\triangle EGD \cong \triangle EGF$ by the SAS Congruence Theorem.

6.4 Practice

1. $D(-4, -2), E(-2, 0), F(-1, -4)$

3. *Sample answer:* Because the slopes of $\overline{EF}$ and $\overline{AC}$ are the same (-4), $\overline{EF} \parallel \overline{AC}$. $EF = \sqrt{17}$ and $AC = 2\sqrt{17}$. Because $\sqrt{17} = \frac{1}{2}(2\sqrt{17})$, $EF = \frac{1}{2}AC$.

5. *Sample answer:* The midpoint of $\overline{OC}$ is $F(p, 0)$. Because the slopes of $\overline{DF}$ and $\overline{BC}$ are the same $\left(-\frac{r}{p-q}\right)$, $\overline{DF} \parallel \overline{BC}$.
$DF = \sqrt{p^2 - 2pq + q^2 + r^2}$ and
$BC = 2\sqrt{p^2 - 2pq + q^2 + r^2}$.
Because $\sqrt{p^2 - 2pq + q^2 + r^2} = \frac{1}{2}\left(2\sqrt{p^2 - 2pq + q^2 + r^2}\right)$, $DF = \frac{1}{2}BC$.

7. $x = 6$ 9. 45 ft

11. a. $(-1, 2), (9, 8), (5, 0)$;
Sample answer: Find the slope of each midsegment. Graph the line parallel to each midsegment passing through the opposite vertex. The intersection of these lines will be the vertices of the original triangle. You can check your answer by finding the midsegments of the triangle.

b. $(2.6, 16.2), (7.4, 13.8), (5.4, 7.8)$
Sample answer: Find the slope of each midsegment. Graph the line parallel to each midsegment passing through the opposite vertex. The intersection of these lines will be the vertices of the original triangle. You can check your answer by finding the midsegments of the triangle.

13. about $1,081,113 \text{ ft}^3$

6.4 Review & Refresh

15. *Sample answer:* $-2 - (-7) = 5$, and $5 > -2$
16. 15
17. $(-4, -4)$
18. nonlinear
19. linear
20. $y = \begin{cases} 12, & \text{if } 0 \leq x \leq 30 \\ 16, & \text{if } 30 < x \leq 60 \\ 20, & \text{if } 60 < x \leq 90 \\ 24, & \text{if } 90 < x \leq 120 \end{cases}$; $20
21. 11

6.5 Practice

1. Assume temporarily that xy is even.
3. Assume temporarily that an odd number is divisible by 4. Let the odd number be represented by $2y + 1$ where y is a positive integer. Then there must be a positive integer x such that $4x = 2y + 1$. However, when you divide each side of the equation by 4, you get $x = \frac{1}{2}y + \frac{1}{4}$, which is not an integer. So, the assumption must be false, and an odd number is not divisible by 4.
5. $m\angle J < m\angle K$
7. $\angle S, \angle R, \angle T$
9. $\overline{AB}, \overline{BC}, \overline{AC}$
11. 7 in. $< x <$ 17 in.
13. 0 m $< x <$ 50 m
15. no; $3 + 6 \not> 9$
17. $\angle L, \angle J, \angle K$
19. a. $x > 76$ km, $x < 1,054$ km
b. *Sample answer:* Because $\angle 2$ is the smallest angle, the distance between Granite Peak and Fort Peck Lake must be the shortest side of the triangle. So, the second inequality becomes $x < 489$ kilometers.
21. *Sample answer:* The right angle of a right triangle must always be the largest angle because the other two will have a sum of $90°$. So, according to the Triangle Larger Angle Theorem, because the right angle is larger than either of the other angles, the side opposite the right angle, which is the hypotenuse, will always have to be longer than either of the legs.
23. *Sample answer:* It is given that $m\angle A > m\angle C$. Assume temporarily that $BC \not> AB$. Then it follows that either $BC < AB$ or $BC = AB$. If $BC < AB$, then $m\angle A < m\angle C$ by the Triangle Longer Side Theorem. If $BC = AB$, then $m\angle A = m\angle C$ by the Base Angles Theorem. Both conclusions contradict the given statement that $m\angle A > m\angle C$. So, the temporary assumption that $BC \not> AB$ cannot be true. This proves that $BC > AB$.

25. greater than 4 and less than 24; *Sample answer:* Because of the Triangle Inequality Theorem, FG must be greater than 2 and less than 8, GH must be greater than 1 and less than 7, and FH must be greater than 1 and less than 9. So, the perimeter must be greater than $2 + 1 + 1 = 4$ and less than $8 + 7 + 9 = 24$.
27. $\frac{1}{2}$
29. no; *Sample answer:* If the length of one side of the triangle is 1.3 inches then that means the sum of the lengths of the two other sides of the triangle is 1.1 inches which is less than the length of the third side. According to the Triangle Inequality Theorem, the sum of the lengths of any two sides of a triangle must be greater than the third side, so it is not possible.

6.5 Review & Refresh

31. $(-4, 1), (0, 2), (-1, -1)$
32. $k = \frac{1}{4}$
33. 15
34. inside; $(0, 4)$
35.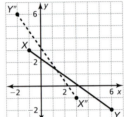

36. yes; HL Congruence Theorem
37. no
38. $x = 12$

6.6 Practice

1. $AC > DC$; *Sample answer:* By the Hinge Theorem, because $\overline{AC}$ is the third side of the triangle with the larger included angle, it is longer than $\overline{DC}$.
3. $m\angle 1 > m\angle 2$; *Sample answer:* By the Converse of the Hinge Theorem, because $\angle 1$ is the included angle in the triangle with the longer third side, its measure is greater than that of $\angle 2$.
5. Flight 1; *Sample answer:* Because $160° > 150°$, the distance the first plane flew is a greater distance than the distance the second plane flew by the Hinge Theorem.
7. $x > \frac{3}{2}$; *Sample answer:* By the Exterior Angle Theorem, $m\angle ABD = m\angle BDC + m\angle C$. So, $m\angle ABD > m\angle BDC$.
$AD > BC$
$4x - 3 > 2x$
$2x > 3$
$x > \frac{3}{2}$

9. *Sample answer:* Because $\overline{BC} \cong \overline{EF}$, $\angle CBP \cong \angle FED$ by construction, and $\overline{BP} \cong \overline{ED}$ by construction, you have $\triangle PBC \cong \triangle DEF$ by the SAS Congruence Theorem.

Because $\overrightarrow{BH}$ bisects $\angle PBA$ by construction, $\angle PBH \cong \angle ABH$. By the Transitive Property of Congruence, $\overline{AB} \cong \overline{PB}$. By the Reflexive Property of Congruence, $\overline{BH} \cong \overline{BH}$. So, $\triangle ABH \cong \triangle PBH$ by the SAS Congruence Theorem.

By the Segment Addition Postulate, $AC = AH + HC$. Because corresponding parts of congruent triangle are congruent, $\overline{AH} \cong \overline{PH}$. By the definition of congruent segments, $AH = PH$. By the Addition Property of Equality, $AH + HC = PH + HC$. By the Triangle Inequality Theorem, $PH + HC > PC$. By substitution, $AH + HC > PC$ and $AC > PC$. Because corresponding parts of congruent triangles are congruent, $\overline{PC} \cong \overline{DF}$. By the definition of congruent segments, $PC = DF$. So, by substitution $AC > DF$.

11. no; *Sample answer:* You would need to know the direct distance the helicopters are away from each other.

6.6 Review & Refresh

13. $x = 72$
14. $x = 17$
15.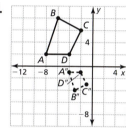

16. no; Because $9 + 11 \not> 21$, by the Triangle Inequality Theorem, the triangle is not possible.

17. **a.** centroid
    b. no; This point is not equidistant from the three cities. the circumcenter would be equidistant from the cities.

Chapter 6 Review

1. 20 2. 23 3. 47°
4. no; *Sample answer:* You would need to know $\overline{RQ} \cong \overline{TQ}$, or one pair of corresponding angles are congruent.
5. $(-3, -3)$ 6. $(4, 3)$ 7. $x = 5$
8. Check students' work. 9. Check students' work.
10. $ED = 6, DC = 12$ 11. $ED = 9, DC = 18$
12. $(-6, 3)$ 13. $(4, -4)$
14. inside; $(3, 5.2)$ 15. outside; $(-6, -1)$
16. $\triangle ABC$ is isosceles.
17. ; *Sample answer:* The orthocenter of any right triangle is the vertex containing the right angle because the legs of the triangle are altitudes.

18. $(-6, 6), (-3, 6), (-3, 4)$ 19. $(0, 3), (2, 0), (-1, -2)$
20. $x = 50$ 21. $x = 14$
22. 1,160 m

23. *Sample answer:* Assume temporarily that $YZ \not> 4$. Then it follows that either $YZ < 4$ or $YZ = 4$. If $YZ < 4$, then $XY + YZ < XZ$ because $4 + YZ < 8$ when $YZ < 4$. If $YZ = 4$, then $XY + YZ = XZ$ because $4 + 4 = 8$. Both conclusions contradict the Triangle Inequality Theorem, which says that $XY + YZ > XZ$. So, the temporary assumption that $YZ \not> 4$ cannot be true. This proves that in $\triangle XYZ$, if $XY = 4$ and $XZ = 8$, then $YZ > 4$.

24. $\overline{FH}, \overline{FG}, \overline{GH}$ 25. $\overline{JK}, \overline{KL}, \overline{JL}$
26. 4 in. $< x <$ 12 in. 27. 3 m $< x <$ 15 m
28. *Sample answer:* Assume temporarily that $\triangle LRT$ has three congruent angles. $LT = 36$ in. and $LR \leq 24$ in., so $LT > LR$. Because $LT > LR$, $m\angle R > m\angle T$ by the Triangle Longer Side Theorem. So, $m\angle R \neq m\angle T$. So, the assumption must be false, which proves that there can be at most two congruent angles of $\triangle LRT$.

29. $QT > ST$ 30. $m\angle QRT > m\angle SRT$
31. second boat; *Sample answer:* Because $170° > 160°$, the distance the second boat traveled is greater than the distance the first boat traveled by the Hinge Theorem.

Chapter 7

Getting Ready for Chapter 7

1. $x = 3$ 2. $x = 4$
3. $a \parallel b, c \perp d$
4. $a \parallel b, c \parallel d, a \perp c, a \perp d, b \perp c, b \perp d$

7.1 Practice

1. 1,260° 3. 2,520° 5. hexagon
7. 16-gon 9. $x = 64$ 11. $x = 99$
13. The right angle was not included and the sum of the angle measures should be 720°, not 540°;
$$x° + 121° + 96° + 101° + 162° + 90° = 720°$$
$$x + 570 = 720$$
$$x = 150$$
15. $m\angle X = m\angle Y = 92°$ 17. $m\angle X = m\angle Y = 135°$
19. $x = 111$ 21. 108°, 72° 23. 172°, 8° 25. 144°; 36°
27. $n = \dfrac{360}{x}$ 29. 24 31. 60
33. 22.5°, 67.5°, 112.5°, 157.5°
35. When $n = 1$, $\dfrac{1(1+1)(2(1)+1)}{6} = 1 = 1^2$. So, the statement is true for $n = 1$. Assume that
$$1^2 + 2^2 + 3^2 + \cdots + k^2 = \dfrac{k(k+1)(2k+1)}{6}$$ for a natural number $k \geq 1$. Then
$$1^2 + 2^2 + 3^2 + \ldots + k^2 + (k+1)^2$$
$$= (1^2 + 2^2 + 3^2 + \ldots + k^2) + (k+1)^2$$
$$= \dfrac{k(k+1)(2k+1)}{6} + (k+1)^2$$
$$= \dfrac{k(k+1)(2k+1) + 6(k+1)^2}{6}$$
$$= \dfrac{(k+1)[(2k+1) + 6(k+1)]}{6}$$
$$= \dfrac{(k+1)(k+2)(2k+3)}{6}.$$
So, the statement is true for all natural numbers $n \geq 1$.

37. In a pentagon, when all the diagonals from one vertex are drawn, the polygon is divided into three triangles. Because the sum of the measures of the interior angles of each triangle is 180°, the sum of the measures of the interior angles of the pentagon is $(5 - 2) \cdot 180° = 3 \cdot 180° = 540°$.

39. a. $h(n) = \dfrac{(n-2) \cdot 180°}{n}$

b. $h(9) = 140°$; $n = 12$

c. 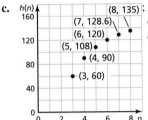 ; As n gets larger, the value of $h(n)$ increases at a decreasing rate.

41. yes; The measure of the angle where the polygon "caves in" is greater than 180° but less than 360°.

43. 90°   **45.** 720°

7.1 Review & Refresh

47. $x = 101$ **48.** $x = 67$
49. $m\angle 2$ **50.** 13 in. $< x <$ 21 in.
51. $y = -2x + 2$ **52.** $x = 14$
53. $(x - 3)(x + 7)$ **54.** 110°

7.2 Practice

1. $d = 126$, $z = 28$ **3.** 129°

5. In a parallelogram, consecutive angles are supplementary; Because quadrilateral STUV is a parallelogram, $\angle S$ and $\angle V$ are supplementary. So, $m\angle V = 180° - 50° = 130°$.

7.

STATEMENTS	REASONS
1. ABCD and CEFD are parallelograms.	1. Given
2. $\overline{AB} \cong \overline{DC}$, $\overline{DC} \cong \overline{FE}$	2. Parallelogram Opposite Sides Theorem
3. $\overline{AB} \cong \overline{FE}$	3. Transitive Property of Segment Congruence

9. (1, 2.5)   **11.** $F(3, 3)$
13. $G(2, 0)$ **15.** 36°, 144°
17. $m\angle R = 114°$, $m\angle S = 66°$, $m\angle T = 114°$

19.

STATEMENTS	REASONS
1. PQRS is a parallelogram.	1. Given
2. $\overline{QR} \parallel \overline{PS}$	2. Definition of parallelogram
3. $\angle Q$ and $\angle P$ are supplementary.	3. Consecutive Interior Angles Theorem
4. $x° + y° = 180°$	4. Definition of supplementary angles

21. 8   **23.** 16°
25. Find the product of the base and the height.
27. *Sample answer:* triangles, regular polygons, pyramids

7.2 Review & Refresh

28. $\overline{DE}, \overline{DF}, \overline{EF}$ **29.** $x = 80$
30. y-axis
31. yes; Alternate Interior Angles Converse
32. $m\angle EGF > m\angle DGE$

7.3 Practice

1. Parallelogram Opposite Angles Converse
3. Parallelogram Diagonals Converse
5. $x = 114$, $y = 66$ **7.** $x = 8$

9. *Sample answer:* Because $BC = AD = 8$, $\overline{BC} \cong \overline{AD}$. Because both $\overline{BC}$ and $\overline{AD}$ are horizontal lines, their slope is 0, and they are parallel. $\overline{BC}$ and $\overline{AD}$ are opposite sides that are both congruent and parallel. So, ABCD is a parallelogram by the Opposite Sides Parallel and Congruent Theorem.

11. In order to be a parallelogram, the quadrilateral must have two pairs of opposite sides that are congruent, not consecutive sides; DEFG is not a parallelogram.

13. $x = 5$

15. A quadrilateral is a parallelogram if and only if both pairs of opposite sides are congruent.

17. Check students' work; Because the diagonals bisect each other, this quadrilateral is a parallelogram by the Parallelogram Diagonals Converse.

19. a. 60°, 120°, 120°
b. Transitive Property of Parallel Lines

21. You can use the Alternate Interior Angles Converse to show that $\overline{AB} \parallel \overline{DC}$ and $\overline{AD} \parallel \overline{BC}$. Because both pairs of opposite sides are parallel, ABCD is a parallelogram by definition.

23. Use the Linear Pair Postulate and the Transitive Property of Equality to show that $\angle DAB \cong \angle BCD$. Use the Alternate Interior Angles Theorem and the Transitive Property of Angle Congruence to show that $\angle B \cong \angle D$. So, ABCD is a parallelogram by the Parallelogram Opposite Angles Converse.

25.

STATEMENTS	REASONS
1. $\overline{QR} \parallel \overline{PS}$, $\overline{QR} \cong \overline{PS}$	1. Given
2. $\angle SQR \cong \angle QSP$	2. Alternate Interior Angles Theorem
3. $\overline{QS} \cong \overline{QS}$	3. Reflexive Property of Segment Congruence
4. $\triangle QRS \cong \triangle SPQ$	4. SAS Congruence Theorem
5. $\angle QSR \cong \angle SQP$	5. Corresponding parts of congruent triangles are congruent.
6. $\overline{QP} \parallel \overline{RS}$	6. Alternate Interior Angles Converse
7. PQRS is a parallelogram.	7. Definition of parallelogram

27.

STATEMENTS	REASONS
1. *DEBF* is a parallelogram. $AE = CF$	1. Given
2. $\overline{DE} \cong \overline{BF}, \overline{FD} \cong \overline{EB}$	2. Parallelogram Opposite Sides Theorem
3. $\angle DFB \cong \angle DEB$	3. Parallelogram Opposite Angles Theorem
4. $\angle AED$ and $\angle DEB$ form a linear pair. $\angle CFB$ and $\angle DFB$ form a linear pair.	4. Definition of linear pair
5. $\angle AED$ and $\angle DEB$ are supplementary. $\angle CFB$ and $\angle DFB$ are supplementary.	5. Linear Pair Postulate
6. $\angle AED \cong \angle CFB$	6. Congruent Supplements Theorem
7. $\overline{AE} \cong \overline{CF}$	7. Definition of congruent segments
8. $\triangle AED \cong \triangle CFB$	8. SAS Congruence Theorem
9. $\overline{AD} \cong \overline{CB}$	9. Corresponding parts of congruent triangles are congruent.
10. $AB = AE + EB$, $DC = CF + FD$	10. Segment Addition Postulate
11. $FD = EB$	11. Definition of congruent segments
12. $AB = CF + FD$	12. Substitution Property of Equality
13. $AB = DC$	13. Transitive Property of Equality
14. $\overline{AB} \cong \overline{DC}$	14. Definition of congruent segments
15. *ABCD* is a parallelogram.	15. Parallelogram Opposite Sides Converse

29. Based on the given information, $\overline{GH}$ is a midsegment of $\triangle EBC$, and $\overline{FJ}$ is a midsegment of $\triangle EAD$. So, by the Triangle Midsegment Theorem, $\overline{GH} \parallel \overline{BC}$, $GH = \frac{1}{2}BC$, $\overline{FJ} \parallel \overline{AD}$, and $FJ = \frac{1}{2}AD$. Also, by the Parallelogram Opposite Sides Theorem and the definition of a parallelogram, $\overline{BC}$ and $\overline{AD}$ are congruent and parallel. So, by the Transitive Property of Parallel Lines, $\overline{AD} \parallel \overline{FJ} \parallel \overline{GH} \parallel \overline{BC}$ and by the Transitive Property of Equality, $\frac{1}{2}BC = GH = FJ = \frac{1}{2}AD$. Because one pair of opposite sides is both congruent and parallel, *FGHJ* is a parallelogram by the Opposite Sides Parallel and Congruent Theorem.

31. about 1,081 pounds

7.3 Review & Refresh

32. 40° **33.** 4 **34.** $x = 100$
35. $3\sqrt{10}$, or about 9.5 units **36.** $(-3, 7)$
37.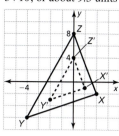
38. $x = 10$ **39.** $AD > CD$

7.4 Practice

1. sometimes; Some rhombuses are squares.

3. always; A rhombus is a parallelogram, and opposite sides of a parallelogram are congruent.

5. square 7. rhombus
9. $m\angle 1 = m\angle 2 = m\angle 4 = 27°$, $m\angle 3 = 90°$, $m\angle 5 = m\angle 6 = 63°$
11. always; All angles of a rectangle are congruent.

13. sometimes; Some rectangles are squares.

15. It is not because all four angles must be congruent.
17. 11 19. 4 21. 53° 23. 16
25. 56° 27. 5 29. 90° 31. 1
33. rectangle, square 35. rhombus, square
37. It is a rectangle, a rhombus, and a square because the diagonals are congruent and perpendicular.
39. It is a rectangle but not a square because adjacent sides are perpendicular and not congruent.
41. always 43. always
45. Measure the diagonals to see if they are congruent.
47. square

49.

STATEMENTS	REASONS
1. PQRS is a parallelogram. $\overline{PR}$ bisects $\angle SPQ$ and $\angle QRS$. $\overline{SQ}$ bisects $\angle PSR$ and $\angle RQP$.	1. Given
2. $\angle QRP \cong \angle SRP$, $\angle QPR \cong \angle SPR$	2. Definition of angle bisector
3. $\overline{RP} \cong \overline{RP}$	3. Reflexive Property of Segment Congruence
4. $\triangle PQR \cong \triangle PSR$	4. ASA Congruence Theorem
5. $\overline{QR} \cong \overline{SR}$	5. Corresponding parts of congruent triangles are congruent.
6. $\overline{QR} \cong \overline{PS}, \overline{PQ} \cong \overline{SR}$	6. Parallelogram Opposite Sides Theorem
7. $\overline{PS} \cong \overline{QR} \cong \overline{SR} \cong \overline{PQ}$	7. Transitive Property of Segment Congruence
8. PQRS is a rhombus.	8. Definition of rhombus

51. If a quadrilateral is a rhombus, then it has four congruent sides; If a quadrilateral has four congruent sides, then it is a rhombus; The conditional statement is true by the definition of rhombus. The converse is true because if a quadrilateral has four congruent sides, then both pairs of opposite sides are congruent. So, by the Parallelogram Opposite Sides Converse, it is a parallelogram with four congruent sides, which is the definition of a rhombus.

53. If a quadrilateral is a square, then it is a rhombus and a rectangle; If a quadrilateral is a rhombus and a rectangle, then it is a square; The conditional statement is true because if a quadrilateral is a square, then by definition of a square, it has four congruent sides, which makes it a rhombus by the Rhombus Corollary, and it has four right angles, which makes it a rectangle by the Rectangle Corollary; The converse is true because if a quadrilateral is a rhombus and a rectangle, then by the Rhombus Corollary, it has four congruent sides, and by the Rectangle Corollary, it has four right angles. So, by the definition, it is a square.

55. a. Not all rhombuses are similar because corresponding angles of two rhombuses might not be congruent.
b. All squares are similar because corresponding angles are congruent and corresponding sides are proportional.

57.

STATEMENTS	REASONS
1. $\triangle XYZ \cong \triangle XWZ$, $\angle XYW \cong \angle ZWY$	1. Given
2. $\angle YXZ \cong \angle WXZ$, $\angle YZX \cong \angle WZX$, $\overline{XY} \cong \overline{XW}, \overline{YZ} \cong \overline{WZ}$	2. Corresponding parts of congruent triangles are congruent.
3. $\overline{XZ}$ bisects $\angle WXY$ and $\angle WZY$.	3. Definition of angle bisector
4. $\angle XWY \cong \angle XYW$, $\angle WYZ \cong \angle ZWY$	4. Base Angles Theorem
5. $\angle XYW \cong \angle WYZ$, $\angle XWY \cong \angle ZWY$	5. Transitive Property of Angle Congruence
6. $\overline{WY}$ bisects $\angle XWZ$ and $\angle XYZ$.	6. Definition of angle bisector
7. WXYZ is a rhombus.	7. Rhombus Opposite Angles Theorem

59.

STATEMENTS	REASONS
1. PQRS is a rectangle.	1. Given
2. PQRS is a parallelogram.	2. Definition of a rectangle
3. $\overline{PS} \cong \overline{QR}$	3. Parallelogram Opposite Sides Theorem
4. $\angle PQR$ and $\angle QPS$ are right angles.	4. Definition of a rectangle
5. $\angle PQR \cong \angle QPS$	5. Right Angles Congruence Theorem
6. $\overline{PQ} \cong \overline{PQ}$	6. Reflexive Property of Segment Congruence
7. $\triangle PQR \cong \triangle QPS$	7. SAS Congruence Theorem
8. $\overline{PR} \cong \overline{SQ}$	8. Corresponding parts of congruent triangles are congruent.

61. *Sample answer:* triangles, quadrilaterals, pentagons

63. Some minerals form crystals due to electron attraction which creates an imbalance in charges, attracting more molecules during the growth process and arranging them in an organized pattern. Those that do not form as crystals lack the ability to arrange atoms and molecules in an organized pattern.

7.4 Review & Refresh

64. $x = 9, y = 26$ **65.** $x = 4, y = 13$
66. 165°, 15°
67. $11 + \sqrt{13}$, or about 14.6 units; 9 square units
68. Parallelogram Opposite Angles Converse
69. $AB = 18$

7.5 Practice

1. slope of $\overline{YZ}$ = slope of $\overline{XW}$ and slope of $\overline{XY} \neq$ slope of $\overline{WZ}$; $XY = WZ$, so WXYZ is isosceles.

3. slope of $\overline{MQ}$ = slope of $\overline{NP}$ and slope of $\overline{MN} \neq$ slope of $\overline{PQ}$; $MN \neq PQ$, so $MNPQ$ is not isosceles.
5. $m\angle L = m\angle M = 62°$, $m\angle K = m\angle J = 118°$
7. 14
9. 4
11. 7.5
13. $3\sqrt{13}$
15. 110°
17. rectangle
19. $x = 3$
21. 18 in., 29 in., 29 in.

23.
STATEMENTS	REASONS
1. $ABCD$ is a kite. $\overline{AB} \cong \overline{CB}$, $\overline{AD} \cong \overline{CD}$	1. Given
2. $\overline{BD} \cong \overline{BD}$, $\overline{ED} \cong \overline{ED}$	2. Reflexive Property of Segment Congruence
3. $\triangle BCD \cong \triangle BAD$	3. SSS Congruence Theorem
4. $\angle CDE \cong \angle ADE$	4. Corresponding parts of congruent triangles are congruent.
5. $\triangle CED \cong \triangle AED$	5. SAS Congruence Theorem
6. $\overline{CE} \cong \overline{AE}$	6. Corresponding parts of congruent triangles are congruent.

25. Given isosceles trapezoid $ABCD$ with $\overline{BC} \parallel \overline{AD}$, construct $\overline{CE}$ parallel to $\overline{BA}$. Then, $ABCE$ is a parallelogram by definition, so $\overline{AB} \cong \overline{EC}$. Because $\overline{AB} \cong \overline{CD}$ by the definition of an isosceles trapezoid, $\overline{CE} \cong \overline{CD}$ by the Transitive Property of Segment Congruence. So, $\angle CED \cong \angle D$ by the Base Angles Theorem and $\angle A \cong \angle CED$ by the Corresponding Angles Theorem. So, $\angle A \cong \angle D$ by the Transitive Property of Angle Congruence. Next, by the Consecutive Interior Angles Theorem, $\angle BCD$ and $\angle D$ are supplementary and so are $\angle B$ and $\angle A$. Because $\angle A$ and $\angle D$ have the same measure, $\angle B$ and $\angle D$ are also supplementary. So, $\angle B \cong \angle BCD$ by the Congruent Supplements Theorem.
27. $y = 2x + 1$
29. a. yes
    b. 75°, 75°, 105°, 105°
31. Given kite $EFGH$ with $\overline{EF} \cong \overline{FG}$ and $\overline{EH} \cong \overline{GH}$, construct diagonal $\overline{FH}$, which is congruent to itself by the Reflexive Property of Segment Congruence. So, $\triangle FGH \cong \triangle FEH$ by the SSS Congruence Theorem, and $\angle E \cong \angle G$ because corresponding parts of congruent triangles are congruent. Next, assume temporarily that $\angle F \cong \angle H$. Then $EFGH$ is a parallelogram by the Parallelogram Opposite Angles Converse, and opposite sides are congruent. However, this contradicts the definition of a kite, which says that opposite sides cannot be congruent. So, the assumption cannot be true and $\angle F$ is not congruent to $\angle H$.
33. By the Triangle Midsegment Theorem, $\overline{BG} \parallel \overline{CD}$, $BG = \frac{1}{2}CD$, $\overline{GE} \parallel \overline{AF}$, and $GE = \frac{1}{2}AF$. By the Transitive Property of Parallel Lines, $\overline{CD} \parallel \overline{BE} \parallel \overline{AF}$. Also, by the Segment Addition Postulate, $BE = BG + GE$. So, by the Substitution Property of Equality, $BE = \frac{1}{2}CD + \frac{1}{2}AF = \frac{1}{2}(CD + AF)$.
35. Sample answer: about 10,000 mi²
37. Sample answer: about 40,000 mi²

7.5 Review & Refresh
38. $3\sqrt{5}$, or about 6.7 units
39. parallelogram
40. 9
41.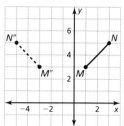
42.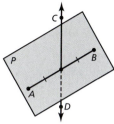
43. Parallelogram Opposite Sides Converse
44. no

Chapter 7 Review
1. 5,040°; 168°; 12°
2. $x = 133$
3. $x = 82$
4. $x = 15$
5. $a = 28$, $b = 87$
6. $c = 6$, $d = 10$
7. $(-2, -1)$
8. $M(2, -2)$
9. Sample answer: $(-6, 9), (-2, -3)$
10. $x = 109$
11. Parallelogram Opposite Sides Converse
12. Parallelogram Diagonals Converse
13. Parallelogram Opposite Angles Converse
14. $x = 1$, $y = 6$
15. $x = 4$
16. a. Opposite Sides Parallel and Congruent Theorem
    b. 3 ft, 123°, 57°, 57°
17. Because $WX = YZ = \sqrt{13}$, $\overline{WX} \cong \overline{YZ}$. Because the slopes of $\overline{WX}$ and $\overline{YZ}$ are both $\frac{2}{3}$, they are parallel. $\overline{WX}$ and $\overline{YZ}$ are opposite sides that are both congruent and parallel. So, $WXYZ$ is a parallelogram by the Opposite Sides Parallel and Congruent Theorem.
18. rhombus
19. parallelogram
20. square
21. 10
22. It is a rectangle, a rhombus, and a square because the diagonals are congruent and perpendicular.
23. $m\angle Z = m\angle Y = 58°$, $m\angle W = m\angle X = 122°$
24. 26
25. $3\sqrt{5}$
26. $x = 15$; the two 105° angles, the 65° angle and the 85° angle
27. By the Consecutive Interior Angles Theorem, the two adjacent angles of a trapezoid with a leg in common are supplementary. By the Congruent Supplements Theorem, two base angles of the trapezoid are congruent. So, the trapezoid is isosceles by the Isosceles Trapezoid Base Angles Converse.
28. trapezoid
29. rhombus
30. rectangle
31. kite
32. 10.5 in.

Chapter 8
Getting Ready for Chapter 8
1. yes
2. yes
3. no
4. no
5. yes
6. yes
7. $k = \frac{3}{7}$
8. $k = \frac{8}{3}$

8.1 Practice
1. $\frac{4}{3}$; $\angle A \cong \angle L$, $\angle B \cong \angle M$, $\angle C \cong \angle N$; $\frac{LM}{AB} = \frac{MN}{BC} = \frac{NL}{CA}$
3. $x = 30$
5. $x = 24$
7. $\frac{2}{3}$
9. 72 cm
11. 350 m
13. 108 ft²

15. The first ratio shows a side length of B divided by a side length of A, but the second ratio shows the perimeter of A divided by the perimeter of B. The second ratio should show the perimeter of B divided by the perimeter of A;
$\frac{5}{10} = \frac{x}{28}$
$x = 14$

17. no
19. no; Corresponding side lengths are not proportional.
21. 8 in.
23.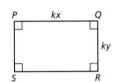

Let KLMN and PQRS be similar rectangles as shown. The ratio of corresponding side lengths is $\frac{KL}{PQ} = \frac{x}{kx} = \frac{1}{k}$. The perimeter of KLMN is $2x + 2y$ and the perimeter of PQRS is $2kx + 2ky$. So, the ratio of the perimeters is
$\frac{2x + 2y}{2kx + 2ky} = \frac{2x + 2y}{k(2x + 2y)} = \frac{1}{k}$. Because both ratios equal $\frac{1}{k}$, the ratios are equal. So,
$\frac{KL + LM + MN + NK}{PQ + QR + RS + SP} = \frac{KL}{PQ} = \frac{LM}{QR} = \frac{MN}{RS} = \frac{NK}{SP}$.

25. sometimes   27. always   29. never

31. The coordinates of the points are $A(-3, 0)$, $B(0, 4)$, $C(6, 0)$, $D(0, -8)$, and $O(0, 0)$. The side lengths are $OA = 3$, $OB = 4$, $AB = 5$, $OC = 6$, $OD = 8$, and $CD = 10$. Corresponding side lengths are proportional with a scale factor of 2. A dilation of △AOB by a scale factor of 2, and a rotation of 180° about the origin maps △AOB onto △COD. Because a similarity transformation maps △AOB onto △COD, △AOB ~ △COD.

33. $x = \frac{1 + \sqrt{5}}{2}$; The ratio of length to the width for PLMS is
$\frac{MS}{SP} = \frac{x}{1} = \frac{\left(\frac{1 + \sqrt{5}}{2}\right)}{1} = \frac{1 + \sqrt{5}}{2} = x$. The ratio of the length to the width for LMRQ is
$\frac{RQ}{QL} = \frac{1}{x - 1} = \frac{1}{\frac{1 + \sqrt{5}}{2} - 1} = \frac{1 + \sqrt{5}}{2} = x$.

35. 4 units, $\frac{16}{3}$ units, $\frac{64}{9}$ units, $\frac{256}{27}$ units

8.1 Review & Refresh
37. $x = 63$ 38. $x = 16$ 39. $x = 97$
40. 9 units   41. $x = \frac{3}{2}$
42. $x = \pm\sqrt{6}$ 43. $k = \frac{1}{16}$
44. $f^{-1}(x) = \sqrt[3]{\frac{x + 4}{2}}$ 45. $f^{-1}(x) = \sqrt{5x}$

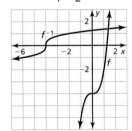 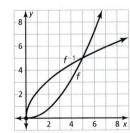

46. exponential   47. 26

8.2 Practice
1. no; $m\angle R \neq m\angle U$
3. $\angle Q \cong \angle MPN$ and $\angle N \cong \angle N$, so △LNQ ~ △MNP by the AA Similarity Theorem.
5. 3 ft 6 in.
7. All the angle measures are 60°. By the Angle-Angle Similarity Theorem, the triangles are similar.
9. a. no; Not all rectangles are similar.
   b. no; Not all rectangles are similar.
11. about 17.1 ft; △AED ~ △CEB, so $\frac{DE}{BE} = \frac{4}{3}$. △DEF ~ △DBC, so $\frac{EF}{30} = \frac{DE}{DB} = \frac{4}{7}$ and $EF = \frac{120}{7}$.
13. Sample answer: △ABC, △DEF, △FGD

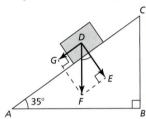

15. Sample answer: no; All three triangles are similar by the AA Similarity Theorem.

8.2 Review & Refresh
16. no
17. a. 135°
    b. 45°
18. 127°   19. 18 m²   20. rectangle

8.3 Practice
1. △RST   3. $x = 4$
5. similar; △DEF ~ △WXY; $\frac{4}{3}$
7. $\frac{12}{18} = \frac{10}{15} = \frac{8}{12} = \frac{2}{3}$
9. $\frac{HG}{HF} = \frac{HJ}{HK} = \frac{GJ}{FK} = \frac{3}{4}$, so △GHJ ~ △FHK by the SSS Similarity Theorem.
11. The similarity statement does not correctly relate the corresponding sides and angles in the triangles. Because $\overline{AB}$ corresponds to $\overline{RQ}$ and $\overline{BC}$ corresponds to $\overline{QP}$, the similarity statement should be △ABC ~ △RQP.
13. yes; $\frac{24}{15} = \frac{8x}{25} = \frac{48}{6x}$ when $x = 5$.
15. a. $\frac{CD}{CE} = \frac{BC}{AC}$
    b. $\angle CBD \cong \angle CAE$
17.

B
D   E
A   F   C

$EF = \frac{1}{2}BA$, $DE = \frac{1}{2}AC$, and $DF = \frac{1}{2}BC$ by the Triangle Midsegment Theorem. So, $\frac{EF}{BA} = \frac{DE}{AC} = \frac{DF}{BC} = \frac{1}{2}$, and △DEF ~ △CAB by the SSS Similarity Theorem. Because corresponding angles of similar figures are congruent, $m\angle CAB = m\angle DEF = 90°$.

A36   Selected Answers

19. *Sample answer:* All similarity transformations preserve angle measure, so the corresponding angles of two similar figures must be congruent.

21.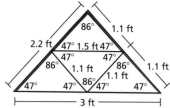

The ratio of the sides of the smaller triangles to the large triangle is $\frac{1.1}{2.2} = \frac{1.5}{3} = \frac{1}{2}$, so the triangles are similar.

23. You are given that $m_\ell = m_n$. By the definition of slope, $m_\ell = \frac{BC}{AC}$ and $m_n = \frac{EF}{DF}$. By the Substitution Property of Equality, $\frac{BC}{AC} = \frac{EF}{DF}$. By the Multiplication Property of Equality, $\frac{BC}{EF} = \frac{AC}{DF}$. By the Right Angles Congruence Theorem, $\angle ACB \cong \angle DFE$. So, $\triangle ABC \sim \triangle DEF$ by the SAS Similarity Theorem. Because corresponding angles of similar triangles are congruent, $\angle BAC \cong \angle EDF$. By the Corresponding Angles Converse, $\ell \parallel n$.

25.

STATEMENTS	REASONS
1. $\ell \perp n$	1. Given
2. $m\angle CAE = 90°$	2. $\ell \perp n$
3. $m\angle CAE = m\angle DAE + m\angle CAD$	3. Angle Addition Postulate
4. $m\angle DAE + m\angle CAD = 90°$	4. Transitive Property of Equality
5. $\angle BCA \cong \angle CAD$	5. Alternate Interior Angles Theorem
6. $m\angle BCA = m\angle CAD$	6. Definition of congruent angles
7. $m\angle DAE + m\angle BCA = 90°$	7. Substitution Property of Equality
8. $m\angle DAE = 90° - m\angle BCA$	8. Solve statement 7 for $m\angle DAE$.
9. $m\angle BCA + m\angle BAC + 90° = 180°$	9. Triangle Sum Theorem
10. $m\angle BAC = 90° - m\angle BCA$	10. Solve statement 9 for $m\angle BAC$.
11. $m\angle DAE = m\angle BAC$	11. Transitive Property of Equality
12. $\angle DAE \cong \angle BAC$	12. Definition of congruent angles
13. $\angle ABC \cong \angle ADE$	13. Right Angles Congruence Theorem
14. $\triangle ABC \sim \triangle ADE$	14. AA Similarity Theorem
15. $\frac{AD}{AB} = \frac{DE}{BC}$	15. Corresponding sides of similar figures are proportional.
16. $\frac{AD}{DE} = \frac{AB}{BC}$	16. Rewrite proportion.
17. $m_\ell = \frac{DE}{AD}, m_n = -\frac{AB}{BC}$	17. Definition of slope.
18. $m_\ell m_n = \frac{DE}{AD} \cdot \left(-\frac{AB}{BC}\right)$	18. Multiplication Property of Equality
19. $m_\ell m_n = \frac{DE}{AD} \cdot \left(-\frac{AD}{DE}\right)$	19. Substitution Property of Equality
20. $m_\ell m_n = -1$	20. Simplify.

27. a. no; Two right trapezoids can have proportional heights and lengths of one base and not be similar.
  b. yes; The fourth pair of sides must be proportional, and the angles must be congruent.
  c. no; The angles might not be congruent.
  d. no; Two kites can have proportional sides and one pair of congruent angles but not be similar.

29. SSS, AA, SAS

31. *Sample answer:* The designer may have used equilateral triangles in order to create a symmetric design. I would have used isosceles triangles.

8.3 Review & Refresh

32. $x = 18$

33. $\angle GEF \cong \angle HDF$ and $\angle F \cong \angle F$, so $\triangle DHF \sim \triangle EGF$.

34. $P(0, -4)$ **35.** $y = -\frac{3}{2}x + 3$

36.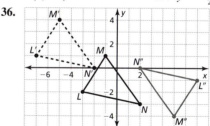

37.

38. yes; SAS Congruence Theorem
39. yes; AAS Congruence Theorem

8.4 Practice

1. 9   **3.** yes   **5.** 6
7. $y = 12$ **9.** $p = 27$ **11.** $x = 5$

13.
STATEMENTS	REASONS
1. $\dfrac{ZY}{YW} = \dfrac{ZX}{XV}$	1. Given
2. $\dfrac{YW}{ZY} = \dfrac{XV}{ZX}$	2. Rewrite the proportion.
3. $\dfrac{YW}{ZY} + 1 = \dfrac{XV}{ZX} + 1$	3. Addition Property of Equality
4. $\dfrac{YW}{ZY} + \dfrac{ZY}{ZY} = \dfrac{XV}{ZX} + \dfrac{ZX}{ZX}$	4. Substitution Property of Equality
5. $\dfrac{YW + ZY}{ZY} = \dfrac{XV + ZX}{ZX}$	5. Add fractions.
6. $ZW = YW + ZY$, $ZV = XV + ZX$	6. Segment Addition Postulate
7. $\dfrac{ZW}{ZY} = \dfrac{ZV}{ZX}$	7. Substitution Property of Equality
8. $\angle Z \cong \angle Z$	8. Reflexive Property of Congruence
9. $\triangle ZWV \sim \triangle ZYX$	9. SAS Similarity Theorem
10. $\angle ZYX \cong \angle ZWV$	10. Corresponding angles of similar triangles are congruent.
11. $\overline{YX} \parallel \overline{WV}$	11. Corresponding Angles Converse

15. $x = 5.25$, $y = 7.5$
17. Because $\overline{WX} \parallel \overline{ZA}$, $\angle XAZ \cong \angle YXW$ by the Corresponding Angles Theorem and $\angle WXZ \cong \angle XZA$ by the Alternate Interior Angles Theorem. So, by the Transitive Property of Congruence, $\angle XAZ \cong \angle XZA$. Then $\overline{XA} \cong \overline{XZ}$ by the Converse of the Base Angles Theorem, and by the Triangle Proportionality Theorem, $\dfrac{YW}{WZ} = \dfrac{XY}{XA}$. Because $XA = XZ$, $\dfrac{YW}{WZ} = \dfrac{XY}{XZ}$.
19. Check students' work.
21. *Sample answer:* The small triangles are all congruent, and are similar to the large triangle.

8.4 Review & Refresh

23.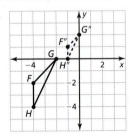

24. The public mailbox is located at point C, which is the circumcenter of the triangle formed by the apartment buildings.

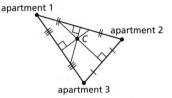

25. $x = 16$ 26. $p = \dfrac{2A}{q}$
27. $\angle A \cong \angle E$ and $\angle B \cong \angle F$, so $\triangle ABC \sim \triangle EFD$.
28. $x = 2$

Chapter 8 Review

1. $\dfrac{2}{3}$; $\angle A \cong \angle E$, $\angle B \cong \angle F$, $\angle C \cong \angle G$, $\angle D \cong \angle H$; $\dfrac{AB}{EF} = \dfrac{BC}{FG} = \dfrac{CD}{GH} = \dfrac{DA}{HE}$
2. $\dfrac{2}{5}$; $\angle X \cong \angle R$, $\angle Y \cong \angle P$, $\angle Z \cong \angle Q$; $\dfrac{RP}{XY} = \dfrac{PQ}{YZ} = \dfrac{RQ}{XZ}$
3. $x = 5$ 4. no   5. yes   6. 81 in.^{2}
7. no; $m\angle H \ne m\angle L$ and $m\angle K \ne m\angle N$
8. yes; $\angle C \cong \angle F$ and $\angle B \cong \angle E$; $\triangle ABC \sim \triangle DEF$
9. $\angle Q \cong \angle T$ and $\angle RSQ \cong \angle UST$, so $\triangle RSQ \sim \triangle UST$.
10. $\angle C \cong \angle F$ and $\angle B \cong \angle E$, so $\triangle ABC \sim \triangle DEF$.
11. 324 ft
12. $\angle C \cong \angle C$ and $\dfrac{CD}{CE} = \dfrac{CB}{CA}$, so $\triangle CBD \sim \triangle CAE$
13. $\dfrac{QU}{QT} = \dfrac{QR}{QS} = \dfrac{UR}{TS}$, so $\triangle QUR \sim \triangle QTS$
14. $x = 4$
15. yes; $\dfrac{20}{25} = \dfrac{8x}{50} = \dfrac{60}{15x}$ when $x = 5$.
16. no; $\triangle ABC$ either has angle measures 50°, 50°, 80°, or angle measures of 65°, 65°, 50°.
17. no   18. yes   19. 11.2
20. *Sample answer:* $VX = 5$, $XZ = 7.5$; $VX = 6$, $XZ = 9$
21. 10.5   22. 7.2
23. 153 m   24. Check students' work.

Chapter 9

Getting Ready for Chapter 9

1. $x = 9$ 2. $x = 7.5$ 3. $x = 32$
4. $x = 9.2$ 5. $x = 2$ 6. $x = 17$
7. $5\sqrt{3}$ 8. $3\sqrt{30}$ 9. $3\sqrt{15}$
10. $\dfrac{2\sqrt{7}}{7}$ 11. $\dfrac{5\sqrt{2}}{2}$ 12. $2\sqrt{6}$

9.1 Practice

1. $x = \sqrt{170} \approx 13.0$; no   3. $x = 15$; yes
5. $\sqrt{199.68}$, or about 14.1 ft
7. yes   9. no   11. yes; acute
13. yes; right   15. yes; acute
17. Each diagonal should form a right triangle with $c^2 = 24^2 + 18^2$, so you can use a yard stick to make each diagonal 30 inches long.
19. 192 ft^2 21. 2 lengths

A38   Selected Answers

23. △CBD ~ △ABC by the AA Similarity Theorem because both triangles have a right angle, and both triangles include ∠B. △ACD ~ △ABC by the AA Similarity Theorem because both triangles have a right angle, and both triangles include ∠A. △ACD ~ △CBD by the AA Similarity Theorem because both triangles have a right angle, and both ∠B and ∠ACD are complementary to ∠BCD, so ∠B ≅ ∠ACD.

STATEMENTS	REASONS
1. △ABC ~ △ACD ~ △CBD	1. Given
2. $\frac{c}{b} = \frac{b}{c-d}, \frac{c}{a} = \frac{a}{d}$	2. Corresponding sides of similar figures are proportional.
3. $c(c - d) = b^2, cd = a^2$	3. Cross Products Property
4. $c^2 - cd = b^2$	4. Distributive Property
5. $c^2 - a^2 = b^2$	5. Substitution Property of Equality
6. $c^2 = a^2 + b^2$	6. Addition Property of Equality

25.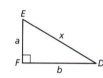

Let △ABC be any triangle so that the square of the length, c, of the longest side of the triangle is equal to the sum of the squares of the lengths, a and b, of the other two sides: $c^2 = a^2 + b^2$. Let △DEF be any right triangle with leg lengths of a and b. Let x represent the length of its hypotenuse. Because △DEF is a right triangle, by the Pythagorean Theorem, $a^2 + b^2 = x^2$. So, by the Transitive Property, $c^2 = x^2$. By taking the positive square root of each side, you get $c = x$. So, △ABC ≅ △DEF by the SSS Congruence Theorem.

27.

STATEMENTS	REASONS
1. In △ABC, $c^2 > a^2 + b^2$, where c is the length of the longest side. △PQR has side lengths a, b, and x, where x is the length of the hypotenuse and ∠R is a right angle.	1. Given
2. $a^2 + b^2 = x^2$	2. Pythagorean Theorem
3. $c^2 > x^2$	3. Substitution Property
4. $c > x$	4. Take the positive square root of each side.
5. $m∠R = 90°$	5. Definition of right angle
6. $m∠C > m∠R$	6. Converse of the Hinge Theorem
7. $m∠C > 90°$	7. Substitution Property
8. ∠C is an obtuse angle.	8. Definition of obtuse angle
9. △ABC is an obtuse triangle.	9. Definition of obtuse triangle

29. $21\sqrt{697}$, or about 554.4 m

9.1 Review & Refresh

31. $x = 10$
32.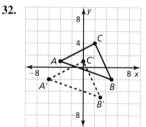
33.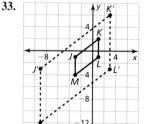
34. Subtract $m∠CBD$ from $m∠ABC$ to find $m∠ABD$.
35. (3, 2) 36. yes
37. $m∠1 = 72°, m∠2 = 108°, m∠3 = 108°$
38. $m∠X = m∠Y = 126°, m∠Z = 54°$

9.2 Practice

1. $x = 7\sqrt{2}$ 3. $x = 3$
5. $x = 12\sqrt{3}, y = 12$ 7. 32 ft²
9. 142 ft; $142\sqrt{2}$, or about 200.82 ft; $142\sqrt{3}$, or about 245.95 ft
11. Because △DEF is a 45°-45°-90° triangle, by the Converse of the Base Angles Theorem, $\overline{DF} \cong \overline{FE}$. So, let $x = DF = FE$. By the Pythagorean Theorem, $x^2 + x^2 = c^2$, where c is the length of the hypotenuse. So, $2x^2 = c^2$ by the Distributive Property. Take the positive square root of each side to get $x\sqrt{2} = c$. So, the hypotenuse is $\sqrt{2}$ times as long as each leg.
13. $2\sqrt{3}$ units

15. $\sqrt{2}, \sqrt{3}, \sqrt{4}, \sqrt{5}, \sqrt{6},\ldots$; The hypotenuse of the *n*th triangle is $\sqrt{n+1}$.

17. one

9.2 Review & Refresh
18. $x = 18$ **19.** yes; obtuse **20.** 15
21. $\left(\frac{1}{2}, 4\right)$ **22.** yes
23. the pieces with side lengths of 5.25 inches and 7 inches
24. $(7, 0)$

9.3 Practice
1. $\triangle HFE \sim \triangle GHE \sim \triangle GFH$
3. $x = 6.72$ **5.** about 11.2 ft   **7.** 16
9. $6\sqrt{30} \approx 32.9$ **11.** $x = 8$ **13.** $z = 45.5625$
15. about 14.9 ft   **17.** $b = 1.5$
19. $x = 16, y = 9, z = 12$

21.

STATEMENTS	REASONS
1. Draw $\triangle ABC$, $\angle BCA$ is a right angle.	1. Given
2. Draw a perpendicular segment (altitude) from C to $\overline{AB}$, and label the new point on $\overline{AB}$ as D.	2. Perpendicular Postulate
3. $\triangle ADC \sim \triangle CDB$	3. Right Triangle Similarity Theorem
4. $\frac{DB}{CB} = \frac{CB}{AB}, \frac{AD}{AC} = \frac{AC}{AB}$	4. Corresponding sides of similar figures are proportional.
5. $CB^2 = DB \cdot AB$, $AC^2 = AD \cdot AB$	5. Cross Products Property

23. $\frac{x+y}{2} \geq \sqrt{xy}$; They are only equal if $x = y$. Otherwise, the arithmetic mean is always greater than or equal to the geometric mean.

25. *Sample answer:* arithmetic mean; The arithmetic mean represents the middle of the areas. The geometric mean is less than most of the areas.

9.3 Review & Refresh
26. $x = 14$ **27.** 8   **28.** 5 ft
29. no   **30.** $y = 14$
31. yes; $\triangle FGH \sim \triangle JKL$

9.4 Practice
1. $\tan R = \frac{45}{28} \approx 1.6071, \tan S = \frac{28}{45} \approx 0.6222$
3. $\tan J = \frac{5}{3} \approx 1.6667, \tan K = \frac{3}{5} = 0.6$
5. $x \approx 13.8$ **7.** 1   **9.** about 555 ft
11. $\frac{5}{12} \approx 0.4167$
13. $\tan A = \frac{a}{b}; \tan B = \frac{b}{a}$; They are reciprocals of each other; complementary
15. Check students' work.   **17.** about 58.4 seconds

9.4 Review & Refresh
18. $x = 4\sqrt{3} \approx 6.9$; no   **19.** $6\sqrt{13} \approx 21.6$
20. 7.5 units^2

21.

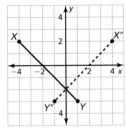

22. $(2, 0)$ **23.** $x = 2\sqrt{3} \approx 3.5$
24. $x = 64$ **25.** $m\angle 2 = 135°$

9.5 Practice
1. $\sin D = \frac{4}{5} = 0.8, \sin E = \frac{3}{5} = 0.6$,
$\cos D = \frac{3}{5} = 0.6, \cos E = \frac{4}{5} = 0.8$
3. $\sin D = \frac{8}{17} \approx 0.4706, \sin E = \frac{15}{17} \approx 0.8824$,
$\cos D = \frac{15}{17} \approx 0.8824, \cos E = \frac{8}{17} \approx 0.4706$
5. $\cos 53°$ **7.** $\sin 31°$ **9.** $\sin 17°$
11. $x \approx 9.5, y \approx 15.3$ **13.** $\cos X, \sin Z, \cos Z$
15. $\sin L, \cos J$ **17.** about 15 ft
19. a. about 23.4 ft
b. no; *Sample answer:* The height is about 24.5 feet when the angle of elevation is 77° and about 25.0 feet when the angle of elevation is 87°. So, as the angle of elevation increases by a constant amount, the height does not increase by a constant amount.
21. You are given the length of the opposite leg and its respective angle measure, so use a sine ratio.
23. a. more than 2,698 yd
b. more than 516.5 yd
25. *Sample answer:* They could use angles of ascent or descent to calculate time and distance to a location.
27. 300 m

9.5 Review & Refresh
28. $x = 8$; yes   **29.** $x = 6\sqrt{2} \approx 8.5$; no
30. $x \approx 6.9$ **31.** about 162.9°, about 17.1°
32. less than   **33.** $x = 10, y = 9$

9.6 Practice
1. about 48.6°   **3.** about 15.6°
5. $x \approx 8.5, m\angle X \approx 70.5°, m\angle Z \approx 19.5°$
7. $m \approx 5.1, k \approx 6.1, m\angle K = 50°$
9. $t \approx 9.7, s \approx 17.9, m\angle T = 33°$
11. no; The body of the dump truck has only been elevated to about 34.8°, which is less than the recommended minimum angle of 45°.

13. 4.76°, 96.4 in., 96.1 in., 8 in.

15. *Sample answer:* $\tan^{-1} 3$; about 71.6°
17. Check students' work.

9.6 Review & Refresh
19. $\sin Y = \frac{56}{65} \approx 0.8615, \cos Y = \frac{33}{65} \approx 0.5077$,
$\tan Y = \frac{56}{33} \approx 1.6970$
20. $\triangle EFG \sim \triangle FHG \sim \triangle EHF; y = 3\sqrt{15} \approx 11.6$
21. $x = 13, y = 9$

22. $m\angle 1 = 138°$; Alternate Exterior Angles Theorem
23. yes; Rotations of 120° and 240° about the center of the model maps the model onto itself.
24. $x = 26$ **25.** $x = 11.1125$ **26.** 138°

9.7 Practice

1. about 0.9903 **3.** about -0.2679
5. about 81.8 square units
7. $m\angle A = 48°, b \approx 25.5, c \approx 18.7$
9. $m\angle B = 66°, a \approx 14.3, b \approx 24.0$
11. $m\angle A \approx 80.9°, m\angle C \approx 43.1°, a \approx 20.2$
13. $a \approx 5.2, m\angle B \approx 50.9°, m\angle C \approx 94.1°$
15. $m\angle A \approx 81.1°, m\angle B \approx 65.3°, m\angle C \approx 33.6°$
17. $b \approx 35.8, m\angle A \approx 46.1°, m\angle C \approx 70.9°$
19. The denominator of the fraction should be $-2bc$, not $-2ab$; $m\angle A \approx 64.2°$
21. Law of Sines; $m\angle A = 45°, b \approx 25.2, c \approx 15.3$
23. Pythagorean Theorem and trigonometric ratios; $b \approx 16.2$, $m\angle A \approx 68.2°, m\angle C \approx 21.8°$
25. about 10.7 ft
27.

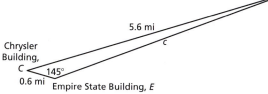

about 5.1 mi
29. a. $x \approx 163.4$ yd; The ball is about 163.4 yards from the hole.
  b. about 3.5°
31. $c^2 = a^2 + b^2$
33. $s = \dfrac{a+b+c}{2}$; area; Substituting $\dfrac{a+b+c}{2}$ for s and simplifying you get
$\sqrt{s(s-a)(s-b)(s-c)} = \dfrac{1}{4}\sqrt{4a^2b^2 - (a^2+b^2-c^2)^2}.$

From the Law of Cosines, $a^2 + b^2 - c^2 = 2ab \cos C$. So,
$\dfrac{1}{4}\sqrt{4a^2b^2 - (a^2+b^2-c^2)^2} = \dfrac{1}{4}\sqrt{4a^2b^2 - (2ab\cos C)^2}$
$= \dfrac{1}{4}\sqrt{4a^2b^2[1-(\cos C)^2]}$
$= \dfrac{1}{2}ab\sqrt{1-(\cos C)^2}$

From the definition of sine and cosine,
$1 - (\cos C)^2 = (\sin C)^2.$
So, $\dfrac{1}{2}ab\sqrt{1-(\cos C)^2} = \dfrac{1}{2}ab\sqrt{(\sin C)^2} = \dfrac{1}{2}ab\sin C$, which is the formula for the area of a triangle.

35. about 523.8 mi
37. One of these 4 options:
  (1) the height of the face
  (2) the length of one of the other sides and the included angle between that side and the base
  (3) the measure of the angle opposite the base and the measure of one of the other angles
  (4) the measure of the angle opposite the base and the length of one of the other sides

9.7 Review & Refresh

39. $x = 66$ **40.** $x \approx 26.7$

41. 7 in. $< x <$ 23 in. **42.** $x \approx 10.8, y \approx 10.4$
43. Parallelogram Diagonals Converse Theorem
44. $x = 8, y = 17$ **45.** (3, 4)
46. $c \approx 9.2, m\angle A \approx 40.6°, m\angle B \approx 49.4°$

Chapter 9 Review

1. $x = 2\sqrt{34} \approx 11.7$; no **2.** $x = 12$; yes
3. $x = 29$; yes **4.** $x = 2\sqrt{30} \approx 11.0$; no
5. yes **6.** no **7.** no **8.** yes
9. yes; acute **10.** yes; right **11.** yes; obtuse
12. yes; *Sample answer:* 24, 70, and 74; 36, 105, and 111
13. acute; Because one of the legs increased from 9 to 10, the sum of the squares of the legs will be greater than the square of the hypotenuse.
14. $x = 3\sqrt{2}, y = 3\sqrt{2}$ **15.** $x = 7$
16. $x = 16\sqrt{3}$ **17.** $x = 16, y = 16\sqrt{2}$
18. Area $= \dfrac{9}{2} + \dfrac{9\sqrt{3}}{2} \approx 12.3$ square units,
Perimeter $= 9 + 3\sqrt{3} + 3\sqrt{2} \approx 18.4$ units
19. $\triangle GFH \sim \triangle FEH \sim \triangle GEF; x = 13.5$
20. $\triangle KLM \sim \triangle JKM \sim \triangle JLK; x = 2\sqrt{6} \approx 4.9$
21. $\triangle QRS \sim \triangle PQS \sim \triangle PRQ; x = 3\sqrt{3} \approx 5.2$
22. $\triangle TUV \sim \triangle STV \sim \triangle SUT; x = 25$
23. 15 **24.** $24\sqrt{3} \approx 41.6$ **25.** 12.2 ft
26. $\tan J = \dfrac{11}{60} \approx 0.1833, \tan L = \dfrac{60}{11} \approx 5.4545$
27. $\tan N = \dfrac{12}{35} \approx 0.3429, \tan P = \dfrac{35}{12} \approx 2.9167$
28. $\tan A = \dfrac{7\sqrt{2}}{8} \approx 1.2374, \tan B = \dfrac{4\sqrt{2}}{7} \approx 0.8081$
29. $\tan M = \dfrac{3}{4} = 0.75, \tan N = \dfrac{4}{3} \approx 1.3333$
30. $x \approx 44.0$ **31.** $x \approx 12.8$
32. $x \approx 9.3$ **33.** $x \approx 30.0$
34. a. about 14.9 ft **b.** about 7.5 ft **c.** about 3.9 ft
35. about 7.9 ft **36.** $\dfrac{8}{15}$
37. The sides may not all have integer lengths. The triangle could be a 3-4-5 triangle (or a multiple), or it could multiply those lengths by a fraction or decimal that does not give all integer lengths.
38. $\sin X = \dfrac{3}{5} = 0.6, \sin Z = \dfrac{4}{5} = 0.8, \cos X = \dfrac{4}{5} = 0.8,$ $\cos Z = \dfrac{3}{5} = 0.6$
39. $\sin X = \dfrac{7\sqrt{149}}{149} \approx 0.5735, \sin Z = \dfrac{10\sqrt{149}}{149} \approx 0.8192,$
$\cos X = \dfrac{10\sqrt{149}}{149} \approx 0.8192, \cos Z = \dfrac{7\sqrt{149}}{149} \approx 0.5735$
40. $\sin X = \dfrac{55}{73} \approx 0.7534, \sin Z = \dfrac{48}{73} \approx 0.6575,$
$\cos X = \dfrac{48}{73} \approx 0.6575, \cos Z = \dfrac{55}{73} \approx 0.7534$
41. $\cos 18°$ **42.** $\sin 61°$
43. $s \approx 31.3, t \approx 13.3$ **44.** $r \approx 4.0, s \approx 2.9$
45. 98 ft **46.** $\angle C$ **47.** $\angle R$
48. $m\angle Q \approx 71.3°$ **49.** $m\angle Q \approx 65.5°$ **50.** $m\angle Q \approx 2.3°$
51. $m\angle A \approx 48.2°, m\angle B \approx 41.8°, a \approx 11.2$
52. $m\angle L = 53°, n \approx 4.5, m \approx 7.5$
53. $m\angle X \approx 46.1°, m\angle Z \approx 43.9°, z \approx 17.3$
54. about 87.1 ft **55.** about 0.6947
56. about -0.5592 **57.** about -0.4663
58. about 41.0 square units **59.** about 42.2 square units

60. $m\angle B \approx 24.3°, m\angle C \approx 43.7°, c \approx 6.7$
61. $m\angle C = 88°, a \approx 25.8, b \approx 49.5$
62. $m\angle A \approx 99.9°, m\angle B \approx 32.1°, a \approx 37.1$
63. $b \approx 5.4, m\angle A \approx 141.5°, m\angle C \approx 13.5°$
64. $m\angle A = 35°, a \approx 12.3, c \approx 14.6$
65. $m\angle A \approx 42.6°, m\angle B \approx 11.7°, m\angle C \approx 125.7°$
66. a.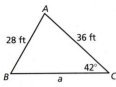
    b. $a \approx 41.0$ ft, $m\angle A \approx 78.6°, m\angle B \approx 59.4°$
    c. 13 gal

Chapter 10

Getting Ready for Chapter 10

1. $x = 1 \pm \sqrt{6}$
2. $r = -5 \pm 3\sqrt{2}$
3. $w = -1, w = 9$
4. $p = -5 \pm \sqrt{29}$
5. $k = 2 \pm \sqrt{11}$
6. $z = 1$
7. $x^2 + 11x + 28$
8. $a^2 - 4a - 5$
9. $3q^2 - 31q + 36$
10. $10v^2 - 33v - 7$
11. $4h^2 + 11h + 6$
12. $18b^2 - 54b + 40$

10.1 Practice

1. $\odot C$
3. $\overline{BH}, \overline{AD}$
5. 1 external
7. 0

9. It is not because $\triangle ABD$ is not a right triangle.
11. 10
13. 16
15. Check students' work.
17. $x = 5$
19. $x = \pm 3$
21. Sample answer: Every point on a circle is the same distance from the center, so the farthest two points can be from each other is opposite sides of the center.
23. about 17.78 in.
25. By the Tangent Line to Circle Theorem, $\overline{PR} \perp \overline{RS}$ and $\overline{PT} \perp \overline{TS}$. By the definition of perpendicular lines, $\angle PRS$ and $\angle PTS$ are right angles. $\overline{PS} \cong \overline{PS}$ by the Reflexive Property of Segment Congruence and $\overline{PR} \cong \overline{PT}$ because radii of a circle are congruent. So, $\triangle PTS \cong \triangle PRS$ by the HL Congruence Theorem. Corresponding parts of congruent triangles are congruent, so $\overline{SR} \cong \overline{ST}$.
27. $2\sqrt{2}$; Sample answer: Using the External Tangent Congruence Theorem, you can determine that $BD = BE = CE = CF = 4$. Using the Pythagorean Theorem, $AE = 8\sqrt{2}$. So, the area of $\triangle ABC$ is $32\sqrt{2}$. If r is the radius of P, then Area of $\triangle APB$ = Area of $\triangle APC = 6r$ and Area of $\triangle BPC = 4r$. Solving $16r = 32\sqrt{2}$ gives $r = 2\sqrt{2}$.
29. It will travel in a straight path rather than a circular path.

10.1 Review & Refresh

31. $m\angle Q = 31°, PR \approx 4.6, PQ \approx 7.7$
32. $m\angle A \approx 27.7°, m\angle B \approx 84.1°, m\angle C \approx 68.2°$
33. neither
34. parallel

35. $LP = 24, PQ = 12$
36. $76°, 104°$
37. about 19.6 ft
38. $MN = 20$

10.2 Practice

1. $\widehat{AB}, 135°; \widehat{ADB}, 225°$
3. $\widehat{JL}, 120°; \widehat{JKL}, 240°$
5. semicircle; 180°
7. minor arc; 131°
9. a. 132°
   b. 147°
   c. 200°
   d. 160°
11. yes; football: 72°, soccer: 108°, volleyball: 54°, cross-country: 72°, none: 54°
13. The red arcs are congruent because they are arcs of the same circle and they have congruent central angles.
15. $x = 70; 110°$
17. $340°; 160°$
19. a. Translate $\odot B$ so that point B maps to point A. The image of $\odot B$ is $\odot B'$ with center A. Because $\overline{AC} \cong \overline{BD}$, this translation maps $\odot B'$ to $\odot A$. A rigid motion maps $\odot B$ to $\odot A$, so $\odot A \cong \odot B$.
    b. Because $\odot A \cong \odot B$, the distance from the center of the circle to a point on the circle is the same for each circle. So, $\overline{AC} \cong \overline{BD}$.
21. yes
23. Sample answer: half of Earth's circumference, or about 12,450 miles

10.2 Review & Refresh

24. $x = -5, x = \frac{2}{3}$
25. $BC \approx 6.6, m\angle B \approx 54.9°, m\angle C \approx 88.1°$
26. $RS \approx 9.0, RT \approx 15.0, m\angle T = 37°$
27. 16
28. $\angle G \cong \angle K$ and $\angle FHG \cong \angle JHK$ because they are vertical angles. So, $\triangle FGH \sim \triangle JKH$ by the AA Similarity Theorem.
29. $x = 135$
30. $x = 8$
31.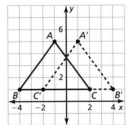
32.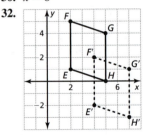

10.3 Practice

1. 75°
3. 170°
5. $x = 7$
7. Draw a segment between each pair of tables. Draw the perpendicular bisectors of the two segments. Place the patio heater where the perpendicular bisectors intersect.
9. It is a diameter because triangles ACB and ADB are congruent, so $\overline{BC} \cong \overline{BD}$. Because $BC = BD$, B lies on the perpendicular bisector of $\overline{CD}$ by the Converse of the Perpendicular Bisector Theorem. So, $\overline{AB}$ is a diameter by the Perpendicular Chord Bisector Converse.
11. 17
13. $\overline{CE}$ is the hypotenuse, not a leg, of $\triangle CGE$.
    $CE^2 = 5^2 + 12^2$
    $CE^2 = 169$
    $CE = 13$
    So, the radius is 13 inches.

15. It is given that $\overline{EG} \perp \overline{DF}$, so $\angle LCD$ and $\angle LCF$ are right angles by the definition of perpendicular lines. By the definition of a right triangle, $\triangle LCD$ and $\triangle LCF$ are right triangles. Because all radii of a circle are congruent, $\overline{LD} \cong \overline{LF}$. By the Reflexive Property of Segment Congruence, $\overline{LC} \cong \overline{LC}$. So, $\triangle LCD \cong \triangle LCF$ by the HL Congruence Theorem. Because corresponding parts of congruent triangles are congruent, $\overline{DC} \cong \overline{FC}$ and $\angle DLC \cong \angle FLC$. So, $\overline{DG} \cong \overline{FG}$ by the Congruent Central Angles Theorem.

17. $\overline{QS}$ is the perpendicular bisector of $\overline{RT}$. Let C be the center of the circle. Because $\overline{CT}$ and $\overline{CR}$ are radii of the same circle, $\overline{CT} \cong \overline{CR}$. By the Converse of the Perpendicular Bisector Theorem, C lies on $\overline{QS}$. So, $\overline{QS}$ is a diameter of the circle by definition.

19.

    Given: $\overline{AB} \cong \overline{CD}$
    Prove: $EF = EG$

    Because $\overline{EG}$ and $\overline{EF}$ are contained in diameters of $\odot E$, $\overline{CG} \cong \overline{DG}$ and $\overline{AF} \cong \overline{BF}$ by the Perpendicular Chord Bisector Theorem. It is also given that $\overline{AB} \cong \overline{CD}$. So, $CG = DG$, $AF = BF$, and $AB = CD$ by the definition of congruent segments. By the Segment Addition Postulate, $AB = AF + BF$ and $CD = CG + DG$. By the Substitution Property of Equality, $AB = AF + AF$ and $CD = CG + CG$. So, $AB = 2AF$ and $CD = 2CG$. Then $2AF = 2CG$ by the Transitive Property of Equality. So, $AF = CG$ by the Division Property of Equality. By the definition of congruent segments, $\overline{AF} \cong \overline{CG}$. Because all radii of a circle are congruent, $\overline{AE} \cong \overline{CE}$. So, $\triangle ECG \cong \triangle EAF$ by the HL Congruence Theorem. Because corresponding parts of congruent triangles are congruent, $\overline{EF} \cong \overline{EG}$. So, $EF = EG$ by the definition of congruent segments.

    Given: $EF = EG$
    Prove: $\overline{AB} \cong \overline{CD}$

    $\overline{EF} \cong \overline{EG}$ by the definition of congruent segments. Because all radii of a circle are congruent, $\overline{EC} \cong \overline{ED} \cong \overline{EA} \cong \overline{EB}$. So, $\triangle AEF \cong \triangle BEF \cong \triangle DEG \cong \triangle CEG$ by the HL Congruence Theorem. Because corresponding parts of congruent triangles are congruent, $\overline{AF} \cong \overline{BF} \cong \overline{DG} \cong \overline{CG}$. So, $AF = BF = DG = CG$ by the definition of congruent segments. By the Segment Addition Postulate, $AB = AF + BF$ and $CD = CG + DG$. By the Substitution Property of Equality, $AB = CG + DG$, and by the Transitive Property of Equality, $AB = CD$. So, $\overline{AB} \cong \overline{CD}$ by the definition of congrent segments.

21. Sample answer: Let $\overline{EM}$ represent a chord of Earth's orbit that passes through the Sun, where point E represents Earth's center. A solar conjunction of Earth and Mars occurs when a line that contains $\overline{EM}$ passes through Mars.

10.3 Review & Refresh
23. 8
24. about 172.1 m
25. 159°
26. 122°
27. similar; The arcs have the same measure but the circles are not congruent.

10.4 Practice
1. 42°
3. 120°
5. 51°
7. $x = 100, y = 85$
9. $a = 20, b = 22$
11. Place the right angle of the carpenter's square on the edge of the circle and connect the points where the sides intersect the edge of the circle.
13. $x = 30, y = 20$; 60°, 60°, 60°
15. Check students' work.
17. a. Because all radii of a circle are congruent, $\overline{QB} \cong \overline{QA}$. So, $\triangle ABQ$ is isosceles by definition. By the Base Angles Theorem, $\angle QBA \cong \angle QAB$, so $m\angle BAQ = x°$. By the Exterior Angles Theorem, $m\angle AQC = 2x°$. Then $m\widehat{AC} = 2x°$ by the definition of the measure of a minor arc. Because $m\angle ABC = x° = \frac{1}{2}(2x)°$, $m\angle ABC = \frac{1}{2}m\widehat{AC}$ by the Substitution Property of Equality.

    b. Case 2
    Given: $\angle ABC$ is inscribed in $\odot Q$. $\overline{DB}$ is a diameter;
    Prove: $m\angle ABC = \frac{1}{2}m\widehat{AC}$;
    By Case 1, proved in part (a), $m\angle ABD = \frac{1}{2}m\widehat{AD}$ and $m\angle CBD = \frac{1}{2}m\widehat{CD}$. By the Arc Addition Postulate, $m\widehat{AD} + m\widehat{CD} = m\widehat{AC}$. By the Angle Addition Postulate, $m\angle ABD + m\angle CBD = m\angle ABC$. Then $m\angle ABC = \frac{1}{2}m\widehat{AD} + \frac{1}{2}m\widehat{CD}$ by the Substitution Property of Equality. By the Distributive Property, $m\angle ABC = \frac{1}{2}(m\widehat{AD} + m\widehat{CD})$. By the Substitution Property of Equality, $m\angle ABC = \frac{1}{2}m\widehat{AC}$.

    Case 3
    Given: $\angle ABC$ is inscribed in $\odot Q$. $\overline{DB}$ is a diameter;
    Prove: $m\angle ABC = \frac{1}{2}m\widehat{AC}$;
    By Case 1, proved in part (a), $m\angle DBA = \frac{1}{2}m\widehat{AD}$ and $m\angle DBC = \frac{1}{2}m\widehat{CD}$. By the Arc Addition Postulate, $m\widehat{AC} + m\widehat{CD} = m\widehat{AD}$, so $m\widehat{AC} = m\widehat{AD} - m\widehat{CD}$ by the Subtraction Property of Equality. By the Angle Addition Postulate, $m\angle DBC + m\angle ABC = m\angle DBA$, so $m\angle ABC = m\angle DBA - m\angle DBC$ by the Subtraction Property of Equality. Then $m\angle ABC = \frac{1}{2}m\widehat{AD} - \frac{1}{2}m\widehat{CD}$ by the Substitution Property of Equality. By the Distributive Property, $m\angle ABC = \frac{1}{2}(m\widehat{AD} - m\widehat{CD})$. By the Substitution Property of Equality $m\angle ABC = \frac{1}{2}m\widehat{AC}$.

19. Conditional: Let right $\triangle ABC$ be inscribed in a circle and $\angle C$ be the right angle. By the Measure of an Inscribed Angle Theorem, $m\widehat{AB} = 2(90°) = 180°$. So, $\widehat{AB}$ is a semicircle, and $\overline{AB}$ is a diameter of the circle by the definition of a semicircle. Converse: Let side $\overline{AB}$ of an inscribed triangle $\triangle ABC$ be a diameter of the circle. Because A and B are endpoints of a diameter, $\widehat{AB}$ is a semicircle by definition. So, $m\widehat{AB} = 180°$. $\angle C$ is an inscribed angle with intercepted arc $\widehat{AB}$. By the Measure of an Inscribed Angle Theorem, $m\angle C = \frac{1}{2}(m\widehat{AB})$. By the Substitution Property of Equality, $m\angle C = \frac{1}{2}(180°) = 90°$. So, $\angle C$ is a right angle by definition and $\triangle ABC$ is a right triangle.

21. Draw the altitude from Point C to $\overline{AB}$. This is a diameter of the smallest circle that passes through C and is perpendicular to $\overline{AB}$. Draw the circle, then draw $\overline{JK}$. Because C is a right angle, $\triangle JKC$ is a right triangle inscribed in the circle, and $\overline{JK}$ is also a diameter of the circle. Then use the Right Triangle Similarity Theorem to find the length of the altitude, which is equal to JK; 2.4 units

23. *Sample answer:* By rolling over logs or using a track with small spherical rocks that allow the larger rock to roll along on top

10.4 Review & Refresh

25. *Sample answer:* Reflect $\triangle ABC$ in the y-axis, then translate 3 units up.

26. 10   **27.** minor arc; 120°   **28.** minor arc; 60°
29. semicircle; 180°   **30.** major arc; 300°   **31.** yes

10.5 Practice

1. 130°   **3.** $x = 115$ **5.** $x = 38$
7. $x = 34$ **9.** about 2.8°
11. yes; When the circumscribed angle is 90°, the central angle is 90°.
13. $0° < m\angle LPJ < 90°$

15.

STATEMENTS	REASONS
1. Chords $\overline{AC}$ and $\overline{BD}$ intersect.	1. Given
2. $m\angle ACB = \frac{1}{2}m\widehat{AB}$ and $m\angle DBC = \frac{1}{2}m\widehat{DC}$	2. Measure of an Inscribed Angle Theorem
3. $m\angle 1 = m\angle DBC + m\angle ACB$	3. Exterior Angle Theorem
4. $m\angle 1 = \frac{1}{2}m\widehat{DC} + \frac{1}{2}m\widehat{AB}$	4. Substitution Property of Equality
5. $m\angle 1 = \frac{1}{2}(m\widehat{DC} + m\widehat{AB})$	5. Distributive Property

17. By the Exterior Angle Theorem, $m\angle 2 = m\angle 1 + m\angle ABC$, so $m\angle 1 = m\angle 2 - m\angle ABC$ by the Subtraction Property of Equality. By the Tangent and Intersected Chord Theorem, $m\angle 2 = \frac{1}{2}m\widehat{BC}$ and by the Measure of an Inscribed Angle Theorem, $m\angle ABC = \frac{1}{2}m\widehat{AC}$. By the Substitution Property of Equality and the Distributive Property, $m\angle 1 = \frac{1}{2}m\widehat{BC} - \frac{1}{2}m\widehat{AC} = \frac{1}{2}(m\widehat{BC} - m\widehat{AC})$;

By the Exterior Angle Theorem, $m\angle 1 = m\angle 2 + m\angle 3$, so $m\angle 2 = m\angle 1 - m\angle 3$ by the Subtraction Property of Equality. By the Tangent and Intersected Chord Theorem, $m\angle 1 = \frac{1}{2}m\widehat{PQR}$ and $m\angle 3 = \frac{1}{2}m\widehat{PR}$. By the Substitution Property of Equality and the Distributive Property, $m\angle 2 = \frac{1}{2}m\widehat{PQR} - \frac{1}{2}m\widehat{PR} = \frac{1}{2}(m\widehat{PQR} - m\widehat{PR})$;

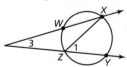

By the Exterior Angle Theorem, $m\angle 1 = m\angle 3 + m\angle WXZ$, so $m\angle 3 = m\angle 1 - m\angle WXZ$ by the Subtraction Property of Equality. By the Measure of an Inscribed Angle Theorem, $m\angle 1 = \frac{1}{2}m\widehat{XY}$ and $m\angle WXZ = \frac{1}{2}m\widehat{WZ}$. By the Substitution Property of Equality and the Distributive Property, $m\angle 3 = \frac{1}{2}m\widehat{XY} - \frac{1}{2}m\widehat{WZ} = \frac{1}{2}(m\widehat{XY} - m\widehat{WZ})$.

19. 20°; *Sample answer:* $m\widehat{WXY} = 160°$ and $m\widehat{WX} = m\widehat{ZY}$, so
$m\angle P = \frac{1}{2}(m\widehat{WZ} - m\widehat{XY})$
$= \frac{1}{2}[(200° - m\widehat{ZY}) - (160° - m\widehat{WX})]$
$= \frac{1}{2}(40°) = 20°$.

21. *Sample answer:* GPS coordinates represent locations on Earth. The 38° 53' 53" N coordinate represents a line of latitude in the Northern hemisphere, while the 77° 2' 12" W coordinate represents a line of longitude west of the Prime Meridian.

23. Check students' work.

10.5 Review & Refresh

24. 40 units; 60 square units   **25.** 67.5°
26. $7 < x < 29$ **27.** 101°   **28.** 130°
29. yes; By the Pythagorean Theorem, $VZ = 6$, so $\overline{WY}$ bisects $\overline{XZ}$. By the Perpendicular Chord Bisector Converse, $\overline{WY}$ is a diameter.

30.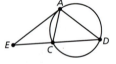

10.6 Practice

1. $x = 5$ **3.** $x = 4$
5. $x = 4$ **7.** $x = 12$
9. $x = 4$ **11.** about 496,494 km

13.

STATEMENTS	REASONS
1. $\overline{EA}$ is a tangent segment and $\overline{ED}$ is a secant segment.	1. Given
2. $\angle E \cong \angle E$	2. Reflexive Property of Angle Congruence
3. $m\angle EAC = \frac{1}{2}m\widehat{AC}$	3. Tangent and Intersected Chord Theorem
4. $m\angle ADC = \frac{1}{2}m\widehat{AC}$	4. Measure of an Inscribed Angle Theorem
5. $m\angle EAC = m\angle ADC$	5. Transitive Property of Equality
6. $\angle EAC \cong \angle ADC$	6. Definition of congruence
7. $\triangle EAC \sim \triangle EDA$	7. AA Similarity Theorem
8. $\dfrac{EA}{ED} = \dfrac{EC}{EA}$	8. Corresponding side lengths of similar triangles are proportional.
9. $EA^2 = EC \cdot ED$	9. Cross Products Property

A44   Selected Answers

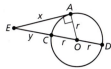

By the Tangent Line to Circle Theorem, $\overline{EA} \perp \overline{AO}$. So, $\angle EAO$ is a right angle by the definition of perpendicular lines, which makes $\triangle AEO$ a right triangle by definition. By the Pythagorean Theorem, $(r + y)^2 = r^2 + x^2$. So, $r^2 + 2yr + y^2 = r^2 + x^2$. By the Subtraction Property of Equality, $2yr + y^2 = x^2$. Then $y(2r + y) = x^2$ by the Distributive Property, so $EC \cdot ED = EA^2$.

15. *Sample answer:* Vehicles will generally be traveling at slower rates of speed in a roundabout.
17. left; The direction in which the third exit leads is left, relative to where you entered the roundabout.

10.6 Review & Refresh
18. 17
19. about 156.3 ft
20. 92°
21. $\angle CBD \cong \angle A$ and $\angle C \cong \angle C$, so $\triangle ACE \sim \triangle BCD$ by the AA Similarity Theorem.
22. $x = 40$
23. 202°

10.7 Practice
1. $x^2 + y^2 = 4$
3. $x^2 + y^2 = 49$
5. $x^2 + y^2 = 36$
7. $(x - 1)^2 + (y - 2)^2 = 9$
9. center: $(0, 0)$, radius: 7
11. center: $(3, 0)$, radius: 4

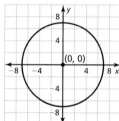
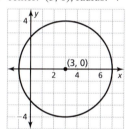

13. The radius of the circle is 8. The distance between $(0, 0)$ and $(2, 3)$ is $\sqrt{(2-0)^2 + (3-0)^2} = \sqrt{13} \neq 8$, so $(2, 3)$ does not lie on the circle.

15. a.

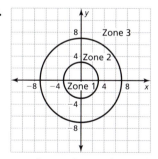

b. zone 2, zone 3, zone 1, zone 1, zone 2

17. *Sample answer:* along the western coast of North and South America, along the eastern coast of Asia, north of Australia
19. Given seismograph data from three different locations, they can graph circles representing the distance between each location and the epicenter. The epicenter will be at the intersection point of the three circles.

10.7 Review & Refresh
20. $x = 120$
21. $x = 5$
22. minor arc; 53°
23. minor arc; 90°
24. minor arc; 127°
25. major arc; 270°
26. semicircle; 180°
27. 26°
28. 51°

10.8 Practice
1. $y = \frac{1}{4}x^2$
3. $x = -\frac{1}{28}y^2$
5. $y = -\frac{3}{32}x^2$

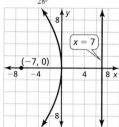
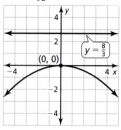

7. $y = -\frac{1}{36}(x - 2)^2 + 3$
9. $x = (y + 1)^2 + 1$

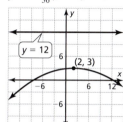
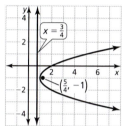

11. The vertex is $(3, 2)$. The focus is $(3, 4)$. The directrix is $y = 0$. The axis of symmetry is $x = 3$. The graph is a vertical shrink by a factor of $\frac{1}{2}$, followed by a translation 3 units right and 2 units up.
13. $y = \frac{1}{32}x^2$
15. $y = \frac{1}{6.8}x^2$; The domain is $-2.9 \leq x \leq 2.9$, and the range is $0 \leq y \leq \frac{841}{680}$; The domain represents the width of the trough, and the range represents the depth of the trough.
17. a. B is the vertex, C is the focus, and A is a point on the directrix.
    b. The focus and directrix will both be shifted down 3 units.
19. Check students' work.
21. It is 2,205 feet above the vertex.

10.8 Review & Refresh
23. $x = 9$
24. $x = -8 + 8\sqrt{2} \approx 3.3$
25. $x = 10$
26. $x = 149$
27. center: $(5, -1)$, radius: 7

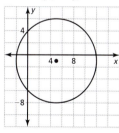

28. $m\angle ORT = 142°$, $m\angle SRT = 38°$
29. $(7, 5)$
30. $x = 12, y = 6\sqrt{3}$
31. 18

32.
33.

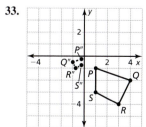

Chapter 10 Review
1. radius
2. chord
3. tangent
4. diameter
5. secant
6. radius
7. 1 internal, 2 external
8. 2 external

9. $a = 2$
10. $r = 12$
11. It is a tangent because the triangle is a right triangle.
12. 100°
13. 60°
14. 160°
15. 80°
16. They are not congruent because the circles are not congruent.
17. They are congruent because the circles are congruent and $m\widehat{AB} = m\widehat{EF}$.
18. a. 64.8° b. 97.2°
    c. 79.2° d. 270°
19. 61°
20. 65°
21. 91°
22. 26
23. $x = 80$
24. $q = 100, r = 20$
25. $d = 5$
26. $m = 44, n = 39$
27.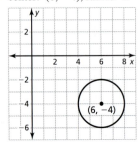

Sample answer: Draw a diameter. By the Inscribed Right Triangle Theorem, the diameter is the hypotenuse of the right triangle. By the 30°-60°-90° Triangle Theorem, the hypotenuse is twice the length of the shorter leg. So, draw a line segment, the length of the radius, from one endpoint of the diameter to a point on the circle. Then connect this point to the other endpoint of the diameter.

28. $x = 120$
29. $x = 25$
30. $x = 106$
31. $x = 16$
32. 120°
33. $x = 9$
34. $x = 3$
35. $x = 5$
36. $x = 10$
37. about 108 ft
38. $x^2 + y^2 = 16$
39. $(x - 4)^2 + (y + 1)^2 = 9$
40. $x^2 + y^2 = 81$
41. $(x - 6)^2 + (y - 21)^2 = 16$
42. $(x + 7)^2 + (y - 6)^2 = 25$
43. center: $(6, -4)$, radius: 2

44. $x = -\frac{1}{8}y^2$
45. $y = -\frac{1}{16}(x - 2)^2 + 6$

46. The focus is (0, 9), the directrix is $y = -9$, and the axis of symmetry is $x = 0$.

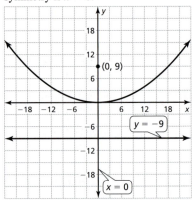

47. The focus is $(-2, 0)$, the directrix is $x = 2$, and the axis of symmetry is $y = 0$.

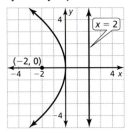

48. $y = \frac{1}{12}x^2$
49. $y = -\frac{1}{4}x^2$
50. $y = \frac{1}{4}(x - 2)^2 - 4$
51. $x = \frac{1}{8}(y - 1)^2 + 3$
52. Sample answer: The microphone is $1\frac{5}{6}$ inches below the opening of the parabolic dish.

Chapter 11
Chapter 11 Getting Ready
1. 27 cm²
2. 19.5 ft²
3. 9 in.
4. 2 cm
5. 12 ft

11.1 Practice
1. $12\pi \approx 37.70$ in.
3. $\frac{63}{\pi} \approx 20.05$ ft
5. about 3.14 ft
7. about 8.58 cm
9. about 182.2 ft
11. about 44.85 units
13. $\frac{7\pi}{18}$ radians
15. 22.5°
17. 8π units
19. $2\frac{1}{3}$
21. Sample answer: Angles 1 and 2 are alternate interior angles, so the arc measure is 7.2°; 28,750 mi

A46 Selected Answers

23. Sample answer:

STATEMENTS	REASONS
1. $\overline{FG} \cong \overline{GH}$, $\angle JFK \cong \angle KFL$	1. Given
2. $FG = GH$	2. Definition of congruent segments
3. $FH = FG + GH$	3. Segment Addition Postulate
4. $FH = 2FG$	4. Substitution Property of Equality
5. $m\angle JFK = m\angle KFL$	5. Definition of congruent angles
6. $m\angle JFL = m\angle JFK + m\angle KFL$	6. Angle Addition Postulate
7. $m\angle JFL = 2m\angle JFK$	7. Substitution Property of Equality
8. $\angle NFG \cong \angle JFL$	8. Vertical Angles Congruence Theorem
9. $m\angle NFG = m\angle JFL$	9. Definition of congruent angles
10. $m\angle NFG = 2m\angle JFK$	10. Substitution Property of Equality
11. arc length of $\widehat{JK}$ $= \dfrac{m\angle JFK}{360°} \cdot 2\pi FH$, arc length of $\widehat{NG}$ $= \dfrac{m\angle NFG}{360°} \cdot 2\pi FG$	11. Formula for arc length
12. arc length of $\widehat{JK}$ $= \dfrac{m\angle JFK}{360°} \cdot 2\pi(2FG)$, arc length of $\widehat{NG}$ $= \dfrac{2m\angle JFK}{360°} \cdot 2\pi FG$	12. Substitution Property of Equality
13. arc length of $\widehat{NG}$ $=$ arc length of $\widehat{JK}$	13. Transitive Property of Equality

25. about 78.5%
27. The same amount of the field is covered.

11.1 Review & Refresh
28. $x = 2$
29. 42 square units
30. $x = \dfrac{-9 + 3\sqrt{21}}{2} \approx 2.4$
31. $y = -\dfrac{1}{50}x^2 + 18$
32. 9 units
33. center: (0, 0), radius: 4

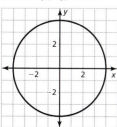

11.2 Practice
1. $25\pi \approx 78.54$ in.²
3. 52 cm
5. about 52.36 in.²; about 261.80 in.²
7. about 66.04 cm²
9. about 19.99 in.
11. about 85.84 in.²
13. about 192.48 ft²
15. about 26,709 km²
17. Sample answer: green: light rain, yellow: moderate rain, red: heavy rain, pink: extreme rain

11.2 Review & Refresh
18. 19.68 ft
19. $CD = 14$, $CE = 21$
20. $\sqrt{52.9}$, or about 7.3 units
21. By the SAS Congruence Theorem, the right triangles that represent each half of the ramp when looking at it from the sides are congruent. Because corresponding parts of congruent triangles are congruent, the lengths of the ramp are the same.
22. 42 units

11.3 Practice
1. 361 square units
3. 70 square units
5. 20°
7. 45°
9. 67.5°
11. about 62.35 square units
13. about 20.87 square units
15. about 342.24 square units
17. about 223.75 square units
19. about 166.28 in.²
21. The area of a kite is equal to half the product of its diagonals, so doubling the length of one diagonal doubles the area of the kite; Doubling the length of both diagonals doubles the area twice, so the area is 4 times greater.
23. yes; about 24.73 in.²; Sample answer: Each side length is 2 inches, and the central angle is 40°.
25. Sample answer: (3, 0); $(2\sqrt{5} + 2\sqrt{13})$ units, 8 square units
27. about 6.60 in.
29. about 64.95 square units; Sample answer: $A = \tfrac{1}{2}aP$; There are fewer calculations.
31. 348°; On a flat surface, the sum of the non-overlapping angles that meet at a vertex have a total measure of 360°, but because the ball is curved, the sum is slightly less.
33. about 290.8 in.²

11.3 Review & Refresh
34. about 43.71 square units
35. about 20.28 in.
36. $y = \tfrac{1}{8}x^2 - 1$
37. yes
38. $x \approx 18.5$
39. $x = 14$
40. $b \approx 3.9$, $m\angle B \approx 29.0°$, $m\angle C \approx 61.0°$
41. $x = 28$
42. 146°

11.4 Practice
1. about 35 people per mi²
3. about 7 mi
5. 50 feet by 50 feet
7. a. 400 knots/in.²
  b. rug in part (a); This rug has a knot density of 350 knots/in.², which is less than 400 knots/in.²
9. Check students' work.
11. about 0.02 employees per square foot

11.4 Review & Refresh
13. about 112.14°
14. about 125.66 yd²; about 326.73 yd²
15. about 181 square units
16. 288 ft, 259.2 ft

17. $a \approx 8.7, b \approx 16.5$ **18.** $2{,}700°$
19. 10

Chapter 11 Review

1. $\dfrac{94.24}{\pi} \approx 30.00$ ft   **2.** about 56.57 cm
3. about 26.09 in.   **4.** about 74.48°
5. $24 + 6\pi \approx 42.8$ units   **6.** $20\pi \approx 62.83$ units
7. $\dfrac{\pi}{12}$ radian   **8.** 108°
9. 2,613.81 in.   **10.** about 169.65 in.^{2}
11. about 17.72 in.^{2} **12.** about 16 in.
13. 130 square units   **14.** 96 square units
15. about 167.11 square units   **16.** about 37.30 square units
17. about 32.73°   **18.** about 173.8 ft^2
19. hexagon   **20.** about 9,903 people per mi^2
21. about 5,747 people per mi^2
22. about 2.5 km   **23.** about 12,000 people
24. 288 ft^2 **25.** about 448,347 seeds

Chapter 12

Getting Ready for Chapter 12

1. 158 ft^2 **2.** 144 m^2 **3.** 5 m^2 **4.** 12 mm^2

12.1 Practice

1. yes; pentagonal pyramid   **3.** yes; trapezoidal prism
5.
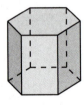

7. pentagonal pyramid   **9.** triangular prism
11. circle
13. The rectangular sides are not the bases. The two triangular faces are bases; The polyhedron has two parallel, identical triangular bases. So, the solid is a triangular prism.
15.   **17.**
rectangle   trapezoid
19. Sample answer:

; yes; The cross section can also be a pentagon with different dimensions or a rectangle.

21. a. 36.5 in.; 59.5 in.^{2}
b. $49\pi \approx 153.94$ in.^{2}; increases by 119 in.^{2}
c. yes; Sample answer: $14\pi \approx 43.98$ in., $49\pi \approx 153.94$ in.^{2}

23.

Solid	tetrahedron	cube	octahedron
Faces, F	4	6	8
Edges, E	6	12	12
Vertices, V	4	8	6

Solid	dodecahedron	icosahedron
Faces, F	12	20
Edges, E	30	30
Vertices, V	20	12

$V - E + F = 2$; Check students' work.
25. no; The plane can intersect the sphere at a single point.
27. The x-ray images show different cross-sections of a human head.
29. A CT scan uses a series of X-ray images, but an MRI uses magnetic fields to create images.

12.1 Review & Refresh

30. First prove that $\overline{BE} \cong \overline{BD}$ using the Converse of the Base Angles Theorem. Then use the Congruent Supplement Theorem to show that $\angle AEB \cong \angle CDB$. $\triangle ABE \cong \triangle CBD$ by the SAS Congruence Theorem. Finally, prove that $\overline{AB} \cong \overline{CB}$ because corresponding parts of congruent triangles are congruent.
31. 12 oz per yd^2
32. yes; Because $32^2 + 60^2 = 68^2$, $\triangle ABC$ is a right triangle. So, $\overline{AB}$ is perpendicular to $\overline{AC}$, and $\overline{AB}$ is tangent to $\odot C$ by the Tangent Line to Circle Theorem.
33. $r = 30, m\angle P \approx 53.1°, m\angle Q \approx 36.9°$
34. $39 + 52 > 64, 52 + 64 > 39, 39 + 64 > 52$; acute
35. 60 square units   **36.** $42.25\pi \approx 132.73$ cm^2

12.2 Practice

1. 12 m^3 **3.** $91.8\pi \approx 288.40$ ft^3
5. 10 ft   **7.** $\dfrac{1{,}211\sqrt{3}}{300} \approx 6.99$ in.
9. 150 ft^3 **11.** $605\pi \approx 1{,}900.66$ in.^{3}
13. $29\frac{1}{3}$ cm^2; 8 cm^3 **15.** about 2,350,000,000 gal
17. 75 in.^{3}; 20 rocks
19. Sample answer: about 3,100 in.^{3}; The bag is approximately cylindrical. The cylinder has a height of about 10 onions and the base is about 5 onions in diameter. If an average onion has a diameter of 2.5 inches, then the cylinder has a diameter of about 12.5 inches and a height of about 25 inches. So, the volume of the bag is about $V = \pi(6.25)^2(25) \approx 3{,}100$ in.^{3}
21. $\dfrac{7\pi}{3} \approx 7.33$ in.^{3}
23. $2{,}000\pi \approx 6{,}283$ m^3 **25.** about 1,659,892 gallons

12.2 Review & Refresh

26. $x = 7, y = 12$ **27.** no
28. yes; rectangular prism   **29.** $x = 4$
30. about 54 people per square mile

12.3 Practice

1. 448 m^3 **3.** $x = 6$ **5.** $x = 12$
7. 4 ft^3 **9.** 72 in.^{3}

11. $47.3671875\sqrt{3} \approx 82.04$ in.^{3}
13. $296,874\frac{2}{3}$ ft^3
15. about 35,563,314.16 cubic feet

12.3 Review & Refresh
16. $x = \frac{10\sqrt{3}}{3} \approx 5.8$ **17.** $x \approx 16.0$
18. $1,215\pi \approx 3,817.04$ m^3 **19.** rectangle
20. no; The campsite is only about 90 feet away from the trail.
21. If it is Thanksgiving, then it is November; true; If it is not November, then it is not Thanksgiving; true
22. about 9.8 mi

12.4 Practice
1. $192\pi \approx 603.19$ in.^{2} **3.** $\frac{1,300\pi}{3} \approx 1,361.36$ mm^3
5. 144π ft^2; 128π ft^3 **7.** $72\pi \approx 226.19$ cm^3
9. $2h$; $r\sqrt{2}$; The original volume is $V = \frac{1}{3}\pi r^2 h$. The new volume is $\frac{2}{3}\pi r^2 h = \frac{1}{3}\pi r^2(2h) = \frac{1}{3}\pi (r\sqrt{2})^2 h$.
11. $V = \frac{1}{3}\pi h(a^2 + ab + b^2)$ **13.** $5\sqrt[3]{4} \approx 7.94$ cm

12.4 Review & Refresh
14. $49\pi \approx 153.94$ ft^2 **15.** 32 m
16. $75.264\pi \approx 236.45$ in.^{3} **17.** 36 in., 81 in.
18. $3\pi \approx 9.42$ in.; $2.25\pi \approx 7.07$ in.^{2}
19. 35 ft^3 **20.** yes

12.5 Practice
1. $64\pi \approx 201.06$ ft^2 **3.** $16\pi \approx 50.27$ ft^2
5. 30 m **7.** $\frac{2,048\pi}{3} \approx 2,144.66$ m^3
9. $\frac{4,000\pi}{3} \approx 4,188.79$ cm^3
11. $75\pi \approx 235.62$ cm^2; $\frac{250\pi}{3} \approx 261.80$ cm^3
13. $42.1875\pi \approx 132.54$ yd^2; $35.15625\pi \approx 110.45$ yd^3
15. $\frac{144}{\pi} \approx 45.84$ in.^{2}; $\frac{288}{\pi^2} \approx 29.18$ in.^{3}
17. $\frac{32\pi}{3} \approx 33.51$ ft^3 **19.** $\frac{425\pi}{3} \approx 445.06$ in.^{3}
21. $\frac{20,000\pi}{3} \approx 20,943.95$ ft^3
23. a.

Radius	Surface Area	Volume
3 in.	36π in.^{2}	36π in.^{3}
4 in.	64π in.^{2}	85.3π in.^{3}
5 in.	100π in.^{2}	166.7π in.^{3}
6 in.	144π in.^{2}	288π in.^{3}

The ratio of the surface areas of any two spheres is equal to the square of the ratio of their radii, and the ratio of the volumes of any two spheres is equal to the cube of the ratio of their radii; The ratios indicate that spheres are always similar, with a scale factor equal to the ratio of the radii.
25. Check students' work.
27. $36\pi \approx 113.10$ in.^{2}; $24\pi \approx 75.40$ in.^{3}
29. a. *Sample answer:* about 140,743,400 mi^2
b. *Sample answer:* about 14,074,340 mi^2

12.5 Review & Refresh
30. 15 in.^{3} **31.** $z = \sqrt{\frac{50}{\pi}} \approx 3.99$ ft
32. 27 units
33. no; $\frac{JK}{KL} \neq \frac{NM}{ML}$, so $\overline{KM}$ is not parallel to $\overline{JN}$.
34. $(9 + 3\sqrt{34})\pi \approx 83.23$ yd^2; $15\pi \approx 47.12$ yd^3

12.6 Practice
1. about 4,551 g
3. a. about 27.5 g
b. increases by about 12.9 in.^{3}; The initial volume is about 3.6 in.^{3} and the volume after 5 weeks is about 16.5 in.^{3}.
5. about 0.021 cm, or 0.21 mm
7. Check students' work; The scales are not linear because they do not increase by constant amounts.
9. *Sample answer:* about 60 times stronger; The average strength of glass is about 300 MPa and the average strength of wood is about 5 MPa.

12.6 Review & Refresh
10. The slope of $\overline{PQ}$ is $-\frac{1}{3}$ and the slope of $\overline{RS}$ is $-\frac{1}{3}$. So $\overline{PQ} \parallel \overline{SR}$. The slope of $\overline{PS}$ is 2 and the slope of $\overline{QR}$ is -5, so $\overline{PS} \nparallel \overline{QR}$. The quadrilateral has exactly one pair of parallel sides, so it is a trapezoid; not isosceles
11. $1,024\pi \approx 3,216.99$ cm^2; $\frac{16,384\pi}{3} \approx 17,157.28$ cm^3
12. $x = 12\sqrt{2}$ **13.** $x = 3\sqrt{3}$
14. yes; The triangles are congruent by the SAS Congruence Theorem.
15. 32 ft^3

12.7 Practice
1. ; cylinder with a height of 8 units and a radius of 8 units

3. ; sphere with a radius of 3 units

5. ; cone with a height of 9 units and a radius of 6 units

7. ; cone with a height of 12 units and a radius of 10 units; $(100 + 20\sqrt{61})\pi \approx 804.89$ square units; $400\pi \approx 1{,}256.64$ cubic units

9. 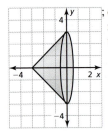 ; cone with a height of 3 units and a radius of 3 units; $9\pi \approx 28.27$ cubic units

11.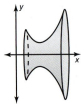

13. *Sample answer:* $x = 0, y = 0, x = 4, y = 4$
15. $16\pi \approx 50.27$ square units
17. Check students' work.

12.7 Review & Refresh
18. about 9 mi
19. about 151.13 g
20. $x = 15$; yes
21. $134.56\pi \approx 422.73$ yd²
22. $\dfrac{77.452\pi}{3} \approx 81.11$ in.³
23. about 62 min 50 sec
24. $x = \dfrac{1}{12}y^2$

Chapter 12 Review
1. rectangle
2. square
3. triangle
4. triangle
5. pentagon
6. rectangle
7. *Sample answer:* rectangle, triangle

8. 11.34 m³
9. $32\pi \approx 100.53$ mm³
10. about 27.53 yd³
11. $294\pi \approx 923.63$ in.³
12. 36 in.
13. $648\pi \approx 2{,}035.75$ in.³
14. $735 - 183.75\pi \approx 157.73$ cm³
15. 504π ft²; $1{,}296\pi$ ft³
16. 189 ft³
17. 300 m³
18. 2,023 m³
19. $2\sqrt{3} \approx 3.46$ in.
20. 3,960 m³
21. 1,152 mm³
22. $216\pi \approx 678.58$ cm²; $324\pi \approx 1{,}017.88$ cm³
23. $(42.25 + 6.5\sqrt{91.25})\pi \approx 327.80$ in.²; $\dfrac{295.75\pi}{3} \approx 309.71$ in.³
24. 15 cm

25. $196\pi \approx 615.75$ in.²; $\dfrac{1{,}372\pi}{3} \approx 1{,}436.76$ in.³
26. $900\pi \approx 2{,}827.43$ ft²; $4{,}500\pi \approx 14{,}137.17$ ft³
27. about 74.8 million km²; about 60.8 billion km³
28. $216 + 18\pi \approx 272.55$ m³
29. a. about 32.38 cm³
   b. no, yes
30. about 103.06 g
31. about 0.50 cm
32. 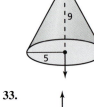 ; cone with a height of 9 units and a radius of 5 units; $(25 + 5\sqrt{106})\pi \approx 240.26$ square units; $75\pi \approx 235.62$ cubic units

33. ; sphere with a radius of 7 units; $196\pi \approx 615.75$ square units; $\dfrac{1{,}372\pi}{3} \approx 1{,}436.76$ cubic units

34. 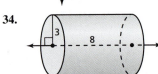 ; cylinder with a radius of 3 units and a height of 8 units; $66\pi \approx 207.35$ square units; $72\pi \approx 226.19$ cubic units

35. ; cone with a height of 6 units and a radius of 8 units and a hemisphere with a radius of 8 units; $208\pi \approx 653.45$ square units; $\dfrac{1{,}408\pi}{3} \approx 1{,}474.45$ cubic units

36.
37.

38.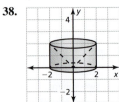

cylinder with a cone removed, both with a height of 2 units and a radius of 2 units; $\dfrac{16\pi}{3} \approx 16.76$ cubic units

39. no; Rotating around the *y*-axis produces a hemisphere.
40. *y*-axis

Chapter 13

Getting Ready for Chapter 13

1. $\frac{6}{30} = \frac{p}{100}$; 20%   2. $\frac{a}{25} = \frac{68}{100}$; 17

3.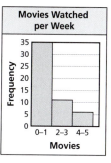

13.1 Practice

1. 6; HP, HP, HW, TP, TP, TW
3. 18; A1, A2, A3, B1, B2, B3, C1, C2, C3, D1, D2, D3, E1, E2, E3, F1, F2, F3
5. $\frac{5}{16}$, or 31.25%
7. a. $\frac{11}{12}$, or about 91.7%   b. $\frac{13}{18}$, or about 72.2%
9. $\frac{2}{7}$, or about 28.6%   11. 4
13. $\frac{6}{35}$, or about 17.1%   15. Check students' work.
17. Check students' work.
19. *Sample answer:* $\frac{1}{3}$, or about 33.3%

13.1 Review & Refresh

20. ; cone with a height of 9 units and a radius of 7 units

21. 540 kg, about 566 kg, about 567 kg, or about 583 kg
22. $192\pi \approx 603.19$ ft²; $\frac{1{,}024\pi}{3} \approx 1{,}072.233$ ft²
23. $(x - 2)^2 + (y - 3)^2 = 25$

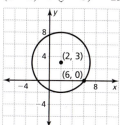

24. $x = 2$ 25. $x = 20$

13.2 Practice

1.

	Age Group		
Response		Child	Adult	Total
Yes	132	151	283
No	39	29	68
Total	171	180	351

351 people were surveyed, 171 children were surveyed, 180 adults were surveyed, 283 people said yes, 68 people said no.

3.

	Age Group		
Response		Child	Adult	Total
Yes	0.376	0.430	0.806
No	0.111	0.083	0.194
Total	0.487	0.513	1

Sample answer: The joint relative frequency 0.430 means that about 43.0% of the people in the survey are adults and wash their hands after using the public restrooms. So, the probability that a randomly selected person from the survey is an adult who washes their hands after using the public restroom is about 43.0%.

Sample answer: The marginal relative frequency 0.487 means that about 48.7% of the people in the survey are children. So, the probability that a randomly selected person from the survey is a child is about 48.7%.

5. a.

	Like Horror Movies	
	Yes	No
Visited Haunted House — Yes	0.534	0.483
Visited Haunted House — No	0.466	0.517

Sample answer: The conditional relative frequency 0.483 means that of the people in the survey who do not like horror movies, about 48.3% have visited a haunted house. So, given that a randomly selected person in the survey who does not like horror movies, the probability that the person has visited a haunted house is about 48.3%.

b.

		Like Horror Movies	
		Yes	No
Visited Haunted House	Yes	0.481	0.519
	No	0.430	0.570

Sample answer: The conditional relative frequency 0.430 means that of the people in the survey who have not visited a haunted house, about 43.0% like horror movies. So, given that a randomly selected person in the survey has not visited a haunted house, the probability that the person likes horror movies is about 43.0%.

7. $\frac{59}{80}$, or 73.75%   9. Check students' work.

11. $\frac{202}{325}$, or about 62.2%; $\frac{89}{353}$, or about 25.2%

13.2 Review & Refresh

13. $\frac{5}{6}$, or about 83.3%

14.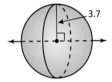
a sphere with a radius of 3.7 units; $54.76\pi \approx 172.03$ square units; $\frac{202.612\pi}{3} \approx 212.17$ cubic units

15. 962.5 kg   16. 98°   17. $x = 3$

13.3 Practice

1. $\frac{1}{2}$, or 50%

3. a. $\frac{7}{8}$, or 87.5%   b. $\frac{12}{19}$, or about 63.2%

5. $\frac{7}{8}$, or 87.5%

7. a. $\frac{23}{43}$, or about 53.5%   b. $\frac{23}{48}$, or about 47.9%

9. Route B; The probability of being on time using Route B is about 78.6%, which is greater than Route A (about 63.6%) and Route C (about 74.9%).

11. $P(B \mid A) = \dfrac{P(A \text{ and } B)}{P(A)}$

$P(B \mid A) \cdot P(A) = \dfrac{P(A \text{ and } B)}{P(A)} \cdot P(A)$

$P(B \mid A) \cdot P(A) = P(A \text{ and } B)$

and

$P(A \mid B) = \dfrac{P(A \text{ and } B)}{P(B)}$

$P(A \mid B) \cdot P(B) = \dfrac{P(A \text{ and } B)}{P(B)} \cdot P(B)$

$P(A \mid B) \cdot P(B) = P(A \text{ and } B)$,

so

$P(B \mid A) \cdot P(A) = P(A \mid B) \cdot P(B)$.

13.

		Cat Owner	
		Yes	No
Dog Owner	Yes	36	57
	No	25	92

$\frac{12}{31}$, about 38.7%

15. Check students' work.

17. Check students' work; *Sample answer:* Movies with a greater number of reviewers tend to have higher ratings.

19. *Sample answer:* about 64.1%; Find the number of movies that were given a mean rating of 4: $24 + 6 + 6 + 6 + 12 + 12 + 18 + 36 + 30 + 36 + 42 + 6 = 234$. Then find the number of movies given a mean rating of 4 that also had 50 or more reviewers: $36 + 30 + 36 + 42 + 6 = 150$. So, $\frac{150}{234} = \frac{25}{39} \approx 0.641$.

13.3 Review & Refresh

20.

		Dominant Hand		
		Left	Right	Total
Grade	10th	0.069	0.429	0.498
	11th	0.104	0.398	0.502
	Total	0.173	0.827	1

21. $\frac{1}{6}$, or about 16.7%; $\frac{4}{15}$, or about 26.7%

22. $14\pi \approx 43.98$ in.   23. $x = 2\sqrt{6} \approx 4.90$

24. 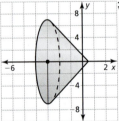 ; cone with a height of 3.5 units and a radius of 7 units; about $\dfrac{171.5\pi}{3} \approx 179.59$ cubic units

13.4 Practice

1. independent   3. not independent
5. not independent   7. independent
9. $\frac{14}{95}$, or about 14.7%
11. a. without replacement   b. with replacement
13. Event A represents rolling at least one 2. Event B represents the dice summing to 5; dependent; $P(A \text{ and } B) = \frac{1}{18}$ and $P(A) \cdot P(B) = \frac{11}{324}$
15. Go for 2 points after the first touchdown, and then go for 1 point if they were successful the first time or 2 points if they were unsuccessful the first time; winning: 44.55%; losing: 30.25%
17. *Sample answer:* about 60%

13.4 Review & Refresh

18. $\frac{1}{12}$, or about 8.3%

19. $m\angle 1 = 36°, m\angle 2 = 36°, m\angle 3 = 108°, m\angle 4 = 36°, m\angle 5 = 36°$

20. $\left(\dfrac{4}{3}, -\dfrac{5}{3}\right)$ **21.** $\dfrac{7\sqrt{2}}{2} \approx 4.95$ units

22.

		Escape Room		
		Yes	No	Total
Age	Adult	35	33	68
	Teenager	29	28	57
	Total	64	61	125

125 people were surveyed, 68 adults were surveyed, 57 teenagers were surveyed, 64 people said yes, 61 people said no.

13.5 Practice

1. $\dfrac{1}{3}$, or about 33.3%   **3.** $\dfrac{2}{3}$; or about 66.7%
5. $\dfrac{7}{12}$, or about 58.3%
7. P(heart and face card) should be subtracted; because there are face cards that are hearts
9. $\dfrac{1}{10}$, or 10%   **11.** 47.42%
13. a. $P(A \text{ or } B \text{ or } C) = P(A) + P(B) + P(C)$
  b. $P(A \text{ or } B \text{ or } C) = P(A) + P(B) + P(C) - P(A \text{ and } B) - P(A \text{ and } C) - P(B \text{ and } C) + P(A \text{ and } B \text{ and } C)$
15. $\dfrac{2{,}007}{33{,}500}$, or about 6%

13.5 Review & Refresh

16. $\dfrac{1}{17}$, or about 5.9%   **17.** yes
18. 180°   **19.** 207°
20. 153°   **21.** $x \approx 9.6, y \approx 12.8$

13.6 Practice

1. a. 24   **3. a.** 5,040
  b. 12   **b.** 42
5. 9   **7.** 990   **9.** $\dfrac{1}{56}$ **11.** 4
13. 5   **15.** 1   **17.** 53,130
19. The factorial in the denominator was left out; $_{11}P_7 = 1{,}663{,}200$
21. $\dfrac{1}{44{,}850}$

23.

	r = 0	r = 1	r = 2	r = 3
$_3P_r$	1	3	6	6
$_3C_r$	1	3	3	1

$_nP_r \geq {_nC_r}$

25. Sample answer: There is only one way to arrange a data set with zero elements.
27. 376
29. a. 11,232,000
  b. 1,402,410,240

13.6 Review & Refresh

31. $x = 2\sqrt{22} \approx 9.4$ **32.** independent
33. 0.25   **34.** 1
35. about 1,727.88 in., or about 144 ft
36. $SQ = 26, QV = 13$ **37.** 109°

13.7 Practice

1.

x (value)	1	2	3
Outcomes	5	3	2
P(x)	$\dfrac{1}{2}$	$\dfrac{3}{10}$	$\dfrac{1}{5}$

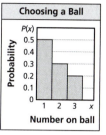

3. a. 2
  b. $\dfrac{5}{8}$, or 62.5%
  c. $\dfrac{9}{64}$, or 14.0625%
5. about 0.002%   **7.** about 0.02%
9. a.

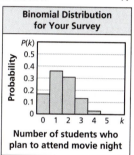

  b. 1 of the 5 students plans to attend movie night.
  c. about 83.7%
11. np successes   **13.** 3.4 kg
15. Sample answer: $\dfrac{110}{2{,}235}$, or about 4.9%

13.7 Review & Refresh

16. 6   **17.** 10   **18.** (5, 0)
19. $m\angle G \approx 45.2°$ **20.** $\dfrac{4}{5}$, or 80%
21. dependent   **22.** $r = 7.5$ units

Chapter 13 Review

1. 8; HB, HB, HG, HG, TB, TB, TG, TG
2. $\dfrac{2}{9}$, or 22.2%; $\dfrac{7}{9}$ or 77.8%   **3.** 20 points
4. $\dfrac{9}{17}$, or about 52.9%
5.

		Class		
		Senior	Junior	Total
Response	Yes	200	230	430
	No	20	40	60
	Total	220	270	490

490 students were surveyed, 430 students said the speaker was impactful, 60 students said the speaker was not impactful, 220 seniors were surveyed, 270 juniors were surveyed.

6. $\dfrac{2}{3}$, or about 66.7%

7. $\frac{2}{3}$, or about 66.7%; $\frac{3}{7}$, or about 42.9%; The probability that a failed rotor is a single rotor is greater than the probability that a passed rotor is a single rotor.
8. $\frac{1}{3}$, or about 33.3%
9. $\frac{5}{64}$, or about 7.8%
10. $\frac{38}{87}$, or about 43.7%
11. 0.68
12. $\frac{1}{50}$, or 0.02
13. 5,040
14. 1,037,836,800
15. 15
16. 70
17. $\frac{1}{12}$
18. $\frac{2}{11}$
19. about 12.1%
20. 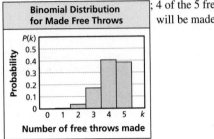 ; 4 of the 5 free throw shots will be made.

21. 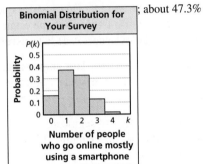 ; about 47.3%

English-Spanish Glossary

English | Spanish

A

acute angle *(p. 35)* An angle that has a measure greater than 0° and less than 90°

adjacent angles *(p. 46)* Two angles that share a common vertex and side, but have no common interior points

adjacent arcs *(p. 517)* Arcs of a circle that have exactly one point in common

alternate exterior angles *(p. 120)* Two angles that are formed by two lines and a transversal that are outside the two lines and on opposite sides of the transversal

alternate interior angles *(p. 120)* Two angles that are formed by two lines and a transversal that are between the two lines and on opposite sides of the transversal

altitude of a triangle *(p. 309)* The perpendicular segment from a vertex of a triangle to the opposite side or to the line that contains the opposite side

angle *(p. 36)* A set of points consisting of two different rays that have the same endpoint

angle bisector *(p. 40)* A ray that divides an angle into two angles that are congruent

angle of depression *(p. 475)* An angle formed by a horizontal line and a line of sight *down* to an object

angle of elevation *(p. 468)* An angle formed by a horizontal line and a line of sight *up* to an object

angle of rotation *(p. 184)* The angle that is formed by rays drawn from the center of rotation to a point and its image

apothem of a regular polygon *(p. 593)* The distance from the center to any side of a regular polygon

arc length *(p. 579)* A portion of the circumference of a circle

axiom *(p. 12)* A rule that is accepted without proof
See postulate.

axis of revolution *(p. 656)* The line around which a two-dimensional shape is rotated to form a three-dimensional figure

ángulo agudo *(p. 35)* Un ángulo que tiene una medida mayor que 0° y menor que 90°

ángulos adyacentes *(p. 46)* Dos ángulos que comparten un vértice y lado en común, pero que no tienen puntos interiores en común

arcos adyacentes *(p. 517)* Arcos de un círculo que tienen exactamente un punto en común

ángulos exteriores alternos *(p. 120)* Dos ángulos que son formados por dos rectas y una transversal que están fuera de las dos rectas y en lados opuestos de la transversal

ángulos interiores alternos *(p. 120)* Dos ángulos que son formados por dos rectas y una transversal que están entre las dos rectas y en lados opuestos de la transversal

altitud de un triángulo *(p. 309)* El segmento perpendicular desde el vértice de un triángulo al lado opuesto o a la recta que contiene el lado opuesto

ángulo *(p. 36)* Un conjunto de puntos que consiste en dos rayos distintos que tienen el mismo punto extremo

bisectriz de un ángulo *(p. 40)* Un rayo que divide un ángulo en dos ángulos congruentes

ángulo de depresión *(p. 475)* El ángulo formado por la recta horizontal y la recta de vista descendente hacia un objeto

ángulo de elevación *(p. 468)* El ángulo formado por la recta horizontal y la recta de vista ascendente hacia un objeto

ángulo de rotación *(p. 184)* El ángulo que está formado por rayos dibujados desde el centro de rotación hacia un punto y su imagen

apotema de un polígono regular *(p. 593)* La distancia desde el centro a cualquier lado de un polígono regular

longitud de arco *(p. 579)* Una porción de la circunferencia de un círculo

axioma *(p. 12)* Una regla que es aceptada sin demostración
Ver postulado.

eje de revolución *(p. 656)* La recta alrededor de la cual una forma bidimensional rota para formar una figura tridimensional

B

base angles of an isosceles triangle *(p. 244)* The two angles adjacent to the base of an isosceles triangle

base angles of a trapezoid *(p. 384)* Either pair of consecutive angles whose common side is a base of a trapezoid

base of an isosceles triangle *(p. 244)* The side of an isosceles triangle that is not one of the legs

bases of a trapezoid *(p. 384)* The parallel sides of a trapezoid

between *(p. 14)* When three points are collinear, one point is between the other two.

biconditional statement *(p. 65)* A statement that contains the phrase "if and only if"

binomial distribution *(p. 718)* A type of probability distribution that shows the probabilities of the outcomes of a binomial experiment

binomial experiment *(p. 718)* An experiment in which there are a fixed number of independent trials, exactly two possible outcomes for each trial, and the probability of success is the same for each trial

ángulos de la base de un triángulo isósceles *(p. 244)* Los dos ángulos adyacentes a la base de un triángulo isósceles

ángulos de la base de un trapecio *(p. 384)* Cualquier par de ángulos consecutivos cuyo lado común es la base de un trapezoide

base de un triángulo isósceles *(p. 244)* El lado de un triángulo isósceles que no es uno de los catetos

bases de un trapecio *(p. 384)* Los lados paralelos de un trapezoide

entre *(p. 14)* Cuando tres puntos son colineales, un punto está entre los otros dos.

enunciado bicondicional *(p. 65)* Un enunciado que contiene la frase "si y sólo si"

distribución del binomio *(p. 718)* Un tipo de distribución de probabilidades que muestra las probabilidades de los resultados posibles de un experimento del binomio

experimento del binomio *(p. 718)* Un experimento en el que hay un número fijo de pruebas independientes, exactamente dos resultados posibles para cada prueba, y la probabilidad de éxito es la misma para cada prueba

C

Cavalieri's Principle *(p. 622)* If two solids have the same height and the same cross-sectional area at every level, then they have the same volume.

center of a circle *(p. 508)* The point from which all points on a circle are equidistant

center of dilation *(p. 200)* The fixed point in a dilation

center of a regular polygon *(p. 593)* The center of a polygon's circumscribed circle

center of rotation *(p. 184)* The fixed point in a rotation

center of symmetry *(p. 187)* The center of rotation in a figure that has rotational symmetry

central angle of a circle *(p. 516)* An angle that is formed by two radii and has a vertex at the center of the circle

central angle of a regular polygon *(p. 593)* An angle formed by two radii drawn to consecutive vertices of a polygon

centroid *(p. 308)* The point of concurrency of the three medians of a triangle

Principio de Cavalieri *(p. 622)* Si dos sólidos tienen la misma altura y la misma área transversal en todo nivel, entonces tienen el mismo volumen.

centro de un círculo *(p. 508)* El punto desde donde todos los puntos en un círculo son equidistantes

centro de dilatación *(p. 200)* El punto fijo en una dilatación

centro de un polígono regular *(p. 593)* El centro del círculo circunscrito de un polígono

centro de rotación *(p. 184)* El punto fijo en una rotación

centro de simetría *(p. 187)* El centro de rotación en una figura que tiene simetría rotacional

ángulo central de un círculo *(p. 516)* Un ángulo que es formado por dos radios y que tiene un vértice en el centro del círculo

ángulo central de un polígono regular *(p. 593)* Un ángulo formado por dos radios extendidos a vértices consecutivos de un polígono

centroide *(p. 308)* El punto de concurrencia de las tres medianas de un triángulo

chord of a circle *(p. 508)* A segment whose endpoints are on a circle

chord of a sphere *(p. 642)* A segment whose endpoints are on the sphere

circle *(p. 508)* The set of all points in a plane that are equidistant from a given point

circumcenter *(p. 298)* The point of concurrency of the three perpendicular bisectors of a triangle

circumference *(p. 578)* The distance around a circle

circumscribed angle *(p. 542)* An angle whose sides are tangent to a circle

circumscribed circle *(p. 534)* A circle that contains all the vertices of an inscribed polygon

collinear points *(p. 4)* Points that lie on the same line

combination *(p. 710)* A selection of objects in which order is not important

common tangent *(p. 509)* A line or segment that is tangent to two coplanar circles

complementary angles *(p. 46)* Two angles whose measures have a sum of 90°

component form *(p. 168)* A form of a vector that combines the horizontal and vertical components

composition of transformations *(p. 170)* The combination of two or more transformations to form a single transformation

compound event *(p. 702)* The union or intersection of two events

concentric circles *(p. 509)* Coplanar circles that have a common center

conclusion *(p. 62)* The "then" part of a conditional statement written in if-then form

concurrent *(p. 298)* Three or more lines, rays, or segments that intersect in the same point

conditional probability *(p. 686)* The probability that event B occurs given that event A has occurred, written as $P(B|A)$

conditional relative frequency *(p. 682)* The ratio of a joint relative frequency to the marginal relative frequency in a two-way table

conditional statement *(p. 62)* A logical statement that has a hypothesis and a conclusion

cuerda de un círculo *(p. 508)* Un segmento cuyos puntos extremos están en un círculo

cuerda de una esfera *(p. 642)* Un segmento cuyos puntos extremos están en la esfera

círculo *(p. 508)* El conjunto de todos los puntos en un plano que son equidistantes de un punto dado

circuncentro *(p. 298)* El punto de concurrencia de las tres bisectrices perpendiculares de un triángulo

circunferencia *(p. 578)* La distancia alrededor de un círculo

ángulo circunscrito *(p. 542)* Un ángulo cuyos lados son tangentes a un círculo

círculo circunscrito *(p. 534)* Un círculo que contiene todos los vértices de un polígono inscrito

puntos colineales *(p. 4)* Puntos que descansan en la misma recta

combinación *(p. 710)* Una selección de objetos en la que el orden no es importante

tangente común *(p. 509)* Una recta o segmento que es tangente a dos círculos coplanarios

ángulos complementarios *(p. 46)* Dos ángulos cuyas medidas suman 90°

forma componente *(p. 168)* Una forma de un vector que combina los componentes horizontales y verticales

composición de transformaciones *(p. 170)* La combinación de dos o más transformaciones para formar una transformación única

evento compuesto *(p. 702)* La unión o intersección de dos eventos

círculos concéntricos *(p. 509)* Círculos coplanarios que tienen un centro en común

conclusión *(p. 62)* La parte después de "entonces" en un enunciado condicional escrito de la forma "si..., entonces..."

concurrente *(p. 298)* Tres o más rectas, rayos o segmentos que se intersectan en el mismo punto

probabilidad condicional *(p. 686)* La probabilidad de que el evento B ocurra dado que el evento A ha ocurrido, escrito como $P(B|A)$

frecuencia relativa condicional *(p. 682)* La razón de una frecuencia relativa conjunta a la frecuencia relativa marginal en una tabla de doble entrada

enunciado condicional *(p. 62)* Un enunciado lógico que tiene una hipótesis y una conclusión

congruence transformation *(p. 193)* A transformation that preserves length and angle measure
See rigid motion.

congruent angles *(p. 38)* Two angles that have the same measure

congruent arcs *(p. 518)* Arcs that have the same measure and are of the same circle or of congruent circles

congruent circles *(p. 518)* Circles that can be mapped onto each other by a rigid motion or a composition of rigid motions

congruent figures *(p. 192)* Geometric figures that have the same size and shape

congruent segments *(p. 13)* Line segments that have the same length

conjecture *(p. 72)* An unproven statement that is based on observations

consecutive interior angles *(p. 120)* Two angles that are formed by two lines and a transversal that lie between the two lines and on the same side of the transversal

construction *(p. 11)* A geometric drawing that uses a limited set of tools, usually a compass and a straightedge

contrapositive *(p. 63)* The statement formed by negating both the hypothesis and conclusion of the converse of a conditional statement

converse *(p. 63)* The statement formed by exchanging the hypothesis and conclusion of a conditional statement

coordinate *(p. 12)* A real number that corresponds to a point on a line

coordinate proof *(p. 274)* A style of proof that involves placing geometric figures in a coordinate plane

coplanar points *(p. 4)* Points that lie in the same plane

corollary to a theorem *(p. 225)* A statement that can be proved easily using the theorem

corresponding angles *(p. 120)* Two angles that are formed by two lines and a transversal that are in corresponding positions

corresponding parts *(p. 230)* A pair of sides or angles that have the same relative position in two congruent figures

cosine *(p. 472)* For an acute angle of a right triangle, the ratio of the length of the leg adjacent to the acute angle to the length of the hypotenuse

transformación de congruencia *(p. 193)* Una transformación que preserva la longitud y medida del ángulo
Ver movimiento rígida.

ángulos congruentes *(p. 38)* Dos ángulos que tienen la misma medida

arcos congruentes *(p. 518)* Arcos que tienen la misma medida y que son del mismo círculo o de círculos congruentes

círculos congruentes *(p. 518)* Círculos que pueden superponerse sobre sí mismos mediante un movimiento rígido o una composición de movimientos rígidos

figuras congruentes *(p. 192)* Figuras geométricas que tienen el mismo tamaño y forma

segmentos congruentes *(p. 13)* Segmentos de rectas que tienen la misma longitud

conjetura *(p. 72)* Una afirmación no comprobada que se basa en observaciones

ángulos interiores consecutivos *(p. 120)* Dos ángulos que son formados por dos rectas y una transversal que descansan entre las dos rectas y en el mismo lado de la transversal

construcción *(p. 11)* Un dibujo geométrico que usa un conjunto limitado de herramientas, generalmente una regla y compás

contrapositivo *(p. 63)* El enunciado formado por la negación de la hipótesis y conclusión del converso de un enunciado condicional

converso *(p. 63)* El enunciado formado por el intercambio de la hipótesis y conclusión de un enunciado condicional

coordenada *(p. 12)* Un número real que corresponde a un punto en una línea

prueba de coordenadas *(p. 274)* Un estilo de prueba que implica colocar figuras geométricas en un plano coordenado

puntos coplanarios *(p. 4)* Puntos que descansan en el mismo plano

corolario de un teorema *(p. 225)* Un enunciado que puede comprobarse fácilmente usando el teorema

ángulos correspondientes *(p. 120)* Dos ángulos que están formados por dos líneas y una transversal que están en las posiciones correspondientes

partes correspondientes *(p. 230)* Un par de lados o ángulos que tienen la misma posición relativa en dos figuras congruentes

coseno *(p. 472)* Para un ángulo agudo de un triángulo rectángulo, la razón de la longitud del cateto adyacente al ángulo agudo a la longitud de la hipotenusa

counterexample (p. 73) A specific case for which a conjecture is false

cross section (p. 615) The intersection of a plane and a solid

contraejemplo (p. 73) Un caso específico para el que una conjetura es falsa

sección transversal (p. 615) La intersección de un plano y un sólido

D

deductive reasoning (p. 74) A process that uses facts, definitions, accepted properties, and the laws of logic to form a logical argument

defined terms (p. 5) Terms that can be described using known words, such as *point* or *line*

density (p. 650) The amount of matter that an object has in a given unit of volume

dependent events (p. 697) Two events in which the occurrence of one event does affect the occurrence of the other event

diagonal (p. 346) A segment that joins two nonconsecutive vertices of a polygon

diameter (p. 508) A chord that contains the center of a circle

dilation (p. 200) A transformation in which a figure is enlarged or reduced with respect to a fixed point

directed line segment (p. 150) A segment that represents moving from point A to point B is called the directed line segment AB.

directrix (p. 560) A fixed line perpendicular to the axis of symmetry, such that the set of all points (x, y) of the parabola are equidistant from the focus and the directrix

disjoint events (p. 702) Two events that have no outcomes in common

distance between two points (p. 12) The absolute value of the difference of two coordinates on a line

distance from a point to a line (p. 140) The length of the perpendicular segment from the point to the line

razonamiento deductivo (p. 74) Un proceso que usa hechos, definiciones, propiedades aceptadas y las leyes de la lógica para formar un argumento lógico

términos definidos (p. 5) Términos que pueden describirse usando palabras conocidas, como *punto* o *línea*

densidad (p. 650) La cantidad de materia que tiene un objeto en una unidad de volumen dada

eventos dependientes (p. 697) Dos eventos en los que la ocurrencia de un evento afecta la ocurrencia del otro evento

diagonal (p. 346) Un segmento que une dos vértices no consecutivos de un polígono

diámetro (p. 508) Una cuerda que contiene el centro de un círculo

dilatación (p. 200) Una transformación en la cual una figura se agranda o reduce con respecto a un punto fijo

segmento de línea dirigido (p. 150) Un segmento que representa el moverse del punto A al punto B se llama el segmento de línea dirigido AB.

directriz (p. 560) Una recta fija perpendicular al eje de simetría de modo tal, que el conjunto de todos los puntos (x, y) de la parábola sean equidistantes del foco y la directriz

eventos disjunto (p. 702) Dos eventos que no tienen resultados en común

distancia entre dos puntos (p. 12) El valor absoluto de la diferencia de dos coordenadas en una recta

distancia desde un punto a una recta (p. 140) La longitud del segmento perpendicular desde el punto a la recta

edge (p. 614) A line segment formed by the intersection of two faces of a polyhedron

endpoints (p. 5) Points that represent the ends of a line segment or ray

enlargement (p. 200) A dilation in which the scale factor is greater than 1

equiangular polygon (p. 348) A polygon in which all angles are congruent

borde (p. 614) Un segmento de línea formado por la intersección de dos caras de un poliedro

puntos extremos (p. 5) Puntos que representan los extremos de una semirrecta o un segmento de recta

agrandamiento (p. 200) Una dilatación en donde el factor de escala es mayor que 1

polígono equiangular (p. 348) Un polígono en donde todos los ángulos son congruentes

English-Spanish Glossary

equidistant *(p. 290)* A point is equidistant from two figures when it is the same distance from each figure.

equilateral polygon *(p. 348)* A polygon in which all sides are congruent

equivalent statements *(p. 63)* Two related conditional statements that are both true or both false

event *(p. 672)* A collection of one or more outcomes in a probability experiment

experimental probability *(p. 675)* The ratio of the number of successes, or favorable outcomes, to the number of trials in a probability experiment

exterior of an angle *(p. 36)* The region that contains all the points outside of an angle

exterior angles *(p. 224)* Angles that form linear pairs with the interior angles of a polygon

external segment *(p. 549)* The part of a secant segment that is outside the circle

equidistante *(p. 290)* Un punto es equidistante desde dos figuras cuando está a la misma distancia de cada figura.

polígono equilátero *(p. 348)* Un polígono en donde todos los lados son congruentes

enunciados equivalentes *(p. 63)* Dos enunciados condicionales relacionados que son ambos verdaderos, o ambos falsos

evento *(p. 672)* Una colección de uno o más resultados en un experimento de probabilidades

probabilidad experimental *(p. 675)* La razón del número de éxitos, o resultados favorables, con respecto al número de pruebas en un experimento de probabilidades

exterior de un ángulo *(p. 36)* La región que contiene todos los puntos fuera de un ángulo

ángulos exteriores *(p. 224)* Ángulos que forman pares lineales con los ángulos interiores de un polígono

segmento externo *(p. 549)* La parte de un segmento secante que está fuera del círculo

face *(p. 614)* A flat surface of a polyhedron

flowchart proof (flow proof) *(p. 100)* A type of proof that uses boxes and arrows to show the flow of a logical argument

focus *(p. 560)* A fixed point in the interior of a parabola, such that the set of all points (x, y) of the parabola are equidistant from the focus and the directrix

cara *(p. 614)* Una superficie plana de un poliedro

prueba de organigrama (prueba de flujo) *(p. 100)* Un tipo de prueba que usa casillas y flechas para mostrar el flujo de un argumento lógico

foco *(p. 560)* Un punto fijo en el interior de una parábola, de tal forma que el conjunto de todos los puntos (x, y) de la parábola sean equidistantes del foco y la directriz

geometric mean *(p. 460)* The positive number x that satisfies $\frac{a}{x} = \frac{x}{b}$

So, $x^2 = ab$ and $x = \sqrt{ab}$.

geometric probability *(p. 682)* A probability found by calculating a ratio of two lengths, areas, or volumes

glide reflection *(p. 178)* A transformation involving a translation followed by a reflection

great circle *(p. 642)* The intersection of a plane and a sphere such that the plane contains the center of the sphere

media geométrica *(p. 460)* El número positivo x que satisface $\frac{a}{x} = \frac{x}{b}$

Entonces, $x^2 = ab$ and $x = \sqrt{ab}$.

probabilidad geométrica *(p. 682)* Una probabilidad hallada al calcular la razón de dos longitudes, áreas o volúmenes

reflexión por deslizamiento *(p. 178)* Una transformación que implica una traslación seguida de una reflexión

gran círculo *(p. 642)* La intersección de un plano y una esfera, de tal forma que el plano contiene el centro de la esfera

hypotenuse *(p. 253)* The side opposite the right angle of a right triangle

hypothesis *(p. 62)* The "if" part of a conditional statement written in if-then form

hipotenusa *(p. 253)* El lado opuesto al ángulo recto de un triángulo recto

hipótesis *(p. 62)* La parte después de "si" en un enunciado condicional escrito de la forma "si..., entonces..."

if-then form *(p. 62)* A conditional statement in the form "if p, then q"

image *(p. 167)* A figure that results from the transformation of a geometric figure

incenter *(p. 301)* The point of concurrency of the angle bisectors of a triangle

independent events *(p. 694)* Two events in which the occurrence of one event does not affect the occurrence of another event

indirect proof *(p. 322)* A style of proof in which you temporarily assume that the desired conclusion is false, then reason logically to a contradiction

This proves that the original statement is true.

inductive reasoning *(p. 72)* A process that includes looking for patterns and making conjectures

inscribed angle *(p. 532)* An angle whose vertex lies on a circle and whose sides contain chords of the circle

inscribed polygon *(p. 534)* A polygon in which all the vertices lie on a circle

intercepted arc *(p. 532)* An arc that lies between two lines, rays, or segments

interior of an angle *(p. 36)* The region that contains all the points between the sides of an angle

interior angles *(p. 224)* Angles of a polygon

intersection *(p. 6)* The set of points two or more geometric figures have in common

inverse *(p. 63)* The statement formed by negating both the hypothesis and conclusion of a conditional statement

inverse cosine *(p. 480)* An inverse trigonometric ratio, abbreviated as $\cos^{-1}$

For acute angle A, if $\cos A = z$, then $\cos^{-1} z = m\angle A$.

inverse sine *(p. 480)* An inverse trigonometric ratio, abbreviated as $\sin^{-1}$

For acute angle A, if $\sin A = y$, then $\sin^{-1} y = m\angle A$.

forma "si..., entonces..." *(p. 62)* Un enunciado condicional en la forma de "si p, entonces q"

imagen *(p. 167)* Una figura que resulta de la transformación de una figura geométrica

incentro *(p. 301)* El punto de concurrencia de las bisectrices de los ángulos de un triángulo

eventos independientes *(p. 694)* Dos eventos en los que la ocurrencia de un evento no afecta la ocurrencia de otro evento

prueba indirecta *(p. 322)* Un estilo de prueba en donde uno asume temporalmente que la conclusión deseada es falsa, luego se razona de forma lógica hasta llegar a una contradicción

Esto prueba que el enunciado original es verdadero.

razonamiento inductivo *(p. 72)* Un proceso que incluye buscar patrones y hacer conjeturas

ángulo inscrito *(p. 532)* Un ángulo cuyo vértice está en un círculo y cuyos lados contienen cuerdas del círculo

polígono inscrito *(p. 534)* Un polígono en donde todos los vértices descansan sobre un círculo

arco interceptado *(p. 532)* Un arco que descansa entre dos rectas, rayos o segmentos

interior de un ángulo *(p. 36)* La región que contiene todos los puntos entre los lados de un ángulo

ángulos interiores *(p. 224)* Los ángulos de un polígono

intersección *(p. 6)* El conjunto de puntos que dos o más figuras geométricas tienen en común

inverso *(p. 63)* El enunciado formado por la negación de la hipótesis y conclusión de un enunciado condicional

coseno inverso *(p. 480)* Una razón trigonométrica inversa, abreviada como $\cos^{-1}$

Para un ángulo agudo A, si $\cos A = z$, entonces $\cos^{-1} z = m\angle A$.

seno inverso *(p. 480)* Una razón trigonométrica inversa, abreviada como $\sin^{-1}$

Para un ángulo agudo A, si $\sin A = y$, entonces $\sin^{-1} y = m\angle A$.

English-Spanish Glossary

inverse tangent (p. 480) An inverse trigonometric ratio, abbreviated as $\tan^{-1}$

For acute angle A, if $\tan A = x$, then $\tan^{-1} x = m\angle A$.

isosceles trapezoid (p. 384) A trapezoid with congruent legs

tangente inversa (p. 480) Una razón trigonométrica inversa, abreviada como $\tan^{-1}$

Para un ángulo agudo A, si $\tan A = x$, entonces $\tan^{-1} x = m\angle A$.

trapecio isósceles (p. 384) Un trapecio con catetos congruentes

---

J

---

joint frequency (p. 680) Each entry in a two-way table

joint relative frequency (p. 681) The ratio of a joint frequency to the total number of values or observations in a two-way table

frecuencia conjunta (p. 680) Cada valor en una tabla de doble entrada

frecuencia relativa conjunta (p. 681) La razón de una frecuencia conjunta al número total de valores y observaciones en una tabla de doble entrada

---

K

---

kite (p. 387) A quadrilateral that has two pairs of consecutive congruent sides, but opposite sides are not congruent

papalote (p. 387) Un cuadrilátero que tiene dos pares de lados congruentes consecutivos, pero los lados opuestos no son congruentes

---

L

---

lateral surface of a cone (p. 636) Consists of all segments that connect the vertex with points on the base edge of a cone

Law of Cosines (p. 489) For $\triangle ABC$ with side lengths of a, b, and c,

$$a^2 = b^2 + c^2 - 2bc \cos A,$$
$$b^2 = a^2 + c^2 - 2ac \cos B, \text{ and}$$
$$c^2 = a^2 + b^2 - 2ab \cos C.$$

Law of Sines (p. 487) For $\triangle ABC$ with side lengths of a, b, and c,

$$\frac{\sin A}{a} = \frac{\sin B}{b} = \frac{\sin C}{c} \text{ and}$$
$$\frac{a}{\sin A} = \frac{b}{\sin B} = \frac{c}{\sin C}.$$

legs of an isosceles triangle (p. 244) The two congruent sides of an isosceles triangle

legs of a right triangle (p. 253) The sides adjacent to the right angle of a right triangle

legs of a trapezoid (p. 384) The nonparallel sies of a trapezoid

line (p. 4) A line has one dimension. It is represented by a line with two arrowheads, but it extends without end.

line perpendicular to a plane (p. 82) A line that intersects the plane in a point and is perpendicular to every line in the plane that intersects it at that point

superficie lateral de un cono (p. 636) Consiste en todos los segmentos que conectan el vértice con puntos en el borde base de un cono

Ley de cosenos (p. 489) Para $\triangle ABC$ con longitudes de lados de a, b, y c,

$$a^2 = b^2 + c^2 - 2bc \cos A,$$
$$b^2 = a^2 + c^2 - 2ac \cos B, \text{ y}$$
$$c^2 = a^2 + b^2 - 2ab \cos C.$$

Ley de senos (p. 487) Para $\triangle ABC$ con longitudes de lados de a, b, y c,

$$\frac{\sin A}{a} = \frac{\sin B}{b} = \frac{\sin C}{c} \text{ y}$$
$$\frac{a}{\sin A} = \frac{b}{\sin B} = \frac{c}{\sin C}.$$

catetos de un triángulo isósceles (p. 244) Los dos lados congruentes de un triángulo isósceles

catetos de un triángulo recto (p. 253) Los lados adyacentes al ángulo recto de un triángulo recto

catetos de un trapecio (p. 384) Los lados no paralelos de un trapezoide

recta (p. 4) Una recta tiene una dimensión. Se representa por una línea con dos flechas, pero se extiende sin fin.

recta perpendicular a un plano (p. 82) Una recta que intersecta el plano en un punto y es perpendicular a cada recta en el plano que la intersecta en ese punto

line of reflection *(p. 176)* A line that acts as a mirror for a reflection

line segment *(p. 5)* A part of a line that consists of two endpoints and all points on the line between the endpoints *See* segment.

line symmetry *(p. 179)* A figure in the plane has line symmetry when the figure can be mapped onto itself by a reflection in a line.

line of symmetry *(p. 179)* A line of reflection that maps a figure onto itself

linear pair *(p. 48)* Two adjacent angles whose noncommon sides are opposite rays

recta de reflexión *(p. 176)* Una recta que actúa como un espejo para una reflexión

segmento de recta *(p. 5)* La parte de una recta que consiste en dos puntos extremos y todos los puntos entre ellos
Ver segmento.

simetría de recta *(p. 179)* Una figura en el plano tiene simetría de recta cuando la figura puede superponerse sobre sí misma por una reflexión en una recta.

recta de simetría *(p. 179)* Una recta de reflexión que superpone una figura sobre sí misma

par lineal *(p. 48)* Dos ángulos adyacentes cuyos lados no comunes son rayos opuestos

major arc *(p. 516)* An arc with a measure greater than 180°

marginal frequency *(p. 680)* The sums of the rows and columns in a two-way table

marginal relative frequency *(p. 681)* The sum of the joint relative frequencies in a row or a column in a two-way table

measure of an angle *(p. 37)* The absolute value of the difference between the real numbers matched with the two rays that form the angle on a protractor

measure of a major arc *(p. 516)* The measure of a major arc's central angle

measure of a minor arc *(p. 516)* The measure of a minor arc's central angle

median of a triangle *(p. 308)* A segment from a vertex of a triangle to the midpoint of the opposite side

midpoint *(p. 20)* The point that divides a segment into two congruent segments

midsegment of a trapezoid *(p. 386)* The segment that connects the midpoints of the legs of a trapezoid

midsegment of a triangle *(p. 316)* A segment that connects the midpoints of two sides of a triangle

minor arc *(p. 516)* An arc with a measure less than 180°

arco mayor *(p. 516)* Un arco con una medida mayor de 180°

frecuencia marginal *(p. 680)* Las sumas de las hileras y columnas en una tabla de doble entrada

frecuencia relativa marginal *(p. 681)* La suma de las frecuencias relativas conjuntas en una hilera o columna en una tabla de doble entrada

medida de un ángulo *(p. 37)* El valor absoluto de la diferencia entre los números reales asociados con los dos rayos que forman el ángulo en un transportador

medida de arco mayor *(p. 516)* La medida del ángulo central de un arco mayor

medida de arco menor *(p. 516)* La medida del ángulo central de un arco menor

mediana de un triángulo *(p. 308)* Un segmento desde el vértice de un triángulo hasta el punto medio del lado opuesto

punto medio *(p. 20)* El punto que divide un segmento en dos segmentos congruentes

segmento medio de un trapezoide *(p. 386)* El segmento que conecta los puntos medios de los catetos de un trapezoide

segmento medio de un triángulo *(p. 316)* Un segmento que conecta los puntos medios de dos lados de un triángulo

arco menor *(p. 516)* Un arco con una medida menor de 180°

n factorial *(p. 709)* The product of the integers from 1 to n, for any positive integer n

factorial de n *(p. 709)* El producto de los números enteros de 1 a n, para cualquier número entero positivo n

English-Spanish Glossary

negation *(p. 62)* The opposite of a statement. If a statement is *p*, then the negation is "not *p*," written ~*p*.

negación *(p. 62)* Lo opuesto de un enunciado o afirmación. Si un enunciado es *p*, entonces la negación es "no *p*," y se escribe ~*p*.

O

obtuse angle *(p. 35)* An angle that has a measure greater than 90° and less than 180°

ángulo obtuso *(p. 35)* Un ángulo que tiene una medida mayor que 90° y menor que 180°

opposite rays *(p. 5)* Two rays that have the same endpoint and form a line

rayos opuestos *(p. 5)* Dos rayos tienen el mismo punto extremo y forman una recta

orthocenter *(p. 309)* The point of concurrency of the lines containing the altitudes of a triangle

ortocentro *(p. 309)* El punto de concurrencia de las líneas que contienen las alturas de un triángulo

outcome *(p. 672)* The possible result of a probability experiment

resultado *(p. 672)* El resultado posible de un experimento de probabilidad

overlapping events *(p. 702)* Two events that have one or more outcomes in common

eventos superpuestos *(p. 702)* Dos eventos que tienen uno o más resultados en común

P

paragraph proof *(p. 103)* A style of proof that presents the statements and reasons as sentences in a paragraph, using words to explain the logical flow of an argument

prueba en forma de párrafo *(p. 103)* Un estilo de prueba que presenta los enunciados y motivos como oraciones en un párrafo, usando palabras para explicar el flujo lógico de un argumento

parallel lines *(p. 118)* Coplanar lines that do not intersect

rectas paralelas *(p. 118)* Rectas coplanarias que no se intersectan

parallel planes *(p. 118)* Planes that do not intersect

planos paralelos *(p. 118)* Planos que no se intersectan

parallelogram *(p. 356)* A quadrilateral with both pairs of opposite sides parallel

paralelogramo *(p. 356)* Un cuadrilátero con ambos pares de lados opuestos paralelos

permutation *(p. 708)* An arrangement of objects in which order is important

permutación *(p. 708)* Una disposición de objetos en la que el orden es importante

perpendicular bisector *(p. 141)* A ray, line, line segment, or plane that is perpendicular to a segment at its midpoint

bisectriz perpendicular *(p. 141)* Un rayo, una recta, un segmento de recta o un plano que es perpendicular a un segmento en su punto medio

perpendicular lines *(p. 64)* Two lines that intersect to form a right angle

rectas perpendiculares *(p. 64)* Dos líneas que se intersectan para formar un ángulo recto

plane *(p. 4)* A flat surface made up of points that has two dimensions and extends without end and is represented by a shape that looks like a floor or wall

plano *(p. 4)* Una superficie plana formada por puntos que tiene dos dimensiones y se extiende sin fin y que está representada por una forma que parece un piso o una pared

point *(p. 4)* A location in space that is represented by a dot and has no dimension

punto *(p. 4)* Un lugar en el espacio que está representado por un punto y no tiene dimensión

point of concurrency *(p. 298)* The point of intersection of concurrent lines, rays, or segments

punto de concurrencia *(p. 298)* El punto de intersección de rectas, rayos o segmentos concurrentes

point of tangency *(p. 508)* The point at which a tangent line intersects a circle

punto de tangencia *(p. 508)* El punto en donde una recta tangente intersecta a un círculo

polyhedron *(p. 614)* A solid that is bounded by polygons

poliedro *(p. 614)* Un sólido que está encerrado por polígonos

population density *(p. 600)* A measure of how many people live within a given area

postulate *(p. 12)* A rule that is accepted without proof See axiom.

preimage *(p. 167)* The original figure before a transformation

probability distribution *(p. 716)* A function that gives the probability of each possible value of a random variable

probability of an event *(p. 673)* A measure of the likelihood, or chance, that an event will occur

probability experiment *(p. 672)* An action, or trial, that has varying results

proof *(p. 94)* A logical argument that uses deductive reasoning to show that a statement is true

Pythagorean triple *(p. 444)* A set of three positive integers a, b, and c that satisfy the equation $c^2 = a^2 + b^2$

densidad de población *(p. 600)* Medición de la cantidad de personas que habitan un área dada

postulado *(p. 12)* Una regla que es aceptada sin demostración Ver axioma.

preimagen *(p. 167)* La figura original antes de una transformación

distribución de probabilidad *(p. 716)* Una función que da la probabilidad de cada valor posible de una variable aleatoria

probabilidad de un evento *(p. 673)* Una medida de la probabilidad o posibilidad de que ocurrirá un evento

experimento de probabilidad *(p. 672)* Una acción o prueba que tiene resultados variables

prueba *(p. 94)* Un argumento lógico que usa el razonamiento deductivo para mostrar que un enunciado es verdadero

triple pitagórico *(p. 444)* Un conjunto de tres números enteros positivos a, b, y c que satisfacen la ecuación $c^2 = a^2 + b^2$

R

radian *(p. 581)* A unit of measurement for angles

radius of a circle *(p. 508)* A segment whose endpoints are the center and any point on a circle

radius of a regular polygon *(p. 593)* The radius of a polygon's circumscribed circle

random variable *(p. 716)* A variable whose value is determined by the outcomes of a probability experiment

ray *(p. 5)* A part of a line that consists of an endpoint and all points on the line on one side of the endpoint

rectangle *(p. 374)* A parallelogram with four right angles

reduction *(p. 200)* A dilation in which the scale factor is greater than 0 and less than 1

reflection *(p. 176)* A transformation that uses a line like a mirror to reflect a figure

regular polygon *(p. 348)* A convex polygon that is both equilateral and equiangular

rhombus *(p. 374)* A parallelogram with four congruent sides

right angle *(p. 35)* An angle that has a measure of 90°

radián *(p. 581)* Una unidad de medida para ángulos

radio de un círculo *(p. 508)* Un segmento cuyos puntos extremos son el centro y cualquier punto en un círculo

radio de un polígono regular *(p. 593)* El radio del círculo circunscrito de un polígono

variable aleatoria *(p. 716)* Una variable cuyo valor está determinado por los resultados de un experimento de probabilidad

rayo *(p. 5)* La parte de una recta que consiste en un punto extremo y todos los puntos de la recta de un lado del punto extremo

rectángulo *(p. 374)* Un paralelogramo con cuatro ángulos rectos

reducción *(p. 200)* Una dilatación en donde el factor de escala es mayor que 0 y menor que 1

reflexión *(p. 176)* Una transformación que usa una recta como un espejo para reflejar una figura

polígono regular *(p. 348)* Un polígono convexo que es tanto equilátero como equiángulo

rombo *(p. 374)* Un paralelogramo con cuatro lados congruentes

ángulo recto *(p. 35)* Un ángulo que tiene una medida de 90°

rigid motion *(p. 170)* A transformation that preserves length and angle measure
See congruence transformation.

rotation *(p. 184)* A transformation in which a figure is turned about a fixed point

rotational symmetry *(p. 187)* A figure has rotational symmetry when the figure can be mapped onto itself by a rotation of 180° or less about a point on the figure.

movimiento rígido *(p. 170)* Una transformación que preserva la longitud y medida del ángulo
Ver transformación de congruencia.

rotación *(p. 184)* Una transformación en la cual una figura gira sobre un punto fijo

simetría de rotación *(p. 187)* Una figura tiene simetría de rotación cuando la figura puede superponerse sobre sí misma mediante una rotación de 180° o menos a un punto de la figura.

S

sample space *(p. 672)* The set of all possible outcomes for an experiment

scale factor *(p. 200)* The ratio of the lengths of the corresponding sides of the image and the preimage of a dilation

secant *(p. 508)* A line that intersects a circle in two points

secant segment *(p. 549)* A segment that contains a chord of a circle and has exactly one endpoint outside the circle

sector of a circle *(p. 587)* The region bounded by two radii of the circle and their intercepted arc

segment *(p. 5)* A part of a line that consists of two endpoints and all points on the line between the endpoints
See line segment.

segment bisector *(p. 20)* A point, ray, line, line segment, or plane that intersects the segment at its midpoint

segments of a chord *(p. 548)* The segments formed from two chords that intersect in the interior of a circle

semicircle *(p. 516)* An arc with endpoints that are the endpoints of a diameter

sides of an angle *(p. 36)* The rays of an angle

similar arcs *(p. 519)* Arcs that have the same measure

similar figures *(p. 208)* Geometric figures that have the same shape but not necessarily the same size; Two geometric figures are similar if and only if there is a similarity transformation that maps one of the figures to the other.

similar solids *(p. 625)* Two solids of the same type with equal ratios of corresponding linear measures

espacio de muestra *(p. 672)* El conjunto de todos los resultados posibles de un experimento

factor de escala *(p. 200)* La razón de las longitudes de los lados correspondientes de la imagen y la preimagen de una dilatación

secante *(p. 508)* Una recta que intersecta a un círculo en dos puntos

segmento de secante *(p. 549)* Un segmento que contiene una cuerda de un círculo y que tiene exactamente un punto extremo fuera del círculo

sector de un círculo *(p. 587)* La región encerrada por dos radios del círculo y su arco interceptado

segmento *(p. 5)* La parte de una línea que consiste en dos puntos extremos y todos los puntos entre ellos
Ver segmento de recta.

bisectriz de segmento *(p. 20)* Un punto, rayo, recta, segmento de recta o plano que intersecta el segmento en su punto medio

segmentos de una cuerda *(p. 548)* Los segmentos formados a partir de dos cuerdas que se intersectan en el interior de un círculo

semicírculo *(p. 516)* Un arco con puntos extremos que son los puntos extremos de un diámetro

lados de un ángulo *(p. 36)* Los rayos de un ángulo

arcos similares *(p. 519)* Arcos que tienen la misma medida

figuras similares *(p. 208)* Figuras geométricas que tienen la misma forma pero no necesariamente el mismo tamaño; Dos figuras geométricas son similares, sí y solo sí hay una transformación de similitud que relaciona una de las figuras con la otra

sólidos similares *(p. 625)* Dos sólidos del mismo tipo con razones iguales de medidas lineales correspondientes

similarity transformation *(p. 208)* A dilation or a composition of rigid motions and dilations

sine *(p. 472)* For an acute angle of a right triangle, the ratio of the length of the leg opposite the acute angle to the length of the hypotenuse

skew lines *(p. 118)* Lines that do not intersect and are not coplanar

solid of revolution *(p. 656)* A three-dimensional figure that is formed by rotating a two-dimensional shape around an axis

solve a right triangle *(p. 481)* To find all unknown side lengths and angle measures of a right triangle

square *(p. 374)* A parallelogram with four congruent sides and four right angles

standard equation of a circle *(p. 554)* $(x - h)^2 + (y - k)^2 = r^2$, where r is the radius and (h, k) is the center

straight angle *(p. 35)* An angle that has a measure of 180°

subtend *(p. 532)* If the endpoints of a chord or arc lie on the sides of an inscribed angle, then the chord or arc is said to subtend the angle.

supplementary angles *(p. 46)* Two angles whose measures have a sum of 180°

transformación de similitud *(p. 208)* Una dilatación o composición de movimientos rígidos y dilataciones

seno *(p. 472)* Para un ángulo agudo de un triángulo rectángulo, la razón de la longitud del cateto enfrente del ángulo agudo a la longitud de la hipotenusa

rectas sesgadas *(p. 118)* Rectas que no se intersectan y que no son coplanarias

sólido de revolución *(p. 656)* Una figura tridimensional que se forma por la rotación de una forma bidimensional alrededor de un eje

resolver un triángulo recto *(p. 481)* Para encontrar todas las longitudes de los lados y las medidas de los ángulos desconocidas de un triángulo recto

cuadrado *(p. 374)* Un paralelogramo con cuatro lados congruentes y cuatro ángulos rectos

ecuación estándar de un círculo *(p. 554)* $(x - h)^2 + (y - k)^2 = r^2$, donde r es el radio y (h, k) es el centro

ángulo llano *(p. 35)* Un ángulo que tiene una medida de 180°

subtender *(p. 532)* Si los puntos extremos de una cuerda o arco descansan en los lados de un ángulo inscrito, entonces se dice que la cuerda o arco subtiende el ángulo.

ángulos suplementarios *(p. 46)* Dos ángulos cuyas medidas suman 180°

tangent *(p. 466)* For an acute angle of a right triangle, the ratio of the length of the leg opposite the acute angle to the length of the leg adjacent to the acute angle

tangent of a circle *(p. 508)* A line in the plane of a circle that intersects the circle in exactly one point

tangent circles *(p. 509)* Coplanar circles that intersect in one point

tangent segment *(p. 549)* A segment that is tangent to a circle at an endpoint

theorem *(p. 95)* A statement that can be proven

theoretical probability *(p. 673)* The ratio of the number of favorable outcomes to the total number of outcomes when all outcomes are equally likely

transformation *(p. 167)* A function that moves or changes a figure in some way to produce a new figure

tangente *(p. 466)* Para un ángulo agudo de un triángulo rectángulo, la razón de la longitud del cateto enfrente del ángulo agudo a la longitud del cateto adyacente al ángulo agudo

tangente de un círculo *(p. 508)* Una recta en el plano de un círculo que intersecta el círculo en exactamente un punto

círculos tangentes *(p. 509)* Círculos coplanarios que se intersectan en un punto

segmento de tangente *(p. 549)* Un segmento que es tangente a un círculo en un punto extremo

teorema *(p. 95)* Un enunciado que puede comprobarse

probabilidad teórica *(p. 673)* La razón del número de resultados favorables con respecto al número total de resultados cuando todos los resultados son igualmente probables

transformación *(p. 167)* Una función que mueve o cambia una figura de cierta manera para producir una nueva figura

English-Spanish Glossary

translation *(p. 168)* A transformation that moves every point of a figure the same distance in the same direction

translation vector *(p. 168)* A vector that describes the direction and magnitude, or size, of a translation

transversal *(p. 120)* A line that intersects two or more coplanar lines at different points

trapezoid *(p. 384)* A quadrilateral with exactly one pair of parallel sides

trigonometric ratio *(p. 466)* A ratio of the lengths of two sides in a right triangle

truth table *(p. 66)* A table that shows the truth values for a hypothesis, conclusion, and conditional statement

truth value *(p. 66)* True (T) or false (F)

two-column proof *(p. 94)* A type of proof that has numbered statements and corresponding reasons that show an argument in a logical order

two-way table *(p. 680)* A frequency table that displays data collected from one source that belong to two different categories

traslación *(p. 168)* Una transformación que mueve cada punto de una figura la misma distancia en la misma dirección

vector de traslación *(p. 168)* Un vector que describe la dirección y magnitud, o tamaño, de una traslación

transversal *(p. 120)* Una recta que intersecta dos o más rectas coplanarias en puntos distintos

trapecio *(p. 384)* Un cuadrilátero con exactamente un par de lados paralelos

razón trigonométrica *(p. 466)* Una razón de las longitudes de dos lados en un triángulo recto

tabla de verdad *(p. 66)* Una tabla que muestra los verdaderos valores para una hipótesis, conclusión y enunciado condicional

valor de verdad *(p. 66)* Verdadero (V) o falso (F)

prueba de dos columnas *(p. 94)* Un tipo de prueba que tiene enunciados numerados y motivos correspondientes que muestran un argumento en un orden lógico

tabla de doble entrada *(p. 680)* Una tabla de frecuencia que muestra los datos recogidos de una fuente que pertenece a dos categorías distintas

undefined terms *(p. 4)* Words that do not have formal definitions, but there is agreement about what they mean
In geometry, the words *point*, *line*, and *plane* are undefined terms.

términos no definidos *(p. 4)* Palabras que no tienen definiciones formales, pero hay un consenso acerca de lo que significan
En geometría, las palabras *punto*, *línea* y *plano* son términos no definidos.

vertex angle *(p. 244)* The angle formed by the legs of an isosceles triangle

vertex of an angle *(p. 36)* The common endpoint of two rays

vertex of a polyhedron *(p. 614)* A point of a polyhedron where three or more edges meet

vertical angles *(p. 48)* Two angles whose sides form two pairs of opposite rays

volume *(p. 622)* The number of cubic units contained in the interior of a solid

ángulo del vértice *(p. 244)* El ángulo formado por los catetos de un triángulo isósceles

vértice de un ángulo *(p. 36)* El punto extremo que dos rayos tienen en común

vértice de un poliedro *(p. 614)* Un punto de un poliedro donde se encuentran tres o más bordes

ángulos verticales *(p. 48)* Dos ángulos cuyos lados forman dos pares de rayos opuestos

volumen *(p. 622)* El número de unidades cúbicas contenidas en el interior de u sólido

Index

A

AA. *See* Angle-Angle
AAS. *See* Angle-Angle-Side
Absolute value, 2
Acute angles
   defined, 35
   measuring, 37
Acute triangles
   circles circumscribed about, 299
   defined, 222
   identifying, 447
   orthocenter of, 309
Addition Property of Equality, 86–87, 89
Adjacent angles, 46, 48
Adjacent arcs, 517
Algebraic Properties of Equality, 85–92
   defined, 86
   using, 86–89
Algebraic reasoning, 85–92
Alternate exterior angles, 120
Alternate Exterior Angles Converse (Thm. 3.7), 134
Alternate Exterior Angles Theorem (Thm. 3.3), 125
Alternate interior angles, 120
Alternate Interior Angles Converse (Thm. 3.6), 133
Alternate Interior Angles Theorem (Thm. 3.2), 124
Altitude of cones, 636
Altitude of triangles, 307–314
   defined, 307, 309, 311
   drawing, 307
   using, 309
Ambiguous case, 493
Angle(s). *See also specific types of angles*
   circumscribed, 542–543
   classifying types of, 35, 37
   constructing, 35–44
      bisecting angles, 40
      copying angles, 38, 270
      inscribed angles, 531
   defined, 36
   identifying, 124
   inscribed, 531–538
      constructing, 531
      defined, 532
      using, 532–533
   interior and exterior of, 36
   interpreting, 49
   measuring (*See* Angle measures)
   naming, 36
   pairs of (*See* Angle pairs)
   proving statements about, 93–98, 100–104
   sides of, 36
   vertex of, 36
Angle Addition Postulate (Post. 1.4), 39, 88
Angle Bisector Theorem (Thm. 6.3), 292
Angle bisectors, 289–296
   constructing, 40
   defined, 40, 292, 311
   drawing, 289
   finding angle measures with, 40
   two-column proof for, 96
   using theorems of, 292
Angle measures, 35–44
   Angle Addition Postulate (Post. 1.4) on, 39, 88
   angle bisectors and, 40
   in angle pairs, 47, 49
   in circles, 540–541
   classification of angles by, 35, 37
   of congruent angles, 38
   defined, 37
   in degrees, 35, 581
   of kites, 387
   of polygons, 345–354
      exterior, 349
      finding sums of, 345–346, 348–349
      finding unknown, 347, 349
      interior, 345–348
      regular, 593
      using, 346–348
   properties of equality with, 88
   in radians, 581
   of rhombuses, 376
   of triangles, 221–228
      analyzing, 221, 321
      classifying triangles by, 222
      comparing, 323, 329–330
      finding, 224–225, 245, 480
      ordering, 324
Angle of climb, 470
Angle of depression, 475
Angle of elevation, 468, 475
Angle of rotation, 184
Angle pairs, 45–52
   adjacent vs. nonadjacent, 46, 48
   complementary, 46–47
   finding angle measures in, 47, 49
   formed by transversals, 117–122
      alternate exterior, 120
      alternate interior, 120
      consecutive interior, 120
      corresponding, 120
   identifying, 45–46, 48
   linear, 48
   supplementary, 46–47
   vertical, 48
Angle-Angle (AA) Similarity Theorem (Thm. 8.3), 411–416
   vs. other similarity theorems, 421
   using, 412–413
Angle-Angle-Side (AAS) Congruence Theorem (Thm. 5.11), 259–266
   proof of, 261
   using, 263
Angles Inside the Circle Theorem (Thm. 10.15), 541
Angles Outside the Circle Theorem (Thm. 10.16), 541
Angle-Side-Angle (ASA) Congruence Theorem (Thm. 5.10), 259–266
   constructing copies of triangles using, 262
   proof of, 260
   using, 262
Apothem, of regular polygons, 591, 593
Arc(s)
   center of, 38
   radius of, 38
Arc Addition Postulate (Post. 10.1), 517
Arc lengths, 577–584
   defined, 579
   finding, 577, 579
   formulas for, 579
   using, 579–580
Arc measures, 515–522
   of adjacent arcs, 517
   of congruent arcs, 518
   finding from angle relationships, 540–541
   finding from congruent chords, 524
   of intercepted arcs, 533
   of minor and major arcs, 516
   of similar arcs, 519
Area. *See also* Surface area
   of circles, 585–590
      finding, 586

formula for, 586
of cross sections, 617
of kites, 592
modeling with, 599–604
of parallelograms, formula for, 29
of polygons
    in coordinate plane, 27–34
    formulas for, 29
    regular, 591–598
    similar, 405, 612
of rectangles, formula for, 29
of rhombuses, 592
of squares, formula for, 29
of triangles
    finding, 2, 486, 576
    formula for, 29, 486

Areal density, 602
Areas of Similar Polygons (Thm. 8.2), 405
Arithmetic mean, 464
Arithmetic sequences, equations for, 60
ASA. *See* Angle-Side-Angle
Axioms, 12. *See also* Postulates
Axis of revolution, 656
Axis of symmetry, 561

B

Base(s)
    of cones, 635–637
    of cylinders, 621, 623
    of isosceles triangles, 244
    of prisms, 614, 621–622
    of pyramids, 614, 616, 630, 633, 635
    of trapezoids, 384
Base angles
    of isosceles triangles, 244
    of trapezoids, 384
Base Angles Theorem (Thm. 5.6), 244–245
Bayes' Theorem, 691
Between, 14
Biconditional statements, 65
Binomial distributions, 715–720
    constructing, 718
    defined, 718
Binomial experiments, 718
Binomials, multiplying, 506
Birthday problem, 713
Bisectors
    angle, 289–296
        constructing, 40
        defined, 40, 292, 311
        drawing, 289
        finding angle measures with, 40
        two-column proof for, 96
        using theorems of, 292

perpendicular, 289–296
    analyzing, 297
    and chords, 525–526
    constructing, 141
    defined, 141, 290, 311
    diagrams of, 290
    drawing, 289
    using theorems of, 291
    writing equations of, 293
segment, 20–21
of triangles, 297–307
    analyzing, 297
    circumcenter and, 298–300
    incenter and, 301–302

C

Cavalieri, Bonaventura, 622
Cavalieri's Principle, 622–623, 644
Center
    of arcs, 38
    of circles, 508
    of regular polygons, 591, 593
    of spheres, 642
Center of dilation, 200, 210
Center of gravity, 314
Center of rotation, 184, 187
Center of symmetry, 187
Central angles
    of circles
        constructing, 531
        defined, 515–516
    of regular polygons, 593
Centroid, of triangles, 308
    defined, 306, 308, 311
    finding, 308
    using, 308
Centroid Theorem (Thm. 6.7), 308
Ceva's Theorem, 433
Chords of circles, 523–530
    defined, 508, 524
    identifying, 508
    making conjectures about, 523
    segments of, 547–552
    using congruent, 524
        to find arc measures, 524
        to find radius, 527
Chords of spheres, 642
Circle(s)
    angle relationships in, 539–546
        angle and arc measures in, 540–541
        circumscribed angles, 542–543
    arcs in (*See* Arc lengths; Arc measures)
    area of, 585–590
        finding, 586
        formula for, 586

center of, 508
chords of (*See* Chords)
circumference of, 577–584
    arc length and, 579
    defined, 578
    formula for, 578
congruent, 518
in coordinate plane, 553–558
as cross sections of cones, 615
as cross sections of spheres, 615
defined, 508
diameter of, 508, 525
equations of, 553–558
    deriving, 553
    writing, 554–555
    graphing, 554–555
great, 92
    defined, 129
    in spherical geometry, 129
inscribed angles and polygons in, 531–538
    constructing, 531
    using, 532–533
inscribed triangles in, 299–300
inscribed within triangles, 302
lines and segments intersecting, 507–514 (*See also* Tangent(s))
    identifying, 508–509
radius of (*See* Radius, of circles)
segment relationships in, 547–552
similar, 519
Circular arcs, 515
Circular cones. *See* Cones
Circumcenter, of triangles
    defined, 298, 311
    finding, 300
    using, 298–300
Circumcenter Theorem (Thm. 6.5), 298
Circumference, 577–584
    arc length and, 579
    defined, 578
    formula for, 578
Circumscribed Angle Theorem (Thm. 10.17), 542
Circumscribed angles, 542–543
    defined, 542
    using, 542–543
Circumscribed circles
    defined, 534
    about polygons, 534–535
    about squares, 535
    about triangles, 299–300
Climb, angle of, 470
Clockwise rotations, 184, 187
Coincident lines, 117
Collinear points, 4

Collinear rays, 5
Collinear segments, 5
Combinations, 707–714
   counting, 710
   defined, 710
   finding probabilities using, 711
   using formula for, 710
Common external tangents, 509
Common internal tangents, 509
Common tangents, 509
Compass, 11, 38, 40
Complementary angles
   defined, 46, 101
   sine and cosine of, 473
   using, 46–47
Complements, of events, 674
   defined, 674
   finding probabilities of, 674
Completing the square, solving quadratic equations by, 506
Component form, of vectors, 169
Composite solids
   surface area of, 638
   volume of, 624, 632, 638, 645, 658
Composition Theorem (Thm. 4.1), 170
Compositions of transformations
   defined, 170
   performing, 170–171
   with rotations, 186
Compound events, 702
Compound inequalities, writing, 288
Concave polygons, 28, 353
Concentric circles, 509
Conclusions, in conditional statements, 61–62
Concurrency, point of, 298
Concurrent lines, 298
Concurrent rays, 298
Concurrent segments, 298
Conditional probabilities, 685–692
   decision making using, 689
   defined, 686
   finding, 685–688
      using formula, 687
      using sample spaces, 686
      using two-way tables, 686
   and independent events, 695
Conditional relative frequencies, 682
Conditional statements, 61–70
   biconditional, 65
   defined, 61–62
   definitions in, 64
   identifying true vs. false, 61, 66
   if-then form of, 61–62
   negation of, 62
   related, 63
   truth value of, 66
   writing, 62–64
      biconditional, 65
      definitions in, 64
      negation of, 62
      related, 63
Cones
   cross sections of, 615
   frustum of, 639
   lateral surface of, 636
   right
      defined, 636
      surface area of, 636
   surface area of, 635–640
      finding, 636
      formula for, 636
      right, 636
   volume of, 635–640
      finding, 635, 637
      formula for, 637
      using, 638
Congruence, properties of
   naming, 95
   proving, 95, 231
   using, 95–96, 231
Congruence statements, 230
Congruence symbol, 13
Congruence transformations, 191–198
   defined, 193
   describing, 193
   theorems about, 194–195
Congruent angles, 38, 100–102, 104
Congruent arcs, 518
Congruent Central Angles Theorem (Thm. 10.4), 518
Congruent chords, using, 524
   to find arc measures, 524
   to find radius, 527
Congruent circles, 518
Congruent Circles Theorem (Thm. 10.3), 518
Congruent Complements Theorem (Thm. 2.5), 102
Congruent Corresponding Chords Theorem (Thm. 10.6), 524
Congruent figures. *See also specific types of figures*
   corresponding parts of, 230–231
   defined, 192, 230
   identifying, 192, 231
   using properties of, 231
Congruent Parts of Parallel Lines Corollary, 361
Congruent polygons, 229–234
   corresponding parts of, 230–231
   proving congruence of, 231
   using properties of, 231
Congruent segments
   defined, 13
   identifying, 13
   midpoints of, 20
Congruent Supplements Theorem (Thm. 2.4), 101
Congruent triangles
   corresponding parts of, 230
   identifying, 261
   proving congruence of
      by ASA and AAS, 259–266
      by Properties of Triangle Congruence (Thm. 5.3), 231–232
      by SAS, 235–242
      by SSS, 251–258
      summary of methods for, 263
   using, 267–272
      for measurement, 269
Conjectures
   about chords, 523
   defined, 71–72
   Goldbach's Conjecture, 98
   making and testing, 73
   about parallel lines, 123
Consecutive integers, 73
Consecutive interior angles, 120
Consecutive Interior Angles Converse (Thm. 3.8), 134
Consecutive Interior Angles Theorem (Thm. 3.4), 125
Consecutive vertices, 346
Constant of proportionality, 581
Constructions
   of binomial distributions, 718
   of bisecting angles, 40
   of bisecting segments, 21
   circumscribing circles about triangles, 300
   copying angles, 38, 270
   copying segments, 11
   copying triangles
      using ASA, 262
      using SAS, 240
      using SSS, 256
   defined, 11
   of dilations, 202
   of equilateral triangles, 246
   of inscribed angles and central angles, 531
   inscribing circles within triangles, 302
   of parallel lines, 133
   of perpendicular bisectors, 141
   of perpendicular lines, 139, 141

of points along directed line
  segments, 429
of probability distributions, 716
proving, 270
of squares inscribed in circles, 535
of tangents to circles, 511
Contingency tables. *See* Two-way
  tables
Contradiction, proof by, 321–328
  defined, 322
  writing, 322
Contrapositive, of conditional
  statements, 63, 66
**Contrapositive of the Triangle
  Proportionality Theorem,**
  429
Converses of conditional statements
  defined, 63
  determining truth of, 131
  truth table for, 66
  writing, 63
Converses of theorems
  Alternate Exterior Angles Converse
    (Thm. 3.7), 134
  Alternate Interior Angles Converse
    (Thm. 3.6), 133
  Consecutive Interior Angles
    Converse (Thm. 3.8), 134
  Converse of the Angle Bisector
    Theorem (Thm. 6.4), 292
  Converse of the Base Angles
    Theorem (Thm. 5.7), 244
  Converse of the Hinge Theorem
    (Thm. 6.13), 330–331
  Converse of the Perpendicular
    Bisector Theorem (Thm. 6.2),
    290
  Converse of the Pythagorean
    Theorem (Thm. 9.2), 446
  Converse of the Triangle
    Proportionality Theorem
    (Thm. 8.7), 428
  Corresponding Angles Converse
    (Thm. 3.5), 132
  Isosceles Trapezoid Base Angles
    Converse (Thm. 7.15), 385
  Parallelogram Diagonals Converse
    (Thm. 7.10), 366
  Parallelogram Opposite Angles
    Converse (Thm. 7.8), 364
  Parallelogram Opposite Sides
    Converse (Thm. 7.7), 364
  Perpendicular Chord Bisector
    Converse (Thm. 10.8), 526
Convex polygons, 28, 346–349
Coordinate (of point), 12
Coordinate geometry, 368, 378

Coordinate plane
  circles in, 553–558
    graphing, 554–555
  figures in
    dilating, 201
    placing, 274
    rotating, 185
    translating, 166, 169
  parallelograms in
    identifying, 368, 378
    using, 359
  polygons in, perimeter and area of,
    27–34
  solids of revolution in, 658
  trapezoids in
    identifying, 384
    using midsegments of, 386
  triangles in
    classifying, 223
    midsegments of, 316
Coordinate proofs, 273–278
  defined, 274
  writing, 273, 275–276
Coordinate rules
  for dilations, 201
  for reflections, 177
  for rotations about the origin, 185
Coplanar circles, 509
Coplanar lines, 5
Coplanar points, 4
Coplanar rays, 5
Coplanar segments, 5
Corollaries to theorems
  Congruent Parts of Parallel Lines
    Corollary, 361
  Corollary to the Base Angles
    Theorem (Cor. 5.2), 245
  Corollary to the Converse of the
    Base Angles Theorem
    (Cor. 5.3), 245
  Corollary to the Polygon Interior
    Angles Theorem (Cor. 7.1),
    347
  Corollary to the Triangle Sum
    Theorem (Cor. 5.1), 225
  defined, 225
  Rectangle Corollary (Cor. 7.3), 375
  Rhombus Corollary (Cor. 7.2), 375
  Square Corollary (Cor. 7.4), 375
Corresponding angles
  of congruent polygons, 230
  defined, 120
  of similar polygons, 402
**Corresponding Angles Converse
  (Thm. 3.5),** 132
**Corresponding Angles Theorem
  (Thm. 3.1),** 124

Corresponding lengths, of similar
  polygons, 403
Corresponding parts
  of congruent polygons, 230–231
  defined, 230
  identifying and using, 230–231
  of similar polygons, 402–403
Corresponding sides, of congruent
  polygons, 230
Cosine ratios, 471–478
  calculating, 471
  of complementary angles, 473
  defined, 472
  finding, 472
  inverse, 480
  of special right triangles, 474
  using, 473–475
Counterclockwise rotations, 184–185,
  187
Counterexamples, 73
Cross sections of solids, 613–620
  defined, 613, 615
  describing, 613, 615
  drawing, 616
  finding perimeter and area of, 617
Cubes
  cross sections of, 615
  sum of, 108
  writing equations for, 619
Cubic units, 622
Cylinders
  cross sections of, 615
  right, volume of, 621
  similar, surface area of, 625
  volume of, 621–628
    finding, 621–623
    formula for, 110, 623

D

Decagrams, 52
Decay, exponential, 228
Decision making, with conditional
  probabilities, 689
Deductive reasoning, 71–78. *See also*
  Proofs
  defined, 74
  vs. inductive reasoning, 75
  using, 74–76
Defined terms, 5
Definitions, writing as conditional
  statements, 64
Degrees
  angle measures in, 35
  converting between radians and, 581
Density
  areal, 602
  defined, 650

finding, 649
formula for, 650
population, 599–604
defined, 600
finding, 600
formula for, 600
Dependent events, 693–700
defined, 697
identifying, 693
probability of, 697
Depression, angle of, 475
Detachment, Law of, 75
Diagonals
of parallelograms
finding lengths of, 367
using properties of, 376–377
of polygons, 346
of quadrilaterals, 373
of rectangles, 377
Diagrams, 79–84
identifying postulates using, 81
interpreting, 49, 79, 82
sketching, 82
Venn, 69
of parallelograms, 374
using, 71
Diameter
of circles
and chords, 525
defined, 508
identifying, 508
of spheres, 642–643
Dilations, 199–206
center of, 200, 210
comparing figures to, 401
constructing, 202
coordinate rule for, 201
defined, 200
identifying, 200
scale factors of, 200
finding, 203
negative, 202
of triangles, 199, 201
Directed line segments
constructing points along, 429
defined, 150
partitioning, 150
Directrix, of parabolas, 560–563
Disjoint events
defined, 702
identifying, 701
probability of, 701–706
Distance
arc length and, 580
from point to line
defined, 140
finding, 140, 153

between points
defined, 12
finding with Distance Formula, 23
Distance Formula, 19–26
defined, 23
using, 220
to find distances between points, 23
to find perimeters and areas, 29
to find side lengths of triangles, 223
Distributive Property, 86–87
Division Property of Equality, 86–87
Dodecagons, 391
Dodecagrams, 52
Dodecahedrons, 619
Domes, geodesic, 242

E

Edges, of polyhedrons, 614
Elevation, angle of, 468, 475
Endpoints, 5
Enlargement, 200
Epidemiologic triangles, 241
Equal sign, 13
Equations. *See also specific types of equations*
solving, 86–87
using structure, 344
with variables on both sides, 60, 220
Equiangular polygons, 348
Equiangular triangles, 222
Equidistant Chords Theorem (Thm. 10.9), 527
Equidistant points, 290
Equilateral polygons, 348
Equilateral triangles, 243–250
constructing, 246
defined, 222
using, 246–247
Equivalent statements, 63, 66
Euclidean geometry, 92, 122
Euclid's proof of Pythagorean Theorem, 272
Even numbers, Goldbach's Conjecture on, 98
Events
complements of, 674
compound, 702
defined, 672
describing, 671
disjoint and overlapping, 701–706
independent and dependent, 693–700

probability of (*See* Probabilities)
Experimental probabilities, 675
Experiments
binomial, 718
probability, 672
Exponential decay, 228
Exponential growth, 228
Exterior, of angles, 36
Exterior Angle Inequality Theorem, 327
Exterior Angle Theorem (Thm. 5.2), 224
Exterior angles
formed by transversals, 120
of polygons, 349
finding sums of, 349
finding unknown, 349
using, 349
of triangles, 224
External segments, 549
External Tangent Congruence Theorem (Thm. 10.2), 510
External tangents, 509

F

Faces, of polyhedrons, 614
Favorable outcomes, 673
Figures. *See also specific types of figures*
comparing to dilations, 401
transformations of (*See* Transformations)
Flow proofs. *See* Flowchart proofs
Flowchart proofs
defined, 100
writing, 99–102
Focus, of parabolas, 560–563
Formulas
for arc lengths, 579
for area
of circles, 586
of kites, 592
of parallelograms, 29
of rectangles, 29
of regular polygons, 594
of rhombuses, 592
of sectors of circles, 587
of squares, 29
of triangles, 29, 486
for circumference, 578
for combinations, 710
for conditional probabilities, 687
for density, 650
Distance Formula, 19–26, 29, 220, 223
Midpoint Formula, 19–26, 220
for permutations, 709

for population density, 600
for surface area
   of cones, 636
   of spheres, 642
   using, 652
for volume
   of cones, 637
   of cylinders, 110, 623
   of prisms, 622
   of pyramids, 630
   of spheres, 644
   using, 650–651

45°-45°-90° (isosceles) right triangles
defined, 452
finding side lengths of, 452
finding sine and cosine of, 474

45°-45°-90° Triangle Theorem (Thm. 9.4), 452

Frequencies
conditional, 682
joint, 680–681
marginal, 680–681
relative, 681–682

Frequency tables. *See* Two-way tables

Frustum
of cones, 639
of pyramids, 633

G

Geodesic domes, 242
Geometric mean, 460–461
and arithmetic mean, 464
defined, 460
using, 461

Geometric Mean (Altitude) Theorem (Thm. 9.7), 460

Geometric Mean (Leg) Theorem (Thm. 9.8), 460

Geometric relationships, proving, 99–108

Geometry
coordinate, 368, 378
Euclidean, 92, 122
hyperbolic, 122
non-Euclidean, 122
spherical, 92, 122, 129

Glide reflections, 178
Goldbach's Conjecture, 98
Golden ratio, 409

Graphing
circles, 554–555
parabolas, 559–566

Gravity, center of, 314

Great circle(s), 92
defined, 129
of spheres, 642
in spherical geometry, 129

Great circle routes, 522
Growth, exponential, 228

H

Height
of cones, 636–638, 656
of cylinders, 621, 623, 638, 656–657
of prisms, 621–622, 624
of pyramids, 630

Hemispheres, 642
Hendecagrams, 52
Hexagonal patterns, 182

Hexagons
as cross sections of prisms, 615
line symmetry of, 179

Hexagrams, 52
Hinge Theorem (Thm. 6.12), 330–331
Histograms, 670
Horizontal axis of symmetry, 561
Horizontal component, of vectors, 169
Horizontal lines, reflecting in, 176
Hyperbolic geometry, 122
Hypotenuse, 253
Hypotenuse-Leg (HL) Congruence Theorem (Thm. 5.9), 253–254

Hypotheses
in conditional statements, 61–62
in proofs, 100

I

Icosahedra, 242, 619
If-then form, of conditional statements, 61–62
Images, 167

Incenter, of triangles
defined, 301, 311
using, 301–302

Incenter Theorem (Thm. 6.6), 301
Included angles, 236

Independent events, 693–700
defined, 694
identifying, 693–696
probability of, 694

Indirect measurements, using geometric mean, 461

Indirect proofs, 321–328
defined, 322
writing, 322

Inductive reasoning, 71–78
vs. deductive reasoning, 75
defined, 72
proving by, 350
using, 72–73, 75

Inequalities
in one triangle, 321–328
in two triangles, 329–334
writing compound, 288

Inscribed angles, 531–538
constructing, 531
defined, 532
using, 532–533

Inscribed Angles of a Circle Theorem (Thm. 10.11), 533

Inscribed circles, within triangles, 302

Inscribed polygons, 531–538
defined, 534
using, 534–535

Inscribed Quadrilateral Theorem (Thm. 10.13), 534

Inscribed Right Triangle Theorem (Thm. 10.12), 534

Integers, consecutive, 73

Intercepted arcs
defined, 532
finding measure of, 533

Interior, of angles, 36

Interior angles
formed by transversals, 120
of polygons, 345–348
   finding sums of, 345–346
   finding unknown, 347
   using, 346–348
of triangles, 224

Internal tangents, 509

Intersecting lines
classifying, 117–118
reflections in, 195

Intersections
defined, 6
describing, 3
of lines and planes, 6
postulates involving, 80–81
of two events, 702
of two planes, 6

Inverse, of conditional statements, 63, 66

Inverse cosine, 480

Inverse of the Triangle Proportionality Theorem, 429

Inverse sine, 480
Inverse tangent, 480
Inverse trigonometric ratios, 480

Isosceles (45°-45°-90°) right triangles
defined, 452
finding side lengths of, 452
finding sine and cosine of, 474
in Spiral of Theodorus, 456

Isosceles Trapezoid Base Angles Converse (Thm. 7.15), 385

Isosceles Trapezoid Base Angles Theorem (Thm. 7.14), 385

Isosceles Trapezoid Diagonals Theorem (Thm. 7.16), 385
Isosceles trapezoids, 384–385
  defined, 384
  using properties of, 385
Isosceles triangles, 243–250
  Base Angles Theorem (Thm. 5.6) on, 244–245
  defined, 222, 244
  legs and base of, 244
  median and altitude of, 311
  reasoning about, 243
  using, 246–247

J

Joint frequencies, 680–681
Joint relative frequencies, 681

K

Kite Diagonals Theorem (Thm. 7.18), 387
Kite Opposite Angles Theorem (Thm. 7.19), 387
Kites, 383–392
  angle measures in, 387
  area of, 592
  defined, 387
  properties of, 383, 387

L

Lateral faces, of pyramids, 616
Lateral surface of cones, 636
Law of Cosines, 485–494
  defined, 489
  solving triangles using, 489–490
Law of Cosines (Thm. 9.10), 489
Law of Detachment, 75
Law of forces. See Parallelogram law of forces
Law of reflection, 265
Law of Sines, 485–494
  ambiguous case of, 493
  defined, 487
  solving triangles using, 487–488
Law of Sines (Thm. 9.9), 487
Law of Syllogism, 75
Laws of Logic, 75
Legs
  of isosceles triangles, 244
  of right triangles
    defined, 253
    finding with sine and cosine ratios, 473–474
    finding with tangent ratios, 467
  of trapezoids, 384

Line(s), 3–10. See also Parallel lines; Perpendicular lines
  coincident, 117
  concurrent, 298
  coplanar, 5
  distance from point to, 140, 153
  horizontal and vertical, reflecting in, 176
  intersecting
    classifying, 117–118
    reflections in, 195
  intersecting circles, 507–514
    (See also Tangent(s))
    identifying, 508–509
  intersections of planes with, 6
  naming, 4
  pairs of, 117–122
    identifying, 118–119
  postulates involving, 80–81
  skew, 117–118
  slope of (See Slope of line)
  as undefined terms, 4
  writing equations of, 116, 152
Line Intersection Postulate (Post. 2.3), 80–81
Line of reflection, 176
Line of symmetry, 179
Line perpendicular to plane, 82
Line segments
  in circles, 547–552
  collinear, 5
  comparing for congruence, 13
  concurrent, 298
  congruent
    defined, 13
    identifying, 13
    midpoints of, 20
  constructing, 11–18
    bisecting segments, 21
    copying segments, 11
  coplanar, 5
  defined, 5
  directed
    constructing points along, 429
    defined, 150
    partitioning of, 150
  finding (measuring) lengths of, 11–18
    with Distance Formula, 19–26
    with Ruler Postulate (Post. 1.1), 12
    with Segment Addition Postulate (Post. 1.2), 14–15, 89
    in triangles, 428
  intersecting circles, 507–514
    (See also Tangent(s))
    identifying, 508–509

  midpoints of, 19–26
    defined, 20
    finding, 19, 22
    segment bisectors at, 20–21
  naming, 5
  properties of equality with, 88–89
  proving statements about, 93–98
  of triangles, finding lengths of, 428
Line symmetry, 179
Linear equations
  slope-intercept form of, 152
  solutions to systems of two, 153
  writing, 116
Linear Pair Perpendicular Theorem (Thm. 3.10), 142
Linear Pair Postulate (Post. 2.8), 103
Linear pairs, of angles, 48
Line-Point Postulate (Post. 2.2), 80
Lines Perpendicular to a Transversal Theorem (Thm. 3.12), 143
Literal equations, rewriting, 60
Logic, Laws of, 75
Logically equivalent statements, 66

M

Magnitude, 168
Major arcs, 516
Marginal frequencies, 680–681
Marginal relative frequencies, 681
Mass, and density, 650–652
Mathematical induction, defined, 350
Measure of an Inscribed Angle Theorem (Thm. 10.10), 532
Measure of major arcs, 516
Measure of minor arcs, 516
Measurements. See also Angle measures; Arc measures
  congruent triangles used for, 269
  indirect, using geometric mean, 461
Medians, of triangles, 307–314
  defined, 306–308, 311
  drawing, 307
  using, 308
Midpoint Formula, 19–26
  defined, 22
  using, 22, 220
Midpoints, of line segments, 19–26
  defined, 20
  finding, 19, 22
  segment bisectors at, 20–21
Midsegment triangles, 316
Midsegments
  of trapezoids, 386
  of triangles, 315–320
    defined, 316
    drawing, 315

Triangle Midsegment Theorem (Thm. 6.8) on, 317–318
    using in coordinate plane, 316
Minor arcs, 516
Modeling
    with area, 599–604
    with solids of revolution, 655
    with surface area and volume, 649–654
Multiplication, of binomials, 506
Multiplication Property of Equality, 86
Mutually exclusive events. *See* Disjoint events

***n* factorial,** 709
Narrative proofs. *See* Paragraph proofs
Negation, of conditional statements, 62
Negative scale factors, 202
***n*-gon,** 28
Nicomachus's Theorem, 108
Nonadjacent angles, 46
Nonagrams, 52
Nonconsecutive vertices, 346
Non-Euclidean geometry, 122
Nonrigid transformations, 208
***n*-pointed stars,** 52
***n*th term of arithmetic sequence,** 60

Obtuse angles
    defined, 35
    finding trigonometric ratios for, 486
    measuring, 37
Obtuse triangles
    circles circumscribed about, 299
    defined, 222
    identifying, 447
    orthocenter of, 309
Octagonal patterns, 182
Octagons
    finding sums of angle measures in, 346
    rotational symmetry of, 187
Octagrams, 52
Octahedrons, 619
Opposite, of conditional statements. *See* Negation, of conditional statements
Opposite rays, 5
Opposite Sides Parallel and Congruent Theorem (Thm. 7.9), 366
Origin
    as center of dilation, 201

    parabolas with vertex at, 561
    rotations about, coordinate rules for, 185
Orthocenter, of triangles, 309–310
    defined, 309, 311
    finding, 309–310
Outcomes
    counting, 707, 715
    defined, 672
    favorable, 673
Overlapping events
    defined, 702
    identifying, 701
    probability of, 701–706

Pairs
    of angles (*See* Angle pairs)
    of lines, 117–122
        identifying, 118–119
Parabolas, 559–566
    defined, 560
    translations of, 562
    writing equations of, 560–563
Parabolic reflectors, 563
Paragraph proofs
    defined, 103
    writing, 103–104
Parallel lines
    constructing, 133
    defined, 118–119
    identifying, 118–119, 134, 151, 344
    proofs with, 131–138
        Alternate Exterior Angles Theorem (Thm. 3.3), 126
        Alternate Interior Angles Converse (Thm. 3.6), 133
        Corresponding Angles Converse (Thm. 3.5), 132
        Slopes of Parallel Lines Theorem (Thm. 3.13), 421
        Transitive Property of Parallel Lines (Thm. 3.9), 135
    reflections in, 194
    symbol of, 118
    three, proportionality with, 430
    and transversals, 123–130
        making conjectures about, 123
        proving theorems about, 126
        using properties of parallel lines with, 125
    writing equations of, 152
Parallel planes, 118
Parallel Postulate (Post. 3.1), 119, 122
Parallelogram(s)
    area of, 29
    in coordinate plane
        identifying, 368, 378

        using, 359
        defined, 355–356
    diagonals of
        finding lengths of, 367
        using properties of, 376–377
    identifying and verifying, 364–367
    lack of line symmetry of, 179
    perimeter of, 29
    properties of, 355–362
        using, 356–358
    proving quadrilaterals are, 363–372
    rotational symmetry of, 187
    side lengths of, 365
    special, 373–382
        classifying, 375
        properties of, 374–377
        types of, 374–375
    symbol of, 30
    writing two-column proof for, 358
Parallelogram Consecutive Angles Theorem (Thm. 7.5), 357
Parallelogram Diagonals Converse (Thm. 7.10), 366
Parallelogram Diagonals Theorem (Thm. 7.6), 356–357
Parallelogram law of forces, 372
Parallelogram Opposite Angles Converse (Thm. 7.8), 364
Parallelogram Opposite Angles Theorem (Thm. 7.4), 356
Parallelogram Opposite Sides Converse (Thm. 7.7), 364
Parallelogram Opposite Sides Theorem (Thm. 7.3), 356
Partitioning, of directed line segments, 150
Patterns
    describing visual, 72
    lines of symmetry in, 182
    venation, 296
Pentagonal prisms, 614
Pentagrams, 52
Percent proportion, 670
Perimeter
    of cross sections, 617
    of polygons
        in coordinate plane, 27–34
        formulas for, 29
        similar, 404
Perimeters of Similar Polygons (Thm. 8.1), 404
Permutations, 707–714
    counting, 708
    defined, 708
    finding probabilities using, 709
    using formula for, 709
Perpendicular Bisector Theorem (Thm. 6.1), 290–291

Perpendicular bisectors, 289–296
   analyzing, 297
   and chords, 525–526
   constructing, 141
   defined, 141, 290, 311
   diagrams of, 290
   drawing, 289
   using theorems of, 291
   writing equations of, 293
Perpendicular Chord Bisector Converse (Thm. 10.8), 526
Perpendicular Chord Bisector Theorem (Thm. 10.7), 525
Perpendicular lines
   constructing, 139, 141
   defined, 64–65, 119
   in Euclidean geometry, 92
   identifying, 119, 151, 344
   proofs with, 139–148
      distance from point to line, 140
      Lines Perpendicular to a Transversal Theorem (Thm. 3.12), 143
      Perpendicular Transversal Theorem (Thm. 3.11), 142
      Slopes of Perpendicular Lines Theorem (Thm. 3.14), 151
   writing equations of, 152, 288
Perpendicular Postulate (Post. 3.2), 119
Perpendicular Transversal Theorem (Thm. 3.11), 142
Plane(s), 3–10
   describing, 3
   intersections of lines with, 6
   intersections of two, 6
   lines perpendicular to, 82
   naming, 4
   parallel, 118
   postulates involving, 80–81
   as undefined terms, 4
Plane figures, 28
Plane Intersection Postulate (Post. 2.7), 80–81
Plane-Line Postulate (Post. 2.6), 80–81
Plane-Point Postulate (Post. 2.5), 80–81
Point(s), 3–10
   coordinate of, 12
   along directed line segments, 429
   distance between, 12, 23
   distance to line from, 140, 153
   equidistant, 290
   naming, 4
   postulates involving, 80–81
   as undefined terms, 4

Point of concurrency, 298
Point of tangency, 508
Polygon Exterior Angles Theorem (Thm. 7.2), 349
Polygon Interior Angles Theorem (Thm. 7.1), 346–347, 350
Polygons. *See also specific types of polygons*
   angle measures of, 345–354
      exterior, 349
      finding sums of, 345–346, 348–349
      finding unknown, 347, 349
      interior, 345–348
      regular, 593
      using, 346–348
   area of
      in coordinate plane, 27–34
      formulas for, 29
      regular, 591–598
      similar, 405
   classifying types of, 28
   concave, 28, 353
   congruent, 229–234
      corresponding parts of, 230–231
      proving congruence of, 231
      using properties of, 231
   convex, 28, 346–349
   corresponding angles of, 230
   defined, 28
   diagonals of, 346
   inscribed, 531–538
      defined, 534
      using, 534–535
   line symmetry of, 179
   naming, 28
   perimeter of
      in coordinate plane, 27–34
      formulas for, 29
      similar, 404
   reflections of, 175
   rotations of, 183
   sides of
      corresponding, 230
      defined, 28
      finding number of, 347
   similar, 401–410
      area of, 405, 612
      corresponding parts of, 402–403
      identifying, 406
      perimeter of, 404
   translations of, 167
   vertices of
      consecutive vs. nonconsecutive, 346
      defined, 28

Polyhedrons
   defined, 614
   in geodesic domes, 242
Population density, 599–604
   defined, 600
   finding, 600
   formula for, 600
Postulates, 79–84
   Angle Addition Postulate (Post. 1.4), 39, 88
   Arc Addition Postulate (Post. 10.1), 517
   defined, 12
   identifying, 80–81
   Line Intersection Postulate (Post. 2.3), 80–81
   Linear Pair Postulate (Post. 2.8), 103
   Line-Point Postulate (Post. 2.2), 80
   Parallel Postulate (Post. 3.1), 119, 122
   Perpendicular Postulate (Post. 3.2), 119
   Plane Intersection Postulate (Post. 2.7), 80–81
   Plane-Line Postulate (Post. 2.6), 80–81
   Plane-Point Postulate (Post. 2.5), 80–81
   Protractor Postulate (Post. 1.3), 37
   Reflection Postulate (Post. 4.2), 178
   Rotation Postulate (Post. 4.3), 186
   Ruler Postulate (Post. 1.1), 12, 29–31
   Segment Addition Postulate (Post. 1.2), 14–15, 89
   Three Point Postulate (Post. 2.4), 80
   Translation Postulate (Post. 4.1), 170
   Two Point Postulate (Post. 2.1), 80
Preimages, 167
Prime numbers, Goldbach's Conjecture on, 98
Prisms
   cross sections of, 615
   naming, 614
   right, volume of, 621
   surface area of, finding, 612
   volume of, 621–628
      finding, 621–623
      formula for, 622
      using, 624
Probabilities
   of complements of events, 674
   of compound events, 702
   conditional, 685–692
   defined, 673
   of dependent events, 697

of disjoint and overlapping events, 701–706
experimental, 675
finding
   using combinations, 711
   using permutations, 709
   using two or more rules, 704
   using two-way tables, 679–684
of independent events, 694
sample spaces and, 671–678
theoretical, 673–674
Probability distributions, 716–718
constructing, 716
defined, 716
interpreting, 717
Probability experiments, 672
Proofs
completing, 93
for constructions, 270
by contradiction, 321–328
coordinate, 273–278
   defined, 274
   writing, 273, 275–276
defined, 93–94
of geometric relationships, 99–108
   flowchart, 99–102
   paragraph, 103–104
by mathematical induction, 350
with parallel lines, 131–138
   Alternate Exterior Angles Theorem (Thm. 3.3), 126
   Alternate Interior Angles Converse (Thm. 3.6), 133
   Corresponding Angles Converse (Thm. 3.5), 132
   Slopes of Parallel Lines Theorem (Thm. 3.13), 421
   Transitive Property of Parallel Lines (Thm. 3.9), 135
with perpendicular lines, 139–148
   distance from point to line, 140
   Lines Perpendicular to a Transversal Theorem (Thm. 3.12), 143
   Perpendicular Transversal Theorem (Thm. 3.11), 142
with segments and angles, 93–98
   flowchart, 99–102
   paragraph, 103–104
   properties of congruence in, 95–96
   two-column, 94–96, 100–101
of similarity, 210
visual, 108
Proofs of theorems
Alternate Exterior Angles Theorem (Thm. 3.3), 126

Angle-Angle-Side (AAS) Congruence Theorem (Thm. 5.11), 261
Angle-Side-Angle (ASA) Congruence Theorem (Thm. 5.10), 260
Circumcenter Theorem (Thm. 6.5), 298
Congruent Supplements Theorem (Thm. 2.4), 101
Converse of the Hinge Theorem (Thm. 6.13), 331
Parallelogram Diagonals Theorem (Thm. 7.6), 358
Parallelogram Opposite Sides Converse (Thm. 7.7), 364
Perpendicular Bisector Theorem (Thm. 6.1), 290
Perpendicular Transversal Theorem (Thm. 3.11), 142
Polygon Interior Angles Theorem (Thm. 7.1), 350
Pythagorean Theorem (Thm. 9.1), 272, 443
Right Angles Congruence Theorem (Thm. 2.3), 100
Side-Angle-Side (SAS) Congruence Theorem (Thm. 5.5), 236
Side-Side-Side (SSS) Congruence Theorem (Thm. 5.8), 252
Side-Side-Side (SSS) Similarity Theorem (Thm. 8.4), 419
Similar Circles Theorem (Thm. 10.5), 519
Slopes of Parallel Lines Theorem (Thm. 3.13), 421
Symmetric Property of Segment Congruence, 95
Triangle Midsegment Theorem (Thm. 6.8), 317
Vertical Angles Congruence Theorem (Thm. 2.6), 103
Properties
Addition Property of Equality, 86–87, 89
Algebraic Properties of Equality, 85–92
Distributive Property, 86–87
Division Property of Equality, 86–87
Multiplication Property of Equality, 86
Reflexive Property, 88
   of Angle Congruence, 96
   of Segment Congruence, 95
Substitution Property of Equality, 86, 88–89

Subtraction Property of Equality, 86–87
Symmetric Property, 88
   of Angle Congruence, 96
   of Segment Congruence, 95
Transitive Property, 88
   of Angle Congruence, 96
   of Segment Congruence, 95
Properties of Angle Congruence (Thm. 2.2), 96
proof of, 96
Properties of Segment Congruence (Thm. 2.1), 95
Properties of Triangle Congruence (Thm. 5.3), 231
Proportion(s)
percent, 670
ratios forming, 400
solving, 442
Proportionality
constant of, 581
finding relationships of, 427
statements of, 402
Proportionality theorems, 427–434
for parallel lines, 430
for triangle angle bisectors, 431
for triangles, 428–429
Protractor Postulate (Post. 1.3), 37
Protractors, 35, 37
Pyramids
cross sections of, 615–616
frustum of, 633
naming, 614
similar, volume of, 632
triangular, 614, 629–631
vertex of, 635
volume of, 629–634
   finding, 629–630
   formula for, 630
   similar, 632
   using, 631
Pythagorean Inequalities Theorem (Thm. 9.3), 447
Pythagorean Theorem (Thm. 9.1), 443–450
converse of, 446
in Distance Formula, 23
proving, 272, 443
using, 444–445, 481, 510, 554, 595, 617
Pythagorean triples, 444

Q

Quadratic equations, solving by completing the square, 506

Quadrilaterals. *See also specific types of quadrilaterals*
  area of, 27
  diagonals of, 373
  dilations of, 201
  identifying, 388
  perimeter of, 27
  proving quadrilaterals are parallelograms, 363–372
  rotations of, 185
  special, 375, 388
  translations of, 169

R

Radians, measuring angles in, 581
Radicals, using properties of, 442
Radius
  of arcs, 38
  of circles
    defined, 508
    finding, 510
    finding with congruent chords, 527
    finding with segments, 550
    identifying, 508
  of regular polygons, 593
  of spheres, 642
Random variables, 716
Ratios
  forming proportions, 400
  golden, 409
  trigonometric (*See* Trigonometric ratios)
Rays
  collinear, 5
  concurrent, 298
  coplanar, 5
  defined, 5
  opposite, 5
Reasoning. *See also* Deductive reasoning; Inductive reasoning
  algebraic, 85–92
  about triangles, 235, 251
    isosceles, 243
Rectangle Corollary (Cor. 7.3), 375
Rectangle Diagonals Theorem (Thm. 7.13), 377
Rectangles
  as cross sections of cubes, 615
  as cross sections of cylinders, 615
  defined, 374
  diagonal lengths in, 377
  finding missing dimensions of, 576
  identifying, 377
  perimeter and area of, 29
Reduction, 200

Reflection(s), 175–182
  coordinate rules for, 177
  defined, 176
  glide, 178
  in horizontal and vertical lines, 176
  law of, 265
  line symmetry in, 179
  in line $y = x$ or $y = -x$, 177
  of triangles, 175
    in lines, 191
Reflection Postulate (Post. 4.2), 178
Reflections in Intersecting Lines Theorem (Thm. 4.3), 195
Reflections in Parallel Lines Theorem (Thm. 4.2), 194
Reflexive Property, 88
  of Angle Congruence, 96
  of Segment Congruence, 95
  of Triangle Congruence, 231
Regular polygons
  angle measures of, 593
  apothem of, 591, 593
  area of, 591–598
  center of, 591, 593
  defined, 348
  radius of, 593
Related conditional statements
  defined, 63
  writing, 63
Relative frequencies, 681–682
  conditional, 682
  finding, 681–682
  joint, 681
  marginal, 681
Revolution, solids of. *See* Solids of revolution
Rewriting
  conditional statements, 62
  literal equations, 60
  trigonometric expressions, 473
Rhombus(es)
  angle measures of, 376
  area of, 592
  defined, 374
Rhombus Corollary (Cor. 7.2), 375
Rhombus Diagonals Theorem (Thm. 7.11), 376
Rhombus Opposite Angles Theorem (Thm. 7.12), 376
Right angles
  defined, 35, 64, 100
  in Euclidean geometry, 92
  measuring, 37
  proving statements about, 64–65, 100
Right Angles Congruence Theorem (Thm. 2.3), 100

Right cones
  defined, 636
  surface area of, 636
Right cylinders, volume of, 621
Right prisms, volume of, 621
Right Triangle Similarity Theorem (Thm. 9.6), 458
Right triangles. *See also* Pythagorean Theorem
  circles circumscribed about, 299
  cosine ratios of, 471–478
    calculating, 471
    of complementary angles, 473
    defined, 472
    finding, 472
    using, 473–475
  defined, 222
  Hypotenuse-Leg (HL) Congruence Theorem (Thm. 5.9) on, 253–254
  identifying, 446–447
  isosceles
    defined, 452
    finding side lengths of, 452
  legs and hypotenuse of, 253
  orthocenter of, 309
  similar, 457–464
    analyzing, 457
    geometric mean and, 460–461
    identifying, 458
  sine ratios of, 471–478
    calculating, 471
    of complementary angles, 473
    defined, 472
    finding, 472
    using, 473–475
  solving, 479–484
    defined, 481
    using inverse trigonometric ratios, 480
  special, 451–456
    finding side lengths of, 451–453
    finding sine and cosine using, 474
    finding tangent using, 467
  in Spiral of Theodorus, 456
  tangent ratios of, 465–470
    calculating, 465
    defined, 466
    finding, 466–467
    using, 466–467
Rigid motions
  composition of, 192, 208
  and congruence transformations, 193
  defined, 170
  describing, 229
  reflections as, 178

rotations as, 186
translations as, 170
Rotation Postulate (Post. 4.3), 186
Rotational symmetry, 187
Rotations, 183–190
  angle of, 184
  center of, 184, 187
  clockwise, 184, 187
  counterclockwise, 184–185, 187
  defined, 184
  about the origin, coordinate rules for, 185
  performing compositions with, 186
  rotational symmetry in, 187
  of triangles, 183–184
Ruler Postulate (Post. 1.1), 12
  using, to find perimeters and areas, 29–31
Rules
  coordinate
    for dilations, 201
    for reflections, 177
    for rotations about the origin, 185
  probability, using two or more, 704

S

Same-Side Interior Angles Theorem.
  See Consecutive Interior Angles Theorem (Thm. 3.4)
Sample spaces, 671–678
  defined, 672
  finding, 671–672
  finding conditional probabilities using, 686
SAS. *See* Side-Angle-Side
Scale factors
  defined, 200
  finding, 203, 400
  negative, 202
  of similar solids, 625, 632, 638
Scalene triangles, 222
Secant segments, 549
Secants
  defined, 508
  identifying, 508
  segments of, 547–552
Sectors of circles
  area of, 585–590
    finding, 585, 587–588
    using, 588
  defined, 587
Segment(s)
  of chords, 548
  of lines, 5 (*See also* Line segments)
Segment Addition Postulate (Post. 1.2), 14–15, 89
Segment bisectors, 20–21

constructing, 21
defined, 20
Segments of Chords Theorem (Thm. 10.18), 548
Segments of Secants and Tangents Theorem (Thm. 10.20), 550
Segments of Secants Theorem (Thm. 10.19), 549
Semicircles, 516
Septagrams, 52
Sequences, arithmetic, equations for, 60
Side(s)
  of angles, 36
  of polygons
    corresponding, 230
    defined, 28
    finding number of, 347
  of triangles, classifying triangles by congruence of, 222
Side lengths
  of parallelograms, 365
  of similar polygons, 403
  of triangles
    comparing, 323, 329–330
    finding, 321, 325, 414, 451–453
    ordering, 324
    special right, 451–453
Side-Angle-Side (SAS) Congruence Theorem (Thm. 5.5), 236–238
  constructing copies of triangles using, 240
  proof of, 236
  and properties of shapes, 237
  using, 237–238
Side-Angle-Side (SAS) Similarity Theorem (Thm. 8.5), 417–426
  vs. other similarity theorems, 421
  using, 420
Side-Side-Side (SSS) Congruence Theorem (Thm. 5.8)
  constructing copies of triangles using, 256
  proof of, 252
  proving triangle congruence by, 251–258
  using, 252
Side-Side-Side (SSS) Similarity Theorem (Thm. 8.4), 417–426
  vs. other similarity theorems, 421
  proof of, 419
  using, 418–419
Similar arcs, 519
Similar circles, 519

Similar Circles Theorem (Thm. 10.5), 519
Similar figures. *See also specific types of figures*
  defined, 207–208
  proving similarity of, 210
  after transformations, 207
Similar polygons, 401–410
  area of, 405, 612
  corresponding parts of, 402–403
  identifying, 406
  perimeter of, 404
Similar solids
  defined, 625
  scale factors of, 625, 632, 638
  surface area of, 625, 638
  volume of, 625, 632, 638
Similar triangles
  identifying, 417
  proving similarity of
    by AA, 411–416
    by SAS, 417–426
    by SSS, 417–426
  proving slope criteria using, 421
  right, 457–464
    analyzing, 457
    geometric mean and, 460–461
    identifying, 458
Similarity statements, 402
Similarity transformations, 207–212
  defined, 208
  describing, 209
  performing, 208
  of triangles, 208
Sine ratios, 471–478
  calculating, 471
  of complementary angles, 473
  defined, 472
  finding, 472
  inverse, 480
  of special right triangles, 474
  using, 473–475
Skew lines, 117–118
Slant height, of right cones, 636
Slope of line
  finding, 116
  parallel, 149–156
  perpendicular, 149–156
  proving criteria using similar triangles, 421
Slope-intercept form, 152
Slopes of Parallel Lines Theorem (Thm. 3.13), 151, 421
Slopes of Perpendicular Lines Theorem (Thm. 3.14), 151
Solids. *See also specific types of solids*
  classifying types of, 614

cross sections of, 613–620
    defined, 615
    describing, 615
    drawing, 616
defined, 614
surface area of (See Surface area)
volume of (See Volume)

Solids of revolution, 655–660
  defined, 656
  forming in coordinate plane, 658
  modeling with, 655
  sketching and describing, 656
  surface area of, 657
  volume of, 657

Solutions, to systems of two linear equations, 153

Special parallelograms, 373–382
  classifying, 375
  properties of, 374–377
  types of, 374–375

Special quadrilaterals, identifying, 375, 388

Special right triangles, 451–456
  finding side lengths of, 451–453
  finding sine and cosine using, 474
  finding tangent using, 467

Spheres
  chords of, 642
  cross sections of, 615
  defined, 642
  diameter of, 642–643
  finding length in, 643
  surface area of, 641–648
    finding, 641–643
    formula for, 642
  volume of, 641–648
    finding, 644–645
    formula for, 644

Spherical geometry, 92, 122, 129
Spherical lunes, 647
Spiral of Theodorus, 456
Square Corollary (Cor. 7.4), 375

Squares
  as cross sections of cubes, 615
  as cross sections of pyramids, 616
  defined, 374
  inscribed in circles, 535
  perimeter and area of, 29
  proving similarity of, 210

SSS. See Side-Side-Side

Standard equations
  of circles
    defined, 554
    writing, 554–555
  of parabolas, 561–562

Stars, n-pointed, 52
Straight angles, 35

Straightedge, 11, 40
Substitution Property of Equality, 86, 88–89
Subtend, 532
Subtraction Property of Equality, 86–87
Successes, 675
Summer Triangle, 250
Supplementary angles
  defined, 46, 101
  proving statements about, 101
  using, 46–47

Surface area
  of composite solids, 638
  of cones, 635–640
    finding, 636
    formula for, 636
    right, 636
  of cylinders, similar, 625
  modeling with, 649–654
  of prisms, finding, 612
  of similar solids, 625, 638
  of solids of revolution, 657
  of spheres, 641–648
    finding, 641–643
    formula for, 642
  using formulas for, 652

Syllogism, Law of, 75
Symbols
  of conditional statements, 62–63
  of congruence, 13
  of equality, 13
  of negation, 62
  of parallel lines, 118
  of parallelograms, 30

Symmetric Property, 88
  of Angle Congruence, 96
  of Segment Congruence, 95
    proof of, 95
  of Triangle Congruence, 231

Symmetry
  horizontal axis of, 561
  line, 179
  rotational, 187
  vertical axis of, 561

Systems of two linear equations, solutions to, 153

T

Tables. See also Two-way tables
  truth, 66
Tangency, point of, 508
Tangent(s)
  constructing, 511
  defined, 465, 508
  drawing, 509
  identifying, 509

  segments of, 548–550
  using properties of, 510–511
  verifying, 510

Tangent and Intersected Chord Theorem (Thm. 10.14), 540
Tangent circles, 509
Tangent Line to Circle Theorem (Thm. 10.1), 510
Tangent ratios, 465–470
  calculating, 465
  defined, 466
  finding, 465–467
  inverse, 480
  of special right triangles, 467
  using, 466–467

Tangent segments, 549
Tetrahedrons, 619
Theodorus, Spiral of, 456
Theorems. See also specific theorems
  Alternate Exterior Angles Theorem (Thm. 3.3), 125
  Alternate Interior Angles Theorem (Thm. 3.2), 124
  Angle Bisector Theorem (Thm. 6.3), 292
  Angle-Angle (AA) Similarity Theorem (Thm. 8.3), 412
  Angle-Angle-Side (AAS) Congruence Theorem (Thm. 5.11), 261
  Angles Inside the Circle Theorem (Thm. 10.15), 541
  Angles Outside the Circle Theorem (Thm. 10.16), 541
  Angle-Side-Angle (ASA) Congruence Theorem (Thm. 5.10), 260
  Areas of Similar Polygons (Thm. 8.2), 405
  Base Angles Theorem (Thm. 5.6), 244–245
  Bayes' Theorem, 691
  Centroid Theorem (Thm. 6.7), 308
  Ceva's Theorem, 433
  Circumcenter Theorem (Thm. 6.5), 298
  Circumscribed Angle Theorem (Thm. 10.17), 542
  Composition Theorem (Thm. 4.1), 170
  Congruent Central Angles Theorem (Thm. 10.4), 518
  Congruent Circles Theorem (Thm. 10.3), 518
  Congruent Complements Theorem (Thm. 2.5), 102

Index **A81**

Congruent Corresponding Chords Theorem (Thm. 10.6), 524
Congruent Supplements Theorem (Thm. 2.4), 101
Consecutive Interior Angles Theorem (Thm. 3.4), 125
Contrapositive of the Triangle Proportionality Theorem, 429
converses of (*See* Converses of theorems)
corollaries to (*See* Corollaries to theorems)
Corresponding Angles Theorem (Thm. 3.1), 124
defined, 12, 95
Equidistant Chords Theorem (Thm. 10.9), 527
Exterior Angle Inequality Theorem, 327
Exterior Angle Theorem (Thm. 5.2), 224
External Tangent Congruence Theorem (Thm. 10.2), 510
45°-45°-90° Triangle Theorem (Thm. 9.4), 452
Geometric Mean (Altitude) Theorem (Thm. 9.7), 460
Geometric Mean (Leg) Theorem (Thm. 9.8), 460
Hinge Theorem (Thm. 6.12), 330–331
Hypotenuse-Leg (HL) Congruence Theorem (Thm. 5.9), 253–254
Incenter Theorem (Thm. 6.6), 301
Inscribed Angles of a Circle Theorem (Thm. 10.11), 533
Inscribed Quadrilateral Theorem (Thm. 10.13), 534
Inscribed Right Triangle Theorem (Thm. 10.12), 534
Inverse of the Triangle Proportionality Theorem, 429
Isosceles Trapezoid Base Angles Theorem (Thm. 7.14), 385
Isosceles Trapezoid Diagonals Theorem (Thm. 7.16), 385
Kite Diagonals Theorem (Thm. 7.18), 387
Kite Opposite Angles Theorem (Thm. 7.19), 387
Law of Cosines (Thm. 9.10), 489
Law of Sines (Thm. 9.9), 487
Linear Pair Perpendicular Theorem (Thm. 3.10), 142
Lines Perpendicular to a Transversal Theorem (Thm. 3.12), 143
Measure of an Inscribed Angle Theorem (Thm. 10.10), 532
Nicomachus's Theorem, 108
Opposite Sides Parallel and Congruent Theorem (Thm. 7.9), 366
Parallelogram Consecutive Angles Theorem (Thm. 7.5), 357
Parallelogram Diagonals Theorem (Thm. 7.6), 356–357
Parallelogram Opposite Angles Theorem (Thm. 7.4), 356, 364
Parallelogram Opposite Sides Theorem (Thm. 7.3), 356, 364
Perimeters of Similar Polygons (Thm. 8.1), 404
Perpendicular Bisector Theorem (Thm. 6.1), 290
Perpendicular Chord Bisector Theorem (Thm. 10.7), 525
Perpendicular Transversal Theorem (Thm. 3.11), 142
Polygon Exterior Angles Theorem (Thm. 7.2), 349
Polygon Interior Angles Theorem (Thm. 7.1), 346–347
proofs of (*See* Proofs of theorems)
Properties of Angle Congruence (Thm. 2.2), 96
Properties of Segment Congruence (Thm. 2.1), 95
Properties of Triangle Congruence (Thm. 5.3), 231
Pythagorean Inequalities Theorem (Thm. 9.3), 447
Pythagorean Theorem (Thm. 9.1), 444
Rectangle Diagonals Theorem (Thm. 7.13), 377
Reflections in Intersecting Lines Theorem (Thm. 4.3), 195
Reflections in Parallel Lines Theorem (Thm. 4.2), 194
Rhombus Diagonals Theorem (Thm. 7.11), 376
Rhombus Opposite Angles Theorem (Thm. 7.12), 376
Right Angles Congruence Theorem (Thm. 2.3), 100
Right Triangle Similarity Theorem (Thm. 9.6), 458
Segments of Chords Theorem (Thm. 10.18), 548
Segments of Secants and Tangents Theorem (Thm. 10.20), 550
Segments of Secants Theorem (Thm. 10.19), 549
Side-Angle-Side (SAS) Congruence Theorem (Thm. 5.5), 236–238
Side-Angle-Side (SAS) Similarity Theorem (Thm. 8.5), 420
Side-Side-Side (SSS) Congruence Theorem (Thm. 5.8), 252
Side-Side-Side (SSS) Similarity Theorem (Thm. 8.4), 418
Similar Circles Theorem (Thm. 10.5), 519
Slopes of Parallel Lines Theorem (Thm. 3.13), 151, 421
Slopes of Perpendicular Lines Theorem (Thm. 3.14), 151
Tangent and Intersected Chord Theorem (Thm. 10.14), 540
Tangent Line to Circle Theorem (Thm. 10.1), 510
Third Angles Theorem (Thm. 5.4), 232
30°-60°-90° Triangle Theorem (Thm. 9.5), 453
Three Parallel Lines Theorem (Thm. 8.8), 430
Transitive Property of Parallel Lines (Thm. 3.9), 135
Trapezoid Midsegment Theorem (Thm. 7.17), 386
Triangle Angle Bisector Theorem (Thm. 8.9), 431
Triangle Inequality Theorem (Thm. 6.11), 325
Triangle Larger Angle Theorem (Thm. 6.10), 323
Triangle Longer Side Theorem (Thm. 6.9), 323
Triangle Midsegment Theorem (Thm. 6.8), 317
Triangle Proportionality Theorem (Thm. 8.6), 428
Triangle Sum Theorem (Thm. 5.1), 224–225
Vertical Angles Congruence Theorem (Thm. 2.6), 103–104
visual proofs of, 108
Theoretical probabilities, 673–674
defined, 673
finding, 673
Third Angles Theorem (Thm. 5.4), 232
30°-60°-90° right triangles
finding side lengths of, 453
finding sine and cosine of, 474
finding tangent of, 467
30°-60°-90° Triangle Theorem (Thm. 9.5), 453

Three Parallel Lines Theorem (Thm. 8.8), 430
Three Point Postulate (Post. 2.4), 80
Three-dimensional figures. *See* Solids
Tick marks, 13
Transformations. *See also* Dilations; Reflections; Rotations; Translations
   compositions of
      defined, 170
      performing, 170–171
      with rotations, 186
   congruence, 191–198
      defined, 193
      describing, 193
      theorems about, 194–195
   defined, 167
   identifying types of, 166
   nonrigid, 208
   similarity, 207–212
      defined, 208
      describing, 209
      performing, 208
      of triangles, 208
Transitive Property, 88
   of Angle Congruence, 96
   of Segment Congruence, 95
   of Triangle Congruence, 231
Transitive Property of Parallel Lines (Thm. 3.9), 135
Translation Postulate (Post. 4.1), 170
Translation vectors
   components of, 169
   defined, 168
   using, 169
Translations, 167–174
   compositions of, 170–171
   defined, 168
   of parabolas, 562
   of polygons, 167
   of quadrilaterals, 169
   of triangles, 166
   with vectors, 169
Transversals
   angles formed by, 117–122
      alternate exterior, 120
      alternate interior, 120
      consecutive interior, 120
      corresponding, 120
   defined, 117, 120
   and parallel lines, 123–130
      making conjectures about, 123
      proving theorems about, 126
      using properties of parallel lines with, 125
Trapezoid Midsegment Theorem (Thm. 7.17), 386

Trapezoids, 383–392
   in coordinate plane
      identifying, 384
      using midsegments of, 386
   as cross sections of prisms, 615
   defined, 384
   isosceles, 384–385
   lack of rotational symmetry of, 187
   line symmetry of, 179
   midsegments of, 386
   properties of, 383–385
Trials, 675
Triangle(s). *See also specific types of triangles*
   altitude of, 307–314
      defined, 307, 309, 311
      drawing, 307
      using, 309
   angle measures of, 221–228
      analyzing, 221, 321
      classifying triangles by, 222
      comparing, 323, 329–330
      finding, 224–225, 245, 480
      ordering, 324
   area of
      finding, 2, 486, 576
      formula for, 29, 486
   bisectors of, 297–307
      analyzing, 297
      circumcenter and, 298–300
      incenter and, 301–302
   centroid of, 306, 308
   circles circumscribed about, 299–300
   circles inscribed within, 302
   circumcenter of
      defined, 298, 311
      finding, 300
      using, 298–300
   classifying types of, 222–223, 447
   comparing, 329–330, 411
   congruent (*See* Congruent triangles)
   constructing copies of
      using ASA, 262
      using SAS, 240
      using SSS, 256
   in coordinate plane
      classifying, 223
      midsegments of, 316
   as cross sections of cubes, 615
   as cross sections of pyramids, 615
   dilations of, 199, 201
   epidemiologic, 241
   incenter of, 301–302
   inequalities in
      in one triangle, 321–328
      in two triangles, 329–334

   medians of, 307–314
   midsegments of, 315–320
   orthocenter of, 309–310
   perimeter of, 29
   polyhedrons formed by, 242
   reasoning about, 235, 251
   reflections of, 175
      in lines, 191
   rotations of, 183–184
   side lengths of
      comparing, 323, 329–330
      finding, 321, 325, 414, 451–453
      ordering, 324
      special right, 451–453
   sides of, classifying triangles by congruence of, 222–223
   similar (*See* Similar triangles)
   similarity transformations of, 208
   in Spiral of Theodorus, 456
   Summer Triangle, 250
   translations of, 166
Triangle Angle Bisector Theorem (Thm. 8.9), 431
Triangle Inequality Theorem (Thm. 6.11), 325
Triangle Larger Angle Theorem (Thm. 6.10), 323
Triangle Longer Side Theorem (Thm. 6.9), 323
Triangle Midsegment Theorem (Thm. 6.8), 317–318
Triangle Proportionality Theorem (Thm. 8.6), 428–429
Triangle similarity. *See* Similar triangles
Triangle Sum Theorem (Thm. 5.1), 224–225
Triangular prisms, 629
Triangular pyramids, 614, 629–631
Trigonometric expressions, rewriting, 473
Trigonometric ratios. *See also* Cosine ratios; Sine ratios; Tangent ratios
   defined, 466
   finding areas of triangles using, 486
   identifying angles from, 480
   inverse, 480
Truth tables, 66
Truth value, of conditional statements, 66
Two Point Postulate (Post. 2.1), 80
Two-column proofs
   defined, 94
   writing
      for angle bisectors, 96
      for angles, 94, 100–101

for parallelograms, 358
Two-dimensional shapes, sketching, 656
Two-way tables, 679–684
   defined, 680
   finding conditional probabilities using, 686
   identifying independent events using, 696
   joint and marginal frequencies in, 680
   making, 680
   relative and conditional relative frequencies in, 681–682

U

Undefined terms, 4
Union, of two events, 702

V

Variable coordinates, 274
Variables, random, 716
Vectors
   components of, 169
   defined, 168
   translating figures using, 169
Venation patterns, 296
Venn diagrams, 69
   of parallelograms, 374
   using, 71
Vertex (vertices)
   of angles, 36
   of cones, 636
   at origin, parabolas with, 561
   of polygons
      consecutive vs. nonconsecutive, 346
      defined, 28
   of polyhedrons, 614
   of pyramids, 635
Vertex angles, of isosceles triangles, 244
Vertical angles, 48
Vertical Angles Congruence Theorem (Thm. 2.6), 103–104
Vertical axis of symmetry, 561
Vertical component, of vectors, 169
Vertical lines, reflecting in, 176
Visual patterns, describing, 72
Visual proofs, 108
Volume
   Cavalieri's Principle on, 622–623, 644
   of composite solids, 624, 632, 638, 645, 658
   of cones, 635–640
      finding, 635, 637

      formula for, 637
      using, 638
   cubic units of, 622
   of cylinders, 621–628
      finding, 621–623
      formula for, 110, 623
   defined, 622
   in density, 650–652
   modeling with, 649–654
   of prisms, 621–628
      finding, 621–623
      formula for, 622
      using, 624
   of pyramids, 629–634
      finding, 629–630
      formula for, 630
      using, 631
   of similar solids, 625, 632, 638
   of solids of revolution, 657
   of spheres, 641–648
      finding, 644–645
      formula for, 644
   using formulas for, 650–651

W

Writing. See also Rewriting
   compound inequalities, 288
   conditional statements, 62–64
      biconditional, 65
      definitions in, 64
      negation of, 62
      related, 63
   coordinate proofs, 273, 275–276
   equations
      of circles, 554–555
      of lines, 116, 152
      of parabolas, 560–563
      of parallel and perpendicular lines, 152, 288
      of perpendicular bisectors, 293
   flowchart proofs, 99–102
   paragraph proofs, 103–104
   two-column proofs
      for angle bisectors, 96
      for angles, 94, 100–101
      for parallelograms, 358

Postulates

1.1 Ruler Postulate (p. 12)
The points on a line can be matched one to one with the real numbers. The real number that corresponds to a point is the coordinate of the point. The distance between points A and B, written as AB, is the absolute value of the difference of the coordinates of A and B.

1.2 Segment Addition Postulate (p. 14)
If B is between A and C, then $AB + BC = AC$.
If $AB + BC = AC$, then B is between A and C.

1.3 Protractor Postulate (p. 37)
Consider $\overleftrightarrow{OB}$ and a point A on one side of $\overleftrightarrow{OB}$. The rays of the form $\overrightarrow{OA}$ can be matched one to one with the real numbers from 0 to 180. The measure of $\angle AOB$, which can be written as $m\angle AOB$, is equal to the absolute value of the difference between the real numbers matched with $\overrightarrow{OA}$ and $\overrightarrow{OB}$ on a protractor.

1.4 Angle Addition Postulate (p. 39)
If P is in the interior of $\angle RST$, then the measure of $\angle RST$ is equal to the sum of the measures of $\angle RSP$ and $\angle PST$.

2.1 Two Point Postulate (p. 80)
Through any two points, there exists exactly one line.

2.2 Line-Point Postulate (p. 80)
A line contains at least two points.

2.3 Line Intersection Postulate (p. 80)
If two lines intersect, then their intersection is exactly one point.

2.4 Three Point Postulate (p. 80)
Through any three noncollinear points, there exists exactly one plane.

2.5 Plane-Point Postulate (p. 80)
A plane contains at least three noncollinear points.

2.6 Plane-Line Postulate (p. 80)
If two points lie in a plane, then the line containing them lies in the plane.

2.7 Plane Intersection Postulate (p. 80)
If two planes intersect, then their intersection is a line.

2.8 Linear Pair Postulate (p. 103)
If two angles form a linear pair, then they are supplementary.

3.1 Parallel Postulate (p. 119)
If there is a line and a point not on the line, then there is exactly one line through the point parallel to the given line.

3.2 Perpendicular Postulate (p. 119)
If there is a line and a point not on the line, then there is exactly one line through the point perpendicular to the given line.

4.1 Translation Postulate (p. 170)
A translation is a rigid motion.

4.2 Reflection Postulate (p. 178)
A reflection is a rigid motion.

4.3 Rotation Postulate (p. 186)
A rotation is a rigid motion.

10.1 Arc Addition Postulate (p. 517)
The measure of an arc formed by two adjacent arcs is the sum of the measures of the two arcs.

Theorems

2.1 Properties of Segment Congruence *(p. 95)*
Segment congruence is reflexive, symmetric, and transitive.
Reflexive For any segment AB, $\overline{AB} \cong \overline{AB}$.
Symmetric If $\overline{AB} \cong \overline{CD}$, then $\overline{CD} \cong \overline{AB}$.
Transitive If $\overline{AB} \cong \overline{CD}$ and $\overline{CD} \cong \overline{EF}$, then $\overline{AB} \cong \overline{EF}$.

2.2 Properties of Angle Congruence *(p. 96)*
Angle congruence is reflexive, symmetric, and transitive.
Reflexive For any angle A, $\angle A \cong \angle A$.
Symmetric If $\angle A \cong \angle B$, then $\angle B \cong \angle A$.
Transitive If $\angle A \cong \angle B$ and $\angle B \cong \angle C$, then $\angle A \cong \angle C$.

2.3 Right Angles Congruence Theorem *(p. 100)*
All right angles are congruent.

2.4 Congruent Supplements Theorem *(p. 101)*
If two angles are supplementary to the same angle (or to congruent angles), then they are congruent.

2.5 Congruent Complements Theorem *(p. 102)*
If two angles are complementary to the same angle (or to congruent angles), then they are congruent.

2.6 Vertical Angles Congruence Theorem *(p. 103)*
Vertical angles are congruent.

3.1 Corresponding Angles Theorem *(p. 124)*
If two parallel lines are cut by a transversal, then the pairs of corresponding angles are congruent.

3.2 Alternate Interior Angles Theorem *(p. 124)*
If two parallel lines are cut by a transversal, then the pairs of alternate interior angles are congruent.

3.3 Alternate Exterior Angles Theorem *(p. 125)*
If two parallel lines are cut by a transversal, then the pairs of alternate exterior angles are congruent.

3.4 Consecutive Interior Angles Theorem *(p. 125)*
If two parallel lines are cut by a transversal, then the pairs of consecutive interior angles are supplementary.

3.5 Corresponding Angles Converse *(p. 132)*
If two lines are cut by a transversal so the corresponding angles are congruent, then the lines are parallel.

3.6 Alternate Interior Angles Converse *(p. 133)*
If two lines are cut by a transversal so the alternate interior angles are congruent, then the lines are parallel.

3.7 Alternate Exterior Angles Converse *(p. 134)*
If two lines are cut by a transversal so the alternate exterior angles are congruent, then the lines are parallel.

3.8 Consecutive Interior Angles Converse *(p. 134)*
If two lines are cut by a transversal so the consecutive interior angles are supplementary, then the lines are parallel.

3.9 Transitive Property of Parallel Lines *(p. 135)*
If two lines are parallel to the same line, then they are parallel to each other.

3.10 Linear Pair Perpendicular Theorem *(p. 142)*
If two lines intersect to form a linear pair of congruent angles, then the lines are perpendicular.

3.11 Perpendicular Transversal Theorem *(p. 142)*
In a plane, if a transversal is perpendicular to one of two parallel lines, then it is perpendicular to the other line.

3.12 Lines Perpendicular to a Transversal Theorem *(p. 143)*
In a plane, if two lines are perpendicular to the same line, then they are parallel to each other.

3.13 Slopes of Parallel Lines *(p. 151)*
In a coordinate plane, two distinct nonvertical lines are parallel if and only if they have the same slope. Any two vertical lines are parallel.

3.14 Slopes of Perpendicular Lines *(p. 151)*
In a coordinate plane, two nonvertical lines are perpendicular if and only if the product of their slopes is -1. Horizontal lines are perpendicular to vertical lines.

4.1 Composition Theorem (p. 170)

The composition of two (or more) rigid motions is a rigid motion.

4.2 Reflections in Parallel Lines Theorem (p. 194)

If lines k and m are parallel, then a reflection in line k followed by a reflection in line m is the same as a translation. If A'' is the image of A, then
1. $\overline{AA''}$ is perpendicular to k and m, and
2. $AA'' = 2d$, where d is the distance between k and m.

4.3 Reflections in Intersecting Lines Theorem (p. 195)

If lines k and m intersect at point P, then a reflection in line k followed by a reflection in line m is the same as a rotation about point P. The angle of rotation is $2x°$, where $x°$ is the measure of the acute or right angle formed by lines k and m.

5.1 Triangle Sum Theorem (p. 224)

The sum of the measures of the interior angles of a triangle is 180°.

5.2 Exterior Angle Theorem (p. 224)

The measure of an exterior angle of a triangle is equal to the sum of the measures of the two nonadjacent interior angles.

Corollary 5.1 Corollary to the Triangle Sum Theorem (p. 225)

The acute angles of a right triangle are complementary.

5.3 Properties of Triangle Congruence (p. 231)

Triangle congruence is reflexive, symmetric, and transitive.
Reflexive For any triangle $\triangle ABC$, $\triangle ABC \cong \triangle ABC$.
Symmetric If $\triangle ABC \cong \triangle DEF$, then $\triangle DEF \cong \triangle ABC$.
Transitive If $\triangle ABC \cong \triangle DEF$ and $\triangle DEF \cong \triangle JKL$, then $\triangle ABC \cong \triangle JKL$.

5.4 Third Angles Theorem (p. 232)

If two angles of one triangle are congruent to two angles of another triangle, then the third angles are also congruent.

5.5 Side-Angle-Side (SAS) Congruence Theorem (p. 236)

If two sides and the included angle of one triangle are congruent to two sides and the included angle of a second triangle, then the two triangles are congruent.

5.6 Base Angles Theorem (p. 244)

If two sides of a triangle are congruent, then the angles opposite them are congruent.

5.7 Converse of the Base Angles Theorem (p. 244)

If two angles of a triangle are congruent, then the sides opposite them are congruent.

Corollary 5.2 Corollary to the Base Angles Theorem (p. 245)

If a triangle is equilateral, then it is equiangular.

Corollary 5.3 Corollary to the Converse of the Base Angles Theorem (p. 245)

If a triangle is equiangular, then it is equilateral.

5.8 Side-Side-Side (SSS) Congruence Theorem (p. 252)

If three sides of one triangle are congruent to three sides of a second triangle, then the two triangles are congruent.

5.9 Hypotenuse-Leg (HL) Congruence Theorem (p. 253)

If the hypotenuse and a leg of a right triangle are congruent to the hypotenuse and a leg of a second right triangle, then the two triangles are congruent.

5.10 Angle-Side-Angle (ASA) Congruence Theorem (p. 260)

If two angles and the included side of one triangle are congruent to two angles and the included side of a second triangle, then the two triangles are congruent.

5.11 Angle-Angle-Side (AAS) Congruence Theorem (p. 261)

If two angles and a non-included side of one triangle are congruent to two angles and the corresponding non-included side of a second triangle, then the two triangles are congruent.

6.1 Perpendicular Bisector Theorem (p. 290)

In a plane, if a point lies on the perpendicular bisector of a segment, then it is equidistant from the endpoints of the segment.

6.2 Converse of the Perpendicular Bisector Theorem (p. 290)

In a plane, if a point is equidistant from the endpoints of a segment, then it lies on the perpendicular bisector of the segment.

6.3 Angle Bisector Theorem (p. 292)

If a point lies on the bisector of an angle, then it is equidistant from the two sides of the angle.

6.4 Converse of the Angle Bisector Theorem (p. 292)

If a point is in the interior of an angle and is equidistant from the two sides of the angle, then it lies on the bisector of the angle.

6.5 Circumcenter Theorem (p. 298)

The circumcenter of a triangle is equidistant from the vertices of the triangle.

6.6 Incenter Theorem (p. 301)

The incenter of a triangle is equidistant from the sides of the triangle.

6.7 Centroid Theorem (p. 308)

The centroid of a triangle is two-thirds of the distance from each vertex to the midpoint of the opposite side.

6.8 Triangle Midsegment Theorem (p. 317)

The segment connecting the midpoints of two sides of a triangle is parallel to the third side and is half as long as that side.

6.9 Triangle Longer Side Theorem (p. 323)

If one side of a triangle is longer than another side, then the angle opposite the longer side is larger than the angle opposite the shorter side.

6.10 Triangle Larger Angle Theorem (p. 323)

If one angle of a triangle is larger than another angle, then the side opposite the larger angle is longer than the side opposite the smaller angle.

6.11 Triangle Inequality Theorem (p. 325)

The sum of the lengths of any two sides of a triangle is greater than the length of the third side.

6.12 Hinge Theorem (p. 330)

If two sides of one triangle are congruent to two sides of another triangle, and the included angle of the first is larger than the included angle of the second, then the third side of the first is longer than the third side of the second.

6.13 Converse of the Hinge Theorem (p. 331)

If two sides of one triangle are congruent to two sides of another triangle, and the third side of the first is longer than the third side of the second, then the included angle of the first is larger than the included angle of the second.

7.1 Polygon Interior Angles Theorem (p. 346)

The sum of the measures of the interior angles of a convex n-gon is $(n - 2) \cdot 180°$.

Corollary 7.1 Corollary to the Polygon Interior Angles Theorem (p. 347)

The sum of the measures of the interior angles of a quadrilateral is 360°.

7.2 Polygon Exterior Angles Theorem (p. 349)

The sum of the measures of the exterior angles of a convex polygon, one angle at each vertex, is 360°.

7.3 Parallelogram Opposite Sides Theorem (p. 356)

If a quadrilateral is a parallelogram, then its opposite sides are congruent.

7.4 Parallelogram Opposite Angles Theorem (p. 356)

If a quadrilateral is a parallelogram, then its opposite angles are congruent.

7.5 Parallelogram Consecutive Angles Theorem (p. 357)

If a quadrilateral is a parallelogram, then its consecutive angles are supplementary.

7.6 Parallelogram Diagonals Theorem (p. 357)

If a quadrilateral is a parallelogram, then its diagonals bisect each other.

7.7 Parallelogram Opposite Sides Converse (p. 364)

If both pairs of opposite sides of a quadrilateral are congruent, then the quadrilateral is a parallelogram.

7.8 Parallelogram Opposite Angles Converse (p. 364)

If both pairs of opposite angles of a quadrilateral are congruent, then the quadrilateral is a parallelogram.

7.9 Opposite Sides Parallel and Congruent Theorem (p. 366)

If one pair of opposite sides of a quadrilateral are parallel and congruent, then the quadrilateral is a parallelogram.

7.10 Parallelogram Diagonals Converse (p. 366)

If the diagonals of a quadrilateral bisect each other, then the quadrilateral is a parallelogram.

Corollary 7.2 Rhombus Corollary (p. 375)

A quadrilateral is a rhombus if and only if it has four congruent sides.

Corollary 7.3 Rectangle Corollary (p. 375)

A quadrilateral is a rectangle if and only if it has four right angles.

Corollary 7.4 Square Corollary (p. 375)

A quadrilateral is a square if and only if it is a rhombus and a rectangle.

7.11 Rhombus Diagonals Theorem (p. 376)

A parallelogram is a rhombus if and only if its diagonals are perpendicular.

7.12 Rhombus Opposite Angles Theorem (p. 376)

A parallelogram is a rhombus if and only if each diagonal bisects a pair of opposite angles.

7.13 Rectangle Diagonals Theorem (p. 377)

A parallelogram is a rectangle if and only if its diagonals are congruent.

7.14 Isosceles Trapezoid Base Angles Theorem (p. 385)

If a trapezoid is isosceles, then each pair of base angles is congruent.

7.15 Isosceles Trapezoid Base Angles Converse (p. 385)

If a trapezoid has a pair of congruent base angles, then it is an isosceles trapezoid.

7.16 Isosceles Trapezoid Diagonals Theorem (p. 385)

A trapezoid is isosceles if and only if its diagonals are congruent.

7.17 Trapezoid Midsegment Theorem (p. 386)

The midsegment of a trapezoid is parallel to each base, and its length is one-half the sum of the lengths of the bases.

7.18 Kite Diagonals Theorem (p. 387)

If a quadrilateral is a kite, then its diagonals are perpendicular.

7.19 Kite Opposite Angles Theorem (p. 387)

If a quadrilateral is a kite, then exactly one pair of opposite angles are congruent.

8.1 Perimeters of Similar Polygons (p. 404)

If two polygons are similar, then the ratio of their perimeters is equal to the ratios of their corresponding side lengths.

8.2 Areas of Similar Polygons (p. 405)

If two polygons are similar, then the ratio of their areas is equal to the squares of the ratios of their corresponding side lengths.

8.3 Angle-Angle (AA) Similarity Theorem (p. 412)

If two angles of one triangle are congruent to two angles of another triangle, then the two triangles are similar.

8.4 Side-Side-Side (SSS) Similarity Theorem (p. 418)

If the corresponding side lengths of two triangles are proportional, then the triangles are similar.

8.5 Side-Angle-Side (SAS) Similarity Theorem (p. 420)

If an angle of one triangle is congruent to an angle of a second triangle and the lengths of the sides including these angles are proportional, then the triangles are similar.

8.6 Triangle Proportionality Theorem (p. 428)

If a line parallel to one side of a triangle intersects the other two sides, then it divides the two sides proportionally.

8.7 Converse of the Triangle Proportionality Theorem (p. 428)

If a line divides two sides of a triangle proportionally, then it is parallel to the third side.

8.8 Three Parallel Lines Theorem (p. 430)

If three parallel lines intersect two transversals, then they divide the transversals proportionally.

8.9 Triangle Angle Bisector Theorem (p. 431)

If a ray bisects an angle of a triangle, then it divides the opposite side into segments whose lengths are proportional to the lengths of the other two sides.

9.1 Pythagorean Theorem (p. 444)

In a right triangle, the square of the length of the hypotenuse is equal to the sum of the squares of the lengths of the legs.

9.2 Converse of the Pythagorean Theorem (p. 446)

If the square of the length of the longest side of a triangle is equal to the sum of the squares of the lengths of the other two sides, then the triangle is a right triangle.

9.3 Pythagorean Inequalities Theorem (p. 447)

For any $\triangle ABC$, where c is the length of the longest side, the following statements are true.
If $c^2 < a^2 + b^2$, then $\triangle ABC$ is acute.
If $c^2 > a^2 + b^2$, then $\triangle ABC$ is obtuse.

9.4 45°-45°-90° Triangle Theorem (p. 452)

In a 45°-45°-90° triangle, the hypotenuse is $\sqrt{2}$ times as long as each leg.

9.5 30°-60°-90° Triangle Theorem (p. 453)
In a 30°-60°-90° triangle, the hypotenuse is twice as long as the shorter leg, and the longer leg is $\sqrt{3}$ times as long as the shorter leg.

9.6 Right Triangle Similarity Theorem (p. 458)
If the altitude is drawn to the hypotenuse of a right triangle, then the two triangles formed are similar to the original triangle and to each other.

9.7 Geometric Mean (Altitude) Theorem (p. 460)
In a right triangle, the altitude to the hypotenuse divides the hypotenuse into two segments. The length of the altitude is the geometric mean of the lengths of the two segments of the hypotenuse.

9.8 Geometric Mean (Leg) Theorem (p. 460)
In a right triangle, the altitude to the hypotenuse divides the hypotenuse into two segments. The length of each leg of the right triangle is the geometric mean of the lengths of the hypotenuse and the segment of the hypotenuse that is adjacent to that leg.

9.9 Law of Sines (p. 487)
The Law of Sines can be written in either of the following forms for $\triangle ABC$ with sides of length a, b, and c.

$$\frac{\sin A}{a} = \frac{\sin B}{b} = \frac{\sin C}{c}$$

$$\frac{a}{\sin A} = \frac{b}{\sin B} = \frac{c}{\sin C}$$

9.10 Law of Cosines (p. 489)
If $\triangle ABC$ has sides of length a, b, and c, then the following are true.
$a^2 = b^2 + c^2 - 2bc \cos A$
$b^2 = a^2 + c^2 - 2ac \cos B$
$c^2 = a^2 + b^2 - 2ab \cos C$

10.1 Tangent Line to Circle Theorem (p. 510)
In a plane, a line is tangent to a circle if and only if the line is perpendicular to a radius of the circle at its endpoint on the circle.

10.2 External Tangent Congruence Theorem (p. 510)
Segments that are tangents to a circle and have common external point are congruent.

10.3 Congruent Circles Theorem (p. 518)
Two circles are congruent circles if and only if they have the same radius.

10.4 Congruent Central Angles Theorem (p. 518)
In the same circle, or in congruent circles, two minor arcs are congruent if and only if their corresponding central angles are congruent.

10.5 Similar Circles Theorem (p. 519)
All circles are similar.

10.6 Congruent Corresponding Chords Theorem (p. 524)
In the same circle, or in congruent circles, two minor arcs are congruent if and only if their corresponding chords are congruent.

10.7 Perpendicular Chord Bisector Theorem (p. 525)
If a diameter of a circle is perpendicular to a chord, then the diameter bisects the chord and its arc.

10.8 Perpendicular Chord Bisector Converse (p. 526)
If one chord of a circle is a perpendicular bisector of another chord, then the first chord is a diameter.

10.9 Equidistant Chords Theorem (p. 527)
In the same circle, or in congruent circles, two chords are congruent if and only if they are equidistant from the center.

10.10 Measure of an Inscribed Angle Theorem (p. 532)
The measure of an inscribed angle is one-half the measure of its intercepted arc.

10.11 Inscribed Angles of a Circle Theorem (p. 533)
If two inscribed angles of a circle intercept the same arc, then the angles are congruent.

10.12 Inscribed Right Triangle Theorem (p. 534)
If a right triangle is inscribed in a circle, then the hypotenuse is a diameter of the circle. Conversely, if one side of an inscribed triangle is a diameter of the circle, then the triangle is a right triangle and the angle opposite the diameter is the right angle.

10.13 Inscribed Quadrilateral Theorem (p. 534)
A quadrilateral can be inscribed in a circle if and only if its opposite angles are supplementary.

10.14 Tangent and Intersected Chord Theorem (p. 540)

If a tangent and a chord intersect at a point on a circle, then the measure of each angle formed is one-half the measure of its intercepted arc.

10.15 Angles Inside the Circle Theorem (p. 541)

If two chords intersect inside a circle, then the measure of each angle is one-half the sum of the measures of the arcs intercepted by the angle and its vertical angle.

10.16 Angles Outside the Circle Theorem (p. 541)

If a tangent and a secant, two tangents, or two secants intersect outside a circle, then the measure of the angle formed is one-half the difference of the measures of the intercepted arcs.

10.17 Circumscribed Angle Theorem (p. 542)

The measure of a circumscribed angle is equal to 180° minus the measure of the central angle that intercepts the same arc.

10.18 Segments of Chords Theorem (p. 548)

If two chords intersect in the interior of a circle, then the product of the lengths of the segments of one chord is equal to the product of the lengths of the segments of the other chord.

10.19 Segments of Secants Theorem (p. 549)

If two secant segments share the same endpoint outside a circle, then the product of the lengths of one secant segment and its external segment equals the product of the lengths of the other secant segment and its external segment.

10.20 Segments of Secants and Tangents Theorem (p. 550)

If a secant segment and a tangent segment share an endpoint outside a circle, then the product of the lengths of the secant segment and its external segment equals the square of the length of the tangent segment.

My Guide to the Standards for Mathematical Practice

SMP.1 Make Sense of Problems and Persevere in Solving Them

I can analyze the given information and find what the problem is asking to help plan a solution pathway.

SMP.2 Reason Abstractly and Quantitatively

I can represent a problem symbolically, or see relationships in numbers or symbols and draw conclusions about a concrete example.

SMP.3 Construct Viable Arguments and Critique the Reasoning of Others

I can make and justify conclusions and decide whether others' arguments are correct or flawed.

SMP.4 Model with Mathematics

I can apply the math I learned to a real-life problem and interpret mathematical results in the context of the situation.

SMP.5 Use Appropriate Tools Strategically

I can think about the tools that are available and how they might help solve a mathematical problem. I can use a tool for its advantages, while being aware of its limitations.

SMP.6 Attend to Precision

I can develop a habit of being careful of how I talk about concepts, label my work, and write my answers.

SMP.7 Look for and Make Use of Structure

I can see structure within a mathematical statement, or step back for an overview to see how individual parts make one single object.

SMP.8 Look for and Express Regularity in Repeated Reasoning

I can recognize patterns and make generalizations while evaluating the reasonableness of answers as I solve problems.

My Guide to Problem Solving

I can apply the mathematics I learn to model and solve real-life problems.

1 Understand the Problem

Before planning a solution, I read the problem carefully.

- What is the problem asking?
- What do I know?
- What do I need to find out?
- Is any information not needed?
- What are some possible entry points to a solution?

2 Make a Plan

I plan my solution pathway before jumping in to solve.

- What variables or relationships can I identify in the situation?
- Do I understand these in the real-life context?
- Are there any constraints that I need to consider?
- Have I solved a problem like this before?
- Which problem-solving strategy will I use?
    - Use a verbal model.
    - Draw a diagram.
    - Write an equation.
    - Solve a simpler problem.
    - Sketch a graph or number line.
    - Make a table.
    - Make a list.
    - Break the problem into parts.

3 Solve and Check

As I solve the problem, I monitor and evaluate my progress.

- How precise does my answer need to be?
- What tools can I use to help model and solve?
- How does my model help me analyze the relationships among the variables?
- How can I interpret my results in terms of the real-life situation?
- Are my answers reasonable mathematically? Do they make sense in the context?
- Am I willing to change course if necessary?
- How will I report on my conclusions and explain my reasoning?

Quick Reference

Properties

Properties of Equality

Addition Property of Equality
If $a = b$, then $a + c = b + c$.

Subtraction Property of Equality
If $a = b$, then $a - c = b - c$.

Multiplication Property of Equality
If $a = b$, then $a \cdot c = b \cdot c, c \neq 0$.

Division Property of Equality
If $a = b$, then $\dfrac{a}{c} = \dfrac{b}{c}, c \neq 0$.

Reflexive Property of Equality
$a = a$

Symmetric Property of Equality
If $a = b$, then $b = a$.

Transitive Property of Equality
If $a = b$ and $b = c$, then $a = c$.

Substitution Property of Equality
If $a = b$, then a can be substituted for b (or b for a) in any equation or expression.

Properties of Segment and Angle Congruence

Reflexive Property of Congruence
For any segment $AB, \overline{AB} \cong \overline{AB}$.

For any angle A, $\angle A \cong \angle A$.

Symmetric Property of Congruence
If $\overline{AB} \cong \overline{CD}$, then $\overline{CD} \cong \overline{AB}$.

If $\angle A \cong \angle B$, then $\angle B \cong \angle A$.

Transitive Property of Congruence
If $\overline{AB} \cong \overline{CD}$ and $\overline{CD} \cong \overline{EF}$, then $\overline{AB} \cong \overline{EF}$.

If $\angle A \cong \angle B$ and $\angle B \cong \angle C$, then $\angle A \cong \angle C$.

Other Properties

Transitive Property of Parallel Lines
If $p \parallel q$ and $q \parallel r$, then $p \parallel r$.

Distributive Property
Sum
$a(b + c) = ab + ac$
Difference
$a(b - c) = ab - ac$

Triangle Inequalities

Triangle Inequality Theorem

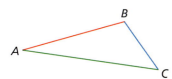

$AB + BC > AC$
$AC + BC > AB$
$AB + AC > BC$

Pythagorean Inequalities Theorem

If $c^2 < a^2 + b^2$, then $\triangle ABC$ is acute.

If $c^2 > a^2 + b^2$, then $\triangle ABC$ is obtuse.

Formulas

Coordinate Geometry

Slope
$m = \dfrac{y_2 - y_1}{x_2 - x_1}$

Slope-intercept form
$y = mx + b$

Point-slope form
$y - y_1 = m(x - x_1)$

Standard form of a linear equation
$Ax + By = C$

Standard equation of a circle
$(x - h)^2 + (y - k)^2 = r^2$, with center (h, k) and radius r

Midpoint Formula
$\left(\dfrac{x_1 + x_2}{2}, \dfrac{y_1 + y_2}{2}\right)$

Distance Formula
$d = \sqrt{(x_2 - x_1)^2 + (y_2 - y_1)^2}$

Polygons

Triangle Sum Theorem

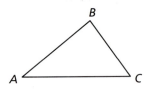

$m\angle A + m\angle B + m\angle C = 180°$

Exterior Angle Theorem

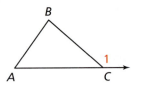

$m\angle 1 = m\angle A + m\angle B$

Triangle Midsegment Theorem

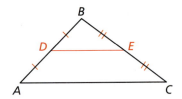

$\overline{DE} \parallel \overline{AC}$, $DE = \frac{1}{2}AC$

Trapezoid Midsegment Theorem

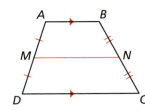

$\overline{MN} \parallel \overline{AB}, \overline{MN} \parallel \overline{DC}, MN = \frac{1}{2}(AB + CD)$

Polygon Interior Angles Theorem

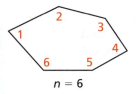

$n = 6$

$m\angle 1 + m\angle 2 + \cdots + m\angle n = (n - 2) \cdot 180°$

Polygon Exterior Angles Theorem

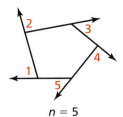

$n = 5$

$m\angle 1 + m\angle 2 + \cdots + m\angle n = 360°$

Geometric Mean (Altitude) Theorem

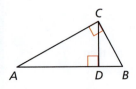

$CD^2 = AD \cdot BD$

Geometric Mean (Leg) Theorem

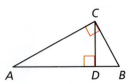

$CB^2 = DB \cdot AB$ $AC^2 = AD \cdot AB$

Right Triangles

Pythagorean Theorem

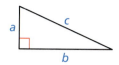

$a^2 + b^2 = c^2$

45°-45°-90° Triangles

hypotenuse = leg · $\sqrt{2}$

30°-60°-90° Triangles

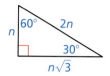

hypotenuse = shorter leg · 2
longer leg = shorter leg · $\sqrt{3}$

Trigonometry

Ratios

$\sin A = \dfrac{BC}{AB}$ $\cos A = \dfrac{AC}{AB}$ $\tan A = \dfrac{BC}{AC}$

$\sin^{-1} \dfrac{BC}{AB} = m\angle A$ $\cos^{-1} \dfrac{AC}{AB} = m\angle A$ $\tan^{-1} \dfrac{BC}{AC} = m\angle A$

Conversion between degrees and radians
180° = π radians

Sine and cosine of complementary angles
Let A and B be complementary angles. Then the following statements are true.
$\sin A = \cos(90° - A) = \cos B$ $\sin B = \cos(90° - B) = \cos A$
$\cos A = \sin(90° - A) = \sin B$ $\cos B = \sin(90° - B) = \sin A$

Any Triangle

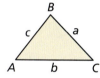 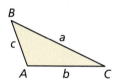

Area

Area = $\dfrac{1}{2} bc \sin A$

Area = $\dfrac{1}{2} ac \sin B$

Area = $\dfrac{1}{2} ab \sin C$

Law of Sines

$\dfrac{\sin A}{a} = \dfrac{\sin B}{b} = \dfrac{\sin C}{c}$

$\dfrac{a}{\sin A} = \dfrac{b}{\sin B} = \dfrac{c}{\sin C}$

Law of Cosines

$a^2 = b^2 + c^2 - 2bc \cos A$
$b^2 = a^2 + c^2 - 2ac \cos B$
$c^2 = a^2 + b^2 - 2ab \cos C$

Circles

Arc length

Arc length of $\widehat{AB} = \dfrac{m\widehat{AB}}{360°} \cdot 2\pi r$

Area of a sector

Area of sector $APB = \dfrac{m\widehat{AB}}{360°} \cdot \pi r^2$

Central angles

$m\angle ACB = m\widehat{AB}$

Inscribed angles

$m\angle ADB = \tfrac{1}{2}(m\widehat{AB})$

Tangent and intersected chord

$m\angle 1 = \tfrac{1}{2}(m\widehat{AB})$

$m\angle 2 = \tfrac{1}{2}(m\widehat{BCA})$

Angles and Segments of Circles

Two chords

$m\angle 1 = \tfrac{1}{2}(m\widehat{AC} + m\widehat{DB})$

$m\angle 2 = \tfrac{1}{2}(m\widehat{AD} + m\widehat{CB})$

$EA \cdot EB = EC \cdot ED$

Two secants

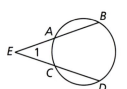

$m\angle 1 = \tfrac{1}{2}(m\widehat{BD} - m\widehat{AC})$

$EA \cdot EB = EC \cdot ED$

Tangent and secant

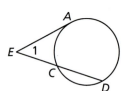

$m\angle 1 = \tfrac{1}{2}(m\widehat{AD} - m\widehat{AC})$

$EA^2 = EC \cdot ED$

Two tangents

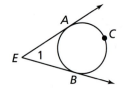

$m\angle 1 = \tfrac{1}{2}(m\widehat{ACB} - m\widehat{AB})$

$EA = EB$

Probability and Combinatorics

Theoretical Probability $= \dfrac{\text{Number of favorable outcomes}}{\text{Total number of outcomes}}$

Experimental Probability $= \dfrac{\text{Number of successes}}{\text{Number of trials}}$

Probability of the complement of an event
$P(\overline{A}) = 1 - P(A)$

Probability of independent events
$P(A \text{ and } B) = P(A) \cdot P(B)$

Probability of dependent events
$P(A \text{ and } B) = P(A) \cdot P(B \mid A)$

Probability of compound events
$P(A \text{ or } B) = P(A) + P(B) - P(A \text{ and } B)$

Permutations
$_nP_r = \dfrac{n!}{(n-r)!}$

Combinations
$_nC_r = \dfrac{n!}{(n-r)! \cdot r!}$

Binomial experiments
$P(k \text{ successes}) = {_nC_k} p^k (1-p)^{n-k}$

Perimeter, Area, and Volume Formulas

Square

$P = 4s$
$A = s^2$

Rectangle
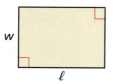
$P = 2\ell + 2w$
$A = \ell w$

Triangle
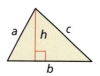
$P = a + b + c$
$A = \frac{1}{2}bh$

Circle
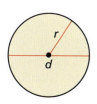
$C = \pi d$ or $C = 2\pi r$
$A = \pi r^2$

Parallelogram
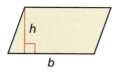
$A = bh$

Trapezoid
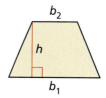
$A = \frac{1}{2}h(b_1 + b_2)$

Rhombus/Kite
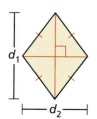 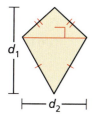
$A = \frac{1}{2}d_1 d_2$

Regular n-gon
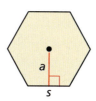
$A = \frac{1}{2}aP$ or $A = \frac{1}{2}a \cdot ns$

Prism

$L = Ph$
$S = 2B + Ph$
$V = Bh$

Cylinder

$L = 2\pi rh$
$S = 2\pi r^2 + 2\pi rh$
$V = \pi r^2 h$

Pyramid
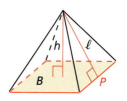
$L = \frac{1}{2}P\ell$
$S = B + \frac{1}{2}P\ell$
$V = \frac{1}{3}Bh$

Cone
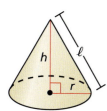
$L = \pi r\ell$
$S = \pi r^2 + \pi r\ell$
$V = \frac{1}{3}\pi r^2 h$

Sphere

$S = 4\pi r^2$
$V = \frac{4}{3}\pi r^3$

Other Formulas

Geometric mean
$x = \sqrt{a \cdot b}$

Quadratic Formula
$$x = \frac{-b \pm \sqrt{b^2 - 4ac}}{2a},$$
where $a \neq 0$ and $b^2 - 4ac \geq 0$

Density
$$\text{Density} = \frac{\text{Mass}}{\text{Volume}}$$

Similar polygons or similar solids with scale factor $a : b$
Ratio of perimeters $= a : b$
Ratio of areas $= a^2 : b^2$
Ratio of volumes $= a^3 : b^3$

Population Density
$$\text{Population density} = \frac{\text{number of people}}{\text{area of land}}$$

Conversions

U.S. Customary
1 foot = 12 inches
1 yard = 3 feet
1 mile = 5,280 feet
1 mile = 1,760 yards
1 acre = 43,560 square feet
1 cup = 8 fluid ounces
1 pint = 2 cups
1 quart = 2 pints
1 gallon = 4 quarts
1 gallon = 231 cubic inches
1 pound = 16 ounces
1 ton = 2,000 pounds
1 cubic foot ≈ 7.5 gallons

U.S. Customary to Metric
1 inch = 2.54 centimeters
1 foot ≈ 0.3 meter
1 mile ≈ 1.61 kilometers
1 quart ≈ 0.95 liter
1 gallon ≈ 3.79 liters
1 cup ≈ 237 milliliters
1 pound ≈ 0.45 kilogram
1 ounce ≈ 28.3 grams
1 gallon ≈ 3,785 cubic centimeters

Time
1 minute = 60 seconds
1 hour = 60 minutes
1 hour = 3,600 seconds
1 year = 52 weeks

Temperature
$C = \frac{5}{9}(F - 32)$
$F = \frac{9}{5}C + 32$

Metric
1 centimeter = 10 millimeters
1 meter = 100 centimeters
1 kilometer = 1,000 meters
1 liter = 1,000 milliliters
1 kiloliter = 1,000 liters
1 milliliter = 1 cubic centimeter
1 liter = 1,000 cubic centimeters
1 cubic millimeter = 0.001 milliliter
1 gram = 1,000 milligrams
1 kilogram = 1,000 grams

Metric to U.S. Customary
1 centimeter ≈ 0.39 inch
1 meter ≈ 3.28 feet
1 meter ≈ 39.37 inches
1 kilometer ≈ 0.62 mile
1 liter ≈ 1.06 quarts
1 liter ≈ 0.26 gallon
1 kilogram ≈ 2.2 pounds
1 gram ≈ 0.035 ounce
1 cubic meter ≈ 264 gallons

Credits

Chapter 1
0 *top* ©Rae Wynn-Grant; *bottom* lassedesignen/Shutterstock.com; **1** Alexey Seafarer/Shutterstock.com, Adapted from poar bear range map, accessed February 23, 2023, https://commons.wikimedia.org/wiki/File:Polar_bear_range_map.png#filehistory; and "Global Polar Bear Population Estimates," Polar Bear Specialist Group, IUCN Species Survival Commission, accessed February 23, 2023, https://pbsg.npolar.no/web/en/status/pb-global-estimate.html.; **3** faestock/Shutterstock.com; **9** *top* virusowy/E+/Getty Images; *right* Yayasya/iStock/Getty Images Plus; **15** Martina Birnbaum/Shutterstock.com; **16** MediaProduction/iStock/Getty Images Plus; **17** wavebreakmedia/Shutterstock.com; **25** *right* Mark Herreid/Shutterstock.com; *bottom* stevanovicigor/iStock/Getty Images Plus; 26 Sean Locke Photography/Shutterstock.com; **27** diogoppr/Shutterstock.com; **31** *left* aoldman/iStock/Getty Images Plus; *right* Albert999/shutterstock.com; **33** *left* JordiStock/iStock/Getty Images Plus; *right* GlobalP/iStock/Getty Images Plus; **36** MAGNIFIER/Shutterstock.com; **38** Ekaterina Romanova/iStock/Getty Images Plus; **42** Lewis Calvert Cooper (gonzoshots.com); **47** OSTILL/iStock/Getty Images Plus; **51** Francisco Javier Alcerreca Gomez/Shutterstock.com; **55** TommL/E+/Getty Images; **56–57** SantiPhotoSS/Shutterstock.com, Andyworks/E+/Getty Images

Chapter 2
58 *top* ©Caroline Quanbeck; *bottom* Sharp/Shutterstock.com; **59** Rebecca Lindsey and Luann Dahlman, "Climate Change: Global Temperature," Climate.gov, January 18, 2023, https://www.climate.gov/news-features/understanding-climate/climate-change-global-temperature.; **63** Rawpixel/iStock/Getty Images Plus; **70** Ink Drop/Shutterstock.com; **78** SounderBruce (translated version), Ariel Provost (French version), Tahc (original version), "Euler diagram of solar system bodies," (https://commons.wikimedia.org/wiki/File:Euler_diagram_of_solar_system_bodies.svg), https://creativecommons.org/licenses/by-sa/3.0/legalcode. Used by permission of the International Astronomical Union.; **79** Elenathewise/iStock/Getty Images Plus; **80** Rawpixel/iStock/Getty Images Plus; **84** *left* Strakovskaya/Shutterstock.com; *right* Adapted from Matt Fussell, "One Point Perspective," The Virtual Instructor, https://thevirtualinstructor.com/onepointperspective.html, accessed May 17, 2023., YamabikaY/Shutterstock.com; **87** Pixel-Shot/Shutterstock.com; **88** Twin Design/Shutterstock.com; **89** SDI Productions/E+/Getty Images; **92** *left* titoOnz/Shutterstock.com; *right* Pavlo S/Shutterstock.com; **93** track5/iStock/Getty Images Plus; **94** Twin Design/Shutterstock.com; **97** Oliver Hoffmann/Shutterstock.com; **98** *left* Constantine Pankin/Shutterstock.com; *right* Adam Cunningham and John Ringland, "Goldbach partitions of the even integers from 4 to 96," Wikimedia Commons, May 24, 2012, https://commons.wikimedia.org/wiki/File:Goldbach_partitions_of_the_even_integers_from_4_to_96.svg), https://creativecommons.org/licenses/by-sa/3.0/legalcode.; **104** caimacanul/Shutterstock.com; **105** Geartooth Productions/Shutterstock.com; **110** Nattstudio/Shutterstock.com; **112–113** imaginima/E+/Getty Images, Kativ/E+/Getty Images

Chapter 3
114 *top* ©Cengage Learning/National Geographic Learning; *bottom* Mateusz Liberra/Shutterstock.com; **115** Diego Barucco/Shutterstock.com; **121** *Exercise 15* Aldona Griskeviciene/shutterstock.com; *Exercise 16* Nastya22/iStock/Getty Images Plus; **127** *top* LIGHT_ONLY/Shutterstock.com, S.Borisov/Shutterstock.com; *bottom* patat/Shutterstock.com; **129** R-Tvist/Shutterstock.com; **130** *left* Gorodenkoff/Shutterstock.com; *center* File:BOS airport diagram.svg: Federal Aviation Administration / * derivative work TilmannR (https://commons.wikimedia.org/wiki/File:BOS_airport_diagram2.svg), "BOS airport diagram2", marked as public domain, more details on Wikimedia Commons: https://commons.wikimedia.org/wiki/Template:PD-US; *right* Good Luck Photo/Shutterstock.com; **135** Sanit Fuangnakhon/Shutterstock.com; **138** Everett Collection/Shutterstock.com; **144** *top* kokouu/iStock/Getty Images Plus; *bottom* Orbon Alija/E+/Getty Images; **145** *left* valio84sl/iStock/Getty Images Plus; *right* gowithstock/Shutterstock.com; **148** LeysanI/Shutterstock.com; **149** Ljupco/iStock/Getty Images Plus; **156** Anatoli Styf/Shutterstock.com; **158** okandilek/iStock/Getty Images Plus; **160–161** Johann Ragnarsson/Shutterstock.com, Mopic/Shutterstock.com, Figure 2-3, "Geothermal Diversity," from GeoVision: Harnessing the Heat Beneath Our Feet, Geothermal Technologies Office, Energy.gov, May 29, 2019, accessed at https://www.energy.gov/eere/geothermal/articles/geovision-harnessing-heat-beneath-our-feet,; **162–163** Adapted from Ephraim George Squier and Edwin Hamilton Davis, Ancient Monuments of the Mississippi Valley: Comprising the Results of Extensive Original Surveys and Explorations (New York: Bartlett & Welford, 1848), p. 365., Zack Frank/Shutterstock.com

Chapter 4
164 *top* ©Aaron Pomerantz/National Geographic Image Collection; *bottom* suns07butterfly/Shutterstock.com, Anton-Burakov/Shutterstock.com;**165** Neo Edmund/Shutterstock.com, sakhorn/Shutterstock.com, Svetlana Foote/Shutterstock.com, Mathisa/Shutterstock.com; **167** *right* oatintro/iStock/Getty Images Plus; *left* Wavebreakmedia/iStock/Getty Images Plus; **171** SLP_London/iStock/Getty Images Plus; **173** Melinda Fawver/Shutterstock.com; **174** Photo by Maria Emelianova, from Colin Stapczynski, "The 10 Best Chess Moves of All Time," Chess.com, https://www.chess.com/article/view/best-chess-moves. Used by permission.; **179** suns07butterfly/Shutterstock.com; **182** *left* Jason Finn/Shutterstock.com; *right* NEW N FRESH/Shutterstock.com; **183** *left* Dean Drobot/Shutterstock.com; *right* Billion Photos/Shutterstock.com; **187** Hans Kim/Shutterstock.com **190** *in order from left to right* oksana2010/Shutterstock.com, Tetiana Rostopira/Shutterstock.com, Plus69/Shutterstock.com, jaroslava V/Shutterstock.com; **191** TimeImage Production/Shutterstock.com; **198** Africa Studio/Shutterstock.com; **199** Andrey_Popov/Shutterstock.com; **203** *top* martin-dm/E+/Getty Images; *left* Federico.Crovetto/Shutterstock.com; *right* Henrik Larsson/Shutterstock.com; **205** *Exercise 16* Protasov AN/Shutterstock.com; *Exercise 17* irin-k/Shutterstock.com; *Exercise 18* photomaster/Shutterstock.com; *Exercise 19* Eric Isselee/Shutterstock.com; **206** *left* Pressmaster/Shutterstock.com; *right* Kalcutta/Shutterstock.com; **207** Kaesler Media/Shutterstock.com; **212** stihii/Shutterstock.com, Data from Wilfred T. Neill, The Last of the Ruling Reptiles, Alligators, Crocodiles and Their Kin (New York: Columbia University Press, 1971).; **215** *top* irin-k/Shutterstock.com; *bottom* FatCamera/E+/Getty Images; **216–217** Flower Studio/Shutterstock.com, Mathee Boonphram/123RF, Thawat Tanhai/123RF, Cosmin Manci/123RF, Geza Farkars/123RF, Geza Farkars/123RF, Vac1/iStock/Getty Images Plus, MarkMirror/iStock/Getty Images Plus, Iuliia Morozova/iStock/Getty Images Plus, Image from the Smithsonian, "Bug Info: Butterflies in the United States" (https://www.si.edu/spotlight/buginfo/butterflyus). Prepared by the Department of Systematic Biology, Entomology Section, National Museum of Natural History, Marco Uliana/123RF, Image from the Smithsonian, "Bug Info: Butterflies in the United States" (https://www.si.edu/spotlight/buginfo/butterflyus). Prepared by the Department of Systematic Biology, Entomology Section, National Museum of Natural History, Onfokus/E+/Getty Images, Olga Danylenko/Shutterstock.com

Chapter 5
218 *top* ©Mark Thiessen/National Geographic Image Collection; *bottom* traffic_analyzer/DigitalVision Vectors/Getty Images; **219** akr11_ss/Shutterstock.com, akr11_ss/Shutterstock.com; **221** *top* tuulijumala/iStock/Getty Images Plus; *bottom* ferlistockphoto/iStock/Getty Images Plus; **222** *top* Goettingen/iStock/Getty Images Plus; *bottom* artisteer/iStock/Getty Images Plus; **225** AndreyPopov/iStock/Getty Images Plus; **228** Anton Balazh/Shutterstock.com; **229** hexvivo/iStock/Getty Images Plus; **234** Aila Images/Shutterstock.com; **235** *right* hocus-focus/E+/Getty Images; *left* tetmc/iStock/Getty Images Plus; **238** *top* Arthur Eugene Preston/Shutterstock.com; *bottom* ritno kurniawan/Shutterstock.com; **242** *left* Zeiss Factory Jena, Germany. Design by Walter Bauersfeld and Franz Dischinger, 1922. IL Archives Stuttgart, Public domain, via Wikimedia Commons.; *right* automation5/Shutterstock.com; **243** OvsiankaStudio/iStock/Getty Images Plus; **247** *left* Pixel-Shot/Shutterstock.com; *right* Colin

D. Young/Shutterstock.com; **248** Leonard Zhukovsky/Shutterstock.com; **250** Cristina Ivan/Shutterstock.com, pixelparticle/Shutterstock.com; **251** *right* OvsiankaStudio/iStock/Getty Images Plus; *left* g-stockstudio/iStock/Getty Images Plus; **254** Troggt/Shutterstock.com; **256** antpkr/Shutterstock.com; **258** *top* U.S. Department of Agriculture; *bottom* style-photography/iStock/Getty Images Plus; **259** *right* tuulijumala/iStock/Getty Images Plus; *left* Luis Molinero/Shutterstock.com; **265** m-imagephotography/iStock/Getty Images Plus; **266** *top* EHStockphoto/Shutterstock.com; *bottom* image_jungle/iStock/Getty Images Plus; **267** Carle Vernet, La Grande Armée de 1812, Public domain, via Wikimedia Commons.; **268** DanCardiff/iStock/Getty Images Plus; **271** pisaphotography/Shutterstock.com; **272** Files.ai/Shutterstock.com; **273** Hogan Imaging/Shutterstock.com; **276** *top* Trexdigital/Shutterstock.com, Sergey Mironov/Shutterstock.com; *bottom* zyxeos30/iStock/Getty Images Plus; **278** *left* Hugo Felix/Shutterstock.com; *right* Alfred Goldberg et al, Pentagon 9/11, Defense Studies Series (Washington, DC: Historical Office of the Secretary of Defense, 2007), p. 19, https://history.defense.gov/Portals/70/Documents/pentagon/Pentagon9-11.pdf?ver=DlercTvMP_fMisVdENP6jg%3d%3d.; **280** Photology1971/Shutterstock.com; **281** Taurus106/Shutterstock.com; **284–285** luismmolina/iStock/Getty Images Plus, ktsimage/iStock/Getty Images Plus, Science Photo Library | KATERYNA KON, Kateryna Kon/Shutterstock.com, Design Cells/iStock/Getty Images Plus, Science Photo Library | KATERYNA KON

Chapter 6
286 *top* ©Amy Gusick/National Geographic Image Collection; *bottom* John Kepchar/Shutterstock.com; **287** *top* Dimitrios Karamitros/Shutterstock.com; *bottom* photo stella/Shuterstock.com; **289** *left* kurhan/Shutterstock.com; *right* tuulijumala/iStock/Getty Images Plus; **290** Pro2sound/iStock/Getty Images Plus; **296** *in order from left to right* Maks Narodenko/Shutterstock.com, Subject Photo/Shutterstock.com, Subject Photo/Shutterstock.com; **297** *left* michaeljung/Shuterstock.com; *right* OvsiankaStudio/iStock/Getty Images Plus; **299** *top* Alex Tuzhiko/Shutterstock.com; *bottom* FG Trade/E+/Getty Images Plus; **303** Wafi Zimamul/Shutterstock.com; **304** amwu/iStock/Getty Images Plus; **305** pedrosala/iStock/Getty Images Plus; **306** *left* hans.slegers/Shutterstock.com; *right* Vitaly Zorkin/Shutterstock.com; **307** *left* Take A Pix Media/shutterstock.com; *right* tuulijumala/iStock/Getty Images Plus; **315** *left* BCFC/Shutterstock.com; *right* tuulijumala/iStock/Getty Images Plus; **319** pics721/Shutterstock.com; **320** *top* jgorzynik/Shutterstock.com; *bottom* frantic00/Shutterstock.com; **321** *right* oatintro/iStock/Getty Images Plus; *bottom left* Dean Drobot/Shutterstock.com; **324** mahiruysal/iStock/Getty Images Plus; **326** Dzm1try/Shutterstock.com; **328** *left* Craig Chaddock/Shutterstock.com; *right* marekuliasz/Shutterstock.com; **329** *right* tuulijumala/iStock/Getty Images Plus; *left* Pixel-Shot/Shutterstock.com; **332** Ridofranz/iStock/Getty Images Plus; **334** *left* michaeljung/Shutterstock.com; *right* Whitevector/Shutterstock.com; **335** stocksolutions/Shutterstock.com; **337** Dan Baciu/Shutterstock.com; **338–339** de_zla/Shutterstock.com, jonnysek/iStock/Getty Images Plus, Dewin ID/Shutterstock.com, sb-borg/iStock/Getty Images Plus, Andrey_Kuzmin/Shutterstock.com; **340–341** codrinn/Shutterstock.com, Paitoon Pornsuksomboon/Shutterstock.com, max dallocco/Shutterstock.com, NASA/Goddard/University of Arizona

Chapter 7
342 *top* ©Rebecca Drobis/National Geographic Image Collection; *bottom* Sergey Nivens/Shutterstock.com; **343** *top* Andrey Prokhorov/Shutterstock.com; *bottom* Jasonfang/E+/Getty Images; **345** iodrakon/iStock/Getty Images Plus; **346** peterspiro/iStock Editorial/Getty Images Plus; **352** FABIO BISPO/iStock/Getty Images Plus; **354** *left* vagabond54/Shutterstock.com; *right* Hank Shiffman/Shutterstock.com; **355** *left* Roman Samborskyi/Shutterstock.com; *right* OvsiankaStudio/iStock/Getty Images Plus; **357** Africa Studio/Shutterstock.com; **362** foto-select/Shutterstock.com; **366** JackF/iStock/Getty Images Plus; **367** AlexRaths/iStock/Getty Images Plus; **368** Boarding1Now/iStock/Getty Images Plus; **370** nonnie192/iStock/Getty Images Plus; **372** Minerva Studio/Shutterstock.com; **373** *left* michaeljung/Shutterstock.com; *right* Roman Samokhin/Shutterstock.com; **379** *Exercise 5* Ksenia Palimski/Shutterstock.com; *Exercise 6* mphillips007/iStock/Getty Images Plus; *Exercise 7* donatas1205/Shutterstock.com; **380** Bahadirkar/iStock/Getty Images Plus; **382** *left* Sebastian Janicki/Shutterstock.com; *right* suesse/Shutterstock.com; **383** *left* Victoria Kisel/Shutterstock.com; *right* OvsiankaStudio/iStock/Getty Images Plus; **385** Roman Tiraspolsky/Shutterstock.com; **392** Schwabenblitz/Shutterstock.com; **396–397** valio84sl/iStock/Getty Images Plus

Chapter 8
398 *top* ©Carter Clinton; *bottom* Creations/Shutterstock.com; **399** Vertyr/Shutterstock.com; **401** *bottom* feedough/iStock/Getty Images Plus; *right* 24Novembers/Shutterstock.com; **404** Photitos2016/iStock/Getty Images Plus; **406** Dean Drobot/Shutterstock.com; **408** Kryuchka Yaroslav/Shutterstock.com; **411** oatintro/iStock/Getty Images Plus; **414** Graeme Dawes/Shutterstock.com; **416** Pressmaster/Shutterstock.com; **417** CostinT/E+/Getty Images; **423** *right* liveslow/iStock/Getty Images Plus; *left* spkphotostock/iStock/Getty Images Plus; **426** © Patrick Reynolds; **427** *right* oatintro/iStock/Getty Images Plus; *bottom* cc-stock/E+/Getty Images; **429** Andregric/iStock/Getty Images Plus, MaleWitch/iStock/Getty Images Plus; **434** *top* From N. Bahcall, J.P. Ostriker, S. Perlmutter, and P. J. Steinhardt, "The Cosmic Triangle: Revealing the State of the Universe," Science, 28 May 1999, vol. 284, issue 5419, pp. 1481-1488. Reprinted with permission from AAAS., M.Aurelius/Shutterstock.com; *bottom* Ryan Herron/iStock/Getty Images Plus; **435** Seregam/Shutterstock.com; **438–439** Tami Heilemann, Department of the Interior, U.S. National Archives., Rodney Leon of AARRIS Architects, African Burial Ground, New York, New York. Photograph in the Carol M. Highsmith Archive, Library of Congress, Prints and Photographs Division.

Chapter 9
440 *top* ©Mark Thiessen/National Geographic Image Collection; *bottom* mjones/Shutterstock.com; **441** Abby Grace Drake et al., "Three-Dimensional Geometric Morphometric Analysis of Fossil Canid Mandibles and Skulls," Scientific Reports 7, 9508 (2017), Figure 1. https://doi.org/10.1038/s41598-017-10232-1.; **443** Ana Blazic Pavlovic/Shutterstock.com; **450** *left* tan_tan/Shutterstock.com; *right* Mummert-und-Ibold/Shutterstock.com; **451** tuulijumala/iStock/Getty Images Plus; **454** aron Kohr/Shutterstock.com; **455** DeborahMaxemow/iStock/Getty Images Plus; **456** David A Litman/Shutterstock.com; **457** Hugo Felix/Shutterstock.com; **462** *left* travelview/Shutterstock.com; *right* et-anan/Shutterstock.com; **463** chinahbzyg/Shutterstock.com, 4x6/iStock/Getty Images Plus, Kamenetskiy Konstantin/Shutterstock.com; **465** *left* Portrait Image Asia/Shutterstock.com; *right* OvsiankaStudio/iStock/Getty Images Plus; **468** DNY59/iStock/Getty Images Plus; **469** Bob Steiner/iStock/Getty Images Plus; **470** *left* Roman Samborskyi/Shutterstock.com; *right* Nerthuz/Shutterstock.com; *bottom* BerndBrueggemann/iStock/Getty Images Plus; **471** *left* Anetlanda/Shutterstock.com; *right* OvsiankaStudio/iStock/Getty Images Plus; **475** George Rudy/Shutterstock.com; **477** *top* David McGill 71/Shutterstock.com; *bottom* Nosyrevy/Shutterstock.com; **478** *left* Aytug askin/Shutterstock.com; *right* Andrey_Kuzmin/Shutterstock.com, pixel creator/Shutterstock.com, Alexey Seafarer/Shutterstock.com; **479** steven parks/Shutterstock.com; **482** WesAbrams/iStock/Getty Images Plus; **484** *left* Tyler Olson/Shutterstock.com; *right* aappp/Shutterstock.com, Troggt/Shutterstock.com, Drazbedel/Shutterstock.com; **485** Sergey Peterman/iStock/Getty Images; **493** *top* Luis Molinero/Shutterstock.com, nickp37/iStock/Getty Images Plus; *bottom right* zoom-zoom/iStock/Getty Images Plus; **494** *left* Shalyapin Ivan/Shutterstock.com; *right* Steve Cukrov/Shutterstock.com; **496** 4x6/iStock/Getty Images Plus, ARTYuSTUDIO/iStock/Getty Images Plus; **497** londoneye/E+/Getty Images; **498** Javen/Shutterstock.com; **499** vchal/Shutterstock.com, michaeljung/Shutterstock.com; **500–501** Escaflowne/E+/Getty Images, Design Cells/iStock/Getty Images Plus, Svitlyk/shutterstock.com, Alexey Kljatov/Shutterstock.com; **502–503** Kostenyukova Nataliya/Shutterstock.com, iconohek/Shutterstock.com, WDnet Creation/Shutterstock.com

Chapter 10
504 *top* ©Mark Thiessen/National Geographic Image Collection; *bottom* CW Pix/Shutterstock.com; **505** Nicholas Grey/Shutterstock.com; **507** Asier Romero/Shutterstock.com; **513** ilyarexi/iStock/Getty Images Plus; **514** *left* vectorfusionart/shutterstock.com; *right* Mi Sketch/Shutterstock.com; *bottom* Nerthuz/iStock/Getty Images Plus; **515** Artpose Adam Borkowski/Shutterstock.com; **526** Tusumaru/Shutterstock.com; **530** Artsiom P/Shutterstock.com; **531** oatintro/iStock/Getty Images Plus; **538** *left* Private Collection © Look and Learn / Bridgeman Images; *right* Jlert

Joseph Lertola, "Stonehenge render," (https://commons.wikimedia.org/wiki/File:Stonehenge_render.jpg).; **539** *left* sheff/Shutterstock.com; *right* tuulijumala/iStock/Getty Images Plus; **546** *left* Mechanik/Shutterstock.com; *right* ixpert/Shutterstock.com; **547** oatintro/iStock/Getty Images Plus; **552** *left* Ljupco Smokovski/Shutterstock.com; *right* Bilanol/Shutterstock.com; **553** A Lot Of People/Shutterstock.com; **557** Timothy Messick/DigitalVision Vectors; **558** NASA, DTAM project team; **559** Apollofoto/Shutterstock.com; **564** bekirevren/Shutterstock.com; **566** *left* topseller/Shuttetstock.com; *right* Fit Ztudio/Shutterstock.com; **571** AlexLMX/Shutterstock.com; **572–573** PTZ Pictures/Shutterstock.com, Nicholas Grey/Shutterstock.com, TonyBaggett/iStock/Getty Images Plus, Gerasimov174/iStock/Getty Images Plus, ipopba/iStock/Getty Images Plus, duncan1890/DigitalVision Vectors/Getty Images, Julia Khimich/Shutterstock.com

Chapter 11

574 *top* ©Alize Carrere/National Geographic Image Collection; *bottom* Angela N Perryman/Shutterstock.com; **575** *left* LukeOnTheRoad/Shutterstock.com; *right* Eric Isselee/Shutterstock.com; *bottom* photomaster/Shutterstock.com; **577** michaeljung/Shutterstock.com; **580** Gwoeii/Shutterstock.com; **582** ©iStockphoto.com/Prill Mediendesign & Fotografie; **583** Gearstd/iStock/Getty Images Plus; **584** Kent Raney/Shutterstock.com; **585** Ranta Images/Shutterstock.com; **588** Prachaya Roekdeethaweesab/Shutterstock.com; **590** *top right* metamorworks/Shutterstock.com; *bottom* Agata Buczek/Shutterstock.com; **591** tuulijumala/iStock/Getty Images Plus; **595** *left* ©iStockphoto.com/Olgertas; *right* keella/Shutterstock.com; **596** Laschon Maximilian/Shutterstock.com; **598** *left* wavebreakmedia/Shutterstock.com; *right* irin-k/Shutterstock.com; **601** Edoma/Shutterstock.com; **602** Hugnoi/iStock/Getty images Plus; **603** inhauscreative/iStock/Getty Images Plus; **604** *left* sirtravelalot/Shutterstock.com; *right* burakyalcin/Shutterstock.com; **605** Ebtikar/Shutterstock.com; **606** *top* ninikas/iStock/Getty Images Plus; *bottom* mipan/iStock/Getty Images Plus; **607** *top* Andrii Yalanskyi/Shutterstock.com; *bottom* Hurst Photo/Shutterstock.com; **608–609** Cecilia Lim H M/Shutterstock.com, BrianBrownImages/iStock/Getty Images Plus, Songbird839/iStock/Getty Images Plus, Sergei Kardashev/Shutterstock.com

Chapter 12

610 *top* ©Daniela Cafaggi Lemus; *bottom* Photoongraphy/Shutterstock.com; **611** All-stock-photos/Shutterstock.com; **613** *left* Luis Molinero/Shutterstock.com; *right* matejmm/iStock/Getty Images Plus, vladimir_karpenyuk/iStock/Getty Images Plus, pamela_d_mcadams/iStock/Getty Images Plus, akepong srichaichana/Shutterstock.com, subjug/E+/Getty Images Plus; **617** popovaphoto/iStock/Getty Images Plus; **620** *right* Fit Ztudio/Shutterstock.com; *left* Tridsanu Thopet/Shutterstock.com; **621** *top* Tatiana Popova/Shutterstock.com; *bottom* Steve Heap/Shutterstock.com; **624** Blade_kostas/iStock/Getty Images Plus; **627** nzfhatipoglu/iStock/Getty Images Plus; **628** *left* M2020/Shutterstock.com; *right* travelview/Shutterstock.com; **631** koya79/iStock/Getty Images Plus; **633** © Richard Lowthian | Dreamstime.com; **634** *left* Mona Lisa, Leonardo da Vinci creator QS:P170,Q762 C2RMF: Galerie de tableaux en très haute définition: image page (https://commons.wikimedia.org/wiki/File:Mona_Lisa,_by_Leonardo_da_Vinci,_from_C2RMF_retouched.jpg), marked as public domain.; *right* Catarina Belova/Shutterstock.com; **640** Vasil_Onyskiv/iStock/Getty Images Plus; **641** Mark Herreid/Shutterstock.com; **646** *in order from left to right* Nomad_Soul/Shutterstock.com, Mark Herreid/Shutterstock.com, Keattikorn/Shutterstock.com; **647** *top right* Nerthuz/iStock/Getty Images Plus; *left* Npeter/Shutterstock.com; *bottom right* KangeStudio/iStock/Getty Images Plus; **648** ixpert/Shutterstock.com; **649** *left* Odua Images/Shutterstock.com; *right* Mega Pixel/Shutterstock.com, JIANG HONGYAN/Shutterstock.com, forest_strider/Shutterstock.com, Mario Savoia/Shutterstock.com; *bottom* Stanislaw Mikulski/Shutterstock.com; **650** witoldkr1/iStock/Getty Images Plus; **651** Simon Dannhauer/Shutterstock.com; **652** *top* karandaev/iStock/Getty Images Plus; *bottom* Suzanne Tucker/Shutterstock.com; **653** paperbees/Shutterstock.com; **654** iodrakon/Shutterstock.com; **655** luckyraccoon/Shutterstock.com; **660** *left* Karen Dole/Shutterstock.com; *right* martin33/Shutterstock.com; *bottom* Mananya Kaewthawee/iStock/Getty Images Plus; **662** aquatarkus/Shutterstock.com; **663** Aerodim/Shutterstock.com; **664** ©iStockphoto.com/mlevy; **665** *left* ThomasVogel/iStock/Getty Images Plus; *right* Chimpinski/iStock/Getty Images Plus; **666–667** Ivan Kurmyshov/Shutterstock.com, Photo courtesy Ryan von Linden/New York Department of Environmental Conservation, Remus86/iStock/Getty Images Plus, IgorCheri/Shutterstock.com

Chapter 13

668 *top* ©Scott Degraw/National Geographic Image Collection; *bottom* Trevor Mayes/Shutterstock.com; **669** Microgen/Shutterstock.com; **671** *left* Apollofoto/Shutterstock.com; *right* Viktor Fedorenko/Shutterstock.com, fotohunter/Shutterstock.com, VIKTOR FEDORENKO/iStock/Getty Images Plus; **672** VIKTOR FEDORENKO/iStock/Getty Images Plus; **676** hobbit/Shutterstock.com; **678** BananyakoSensei/Shutterstock.com; **679** V.S.Anandhakrishna/Shutterstock.com; **683** Antonio_Diaz/iStock/Getty Images Plus; **684** Everett Collection/Shutterstock.com; **688** Africa Studio/Shutterstock.com; **689** 4x6/iStock/Getty Images Plus; **690** *right* Harvepino/iStock/Getty Images Plus; *bottom left* Ody_Stocker/Shutterstock.com; **692** Apollofoto/Shutterstock.com, "F. Maxwell Harper and Joseph A. Konstan, ""The MovieLens Datasets: History and Context,"" ACM Transactions on Interactive Intelligent Systems 5, no. 4, Article 19 (December 22, 2015), http://dx.doi.org/10.1145/2827872."; **693** Pixel-Shot/Shutterstock.com; **695** Mega Pixel/Shutterstock.com; **697** 1550539/iStock/Getty Images Plus, NoDerog/iStock/Getty Images Plus, Pongasn68/iStock/Getty Images Plus; **700** BananyakoSensei/Shutterstock.com; **701** *right* empire331/iStock/Getty Images Plus; *left* Ridofranz/iStock/Getty Images Plus; **703** marekuliasz/iStock/Getty Images Plus; **704** Dmitry Lobanov/Shutterstock.com; **707** *right* Silense/iStock/Getty Images Plus, Africa Studio/Shutterstock.com, purple_queue/iStock/Getty Images Plus, GlobalP/iStock/Getty Images Plus; *left* ESB Professional/Shutterstock.com; **711** nojustice/iStock/Getty Images Plus, IPGGutenbergUKLtd/iStock/Getty Images Plus; **712** Yganko/Shutterstock.com; **714** Vector Tradition/Shutterstock.com; **715** *left* NaMong Productions92/Shutterstock.com; *right* Viktor Fedorenko/Shutterstock.com; **717** Undorik/Shutterstock.com; **719** Boarding1Now/iStock/Getty Images Plus; **722** vchal/Shutterstock.com; **723** Alexander Kondratenko/Shutterstock.com; **724–725** krystiannawrocki/iStock/Getty Images Plus, momnoi/iStock/Getty Images Plus, mofles/iStock/Getty Images Plus, alice-photo/iStock/Getty Images Plus, arogant/iStock/Getty Images Plus, yannp/iStock/Getty Images Plus, Lefteris_/iStock/Getty Images Plus, kovalvs/iStock/Getty Images Plus, Comstock/Stockbyte/Getty Images, Orchidpoet/E+/Getty Images, Anton Starikov/Shutterstock.com, Zurbagan/Shutterstock.com, Teerapong Teerapong/Shutterstock.com; **726–727** feygraphy/Shutterstock.com, BananyakoSensei/Shutterstock.com

Special thanks to Thurner Photography.